Lecture Notes in Artificial Intelligence 2111

Subseries of Lecture Notes in Computer Science
Edited by J. G. Carbonell and J. Siekmann

Lecture Notes in Computer Science
Edited by G. Goos, J. Hartmanis and J. van Leeuwen

Springer
Berlin
Heidelberg
New York
Barcelona
Hong Kong
London
Milan
Paris
Singapore
Tokyo

David Helmbold Bob Williamson (Eds.)

Computational Learning Theory

14th Annual Conference
on Computational Learning Theory, COLT 2001
and 5th European Conference
on Computational Learning Theory, EuroCOLT 2001
Amsterdam, The Netherlands, July 16-19, 2001
Proceedings

Series Editors

Jaime G. Carbonell, Carnegie Mellon University, Pittsburgh, PA, USA
Jörg Siekmann, University of Saarland, Saarbrücken, Germany

Volume Editors

David Helmbold
University of California, Santa Cruz
School of Engineering, Department of Computer Science
Santa Cruz, CA 95064, USA
E-mail: dph@cse.ucsc.edu

Bob Williamson
Australian National University
Research School of Information Sciences and Engineering
Department of Telecommunications Engineering
Canberra 0200, Australia
E-mail: Bob.Williamson@anu.edu.au

Cataloging-in-Publication Data applied for

Die Deutsche Bibliothek - CIP-Einheitsaufnahme

Computational learning theory : proceedings / 14th Annual Conference on Computational Learning Theory, COLT 2001 and 5th European Conference on Computational Learning Theory, EuroCOLT 2001, Amsterdam, The Netherlands, July 16 - 19, 2001. David Helmbold ; Bob Williamson (ed.). - Berlin ; Heidelberg ; New York ; Barcelona ; Hong Kong ; London ; Milan ; Paris ; Singapore ; Tokyo : Springer, 2001
(Lecture notes in computer science ; Vol. 2111 : Lecture notes in artificial intelligence)
ISBN 3-540-42343-5

CR Subject Classification (1998): I.2.6, I.2.3, F.4.1, F.1.1, F.2

ISBN 3-540-42343-5 Springer-Verlag Berlin Heidelberg New York

Springer-Verlag Berlin Heidelberg New York
a member of BertelsmannSpringer Science+Business Media GmbH

http://www.springer.de

Typesetting: Camera-ready by author
Printed on acid-free paper SPIN: 10839809 06/3142 5 4 3 2 1 0

Preface

This volume contains papers presented at the joint 14th Annual Conference on Computational Learning Theory and 5th European Conference on Computational Learning Theory, held at the Trippenhuis in Amsterdam, The Netherlands from July 16 to 19, 2001.

The technical program contained 40 papers selected from 69 submissions. In addition, David Stork (Ricoh California Research Center) was invited to give an invited lecture and make a written contribution to the proceedings.

The Mark Fulk Award is presented annually for the best paper co-authored by a student. This year's award was won by Olivier Bousquet for the paper "Tracking a Small Set of Modes by Mixing Past Posteriors" (co-authored with Manfred K. Warmuth).

We gratefully thank all of the individuals and organizations responsible for the success of the conference. We are especially grateful to the program committee: Dana Angluin (Yale), Peter Auer (Univ. of Technology, Graz), Nello Christianini (Royal Holloway), Claudio Gentile (Università di Milano), Lisa Hellerstein (Polytechnic Univ.), Jyrki Kivinen (Univ. of Helsinki), Phil Long (National Univ. of Singapore), Manfred Opper (Aston Univ.), John Shawe-Taylor (Royal Holloway), Yoram Singer (Hebrew Univ.), Bob Sloan (Univ. of Illinois at Chicago), Carl Smith (Univ. of Maryland), Alex Smola (Australian National Univ.), and Frank Stephan (Univ. of Heidelberg), for their efforts in reviewing and selecting the papers in this volume.

Special thanks go to our conference co-chairs, Peter Grünwald and Paul Vitányi, as well as Marja Hegt. Together they handled the conference publicity and all the local arrangements to ensure a successful conference. We would also like to thank ACM SIGACT for the software used in the program committee deliberations and Stephen Kwek for maintaining the COLT web site.

Finally, we would like to thank The National Research Institute for Mathematics and Computer Science in the Netherlands (CWI), The Amsterdam Historical Museum, and The Netherlands Organization for Scientific Research (NWO) for their sponsorship of the conference.

May 2001

David Helmbold
Bob Williamson
Program Co-chairs
COLT/EuroCOLT 2001

Table of Contents

How Many Queries Are Needed to Learn One Bit of Information?*

Hans Ulrich Simon[1]

Fakultät für Mathematik, Ruhr-Universität Bochum, D-44780 Bochum, Germany
simon@lmi.ruhr-uni-bochum.de

Abstract. In this paper we study the question how many queries are needed to "halve a given version space". In other words: how many queries are needed to extract from the learning environment the one bit of information that rules out fifty percent of the concepts which are still candidates for the unknown target concept. We relate this problem to the classical exact learning problem. For instance, we show that lower bounds on the number of queries needed to halve a version space also apply to randomized learners (whereas the classical adversary arguments do not readily apply). Furthermore, we introduce two new combinatorial parameters, the halving dimension and the strong halving dimension, which determine the halving complexity (modulo a small constant factor) for two popular models of query learning: learning by a minimum adequate teacher (equivalence queries combined with membership queries) and learning by counterexamples (equivalence queries alone). These parameters are finally used to characterize the additional power provided by membership queries (compared to the power of equivalence queries alone). All investigations are purely information-theoretic and ignore computational issues.

1 Introduction

The exact learning model was introduced by Angluin in [1]. In this model, a learner A tries to identify an unknown target concept C_* (of the form $C_* : X \rightarrow \{0,1\}$ for a finite set X) by means of queries that must be honestly answered by an oracle. Although the oracle must not lie, it may select its answers in a worstcase fashion such as to slow down the learning process as much as possible. In the (worstcase) analysis of A, we assume that the oracle is indeed an adversary of A that makes full use of this freedom. (In the sequel, we sometimes say "adversary" instead of "oracle" for this reason.) Furthermore, A must be able to identify any target concept selected from a (known) concept class $\mathcal{C}$. Again, A is subjected to a worstcase analysis, i.e., we count the number of queries needed to identify the hardest concept from $\mathcal{C}$ (that is the concept that forces A to invest a maximal number of queries).

Among the most popular query types are the following ones:

* This work has been supported in part by the ESPRIT Working Group in Neural and Computational Learning II, NeuroCOLT2, No. 27150. The author was also supported by the Deutsche Forschungsgemeinschaft Grant SI 498/4-1.

D. Helmbold and B. Williamson (Eds.): COLT/EuroCOLT 2001, LNAI 2111, pp. 1–13, 2001.

Equivalence Queries. A selects a hypothesis H from its hypothesis class $\mathcal{H}$. (Typically, $\mathcal{H} = \mathcal{C}$ or $\mathcal{H}$ is a superset of $\mathcal{C}$.) If $H = C_*$, the oracle answers "YES" (signifying that A suceeded to identify the target concept). Otherwise, the oracle returns a counterexample, i.e., an $x \in X$ such that $H(x) \neq C_*(x)$.

Membership Queries. A selects an $x \in X$ and receives label $C_*(x)$ from the oracle.

At each time of the learning process, the so-called version space $\mathcal{V}$ contains all concepts from $\mathcal{C}$ that do not contradict to the answers that have been received so far. Clearly, the learner succeeded to identify C_* as soon as $\mathcal{V} = \{C_*\}$. It is well-known in the learning community that the task of identifying an unknown but fixed target concept from $\mathcal{C}$ is equivalent to the task of playing against another adversary who need not to commit itself to a target concept in the beginning. The answers of this adversary are considered as honest as long as they do not lead to an empty version space. The learner still tries to shrink the version space to a singleton and thereby to issue as few queries as possible. We will refer to this task as the "contraction task" (or the "contraction game"). At first glance, the contraction task seems to give more power to the adversary. However, if we assume that A is deterministic, both tasks require the same number of queries: since A is deterministic, one can "predict" which concept C_* will form the final (singleton) version space in the hardest scenario of the contraction task. Now, it does not hurt the adversary, to commit itself to C_* as the target concept in the beginning.

Since randomized learning complexity will be an issue in this paper, we briefly illustrate that the initial commitment to a target concept is relevant when we allow randomized learners:

Example 1. Consider the model of learning by means of equivalence queries. Let the concept and hypothesis class coincide with the set of all functions from X to $\{0,1\}$, where $X = \{1, \ldots, d\}$. Clearly, the contraction task forces each deterministic (or randomized) algorithm to issue d equivalence queries because each (non-redundant) query halves the version space. As for deterministic algorithms, the same remark is valid for the learning task. However the following randomized learning algorithm needs in the average only $d/2$ queries:
Pick a first hypothesis $H_0 : X \to \{0,1\}$ uniformly at random. Given that the current hypothesis is H and that counterexample $x \in X$ is received, let the next hypothesis H' coincide with H on $X \setminus \{x\}$ and set $H'(x) \stackrel{\triangle}{=} 1 - H(x)$.
The number of queries needed to identify an arbitrary (but fixed) target concept C_* equals the number of instances on which C_* and H_0 disagree. This is $d/2$ in the average.

This example demonstrates that the typical adversary arguments, that are used in the literature for proving lower bounds on the number of queries, do not readily apply to randomized learners.[1]

[1] To the best of our knowledge, almost all papers devoted to query learning assume deterministic learning algorithms. A notable exception is the paper [5] of Maass that

The main issue in this paper is the number of queries needed to halve (as opposed to contract) an initial version space $\mathcal{V}_0$. There are several reasons for this kind of research:

- Contraction of the version space by iterated halving is considered as very efficient. Iterated halving is an important building stone of well known strategies such as the "Majority Vote Strategy", for instance. The binary search paradigm is based on halving. Halving may therefore be considered as an interesting problem in its own right.
- Halving the version space yields exactly one bit of information. In this sense, we explore the hardness to extract one bit of information from the learning environment. This sounds like an elementary and natural problem.
- Although the contraction task is not meaningful for randomized learners, we will be able to show that the halving task is meaningful. This makes adversary arguments applicable to randomized learning algorithms.
- We can characterize the halving complexity for two popular query types (equivalence and membership queries) by tight combinatorial bounds (leaving almost no gap).[2] These bounds can be used to characterize the additional power provided by membership queries (compared to the power of equivalence queries alone).

The paper is organized as follows. In Section 2, we present the basic definitions and notations. In Section 3, we view the tasks of learning, contraction and halving as a game between the learner (contraction algorithm, halving algorithm, respectively) and an adversary. In Section 4, we investigate the relation between halving and learning complexity (including randomized learning complexity). In Section 5, we present the combinatorial (lower and upper) bounds on the halving complexity. In Section 6, these bounds are used to characterize the additional power provided by membership queries (compared to the power of equivalence queries alone).

2 Basic Definitions and Notations

Let X be a finite set and $\mathcal{C}, \mathcal{H}$ be two families of functions from X to $\{0, 1\}$. In the sequel, we refer to X as the *instance space*, to $\mathcal{C}$ as the *concept class*, and to $\mathcal{H}$ as the *hypothesis class*. It is assumed that $\mathcal{C} \subseteq \mathcal{H}$. A labeled instance $(x, b) \in X \times \{0, 1\}$ is called a *sample-point*. A *sample* is a collection of sample-points. For convenience, we represent each sample S as a partially defined binary

demonstrates the significance of supporting examples in the on-line learning model, when the learner is randomized and the learning environment is oblivious.

[2] The derivation of these bounds is based on ideas and results from [4,2], where bounds on the number of queries needed for learning (i.e, for contracting the version space) are presented. These bounds, however, leave a gap. It seems that the most accurate combinatorial bounds are found on the level of the halving task. (See also [3] for a survey on papers presenting upper and lower bounds on query complexity.)

function over domain X. More formally, S is of the form $S : X \to \{0, 1, ?\}$, where $S(x) =?$ indicates that S is undefined on instance x. The set

$$\mathrm{supp}(S) \triangleq \{x \in X : S(x) \neq ?\} \tag{1}$$

is called the *support* of S. Note that a concept or hypothesis can be viewed as a sample with full support. The *size* of S is the number of instances in its support. S' is called *subsample* of S, denoted as $S' \sqsubseteq S$, if $\mathrm{supp}(S') \subseteq \mathrm{supp}(S)$ and $S'(x) = S(x)$ for each instance $x \in \mathrm{supp}(S')$. We say that sample S and concept C are *consistent* if $S \sqsubseteq C$. We say that S *has a consistent explanation in* $\mathcal{C}$ if there exists a concept $C \in \mathcal{C}$ such that S and C are consistent. The terminology for hypotheses is analogous.

In the exact learning model, a *learner (learning algorithm)* A has to identify an unknown *target concept* $C_* \in \mathcal{C}$ by means of queries. The query learning process can be informally described as follows. Each query must be honestly answered by an oracle. Learning proceeds in rounds. In each round, A issues the next query and obtains an honest answer from the oracle. The current *version space* $\mathcal{V}$ is the set of concepts from $\mathcal{C}$ that do not contradict to the answers received so far. Initially, $\mathcal{V} = \mathcal{C}$. From round to round, $\mathcal{V}$ shrinks. However, at least the target concept C_* always belongs to $\mathcal{V}$ because the answers given by the oracle are honest. The learning process stops when $\mathcal{V} = \{C_*\}$.

For the sake of simplicity, we formalize this general framework only for the following popular models of exact learning:

Equivalence Query Learning (EQ-Learning). Each allowed query can be identified with a hypothesis $H \in \mathcal{H}$. If $H = C_*$, the only honest answer is "YES" (signifying that the target concept has been exactly identified by A). Otherwise, an honest answer is a *counterexample* to H, i.e., an instance x such that $H(x) \neq C_*(x)$.

Membership Query Learning (MQ-Learning). Each allowed query can be identified with an instance $x \in X$. The only honest answer is $C_*(x)$.

EQ-MQ-Learning. The learner may issue both types of queries.

Let $\mathcal{V}$ be the current version space. If A issues a membership query with instance x and receives the binary label b, then the subsequent version space is given by

$$\mathcal{V}[x, b] \triangleq \{C \in \mathcal{V} : C(x) = b\}. \tag{2}$$

Similarly, if A issues an equivalence query with hypothesis H and receives the counterexample x, then the subsequent version space is given by

$$\mathcal{V}[H, x] \triangleq \{C \in \mathcal{V} : C(x) \neq H(x)\}. \tag{3}$$

Clearly, answer "YES" to an equivalence query immediately leads to the final version space $\{C_*\}$.

In general, $\mathcal{V}[Q, R]$ denotes the version space resulting from the current version space $\mathcal{V}$ when A issues query Q and receives answer R. We denote by $\mathcal{Q}$

the set of queries from which Q must be selected. Given $\mathcal{C}, \mathcal{H}$, a collection $\mathcal{Q}$ of allowed queries, and a deterministic learner A, we define $\mathrm{DLC}_A^{\mathcal{Q}}(\mathcal{C}, \mathcal{H})$ as the following unique number q:

- There exists a target concept $C_* \in \mathcal{C}$ and a sequence of honest answers to the queries selected by A such that the learning process does not stop before round q.
- For each target concept $C_* \in \mathcal{C}$ and each sequence of honest answers to the queries selected by A, the learning process stops after round q or earlier.

In other words, $\mathrm{DLC}_A^{\mathcal{Q}}(\mathcal{C}, \mathcal{H})$ is the smallest number q of queries such that A is guaranteed to identify any target concept from $\mathcal{C}$ with hypotheses from $\mathcal{H}$ using q queries from $\mathcal{Q}$. The *deterministic learning complexity* associated with $\mathcal{C}, \mathcal{H}, \mathcal{Q}$ is given by

$$\mathrm{DLC}^{\mathcal{Q}}(\mathcal{C}, \mathcal{H}) \triangleq \min_A \mathrm{DLC}_A^{\mathcal{Q}}(\mathcal{C}, \mathcal{H}), \tag{4}$$

where A varies over all deterministic learners.

3 Games Related to Learning

Since we measure the number of queries needed by the learner in a worstcase fashion, we can model the learning process as a game between two players: the learner A and its adversary ADV. We use the notation ADV_A to indicate the strongest possible adversary of A. We begin with a rather straightforward interpretation of exact learning as a game.

3.1 The Learning Game

$\mathcal{C}, \mathcal{H}$ and $\mathcal{Q}$ are fixed and known to both players. The game proceeds as follows. In a first move (invisible to A), ADV picks the target concept C_* from C. Afterwards, both players proceed in rounds. In each round, first player A makes its move by selecting a query from $\mathcal{Q}$. Then, ADV makes its move by selecting an honest answer. The game is over when the current version space does not contain any concept different from C_*. The goal of A is to finish the game as soon as possible, whereas the goal of ADV is to continue playing as long as possible. A is evaluated against the strongest adversary ADV_A that forces A to make a maximum number of moves (or the maximum expected number of moves in the case of a randomized learner).

It should be evident that the number of rounds in the learning game between a deterministic learner A and ADV_A coincides with the quantity $\mathrm{DLC}_A^{\mathcal{Q}}(\mathcal{C}, \mathcal{H})$ that was defined in the previous section. Thus, $\mathrm{DLC}^{\mathcal{Q}}(\mathcal{C}, \mathcal{H})$ coincides with the number of rounds in the learning game between the best deterministic learner and its adversary.

We define $\mathrm{RLC}_A^{\mathcal{Q}}(\mathcal{C}, \mathcal{H})$ as the expected number of rounds in the learning game between the (potentially) randomized learner A and its strongest adversary

ADV_A.[3] The *randomized learning complexity* associated with $\mathcal{C}, \mathcal{H}, \mathcal{Q}$ is given by

$$\mathrm{RLC}^{\mathcal{Q}}(\mathcal{C},\mathcal{H}) \triangleq \min_A \mathrm{RLC}^{\mathcal{Q}}_A(\mathcal{C},\mathcal{H}), \tag{5}$$

where A varies over all (potentially) randomized learners.

3.2 The Contraction Game

It is well known that, in the case of deterministic learners A, the learning game can be replaced by a conceptually simpler game, differing from the learning game as follows:

- The first move of ADV is omitted, i.e., ADV makes no commitment about the target concept in the beginning.
- Each (syntactically correct)[4] answer that does not lead to an empty version space is honest.
- The game is over when the version space is a singleton.

Again, the goal of player A is to finish the game as soon as possible, whereas the goal of the adversary is to finish as late as possible. A is evaluated against its strongest adversary ADV_A. We will refer to this new game as the contraction game and to A as a contraction algorithm.

The following lemmas recall some well known facts (in a slightly more general setting).

Lemma 1. *As for the contraction game, there exist two deterministic optimal players A_* and ADV_*, i.e., the following holds:*

1. *Let A be any (potentially randomized) contraction algorithm. Then, ADV_* forces A to make at least as many moves as A_*.*
2. *Let ADV be any (potentially randomized) oracle. Then A_* needs no more moves against ADV than against ADV_*.*

The proof uses a standard argument which is given here for sake of completeness.

Proof. Consider the decision tree T that models the moves of both players. Each node of T is of type either $\mathcal{Q}$ or $\mathcal{R}$ (signifying which player makes the next move). Each node of type $\mathcal{Q}$ is marked by a version space (reflecting the actual configuration of the contraction game), and each node of type $\mathcal{R}$ is marked by a version space and a question (again reflecting the actual configuration of the game including the last question of A). The structure of T can be inductively described as follows:

---

[3] Here, ADV_A knows the program of A, but A determines its next move by means of secret random bits. Thus, ADV_A knows the probability distribution of the future moves, but cannot exactly predict them. This corresponds to what is called "weakly oblivious environment" in [5].

[4] E.g., the answer to an equivalence (or membership) query must be an instance from X (or a binary label, respectively).

- Its root is of type $\mathcal{Q}$ and marked $\mathcal{C}$ (the initial version space in the contraction game).
- A node of type $\mathcal{Q}$ that is marked by a singleton (version space of size 1) is a leaf (signifying that the game is over).
- Each inner node v of type $\mathcal{Q}$ that is marked $\mathcal{V}$ has k children $v[Q_1], \ldots, v[Q_k]$, where $Q_1, \ldots, Q_k$ denote the non-redundant questions that A is allowed to issue at this stage. Node $v[Q_i]$ is of type $\mathcal{R}$ and marked $(\mathcal{V}, Q_i)$.
- Each inner node w of type $\mathcal{R}$ that is marked $(\mathcal{V}, Q)$ has l children $w[R_1], \ldots, w[R_l]$, where $R_1, \ldots, R_l$ denote the honest answers of ADV to question Q at this stage. Node $w[R_j]$ is of type $\mathcal{Q}$ and marked $\mathcal{V}[Q, R_j]$ (the version space resulting from $\mathcal{V}$ when A issues query Q and receives answer R_j).

It is easy to describe deterministic optimal strategies for both players in a bottom-up fashion. At each node of T, the optimal decisions for A and ADV result from the following rules:

- Each leaf is labeled 0 (signifying that no more moves of A are needed to finish the game).
- If a node w of type $\mathcal{R}$ that is labeled $(\mathcal{V}, Q)$ has children $w[R_1], \ldots, w[R_l]$ labeled $(n_1, \ldots, n_l)$, respectively, and $n_j = \max\{n_1, \ldots, n_l\}$, then w is labeled n_j. Furthermore, ADV should answer R_j to question Q, given that $\mathcal{V}$ is the current version space.
- If a node v of type $\mathcal{Q}$ that is labeled $\mathcal{V}$ has children $v[Q_1], \ldots, v[Q_k]$ labeled $(m_1, \ldots, m_k)$, respectively, and $m_i = \min\{m_1, \ldots, m_k\}$, then v is labeled $1 + m_i$. Furthermore, A should ask question Q_i, given that $\mathcal{V}$ is the current version space.

Note that these rules can be made deterministic by resolving the ties in an arbitrary deterministic fashion. It is easy to prove for each node v of T (by induction on the height of v) that the following holds:
If v is marked $\mathcal{V}$, then the rules specify two deterministic optimal players (in the sense of Lemma 1) for the partial contraction game that starts with initial version space $\mathcal{V}$. The bottom-up label associated with v specifies the number of rounds in this partial game when both player follow the rules.
The extrapolation of this claim to the root node of T yields Lemma 1.

Lemma 1 implies that A_* is the best contraction algorithm among all (possibly randomized) algorithms. (Remember that each algorithm A is evaluated against its strongest adversary ADV_A.) It implies also that ADV_* is the strongest adversary of A_*.

Lemma 2. *$DLC^{\mathcal{Q}}(\mathcal{C}, \mathcal{H})$ coincides with the number of rounds, say q_*, in the contraction game between A_* and ADV_*.*

The proof of this lemma (given here for sake of completeness) is well known in the learning community and is, in fact, the justification of the popular adversary arguments within the derivation of lower bounds on the number of queries needed by deterministic learners.

Proof. The contraction game coincides with the learning game, except for the commitment that the adversary has to make in the first step of the learning game: the selection of a target concept $C_* \in \mathcal{C}$. Thus, $\mathrm{DLC}^{\mathcal{Q}}(\mathcal{C},\mathcal{H}) \leq q^*$. It suffices therefore to show that for each deterministic learner A there exists an adversary ADV_A that forces at least q_* moves of A.

To this end, let A be an arbitrary, but fixed, deterministic learner. Let ADV_* be the optimal deterministic adversary in the contraction game that was described in the proof of Lemma 1. Let A play against ADV_* in the contraction game.[5] Let $q \geq q_*$ be the number of queries needed by A to finish the contraction game against player ADV_*, and let C_* be the unique concept in the final (singleton) version space. Now we may use an adversary ADV_A in the learning game that selects C_* as a target concept in the beginning and then simulates ADV_*. Since A is deterministic, this will lead to the same sequence of moves as in the contraction game. Thus, ADV can force $q \geq q^*$ moves of A.
Note that a lower bound argument can deal with a sub-optimal (but, may be, easier to analyze) adversary ADV (instead of ADV_*). Symmetrically, an upper bound argument may use a sub-optimal (but, may be, easier to analyze) contraction algorithm A (instead of A_*).

We briefly remind the reader to Example 1. If $\mathcal{C}$ contains all functions from $\{1,\ldots,d\}$ to $\{0,1\}$, then Example 1 shows that

$$\mathrm{DLC}^{EQ}(\mathcal{C},\mathcal{C}) = d \text{ and } \mathrm{RLC}^{EQ}(\mathcal{C},\mathcal{C}) \leq d/2.$$

In the light of Lemmas 1 and 2, this demonstrates that the contraction game does not model the learning game when randomized learners are allowed.

3.3 The Halving Game

The halving game is defined like the contraction game except that it may start with an arbitrary initial version space $\mathcal{V}_0 \subseteq \mathcal{C}$ (known to both players), and it is over as soon as the current version space $\mathcal{V}$ contains at most half of the concepts of $\mathcal{V}_0$. Player A (called halving algorithm in this context) tries to halve $\mathcal{V}_0$ as fast as possible. Player ADV_A is its strongest adversary.

Like in the contraction game, there exist two optimal deterministic players: A_* (representing the optimal halving algorithm) and ADV_* (wich is also the strongest adversary for A_*). (Compare with Lemma 1.) Let $\mathrm{HC}^{\mathcal{Q}}(\mathcal{V}_0,\mathcal{H})$ be defined as the number of rounds in the halving game between A_* and ADV_*. In other words, $\mathrm{HC}^{\mathcal{Q}}(\mathcal{V}_0,\mathcal{H})$ is the smallest number of queries that suffices to halve the initial version space $\mathcal{V}_0$ when all queries are answered in a worstcase fashion. This parameter has the disadvantage of being not monotonic: a subset of $\mathcal{V}_0$ might be harder to halve than $\mathcal{V}_0$ itself. In order to force monotonicity, we define the *halving complexity* associated with $\mathcal{C},\mathcal{H},\mathcal{Q}$ as follows:

$$\mathrm{HC}^{\mathcal{Q}}_*(\mathcal{C},\mathcal{H}) = \max\{\mathrm{HC}^{\mathcal{Q}}(\mathcal{V},\mathcal{H}) : \mathcal{V} \subseteq \mathcal{C}\} \tag{6}$$

[5] This looks like a dirty trick because A is an algorithm that expects to play the learning game. We will however argue later that A cannot distinguish the communication with ADV_* from the communication with an adversary ADV in the learning game.

The relation between halving and learning is the central issue of the next section.

4 Halving and Learning Complexity

Theorem 1. *The following chain of inequalities is valid:*

$$\begin{aligned}\frac{1}{2}\cdot HC_*^Q(\mathcal{C},\mathcal{H}) &< RLC^Q(\mathcal{C},\mathcal{H}) &(7)\\ &\le \max\left\{HC_*^Q(\mathcal{C},\mathcal{H}), RLC^Q(\mathcal{C},\mathcal{H})\right\} &(8)\\ &\le DLC^Q(\mathcal{C},\mathcal{H}) &(9)\\ &\le \lfloor\log|\mathcal{C}|\rfloor\cdot HC_*^Q(\mathcal{C},\mathcal{H}). &(10)\end{aligned}$$

Proof. We begin with the proof of inequality (7). Let A be an arbitrary (potentially randomized) learning algorithm. Let $\mathcal{V}_* \subseteq \mathcal{C}$ be the version space such that

$$q_* \triangleq \mathrm{HC}_*^Q(\mathcal{C},\mathcal{H}) = \mathrm{HC}^Q(\mathcal{V}_*,\mathcal{H}).$$

Let ADV_* be the optimal deterministic adversary for the problem of halving $\mathcal{V}_*$. Thus, ADV_* forces each halving algorithm to issue at least q^* queries. In order to derive a lower bound on $\mathrm{RLC}^Q(\mathcal{C},\mathcal{H})$, we use an adversary ADV that proceeds as follows:

First move. Pick a target concept $C_* \in \mathcal{V}_*$ uniformly at random. Release the information that the target concept is taken from $\mathcal{V}_*$ to A.

Subsequent moves. Simulate ADV_* as long as its answers do not exclude target concept $\mathcal{C}_*$ from the resulting version space. As soon as $\mathcal{C}_*$ would be excluded, abort the simulation and give up.

We say that the learning algorithm A "wins" in q moves against ADV if it takes q moves until A either has identified the target concept $\mathcal{C}_*$ or forced ADV to give up. It suffices to show that the expected number of moves needed for A to win against ADV is larger than $q^*/2$.

Note that the behaviour of ADV_* does not depend on the first move of ADV. We may therefore alternatively run the complete simulation of ADV_* in a first stage, pick the target concept $C_* \in \mathcal{V}$ uniformly at random in a second stage, and undo the final illegal rounds with $\mathcal{C}_*$ not belonging to the version space in a third stage. Let q be the number of rounds in stage 1, and let $\mathcal{V}_i$ be the version space after i rounds. Since the halving game stops as soon as the initial version space $\mathcal{V}_*$ is halved, $\mathcal{V}_{q-1}$ still contains more than half of the concepts in $\mathcal{V}$. Thus, with a probability exceeding $1/2$, the target concept $\mathcal{C}_*$ is taken from $\mathcal{V}_{q-1}$. In this case, the learning algorithm A cannot win in fewer than q rounds. It follows that the expected number of rounds until the learner wins is larger than $q^*/2$.

We proceed with the proof of inequality (9). Deterministic query learning is correctly modelled by the contraction game. Since the contraction of an initial version space $\mathcal{V}_*$ cannot be easier than halving $\mathcal{V}_*$, we get $\mathrm{DLC}^Q(\mathcal{C},\mathcal{H}) \geq \mathrm{HC}_*^Q(\mathcal{C},\mathcal{H})$. Clearly, $\mathrm{DLC}^Q(\mathcal{C},\mathcal{H}) \geq \mathrm{RLC}^Q(\mathcal{C},\mathcal{H})$. Thus, inequality (9) is valid.

We move on to inequality (10). Contraction of the initial version space $\mathcal{C}$ is obtained after $\lfloor \log |\mathcal{C}| \rfloor$ halvings. A learning algorithm A may therefore proceed in $\lfloor \log |\mathcal{C}| \rfloor$ phases and apply, in each phase with current version space $\mathcal{V}$, the optimal deterministic halving strategy w.r.t. initial version space $\mathcal{V}$. In each phase, at most $\mathrm{HC}_*^{\mathcal{Q}}(\mathcal{C},\mathcal{H})$ queries are issued.

Since inequality (8) is trivial, we are done.

5 Bounds on the Halving Complexity

For $\mathcal{Q} = \{\mathrm{EQ},\mathrm{MQ}\}$ or $\mathcal{Q} = \{\mathrm{EQ}\}$, the halving complexity can be characterized by combinatorial parameters that we call "halving dimension" and "strong halving dimension".[6] These parameters are closely related to the "consistency dimension" and "strong consistency dimension" that were used in [2] for describing lower and upper bounds on the deterministic learning complexity. The bounds in [2] left a gap of size $\theta(\log |\mathcal{C}|)$. The bounds that we derive in the course of this section are (almost) tight.

Definition 1. *1. The parameter $Hdim(\mathcal{V},\mathcal{H})$ denotes the smallest number d with the following property. If a function $S : X \to \{0,1\}$ (sample with full support) does not belong to $\mathcal{H}$, then there exists a subsample $S' \sqsubseteq S$ of size at most d such that the fraction of concepts in $\mathcal{V}$ that are consistent with S' is at most $1/2$. The* halving dimension *associated with $\mathcal{C}$ and $\mathcal{H}$ is given by*

$$Hdim_*(\mathcal{C},\mathcal{H}) \triangleq \max\{Hdim(\mathcal{V},\mathcal{H}) : \mathcal{V} \subseteq \mathcal{C}\}. \tag{11}$$

2. The parameter $SHdim(\mathcal{V},\mathcal{H})$ denotes the smallest number d with the following property. If a sample $S : X \to \{0,1,?\}$ has no consistent explanation in $\mathcal{H}$, then there exists a a subsample $S' \sqsubseteq S$ of size at most d such that the fraction of concepts in $\mathcal{V}$ that are consistent with S' is at most $1/2$. The strong halving dimension *associated with $\mathcal{C},\mathcal{H},\mathcal{Q}$ is given by*

$$SHdim_*(\mathcal{C},\mathcal{H}) \triangleq \max\{SHdim(\mathcal{V},\mathcal{H}) : \mathcal{V} \subseteq \mathcal{C}\}. \tag{12}$$

Note that both definitions are almost identical, except for the subtle fact that the first definition ranges over samples with full support, whereas the second definition ranges over all samples. The next theorems show that the halving dimension characterizes the halving complexity when $\mathcal{Q} = \{\mathrm{EQ},\mathrm{MQ}\}$, and the strong halving dimension characterizes the halving complexity when $\mathcal{Q} = \{\mathrm{EQ}\}$.

Theorem 2. *$HC^{EQ,MQ}(\mathcal{V},\mathcal{H}) = Hdim(\mathcal{V},\mathcal{H})$.*

Proof. For sake of simplicity, set $q \triangleq \mathrm{HC}^{EQ,MQ}(\mathcal{V},\mathcal{H})$ and $d \triangleq \mathrm{Hdim}(\mathcal{V},\mathcal{H})$.

First, we show that $q \geq d$. The minimality of d implies that there exists a function $C : X \to \{0,1\} \notin \mathcal{H}$ such that each subsample $S \sqsubseteq C$ of size at most $d-1$ is consistent with more than half of the concepts in $\mathcal{V}$. Thus, any

[6] Note that the case $\mathcal{Q} = \{\mathrm{EQ},\mathrm{MQ}\}$ and $\mathcal{H} = \emptyset$ covers also the case $\mathcal{Q} = \{\mathrm{MQ}\}$.

halving algorithm issuing equivalence queries with hypotheses from $\mathcal{H}$ fails to be consistent with C and may obtain counterexamples taken from C. If, in addition, each membership query is answered in accordance with C, then the sample points, returned after up to $d-1$ queries, form a subsample $S \sqsubseteq C$ of size at most $d-1$. Hence, at least one additional query is needed for halving the initial version space $\mathcal{V}$.

Second, we show that $q \le d$. Let $M : X \to \{0,1\}$ be a function that goes with the majority of the concepts in $\mathcal{V}$ on each instance $x \in X$ (breaking ties arbitrarily). If $M \in \mathcal{H}$, then $q = 1$ because the equivalence query with hypothesis M will halve the version space $\mathcal{V}$. Clearly, $d \ge 1$. We may therefore assume wlog. that $M \notin \mathcal{H}$. It follows that there exists a subsample $S \sqsubseteq M$ of size at most d that is inconsistent to at least half of the concepts in $\mathcal{V}$. The crucial observation is that $q \le |S| \le d$ since $\mathcal{V}$ can be halved by issuing the $|S|$ membership queries for all instances in S: The adversary either fails to go with the majority of the concepts in $\mathcal{V}$ on some $x \in S$ (which immediately halves $\mathcal{V}$) or goes with the majority on all $x \in S$. In the latter case, $\mathcal{V}$ is halved after all $|S|$ membership queries have been issued.

Corollary 1. $HC_*^{EQ,MQ}(\mathcal{C},\mathcal{H}) = Hdim_*(\mathcal{C},\mathcal{H})$.

Theorem 3. $SHdim(\mathcal{V},\mathcal{H}) \le HC^{EQ}(\mathcal{V},\mathcal{H}) \le \lceil \ln(4) \cdot SHdim(\mathcal{V},\mathcal{H}) \rceil$.

Proof. For sake of simplicity, set $q \triangleq \mathrm{HC}^{EQ}(\mathcal{V},\mathcal{H})$ and $d \triangleq \mathrm{SHdim}(\mathcal{V},\mathcal{H})$.

First, we show that $q \ge d$. The minimality of d implies that there exists a sample $C : X \to \{0,1,?\}$ without consistent explanation in $\mathcal{H}$ such that each subsample $S \sqsubseteq C$ of size at most $d-1$ is consistent with more than half of the concepts in $\mathcal{V}$. Thus, any halving algorithm issuing equivalence queries with hypotheses from $\mathcal{H}$ fails to be consistent with C and may obtain counterexamples taken from C. After up to $d-1$ queries, these counterexamples form a subsample $S \sqsubseteq C$ of size at most $d-1$. Hence, at least one additional query is needed for halving the initial version space $\mathcal{V}$.

In order to prove $q \le \lceil \ln(4) \cdot d \rceil$, we describe an appropriate halving algorithm A. A keeps track of the current version space $\mathcal{W}$ (which is $\mathcal{V}$ initially). For $i = 0,1$, let $M_{\mathcal{W}}^i$ be the set

$$\left\{ x \in X : \text{the fraction of concepts } C \in \mathcal{W} \text{ with } C(x) = 1 - i \text{ is less than} \frac{1}{2d} \right\}.$$

In other words, a very large fraction (at least $1-1/(2d)$) of the concepts in $\mathcal{V}$ votes for output label i on instances from $M_{\mathcal{W}}^i$. Let $M_{\mathcal{W}}$ be the sample assigning label $i \in \{0,1\}$ to all instances from $M_{\mathcal{W}}^i$ and label "?" to all remaining instances (those without a so clear majority). Let $S \sqsubseteq M_{\mathcal{W}}$ be an arbitrary but fixed subsample of size at most d. The definition of $M_{\mathcal{W}}^i$ implies (through some easy-to-check counting) that more than half of the concepts in $\mathcal{W}$ are consistent with S. The definition of the strong halving dimension implies that $M_{\mathcal{W}}$ has a consistent explanation, say $H_{\mathcal{W}}$, in $\mathcal{H}$.

The punchline of this discussion is: if A issues the the equivalence query with hypothesis $H_{\mathcal{W}}$ (for the current version space $\mathcal{W}$), then the next counterexample will shrink $\mathcal{W}$ by a factor $1 - 1/(2d)$ (or by a smaller factor). For the purpose of halving the initial version space $\mathcal{V}$, a sufficiently large number of equivalence queries is therefore obtained by solving

$$\left(1 - \frac{1}{2d}\right)^{q'} \cdot |\mathcal{V}| < e^{-q'/(2d)} \cdot |\mathcal{V}| \leq \frac{1}{2} \cdot |\mathcal{V}|$$

for q'. Clearly, $q = \lceil \ln(4) \cdot d \rceil$ is sufficiently large.

Corollary 2. *$SHdim_*(\mathcal{C}, \mathcal{H}) \leq HC_*^{EQ}(\mathcal{C}, \mathcal{H}) \leq \lceil \ln(4) \cdot SHdim_*(\mathcal{C}, \mathcal{H}) \rceil$.*

6 An Application of the Halving Dimension

In this section, we show that the number equivalence queries needed to halve a given version space $\mathcal{V}$ (roughly) equals the total number of equivalence and membership queries needed to halve $\mathcal{V}$ on the "hardest subdomain" K of X. Loosely speaking, there is always a subdomain K of X that leaves the problem of halving $\mathcal{V}$ by means of equivalence queries as as hard as before, but which renders membership queries useless. A similar result was shown in [2] for contraction (deterministic exact learning). However, this result left a gap of size $\theta(\log |\mathcal{C}|)$. The result proven here leaves only a (small) constant gap.

Let $K \subseteq X$. For each function $F : X \rightarrow \{0, 1\}$, let F_K denote the restriction of F to subdomain K. For each class $\mathcal{F}$ of functions from X to $\{0, 1\}$, we define $\mathcal{F}_K \triangleq \{F_K : F \in \mathcal{F}\}$. Then the following holds:

Lemma 3. *$SHdim(\mathcal{V}, \mathcal{H}) = \max_{K \subseteq X} Hdim(\mathcal{V}_K, \mathcal{H}_K)$.*

Proof. Set $d \triangleq \mathrm{SHdim}(\mathcal{V}, \mathcal{H})$. Remember that d is the smallest number such that for all samples $S : X \rightarrow \{0, 1, ?\}$ the condition described in the second part of Definition 1 is satisfied. Let d_K be the corresponding number when we restrict ourselves to samples S with support K. It is evident that $d = \max_{K \subseteq X} d_K$ and $d_K = \mathrm{Hdim}(\mathcal{V}_K, \mathcal{H}_K)$, which completes the proof of the lemma.

Combining Lemma 3, Corollary 1 and Corollary 2, we get

Corollary 3.

$$\max_{K \subseteq X} HC^{EQ,MQ}(\mathcal{V}_K, \mathcal{H}_K) \leq HC^{EQ}(\mathcal{V}, \mathcal{H}) \leq \ln(4) \cdot \max_{K \subseteq X} HC^{EQ,MQ}(\mathcal{V}_K, \mathcal{H}_K).$$

Among the obvious open problems are the following-ones:

- The relation between halving and learning complexity that is proven in this paper leaves a gap. Can this gap be removed (at least for some concrete popular classes)?
- Can the (strong) halving dimension be determined for some popular concept and hypothesis classes?

References

1. Dana Angluin. Queries and concept learning. *Machine Learning*, 2(4):319–342, 1988.
2. José L. Balcázar, Jorge Castro, David Guijarro, and Hans U. Simon. The consistency dimension and distribution-dependent learning from queries. In *Proceedings of the 10th International Workshop on Algorithmic Learning Theory*, pages 77–92. Springer Verlag, 1999.
3. Tibor Hegedüs. Generalized teaching dimensions and the query complexity of learning. In *Proceedings of the 8th Annual Workshop on Computational Learning Theory*, pages 108–117. ACM Press, 1995.
4. Lisa Hellerstein, Krishnan Pillaipakkamnatt, Vijay Raghavan, and Dawn Wilkins. How many queries are needed to learn? *Journal of the Association on Computing Machinery*, 43(5):840–862, 1996.
5. Wolfgang Maass. On-line with an oblivious environment and the power of randomization. In *Proceedings of the 4th Annual Workshop on Computational Learning Theory*, pages 167–175, 1991.

Radial Basis Function Neural Networks Have Superlinear VC Dimension*

Michael Schmitt

Lehrstuhl Mathematik und Informatik, Fakultät für Mathematik
Ruhr-Universität Bochum, D–44780 Bochum, Germany
http://www.ruhr-uni-bochum.de/lmi/mschmitt/
mschmitt@lmi.ruhr-uni-bochum.de

Abstract. We establish superlinear lower bounds on the Vapnik-Chervonenkis (VC) dimension of neural networks with one hidden layer and local receptive field neurons. As the main result we show that every reasonably sized standard network of radial basis function (RBF) neurons has VC dimension $\Omega(W \log k)$, where W is the number of parameters and k the number of nodes. This significantly improves the previously known linear bound. We also derive superlinear lower bounds for networks of discrete and continuous variants of center-surround neurons. The constants in all bounds are larger than those obtained thus far for sigmoidal neural networks with constant depth.

The results have several implications with regard to the computational power and learning capabilities of neural networks with local receptive fields. In particular, they imply that the pseudo dimension and the fat-shattering dimension of these networks is superlinear as well, and they yield lower bounds even when the input dimension is fixed. The methods developed here appear suitable for obtaining similar results for other kernel-based function classes.

1 Introduction

Although there exists already a large collection of Vapnik-Chervonenkis (VC) dimension bounds for neural networks, it has not been known thus far whether the VC dimension of radial basis function (RBF) neural networks is superlinear. Major reasons for this might be that previous results establishing superlinear bounds are based on methods geared to sigmoidal neurons or consider networks having an unrestricted number of layers [3,10,13,22]. RBF neural networks, however, differ from other neural network types in two characteristic features (see, e.g., Bishop [4], Ripley [21]): There is only one hidden layer and the neurons have local receptive fields. In particular, the neurons are not of the sigmoidal type (see Koiran and Sontag [10] for a rather general definition of a sigmoidal activation function that does not capture radial basis functions).

* This work has been supported in part by the ESPRIT Working Group in Neural and Computational Learning II, NeuroCOLT2, No. 27150.

D. Helmbold and B. Williamson (Eds.): COLT/EuroCOLT 2001, LNAI 2111, pp. 14–30, 2001.

Beside sigmoidal networks, RBF networks are among the major neural network types used in practice. They are appreciated because of their impressive capabilities in function approximation and learning that have been well studied in theory and practice (see, e.g., [5,9,15,16,18,19,20]). Sigmoidal neural networks are known having VC dimension that is superlinear in the number of network parameters, even when there is only one hidden layer [22]. Since the VC dimension of single neurons is linear, this superlinearity witnesses the enormous computational capabilities that emerge when neurons cooperate in networks. The VC dimension of RBF networks has been studied earlier by Anthony and Holden [2], Lee et al. [11,12], and Erlich et al. [7]. In particular, Erlich et al. [7] established a linear lower bound, and Anthony and Holden [2] posed as an open problem whether a superlinear bound can be shown.

In this paper we prove that the VC dimension of RBF networks is indeed superlinear. Precisely, we show that every network with n input nodes, W parameters, and one hidden layer of k RBF neurons, where $k \leq 2^{(n+2)/2}$, has VC dimension at least $(W/12)\log(k/8)$. Thus, the cooperative network effect enhancing the computational power of sigmoidal networks is now confirmed for RBF networks, too. Furthermore, the result has consequences for the complexity of learning with RBF networks, all the more since it entails the same lower bound for the pseudo dimension and the fat-shattering dimension. (See Anthony and Bartlett [1] for implications of VC dimension bounds, and the relationship between the VC dimension, the pseudo dimension, and the fat-shattering dimension.)

We do not derive the result for RBF networks directly but take a major detour. We first consider networks consisting of a different type of locally processing units, the so-called binary center-surround receptive field (CSRF) neurons. These are discrete models of neurons found in the visual system of mammals (see, e.g., Nicholls et al. [17, Chapter 16], Tessier-Lavigne [23]). In Section 3 we establish a superlinear VC dimension bound for CSRF neural networks showing that every network having W parameters and k hidden nodes has VC dimension at least $(W/5)\log(k/4)$, where $k \leq 2^{n/2}$. Then in Section 4 we look at a continuous variant of the CSRF neuron known as the difference-of-Gaussians (DOG) neuron, which computes the weighted difference of two concentric Gaussians. This type of unit is widely used as a continuous model of neurons in the visual pathway (see, e.g., Glezer [8], Marr [14]). Utilizing the result for CSRF networks we show that DOG networks have VC dimension at least $(W/5)\log(k/4)$ as well. Finally, the above claimed lower bound for RBF networks is then immediately obtained.

We note that regarding the constants, the bounds for CSRF and DOG networks are larger than for RBF networks. Further, all bounds we derive for networks of local receptive field neurons have larger constant factors than those known for sigmoidal networks of constant depth thus far. For comparison, sigmoidal networks are known that have one hidden layer and VC dimension at least $(W/32)\log(k/4)$; for two hidden layers a VC dimension of at least $(W/132)\log(k/16)$ has been found (see Anthony and Bartlett [1, Section 6.3]).

Finally, the results obtained here give rise to linear lower bounds for local receptive field neural networks when the input dimension is fixed.

2 Definitions and Notation

Let $||u||$ denote the Euclidean norm of vector u. A *Gaussian radial basis function (RBF) neuron* computes a function $g_{\mathrm{RBF}} : \mathbb{R}^{2n+1} \to \mathbb{R}$ defined as

$$g_{\mathrm{RBF}}(c, \sigma, x) = \exp\left(-\frac{\|x - c\|^2}{\sigma^2}\right) ,$$

with input variables $x_1, \ldots, x_n$, and parameters $c_1, \ldots, c_n$ (the *center*) and $\sigma > 0$ (the *width*). A *difference-of-Gaussians (DOG) neuron* is defined as a function $g_{\mathrm{DOG}} : \mathbb{R}^{2n+4} \to \mathbb{R}$ computed by the weighted difference of two RBF neurons with equal centers, that is,

$$g_{\mathrm{DOG}}(c, \sigma, \tau, \alpha, \beta, x) = \alpha g_{\mathrm{RBF}}(c, \sigma, x) - \beta g_{\mathrm{RBF}}(c, \tau, x) .$$

A *binary center-surround receptive field (CSRF) neuron* computes a function $g_{\mathrm{CSRF}} : \mathbb{R}^{2n+2} \to \{0, 1\}$ defined as

$$g_{\mathrm{CSRF}}(c, a, b, x) = 1 \Longleftrightarrow a \leq \|x - c\| \leq b$$

with *center* $(c_1, \ldots, c_n)$, *center radius* $a > 0$, and *surround radius* $b > a$. We also refer to it as *off-center on-surround neuron* and call for given parameters c, a, b the set $\{x : g_{\mathrm{CSRF}}(c, a, b, x) = 1\}$ the *surround region* of the neuron.

We consider *neural networks with one hidden layer* computing functions of the form $f : \mathbb{R}^{W+n} \to \mathbb{R}$, where W is the number of network parameters, n the number of input nodes, and

$$f(w, y, x) = w_0 + w_1 h_1(y, x) + \cdots + w_k h_k(y, x) .$$

The k hidden nodes compute functions $h_1, \ldots, h_k \in \{g_{\mathrm{RBF}}, g_{\mathrm{DOG}}, g_{\mathrm{CSRF}}\}$. (Each hidden node "selects" its parameters from y, which comprises all parameters of the hidden nodes.) Note that if $h_i = g_{\mathrm{RBF}}$ for $i = 1, \ldots, k$, this is the standard form of a radial basis function neural network. The network has a linear output node with parameters $w_0, \ldots, w_k$ also known as the *output weights*. For simplicity we sometimes refer to all network parameters as weights.

An $(n-1)$-dimensional *hyperplane* in $\mathbb{R}^n$ is given by a vector $(w_0, \ldots, w_n) \in \mathbb{R}^{n+1}$ and defined as the set

$$\{x \in \mathbb{R}^n : w_0 + w_1 x_1 + \cdots + w_n x_n = 0\} .$$

An $(n-1)$-dimensional *hypersphere* in $\mathbb{R}^n$ is represented by a center $c \in \mathbb{R}^n$ and a radius $r > 0$, and defined as the set

$$\{x \in \mathbb{R}^n : \|x - c\| = r\} .$$

We also consider hyperplanes and hyperspheres in $\mathbb{R}^n$ with a dimension $k < n-1$. In this case, a k-dimensional hyperplane (hypersphere) is the intersection of two $(k+1)$-dimensional hyperplanes (hyperspheres), assuming that the intersection is non-empty. (For hyperspheres we additionally require that the intersection is not a single point.)

A *dichotomy* of a set $S \subseteq \mathbb{R}^n$ is a pair (S_0, S_1) of subsets such that $S_0 \cap S_1 = \emptyset$ and $S_0 \cup S_1 = S$. A class $\mathcal{F}$ of functions mapping $\mathbb{R}^n$ to $\{0,1\}$ *shatters* S if every dichotomy (S_0, S_1) of S is *induced* by some $f \in \mathcal{F}$ (i.e., satisfying $f(S_0) \subseteq \{0\}$ and $f(S_1) \subseteq \{1\}$). The *Vapnik-Chervonenkis (VC) dimension* of $\mathcal{F}$ is the cardinality of the largest set shattered by $\mathcal{F}$. The VC dimension of a neural network $\mathcal{N}$ is defined as the VC dimension of the class of functions computed by $\mathcal{N}$, where the output is made binary using some threshold.

We use "ln" to denote the natural logarithm and "log" for the logarithm to base 2.

3 Lower Bounds for CSRF Networks

In this section we consider one-hidden-layer networks of binary center-surround receptive field neurons. The main result requires a property of certain finite sets of points.

Definition. *A set S of m points in $\mathbb{R}^n$ is said to be* in spherically general position *if the following two conditions are satisfied:*

(1) For every $k \leq \min(n, m-1)$ and every $(k+1)$-element subset $P \subseteq S$, there is no $(k-1)$-dimensional hyperplane containing all points in P.
(2) For every $l \leq \min(n, m-2)$ and every $(l+2)$-element subset $Q \subseteq S$, there is no $(l-1)$-dimensional hypersphere containing all points in Q.

Sets satisfying condition (1) are commonly referred to as being "in general position" (see, e.g., Cover [6]). For the VC dimension bounds we require sufficiently large sets in spherically general position. It is not hard to show that such sets exist.

Proposition 1. *For every $n, m \geq 1$ there exists a set $S \subseteq \mathbb{R}^n$ of m points in spherically general position.*

Proof. We perform induction on m. Clearly, every single point trivially satisfies conditions (1) and (2). Assume that some set $S \subseteq \mathbb{R}^n$ of cardinality m has been constructed. Then by the induction hypothesis, for every $k \leq \min(n, m)$, every k-element subset $P \subseteq S$ does not lie on a hyperplane of dimension less than $k-1$. Hence, every $P \subseteq S$, $|P| = k \leq \min(n, m)$, uniquely specifies a $(k-1)$-dimensional hyperplane H_P that includes P. The induction hypothesis implies further that no point in $S \setminus P$ lies on H_P. Analogously, for every $l \leq \min(n, m-1)$, every $(l+1)$-element subset $Q \subseteq S$ does not lie on a hypersphere of dimension less than $l-1$. Thus, every $Q \subseteq S$, $|Q| = l+1 \leq \min(n, m-1)+1$, uniquely determines an $(l-1)$-dimensional hypersphere B_Q containing all points in Q and none of the points in $S \setminus Q$.

To obtain a set of cardinality $m+1$ in spherically general position we observe that the union of all hyperplanes and hyperspheres considered above, that is, the union of all H_P and all B_Q for all subsets P and Q, has Lebesgue measure 0. Hence, there is some point $s \in \mathbb{R}^n$ not contained in any hyperplane H_P and not contained in any hypersphere B_Q. By adding s to S we then obtain a set of cardinality $m+1$ in spherically general position. □

The following theorem establishes the major step for the superlinear lower bound.

Theorem 2. *Let $h, q, m \geq 1$ be arbitrary natural numbers. Suppose $\mathcal{N}$ is a network with one hidden layer consisting of binary CSRF neurons, where the number of hidden nodes is $h+2^q$ and the number of input nodes is $m+q$. Assume further that the output node is linear. Then there exists a set of cardinality $hq(m+1)$ shattered by $\mathcal{N}$. This even holds if the output weights of $\mathcal{N}$ are fixed to* 1.

Proof. Before starting with the details we give a brief outline. The main idea is to imagine the set we want to shatter as being composed of groups of vectors, where the groups are distinguished by means of the first m components and the remaining q components identify the group members. We catch these groups by hyperspheres such that each hypersphere is responsible for up to $m+1$ groups. The condition of spherically general position will ensure that this works. The hyperspheres are then expanded to become surround regions of CSRF neurons. To induce a dichotomy of the given set, we split the groups. We do this for each group using the q last components in such a way that the points with designated output 1 stay within the surround region of the respective neuron and the points with designated output 0 are expelled from it. In order for this to succeed, we have to make sure that the displaced points do not fall into the surround region of some other neuron. The verification of the split operation will constitute the major part of the proof.

By means of Proposition 1 let $\{s_1, \ldots, s_{h(m+1)}\} \subseteq \mathbb{R}^m$ be in spherically general position. Let $e_1, \ldots, e_q$ denote the unit vectors in $\mathbb{R}^q$, that is, with a 1 in exactly one component and 0 elsewhere. We define the set S by

$$S = \{s_i : i = 1, \ldots, h(m+1)\} \times \{e_j : j = 1, \ldots, q\} .$$

Clearly, S is a subset of $\mathbb{R}^{m+q}$ and has cardinality $hq(m+1)$. To show that S is shattered by $\mathcal{N}$, let (S_0, S_1) be some arbitrary dichotomy of S. Consider an enumeration $M_1, \ldots, M_{2^q}$ of all subsets of the set $\{1, \ldots, q\}$. Let the function $f : \{1, \ldots, h(m+1)\} \to \{1, \ldots, 2^q\}$ be defined by

$$M_{f(i)} = \{j : s_i e_j \in S_1\} ,$$

where $s_i e_j$ denotes the vector resulting from the concatenation of s_i and e_j. We use f to define a partition of $\{s_1, \ldots, s_{h(m+1)}\}$ into sets T_k for $k = 1, \ldots, 2^q$ by

$$T_k = \{s_i : f(i) = k\} .$$

We further partition each set T_k into subsets $T_{k,p}$ for $p = 1, \dots, \lceil |T_k|/(m+1) \rceil$, where each subset $T_{k,p}$ has cardinality $m+1$, except if $m+1$ does not divide $|T_k|$, in which case there is exactly one subset of cardinality less than $m+1$. Since there are at most $h(m+1)$ elements s_i, the partitioning of all T_k results in no more than h subsets of cardinality $m+1$. Further, the fact $k \leq 2^q$ permits at most 2^q subsets of cardinality less than $m+1$. Thus, there are no more than $h + 2^q$ subsets $T_{k,p}$.

We employ one hidden node $H_{k,p}$ for each subset $T_{k,p}$. Thus the $h+2^q$ hidden nodes of $\mathcal{N}$ suffice. Since $\{s_1, \dots, s_{h(m+1)}\}$ is in spherically general position, there exists for each $T_{k,p}$ an $(m-1)$-dimensional hypersphere containing all points in $T_{k,p}$ and no other point. If $|T_{k,p}| = m+1$, this hypersphere is unique; if $|T_{k,p}| < m+1$, there is a unique $(|T_{k,p}|-2)$-dimensional hypersphere which can be extended to an $(m-1)$-dimensional hypersphere that does not contain any further point. (Here we require condition (1) from the definition of spherically general position, otherwise no hypersphere of dimension $|T_{k,p}| - 2$ including all points of $T_{k,p}$ might exist.) Clearly, if $|T_{k,p}| = 1$, we can also extend this single point to an $(m-1)$-dimensional hypersphere not including any further point.

Suppose that $(c_{k,p}, r_{k,p})$ with center $c_{k,p}$ and radius $r_{k,p}$ represents the hypersphere associated with subset $T_{k,p}$. It is obvious from the construction above that all radii satisfy $r_{k,p} > 0$. Further, since the subsets $T_{k,p}$ are pairwise disjoint, there is some $\varepsilon > 0$ such that every point $s_i \in \{s_1, \dots, s_{h(m+1)}\}$ and every just defined hypersphere $(c_{k,p}, r_{k,p})$ satisfy

$$\text{if } s_i \notin T_{k,p} \text{ then } \big| \|s_i - c_{k,p}\| - r_{k,p} \big| > \varepsilon \ . \tag{1}$$

In other words, ε is smaller than the distance between any s_i and any hypersphere $(c_{k,p}, r_{k,p})$ that does not contain s_i. Without loss of generality we assume that ε is sufficiently small such that

$$\varepsilon \leq \min_{k,p} r_{k,p} \ . \tag{2}$$

The parameters of the hidden nodes are adjusted as follows: We define the center $\widehat{c}_{k,p} = (\widehat{c}_{k,p,1}, \dots, \widehat{c}_{k,p,m+q})$ of hidden node $H_{k,p}$ by assigning the vector $c_{k,p}$ to the first m components and specifying the remaining ones by

$$\widehat{c}_{k,p,m+j} = \begin{cases} 0 & \text{if} j \in M_k \ , \\ -\varepsilon^2/4 & \text{otherwise} \ , \end{cases}$$

for $j = 1, \dots, q$. We further define new radii $\widehat{r}_{k,p}$ by

$$\widehat{r}_{k,p} = \sqrt{r_{k,p}^2 + (q - |M_k|)\left(\frac{\varepsilon}{2}\right)^4 + 1}$$

and choose some $\gamma > 0$ satisfying

$$\gamma \leq \min_{k,p} \frac{\varepsilon^2}{8\widehat{r}_{k,p}} \ . \tag{3}$$

The center and surround radii $\widehat{a}_{k,p}, \widehat{b}_{k,p}$ of the hidden nodes are then specified as

$$\widehat{a}_{k,p} = \widehat{r}_{k,p} - \gamma \ ,$$
$$\widehat{b}_{k,p} = \widehat{r}_{k,p} + \gamma \ .$$

Note that $\widehat{a}_{k,p} > 0$ holds, because $\varepsilon^2 < \widehat{r}^2_{k,p}$ implies $\gamma < \widehat{r}_{k,p}$.

This completes the assignment of parameters to the hidden nodes $H_{k,p}$. We now derive two inequalities concerning the relationship between ε and γ that we need in the following. First, we estimate $\varepsilon^2/2$ from below by

$$\begin{aligned} \frac{\varepsilon^2}{2} &> \frac{\varepsilon^2}{4} + \frac{\varepsilon^2}{64} \\ &> \frac{\varepsilon^2}{4} + \frac{\varepsilon^4}{(8\widehat{r}_{k,p})^2} \quad \text{for all } k,p \ , \end{aligned}$$

where the last inequality is obtained from $\varepsilon^2 < \widehat{r}^2_{k,p}$. Using (3) for both terms on the right-hand side, we get

$$\frac{\varepsilon^2}{2} > 2\widehat{r}_{k,p}\gamma + \gamma^2 \quad \text{for all } k,p \ . \tag{4}$$

Second, from (2) we get

$$-r_{k,p}\varepsilon + \frac{\varepsilon^2}{2} < -\frac{\varepsilon^2}{4} \quad \text{for all } k,p \ ,$$

and (3) yields

$$-\frac{\varepsilon^2}{4} < -2\widehat{r}_{k,p}\gamma \quad \text{for all } k,p \ .$$

Putting the last two inequalities together and adding γ^2 to the right-hand side, we obtain

$$-r_{k,p}\varepsilon + \frac{\varepsilon^2}{2} < -2\widehat{r}_{k,p}\gamma + \gamma^2 \quad \text{for all } k,p \ . \tag{5}$$

We next establish three facts about the hidden nodes.

Claim 1. *Let $s_i e_j$ be some point and $T_{k,p}$ some subset where $s_i \in T_{k,p}$ and $j \in M_k$. Then hidden node $H_{k,p}$ outputs 1 on $s_i e_j$.*

According to the definition of $\widehat{c}_{k,p}$, if $j \in M_k$, we have

$$\|s_i e_j - \widehat{c}_{k,p}\|^2 = \|s_i - c_{k,p}\|^2 + (q - |M_k|)\left(\frac{\varepsilon}{2}\right)^4 + 1 \ .$$

The condition $s_i \in T_{k,p}$ implies $\|s_i - c_{k,p}\|^2 = r^2_{k,p}$, and thus

$$\begin{aligned} \|s_i e_j - \widehat{c}_{k,p}\|^2 &= r^2_{k,p} + (q - |M_k|)\left(\frac{\varepsilon}{2}\right)^4 + 1 \\ &= \widehat{r}^2_{k,p} \ . \end{aligned}$$

It follows that $\|s_i e_j - \widehat{c}_{k,p}\| = \widehat{r}_{k,p}$, and since $\widehat{a}_{k,p} < \widehat{r}_{k,p} < \widehat{b}_{k,p}$, point $s_i e_j$ lies within the surround region of node $H_{k,p}$. Hence, Claim 1 is shown.

Claim 2. *Let $s_i e_j$ and $T_{k,p}$ satisfy $s_i \in T_{k,p}$ and $j \notin M_k$. Then hidden node $H_{k,p}$ outputs 0 on $s_i e_j$.*

From the assumptions we get here

$$\begin{aligned}\|s_i e_j - \widehat{c}_{k,p}\|^2 &= \|s_i - c_{k,p}\|^2 + (q - |M_k| - 1)\left(\frac{\varepsilon}{2}\right)^4 + \left(1 + \frac{\varepsilon^2}{4}\right)^2 \\ &= r_{k,p}^2 + (q - |M_k|)\left(\frac{\varepsilon}{2}\right)^4 + 1 + \frac{\varepsilon^2}{2} \\ &= \widehat{r}_{k,p}^2 + \frac{\varepsilon^2}{2} \ .\end{aligned}$$

Employing (4) on the right-hand side results in

$$\|s_i e_j - \widehat{c}_{k,p}\|^2 > \widehat{r}_{k,p}^2 + 2\widehat{r}_{k,p}\gamma + \gamma^2 \ .$$

Hence, taking square roots we have $\|s_i e_j - \widehat{c}_{k,p}\| > \widehat{r}_{k,p} + \gamma$, implying that $s_i e_j$ lies outside the surround region of $H_{k,p}$. Thus, Claim 2 follows.

Claim 3. *Let $s_i e_j$ be some point and $T_{k,p}$ some subset such that $s_i \in T_{k,p}$. Then every hidden node $H_{k',p'}$ with $(k',p') \neq (k,p)$ outputs 0 on $s_i e_j$.*

Since $s_i \in T_{k,p}$ and s_i is not contained in any other subset $T_{k',p'}$, condition (1) implies

$$\|s_i - c_{k',p'}\|^2 > (r_{k',p'} + \varepsilon)^2 \ \text{ or } \|s_i - c_{k',p'}\|^2 < (r_{k',p'} - \varepsilon)^2 \ . \tag{6}$$

We distinguish between two cases: whether $j \in M_{k'}$ or not.

Case 1. If $j \in M_{k'}$ then by the definition of $\widehat{c}_{k',p'}$ we have

$$\|s_i e_j - \widehat{c}_{k',p'}\|^2 = \|s_i - c_{k',p'}\|^2 + (q - |M_{k'}|)\left(\frac{\varepsilon}{2}\right)^4 + 1 \ .$$

From this, using (6) and the definition of $\widehat{r}_{k',p'}$ we obtain

$$\begin{gathered}\|s_i e_j - \widehat{c}_{k',p'}\|^2 > \widehat{r}_{k',p'}^2 + 2r_{k',p'}\varepsilon + \varepsilon^2 \\ \text{or} \\ \|s_i e_j - \widehat{c}_{k',p'}\|^2 < \widehat{r}_{k',p'}^2 - 2r_{k',p'}\varepsilon + \varepsilon^2 \ .\end{gathered} \tag{7}$$

We derive bounds for the right-hand sides of these inequalities as follows. From (4) we have

$$\varepsilon^2 > 4\widehat{r}_{k',p'}\gamma + 2\gamma^2 \ ,$$

which, after adding $2r_{k',p'}\varepsilon$ to the left-hand side and halving the right-hand side, gives

$$2r_{k',p'}\varepsilon + \varepsilon^2 > 2\widehat{r}_{k',p'}\gamma + \gamma^2 \ . \tag{8}$$

From (2) we get $\varepsilon^2/2 < r_{k',p'}\varepsilon$, that is, the left-hand side of (5) is negative. Hence, we may double it to obtain from (5)

$$-2r_{k',p'}\varepsilon + \varepsilon^2 < -2\widehat{r}_{k',p'}\gamma + \gamma^2 \ .$$

Using this and (8) in (7) leads to

$$\|s_i e_j - \widehat{c}_{k',p'}\|^2 > (\widehat{r}_{k',p'} + \gamma)^2 \ \text{ or } \|s_i e_j - \widehat{c}_{k',p'}\|^2 < (\widehat{r}_{k',p'} - \gamma)^2 \ .$$

And this is equivalent to

$$\|s_i e_j - \widehat{c}_{k',p'}\| > \widehat{b}_{k',p'} \ \text{ or } \|s_i e_j - \widehat{c}_{k',p'}\| < \widehat{a}_{k',p'} \ ,$$

meaning that $H_{k',p'}$ outputs 0.

Case 2. If $j \notin M_{k'}$ then

$$\|s_i e_j - \widehat{c}_{k',p'}\|^2 = \|s_i - c_{k',p'}\|^2 + (q - |M_{k'}|)\left(\frac{\varepsilon}{2}\right)^4 + 1 + \frac{\varepsilon^2}{2} \ .$$

As a consequence of this together with (6) and the definition of $\widehat{r}_{k',p'}$ we get

$$\begin{aligned} \|s_i e_j - \widehat{c}_{k',p'}\|^2 &> \widehat{r}^2_{k',p'} + 2r_{k',p'}\varepsilon + \varepsilon^2 + \frac{\varepsilon^2}{2} \\ &\text{or} \\ \|s_i e_j - \widehat{c}_{k',p'}\|^2 &< \widehat{r}^2_{k',p'} - 2r_{k',p'}\varepsilon + \varepsilon^2 + \frac{\varepsilon^2}{2} \ , \end{aligned}$$

from which we derive, using for the second inequality $\varepsilon \le r_{k',p'}$ from (2),

$$\begin{aligned} \|s_i e_j - \widehat{c}_{k',p'}\|^2 &> \widehat{r}^2_{k',p'} + r_{k',p'}\varepsilon + \frac{\varepsilon^2}{2} \\ &\text{or} \\ \|s_i e_j - \widehat{c}_{k',p'}\|^2 &< \widehat{r}^2_{k',p'} - r_{k',p'}\varepsilon + \frac{\varepsilon^2}{2} \ . \end{aligned} \tag{9}$$

Finally, from (4) we have

$$r_{k',p'}\varepsilon + \frac{\varepsilon^2}{2} > 2\widehat{r}_{k',p'} + \gamma^2 \ ,$$

and, employing this together with (5), we obtain from (9)

$$\|s_i e_j - \widehat{c}_{k',p'}\|^2 > (\widehat{r}_{k',p'} + \gamma)^2 \ \text{ or } \|s_i e_j - \widehat{c}_{k',p'}\|^2 < (\widehat{r}_{k',p'} - \gamma)^2 \ ,$$

which holds if and only if

$$\|s_i e_j - \widehat{c}_{k',p'}\| > \widehat{b}_{k',p'} \text{ or } \|s_i e_j - \widehat{c}_{k',p'}\| < \widehat{a}_{k',p'} .$$

This shows that $H_{k',p'}$ outputs 0 also in this case. Thus, Claim 3 is established.

We complete the construction of $\mathcal{N}$ by connecting every hidden node with weight 1 to the output node, which then computes the sum of the hidden node output values.

We finally show that we have indeed obtained a network that induces the dichotomy (S_0, S_1). Assume that $s_i e_j \in S_1$. Claims 1, 2, and 3 imply that there is exactly one hidden node $H_{k,p}$, namely one satisfying $k = f(i)$ by the definition of f, that outputs 1 on $s_i e_j$. Hence, the network outputs 1 as well. On the other hand, if $s_i e_j \in S_0$, it follows from Claims 2 and 3 that none of the hidden nodes outputs 1. Therefore, the network output is 0. Thus, $\mathcal{N}$ shatters S with threshold $1/2$ and the theorem is proven. □

The construction in the previous proof was based on the assumption that the difference between center radius and surround radius, given by the value 2γ, can be made sufficiently small. This may require constraints for the precision of computation that are not available in natural or artificial systems. It is possible, however, to obtain the same result even if there is a lower bound on γ by simply scaling the elements of the shattered set using a sufficiently large factor.

In the following we obtain a superlinear lower bound for the VC dimension of networks with center-surround receptive field neurons. By $\lfloor x \rfloor$ we denote the largest integer less or equal to x.

Corollary 3. *Suppose $\mathcal{N}$ is a network with one hidden layer of k binary CSRF neurons and input dimension $n \geq 2$, where $k \leq 2^n$, and assume that the output node is linear. Then $\mathcal{N}$ has VC dimension at least*

$$\left\lfloor \frac{k}{2} \right\rfloor \cdot \left\lfloor \log\left(\frac{k}{2}\right) \right\rfloor \cdot \left(n - \left\lfloor \log\left(\frac{k}{2}\right) \right\rfloor + 1\right) .$$

This even holds if the weights of the output node are not adjustable.

Proof. We use Theorem 2 with $h = \lfloor k/2 \rfloor$, $q = \lfloor \log(k/2) \rfloor$, and $m = n - \lfloor \log(k/2) \rfloor$. The condition $k \leq 2^n$ guarantees that $m \geq 1$. Then there is a set of cardinality

$$hq(m+1) = \left\lfloor \frac{k}{2} \right\rfloor \cdot \left\lfloor \log\left(\frac{k}{2}\right) \right\rfloor \cdot \left(n - \left\lfloor \log\left(\frac{k}{2}\right) \right\rfloor + 1\right) .$$

that is shattered by the network specified in Theorem 2. Since the number of hidden nodes is $h + 2^q \leq k$ and the input dimension is $m + q = n$, the network satisfies the required conditions. Furthermore, it was shown in the proof of Theorem 2 that all weights of the output node can be fixed to 1. Hence, they need not be adjustable. □

Corollary 3 immediately implies the following statement, which gives a superlinear lower bound in terms of the number of weights and the number of hidden nodes.

Corollary 4. *Consider a network $\mathcal{N}$ with input dimension $n \geq 2$, one hidden layer of k binary CSRF neurons, where $k \leq 2^{n/2}$, and a linear output node. Let $W = k(n+2)+k+1$ denote the number of weights. Then $\mathcal{N}$ has VC dimension at least*

$$\frac{W}{5}\log\left(\frac{k}{4}\right) .$$

This even holds if the weights of the output node are fixed.

Proof. According to Corollary 3, $\mathcal{N}$ has VC dimension at least $\lfloor k/2 \rfloor \cdot \lfloor \log(k/2) \rfloor \cdot (n - \lfloor \log(k/2) \rfloor + 1)$. The condition $k \leq 2^{n/2}$ implies

$$n - \left\lfloor \log\left(\frac{k}{2}\right)\right\rfloor + 1 \geq \frac{n+4}{2} .$$

We may assume that $k \geq 5$. (The statement is trivial for $k \leq 4$.) It follows, using $\lfloor k/2 \rfloor \geq (k-1)/2$ and $k/10 \geq 1/2$, that

$$\left\lfloor \frac{k}{2} \right\rfloor \geq \frac{2k}{5} .$$

Finally, we have

$$\left\lfloor \log\left(\frac{k}{2}\right)\right\rfloor \geq \log\left(\frac{k}{2}\right) - 1 = \log\left(\frac{k}{4}\right) .$$

Hence, $\mathcal{N}$ has VC dimension at least $(n+4)(k/5)\log(k/4)$, which is at least as large as the claimed bound $(W/5)\log(k/4)$. □

In the networks considered thus far the input dimension was assumed to be variable. It is an easy consequence of Theorem 2 that even when n is constant, the VC dimension grows still linearly in terms of the network size.

Corollary 5. *Assume that the input dimension is fixed and consider a network $\mathcal{N}$ with one hidden layer of binary CSRF neurons and a linear output node. Then the VC dimension of $\mathcal{N}$ is $\Omega(k)$ and $\Omega(W)$, where k is the number of hidden nodes and W the number of weights. This even holds in the case of fixed output weights.*

Proof. Choose $m, q \geq 1$ such that $m + q \leq n$, and let $h = k - 2^q$. Since n is constant, $hq(m+1)$ is $\Omega(k)$. Thus, according to Theorem 2, there is a set of cardinality $\Omega(k)$ shattered by $\mathcal{N}$. Since the number of weights is $O(k)$, the bound $\Omega(W)$ also follows. □

4 Lower Bounds for RBF and DOG Networks

In the following we present the lower bounds for networks with one hidden layer of Gaussian radial basis function neurons and difference-of-Gaussians neurons, respectively. We first consider the latter type.

Theorem 6. *Let $h, q, m \geq 1$ be arbitrary natural numbers. Suppose $\mathcal{N}$ is a network with $m+q$ input nodes, one hidden layer of $h + 2^q$ DOG neurons, and a linear output node. Then there is a set of cardinality $hq(m+1)$ shattered by $\mathcal{N}$.*

Proof. We use ideas and results from the proof of Theorem 2. In particular, we show that the set constructed there can be shattered by a network of new model neurons, the so-called extended Gaussian neurons which we introduce below. Then we demonstrate that a network of these extended Gaussian neurons can be simulated by a network of DOG neurons, which establishes the statement of the theorem.

We define an extended Gaussian neuron with n inputs to compute the function $\tilde{g} : \mathbb{R}^{2n+2} \to \mathbb{R}$ with

$$\tilde{g}(c, \sigma, \alpha, x) = 1 - \left(\alpha \exp\left(-\frac{\|x - c\|^2}{\sigma^2}\right) - 1\right)^2 ,$$

where $x_1, \ldots, x_n$ are the input variables, $c_1, \ldots, c_n$, α, and $\sigma > 0$ are real-valued parameters. Thus, the computation of an extended Gaussian neuron is performed by scaling the output of a Gaussian RBF neuron with α, squaring the difference to 1, and comparing this value with 1.

Let $S \subseteq \mathbb{R}^{m+q}$ be the set of cardinality $hq(m+1)$ constructed in the proof of Theorem 2. In particular, S has the form

$$S = \{s_i e_j : i = 1, \ldots, h(m+1); j = 1, \ldots, q\} .$$

We have also defined in that proof binary CSRF neurons $H_{k,p}$ as hidden nodes in terms of parameters $\widehat{c}_{k,p} \in \mathbb{R}^{m+q}$, which became the centers of the neurons, and $\widehat{r}_{k,p} \in \mathbb{R}$, which gave the center radii $\widehat{a}_{k,p} = \widehat{r}_{k,p} - \gamma$ and the surround radii $\widehat{b}_{k,p} = \widehat{r}_{k,p} + \gamma$ using some $\gamma > 0$. The number of hidden nodes was not larger than $h + 2^q$. We replace the CSRF neurons by extended Gaussian neurons $G_{k,p}$ with parameters $c_{k,p}, \sigma_{k,p}, \alpha_{k,p}$ defined as follows. Assume some $\sigma > 0$ that will be specified later. We let

$$\begin{aligned} c_{k,p} &= \widehat{c}_{k,p} , \\ \sigma_{k,p} &= \sigma , \\ \alpha_{k,p} &= \exp\left(\frac{\widehat{r}_{k,p}^2}{\sigma^2}\right) . \end{aligned}$$

These hidden nodes are connected to the output node with all weights being 1. We call this network $\mathcal{N}'$ and claim that it shatters S. Consider some arbitrary dichotomy (S_0, S_1) of S and some $s_i e_j \in S$. Then node $G_{k,p}$ computes

$$\begin{aligned}\tilde{g}(c_{k,p}, \sigma_{k,p}, \alpha_{k,p}, s_i e_j) &= 1 - \left(\alpha_{k,p} \exp\left(-\frac{\|s_i e_j - c_{k,p}\|^2}{\sigma_{k,p}^2}\right) - 1\right)^2 \\ &= 1 - \left(\exp\left(\frac{\widehat{r}_{k,p}^2}{\sigma^2}\right) \cdot \exp\left(-\frac{\|s_i e_j - \widehat{c}_{k,p}\|^2}{\sigma^2}\right) - 1\right)^2 \\ &= 1 - \left(\exp\left(-\frac{\|s_i e_j - \widehat{c}_{k,p}\|^2 - \widehat{r}_{k,p}^2}{\sigma^2}\right) - 1\right)^2 . \qquad (10)\end{aligned}$$

Suppose first that $s_i e_j \in S_1$. It was shown by Claims 1, 2, and 3 in the proof of Theorem 2 that there is exactly one hidden node $H_{k,p}$ that outputs 1 on $s_i e_j$. In particular, the proof of Claim 1 established that this node satisfies

$$\|s_i e_j - \widehat{c}_{k,p}\|^2 = \widehat{r}_{k,p}^2 .$$

Hence, according to (10) node $G_{k,p}$ outputs 1. We note that this holds for all values of σ. Further, the proofs of Claims 2 and 3 yielded that those nodes $H_{k,p}$ that output 0 on $s_i e_j$ satisfy

$$\|s_i e_j - \widehat{c}_{k,p}\|^2 > (\widehat{r}_{k,p} + \gamma)^2 \ \text{ or } \|s_i e_j - \widehat{c}_{k,p}\|^2 < (\widehat{r}_{k,p} - \gamma)^2 .$$

This implies for the computation of $G_{k,p}$ that in (10) we can make the expression

$$\exp\left(-\frac{\|s_i e_j - \widehat{c}_{k,p}\|^2 - \widehat{r}_{k,p}^2}{\sigma^2}\right)$$

as close to 0 as necessary by choosing σ sufficiently small. Since this does not affect the node that outputs 1, network $\mathcal{N}'$ computes a value close to 1 on $s_i e_j$.

On the other hand, for the case $s_i e_j \in S_0$ it was shown in Theorem 2 that all nodes $H_{k,p}$ output 0. Thus, if σ is sufficiently small, each node $G_{k,p}$, and hence $\mathcal{N}'$, outputs a value close to 0. Hence, S is shattered by thresholding the output of $\mathcal{N}'$ at 1/2.

Finally, we show that S can be shattered by a network $\mathcal{N}$ of the same size with DOG neurons as hidden nodes. The computation of an extended Gaussian neuron can be rewritten as

$$\begin{aligned}\tilde{g}(c, \sigma, \alpha, x) &= 1 - \left(\alpha \exp\left(-\frac{\|x - c\|^2}{\sigma^2}\right) - 1\right)^2 \\ &= 1 - \left(\alpha^2 \exp\left(-\frac{2\|x - c\|^2}{\sigma^2}\right) - 2\alpha \exp\left(-\frac{\|x - c\|^2}{\sigma^2}\right) + 1\right) \\ &= 2\alpha \exp\left(-\frac{\|x - c\|^2}{\sigma^2}\right) - \alpha^2 \exp\left(-\frac{2\|x - c\|^2}{\sigma^2}\right) \\ &= g_{\mathrm{DOG}}(c, \sigma, \sigma/\sqrt{2}, 2\alpha, \alpha^2, x) .\end{aligned}$$

Hence, the extended Gaussian neuron is equivalent to a weighted difference of two Gaussian neurons with center c, widths $\sigma, \sigma/\sqrt{2}$ and weights $2\alpha, \alpha^2$, respectively. Thus, the extended Gaussian neurons can be replaced by the same number of DOG neurons. □

We note that the network of extended Gaussian neurons constructed in the previous proof has all output weights fixed, whereas the output weights of the DOG neurons, that is, the parameters α and β in the notation of Section 2, are calculated from the parameters of the extended Gaussian neurons and, therefore, depend on the particular dichotomy to be implemented. (It is trivial for a DOG network to have an output node with fixed weights since the DOG neurons have built-in output weights.)

We are now able to deduce a superlinear lower bound on the VC dimension of DOG networks.

Corollary 7. *Suppose $\mathcal{N}$ is a network with one hidden layer of DOG neurons and a linear output node. Let $\mathcal{N}$ have k hidden nodes and input dimension $n \geq 2$, where $k \leq 2^n$. Then $\mathcal{N}$ has VC dimension at least*

$$\left\lfloor \frac{k}{2} \right\rfloor \cdot \left\lfloor \log\left(\frac{k}{2}\right) \right\rfloor \cdot \left(n - \left\lfloor \log\left(\frac{k}{2}\right) \right\rfloor + 1\right) .$$

Let W denote the number of weights and assume that $k \leq 2^{n/2}$. Then the VC dimension of $\mathcal{N}$ is at least

$$\frac{W}{5} \log\left(\frac{k}{4}\right) .$$

For fixed input dimension the VC dimension of $\mathcal{N}$ is bounded by $\Omega(k)$ and $\Omega(W)$.

Proof. The results are implied by Theorem 6 in the same way as Corollaries 3, 4, and 5 follow from Theorem 2. □

Finally, we have the lower bound for Gaussian RBF networks.

Theorem 8. *Suppose $\mathcal{N}$ is a network with one hidden layer of Gaussian RBF neurons and a linear output node. Let k be the number of hidden nodes and n the input dimension, where $n \geq 2$ and $k \leq 2^{n+1}$. Then $\mathcal{N}$ has VC dimension at least*

$$\left\lfloor \frac{k}{4} \right\rfloor \cdot \left\lfloor \log\left(\frac{k}{4}\right) \right\rfloor \cdot \left(n - \left\lfloor \log\left(\frac{k}{4}\right) \right\rfloor + 1\right) .$$

Let W denote the number of weights and assume that $k \leq 2^{(n+2)/2}$. Then the VC dimension of $\mathcal{N}$ is at least

$$\frac{W}{12} \log\left(\frac{k}{8}\right) .$$

For fixed input dimension $n \geq 2$ the VC dimension of $\mathcal{N}$ satisfies the bounds $\Omega(k)$ and $\Omega(W)$.

Proof. Clearly, a DOG neuron can be simulated by two weighted Gaussian RBF Neurons. Thus, by virtue of Theorem 6 there is a network $\mathcal{N}$ with $m+q$ input nodes and one hidden layer of $2(h+2^q)$ Gaussian RBF neurons that shatters some set of cardinality $hq(m+1)$. Choosing $h = \lfloor k/4 \rfloor, q = \lfloor \log(k/4) \rfloor$, and $m = n - \lfloor \log(k/4) \rfloor$ we obtain similarly to Corollary 3 the claimed lower bound in terms of n and k. Furthermore, the stated bound in terms of W and k follows by analogy to Corollary 4. The bound for fixed input dimension is obvious, as in the proof of Corollary 5. □

Some radial basis function networks studied theoretically or used in practice have no adjustable width parameters (for instance in [5,20]). Therefore, a natural question is whether the previous result also holds for networks with fixed width parameters. The values of the width parameters for Theorem 8 arise from the widths of DOG neurons specified in Theorem 6. The two width parameters of each DOG neuron have the form σ and $\sigma/\sqrt{2}$ where σ is common to all DOG neurons and is only required to be sufficiently small. Hence, we can choose a single σ that is sufficiently small for all dichotomies to be induced. Thus, for the RBF network we not only have that the width parameters can be fixed, but even that there need to be only two different width values—solely depending on the architecture and not on the particular dichotomy.

Corollary 9. *Let $\mathcal{N}$ be a Gaussian RBF network with n input nodes and k hidden nodes satisfying the conditions of Theorem 8. Then there exists a real number $\sigma_{n,k} > 0$ such that the VC dimension bounds stated in Theorem 8 hold for $\mathcal{N}$ with each RBF neuron having fixed width $\sigma_{k,n}$ or $\sigma_{k,n}/\sqrt{2}$.*

With regard to Theorem 8 we further remark that k has been previously established as lower bound for RBF networks by Anthony and Holden [2]. Further, also Theorem 19 of Lee et al. [11] in connection with the result of Erlich et al. [7] implies the lower bound $\Omega(nk)$, and hence $\Omega(k)$ for fixed input dimension. By means of Theorem 8 we are now able to present a lower bound that is even superlinear in k.

Corollary 10. *Let $n \geq 2$ and $\mathcal{N}$ be the network with $k = 2^{n+1}$ hidden Gaussian RBF neurons. Then $\mathcal{N}$ has VC dimension at least*

$$\frac{k}{3} \log\left(\frac{k}{8}\right) .$$

Proof. Since $k = 2^{n+1}$, we may substitute $n = \log k - 1$ in the first bound of Theorem 8. Hence, the VC dimension of $\mathcal{N}$ is at least

$$\left\lfloor \frac{k}{4} \right\rfloor \cdot \left\lfloor \log\left(\frac{k}{4}\right) \right\rfloor \cdot \left(\log k - \left\lfloor \log\left(\frac{k}{4}\right) \right\rfloor\right) \geq 2 \left\lfloor \frac{k}{4} \right\rfloor \cdot \left\lfloor \log\left(\frac{k}{4}\right) \right\rfloor .$$

Using $\lfloor k/4 \rfloor \geq k/6$ and $\lfloor \log(k/4) \rfloor \geq \log(k/8)$ yields the claimed bound. □

5 Concluding Remarks

We have shown that the VC dimension of every reasonably sized one-hidden-layer network of RBF, DOG, and binary CSRF neurons is superlinear. It is not difficult to deduce that the bound for binary CSRF networks is asymptotically tight. For RBF and DOG networks, however, the currently available methods give only rise to the upper bound $O(W^2k^2)$. To narrow the gap between upper and lower bounds for these networks is an interesting open problem.

It is also easy to obtain a linear upper bound for the single neuron in the RBF and binary CSRF case, whereas for the DOG neuron the upper bound is quadratic. We conjecture that also the DOG neuron has a linear VC dimension, but the methods currently available do not seem to permit an answer.

The bounds we have derived involve constant factors that are the largest known for any standard neural network with one hidden layer. This fact could be evidence of the higher cooperative computational capabilities of local receptive field neurons in comparison to other neuron types. This statement, however, must be taken with care since the constants involved in the bounds are not yet known to be tight.

RBF neural networks compute a particular type of kernel-based functions. The method we have developed for obtaining the results presented here is of quite general nature. We expect it therefore to be applicable for other kernel-based function classes as well.

References

1. Martin Anthony and Peter L. Bartlett. *Neural Network Learning: Theoretical Foundations.* Cambridge University Press, Cambridge, 1999.
2. Martin Anthony and Sean B. Holden. Quantifying generalization in linearly weighted neural networks. *Complex Systems*, 8:91–114, 1994.
3. Peter L. Bartlett, Vitaly Maiorov, and Ron Meir. Almost linear VC dimension bounds for piecewise polynomial networks. *Neural Computation*, 10:2159–2173, 1998.
4. Christopher M. Bishop. *Neural Networks for Pattern Recognition.* Clarendon Press, Oxford, 1995.
5. D. S. Broomhead and David Lowe. Multivariable functional interpolation and adaptive networks. *Complex Systems*, 2:321–355, 1988.
6. Thomas M. Cover. Geometrical and statistical properties of systems of linear inequalities with applications in pattern recognition. *IEEE Transactions on Electronic Computers*, 14:326–334, 1965.
7. Yossi Erlich, Dan Chazan, Scott Petrack, and Avraham Levy. Lower bound on VC-dimension by local shattering. *Neural Computation*, 9:771–776, 1997.
8. Vadim D. Glezer. *Vision and Mind: Modeling Mental Functions.* Lawrence Erlbaum, Mahwah, New Jersey, 1995.
9. Eric J. Hartman, James D. Keeler, and Jacek M. Kowalski. Layered neural networks with Gaussian hidden units as universal approximations. *Neural Computation*, 2:210–215, 1990.
10. Pascal Koiran and Eduardo D. Sontag. Neural networks with quadratic VC dimension. *Journal of Computer and System Sciences*, 54:190–198, 1997.

11. Wee Sun Lee, Peter L. Bartlett, and Robert C. Williamson. Lower bounds on the VC dimension of smoothly parameterized function classes. *Neural Computation*, 7:1040–1053, 1995.
12. Wee Sun Lee, Peter L. Bartlett, and Robert C. Williamson. Correction to "Lower bounds on VC-dimension of smoothly parameterized function classes". *Neural Computation*, 9:765–769, 1997.
13. Wolfgang Maass. Neural nets with super-linear VC-dimension. *Neural Computation*, 6:877–884, 1994.
14. David Marr. *Vision: A Computational Investigation into the Human Representation and Processing of Visual Information.* Freeman, New York, 1982.
15. H. N. Mhaskar. Neural networks for optimal approximation of smooth and analytic functions. *Neural Computation*, 8:164–177, 1996.
16. John Moody and Christian J. Darken. Fast learning in networks of locally-tuned processing units. *Neural Computation*, 1:281–294, 1989.
17. John G. Nicholls, A. Robert Martin, and Bruce G. Wallace. *From Neuron to Brain: A Cellular and Molecular Approach to the Function of the Nervous System.* Sinauer Associates, Sunderland, Mass., third edition, 1992.
18. Jooyoung Park and Irwin W. Sandberg. Approximation and radial-basis-function networks. *Neural Computation*, 5:305–316, 1993.
19. Tomaso Poggio and Federico Girosi. Networks for approximation and learning. *Proceedings of the IEEE*, 78:1481–1497, 1990.
20. M. J. D. Powell. The theory of radial basis function approximation in 1990. In Will Light, editor, *Advances in Numerical Analysis II: Wavelets, Subdivision Algorithms, and Radial Basis Functions*, chapter 3, pages 105–210. Clarendon Press, Oxford, 1992.
21. B. D. Ripley. *Pattern Recognition and Neural Networks.* Cambridge University Press, Cambridge, 1996.
22. Akito Sakurai. Tighter bounds of the VC-dimension of three layer networks. In *Proceedings of the World Congress on Neural Networks*, volume 3, pages 540–543. Erlbaum, Hillsdale, New Jersey, 1993.
23. Marc Tessier-Lavigne. Phototransduction and information processing in the retina. In Eric R. Kandel, James H. Schwartz, and Thomas M. Jessell, editors, *Principles of Neural Science*, chapter 28, pages 400–418. Prentice Hall, Englewood Cliffs, New Jersey, third edition, 1991.

Tracking a Small Set of Experts by Mixing Past Posteriors*

Olivier Bousquet[1] and Manfred K. Warmuth[2]

[1] Centre de Mathématiques Appliquées
Ecole Polytechnique
91128 Palaiseau
France
bousquet@cmapx.polytechnique.fr
[2] Computer Science Department
University of California, Santa Cruz
Santa Cruz, CA 95064
U.S.A.
manfred@cse.ucsc.edu

Abstract. In this paper, we examine on-line learning problems in which the target concept is allowed to change over time. In each trial a master algorithm receives predictions from a large set of n experts. Its goal is to predict almost as well as the best sequence of such experts chosen off-line by partitioning the training sequence into $k+1$ sections and then choosing the best expert for each section. We build on methods developed by Herbster and Warmuth and consider an open problem posed by Freund where the experts in the best partition are from a small pool of size m. Since $k >> m$ the best expert shifts back and forth between the experts of the small pool. We propose algorithms that solve this open problem by mixing the past posteriors maintained by the master algorithm. We relate the number of bits needed for encoding the best partition to the loss bounds of the algorithms. Instead of paying $\log n$ for choosing the best expert in each section we first pay $\log \binom{n}{m}$ bits in the bounds for identifying the pool of m experts and then $\log m$ bits per new section. In the bounds we also pay twice for encoding the boundaries of the sections.

1 Introduction

We consider the following standard on-line learning model in which a master algorithm has to combine the predictions from a set of experts [12,15,3,11]. Learning proceeds in trials. In each trial the master receives the predictions from n experts and uses them to form its own prediction. At the end of the trial both the master and the experts receive the true outcome and incur a loss measuring the discrepancy between their predictions and the outcome. The master maintains a weight for each of its experts. The weight of an expert is

* Supported by NSF grant CCR 9821087. This research was done while the first author was visiting UC Santa Cruz

D. Helmbold and B. Williamson (Eds.): COLT/EuroCOLT 2001, LNAI 2111, pp. 31–47, 2001.

an estimate of the "quality" of this expert's predictions and the master forms its prediction based on a weighted combination of the expert's predictions. The master updates the expert's weights at the end of each trial based on the losses of the experts and master.

The goal is to design weight updates that guarantee that the loss of the master is never much larger than the loss of the best expert or the best convex combination of the losses of the experts. So here the best expert or convex combination serves as a comparator.

A more challenging goal is to learn well when the comparator changes over time. So now the sequence of trials is partitioned into sections. In each section the loss of the algorithm is compared to the loss of a particular expert and this expert changes at the beginning of a new section. The goal of the master now is to do almost as well as the best partition. Bounds of this type were first investigated by Littlestone and Warmuth [12] and then studied in more detail by Herbster and Warmuth [9] and Vovk [17]. Other work on learning in relation to a shifting comparator but not in the expert setting appears in [2,10,14].

In this paper we want to model situations where the comparators are from a small pool of m convex combinations of the n experts each represented by a probability vector $\tilde{\boldsymbol{u}}_j$, $(1 \leq j \leq m)$. In the initial segment a convex combination $\tilde{\boldsymbol{u}}_1$ might be the best comparator. Then at some point there is a shift and $\tilde{\boldsymbol{u}}_2$ does well. In a third section, $\tilde{\boldsymbol{u}}_1$ might again be best and so forth. The pool size is small $(m << n)$ and the best comparator switches back and forth between the few convex combinations in the pool $(m << k$, where k is the number of shifts). Of course, the convex combinations of the pool are not known to the master algorithm.

This type of setting was popularized by an open problem posed by Yoav Freund [5]. In his version of the problem he focused on the special case where the pool consists of single experts (i.e. the convex combinations in the pool are unit vectors). Thus the goal is to develop bounds for the case when the comparator shifts back and forth within a pool of m out a much larger set of n experts.

In [9] bounds were developed where the additional loss of the algorithm over the loss of the best comparator partition is proportional to the number of bits needed to encode the partition. Following this approach Freund suggests the following additional loss bound for his open problem: $\log \binom{n}{m} \approx m \log \frac{n}{m}$ bits for choosing the pool of m experts, $\log m$ bits per segment for choosing an expert from the pool, and $\log \binom{T-1}{k} \approx k \log \frac{T}{k}$ bits for specifying the k boundaries of the segments (where T is the total number of trials).

In this paper we solve Freund's open problem. Our methods build on those developed by Herbster and Warmuth [9]. There are two types of updates: a *Loss Update* followed by a *Mixing Update*. The Loss Update is the standard update used for the expert setting [12,15,7,11] in which the weights of the experts decay exponentially with the loss. In the case of the log loss this becomes Bayes rule for computing the posterior weights for the experts. In the new Mixing Update the weight vector in the next trial becomes a mixture of all the past posteriors where the current posterior always has the largest mixture coefficient.

The key insight of our paper is to design the mixture coefficients for the past posteriors. In our main scheme the coefficient for the current posterior is $1-\alpha$ for some small $\alpha \in [0,1]$ and the coefficient for the posterior d trials in the past is proportional to α/d. Curiously enough this scheme solves Freund's open problem: When the comparators are single experts then the additional loss of our algorithms over the loss of the best comparator partition is order of the number of bits needed to encode the partition. For this scheme all past posteriors need to be stored requiring time and space $O(nt)$ at trial t. However, we show how this mixing scheme can be approximated in time and space $O(n \ln t)$. The simplest scheme has slightly weaker bounds: The coefficients of all past posteriors (there are t of them at trial t) are $\alpha\frac{1}{t}$. Now only the average of the past posteriors needs to be maintained requiring time and space $O(n)$.

We begin by reviewing some preliminaries about the expert setting and then give our main algorithm in Section 3. This algorithm contains the main schemes for choosing the mixture coefficients. In Section 4 we prove bounds for the various mixing schemes. In particular, we discuss the optimality of the bounds in relation to the number of bits needed to encode the best partition. We then discuss alternates to our main algorithm in Section 5 and experimentally compare the algorithms in Section 6. We conclude with a number of open problems.

2 Preliminaries

Let T denote the number of trials and n the number of experts. We will refer to the experts by their index $i \in \{1,\ldots,n\}$. At trial $t = 1,\ldots,T$, the master receives a vector $\boldsymbol{x}_t$ of n predictions, where $x_{t,i}$ is the prediction of the i-th expert. The master then must produce a prediction $\hat{y}_t$ and, following that, receives the true outcome y_t for trial t. We assume that $x_{t,i}, \hat{y}_t, y_t \in [0,1]$.

A loss function $L : [0,1] \times [0,1] \to [0,\infty]$ is used to measure the discrepancy between the true outcome and the predictions. Expert i incurs loss $L_{t,i} = L(y_t, x_{t,i})$ at trial t and the master algorithm A incurs loss $L_{t,A} = L(y_t, \hat{y}_t)$. For the cumulative loss over a sequence, we will use the shorthand notation $L_{1..T,A} = \sum_{t=1}^{T} L_{t,A}$.

The weight vector maintained by the algorithm at trial t is denoted by $\boldsymbol{v}_t$. Its elements are non-negative and sum to one, i.e. $\boldsymbol{v}_t$ is in the n-dimensional probability simplex denoted by $\mathcal{P}_n$.

Based on the current weight vector $\boldsymbol{v}_t$, and the experts predictions $\boldsymbol{x}_t$, the master algorithm uses a *prediction function* $\texttt{pred} : \mathcal{P}_n \times [0,1]^n \to [0,1]$ to compute its prediction for trial t: $\hat{y}_t = \texttt{pred}(\boldsymbol{v}_t, \boldsymbol{x}_t)$. In the simplest case the prediction function is an average of the experts predictions $\texttt{pred}(\boldsymbol{v}, \boldsymbol{x}) = \boldsymbol{v} \cdot \boldsymbol{x}$ (See [11]). Refined prediction functions can be defined depending on the loss function used [15]. The loss and prediction functions are characterized by the following definition.

Definition 1. *([7,16]) Let $c, \eta > 0$. A loss function L and prediction function* `pred` *are (c,η)-realizable if, for any weight vector $\boldsymbol{v} \in \mathcal{P}_n$, prediction vector $\boldsymbol{x}$ and outcome y,*

$$L(y, \texttt{pred}(\boldsymbol{v}, \boldsymbol{x})) \leq -c \ln \sum_{i=1}^{n} v_i e^{-\eta L(y, x_i)} \ . \tag{1}$$

For example, with the prediction function $\texttt{pred}(\boldsymbol{v}, \boldsymbol{x}) = \boldsymbol{v} \cdot \boldsymbol{x}$ the quadratic loss $L_{sq}(y, \hat{y}) = (y - \hat{y})^2$ satisfies[1] (1) with $(c, \eta) = (2, \frac{1}{2})$ and the entropic loss $L_{ent}(y, \hat{y}) = y \ln \frac{y}{\hat{y}} + (1 - y) \ln \frac{1-y}{1-\hat{y}}$ satisfies (1) with $(c, \eta) = (1, 1)$.

In the remainder we will assume the loss and prediction functions that we use are $(c, 1/c)$-realizable so that $c\eta = 1$. The two examples given above satisfy this criterion. This does not include the case of the absolute loss. However, the results here can essentially be extended to this loss as was done in [9].

3 The Algorithms

Learning proceeds in trials. At the beginning of each trial t (see Figure 1) the master algorithm receives the prediction vector $\boldsymbol{x}_t$ from the experts and forms is own prediction $\hat{y}_t$. It then receives the correct outcome y_t and performs two weight updates. The first update is the standard *Loss Update* which is the basis for all the work in the expert framework [12,15]. This update, which produces an intermediate weight vector $\boldsymbol{v}_t^m$, may be seen as a generalization of Bayes rule for updating a posterior. Indeed when $y_t \in \{0, 1\}$, the learning rate η is one and the loss is the log loss then this update becomes Bayes rule.[2]

The Loss Update allows us to prove bounds on the loss of the master algorithm in terms of the loss of the best expert [12,15] or the best convex combination $\tilde{\boldsymbol{u}} \in \mathcal{P}_n$ of the losses of the experts [11]. However in this paper the comparator convex combination is allowed to change with the trial t. Let $\boldsymbol{u}_t$ be the convex combination used in trial t. The beliefs of the algorithm about the comparator sequence are modeled with a probability distribution $\beta_{t+1}(.)$. At the end of each trial t the master algorithm might need to "pick up" the computation from some previous trial. For $0 \leq q \leq t$, let $\beta_{t+1}(q)$ be the coefficient/probability given to weight vector $\boldsymbol{v}_q^m$ of trial q. Intuitively, if q is the last trial in which the comparator $\boldsymbol{u}_{t+1}$ is used then $\beta_{t+1}(q)$ should be high. In particular, $\beta_{t+1}(t)$ should be high if the comparison vector remains unchanged, i.e. $\boldsymbol{u}_t = \boldsymbol{u}_{t+1}$. Also if the comparison vector $\boldsymbol{u}_{t+1}$ has never appeared before

---

[1] A slightly more involved prediction function shows that the quadratic loss is $(\frac{1}{2}, 2)$-realizable [15].

[2] Assume E_t is the random variable naming the expert generating the label y_t and $x_{t,i} = P(y_t = 1 | E_t = i, \boldsymbol{y}_{t-1})$ then $L_{ent}(y_t, x_{t,i}) = -\ln P(y_t | E_t = i, \boldsymbol{y}_{t-1})$, i.e the entropic loss becomes the log-loss. Now if $v_{t,i}$ is the prior $P(E_t = i | \boldsymbol{y}_{t-1})$ at the beginning of trial t then $v_{t,i}^m = P(E_t = i | \boldsymbol{y}_t)$. Also in this case the prediction $\boldsymbol{v}_t \cdot \boldsymbol{x}_t$ is the mean posterior $P(y_t = 1 | \boldsymbol{v}_{t-1})$ and $-\ln P(y_t | \boldsymbol{y}_{t-1}) = L_{ent}(y_t, \boldsymbol{v}_t \cdot \boldsymbol{x}_t) = -\ln \sum_{i=1}^{n} v_{t,i} e^{-L_{ent}(y_t, x_{t,i})}$.

Parameters: $0 < \eta, c$ and $0 \le \alpha \le 1$
Initialization: Initialize the weight to $\boldsymbol{v}_1 = \frac{1}{n}\mathbf{1}$ and denote $\boldsymbol{v}_0^m = \frac{1}{n}\mathbf{1}$
FOR $t = 1$ **TO** T **DO**

- **Prediction:** After receiving the vector of experts predictions $\boldsymbol{x}_t$, predict with

$$\hat{y}_t = \texttt{pred}(\boldsymbol{v}_t, \boldsymbol{x}_t) \ .$$

- **Loss Update:** After receiving the outcome y_t, compute for $1 \le i \le n$,

$$v_{t,i}^m = \frac{v_{t,i}e^{-\eta L_{t,i}}}{\sum_{j=1}^n v_{t,j}e^{-\eta L_{t,j}}}, \quad \text{where } L_{t,i} = L(y_t, x_{t,i}) \ .$$

- **Mixing Update:** Choose mixture coefficients $\beta_{t+1}(q)$ $(q = 0, \ldots, t)$ such that $\sum_{q=0}^t \beta_{t+1}(q) = 1$ and compute

$$\boldsymbol{v}_{t+1} = \sum_{q=0}^t \beta_{t+1}(q)\boldsymbol{v}_q^m \ .$$

Fig. 1. The Mixing Algorithm

then the coefficient $\beta_{t+1}(0)$ should be high because a section needs to be started with the initial weight v_0^m. Thus the second update (called the *Mixing Update*) "mixes" the previous weight vectors $\boldsymbol{v}_t^m$. In the case of log loss the update mixes the current and the previous posteriors. However note that all posteriors are influenced by mixing that occurred in previous trials.

The probabilities $\beta_{t+1}(q)$ are specified by the specific mixing scheme to be used (see Table 1). The simplest case occurs when $\beta_{t+1}(t) = 1$ and the remaining coefficients are zero. Thus $\boldsymbol{v}_{t+1}$ simply becomes $\boldsymbol{v}_t^m$. Following [9] we call this the Static Experts case. This choice is the setup suitable when the comparator is the loss of a fixed expert (e.g. [12,15]) or a fixed convex combination of the losses of the experts [11].

Table 1. The Mixing Schemes

Name	Coefficients
Static Experts	$\beta_{t+1}(t) = 1$ and $\beta_{t+1}(q) = 0$ for $0 \le q < t$
Fixed-Share Update	$\beta_{t+1}(t) = 1 - \alpha$ and $\sum_{q=0}^{t-1} \beta_{t+1}(q) = \alpha$
• To Start Vector	$\beta_{t+1}(0) = \alpha$
• To Past	
• Uniform Past	$\beta_{t+1}(q) = \alpha\,\frac{1}{t}$ for $0 \le q < t$
• Decaying Past	$\beta_{t+1}(q) = \alpha\,\frac{1}{(t-q)^\gamma}\,\frac{1}{Z_t}$ for $0 \le q < t$, with $Z_t = \sum_{q=0}^{t-1} \frac{1}{(t-q)^\gamma}$ and $\gamma \ge 0$

Even in the case when shifting occurs then the largest coefficient is naturally $\beta_{t+1}(t)$ signifying that the computation is most likely going to continue from the weight vector at the current trial t. We call any update where $\beta_{t+1}(t) = 1-\alpha$ for some fixed small α by the name *Fixed-Share Update*. In contrast to the Static Update when $\boldsymbol{v}_{t+1}$ simply becomes the current posterior $\boldsymbol{v}_t^m$, each expert first "shares" a fraction of α of its weight $v_{t,i}^m$ and the total shared weight α is then distributed among the earlier posteriors (i.e. $\sum_{q=0}^{t-1} \beta_{t+1}(q) = 1 - \beta_{t+1}(t) = \alpha$).

In the simplest case all of the shared weight α goes to the uniform weight vector $\frac{1}{n}\mathbf{1} = \boldsymbol{v}_0^m$ leading to essentially the Fixed-Share Algorithm analyzed in [9]. The main contribution of this paper is to show that other choices of distributing the shared weight to the past posteriors give useful bounds. A simple choice is the average of the past weight vectors (*Uniform Past*), i.e. $\beta_{t+1}(q) = \alpha\,\frac{1}{t}$, for $0 \le q < t$. Instead of the average a decaying sequence of coefficients leads to better bounds. The more recent weight vectors receive higher coefficients. In the case of the *Decaying Past* mixing scheme, $\beta_{t+1}(q) \approx \alpha\,\frac{1}{(t-q)^\gamma}$, for $\gamma \ge 0$.

4 Analysis of the Algorithms

In this paper we stress the bounds where the loss of the algorithm is compared to some convex combination of the losses of the experts (see e.g. [11]) rather than the loss of a single expert. Let $\beta_1(0) = 1$, $\Delta(.,.)$ be the relative entropy and L_t be the vector of the losses $L_{t,i}$ of the experts at trial t.

Lemma 1. *For any trial t, any $0 \le q \le t-1$ and any comparison vector $\boldsymbol{u}_t \in \mathcal{P}_n$*

$$\begin{aligned} L_{t,A} &\le L_t \cdot \boldsymbol{u}_t + c\,\Delta(\boldsymbol{u}_t, \boldsymbol{v}_t) - c\,\Delta(\boldsymbol{u}_t, \boldsymbol{v}_t^m) \\ &\le L_t \cdot \boldsymbol{u}_t + c\,\Delta(\boldsymbol{u}_t, \boldsymbol{v}_q^m) - c\,\Delta(\boldsymbol{u}_t, \boldsymbol{v}_t^m) + c\ln\frac{1}{\beta_t(q)} \ . \end{aligned}$$

Proof. The r.h.s. of the first inequality is equal to r.h.s. of (1). The second inequality follows from the fact that $\boldsymbol{v}_t = \sum_{q'=0}^{t-1} \beta_t(q')\boldsymbol{v}_{q'}^m \ge \beta_t(q)\boldsymbol{v}_q^m$ (Note that "$\ge$" holds component-wise). □

4.1 Comparison to a Fixed Convex Combination

Here we consider the case when the comparison vector $\boldsymbol{u}_t = \tilde{\boldsymbol{u}}$ remains unchanged. We will thus use the Static Experts mixing scheme, i.e. $\beta_{t+1}(t) = 1$ and $\beta_{t+1}(q) = 0$ for $0 \le q < t$. This is exactly the Static Experts Algorithm since $\boldsymbol{v}_t^m$ becomes the weight vector used in the next trial, i.e. $\boldsymbol{v}_{t+1} = \boldsymbol{v}_t^m$. By summing Lemma 1 over all trials we get the following bound (see e.g. [11]).

Lemma 2. *For the Mixing Algorithm with the Static Expert mixing scheme (i.e. no mixing) and any $\tilde{\boldsymbol{u}} \in \mathcal{P}_n$,*

$$L_{1..T,A} \le \sum_{t=1}^{T} L_t \cdot \tilde{\boldsymbol{u}} + c\,\Delta(\tilde{\boldsymbol{u}}, \boldsymbol{v}_1) - c\,\Delta(\tilde{\boldsymbol{u}}, \boldsymbol{v}_T^m) \ .$$

Proof. We apply Lemma 1 to each trial $t = 2, \dots, T$ and use the fact that $\boldsymbol{v}_t = \boldsymbol{v}^m_{t-1}$. The sum of divergences telescopes so that only the first and last terms remain. □

Note that the r.h.s. is the same for all $\tilde{\boldsymbol{u}}$. To obtain upper bounds we often choose a particular $\tilde{\boldsymbol{u}}$ and drop the $-\Delta(\tilde{\boldsymbol{u}}, \boldsymbol{v}^m_T)$ term which is always negative. The start vector is always uniform, i.e. $\boldsymbol{v}_1 = \frac{1}{n}\mathbf{1}$. If the best expert has loss L^* and $\tilde{\boldsymbol{u}}$ is the unit probability vector for this expert then $\Delta(\tilde{\boldsymbol{u}}, \frac{1}{n}\mathbf{1}) = \ln n$ and the above bound is at most $L^* + c\ln n$. However if k experts have loss L^* then by choosing $\tilde{\boldsymbol{u}}$ uniform over these experts (and zero on the remaining experts) the bound becomes $L^* + c\ln\frac{n}{k}$. This improvement was first pointed out in [12].

4.2 Comparison to a Sequence with k Shifts

Now, we consider the situation where the comparison vector $\boldsymbol{u}_t$ of trial t is allowed to change/shift from trial to trial. A sequence of comparison vectors $\boldsymbol{u}_1, \dots, \boldsymbol{u}_T \in \mathcal{P}_n$ *has k shifts* if there is a subsequence of k trials $t_1, \dots, t_k$ where $\boldsymbol{u}_{t_j} \neq \boldsymbol{u}_{t_j-1}$ and $\boldsymbol{u}_{t-1} = \boldsymbol{u}_t$ for all other trials $t > 1$. We define $t_0 = 1$ and $t_{k+1} = T + 1$. We now apply Lemma 1 to the case when all of the lost weight α goes to the original posterior $\frac{1}{n}\mathbf{1}$. This essentially becomes the Fixed-Share Algorithm of [9].

Lemma 3. *For the Mixing Algorithm A with the Fixed-Share to the Start Vector mixing scheme and any sequence of T comparison vectors $\boldsymbol{u}_t$ with k shifts,*

$$L_{1..T,A} \le \sum_{t=1}^{T} L_t \cdot \boldsymbol{u}_t + c\sum_{j=0}^{k}\left(\Delta(\boldsymbol{u}_{t_j}, \frac{1}{n}\mathbf{1}) - \Delta(\boldsymbol{u}_{t_j}, \boldsymbol{v}^m_{t_{j+1}-1})\right)$$
$$+ck\ln\frac{1}{\alpha} + c(T-k-1)\ln\frac{1}{1-\alpha} \; .$$

Proof. We apply Lemma 1 for each trial. Whenever $\boldsymbol{u}_t = \boldsymbol{u}_{t-1}$ then we use $q = t-1$ and $\beta_t(t-1) = 1-\alpha$, i.e.

$$L_{A,t} \le L_t \cdot \boldsymbol{u}_t + c\,\Delta(\boldsymbol{u}_t, \boldsymbol{v}^m_{t-1}) - c\,\Delta(\boldsymbol{u}_t, \boldsymbol{v}^m_t) + c\ln\frac{1}{1-\alpha} \; .$$

For the first trial we use $q = 0$, $\beta_1(0) = 1$, and $\boldsymbol{v}^m_0 = \frac{1}{n}\mathbf{1}$:

$$L_{A,1} \le L_1 \cdot \boldsymbol{u}_1 + c\,\Delta(\boldsymbol{u}_1, \frac{1}{n}\mathbf{1}) - c\,\Delta(\boldsymbol{u}_1, \boldsymbol{v}^m_1) \; .$$

For all other beginnings of sections, i.e. the trials $t = t_j$ $(1 \le j \le k)$ we use $q = 0$, $\beta_{t_j}(0) = \alpha$, and $v^m_0 = \frac{1}{n}\mathbf{1}$:

$$L_{A,t_j} \le L_{t_j} \cdot \boldsymbol{u}_{t_j} + c\,\Delta(\boldsymbol{u}_{t_j}, \frac{1}{n}\mathbf{1}) - c\,\Delta(\boldsymbol{u}_{t_j}, \boldsymbol{v}^m_{t_j}) + c\ln\frac{1}{\alpha} \; .$$

Now we sum over all trials. The entropy terms within the sections telescope and only for the beginning and the end of each section a positive and a negative entropy term remains, respectively. The beginnings of the k sections each incur an additional term of $c \ln \frac{1}{\alpha}$. Also $T-k+1$ times $\boldsymbol{u}_t = \boldsymbol{u}_{t-1}$ and an additional term of $c \ln \frac{1}{1-\alpha}$ is incurred. The initial trial ($t=1$) has no additional term. □

If we restrict ourselves to the case when the comparison vectors are focused on single experts then we essentially obtain the basic bound of [9] for the Fixed Share to the Start Vector mixing scheme.

4.3 Comparison to a Sequence with k Shifts and a Pool of Size m

As in the previous section we let $t_1, \ldots, t_k$ be the subsequence of indices in the sequence of comparators $\boldsymbol{u}_1, \ldots, \boldsymbol{u}_T$ where shifting occurs (Also $t_0 = 1$, $t_{k+1} = T+1$ and $u_{T+1} = u_T$). Let $\tilde{\boldsymbol{u}}_1, \ldots, \tilde{\boldsymbol{u}}_m$ be the pool of m distinct convex combinations in $\{\boldsymbol{u}_{t_1}, \ldots, \boldsymbol{u}_{t_k}\}$. At trial $t_0 = 1$ a the first convex combination from the pool is selected. At the remaining starting points $\boldsymbol{u}_{t_j}$ $(1 \le j \le k)$ of sections either a new convex combination is selected from the pool ($m-1$ times) or the convex combination $\boldsymbol{u}_{t_j}$ has appeared before in $\{\boldsymbol{u}_{t_1}, \ldots, \boldsymbol{u}_{t_{j-1}}\}$. In the latter case ($k-m+1$ times) the convex combination *shifts back* to the end of the last section where this convex combination from the pool was the comparator. We assume that $m << k$ and thus most of the shifts ($k+1-m$ of them) are shift backs. Curiously enough the entropy terms for all trials belonging to the same convex combination telescope.

Theorem 1. *For the Mixing Algorithm A and for any sequence of T comparison vectors $\boldsymbol{u}_t$ with k shifts from a pool $\{\tilde{\boldsymbol{u}}_1, \ldots, \tilde{\boldsymbol{u}}_m\}$ of m convex combinations, we have (recall $\beta_1(0) = 1$)*

$$L_{1..T,A} \le \sum_{t=1}^{T} L_t \cdot \boldsymbol{u}_t + c \sum_{j=1}^{m} \left(\Delta(\tilde{\boldsymbol{u}}_j, \frac{1}{n}\mathbf{1}) - \Delta(\tilde{\boldsymbol{u}}_j, \boldsymbol{v}^m_{\ell_j}) \right) + c \sum_{t=1}^{T} \ln \frac{1}{\beta_t(q_{t-1})} ,$$

where ℓ_j is the last trial such that $\boldsymbol{u}_t = \tilde{\boldsymbol{u}}_j$ and q_t is the last of the trials $t, t-1, \ldots, 1$ such that $\boldsymbol{u}_{t+1} = \boldsymbol{u}_q$ (we let $q_t = 0$ when no such trial exists).

Proof. We apply Lemma 1 to all trials using $q = q_{t-1}$:

$$L_{t,A} \le L_t \cdot \boldsymbol{u}_t + c\,\Delta(\boldsymbol{u}_t, \boldsymbol{v}^m_{q_{t-1}}) - c\,\Delta(\boldsymbol{u}_t, \boldsymbol{v}^m_t) + c \ln \frac{1}{\beta_t(q_{t-1})} .$$

We claim that summing the above over all trials proves the theorem. First note that the comparator remains constant within each section. So as before the entropy terms within each section telescope and only for the beginning and end of each section a positive and a negative entropy term remains, respectively. Furthermore, the ending and beginning terms belonging to successive sections of the same convex combination from the pool also telescope. So for each element of the pool only two entropy terms survive: one for the beginning of the first section where it appears and one for the end of its last section. More precisely, the beginning of the first section of convex combination $\tilde{\boldsymbol{u}}_j$ contributes $\Delta(\tilde{\boldsymbol{u}}_j, \frac{1}{n}\mathbf{1})$ because then $q_{t-1} = 0$ by definition. Also the last trial ℓ_j of $\tilde{\boldsymbol{u}}_j$ contributes $-\Delta(\tilde{\boldsymbol{u}}_j, \boldsymbol{v}^m_{\ell_j})$. □

The challenge is to design the mixing coefficients $\beta_{t+1}(q)$ so that the last sum in the above theorem is minimized. We give some reasonable choices below and discuss time and space trade offs.

Bound for the Fixed Share to Uniform Past Mixing Scheme. Consider a mixing scheme that equally penalizes all vectors in the past: $\beta_{t+1}(q) = \alpha\,\frac{1}{t}\ (q = 0..t-1)$.

Corollary 1. *For the Mixing Algorithm A with the Fixed Share to Uniform Past mixing scheme and for any sequence of T comparison vectors $\boldsymbol{u}_t$ with k shifts from a pool $\{\tilde{\boldsymbol{u}}_1, \ldots, \tilde{\boldsymbol{u}}_m\}$ of m convex combinations, we have*

$$L_{1..T,A} \le \sum_{t=1}^{T} L_t \cdot \boldsymbol{u}_t + c\sum_{j=1}^{m}\left(\Delta(\tilde{\boldsymbol{u}}_j, \frac{1}{n}\boldsymbol{1}) - \Delta(\tilde{\boldsymbol{u}}_j, \boldsymbol{v}^m_{\ell_j})\right)$$
$$+ck\ln\frac{1}{\alpha} + c(T-k-1)\ln\frac{1}{1-\alpha} + ck\ln(T-1)\ ,$$

where ℓ_j denotes the last trial such that $\boldsymbol{u}_t = \tilde{\boldsymbol{u}}_j$.

Proof. We simply bound the last term in the inequality of Theorem 1 by the last line in the inequality above. There are $T-k-1$ trials such that $\boldsymbol{u}_t = \boldsymbol{u}_{t-1}$. For all these trials $\beta_t(q_{t-1}) = \beta_t(t-1) = 1-\alpha$ contributing a total cost of $c(T-k-1)\ln\frac{1}{1-\alpha}$. In all the remaining trials a section is starting. For the first trial $\beta_1(0) = 1$ and no cost is incurred. For all k other trials t starting sections, $\beta_t(q_{t-1}) = \alpha\,\frac{1}{t-1}$. Thus these trials contribute at most $ck\ln\frac{1}{\alpha} + ck\ln(T-1)$. □

Bound for the Fixed Share to Decaying Past Mixing Scheme. We now show that an improvement of the above corollary is possible by choosing $\beta_{t+1}(q) = \alpha\frac{1}{(t-q)^\gamma Z_t}$ for $0 \le q \le t-1$, with $Z_t = \sum_{q=0}^{t-1}\frac{1}{(t-q)^\gamma}$.

Corollary 2. *For the Mixing Algorithm A with the Fixed Share to Decaying Past mixing scheme with $\gamma = 1$ and for any sequence of T comparison vectors $\boldsymbol{u}_t$ with k shifts from a pool $\{\tilde{\boldsymbol{u}}_1, \ldots, \tilde{\boldsymbol{u}}_m\}$ of m convex combinations, we have*

$$L_{1..T,A} \le \sum_{t=1}^{T} L_t \cdot \boldsymbol{u}_t + c\sum_{j=1}^{m}\left(\Delta(\tilde{\boldsymbol{u}}_j, \frac{1}{n}\boldsymbol{1}) - \Delta(\tilde{\boldsymbol{u}}_j, \boldsymbol{v}^m_{\ell_j})\right) + ck\ln\frac{1}{\alpha}$$
$$+c(T-k-1)\ln\frac{1}{1-\alpha} + ck\ln\frac{(T-1)(m-1)}{k} + ck\ln\ln(eT)\ ,$$

where ℓ_j denotes the last trial such that $\boldsymbol{u}_t = \tilde{\boldsymbol{u}}_j$.

Proof. The proof follows the proof of Corollary 1. □

4.4 Relating the Bounds to the Number of Bits

In this section we assume the comparison vectors $\boldsymbol{u}_t$ are unit vectors. The number of bits (measured with respect to $c\ln$ instead of log) for encoding a partition with k shifts from a pool of size m is the following:

$$c\ln\binom{n}{m} + c\ln\binom{T-1}{k} + c\ln m + ck\ln(m-1) \approx cm\ln\frac{n}{m} + ck\ln\frac{T}{k} + ck\ln m. \quad (2)$$

The first term is for selecting the m experts of the pool, the second term for encoding the boundaries of the k shifts and the last term for naming members of the pool belonging to the $k+1$ sections.

Now consider the following "direct" algorithm proposed by Freund. Run the Mixing Algorithm with the Fixed Share to Start Vector mixing scheme (i.e. the Fixed Share Algorithm of [9]) on every pool/subset of m out of the n experts. Each run becomes an expert that feeds into the Mixing Algorithm with the Static Expert mixing scheme. If $\boldsymbol{u}_t$ is the comparator sequence of the best partition with k shifts from a pool of m experts then the loss of this algorithm is at most $\sum_{t=1}^T L_t \cdot \boldsymbol{u}_t$ plus the number of bits (2). However this algorithm requires $\binom{n}{m}n$ weights which is unrealistic.

In contrast, our algorithms are efficient and the bounds are still close to optimal. For example, if $\alpha = \frac{k}{T-1}$ then the bound of the Mixing Algorithm with the Fixed Share to Decaying Past ($\gamma = 1$) mixing scheme (see Corollary 2) is the loss of the best partition plus approximately

$$cm \ln n + ck \ln \frac{T}{k} + ck \ln \frac{Tm}{k} + ck \ln \ln(eT).$$

If we omit the last term, then this is at most twice the number of bits (2) and thus we solved Freund's open problem. Also note that the above bound is essentially $ck \ln \frac{T}{k} + cm \ln m$ larger than the number of bits. In the dominating first term we are paying a second time for encoding the boundaries. The same bound with the Uniform Past mixing scheme is not a constant times larger than the number of bits. Thus it seems that the mixing coefficients need to decay towards the past to obtain the best bounds.

The better Decaying Past scheme requires us to store all previous posteriors, i.e. nt weights at trial t. However in the appendix we describe a way to approximate this scheme with $O(n \log t)$ weights. The Uniform Past scheme only needs to store the current and the average of the past posterior ($2n$ weights).

5 Additional Observations

Generalized Mixing Schemes. Notice that our main result (Theorem 1) relies on the following simple property of the Mixing Update:

$$\forall q = 0, \ldots, t: \quad \boldsymbol{v}_{t+1} \geq \beta_{t+1}(q) \boldsymbol{v}_q^m \ . \tag{3}$$

The following update (called *Max Mixing Update*) also has this property and thus all bounds proven in the paper immediately hold for this update as well:

$$\boldsymbol{v}_{t+1} = \frac{1}{Z_t} \max_{q=0}^{t} \left(\beta_{t+1}(q) \boldsymbol{v}_q^m \right) \ ,$$

where Z_t is the normalization and the max is component-wise. Since $\max(a,b) \leq a+b$ for positive a and b one can show that $Z_t \leq 1$ and thus (3) is satisfied.

More generally, we can replace the maximum by other functions. For example, for any $p \geq 1$, we can use $f(a,b) = (a^p + b^p)^{1/p}$. Since we have $a^p + b^p \leq (a+b)^p$ for any $a, b \geq 0$, we can see the condition (3) will still hold.

Another possible update is to minimize the relative entropy subject to the constraint defined by (3), i.e.

$$\boldsymbol{v}_{t+1} = \arg \min_{\boldsymbol{v} \in C_t \cap \mathcal{P}_n} \Delta(\boldsymbol{v}, \boldsymbol{v}_t^m) ,$$

where C_t is the set of vectors satisfying (3). We call this the *Projection Mixing Update.* Such updates have been used by Herbster and Warmuth to obtain bounds for shifting in a regression setting [10].

Notice for all generalized mixing schemes described above we can still use the technique sketched in the appendix for reducing the number of weights at trial t from $O(nt)$ to $O(n \log t)$.

Variable Share and Lazy Mixing Updates. Inspired by the Variable Share Algorithm of [9] we define the following *Variable Share Mixing Update.* As we shall see in the next section this algorithm is better in the experiments than the Mixing Update when the same mixing scheme is used.

$$v_{t+1,i} = \beta_{t+1}(t)^{L_{t,i}} v_{t,i}^m + F_t \sum_{q=0}^{t-1} \beta_{t+1}(q) v_{q,i}^m ,$$

where the losses $L_{t,i}$ must be in $[0,1]$ and F_t is a factor that assures that the $v_{t+1,i}$ sum to one. Note that the standard Mixing update can be written as

$$v_{t+1,i} = \beta_{t+1}(t) v_{t,i}^m + \sum_{q=0}^{t-1} \beta_{t+1}(q) v_{q,i}^m .$$

Thus when all $L_{t,i}$ are one then $F_t = 1$ and both updates agree. Also when all $L_{t,i}$ are zero then $F_t = 0$ and $\boldsymbol{v}_{t+1} = \boldsymbol{v}_t^m = \boldsymbol{v}_t$ which is the Static Experts Update. This shows that the new update interpolates between the Mixing Update and the Static Experts Update. In some sense this update uses a small loss of the experts as an indicator that no shift is occurring.

Another such indicator is the loss of the master algorithm itself. Indeed, when the master performs well, it is likely that no shift is occurring and there is no need to mix the posteriors. This idea leads to the *Lazy Mixing Update* which works as follows. We use a variable B_t to accumulate the loss of the master algorithm: we initialize B_1 to 0 and update with $B_{t+1} = B_t + L_{t,A}$. Only if $B_{t+1} \geq 1$ then we perform the Mixing Update and reset B_{t+1} to 0.

NP-Completeness.

Theorem 2. *The following off-line problem is NP-complete.*

Input: A number of trials T, a number of experts n, a number of shifts k, a pool size m, binary predictions $x_{t,i}$ for each expert i and trial t, and binary labels y_t for each trial t.

Question: Is there a partition of the T trials with k shifts from a pool of m convex combinations that has loss zero.

Proof. The problem reduces to three-dimensional matching ([6], page 221): We have $T = 3q$ trials. Trials $1, 2, \ldots, 3q$ correspond to the elements $w_1, w_2, \ldots, w_q$, $r_1, r_2, \ldots, r_q, s_1, s_2, \ldots, s_q$, respectively. Choose the $x_{t,i}$ and y_t so that each triplet (w_j, r_k, s_ℓ) corresponds to an expert that only predicts correctly in trials j, $k+q$ and $\ell+2q$, respectively. The number of convex combinations m is q and the number of shifts k is $3q-1$.

One now can now show that a partition of loss zero corresponds to a matching and vice versa. □

6 Experiments

In this section we discuss experiments performed on artificial data. The setup is similar to the one used in [9]. We choose the square loss as the loss function and the simple average prediction function with $c = 2$ and $\eta = 1/2$. We use $T = 2800$ trials and $n = 200$ experts, $m = 3$ of which constitute the experts (unit vectors) in the pool $\{\tilde{\boldsymbol{u}}_1, \tilde{\boldsymbol{u}}_2, \tilde{\boldsymbol{u}}_3\}$. The predictions of the experts are generated randomly and are always in $[0, 1]$. An expert from the pool has (when active) an expected loss of $1/360$ per trial while the other $n-1$ (non-active) experts have an expected loss of $1/12$ per trial. The sequence of comparators is $\tilde{\boldsymbol{u}}_1, \tilde{\boldsymbol{u}}_2, \tilde{\boldsymbol{u}}_1, \tilde{\boldsymbol{u}}_2, \tilde{\boldsymbol{u}}_3, \tilde{\boldsymbol{u}}_1, \tilde{\boldsymbol{u}}_2$ and the shifts occur every 400 trials. This means that at trials 1, $t_1 = 401$ and $t_4 = 2001$ the three experts of the pool are introduced, while at trials 801, 1201, 1601 and 2401 we are shifting back to a previously used expert from the pool. We considered the different mixing schemes studied in this paper when the α parameter was set to the optimal rate $\frac{T-1}{k}$. In figures 2 and 3 we plot the total loss of the different algorithms as a function of the trial number. The top curve is the total loss of a typical expert and the bottom curve is the total loss of the best partition. The slope always corresponds to the loss per trial. As expected (see Fig. 2), the Static Experts Algorithm simply learns the weight of the expert belonging to the first section and then "gets stuck" with that expert. It has the optimal rate of loss (slope of bottom curve) in all later segments in which the first expert is active and the slope of the top curve in the remaining sections. The total loss curve of the Fixed Share to Start Vector mixing scheme has a bump at the beginning of each section but is able to recover to the optimum slope after each shift.

The bumps in its total loss curve are roughly of equal size. However note that the Fixed Share to Decaying Past mixing scheme is able to recover faster when the sequence shifts back to a previously active expert from the pool. Thus in trials 801, 1201, 1601 and 2401 the bumps in its total loss curve are smaller than the bumps in the curve for the Fixed Share to Start Vector mixing scheme. We also depicted the log weights maintained by the algorithms in Figure 4 and these plots support the above explanation. The log weight plot of the Fixed Share to Decaying Past mixing scheme shows that if an expert of the pool was active

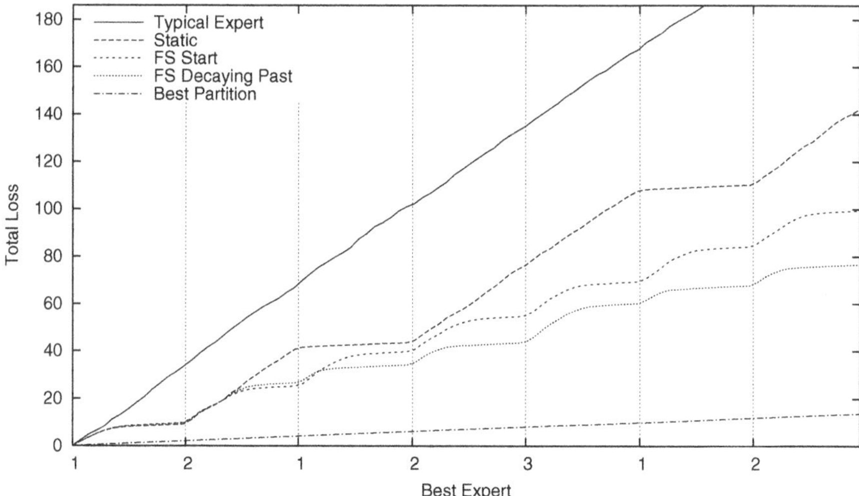

Fig. 2. Total losses obtained by the different mixing schemes. The parameters are $T = 2800$, $n = 200$, $k = 6$, $m = 3$ and α is tuned optimally. The numbers below the x-axis indicate the index of the best expert in the segment.

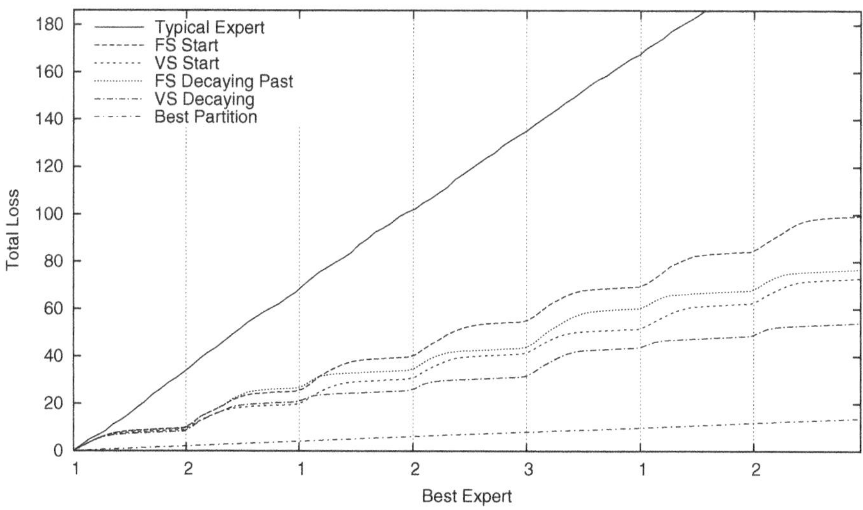

Fig. 3. Comparison between Fixed Share and Variable Share mixing schemes

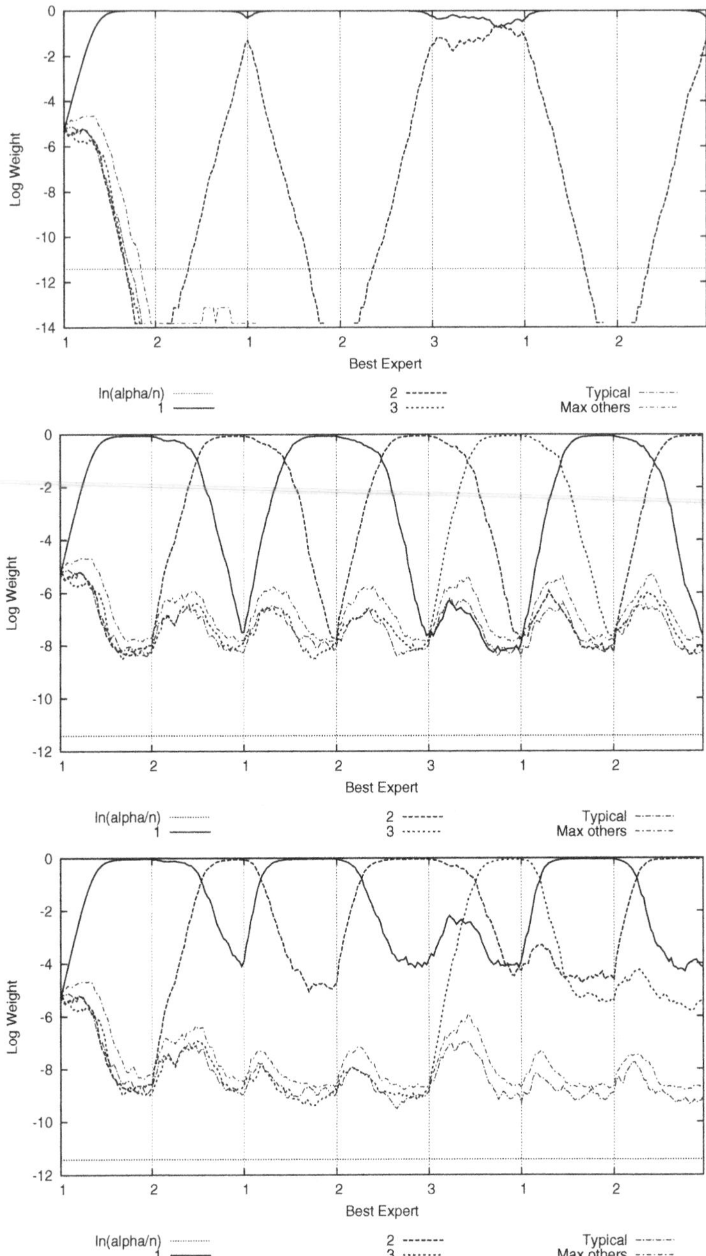

Fig. 4. Log weights for the different updates (top: Static Experts Algorithm, middle: Fixed Share to Start Vector, bottom: Fixed Share to Decaying Past). The line marked "1" depicts the log weight of expert $\tilde{\boldsymbol{u}}_1$. "Typical" is the log weight of an expert outside the pool and "max others" the maximum log weight of any expert outside the pool.

then its weight remains at an elevated level above the maximum weight of all $n-3$ experts outside the pool. From the elevated level the weight can be picked up quickly when the same expert becomes active again. This corresponds to the smaller bumps in the total loss curve of the Decaying Past mixing scheme for the sections when an expert becomes active again.

In our experiments (plots not shown) the Uniform Past mixing scheme essentially has the same performance as the Decaying Past mixing scheme, although the bounds we proved for the former scheme are slightly worse than those for the latter scheme. Similar performance was also obtained with the Max Mixing Updates. However, as expected, we got some improvement by using the Variable Share modification of the updates[3] (see Fig. 3).

7 Conclusion

Building on the work of Herbster and Warmuth, we have shown that by mixing the past posteriors, we can significantly reduce the cost of comparator shifts when the comparators are from a small pool of convex combinations of the experts. We showed that the total loss for the Fixed Share to Decaying Past mixing scheme is at most the loss of the best partition plus the number of bits needed to encode the best partition (including the boundaries of the sections) plus (a second time) the number of bits needed to encode the boundaries. A good approximation of this mixing scheme requires time and space $O(n \ln t)$ at trial t.

We are investigating whether the cost of paying for the boundaries a second time can be can be reduced. However the off-line problem of finding a partition with k shifts from a pool of m convex combinations and small loss is NP-hard. Therefore no significant improvement of the loss bounds may be achievable with efficient algorithms.

Another theoretical question is whether the new mixing schemes can be explained in terms of priors over partition experts. Indeed, for the Fixed Share Algorithm of [9] (called Fixed Share to Start Vector mixing scheme in this paper) it has been proven [17,8] that using one weight per partition gives an update that collapses to the latter efficient algorithm.

The mixing schemes we propose can be extended in various ways. For example one could cluster the past weight vectors in order to limit the number of weights to be stored and to improve the identification of the convex combinations in the best comparator sequence. Also, one could incorporate prior and on-line knowledge about how the best convex combination is changing into the mixing schemes.

Another open question is whether the parameters α, γ, and (in the case of absolute loss) η can be tuned on-line using techniques from on-line learning [4, 1] and universal coding [18,13]. Finally, following [9], slightly improved upper bounds should be obtainable for the Variable Share modification of the updates when the losses of the experts lie in $[0,1]$. Also it should be possible to formally

[3] Note that for our experiment the losses of the expert lie in $[0,1]$.

prove lower bounds on the loss of any on-line algorithm in terms of the number of bits needed to encode the partition.

Acknowledgments

The authors are grateful to Yoav Freund and Mark Herbster for many inspiring discussions.

References

1. P. Auer, N. Cesa-Bianchi, and C. Gentile. Adaptive and self-confident on-line learning algorithms. NeuroCOLT Technical Report NC-TR-00-083, 2000. An extended abstract appeared in *Proc. 13th Ann. Conf. Computational Learning Theory.*
2. P. Auer and M. K. Warmuth. Tracking the best disjunction. *Journal of Machine Learning*, 32(2):127–150, August 1998. Special issue on concept drift.
3. N. Cesa-Bianchi, Y. Freund, D. Haussler, D. P. Helmbold, R. E. Schapire, and M. K. Warmuth. How to use expert advice. *Journal of the ACM*, 44(3):427–485, 1997.
4. N. Cesa-Bianchi, D. P. Helmbold, and S. Panizza. On Bayes methods for on-line boolean prediction *Algorithmica*, 22(1/2):112–137, 1998.
5. Y. Freund. Private Communication, 2000.
Also posted on `http://www.learning-theory.org/`.
6. M. R. Garey and D. J. Johnson. Computers and intractability: a guide to the theory of NP-completeness. W. H. Freeman, 1979.
7. D. Haussler, J. Kivinen, and M. K. Warmuth. Sequential prediction of individual sequences under general loss functions. IEEE Transactions on Information Theory, 44(2):1906–1925, September 1998.
8. M. Herbster. Private Communication, 1998.
9. M. Herbster and M. K. Warmuth. Tracking the best expert. *Journal of Machine Learning*, 32(2):151–178, August 1998. Special issue on concept drift.
10. M. Herbster and M. K. Warmuth. Tracking the best regressor. In *Proc. 11th Annu. Conf. on Comput. Learning Theory*, pages 24–31. ACM Press, New York, NY, 1998.
11. J. Kivinen and M. K. Warmuth. Averaging expert predictions. In Paul Fischer and Hans Ulrich Simon, editors, *Computational Learning Theory: 4th European Conference (EuroCOLT '99)*, pages 153–167, Berlin, March 1999. Springer.
12. N. Littlestone and M. K. Warmuth. The weighted majority algorithm. *Information and Computation*, 108(2):212–261, 1994.
13. G. Shamir and N. Merhav. Low complexity sequential lossless coding for piecewise stationary memoryless sources. *IEEE Trans. Info. Theory*, 45:1498–1519, 1999.
14. Y. Singer. Switching portfolios. In *Proceedings of the 14th Conference on Uncertainty in Artificial Intelligence (UAI'98)*, pages 488–495, Morgan Kaufmann, San Francisco, CA, 1998.
15. V. Vovk. Aggregating strategies. In *Proc. 3rd Annu. Workshop on Comput. Learning Theory*, pages 371–383. Morgan Kaufmann, 1990.
16. V. G. Vovk. A game of prediction with expert advice. In *Proc. 8th Annu. Conf. on Comput. Learning Theory*, pages 51–60. ACM Press, New York, NY, 1995.

17. V. Vovk. Derandomizing stochastic prediction strategies. In *Proc. 10th Annu. Workshop on Comput. Learning Theory.* ACM Press, New York, NY, 1997.
18. F. M. J. Willems. Coding for a binary independent piecewise-identically-distributed source. *IEEE Trans. Info. Theory*, 42(6):2210–2217, 1996.

Appendix: Keeping the Number of Weights Small

For the Fixed Share to Uniform Past mixing scheme it suffices to store the average of the past vectors $\boldsymbol{v}_q^m$ (for $0 \le q < t$), that is,

$$\boldsymbol{v}_{t+1} = (1-\alpha)\boldsymbol{v}_t^m + \alpha \boldsymbol{r}_t \ ,$$

where the average $\boldsymbol{r}_t$ is computed via

$$\boldsymbol{r}_{t+1} = \frac{(t-1)\boldsymbol{r}_t + \boldsymbol{v}_t^m}{t} \ .$$

The Fixed Share Update to Decaying Past mixing scheme has slightly better bounds but now all past weight vectors need to be stored and thus the number of weights at trial t is $O(nt)$. However, we will sketch an approximate version of this update which has essentially the same bound while requiring only $O(n \ln t)$ weights to be stored.

In the case of the Uniform Past mixing scheme all past weight vectors have the same coefficient and thus can be collapsed into an average weight vector. For the best bounds we need some decaying towards the past. However the value of the coefficients for the past posteriors only enters logarithmically into the bounds. So we can group past posteriors into large blocks. For each block we only keep the average weight vector and the mixture coefficient for the whole block is the smallest mixture coefficient of all vectors in the block.

We maintain a linked list of blocks whose lengths are powers of 2. This list contains at most two blocks for each power of 2 and at least one block for each power (up to the maximal power). For each block only the average weight vector is stored. Each time a new weight vector is added, a new block with power zero is created and added to the end of the list. If there are already three blocks of power 0, then the previous two blocks of power 0 are collapsed into a block with power 1. The algorithm proceeds down the list. If a third block of power q is created, then the previous two are collapsed into a block of power $q+1$. Whenever two blocks are collapsed, their weight vectors are averaged.

It can be proven that the maximum number of nodes in the list is $1+2\lfloor \log t \rfloor$. Also the cost per boundary in Theorem 1 is $\ln \frac{1}{\beta_{t+1}(q_t)}$ and when applying the above method to the Decaying Past mixing scheme this cost is increased by at most $\gamma c \ln 2$.

Potential-Based Algorithms in Online Prediction and Game Theory*

Nicolò Cesa-Bianchi[1] and Gábor Lugosi[2]

[1] Dept. of Information Technologies,
University of Milan
Via Bramante 65,
26013 Crema, Italy
cesa-bianchi@dti.unimi.it

[2] Department of Economics,
Pompeu Fabra University
Ramon Trias Fargas 25-27,
08005 Barcelona, Spain
lugosi@upf.es

Abstract. In this paper we show that several known algorithms for sequential prediction problems (including the quasi-additive family of Grove *et al.* and Littlestone and Warmuth's Weighted Majority), for playing iterated games (including Freund and Schapire's Hedge and MW, as well as the Λ-strategies of Hart and Mas-Colell), and for boosting (including AdaBoost) are special cases of a general decision strategy based on the notion of potential. By analyzing this strategy we derive known performance bounds, as well as new bounds, as simple corollaries of a single general theorem. Besides offering a new and unified view on a large family of algorithms, we establish a connection between potential-based analysis in learning and their counterparts independently developed in game theory. By exploiting this connection, we show that certain learning problems are instances of more general game-theoretic problems. In particular, we describe a notion of generalized regret and show its applications in learning theory.

Keywords and phrases: universal prediction, on-line learning, Blackwell's strategy, Perceptron algorithm, weighted average predictors, internal regret, boosting.

* Both authors gratefully acknowledge support of ESPRIT Working Group EP 27150, Neural and Computational Learning II (NeuroCOLT II). The work of the second author was also supported by DGI grant BMF2000-0807.

D. Helmbold and B. Williamson (Eds.): COLT/EuroCOLT 2001, LNAI 2111, pp. 48–64, 2001.

1 Introduction

We begin by describing an abstract sequential decision problem and a general strategy to solve it. As we will see in detail in the subsequent sections, several previously known algorithms for more specific decision problems turn out to be special cases of this strategy.

The problem is parametrized by a *decision space* $\mathcal{X}$, by an *outcome space* $\mathcal{Y}$, and by a convex and twice differentiable *potential function* $\Phi : \mathbb{R}^N \to \mathbb{R}^+$. At each step $t = 1, 2, \ldots$, the current state is represented by a point $\boldsymbol{R}_{t-1} \in \mathbb{R}^N$, where $\boldsymbol{R}_0 = \mathbf{0}$. The decision maker observes a vector-valued *drift function* $\boldsymbol{r}_t : \mathcal{X} \times \mathcal{Y} \to \mathbb{R}^N$ and selects an element $\widehat{y}_t$ from the decision space $\mathcal{X}$. In return, an outcome $y_t \in \mathcal{Y}$ is received, and the new state of the problem is the "drifted point" $\boldsymbol{R}_t = \boldsymbol{R}_{t-1} + \boldsymbol{r}_t(y_t, \widehat{y}_t)$. The goal of the decision maker is to minimize the potential $\Phi(\boldsymbol{R}_t)$ for a given t (which might be known or unknown to the decision maker).

Example 1. Consider an on-line prediction problem in the experts' framework of [4]. Here, the decision maker is a predictor whose goal is to forecast a hidden sequence $y_1, y_2, \ldots$ of elements in the outcome space $\mathcal{Y}$. At each time t, the predictor computes its guess $\widehat{y}_t \in \mathcal{X}$ for the next outcome y_t. This guess is based on the advice $f_{1,t}, \ldots, f_{N,t} \in \mathcal{X}$ of N reference predictors, or *experts* from a fixed pool. The guesses of the predictor and the experts are then individually scored using a *loss function* $\ell : \mathcal{X} \times \mathcal{Y} \to \mathbb{R}$. The predictor's goal is to keep as small as possible the *cumulative regret* with respect to each expert. This quantity is defined, for expert i, by the sum

$$\sum_{s=1}^{t} \left(\ell(\widehat{y}_s, y_s) - \ell(f_{i,s}, y_s)\right) .$$

This can be easily modeled within our abstract decision problem by associating a coordinate to each expert and by defining the components $r_{i,t}$ of the drift function $\boldsymbol{r}_t$ by $r_{i,t}(\widehat{y}_t, y_t) = \ell(\widehat{y}_t, y_t) - \ell(f_{i,t}, y_t)$ for $i = 1, \ldots, N$.

In this work, we will restrict our attention to instances of our abstract decision problem satisfying the following two assumptions. The notation $\boldsymbol{u} \cdot \boldsymbol{v}$ stands for the inner product of two vectors defined by $\boldsymbol{u} \cdot \boldsymbol{v} = u_1 v_1 + \ldots + u_N v_N$.

1. **Generalized Blackwell's condition.** At each time t, a decision $\widehat{y}_t \in \mathcal{X}$ exists such that
$$\sup_{y_t \in \mathcal{Y}} \nabla\Phi(\boldsymbol{R}_{t-1}) \cdot \boldsymbol{r}_t(\widehat{y}_t, y_t) \leq 0 , \tag{1}$$
2. **Additive potential.** The potential Φ can be written as $\Phi(\boldsymbol{u}) = \sum_{i=1}^{N} \phi(u_i)$ for all $\boldsymbol{u} = (u_1, \ldots, u_N) \in \mathbb{R}^N$, where $\phi : \mathbb{R} \to \mathbb{R}^+$ is a nonnegative function of one variable. Typically, ϕ will be monotonically increasing and convex on $\mathbb{R}^+$.

Remark 2. Strategies satisfying condition (1) tend to keep the point $\boldsymbol{R}_t$ as close as possible to the minimum of the potential by forcing the drift vector to point away from the gradient of the current potential. This gradient descent approach to sequential decision problems is not new. A prominent example of a decision strategy of this type is the one used by Blackwell to prove his celebrated approachability theorem [1], generalizing to vector-valued payoffs von Neumann's minimax theorem. The application of Blackwell's strategy to sequential decision problems, and its generalization to arbitrary potentials, is due to a series of papers by Hart and Mas-Colell [18, 19], where condition (1) was first introduced (though in a somewhat more restricted context). Condition (1) has been independently introduced by Grove, Littlestone and Schuurmans [15], who used it to define and analyze a new family of algorithms for solving on-line binary classification problems. This family includes, as special cases, the Perceptron [25] and the zero-threshold Winnow algorithm [23]. Finally, our abstract decision problem bears some similarities with Schapire's drifting game [26] (discussed in the full paper).

2 General Bounds

In this section we describe a general upper bound on the potential of the location reached by the drifting point when the decision maker uses a strategy satisfying condition (1). This result is inspired by, and partially builds on, Hart and Mas-Colell's analysis of their Λ-strategies [18] for playing iterated games and Grove *et al.*'s analysis of quasi-additive algorithms [15] for binary classification.

Theorem 3. *Let Φ be a twice differentiable additive potential function and let $\boldsymbol{r}_1, \boldsymbol{r}_2, \ldots \in \mathbb{R}^N$ be such that*

$$\nabla\Phi(\boldsymbol{R}_{t-1}) \cdot \boldsymbol{r}_t \le 0$$

for all $t \ge 1$, where $\boldsymbol{R}_t = \boldsymbol{r}_1 + \ldots + \boldsymbol{r}_t$. Let $f : \mathbb{R}^+ \to \mathbb{R}^+$ be an increasing, concave, and twice differentiable auxiliary function such that, for all $t = 1, 2, \ldots$,

$$\sup_{\boldsymbol{u} \in \mathbb{R}^N} f'(\Phi(\boldsymbol{u})) \sum_{i=1}^{N} \phi''(u_i) r_{i,t}^2 \le C(\boldsymbol{r}_t)$$

for some nonegative function $C : \mathbb{R}^N \to \mathbb{R}^+$. Then, for all $t = 1, 2, \ldots$,

$$f(\Phi(\boldsymbol{R}_t)) \le f(\Phi(\boldsymbol{0})) + \frac{1}{2} \sum_{s=1}^{t} C(\boldsymbol{r}_s) \ .$$

Proof. We estimate $f(\Phi(\boldsymbol{R}_t))$ in terms of $f(\Phi(\boldsymbol{R}_{t-1}))$ using Taylor's theorem. Note that $\nabla f(\Phi(\boldsymbol{R}_{t-1})) = f'(\Phi(\boldsymbol{R}_{t-1}))\nabla\Phi(\boldsymbol{R}_{t-1})$. So we obtain

$$\begin{aligned} f(\Phi(\boldsymbol{R}_t)) &= f(\Phi(\boldsymbol{R}_{t-1} + \boldsymbol{r}_t)) \\ &= f(\Phi(\boldsymbol{R}_{t-1})) + f'(\Phi(\boldsymbol{R}_{t-1}))\ \nabla(\Phi(\boldsymbol{R}_{t-1})) \cdot \boldsymbol{r}_t + \frac{1}{2} \sum_{i=1}^{N} \sum_{j=1}^{N} \left. \frac{\partial^2 f(\Phi)}{\partial u_i \partial u_j} \right|_{\boldsymbol{\xi}} r_{i,t} r_{j,t} \end{aligned}$$

(where $\boldsymbol{\xi}$ is some vector between $\boldsymbol{R}_{t-1}$ and $\boldsymbol{R}_t$)

$$\leq f\left(\Phi(\boldsymbol{R}_{t-1})\right) + \frac{1}{2}\sum_{i=1}^{N}\sum_{j=1}^{N} \left.\frac{\partial^2 f(\Phi)}{\partial u_i \partial u_j}\right|_{\boldsymbol{\xi}} r_{i,t} r_{j,t}$$

where the inequality follows by (1) and the fact that $f' \geq 0$. Since Φ is additive, straightforward calculation shows that

$$\begin{aligned}
&\sum_{i=1}^{N}\sum_{j=1}^{N} \left.\frac{\partial^2 f(\Phi)}{\partial u_i \partial u_j}\right|_{\boldsymbol{\xi}} r_{i,t} r_{j,t} \\
&= f''\left(\Phi(\boldsymbol{\xi})\right) \sum_{i=1}^{N}\sum_{j=1}^{N} \phi'(\xi_i)\phi'(\xi_j) r_{i,t} r_{j,t} + f'\left(\Phi(\boldsymbol{\xi})\right) \sum_{i=1}^{N} \phi''(\xi_i) r_{i,t}^2 \\
&= f''\left(\Phi(\boldsymbol{\xi})\right) \left(\sum_{i=1}^{N} \phi'(\xi_i) r_{i,t}\right)^2 + f'\left(\Phi(\boldsymbol{\xi})\right) \sum_{i=1}^{N} \phi''(\xi_i) r_{i,t}^2 \\
&\leq f'\left(\Phi(\boldsymbol{\xi})\right) \sum_{i=1}^{N} \phi''(\xi_i) r_{i,t}^2 \qquad \text{(since } f \text{ is concave)} \\
&\leq C(\boldsymbol{r}_t)
\end{aligned}$$

where at the last step we used the hypothesis of the theorem. Thus, we have obtained $f(\Phi(\boldsymbol{R}_t)) \leq f(\Phi(\boldsymbol{R}_{t-1})) + C(\boldsymbol{r}_t)/2$. The proof is finished by iterating the argument. □

In what follows, we will often write $\boldsymbol{r}_t$ instead of $\boldsymbol{r}_t(\widehat{y}_t, y_t)$ when $\widehat{y}_t$ and y_t are taken as arbitrary elements of, respectively, $\mathcal{X}$ and $\mathcal{Y}$. Moreover, we will always use $\boldsymbol{R}_t$ to denote $\boldsymbol{r}_1(\widehat{y}_1, y_1) + \ldots + \boldsymbol{r}_t(\widehat{y}_t, y_t)$.

We now review two simple applications of Theorem 3. The first is for polynomial potential functions. For $p \geq 1$, define the p-norm of a vector $\boldsymbol{u}$ by

$$\|\boldsymbol{u}\|_p = \left(\sum_{i=1}^{N} |u_i|^p\right)^{1/p} .$$

Corollary 4. *Assume that a prediction algorithm satisfies condition (1) with the potential function*

$$\Phi(\boldsymbol{u}) = \sum_{i=1}^{N} |u_i|^p , \tag{2}$$

where $p \geq 2$. Then

$$\Phi(\boldsymbol{R}_t)^{2/p} \leq (p-1)\sum_{s=1}^{t} \|\boldsymbol{r}_s\|_p^2 \qquad \text{and} \qquad \max_{1\leq i\leq N} R_{i,t} \leq \sqrt{(p-1)\sum_{s=1}^{t} \|\boldsymbol{r}_s\|_p^2} .$$

Proof. Apply Theorem 3 with $f(x) = x^{2/p}$ and $\phi(x) = |x|^p$. By straightforward calculation,

$$f'(x) = \frac{2}{p x^{(p-2)/p}} .$$

On the other hand, since $\phi''(x) = p(p-1)|x|^{p-2}$, by Hölder's inequality,

$$\sum_{i=1}^{N} \phi''(u_i) r_{i,t}^2 = p(p-1) \sum_{i=1}^{N} |u_i|^{p-2} r_{i,t}^2$$
$$\leq p(p-1) \left(\sum_{i=1}^{N} \left(|u_i|^{p-2}\right)^{p/(p-2)} \right)^{(p-2)/p} \left(\sum_{i=1}^{N} |r_{i,t}|^p \right)^{2/p} .$$

Thus,

$$f'(\Phi(\boldsymbol{u})) \sum_{i=1}^{N} \phi''(u_i) r_{i,t}^2 \leq (p-1) \left(\sum_{i=1}^{N} |r_{i,t}|^p \right)^{2/p} .$$

The conditions of Theorem 3 are then satisfied with $C(\boldsymbol{r}_t) = (p-1) \|\boldsymbol{r}_t\|_p^2$. Since $\Phi(\boldsymbol{0}) = 0$, Theorem 3 implies the result. □

Another simple and important choice for the potential function is the *exponential potential*, treated in the next corollary.

Corollary 5. *Assume that a prediction algorithm satisfies condition (1) with the potential function*

$$\Phi(\boldsymbol{u}) = \sum_{i=1}^{N} e^{\eta u_i} , \tag{3}$$

where $\eta > 0$ is a parameter. Then

$$\ln \Phi(\boldsymbol{R}_t) \leq \ln N + \frac{\eta^2}{2} \sum_{s=1}^{t} \max_{1 \leq i \leq N} r_{i,s}^2$$

and

$$\max_{1 \leq i \leq N} R_{i,t} \leq \frac{\ln N}{\eta} + \frac{\eta}{2} \sum_{s=1}^{t} \max_{1 \leq i \leq N} r_{i,s}^2 .$$

Proof. Choosing $f(x) = (1/\eta) \ln x$ and $\phi(x) = e^{\eta x}$, the conditions of Theorem 3 are satisfied with $C(\boldsymbol{r}_t) = \eta \max_{1 \leq i \leq N} r_{i,t}^2$. Using $\Phi(\boldsymbol{0}) = N$ then yields the result. □

Remark 6. The polynomial potential was considered in [18] and, in the context of binary classification, in [15], where it was used to define the p-norm Perceptron. In game theory, the exponential potential is viewed as a form of smooth fictitious play (in fictitious play, the player chooses the pure strategy that is best given the past distribution of the adversary's plays; smoothing this choice amounts to introduce randomization). In learning theory, algorithms based on the exponential potential have been intensively studied and applied to a variety of problems (see, e.g., [4, 8, 28, 29]).

If $\boldsymbol{r}_t \in [-1,1]^N$ for all t, then the choice $p = 2\ln N$ for the polynomial potential yields the bound

$$\max_{1\le i\le N} R_{i,t} \le \sqrt{(2\ln N - 1)\sum_{s=1}^{t}\left(\sum_{i=1}^{N}|u_i|^{2\ln N}\right)^{1/\ln N}}$$
$$\le \sqrt{(2\ln N - 1)N^{1/\ln N}t} = \sqrt{(2\ln N - 1)et}\ .$$

(This choice of p was also suggested in [13] in the context of p-norm perceptron algorithms.) A similar bound can be obtained, under the same assumption on the $\boldsymbol{r}_t$'s, by setting $\eta = \sqrt{2\ln N/t}$ in the exponential potential. Note that this tuning of η requires knowledge of the horizon t.

3 Weighted Average Predictors

In this section, we consider one of the main applications of the potential-based strategy induced by the generalized Blackwell condition, that is, the experts' framework mentioned in Section 1. Recall that, in this framework, the i-th component of the drift vector at time t takes the form of a regret

$$r_{i,t}(\widehat{y}_t, y_t) = \ell(\widehat{y}_t, y_t) - \ell(f_{i,t}, y_t)$$

where $\ell(\widehat{y}_t, y_t)$ is the loss of the predictor and $\ell(f_{i,t}, y_t)$ is the loss of the i-th expert. Denote $\partial\Phi(\boldsymbol{u})/\partial u_i$ by $\nabla_i\Phi(\boldsymbol{u})$ and assume $\nabla_i\Phi(\boldsymbol{u}) \ge 0$ for all $\boldsymbol{u} \in \mathbb{R}^N$. A remarkable fact in this application is that, if $\mathcal{X}$ is a convex subset of a vector space and the loss function ℓ is convex in its first component, then a predictor satisfying condition (1) is always obtained by averaging the experts' predictions weighted by the normalized potential gradient. Indeed, note that condition (1) is equivalent to

$$(\forall y \in \mathcal{Y}) \qquad \ell(\widehat{y}_t, y) \le \frac{\sum_{i=1}^N \nabla_i\Phi(\boldsymbol{R}_{t-1})\ell(f_{i,t}, y)}{\sum_{j=1}^N \nabla_j\Phi(\boldsymbol{R}_{t-1})} \tag{4}$$

Now by convexity of ℓ, we have that (4) is implied by

$$(\forall y \in \mathcal{Y}) \qquad \ell(\widehat{y}_t, y) \le \ell\left(\frac{\sum_{i=1}^N \nabla_i\Phi(\boldsymbol{R}_{t-1})f_{i,t}}{\sum_{j=1}^N \nabla_j\Phi(\boldsymbol{R}_{t-1})}, y\right)$$

which is clearly satisfied by choosing

$$\widehat{y}_t = \frac{\sum_{i=1}^N \nabla_i\Phi(\boldsymbol{R}_{t-1})f_{i,t}}{\sum_{j=1}^N \nabla_j\Phi(\boldsymbol{R}_{t-1})}\ .$$

Example 7. Consider the exponential potential function of Corollary 5. In this case, the weighted average predictor described above simplifies to

$$\widehat{y}_t = \frac{\sum_{i=1}^N \exp\left(\eta \sum_{s=1}^{t-1} \left(\ell(\widehat{y}_s, y_s) - \ell(f_{i,s}, y_s)\right)\right) f_{i,t}}{\sum_{i=1}^N \exp\left(\eta \sum_{s=1}^{t-1} \left(\ell(\widehat{y}_s, y_s) - \ell(f_{i,s}, y_s)\right)\right)}$$
$$= \frac{\sum_{i=1}^N \exp\left(-\eta \sum_{s=1}^{t-1} \ell(f_{i,s}, y_s)\right) f_{i,t}}{\sum_{i=1}^N \exp\left(-\eta \sum_{s=1}^{t-1} \ell(f_{i,s}, y_s)\right)} . \qquad (5)$$

This is the well-known Weighted Majority predictor of [22], and Corollary 5 recovers, up to constant factors, previously known performance bounds (see, e.g., [3]). Similarly, Corollary 4 may be used to derive performance bounds for the predictor

$$\widehat{y}_t = \frac{\sum_{i=1}^N \max\left\{0,\ \sum_{s=1}^{t-1} \left(\ell(\widehat{y}_s, y_s) - \ell(f_{i,s}, y_s)\right)\right\}^{p-1} f_{i,t}}{\sum_{i=1}^N \max\left\{0,\ \sum_{s=1}^{t-1} \left(\ell(\widehat{y}_s, y_s) - \ell(f_{i,s}, y_s)\right)\right\}^{p-1}} . \qquad (6)$$

based on a slight modification of the polynomial potential (2).

These results are summarized as follows.

Corollary 8. *Assume that the decision space $\mathcal{X}$ is a convex subset of a vector space and let ℓ be a loss function which is convex in its first component and bounded between 0 and 1. Then the exponential weighted average predictor (5) with parameter $\eta = \sqrt{2 \ln N / t}$ satisfies, for all sequences $y_1, y_2, \ldots$,*

$$\sum_{s=1}^t \ell(\widehat{y}_s, y_s) \le \min_{i=1,\ldots,N} \sum_{s=1}^t \ell(f_{i,s}, y_s) + \sqrt{2t \ln N} ,$$

and the polynomial weighted average predictor (6) with parameter $p = 2 \ln N$ satisfies, for all sequences $y_1, y_2, \ldots$,

$$\sum_{s=1}^t \ell(\widehat{y}_s, y_s) \le \min_{i=1,\ldots,N} \sum_{s=1}^t \ell(f_{i,s}, y_s) + \sqrt{te(2 \ln N - 1)} .$$

The beauty of the Weighted Majority predictor of Corollary 8 is that it only depends on the past performance of the experts, whereas the predictions made using polynomial (and other general) potentials depend on the past predictions $\widehat{y}_s$, $s < t$ as well.

Remark 9. In some cases Theorem 3 gives suboptimal bounds. In fact, the arguments of Theorem 3 use Taylor's theorem to bound the increase of the potential function. However, in some situations the value of the potential function is actually nonincreasing. The following property is proven by repeating an argument of Kivinen and Warmuth [20].

Proposition 10. *Consider the weighted majority predictor (5). If the loss function ℓ is such that the function $F(z) = e^{-\eta\ell(z,y)}$ is concave for all $y \in \mathcal{Y}$, then for all $t \geq 1$, $\Phi(\boldsymbol{R}_t) \leq \Phi(\boldsymbol{0})$ where Φ is the exponential potential function (3). In particular, since $\Phi(\boldsymbol{0}) = N$, we have* $\max_{i=1,\ldots,N} R_{i,t} \leq \ln(N)/\eta$.

Proof. It suffices to show that $\Phi(\boldsymbol{R}_t) \leq \Phi(\boldsymbol{R}_{t-1})$ or, equivalently, that

$$\sum_{i=1}^{N} \exp\left(-\eta \sum_{s=1}^{t-1} \ell(f_{i,s}, y_s)\right) e^{\eta(\ell(\hat{y}_t,y_t)-\ell(f_{i,t},y_t))} \leq \sum_{i=1}^{N} \exp\left(-\eta \sum_{s=1}^{t-1} \ell(f_{i,s}, y_s)\right) ,$$

which, denoting $w_{i,t-1} = \exp\left(-\eta \sum_{s=1}^{t-1} \ell(f_{i,s}, y_s)\right)$, may be written as

$$e^{-\eta\ell(\hat{y}_t,y_t)} \geq \frac{\sum_{i=1}^{N} w_{i,t-1} e^{-\eta\ell(f_{i,t},y_t)}}{\sum_{i=1}^{N} w_{i,t-1}} .$$

But since $\widehat{y}_t = \sum_{i=1}^{N} w_{i,t-1} f_{i,t} \Big/ \sum_{i=1}^{N} w_{i,t-1}$, this follows by the concavity of $F(z)$ and Jensen's inequality. □

Simple and common examples of loss functions satisfying the concavity assumption of the proposition include the squared loss $\ell(z,y) = (z-y)^2$ for $\mathcal{X} = \mathcal{Y} = [0,1]$ with $\eta = 1/2$ and the logarithmic loss with $\eta = 1$. For more information on this type of prediction problems we refer to Vovk [30], Haussler, Kivinen, and Warmuth [17] and Kivinen and Warmuth [20]. Observe that the proof of the proposition does not make explicit use of the generalized Blackwell condition.

4 The Quasi-Additive Algorithm

In this section, we show that the quasi-additive algorithm of Grove, Littlestone and Schuurmans (whose specific instances are the p-norm Perceptron [13, 15], the classical Perceptron [2, 24, 25], and the zero-threshold Winnow algorithm [23]) is a special case of our general decision strategy. Then, we derive performance bounds as corollaries of our Theorem 3.

We recall that the quasi-additive algorithm performs binary classification of *attribute vectors* $\boldsymbol{x} = (x_1, \ldots, x_N) \in \mathbb{R}^N$ by incrementally adjusting a vector $\boldsymbol{w} \in \mathbb{R}^N$ of *weights*. If $\boldsymbol{w}_t$ is the weight vector before observing the t-th attribute vector $\boldsymbol{x}_t$, then the quasi-additive algorithm predicts the unknown label $y_t \in \{-1,1\}$ of $\boldsymbol{x}_t$ with the thresholded linear function $\widehat{y}_t = \text{SGN}(\boldsymbol{x}_t \cdot \boldsymbol{w}_t)$. If the correct label y_t is different from $\widehat{y}_t$, then the weight vector is updated, and the precise way this update occurs distinguishes the various instances of the quasi-additive algorithm.

To fit and analyze the quasi-additive algorithm in our framework, we specialize the abstract decision problem of Section 1 as follows. The decision space $\mathcal{X}$ and the outcome space $\mathcal{Y}$ are both set equal to $\{-1,1\}$. The drift vector at time t is the function $\boldsymbol{r}_t(\widehat{y}_t, y_t) = \mathbb{1}_{\{y_t \neq \widehat{y}_t\}} y_t \boldsymbol{x}_t$ where $\mathbb{1}_{\{E\}}$ is the indicator function of event E. Instances of the quasi-additive algorithm are parametrized by a potential function Φ and use the gradient of the current potential as weight vector, that is, $\boldsymbol{w}_t = \nabla\Phi(\boldsymbol{R}_{t-1})$. Hence, the weight update is defined by

$$\boldsymbol{w}_{t+i} = \nabla\Phi\left((\nabla\Phi)^{-1}(\boldsymbol{w}_t) + r_{i,t}\right)$$

where $(\nabla\Phi)^{-1}$, when it exists, is the functional inverse of $\nabla\Phi$. We now check that condition (1) is satisfied. If $\widehat{y}_t = y_t$, then $\boldsymbol{r}_t(\widehat{y}_t, y_t) = \mathbf{0}$ and the condition is satisfied. Otherwise, $\boldsymbol{r}_t \cdot \nabla\Phi(\boldsymbol{R}_{t-1}) = \mathbb{1}_{\{y_t \neq \widehat{y}_t\}} y_t \boldsymbol{x}_t \cdot \boldsymbol{w}_t \leq 0$, and the condition is satisfied in this case as well.

In the rest of this section, we denote by $M_t = \sum_{s=1}^{t} \mathbb{1}_{\{y_t \neq \widehat{y}_t\}}$ the total number of mistakes made by the specific quasi-additive algorithm being considered.

4.1 The p-Norm Perceptron

As defined in [15], the p-norm Perceptron uses the polynomial potential (2). We now derive a generalization of the Perceptron convergence theorem [2, 24] (a version slightly stronger than ours was proven in [13]).

Fix $\boldsymbol{v}_0 \in \mathbb{R}^N$ and $\gamma > 0$. For an arbitrary sequence $(\boldsymbol{x}_1, y_1), \ldots, (\boldsymbol{x}_t, y_t)$ of labeled attribute vectors, let $D_t = \sum_{s=1}^{t} \max\{0, \gamma - y_t \boldsymbol{x}_t \cdot \boldsymbol{v}_0\}$ be the total *deviation* [9, 13, 14] of $\boldsymbol{v}_0$ with respect to margin $\gamma > 0$. Each term in the sum defining D_t tells whether, and by how much, the linear threshold classifier based on weight vector $\boldsymbol{v}_0$ missed to classify, to within a certain margin, the corresponding example. Thus D_t measures a notion of loss, called *hinge loss* in [14], different from the number of misclassifications, associated to the weight vector $\boldsymbol{v}_0$.

Corollary 11. *Let $(\boldsymbol{x}_1, y_1), (\boldsymbol{x}_2, y_2), \ldots \in \mathbb{R}^N \times \{-1, 1\}$ be any sequence of labeled attribute vectors. Then the number M_t of mistakes made by the p-norm Perceptron on a prefix of arbitrary length t of this sequence such that $\|\boldsymbol{x}_s\|_p \leq X_p$ for some X_p and for all $s \leq t$ is at most*

$$M_t \leq \frac{D_t}{\gamma} + \frac{p-1}{2}\left(\frac{X_p}{\gamma}\right)^2 + \sqrt{\frac{(p-1)^2 X_p^4 + 4(p-1)\gamma D_t X_p^2}{4\gamma^4}}$$

where D_t is the deviation of $\boldsymbol{v}_0$ with respect to margin γ for any $\boldsymbol{v}_0$ of unit q-norm (q being the dual norm of p) and any $\gamma > 0$.

Proof. Corollary 4 and the bound on $\|\boldsymbol{x}_t\|_p$ implies that $\|\boldsymbol{R}_t\|_p^2 \leq (p-1) X_p^2 M_t$. On the other hand, let $\boldsymbol{v}_0 \in \mathbb{R}^N$ be any vector such that $\|\boldsymbol{v}_0\|_q = 1$. Then

$$\begin{aligned}
\|\boldsymbol{R}_t\|_p &\geq \boldsymbol{R}_t \cdot \boldsymbol{v}_0 \quad \text{(by Hölder's inequality)} \\
&= \boldsymbol{R}_{t-1} \cdot \boldsymbol{v}_0 + \mathbb{1}_{\{y_t \neq \widehat{y}_t\}} y_t \boldsymbol{x}_t \cdot \boldsymbol{v}_0 \\
&\geq \boldsymbol{R}_{t-1} \cdot \boldsymbol{v}_0 + \mathbb{1}_{\{y_t \neq \widehat{y}_t\}} (\gamma - d_t) \\
&= \cdots \quad \geq \gamma M_t - D_t\ .
\end{aligned}$$

Piecing together the two inequalities, and solving the resulting equation for M_t, yields the desired result. □

4.2 Zero-Threshold Winnow

The zero-threshold Winnow algorithm uses the exponential potential (3). As we did for the p-norm Perceptron, we derive as a corollary (proof shown in the appendix) a robust version of the bound shown by Grove, Littlestone and Schuurmans [15]. Let D_t be the same as in Corollary 11.

Corollary 12. *Let $(\boldsymbol{x}_1, y_1), (\boldsymbol{x}_2, y_2), \ldots \in \mathbb{R}^N \times \{-1, 1\}$ be any sequence of labeled attribute vectors. On a prefix of arbitrary length t of this sequence such that*

$$\begin{aligned} \|\boldsymbol{x}_s\|_\infty &\le X_\infty \quad \text{for some } X_\infty \text{ and for all } s \le t, \\ L &\ge D_t/\gamma \quad \text{for some probability vector } \boldsymbol{v}_0 \text{ and for some } L, \gamma > 0, \end{aligned}$$

the number M_t of mistakes made by zero-threshold Winnow tuned with

$$\eta = \begin{cases} \gamma/(X_\infty^2) & \text{if } L < 2(X_\infty/\gamma)^2 \ln N \\ \sqrt{\dfrac{2\ln N}{X_\infty^2 L}} & \text{otherwise} \end{cases}$$

is at most $6\left(X_\infty/\gamma\right)^2 \ln N$ if $L < 2(X_\infty/\gamma)^2 \ln N$, and at most

$$\frac{D_t}{\gamma} + \sqrt{2L\left(\frac{X_\infty}{\gamma}\right)^2 \ln N + 2\left(\frac{X_\infty}{\gamma}\right)^2 \ln N} \; .$$

otherwise.

Remark 13. Performance bounds similar to those shown in this section and in Section 3 can be obtained, for the same algorithms, via an analysis based on the Bregman divergence of Φ. Though Bregman divergences are a very versatile tool [13], their applicability seems to be limited to weighted average predictors (and to certain losses only). Hence, it is an interesting open problem to understand whether more complex predictors, like the ones analyzed in the Section 6, could be analyzed in this way.

5 Boosting

Boosting algorithms for $\{-1, 1\}$ classification problems receive in input a labeled sample $(v_1, \ell_1), \ldots, (v_N, \ell_N) \in \mathcal{V} \times \{-1, 1\}$, where $\mathcal{V}$ is a generic instance space, and return classifiers of the form $\text{SGN}\left(\sum_{s=1}^t \alpha_s h_s\right)$, where $\alpha_s \in \mathbb{R}$ and the functions $h_s : \mathcal{V} \to [-1, 1]$ belong to a fixed *hypothesis space* $\mathcal{H}$. In the *boosting by resampling* schema, the classifier is built incrementally: at each step t, the booster weighs the sample and calls an oracle (the so-called *weak learner*) that returns some $h_t \in \mathcal{H}$. Then the booster chooses α_t based on the performance of h_t on the weighted sample and adds $\alpha_t h_t$ to the thresholded sum. Boosting by resampling can be easily fitted in our framework by letting, at each round t, α_t be the decision maker's choice ($\mathcal{X} = \mathbb{R}$) and h_t be the outcome ($\mathcal{Y} = \mathcal{H}$). The drift function $\boldsymbol{r}_t$ is defined by $r_{i,t}(\alpha_t, h_t) = -\alpha_t \ell_i h_t(v_i)$ for each $i = 1, \dots, N$, and condition (1) takes the form

$$\nabla \Phi(\boldsymbol{R}_{t-1}) \cdot \boldsymbol{r}_t = -\alpha_t \sum_{i=1}^{N} \ell_i h_t(v_i) \nabla_i \Phi(\boldsymbol{R}_{t-1}) \leq 0 .$$

Define $\sum_{i=1}^{N} \ell_i h_t(v_i) \nabla_i \Phi(\boldsymbol{R}_{t-1})$ as the *weighted functional margin* of h_t, denoted by $\overline{m}(h_t)$. We see that (1) corresponds to $\alpha_t \overline{m}(h_t) \geq 0$. Freund and Schapire's AdaBoost [8] is a special case of this schema where the potential is exponential and α_t is chosen in a way such that (1) is satisfied. We recover (to within constants) the known bound on the accuracy of the classifier output by AdaBoost as a special case of our main result.

Corollary 14. *For every training set* $(v_1, \ell_1), \dots, (v_N, \ell_N) \in \mathcal{V} \times \{-1, 1\}$, *and for every sequence* $h_1, h_2, \dots$ *of functions* $h_t : \mathcal{V} \to [-1, 1]$, *if* Φ *is the exponential potential (2) with* $\eta = 1$, *then the classifier* $f = \mathrm{SGN}\left(\sum_{s=1}^{t} \widetilde{\alpha}_s h_s\right)$ *achieves*

$$\frac{1}{N} \sum_{i=1}^{N} \mathbb{1}_{\{f(v_i) \neq \ell_i\}} \leq \exp\left(-\frac{1}{4} \sum_{s=1}^{t} \widetilde{\alpha}_s^2\right) ,$$

where $\widetilde{\alpha}_s = \overline{m}(h_s) / \left(2 \sum_{i=1}^{N} \exp(R_{i,t-1})\right)$.

Proof. The result does not follow directly from Corollary 5. We need to slightly modify the proof of Theorem 3 when the negative term $f'(\Phi(\boldsymbol{R}_{t-1})) \nabla \Phi(\boldsymbol{R}_{t-1}) \cdot \boldsymbol{r}_t$ was dropped. Here, that term is $-\alpha_t \overline{m}(h_t) / \left(\sum_{i=1}^{N} \exp(R_{i,t-1})\right)$, where

$$\overline{m}(h_t) = \sum_{i=1}^{N} \ell_i h_t(v_i) \exp(R_{i,t-1}) .$$

Keeping this term around, and noting that $C(\boldsymbol{r}_t) \leq \alpha_t^2$, we can choose $\alpha_t = \widetilde{\alpha}_t$ and, proceeding as in the proof of Corollary 5, obtain

$$\ln \Phi(\boldsymbol{R}_t) \leq \ln N - \frac{1}{4} \sum_{s=1}^{t} \widetilde{\alpha}_s^2 .$$

By rearranging and exponentiating we get

$$\frac{\Phi(\boldsymbol{R}_t)}{N} \leq \exp\left(-\frac{1}{4} \sum_{s=1}^{t} \widetilde{\alpha}_s^2\right) .$$

As, for the exponential potential, $\Phi(\boldsymbol{R}_t)/N$ upper bounds the fraction of misclassified examples, we get the desired result. □

6 Potential-Based Algorithms in Game Theory

Our abstract decision problem can be applied to the problem of playing repeated games. Consider a game between a player and an adversary. At each round of the game, the player chooses an action (or pure strategy) $i \in \{1, \ldots, m\}$ and, independently, the adversary chooses an action $y \in \mathcal{Y}$. The player's loss $L(i, y)$ is the value of a loss function $L : \{1, \ldots, m\} \times \mathcal{Y} \to \mathbb{R}^+$, where $L(i, y) < M$ for some $M < \infty$ and for all $(i, y) \in \{1, \ldots, m\} \times \mathcal{Y}$. Now suppose that, at the t-th round of the game, the player chooses an action according to the mixed strategy (i.e., probability distribution over actions) $\boldsymbol{p}_t = (p_{1,t}, \ldots, p_{m,t})$, and suppose the adversary chooses action $y \in \mathcal{Y}$. Then the regret for the player is the vector $\boldsymbol{r}_t \in \mathbb{R}^m$, whose j-th component is

$$r_{j,t}(\boldsymbol{p}_t, y) = \sum_{k=1}^{m} p_{k,t} \left(L(k, y) - L(j, y) \right) . \tag{7}$$

This quantity measures the expected change in the player loss if it were to deterministically choose action k, and the adversary did not change his action. A player is *Hannan consistent* [16] if the per-round regret vector $\boldsymbol{R}_t / t = (\boldsymbol{r}_1 + \ldots + \boldsymbol{r}_t)/t$ converges to the zero vector as t grows to infinity.

Our general decision strategy can be used to play repeated games of this type by letting the decision space $\mathcal{X}$ be the set of distributions on the player set $\{1, \ldots, m\}$ of actions and the drift vector be the regret vector (7). It is not hard to see that, in this setting, condition (1) yields the mixed strategy $\boldsymbol{p}_t$ defined, for $\nabla \Phi \geq \mathbf{0}$, by

$$p_{i,t} = \frac{\nabla_i \Phi(\boldsymbol{R}_{t-1})}{\sum_{k=1}^{m} \nabla_k \Phi(\boldsymbol{R}_{t-1})} . \tag{8}$$

Freund and Schapire's Hedge algorithm [8] and the strategy in Blackwell's proof of the approachability theorem are special cases of (8) for, respectively, the exponential potential (3) and the polynomial potential (2) with $p = 2$. Hart and Mas-Colell [18] characterize the whole class of potentials for which condition (1) yields a Hannan consistent player.

Remark 15. Freund and Schapire [10] discuss a more general setup where the game is defined by an $N \times M$ loss matrix S of entries in $[0, 1]$. In each round t the row player chooses a row of M according to a mixed strategy $\boldsymbol{p}_t = (p_{1,t}, \ldots, p_{N,t})$ and the column player chooses a column of M according to the mixed strategy $\boldsymbol{q}_t = (q_{1,t}, \ldots, q_{M,t})$. The row player's loss at time t is $S(\boldsymbol{p}_t, \boldsymbol{q}_t) = \sum_{i=1}^{N} \sum_{j=1}^{M} p_{i,t} q_{j,t} S(i, j)$ and its goal is to achieve a cumulative loss $\sum_{s=1}^{t} S(\boldsymbol{p}_t, \boldsymbol{q}_t)$ almost as small as the cumulative loss of the best fixed mixed strategy $\min_{\boldsymbol{p}} \sum_{s=1}^{t} S(\boldsymbol{p}, \boldsymbol{q}_t)$. Freund and Schapire introduce an algorithm MW and show that it achieves the desired goal. They also provide finite-sample bounds for the cumulative loss of their algorithm and show that it is, in a certain sense, optimal. Defining the regret $r_{i,t} = S(\boldsymbol{p}_t, \boldsymbol{q}_t) - S(i, \boldsymbol{q}_t)$ it is easy to show that the MW algorithm satisfies condition (1) with the exponential potential.

Also, it is easy to see that the bound in [10] follows from Corollary 5 together with the log-sum inequality used as in the proof of Corollary 12.

6.1 Generalized Regret in Learning with Experts

In this section we will consider a more general notion of regret, which we call "generalized regret", introduced in [21]. As we will see, generalized regret has several other notions of regret, such as those defined in [12, 6], as special cases. According to our definition, a repeated game can be viewed as an on-line prediction problem with a randomized predictor. Hence, we can use generalized regret to analyze such on-line prediction problems. Consider the prediction with experts framework, where $f_{1,t}, \ldots, f_{N,t} \in \{1, \ldots, m\}$ denote the predictions of the experts at time t. For each expert $i = 1, \ldots, N$, define an *activation function* $A_i : \{1, \ldots, m\} \times \mathbb{N} \to \{0, 1\}$. The activation function determines whether the corresponding expert is active at the current prediction step. At each time instant t, the values $A_i(k, t)$, $i = 1, \ldots, N$, $k = 1, \ldots, m$ of the activation function are revealed to the predictor who then decides on his guess $\boldsymbol{p}_t = (p_{1,t}, \ldots, p_{m,t})$. Define the *generalized regret* of a randomized predictor with respect to expert i at round t by

$$r_{i,t}(\boldsymbol{p}_t, y) = \sum_{k=1}^{m} p_{k,t} \, A_i(k, t) \, (L(k, y) - L(f_{i,t}, y)) \ . \tag{9}$$

Hence, the generalized regret with respect to expert i is nonzero only if expert i is active, and the expert is active based on the current step t and, possibly, on the predictor's guess k. Variants of the learning with experts framework, such as "shifting experts" or the more general "specialists" [11] can be analyzed using generalized regret.

Example 16. An important special case of the generalized regret (9) is the so-called "internal" or "conditional" regret [19] (see also [7] for a survey). In this case the $N = m(m-1)$ experts are labeled by pairs (i, j) for $i \neq j$. Expert (i, j) predicts always i, that is, $f_{(i,j),t} = i$ for all t, and it is active only when the predictor's guess is j, that is, $A_{(i,j)}(k, t) = 1$ if and only if $k = j$. Thus, component (i, j) of the generalized regret vector $\boldsymbol{r}_t(\boldsymbol{p}_t, y) \in \mathbb{R}^N$ becomes

$$r_{(i,j),t}(\boldsymbol{p}_t, y) = p_{j,t}(L(j, y) - L(i, y)) \ .$$

Hence, the cumulative internal regret with respect to expert (i, j), $R_{(i,j),t} = r_{(i,j),1} + \ldots + r_{(i,j),t}$, may be interpreted as the regret the predictor feels of not having predicted i each time he predicted j. It is easy to see that this notion of regret is stronger than the usual regret (7). Indeed, assume that $\max\{0, R_{(i,j),t}\} \le a_t = o(t)$ for all possible pairs (i, j) and for some sequence $a_t \ge 0$, $t \ge 1$. Let $k \in \{1, \ldots, m\}$ be the action with minimal cumulative loss, that is, $\sum_{s=1}^{t} L(k, y_s) = \min_{1 \le i \le m} \sum_{s=1}^{t} L(i, y_s)$. Then the cumulative regret based on (7) is just

$$\sum_{s=1}^{t}\left(\sum_{j=1}^{m} p_{j,t}L(j,y_s) - L(k,y_s)\right) = \sum_{j=1}^{m} R_{(k,j),t} \le m a_t = o(t) .$$

Thus, small cumulative internal regret implies small cumulative regret of the form considered in the experts' framework. On the other hand, it is easy to show by example that, for $m \ge 3$, small cumulative regret does not imply small internal regret.

We now state the extension of (8) to generalized regret. The proof, which we relegate to the appendix, is a generalization of a proof contained in [19].

Theorem 17. *Consider an abstract decision problem with drift function (9) and potential Φ, where $\nabla\Phi \ge \mathbf{0}$. Then a randomized predictor satisfying condition (1) is defined by the unique solution to the set of m linear equations*

$$p_{k,t} = \frac{\sum_{j=1}^{m} p_{j,t} \sum_{i=1}^{N} \mathbb{1}_{\{f_{i,t}=k\}}\, A_i(j,t)\, \nabla_i\Phi(\boldsymbol{R}_{t-1})}{\sum_{i=1}^{N} A_i(k,t)\, \nabla_i\Phi(\boldsymbol{R}_{t-1})} \qquad k = 1,\ldots,m.$$

As an example, we may apply Theorem 17 to the internal regret with exponential potential.

Corollary 18. *If the randomized predictor of Theorem 17 is run with the exponential potential (3) and parameter $\eta = \sqrt{4\ln m/t}$, then for all sequences $y_1, y_2, \ldots \in \mathcal{Y}$ its internal regret satisfies*

$$\max_{j,k} R_{(j,k),t} \le 2\sqrt{t \ln m} .$$

For large values of m this bound is a significant improvement on the bound $O(\sqrt{tm})$, obtainable with the polynomial potential (with $p = 2$) used by Hart and Mas-Colell to show that $\max_{j,k} R_{(j,k),t} = o(t)$.

Appendix

Proof of Theorem 17. We write condition (1) as follows:

$$\begin{aligned}
&\nabla\Phi(\boldsymbol{R}_{t-1}) \cdot \boldsymbol{r}_t \\
&= \sum_{i=1}^{N} \nabla_i\Phi(\boldsymbol{R}_{t-1}) \sum_{k=1}^{m} p_{k,t} A_i(k,t)\,[L(k,y_t) - L(f_{i,t},y_t)] \\
&= \sum_{k=1}^{m}\sum_{j=1}^{m}\sum_{i=1}^{N} \mathbb{1}_{\{f_{i,t}=j\}} \nabla_i\Phi(\boldsymbol{R}_{t-1}) p_{k,t} A_i(k,t)\,[L(k,y_t) - L(f_{i,t},y_t)] \\
&= \sum_{k=1}^{m}\sum_{j=1}^{m}\sum_{i=1}^{N} \mathbb{1}_{\{f_{i,t}=j\}} \nabla_i\Phi(\boldsymbol{R}_{t-1}) p_{k,t} A_i(k,t) L(k,y_t)
\end{aligned}$$

$$
\begin{aligned}
&-\sum_{k=1}^{m}\sum_{j=1}^{m}\sum_{i=1}^{N} \mathbb{1}_{\{f_{i,t}=j\}} \nabla_i \Phi(\boldsymbol{R}_{t-1}) p_{k,t} A_i(k,t) L(f_{i,t}, y_t) \\
&= \sum_{k=1}^{m}\sum_{j=1}^{m}\sum_{i=1}^{N} \mathbb{1}_{\{f_{i,t}=j\}} \nabla_i \Phi(\boldsymbol{R}_{t-1}) p_{k,t} A_i(k,t) L(k, y_t) \\
&-\sum_{k=1}^{m}\sum_{j=1}^{m}\sum_{i=1}^{N} \mathbb{1}_{\{f_{i,t}=k\}} \nabla_i \Phi(\boldsymbol{R}_{t-1}) p_{j,t} A_i(j,t) L(k, y_t) \\
&= \sum_{k=1}^{m} L(k,y_t) \left[\sum_{i=1}^{N} \nabla_i \Phi(\boldsymbol{R}_{t-1}) p_{k,t} A_i(k,t) \right. \\
&\left. -\sum_{j=1}^{m}\sum_{i=1}^{N} \mathbb{1}_{\{f_{i,t}=k\}} \nabla_i \Phi(\boldsymbol{R}_{t-1}) p_{j,t} A_i(j,t) \right] \le 0 \,.
\end{aligned}
$$

Since the $L(k, y_t)$ are arbitrary and nonnegative, the above is implied by

$$
\sum_{i=1}^{N} \nabla_i \Phi(\boldsymbol{R}_{t-1}) p_{k,t} A_i(k,t) - \sum_{j=1}^{m}\sum_{i=1}^{N} \mathbb{1}_{\{f_{i,t}=k\}} \nabla_i \Phi(\boldsymbol{R}_{t-1}) p_{j,t} A_i(j,t) \le 0 \qquad (10)
$$

for each $k = 1, \ldots, m$. Solving for $p_{k,t}$ yields the result.

We now check that such a predictor always exists. Let M be the $(m \times m)$ matrix whose entries are

$$
M_{k,j} = \frac{\sum_{i=1}^{N} \mathbb{1}_{\{f_{i,t}=k\}} \nabla_i \Phi(\boldsymbol{R}_{t-1}) A_i(j,t)}{\sum_{i=1}^{N} \nabla_i \Phi(\boldsymbol{R}_{t-1}) A_i(k,t)} \,.
$$

Then condition (10) is implied by $M\boldsymbol{p} = \boldsymbol{p}$. As $\nabla\Phi \ge \boldsymbol{0}$, M is nonnegative, and thus the eigenvector equation $M\boldsymbol{p} = \boldsymbol{p}$ has a positive solution by the Perron-Frobenius theorem [27].

Proof of Corollary 12. Corollary 5 implies $\ln \Phi(\boldsymbol{R}_t) \le \ln N + (\eta^2/2) X_\infty^2 M_t$. To obtain a lower bound on $\ln \Phi(\boldsymbol{R}_t)$, consider any vector $\boldsymbol{v}_0$ of convex coefficients. Then we use the well-known "log sum inequality" (see [5, page 29]) which implies that, for any vectors $\boldsymbol{u}, \boldsymbol{v} \in \mathbb{R}^N$ of nonnegative numbers with $\sum_{i=1}^{N} v_i = 1$,

$$
\ln \sum_{i=1}^{N} u_i \ge \sum_{i=1}^{N} v_i \ln u_i + H(\boldsymbol{v}) \,,
$$

where $H(\boldsymbol{v}) = -\sum_{i=1}^{N} v_i \ln v_i$ is the *entropy* of $\boldsymbol{v}$. Therefore, for any vector $\boldsymbol{v}_0$ of convex coefficients such that $y_s \boldsymbol{v}_0 \cdot \boldsymbol{x}_s \ge \gamma$ for all $s = 1, \ldots, t$,

$$
\ln \Phi(\boldsymbol{R}_t) = \ln \sum_{i=1}^{N} e^{\eta R_{i,t}} \ge \eta \boldsymbol{R}_t \cdot \boldsymbol{v}_0 + H(\boldsymbol{v}_0) \ge \eta\,(\gamma M_t - D_t) + H(\boldsymbol{v}_0)
$$

where in the last step we proceeded just like in the proof of Corollary 11. Putting the upper and lower bounds for $\ln \Phi(\boldsymbol{R}_t)$ together we obtain

$$\eta\,(\gamma M_t - D_t) + H(\boldsymbol{v}_0) \le \ln N + (\eta^2/2)X_\infty^2 M_t$$

which, dropping the positive term $H(\boldsymbol{v}_0)$, implies

$$M_t\left(1 - \frac{\eta}{2}\frac{X_\infty^2}{\gamma}\right) \le \frac{D_t}{\gamma} + \frac{\ln N}{\eta\gamma}\,. \tag{11}$$

We prove only the case $L \ge 2(X_\infty/\gamma)^2 \ln N$. Letting $\beta = (\eta X_\infty^2)/(2\gamma)$, and verifying that $\beta < 1$, we may rearrange (11) as follows

$$\begin{aligned}
M_t &\le \frac{1}{1-\beta}\left(\frac{D_t}{\gamma} + \frac{1}{2\beta}\left(\frac{X_\infty}{\gamma}\right)^2 \ln N\right) \\
&\le \frac{D_t}{\gamma} + \frac{1}{1-\beta}\left(\beta\frac{D_t}{\gamma} + \frac{1}{\beta}\frac{A}{2}\right) \quad \text{where we set } A = (X_\infty/\gamma)^2 \ln N \\
&\le \frac{D_t}{\gamma} + \frac{1}{1-\beta}\left(\beta L + \frac{1}{\beta}\frac{A}{2}\right) \quad \text{since } L \ge D_t/\gamma \text{ by hypothesis} \\
&\le \frac{D_t}{\gamma} + \frac{\sqrt{2AL}}{1-\sqrt{A/(2L)}} \quad \text{since } \beta = \sqrt{(A\gamma)/(2L)} \text{ by our choice of } \eta \\
&\le \frac{D_t}{\gamma} + \sqrt{2AL} + 2A
\end{aligned}$$

whenever $L \ge 2A$, which holds by hypothesis.

References

[1] D. Blackwell. An analog of the minimax theorem for vector payoffs. *Pacific Journal of Mathematics*, 6:1–8, 1956.

[2] H.D. Block. The Perceptron: a model for brain functioning. *Review of Modern Physics*, 34:123–135, 1962.

[3] N. Cesa-Bianchi. Analysis of two gradient-based algorithms for on-line regression. *Journal of Computer and System Sciences*, 59(3):392-411, 1999.

[4] N. Cesa-Bianchi, Y. Freund, D.P. Helmbold, D. Haussler, R. Schapire, and M.K. Warmuth. How to use expert advice. *Journal of the ACM*, 44(3):427–485, 1997.

[5] T.M. Cover and J.A. Thomas. *Elements of Information Theory*. John Wiley, New York, 1991.

[6] D. Foster and R. Vohra. Calibrated learning and correlated equilibrium. *Games and Economic Behaviour*, 21:40–55, 1997.

[7] D. Foster and R. Vohra. Regret in the on-line decision problem. *Games and Economic Behavior*, 29:7–36, 1999.

[8] Y. Freund and R. Schapire. A decision-theoretic generalization of on-line learning and an application to boosting. *Journal of Computer and System Sciences*, 55(1):119–139, 1997.

[9] Y. Freund and R. Schapire. Large margin classification using the Perceptron algorithm. *Machine Learning*, 22:277–296, 1999.

[10] Y. Freund and R. Schapire. Adaptive game playing using multiplicative weights. *Games and Economic Behavior*, 29:79, 1999.

[11] Y. Freund, R. Schapire, Y. Singer, and M. Warmuth. Using and combining predictors that specialize. In *Proceedings of the 29th Annual ACM Symposium on the Theory of Computing*, page 334–343. ACM Press, 1997.

[12] D. Fudenberg and D. Levine. Conditional universal consistency. *Games and Economic Behaviour*, 29:7–35, 1999.

[13] C. Gentile The robustness of the *p*-norm algorithms. Manuscript, 2001. An extended abstract (co-authored with N. Littlestone) appeared in the *Proceedings of the 12th Annual Conference on Computational Learning Theory*, pages 1–11. ACM Press, 1999.

[14] C. Gentile and M. Warmuth. Linear hinge loss and average margin. In *Advances in Neural Information Processing Systems 11*, pages 225–231, MIT Press, 1998.

[15] A.J. Grove, N. Littlestone, and D. Schuurmans. General convergence results for linear discriminant updates. In *Proceedings of the 10th Annual Conference on Computational Learning Theory*, pages 171–183. ACM Press, 1997.

[16] J. Hannan. Approximation to Bayes risk in repeated play. *Contributions to the theory of games*, 3:97–139, 1957.

[17] D. Haussler, J. Kivinen, and M.K. Warmuth. Sequential prediction of individual sequences under general loss functions. *IEEE Transactions on Information Theory*, 44:1906–1925, 1998.

[18] S. Hart and A. Mas-Colell. A general class of adaptive strategies. *Journal of Economic Theory*, to appear, 2000.

[19] S. Hart and A. Mas-Colell. A simple adaptive procedure leading to correlated equilibrium. *Econometrica*, 68:1127–1150, 2000.

[20] J. Kivinen and M.K. Warmuth. Averaging expert predictions. In *Proceedings of the Fourth European Conference on Computational Learning Theory*, pages 153–167. Lecture Notes in Artificial Intelligence 1572. Springer, Berlin, 1999.

[21] E. Lehrer. A wide range no-regret theorem. Unpublished manuscript, 2000.

[22] N. Littlestone and M. K. Warmuth. The weighted majority algorithm. *Information and Computation*, 108:212–261, 1994.

[23] N. Littlestone. *Mistake bounds and linear-threshold learning algorithms.* PhD Thesis, University of California, Santa Cruz, 1989. Technical Report UCSC-CRL-89-11.

[24] A.B.J. Novikov. On convergence proofs on Perceptrons. In *Proceedings of the Symposium of the Mathematical Theory of Automata*, volume XII, pages 615–622, 1962.

[25] F. Rosenblatt. *Principles of Neurodynamics: Perceptrons and the Theory of Brain Mechanisms.* Spartan Books, Washington, DC, 1962.

[26] R. Schapire. Drifting games. *Machine Learning*, 2001. To appear.

[27] E. Seneta. *Non-negative Matrices and Markov Chains.* Springer, New York, 1981.

[28] V.G. Vovk. Aggregating strategies. In *Proceedings of the Third Annual Workshop on Computational Learning Theory*, pages 372–383. Association of Computing Machinery, New York, 1990.

[29] V.G. Vovk. A game of prediction with expert advice. In *Journal of Computer and System Sciences*, 56(2):153–173, 1998.

[30] V.G. Vovk Competitive on-line statistics. *International Statistical Review*, 2001. To appear.

A Sequential Approximation Bound for Some Sample-Dependent Convex Optimization Problems with Applications in Learning

Tong Zhang

IBM T.J. Watson Research Center
Yorktown Heights, NY 10598
tzhang@watson.ibm.com

Abstract. In this paper, we study a class of sample dependent convex optimization problems, and derive a general sequential approximation bound for their solutions. This analysis is closely related to the regret bound framework in online learning. However we apply it to batch learning algorithms instead of online stochastic gradient decent methods. Applications of this analysis in some classification and regression problems will be illustrated.

1 Introduction

An important aspect of a machine learning algorithm is its generalization ability. In the batch learning framework, an algorithm obtains a hypothesis from a finite number of training data. The generalization ability is measured by the accuracy of the learned hypothesis when it is tested on some previously unobserved data.

A popular method to derive generalization bounds is the so-called Vapnik-Chervonenkis (VC) style analysis [11]. This method depends on the uniform convergence of observed errors of the hypothesis family to their true errors. The rate of uniform convergence depends on an estimate of certain sample-dependent covering numbers (growth numbers) for the underlying hypothesis family. Although this framework is quite general and powerful, it also has many disadvantages. For example, the derived generalization bounds are often very loose.

Because of various disadvantages of VC analysis, other methods to estimate generalization performance have been introduced. In this paper, we propose a new style of analysis that is suitable for certain sample dependent convex optimization problems. This type of bounds are closely related to the leave-one-out analysis, which has received much attention recently. For example, see [3,7,8,13] and some references therein. However, instead of estimating the leave-one-out cross-validation error, we estimate the convergence of the estimated parameter averaged over a sequence of data. This is closely related to the online regret bound framework (for example, see [1,9]). However, we study the learning problems in batch setting. Another important technical difference is that since an

D. Helmbold and B. Williamson (Eds.): COLT/EuroCOLT 2001, LNAI 2111, pp. 65–81, 2001.

explicit regularization condition is used in a batch-form sample-dependent optimization formulation, we can avoid the limitation of "matching loss" and the "learning rate" parameter which requires to be adjusted in online learning analysis.

Our analysis also indicates that even though some gradient descent type online learning algorithms achieve good worst-case regret bounds, in practice they could still be inferior to the corresponding batch algorithms. This also justifies why practitioners apply an online algorithm repeatedly over the training data so that it effectively converges to the solution of a sample dependent optimization problem, although the online mistake bound analysis implies that this is not helpful. In addition, the sequential approximation analysis complements the leave-one-out analysis in batch learning. In many cases it can give better bounds than those from the leave-one-out analysis. The latter analysis may not yield bounds that are asymptotically tight.

We organize the paper as follows. In Section 2, we prove a sequential approximation bound for a class of sample dependent optimization problems. This bound is the foundation of our analysis. Section 3 applies this bound to a general formulation of linear learning machines. Section 4 and Section 5 contain specific results of this analysis on some classification and regression problems. Concluding remarks are given in Section 6.

2 A Generic Sequential Approximation Bound

In many machine learning problems, we are given a training set of input variable x and output variable y. Our goal is to find a function that can predict y based on x. Typically, one needs to restrict the hypothesis function family size so that a stable estimate within the function family can be obtained from a finite number of samples. We assume that the function family can be specified by a vector parameter $w \in H$, where H is a Hilbert space. The inner product of two vectors $w_1, w_2 \in H$ is denoted by $w_1^T w_2$. We also let $w^2 = w^T w$ and $\|w\| = (w^T w)^{1/2}$.

We consider a "learning" algorithm that determines a parameter estimate w_n from training samples $(x_1, y_1), \ldots, (x_n, y_n)$ by solving the following sample-dependent optimization problem:

$$w_n = \arg\min_{w} w^2 \tag{1}$$

$$\text{s.t.} \quad w \in C_n(x_1, y_1, \ldots, x_n, y_n). \tag{2}$$

We assume that C_n is a sample-dependent weakly closed convex set in H. That is,

- $\forall\, w \in H$: if $\exists$ sequence $\{w_i\}_{i=1,2,\ldots} \in C_n$ such that $\lim_{i\to\infty} w_i^T x = w^T x$ for all $x \in H$,[1] then $w \in C_n$.
- $\forall w_1, w_2 \in C_n$ and $\theta \in [0,1]$, we have $\theta w_1 + (1-\theta) w_2 \in C_n$.

[1] We say that the sequence $\{w_i\}$ converges weakly to w.

Under the above assumptions, the optimization problem (1) becomes a convex programming problem. The following proposition shows that it has a unique solution.

Proposition 1. *If $C_n(x_1, y_1, \ldots, x_n, y_n)$ is non-empty, then optimization problem (1) has a unique solution that belongs to $C_n(x_1, y_1, \ldots, x_n, y_n)$.*

Proof. Since C_n is non-empty, there exists a sequence $\{w_i\}_{i=1,2,\ldots}$ such that $\lim_{i\to\infty} w_i^2 = \inf_{w\in C_n} w^2$. Note that since the sequence $\{w_i^2\}$ converges, it is bounded. Therefore it contains a weakly convergent subsequence (cf. Proposition 66.4 in [6]). Without loss of generality, we assume the weakly convergent subsequence is the sequence $\{w_i\}$ itself. Denote its weak limit by w_*, then by the weakly closedness of C_n, we have $w_* \in C_n$. Also

$$w_*^2 = \lim_{i\to\infty} w*^T w_i \le (w_*^2 \lim_{i\to\infty} w_i^2)^{1/2} \le (w_*^2 \inf_{w\in C_n} w^2)^{1/2} \le w_*^2.$$

This implies that w_* is a solution of (1).

To see that the solution is unique, we simply assume that there are two solutions denoted by $w_1 \in C_n$ and $w_2 \in C_n$. Note that $0.5w_1 + 0.5w_2 \in C_n$ by the convexity of C_n. We thus have $(0.5w_1 + 0.5w_2)^2 \ge 0.5w_1^2 + 0.5w_2^2$ by the definition of w_1 and w_2 as solutions of (1). This inequality is satisfied only when $w_1 = w_2$.

The following lemma, although simple to prove, is the foundation of our analysis.

Lemma 1. *Let $(x_1, y_1), \ldots, (x_n, y_n)$ be a sequence of observations. Assume that*

$$C_n(x_1, y_1, \ldots, x_n, y_n) \subseteq C_{n-1}(x_1, y_1, \ldots, x_{n-1}, y_{n-1}).$$

Let w_k be the solution of (1) with respect to samples $(x_1, y_1), \ldots, (x_k, y_k)$ where $(k = n-1, n)$,[2] *then if C_n is non-empty, we have the following one-step approximation bound:*

$$(w_n - w_{n-1})^2 \le w_n^2 - w_{n-1}^2.$$

Proof. Since $w_n^2 = w_{n-1}^2 + (w_n - w_{n-1})^2 + 2(w_n - w_{n-1})^T w_{n-1}$, to prove the lemma we only need to show $(w_n - w_{n-1})^T w_{n-1} \ge 0$. If this is not true, then assume $z = (w_n - w_{n-1})^T w_{n-1} < 0$. Let $\theta = \min(1, -z/(w_n - w_{n-1})^2)$, then $\theta \in (0, 1]$ and by the convexity of C_{n-1}, we know $w_{n-1} + \theta(w_n - w_{n-1}) \in C_{n-1}$. However,

$$\begin{aligned}
&(w_{n-1} + \theta(w_n - w_{n-1}))^2 \\
&= w_{n-1}^2 + \theta^2(w_n - w_{n-1})^2 + 2\theta(w_n - w_{n-1})^T w_{n-1} \\
&\le w_{n-1}^2 + \theta z < w_{n-1}^2,
\end{aligned}$$

which contradicts the definition of w_{n-1}. Therefore the lemma holds.

[2] There is a little abuse of notation. We need to change the subscripts of n to k in (1) to define w_k. This convention, also used in later parts of the paper, should not cause any confusion.

Theorem 1. *Let $(x_1, y_1), \ldots, (x_n, y_n)$ be a sequence of observations. Let $C_0 = H$, and assume that for all $k = m, \ldots, n$,*

$$C_k(x_1, y_1, \ldots, x_k, y_k) \subseteq C_{k-1}(x_1, y_1, \ldots, x_{k-1}, y_{k-1}).$$

Let w_k be the solution of (1) with respect to samples $(x_1, y_1), \ldots, (x_k, y_k)$ where $(k = m-1, \ldots, n)$, then we have the following sequential approximation bound:

$$\sum_{i=m}^{n} (w_i - w_{i-1})^2 \leq w_n^2 - w_{m-1}^2.$$

Proof. By Lemma 2, we have $(w_i - w_{i-1})^2 \leq w_i^2 - w_{i-1}^2$ for all $i = 1, \ldots, n$. Summing over $i = m, \ldots, n$, we obtain the theorem.

Note that the style of the above bound is similar to techniques widely used in online learning [1,9,4,5]. However, the formulation we consider here is significantly different than what has been considered in the existing online learning literature. Furthermore, from a technical point of view, instead of bounding the regret loss as in online learning analysis, we directly bound the sum of squared distances of consecutive parameter estimates in a batch learning setting. Therefore our bound indicates the convergence of estimated parameter itself, which can then be used to bound the regret with respect to any loss function. The reason we can prove the convergence of parameter itself is due to our explicit use of regularization that minimizes w_n^2 in (1).

The concept of convergence of the estimated parameter has been widely used in traditional numerical mathematics and statistics. However, it has only recently been applied to analyzing learning problems. For example, techniques related to what we use here have also been applied in [12,13]. The former leads to PAC style probability bounds, while the latter gives leave-one-out estimates. The convergence of the estimated parameter is also related to the algorithmic stability concept in [8]. However, the former condition is stronger. Consequently, better bounds can usually be obtained if we can show the convergence of the estimated parameter.

3 Linear Learning Methods

3.1 Linear Learning Formulations

To apply the general sequential approximation bound, we consider the linear prediction model where y is predicted as $y \approx w^T x$. We assume that $x \in H$ for all sample x. Given a training set of $(x_1, y_1), \ldots, (x_n, y_n)$, the parameter estimate w_n is obtained from (1) with the set C_n defined by the following type of constraints:

$$\begin{aligned} & C_n(x_1, y_1, \ldots, x_n, y_n) \\ &= \{w \in H : c_{n,k}(w^T x_1, x_1, y_1 \ldots, w^T x_n, x_n, y_n) \leq 0, (k = 1, \ldots, s_n)\}, \quad (3) \end{aligned}$$

where each $c_{n,k}$ is a continuous convex function of w.

Proposition 2. *The set C_n defined in (3) is convex and weakly closed.*

Proof. It is easy to check that the set C_n defined above is convex. C_n is also weakly closed since if a sequence $\{w_i\} \in C_n$ converges weakly to $w \in H$, then $\forall k$, by the continuity of $c_{n,k}$:

$$\begin{aligned} & c_{n,k}(w^T x_1, x_1, y_1, \ldots, w^T x_n, x_n, y_n) \\ = & c_{n,k}(\lim_i w_i^T x_1, x_1, y_1, \ldots, \lim_i w_i^T x_n, x_n, y_n) \\ = & \lim_i c_{n,k}(w_i^T x_1, x_1, y_1, \ldots, w_i^T x_n, x_n, y_n) \leq 0. \end{aligned}$$

This means that $w \in C_n$.

For all concrete examples in this paper, we only consider the following functional form of $c_{n,k}$ in (3):

$$c_{n,k}(w^T x_1, x_1, y_1, \ldots, w^T x_n, x_n, y_n) = \sum_{i=1}^{n} f_{k,i}(w^T x_i, x_i, y_i),$$

where $f_{k,i}(a, b_1, b_2)$ is a continuous convex function of a. Specifically, we consider the following two choices of C_n. The first choice is

$$C_n = \{w \in H : a(x_i, y_i) \leq w^T x_i \leq b(x_i, y_i), \quad (i = 1, \ldots, n)\}. \tag{4}$$

Both $a(\cdot)$ and $b(\cdot)$ are functions that can take $\pm\infty$ as their values. The second choice is

$$C_n = \{w \in H : \sum_{i=1}^{k} L(w^T x_i, x_i, y_i) \leq s\}, \tag{5}$$

where $L(a, b_1, b_2) \geq 0$ is a continuous convex function of a. $s \geq 0$ is a fixed parameter.

Clearly, either of the above choices of C_n satisfies the condition $C_k \subseteq C_{k-1}$. Hence Theorem 1 can be applied.

3.2 An Equivalent Formulation

From the numerical point of view, the parameter estimate w_n in (1) with C_n defined in (5) is closely related to the solution $\tilde{w}_n$ of the following penalized optimization formulation more commonly used in statistics:

$$\tilde{w}_n = \arg\min_{w \in H} [w^2 + C \sum_{i=1}^{k} L(w^T x_i, x_i, y_i)], \tag{6}$$

where $C > 0$ is a parameter. In fact, $\forall C$ in (6), if we let $s = \sum_{i=1}^{n} L(\tilde{w}^T x_i, x_i, y_i)$, then the solution w_n with C_n given in (5) is the same as $\tilde{w}_n$ in (6). To see this, just note that by the definition of w_n, we have $w_n^2 \leq \tilde{w}_n^2$. Now compare (6) at

$w = w_n$ and $w = \tilde{w}_n$, we obtain $w_n^2 \geq \tilde{w}_n^2$. This means that $\tilde{w}_n$ is the solution of (1) with C_n given in (5). Due to the uniqueness of solution, $w_n = \tilde{w}_n$.

This equivalence suggests that our analysis of the constrained formulation (1) with C_n defined in (5) can provide useful insights into the penalty type formulation (6). However in reality, there are some complications since typically the parameter C in (6) or s in (5) is determined by data-dependent cross-validation. A typical analysis either fixes C in (6) or fixes s in (5). These choices are not equivalent any more. An advantage of using (6) is that we do not need to worry about the feasibility condition (C_n is non-empty), although for many practical problems (even for problems with noise), the feasibility condition itself can be generally satisfied. The readers should be aware that although bounds given later in the paper assume that C_n is always non-empty, it is not difficult to generalize the bounds to handle the case where C_n may become empty with small probability.

There is no difficulty analyzing (6) directly using the same technique developed in this paper. We only need a slight generalization of Lemma 2 that allows a general penalized convex formulation in the objective function. Note that the proof of Lemma 2 essentially relies on the KKT condition of (1) at the optimal solution. In the more general situation, a similar KKT condition can be used to yield a desired inequality.

It is also easy to generalize the scheme to analyze non-square regularization conditions. Furthermore, by introducing slack variables (for example, this is done in the standard SVM formulation), it is not hard to rewrite general penalty type regularization formulations such as (6) as constrained regularization formulations such as (1), where we replace the minimization of w^2 by the minimization of an arbitrary convex function $g(w, \xi)$ of the weight vector w and the slack variable vector ξ. This provides a systematic approach to a very general learning formulation.

It is also possible to use a different technique to bound the squared distance of consecutive parameter estimates as in [13]. Although the method will yield a similar sequential approximation bound for penalty type formulation (6), it is not suitable for analyzing constrained formulation (1) which we study in this paper. In a related work, mistake bounds for some ridge-regression like online algorithms are derived in [4]. The resulting bounds are similar to what can be obtained by using our technique.

In this paper, we do not consider the general formulation which includes (6). We shall only mention that while our current approach is more suitable for the small noise situation (that is, s small, or equivalently C large), a direct analysis for (6) is more suitable for the large noise situation (that is, C small, or equivalently s large).

3.3 Kernel Learning Machines

Proposition 3. *The solution w_n of (1) with C_n defined in (3) belongs to X_n where X_n is the subspace of H that is spanned by x_i $(i = 1, \ldots, n)$.*

Proof. Let $\bar{w}_n$ be the orthonormal projection of w_n onto X_n, then $\bar{w}_n^T x_i = w_n^T x_i$ for $i = 1, \ldots, n$. This implies that $\bar{w}_n \in C_n$. Since $\bar{w}_n^2 \leq w_n^2$, by Proposition 1, we have $w_n = \bar{w}_n$.

Under the assumption of Proposition 3, we can assume a representation of w as $w = \sum_{i=1}^n \alpha_i x_i$ in the optimization of (1). Using this representation, $w^T x = \sum_{i=1}^n \alpha_i x_i^T x$, and $w^2 = \sum_{i=1}^n \sum_{j=1}^n \alpha_i \alpha_j x_i^T x_j$. Therefore the only property we need to know about the Hilbert space H is a representation of its inner product $x^T y$. We may replace $x^T y$ by a symmetric positive-definite kernel function $K(x, y)$, which leads to a corresponding kernel method as follows:

$$\hat{\alpha} = \arg\min_{\alpha} \sum_{i=1}^{n} \sum_{j=1}^{n} \alpha_i \alpha_j K(x_i, x_j) \tag{7}$$

$$\text{s.t.} \quad c_{n,k}(\sum_{i=1}^{n} \alpha_i K(x_i, x_1), x_1, y_1 \ldots, \sum_{i=1}^{n} \alpha_i K(x_i, x_n), x_n, y_n) \leq 0 \quad k = 1, \ldots$$

A properly behaved kernel function induces a Hilbert space (reproducing kernel Hilbert space) that consists of the closure of functions $f(x)$ of the form $\sum_i \alpha_i K(x_i, x)$. We can represent the functions linearly in a feature space as $f(x) = \sum_{i=1}^{\infty} w_i \phi_i(x)$. The inner product is $K(x, y) = \sum_{i=1}^{\infty} \lambda_i \phi_i(x) \phi_i(y)$, where $\lambda_i > 0$ are eigenvalues. See [2], chapter 3 for more details on kernel induced feature spaces. Our analysis in the reproducing kernel Hilbert space can thus be applied to study the general kernel method in (7).

4 Regression

4.1 Sequential-Validation Bounds

We consider regression problems. For simplicity, we only consider the q-norm loss with $1 \leq q \leq 2$. Our goal is to estimate w from the training data so that it has a small expected loss:

$$Q(w) = E_{(x,y) \sim D} |w^T x - y|^q,$$

where the expectation E is taken over an unknown distribution D. $1 \leq q \leq 2$ is a fixed parameter. The training samples (x_i, y_i) for $i = 1, \ldots, n$ are independently drawn from D.

Given the training data, we define the empirical expected loss as

$$Q_n(w, x_1, y_1, \ldots, x_n, y_n) = \frac{1}{n} \sum_{i=1}^{n} |w^T x_i - y_i|^q.$$

We use algorithm (1) to compute an estimate of w_n from the training data. We consider two formulations of C_n in (1). The first employs

$$C_n = \{w \in H : |w^T x_i - y_i| \leq \epsilon(x_i, y_i), \quad (i = 1, \ldots, n)\}, \tag{8}$$

where $\epsilon(x,y) \geq 0$ is a pre-defined noise tolerance parameter. The second employs

$$C_n = \{w \in H : \sum_{i=1}^{n} |w^T x_i - y_i|^q \leq s\}, \tag{9}$$

where s is a data independent parameter. If a solution does not exist in one of the above formulations (that is, C_n is empty), then we let $w_n = 0$. In the following, we only consider the case that C_n is always non-empty for clarity. However as we have mentioned earlier, it is possible to deal with the situation that C_n is empty with a small probability.

Theorem 2. *Assume for all training data C_{n+1} is non-empty, and $C_k \subseteq C_{k-1}$ for $k = m, \ldots, n+1$. For each k, w_k is computed from $(x_1, y_1), \ldots, (x_k, y_k)$ using (1). We have the following sequential expected generalization bound ($1 \leq q \leq 2$):*

$$[\sum_{i=m}^{n} E\, Q(w_i)]^{1/q} \leq E^{1/q} \sum_{i=m+1}^{n+1} Q_i(w_i, x_1, y_1, \ldots, x_i, y_i) +$$
$$E^{1/q}\, [\|w_{n+1}\|^q (\sum_{i=m}^{n} \|x_{i+1}\|^{2q/(2-q)})^{(2-q)/2}].$$

The expectation E is with respect to $n+1$ independent random training samples $(x_1, y_1), \ldots, (x_{n+1}, y_{n+1})$ from D.

Proof. Consider training samples $(x_1, y_1), \ldots, (x_{n+1}, y_{n+1})$.

$$\begin{aligned}
&(\sum_{i=m}^{n} |w_i^T x_{i+1} - y_{i+1}|^q)^{1/q} \\
=&(\sum_{i=m}^{n} |w_{i+1}^T x_{i+1} - y_{i+1} + (w_i - w_{i+1})^T x_{i+1}|^q)^{1/q} \\
\leq&[\sum_{i=m}^{n} |w_{i+1}^T x_{i+1} - y_{i+1}|^q]^{1/q} + [\sum_{i=m}^{n} |(w_i - w_{i+1})^T x_{i+1}|^q]^{1/q} \\
\leq&(\sum_{i=m}^{n} |w_{i+1}^T x_{i+1} - y_{i+1}|^q)^{1/q} + (\sum_{i=m}^{n} (w_i - w_{i+1})^2)^{1/2} (\sum_{i=m}^{n} \|x_{i+1}\|^{\frac{2q}{2-q}})^{\frac{2-q}{2q}}.
\end{aligned}$$

The first inequality follows from the Minkowski inequality. The second inequality follows from the Hölder's inequality.

By taking expectation E and again applying the Minkowski inequality, we obtain

$$\begin{aligned}
&[\sum_{i=m}^{n} E\, Q(w_i)]^{1/q} \\
=&[E \sum_{i=m}^{n} |w_i^T x_{i+1} - y_{i+1}|^q]^{1/q}
\end{aligned}$$

$$\leq E^{\frac{1}{q}}[(\sum_{i=m}^{n}|w_{i+1}^T x_{i+1} - y_{i+1}|^q)^{\frac{1}{q}} + (\sum_{i=m}^{n}(w_i - w_{i+1})^2)^{\frac{1}{2}}(\sum_{i=m}^{n}\|x_{i+1}\|^{\frac{2q}{2-q}})^{\frac{2-q}{2q}}]^q$$

$$\leq E^{\frac{1}{q}}\sum_{i=m}^{n}|w_{i+1}^T x_{i+1} - y_{i+1}|^q + E^{\frac{1}{q}}[(\sum_{i=m}^{n}(w_i - w_{i+1})^2)^{\frac{q}{2}}(\sum_{i=m}^{n}\|x_{i+1}\|^{\frac{2q}{2-q}})^{\frac{2-q}{2}}].$$

By Theorem 1, we have $(\sum_{i=m}^{n}(w_i - w_{i+1})^2)^{q/2} \leq \|w_{n+1}\|^q$. Also observe that

$$E\,(w_{i+1}^T x_{i+1} - y_{i+1})^q = E\,Q_{i+1}(w_{i+1}, x_1, y_1, \ldots, x_{i+1}, y_{i+1}).$$

We thus obtain the theorem.

Corollary 1. *Using formulation (8), we have*

$$[\frac{1}{n+1}\sum_{i=0}^{n} E\,Q(w_i)]^{1/q}$$
$$\leq [E_{(x,y)\sim D}\,\epsilon^q(x,y)]^{1/q} + E^{1/q}[\frac{\|w_{n+1}\|^q}{(n+1)^{q/2}}(\sum_{i=1}^{n+1}\frac{\|x_i\|^{2q/(2-q)}}{n+1})^{(2-q)/2}].$$

Using formulation (9), we have

$$[\frac{1}{n-m}\sum_{i=m+1}^{n} E\,Q(w_i)]^{1/q}$$
$$\leq [\frac{1}{n-m}\sum_{i=m+2}^{n+1}\frac{s}{i}]^{1/q} + E^{1/q}[\frac{\|w_{n+1}\|^q}{(n-m)^{q/2}}(\sum_{i=m+2}^{n+1}\frac{\|x_i\|^{2q/(2-q)}}{n-m})^{(2-q)/2}].$$

Proof. From formulation (8), we obtain

$$EQ_k(w_k, x_1, y_1, \ldots, x_k, y_k) \leq E\frac{1}{k}\sum_{i=1}^{k}\epsilon(x_i, y_i)^q = E_{(x,y)\sim D}\epsilon(x,y)^q.$$

From formulation (9), we obtain

$$Q_k(w_k, x_1, y_1, \ldots, x_k, y_k) \leq \frac{s}{k}.$$

The bounds follow from Theorem 2.

Corollary 2. *Using formulation (8), we have*

$$[\frac{1}{n+1}\sum_{i=0}^{n} E\,Q(w_i)]^{1/q}$$
$$\leq [E_{(x,y)\sim D}\,\epsilon^q(x,y)]^{1/q} + \frac{\sup\|w_{n+1}\|}{(n+1)^{1/2}}E_{x\sim D}^{(2-q)/2q}\|x\|^{2q/(2-q)}.$$

Using formulation (9), we have

$$[\frac{1}{n-m}\sum_{i=m+1}^{n} E\,Q(w_i)]^{1/q} \leq [\frac{s}{m+2}]^{1/q} + \frac{\sup\|w_{n+1}\|}{(n-m)^{1/2}} E_{x\sim D}^{(2-q)/2q}\|x\|^{2q/(2-q)}.$$

Proof. We have

$$\begin{aligned} &E^{1/q}\,[\|w_{n+1}\|^q(\sum_{i=m+2}^{n+1}\frac{\|x_i\|^{2q/(2-q)}}{n-m})^{(2-q)/2}] \\ \leq &\sup\|w_{n+1}\|E^{1/q}\,(\sum_{i=m+2}^{n+1}\frac{\|x_i\|^{2q/(2-q)}}{n-m})^{(2-q)/2} \\ \leq &\sup\|w_{n+1}\|E^{(2-q)/2q}\,(\sum_{i=m+2}^{n+1}\frac{\|x_i\|^{2q/(2-q)}}{n-m}) \\ = &\sup\|w_{n+1}\|E_{x\sim D}^{(2-q)/2q}\,\|x\|^{2q/(2-q)}. \end{aligned}$$

The second inequality above follows from the Jensen's inequality. Note also $\frac{1}{n-m}\sum_{i=m+2}^{n+1}\frac{s}{i} \leq \frac{s}{m+2}$. The bounds follow from Corollary 1.

Note that in Corollary 2, $\sup\|w_{n+1}\|$ is with respect to all instances of training data. It is useful when there exists a "target" vector such that the imposed constraints are satisfied. In this case, $\sup\|w_{n+1}\|$ is well-bounded. In the following, we briefly discuss some consequences of our bounds.

Consider the bound for formulation (8) in Corollary 2. If there exists a "target" vector $w_* \in H$ such that $|w_*^T x - y| \leq \epsilon(x,y)$ for all data, then there exists $k \leq n$ such that

$$(E\,Q(w_k))^{1/q} \leq [E_{(x,y)\sim D}\,\epsilon^q(x,y)]^{1/q} + \frac{\|w_*\|}{(n+1)^{1/2}}E_{x\sim D}^{(2-q)/2q}\,\|x\|^{2q/(2-q)}. \quad (10)$$

We can further define an estimator $\bar{w}_n = \frac{1}{n+1}\sum_{i=0}^{n} w_i$, then we obtain from the Jensen's inequality that

$$Q(\bar{w}_n) \leq \frac{1}{n+1}\sum_{i=0}^{n} Q(w_i).$$

Therefore from Corollary 1, we have

$$(E\,Q(\bar{w}_n))^{1/q} \leq [E_{(x,y)\sim D}\,\epsilon^q(x,y)]^{1/q} + \frac{\|w_*\|}{(n+1)^{1/2}}E_{x\sim D}^{(2-q)/2q}\,\|x\|^{2q/(2-q)}.$$

Although the estimator $\bar{w}_n$ gives a worst case expected bound that is as good as we can obtain for w_n using a leave-one-out cross validation analysis,[3] it is likely to be inferior to the estimator w_n. This is because the performance of $\bar{w}_n$ is comparable to the average performance of w_k for $k = 0, \ldots, n$. However, in practice, we can make the very reasonable assumption that with more training data, we obtain better estimates. Under this assumption, w_n should perform much better than this average bound.

Another observation we can make from (10) is that if we let $q = 2$, then we have to assume that $\|x\|$ is bounded almost everywhere to make the second term of right hand side bounded. However, if we use a formulation with $q < 2$, then we only require the moment $E_{x \sim D}\|x\|^{2q/(2-q)}$ to be bounded. This implies that the formulation with $q < 2$ is more robust to large data than the squared loss formulation is.

We may also consider bounds for formulation (9) in Corollary 2 and obtain similar results. In this case, we shall seek m that approximately minimizes the bound. For example, consider $q = 2$ and assume $\|x\| \leq M$ for all x. We let $m \approx (n+2)s^{1/3}(s^{1/3} + (\sup \|w_{n+1}\|M)^{2/3})^{-1} - 2$, then the bound in Corollary 2 is approximately

$$(n+2)^{-1/2}(s^{1/3} + (\sup \|w_{n+1}\|M)^{2/3})^{3/2}. \tag{11}$$

To interpret this result, we consider the following scenario. Let w be any fixed vector such that $Q(w) \leq A$. By the law of large numbers, we can find $\epsilon_n \to 0$ as $n \to \infty$ such that $P(Q_n(w, x_1, y_1, \ldots, x_n, y_n) > A+\epsilon_n) = o(1/\sqrt{n})$. If we let $s = n(A+\epsilon_n)$, then with large probability, the inequality $Q_n(w, x_1, y_1, \ldots, x_n, y_n) \leq s$ can be satisfied. Technically, under appropriate regularity assumptions, data such that $Q_n(w, x_1, y_1, \ldots, x_n, y_n) > s$ contribute an additional $o(1/\sqrt{n})$ term (which we can ignore) to the expected generalization error. The expected generalization performance is dominated by those training data for which the condition $Q_n(w, x_1, y_1, \ldots, x_n, y_n) \leq s$ is satisfied. This can be obtained from (11), which now becomes

$$(A+\epsilon_n)^{1/2}(1 + O((n(A+\epsilon_n))^{-1/3}(\|w\|M)^{2/3})$$

as $n \to \infty$. Assume that A is not small, then this bound, in a style of $A + \epsilon_n + O(n^{-1/3})$, is not optimal as $n \to \infty$. A better bound in the style of $A + O(n^{1/2})$ can be obtained by directly dealing with formulation (6), which we do not consider in this paper. However, this bound is good when A is small. It also clearly implies that if $\inf_w Q(w) = 0$, then we can choose $A \to 0$ (or equivalently $s = o(n)$) such that there is a sequence of increasing sample size k: $\lim_{k\to\infty} E\,Q(w_k) = 0$. Note that $\inf_w Q(w) = 0$ does not imply that there exists w such that $Q(w) = 0$. Many Hilbert functional spaces H (such as those generated by various kernels) are dense in the set of continuous functions. On the other hand, an arbitrary continuous target function does not correspond to a vector $w \in H$.

[3] We do not give a thorough comparison here due to the limitation of space and a lack of previous leave-one-out results for similar regression problems that we can cite.

It is useful to mention that in many cases (for example, in many kernel methods such as the exponential kernel $K(x, y) = \exp(-(x-y)^2))$, C_n in (8) is not empty as long as either the training data x_i are non-duplicate or y is a function of x. The noise tolerance $\epsilon(x, y)$ in (10) (or s in (11)) can be used to trade-off the two terms on the right-hand-side of the bound in (10) (or the two terms in (11)): when we increase ϵ (or s), we increase the first term but decrease $\|w\|$ in the second term.

4.2 Noise-Free Formulation

Assume y is generated from the following exact formulation $y = w_*^T x$. Where $w_* \in H$ is the target weight vector. We consider the following noise free estimation formulation:

$$C_n = \{w \in H : w^T x_i = y_i \quad (i = 1, \ldots, n)\}.$$

For simplicity, we assume that $\|x\| \le M$, and let $q = 2$. Our sequential approximation bound implies

$$\sum_{i=0}^{n} (w_i^T x_{i+1} - y_{i+1})^2 \le \|w_*\|^2 M^2. \tag{12}$$

The above bound is similar to the regret bound using a stochastic gradient descent rule from $i = 0, \ldots, n$ (we let $w_0' = 0$):

$$w_{i+1}' = w_i' - \frac{1}{x_{i+1}^2}(w_i'^T x_{i+1} - y_{i+1}) x_{i+1}. \tag{13}$$

Using techniques in [1], we may consider the following equality:

$$(w_{i+1}' - w_*)^2 = (w_i' - w_*)^2 - \frac{1}{x_{i+1}^2}(w_i'^T x_{i+1} - y_{i+1})^2.$$

Summing over i, we obtain

$$\sum_{i=0}^{n} (w_i'^T x_{i+1} - y_{i+1})^2 \le \|w_*\|^2 M^2. \tag{14}$$

Both (12) and (14) can be achieved with a set of orthonormal vectors x_i and $y_i = 1$. So both bounds are tight in the worst case. However, in practice w_n is likely to be a better estimator than w_n'. We illustrate this in the following.

Observe that $w_n = P_{x_1,\ldots,x_n}(w_*)$, where P is the orthogonal projection operator onto the subspace of H spanned by $x_1, \ldots, x_n$. We also denote $w - P_{x_1,\ldots,x_n}(w)$ by $P_{x_1,\ldots,x_n}^{\perp}(w)$. We have the following inequality:

$$\begin{aligned}(w_i^T x_{i+1} - y_{i+1})^2 &= (P_{x_1,\ldots,x_i}^{\perp}(w_*)^T P_{x_1,\ldots,x_i}^{\perp}(x_{i+1}))^2 \\ &\le P_{x_1,\ldots,x_i}^{\perp}(w_*)^2 P_{x_1,\ldots,x_i}^{\perp}(x_{i+1})^2.\end{aligned}$$

The effective length of x_{i+1} is thus $P^{\perp}_{x_1,\ldots,x_i}(x_{i+1})$ which can be substantially smaller than M. As an extreme, we can bound $EQ(w_n)$ using the following inequality:

$$E\,Q(w_n) \le w_*^2 E\,P^{\perp}_{x_1,\ldots,x_n}(x_{n+1})^2.$$

Now, we assume x_i is in an d-dimensional space, and the training data $x_1, \ldots, x_n$ ($n \ge d$) have rank d with probability 1, then $E\,Q(w_n) = 0$. Clearly in general we still have $E\,Q(w'_n) > 0$. In practice, even though the data may not lie in finite dimension, the effective dimension measured by $E\,P^{\perp}_{x_1,\ldots,x_n}(x_{n+1})^2$ can decrease rapidly as $n \to \infty$. In this case, the estimator w_n will be superior to w'_n although both have the same worst-case regret bounds.

This also justifies why in practice, one often run an online method repeatedly over the data. In the noise-free squared loss regression case, if $w'_{n,m}$ is obtained by applying (13) repeatedly m times over the training data, then $w'_{n,m} \to w_n$ as $m \to \infty$. This is because $\lim_{m\to 0} {w'}^T_{n,m} x_i = y_i = w_n^T x_i$, which easily follows from the regret bound of $w'_{n,m}$. This means $w'_{n,m}$ converges weakly to w_n, which also implies strong convergence since the vectors are in the finite dimensional subspace of H spanned by x_i ($i = 1, \ldots, n$).

5 Classification

5.1 Sequential-Validation Bounds

We consider the classification problem: to find w that minimizes the classification error

$$Q(w) = E_{(x,y)\sim D} I(w^T xy \le 0),$$

where D is an unknown distribution. $I(z \le 0)$ is the indicator function: $I(z \le 0) = 1$ if $z \le 0$ and $I(z \le 0) = 0$ otherwise.

Given the training data, we define the empirical expected loss with margin $\gamma > 0$ as:

$$Q_n^{\gamma}(w, x_1, y_1, \ldots, x_n, y_n) = \frac{1}{n}\sum_{i=1}^{n} I(w^T xy < \gamma).$$

We consider two formulations of C_n in (1). The first formulation is the maximum margin algorithm in [11] (also know as the separable SVM) that employs the following hard-margin constraints:

$$C_n = \{w \in H : w^T x_i y_i \ge 1, \quad (i = 1, \ldots, n)\}. \tag{15}$$

The second formulation employs a soft-margin constraint:

$$C_n = \{w \in H : \sum_{i=1}^{n} L(w^T x_i y_i) \le s\}, \tag{16}$$

where s is a data independent parameter and L is a non-negative and non-increasing convex function. If a solution does not exist in one of the above formulations (that is, C_n is empty), then we let $w_n = 0$. In the following discussion, we only consider the case that C_n is non-empty for all training data.

Theorem 3. *Assume for all training data C_n is non-empty, and $C_k \subseteq C_{k-1}$ for all $k = m, \ldots, n$. For each k, w_k is computed from samples $(x_1, y_1), \ldots, (x_k, y_k)$ using (1). We have the following average expected generalization bound ($1 \leq q \leq 2$):*

$$\sum_{i=m}^{n} E\,Q(w_i)$$
$$\leq \sum_{i=m+1}^{n+1} E\,Q_i^{\gamma}(w_i, x_1, y_1, \ldots, x_i, y_i) + E\,[\frac{\|w_{n+1}\|^q}{\gamma^q}(\sum_{i=m}^{n} |x_{i+1}|^{2q/(2-q)})^{(2-q)/2}].$$

The expectation E is with respect to $n+1$ independent random training samples $(x_1, y_1), \ldots, (x_{n+1}, y_{n+1})$ from D. Note that $\gamma > 0$ can be a function of $(x_1, y_1), \ldots, (x_{n+1}, y_{n+1})$.

Proof. Note that

$$I(w_i x_{i+1} y_{i+1} \leq 0) \leq I(w_{i+1}^T x_{i+1} y_{i+1} < \gamma) + \frac{1}{\gamma^q}|(w_{i+1} - w_i)^T x_{i+1}|^q.$$

Summing over $i = m, \ldots, n$, and using the Hölder's inequality, we have

$$\sum_{i=m}^{n} I(w_i x_{i+1} y_{i+1} \leq 0)$$
$$\leq \sum_{i=m}^{n} I(w_{i+1}^T x_{i+1} y_{i+1} < \gamma) + \frac{1}{\gamma^q}(\sum_{i=m}^{n}(w_i - w_{i+1})^2)^{\frac{q}{2}}(\sum_{i=m}^{n} \|x_{i+1}\|^{\frac{2q}{2-q}})^{\frac{2-q}{2}}.$$

Taking expectation E, we obtain

$$\sum_{i=m}^{n} E\,Q(w_i)$$
$$\leq \sum_{i=m}^{n} E\,I(w_{i+1}^T x_{i+1} y_{i+1} < \gamma) + E\frac{1}{\gamma^q}(\sum_{i=m}^{n}(w_i - w_{i+1})^2)^{\frac{q}{2}}(\sum_{i=m}^{n} \|x_{i+1}\|^{\frac{2q}{2-q}})^{\frac{2-q}{2}}.$$

From Theorem 1, we have $(\sum_{i=m}^{n}(w_i - w_{i+1})^2)^{q/2} \leq \|w_{n+1}\|^q$. Also observe that

$$E\,I(w_{i+1}^T x_{i+1} y_{i+1} < \gamma) = E\,Q_{i+1}^{\gamma}(w_{i+1}, x_1, y_1, \ldots, x_{i+1}, y_{i+1}).$$

We thus obtain the theorem.

Corollary 3. *Using formulation (15), we have*

$$\sum_{i=0}^{n} E\,Q(w_i) \leq E\,[\|w_{n+1}\|^q(\sum_{i=1}^{n+1} |x_i|^{2q/(2-q)})^{(2-q)/2}].$$

Using formulation (16), we have

$$\sum_{i=m+1}^{n} E\,Q(w_i) \leq \sum_{i=m+2}^{n+1} \frac{s}{i} E\,\frac{1}{L(\gamma)} + E\,[\frac{\|w_{n+1}\|^q}{\gamma^q}(\sum_{i=m+1}^{n} |x_{i+1}|^{2q/(2-q)})^{(2-q)/2}].$$

Proof. If $\gamma = 1$, we obtain from formulation (15)

$$Q_k^{\gamma}(w_k, x_1, y_1, \ldots, x_k, y_k) = 0.$$

From formulation (16), we obtain

$$Q_k^{\gamma}(w_k, x_1, y_1, \ldots, x_k, y_k) \leq \frac{1}{k}\sum_{i=1}^{k} \frac{L(w_k^T x_i y_i)}{L(\gamma)} \leq \frac{s}{kL(\gamma)}.$$

The bounds follow from Theorem 3.

Corollary 4. *Using formulation (15), we have*

$$\frac{1}{n+1}\sum_{i=0}^{n} E\,Q(w_i) \leq \frac{\sup\|w_{n+1}\|^q}{(n+1)^{q/2}} E_{x\sim D}^{(2-q)/2}\|x\|^{2q/(2-q)}.$$

Using formulation (16), with fixed γ, we have

$$\frac{1}{n-m}\sum_{i=m+1}^{n} E\,Q(w_i) \leq \frac{s}{(m+2)L(\gamma)} + \frac{\sup\|w_{n+1}\|^q}{(n-m)^{q/2}\gamma^q} E_{x\sim D}^{(2-q)/2}\|x\|^{2q/(2-q)}.$$

Proof. Using Corollary 3, the proof is the essentially the same as that of Corollary 2.

The separable case (15) has also been considered in [10], where they derived a result that is similar to the corresponding bound in Corollary 4 with $q = 2$.

We shall mention that in most of previous theoretical studies, the quantity $\|x\|$ were assumed to be bounded. However, our bounds can still be applied when $\|x\|$ is not bounded, as long as there exists $1 \leq q < 2$ such that the moment $E_{x\sim D}\|x\|^{2q/(2-q)}$ is finite. On the other hand, this causes a slow down of convergence in our bounds.

Consider formulation (16) in Corollary 4. We may seek m to approximately minimize the bound. For example, consider $q = 2$ and assume $\|x\| \leq M$ for all x. We let $m \approx (n+2)s^{1/2}L(\gamma)^{1/2}(s^{1/2} + L(\gamma)^{1/2}\sup\|w_{n+1}\|M\gamma^{-1})^{-1} - 2$, then the bound in Corollary 2 is approximately

$$(n+2)^{-1}(s^{1/2}L(\gamma)^{-1/2} + \sup\|w_{n+1}\|M\gamma^{-1})^2. \tag{17}$$

Similar to the discussion after (11), the above bound can be improved by directly analyzing the penalty type formulation (6) if the problem is not linearly separable. On the other hand, the bound is good if the problem is nearly separable. If $\inf_w Q(w) = 0$, then we can find $s = o(n)$ such that there is a sequence of increasing sample size k: $\lim_{k\to\infty} E\,Q(w_k) = 0$.

5.2 Separable Linear Classification

We consider the separable case using formulation (15). Similar to the regression case, we may compare our results with the perceptron mistake bound. However, in this section we consider the comparison with Vapnik's leave-one-out bound in [11] and illustrate why our sequential validation analysis can provide useful information that cannot be obtained by using the leave-one-out bound alone.

To be compatible with Vapnik's result, we consider the special case of $q = 2$ in Corollary 3:

$$\sum_{i=0}^{n} E\, Q(w_i) \leq E\, w_{n+1}^2 \max_{i=1,\ldots,n+1} x_i^2.$$

This implies the following: there exists a sample size $k \leq n$ such that

$$E\, Q(w_k) \leq \frac{1}{n+1} E\, w_{n+1}^2 \max_{i=1,\ldots,n+1} x_i^2.$$

This can be compared with Vapnik's leave-one-out bound in [11], which can be expressed as:

$$E\, Q(w_n) \leq \frac{1}{n+1} E\, w_{n+1}^2 \max_{i=1,\ldots,n+1} x_i^2.$$

Using our bound, we may also consider an estimator w'_n that is randomly selected among w_i from $i = 0, \ldots, n$. Clearly,

$$E\, Q(w'_n) \leq \frac{1}{n+1} E\, w_{n+1}^2 \max_{i=1,\ldots,n+1} x_i^2.$$

This gives a comparable bound as the leave-one-out bound of w_n. However, as we have argued before, despite of the same worst case bound, w'_n is likely to be inferior to w_n. If we make the reasonable assumption that with more training data, one can obtain better results, than our sequential validation result implies that the performance of w_n should be better than what is implied by the leave-one-out bound.

Specifically, we consider the situation that there exists an estimator M such that $\|x\| \leq M$ and there exists a weight parameter w_* so that the condition $w_*^T xy \geq 1$ is always satisfied. Vapnik's bounds implies that

$$E\, Q(w_n) \leq \frac{1}{n} w_*^2 M^2.$$

That is, the expected generalization error decreases at an order of $O(1/n)$. However, our bound implies that

$$\sum_{n=0}^{\infty} E\, Q(w_n) \leq w_*^2 M^2.$$

This implies that asymptotically the expected generalization error decreases faster than $O(1/n)$ since $\sum_{n=1}^{\infty} 1/n = \infty$.

This example shows that the sequential approximation analysis proposed in this paper provides useful insights into classification problems that cannot be obtained by using the leave-one-out analysis.

6 Summary

In this paper, we derived a general sequential approximation bound for a class of sample dependent convex optimization problems. Based on this bound, we are able to obtain sequential cross validation bounds for some learning formulations. A unique aspect that distinguishes this work from many previous works on mistake bound analysis is that we directly bound the convergence of consecutive parameter estimates in a batch learning setting.

The specific analysis given in this paper for constrained regularization formulation is more suitable for problems that contain small noise. However, it is easy to generalize the idea to analyze penalty type regularization formulations including the standard forms of Gaussian processes and soft-margin support vector machines. A direct analysis of penalty type regularization formulations is more suitable for large noise problems. Note that we have already demonstrated in the paper that the constrained regularization formulation considered here is numerically equivalent to the penalty type regularization formulation.

References

1. N. Cesa-Bianchi, P. Long, and M. K. Warmuth. Worst-case quadratic loss bounds for prediction using linear functions and gradient descent. *IEEE Transactions on Neural Networks*, 7:604–619, 1996.
2. Nello Cristianini and John Shawe-Taylor. *An Introduction to Support Vector Machines and other Kernel-based Learning Methods.* Cambridge University Press, 2000.
3. Jüergen Forster and Manfred Warmuth. Relative expected instantaneous loss bounds. In *COLT 00*, pages 90–99, 2000.
4. Jüergen Forster and Manfred Warmuth. Relative loss bounds for temporal-difference learning. In *ICML 00*, pages 295–302, 2000.
5. Geoffrey J. Gordon. Regret bounds for prediction problems. In *COLT 99*, pages 29–40, 1999.
6. Harro G. Heuser. *Functional analysis.* John Wiley & Sons Ltd., Chichester, 1982. Translated from the German by John Horváth, A Wiley-Interscience Publication.
7. T. Jaakkola and D. Haussler. Probabilistic kernel regression models. In *Proceedings of the 1999 Conference on AI and Statistics*, 1999.
8. Michael Kearns and Dana Ron. Algorithmic stability and sanity-check bounds for leave-one-out cross-validation. *Neural Computation*, 11(6):1427–1453, 1999.
9. J. Kivinen and M.K. Warmuth. Additive versus exponentiated gradient updates for linear prediction. *Journal of Information and Computation*, 132:1–64, 1997.
10. Yi Li and Philip M. Long. The relaxed online maximum margin algorithm. In S.A. Solla, T.K. Leen, and K.-R. Müller, editors, *Advances in Neural Information Processing Systems 12*, pages 498–504. MIT Press, 2000.
11. V.N. Vapnik. *Statistical learning theory.* John Wiley & Sons, New York, 1998.
12. Tong Zhang. Convergence of large margin separable linear classification. In *Advances in Neural Information Processing Systems 13*, pages 357–363, 2001.
13. Tong Zhang. A leave-one-out cross validation bound for kernel methods with applications in learning. In *COLT*, 2001.

Efficiently Approximating Weighted Sums with Exponentially Many Terms*

Deepak Chawla, Lin Li, and Stephen Scott

Dept. of Computer Science, University of Nebraska, Lincoln, NE 68588-0115, USA
{dchawla,lili,sscott}@cse.unl.edu

Abstract. We explore applications of Markov chain Monte Carlo methods for weight estimation over inputs to the Weighted Majority (WM) and Winnow algorithms. This is useful when there are exponentially many such inputs and no apparent means to efficiently compute their weighted sum. The applications we examine are pruning classifier ensembles using WM and learning general DNF formulas using Winnow. These uses require exponentially many inputs, so we define Markov chains over the inputs to approximate the weighted sums. We state performance guarantees for our algorithms and present preliminary empirical results.

1 Introduction

Multiplicative weight-update algorithms (e.g. [11,13,3]) have been studied extensively due to their on-line mistake bounds' logarithmic dependence on N, the total number of inputs. This *attribute efficiency* allows them to be applied to problems where N is exponential in the input size, which is the case in the problems we study here: using the Weighted Majority algorithm (WM [13]) to predict nearly as well as the best pruning of a classifier ensemble (from e.g. boosting) and using Winnow [11] to learn DNF formulas in unrestricted domains. However, a large N requires techniques to efficiently compute the weighted sums of inputs to WM and Winnow. One method is to exploit commonalities among the inputs, partitioning them into a polynomial number of groups such that given a single member of each group, the total weight contribution of that group can be efficiently computed [14,6,7,8,18,20]. But many WM and Winnow applications do not appear to exhibit such structure, so it seems that a brute-force implementation is the only option to guarantee complete correctness.[1] Thus we explore applications of Markov chain Monte Carlo (MCMC) methods to estimate the total weight without the need for special structure in the problem.

First we study pruning a classifier ensemble (from e.g. boosting), which can reduce overfitting and time for evaluation [15,21]. We use the Weighted Majority algorithm, using all possible prunings as experts. WM is guaranteed to not

* This work was supported in part by NSF grant CCR-9877080 with matching funds from CCIS and a Layman grant, and was completed in part utilizing the Research Computing Facility of the University of Nebraska-Lincoln.

[1] For additive weight-update algorithms, kernels can be used to exactly compute the weighted sums (e.g. [4]).

D. Helmbold and B. Williamson (Eds.): COLT/EuroCOLT 2001, LNAI 2111, pp. 82–98, 2001.

make many more prediction mistakes than the best expert, so we know that a brute-force WM will perform nearly as well as the best pruning. However, the exponential number of prunings motivates us to use an MCMC approach to approximate the weighted sum of the experts' predictions.

Another problem we investigate is learning DNF formulas using Winnow [11]. Our algorithm implicitly enumerates all possible DNF terms and uses Winnow to learn a monotone disjunction over these terms, which it can do while making $O(k \log N)$ prediction mistakes, where k is the number of relevant terms and N is the total number of terms. So a brute-force implementation of Winnow makes a polynomial number of errors on arbitrary examples (with no distributional assumptions) and does not require membership queries. However, a brute-force implementation requires exponential time to compute the weighted sum of the inputs. So we apply MCMC methods to estimate this sum.

MCMC methods [9] have been applied to problems in approximate discrete integration, where the goal is to approximate $W = \sum_{x \in \Omega} w(x)$, where w is a positive function and Ω is a finite set of combinatorial structures. It involves defining an ergodic Markov chain $\mathcal{M}$ with state space Ω and stationary distribution π. Then repeatedly simulate $\mathcal{M}$ to draw samples almost according to π. Under appropriate conditions, these samples yield accuracy guarantees. E.g. in approximate discrete integration, sometimes one can guarantee that the estimate of the sum is within a factor ϵ of the true value (w.h.p.). When this is true and the estimation algorithm requires only polynomial time in the problem size and $1/\epsilon$, the algorithm is called a *fully polynomial randomized approximation scheme* (FPRAS). In certain cases a similar argument can be made about combinatorial optimization problems, i.e. that the algorithm's solution is within a factor of ϵ of the true maximum or minimum (in this case the chain is called a *Metropolis process* [16]). In this paper we combine two known approximators for application to WM and Winnow: one is for the *approximate knapsack problem* [17,5], where given a positive real vector $\mathbf{x}$ and real number b, the goal is to estimate $|\Omega|$ within a multiplicative factor of ϵ, where $\Omega = \{\mathbf{p} \in \{0,1\}^n : \mathbf{x} \cdot \mathbf{p} \leq b\}$. The other is for computing the sum of the weights of a *weighted matching* of a graph: for a graph G and $\lambda \geq 0$, approximate $Z_G(\lambda) = \sum_{k=0}^{n} m_k \lambda^k$, where m_k is the number of matchings in G of size k and n is the number of nodes. Each of these problems has an FPRAS [9,17]. In combining the results from these two problems, we make several non-trivial changes. We also propose Metropolis processes to find prunings in WM and terms in Winnow with high weight, allowing us to output hypotheses that do not require MCMC simulations to evaluate them.

1.1 Summary of Results

Theorems 2 and 7 give bounds on the error of our approximations of the weighted sums of the inputs to WM and Winnow for the problems (respectively) of predicting nearly as well as the best ensemble pruning and learning DNF formulas. Specifically, we show that the weighted sums can be approximated to within a factor of $1 \pm \epsilon$ with probability at least $1 - \delta$. The theorems hold if the Markov chains used are simulated sufficiently long such that the resultant simulated probability distribution is "close" to the chain's true stationary distribution. If these *mixing times* are polynomial in all relevant inputs, then we get FPRASs for these problems. This is the case for WM under appropriate conditions, as described in Theorem 5. Based on our empirical evidence, we also believe that both Winnow and WM have polynomial mixing time bounds for more general cases. However, even if an FPRAS exists for these problems, then while we can guarantee correctness of our algorithms in the PAC sense, we cannot necessarily guarantee efficiency. This is because in the worst case, the weighted sum for Winnow might be exponentially close to the threshold. Thus unless we make ϵ exponentially small, an adversary can force the on-line version of each of our algorithms to make an arbitrary number of mistakes, since when ϵ is too large, we can never be certain that our algorithm is behaving the same as brute-force Winnow. A similar situation can occur for WM. (Corollaries 4 and 8 formalize this.) It is an open problem as to whether this can be avoided when there are specific probability distributions over the examples and/or restricted cases of the problems.[2]

Section 2 gives our algorithms and Markov chains for pruning ensembles and learning DNF formulas, and some preliminary empirical results appear in Sect. 3. Finally, we conclude in Sect. 4 with a description of future and ongoing work.

2 The Algorithms and Markov Chains

2.1 Pruning Ensembles of Classifiers

We start by exploring methods for pruning an ensemble produced by e.g. AdaBoost [19]. AdaBoost's output is a set of functions $h_i : \mathcal{X} \rightarrow \mathrm{Re}$, where $i \in \{1, \ldots, n\}$ and $\mathcal{X}$ is the instance space. Each h_i is trained on a different distribution over the training examples and is associated with a parameter $\beta_i \in \mathrm{Re}$ that weights its predictions. Given an instance $\mathbf{x} \in \mathcal{X}$, the ensemble's prediction is $H(\mathbf{x}) = \mathrm{sign}\left(\sum_{i=1}^{n} \beta_i h_i(\mathbf{x})\right)$. Thus $\mathrm{sign}\left(h_i(\mathbf{x})\right)$ is h_i's prediction on $\mathbf{x}$, $|h_i(\mathbf{x})|$ is its confidence in its prediction, and β_i weights AdaBoost's confidence in h_i. It has been shown that if each h_i has error less than $1/2$ on its distribution, then the error on the training set and the generalization error of $H(\cdot)$ can be bounded. Strong bounds on $H(\cdot)$'s generalization error can also be shown. However, overfitting can still occur [15], i.e. sometimes better generalization can be achieved if some of the h_i's are discarded. So our first goal is to find a weighted combination of all possible prunings that performs not much worse in terms of generalization error than the best single pruning. Since another motivation for pruning an ensemble is to reduce its size, we also explore methods for choosing a single good pruning.

The typical approach to predicting nearly as well as the best pruning of classifiers (e.g. [18,20]) uses recent results from [3] on predicting with expert advice, where each possible pruning is an expert. If there is an efficient way to make predictions, then the expert-based algorithm's mistake bound yields an

[2] It is unlikely that an efficient distribution-free DNF-learning algorithm exists [2,1].

efficient algorithm. We take a similar approach, but for simplicity we use the more straightforward WM.

To predict nearly as well as the best pruning, we place every possible pruning in a pool (so $N = 2^n$) and run WM for binary predictions. We start by computing W_t^+ and W_t^-, which are, respectively, the sums of the weights of the experts predicting a positive and a negative label on example $\mathbf{x}_t$. Then WM predicts $+1$ if $W_t^+ > W_t^-$ and -1 otherwise. Whenever WM makes a prediction mistake, it reduces the weights of all experts that predicted incorrectly by dividing them by some constant $\alpha > 1$. It has been shown that if the best expert makes at most M mistakes, then WM has a mistake bound of $2.41(M + \log_2 N)$.

We use WM in the following way. Given an example $\mathbf{x}_t \in \mathcal{X}$, we compute $h_i(\mathbf{x}_t)$ for all $i \in \{1, \ldots, n\}$. We then use an MCMC procedure to compute $\hat{W}_t^+$, an estimate of $W_t^+ = \sum_{\mathbf{p}_j \in \Omega_t^+} w_j$, where $\Omega_t^+ = \{\mathbf{p} \in \{0,1\}^n : \sum_{i=1}^n p_i \beta_i h_i(\mathbf{x}_t) \geq 0\}$. A similar procedure is used to compute $\hat{W}_t^-$. Then WM predicts $+1$ if $\hat{W}_t^+ > \hat{W}_t^-$ and -1 otherwise.

Define $\mathcal{M}_{\mathrm{WM},t}^+$ as a Markov chain with state space Ω_t^+ that makes transitions from state $\mathbf{p} = (p_0, \ldots, p_{n-1}) \in \Omega_t^+$ to state $\mathbf{q} \in \Omega_t^+$ by the following rules.[3] (1) With probability $1/2$ let $\mathbf{q} = \mathbf{p}$. Otherwise, (2) select i uniformly at random from $\{0, \ldots, n-1\}$ and let $\mathbf{p}' = (p_0, \ldots, p_{i-1}, 1 - p_i, p_{i+1}, \ldots, p_{n-1})$. (3) If $\mathbf{p}' \in \Omega_t^+$ (i.e. if the new pruning also predicts positive on $\mathbf{x}_t$), then let $\mathbf{p}'' = \mathbf{p}'$, else let $\mathbf{p}'' = \mathbf{p}$. (4) With probability $\min\left\{1, \alpha^{v_t(\mathbf{p}) - v_t(\mathbf{p}'')}\right\}$, let $\mathbf{q} = \mathbf{p}''$, else let $\mathbf{q} = \mathbf{p}$. Here $v_t(\mathbf{p})$ is the number of prediction mistakes made on trials 1 through $t-1$ by the pruning represented by $\mathbf{p}$.

Lemma 1. *$\mathcal{M}_{WM,t}^+$ is ergodic with stationary distribution*

$$\pi_{\alpha,t}^+(\mathbf{p}) = \frac{\alpha^{-v_t(\mathbf{p})}}{W_t^+(\alpha)} ,$$

where $W_t^+(\alpha) = \sum_{\mathbf{p} \in \Omega_t^+} \alpha^{-v_t(\mathbf{p})}$, i.e. the sum of the weights of the prunings in Ω_t^+ assuming α was the update factor for all previous trials.

Proof. In $\mathcal{M}_{\mathrm{WM},t}^+$, all pairs of states can communicate. To see this, note that to move from $\mathbf{p} \in \Omega_t^+$ to $\mathbf{q} \in \Omega_t^+$, first add to $\mathbf{p}$ all bits i in $\mathbf{q}$ and not in $\mathbf{p}$ that correspond to positions where $\beta_i h_i(x) \geq 0$. Then delete from $\mathbf{p}$ all bits i in $\mathbf{p}$ and not in $\mathbf{q}$ that correspond to positions where $\beta_i h_i(x) < 0$. Then delete the unnecessary "positive bits" and add the necessary "negative bits". All states between $\mathbf{p}$ and $\mathbf{q}$ are in Ω_t^+. Thus $\mathcal{M}_{\mathrm{WM},t}^+$ is irreducible. Also, the self-loop of Step 1 ensures aperiodicity. Finally, $\mathcal{M}_{\mathrm{WM},t}^+$ is reversible since the transition probabilities $P(\mathbf{p}, \mathbf{q}) = \min\{1, \alpha^{v_t(\mathbf{q})}/\alpha^{v_t(\mathbf{p})}\}/(2n) = \min\{1, \pi_{\alpha,t}^+(\mathbf{q})/\pi_{\alpha,t}^+(\mathbf{p})\}/(2n)$ satisfy the detailed balance condition $\pi_{\alpha,t}^+(\mathbf{p})P(\mathbf{p}, \mathbf{q}) = \pi_{\alpha,t}^+(\mathbf{q})P(\mathbf{q}, \mathbf{p})$. So $\mathcal{M}_{\mathrm{WM},t}^+$ is ergodic with the stated stationary distribution. □

[3] The chain $\mathcal{M}_{\mathrm{WM},t}^-$ is defined similarly with respect to Ω_t^-.

Let r_t be the smallest integer s.t. $(1+1/B)^{r_t-1} \geq \alpha$ and $r_t \geq 1+\log_2 \alpha$, where B is the total number of prediction mistakes made by WM. Then $r_t \leq 1+2B\ln\alpha$. Also, let $m_t = 1/\left(\alpha^{1/(r_t-1)}-1\right) \geq B$ and $\alpha_{i,t} = (1+1/m_t)^{i-1} = \alpha^{(i-1)/(r_t-1)}$ for $0 \leq i \leq r_t$ (so $\alpha_{r_t,t} = \alpha$). Now define $f_{i,t}^{\mathrm{WM}}(\mathbf{p}) = (\alpha_{i,t}/\alpha_{i-1,t})^{-v_t(\mathbf{p})}$, where $\mathbf{p}$ is chosen according to $\pi^+_{\alpha_{i,t}}$. Then

$$\mathrm{E}\left[f_{i,t}^{\mathrm{WM}}\right] = \sum_{\mathbf{p}\in\Omega_t^+} \left(\frac{\alpha_{i,t}}{\alpha_{i-1,t}}\right)^{-v_t(\mathbf{p})} \frac{\alpha_{i,t}^{-v_t(\mathbf{p})}}{W_t^+(\alpha_{i,t})} = \frac{W_t^+(\alpha_{i+1,t})}{W_t^+(\alpha_{i,t})} \ .$$

So we can estimate $W_t^+(\alpha_{i+1,t})/W_t^+(\alpha_{i,t})$ by sampling points from $\mathcal{M}^+_{\mathrm{WM},t}$ and computing the sample mean of $f_{i,t}^{\mathrm{WM}}$. Note that

$$W_t^+(\alpha) = \left(\frac{W_t^+(\alpha_{r_t,t})}{W_t^+(\alpha_{r_t-1,t})}\right)\left(\frac{W_t^+(\alpha_{r_t-1,t})}{W_t^+(\alpha_{r_t-2,t})}\right)\cdots\left(\frac{W_t^+(\alpha_{2,t})}{W_t^+(\alpha_{1,t})}\right) W_t^+(\alpha_{1,t}) \ ,$$

where $W_t^+(\alpha_{1,t}) = W_t^+(1) = |\Omega_t^+|$. So for each value $\alpha_{1,t},\ldots,\alpha_{r_t-1,t}$, we run S_t independent simulations of $\mathcal{M}^+_{\mathrm{WM},t}$, each of length $T_{i,t}$, and let $X_{i,t}$ be the sample mean of $(\alpha_{i,t}/\alpha_{i-1,t})^{-v_t(\mathbf{p})}$. Then our estimate is[4]

$$\hat{W}_t^+(\alpha) = W_t^+(\alpha_{1,t}) \prod_{i=1}^{r_t-1} X_{i,t} = |\Omega_t^+| \prod_{i=1}^{r_t-1} X_{i,t} \ . \qquad (1)$$

Theorem 2's proof is a hybrid of those of Jerrum and Sinclair [9] for weighted matchings and the knapsack problem, with several non-trivial extensions. The theorem uses *variation distance*, a distance measure between a chain's simulated and stationary distributions, defined as $\max_{U\subseteq\Omega} |P^\tau(\mathbf{p},U) - \pi(U)|$, where $P^\tau(\mathbf{p},\cdot)$ is the distribution of a chain's state at simulation step τ given that the simulation started in state $\mathbf{p}\in\Omega$, and π is the stationary distribution.

Theorem 2. *Let $\epsilon' = 2(1+\epsilon)^{1/3} - 2$, the sample size $S_t = \left\lceil 520 r_t e/\epsilon'^2 \right\rceil$, $|\Omega_t^+|$'s estimate be within $\epsilon'/2$ of its true value with probability $\geq 3/4$, and $\mathcal{M}^+_{WM,t}$ be simulated long enough ($T_{i,t}$ steps) for each sample s.t. the variation distance is $\leq \epsilon'/(10er_t)$. Then $\hat{W}_t^+(\alpha)$ satisfies*

$$\Pr\left[(1-\epsilon)\,W_t^+(\alpha) \leq \hat{W}_t^+(\alpha) \leq (1+\epsilon)\,W_t^+(\alpha)\right] \geq 1/2 \ .$$

In addition, the $1/2$ can be made arbitrarily close to $1-\delta$ for any $\delta > 0$.

We start with a lemma to bound $f_{i,t}^{\mathrm{WM}}$'s variance relative to its expectation.

Lemma 3.

$$\frac{\mathrm{Var}\left[f_{i,t}^{WM}\right]}{\left(\mathrm{E}\left[f_{i,t}^{WM}\right]\right)^2} \leq \frac{1}{\mathrm{E}\left[f_{i,t}^{WM}\right]} < e \ .$$

[4] Since computing $|\Omega_t^+|$ is #P-complete [22], we use a variation of the knapsack FPRAS [17,9] to estimate $|\Omega_t^+|$.

Proof. The first inequality follows from

$$\begin{aligned}
\mathrm{Var}\left[f_{i,t}^{\mathrm{WM}}\right] &= \mathrm{E}\left[\left(f_{i,t}^{\mathrm{WM}}\right)^2\right] - \left(\mathrm{E}\left[f_{i,t}^{\mathrm{WM}}\right]\right)^2 \\
&= \sum_{\mathbf{p}\in\Omega_t^+} \left(\frac{\alpha_{i,t}}{\alpha_{i-1,t}}\right)^{-2v_t(\mathbf{p})} \frac{\alpha_{i,t}^{-v_t(\mathbf{p})}}{W_t^+(\alpha_{i,t})} - \frac{W_t^+(\alpha_{i+1,t})^2}{W_t^+(\alpha_{i,t})^2} \\
&\leq \frac{1}{W_t^+(\alpha_{i,t})} \sum_{\mathbf{p}\in\Omega_t^+} \left(\frac{\alpha_{i,t}^2}{\alpha_{i-1,t}}\right)^{-v_t(\mathbf{p})} - \frac{W_t^+(\alpha_{i+1,t})^2}{W_t^+(\alpha_{i,t})^2} \\
&= \frac{W_t^+(\alpha_{i+1,t})}{W_t^+(\alpha_{i,t})} - \frac{W_t^+(\alpha_{i+1,t})^2}{W_t^+(\alpha_{i,t})^2} < \mathrm{E}\left[f_{i,t}^{\mathrm{WM}}\right] .
\end{aligned}$$

Thus for all $1 \leq i \leq r_t - 1$,

$$\begin{aligned}
\frac{\mathrm{Var}\left[f_{i,t}\right]}{\left(\mathrm{E}\left[f_{i,t}\right]\right)^2} &< \frac{1}{\mathrm{E}\left[f_{i,t}\right]} = \frac{W_t^+(\alpha_{i,t})}{W_t^+(\alpha_{i+1,t})} = \frac{\sum_{\mathbf{p}\in\Omega_t^+} \alpha_{i,t}^{-v_t(\mathbf{p})}}{\sum_{\mathbf{p}\in\Omega_t^+} \alpha_{i+1,t}^{-v_t(\mathbf{p})}} \\
&= \frac{\left(\frac{1}{\alpha_{i,t}}\right)^B \left(\sum_{\mathbf{p}\in\Omega_t^+} \left(\frac{1}{\alpha_{i,t}}\right)^{v_t(\mathbf{p})-B}\right)}{\left(\frac{1}{\alpha_{i+1,t}}\right)^B \left(\sum_{\mathbf{p}\in\Omega_t^+} \left(\frac{1}{\alpha_{i+1,t}}\right)^{v_t(\mathbf{p})-B}\right)} \\
&\leq \left(\frac{\alpha_{i+1,t}}{\alpha_{i,t}}\right)^B = \left(1 + 1/m_t\right)^B \leq e .
\end{aligned}$$

□

Proof (of Theorem 2). Let the distribution $\hat{\pi}_{\alpha_{i,t}}^+$ be the one resulting from a length-$T_{i,t}$ simulation of $\mathcal{M}_{\mathrm{WM},t}^+$, and assume that the variation distance $\left\|\hat{\pi}_{\alpha_{i,t}}^+ - \pi_{\alpha_{i,t}}^+\right\| \leq \epsilon'/(10er_t)$. Now consider the random variable $\hat{f}_{i,t}^{\mathrm{WM}}$, which is the same as $f_{i,t}^{\mathrm{WM}}$ except that the terms are selected according to $\hat{\pi}_{\alpha_{i,t}}^+$. Since $\hat{f}_{i,t}^{\mathrm{WM}} \in (0,1]$, $\left|\mathrm{E}\left[\hat{f}_{i,t}^{\mathrm{WM}}\right] - \mathrm{E}\left[f_{i,t}^{\mathrm{WM}}\right]\right| \leq \epsilon'/(10er_t)$, which implies $\mathrm{E}\left[f_{i,t}^{\mathrm{WM}}\right] - \epsilon'/(10er_t) \leq \mathrm{E}\left[\hat{f}_{i,t}^{\mathrm{WM}}\right] \leq \mathrm{E}\left[f_{i,t}^{\mathrm{WM}}\right] + \epsilon'/(10er_t)$. Factoring out $\mathrm{E}\left[f_{i,t}^{\mathrm{WM}}\right]$ and applying Lemma 3 yields

$$\left(1 - \frac{\epsilon'}{10r_t}\right) \mathrm{E}\left[f_{i,t}^{\mathrm{WM}}\right] \leq \mathrm{E}\left[\hat{f}_{i,t}^{\mathrm{WM}}\right] \leq \left(1 + \frac{\epsilon'}{10r_t}\right) \mathrm{E}\left[f_{i,t}^{\mathrm{WM}}\right] . \tag{2}$$

This allows us to conclude that $\mathrm{E}\left[\hat{f}_{i,t}^{\mathrm{WM}}\right] \geq \mathrm{E}\left[f_{i,t}^{\mathrm{WM}}\right]/2$. Also, slight modifications of Lemma 3's proof show $\mathrm{Var}\left[\hat{f}_{i,t}^{\mathrm{WM}}\right] \leq \mathrm{E}\left[\hat{f}_{i,t}^{\mathrm{WM}}\right]$. Using this and again applying Lemma 3 yields

$$\frac{\mathrm{Var}\left[\hat{f}_{i,t}^{\mathrm{WM}}\right]}{\left(\mathrm{E}\left[\hat{f}_{i,t}^{\mathrm{WM}}\right]\right)^2} \leq \frac{1}{\left(\mathrm{E}\left[\hat{f}_{i,t}^{\mathrm{WM}}\right]\right)} \leq \frac{2}{\mathrm{E}\left[f_{i,t}^{\mathrm{WM}}\right]} \leq 2e . \tag{3}$$

Let $X_{i,t}^{(1)}, \ldots, X_{i,t}^{(S_t)}$ be a sequence of S_t independent copies of $\hat{f}_{i,t}^{\mathrm{WM}}$, and let $\bar{X}_{i,t} = \left(\sum_{j=1}^{S_t} X_{i,t}^{(j)}\right)/S_t$. Then $\mathrm{E}\left[\bar{X}_{i,t}\right] = \mathrm{E}\left[\hat{f}_{i,t}^{\mathrm{WM}}\right]$ and $\mathrm{Var}\left[\bar{X}_{i,t}\right] = \frac{\mathrm{Var}\left[\hat{f}_{i,t}^{\mathrm{WM}}\right]}{S_t}$. The estimator of $W_t^+(\alpha)$ is $\hat{W}_t^+(\alpha_{1,t})X_t = \hat{W}_t^+(\alpha_{1,t})\prod_{i=1}^{r_t-1}\bar{X}_{i,t}$, where $\hat{W}_t^+(\alpha_{1,t})$ is an estimate of $|\Omega_t^+|$, which by assumption is within $\epsilon'/2$ of the true value. Since the $\bar{X}_{i,t}$'s are independent, $\mathrm{E}\left[X_t\right] = \prod_{i=1}^{r_t-1}\mathrm{E}\left[\bar{X}_{i,t}\right] = \prod_{i=1}^{r_t-1}\mathrm{E}\left[\hat{f}_{i,t}^{\mathrm{WM}}\right]$ and $\mathrm{E}\left[X_t^2\right] = \prod_{i=1}^{r_t-1}\mathrm{E}\left[\bar{X}_{i,t}^2\right]$. Let $\rho = \prod_{i=1}^{r_t-1}\frac{W_t^+(\alpha_{i+1,t})}{W_t^+(\alpha_{i,t})}$, (i.e. what we are estimating with X_t) and $\hat{\rho} = \mathrm{E}\left[X_t\right]$. Then applying (2) gives

$$\left(1-\frac{\epsilon'}{10r_t}\right)^{r_t}\rho \le \hat{\rho} \le \rho\left(1+\frac{\epsilon'}{10r_t}\right)^{r_t} .$$

Since $\lim_{r_t\to\infty}\left(1+\epsilon'/(10r_t)\right)^{r_t} = e^{\epsilon'/10} \le 1+\epsilon'/8$ and $\left(1-\epsilon'/(10r_t)\right)^{r_t}$ is minimized at $r_t = 1$, we get

$$\left(1-\frac{\epsilon'}{8}\right)\rho \le \hat{\rho} \le \left(1+\frac{\epsilon'}{8}\right)\rho .$$

Since $\mathrm{Var}\left[X_t\right] = \mathrm{E}\left[X_{i,t}^2\right] - \left(\mathrm{E}\left[X_{i,t}\right]\right)^2$, we have

$$\begin{aligned}
\frac{\mathrm{Var}\left[X_t\right]}{\left(\mathrm{E}\left[X_t\right]\right)^2} &= \prod_{i=1}^{r_t-1}\left(1+\frac{\mathrm{Var}\left[\bar{X}_{i,t}\right]}{\left(\mathrm{E}\left[\bar{X}_{i,t}\right]\right)^2}\right) - 1 \\
&\le \left(1+\frac{2e}{S_t}\right)^{r_t-1} - 1 \qquad \text{(By (3))} \\
&\le \left(1+\frac{\epsilon'^2}{260r_t}\right)^{r_t} - 1 \le \exp\left(\epsilon'^2/260\right) - 1 \le \epsilon'^2/256 .
\end{aligned}$$

We now apply Chebyshev's inequality to X_t with standard deviation $\epsilon'\hat{\rho}/16$:

$$\Pr\left[|X_t - \hat{\rho}| > \epsilon'\hat{\rho}/8\right] \le 1/4 .$$

So with probability at least 3/4 we get

$$\left(1-\frac{\epsilon'}{8}\right)\hat{\rho} \le X_t \le \left(1+\frac{\epsilon'}{8}\right)\hat{\rho} ,$$

which implies that with probability at least 3/4

$$\left(1-\frac{\epsilon'}{8}\right)^2\rho \le X_t \le \left(1+\frac{\epsilon'}{8}\right)^2\rho .$$

Given that

$$|\Omega^+|\left(1-\frac{\epsilon'}{2}\right) \le \hat{W}_t^+(\alpha_{1,t}) \le |\Omega^+|\left(1+\frac{\epsilon'}{2}\right)$$

with probability $\geq 3/4$, we get

$$|\Omega^+|\left(1-\frac{\epsilon'}{2}\right)\rho\left(1-\frac{\epsilon'}{8}\right)^2 \leq \hat{W}_t^+(\alpha_{1,t})X_t \leq |\Omega^+|\left(1+\frac{\epsilon'}{2}\right)\rho\left(1+\frac{\epsilon'}{8}\right)^2$$

with probability $\geq 1/2$. Thus

$$W_t^+(\alpha)\left(1-\frac{\epsilon'}{2}\right)^3 \leq \hat{W}_t^+(\alpha_t) \leq W_t^+(\alpha)\left(1+\frac{\epsilon'}{2}\right)^3$$

with probability $\geq 1/2$. Substituting for ϵ' completes the proof of the first part of the theorem. Making these approximations with probability $\geq 1-\delta$ for any $\delta > 0$ is done by rerunning the procedures for estimating $|\Omega_t^+|$ and X_t each $O(\ln 2/\delta)$ times and taking the median of the results [10]. □

Note that if $W_t^+(\alpha)/W_t^-(\alpha) \notin [\frac{1-\epsilon}{1+\epsilon}, \frac{1+\epsilon}{1-\epsilon}]$ for all t, then our version of WM runs identically to the brute-force version, and we can apply WM's mistake bounds. This yields the following corollary.

Corollary 4. *Using the assumptions of Theorem 2, if $W_t^+(\alpha)/W_t^-(\alpha) \notin [\frac{1-\epsilon}{1+\epsilon}, \frac{1+\epsilon}{1-\epsilon}]$ for all t, then (w.h.p.) the number of prediction mistakes made by this algorithm on any sequence of examples is $B \leq 2.41(M+n)$, where n is the number of hypotheses in the ensemble and M is the number of mistakes made by the best pruning. Thus $r_t \leq 1+4.82(M+n)\ln\alpha$ and $S_t = O((M+n)(\ln\alpha)/\epsilon'^2)$.*

We now investigate bounding the mixing time of $\mathcal{M}_{\mathrm{WM},t}^+$ under restricted conditions using the *canonical paths* method [9]. The first condition is that we use AdaBoost's confidences in the weight updates by multiplying pruning $\mathbf{p}$'s weight by $\alpha^{z_{\mathbf{p},t}}$, where $z_{\mathbf{p},t} = \ell_t \sum_{h_i \in \mathbf{p}} \beta_i h_i(\mathbf{x}_t)$ and ℓ_t is $\mathbf{x}_t$'s true label. The second condition is that Ω_t^+ be the entire set of prunings. The final condition is that $|z_{\mathbf{p},t} - z_{\mathbf{q},t}| = O(\log n)$ for any two neighboring prunings $\mathbf{p}$ and $\mathbf{q}$ (differing in one bit). If these conditions hold, then $\mathcal{M}_{\mathrm{WM},t}^+$'s mixing time is bounded by a polynomial in all relevant parameters. Theorem 5's proof is deferred to the full version of the paper.

Theorem 5. *If WM's weights are updated as described above, $\Omega_t^+ = \{0,1\}^n$, and for all t and neighbors $\mathbf{p},\mathbf{q} \in \Omega_t^+$, $|z_{\mathbf{p},t} - z_{\mathbf{q},t}| \leq \log_\alpha n^c$ for a constant c, then a simulation of $\mathcal{M}_{WM,t}^+$ of length*

$$T_{i,t} = 2n^{c+2}\left(n\ln 2 + 2nc\ln n + \ln\left(10er_t/\epsilon'\right)\right)$$

will draw samples from $\hat{\pi}_{\alpha_{i,t}}^+$ such that $\left\|\hat{\pi}_{\alpha_{i,t}}^+ - \pi_{\alpha_{i,t}}^+\right\| \leq \epsilon'/(10er_t)$.

Combining Theorems 2 and 5 yields an FPRAS for ensemble pruning under the conditions of Theorem 5. To get a general FPRAS, we need to eliminate the conditions of Theorem 5. The first condition is to simplify the proof and should not be difficult to remove. The second condition can probably be removed by adapting the proof of Morris and Sinclair [17] that solved the long-standing open problem of finding an FPRAS for knapsack. However, it is open whether the final condition (that neighboring prunings be close in magnitude of weight changes) can be removed. In the meantime, one can meet this condition in general by artificially bounding the changes any weight undergoes, similar to the procedure for tracking a shifting concept [13].

Since one of the goals of pruning an ensemble of classifiers is to reduce its size, one may adopt one of several heuristics, such as choosing the pruning that has highest weight in WM or the highest product of weight and diversity, where diversity is measured by e.g. KL divergence [15]. Let $f(\mathbf{p})$ be the function that we want to maximize. Then our goal is to find the $\mathbf{p} \in \{0,1\}^n$ that approximately maximizes f. To do this we define a new Markov chain $\mathcal{M}_{\text{WM}}^{\max}$ whose transition probabilities are the same as for $\mathcal{M}_{\text{WM},t}^{+}$ except that step 3 is irrelevant and in step 4, we substitute $f(\cdot)$ for $(-v_t(\cdot))$ and substitute η for α, where η is a parameter that governs the shape of the stationary distribution. Lemma 1 obviously holds for $\mathcal{M}_{\text{WM}}^{\max}$, i.e. it is ergodic with stationary distribution $\pi_\eta(\mathbf{p}) = \eta^{f(\mathbf{p})}/W(\eta)$, where $W(\eta) = \sum_{\mathbf{p}\in\{0,1\}^n} \eta^{f(\mathbf{p})}$. However, the existence of an FPRAS is still open.

2.2 Learning DNF Formulas

We first note the well-known reduction from learning DNF to learning monotone DNF, where no variable in the target function is negated. If the DNF formula is defined over n variables, we convert each example $\mathbf{x} = x_1 \cdots x_n$ to $\mathbf{x}' = x_1 \cdots x_n \bar{x}_1 \cdots \bar{x}_n$. It is easy to see that by giving $\mathbf{x}'$ to a learning algorithm for monotone DNF, we automatically get an algorithm for learning DNF. Thus we focus on learning monotone DNF, though our empirical results are based on a more general definition (Sect. 3.1).

To learn monotone DNF, one can use Winnow, which maintains a weight vector $\mathbf{w}_t \in \text{Re}^{+N}$ (N-dimensional positive real space). Upon receiving an instance $\mathbf{x}_t \in \{0,1\}^N$, Winnow makes its prediction $\hat{y}_t = 1$ if $W_t = \mathbf{w}_t \cdot \mathbf{x}_t \geq \theta$ and 0 otherwise ($\theta > 0$ is a threshold). Given the true label y_t, the weights are updated as follows: $w_{t+1,i} = w_{t,i}\alpha^{x_{t,i}(y_t - \hat{y}_t)}$ for some $\alpha > 1$. If $w_{t+1,i} > w_{t,i}$ we call it a *promotion* and if $w_{t+1,i} < w_{t,i}$ we call it a *demotion*. Littlestone [11] showed that if the target function f is a monotone disjunction of K of the N inputs, then Winnow can learn f while making only $2 + 2K \log_2 N$ prediction mistakes. So using the 2^n possible terms as Winnow's inputs, it can learn k-term monotone DNF with only $2 + 2kn$ prediction mistakes. However, computing $\hat{y}_t$ and updating the weights for each trial t takes exponential time. So we estimate W_t by associating each term with a state in a Markov chain, representing it by a string over $\{0,1\}^n$. Since W_t is a weighted sum of the terms satisfied by example $\mathbf{x}_t$, we want to estimate the sum of the weights of the strings $\mathbf{p} \in \{0,1\}^n$ that satisfy $\mathbf{x}_t \cdot \mathbf{p} = \sum_{i=0}^{n-1} x_{t,i} p_i = \|\mathbf{p}\|_1$, where $\|\mathbf{p}\|_1 = \sum_{i=0}^{n-1} p_i$.

The state space for our Markov chain $\mathcal{M}_{\text{DNF},t}$ is $\Omega_t = \{\mathbf{p} \in \{0,1\}^n : \mathbf{x}_t \cdot \mathbf{p} = \|\mathbf{p}\|_1\}$. Transitions from state $\mathbf{p} = (p_0, \ldots, p_{n-1}) \in \Omega_t$ to state $\mathbf{q} \in \Omega_t$ are given by the following rules. (1) With probability 1/2 let $\mathbf{q} =$

$\mathbf{p}$. Otherwise, (2) select i uniformly at random from $\{0, \ldots, n-1\}$ and let $\mathbf{q}' = (p_0, \ldots, p_{i-1}, 1-p_i, p_{i+1}, \ldots, p_{n-1})$. (3) If $\mathbf{x}_t$ satisfies the term represented by $\mathbf{q}'$, let $\mathbf{q}'' = \mathbf{q}'$, else let $\mathbf{q}'' = \mathbf{p}$. (4) Let $\mathbf{q} = \mathbf{q}''$ with probability $\min\left\{1, \alpha^{u_t(\mathbf{q}'')-v_t(\mathbf{q}'')-u_t(\mathbf{p})+v_t(\mathbf{p})}\right\}$, else let $\mathbf{q} = \mathbf{p}$. Here $u_t(\mathbf{p})$ is the number of promotions of $\mathbf{p}$ so far, and $v_t(\mathbf{p})$ is the number of demotions. Lemma 1 holds for $\mathcal{M}_{\mathrm{DNF},t}$ as well: it is ergodic with stationary distribution $\pi_{\alpha,t}(\mathbf{p}) = \alpha^{u_t(\mathbf{p})-v_t(\mathbf{p})}/W_t(\alpha)$, where $W_t(\alpha) = \sum_{\mathbf{p}\in\Omega_t} \alpha^{u_t(\mathbf{p})-v_t(\mathbf{p})}$.

We now describe how to estimate $W_t(\alpha)$. Let $m_t = \sum_{\tau=1}^{t-1} u_\tau(\mathbf{p}_e) + v_\tau(\mathbf{p}_e)$, $\alpha_{i,t} = (1+1/m_t)^{i-1}$ for $1 \le i < r_t$, where r_t is the smallest integer such that $(1+1/m_t)^{r_t-1} \ge \alpha$ (thus $r_t \le 1 + 2m_t \ln \alpha$) and $\mathbf{p}_e = \mathbf{0}$, the "empty" (always satisfied) term. Also, set $\alpha_{r,t} = \alpha$. Now define $f_{i,t}(\mathbf{p}) = (\alpha_{i-1,t}/\alpha_{i,t})^{u_t(\mathbf{p})-v_t(\mathbf{p})}$, where $\mathbf{p}$ is chosen according to distribution $\pi_{\alpha_{i,t},t}$. Then

$$\mathrm{E}\left[f_{i,t}\right] = \sum_{\mathbf{p}\in\Omega_t} \left(\frac{\alpha_{i-1,t}}{\alpha_{i,t}}\right)^{u_t(\mathbf{p})-v_t(\mathbf{p})} \frac{\alpha_{i,t}^{u_t(\mathbf{p})-v_t(\mathbf{p})}}{W_t(\alpha_{i,t})} = \frac{W_t(\alpha_{i-1,t})}{W_t(\alpha_{i,t})} \ .$$

So we can estimate $W_t(\alpha_{i-1,t})/W_t(\alpha_{i,t})$ by sampling points from $\mathcal{M}_{\mathrm{DNF},t}$ and computing the sample mean of $f_{i,t}$, which allows us to compute $W_t(\alpha)$ since

$$W_t(\alpha) = \left(\frac{W_t(\alpha_{r,t})}{W_t(\alpha_{r-1,t})}\right)\left(\frac{W_t(\alpha_{r-1,t})}{W_t(\alpha_{r-2,t})}\right)\cdots\left(\frac{W_t(\alpha_{2,t})}{W_t(\alpha_{1,t})}\right) W_t(\alpha_{1,t})$$

and $W_t(\alpha_{1,t}) = W(1) = |\Omega| = 2^{\|\mathbf{x}_t\|_1}$. Therefore, for each value $\alpha_{2,t}, \ldots, \alpha_{r,t}$, we run S_t independent simulations of $\mathcal{M}_{\mathrm{DNF},t}$, each of length $T_{i,t}$, and let $X_{i,t}$ be the sample mean of $(\alpha_{i-1,t}/\alpha_{i,t})^{u_t(\mathbf{x})-v_t(\mathbf{x})}$. Then our estimate of $W_t(\alpha)$ is

$$\hat{W}_t(\alpha) = 2^{\|\mathbf{x}_t\|_1} \prod_{i=2}^{r_t} 1/X_{i,t} \ .$$

Below we show results similar to Theorem 2 for $\mathcal{M}_{\mathrm{DNF},t}$. We start by bounding the variance of $f_{i,t}^{\mathrm{DNF}}$ relative to its expectation. The proof is slightly different since $f_{i,t}^{\mathrm{DNF}}$ can take on values greater than 1 (specifically, $f_{i,t}^{\mathrm{DNF}} \in [1/e, e]$).

Lemma 6.

$$\frac{\mathrm{Var}\left[f_{i,t}^{DNF}\right]}{\left(\mathrm{E}\left[f_{i,t}^{DNF}\right]\right)^2} \le e, \quad \frac{1}{\mathrm{E}\left[f_{i,t}^{DNF}\right]} < e, \quad \text{and} \quad \mathrm{Var}\left[f_{i,t}^{DNF}\right] \le e^2 \mathrm{E}\left[f_{i,t}^{DNF}\right] \ .$$

Proof. Let $P_t^{\min} = \min_{\mathbf{p}}\{u_t(\mathbf{p}) - v_t(\mathbf{p})\}$ and $P_t^{\max} = \max_{\mathbf{p}}\{u_t(\mathbf{p}) - v_t(\mathbf{p})\}$, i.e. the minimum and maximum (respectively) number of net promotions over all terms at trial t. The first inequality of the lemma follows from

$$\frac{\mathrm{Var}\left[f_{i,t}^{\mathrm{DNF}}\right]}{\left(\mathrm{E}\left[f_{i,t}^{\mathrm{DNF}}\right]\right)^2} = \frac{\sum_{\mathbf{p}\in\Omega_t} \left(\frac{\alpha_{i-1,t}}{\alpha_{i,t}}\right)^{-2(u_t(\mathbf{p})-v_t(\mathbf{p}))} \frac{\alpha_{i,t}^{u_t(\mathbf{p})-v_t(\mathbf{p})}}{W_t(\alpha_{i,t})} - \frac{W_t(\alpha_{i-1,t})^2}{W_t(\alpha_{i,t})^2}}{W_t(\alpha_{i-1,t})^2/W_t(\alpha_{i,t})^2}$$

$$< \frac{W_t(\alpha_{i,t}) \sum_{\mathbf{p}\in\Omega_t} \left(\frac{\alpha_{i-1,t}^2}{\alpha_{i,t}}\right)^{u_t(\mathbf{p})-v_t(\mathbf{p})}}{W_t(\alpha_{i-1,t})^2}$$

$$= \frac{\left[\sum_{\mathbf{p}\in\Omega_t} (\alpha_{i,t})^{u_t(\mathbf{p})-v_t(\mathbf{p})}\right] \left[\sum_{\mathbf{p}\in\Omega_t} (\alpha_{i-2,t})^{u_t(\mathbf{p})-v_t(\mathbf{p})}\right]}{\left[\sum_{\mathbf{p}\in\Omega_t} (\alpha_{i-1,t})^{u_t(\mathbf{p})-v_t(\mathbf{p})}\right] \left[\sum_{\mathbf{p}\in\Omega_t} (\alpha_{i-1,t})^{u_t(\mathbf{p})-v_t(\mathbf{p})}\right]}$$

$$\leq \frac{\sum_{\mathbf{p}\in\Omega_t} (\alpha_{i-2,t})^{u_t(\mathbf{p})-v_t(\mathbf{p})-P_t^{\max}}}{\sum_{\mathbf{p}\in\Omega_t} (\alpha_{i-1,t})^{u_t(\mathbf{p})-v_t(\mathbf{p})-P_t^{\max}}} .$$

Since the series of exponents is the same in the numerator and denominator, $\alpha_{i,t} \geq 1$ for all $i \geq 1$, and $m_t \geq P_t^{\max} - P_t^{\min}$, we get

$$\frac{\sum_{\mathbf{p}\in\Omega_t} (\alpha_{i-2,t})^{u_t(\mathbf{p})-v_t(\mathbf{p})-P_t^{\max}}}{\sum_{\mathbf{p}\in\Omega_t} (\alpha_{i-1,t})^{u_t(\mathbf{p})-v_t(\mathbf{p})-P_t^{\max}}} \leq \frac{\sum_{\mathbf{p}\in\Omega_t} (\alpha_{i-2,t})^{P_t^{\min}-P_t^{\max}}}{\sum_{\forall \mathbf{p}\in\Omega_t} (\alpha_{i-1,t})^{P_t^{\min}-P_t^{\max}}}$$

$$= (1+1/m_t)^{P_t^{\max}-P_t^{\min}} \leq e . \qquad (4)$$

To prove the lemma's second inequality, note that

$$\frac{1}{\mathrm{E}\left[f_{i,t}^{\mathrm{DNF}}\right]} = \frac{\sum_{\mathbf{p}\in\Omega_t} (\alpha_{i,t})^{u_t(\mathbf{p})-v_t(\mathbf{p})}}{\sum_{\mathbf{p}\in\Omega_t} (\alpha_{i-1,t})^{u_t(\mathbf{p})-v_t(\mathbf{p})}} = \frac{\alpha_{i,t}^{P_t^{\max}} \sum_{\mathbf{p}\in\Omega_t} (\alpha_{i,t})^{u_t(\mathbf{p})-v_t(\mathbf{p})-P_t^{\max}}}{\alpha_{i-1,t}^{P_t^{\max}} \sum_{\mathbf{p}\in\Omega_t} (\alpha_{i-1,t})^{u_t(\mathbf{p})-v_t(\mathbf{p})-P_t^{\max}}}$$

$$= (1+1/m_t)^{P_t^{\max}} \frac{\sum_{\mathbf{p}\in\Omega_t} (\alpha_{i,t})^{u_t(\mathbf{p})-v_t(\mathbf{p})-P_t^{\max}}}{\sum_{\mathbf{p}\in\Omega_t} (\alpha_{i-1,t})^{u_t(\mathbf{p})-v_t(\mathbf{p})-P_t^{\max}}} \leq e .$$

Since $\mathrm{Var}\left[f_{i,t}^{\mathrm{DNF}}\right] < W_t(\alpha_{i-2,t})/W_t(\alpha_{i,t})$ and $\mathrm{E}\left[f_{i,t}^{\mathrm{DNF}}\right] = W_t(\alpha_{i-1,t})/W_t(\alpha_{i,t})$, showing $W_t(\alpha_{i-2,t}) \leq e^2 W_t(\alpha_{i-1,t})$ proves the third part of this lemma. Applying (4) yields

$$\frac{W_t(\alpha_{i-2,t})}{W_t(\alpha_{i-1,t})} = \frac{\alpha_{i-2,t}^{P_t^{\max}} \sum_{\mathbf{p}\in\Omega_t} (\alpha_{i-2,t})^{u_t(\mathbf{p})-v_t(\mathbf{p})-P_t^{\max}}}{\alpha_{i-1,t}^{P_t^{\max}} \sum_{\mathbf{p}\in\Omega_t} (\alpha_{i-1,t})^{u_t(\mathbf{p})-v_t(\mathbf{p})-P_t^{\max}}} \leq \frac{e}{(1+1/m_t)^{P_t^{\max}}} .$$

If $P_t^{\max} \geq 0$, the above quantity is at most e. Otherwise, it is at most $e(1 + 1/m_t)^{|P_t^{\max}|} \leq e^2$. □

The proof to the following theorem is similar to that of Theorem 2, but also accounts for the fact that $f_{i,t}^{\mathrm{DNF}}$ can be greater than 1.

Theorem 7. *Let the sample size* $S_t = \lceil 130 r_t e^3/\epsilon^2 \rceil$ *and* $\mathcal{M}_{DNF,t}$ *be simulated long enough (*$T_{i,t}$ *steps) for each sample s.t. the variation distance between the empirical distribution and* $\pi_{\alpha_{i,t}}$ *is* $\leq \epsilon/(5e^2 r_t)$*. Then* $\hat{W}_t(\alpha)$ *satisfies* $\Pr\left[(1-\epsilon)W_t(\alpha) \leq \hat{W}_t(\alpha) \leq (1+\epsilon)W_t(\alpha)\right] \geq 3/4$*. In addition, the 3/4 can be made arbitrarily close to* $1-\delta$ *for any* $\delta > 0$*.*

As stated in the following corollary, our algorithm's behavior is the same as Winnow's if the weighted sums are not too close to θ for any input. It is easy to extend this result to tolerate a bounded number of trials with weighted sums near θ by thinking of the potential mispredictions as noise [12].

Corollary 8. *Using the assumptions of Theorem 7, if* $W_t(\alpha) \notin [\frac{\theta}{(1+\epsilon)}, \frac{\theta}{(1-\epsilon)}]$ *for all* t*, then (w.h.p.) the number of mistakes made by Winnow on any sequence of examples is at most* $2+2kn$*. Thus for all* t*,* $m_t \leq 2+2kn$*,* $r_t \leq 1+(4+4kn)\ln\alpha$*, and* $S_t = O((kn\log\alpha)/\epsilon^2)$*.*

We have not yet shown that $\mathcal{M}_{\mathrm{DNF},t}$ mixes rapidly, but Theorem 5 and our preliminary empirical results (Sect. 3.1) lead us to believe that it does, at least under appropriate conditions.

One issue with this algorithm is that after training, we still require the training examples and running $\mathcal{M}_{\mathrm{DNF},t}$ to evaluate the hypothesis on a new example. In lieu of this, we can, after training, run a Metropolis process to find the terms with the largest weights. The result is a set of rules, and the prediction on a new example can be a thresholded sum of weights of satisfied rules, using the same threshold θ. The only issue then is to determine how many terms to select. If we focus on the generalized DNF representations of Sect. 3.1, then each example satisfies exactly 2^n terms (out of $\prod_{i=1}^{n}(k_i+1)$). Thus for an example to be classified as positive, the average weight of its satisfied terms must be at least $\theta/2^n$. Thus one heuristic is to use the Metropolis process to choose as many terms as possible with weight at least $\theta/2^n$. Using this pruned set of rules, no additional false positives will occur, and in fact the number will likely be reduced. The only concern is causing extra false negatives.

3 Preliminary Empirical Results

3.1 Learning DNF Formulas

In our DNF experiments, we used generalized DNF representations. The set of terms and the instance space were both $\prod_{i=0}^{n-1}\{0,\ldots,k_i\}$, where k_i is the number of values for feature i. A term $\mathbf{p} = (p_0,\ldots,p_{n-1})$ is satisfied by example $\mathbf{x} = (x_0,\ldots,x_{n-1})$ iff $\forall\, p_i > 0$, $p_i = x_i$. So $p_i = 0 \Rightarrow x_i$ is irrelevant for term $\mathbf{p}$ and $p_i > 0 \Rightarrow x_i$ must equal p_i for $\mathbf{p}$ to be satisfied. If $x_i = 0$ for some i then we assume it is unspecified.

We generated random (from a uniform distribution) 5-term DNF formulas, using $n \in \{10, 15, 20\}$, with $k_i = 2$ for all i. So the total number of Winnow inputs was $3^{10} = 59049$, $3^{15} = 1.43\times10^7$, and $3^{20} = 3.49\times10^9$. For each value of n there were nine training/testing set combinations, each with 50 training examples and 50 testing examples. Examples were generated uniformly at random.

Table 1 gives averaged[5] results for $n = 10$, indexed by S and T ("BF" means brute-force). "GUESS" is the average error of the estimates. "LOW" is

[5] The number of weight estimations made per row in the table varied due to a varying number of training rounds, but typically was around 3000.

the fraction of guesses that were $< \theta$ when the actual value was $> \theta$, and "HIGH" is symmetric. These are the only times our algorithm deviates from brute-force. "PRED" is the prediction error on the test set and "S_{theo}" is S from Theorem 7 that guarantees an error of GUESS given the values of r_t in our simulations.

Both GUESS and HIGH are very sensitive to T but not as sensitive to S. LOW was negligible due to the distribution of weights as training progressed: the term $\mathbf{p}_e = \mathbf{0}$ (satisfied by all examples) had high weights. Since all computations started at $\mathbf{0}$ and $\mathcal{M}_{\mathrm{DNF},t}$ seeks out nodes with high weights, the estimates tended to be too high rather than too low. But this is less significant as S and T increase. In addition, note that PRED does not appear correlated to the accuracy of the weight guesses, and most of them are very near that for brute-force. We feel that this is coincidental, and that the only way to ensure a good hypothesis is to choose S and T sufficiently large such that GUESS, LOW, and HIGH are small, e.g. $S = 100$ and $T = 300$. For these values, training and testing took an average of 10.286 minutes per example, while brute-force took 0.095 min/example. So for $n = 10$, $\mathcal{M}_{\mathrm{DNF},t}$ is slower than brute-force by a factor of over 108. Finally, we note that in our runs with $S = 100$ and $T = 300$, the values of r_t used ranged from 19–26 and averaged 21.6.

Table 1. $\mathcal{M}_{\mathrm{DNF},t}$ results for $n = 10$ and r chosen as in Sect. 2.2

S	T	**GUESS**	**LOW**	**HIGH**	**PRED**	S_{theo}
100	100	0.4713	0.0000	0.1674	0.0600	2.23×10^5
100	200	0.1252	0.0017	0.0350	0.0533	3.16×10^6
100	300	0.0634	0.0041	0.0172	0.0711	1.23×10^7
100	500	0.0484	0.0091	0.0078	0.0844	2.11×10^7
500	100	0.4826	0.0000	0.1594	0.1000	2.13×10^5
500	200	0.1174	0.0000	0.0314	0.0600	3.60×10^6
500	300	0.0441	0.0043	0.0145	0.0867	2.55×10^7
500	500	0.0232	0.0034	0.0064	0.0800	9.16×10^7
BF					0.0730	

Since the run time of our algorithm varies linearly in r, we ran some experiments where we fixed r rather than letting it be set as in Sect. 2.2. We set $S = 100$, $T = 300$ and $r \in \{5, 10, 15, 20\}$. The results are in Table 2. This indicates that for the given parameter values, r can be reduced a little below that which is stipulated in Sect. 2.2.

Results for $n = 15$ appear in Table 3. The trends for $n = 15$ are similar to those for $n = 10$. Brute-force is faster than $\mathcal{M}_{\mathrm{DNF},t}$ at $S = 500$ and $T = 1500$, but only by a factor of 16. Finally, we note that in our runs with $S = 500$ and $T = 1500$, the values of r_t used ranged from 26–40 (average was 33.2).

As with $n = 10$, r can be reduced to speed up the algorithm, but at a cost of increasing the errors of the predictions (e.g. see Table 4(a)). We ran the same

Table 2. $\mathcal{M}_{\mathrm{DNF},t}$ results for $n = 10$, $S = 100$, and $T = 300$

r	**GUESS**	**LOW**	**HIGH**	**PRED**
5	0.1279	0.0119	0.0203	0.0844
10	0.0837	0.0095	0.0189	0.0867
15	0.0711	0.0058	0.0159	0.0800
20	0.0638	0.0042	0.0127	0.0889
BF				0.0730

Table 3. $\mathcal{M}_{\mathrm{DNF},t}$ results for $n = 15$ and r chosen as in Sect. 2.2

S	T	**GUESS**	**LOW**	**HIGH**	**PRED**	S_{theo}
500	1500	0.0368	0.0028	0.0099	0.0700	5.01×10^7
500	1800	0.0333	0.0040	0.0049	0.0675	6.12×10^7
500	2000	0.0296	0.0035	0.0023	0.0675	7.68×10^7
1000	1500	0.0388	0.0015	0.0042	0.0650	4.51×10^7
1000	1800	0.0253	0.0006	0.0038	0.0775	1.06×10^8
1000	2000	0.0207	0.0025	0.0020	0.0800	1.58×10^8
BF					0.0800	

experiments with a training set of size 100 rather than 50 (the test set was still of size 50), summarized in Table 4(b). As expected, error on the guesses changes little, but prediction error is decreased.

Table 4. $\mathcal{M}_{\mathrm{DNF},t}$ results for $n = 15$, $S = 500$, and $T = 1500$, and a training set of size (a) 50 and (b) 100

(a)

r	**GUESS**	**LOW**	**HIGH**	**PRED**
10	0.0572	0.0049	0.0132	0.1075
20	0.0444	0.0033	0.0063	0.0756
30	0.0407	0.0022	0.0047	0.0822
BF				0.0800

(b)

r	**GUESS**	**LOW**	**HIGH**	**PRED**
10	0.0577	0.0046	0.0478	0.0511
20	0.0456	0.0032	0.0073	0.0733
30	0.0405	0.0044	0.0081	0.0689
BF				0.0356

For $n = 20$, no exact (brute-force) sums were computed since there are over 3 billion inputs. So we only examined the prediction error of our algorithm. The average error over all runs was 0.11 with $S = 1000$, $T = 2000$, r set as in Sect. 2.2, and a training set of size 100. The average value of r used was 55 (range was 26–78), and the run time was approximately 30 minutes/example.[6] Brute-force evaluation on a few examples required roughly 135 hours/example, a 270-fold slowdown. Thus for this case our algorithm provides a significant speed advantage. When running our algorithm with a fixed value of $r = 30$ (reducing time per example by almost a factor of 2), prediction error increases to 0.1833.

In summary, even though our experiments are for small values of n, they indicate that relatively small values of S, T, and r are sufficient to minimize our algorithm's deviations from brute-force Winnow. Thus we conjecture that $\mathcal{M}_{\mathrm{DNF},t}$ does mix rapidly, at least for the uniformly random data in our experiments. In addition, our algorithm becomes significantly faster than that of brute-force somewhere between $n = 15$ and $n = 20$, which is small for a machine learning problem. However, our implementation is still extremely slow, taking several days or longer to finish training when $n = 20$ (evaluating the learned hypothesis is also slow). Thus we are actively seeking heuristics to speed up learning and evaluation, including parallelization of the independent Markov chain simulations and using a Metropolis process (Sect. 2.2) after training to return as a hypothesis only the subset of high-weight terms.

3.2 Pruning an Ensemble

For the Weighted Majority experiments, we used AdaBoost over decision shrubs (depth-2 decision trees) generated by C4.5 to learn hypotheses for an artificial two-dimensional data set. The target concept is a circle and the examples are distributed around its circumference, each point's distance from the circle normally distributed with zero mean and unit variance. We created an ensemble of 10 classifiers and simulated WM with[7] $S \in \{50, 75, 100\}$ and $T \in \{500, 750, 1000\}$ on the set of 2^{10} prunings and compared the values computed for (1) to the true values from brute-force WM. The results are in Table 5: "$|\Omega_t^+|$" denotes the error of our estimates of $|\Omega^+|$, "$X_{i,t}$" denotes the error of our estimates of the ratios $W_t^+(\alpha_{i,t})/W_t^+(\alpha_{i-1,t})$, and "$\hat{W}_t^+(\alpha)$" denotes the error of our estimates of $W_t^+(\alpha)$. Finally, "DEPARTURE" indicates our algorithm's departure from brute-force WM, i.e. in these experiments our algorithm perferctly emulated brute-force. Finally, we note that other early results show that for $n = 30$, $S = 200$, and $T = 2000$, our algorithm takes about 4.5 hours/example to run, while brute-force takes about 2.8 hours/example. Thus we expect our algorithm to run faster than brute-force at about $n = 31$ or $n = 32$.

4 Conclusions and Future Work

We have shown how MCMC methods can be used to approximate the weighted sums for multiplicative weight update algorithms, particularly when applying

---

[6] Runs for $n = 20$ were on a different machine than those for $n = 10$.

[7] Note that the estimation of $|\Omega_t^+|$ required an order of magnitude larger values of S and T than did the estimation of the ratios to get sufficiently low error rates.

Table 5. $\mathcal{M}^{+}_{\mathrm{WM},t}$ results for $n = 10$ and r chosen as in Sect. 2.1

S	T	$\lvert\Omega_t^+\rvert$	$X_{i,t}$	$\hat{W}_t^+(\alpha)$	**DEPARTURE**
50	500	0.0423	0.00050	0.0071	0.0000
50	750	0.0332	0.00069	0.0061	0.0000
50	1000	0.0419	0.00068	0.0070	0.0000
75	500	0.0223	0.00067	0.0050	0.0000
75	750	0.0197	0.00047	0.0047	0.0000
75	1000	0.0276	0.00058	0.0055	0.0000
100	500	0.0185	0.00040	0.0047	0.0000
100	750	0.0215	0.00055	0.0050	0.0000
100	1000	0.0288	0.00044	0.0056	0.0000

WM to ensemble pruning and applying Winnow to learning DNF formulas. We presented some theoretical and preliminary empirical results.

One obvious avenue of future work is to more generally bound the mixing times of our Markov chains and to prove theoretical results of our Metropolis processes. Based on our current theoretical and empirical results, we believe that both chains mix rapidly under appropriate conditions. There is also the question of how to elegantly choose S and T for empirical use to balance time complexity and precision. While it is important to accurately estimate the weighted sums in order to properly simulate WM and Winnow, some imperfections in simulation can be handled since incorrect simulation decisions can be treated as noise, which Winnow and WM can tolerate. Ideally, the algorithms would intelligently choose S and T based on past performance, perhaps (for Winnow) utilizing the brute-force upper bound of $\alpha\,\theta$ on all weights (since no promotions can occur past that point). So $\forall\,\mathbf{p}$, $u_t(\mathbf{p}) - v_t(\mathbf{p}) \leq 1 + \lfloor \log_\alpha \theta \rfloor$. If this bound is exceeded during a run of Winnow, then we can increase S and T and run again. Finally, we are exploring heuristics to accelerate learning and hypothesis evaluation in our implementations (Sect. 3.1).

Acknowledgments

The authors thank Jeff Jackson, Mark Jerrum, and Alistair Sinclair for their discussions and the COLT reviewers for their helpful comments. We also thank Jeff Jackson for presenting this paper at COLT.

References

[1] A. Blum, P. Chalasani, and J. Jackson. On learning embedded symmetric concepts. In *Proc. 6th Annu. Workshop on Comput. Learning Theory*, pages 337–346. ACM Press, New York, NY, 1993.

[2] A. Blum, M. Furst, J. Jackson, M. Kearns, Y. Mansour, and S. Rudich. Weakly learning DNF and characterizing statistical query learning using fourier analysis. In *Proceedings of Twenty-sixth ACM Symposium on Theory of Computing*, 1994.
[3] N. Cesa-Bianchi, Y. Freund, D. Helmbold, D. Haussler, R. Schapire, and M. Warmuth. How to use expert advice. *J. of the ACM*, 44(3):427–485, 1997.
[4] N. Cristianini and J. Shawe-Taylor. *An Introduction to Support Vector Machines and Other Kernel-Based Learning Methods.* Cambridge University Press, 2000.
[5] M. Dyer, A. Frieze, R. Kannan, A. Kapoor, and U. Vazirani. A mildly exponential time algorithm for approximating the number of solutions to a multidimensional knapsack problem. *Combinatorics, Prob. and Computing*, 2:271–284, 1993.
[6] S. A. Goldman, S. K. Kwek, and S. D. Scott. Agnostic learning of geometric patterns. *Journal of Computer and System Sciences*, 6(1):123–151, February 2001.
[7] S. A. Goldman and S. D. Scott. Multiple-instance learning of real-valued geometric patterns. *Annals of Mathematics and Artificial Intelligence*, to appear. Early version in technical report UNL-CSE-99-006, University of Nebraska.
[8] D. P. Helmbold and R. E. Schapire. Predicting nearly as well as the best pruning of a decision tree. *Machine Learning*, 27(1):51–68, 1997.
[9] M. Jerrum and A. Sinclair. The Markov chain Monte Carlo method: An approach to approximate counting and integration. In D. Hochbaum, editor, *Approximation Algorithms for NP-Hard Problems*, chapter 12, pages 482–520. PWS Pub., 1996.
[10] M. R. Jerrum, L. G. Valiant, and V. V. Vazirani. Random generation of combinatorial structures from a uniform distribution. *Theoretical Computer Science*, 43:169–188, 1986.
[11] N. Littlestone. Learning quickly when irrelevant attributes abound: A new linear-threshold algorithm. *Machine Learning*, 2:285–318, 1988.
[12] N. Littlestone. Redundant noisy attributes, attribute errors, and linear threshold learning using Winnow. In *Proc. 4th Annu. Workshop on Comput. Learning Theory*, pages 147–156, San Mateo, CA, 1991. Morgan Kaufmann.
[13] N. Littlestone and M. K. Warmuth. The weighted majority algorithm. *Information and Computation*, 108(2):212–261, 1994.
[14] W. Maass and M. K. Warmuth. Efficient learning with virtual threshold gates. *Information and Computation*, 141(1):66–83, 1998.
[15] D. D. Margineantu and T. G. Dietterich. Pruning adaptive boosting. In *Proc. 14th International Conference on Machine Learning*, pages 211–218. Morgan Kaufmann, 1997.
[16] N. Metropolis, A. W. Rosenbluth, M. N. Rosenbluth, A. H. Teller, and E. Teller. Equation of state calculation by fast computing machines. *J. of Chemical Physics*, 21:1087–1092, 1953.
[17] B. Morris and A. Sinclair. Random walks on truncated cubes and sampling 0-1 knapsack solutions. In *Proc. of 40th Symp. on Foundations of Comp. Sci.*, 1999.
[18] F. Pereira and Y. Singer. An efficient extension to mixture techniques for prediction and decision trees. *Machine Learning*, 36(3):183–199, September 1999.
[19] R. E. Schapire and Y. Singer. Improved boosting algorithms using confidence-rated predictions. *Machine Learning*, 38(3):297–336, 1999.
[20] E. Takimoto and M. Warmuth. Predicting nearly as well as the best pruning of a planar decision graph. In *Proc. of the Tenth International Conference on Algorithmic Learning Theory*, 1999.
[21] C. Tamon and J. Xiang. On the boosting pruning problem. In *Proceedings of the Eleventh European Conference on Machine Learning*, pages 404–412, 2000.
[22] L. G. Valiant. The complexity of enumeration and reliability problems. *SIAM Journal of Computing*, 8:410–421, 1979.

Ultraconservative Online Algorithms for Multiclass Problems

Koby Crammer and Yoram Singer

School of Computer Science & Engineering
The Hebrew University, Jerusalem 91904, Israel
{kobics,singer}@cs.huji.ac.il

Abstract. In this paper we study online classification algorithms for multiclass problems in the mistake bound model. The hypotheses we use maintain one prototype vector per class. Given an input instance, a multiclass hypothesis computes a similarity-score between each prototype and the input instance and then sets the predicted label to be the index of the prototype achieving the highest similarity. To design and analyze the learning algorithms in this paper we introduce the notion of *ultraconservativeness.* Ultraconservative algorithms are algorithms that update only the prototypes attaining similarity-scores which are higher than the score of the correct label's prototype. We start by describing a family of additive ultraconservative algorithms where each algorithm in the family updates its prototypes by finding a feasible solution for a set of linear constraints that depend on the instantaneous similarity-scores. We then discuss a specific online algorithm that seeks a set of prototypes which have a small norm. The resulting algorithm, which we term MIRA (for Margin Infused Relaxed Algorithm) is ultraconservative as well. We derive mistake bounds for all the algorithms and provide further analysis of MIRA using a generalized notion of the margin for multiclass problems.

1 Introduction

In this paper we present a general approach for deriving algorithms for multiclass prediction problems. In multiclass problems the goal is to assign one of k labels to each input instance. Many machine learning problems can be phrased as a multiclass categorization problem. Examples to such problems include optical character recognition (OCR), text classification, and medical analysis. There are numerous specialized solutions for multiclass problems for specific models such as decision trees [3,16] and neural networks. Another general approach is based on reducing a multiclass problem to multiple binary problems using output coding [6,1]. An example of a reduction that falls into the above framework is the "one-against-rest" approach. In one-against-rest a set of binary classifiers is trained, one classifier for each class. The ith classifier is trained to distinguish between the ith class and the rest of the classes. New instances are classified by setting the predicted label to be the index of the classifier attaining the highest score in its prediction. We present a unified approach that operates directly on

D. Helmbold and B. Williamson (Eds.): COLT/EuroCOLT 2001, LNAI 2111, pp. 99–115, 2001.

the multiclass problem by imposing constraints on the updates for the various classes. Thus, our approach is inherently different from methods based on output coding.

Our framework for analyzing the algorithms is the mistake bound model. The algorithms we study work in rounds. On each round the proposed algorithms get a new instance and output a prediction for the instance. They then receive the correct label and update their predication rule in case they made a prediction error. The goal of the algorithms is to minimize the number of mistakes they made compared to the minimal number of errors that an hypothesis, built offline, can achieve.

The algorithms we consider in this paper maintain one prototype vector for each class. Given a new instance we compare each prototype to the instance by computing the similarity-score between the instance and each of the prototypes for the different classes. We then predict the class which achieves the highest similarity-score. In binary problems, this scheme reduces (under mild conditions) to a linear discriminator. After the algorithm makes a prediction it receives the correct label of the input instance and updates the set of prototypes. For a given input instance, the set of labels that attain similarity-scores higher than the score of correct label is called the *error set.* The algorithms we describe share a common feature: they all update only the prototypes from the error sets and the prototype of the correct label. We call such algorithms *ultraconservative.*

We start in Sec. 3 in which we provide a motivation for our framework. We do that by revisiting the well known perceptron algorithm and give a new account of the algorithm using two prototype vectors, one for each class. We then extend the algorithm to a multiclass setting using the notion of ultraconservativeness. In Sec. 4 we further generalize the multiclass version of the extended perceptron algorithm and describe a new family of ultraconservative algorithms that we obtain by replacing the perceptron's update with a set of linear equations. We give a few illustrative examples of specific updates from this family of algorithms. Going back to the perceptron algorithm, we show that in the binary case all the different updates reduce to the perceptron algorithm. We finish Sec. 4 by deriving a mistake bound that is common to all the additive algorithms in the family. We analyze both the separable and the non-separable case.

The fact that all algorithms from Sec. 4 achieve the same mistake bound implies that there are some undetermined degrees of freedom. We present in Sec. 5 a new online algorithm that gives a unique update and is based on a relaxation of the set of linear constraints employed by the family of algorithms from Sec. 4. The algorithm is derived by adding an objective function that incorporates the norm of the new matrix of prototypes and minimizing it subject to a subset of the linear constraints. Following recent trend, we call the new algorithm MIRA for Margin Infused Relaxed Algorithm. We analyze MIRA and give a mistake bound related to the instantaneous margin of individual examples. This analysis leads to modification of MIRA which incorporates the margin into the update rule. Both MIRA and of the additive algorithms from Sec. 4 can be combined with kernels techniques and voting methods.

The algorithms presented in this paper underscore a general framework for deriving ultraconservative multiclass algorithms. This framework can be used in combination with other online techniques. To conclude, we outline some of our current research directions. Due to the lack of space many of the proofs and some of the results have omitted. They will appear in a forthcoming long version of this paper.

Related Work. Multiclass extensions to binary approaches by maintaining multiple prototypes are by no means new. The widely read and cited book by Duda and Hart [7] describes a multiclass extension to the perceptron that employs multiple vectors. However, direct methods for online learning of multiclass problems in the mistake bound model have received relatively little attention.

A question that is common to numerous online algorithms is how to compromise the following two demands. On one hand, we want to update the classifier we learn so that it will better predict the current input instance, in particular if an error occurs when using the current classifier. On the other hand, we do not want to change the current classifier too radically, especially if it classifies well most of the previously observed instances. The good old perceptron algorithm suggested by Rosenblatt [17] copes with these two requirements by replacing the classifier with a linear combination of the current hyperplane and the current instance vector. Although the algorithm uses a simple update rule, it performs well on many synthetic and real-world problems. The perceptron algorithm spurred voluminous work which clearly cannot be covered here. For an overview of numerous additive and multiplicative online algorithms see the paper by Kivinen and Warmuth [12]. We outline below some of the research that is more relevant to the work presented in this paper.

Kivinen and Warmuth [12] presented numerous online algorithms for regression. Their algorithms are based on minimization of an objective function which is a sum of two terms. The first term is equal to the distance between the new classifier and the current classifier while the second term is the loss on the current example. The resulting update rule can be viewed as a gradient-descent method. Although multiclass classification problems are a special case of regression problems, the algorithms for regression put emphasis on smooth loss functions which might not be suitable for classification problems.

The idea of seeking a hyperplane of a small norm is a primary goal in support vector machines (SVM) [4,18]. Algorithms for constructing support vector machines solve optimization problems with a quadratic objective function and linear constraints. The work in [2,9] suggests to minimize the objective function in a gradient-decent method, which can be performed by going over the sample sequentially. Algorithms with a similar approach include the Sequential Minimization Optimization (SMO) algorithm introduced by Platt [15]. SMO works on rounds, on each round it chooses two examples of the sample and minimizes the objective function by modifying variables relevant only to these two examples. While these algorithms share some similarities with the algorithmic approaches described in this paper, they were all designed for batch problems and were not analyzed in the mistake bound model.

Another approach to the problem of designing an update rule which results in a linear classifier of a small norm was suggested by Li and Long [13]. The algorithm Li and Long proposed, called ROMMA, tackles the problem by finding a hyperplane with a minimal norm under two linear constraints. The first constraint is presented so that the new classifier will classify well previous examples, while the second rule demands that the hyperplane will classify correctly the current new instance. Solving this minimization problem leads to an additive update rule with adaptive coefficients.

Grove, Littlestone and Schuurmans [11] introduced a general framework of quasi-additive binary algorithms, which contain the perceptron and Winnow as special cases. In [10] Gentile proposed an extension to a subset of the quasi-additive algorithms, which uses an additive conservative update rule with decreasing learning rates.

The algorithms presented in this paper are reminiscent of some of the widely used methods for constructing classifiers in multiclass problems. As mentioned above, a popular approach for solving classification problems with many classes is to learn a set of binary classifiers where each classifier is designed to separate one class from the rest of classes. If we use the perceptron algorithm to learn the binary classifiers, we need to maintain and update one vector for each possible class. This approach shares the same form of hypothesis as the algorithms presented in this paper, which maintain one prototype per class. Nonetheless, there is one major difference between the ultraconservative algorithms we present and the one-against-rest approach. In one-against-rest we update and change each of the classifiers *independently* of the others. In fact we can construct them one after the other by re-running over the data. In contrast, ultraconservative algorithms update all the prototypes in tandem thus updating one prototype has a global effect on the other prototypes. There are situations in which there is an error due to some classes, but not all the respective prototypes should be updated. Put another way, we might perform milder changes to the set of classifiers by changing them together with the prototypes so as to achieve the same goal. As a result we get better mistake bounds and empirically better algorithms.

2 Preliminaries

The focus of this paper is online algorithms for multiclass prediction problems. We observe a sequence $(\bar{x}^1, y^1), \ldots, (\bar{x}^t, y^t), \ldots$ of instance-label pairs. Each instance $\bar{x}^t$ is in $\mathbb{R}^n$ and each label belongs to a finite set $\mathcal{Y}$ of size k. We assume without loss of generality that $\mathcal{Y} = \{1, 2, \ldots, k\}$. A *multiclass classifier* is a function $H(\bar{x})$ that maps instances from $\mathbb{R}^n$ into one of the possible labels in $\mathcal{Y}$. In this paper we focus on classifiers of the form $H(\bar{x}) = \arg\max_{r=1}^{k}\{\bar{M}_r \cdot \bar{x}\}$, where $\mathbf{M}$ is a $k \times n$ matrix over the reals and $\bar{M}_r \in \mathbb{R}^n$ denotes the rth row of $\mathbf{M}$. We call the inner product of $\bar{M}_r$ with the instance $\bar{x}$, the *similarity-score* for class r. Thus, the classifiers we consider in this paper set the label of an instance to be the index of the row of $\mathbf{M}$ which achieves the highest similarity-score. The margin of H on $\bar{x}$ is the difference between the similarity-score of the correct label y and the maximum among the similarity-scores of the rest of the rows of $\mathbf{M}$. Formally, the margin that $\mathbf{M}$ achieves on $(\bar{x}, y)$ is,

$$\bar{M}_y \cdot \bar{x} - \max_{r \neq y}\{\bar{M}_r \cdot \bar{x}\} \ .$$

The l_p norm of a vector $\bar{u} = (u_1, \ldots, u_l)$ in $\mathbb{R}^l$ is $\|\bar{u}\|_p = \left(\sum_{i=1}^{l} |u_i|^p\right)^{\frac{1}{p}}$. We define the l_p vector-norm of a matrix $\mathbf{M}$ to be the l_p norm of the vector we get by concatenating the rows of $\mathbf{M}$, that is,

$$\|\mathbf{M}\|_p = \|(\bar{M}_1, \ldots, \bar{M}_k)\|_p \ .$$

The framework that we use in this paper is the mistake bound model for online learning. The algorithms we consider work in rounds. On round t an online learning algorithm gets an instance $\bar{x}^t$. Given $\bar{x}^t$, the learning algorithm outputs a prediction, $\hat{y}^t = \arg\max_r\{\bar{M}_r \cdot \bar{x}^t\}$. It then receives the correct label y^t and updates its classification rule by modifying the matrix $\mathbf{M}$. We say that the algorithm made a (multiclass) prediction error if $\hat{y}^t \neq y^t$. Our goal is to make as few prediction errors as possible. When the algorithm makes a prediction error there might be more than one row of $\mathbf{M}$ achieving a score higher than the score of the row corresponding to the correct label. We define the *error-set* for $(\bar{x}, y)$ using a matrix $\mathbf{M}$ to be the index of all the rows in $\mathbf{M}$ which achieve such high scores. Formally, the error-set for a matrix $\mathbf{M}$ on an instance-label pair $(\bar{x}, y)$ is,

$$E = \{r \neq y : \bar{M}_r \cdot \bar{x} \geq \bar{M}_y \cdot \bar{x}\} \ .$$

Many online algorithms update their prediction rule only on rounds on which they made a prediction error. Such algorithms are called *conservative*. We give a definition that extends the notion of conservativeness to multiclass settings.

Definition 1 (Ultraconservative). *An online multiclass algorithm of the form $H(\bar{x}) = \arg\max_r\{\bar{M}_r \cdot \bar{x}\}$ is ultraconservative if it modifies $\mathbf{M}$ only when the error-set E for $(\bar{x}, y)$ is not empty and the indices of the rows that are modified are from $E \cup \{y\}$.*

Note that our definition implies that an ultraconservative algorithm is also conservative. For binary problems the two definitions coincide.

3 From Binary to Multiclass

Roseneblatt's perceptron algorithm [17] is a well known online algorithm for binary classification problems. The algorithm maintains a weight vector $\bar{w} \in \mathbb{R}^n$ that is used for prediction. To motivate our multiclass algorithms let us now describe the perceptron algorithm using the notation employed in this paper. In our setting the label of each instance belongs to the set $\{1, 2\}$. Given an input instance $\bar{x}$ the perceptron algorithm predicts that its label is $\hat{y} = 1$ iff $\bar{w} \cdot \bar{x} \geq 0$ and otherwise it predicts $\hat{y} = 2$. The algorithm modifies $\bar{w}$ only on rounds with

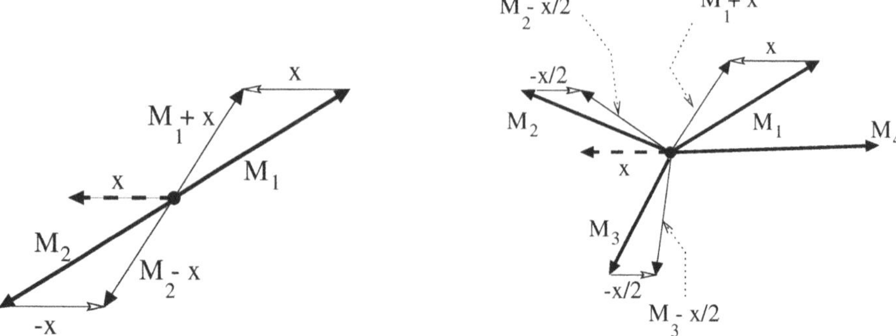

Fig. 1. A geometrical illustration of the update for a binary problem (left) and a four-class problem (right) using the extended perceptron algorithm.

prediction errors and is thus conservative. On such rounds $\bar{w}$ is changed to $\bar{w}+\bar{x}$ if the correct label is $y=1$ and to $\bar{w}-\bar{x}$ if $y=2$.

To implement the perceptron algorithm using a prototype matrix $\mathbf{M}$ with one row (prototype) per class, we set the first row $\bar{M}_1$ to $\bar{w}$ and the second row $\bar{M}_2$ to $-\bar{w}$. We now modify $\mathbf{M}$ every time the algorithm misclassifies $\bar{x}$ as follows. If the correct label is 1 we replace $\bar{M}_1$ with $\bar{M}_1+\bar{x}$ and $\bar{M}_2$ with $\bar{M}_2-\bar{x}$. Similarly, we replace $\bar{M}_1$ with $\bar{M}_1-\bar{x}$ and $\bar{M}_2$ with $\bar{M}_2+\bar{x}$ when the correct label is 2 and $\bar{x}$ is misclassified. Thus, the row $\bar{M}_y$ is moved toward the misclassified instance $\bar{x}$ while the other row is moved away from $\bar{x}$. Note that this update implies that the total change to the two prototypes is zero. An illustration of this geometrical interpretation is given on the left-hand side of Fig. 1. It is straightforward to verify that the algorithm is equivalent to the perceptron algorithm.

We can now use this interpretation and generalize the perceptron algorithm to multiclass problems as follows. For k classes maintain a matrix $\mathbf{M}$ of k rows, one row per class. For each input instance $\bar{x}$, the multiclass generalization of the perceptron calculates the similarity-score between the instance and each of the k prototypes. The predicted label, $\hat{y}$, is the index of the row (prototype) of $\mathbf{M}$ which achieves the highest score, that is, $\hat{y}=\arg\max_r\{\bar{M}_r\cdot\bar{x}\}$. If $\hat{y}\neq y$ the algorithm moves $\bar{M}_y$ toward $\bar{x}$ by replacing $\bar{M}_y$ with $\bar{M}_y+\bar{x}$. In addition, the algorithm moves each row $\bar{M}_r$ $(r\neq y)$ for which $\bar{M}_r\cdot\bar{x}\geq\bar{M}_y\cdot\bar{x}$ away from $\bar{x}$. The indices of these rows constitute the error set E. The algorithms presented in this paper, and in particular the multiclass version of the perceptron algorithm, modify $\mathbf{M}$ such that the following property holds: The total change in units of $\bar{x}$ in the rows of $\mathbf{M}$ that are moved away from $\bar{x}$ is equal to the change of $\bar{M}_y$, (in units of $\bar{x}$). Specifically, for the multiclass perceptron we replace $\bar{M}_y$ with $\bar{M}_y+\bar{x}$ and for each r in E we replace $\bar{M}_r$ with $\bar{M}_r-\bar{x}/|E|$. A geometric illustration of this update is given in the right-hand side of Fig. 1. There are four classes in the example appearing in the figure. The correct label of $\bar{x}$ is $y=1$ and since $\bar{M}_1$ is not the most similar vector to $\bar{x}$, it is moved toward $\bar{x}$. The rows $\bar{M}_2$ and $\bar{M}_3$ are also modified by subtracting $\bar{x}/2$ from each one. The last row $\bar{M}_4$ is not in the error-set since $\bar{M}_1 \cdot \bar{x} > \bar{M}_4 \cdot \bar{x}$ and therefore it is not modified. We defer the analysis of the algorithm to the next section in which we describe and analyze a family of online multiclass algorithms that also includes this algorithm.

4 A Family of Additive Multiclass Algorithms

We describe a family of ultraconservative algorithms by using the algorithm of the previous section as our starting point. The algorithm is ultraconservative and thus updates $\mathbf{M}$ only on rounds with predictions errors. The row $\bar{M}_y$ is changed to $\bar{M}_y + \bar{x}$ while for each $r \in E$ we modify $\bar{M}_r$ to $\bar{M}_r - \bar{x}/|E|$. Let us introduce a vector of weights $\bar{\tau} = (\tau_1, \ldots, \tau_k)$ and rewrite the update of the rth row as $\bar{M}_r + \tau_r \bar{x}$. Thus, for $r = y$ we have $\tau_r = 1$, for $r \in E$ we set $\tau_r = -1/|E|$, and for $r \notin E \cup \{y\}$, τ_r is zero. The weights $\bar{\tau}$ were chosen such that the total change of the rows of $\mathbf{M}$ whose indices are from E are equal to the change in $\bar{M}_y$, that is, $1 = \tau_y = -\sum_{r \in E} \tau_r$. If we do not impose the condition that for $r \in E$ all the τ_r's attain the same value, then the constraints on $\bar{\tau}$ become $\sum_{r \in E \cup \{y\}} \tau_r = 0$. This constraint enables us to move the prototypes from the error-set E away from $\bar{x}$ in different proportions as long as the total change is sum to one. The result is a whole family of multiclass algorithms. A pseudo-code of the family of algorithms is provided in Fig. 2. Note that the constraints on $\bar{\tau}$ are redundant and we could have used less constraints. We make use of this more elaborate set of constraints in the next section.

Before analyzing the family of algorithms we have just introduced, we give a few examples of specific schemes to set $\bar{\tau}$. We have already described one update above which sets $\bar{\tau}$ to,

$$\tau_r = \begin{cases} -\frac{1}{|E|} & r \in E \\ 1 & r = y \\ 0 & \text{otherwise} \end{cases} .$$

Since all the τ's for rows in the error-set are equal, we call this the *uniform* multiclass update. We can also be further conservative and modify in addition to $\bar{M}_y$ only one other row in $\mathbf{M}$. A reasonable choice is to modify the row that achieves the highest similarity-score. That is, we set $\bar{\tau}$ to,

$$\tau_r = \begin{cases} -1 & r = \arg\max_s \{\bar{M}_s \cdot \bar{x}\} \\ 1 & r = y \\ 0 & \text{otherwise} \end{cases} .$$

We call this form of updating $\bar{\tau}$ the *worst-margin* multiclass update. The two examples above set τ_r for $r \in E$ to a fixed value, ignoring the actual values of similarity-scores each row achieves. We can also set $\bar{\tau}$ in promotion to the excess in the similarity-score of each row in the error set (with respect to $\bar{M}_y$). For instance, we can set $\bar{\tau}$ to be,

$$\tau_r = \begin{cases} -\frac{[\bar{M}_r \cdot \bar{x} - \bar{M}_y \cdot \bar{x}]_+}{\sum_{r=1}^{k} [\bar{M}_r \cdot \bar{x} - \bar{M}_y \bar{x}]_+} & r \neq y \\ 1 & r = y \end{cases} ,$$

Initialize: Set $\mathbf{M} = 0$ $(\mathbf{M} \in \mathbb{R}^{k \times n})$.
Loop: For $t = 1, 2, \ldots, T$

- Get a new instance $\bar{x}^t \in \mathbb{R}^n$.
- Predict $\hat{y}^t = \arg \max_{r=1}^{k} \{\bar{M}_r \cdot \bar{x}^t\}$.
- Get a new label y^t.
- Set $E = \{r \neq y^t \ : \bar{M}_r \cdot \bar{x}^t \geq \bar{M}_{y^t} \cdot \bar{x}^t\}$.
- If $E \neq \emptyset$ update $\mathbf{M}$ by choosing any $\tau_1^t, \ldots, \tau_k^t$ that satisfy:
  1. $\tau_r^t \leq \delta_{r,y^t}$ for $r = 1, \ldots, k$.
  2. $\sum_{r=1}^{k} \tau_r^t = 0$.
  3. $\tau_r^t = 0$ for $r \notin E \cup \{y^t\}$.
  4. $\tau_{y^t}^t = 1$.
- For $r = 1, 2, \ldots, k$ update: $\bar{M}_r \leftarrow \bar{M}_r + \tau_r^t \, \bar{x}^t$.

Output : $H(\bar{x}) = \arg \max_r \{\bar{M}_r \cdot \bar{x}\}$.

Fig. 2. A family of additive multiclass algorithms.

where $[x]_+$ is equal to x if $x \geq 0$ and zero otherwise. Note that the above update implies that $\tau_r = 0$ for $r \notin E \cup \{y\}$. We now proceed to analyze the algorithms.

4.1 Analysis

In the analysis of the algorithms of Fig. 2 we use the following auxiliary lemma.

Lemma 1. *For any set $\{\tau_1, \ldots, \tau_k\}$ such that, $\sum_{r=1}^{k} \tau_r = 0$ and $\tau_r \leq \delta_{r,y}$ for $r = 1, \ldots, k$, then $\sum_r \tau_r^2 \leq 2\tau_y \leq 2$.*

We now give the main theorem of this section.

Theorem 1. *Let $(\bar{x}^1, y^1), \ldots, (\bar{x}^T, y^T)$ be an input sequence for any multiclass algorithm from the family described in Fig. 2 where $\bar{x}^t \in \mathbb{R}^n$ and $y^t \in \{1, 2, \ldots, k\}$. Denote by $R^2 = \max_t \|\bar{x}^t\|^2$. Assume that there is a matrix $\mathbf{M}^*$ of a unit vector-norm, $\|\mathbf{M}^*\| = 1$, that classifies the entire sequence correctly with margin $\gamma = \min_t \{\bar{M}_{y^t}^* \cdot \bar{x}^t - \max_{r \neq y^t} \bar{M}_r^* \cdot \bar{x}^t\} > 0$. Then, the number of mistakes that the algorithm makes is at most $2R^2/\gamma^2$.*

Proof. Assume that an error occurred when classifying the tth example $(\bar{x}^t, y^t)$ using the matrix $\mathbf{M}$. Denote by $\mathbf{M}^{'}$ the updated matrix after round t. That is, for $r = 1, 2, \ldots, k$ we have $\bar{M}_r^{'} = \bar{M}_r + \tau_r^t \, \bar{x}^t$. To prove the theorem we bound $\|\mathbf{M}\|_2^2$ from above and below. First, we derive a lower bound on $\|\mathbf{M}\|^2$ by bounding the term,

$$
\begin{aligned}
\sum_{r=1}^{k} \bar{M}_r^* \cdot \bar{M}_r^{'} &= \sum_{r=1}^{k} \bar{M}_r^* \cdot (\bar{M}_r + \tau_r^t \bar{x}^t) \\
&= \sum_{r=1}^{k} \bar{M}_r^* \cdot \bar{M}_r + \sum_r \tau_r^t \left(\bar{M}_r^* \cdot \bar{x}^t\right) \ . \qquad (1)
\end{aligned}
$$

We further develop the second term of Eq. (1) using the second constraint of the algorithm $\left(\sum_{r=1}^{k} \tau_r^t = 0\right)$. Substituting $\tau_{y^t} = -\sum_{r \neq y^t} \tau_r^t$ we get,

$$\begin{aligned}\sum_r \tau_r^t \left(\bar{M}_r^* \cdot \bar{x}^t\right) &= \sum_{r \neq y^t} \tau_r^t \left(\bar{M}_r^* \cdot \bar{x}^t\right) + \tau_{y^t} \left(\bar{M}_{y^t}^* \cdot \bar{x}^t\right) \\ &= \sum_{r \neq y^t} \tau_r^t \left(\bar{M}_r^* \cdot \bar{x}^t\right) - \sum_{r \neq y^t} \tau_r^t \left(\bar{M}_{y^t}^* \cdot \bar{x}^t\right) \\ &= \sum_{r \neq y^t} \left(-\tau_r^t\right) \left(\bar{M}_{y^t}^* - \bar{M}_r^*\right) \cdot \bar{x}^t . \end{aligned} \tag{2}$$

Using the assumption that $\mathbf{M}^*$ classifies each instance with a margin of at least γ and that $\tau_y = 1$ (fourth constraint) we obtain,

$$\sum_r \tau_r^t \left(\bar{M}_r^* \cdot \bar{x}^t\right) \geq \sum_{r \neq y^t} \left(-\tau_r^t\right) \gamma = \tau_{y^t}^t \gamma = \gamma . \tag{3}$$

Combining Eq. (1) and Eq. (3) we get, $\sum_r \bar{M}_r^* \cdot \bar{M}_r' \geq \sum_r \bar{M}_r^* \cdot \bar{M}_r + \gamma$. Thus, if the algorithm made m mistakes in T rounds then the matrix $\mathbf{M}$ satisfies,

$$\sum_r \bar{M}_r^* \cdot \bar{M}_r \geq m\gamma \tag{4}$$

Using the vector-norm definition and applying the Cauchy-Schwartz inequality we get,

$$\begin{aligned}\|\mathbf{M}\|^2 \|\mathbf{M}^*\|^2 &= \left(\sum_{r=1}^{k} \|\bar{M}_r\|^2\right) \left(\sum_{r=1}^{k} \|\bar{M}_r^*\|^2\right) \\ &\geq \left(\bar{M}_1 \cdot \bar{M}_1^* + \ldots + \bar{M}_k \cdot \bar{M}_k^*\right)^2 \quad = \left(\sum_{r=1}^{k} \bar{M}_r \cdot \bar{M}_r^*\right)^2 . \end{aligned} \tag{5}$$

Plugging Eq. (4) into Eq. (5) and using the assumption that $\mathbf{M}^*$ is of a unit vector-norm we get the following lower bound,

$$\|\mathbf{M}\|^2 \geq m^2 \gamma^2 . \tag{6}$$

Next, we bound the vector-norm of $\mathbf{M}$ from above. As before, assume that an error occurred when classifying the example $(\bar{x}^t, y^t)$ using the matrix $\mathbf{M}$ and denote by $\mathbf{M}'$ the matrix after the update. Then,

$$\begin{aligned}\|\mathbf{M}'\|^2 = \sum_r \|\bar{M}_r'\|^2 &= \sum_r \|\bar{M}_r + \tau_r^t \bar{x}^t\|^2 \\ &= \sum_r \|\bar{M}_r\|^2 + 2\sum_r \tau_r^t \left(\bar{M}_r \cdot \bar{x}^t\right) + \sum_r \|\tau_r^t \bar{x}^t\|^2 \\ &= \|\mathbf{M}\|^2 + 2\sum_r \tau_r^t \left(\bar{M}_r \cdot \bar{x}^t\right) + \|\bar{x}^t\|^2 \sum_r (\tau_r^t)^2 . \end{aligned} \tag{7}$$

We further develop the second term using the second constraint of the algorithm and analogously to Eq. (2) we get,

$$\sum_r \tau_r^t \left(\bar{M}_r \cdot \bar{x}^t\right) = \sum_{r \neq y^t} (-\tau_r^t) \left(\bar{M}_{y^t} - \bar{M}_r\right) \cdot \bar{x}^t .$$

Since $\bar{x}^t$ was misclassified we need to consider the following two cases. The first case is when the label r was not the source of the error, that is $(\bar{M}_{y^t} - \bar{M}_r)\cdot\bar{x}^t > 0$. Then, using the third constraint ($r \notin E \cup \{y^t\} \Rightarrow \tau_r^t = 0$) we get that $\tau_r^t = 0$ and thus $(-\tau_r^t)\left(\bar{M}_{y^t} - \bar{M}_r\right)\cdot\bar{x}^t = 0$. The second case is when one of the sources of error was the label r. In that case $(\bar{M}_{y^t} - \bar{M}_r)\cdot\bar{x}^t \le 0$. Using the first constraint of the algorithm we know that $\tau_r^t \le 0$ and thus $(-\tau_r^t)\left(\bar{M}_{y^t} - \bar{M}_r\right)\cdot\bar{x}^t \le 0$. Finally, summing over all r we get,

$$\sum_r \tau_r^t \left(\bar{M}_r \cdot \bar{x}^t\right) \le 0 \; . \tag{8}$$

Plugging Eq. (8) into Eq. (7) we get, $\|\mathbf{M}^{'}\|^2 \le \|\mathbf{M}\|^2 + \|\bar{x}^t\|^2 \sum_r (\tau_r^t)^2$. Using the bound $\|\bar{x}^t\|^2 \le R^2$ and Lemma 1 we obtain,

$$\|\mathbf{M}^{'}\|^2 \le \|\mathbf{M}\|^2 + 2\|R\|^2 \; . \tag{9}$$

Thus, if the algorithm made m mistakes in T rounds, the matrix $\mathbf{M}$ satisfies,

$$\|\mathbf{M}\|^2 \le 2m\|R\|^2 \; . \tag{10}$$

Combining Eq. (6) and Eq. (10), we have that, $m^2\gamma^2 \le \|\mathbf{M}\|^2 \le 2m\|R\|^2$, and therefore, $m \le 2R^2/\gamma^2$. ∎

We would like to note that the bound of the above theorem reduces to the perceptrons mistake bound in the binary case ($k = 2$). To conclude this section we analyze the non-separable case by generalizing Thm. 2 of Freund and Schapire [8] to a multiclass setting.

Theorem 2. *Let $(\bar{x}^1, y^1), \ldots, (\bar{x}^T, y^T)$ be an input sequence for any multiclass algorithm from the family described in Fig. 2, where $\bar{x}^t \in \mathbb{R}^n$ and $y^t \in \{1, 2, \ldots, k\}$. Denote by $R^2 = \max_t \|\bar{x}^t\|^2$. Let $\mathbf{M}^*$ be a prototype matrix of a unit vector-norm, $\|\mathbf{M}^*\| = 1$, and define, $d^t = \max\left\{0,\ \gamma - \left[\bar{M}^*_{y^t}\cdot\bar{x}^t - \max_{r\neq y^t} \bar{M}^*_r\cdot\bar{x}^t\right]\right\}$. Denote by $D^2 = \sum_{t=1}^T (d^t)^2$ and fix some $\gamma > 0$. Then the number of mistakes the algorithm makes is at most $2(R+D)^2/\gamma^2$.*

Proof. The case $D = 0$ follows from Thm. 1 thus we can assume that $D > 0$. The theorem is proved by transforming the non-separable setting to a separable one. To do so, we extend each instance $\bar{x}^t \in \mathbb{R}^n$ to $\bar{z}^t \in \mathbb{R}^{n+T}$ as follows. The first n coordinates of $\bar{z}^t$ are set to $\bar{x}^t$. The $n+t$ coordinate of $\bar{z}^t$ is set to Δ, which is a positive real number whose value is determined later; the rest of the coordinates of $\bar{z}^t$ are set to zero. We similarly extend the matrix $\mathbf{M}^*$ to $\mathbf{W}^* \in \mathbb{R}^{k\times(n+T)}$ as follows. We set the first n columns $\mathbf{W}^*$ to be $\frac{1}{Z}\mathbf{M}^*$. For each row r we set $W^*_{r,n+t}$ to $\frac{d^t}{Z\Delta}$ if $y^t = r$ and zero otherwise. We choose the value of Z so that $\|\mathbf{W}^*\|_2 = 1$, hence, $1 = \|\mathbf{W}^*\|_2^2 = \frac{1}{Z^2}\left(1 + \frac{D^2}{\Delta^2}\right)$ which gives that, $Z = \sqrt{1 + \frac{D^2}{\Delta^2}}$. We now show that $\mathbf{W}^*$ achieves a margin of $\frac{\gamma}{Z}$ on the extended data sequence. Note that for all r and t, $\bar{W}^*_r \cdot \bar{z}^t = \frac{1}{Z}\left(\bar{M}^*_r \cdot \bar{x}^t + \delta_{r,y^t} d^t\right)$. Now, using the definition of d^t we get,

$$\begin{aligned}
\bar{W}^*_{y^t} \cdot \bar{z}^t - \max_{r \neq y^t}\left\{\bar{W}^*_r \cdot \bar{z}^t\right\} &= \frac{1}{Z}\left(\bar{M}^*_{y^t} \cdot \bar{x}^t + d^t\right) - \max_{r \neq y^t}\left\{\frac{1}{Z}\left(\bar{M}^*_r \cdot \bar{x}^t\right)\right\} \\
&= \frac{1}{Z} d^t + \frac{1}{Z}\left[\bar{M}^*_{y^t} \cdot \bar{x}^t - \max_{r \neq y^t}\left\{\bar{M}^*_r \cdot \bar{x}^t\right\}\right] \\
&\geq \frac{1}{Z}\left(\gamma - \left[\bar{M}^*_{y^t} \cdot \bar{x}^t - \max_{r \neq y^t}\left\{\bar{M}^*_r \cdot \bar{x}^t\right\}\right]\right) \\
&\quad + \frac{1}{Z}\left[\bar{M}^*_{y^t} \cdot \bar{x}^t - \max_{r \neq y^t}\left\{\bar{M}^*_r \cdot \bar{x}^t\right\}\right] \\
&= \frac{\gamma}{Z} \cdot
\end{aligned} \tag{11}$$

We also have that,

$$\|\bar{z}^t\|^2 = \|\bar{x}^t\|^2 + \Delta^2 \leq R^2 + \Delta^2 . \tag{12}$$

In summary, Eq. (11) and Eq. (12) imply that the sequence $(\bar{z}^1, y^1), \ldots, (\bar{z}^T, y^T)$ is classified correctly with margin $\frac{\gamma}{Z}$ and each instance $\bar{z}^t$ is bounded above by $R^2 + \Delta^2$. Thus, we can use Thm. 1 and conclude that the number of mistakes that the algorithm makes on $(\bar{z}^1, y^1), \ldots, (\bar{z}^T, y^T)$ is bounded from above by,

$$2\frac{R^2 + \Delta^2}{\left(\frac{\gamma}{Z}\right)^2} . \tag{13}$$

Minimizing Eq. (13) over Δ we get that the optimal value for Δ is $\sqrt{DR}$ and the tightest mistake bound is, $2(D+R)^2/\gamma^2$. To complete the proof we show that the prediction of the algorithm in the extended space and in the original space are equal. Namely, let $\mathbf{M}^t$ and $\mathbf{W}^t$ be the value of the parameter matrix just before receiving $\bar{x}^t$ and $\bar{z}^t$, respectively. We need to show that the following conditions hold for $t = 1, \ldots, T$:

1. The first n columns of $\mathbf{W}^t$ are equal to $\mathbf{M}^t$.
2. The $(n+t)$th column of $\mathbf{W}^t$ is equal zero.
3. $\bar{M}^t_r \cdot \bar{x}^t = \bar{W}^t_r \cdot \bar{z}^t$ for $r = 1, \ldots, k$.

The proof of these conditions is straightforward by induction on t. ■

5 A Norm-Optimized Multiclass Algorithm

In the previous section we have described a family of algorithms where each algorithm of the family achieves the same mistake bound given by Thm. 1 and Thm. 2. This variety of equivalent algorithms suggests that there are some degrees of freedom that we might be able to exploit. In this section we describe an online algorithm that chooses a feasible vector $\bar{\tau}^t$ such that the vector-norm of the matrix $\mathbf{M}$ will be as small as possible.

Initialize: Set $\mathbf{M} \neq 0 \;\; \mathbf{M} \in \mathbb{R}^{k\times n}$.
Loop: For $t = 1, 2, \ldots, T$

- Get a new instance $\bar{x}^t$.
- Predict $\hat{y}^t = \arg\max_r\{\bar{M}_r \cdot \bar{x}^t\}$.
- Get a new label y^t.
- Find $\bar{\tau}^t$ that solves the following optimization problem:

$$\begin{aligned} &\min_{\bar{\tau}} \tfrac{1}{2} \textstyle\sum_r \|\bar{M}_r + \tau_r\, \bar{x}^t\|_2^2 \\ &\text{subject to : } (1)\ \tau_r \leq \delta_{r,y^t} \text{ for } r = 1, \ldots, k \\ &\qquad\qquad\quad (2)\ \textstyle\sum_{r=1}^k \tau_r = 0 \end{aligned}$$

- Update : $\bar{M}_r \leftarrow \bar{M}_r + \tau_r^t\, \bar{x}^t \;\;$ for $\;r = 1, 2, \ldots, k$.

Output : $H(\bar{x}) = \arg\max_r\{\bar{M}_r \cdot \bar{x}\}$.

Fig. 3. The Margin Infused Relaxed Algorithm (MIRA).

To derive the new algorithm we omit the fourth constraint ($\tau_y = 1$) and thus allow more flexibility in choosing $\bar{\tau}^t$, or smaller changes in the prototype matrix. Previous bounds provides motivation for the algorithms in this section. We choose a vector $\bar{\tau}^t$ which minimizes the vector-norm of the new matrix $\mathbf{M}$ subject to the first two constraints only. As we show in the sequel, the solution of the optimization problem automatically satisfies the third constraint. The algorithm attempts to update the matrix $\mathbf{M}$ on *each* round regardless of whether there was a prediction error or not. We show below that the algorithm is ultraconservative and thus $\bar{\tau}^t$ is the zero vector if $\bar{x}^t$ is correctly classified (and no update takes place). Following the trend set by Li and Long [13] and Gentile [10], we term our algorithm MIRA for Margin Infused Relaxed Algorithm. The algorithm is described in Fig. 3.

Before investigating the properties of the algorithm, we rewrite the optimization problem that MIRA solves on each round in a more convenient form. Omitting the example index t the objective function becomes,

$$\frac{1}{2}\sum_r \|\bar{M}_r + \tau_r \bar{x}\|^2 = \frac{1}{2}\sum_r \|\bar{M}_r\|^2 + \sum_r \tau_r \left(\bar{M}_r \cdot \bar{x}\right) + \frac{1}{2}\sum_r \tau_r^2 \|\bar{x}\|^2 \;\; .$$

Omitting $\frac{1}{2}\sum_r \|\bar{M}_r\|^2$ which is constant, the quadratic optimization problem becomes,

$$\min_{\tau} \;\; Q(\tau) = \frac{1}{2} A \sum_{r=1}^{k} \tau_r^2 + \sum_{r=1}^{k} B_r \tau_r \tag{14}$$
$$\text{subject to : } \;\forall r \quad \tau_r \leq \delta_{r,y} \quad \text{and} \quad \textstyle\sum_r \tau_r = 0$$

where,

$$A = \|\bar{x}\|^2 \quad \text{and} \quad B_r = \bar{M}_r \cdot \bar{x} \; . \tag{15}$$

Since $\mathcal{Q}$ is a quadratic function, and thus convex, and the constraints are linear, the problem has a unique solution.

We now show that MIRA automatically satisfies the third constraint of the family of algorithms from Sec. 4, which implies that it is ultraconservative. We use the following auxiliary lemma.

Lemma 2. *Let $\bar{\tau}$ be the optimal solution of the constrained optimization problem given by Eq. (14) for an instance-label pair $(\bar{x}, y)$. For each $r \neq y$ such that $B_r \leq B_y$ we have $\tau_r = 0$.*

The lemma implies that if a label r is not a source of error, then the rth prototype, $\bar{M}_r$, is not updated after $(\bar{x}, y)$ has been observed. In other words, the solution of Eq. (14) satisfies that $\tau_r = 0$ for all $r \neq y$ with $\left(\bar{M}_r \cdot \bar{x} \leq \bar{M}_y \cdot \bar{x}\right)$.

Corollary 1. *MIRA is ultraconservative.*

Proof. Let $(\bar{x}, y)$ be a new example fed to the algorithm. And let $\bar{\tau}$ be the coefficients found by the algorithm. From Lemma 2 we get that for each label r whose score $(\bar{M}_r \cdot \bar{x})$ is not larger than the score of the correct label $(\bar{M}_y \cdot \bar{x})$ its corresponding value τ_r is set to zero. This implies that only the indices which belong to the set $E \cup \{y\} = \{r \neq y : \bar{M}_r \cdot \bar{x} \geq \bar{M}_y \cdot \bar{x}\} \cup \{y\}$ may be updated. Furthermore, if the algorithm predicts correctly that the label is y, we get that $E = \emptyset$ and $\tau_r = 0$ for all $r \neq y$. In this case τ_y is set to zero due to the constraint $\sum_r \tau_r = \tau_y + \sum_{r \neq y} \tau_r = 0$. Hence, $\bar{\tau} = 0$ and the algorithm does not modify $\mathbf{M}$ on $(\bar{x}, y)$. Thus, the conditions required for ultraconservativeness are satisfied. ■

In Sec. 5.2 we give a detailed analysis of MIRA that incorporates the margin achieved on each example, and can be used to derive a mistake bound. Let us first show that the cumulative l_1-norm of the coefficients $\bar{\tau}^t$ is bounded.

Theorem 3. *Let $(\bar{x}^1, y^1), \ldots, (\bar{x}^T, y^T)$ be an input sequence to MIRA where $\bar{x}^t \in \mathbb{R}^n$ and $y^t \in \{1, 2, \ldots, k\}$. Let $R = \max_t \|\bar{x}^t\|^2$ and assume that there is a prototype matrix $\mathbf{M}^*$ of a unit vector-norm, $\|\mathbf{M}^*\| = 1$, which classifies the entire sequence correctly with margin $\gamma = \min_t\{\bar{M}^*_{y^t} \cdot \bar{x}^t - \max_{r \neq y^t} \bar{M}^*_r \cdot \bar{x}^t\} > 0$. Let $\bar{\tau}^t$ be the coefficients that MIRA finds for $(\bar{x}^t, y^t)$. Then, $\sum_{t=1}^{T} \|\bar{\tau}^t\|_1 \leq 4R^2/\gamma^2$.*

The proof is omitted due to lack of space.

5.1 Characteristics of the Solution

Let us now further examine the characteristics of the solution obtained by MIRA. In [5] we investigated a related setting that uses error correcting output codes for multiclass problems. Using the results from [5] it is simple to show that the optimal $\bar{\tau}$ in Eq. (14) is given by

$$\tau_r = \min\{\theta^* - \frac{B_r}{A}, \delta_{y,r}\} \tag{16}$$

where $A = \|\bar{x}\|^2$ and $B_r = \bar{M}_r \cdot \bar{x}$ is the similarity-score of $(\bar{x}, y)$ for label r, as defined by Eq. (15). The optimal value θ^* is uniquely defined by the equality constraint $\sum_r \tau_r = 0$ of Eq. (14) and satisfies, $\sum_{r=1}^{k} \min\{\theta^* - \frac{B_r}{A}, \delta_{y,r}\} = 0$. We now can view MIRA in the following alternative light. Assume that the instance $(\bar{x}, y)$ was misclassified by MIRA and set $E = \{r \neq y \; : \bar{M}_r \cdot \bar{x} \geq \bar{M}_y \cdot \bar{x}\} \neq \emptyset$. The similarity-score for label r of the new matrix on the current instance $\bar{x}$ is,

$$(\bar{M}_r + \tau \bar{x}) \cdot \bar{x} = B_r + \tau_r A \; . \tag{17}$$

Plugging Eq. (16) into Eq. (17) we get that the similarity-score for class r on the current instance is, $\min\{A\theta^*, B_r + A\delta_{y,r}\}$. Since $\tau_r \leq \delta_{y,r}$, the maximal similarity score the updated matrix can attain on $\bar{x}$ is $B_r + A\delta_{r,y}$. Thus, the similarity-score for class r after the update is either a constant that is common to all classes, $A\theta^*$, or the largest similarity-score the class r can attain, $B_r + A\delta_{r,y}$. The constant $A\theta^*$ places an upper bound on the similarity-score for all classes after the update. This bound is tight, that is at least one similarity-score value is equal to $A\theta^*$.

5.2 Margin Analysis of MIRA

In this section we further analyze MIRA by relating its mistake bound to the instantaneous margin of the individual examples. The margin analysis we present in this section sheds some more light on the source of difficulty in achieving a mistake bound for MIRA. Our analysis here also leads to an alternative version of MIRA that incorporates the margin into the quadratic optimization problem that we need to solve on each round. Our starting point is Thm. 3. We first give a lower bound on τ_y on each round. If MIRA made a mistake on $(\bar{x}, y)$, then we know that $\max_{r \neq y} B_r - B_y > 0$. Therefore, we can bound the minimal value of τ_y by a function of the (negative) margin, $B_y - \max_{r \neq y} B_r$.

Lemma 3. *Let $\bar{\tau}$ be the optimal solution of the constrained optimization problem given by Eq. (14) for an instance-label pair $(\bar{x}, y)$ with $A \leq R^2$. Assume that the margin $B_y - \max_{r \neq y} B_r$ is bounded from above by $-\beta$, where $0 < \beta \leq 2R^2$. Then τ_y is at least $\beta/(2R^2)$.*

We would like to note that for the above lemma if $\beta \geq 2R^2$ then $\tau_y = 1$ regardless of the margin achieved. We are now ready to prove the main result of this section.

Theorem 4. *Let $(\bar{x}^1, y^1), \ldots, (\bar{x}^T, y^T)$ be an input sequence to MIRA where $\bar{x}^t \in \mathbb{R}^n$ and $y^t \in \{1, 2, \ldots, k\}$. Denote by $R = \max_t \|\bar{x}^t\|$ and assume that there is a prototype matrix $\mathbf{M}^*$ of a unit vector-norm, $\|\mathbf{M}^*\|_2 = 1$, which classifies the entire sequence correctly with margin $\gamma = \min_t\{\bar{M}^*_{y^t} \cdot \bar{x}^t - \max_{r \neq y^t} \bar{M}^*_r \cdot \bar{x}^t\} > 0$. Denote by n_β the number of rounds for which $B_{y^t} - \max_{r \neq y^t} B_r \leq -\beta$, for some $0 < \beta \leq 2R^2$. Then the following bound holds, $n_\beta \leq 4R^4/(\beta\gamma^2)$.*

Proof. The proof is a simple application of Thm. 3 and Lemma 3. Using the second constraint of MIRA ($\sum_r \tau_r = 0$) and Thm. 3 we get that,

$$\sum_{t=1}^{T} \tau^t_{y^t} \leq 2\frac{R^2}{\gamma^2} \; . \tag{18}$$

From Lemma 3 we know that whenever $\max_{r \neq y^t} B_r - B_{y^t} \geq \beta$ then $1 \leq \frac{2R^2}{\beta} \tau^t_{y^t}$ and therefore,

$$n_\beta \leq \sum_{t=1}^{T} \frac{2R^2}{\beta} \tau^t_{y^t} \ . \tag{19}$$

Combining Eq. (18) and Eq. (19) we obtain the required bound,

$$n_\beta \leq 2\frac{R^2}{\beta} \sum_{t=1}^{T} \tau^t_{y^t} \leq 2\frac{R^2}{\beta} 2\frac{R^2}{\gamma^2} \leq 4\frac{R^4}{\beta\gamma^2} \ .$$

■

Note that Thm. 4 still does not provide a mistake bound for MIRA since in the limit of $\beta \rightarrow 0$ the bound diverges. Note also that for $\beta = 2R^2$ the bound reduces to the bounds of Thm. 1 and Thm. 3. The source of the difficulty in obtaining a mistake bound is rounds on which MIRA achieves a small negative margin and thus makes small changes to $\mathbf{M}$. On such rounds τ_y can be arbitrarily small and we cannot translate the bound on $\sum_t \tau^t_{y^t}$ into a mistake bound. This implies that MIRA is not robust to small changes in the input instances. We therefore describe now a simple modification to MIRA for which we can prove a mistake bound and, as we will see later, performs better empirically.

The modified MIRA aggressively updates $\mathbf{M}$ on every round for which the margin is smaller than some predefined value denoted again by β. This technique is by no means new, see for instance [13]. The result is a mixed algorithm which is both aggressive and ultraconservative. On one hand, the algorithm updates $\mathbf{M}$ whenever a minimal margin is not achieved, including rounds on which $(\bar{x}, y)$ is classified correctly but with a small margin. On the other hand, on each update of $\mathbf{M}$ only the rows whose corresponding similarity-scores are mistakenly too high are updated. We now describe how to modify MIRA along these lines.

To achieve a minimal margin of at least $\beta \leq 2R^2$ we modify the optimization problem given by Eq. (14). A minimal margin of β is achieved if for all r we require $\bar{M}_y \cdot \bar{x} - \bar{M}_r \cdot \bar{x} \geq \beta$ or, alternatively, $(\bar{M}_y \cdot \bar{x} - \beta) - (\bar{M}_r \cdot \bar{x}) \geq 0$. Thus, if we replace B_y with $B_y - \beta$, $\mathbf{M}$ will be updated whenever the margin is smaller than β. We thus let MIRA solve for each example $(\bar{x}, y)$ the following constrained optimization problem,

$$\min_{\tau} \quad \mathcal{Q}(\tau) = \frac{1}{2}\tilde{A}\sum_{r=1}^{k} \tau_r^2 + \sum_{r=1}^{k} \tilde{B}_r \tau_r \tag{20}$$

$$\text{subject to}: \ \forall r \quad \tau_r \leq \delta_{r,y} \quad \text{and} \quad \textstyle\sum_r \tau_r = 0$$

$$\text{where}: \ \tilde{A} = A = \|\bar{x}\|^2 \ ; \ \tilde{B}_r = B_r - \beta\delta_{y,r} = \bar{M}_r \cdot \bar{x} - \beta\delta_{y,r} \ .$$

To get a mistake bound for this modified version of MIRA we apply Thm. 4 almost verbatim by replacing B_r with $\tilde{B}_r$ in the theorem. Note that if $\tilde{B}_y - \max_{r \neq y} \tilde{B}_r \leq -\beta$ then $B_y - \beta - \max_{r \neq y} B_r \leq -\beta$ and hence $B_y - \max_{r \neq y} B_r \leq 0$. Therefore, for any $0 \leq \beta \leq 2R^2$ we get that the number of mistakes of the modified algorithm is equal to n_β which is bounded by $4R^4/\beta\gamma^2$. This gives the following corollary.

Corollary 2. *Let* $(\bar{x}^1, y^1), \ldots, (\bar{x}^T, y^T)$ *be an input sequence to the aggressive version of MIRA with margin* β*, where* $\bar{x}^t \in \mathbb{R}^n$ *and* $y^t \in \{1, 2, \ldots, k\}$*. Denote by* $R = \max_t \|\bar{x}^t\|$ *and assume that there is a prototype matrix* $\mathbf{M}^*$ *of a unit vector-norm,* $\|\mathbf{M}^*\|_2 = 1$*, which classifies the entire sequence correctly with margin* $\gamma = \min_t\{\bar{M}^*_{y^t} \cdot \bar{x}^t - \max_{r \neq y^t} \bar{M}^*_r \cdot \bar{x}^t\} > 0$*. Then, the number of mistakes the algorithm makes is bounded above by,* $4R^4/(\beta\gamma^2)$.

Note that the bound is a decreasing function of β. This means that the more aggressive we are by requiring a minimal margin the smaller the bound on the number of mistakes the aggressively modified MIRA makes. However, this also implies that the algorithm will update $\mathbf{M}$ more often and the solution will be less sparse.

6 Discussion and Current Research Directions

In this paper we described a general framework for deriving ultraconservative algorithms for multiclass categorization problems and analyzed the proposed algorithms in the mistake bound model. We investigated in detail an additive family of online algorithms. The entire family reduces to the perceptron algorithm in the binary case. In addition, we gave a method for choosing a unique member of the family by imposing a quadratic objective function that minimizes the norm of the prototype matrix after each update. Note that the similarity-score of a new instance is a linear combination of inner-products between pairs of instances. Therefore, all the algorithms we presented can be straightforwardly combined with kernel methods [18].

An interesting direction we are currently working on is combining our framework with other online learning algorithms for binary problems. Specifically, we have been able to combine Winnow [14] and Li and Long's ROMMA algorithm [13] with our framework, and to construct a multiclass version for those algorithms. A question that remains open is how to impose constraints similar to the one MIRA employs in both cases.

An interesting question in this case is whether our framework can be combined with the family of quasi-additive binary algorithms of Grove, Littlestone and Schuurmans [11] and other p-norm algorithms [10]. Another interesting direction that generalizes our framework is algorithms that maintain multiple prototypes per class. It is not clear in this case what form the updates should take.

We have performed preliminary experiments on synthetic data that show the advantages in using our proposed framework over previously studied online algorithms for multiclass problems. A complete description of the results obtained in the various experiments will appear in a forthcoming full version.

A current research direction we are pursuing is methods for reducing the number of updates MIRA performs, and thus the number of instances that are used in building the classifier. We are currently working on the design of o post processing stage of the algorithms. Combining the algorithms presented in this paper with a post processing can be used in batch setting. Preliminary results show that this direction may give a viable algorithmic alternative for building support vector machines.

Acknowledgements. We would like to thank Elisheva Bonchek for carefully reading a draft of the manuscript and to Noam Slonim for useful comments.

References

1. E.L. Allwein, R.E. Schapire, and Y. Singer. Reducing multiclass to binary: A unifying approach for margin classifiers. In *Machine Learning: Proceedings of the Seventeenth International Conference*, 2000.
2. J. K. Anlauf and M. Biehl. The adatron: an adaptive perceptron algorithm. *Europhysics Letters*, 10(7):687–692, Dec 1989.
3. Leo Breiman, Jerome H. Friedman, Richard A. Olshen, and Charles J. Stone. *Classification and Regression Trees.* Wadsworth & Brooks, 1984.
4. Corinna Cortes and Vladimir Vapnik. Support-vector networks. *Machine Learning*, 20(3):273–297, September 1995.
5. Koby Crammer and Yoram Singer. On the learnability and design of output codes for multiclass problems. In *Proceedings of the Thirteenth Annual Conference on Computational Learning Theory*, 2000.
6. T.G. Dietterich and G. Bakiri. Solving multiclass learning problems via error-correcting output codes. *J. of Artificial Intelligence Research*, 2:263–286, 1995.
7. R.O. Duda and P.E. Hart. *Pattern Classification and Scene Analysis.* Wiley, 1973.
8. Yoav Freund and Robert E. Schapire. Large margin classification using the perceptron algorithm. In *Proceedings of the Eleventh Annual Conference on Computational Learning Theory*, 1998. To appear, *Machine Learning.*
9. Thilo Friess, Nello Cristianini, and Colin Campbell. The kernel-adatron: A fast and simple learning procedure for support vector machines. In *Machine Learning: Proceedings of the Fifteenth International Conference*, 1998.
10. Claudio Gentile. Approximate maximal margin classification with respect to an arbitrary norm. In *Advances in Neural Information Processing Systems 14*, 2000.
11. Adam J. Grove, Nick Littlestone, and Dale Schuurmans. General convergence results for linear discriminant updates. In *Proceedings of the Tenth Annual Conference on Computational Learning Theory*, 1997.
12. Jyrki Kivinen and Manfred K. Warmuth. Additive versus exponentiated gradient updates for linear prediction. *Information and Computation*, 132(1):1–64, 1997.
13. Yi Li and Phil M. Long. The relaxed online maximum margin algorithm. In *Advances in Neural Information Processing Systems 13*, 1999.
14. Nick Littlestone. Learning when irrelevant attributes abound. In *28th Annual Symposium on Foundations of Computer Science*, pages 68–77, October 1987.
15. J.C. Platt. Fast training of Support Vector Machines using sequential minimal optimization. In B. Schölkopf, C. Burges, and A. Smola, editors, *Advances in Kernel Methods - Support Vector Learning.* MIT Press, 1998.
16. J. Ross Quinlan. *C4.5: Programs for Machine Learning.* Morgan Kaufmann, 1993.
17. F. Rosenblatt. The perceptron: A probabilistic model for information storage and organization in the brain. *Psychological Review*, 65:386–407, 1958.
18. Vladimir N. Vapnik. *Statistical Learning Theory.* Wiley, 1998.

Estimating a Boolean Perceptron from Its Average Satisfying Assignment: A Bound on the Precision Required

Paul W. Goldberg*

Dept. of Computer Science, University of Warwick, Coventry CV4 7AL, U.K.
pwg@dcs.warwick.ac.uk

Abstract. A boolean perceptron is a linear threshold function over the discrete boolean domain $\{0,1\}^n$. That is, it maps any binary vector to 0 or 1 depending on whether the vector's components satisfy some linear inequality. In 1961, Chow [9] showed that any boolean perceptron is determined by the average or "center of gravity" of its "true" vectors (those that are mapped to 1). Moreover, this average distinguishes the function from any other boolean function, not just other boolean perceptrons.
We address an associated statistical question of whether an empirical estimate of this average is likely to provide a good approximation to the perceptron. In this paper we show that an estimate that is accurate to within additive error $(\epsilon/n)^{O(\log(1/\epsilon))}$ determines a boolean perceptron that is accurate to within error ϵ (the fraction of misclassified vectors). This provides a mildly super-polynomial bound on the sample complexity of learning boolean perceptrons in the "restricted focus of attention" setting. In the process we also find some interesting geometrical properties of the vertices of the unit hypercube.

1 Introduction

A *boolean perceptron* is a linear threshold function over the domain of 0/1-vectors. (Subsequently we usually just say "perceptron", and omit the adjective "boolean".) Thus it is specifed by a weight vector $\mathbf{w} = (w_1, \ldots, w_n)$ of real numbers and a real-valued threshold t, and it maps a binary vector $\mathbf{x}$ to the output value 1 provided that $\mathbf{w}.\mathbf{x} \geq t$, otherwise it maps $\mathbf{x}$ to 0.

In this paper we consider the problem of estimating a perceptron from an approximate value of the mean, or "center of gravity" of its satisfying assignments. Chow [9] originally showed that the exact value of the average of the satisfying assignments of a boolean perceptron determines it, in that there are no other boolean functions of any kind for which the average satisfying assignment is the same. (Bruck [8] also gives a more general result.) The question of the extent to which an approximation to the average determines the perceptron, is equivalent to a problem of learning boolean perceptrons in the "restricted focus of attention" setting, described below.

* Partially supported by the IST Programme of the EU under contract number IST-1999-14186 (ALCOM-FT).

D. Helmbold and B. Williamson (Eds.): COLT/EuroCOLT 2001, LNAI 2111, pp. 116–127, 2001.

The *Chow parameters* of a boolean perceptron are the coordinates of the vector sum of the satisfying vectors, together with the number of satisfying vectors. Subject to a uniform distribution over boolean vectors, these are essentially equivalent to the conditional probabilities of the output value 1, conditioned on some input value being set to either 0 or 1. Letting y denote the output value and $\mathbf{x} = (x_1, \ldots, x_n)$, these are the probabilities $Pr(y = 1 \mid x_i = 1)$, for $i = 1, \ldots, n$, together with the value $Pr(y = 1)$.[1] These values determine the functional behavior on binary input vectors, obviously there may some amount of freedom to vary the values of $\mathbf{w}$ and t while preserving the output for any binary input.

In this paper we show that additive approximations of the Chow parameters determine the approximate behavior of the function, to within a mildly super-polynomial factor. That is in contrast to the situation for the weights-based parameterization of a perceptron, for which a tiny perturbation of some parameter may result in a large change to the set of points that are mapped to output value 1. Thus in a sense the Chow parameters are a more robust parameterization.

1.1 Learning-Theoretic Background and Results

The related literature can be divided into three parts: some earlier papers that follow on from Chow's paper, work on boolean perceptron learning in general, and work on learning in the so-called "restricted focus of attention" setting.

Earlier work that followed on from [9] includes an algorithm by Kaszerman [14] for recovering a linear threshold function from its Chow parameters. The algorithm is iterative and somewhat related to the perceptron algorithm [17]; it does not have a good bound on the number of iterations and assumes exact values of the parameters are given. A paper of Winder [18] compares 7 functions (4 of which were proposed in previous papers) for rescaling Chow parameters to obtains weights for a linear-threshold function. None of these functions has perfect performance, and it is uncertain that any function exists from individual Chow parameters to good weights – it may be necessary to deal with them collectively rather than individually. A further paper by Winder [19] investigates the class of boolean functions that are uniquely defined by their Chow parameters, and shows among other things that it lies properly between the class of linear threshold functions and the class of monotonic functions.

There is much known about learning boolean perceptrons in various settings, for example irrelevant attributes [15], classification noise [6] and learning from a source of "helpful" examples [2]. Special cases include monomials, decision lists [16,12] and boolean threshold functions. Further knowledge on this topic occurs in the more general context of perceptrons over the real as opposed to the boolean domain. An example is that they may be PAC-learned in time

[1] If the coordinates of the sum of all satisfying vectors are rescaled down by the number of satisfying vectors, one obtains the average satisfying assignment, whose coordinates are the probabilities $Pr(y = 1 \mid x_i = 1)$. The Chow parameters are recovered by multiplying this average by $2^n \cdot Pr(y = 1)$.

polynomial in the dimension n and the PAC parameters ϵ and δ, using the VC dimension theory [7]. Chapter 24 of [1] and references therein is a good introduction to results on learning boolean perceptrons.

Restricted focus of attention (RFA) learning was introduced and developed in the papers [3,4,5]. The k-RFA setting (where k is a positive integer) allows the learner to see only a subset of size k of the input attributes of any training example. The usual assumption has been that the input distribution is known to be a product distribution (with no other information given about it). In [13] we studied in detail the problem of learning linear-threshold functions over the real domain in the 1-RFA setting, so that each example of input/output behavior of the target function, has only a single input component value, together with the binary value of the output, revealed to the learner. We showed that the input distribution (in [13], not necessarily a product distribution) needs to be at least partly known, and that the sample-size required for learning depends sensitively on the input distribution. We identified measures of "well-behavedness" of the input distribution and gave sample size bounds in terms of these measures.

This paper addresses the topic of 1-RFA learning of perceptrons where the input distribution is uniform over V, the vertices of the unit hypercube. This learning-theoretic characterization is equivalent because from [5] we have that a random sample of 1-RFA data is equivalent, in terms of the information it conveys, to approximations of the conditional probabilities $Pr(y = 1 \mid x_i = b)$, for $b \in \{0, 1\}$, together with the probability $Pr(y = 1)$, and these approximations have additive error inversely proportional to the sample size. "1-RFA data" means observations of the input/output behavior of the target perceptron in which only one out of the n input values (entry of input vector $\mathbf{x}$) in any training example is made available to the learner, and that entry is chosen by the learner without any other information about that example (equivalently for polynomial learnability, is chosen uniformly at random). The reason why this special case (for which bounds of [13] are inapplicable) is of particular interest is that the uniform distribution over V is the most interesting and widely studied input distribution from the perspective of computational learning theory. The question of whether this learning problem is solvable with polynomial time or sample size is previously discussed in [10] and [13]. Birkendorf et al [5] suggest the following rule: for $1 \leq i \leq n$ and $b \in \{0, 1\}$, let p_b^i be the conditional probability $Pr(y = 1 \mid x_i = b)$ and let $p = Pr(y = 1)$. Then take $\mathbf{x}$ to be a positive instance if $\frac{1}{n}\sum_{i=1}^{n} p_{x_i}^i > p$, otherwise label $\mathbf{x}$ as negative. It is left as an open problem whether the rule is valid.

The computational learning-theoretic result that we obtain is a mildly super-polynomial bound (of the order of $\log(\delta^{-1})(n/\epsilon)^{-\log\epsilon}$) on the sample complexity of learning a perceptron from 1-RFA data. This is a purely "information-theoretic" result; we do not have any algorithm whose guaranteed time complexity improves substantially on a brute-force approach.

1.2 Some Notation and Terminology

Let V be the input domain, *i.e.* the vertices of the unit hypercube, or 0/1-vectors.

Let F and G be two boolean perceptrons, where generally F will denote the target function and G some alternative function, such as a hypothesis returned by an algorithm. The *positive* (resp. *negative*) examples of a function are those that are mapped to 1 (resp. 0). Let $pos(F)$, $neg(F)$, $pos(G)$, $neg(G)$ denote the positive and negative examples of F and G. (So $pos(F) = F^{-1}(1)$, etc.) F and G divide V into 4 subsets defined as follows.

$$\begin{array}{ll} V_{00} = neg(F) \cap neg(G) & V_{01} = neg(F) \cap pos(G) \\ V_{10} = pos(F) \cap neg(G) & V_{11} = pos(F) \cap pos(G) \end{array}$$

For $R \subseteq \mathbf{R}^n$, let $m(R)$ be the number of elements of V that lie in R. Let $a(R)$ be the vector sum of elements of $V \cap R$. Let $\mu(R)$ denote the (unweighted) average of members of V that lie in the region R, so that $\mu(R) = a(R)/m(R)$, well-defined provided that $m(R) > 0$. For any boolean function f, let $\mu(f)$ be the (unweighted) average of its satisfying assignments. The region of disagreement of F and G is $V_{01} \cup V_{10}$; thus the disagreement rate between F and G, over the uniform distribution on V, is $(m(V_{01}) + m(V_{10}))/2^n$.

2 Geometric Results

In this section we give various geometric results about the vertices of the unit hypercube, which we use in section 3 to deduce the sample-complexity bound. We summarize the results of this section:

1. Lemma 1 gives a simple upper bound on the number of elements of V contained in a linear subspace, in terms of the dimension of that subspace.
2. Theorem 1 gives a bound on the bit complexity of the parameters of a hyperplane, in terms of the number of elements of V contained in that hyperplane (the more elements of V contained, the less bit complexity is needed for the parameters).
3. Theorem 2 uses theorem 1 to show that any hyperplane that "narrowly misses" a large fraction of V can be perturbed slightly so that it actually contains all those vertices. The resulting hyperplane does no longer "narrowly miss" any other vertices. More precisely, if a hyperplane comes within distance $2\alpha/n^2$ of a fraction α of the 2^n vertices, then all those $\alpha \cdot 2^n$ vertices lie on the perturbed hyperplane. That result is then used to show limits on the bit complexity of boolean perceptrons that satisfy certain conditions.
4. Theorem 3 derives a lower bound on the distance between $\mu(V_{01})$ and $\mu(V_{10})$ (the means of the two regions of disagreement between a pair of perceptrons) in terms of their disagreement rate $m(V_{01} \cup V_{10})/2^n$.

We generally assume that weight vectors of linear threshold functions are normalized, *i.e.* weights and thresholds are rescaled so that the weight vector is of length 1. By a *vertex* we mean a member of V, *i.e.* a 0/1-vector of length n.

Throughout, when we refer to subspaces, or spanning, or dimension, we mean in the affine sense, so that a "subspace" does not necessarily contain the origin, and a spanning set of S is a set of points in S such that any other point in S is expressible as the sum of one member of the spanning set plus a weighted sum of differences between pairs of points in the spanning set.

Lemma 1. *Any affine subspace S of $\mathbf{R}^n$ of affine dimension d contains at most 2^d elements of V.*

Proof. Proof by induction on d. It clearly holds for $d = 0$, when the subspace consists of a single point.

For $d > 0$ we consider 2 cases. Suppose some subcube of V of dimension d has all its 2^d points in S. Then S cannot contain any other points in V, since then S would have dimension $> d$.

Alternatively, we can divide V into 2 subcubes V_0 and V_1 such that each subcube contains some elements of S and in addition each subcube contains some non-elements of S. S restricted to the span of V_0 (similarly V_1) is a subspace of dimension $d-1$. The inductive hypothesis says that each of these intersections has at most 2^{d-1} points. $\diamondsuit$

The following theorem tells us that when a large fraction of vertices of the unit hypercube span a hyperplane, then the hyperplane must be defined by a linear equation with "simple" coefficients (low bit complexity). The subsequent corollary shows that when a large fraction of vertices span a lower-dimensional subspace, then it can be expressed as the intersection of a set of hyperplanes with simple coefficients. In what follows, logarithms are to the base 2.

Theorem 1. *Let S be a hyperplane of $\mathbf{R}^n$, and suppose that S contains a fraction α of the vertices of the unit hypercube. Assume that the vertices contained by S span S. Suppose that S is the set of points $\{\mathbf{x} : \mathbf{w}.\mathbf{x} = t\}$, where $\mathbf{w} = (w_1, \ldots, w_n)$, $w_1 = 1$ and $0 \leq w_i \leq 1$ for $i = 2, \ldots n$. Then the bit complexity of w_i for $i = 2, \ldots, n$ is at most $\lceil \log(1/\alpha) \rceil$. Hence all the w_i are integer multiples of some constant at least $\alpha/2$.*

Proof. We construct a linear system that must be satisfied by the weights $w_2, \ldots, w_n$, such that when we solve it (invert a matrix) the inverse does not contain numbers of excessive bit complexity.

We have a set $\mathcal{E}$ of $2^n \cdot \alpha$ distinct equations of the form $\mathbf{w}.\mathbf{x} = t$ where $\mathbf{x}$ is a $0/1$ vector (a vertex of the hypercube). By our assumption that vertices in S do in fact span S, we have that $\mathcal{E}$ is a linear system that specifies $\mathbf{w}$. Essentially, we want to make a careful choice of just n equations in $\mathcal{E}$ that specify $\mathbf{w}$ and also define a linear system that does not result in numbers with high bit complexity when it is solved. Observe that for two distinct vertices $\mathbf{x}$ and $\mathbf{x}'$ we have $\mathbf{w}.(\mathbf{x} - \mathbf{x}') = 0$, and if we let $\mathbf{w}^- = (w_2, \ldots w_n)$ then (since $w_1 = 1$) we can derive an equation of the form $\mathbf{z}.\mathbf{w}^- = k$ where $\mathbf{z} \in \{0, 1, -1\}^{n-1}$ and k is either 0 or 1. Let $\mathcal{F}$ be the set of all possible equations we can construct in this way.

The linear system we construct will be satisfied by a vector $\mathbf{w}^+$ whose entries $(w_1^+, \ldots, w_{n-1}^+)$ are a permutation of the weights $w_2, \ldots, w_n$, the entries of $\mathbf{w}^-$. The re-ordering of the weights results from the following procedure.

Procedure for Constructing the Linear System:
The following procedure is iterative and we show below that it can continue for at least $n - \lfloor \log(1/\alpha) \rfloor$ iterations. We describe the first three iterations before giving a general description of the k-th iteration.

- Iteration 1: Choose any two equations from $\mathcal{E}$ that differ in the coefficient of some weight w_i, $2 \leq i \leq n$ (which becomes w_1^+, the first weight of $\mathbf{w}^+$), take their difference as described above, and we get an equation (in $\mathcal{F}$) for which the coefficient of w_i (*i.e.* w_1^+) is 1 or -1.
- Iteration 2: Choose any two equations in $\mathcal{E}$ with the same coefficients of w_1^+, identify a weight where they differ, which becomes w_2^+, and their difference gives us a member of $\mathcal{F}$ whose coefficient of w_1^+ is 0 and whose coefficient of w_2^+ is 1 or -1.
- Iteration 3: Choose any two equations in $\mathcal{E}$ with the same coefficients of w_1^+ and w_2^+, identify a weight where they differ, which becomes w_3^+, and their difference gives us a member of $\mathcal{F}$ whose coefficients of w_1^+ and w_2^+ are 0 and whose coefficient of w_3^+ is 1 or -1.
- Iteration k: Choose any two members of $\mathcal{E}$ whose coefficients agree on $w_1^+, \ldots$ w_{k-1}^+, find a weight where they differ, which becomes w_k^+, deduce a member of $\mathcal{F}$ whose first $k-1$ coefficients are 0 and whose k-th coefficient is 1 or -1.

By the pigeon-hole principle, we claim we can continue with this procedure until k exceeds $n - \log(1/\alpha)$. At the k-th iteration there are 2^{k-1} possible vectors of coefficients of $w_1^+, \ldots, w_{k-1}^+$, and $2^n \cdot \alpha$ equations in $\mathcal{E}$ to choose from. Provided that $2^n \cdot \alpha > 2^{k-1}$ we can find a pair of members of $\mathcal{E}$ that agree on these coefficients. Since all members of $\mathcal{E}$ are distinct, they will differ on some other coefficient. The condition $1/\alpha < 2^{n+1-k}$ indicates that for k less than $n + 1 - \log(1/\alpha)$ we can continue.

When we can continue no longer, we supplement our set of $n - \lfloor \log(1/\alpha) \rfloor$ members of $\mathcal{F}$ by any other members of $\mathcal{F}$ that are linearly independent of them. We have constructed a linear system $A.\mathbf{w}^+ = \mathbf{v}$ where

1. A is an invertible $(0/1/-1)$-matrix
2. the submatrix of A that excludes the last $\lfloor \log(1/\alpha) \rfloor$ rows and columns, is upper triangular
3. $\mathbf{v} \in \{0, 1, -1\}^n$, *i.e.* $\mathbf{v}$ is a $(0/1/-1)$-vector.

Hence $\mathbf{w}^+ = A^{-1}\mathbf{v}$. We invert A by Gaussian elimination, identifying a set of linear operations on the rows of A which convert it to the identity matrix I, and then the application of the same operations to I gives A^{-1}. The operations will not create excessively large/small numbers when applied to I.

Procedure for Inverting the Matrix A

- We start by eliminating the non-zero entries of the upper triangle of the upper triangular submatrix we noted earlier (that is, rows and columns $1, \ldots, n - \lfloor \log(1/\alpha) \rfloor$ of A). This is done by adding or subtracting row $n - \lfloor \log(1/\alpha) \rfloor - 1$ from rows above so as to eliminate non-zero entries in column $n - \lfloor \log(1/\alpha) \rfloor - 1$, then doing the same for row $n - \lfloor \log(1/\alpha) \rfloor - 2$, and so on.
- We then eliminate the region below this submatrix by adding or subtracting copies of the first $n - \lfloor \log(1/\alpha) \rfloor$ rows to/from the bottom rows.
- Then we diagonalize the bottom-right hand submatrix of size $\lceil \log(1/\alpha) \rceil \times \lceil \log(1/\alpha) \rceil$, which may lead to entries of size $1/\alpha$ being created in the diagonal. Re-scale the bottom rows to make the diagonal entries equal to 1.
- Finally we eliminate the region above this bottom-right hand submatrix by adding or subtracting the bottom $\lceil \log(1/\alpha) \rceil$ rows to/from the rows above.

Applying these operations to the identity matrix leads to entries that differ by a factor of at most $2^{\lceil \log(1/\alpha) \rceil}$, hence the bit complexity of entries of A^{-1} is at most $\log(2/\alpha)$. $\diamondsuit$

We use theorem 1 to prove the following result.

Theorem 2. *Let $\alpha \in (0, 1)$, and let $\beta \leq 2\alpha/n^2$. Given any affine subspace of $\mathbf{R}^n$ whose β-neighborhood contains a fraction α of points on the unit hypercube, there exists an affine subspace which itself contains all those $2^n \cdot \alpha$ points.*

Proof. Let $V_S \subseteq V$ be the set of vertices within a β-neighborhood of S, where by our assumption, $|V_S| = 2^n \cdot \alpha$. We assume that S is a hyperplane – if it is of lower dimension we can choose some arbitrary hyperplane that contains it.

Let $S = \{\mathbf{x} : \mathbf{w}.\mathbf{x} = t\}$, where by rescaling we can choose $\|\mathbf{w}\| = 1$. For $\mathbf{x} \in V_S$, we have $\mathbf{w}.\mathbf{x} \in [t - \beta, t + \beta]$.

Define a new weight vector $\mathbf{w}'$ derived from $\mathbf{w}$ by taking each weight in $\mathbf{w}$ and rounding it off to the nearest integer multiple of β. Then products $\{\mathbf{w}'.\mathbf{x} : \mathbf{x} \in V_S\}$ can take n possible values. To see this, observe that the value of $\mathbf{w}'.\mathbf{x}$ must be an integer multiple of β, and the rounding error (absolute difference $|\mathbf{w}'.\mathbf{x} - \mathbf{w}.\mathbf{x}|$ *i.e.* $|\mathbf{w}'.\mathbf{x} - t|$) is at most $\beta n/2$. Let T be the set of these n values.

Let t' be the member of T which maximizes the number of vertices $\mathbf{x}$ satisfying $\mathbf{w}'.\mathbf{x} = t'$. Then there are at least $2^n \cdot \alpha/n$ vertices $\mathbf{x}$ of the unit hypercube that satisfy $\mathbf{w}'.\mathbf{x} = t'$. We will use this observation to prove that in fact there are no vertices $\mathbf{x} \in V$ for which $\mathbf{w}'.\mathbf{x}$ "narrowly misses" t', in particular this will show that no other element $t'' \in T$ with $t'' \neq t'$ satisfies $\mathbf{w}'.\mathbf{x} = t''$ for any vertex $\mathbf{x}$.

Let S' be a hyperplane containing all points $\mathbf{x}$ that satisfy $\mathbf{w}'.\mathbf{x} = t'$. Suppose that $S' \cap V$ spans the hyperplane S'. (Below we show how to handle the alternative.)

$|S' \cap V| \geq 2^n \cdot \alpha/n$. By theorem 1 we have that for all vertices $\mathbf{v} \in S'$, $\mathbf{w}'.\mathbf{v} - t'$ is an integer multiple of α/n. (Theorem 1 applies to weight vectors $\mathbf{w}$

whose maximum component is 1. They can be normalized by rescaling by a factor of at most n.) Now consider members of V_S that do not lie in S'. These points $\mathbf{v}$ satisfy $\mathbf{w}'.\mathbf{v} - t' \in [-n\beta/2, n\beta/2]$. We chose $\beta \leq 2\alpha/n^2$, and consequently for $\mathbf{v} \in V_S$ to satisfy these two properties, $\mathbf{w}'.\mathbf{v} - t' = 0$. Hence all elements of V_S lie in S.

Now suppose that $S' \cap V$ spans a proper subspace of S'. In this case we embed V in $\mathbf{R}^{n+1}$: let V be the vertices of the unit hypercube of $\mathbf{R}^{n+1}$ for which $x_{n+1} = 0$ and let V' be those for which $x_{n+1} = 1$. $S' \cap V$ spans a subspace of $\mathbf{R}^{n+1}$ of affine dimension d, where $d < n-1$. Choose $n-d$ vertices from V' in general position, and these vertices together with $S' \cap V$ span a hyperplane H of $\mathbf{R}^{n+1}$. Moreover any element of V is at least as close to H as it is to S'. The argument for the first case (where $S' \cap V$ spans S') can now be applied. ♢

The following lemma is used in theorem 3 below.

Lemma 2. *Given boolean perceptrons F and G with V_{01} and V_{10} as defined in section 1.2, suppose we have subspaces $S' \subset S \subseteq \mathbf{R}^n$ with $\dim(S') = dim(S) - 1$ where $S' \cap (V_{01} \cup V_{10})$ contains at least $2^n\alpha$ points, and $\mu(S' \cap V_{01})$ differs from $\mu(S' \cap V_{10})$ by L_2 distance d. Suppose also that S' divides S into 2 connected components such that on each side, F gives the same label to points on that side. Then $\mu(S \cap V_{01})$ differs from $\mu(S \cap V_{10})$ by L_2 distance $d(\alpha/2\sqrt{n})$.*

Proof. We have assumed a gap between the means of points in V_{01} and V_{10} that also belong to S', and we will upper-bound the extent to which points in V_{01} and V_{10} that also belong to $S \setminus S'$ can bring the overall averages together.

The general observation is that if the points in $(S \setminus S') \cap (V_{01} \cup V_{10})$ cause the overall means to come closer together, they do in the process displace those means away from S', due to the fact that points in $(S \setminus S') \cap (V_{01} \cup V_{10})$ must lie within distance $\sqrt(n)$ of any point in V, but also are at least a distance $\alpha/2$ from S', due to theorem 1. (This also uses the assumption that one side of $S \setminus S'$ contains only points from V_{01} but not V_{10} and the other contains points from V_{10} but not V_{01}.) ♢

Theorem 3. *Let F and G be boolean perceptrons that disagree on a fraction ϵ of the 2^n members of V. Then the Euclidean distance between $\mu(V_{01})$ and $\mu(V_{10})$ is at least $(\epsilon/n)^{O(\log(1/\epsilon))}$.*

Proof. By a *line* we mean a 1-dimensional affine subspace. If l is a line and S is a set of points, let $l(S)$ denote the set of points obtained by projecting elements of S onto their closest points on l.

Let l be a line normal to P_F, a hyperplane defining F.

Observe that members of $l(V_{01})$ are separated from members of $l(V_{10})$ by the point of intersection of l and P_F (which itself is $l(P_F)$).

Two cases:

Case 1: Suppose at least a fraction ϵ of the members of $V_{01} \cup V_{10}$ (*i.e.* at least $2^n\epsilon^2$ points altogether) have projections onto l that are more than ϵ/n^2 distant from $l(P_F)$. In this case we have

$$|\mu(V_{01}) - \mu(V_{10})| \geq \epsilon^2/n^2.$$

Case 2: in which more than a fraction $(1-\epsilon)$ of points in $V_{01} \cup V_{10}$ lie within distance ϵ/n^2 of $l(P_F)$.

In this case we apply theorem 2 to obtain a hyperplane P' that contains all but a fraction ϵ of points in $V_{01} \cup V_{10}$.

Choose an affine subspace of P' that separates members of V_{01} lying in P' from members of V_{10} lying in P'. Let $l' \subseteq P'$ be a line normal to that subspace.

Two cases (similar to before):

Case 2a: At least a fraction ϵ of the members of $(V_{01} \cup V_{10}) \cap P'$ have projections onto l' that are more than ϵ/n^2 distant from the boundary $l'(P')$. Then the distance between the means of points in P' is at least ϵ^2/n^2. All points in $V_{01} \cup V_{10}$ *not* in P' lie at least ϵ from P' by theorem 1 (coefficients of P' have a common factor approximately ϵ). We claim that the overall distance between $\mu(V_{01})$ and $\mu(V_{10})$ is at least $(\epsilon^2/n^2)(\epsilon(1-\epsilon)/2\sqrt{n})$. This claim follows using lemma 2.

Case 2b: Alternatively, all but a fraction ϵ of these points lie in some subspace of $P'' \subset P'$. We look in that subspace for a similar difference between means of members of V_{01} and members of V_{10} in P''. As before let $l'' \subseteq P''$ be a line constructed in a similar way to l'. Either we find a fraction ϵ of points $\mathbf{x}$ with $l''(\mathbf{x})$ more than ϵ/n^2 from the boundary between $V_{01} \cap P''$ and $V_{10} \cap P''$ or we continue by looking in a subspace of P'' that now contains at least a fraction $(1-\epsilon)^2$ of points in $V_{01} \cap V_{10}$. By lemma 1 this process only continues for $\log(\epsilon^{-1})$ iterations before subspaces do not have sufficient dimension to hold a fraction ϵ of elements of V. $\diamond$

3 Computational Learning-Theoretic Consequences

Recall that 1-RFA data refers to the special case of RFA learning where each training example has just a single input attribute revealed to the learner, together with the (binary) output value. In the case of boolean functions, a training example is essentially a member of $\{1,\ldots n\} \times \{0,1\} \times \{0,1\}$, the identity of one of the n attributes, together with its binary value, together with the binary value of the output. The identity of the observed attribute is assumed to be chosen by the learner, which as noted in [13] is equivalent (for the purpose of polynomial bounds) to the assumption that it is chosen at random.

We continue by using the preceding results to obtain a bound on learning boolean perceptrons in the 1-RFA setting. We first show how to determine (using 1-RFA data) which of any given pair of candidate hypotheses F and G that have a disagreement rate of ϵ, is the target function, using time and sample complexity $\log \delta(n/\epsilon)^{-\log \epsilon}$, where δ is the allowed probability that the learner's choice is incorrect. We then show how a computationally unbounded learner can select a good hypothesis from the entire set of boolean perceptrons, using sample size $\log \delta(n/\epsilon)^{-\log \epsilon}$, where δ is the probability that the hypothesis has error $> \epsilon$.

3.1 Distinguishing between Two Candidate Functions

Remark 1. Given any perceptron F we may estimate $Pr(F(\mathbf{x}) = 1)$ and $Pr(F(\mathbf{x}) = 1 \mid x_i = 1)$ within additive error ϵ and with uncertainty δ, in time polynomial in ϵ^{-1} and δ^{-1}.

Proof. This can be done by generating $poly(n, \epsilon^{-1}, \delta^{-1})$ elements $\mathbf{x}$ of V uniformly at random and taking empirical estimates of the relevant probabilities. $\diamondsuit$

It is worth noting that computing these quantities exactly is $\sharp P$-hard as it is the 0/1 knapsack problem [11]. The following fact is noted in [5], with regard to the problem of PAC-learning boolean perceptrons:

Remark 2. Learning from 1-RFA data with respect to the uniform distribution is equivalent to reconstructing a boolean function from empirical estimates of the components of its average satisfying assignment.

These two facts together with the geometric results of the previous section are used to solve the following learning problem: Given two perceptrons F and G, one of which is the target function, and which have a disagreement rate of ϵ, decide which of the two is the target function.

There are two cases that we consider: either the difference between $Pr(V_{01})$ and $Pr(V_{10})$ exceeds ϵ^2/n, or not. In the first case, assume that the difference is more than ϵ^2/n, and consequently $Pr(pos(F))$ and $Pr(pos(G))$ also differ by ϵ^2/n. A simple Chernoff bound analysis shows that a sample size of $O(\log(\delta^{-1}) \cdot \epsilon^2/n)$ is sufficient to distinguish F from G using the relative frequency of positive examples.

Now in the second case, we derive a lower bound on the distance between the means $\mu(pos(F))$ and $\mu(pos(G))$ (using the lower bound on the distance between $\mu(V_{01})$ and $\mu(V_{01})$ in conjunction with the upper bound of ϵ^2/n on the difference between $Pr(V_{10})$ and $Pr(V_{01})$.

We show that the distance between $\mu(V_{01})$ and $\mu(V_{10})$ is at least $\epsilon^{-1} \cdot (\epsilon/n)^{-\log\epsilon}$. This allows us to deduce the distance of $(\epsilon/n)^{-\log\epsilon}$ between $\mu(pos(F))$ and $\mu(pos(G))$ as follows.

$$\mu(pos(F)) = \lambda \cdot \mu(V_{11}) + (1 - \lambda)\mu(V_{10})$$

where $\lambda \geq \epsilon/2$. Similarly

$$\mu(pos(G)) = \lambda' \cdot \mu(V_{11}) + (1 - \lambda')\mu(V_{01})$$

where $\lambda' \geq \epsilon/2$. Hence

$$\mu(pos(F)) - \mu(pos(G)) = \lambda(\mu(V_{01}) - \mu(V_{01})) + (\lambda - \lambda')(\mu(V_{01}) - \mu(V_{11}).$$

By the assumption (of this second case) that V_{01} and V_{10} differ in size by at most a fraction ϵ^2/n elements, we have that $|\lambda - \lambda'| \leq \epsilon^2$. Hence

$$\mu(pos(F)) - \mu(pos(G)) \geq \epsilon(\mu(V_{01}) - \mu(V_{01})).$$

We now use theorem 3 to say that in this case, there is a difference between the means of V_{01} and V_{10} at least $(\epsilon/n)^{O(\log(1/\epsilon))}$, and hence a difference between the means of positive examples of the order of $(\epsilon/n)^{O(\log(1/\epsilon))}$, so that (in conjunction with remark 2) a sample size of $\log(\delta^{-1}) \cdot (n/\epsilon)^{O(\log(1/\epsilon))}$ is sufficient to identify (with probability $1-\delta$ of correctness) which of the two candidate means is the correct one.

3.2 Estimating a Target Function from the Set of All Possible Perceptrons

We have shown how to identify which of two given perceptrons is correct, using time and sample size of the order of $\log\delta(n/\epsilon)^{O(\log(1/\epsilon))}$. A computationally unbounded learner may identify (for target perceptron F) a hypothesis G as follows.

Obtain empirical estimates of the Chow parameters of F using a sample size of $O(\log\delta(n/\epsilon)^{\log(1/\epsilon)})$. Evaluate the Chow parameters of every boolean perceptron, and output any perceptron G whose Chow parameters are all within $(n/\epsilon)^{\log(1/\epsilon)}$ of the observed parameters.

With probability $1-\delta$, the observed Chow parameters differ from the correct Chow parameters of F by no more than the above margin of $(n/\epsilon)^{\log(1/\epsilon)}$. We have also shown that any G with a disagreement rate of $\geq \epsilon$ with F, must have Chow parameters that differ by more than this margin, so that any hypothesis that is eligible to be chosen according to our rule, does in fact have error less than ϵ.

3.3 Conclusions and Open Problems

The problem of PAC-learning a boolean perceptron from empirical estimates of its Chow parameters has been raised in various papers in computational learning theory. We have so far just shown a bound on sample complexity only (the problem of how to best select the right hypothesis given sufficient data having not been addressed), and that bound is still super-polynomial. The next step would appear to be to find a bound on the sample complexity that is polynomial in the parameters n, ϵ^{-1} and δ^{-1}. The geometrical results we have found may well assist with further progress.

References

1. M. Anthony and P.L. Bartlett (1999). *Neural Network Learning: Theoretical Foundations*, Cambridge University Press, Cambridge.
2. M. Anthony, G. Brightwell and J. Shawe-Taylor (1995). On Specifying Boolean Functions by Labelled Examples. *Discrete Applied Mathematics* **61**, pp. 1-25.
3. S. Ben-David and E. Dichterman (1998). Learning with Restricted Focus of Attention, *J. of Computer and System Sciences*, **56**(3), pp. 277-298. (earlier version in COLT'93)

4. S. Ben-David and E. Dichterman (1994). Learnability with restricted focus of attention guarantees noise-tolerance, *5th International Workshop on Algorithmic Learning Theory*, pp. 248-259.
5. A. Birkendorf, E. Dichterman, J. Jackson, N. Klasner and H.U. Simon (1998). On restricted-focus-of-attention learnability of Boolean functions, *Machine Learning*, **30**, 89-123. (earlier version in COLT'96)
6. A. Blum, A. Frieze, R. Kannan and S. Vempala (1998). A Polynomial-time Algorithm for Learning Noisy Linear Threshold Functions. *Algorithmica* **22**: pp. 35-52.
7. A. Blumer, A. Ehrenfeucht, D. Haussler and M.K. Warmuth (1989). Learnability and the Vapnik-Chervonenkis Dimension, J.ACM **36**, 929-965.
8. J. Bruck (1990). Harmonic analysis of polynomial threshold functions. *SIAM Journal of Discrete Mathematics*, **3** (2), 168-177.
9. C.K. Chow (1961). On the characterization of threshold functions. *Proc. Symp. on Switching Circuit Theory and Logical Design*, 34-38.
10. E. Dichterman (1998). Learning with Limited Visibility. *CDAM Research Reports Series, LSE-CDAM-98-01* 44pp.
11. M. E. Dyer, A. M. Frieze, R. Kannan, A. Kapoor, L. Perkovic and U. Vazirani (1993). A mildly exponential time algorithm for approximating the number of solutions to a multidimensional knapsack problem. *Combinatorics, Probability and Computing* **2**, 271-284.
12. T. Eiter, T. Ibaraki and K. Makino (1998). Decision Lists and Related Boolean Functions. *Institut Für Informatik JLU Giessen (IFIG) Research Reports 9804.*
13. P.W. Goldberg (1999). Learning Fixed-dimension Linear Thresholds from Fragmented Data. *Warwick CS dept. tech. report RR362*, Sept. 99, accepted for publication in *Information and Computation* as of Dec. 2000. A preliminary version is in Procs of the 1999 Conference on Computational Learning Theory, pp. 88-99 July 1999.
14. P. Kaszerman (1963). A geometric test-synthesis procedure for a threshold device. *Information and Control* **6**(4), 381-398.
15. N. Littlestone (1988). Learning Quickly When Irrelevant Attributes Abound: A New Linear-threshold Algorithm. *Machine Learning* **2**, pp. 285-318.
16. R. L. Rivest (1996). Learning Decision Lists. *Machine Learning* **2** pp. 229–246.
17. F. Rosenblatt (1962). *Principles of Neurodynamics.* Spartan Books, New York, 1962.
18. R.O. Winder (1969). Threshold Gate Approximations Based on Chow Parameters. *IEEE Transactions on Computers* **18**, pp. 372-5.
19. R.O. Winder (1971). Chow Parameters in Threshold Logic. *Journal of the ACM* **18**(2), pp. 265-89.

Adaptive Strategies and Regret Minimization in Arbitrarily Varying Markov Environments

Shie Mannor and Nahum Shimkin

Department of Electrical Engineering
Technion, Haifa 32000
Israel
{shie,shimkin}@{tx,ee}.technion.ac.il

Abstract. We consider the problem of maximizing the average reward in a controlled Markov environment, which also contains some arbitrarily varying elements. This problem is captured by a two-person stochastic game model involving the reward maximizing agent and a second player, which is free to use an arbitrary (non-stationary and unpredictable) control strategy. While the minimax value of the associated zero-sum game provides a guaranteed performance level, the fact that the second player's behavior is observed as the game unfolds opens up the opportunity to improve upon this minimax value if the second player is not playing a worst-case strategy. This basic idea has been formalized in the context of repeated matrix games by the classical notions of regret minimization with respect to the Bayes envelope, where an attainable performance goal is defined in terms of the empirical frequencies of the opponent's actions. This paper presents an extension of these ideas to problems with Markovian dynamics, under appropriate recurrence conditions. The Bayes envelope is first defined in a natural way in terms of the observed state action frequencies. As this envelope may not be attained in general, we define a proper convexification thereof as an attainable solution concept. In the specific case of single-controller games, where the opponent alone controls the state transitions, the Bayes envelope itself turns out to be convex and attainable. Some concrete examples are shown to fit in this framework.

1 Introduction

Stochastic games are a flexible model for conflict situations in which agents interact in a dynamic environment (cf. [6]). Building upon an extensive theoretical foundation and major application areas in economic analysis and operations research, there has been much recent interest in stochastic game models in the context of artificial intelligence and machine learning, see e.g. [3,12,16,18].

An average-reward stochastic game is used here to model the situation where a reward-maximizing agent is facing a controlled Markovian environment which also contains some arbitrarily varying elements. These elements, which are modelled by a second player, may stand for the actions of other, non-cooperative agents, or for non-stationary moves of nature. While these elements may be

D. Helmbold and B. Williamson (Eds.): COLT/EuroCOLT 2001, LNAI 2111, pp. 128–142, 2001.

unpredictable, they need not be hostile. Thus, the security level offered by the minimax value of the associated zero-sum game is in general too conservative. One is therefore lead to look for adaptive strategies, which allow the reward-maximizing agent to exceed the minimax value when the strategy of the second player, as revealed in time, is not adversarial. At the same time, such a strategy should ensure that the average reward never falls below the minimax value.

An elegant formulation of this goal is offered by the empirical Bayes envelope, that was introduced in the context repeated games with average reward. The Bayes envelope is the maximal reward rate a player could achieve had he known in advance the relative frequencies of the other players. It was originally established by Hannan ([9]) that the Bayes envelope may be asymptotically attained in such games. This result was subsequently proved by Blackwell [5] using his theory of approachability. Policies that attain the Bayes envelope are referred to as regret-minimizing. These classical results rely on a complete observation of the opponent's action in each stage game. Recently, these results have been extended to the case where complete observations of the opponents' actions are not available, but rather some related signals [2,7,19].

In this paper we seek to extend the regret minimization framework to stochastic games. The empirical frequencies of the opponent are now replaced by the state action frequencies, and the empirical Bayes envelope is defined in terms of these frequencies. As the average reward presented by this envelope is not attainable in general, we define a convexification of this envelope as our main solution concept, and show that it is both attainable and provides appropriate performance guarantees. Our basic tool of analysis in an extension of Blackwell's Approachability theory to stochastic games.

A specific case of interest is the single-controller game, where the second player alone determines the state transitions. It is shown that in this case the Bayes envelope itself is convex, hence attainable. Some applications of this model will be briefly discussed, including prediction with expert advice and the k-th order Bayes envelope.

The paper is organized as follows. Section 2 presents the stochastic game model. Section 3 recalls the basic results from the theory of approachability that are required in the ensuing analysis. In Section 4 we introduce the empirical Bayes envelope for stochastic games, and establish its basic properties. Section 5 considers the single-controller case. Some concluding remarks are drawn in Section 6. The appendix contains the technical proofs of the various results in this paper.

2 The Game Model

We consider a two-person stochastic game with finite state and action spaces. We refer to the players as P1 (the regret-minimizing player) and P2 (the opponent, or arbitrary player). Let $\mathcal{S}$ denote the state space, and let $\mathcal{A}$ and $\mathcal{B}$ denote the action spaces for P1 and P2, respectively. At each time instant $n = 0, 1, \ldots$, both players observe the current state $s_n \in S$, and then simultaneously choose their actions $a_n \in \mathcal{A}$ and $b_n \in \mathcal{B}$. As a result P1 receives a reward $r_n = r(s_n, a_n, b_n)$, where r is a given reward function, and the next state is chosen according to the probability vector $P(\cdot|s_n, a_n, b_n)$ over S, where P is a the state transition kernel. It is assumed that both players observe and recall all actions and states as they occur. A strategy $\sigma_1 \in \Sigma_1$ for P1 is a mapping from all possible histories to the mixed action Δ^A, where Δ^A is the set of all probability measures over $\mathcal{A}$. Similarly, a strategy $\sigma_2 \in \Sigma_2$ for P2 is a mapping from all possible histories to the mixed action Δ^B. A strategy of either player is *stationary* if the mixed action it prescribes at any time n depends only on current state s_n. The set of stationary strategies of P1 (resp. P2) is denoted by F (resp. G). Let $P^s_{\sigma_1,\sigma_2}$ denote the probability measure induced on the sequence of states and actions by the strategy pair σ_1 and σ_2 and initial state $s_0 = s$, and let $E^s_{\sigma_1,\sigma_2}$ denote the corresponding expectation operator. The n-stage average reward is given by $\hat{r}_n = \frac{1}{n}\sum_{t=0}^{n-1} r_t$. P1's general goal is to maximize the long-term average reward. This will be made precise in Section 4.

We shall assume throughout that the following recurrence condition holds. Recall that a state s is recurrent in a Markov process if a return to that state is guaranteed with probability 1 in finite time (e.g. [6]).

Assumption 1 *There exists a state $s^* \in \mathcal{S}$ that is recurrent under any pair (f, g) of stationary non-randomized strategies.*

This assumption is usually straightforward to verify by inspecting the state transition structure. The results of this paper still hold if the assumption is considerably relaxed, see [13] for details.

3 Approachability for Stochastic Games

We briefly recall here some results from approachability theory that will be needed in the sequel. As these results are only used in the proof of Theorem 3, this section may be skipped without loss of continuity.

A theory of approachability for repeated matrix games with vector-valued payoffs was introduced by Blackwell in [4]. It has since found various uses in game theory and related applications; see, e.g., [8,10,11,21] and the recent special issue [1]. An extension to stochastic games was presented in [20], under Assumption 1. Further results that relax this recurrence requirement can be found in [13].

Consider the stochastic game model as above, except that the scalar reward function $r = r(s, a, b)$ is replaced by a vector-valued reward $m = m(s, a, b)$ in $\mathbb{R}^k$. Let $m_n = m(s_n, a_n, b_n)$ and $\hat{m}_n = \frac{1}{n}\sum_{t=0}^{n-1} m_t$. In the following definition of an approachable set, $d(\cdot,\cdot)$ denotes the Euclidean point-to-set distance in $\mathbb{R}^k$.

Definition 1. *A set $B \subseteq \mathbb{R}^k$ is* approachable *by P1 from state s if there exists a B-*approaching *strategy σ_1^* of P1 such that*

$$d(\hat{m}_n, B) \to 0 \quad P^s_{\sigma_1^*,\sigma_2}\text{-a.s.,} \quad \text{for every } \sigma_2 \in \Sigma_2$$

Furthermore, the convergence rate is required to be uniform over all policies $\sigma_2 \in \Sigma_2$ of P2.

A strategy of P1 that satisfies this definition is termed *B-approaching.* Such a strategy ensures that the average reward vector $\hat{m}_n$ converges to the set B, irrespective of P2's strategy.

To present conditions for approachability, we consider some related games with scalar rewards. Given a unit vector $u \in \mathbb{R}^k$, the u-projected stochastic game $\Gamma(u)$ is defined similarly to the game model in interest, but with the scalar reward function $r^u = m \cdot u$ ($\cdot$ is inner product in $\mathbb{R}^k$). We consider this stochastic game as average-reward zero-sum game, with P1 the maximizer. Recall that under Assumption 1 the (minimax) value of this game exists and is independent of the initial state ([15]); denote this value by $\mathrm{v}\Gamma(u)$. Furthermore, under that assumption both players posses optimal (saddle point) strategies which are stationary.

The next theorem characterizes convex approachable sets, and constructs an approaching strategy. We note that a similar condition is *sufficient* for general sets, however this will not be required here.

Theorem 1 ([20]). *Let Assumption 1 hold. Let B be a convex set in $\mathbb{R}^k$.*

(i) B is approachable if and only if $\mathrm{v}\Gamma(u) \geq \inf_{y \in B}(y \cdot u)$ for every unit vector $u \in \mathbb{R}^k$.

(ii) If B is approachable, an approaching strategy for P1 is given as follows: Whenever the reference state s^* is hit, namely $s_n = s^*$, inspect the average reward vector $\hat{m}_n$. If $\hat{m}_n \notin B$, then play an optimal strategy in the game $\Gamma(u_n)$ until the next time s^* is hit, where u_n is the unit vector that points from m_n in the direction of the shortest distance to B. Otherwise, if $\hat{m}_n \in B$, play arbitrarily.

This result is based on the geometric idea of "steering" the average reward vector towards the required set B. A dual characterization may be given (for convex sets only), which can be considered a generalization of the minimax theorem to vector-valued games ([4]). To state this condition, let

$$M(f, g) = \lim_{n \to \infty} E^s_{f,g}(\frac{1}{n} \sum_{t=0}^{n-1} m_t) \tag{1}$$

denote the long-term average reward vector under a pair of *stationary* policies $f \in F$ and $g \in G$. Note that under Assumption 1 this limit is well defined and does not depend on the initial state. Finally, for any $g \in G$ define the set $M(F, g) \stackrel{\triangle}{=} \{M(f, g) : f \in F\} \subset \mathbb{R}^k$, which is the (closed convex) set of average reward vectors that are achievable by P1 against g.

Theorem 2 ([20]). *Let Assumption 1 hold, and let B be a closed convex set in $\mathbb{R}^k$. Then B is approachable if and only if $M(F, g) \cap B \neq \emptyset$ for every stationary strategy $g \in G$.*

The necessity of this condition is evident, as P2 can prevent B from being approached simply by maintaining the stationary strategy g that violates this condition.

4 The Empirical Bayes Envelope for Stochastic Games

In this section we define the empirical Bayes envelope for stochastic games and analyze its properties. To motivate the proposed approach we first consider the standard definitions for repeated matrix games.

A repeated matrix game may be viewed as a single-state stochastic game. Note that stationary policies in this game coincide with mixed actions in the one-shot matrix game. Omitting the state symbol but retaining all other notation, let

$$g_n(b) = \frac{1}{n}\sum_{t=0}^{n-1} 1\{b_t = b\}$$

denote the n-step relative frequency of P2's action b, and let $g_n \in \Delta^B$ be the corresponding frequency vector. Now,

$$r^*(g) = \max_{f\in\Delta^A} r(f,g) \triangleq \max_{f\in\Delta^A} \sum_{a,b} f(a)g(b)r(a,b)$$

is the expected reward that P1 could secure in the one-shot matrix game had he known in advance that P2's mixed action is g; $r^*(\cdot)$ defines the *Bayes envelope* of the matrix game. Equivalently, $r^*(g_n)$ is the best n-stage average reward that P1 could secure by playing a *stationary* policy f. A strategy σ_1 of P1 is said to be *regret minimizing* (or to attain the Bayes envelope) if it guarantees that, in the long run, the average reward will be as high as the current Bayes envelope; that is $\liminf_{n\to\infty}(\hat{r}_n - r^*(g_n)) \geq 0$ (a.s.) for *any* strategy of P2.

Obviously, if $P2$ is restricted to stationary strategies, then the Bayes envelope is readily attainable: here g_n is a consistent estimate of P2's stationary strategy, and P1 can simply choose the best reply to $\hat{g}_n$ at each stage. However, when P2 is non-stationary this simple best-response strategy easily fails and even lead to average reward that falls short of the minimax value of the game. The point is, then, that the Bayes envelope may be achieved without any restriction on the opponent's strategy, save for causality.

Returning to the stochastic game problem, we will again use the observations (which now include both states and actions) to form an estimated stationary strategy g_n of P2. Denote by $\pi_n(s,b)$ the empirical frequency of the state action pair by time n, namely

$$\pi_n(s,b) = \frac{1}{n}\sum_{t=0}^{n-1} 1\{s_t = s, b_t = b\}\,,$$

and by $\pi_n \in \Delta^{SB}$ the corresponding vector of state action frequencies.

Given $\pi_n = \pi$, and assuming for the moment that $\pi(s) \triangleq \sum_b \pi(s,b) \neq 0$ for all s, the relative frequency of P2's action b at state s is defined by

$$g(\pi)(b|s) \triangleq \frac{\pi(s,b)}{\pi(s)}, \tag{2}$$

intuitively, $g(\pi)$ may be viewed as an estimate for a stationary strategy of P2. A natural definition for the Bayes envelope r^* in terms of the observed frequencies vector π is then

$$r^*(\pi) = \max_{f \in F} r(f, g(\pi))$$

where $r(f,g)$ is the expected average reward of the two stationary strategies f and g. Note that $r(f,g)$ is well defined under Assumption 1 and does not depend on the reference state. Thus, $r^*(\pi)$ is the best-response average reward for P1, given the stationary strategy $g(\pi)$ of P2.

When $\pi(s) = 0$ for some state s, there is no data available for estimating P2's strategy at this state. In that case we modify the last definitions by considering the set of all possible strategies that are consistent with π, that is:

$$G(\pi) = \{g \in G : \pi(s)g(b|s) = \pi(s,b)\,, \ \ \forall (s,b) \in \mathcal{S} \times \mathcal{B}\}\,. \tag{3}$$

$G(\pi)$ is a singleton and coincides with $g(\pi)$ as defined above when every state has been visited, and in any case is a convex and closed set. By considering the worst-case over all possible strategies in $G(\pi)$, the Bayes envelope (BE) can now be defined in general as:

$$r^*(\pi) = \max_{f \in F} \min_{g \in G(\pi)} r(f,g)\,. \tag{4}$$

It is obvious that $r^*(\pi)$ is never below the minimax value of the game, since the minimum in (4) is over a subset of G. It is strictly above the value if $G(\pi)$ does not contain an optimal strategy for P2. Note that r^* reduces to its definition for repeated matrix games when the state space is a singleton.

We can make a first attempt at defining a possible goal for regret minimization.

Definition 2. *The Bayes envelope r^* is* weakly attainable *by P1 if there exists a strategy σ_1 of P1 such that*

$$\liminf_{n \to \infty} (\hat{r}_n - r^*(\pi_n)) \geq 0 \quad (a.s.)$$

for every strategy $\sigma_2 \in \Sigma_2$ of P2 and every initial state s. r^* is attainable *if the convergence rate is uniform in σ_2 and s, namely that for any $\epsilon > 0$,*

$$\sup_{\sigma_2,\, s} P\left\{ \inf_{t \geq n} (\hat{r}_t - r^*(\pi_t)) < -\epsilon \right\} \longrightarrow 0 \quad \text{as } n \to \infty\,.$$

Unfortunately the envelope BE just defined need not be attainable (or even weakly attainable); counter-examples may be found in [13,14]. The problem may be attributed to non-convexity of r^* in its variable π. We shall therefore consider a modified definition, which presents a less ambitious yet attainable goal.

The *Convex Bayes Envelope (CBE)*, which we denote by $r^c(\pi)$, is defined as the lower convex hull of $r^*(\pi)$, where both are viewed as functions over $\pi \in \Delta^{SB}$.

Attainability of the CBE may be defined similarly to that of the BE. We can now state our main result concerning this envelope.

Theorem 3. *Suppose Assumption 1 holds. Then the CBE, r^c, is attainable by P1.*

Before presenting the proof, we mention some continuity properties of the above envelopes. The proof of these properties may be found in [13].

Proposition 1. *r^c is continuous on its entire domain.*

Proof of Theorem 3: The proof relies on the approachability results quoted above. In order to fit in this framework, we introduce the following vector-valued reward function for the stochastic game. Define the $(1+SB)$ dimensional reward vector $m = (r, m_\pi) \in \mathbb{R} \times \Delta^{SB}$, where r coincides with the actual (scalar) reward of the game. m_π is a vector indexed by the state action pairs (s, b), with $m_\pi(s, a, b)$ a unit vector with 1 at the entry corresponding to (s, b) and 0 at all others. Thus, the average reward vector $\hat{m}_n = \frac{1}{n}\sum_{t=0}^{n-1} m_t$ is given by $\hat{m}_n = (\hat{r}_n, \pi_n)$, namely the average scalar reward followed by the vector of state action frequencies. For a pair of stationary strategies f of P1 and g of P2 we denote the average reward vector by $m(f, g)$.

We now claim that attainability of the CBE, r^c, is equivalent to approachability of the following set B_{CBE} with respect to the vector reward m:

$$B_{CBE} = \{(r, \pi) : r \geq r^c(\pi)\} \subset R \times \Delta^{SB}. \tag{5}$$

Indeed, approachability requires that the Euclidean distance of $\hat{m}_m = (\hat{r}_n, \pi_n)$ from B_{CBE} converges to zero, while attainability requires the difference $\hat{r}_n - r^c(\pi_n)$ in the scalar reward coordinate to become non-negative. It is easily seen from these respective definitions that attainability implies approachability, while the reverse implication follows by adding the continuity of r^c, as per Proposition 1.

It remains to show that B_{CBE} is approachable by P1. Since r^c is convex, it follows that B_{CBE} (its epigraph) is a convex set. By Theorem 2, it suffices to prove that $M(F, g) \cap CBE \neq \emptyset$ for every $g \in G$. Fix $g^* \in G$. In the original scalar game P1 has a best-response stationary (deterministic) strategy $f^* \in F$ against g^*. Consider the state action frequency π that is the invariant measure corresponding to f^* and g^*. We now show that the point $m^* \triangleq (r(f^*, g^*), \pi) \in M(F, g^*)$ is in B_{CBE}. In fact we will show that $r(f^*, g^*) \geq r^*(\pi)$, and since $r^* \geq r^c$ by definition of the latter, the required inclusion follows. By (3) and the definition of π, $g^* \in G(\pi)$. The reward $r^*(\pi)$ thus satisfies

$$r^*(\pi) = \max_{f \in F} \min_{g \in G(\pi)} r(f, g) \leq \max_{f \in F} r(f, g^*) = r(f^*, g^*) \tag{6}$$

which concludes the argument. □

We now turn to consider the performance guarantees that are provided to P1 by attaining the CBE, r^c. Since $r^*(\pi) \geq \mathrm{v}$ (where v is the min-max value of the game), the same it obviously true for r^c as the lower convex hull of r^*. Thus, the guaranteed average reward is never below the value. We would like to show that the reward exceeds the value when the when the relative frequencies of P2's actions deviate from a worst-case policy. We shall establish that for the class of *irreducible* stochastic games. Recall that a stochastic game is irreducible if all states are recurrent under every pair of (deterministic) stationary strategies. In particular, if Π_0 is the set of feasible limiting state action frequencies, then $\pi(s) > 0$ for every s and $\pi \in \Pi_0$. It follows that each feasible $\pi \in \Pi_0$ induces a single stationary strategy $g(\pi)$, according to (2).

Proposition 2. *Suppose the game is irreducible. Let G^* denote the set of stationary min-max optimal strategies for P2. Then*

(i) $r^c(\pi) > \mathrm{v}$ *for any* $\pi \in \Pi_0$ *such that* $g(\pi) \notin G^*$.
(ii) Moreover, for any $g \notin G^*$, *let* $\Pi(g) = \{\pi \in \Pi_0 : g(\pi) = g\}$ *denote the collection of state action frequency vectors that induce* g. *Then* $\tilde{r}(g) \stackrel{\triangle}{=} \inf_{\pi \in \Pi(g)} r^c(\pi) > \mathrm{v}$.

The proof of this claim is provided in the appendix.

5 Single Controller Games

In this section we consider the special case in which P1 does not affect the state transitions, that is $P(s'|s,a,b) = P(s'|s,b)$. The resulting model can be considered as a sequence of matrix games where the next game to be played is determined only by P2's action. Such a model have been termed a "single controller games" ([6]), since only one of the players controls the state transitions. As it turns out, the Bayes envelope r^* itself is convex, hence attainable by P1. We first show how this follows from our general framework. We then establish this result under weaker assumptions by partitioning the stochastic game into a sequence of interleaved repeated matrix games. Finally, we briefly mention two applications that fall into this framework - prediction with expert advice and the k-th order Bayes envelope for repeated matrix games.

Proposition 3. *Let Assumption 1 hold. Suppose that P1 does not effect the state transitions, i.e.* $P(s'|s,a,b) = P(s'|s,b)$. *Then BE is convex, hence attainable by P1.*

Proof. Under the assumption that $P(s'|s,a,b) = P(s'|s,b)$, the stochastic game dynamics reduces to that of a Markov decision process with a single decision maker. Let $\Pi_0 \subset \Delta^{SB}$ be the set of possible state action frequencies for P2. It is well known (e.g. [17, Theorem 8.9.4]) that Π_0 is a convex set. Since only P2 affects the transition dynamics, then for a given π each $g \in G(\pi)$ induces the same state action frequency for every $f \in F$. Recall that the reward $r(f,g)$

can be written as the sum: $r(f,g) = \sum_{s,a,b} \pi(s,b) f(a|s) r(s,a,b)$, where $f(a|s)$ is the probability of playing action a at state s under the stationary strategy f. It follows that the Bayes reward $r^*(\pi)$ as defined in (4) reduces to: $r^*(\pi) = \max_{f \in F} \sum_{s,a,b} \pi(s,b) f(a|s) r(s,a,b)$. This implies that BE is in fact a convex since it is the maximum of linear functions. Since BE is convex it equals CBE and we can use Theorem 3 to conclude that BE is attainable. □

An alternative method to attain BE which does not rely on Assumption 1 can be devised. The idea is to take advantage of the fact that the single controller game can be effectively partitioned into a set of repeated matrix games, each corresponding to a single state. Let us re-define $r^*(\pi)$ (and BE) so that it is well defined without any assumptions on the game dynamics:

$$r^*(\pi) \triangleq \max_{f \in F} \sum_{s,a,b} \pi(s,b) f(a|s) r(s,a,b) \,. \tag{7}$$

If Assumption 1 holds, then for single controller games the original definition of r^* in (4) equals the one of (7), as shown in the proof of Proposition 3. The algorithm used to attain BE is to play a regret minimizing strategy (such as [7]) for every state separately (considering only the rewards that are received at that state). The next theorem shows that this algorithm attains r^*.

Theorem 4. *Assume that P1 does not affect the state transitions and that P1 plays a regret minimizing strategy in every state separately. Then BE is attained.*

We note that results that are related to the convergence rate may be developed, these results depend on the properties of the specific regret minimizing strategy which is employed per state. For example, if the scheme of [7] is used, then it can be shown that $r^*(\pi_t) - \hat{r}_t \leq Ct^{-1/3}$ (a.s.).

We now provide two examples for applications of single controller games, both examples are discussed in detail in [13].

a. Prediction with expert advice. In this problem (e.g. [22]) a single decision maker is repeatedly predicting the next outcome of an unknown channel. The decision maker is given advice from a finite number of experts before each prediction. The decision maker's goal is to have his long term average performance as good as the best expert. This problem can be formulated as a single controller stochastic game which satisfies our assumptions and therefore regret minimizing strategies exist. No assumptions are made regarding the experts and the channel - they may collaborate and for convenience are unified as a single player. We provide the details in the appendix for completion.

Proposition 4. *There exists a strategy that guarantees that the reward rate is not lower than the best expert, almost surely.*

A noted feature of the proof method (see the appendix) is the ability to easily generalize to other games with similar structure, in which only P2 (experts and channel) determine a state of nature. For example, one may consider a case in which if a certain letter appears in the channel then the stakes of the next stage game are doubled. Since in this case as well, the state action frequencies are determined only by P2, BE is attainable by P1.

b. The k-order Bayes envelope for matrix games: The standard Bayes envelope for matrix games uses the relative frequencies of the opponent's actions to form the "best response" performance envelope. An immediate refinement would be to define the required performance on the basis of the relative frequencies of k-tuples of the opponent's action. Obviously this would lead to a higher improved performance goal, especially if there are significant correlations in the opponent's action sequence. For example, in a sequential prediction problem, the k-th order Bayes envelope would be equivalent to the best k-th order Markovian predictor for the sequence. Now, since subsequent action k-tuples only differ in one symbol, they don't fall in the standard repeated matrix game framework, but rather in the single-controlled framework of this section. Application of our results show that indeed the k-th order BE is attainable.

6 Concluding Remarks

The goal of this paper has been to present adaptive strategies that improve upon the minimax value when the opponent deviates from a worst-case behavior. We have presented an approach to this problem that relies on the state action frequencies for formulating an achievable goal, namely the Convex Bayes Envelope. Let us briefly outline a few issues that need further consideration in this regard.

Existence of strategies which attain the CBE has been established using results from Approachability theory. While this approach is constructive, as it stands, it involves some complex geometric calculations which have not been explicated. In particular, this concerns the steering directions which are at the heart of approaching strategies. It turns out that these geometric quantities can be given an explicit analytical form for CBE. The details of this construction will be presented elsewhere.

While CBE presents performance guarantees against general strategies of the opponent, it may fail to obtain the best-response reward even when the opponent in effect employs a stationary strategy. This best-response property was essentially lost through the convexification of the basic Bayes envelope in the empirical frequencies space, which was necessary since the latter is not attainable in general. It thus seems that to retain the best-response property one must look for other solution concepts that do not rely on state action frequencies alone. Some feasible alternatives in this vein have been outlined in [13], based on ideas from [7]. However, these initial schemes are extremely complex and slow as they operate in the strategy space. Additional research is required.

Returning to the framework of this paper, the CBE need not be the least conservative attainable envelope in the space of state action frequencies. The construction of performance envelopes that are optimal in some sense is of obvious interest. Additional topics for investigation include other applications of the theory to specific problems, and the incorporation of these ideas in on-line learning algorithms in the style of Reinforcement Learning.

Acknowledgement

This research was supported by the fund for the promotion of research at the Technion.

References

1. Special issue on learning in games. *Games and Economic Behavior*, 29(1), November 1999.
2. P. Auer, N. Cesa-Bianchi, Y. Freund, and R. E. Schapire. Gambling in a rigged casino: The adversarial multi armed bandit problem. In *Proc. 36th Annual Symposium on Foundations of Computer Science*, pages 322–331. IEEE Computer Society Press, 1995.
3. D.P. Bertsekas and J.N. Tsitsiklis. *Neuro-Dynamic Programming.* Athena Scientific, 1995.
4. D. Blackwell. An analog of the minimax theorem for vector payoffs. *Pacific J. Math.*, 6(1):1–8, 1956.
5. D. Blackwell. Controlled random walks. In *Proc. International Congress of Mathematicians, 1954*, volume III, pages 336–338. North-Holland, 1956.
6. J. Filar and K. Vrieze. *Competitive Markov Decision Processes.* Springer Verlag, 1996.
7. Y. Freund and R. Schapire. Adaptive game playing using multiplicative weights. *Games and Economic Behavior*, 29:79–103, November 1999.
8. D. Fudenberg and D. Levine. Universal consistency and cautious fictitious play. *Journal of Economic Dynamic and Control*, 19:1065–1990, 1995.
9. J. Hannan. Approximation to bayes risk in repeated play. In M. Dresher, A. W. Tucker, and P. Wolde, editors, *Contribution to The Theory of Games, III*, pages 97–139. Princeton University Press, 1957.
10. S. Hart and A. Mas-Colell. A simple adaptive procedure leading to correlated equilibrium. DP 166, The Hebrew University of Jerusalem, Center for Rationality, 1998.
11. E. Lehrer. Approachability in infinite dimensional spaces and an application: A universal algorithm for generating extended normal numbers. Preprint, May 1998.
12. M.L. Littman. Markov games as a framework for multi-agent reinforcement learning. In Morgan Kaufman, editor, *Eleventh International Conference on Machine Learning*, pages 157–163, 1994.
13. S. Mannor and N. Shimkin. The empirical bayes envelope approach to regret minimization in stochastic games. Technical report EE- 1262, Faculty of Electrical Engineering, Technion, Israel, October 2000. available from: http://tiger.technion.ac.il/~shie/Public/drmOct23techreport.ps.gz.
14. S. Mannor and N. Shimkin. Regret minimization in signal space for repeated matrix games with partial observations. Technical report EE- 1242, Faculty of Electrical Engineering, Technion, Israel, March 2000. available from: http://tiger.technion.ac.il/~shie/Public/beMar16.ps.gz.
15. T. Parthasarathy and M. Stern. Markov games - a survey. *Differential Games and Control Theory*, 1977.
16. S.D. Patek. *Stochastic Shortest Path Games.* PhD thesis, LIDS MIT, January 1997.
17. M. Puterman. *Markov Decision Processes.* Wiley-Interscience, 1994.

18. E. Rasmunsen. *Games and Information : An Introduction to Game Theory.* Blackwell, 1994.
19. A. Rustichini. Minimizing regret: the general case. *Games and Economic Behavior*, 29:224–243, November 1999.
20. N. Shimkin and A. Shwartz. Guaranteed performance regions in markovian systems with competing decision makers. *IEEE Trans. on Automatic Control*, 38(1):84–95, January 1993.
21. X. Spiant. An approachability condition for general sets. Technical Report 496, Ecole Polytechnique, Paris, 1999.
22. V. Vovk. A game of prediction with experts advice. *Journal of Computer and Systems Sciences*, 56(2):153–173, April 1998.

A Proof of Proposition 2

The proof relies on the structure of the set G^* of maximin optimal strategies for P2 under the irreducibility assumption. We first show that G^* is a Cartesian product of optimal (convex) sets of actions at each state. From [16, Proposition 5.1] we know that there is a unique (up to an additive constant) $w^* \in \mathbb{R}^S$ such that $\forall s \in \mathcal{S}$

$$\min_{g\in G}\max_{f\in F}\Big(\sum_a\sum_b f(a|s)g(b|s)r(s,a,b) + \sum_a\sum_b\sum_{s'} P(s'|s,a,b)w^*(s')\Big) = w^*(s) + \mathrm{v}\,, \tag{8}$$

where v is the value of the game. We now apply [6, Lemma 5.3.1] twice. First, note that the assumptions of Lemma 5.3.1 holds since the game is irreducible. We claim that $g \in G^*$ if and only if for every s the mixed action $\{g(s,\cdot)\}$ is in the set $G^*(s)$ of optimal strategies in the matrix game with the following reward for actions a, b:

$$r_{ab}(s) = \sum_a\sum_b r(s,a,b) + \sum_{s'=1}^{S} p(s'|s,a,b)w^*(s')\,. \tag{9}$$

Suppose g is optimal in every such game. Then from part (iii) of Lemma 5.3.1, for every $f \in F$ we have that $r(f,g) \le \mathrm{v}$, so that g is optimal. Suppose that g is not optimal for a matrix game that is induced by some state s'. There is a strategy for P1, f^* that promises a higher reward than the value of the game defined in (9) for P1. Using the other direction of part (iii) of Lemma 5.3.1 (for P1) we have that $r(f^*,g) \ge \mathrm{v}$, but from part (iv) of Lemma 5.3.1 we get that $r(f,g) > \mathrm{v}$ since equality does not hold for all states. As a result the set G^* is a Cartesian product of the optimal strategy sets at each state, namely $G^* = \bigotimes_s G^*(s)$. Furthermore each set $G^*(s)$ is convex, which follows from the well known fact that for a zero sum matrix game the set of optimal strategies is convex.

Suppose $g \notin G^*$ and let $(r,\pi) \in B_{CBE}$ (B_{CBE} is defined in (5)) such that $g(\pi) = g$. Since $g \notin G^*$, then $r^*(\pi) > \mathrm{v}$. Since for any point in BE the reward is not less than the value we have that if $(\mathrm{v}, \pi) \in B_{CBE}$ then there exist at most k ($k \leq SB+1$) points in BE, $\{(\mathrm{v}, \pi_i)\}_{i=1}^k$ such that $g(\pi_i) \in G^*$ and for some $0 < \alpha_i < 1$ we have that $\pi = \sum_{i=1}^k \alpha_i \pi_i$. It can be verified by trivial algebra that if $\pi = \sum_{i=1}^k \alpha_i \pi_i$ then $\forall s$ such that $\pi(s) > 0$ we have that there exists β_i such that $0 \leq \beta_i \leq 1$, $\sum_{i=1}^k \beta_i = 1$ and $\forall b$:

$$g(\pi)(b|s) = \sum_{i=1}^{k} \beta_i g(\pi_i)(b|s) \,,$$

specifically $\beta_i = \frac{\alpha_i \pi_i(s)}{\sum_{i=1}^k \alpha_i \pi_i(s)}$. The result follows since G^* is a Cartesian product and if $g(\pi_i)$ belong to G^* so does any strategy in the SB dimensional box between them.

The second part of the Proposition follows immediately from the first part and by noting that for an irreducible game $G(\pi)$ contains a single element. □

B Proof of Proposition 4

Let us define the stochastic game between the decision maker (P1) and the experts and channel (P2). The game is played in two phases for each prediction. Assume that the prediction is of letters from a finite alphabet $\mathcal{A} = \{1, \ldots, A\}$. At the first phase the k experts state their predictions, and then, knowing their predictions P1 makes his own prediction $a_n \in \mathcal{A}$ and simultaneously (i.e. not knowing P1's prediction), P2 chooses the actual letter $b_n \in \mathcal{A}$. The reward obtained by P1 is $r(a_n, b_n) \in \mathbb{R}$. Although usually in prediction problems of finite alphabets, the reward is assumed a zero-one prediction error reward, we do not restrict the model by this assumption.

We actually prove a somewhat stronger result, we prove that the reward rate is not lower than the reward for any specific stationary strategy that relies on the experts' (mutual) advice. The prediction with expert advice is embedded in the following stochastic game that is defined by:

1. $\mathcal{S} = \{s^*, 1, \ldots, A^k\}$. State s^* is the first phase state and the other A^k states are the second phase states - one for every possible assignment of the joined experts advice.
2. The actions of P1 in state s^* are $\mathcal{A}(s^*) = \{0\}$, that is no choice state s^*. In the second phase, P1 predicts that channel letter, so for $1 \leq s \leq A^k$, P1's action are $\mathcal{A}(s) = \{1, \ldots, A\}$ which corresponds to P1's prediction.
3. The actions of P2 in state s^* are all possible joint expert opinion, that is $\mathcal{B}(s^*) = \{1, 2, \ldots, A^k\}$. The possible actions of P2 at states $1 \leq s \leq A^k$, are $\mathcal{B}(i) = \{1, \ldots, A\}$ which corresponds to the actual letter that appears in the channel.
4. The transition probabilities are in $\{0, 1\}$, when moving from state s^* to each $1 \leq i \leq A^k$, the transition is deterministic and determined by P2's action. When moving from $1 \leq i \leq A^k$ back to s^* the state transition happens with probability 1.

5. The reward at the first phase is 0, i.e. $r(s^*,\cdot,\cdot)=0$ and the reward at the second stage is $r(s,a,b)=2r(a,b)$. That is twice as much as the prediction cost.

This stochastic game obviously has a constant cycle time $\tau=2$ and state s^* is a recurrent reference state. As a result of Theorem 3 BE is attainable. That is:

$$\liminf_{n\to\infty}(\hat{r}_t - r^*(\pi_t)) \geq 0 \text{ P-a.s.}\,, \tag{10}$$

where P is the probability measure that is induced by P1 play of a regret minimizing strategy and by P2 playing any strategy $\sigma_2\in\Sigma_2$. The strategies that participate in the maximum for $r^*(\pi_t)$, certainly include the k strategies that always agree with expert i, $1\leq i\leq k$. □

C Proof of Theorem 4

BE is attained if the average reward $\hat{r}_t$ and the state action frequencies π_t satisfy that

$$\liminf_{n\to\infty}(\hat{r}_t - r^*(\pi_t)) \geq 0 \text{ P-a.s.}\,. \tag{11}$$

Note that since this is a single controller game then $\pi(f,g)=\pi(g)$, that is the state action frequencies generated by the strategies f for P1 and g for P2 depend only on P2's strategy. Starting from equation (7), we have that:

$$\begin{aligned}\hat{r}_t - r^*(\pi_t) &= \hat{r}_t - \sum_s \max_{f\in F}\sum_b\sum_a \pi_t(s,b)f(a|s)r(s,a,b)\\ &= \hat{r}_t - \sum_s \max_a \sum_b \pi_t(s,b)f(a|s)r(s,a,b)\,,\end{aligned} \tag{12}$$

where $\pi_t(s,b)$ is the relative frequency of state s and action b as measured at time t. The last equality is justified since f affects the inner sum only through the actions at state s. But $\hat{r}_t=\sum_s\sum_b\sum_a \pi_t(s,b)f(a|s)r(s,a,b)$ so

$$\begin{aligned}\hat{r}_t - r^*(\pi_t) = \sum_s \pi_t(s)(&\sum_b\sum_a g_t(b|s)f(a|s)r(s,a,b) -\\ &\max_a\sum_b g_t(b|s)f(a|s)r(s,a,b))\,,\end{aligned} \tag{13}$$

where $g_t(b|s)\triangleq\frac{\pi_t(s,b)}{\pi_t(s)}$ and $\pi_t(s)=\sum_b\pi_t(s,b)$. Suppose P1's strategy is to play a regret minimizing strategy for every state s separately for the game in which P1's actions are $a\in\mathcal{A}$, P2's actions are $b\in\mathcal{B}$ and the expected reward is $r(s,a,b)$. In that case, (13) becomes the sum of elements that tend to zero as $t\to\infty$ (if the state is visited often enough). We have that

$$\hat{r}_t - r^*(\pi_t) \geq \sum_s \pi_t(s)R_t(s)\,, \tag{14}$$

where $R_t(s)$ is the regret of the s game by time t:

$$R_t(s) \triangleq \sum_b \sum_a g_t(b|s) f(a|s) r(s,a,b) - \max_a \sum_b g_t(b|s) f(a|s) r(s,a,b) .$$

Now, P1's strategy ensures that $R_t(s) \to 0$ almost surely for every state s that is visited infinitely often, while $\pi_t(s) \to 0$ for the other states. It easily follows from (14) that (11) holds. □

Robust Learning — Rich and Poor

John Case[1], Sanjay Jain *[2], Frank Stephan**[3], and Rolf Wiehagen[4]

[1] Computer and Information Sciences Department, University of Delaware, Newark, DE 19716, USA, case@cis.udel.edu
[2] School of Computing, National University of Singapore, Singapore 119260, sanjay@comp.nus.edu.sg
[3] Mathematisches Institut, Im Neuenheimer Feld 294, Ruprecht-Karls-Universität Heidelberg, 69120 Heidelberg, Germany, fstephan@math.uni-heidelberg.de
[4] Department of Computer Science, University of Kaiserslautern, 67653 Kaiserslautern, Germany, wiehagen@informatik.uni-kl.de

Abstract. A class $\mathcal{C}$ of recursive functions is called *robustly learnable* in the sense **I** (where **I** is any success criterion of learning) if not only $\mathcal{C}$ itself but even all transformed classes $\Theta(\mathcal{C})$ where Θ is any general recursive operator, are learnable in the sense **I**. It was already shown before, see [14,19], that for **I** = **Ex** (learning in the limit) robust learning is rich in that there are classes being both not contained in any recursively enumerable class of recursive functions and, nevertheless, robustly learnable. For several criteria **I**, the present paper makes much more precise *where* we *can* hope for robustly learnable classes and where we can*not*. This is achieved in two ways. First, for **I** = **Ex**, it is shown that only *consistently* learnable classes can be uniformly robustly learnable. Second, some other learning types **I** are classified as to whether or not they contain rich robustly learnable classes. Moreover, the first results on separating robust learning from uniformly robust learning are derived.

1 Introduction

Robust learning has attracted much attention recently. Intuitively, a class of objects is *robustly learnable* if not only this class itself is learnable but all of its effective transformations remain learnable as well. In this sense, being learnable robustly seems to be a desirable property in all fields of learning. In inductive inference, i.e., informally, learning of recursive functions in the limit, a large collection of function classes was already known to be robustly learnable. Actually, in [15] any *recursively enumerable* class of recursive functions was shown to be learnable. This was achieved even by one and the same learning algorithm, the so-called identification by enumeration, see [15]. Moreover, any reasonable model of effective transformations maps any recursively enumerable class again to a recursively enumerable and, hence, learnable class. Consequently, all these classes

* Supported in part by NUS grant number RP3992710.
** Supported by the Deutsche Forschungsgemeinschaft (DFG) under the Heisenberg grant Ste 967/1-1

D. Helmbold and B. Williamson (Eds.): COLT/EuroCOLT 2001, LNAI 2111, pp. 143–159, 2001.

are *robustly* learnable. Clearly, the same is true for all *sub*classes of recursively enumerable classes. Thus, the challenging remaining question was if robust learning is even possible *outside* the world of the recursively enumerable classes. This question remained open for about 20 years, until it has been answered positively! [14,19] showed that there are classes of recursive functions which are both "algorithmically rich" and robustly learnable, where *algorithmically rich* means being not contained in any recursively enumerable class of recursive functions. Earliest examples of (large) algorithmically rich classes featured direct self-referential coding. Though ensuring the learnability of these classes themselves, these direct codings could be destroyed already by simple effective transformations, thus proving that these classes are *not* robustly learnable. An early motivation from Bārzdiņš for studying robustness was just to examine what happens to learnability when at least the then known direct codings are destroyed (by the effective transformations). Later examples of algorithmically rich classes, including some indeed *robustly* learnable examples, featured more indirect, "topological" coding. [14,19] mainly had focussed on the *existence* of rich *and* robustly learnable classes; however, in the present paper we want to make much more precise *where* we *can* hope for robustly learnable classes and where we can*not*. In order to reach this goal we will follow two lines.

The first line, outlined in Section 3, consists in exhibiting a "borderline" that separates the region where robustly learnable classes do exist from the region where robustly learnable classes provably cannot exist. More exactly, for the basic type **Ex** of learning in the limit, such a borderline is given just by the type **Cons** of learning in the limit *consistently* (i.e., each hypothesis correctly and completely reflects all the data seen so far). Actually, in Theorem 16 we show that all the uniformly robustly **Ex**-learnable classes must be already contained in **Cons**, and hence the complementary region **Ex** – **Cons** is free of any such classes. Notice that **Ex** – **Cons** is far from being empty, since it was shown before that **Cons** is a *proper* subset of **Ex**, see [3,6,32]; the latter is also known as *inconsistency phenomenon*, see [35,30,10] where it has been shown that this phenomenon is present in polynomial-time learning as well. We were surprised to find the "robustness phenomenon" and the inconsistency phenomenon so closely related this way. There is another interpretation suggested by Theorem 16 which in a sense nicely contrasts the results on robust learning from [19]. All the robustly learnable classes exhibited in that paper were of some non-trivial topological complexity, see [19] for details. On the other hand, Theorem 16 intuitively says that uniformly robustly learnable classes may not be "too complex", as they all are located in the "lower part" **Cons** of the type **Ex**. Finally, this location in **Cons** in turn seems useful in that just consistent learning plays an important role not only in inductive inference, see [13,20,24,36], but also in various other fields of learning such as PAC learning, machine learning and statistical learning, see the books [2,26,31], respectively.

In Section 4, we follow another line to solve the problem where rich robustly learnable classes can be found and where they cannot. Therefore let us call any type **I** of learning such as **I** = **Ex**, **Cons** etc. *robustly rich* if **I** contains rich classes being robustly learnable in the sense **I** (where "rich" is understood as above, i.e., a class is rich if it is not contained in any recursively enumerable class); otherwise, the type **I** is said to be *robustly poor*. Then, for a few types, it was already known if they are robustly rich or robustly poor. The first results in this direction are due to Zeugmann [37] where the types $\mathbf{Ex}_0$ (**Ex**-learning without any mind change) and **Reliable** (see Definition 7) were proved to be robustly poor. In [14,19] the type **Ex** was shown robustly rich. Below we classify several other types as to whether they are robustly rich or poor, respectively. We exhibit types of both categories, rich ones (hence the first rich ones after **Ex**) and poor ones, thus making the whole picture noticeably more complete. This might even serve as an appropriate starting point for solving the currently open problem to derive conditions (necessary, sufficient, both) for when a type is of which category. Notice that in proving types robustly rich below, in general, we show some stronger results, namely, we *robustly separate* the corresponding types from some other "close" types, thereby strengthening known separations in a robust way. From these separations, the corresponding richness results follow easily.

In Section 5, we deal with a problem which was competely open up to now, namely, separating robust learning from uniformly robust learning. While in robust learning any transformed class is required to be learnable in the mere sense that there *exists* a learning machine for it, uniformly robust learning intuitively requires to get such a learning machine for the transformed class *effectively at hand*, see Definition 13. As it turns out by our results, this additional requirement can really lead to a difference. Actually, for a number of learning types, we show that uniformly robust learning is stronger than robust learning. Notice that fixing this difference is also interesting for the following reason. As said above, in Theorem 16 all the uniformly robustly **Ex**-learnable classes are shown to be learnable consistently. However, at present, it is open if this result remains valid when uniform robustness will be replaced by robustness only. Some results of Section 5 can be considered as first steps to attack this apparently difficult problem.

Recently, several papers were published that deal with robustness in inductive inference, see [8,14,17,19,22,23,28,37]. Each of them has contributed interesting points to a better understanding of the challenging phenomenon of robust learning. [14,19,37] are already quoted above. In addition, notice that in [19] the mind change hierarchy for **Ex**-type learning is proved to stand robustly. This contrasts the result from [14] that the anomaly hierarchy for **Ex**-type learning does *not* hold robustly. In [22,23] the authors were dealing with so-called Bārzdiņš' Conjecture which, intuitively, stated that the type **Ex** is robustly poor. In [8] robust learning has been studied for another specific learning scenario, namely learning aided by context. The intuition behind this model is to present the functions to be learned not in a pure fashion to the learner, but together with some "context" which is intended to help in learning. It is shown that within this scenario several results hold robustly as well. In [28] the notion of hyperrobust learning is introduced. A class of recursive functions is called *hyperrobustly learnable* if there is one and the same learner which learns not only this class itself but also all of its images under all *primitive* recursive operators. Hence this learner must be capable to learn the *union* of all these images. This definition is then justified by the following results. First, it is shown that the power of hyperrobust learning does not change if the class of primitive recursive operators is replaced by any larger, still recursively enumerable class of general recursive operators. Second, based on this stronger definition, Bārzdiņš' Conjecture is proved by showing that a class of recursive functions is hyperrobustly **Ex**-learnable iff this class is contained in a recursively enumerable class of recursive functions. From [28] hyperrobustness destroys both direct and topological coding tricks. In [8] it is noted that hyperrobustness destroys any advantage of context, but, since, empirically, context does help, this provides evidence that the real world, in a sense, has codes for some things buried inside others. In [17] another basic type of inductive inference, namely **Bc**, has been robustly separated from **Ex**, thus solving an open problem from [14]. While in the present paper general recursive operators are taken in order to realize the transformations of the classes under consideration (the reason for this choice is mainly a technical one, namely, that these operators "automatically" map any class of recursive functions to a class of recursive functions again), in some of the papers above other types of operators are used such as effective, recursive, primitive recursive operators, respectively. At this moment, we do not see any choice to this end that seems to be superior to the others. Indeed, each approach appears justified if it yields interesting results.

For references surveying the theory of learning recursive functions, the reader is referred to [1,6,9,11,18,21,27]. Due to lack of space we omit most of the proofs in the present paper.

2 Notation and Preliminaries

Recursion-theoretic concepts not explained below are treated in [29]. N denotes the set of natural numbers. $*$ denotes a non-member of N and is assumed to satisfy $(\forall n)[n < * < \infty]$. Let $\in, \subseteq, \subset, \supseteq, \supset$, respectively denote the membership, subset, proper subset, superset and proper superset relations for sets. The empty set is denoted by $\emptyset$. We let $\mathrm{card}(S)$ denote the cardinality of the set S. So "$\mathrm{card}(S) \leq *$" means that $\mathrm{card}(S)$ is finite. The minimum and maximum of a set S are denoted by $\min(S)$ and $\max(S)$, respectively. We take $\max(\emptyset)$ to be 0 and $\min(\emptyset)$ to be ∞. χ_A denotes the characteristic function of A, that is, $\chi_A(x) = 1$, if $x \in A$, and 0 otherwise.

$\langle\cdot,\cdot\rangle$ denotes a 1-1 computable mapping from pairs of natural numbers onto natural numbers. π_1, π_2 are the corresponding projection functions. $\langle\cdot,\cdot\rangle$ is extended to n-tuples of natural numbers in a natural way. Λ denotes the empty function. η, with or without subscripts, superscripts, primes and the like, ranges over partial functions. If η_1 and η_2 are both undefined on input x, then, we take

$\eta_1(x) = \eta_2(x)$. We say that $\eta_1 \subseteq \eta_2$ iff for all x in domain of η_1, $\eta_1(x) = \eta_2(x)$. We let domain(η) and range(η) respectively denote the domain and range of the partial function η. $\eta(x)\downarrow$ denotes that $\eta(x)$ is defined. $\eta(x)\uparrow$ denotes that $\eta(x)$ is undefined.

We say that a partial function η is *conforming* with η' iff for all $x \in$ domain(η) $\cap$ domain(η'), $\eta(x) = \eta(x')$. $\eta \sim \eta'$ denotes that η is conforming with η'. η is *non-conforming* with η' iff there exists an x such that $\eta(x)\downarrow \neq \eta'(x)\downarrow$. $\eta \not\sim \eta'$ denotes that η is non-conforming with η'.

For $r \in N$, r-extension of η denotes the function f defined as follows:

$$f(x) = \begin{cases} \eta(x), & \text{if } x \in \text{domain}(\eta); \\ r, & \text{otherwise.} \end{cases}$$

f, g, h, F and H, with or without subscripts, superscripts, primes and the like, range over total functions. $\mathcal{R}$ denotes the class of all *recursive* functions, i.e., total computable functions with arguments and values from N. $\mathcal{T}$ denotes the class of all *total* functions. $\mathcal{R}_{0,1}$ ($\mathcal{T}_{0,1}$) denotes the class of all *recursive* functions (total functions) with range contained in $\{0,1\}$. $\mathcal{C}$ and $\mathcal{S}$, with or without subscripts, superscripts, primes and the like, range over subsets of $\mathcal{R}$. $\mathcal{P}$ denotes the class of all *partial recursive* functions over N. φ denotes a *fixed* acceptable programming system. φ_i denotes the partial recursive function computed by program i in the φ-system. Note that in this paper all programs are interpreted with respect to the φ-system. We let Φ be an arbitrary Blum complexity measure [7] associated with the acceptable programming system φ; many such measures exist for any acceptable programming system [7]. We assume without loss of generality that $\Phi_i(x) \geq x$, for all i, x. $\varphi_{i,s}$ is defined as follows:

$$\varphi_{i,s}(x) = \begin{cases} \varphi_i(x), & \text{if } x < s \text{ and } \Phi_i(x) < s; \\ \uparrow, & \text{otherwise.} \end{cases}$$

For a given partial computable function η, we define MinProg(η) $= \min(\{i \mid \varphi_i = \eta\})$.

A class $\mathcal{C} \subseteq \mathcal{R}$ is said to be recursively enumerable iff there exists an r.e. set X such that $\mathcal{C} = \{\varphi_i \mid i \in X\}$. For any non-empty recursively enumerable class $\mathcal{C}$, there exists a recursive function f such that $\mathcal{C} = \{\varphi_{f(i)} \mid i \in N\}$.

The following classes are commonly considered below. CONST $= \{f \mid (\forall x)[f(x) = f(0)]\}$ denotes the class of the constant functions. FINSUP $= \{f \mid (\forall^\infty x)[f(x) = 0]\}$ denotes the class of all recursive functions of finite support.

2.1 Function Identification

We first describe inductive inference machines. We assume, that the graph of a function is fed to a machine in canonical order.

For $f \in \mathcal{R}$ and $n \in N$, we let $f[n]$ denote $f(0)f(1)\dots f(n-1)$, the finite initial segment of f of length n. Clearly, $f[0]$ denotes the empty segment. SEG denotes the set of all finite initial segments, $\{f[n] \mid f \in \mathcal{R} \wedge n \in N\}$. SEG$_{0,1}$ $= \{f[n] \mid f \in \mathcal{R}_{0,1} \wedge n \in N\}$. We let σ, τ and γ, with or without subscripts, superscripts, primes and the like, range over SEG. Λ denotes the empty sequence. We assume some computable ordering of elements of SEG. $\sigma < \tau$, if σ appears before τ in this ordering. Similarly one can talk about least element of a subset of SEG.

We let $\sigma \cdot \tau$ denote the concatenation of σ and τ. We identify $\sigma = a_0 a_1 \ldots a_{n-1}$ with the partial function

$$\sigma(x) = \begin{cases} a_i, & \text{if } x < n; \\ \uparrow, & \text{otherwise.} \end{cases}$$

Similarly a total function g is identified with the infinite sequence $g(0)g(1)g(2)\ldots$ of its values. Thus, for example, 0^∞ is the function mapping all numbers to 0.

Let $|\sigma|$ denote the length of σ. If $|\sigma| \geq n$, then we let $\sigma[n]$ denote the prefix of σ of length n. $\sigma \subseteq \tau$ denotes that σ is a prefix of τ. An *inductive inference machine* (IIM) [15] is an algorithmic device that computes a (possibly partial) mapping from SEG into N. Since the set of all finite initial segments, SEG, can be coded onto N, we can view these machines as taking natural numbers as input and emitting natural numbers as output. We say that $\mathbf{M}(f)$ converges to i (written: $\mathbf{M}(f)\!\downarrow = i$) iff $(\forall^\infty n)[\mathbf{M}(f[n]) = i]$; $\mathbf{M}(f)$ is undefined if no such i exists. $\mathbf{M}_0, \mathbf{M}_1, \ldots$ denotes a recursive enumeration of all the IIMs. The next definitions describe several criteria of function identification. Note that — as a variable for learners — $\mathbf{M}$ always ranges over partial computable machines.

Definition 1. [15] Let $f \in \mathcal{R}$ and $\mathcal{S} \subseteq \mathcal{R}$.

(a) $\mathbf{M}$ **Ex**-*identifies* f (written: $f \in \mathbf{Ex}(\mathbf{M})$) just in case there exists a program i for f such that $\mathbf{M}(f)\!\downarrow = i$.
(b) $\mathbf{M}$ **Ex**-*identifies* $\mathcal{S}$ iff $\mathbf{M}$ **Ex**-identifies each $f \in \mathcal{S}$.
(c) $\mathbf{Ex} = \{\mathcal{S} \subseteq \mathcal{R} \mid (\exists \mathbf{M})\, [\mathcal{S} \subseteq \mathbf{Ex}(\mathbf{M})]\}$.

By the definition of convergence, only finitely many data points from a function f have been observed by an IIM $\mathbf{M}$ at the (unknown) point of convergence. Hence, some form of learning must take place in order for $\mathbf{M}$ to learn f. For this reason, hereafter the terms *identify*, *learn* and *infer* are used interchangeably.

Definition 2. [3] $\mathbf{M}$ is said to be *consistent* on f iff, for all n, $\mathbf{M}(f[n])\!\downarrow$ and $f[n] \subseteq \varphi_{\mathbf{M}(f[n])}$.

Definition 3. [33] $\mathbf{M}$ is said to be *conforming* on f iff, for all n, $\mathbf{M}(f[n])\!\downarrow$ and $f[n] \sim \varphi_{\mathbf{M}(f[n])}$.

Definition 4. (a) [3] $\mathbf{M}$ **Cons**-*identifies* f iff $\mathbf{M}$ is consistent on f, and $\mathbf{M}$ **Ex**-identifies f.
(b.1) [3] $\mathbf{M}$ **Cons**-*identifies* $\mathcal{C}$ iff $\mathbf{M}$ **Cons**-identifies each $f \in \mathcal{C}$.
(b.2) $\mathbf{Cons} = \{\mathcal{C} \mid (\exists \mathbf{M})[\mathbf{M}$ **Cons**-identifies $\mathcal{C}]\}$.
(c.1) [20] $\mathbf{M}$ $\mathcal{R}$**Cons**-*identifies* $\mathcal{C}$ iff $\mathbf{M}$ is total, and $\mathbf{M}$ **Cons**-identifies $\mathcal{C}$.
(c.2) $\mathcal{R}\mathbf{Cons} = \{\mathcal{C} \mid (\exists \mathbf{M})[\mathbf{M}$ $\mathcal{R}$**Cons**-identifies $\mathcal{C}]\}$.
(d.1) [34] $\mathbf{M}$ $\mathcal{T}$**Cons**-*identifies* $\mathcal{C}$ iff $\mathbf{M}$ is consistent on each $f \in \mathcal{T}$, and $\mathbf{M}$ **Cons**-identifies $\mathcal{C}$.
(d.2) $\mathcal{T}\mathbf{Cons} = \{\mathcal{C} \mid (\exists \mathbf{M})[\mathbf{M}$ $\mathcal{T}$**Cons**-identifies $\mathcal{C}]\}$.

Note that for **M** to **Cons**-identify a function f, it must be defined on each initial segment of f. Similarly for **Conf**-identification below.

Definition 5. (a) [33] **M Conf**-*identifies* f iff **M** is conforming on f, and **M** **Ex**-identifies f.
(b.1) [33] **M Conf**-*identifies* $\mathcal{C}$ iff **M Conf**-identifies each $f \in \mathcal{C}$.
(b.2) **Conf** $= \{\mathcal{C} \mid (\exists \mathbf{M})[\mathbf{M}$ **Conf**-identifies $\mathcal{C}]\}$.
(c.1) **M** $\mathcal{R}$**Conf**-*identifies* $\mathcal{C}$ iff **M** is total, and **M Conf**-identifies $\mathcal{C}$.
(c.2) $\mathcal{R}$**Conf** $= \{\mathcal{C} \mid (\exists \mathbf{M})[\mathbf{M}$ $\mathcal{R}$**Conf**-identifies $\mathcal{C}]\}$.
(d.1) [13] **M** $\mathcal{T}$**Conf**-*identifies* $\mathcal{C}$ iff **M** is conforming on each $f \in \mathcal{T}$, and **M** **Conf**-identifies $\mathcal{C}$.
(d.2) $\mathcal{T}$**Conf** $= \{\mathcal{C} \mid (\exists \mathbf{M})[\mathbf{M}$ $\mathcal{T}$**Conf**-identifies $\mathcal{C}]\}$.

Definition 6. [27] **M** is *confident* iff for all total f, $\mathbf{M}(f)\downarrow$.
M Confident-*identifies* $\mathcal{C}$ iff **M** is confident and **M Ex**-identifies $\mathcal{C}$.
Confident $= \{\mathcal{C} \mid (\exists \mathbf{M})[\mathbf{M}$ **Confident**-identifies $\mathcal{C}]\}$.

Definition 7. [6,25] **M** is *reliable* iff **M** is total and for all total f, $\mathbf{M}(f)\downarrow \Rightarrow$ **M Ex**-identifies f.
M Reliable-*identifies* $\mathcal{C}$ iff **M** is reliable and **M Ex**-identifies $\mathcal{C}$.
Reliable $= \{\mathcal{C} \mid (\exists \mathbf{M})[\mathbf{M}$ **Reliable**-identifies $\mathcal{C}]\}$.

Definition 8. **NUM** $= \{\mathcal{C} \mid (\exists \mathcal{C}' \mid \mathcal{C} \subseteq \mathcal{C}' \subseteq \mathcal{R})[\mathcal{C}'$ is recursively enumerable$]\}$.

For references on inductive inference within **NUM**, the set of all recursively enumerable classes and their subclasses, the reader is referred to [5,12,15]. The next theorem summarizes the main relations between the notions discussed in this paper. A major question of our research is, how these inclusions and non-inclusions change, if robustness is required on the left side of an inclusion or non-inclusion, for example we show for case (d), that there is also a class in **RobustCons** which is not in $\mathcal{R}$**Conf**, see Theorem 20 below.

Theorem 9. [3,4,6,13,16,32,33,34,36]

(a) **NUM** $\subset$ $\mathcal{T}$**Cons** $=$ $\mathcal{T}$**Conf** $\subset$ $\mathcal{R}$**Cons** $\subset$ $\mathcal{R}$**Conf** $\subset$ **Conf** $\subset$ **Ex**.
(b) $\mathcal{R}$**Cons** $\subset$ **Cons** $\subset$ **Conf**.
(c) $\mathcal{R}$**Conf** $\not\subseteq$ **Cons**.
(d) **Cons** $\not\subseteq$ $\mathcal{R}$**Conf**.
(e) $\mathcal{T}$**Cons** $\subset$ **Reliable** $\subset$ **Ex**.
(f) **Reliable** $\not\subseteq$ **Conf**.
(g) $\mathcal{R}$**Cons** $\not\subseteq$ **Reliable**.
(h) **NUM** $\not\subseteq$ **Confident**.
(i) **Confident** $\not\subseteq$ **Conf**.
(j) **Confident** $\not\subseteq$ **Reliable**.

2.2 Operators

The basic idea of robust learning is that not only a given class $\mathcal{S}$ but also every image of $\mathcal{S}$ under a given operator should be learnable. At the beginning of the study of robust learning it was not clear which operators to use; but later the discussion stabilized on using general recursive operators. Although this choice has some disadvantage, there was a feeling in the community that this disadvantage could not be overcome by choosing a larger class of operators.

Definition 10. [29] A *recursive operator* is an effective total mapping, Θ, from (possibly partial) functions to (possibly partial) functions, which satisfies the following properties:

(a) Monotonicity: For all functions η, η', if $\eta \subseteq \eta'$ then $\Theta(\eta) \subseteq \Theta(\eta')$.
(b) Compactness: For all η, if $(x, y) \in \Theta(\eta)$, then there exists a finite function $\alpha \subseteq \eta$ such that $(x, y) \in \Theta(\alpha)$.
(c) Recursiveness: For all finite functions α, one can effectively enumerate (in α) all $(x, y) \in \Theta(\alpha)$.

Definition 11. [29] A recursive operator Θ is called *general recursive* iff Θ maps all total functions to total functions.

For each recursive operator Θ, we can effectively (from Θ) find a recursive operator Θ' satisfying two further constraints (d) and (e).

(d) for each finite function α, $\Theta'(\alpha)$ is finite, and its canonical index can be effectively determined from α; furthermore if $\alpha \in \mathrm{SEG}$ then $\Theta'(\alpha) \in \mathrm{SEG}$.
(e) for all total functions f, $\Theta'(f) = \Theta(f)$.

This allows us to get a nice effective sequence of recursive operators.

Proposition 12. [19] *There exists an effective enumeration, $\Theta_0, \Theta_1, \ldots$, of recursive operators satisfying condition* (d) *above such that, for all recursive operators Θ, there exists an $i \in N$ satisfying:*

$$\text{for all total functions } f,\ \Theta(f) = \Theta_i(f).$$

Since we will be mainly concerned with the properties of operators on total functions, for diagonalization purposes, one can restrict attention to operators in the above enumeration $\Theta_0, \Theta_1, \ldots$.

Definition 13. [14,19]
RobustEx $= \{\mathcal{C} \mid (\forall$ general recursive operators $\Theta)[\Theta(\mathcal{C}) \in \mathbf{Ex}]\}$.
UniformRobustEx $= \{\mathcal{C} \mid (\exists g \in \mathcal{R})(\forall e \mid \Theta_e$ is general recursive$)[\Theta_e(\mathcal{C}) \subseteq \mathbf{Ex}(\mathbf{M}_{g(e)})]\}$.

One can similarly define **RobustI** and **UniformRobustI**, for other criteria **I** of learning considered in this paper.

Proposition 14. [19,37] **NUM** = **RobustNUM**.

Corollary 15. (a) **NUM** $\subseteq$ **Robust$\mathcal{T}$Cons** $\subseteq$ **RobustReliable**.
(b) **NUM** $\subseteq$ **UniformRobust$\mathcal{T}$Cons**.

3 Robust Learning and Consistency

The main result of this section is **UniformRobustEx** $\subseteq$ **Cons**, see Theorem 16. Hence, all the uniformly robustly **Ex**-learnable classes are contained in the "lower part" **Cons** of **Ex**; recall that **Cons** is a *proper* subset of **Ex**, see [3,6,32]. This nicely relates two surprising phenomena of learning, namely the robustness phenomenon and the inconsistency phenomenon. On the other hand, despite the fact that every uniformly robustly **Ex**-learnable class is located in that lower part of **Ex**, **UniformRobustEx** contains "algorithmically rich" classes, since, by Corollary 19, **UniformRobustEx** $\supset$ **NUM**. Note that the non-robust version of Theorem 16 still is open, that is, it is unknown whether **RobustEx** $\subseteq$ **Cons**.

Theorem 16. UniformRobustEx $\subseteq$ **Cons**.

The (omitted) proof even shows that given any recursive g, one can *effectively* construct an $\mathbf{M}$ such that, for any $\mathcal{C}$, if

$$\text{for all } e \text{ such that } \Theta_e \text{ is general recursive, } \Theta_e(\mathcal{C}) \subseteq \mathbf{Ex}(\mathbf{M}_{g(e)})$$

then $\mathbf{M}$ **Cons**-identifies $\mathcal{C}$. Thus we have that

$$\mathbf{UniformRobustEx} \subseteq \mathbf{UniformRobustCons}.$$

Since the reverse inclusion holds by definition, it follows that,

Corollary 17. UniformRobustEx $=$ **UniformRobustCons**.

Now we investigate the links between boundedness and uniform robust learnability of classes of functions. We say that a class $\mathcal{S}$ is *bounded* iff there is a recursive function g such that g dominates all $f \in \mathcal{S}$: $(\forall f \in \mathcal{S})\,(\forall^\infty x)\,[f(x) \leq g(x)]$. For example, every class in **NUM** is bounded. The next theorem states, that although every class in **UniformRobustEx** is bounded by a non-recursive function, there are classes $\mathcal{S} \in$ **UniformRobustEx** which are not bounded by a recursive function. As a consequence, we derive that **UniformRobustEx** contains algorithmically rich classes, see Corollary 19 below.

Theorem 18. *If* $\mathcal{S} \in$ **UniformRobustEx** $-$ **NUM** *then* $g_\mathcal{S}(x) = \max(\{f(x) \mid f \in \mathcal{S}\})$ *is a total function and satisfies that* $g_\mathcal{S}(x) < \infty$ *for all* x.
There is $\mathcal{S} \in$ **UniformRobustEx** *such that* $\mathcal{S}$ *is unbounded; in particular, the above defined* $g_\mathcal{S}$ *is not recursive and* $\mathcal{S} \notin$ **NUM**.

Corollary 19. UniformRobustEx $\supset$ **NUM**.

4 Robustly Rich and Robustly Poor Learning

In this section, we show for several learning types that they are "robustly rich"; that is, these types contain classes being both robustly learnable and not contained in any recursively enumerable class. Notice that in proving these types robustly rich below, in general, we show some stronger results, namely, we *robustly separate* (or even *uniformly* robustly separate) the corresponding types from some other types, thereby strengthening known separations in a (uniformly) robust way. From these separations, the corresponding richness results follow easily by applying Theorem 9. On the other hand, there are also "robustly poor" learning types; that is, every robustly learnable class of these types is contained in a recursively enumerable class. Some further robustly poor types will be exhibited in Section 5.

Theorem 20. UniformRobustCons $\not\subseteq$ $\mathcal{R}$Conf.

Theorem 21. Robust$\mathcal{R}$Cons $\not\subseteq$ $\mathcal{T}$Cons.

Theorem 22. Robust$\mathcal{R}$Conf $\not\subseteq$ $\mathcal{R}$Cons.

It should be noted that in the three preceding theorems, the separating class can always be taken from $\mathcal{R}_{0,1}$, that is, it consists of $\{0,1\}$-valued functions. Furthermore, one gets that the learning criteria **$\mathcal{R}$Cons** and **$\mathcal{R}$Conf** are robustly rich. As a consequence also the criteria **Cons** and **Conf** are robustly rich. Zeugmann [37] proved that **RobustReliable** = **NUM** which directly implies the corresponding result for **Robust$\mathcal{T}$Cons**.

Theorem 23. [37] **RobustReliable = NUM.**
Robust$\mathcal{T}$Cons = NUM.

This gives then that the following hierarchy corresponding to Theorem 9 (a) and (b) holds. The equality of **$\mathcal{T}$Cons** and **$\mathcal{T}$Conf** inherits from the non-robust case and so **$\mathcal{T}$Cons** and **$\mathcal{T}$Conf** are robustly poor.

Corollary 24. NUM = Robust$\mathcal{T}$Cons = Robust$\mathcal{T}$Conf.
NUM $\subset$ Robust$\mathcal{R}$Cons $\subset$ RobustCons.
NUM $\subset$ Robust$\mathcal{R}$Cons $\subset$ Robust$\mathcal{R}$Conf $\subset$ RobustConf.

Furthermore, one can also separate the notions **NUM** and **Confident** robustly and conclude, that confidence is a robustly rich learning criteria.

Proposition 25. UniformRobustConfident $\not\subseteq$ $\mathcal{R}$Conf.

Corollary 26. UniformRobustConfident $\not\subseteq$ NUM.

Note that by Theorem 9(h), **NUM** $\not\subseteq$ **Confident**. Thus using Corollary 26, **NUM** and **Confident** are incomparable. The following proposition strengthens Corollary 19.

Proposition 27. UniformRobustEx $\not\subseteq$ Confident $\cup$ NUM.

5 Robust Learning versus Uniformly Robust Learning

While in robust learning any transformed class is required to be learnable in the mere sense that there *exists* a learning machine for it, uniformly learning requires to get such a machine for the transformed class *effectively at hand*. For a number of learning types, we now show that uniformly robust learning is indeed stronger than robust learning.

Theorem 28. UniformRobustConfident $\subset$ **RobustConfident**.

For identification with mind changes, we assume **M** to be a mapping from SEG to $N \cup \{?\}$. This is to avoid biasing the number of mind changes made by the machine [9].

Definition 29. [6,9,15] Let $b \in N \cup \{*\}$. Let $f \in \mathcal{R}$.

M $\mathbf{Ex}_b$*-identifies* f (written: $f \in \mathbf{Ex}_b(\mathbf{M})$) just in case **M** **Ex**-identifies f, and $\text{card}(\{n \mid ? \neq \mathbf{M}(f[n]) \neq \mathbf{M}(f[n+1])\}) \leq b$ (i.e., **M** makes no more than b mind changes on f).
M $\mathbf{Ex}_b$*-identifies* $\mathcal{S}$ iff **M** $\mathbf{Ex}_b$-identifies each $f \in \mathcal{S}$.
$\mathbf{Ex}_b = \{\mathcal{S} \subseteq \mathcal{R} \mid (\exists \mathbf{M})[\mathcal{S} \subseteq \mathbf{Ex}_b(\mathbf{M})]\}$.

Zeugmann [37] showed that a class of functions is robustly learnable without mind changes iff it is finite.

Proposition 30. [19,37] *For any* $\mathcal{C} \subseteq \mathcal{R}$*,* $\mathcal{C} \in \mathbf{RobustEx}_0$ *iff* $\mathcal{C}$ *is finite.*

Thus, the type $\mathbf{Ex}_0$ of learning without any mind change is robustly poor, since every finite class is recursively enumerable. Somehow, uniformly robust learning with up to n mind changes even turns out to be more restrictive than robust learning with 0 mind changes: the cardinality of such classes is strictly less than 2^{n+1}. This forms a contrast to the fact that $\mathbf{RobustEx}_1$ contains infinite classes [19]. On the other hand, there is a nice connection between $\mathbf{RobustEx}_0$ and the classes in $\mathbf{UniformRobustEx}_n$.

Theorem 31. *For any* $n \in N$ *and* $\mathcal{C} \subseteq \mathcal{R}$*,* $\mathcal{C} \in \mathbf{UniformRobustEx}_n$ *iff* $\text{card}(\mathcal{C}) < 2^{n+1}$.
In particular, $\mathbf{RobustEx}_0 = \bigcup_{n \in N} \mathbf{UniformRobustEx}_n$.

The following Propositions 32 and 33 are needed in proving one of the main results, namely Theorem 36 below. From this theorem, we then derive that uniformly robust learning is stronger than robust learning for each of the types **Cons**, **Ex** and **Bc** (the latter defined below).

Proposition 32. *There exists a* K*-recursive sequence of initial segments,* $\sigma_0, \sigma_1, \ldots \in SEG_{0,1}$*, such that for all* $e \in N$*, the following are satisfied.*

(a) $0^e 1 \subseteq \sigma_e$.
(b) *For all* $e' \leq e$*, if* $\Theta_{e'}$ *is general recursive, then either* $\Theta_{e'}(\sigma_e) \not\sim \Theta_{e'}(0^{|\sigma_e|})$ *or for all* $f \in \mathcal{T}_{0,1}$ *extending* σ_e*,* $\Theta_{e'}(f) = \Theta_{e'}(0^\infty)$.

Proof. We define σ_e (using oracle for K) as follows. Initially, let $\sigma_e^0 = 0^e1$. For $e' \leq e$, define $\sigma_e^{e'+1}$ as follows: if there exists an extension $\tau \in \mathrm{SEG}_{0,1}$ of $\sigma_e^{e'}$, such that $\Theta_{e'}(\tau) \not\sim \Theta_{e'}(0^{|\tau|})$, then let $\sigma_e^{e'+1} = \tau$; otherwise, let $\sigma_e^{e'+1} = \sigma_e^{e'}$.

Now let $\sigma_e = \sigma_e^{e+1}$ as defined above. It is easy to verify that the proposition is satisfied. ∎

Proposition 33. *There exists an infinite increasing sequence $a_0, a_1, \ldots$ of natural numbers such that for $A = \{a_i \mid i \in N\}$, the following properties are satisfied for all $k \in N$.*

(a) *The complement of A is recursively enumerable relative to K.*
(b) *φ_{a_k} is total.*
(c) *For all $e \leq a_k$ such that φ_e is total, $\varphi_e(x) \leq \varphi_{a_{k+1}}(x)$ for all $x \in N$.*
(d) *For σ_e as defined in Proposition 32, $|\sigma_{a_k}| \leq a_{k+1}$.*

Proof. The construction of a_i's is done using movable markers (using oracle for K). Let a_i^s denote the value of a_i at the beginning of stage s in the construction. It will be the case that, for all s and i, either $a_i^s = a_i^{s+1}$, or $a_i^{s+1} > s$. This allows us to ensure property (a). The construction itself directly implements properties (b) to (d). Let *pad* be a 1–1 padding function [29] such that for all i, j, $\varphi_{pad(i,j)} = \varphi_i$, and $pad(i,j) \geq i + j$.

We assume without loss of generality that φ_0 is total. Initially, let $a_0^0 = 0$, and $a_{i+1}^0 = pad(0, |\sigma_{a_i^0}|)$ (this ensures $a_{i+1}^0 \geq |\sigma_{a_i^0}| > a_i^0$). Go to stage 0.

Stage s
1. If there exist a k, $0 < k \leq s$, and $x \leq s$ such that:
   (I) $\varphi_{a_k^s}(x)\uparrow$ or
   (II) for some $e \leq a_{k-1}^s$, $[(\forall y \leq s)[\varphi_e(y)\downarrow]$ and $\varphi_e(x) > \varphi_{a_k^s}(x)]$
2. Then pick least such k and go to step 3. If there is no such k, then for all i, let $a_i^{s+1} = a_i^s$, and go to stage $s+1$.
3 For $i < k$, let $a_i^{s+1} = a_i^s$.
4. Let j be the least number such that
   (I) $(\forall y \leq s)[\varphi_j(y)\downarrow]$ and
   (II) for all $e \leq a_{k-1}^s$, if for all $y \leq s$, $\varphi_e(y)\downarrow$, then for all $y \leq s$, $\varphi_j(y) \geq \varphi_e(y)$.
   Let $a_k^{s+1} = pad(j, |\sigma_{a_{k-1}^s}| + s + 1)$.
5. For $i > k$, let $a_i^{s+1} = pad(0, |\sigma_{a_{i-1}^{s+1}}| + s + 1)$.
6. Go to stage $s+1$.
End stage s

We claim (by induction on k) that $\lim_{s\to\infty} a_k^s\downarrow$ for each k. To see this, note that once all the a_i, $i < k$, have stabilized, step 4 would eventually pick a j such that φ_j is total, and for all $e \leq a_{k-1}$, if φ_e is total then $\varphi_e \leq \varphi_j$. Thereafter a_k would not be changed.

We now show the various properties claimed in the proposition. One can enumerate $\overline{A}$ (using oracle for K) using the following property: $x \in \overline{A}$ iff there exists a stage $s > x$ such that, for all $i \leq x$, $a_i^s \neq x$. Thus (a) holds. (b) and (c) hold due to the check in step 1. (d) trivially holds due to padding used for definition of a_i^s for all s. ∎

Definition 34. Suppose $h \in \mathcal{R}$. Let $\mathcal{B}_h = \{\varphi_e \mid \varphi_e \in \mathcal{R} \wedge (\forall^\infty x)[\Phi_e(x) \leq h(x)]\}$.

Intuitively, $\mathcal{B}_h$ denotes the class of recursive functions whose complexity is almost everywhere bounded by h. We assume without loss of generality that FINSUP $\subseteq \mathcal{B}_{\varphi_0}$. Thus for a_i as in Proposition 33, FINSUP $\subseteq \mathcal{B}_{\varphi_{a_i}}$, for all i.

The notion of behaviourally correct learning does not require syntactical convergence as explanatory learning but only that almost all hypotheses compute the function to be learned.

Definition 35. [4,9] **M Bc**-*identifies* a function $f \in \mathcal{R}$ (written: $f \in \mathbf{Bc}(\mathbf{M})$) iff, for all but finitely many $n \in N$, $\mathbf{M}(f[n])$ is defined and is a program for f.
M Bc-*identifies* $\mathcal{S}$ iff **M Bc**-identifies each $f \in \mathcal{S}$.
$\mathbf{Bc} = \{\mathcal{S} \subseteq \mathcal{R} \mid (\exists \mathbf{M})\,[\mathcal{S} \subseteq \mathbf{Bc}(\mathbf{M})]\}$.

By the way, whenever $\mathcal{S} \in \mathbf{Bc}$ then there is also a total machine **M** such that $\mathcal{S} \in \mathbf{Bc}(\mathbf{M})$. Thus one can require without loss of generality, that **Bc**-learners are total.

Theorem 36. RobustCons $\not\subseteq$ UniformRobustBc.

Proof. Fix $\sigma_0, \sigma_1, \ldots$ as in Proposition 32, and $a_0, a_1, \ldots$ as in Proposition 33.

Let $G_k = \mathcal{B}_{\varphi_{a_k}} \cap \{f \mid \sigma_{a_k} \subseteq f\}$.

The main idea of the construction is to construct the diagonalizing class by taking at most finitely many functions from each G_k.

Let Θ_{b_k} be defined as

$$\Theta_{b_k}(f[n]) = \begin{cases} \Lambda, & \text{if } n < |\sigma_{a_k}|; \\ f(|\sigma_{a_k}|)f(|\sigma_{a_k}|+1)\ldots f(n-1), & \text{if } \sigma_{a_k} \subseteq f[n]; \\ f[n], & \text{otherwise.} \end{cases}$$

Note that Θ_{b_k} is general recursive.

Claim. $\bigcup_{i \geq k} \Theta_{b_k}(G_i) \notin \mathbf{Bc}$.

Proof. Suppose by way of contradiction that **M Bc**-identifies $\bigcup_{i \geq k} \Theta_{b_k}(G_i)$. Then, clearly **M** must **Bc**-identify FINSUP (since FINSUP $\subseteq \Theta_{b_k}(G_k)$). Thus, for all $\tau \in \mathrm{SEG}_{0,1}$, there exists an n such that, for all $m \geq n$, $\varphi_{\mathbf{M}(\tau 0^m)}(|\tau|+m) = 0$. Thus, there exists a recursive function g such that, for all $\tau \in \mathrm{SEG}_{0,1}$ satisfying $|\tau| \leq n$, $\varphi_{\mathbf{M}(\tau 0^{g(n)})}(|\tau| + g(n)) = 0$. Now for each τ, define f_τ inductively by letting $\eta_0 = \tau$, $\eta_{n+1} = \eta_n 0^{g(|\eta_n|)} 1$ and $f_\tau = \bigcup_n \eta_n$. Note that **M** does not **Bc**-identify any f_τ. Also, f_τ is uniformly (in τ) computable and thus $\{f_\tau \mid \tau \in \mathrm{SEG}_{0,1}\} \subseteq \mathcal{B}_h$, for some recursive h. Thus, for sufficiently large j, $\{f_\tau \mid \tau \in \mathrm{SEG}_{0,1}\} \subseteq \mathcal{B}_{\varphi_{a_j}}$. Thus, for almost all $j > k$, $f_{\sigma_{a_j}} \in G_j = \Theta_{b_k}(G_j)$.

Since **M** does not **Bc**-identify $f_{\sigma_{a_j}}$, claim follows. □

Let g' be a function dominating all K'-recursive functions. For each $k \in N$ and $e \leq g'(k)$, let $f_{k,e}$ denote a function in $\bigcup_{i \geq k} G_i$, such that $\mathbf{M}_e$ does not **Bc**-identify $\Theta_{b_k}(f_{k,e})$.

Let $\mathcal{S} = \{f_{k,e} \mid k \in N, e \leq g'(k)\}$. Let $F_k = \mathcal{S} \cap G_k$. It is easy to verify that F_k is finite (since $f_{k,e} \notin \bigcup_{i<k} G_i$).

Claim. $\mathcal{S} \notin$ **UniformRobustBc**.

Proof. Suppose by way of contradiction that h is a recursive function such that $\mathbf{M}_{h(e)}$ **Bc**-identifies $\Theta_e(\mathcal{S})$. Note that b_k can be recursively computed using oracle for K. Thus, $h(b_k)$ can be recursively computed using oracle for K. Hence, for all but finitely many k, $h(b_k) \leq g'(k)$. Consequently, $\mathbf{M}_{h(b_k)}$ does not **Bc**-identify $\Theta_{b_k}(f_{k,h(b_k)}) \in \Theta_{b_k}(\mathcal{S})$. A contradiction. □

Claim. $\mathcal{S} \in$ **RobustCons**.

Proof. Suppose $\Theta = \Theta_k$ is general recursive. We need to show that $\Theta_k(\mathcal{S}) \in$ **Cons**. Let $A = \{a_i \mid i \in N\}$. Since $\overline{A}$ is r.e. in K, there exists a recursive sequence $c_0, c_1, \ldots$, such that each $a \in A$, $a > a_k$, appears infinitely often in the sequence, and each $a \notin A$ or $a \leq a_k$, appears only finitely often in the sequence. Let $\sigma_{e,t} \in \mathrm{SEG}_{0,1}$ be such that $\sigma_{e,t} \supseteq 0^e 1$, and $\sigma_{e,t}$ can be obtained effectively from e, t, and $\lim_{t \to \infty} \sigma_{e,t} = \sigma_e$. Note that there exist such $\sigma_{e,t}$ due to K-recursiveness of the sequence $\sigma_0, \sigma_1, \ldots$.

Note that there exists a recursive h such that, if φ_e is recursive then, $\mathbf{M}_{h(e)}$ **Cons**-identifies $\Theta(\mathcal{B}_{\varphi_e})$. Fix such recursive h.

Let $F = \{0^\infty\} \cup F_0 \cup F_1 \cup \ldots \cup F_k$. F and $\Theta(F)$ are finite sets of total recursive functions.

Define **M** as follows.

$\mathbf{M}(f[n])$

1. If for some $g \in \Theta(F)$, $g[n] = f[n]$, then output a canonical program for one such g.
2. Else, let $t \leq n$ be the largest number such that $\Theta(\sigma_{c_t,n}) \sim f[n]$, and $\Theta(\sigma_{c_t,n}) \not\sim \Theta(0^\infty)$.
   Dovetail the following steps until one of them succeeds. If steps 2.1 or 2.2 succeed, then go to step 3. If step 2.3 succeeds, then go to step 4.
   2.1 There exists an $s > n$, such that $c_s \neq c_t$, and $\Theta(\sigma_{c_s,s}) \sim f[n]$, and $\Theta(\sigma_{c_s,s}) \not\sim \Theta(0^\infty)$.
   2.2 There exists an $s > n$, such that $\sigma_{c_t,s} \neq \sigma_{c_t,n}$.
   2.3 $\mathbf{M}_{h(c_t)}(f[n])\downarrow$, and $f[n] \subseteq \varphi_{\mathbf{M}_{h(c_t)}(f[n])}$.
3. Output a program for $f[n]0^\infty$.
4. Output $\mathbf{M}_{h(c_t)}(f[n])$.

End

It is easy to verify that whenever $\mathbf{M}(f[n])$ is defined, $f[n] \subseteq \varphi_{\mathbf{M}(f[n])}$. Also, if $f \in \Theta(F)$, then $\mathbf{M}$ **Cons**-identifies f.

Now, consider any $f \in \Theta(\mathcal{S}) - \Theta(F)$. Note that there exists a unique $i > k$ such that $f \sim \Theta(\sigma_{a_i})$ and $\Theta(\sigma_{a_i}) \not\sim \Theta(0^\infty)$ (due to definition of σ_{a_j}'s). Fix such i. Also, since $f \neq \Theta(0^\infty)$, there exist only finitely many e such that $f \sim \Theta(0^e 1)$.

We first claim that $\mathbf{M}(f[n])$ is defined for all n. To see this, note that if $c_t \neq a_i$ or $\sigma_{c_t,n} \neq \sigma_{a_i}$, then step 2.1 or step 2.2 would eventually succeed. Otherwise, since $f \in \Theta(F_i) \subseteq \Theta(\mathcal{B}_{\varphi_{a_i}})$, step 2.3 would eventually succeed (since $\mathbf{M}_{h(a_i)}$ **Cons**-identifies $\Theta(\mathcal{B}_{\varphi_{a_i}})$).

Thus, it suffices to show that $\mathbf{M}$ **Ex**-identifies f. Let r be such that $f \not\sim \Theta(0^r)$. Let m and $n > m$ be large enough such that (I) to (IV) hold.

(I) $f[n] \not\sim \Theta(0^r)$.
(II) $c_m = a_i$, and for all $s \geq m$, $\sigma_{a_i,s} = \sigma_{a_i,m}$.
(III) For all $e < r$ and $t > m$, if $e \notin A$ or $e \leq a_k$, then $c_t \neq e$.
(IV) For all $e < r$ and $t > m$, if $e \in A - \{a_i\}$ and $e > a_k$, then $\Theta(\sigma_{e,t}) \not\sim f[n]$ or $\Theta(\sigma_{e,t}) \sim \Theta(0^\infty)$.

Note that there exist such m, n. Thus, for all $n' \geq n$, in computation of $\mathbf{M}(f[n'])$, c_t would be a_i, and step 2.1 and step 2.2 would not succeed. Thus step 2.3 would succeed, and $\mathbf{M}$ would output $\mathbf{M}_{h(a_i)}(f[n'])$. Thus $\mathbf{M}$ **Ex**-identifies f, since $\mathbf{M}_{h(a_i)}$ **Ex**-identifies f. □

Theorem follows from above claims. ∎

Corollary 37. UniformRobustCons ⊂ RobustCons.
UniformRobustEx ⊂ RobustEx.
UniformRobustBc ⊂ RobustBc.

References

1. D. Angluin and C. Smith. Inductive inference: Theory and methods. *Computing Surveys*, 15:237–289, 1983.
2. M. Anthony and N. Biggs. *Computational Learning Theory.* Cambridge University Press, 1992.
3. J. Bārzdiņš. Inductive inference of automata, functions and programs. In *Int. Math. Congress, Vancouver*, pages 771–776, 1974.
4. J. Bārzdiņš. Two theorems on the limiting synthesis of functions. In *Theory of Algorithms and Programs, vol. 1*, pages 82–88. Latvian State University, 1974. In Russian.
5. J. Bārzdiņš and R. Freivalds. Prediction and limiting synthesis of recursively enumerable classes of functions. *Latvijas Valsts Univ. Zimatm. Raksti*, 210:101–111, 1974.
6. L. Blum and M. Blum. Toward a mathematical theory of inductive inference. *Information and Control*, 28:125–155, 1975.
7. M. Blum. A machine-independent theory of the complexity of recursive functions. *Journal of the ACM*, 14:322–336, 1967.

8. J. Case, S. Jain, M. Ott, A. Sharma, and F. Stephan. Robust learning aided by context. *Journal of Computer and System Sciences (Special Issue for COLT'98)*, 60:234–257, 2000.
9. J. Case and C. Smith. Comparison of identification criteria for machine inductive inference. *Theoretical Computer Science*, 25:193–220, 1983.
10. C. C. Florencio. Consistent identification in the limit of some Penn and Buszkowski's classes is NP-hard. In *Proceedings of the International Conference on Computational Linguistics*, 1999.
11. R. Freivalds. Inductive inference of recursive functions: Qualitative theory. In J. Bārzdiņš and D. Bjorner, editors, *Baltic Computer Science*, volume 502 of *Lecture Notes in Computer Science*, pages 77–110. Springer-Verlag, 1991.
12. R. Freivalds, J. Bārzdiņš, and K. Podnieks. Inductive inference of recursive functions: Complexity bounds. In J. Bārzdiņš and D. Bjørner, editors, *Baltic Computer Science*, volume 502 of *Lecture Notes in Computer Science*, pages 111–155. Springer-Verlag, 1991.
13. M. Fulk. Saving the phenomenon: Requirements that inductive machines not contradict known data. *Information and Computation*, 79:193–209, 1988.
14. M. Fulk. Robust separations in inductive inference. In *31st Annual IEEE Symposium on Foundations of Computer Science*, pages 405–410. IEEE Computer Society Press, 1990.
15. E. M. Gold. Language identification in the limit. *Information and Control*, 10:447–474, 1967.
16. J. Grabowski. Starke Erkennung. In R. Lindner and H. Thiele, editors, *Strukturerkennung diskreter kybernetischer Systeme, Teil I*, pages 168–184. Seminarbericht Nr.82, Department of Mathematics, Humboldt University of Berlin, 1986. In German.
17. S. Jain. Robust behaviorally correct learning. *Information and Computation*, 153(2):238–248, September 1999.
18. S. Jain, D. Osherson, J. Royer, and A. Sharma. *Systems that Learn: An Introduction to Learning Theory*. MIT Press, Cambridge, Mass., second edition, 1999.
19. S. Jain, C. Smith, and R. Wiehagen. On the power of learning robustly. In *Proceedings of the Eleventh Annual Conference on Computational Learning Theory*, pages 187–197. ACM Press, 1998.
20. K. P. Jantke and H.-R. Beick. Combining postulates of naturalness in inductive inference. *Journal of Information Processing and Cybernetics (EIK)*, 17:465–484, 1981.
21. R. Klette and R. Wiehagen. Research in the theory of inductive inference by GDR mathematicians – A survey. *Information Sciences*, 22:149–169, 1980.
22. S. Kurtz and C. Smith. On the role of search for learning. In R. Rivest, D. Haussler, and M. Warmuth, editors, *Proceedings of the Second Annual Workshop on Computational Learning Theory*, pages 303–311. Morgan Kaufmann, 1989.
23. S. Kurtz and C. Smith. A refutation of Bārzdiņš' conjecture. In K. P. Jantke, editor, *Analogical and Inductive Inference, Proceedings of the Second International Workshop (AII '89)*, volume 397 of *Lecture Notes in Artificial Intelligence*, pages 171–176. Springer-Verlag, 1989.
24. S. Lange. Consistent polynomial-time inference of k-variable pattern languages. In J. Dix, K. P. Jantke, and P. Schmitt, editors, *Nonmonotonic and Inductive Logic, 1st International Workshop, Karlsruhe, Germany*, volume 543 of *Lecture Notes in Computer Science*, pages 178–183. Springer-Verlag, 1990.
25. E. Minicozzi. Some natural properties of strong identification in inductive inference. *Theoretical Computer Science*, 2:345–360, 1976.

26. T. Mitchell. *Machine Learning.* McGraw Hill, 1997.
27. D. Osherson, M. Stob, and S. Weinstein. *Systems that Learn: An Introduction to Learning Theory for Cognitive and Computer Scientists.* MIT Press, 1986.
28. M. Ott and F. Stephan. Avoiding coding tricks by hyperrobust learning. In P. Vitányi, editor, *Fourth European Conference on Computational Learning Theory,* volume 1572 of *Lecture Notes in Artificial Intelligence,* pages 183–197. Springer-Verlag, 1999.
29. H. Rogers. *Theory of Recursive Functions and Effective Computability.* McGraw-Hill, 1967. Reprinted by MIT Press in 1987.
30. W. Stein. Consistent polynomial identification in the limit. In M. M. Richter, C. H. Smith, R. Wiehagen, and T. Zeugmann, editors, *Algorithmic Learning Theory: Ninth International Conference (ALT' 98),* volume 1501 of *Lecture Notes in Artificial Intelligence,* pages 424–438. Springer-Verlag, 1998.
31. V. N. Vapnik. *The Nature of Statistical Learning Theory. Second Edition.* Springer-Verlag, 2000.
32. R. Wiehagen. Limes-Erkennung rekursiver Funktionen durch spezielle Strategien. *Journal of Information Processing and Cybernetics (EIK),* 12:93–99, 1976.
33. R. Wiehagen. *Zur Theorie der Algorithmischen Erkennung.* Dissertation B, Humboldt University of Berlin, 1978.
34. R. Wiehagen and W. Liepe. Charakteristische Eigenschaften von erkennbaren Klassen rekursiver Funktionen. *Journal of Information Processing and Cybernetics (EIK),* 12:421–438, 1976.
35. R. Wiehagen and T. Zeugmann. Ignoring data may be the only way to learn efficiently. *Journal of Experimental and Theoretical Artificial Intelligence,* 6:131–144, 1994.
36. R. Wiehagen and T. Zeugmann. Learning and consistency. In K. P. Jantke and S. Lange, editors, *Algorithmic Learning for Knowledge-Based Systems,* volume 961 of *Lecture Notes in Artificial Intelligence,* pages 1–24. Springer-Verlag, 1995.
37. T. Zeugmann. On Bārzdiņš' conjecture. In K. P. Jantke, editor, *Analogical and Inductive Inference, Proceedings of the International Workshop,* volume 265 of *Lecture Notes in Computer Science,* pages 220–227. Springer-Verlag, 1986.

On the Synthesis of Strategies Identifying Recursive Functions

Sandra Zilles

Fachbereich Informatik
Universität Kaiserslautern
Postfach 3049
D - 67653 Kaiserslautern
zilles@informatik.uni-kl.de

Abstract. A classical learning problem in Inductive Inference consists of identifying each function of a given class of recursive functions from a finite number of its output values. Uniform learning is concerned with the design of single programs solving infinitely many classical learning problems. For that purpose the program reads a description of an identification problem and is supposed to construct a technique for solving the particular problem.
As can be proved, uniform solvability of collections of solvable identification problems is rather influenced by the description of the problems than by the particular problems themselves. When prescribing a specific inference criterion (for example learning in the limit), a clever choice of descriptions allows uniform solvability of all solvable problems, whereas even the most simple classes of recursive functions are not uniformly learnable without restricting the set of possible descriptions. Furthermore the influence of the hypothesis spaces on uniform learnability is analysed.

1 Introduction

Inductive Inference is concerned with methods of identifying objects in a target class from incomplete information. The learning model is based on a recursion-theoretic background, i.e. target objects as well as learners are represented by computable functions. From an input sequence consisting of finite subgraphs of the graph of a target function the learner produces a sequence of hypotheses interpreted as indices of functions enumerated by a partial-recursive numbering. In the initial approach of identification in the limit introduced by Gold in [6] that sequence of hypotheses is supposed to converge to a correct index of the target function. Several further identification criteria have been introduced and analysed in [2], [3] and [5]. In general, a learning problem is given by

- a class U of recursive functions,
- a hypothesis space ψ and
- an identification criterion I.

D. Helmbold and B. Williamson (Eds.): COLT/EuroCOLT 2001, LNAI 2111, pp. 160–176, 2001.

The aim is to find a learner identifying *each* function in the class U with respect to ψ within the scope of the criterion I.

Now imagine a collection of infinitely many learning problems solvable according to a given criterion. Uniform Inductive Inference is concerned with the question, whether there exists a single program which – given a description of a special learning problem of our collection – synthesizes an appropriate learner solving the actual problem. Such a program may be interpreted as a very "intelligent" learner able to simulate infinitely many learners of the classical type. Instead of tackling each problem in a specific way we want to use a kind of uniform strategy coping with the whole accumulation of problems.

Jantke's work [7] is concerned with the uniform identification of classes of recursive functions in the limit, particularly for the case that in each learning step the intermediate hypothesis generated by the learner is consistent with the information received up to the actual time of the learning process. Jantke proved that his model of uniform identification does not allow the synthesis of a program learning a class consisting of just a single recursive function, as long as the synthesizer is supposed to cope with any possible description of such a class. His negative result indicates that the concept of uniform learning might be rather fruitless. But this suggestion is mitigated by the results on uniform identification of classes of languages – a concept which is studied for example in [10], [9] and [4]. Especially [4] contains lots of positive results allowing a more optimistic point of view concerning the fruitfulness of the uniform identification model. The work of Osherson, Stob and Weinstein additionally deals with several possibilities for the description of learning problems.

The present paper provides its own definition of uniform identifiability with the special feature that any of the learning problems described may be solved with respect to any appropriate hypothesis space without requiring the synthesis of the particular hypothesis spaces. The first result in Section 4 shows the existence of a special set of descriptions accumulating all learning problems solvable according to a given criterion I, such that synthesizing learners successful with respect to I is possible. The trick is to encode programs for the learners within the descriptions. Of course in general such tricks should be avoided, for example by fixing the set of descriptions in advance. But then it is still possible to use tricks by a clever choice of the hypothesis spaces. The results in Section 5 show that such tricks provide a uniform strategy for behaviourally correct identification[1] of any class learnable according to that criterion, even coping with any description of such a class. Nevertheless the free choice of the hypothesis spaces does not trivialize uniform learning in the limit. For example the collection of all descriptions of classes consisting of just two recursive functions is not suitable in that sense, i.e. there is no uniform strategy constructing a successful program for learning in the limit from such a description. Unfortunately, those results are rather negative: either uniform learnability is achieved by tricks and thus becomes trivial or it cannot be achieved at all. When fixing the hypothesis spaces in advance, our situation gets even worse. Jantke's result is strengthened

[1] For the definitions of inference criteria mentioned here see Section 2.

by proving that there is no uniform learner for behaviourally correct identification with respect to an acceptable numbering coping with all descriptions of sets of just one recursive function. The same collection of learning problems becomes unsolvable even for behaviourally correct identification with anomalies, if we further tighten our demands concerning the hypothesis spaces.

On the other hand we also present some quite positive results, which at least seem to justify some further research on uniform learning. For example, if the descriptions of the learning problems fulfill some special topological conditions, one can uniformly construct strategies learning the corresponding classes in the limit – even with total and consistent intermediate hypotheses[2]. Results of this kind strongly substantiate the suggestion that uniform identification is indeed a model of rich learning power. The negative results mentioned above just have to be interpreted carefully. The reason for the failure of uniform learners is most often not a substantial lack of power, but lies in the choice of unsuitable descriptions. So our model really seems worthy of investigation. In general, Section 2 provides preliminaries and Section 3 deals with the notion of uniform identification as well as basic results. General results are presented in Section 4, followed by results on particular description sets in Section 5. Finally Section 6 is concerned with the influence of the choice of the hypothesis spaces. We also transfer Wiehagen's characterizations of classes identifiable in the limit (see [13]) to the case of uniform learning.

2 Preliminaries

First we fix some notions that will be used in this paper. All conceptions in the context of recursion theory not explicitly introduced here can be found in [12].

We denote the set of (nonnegative) integers by $\mathbb{N}$ and write $\mathbb{N}^*$ for the set of all finite tuples of elements of $\mathbb{N}$. If n is any integer, we refer to the set of all n-tuples of integers by $\mathbb{N}^n$. By means of a bijective and computable mapping from $\mathbb{N}^n$ onto $\mathbb{N}$ we identify n-tuples of integers with elements in $\mathbb{N}$. Between $\mathbb{N}^*$ and $\mathbb{N}$ we also choose a bijective, computable mapping and denote it by $\text{cod} : \mathbb{N}^* \to \mathbb{N}$. Thus we may use α to refer to $\text{cod}(\alpha)$, where $\alpha \in \mathbb{N}^*$. The quantifiers $\forall$ and $\exists$ are used in the common way. Quantifying an expression with $\forall^\infty n$ indicates that the expression is true for all but finitely many $n \in \mathbb{N}$.

Inclusion of sets is expressed by the symbol $\subseteq$, proper inclusion by $\subset$. card X serves as a notation for the cardinality of a set X, and we write card $X = \infty$, whenever X is an infinite set. The set of all subsets of X is referred to by $\wp X$.

$\mathcal{P}^n$ denotes the class of all partial-recursive functions of n variables. Its subclass of total functions (called recursive functions) is denoted by $\mathcal{R}^n$. Whenever the number of arguments is of no special interest, we omit the superscripts. For any function $f \in \mathcal{P}$ and any integer n the notation $f[n]$ refers to the coding $\text{cod}(f(0), \dots, f(n))$ of the initial segment of length $n+1$ of f, as long as the values $f(0), \dots, f(n)$ are all defined. For $f \in \mathcal{P}$ and $x \in \mathbb{N}$ we write $f(x)\downarrow$, if f is defined for the argument x; $f(x)\uparrow$, if f is not defined for the argument x.

[2] See Section 6 for definitions.

For piecewise comparison of two functions $f, g \in \mathcal{P}$ we agree on the notation $f =_n g$, if $\{(x, f(x)) \mid x \leq n \text{ and } f(x)\downarrow\} = \{(x, g(x)) \mid x \leq n \text{ and } g(x)\downarrow\}$; otherwise $f \neq_n g$. If the set of arguments on which the functions $f, g \in \mathcal{P}$ disagree is finite, i.e. if $[[f(n)\uparrow \wedge g(n)\uparrow]$ or $[f(n)\downarrow \wedge g(n)\downarrow \wedge f(n) = g(n)]]$ for all but finitely many $n \in \mathbb{N}$, we write $f =^* g$.

A function f may be identified with the sequence $(f(n))_{n \in \mathbb{N}}$ of its values, which yields notations like e.g. $f = 0^k\uparrow^\infty$ or $g = 0^k12^\infty$. A finite tuple $\alpha \in \mathbb{N}^*$ is often regarded as the function $\alpha\uparrow^\infty$ implicitly. For two functions f, g the notation $f \sqsubseteq g$ means that $\{(x, f(x)) \mid x \in \mathbb{N},\ f(x)\downarrow\} \subseteq \{(x, g(x)) \mid x \in \mathbb{N},\ g(x)\downarrow\}$.

Any $\psi \in \mathcal{P}^{n+1}$ $(n \in \mathbb{N})$ is used as a numbering for the set $\mathcal{P}_\psi := \{\psi_i \mid i \in \mathbb{N}\}$ by means of the definition $\psi_i(x) := \psi(i, x)$ for all $i \in \mathbb{N},\ x \in \mathbb{N}^n$. The index $i \in \mathbb{N}$ is called ψ-number of the function ψ_i.

Given $\psi \in \mathcal{P}^{n+2}$ $(n \in \mathbb{N})$, every integer $b \in \mathbb{N}$ "describes" a partial-recursive numbering, which we will denote by ψ^b. We set $\psi^b(i, x) := \psi(b, i, x)$ for all $i \in \mathbb{N},\ x \in \mathbb{N}^n$ and thus write by analogy with the notations above: $\psi^b_i(x) := \psi^b(i, x)$ for all $i \in \mathbb{N},\ x \in \mathbb{N}^n$.

For any $\psi \in \mathcal{P}^{n+1}$, $n \in \mathbb{N}$ we will often refer to the entirety of total functions in $\mathcal{P}_\psi$, which will be called the "recursive core" or "$\mathcal{R}$-core" of $\mathcal{P}_\psi$ (abbreviated by $\mathcal{R}_\psi$). Hence $\mathcal{R}_\psi = \mathcal{R} \cap \mathcal{P}_\psi$.

Identification in the limit[3] provides the fundamentals for learning models examined in Inductive Inference and has first been analysed by Gold in [6].

Definition 1. *Let $U \subseteq \mathcal{R}$, $\psi \in \mathcal{P}^2$. The class U is an element of EX_ψ and called identifiable in the limit with respect to ψ iff there is a function $S \in \mathcal{P}$ (called strategy) such that for any $f \in U$:*

1. $\forall n \in \mathbb{N}\ [S(f[n])\downarrow]$ *($S(f[n])$ is called hypothesis on $f[n]$),*
2. $\exists j \in \mathbb{N}\ [\psi_j = f$ *and* $\forall^\infty n\ [S(f[n]) = j]]$.

If S is given, we also write $U \in EX_\psi(S)$. We set $EX := \bigcup_{\psi \in \mathcal{P}^2} EX_\psi$.

On every function $f \in U$ the strategy S generates a sequence of indices converging to a ψ-number of f. [13] supplies the following characterization of the classes learnable in the limit, which will be useful for us later on.

Theorem 1. *Let $U \subseteq \mathcal{R}$. $U \in EX$ iff there exist $\psi \in \mathcal{P}^2$ and $d \in \mathcal{R}^2$ such that*

1. $U \subseteq \mathcal{P}_\psi$,
2. $\forall i, j \in \mathbb{N}\ [i \neq j \Rightarrow \psi_i \neq_{d(i,j)} \psi_j]$.

If we omit the demand for convergence to *a single* hypothesis, we talk of "behaviourally correct" identification, defined for example in [2].

Definition 2. *Let $U \subseteq \mathcal{R}$, $\psi \in \mathcal{P}^2$. U is called BC-identifiable wrt ψ iff there exists an $S \in \mathcal{P}$, such that for all $f \in U$ the following conditions are fulfilled:*

1. $\forall n \in \mathbb{N}\ [S(f[n])\downarrow]$,

[3] We also use the term "explanatory identification", abbreviated by EX-identification.

2. $\forall^\infty n\ [\psi_{S(f[n])} = f]$.

We also write $U \in BC_\psi(S)$ and define BC_ψ and BC as usual.

BC-identifiability has also been characterized in [13]. But for our purpose the following characterization proved in [11] is more useful.

Theorem 2. *Let $U \subseteq \mathcal{R}$. $U \in BC$ iff there exist $\psi \in \mathcal{P}^2$ and $d \in \mathcal{R}^2$ satisfying*

1. $U \subseteq \mathcal{P}_\psi$,
2. $\forall i, j \in \mathbb{N}\ [\psi_i = \psi_j \iff \psi_i =_{d(i,j)} \psi_j]$.

Though BC-identification provides more learning power than EX-identification – a proof can be found in [2] – there are still classes of recursive functions which are not in BC. In [5] we find a variation of BC-identification, which allows learnability of the whole class $\mathcal{R}$.

Definition 3. *Let $U \subseteq \mathcal{R}$, $\psi \in \mathcal{P}^2$. U is called BC-identifiable with finitely many anomalies wrt ψ iff there exists an $S \in \mathcal{P}$, such that for all $f \in U$ the following conditions are fulfilled:*

1. $\forall n \in \mathbb{N}\ [S(f[n])\downarrow]$,
2. $\forall^\infty n\ [\psi_{S(f[n])} =^* f]$.

We write $U \in BC^*_\psi(S)$ and use the notations BC^*_ψ and BC^* in the usual way.

From now on let $\mathcal{I} := \{\mathrm{EX}, \mathrm{BC}, \mathrm{BC}^*\}$ denote the set of all previously declared inference criteria. The following results have been proved (see [2] and [5]):

Theorem 3. *$EX \subset BC \subset BC^* = \wp\mathcal{R}$.*

3 Uniform Learning – Model and Basic Results

Throughout this paper let $\varphi \in \mathcal{P}^3$ be a fixed acceptable numbering of $\mathcal{P}^2$. If we choose a number $b \in \mathbb{N}$, we may interpret it as an index for the partial-recursive numbering $\varphi^b \in \mathcal{P}^2$, which assigns the value $\varphi(b, x, y)$ to each pair (x, y) of integers. Thus we can regard b as a description of a class of recursive functions, namely the recursive core of $\mathcal{P}_{\varphi^b}$. We will denote this class by $\mathcal{R}_b$, i.e. $\mathcal{R}_b := \mathcal{R}_{\varphi^b} = \mathcal{R} \cap \mathcal{P}_{\varphi^b}$ for $b \in \mathbb{N}$. Similarly each set $B \subseteq \mathbb{N}$ describes a set $\mathcal{R}_B := \{\mathcal{R}_b \mid b \in B\}$ of classes of recursive functions.

If V and W are sets of sets, we will write $V \preceq W$ if and only if for all $X \in V$ there exists a set $Y \in W$ such that $X \subseteq Y$.

Definition 4. *Let I, I' be elements of $\mathcal{I}$ satisfying $I \subseteq I'$. A set $J \subseteq \wp\mathcal{R}$ of classes of recursive functions is said to be uniformly learnable with respect to I and I' iff there exists a set $B \subseteq \mathbb{N}$ such that the following conditions are fulfilled:*

1. $J \preceq \mathcal{R}_B$,
2. $\mathcal{R}_B \subseteq I$,
3. $\exists S \in \mathcal{P}^2\ \forall b \in B\ \exists \psi \in \mathcal{P}^2\ [\mathcal{R}_b \in I'_\psi(\lambda x.S(b, x))]$.

We refer to this definition by $J \in uni(I, I')$.

So $J \in \text{uni}(I, I')$ iff there is a set B of indices of numberings such that

- every class in J is contained in some recursive core $\mathcal{R}_b$ corresponding to an index $b \in B$;
- every recursive core $\mathcal{R}_b$ described by some $b \in B$ is learnable under the criterion I;
- there is a uniform strategy S which, given $b \in B$, learns $\mathcal{R}_b$ under the criterion I' with respect to some appropriate hypothesis space ψ.

The set B is called *description set* for J, I, I'. We also write $J \in \text{uni}_B(I, I')$, $J \in \text{uni}(I, I')(S)$ or $J \in \text{uni}_B(I, I')(S)$, whenever the description set B, the uniform strategy S or both of them are fixed.

In order to prove the uniform learnability of a subset $J \subseteq \wp\mathcal{R}$ wrt $I, I' \in \mathcal{I}$ we first have to specify the set $B \subseteq \mathbb{N}$ describing the classes to be learned, secondly the (possibly distinct) numberings $\psi \in \mathcal{P}^2$ serving as hypothesis spaces for the particular classes $\mathcal{R}_b$ $(b \in B)$ and finally the strategy $S \in \mathcal{P}^2$ designed to do the actual "learning job". Starting from this point of view two main questions arise:

1. Which classes $J \subseteq \wp\mathcal{R}$ are uniformly learnable wrt given criteria I, I' at all?
2. Which classes $J \subseteq \wp\mathcal{R}$ remain learnable in the sense of $\text{uni}(I, I')$, if we specify in advance one of the parameters mentioned above?

Of course these questions are much too general to be answered exhaustively in this paper. Nevertheless some characterizations and interesting special cases are considered.

On condition that $J \in \text{uni}_B(I, I')$ we obviously obtain $\mathcal{R}_B \in \text{uni}_B(I, I')$. As all classes in $\mathcal{I}$ are closed under inclusion, we also verify that $\mathcal{R}_B \in \text{uni}_B(I, I')$ implies $J \in \text{uni}_B(I, I')$ for all $J \preceq \mathcal{R}_B$. Therefore the sets $J \in \text{uni}(I, I')$ are characterized by those description sets $B \subseteq \mathbb{N}$ which are suitable for uniform learning of *some* set $J' \subseteq \wp\mathcal{R}$:

Lemma 1. *Assume $I, I' \in \mathcal{I}$, $J \subseteq \wp\mathcal{R}$. Then $J \in uni(I, I')$ if and only if there exists a set $B \subseteq \mathbb{N}$ satisfying $\mathcal{R}_B \in uni_B(I, I')$ and $J \preceq \mathcal{R}_B$.*

For that reason the appropriate description sets for uniform learning are of particular interest for our further research. Now consider a set $\mathcal{R}_B$ of recursive cores described by a set $B \subseteq \mathbb{N}$. The mere statement that $\mathcal{R}_B \in \text{uni}(I, I')$ for some $I, I' \in \mathcal{I}$ does *not* imply the uniform learnability of $\mathcal{R}_B$ wrt I, I' *from* B. It is quite conceivable that $\mathcal{R}_B$ might be uniformly learnable from a description set $B' \subseteq \mathbb{N}$, but *not* from the description set B. This would as well involve that *no* set $J \subseteq \wp\mathcal{R}$ was uniformly learnable wrt I, I' from description set B at all; thus we might consider the description set B to be unsuitable for uniform learning with respect to I and I'.

Definition 5. *Let $I, I' \in \mathcal{I}$, $B \subseteq \mathbb{N}$. The description set B is said to be suitable for uniform learning with respect to I and I' if $\mathcal{R}_B \in uni_B(I, I')$. The class of all description sets suitable in that sense will be denoted by $suit(I, I')$.*

These considerations raise the question whether there are certain specific properties characterizing our appropriate description sets $B \in \mathrm{suit}(I, I')$.

Definition 6. *Fix $I, I' \in \mathcal{I}$, $h : \mathbb{N} \to \mathbb{N}$. A set $J \subseteq \wp\mathcal{R}$ is called uniformly learnable wrt I and I' by the interpretation function h, iff there exist $B \subseteq \mathbb{N}$ and $S \in \mathcal{P}^2$ such that:*

1. *$J \in uni_B(I, I')(S)$,*
2. *$\forall b \in B\ [\mathcal{R}_b \in I'_{\varphi^{h(b)}}(\lambda x.S(b, x))]$.*

We abbreviate this formulation by $J \in uni_{[h]}(I, I')$. If additionally there is a numbering $\tau \in \mathcal{P}^2$ satisfying $\varphi^{h(b)} = \tau$ for all $b \in \mathbb{N}$, we write $J \in uni_\tau(I, I')$ instead.

Note that the interpretation function h in our definition is not necessarily computable or total. Of course we might wish to fix both our hypothesis spaces by means of an interpretation function h *and* our description set B in advance. In that case we use the notions $\mathrm{uni}_{B,[h]}(I, I')$ as well as $\mathrm{uni}_{B,\tau}(I, I')$ by analogy. In the usual way we may also refer to fixed uniform strategies in our notations. Via the function h each description $b \in B$ obtains an associated hypothesis space $\varphi^{h(b)}$, by means of which we can interpret the hypotheses produced by the strategy $\lambda x.S(b, x)$. Regarding practical aspects we are interested especially in computable interpretation functions, such as for example the identity function $id : \mathbb{N} \to \mathbb{N}$ defined by $id(x) = (x)$ for all $x \in \mathbb{N}$.

We are now able to formulate some basic results on uniform learning. Although the corresponding proofs are quite simple, these results will be useful for our further examinations. First we state a necessary condition for uniform learnability of a subset of $\wp\mathcal{R}$. For the proof of Proposition 1 note that all classes $I \in \mathcal{I}$ are closed with respect to the inclusion of sets.

Proposition 1. *Let $I, I' \in \mathcal{I}$, $I \subseteq I'$, $J \subseteq \wp\mathcal{R}$. If $J \in uni(I, I')$, then $J \subseteq I$.*

Proof. Let $J \in \mathrm{uni}(I, I')$. Then there is a set $B \subseteq \mathbb{N}$ which fulfills $J \in \mathrm{uni}_B(I, I')$. This implies $\mathcal{R}_B \subseteq I$ and $J \preceq \mathcal{R}_B$. Thus for all $U \in J$ there exists $b \in B$ such that $U \subseteq \mathcal{R}_b \in I$. So $J \subseteq I$, because I is closed under inclusion. □

From Proposition 1 and the definition of uniform learning we conclude:

Corollary 1. *Let $I, I' \in \mathcal{I}$, $I \subseteq I'$. Then $uni(I, I) \subseteq uni(I, I') \subseteq \wp I$.*

Any strategy identifying a class $U \subseteq \mathcal{R}$ with respect to some criterion $I \in \mathcal{I}$ can be replaced by a *total* recursive strategy without loss of learning power. This new strategy is defined by computing the values of the old strategy for a bounded number of steps and a bounded number of input examples with increasing bounds. As long as there is no hypothesis found, some temporary hypothesis is produced. Afterwards the hypotheses of the former strategy are put out "with delay". Now we transfer these observations to the level of uniform learning and get:

Proposition 2. *Let $I, I' \in \mathcal{I}$, $B \subseteq \mathbb{N}$ and let $h : \mathbb{N} \to \mathbb{N}$ be any function. Assume $\mathcal{R}_B \in uni_{B,[h]}(I, I')$. Then there exists a total recursive function S satisfying $\mathcal{R}_B \in uni_{B,[h]}(I, I')(S)$.*

We will use this result implicitly in the forthcoming proofs.

Proposition 3. *Let $I \in \mathcal{I}$, $h : \mathbb{N} \to \mathbb{N}$. If $B \subseteq \mathbb{N}$ is a finite set with $\mathcal{R}_b \in I_{\varphi^{h(b)}}$ for all $b \in B$, then $\mathcal{R}_B \in uni_{B,[h]}(I, I)$.*

The proof is obvious: a finite number of strategies – each learning one of the given $\mathcal{R}$-cores wrt I – can be merged to a single computable uniform strategy.

4 Uniform Learning without Specification of the Model Parameters

First we deal with uniform learning according to Definition 4 without specifying the description set B or the hypothesis spaces ψ in advance. We choose two inference criteria $I, I' \in \mathcal{I}$ satisfying $I \subseteq I'$ and try to characterize the subsets $J \subseteq \wp\mathcal{R}$ contained in $\text{uni}(I, I')$. From Corollary 1 we already know that these sets must be subsets of I. Now we will even prove the sufficiency of that simple condition.

Theorem 4. *If $I, I' \in \mathcal{I}$, $I \subseteq I'$, then $uni(I, I) = uni(I, I') = \wp I$.*

Proof. Assume $I, I' \in \mathcal{I}$, $I \subseteq I'$. Applying Corollary 1 we only have to show $\wp I \subseteq \text{uni}(I, I)$. Assume $J \in \wp I$. For each $U \in J$ there is a numbering $\psi \in \mathcal{P}^2$ such that $U \subseteq \mathcal{P}_\psi$ and $\mathcal{R}_\psi \in I$ (a proof can be derived from $\mathcal{R} \in \text{BC}^*$ and the characterizations in Theorems 1 and 2 quite easily). Let $C \subseteq \mathbb{N}$ be the set of φ-indices of all these numberings. Fix an acceptable numbering $\tau \in \mathcal{P}^2$.

For each $c \in C$ there is a τ-index k_c of a strategy $S_c \in \mathcal{P}$, which identifies $\mathcal{R}_c$ in the limit with respect to τ according to the criterion I.

These τ-indices can now be coded within our hypothesis spaces φ^c by simply integrating the function $k_c\uparrow^\infty$ into the numberings. Thus we achieve that our new numberings obtain two very useful properties. Firstly, their recursive cores are learnable with respect to the criterion I, because we do not change the recursive cores by integrating functions of the shape $k_c\uparrow^\infty$. Secondly, they contain τ-indices for strategies identifying their recursive cores according to I.

Our suitable description set is the set of all indices of numberings achieved by modification of the numberings described by C. A uniform I-learner for the target class J just has to read the indices of the particular strategies and then simulate their jobs with the help of the functions associated by τ. We obtain $J \in \text{uni}(I, I)$ as claimed. □

Note that we even obtain $\text{uni}_\tau(I, I')$=$\text{uni}(I, I')$= $\wp I$ for any acceptable numbering τ. Now we can easily compare the power of uniform learning criteria resulting in the choice of particular criteria $I, I' \in \mathcal{I}$:

Corollary 2. *Let $I, I' \in \mathcal{I}$, $I \subset I'$. Then uni$(I, I) =$ uni$(I, I') \subset$ uni(I', I').*

Proof. By Theorem 4 we know $\text{uni}(I, I) = \text{uni}(I, I')$. As $\text{uni}(I, I') \subseteq \text{uni}(I', I')$, it remains to prove that $\text{uni}(I', I')$ is *not* a subset of $\text{uni}(I, I')$. For this purpose we simply choose any class $U \in I' \backslash I$ and obtain a class $J \in \text{uni}(I', I') \backslash \text{uni}(I, I')$ by defining $J := \{U\}$. □

Intuitively, our uniform strategy defined in the proof of Theorem 4 does not really *learn* anything, because the programs for learning the described classes are coded within the described numberings in advance. In the following sections we will see some more examples for such easy "tricks" simplifying the work of uniform strategies. But as we will see later, there are also non-trivial sets of classes of recursive functions uniformly learnable by really "labouring" strategies.

5 Uniform Learning from Special Description Sets

Now we investigate the suitability of given description sets B, i.e. the uniform learnability of $\mathcal{R}_B$ from B wrt some criteria $I, I' \in \mathcal{I}$. We start with a simple but useful observation.

Proposition 4. *Let $I, I' \in \mathcal{I}$ and $B \subseteq \mathbb{N}$ such that $\mathcal{R}_b \in I$ for all $b \in B$. If $\bigcup_{b \in B} \mathcal{R}_b \in I'$, then $B \in$ suit(I, I').*

The proof of Proposition 4 is straightforward from the definitions. As a direct consequence we obtain a simple characterization of the description sets suitable for uniform learning with BC*-strategies:

Theorem 5. *suit$(I, BC^*) = \{B \subseteq \mathbb{N} \mid \mathcal{R}_B \subseteq I\}$ for $I \in \mathcal{I}$. In particular suit$(BC^*, BC^*) = \wp\mathbb{N}$.*

Since BC is not closed under union of sets, the proof of a corresponding characterization for $\text{suit}(I, \text{BC})$ cannot be based on Proposition 4. Instead – as in the proof of Theorem 4 – we make use of special "tricks", such that the resulting strategy does not really have to do any work.

Theorem 6. *Set $B := \{b \in \mathbb{N} \mid \mathcal{R}_b \in BC\}$. Then $B \in$ suit(BC, BC) and thus suit$(I, BC) = \{B \subseteq \mathbb{N} \mid \mathcal{R}_B \subseteq I\}$ for all $I \in \{EX, BC\}$.*

Proof. Fix an acceptable numbering $\tau \in \mathcal{P}^2$. Each class learnable in the sense of BC can be identified wrt τ by a *total* strategy, i.e. for all $b \in B$ there is an $S_b \in \mathcal{R}$ such that $\mathcal{R}_b \in \text{BC}_\tau(S_b)$.

Given any element $b \in B$ we can now list *all* hypotheses produced by S_b on *all* initial segments of recursive functions in a computable way. If we interpret these hypotheses as τ-indices, we obtain a numbering of all candidate functions suggested by S_b.

More formally: for each $b \in B$ we define $\psi^{[b]} \in \mathcal{P}^2$ by $\psi_i^{[b]}(x) := \tau_{S_b(i)}(x)$ for any $i, x \in \mathbb{N}$. If $f \in \mathcal{R}$, $n \in \mathbb{N}$, then the index $f[n]$ via $\psi^{[b]}$ represents exactly the function "suggested" by S_b on input $f[n]$. This property can be used by a uniform BC-strategy: for $b, n \in \mathbb{N}$ and $f \in \mathcal{R}$ we set $S(b, f[n]) := f[n]$ and obtain

$$\psi^{[b]}_{S(b,f[n])} = \psi^{[b]}_{f[n]} = \tau_{S_b(f[n])} \text{ for any } b \in B,\ f \in \mathcal{R}_b,\ n \in \mathbb{N}\ .$$

Let $b \in B$. Since $\mathcal{R}_b \in \mathrm{BC}_\tau(S_b)$, we conclude $\mathcal{R}_b \in \mathrm{BC}_{\psi^{[b]}}(\lambda x.S(b,x))$. This implies $B \in \mathrm{suit}(\mathrm{BC},\mathrm{BC})$. The second claim follows immediately. □

As we have seen, the trick of encoding much information within the description sets or within the hypothesis spaces often supplies quite simple uniform strategies with a huge learning power. But nevertheless, our following results will make sure that uniform learning procedures cannot always be simplified to such a trivial level. On the one hand we can easily find a trick to design a uniform EX-strategy identifying *any* recursive core consisting of just a single element from its description, but on the other hand there is *no* uniform EX-strategy identifying all recursive cores consisting of two elements from their descriptions. In view of classical learning problems any classes consisting of just two elements are not more complex than classes consisting of one element, whereas their complexity is very different regarding uniform learning problems.

Proposition 5. *$\{b \in \mathbb{N} \mid \mathit{card}\ \mathcal{R}_b = 1\} \in \mathit{suit}(EX, EX)$.*

Proof. Let $B := \{b \in \mathbb{N} \mid \text{card } \mathcal{R}_b = 1\}$. Then of course $\mathcal{R}_b \in \mathrm{EX}$ for all $b \in B$, i.e. $\mathcal{R}_B \subseteq \mathrm{EX}$. Since for all $f \in \mathcal{R}$ there exists a numbering $\psi \in \mathcal{P}^2$ with $\psi_0 = f$, the function constantly zero learns $\mathcal{R}_B$ uniformly from B wrt EX and EX. □

Now, in contrast to Proposition 5 we can prove that no kind of trick can help a strategy to uniformly identify all recursive cores consisting of up to two elements from their descriptions. In particular we observe that there are collections of quite simple identification problems, which even cannot be solved uniformly by encoding information within the hypothesis spaces.

Theorem 7. *$\{b \in \mathbb{N} \mid \mathit{card}\ \{i \in \mathbb{N} | \varphi^b_i \in \mathcal{R}\} \leq 2\} \notin \mathit{suit}(EX, EX)$.*

We omit the proof which can be found in [14]. The idea is to proceed indirectly. Let $B := \{b \in \mathbb{N} \mid \text{card } \{i \in \mathbb{N} | \varphi^b_i \in \mathcal{R}\} \leq 2\}$. Assuming $B \in \mathrm{suit}(\mathrm{EX},\mathrm{EX})$ implies the existence of an $S \in \mathcal{R}^2$ satisfying $\mathcal{R}_b \in \mathrm{EX}(\lambda x.S(b,x))$ for all $b \in B$. But it is possible to construct $b_0 \in B$ describing an $\mathcal{R}$-core which cannot be identified in the limit by $\lambda x.S(b_0,x)$. This strategy fails for at least one function $f \in \mathcal{R}_{b_0}$ by either converging to an incorrect hypothesis or by diverging.

The following corollaries are direct consequences of Theorem 7.

Corollary 3. *$\{b \in \mathbb{N} \mid \mathcal{R}_b \text{ is finite}\} \notin \mathit{suit}(EX, EX)$.*

Corollary 4. *$\mathit{suit}(EX, EX) \subset \mathit{suit}(EX, BC)$.*

Proof. Obviously suit(EX, EX) $\subseteq$ suit(EX, BC). From Theorem 6 and Corollary 3 we conclude $\{b \in \mathbb{N} \mid \mathcal{R}_b \text{ is finite}\} \in$ suit(EX, BC)\suit(EX, EX). □

Theorem 8 is a summary of our main results in this section.

Theorem 8. *Fix a criterion $I \in \mathcal{I}$. The following conditions are equivalent:*

1. *suit*$(I, I) = \{B \subseteq \mathbb{N} \mid \mathcal{R}_B \subseteq I\}$,
2. *suit*$(EX, I) = \{B \subseteq \mathbb{N} \mid \mathcal{R}_B \subseteq EX\}$,
3. $I \in \{BC, BC^*\}$.

In order to characterize the sets in suit(EX, EX) we use Theorem 1 with arguments like those presented in [13], which can be transferred to the case of uniform learning quite easily (the proof is left out, but can be found in [14]). Note the similarity of our properties to the conditions for identification of languages in the limit from text, introduced in [1].

Theorem 9. *A set $B \subseteq \mathbb{N}$ belongs to suit(EX, EX) iff $\exists d \in \mathcal{R}^2\ \forall b \in B\ \exists \psi \in \mathcal{P}^2$*

1. $\mathcal{R}_b \subseteq \mathcal{P}_\psi$,
2. $\forall i \in \mathbb{N}\ [d(b,i) \sqsubseteq \psi_i]$,
3. $\forall i, j \in \mathbb{N}\ [d(b,i) \sqsubseteq d(b,j) \sqsubseteq \psi_i \Rightarrow i = j]$.

6 Uniform Learning with Special Hypothesis Spaces

The trick of encoding information within the hypothesis spaces supplies a strategy uniformly identifying all BC-identifiable recursive cores from their corresponding descriptions. This is a consequence of the freedom of choosing the hypothesis spaces in the definition of uniform learnability. The question arises, to what extent the learning power of uniform strategies is influenced by fixing special hypothesis spaces – for example acceptable numberings – in advance. From Jantke's work [7] we already know that the set of descriptions of $\mathcal{R}$-cores consisting of just a single function is not suitable for uniform EX-identification, if we demand the hypotheses to be correct with respect to an acceptable numbering. Here we tighten Jantke's result by proving that for the same set of descriptions even BC-identification is not strong enough.

Theorem 10. *Assume $B := \{b \in \mathbb{N} \mid card\ \{i \in \mathbb{N} | \varphi_i^b \in \mathcal{R}\} = 1\}$ and let $\tau \in \mathcal{P}^2$ be an acceptable numbering. Then $\mathcal{R}_B \notin uni_{B,\tau}(BC, BC)$.*

An indirect proof is contained in [14]. The assumption $\mathcal{R}_B \in \text{uni}_{B,\tau}(\text{BC}, \text{BC})$ implies the existence of $S \in \mathcal{R}^2$ satisfying $\mathcal{R}_b \in \text{BC}_\tau(\lambda x.S(b,x))$ for all $b \in B$. A contradiction is obtained by construction of an index $b_0 \in B$, such that $\lambda x.S(b_0, x)$ produces infinitely many hypotheses incorrect wrt τ for the only function in $\mathcal{R}_{b_0}$.

Let B be the description set defined in Theorem 10. Since $\mathcal{R} \in \text{BC}^*_\tau$ for any acceptable numbering τ, we obtain $\mathcal{R}_B \in \text{uni}_{B,\tau}(\text{EX}, \text{BC}^*) \backslash \text{uni}_{B,\tau}(\text{EX}, \text{BC})$, but we can prove that our set B is not suitable for uniform BC*-identification with respect to the hypothesis spaces φ^b, $b \in B$ given *a priori*:

Corollary 5. *Let* $B := \{b \in \mathbb{N} \mid card\,\{i \in \mathbb{N} | \varphi_i^b \in \mathcal{R}\} = 1\}$. *Then* $\mathcal{R}_B \notin uni_{B,[id]}(EX, BC^*)$.

Proof. Assume $\mathcal{R}_B \in \mathrm{uni}_{B,[id]}(\mathrm{EX}, \mathrm{BC}^*)$. Then there exists $S \in \mathcal{R}^2$ which provides $\mathcal{R}_b \in \mathrm{BC}^*_{\varphi^b}(\lambda x.S(b,x))$ for all $b \in B$. Let $\tau \in \mathcal{P}^2$ be acceptable. We will define a strategy $T \in \mathcal{P}^2$ satisfying $\mathcal{R}_b \in \mathrm{EX}_\tau(\lambda x.T(b,x))$ for all $b \in B$. For that purpose we choose $g \in \mathcal{R}$, such that

$$\varphi_i^{g(b)}(j) := \begin{cases} \varphi_i^b(j) & \forall x \leq j\ [\varphi_i^b(x)\downarrow] \\ \uparrow & \text{otherwise} \end{cases} \quad \text{for all } b, i, j \in \mathbb{N}\,.$$

Fix $c \in \mathcal{R}^2$ such that $\tau_{c(b,i)} = \varphi_i^{g(b)}$ for all $b, i \in \mathbb{N}$. Provided $b \in B$ we observe $g(b) \in B$ and

$$\exists n_b \in \mathbb{N}\ \forall i \in \mathbb{N}\backslash\{n_b\}\ [\varphi_i^{g(b)} \text{ initial}]\,.$$

Let f_b denote the function in $\mathcal{R}_{g(b)}$, $b \in B$. Since $\mathcal{R}_{g(b)} \in \mathrm{BC}^*_{\varphi^{g(b)}}(\lambda x.S(g(b),x))$, we conclude $S(g(b), f_b[n]) = n_b$ for all but finitely many $n \in \mathbb{N}$. This can be explained by the fact that $\varphi_i^{g(b)}$ is initial and thus $\varphi_i^{g(b)} \neq^* f_b$ for all $i \neq n_b$. Therefore $\mathcal{R}_{g(b)} \in \mathrm{EX}_{\varphi^{g(b)}}(\lambda x.S(g(b),x))$. If we define $T(b, f^n) := c(b, S(g(b), f^n))$ for all $b, n \in \mathbb{N}$, $f \in \mathcal{R}$, we obtain $\mathcal{R}_B \in \mathrm{uni}_{B,\tau}(\mathrm{EX}, \mathrm{EX})$ in contradiction to Theorem 10. Thus the assumption $\mathcal{R}_B \in \mathrm{uni}_{B,[id]}(\mathrm{EX}, \mathrm{BC}^*)$ has been wrong.□

One might reason that uniform learning from the description set B and with respect to the hypothesis spaces φ^b given above is so hard, because in each numbering φ^b the element of the recursive core possesses only one index. But even if we allow infinitely many φ^b-numbers for the functions to be learned, our situation does not improve:

Corollary 6. *If* $C := \{b \mid card\,\mathcal{R}_b = 1 \wedge card\,\{i | \varphi_i^b \in \mathcal{R}\} = \infty\}$, *then* $\mathcal{R}_C \notin uni_{C,[id]}(EX, BC^*)$.

Proof. We use Corollary 5. For this purpose assume $\mathcal{R}_C \in \mathrm{uni}_{C,[id]}(\mathrm{EX}, \mathrm{BC}^*)(S)$ for some appropriate strategy $S \in \mathcal{R}^2$. We will construct a uniform BC*-strategy for our class $\mathcal{R}_B$, where B denotes the description set defined in Corollary 5. There is a function $g \in \mathcal{R}$ satisfying

$$\begin{aligned} &\varphi_0^{g(b)} = \varphi_0^b, \\ &\varphi_1^{g(b)} = \varphi_0^b,\ \varphi_2^{g(b)} = \varphi_1^b, \\ &\varphi_3^{g(b)} = \varphi_0^b,\ \varphi_4^{g(b)} = \varphi_1^b,\ \varphi_5^{g(b)} = \varphi_2^b, \ldots \end{aligned}$$

for all $b \in \mathbb{N}$. The following properties can be verified easily:

1. $\forall b \in \mathbb{N}\ [\mathcal{R}_{g(b)} = \mathcal{R}_b]$.
2. $\forall b \in \mathbb{N}\ \forall f \in \mathcal{P}_{\varphi^{g(b)}}\ [\mathrm{card}\,\{i \in \mathbb{N} \mid \varphi_i^{g(b)} = f\} = \infty]$, i.e. each function in $\mathcal{P}_{\varphi^{g(b)}}$ possesses infinitely many $\varphi^{g(b)}$-indices.

3. $\exists e \in \mathcal{R}\ \forall b \in \mathbb{N}\ \forall i \in \mathbb{N}\ [\varphi_i^{g(b)} = \varphi_{e(i)}^b]$, i.e. $\varphi^{g(b)}$-indices can be translated effectively into φ^b-indices with a uniform method.

Considering our problem we observe that $g(b) \in C$ whenever $b \in B$. Therefore $T(b,x) := e(S(g(b),x))$ (for $b, x \in \mathbb{N}$) yields a computable strategy satisfying $\mathcal{R}_B \in \text{uni}_{B,[id]}(\text{EX}, \text{BC}^*)(T)$. That contradiction to Corollary 5 now forces us to reject our assumption. This implies $\mathcal{R}_C \notin \text{uni}_{C,[id]}(\text{EX}, \text{BC}^*)$. □

To characterize uniform learning with respect to acceptable numberings, we use Theorems 1 and 2. We omit the proofs which can be easily transferred from the non-uniform case.

Theorem 11. *Let $B \subseteq \mathbb{N}$ fulfill $\mathcal{R}_b \in EX$ for all $b \in B$. Furthermore, let $\tau \in \mathcal{P}^2$ be acceptable. Then $\mathcal{R}_B \in uni_{B,\tau}(EX, EX) \iff \exists \psi \in \mathcal{P}^3\ \exists d \in \mathcal{R}^3\ \forall b \in B$*

1. $\mathcal{R}_b \subseteq \mathcal{P}_{\psi^b}$,
2. $\forall i, j \in \mathbb{N}\ [i \neq j \Rightarrow \psi_i^b \neq_{d(b,i,j)} \psi_j^b]$.

Theorem 12. *Fix $I \in \{EX, BC\}$. Let $B \subseteq \mathbb{N}$ fulfill $\mathcal{R}_b \in I$ for all $b \in B$. Furthermore, let $\tau \in \mathcal{P}^2$ be an acceptable numbering. Then $\mathcal{R}_B \in uni_{B,\tau}(I, BC)$ $\iff \exists \psi \in \mathcal{P}^3\ \exists d \in \mathcal{R}^2\ \forall b \in B$*

1. $\mathcal{R}_b \subseteq \mathcal{P}_{\psi^b}$,
2. $\forall i, j \in \mathbb{N}\ [\psi_i^b =_{\max\{d(b,i),d(b,j)\}} \psi_j^b \iff \psi_i^b = \psi_j^b]$.

Since $\mathcal{R} \in \text{BC}_\tau^*$ for any acceptable numbering τ, we can use the same reasoning as in Proposition 4 to prove our characterization in Theorem 13.

Theorem 13. *Fix $I \in \mathcal{I}$ and $B \subseteq \mathbb{N}$. Furthermore, let $\tau \in \mathcal{P}^2$ be an acceptable numbering. Then $\mathcal{R}_B \in uni_{B,\tau}(I, BC^*) \iff [\mathcal{R}_b \in I$ for all $b \in B]$.*

A very natural learning behaviour is to construct only consistent intermediate hypotheses, i.e. hypotheses agreeing with the information received so far (cf. [3]).

Definition 7. *Assume $U \in \mathcal{R}$, $\psi \in \mathcal{P}^2$. U is called identifiable consistently wrt ψ iff there is an $S \in \mathcal{P}$ satisfying $U \in EX_\psi(S)$, such that $\psi_{S(f[n])} =_n f$ for all $f \in U$, $n \in \mathbb{N}$. We use the notions CONS, $CONS_\psi$, $CONS_\psi(S)$ for that criterion in the common way.*

Furthermore it is reasonable to demand just total functions to be described by the intermediate hypotheses (see [8]).

Definition 8. *Assume $U \in \mathcal{R}$, $\psi \in \mathcal{P}^2$. U is called identifiable with consistent and total hypotheses wrt ψ iff there is an $S \in \mathcal{P}$ satisfying $U \in CONS_\psi(S)$, such that $\psi_{S(f[n])} \in \mathcal{R}$ for all $f \in U$, $n \in \mathbb{N}$. The notions CT, CT_ψ, $CT_\psi(S)$ are used for that criterion in the usual manner.*

Definitions 4, 5 and 6 can be reformulated for the inference criteria CONS and CT. A quite simple result, based on Identification by Enumeration as has been introduced in [6], is presented in [10]:

Theorem 14. *If* $B \subseteq \mathbb{N}$, $\varphi^b \in \mathcal{R}^2$ *for all* $b \in B$, *then* $\mathcal{R}_B \in uni_{B,[id]}(CT, CT)$.

For uniform learning with respect to "meaningful" hypothesis spaces, i.e. in such a way, that all hypotheses produced by the strategy can be "interpreted" by the user, most of our results have been negative. Even very "simple" classes yield bad results. To show that there still remains a sense in the definition of uniform learning, we present some intuitively more complex description sets suitable for uniform learning in the limit – even with consistent and total intermediate hypotheses – with respect to any acceptable numbering.

Definition 9. *A set* $D \subseteq \mathcal{P}$ *is called discrete iff for any* $f \in D$ *there is an* $n \in \mathbb{N}$, *such that* $f \neq_n g$ *for all functions* $g \in D \backslash \{f\}$. *This* $n \in \mathbb{N}$ *is then called discreteness point for* f *wrt* D.

Theorem 15. *Let* $\tau \in \mathcal{P}^2$ *be an acceptable numbering,* $B \subseteq \mathbb{N}$. *Assume that* $\mathcal{P}_{\varphi^b}$ *is discrete for all* $b \in B$. *Then* $\mathcal{R}_B \in uni_{B,\tau}(CT, CT)$.

Proof. Provided that B fulfills the conditions requested above we first construct appropriate hypothesis spaces uniformly in $b \in B$. Of course their indices may then be transformed to equivalent programs in τ effectively. For that purpose we will fix $b \in B$ and collect all initial segments of functions in $\mathcal{P}_{\varphi^b}$ in order to use them as initial segments for the functions in our new hypothesis space. We will try to extend these initial segments to computable functions, such that finally all functions of the recursive core $\mathcal{R}_b$ have indices in our constructed numbering. The uniform strategy defined afterwards works iteratively. It always starts with a consistent hypothesis and in each following inference step it tests whether its previous hypothesis is still consistent with the new information received or not. In the first case the previous hypothesis is maintained, otherwise a new consistent hypothesis is constructed.

For the definition of our new hypothesis spaces ψ^b, $b \in B$ we need a function *extend* $\in \mathcal{P}$, which indicates suitable extensions of initial segments. For $b, n, x, k \in \mathbb{N}$ and $f \in \mathcal{R}$ define

$$extend(b, f[n], x, k) := \begin{cases} 1 & \varphi_k^b(0)\downarrow, \ldots, \varphi_k^b(x)\downarrow \text{ and } \varphi_k^b[n] = f[n] \\ \uparrow & \text{otherwise} \end{cases}$$

Thus *extend*$(b, f[n], x, k)$ is defined if and only if $\varphi_k^b[x]$ is an "extension" of $f[n]$.

Definition of $\psi \in \mathcal{P}^3$ *with* $\mathcal{R}_b \in CT_{\psi^b}$ *for all* $b \in B$*:*
Let $b, n, x \in \mathbb{N}$, $f \in \mathcal{R}$. We define

$$\psi(b, f[n], x) := \begin{cases} f(x) & x \leq n \\ \varphi_k^b(x) & x > n \text{ and } k \in \mathbb{N} \text{ may be found,} \\ & \quad \text{such that } extend(b, f[n], x, k) = 1 \\ \uparrow & \text{otherwise} \end{cases}$$

Obviously ψ is computable. For any $b \in B$ we observe the following properties:

Claim 1. If $f \in \mathcal{R}_b$ and $n \in \mathbb{N}$ is any integer, then $\psi^b_{f[n]} \in \mathcal{R}$.
Claim 2. If $f \in \mathcal{R}_b$ and n_f is a discreteness point of f wrt $\mathcal{P}_{\varphi^b}$, then $\psi^b_{f[n_f]} = f$.
Claim 3. $\mathcal{R}_b \subseteq \mathcal{P}_{\psi^b}$.

Proof of Claim 1. Since $f \in \mathcal{P}_{\varphi^b}$, we know that for all $x \in \mathbb{N}$ there is an "extension" of $f[n]$, i.e. $\forall x \in \mathbb{N}\ \exists k \in \mathbb{N}\ [extend(b, f[n], x, k) = 1]$. As there *is* an extension, it may also be found within a finite amount of time. The definition of ψ then implies that for all $n \in \mathbb{N}$ the function $\psi^b_{f[n]}$ is total and thus recursive.

Proof of Claim 2. For all arguments less than or equal to n_f the values of $\psi^b_{f[n_f]}$ and f must agree, because those arguments match the first case in the definition of ψ^b. For all arguments greater than n_f the existence of an "extension" of $f[n_f]$ is checked. As $f \in \mathcal{R}$, we observe that this check will always stop with a positive answer. Since n_f is a discreteness point for f wrt $\mathcal{P}_{\varphi^b}$, the only function in $\mathcal{P}_{\varphi^b}$ extending $f[n_f]$ is f. Hence $\psi^b_{f[n_f]} = f$.

Proof of Claim 3. Let $f \in \mathcal{R}_b$ and let n_f be a discreteness point of f wrt $\mathcal{P}_{\varphi^b}$. As $\mathcal{P}_{\varphi^b}$ is discrete, n_f exists. Claim 2 then implies $\psi^b_{f[n_f]} = f$, hence $f \in \mathcal{P}_{\psi^b}$.

Now let $c \in \mathcal{R}^2$ be a recursive function satisfying $\tau_{c(b,y)} = \psi^b_y$ for all $b, y \in \mathbb{N}$.

Definition of a strategy $S \in \mathcal{P}^2$ with $\mathcal{R}_b \in CT_\tau(\lambda x.S(b,x))$ for all $b \in B$:
Let $f \in \mathcal{R}$, $b, n \in \mathbb{N}$. We define $S(b, f[0]) := c(b, f[0])$ and

$$S(b, f[n+1]) := \begin{cases} \uparrow & \exists x \leq n+1\ [\tau_{S(b,f[n])}(x)\uparrow] \\ S(b, f[n]) & \tau_{S(b,f[n])} =_{n+1} f \\ c(b, f[n+1]) & \text{otherwise} \end{cases}$$

Now we prove that for all $b \in B$ and all initial segments of functions in $\mathcal{R}_b$ our strategy returns consistent indices of total functions. Furthermore we will show that for any function in $\mathcal{R}_b$ the sequence of hypotheses converges. From consistency we thus obtain convergence to a *correct* index. We have to verify:

(*i*) $\forall b \in B\ \forall f \in \mathcal{R}_b\ \forall n \in \mathbb{N}\ [S(b, f[n])\downarrow]$.
(*ii*) $\forall b \in B\ \forall f \in \mathcal{R}_b\ \forall n \in \mathbb{N}\ [\tau_{(b,S(b,f[n]))} =_n f]$.
(*iii*) $\forall b \in B\ \forall f \in \mathcal{R}_b\ \forall n \in \mathbb{N}\ [\tau_{(b,S(b,f[n]))} \in \mathcal{R}]$.
(*iv*) $\forall b \in B\ \forall f \in \mathcal{R}_b\ \exists n_0 \in \mathbb{N}\ \forall n \geq n_0\ [S(b, f[n]) = S(b, f[n_0])]$.

Proof of (i), (ii) and (iii). Let $b \in B$, $f \in \mathcal{R}_b$. We use induction on n.
First assume $n = 0$. Obviously $S(b, f[0]) = c(b, f[0])$ is defined. Furthermore, from the definitions of S, *extend*, ψ and c we observe that

$$\tau_{S(b,f[0])} = \tau_{c(b,f[0])} = \psi^b_{f[0]} =_0 f\ .$$

This proves the consistency of the hypothesis $S(b, f[0])$. Since $f \in \mathcal{R}_b$, we observe from Claim 1 with $n = 0$, that $\tau_{S(b,f[0])} = \tau_{c(b,f[0])} = \psi^b_{f[0]} \in \mathcal{R}$.

Assume for a fixed $n \in \mathbb{N}$, that $S(b, f[n])$ is defined, consistent for $f[n]$ and a τ-index of a total function. From this situation we want to deduce that also $S(b, f[n+1])$ is defined, consistent for $f[n+1]$ and a τ-index of a total function. Since $\tau_{S(b,f[n])}$ is total, we can test effectively whether $\tau_{S(b,f[n])} =_{n+1} f$ or not. If the first case occurs, the hypothesis is maintained. Then the new hypothesis is still defined, consistent and an index of a total function. Otherwise, if the second case occurs, our previous hypothesis must have been wrong. We obtain

$$\tau_{S(b,f[n+1])} = \tau_{c(b,f[n+1])} = \psi^b_{f[n+1]} =_{n+1} f .$$

So $S(b, f[n+1])$ is consistent for $f[n+1]$. Claim 1 now yields $\tau_{S(b,f[n+1])} \in \mathcal{R}$. Anyway the hypothesis produced by S fulfills the conditions (i), (ii) and (iii).

Proof of (iv). Again assume $b \in B$, $f \in \mathcal{R}_b$. If there exists an $n_0 \in \mathbb{N}$, such that for all $n \geq n_0$ the first case in the definition of $S(b, f[n])$ occurs, the hypothesis $S(b, f[n_0])$ will never be changed and the sequence of hypotheses converges. Provided such an n_0 does *not* exist, we may deduce a contradiction as follows:

As $\mathcal{P}_{\varphi^b}$ is discrete, there is an $n_f \in \mathbb{N}$ satisfying $[\varphi^b_i =_{n_f} f \iff \varphi^b_i = f]$ for all $i \in \mathbb{N}$. From (ii) we already know $\tau_{S(b,f[n_f])} =_{n_f} f$. Since according to our assumption there exists a number $n > n_f$, such that the second case in the definition of $S(b, f[n])$ occurs, the hypothesis put out by S on input $(b, f[n])$ equals $c(b, f[n])$. Since $n > n_f$, the number n is a discreteness point of f wrt $\mathcal{P}_{\varphi^b}$. Claim 2 now implies $f = \psi^b_{f[n]} = \tau_{c(b,f[n])} = \tau_{S(b,f[n])}$. Thus S has found a correct hypothesis. But correct hypotheses must be consistent for all further inputs; therefore the first case in the definition of S will occur for all following input segments. Hence we reach the desired contradiction. This implies (iv).

From conditions (i),(ii) and (iv) we conclude, that the output of our uniform strategy converges to a correct hypothesis for all "interesting" input sequences. Together with condition (iii) we finally obtain $\mathcal{R}_b \in \mathrm{CT}_{\psi^b}(\lambda x.S(b,x))$ for all $b \in B$. This completes the proof. □

By comparison of Theorem 15 with our previous results we conclude that the way the recursive cores are described has much more influence upon their uniform learnability than the $\mathcal{R}$-cores themselves. We know from the proof of Theorem 4 that from appropriate descriptions even for the entirety of all classes in EX uniform learning with respect to acceptable numberings is possible. Because of Theorem 15 the set $B_{discrete} := \{b \in \mathbb{N} \mid \mathcal{P}_{\varphi^b} \text{ is discrete}\}$ is suitable for uniform CT-identification with respect to any acceptable numbering. On the other hand, there are sets describing finite – and thus very "simple" – recursive cores which are not suitable for uniform learning with respect to EX at all, even if we allow free choice of the hypothesis spaces. The reason for the failure of all uniform strategies might be the inappropriate topological features of the described numberings. Now if a set B even describes functions φ^b enumerating discrete sets *without repetitions*, we observe that B is suitable for uniform learning with respect to the hypothesis spaces φ^b given a priori. Unfortunately, to prove that result we will abandon our demand for total intermediate hypotheses. Theorems 15 and 16 give rise to a more optimistic view regarding the learning power of uniform identification models. Indeed, our concept is not as poor or trivial as our previous results might have suggested.

Definition 10. *A numbering* $\psi \in \mathcal{P}^2$ *is called absolutely discrete iff* $\mathcal{P}_\psi$ *is discrete and each function in* $\mathcal{P}_\psi$ *has exactly one* ψ*-number.*

Theorem 16. *Fix* $B \subseteq \mathbb{N}$*. Assume that* φ^b *is an absolutely discrete numbering for all* $b \in B$*. Then* $\mathcal{R}_B \in uni_{B,[id]}(CT, CONS)$*.*

Proof. From Theorem 15 we know that $\mathcal{R}_b \in$ CT for all $b \in B$. For any $f \in \mathcal{R}$, $n, b \in \mathbb{N}$ a uniform strategy $S \in \mathcal{P}^2$ may look for a number $i \in \mathbb{N}$ with $\varphi_i^b =_n f$ and then return i. As this strategy S works consistently and B describes absolutely discrete numberings only, we obtain $\mathcal{R}_B \in \mathrm{uni}_{B,[id]}(\mathrm{CT}, \mathrm{CONS})(S)$. □

References

1. Angluin, D.; *Inductive Inference of Formal Languages from Positive Data*, Information and Control 45, 117-135 (1980).
2. Barzdins, J.; *Two Theorems on the Limiting Synthesis of Functions*, Theory of Algorithms and Programs, Latvian State University, Riga 210, 82-88 (1974) (in Russian).
3. Barzdins, J.; *Inductive Inference of Automata, Functions and Programs*, In: Proceedings International Congress of Math., Vancouver, 455-460 (1974).
4. Baliga, G.; Case, J.; Jain, S.; *Synthesizing Enumeration Techniques for Language Learning*, In: Proceedings of the Ninth Annual Conference on Computational Learning Theory, ACM Press, 169-180 (1996).
5. Case, J.; Smith, C.; *Comparison of Identification Criteria for Machine Inductive Inference*, Theoretical Computer Science 25, 193-220 (1983).
6. Gold, E.M.; *Language Identification in the Limit*, Information and Control 10, 447-474 (1967).
7. Jantke, K.; *Natural Properties of Strategies Identifying Recursive Functions*, Elektronische Informationsverarbeitung und Kybernetik 15, 487-496 (1979).
8. Jantke, K.; Beick, H.; *Combining Postulates of Naturalness in Inductive Inference*, Elektronische Informationsverarbeitung und Kybernetik 17, 465-484 (1981).
9. Kapur, S.; Bilardi, G.; *On uniform learnability of language families*, Information Processing Letters 44, 35-38 (1992).
10. Osherson, D.N.; Stob, M.; Weinstein, S.; *Synthesizing Inductive Expertise*, Information and Computation 77, 138-161 (1988).
11. Oymanns, L.; *Lernen von rekursiven Funktionen mit guten Beispielen*, Diploma Thesis, University of Kaiserslautern (1998) (in German).
12. Rogers, H.; *Theory of Recursive Functions and Effective Computability*, MIT Press, Cambridge, Massachusetts (1987).
13. Wiehagen, R.; *Zur Theorie der algorithmischen Erkennung*, Dissertation B, Humboldt-University, Berlin (1978) (in German).
14. Zilles, S.; *On Uniform Learning of Classes of Recursive Functions*, Technical Report LSA-2000-05E, Centre for Learning Systems and Applications, University of Kaiserslautern (2000).

Intrinsic Complexity of Learning Geometrical Concepts from Positive Data

Sanjay Jain *[1] and Efim Kinber **[2]

[1] School of Computing, National University of Singapore, Singapore 119260. sanjay@comp.nus.edu.sg

[2] Department of Computer Science, Sacred Heart University, Fairfield, CT 06432-1000, U.S.A. kinbere@sacredheart.edu

Abstract. Intrinsic complexity is used to measure complexity of learning areas limited by broken-straight lines (called *open semi-hulls*)[1] and intersections of such areas. Any strategy learning such geometrical concept can be viewed as a sequence of *primitive basic* strategies. Thus, the length of such a sequence together with complexities of primitive strategies used can be regarded as complexity of learning the concept in question. We obtained best possible lower and upper bounds on learning open semi-hulls, as well as matching upper and lower bounds on complexity of learning intersections of such areas. Surprisingly, upper bounds in both cases turn out to be much lower than those provided by natural learning strategies. Another surprising result is that learning intersections of open semi-hulls (and their complements) turns out to be easier than learning open semi-hulls themselves.

1 Introduction

Learning geometrical concepts from examples is a popular topic in Computational Learning Theory (see for example, [2,8,7,16,20,15,17,19,10,12,3,18]). The goal of this paper is to quantify complexity of algorithmic learning *infinite* geometrical concepts from growing finite segments. Note that, ideas and techinques used to study learning finite geometrical concepts in the papers cited just above are not applicable to infinite concepts. Consider, for example, an *open semi-hull* representing the space consisting of all points (x, y) with integer components x, y in the first quadrant of the plane bounded by the y-axis and the "broken" line passing through some points $(a_0, c_0), (a_1, c_1), \ldots, (a_n, c_n), a_i, c_i \in N, a_i < a_{i+1}, 0 \leq i < n$. The line is straight between any points $(a_i, c_i), (a_{i+1}, c_{i+1}))$ and begins at $(a_0, c_0) = (0, 0)$; further we assume that the slope of the broken line is monotonically non-decreasing — that is $(c_{i+1} - c_i)/(a_{i+1} - a_i)$ is non-decreasing in i (we need this for learnability of the semi-hull). For technical ease we further assume that the first line segment $(0, 0), (a_1, c_1)$ is adjacent to the x-axis, that is, $c_1 = 0$. (See example semi-hull figure in Figure 1.)

* Supported in part by NUS grant number RP3992710.

** Supported in part by the URCG grant of Sacred Heart University.

[1] We thank Mohan Kankanhalli who suggested the name semi-hull.

D. Helmbold and B. Williamson (Eds.): COLT/EuroCOLT 2001, LNAI 2111, pp. 177–193, 2001.

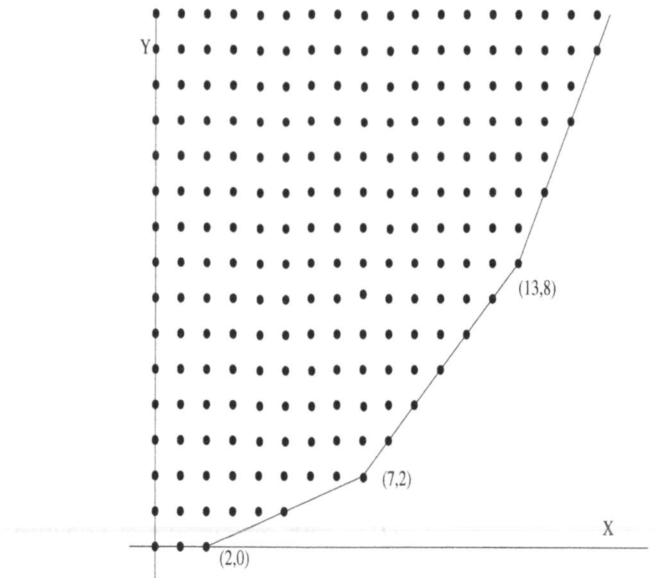

Fig. 1. Open Semi Hull

Any such open semi-hull can be easily learned in the limit by the following strategy: given growing finite sets of points in the open semi-hull (potentially getting all points), learn the first "break" point (a_1, c_1), then the first slope $(c_2 - c_1)/(a_2 - a_1)$, then the second "break" point (a_2, c_2), then the second slope $(c_3 - c_2)/(a_3 - a_2)$, etc. Is this strategy optimal? Do there exist "easier" strategies of learning such geometrical concepts? How to measure complexity of learning such concepts? The theory of inductive inference (learning from growing finite segments) suggests several ways to quantify complexity of learning. Among them are:

a) counting the number of *mind changes* [1,6,27] the learner makes before arriving to the correct hypothesis;

b) measuring the amount of so-called *long-term* memory the learner uses [25, 26];

c) reductions between different learning problems (classes of languages) and respective degrees of so-called *intrinsic* complexity [13,23,24].

There have been other notions of complexity of learning in the limit considered in literature (for example see [14,9,31]).

The first two approaches, however, cannot capture the complexity of learning open semi-hulls with different numbers of "angles": the number of mind changes cannot be bounded by any constant, and the long-term memory is maximum (linear) even for one "angle". Thus, we have chosen reductions as the way to measure (relative) complexity of geometrical concepts like open semi-hulls. An important issue here is which classes of languages can be used as a *scale* for quantifying complexity of open semi-hulls. One such scale, that turned out to be appropriate for our goal, had been suggested in [22]. This scale is a hierarchy of degrees of intrinsic complexity composed of simple natural "ground" degrees. Every such natural "ground" degree represents a natural type of learning strategy. For example, the degree INIT represents a strategy that tries to use a sequence of hypotheses "equivalent" to a sequence of monotonically growing finite sets. Another such ground degree, COINIT, tries to use a sequence of hypotheses "equivalent" to a sequence of monotonically growing sets $N_a = \{x|x \in N, x \geq a\}$. Intuitively, capabilities of INIT and COINIT-strategies must be different, and it has been formally established in [23]. It has been also demonstrated in [23] that many important "simple" learning problems (in particular, *pattern languages*) can be handled by strategies of these basic types. Now, the corresponding degrees of complexity INIT and COINIT can be used to form a complex hierarchy of degrees/strategies as follows. Imagine a "three-dimensional" language L. Suppose an INIT-type strategy M_1 can be used to learn its first "dimension", L_1. Once this "dimension" has been learned, a strategy of a different (or even same) type, say, COINIT can pick the grammar learned by M_1 and use this information to learn the second "dimension" L_2. Consequently, the grammar learned by the COINIT-strategy M_2 can be used to learn the third "dimension" L_3 by a strategy M_3 of type, say, INIT. Thus, we get a strategy of the type (INIT, COINIT, INIT), where information learned by the learner M_i is relayed to the learner M_{i+1} making it possible to learn the next "dimension". This idea can be naturally extended to any (finite) number of "dimensions" and to any sequences $Q = (q_1, q_1, ..., q_k)$ of strategies $q_i \in \{\text{INIT}, \text{COINIT}\}$. It has been shown in [22] that the degrees of complexity (classes of languages) corresponding to such Q-strategies form a rich hierarchy. For example, some classes learnable by (INIT, COINIT, INIT)-type strategies cannot be learned by any (INIT, COINIT)-strategy. Placing a learning problem SEMI_HULL (representing the above open semi-hulls) into this hierarchy, that is, finding a Q such that SEMI_HULL $\equiv Q$, or finding Q_1, Q_2 such that SEMI_HULL is "between" Q_1, Q_2 (where Q_1, Q_2 would be as "close" as possible), would determine what is the most "efficient" learning strategy for open semi-hulls of the above type, and which strategies cannot learn them. The reader may have noticed that learning every "break" point and every slope requires a "simple" strategy of certain type, and they can be learned only in certain order, with information learned on any step being used by the next learning strategy. Thus, we hope it will not be surprising that open semi-hulls will fit well into the above Q-hierarchy. What will be surprising, though, is the fact that the natural learning strategy for open semi-hulls, as described in the second paragraph, is not "optimal". For example, we show (Theorem 2) that open semi-hulls with two "angles" are in the class (INIT, COINIT, INIT, COINIT). That is, there exists a learning strategy for these figures that first works as INIT-like, then "changes its mind" to an COINIT-like strategy, then back to an INIT-like strategy, and then again to INIT. It turns out that this strategy is somewhat more "efficient" than the one suggested in the first paragraph. On the other hand, say, no (COINIT, INIT, COINIT, INIT)-strategy, can possibly learn two-angle open semi-hulls (Theorem 3).

The paper has the following structure. Section 2 introduces notations and preliminaries. In Section 3 we give formal definition of Q-classes and degrees. This definition extends the definition of Q-classes in [22]: in addition to classes INIT and COINIT, we use in vectors Q a new class of strategies/languages HALF that turns out to be different from INIT and COINIT and useful for classifying geometrical concepts. In Section 3 we also show that Q-hierarchy can be appropriately extended to class of learning strategies/languages HALF. In Section 4 we define our main concept, the classes of the type SEMI_HULL that formalize intuitive geometrical concept described above. We also establish upper and lower bounds for the SEMI_HULL degrees in terms of Q-hierarchy. We also show that although the bounds do not match, no better lower or upper bounds can be achieved (in terms of Q-hierarchy). In Section 5 we introduce the classes coSEMI_HULL that consist of complements of languages in SEMI_HULL. We also establish lower and upper bounds for coSEMI_HULLs in terms of Q-hierarchy. Upper and lower bounds for SEMI_HULLs and coSEMI_HULLs come close, but do not match (though, upper bounds are much "lower" than the ones suggested by "intuitive" strategies learning classes in question). In Section 6 we define classes of *open hulls* formed by intersections of languages in SEMI_HULLs adjacent to x and y-axis; Figure 2 shows an example of open hull; for these classes we have established matching upper and lower bounds on complexity of their learning in terms of Q-hierarchy. In Section 6 we also define the classes of languages formed by complements of open hulls and establish matching upper and lower bounds for the corresponding degrees of intrinsic complexity. All the abovementioned upper bounds are much "lower" that the ones suggested by intuitive learning strategies.

Due to space restrictions, most proofs are omitted. Readers interested in proofs may see the Technical Report [21].

2 Notation and Preliminaries

Any unexplained recursion theoretic notation is from [30]. The symbol N denotes the set of natural numbers, $\{0, 1, 2, 3, \ldots\}$. Z denotes the set of integers. Z^- denotes the set of negative integers. $i \dot{-} j$ is defined as follows: if $i \geq j$, then $i \dot{-} j = i - j$; $i \dot{-} j = 0$ otherwise.

We let $\langle \cdot, \cdot \rangle$ stand for an arbitrary, computable, bijective mapping from $N \times N$ onto N [30]. We assume without loss of generality that $\langle \cdot, \cdot \rangle$ is monotonically increasing in both its arguments. $\langle \cdot, \cdot \rangle$ can be extended to n-tuples in a natural way (including $n = 1$, where $\langle x \rangle$ may be taken to be x). Due to above isomorphism between N^k and N, we often identify $(x_1, \cdots, x_n)$ with $\langle x_1, \cdots, x_n \rangle$. Thus we can say $L_1 \times L_2 = \{\langle x, y \rangle \mid x \in L_1, y \in L_2\}$.

By φ we denote a fixed *acceptable* programming system for the partial computable functions: $N \rightarrow N$ [30,28]. By φ_i we denote the partial computable function computed by the program with number i in the φ-system. By W_i we denote domain(φ_i). We also say that i is a grammar for W_i. Symbol $\mathcal{E}$ will de-

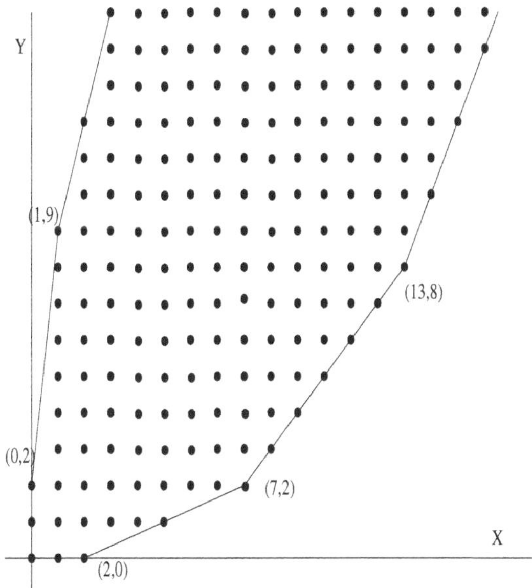

Fig. 2. Open Hull

note the set of all r.e. languages. Symbol L ranges over $\mathcal{E}$. By $\overline{L}$, we denote the complement of L, that is $N - L$. Symbol $\mathcal{L}$ ranges over subsets of $\mathcal{E}$.

We now present concepts from language learning theory. A *finite sequence* σ is a mapping from an initial segment of N into $(N \cup \{\#\})$. The empty sequence is denoted by Λ. The *content* of a finite sequence σ, denoted content(σ), is the set of natural numbers in the range of σ. The *length* of σ, denoted by $|\sigma|$, is the number of elements in σ. So, $|\Lambda| = 0$. For $n \leq |\sigma|$, the initial sequence of σ of length n is denoted by $\sigma[n]$. So, $\sigma[0]$ is Λ. Intuitively, #'s represent pauses in the presentation of data. We let σ, τ, and γ range over finite sequences. SEQ denotes the set of all finite sequences.

A *text* T for a language L is a mapping from N into $(N \cup \{\#\})$ such that L is the set of natural numbers in the range of T ([14]). The *content* of a text T, denoted content(T), is the set of natural numbers in the range of T. $T[n]$ denotes the finite initial sequence of T with length n. We let T range over texts. We let $\mathcal{T}$ range over sets of texts.

A *language learning machine* [14] is an algorithmic device which computes a mapping from SEQ into N. We let $\mathbf{M}$ range over learning machines. $\mathbf{M}(T[n])$ is interpreted as the grammar (index for an accepting program) conjectured by the learning machine $\mathbf{M}$ on the initial sequence $T[n]$. We say that $\mathbf{M}$ converges on T to i, (written $\mathbf{M}(T)\downarrow = i$) iff $(\overset{\infty}{\forall} n)[\mathbf{M}(T[n]) = i]$.

There are several criteria for a learning machine to be successful on a language. Below we define identification in the limit introduced by Gold [14].

Definition 1. [14,6]

(a) **M** **TxtEx**-identifies a text T just in case $(\exists i \mid W_i = \text{content}(T))$ $(\overset{\infty}{\forall} n)[\mathbf{M}(T[n]) = i]$.

(b) **M** **TxtEx**-identifies an r.e. language L (written: $L \in \mathbf{TxtEx}(\mathbf{M})$) just in case **M** **TxtEx**-identifies each text for L.

(c) **M** **TxtEx**-identifies a class $\mathcal{L}$ of r.e. languages (written: $\mathcal{L} \subseteq \mathbf{TxtEx}(\mathbf{M})$) iff **M** **TxtEx**-identifies each $L \in \mathcal{L}$.

(d) **TxtEx** $= \{\mathcal{L} \subseteq \mathcal{E} \mid (\exists \mathbf{M})[\mathcal{L} \subseteq \mathbf{TxtEx}(\mathbf{M})]\}$.

Other criteria of success are finite identification [14], behaviorally correct identification [11,29,5], and vacillatory identification [29,4]. In the present paper, we only discuss results about **TxtEx**-identification.

We write $\sigma \subseteq \tau$ if σ is an initial segment of τ, and $\sigma \subset \tau$ if σ is a proper initial segment of τ. Likewise, we write $\sigma \subset T$ if σ is an initial finite sequence of text T. Let finite sequences $\sigma^0, \sigma^1, \ldots$ be given such that $\sigma^0 \subseteq \sigma^1 \subseteq \cdots$ and $\lim_{i\to\infty} |\sigma^i| = \infty$. Then there is a unique text T such that for all $n \in N$, $\sigma^n = T[|\sigma^n|]$. This text is denoted by $\bigcup_n \sigma^n$. Let $\mathbf{T}$ denote the set of all texts, that is, the set of all infinite sequences over $N \cup \{\#\}$.

We define an *enumeration operator* (or just operator), Θ, to be an algorithmic mapping from SEQ into SEQ such that for all $\sigma, \tau \in$ SEQ, if $\sigma \subseteq \tau$, then $\Theta(\sigma) \subseteq \Theta(\tau)$. We further assume that for all texts T, $\lim_{n\to\infty} |\Theta(T[n])| = \infty$. By extension, we think of Θ as also defining a mapping from $\mathbf{T}$ into $\mathbf{T}$ such that $\Theta(T) = \bigcup_n \Theta(T[n])$. A final notation about the operator Θ. If for a language L, there exists an L' such that for each text T for L, $\Theta(T)$ is a text for L', then we write $\Theta(L) = L'$, else we say that $\Theta(L)$ is undefined. The reader should note the overloading of this notation because the type of the argument to Θ could be a sequence, a text, or a language; it will be clear from the context which usage is intended. We let $\Theta(\mathcal{T}) = \{\Theta(T) \mid T \in \mathcal{T}\}$, and $\Theta(\mathcal{L}) = \{\Theta(L) \mid L \in \mathcal{L}\}$.

We also need the notion of an infinite sequence of grammars. We let α range over infinite sequences of grammars. From the discussion in the previous section it is clear that infinite sequences of grammars are essentially infinite sequences over N. Hence, we adopt the machinery defined for sequences and texts over to finite sequences of grammars and infinite sequences of grammars. So, if $\alpha = i_0, i_1, i_2, i_3, \ldots$, then $\alpha[3]$ denotes the sequence i_0, i_1, i_2, and $\alpha(3)$ is i_3. Furthermore, we say that α converges to i if there exists an n such that, for all $n' \geq n$, $i_{n'} = i$.

Let **I** be any criterion for language identification from texts, for example **I** = **TxtEx**. We say that an infinite sequence α of grammars is **I**-*admissible* for text T just in case α witnesses **I**-identification of text T. So, if $\alpha = i_0, i_1, i_2, \ldots$ is a **TxtEx**-admissible sequence for T, then α converges to some i such that $W_i = \text{content}(T)$; that is, the limit i of the sequence α is a grammar for the language content(T).

We now formally introduce our reductions. Although in this paper we will only be concerned with **TxtEx**-identification, we present the general case of the definition.

Definition 2. [23] Let $\mathcal{L}_1 \subseteq \mathcal{E}$ and $\mathcal{L}_2 \subseteq \mathcal{E}$ be given. Let identification criterion **I** be given. Let $\mathcal{T}_1 = \{T \mid T \text{ is a text for } L \in \mathcal{L}_1\}$. Let $\mathcal{T}_2 = \{T \mid$

T is a text for $L \in \mathcal{L}_2\}$. We say that $\mathcal{L}_1 \leq^{\mathbf{I}} \mathcal{L}_2$ just in case there exist operators Θ and Ψ such that for all $T, T' \in \mathcal{T}_1$ and for all infinite sequences α of grammars the following hold:

(a) $\Theta(T) \in \mathcal{T}_2$ and

(b) if α is an **I**-admissible sequence for $\Theta(T)$, then $\Psi(\alpha)$ is an **I**-admissible sequence for T.

(c) if content(T) = content(T') then content$(\Theta(T))$ = content$(\Theta(T'))$.

We say that $\mathcal{L}_1 \equiv^{\mathbf{I}} \mathcal{L}_2$ iff $\mathcal{L}_1 \leq^{\mathbf{I}} \mathcal{L}_2$ and $\mathcal{L}_2 \leq^{\mathbf{I}} \mathcal{L}_1$.

Intuitively, $\mathcal{L}_1 \leq^{\mathbf{I}} \mathcal{L}_2$ just in case there exists an operator Θ that transforms texts for languages in $\mathcal{L}_1$ into texts for languages in $\mathcal{L}_2$ and there exists another operator Ψ that behaves as follows: if Θ transforms text T (for a language in $\mathcal{L}_1$) to text T' (for a language in $\mathcal{L}_2$), then Ψ transforms **I**-admissible sequences for T' into **I**-admissible sequences for T. Additionally different texts for some language $L \in \mathcal{L}_1$, are transformed into (possibly different) texts for same language $L' \in \mathcal{L}_2$.

Intuitively, for many identification criteria **I** such as **TxtEx**, if $\mathcal{L}_1 \leq^{\mathbf{I}} \mathcal{L}_2$ then the problem of identifying $\mathcal{L}_2$ in the sense of **I** is at least as hard as the problem of identifying $\mathcal{L}_1$ in the sense of **I**, since the solvability of the former problem implies the solvability of the latter one. That is given any machine $\mathbf{M}_2$ which **I**-identifies $\mathcal{L}_2$, one can construct a machine $\mathbf{M}_1$ which **I**-identifies $\mathcal{L}_1$. To see this, for $\mathbf{I} = \mathbf{TxtEx}$, suppose Θ and Ψ witness $\mathcal{L}_1 \leq^{\mathbf{I}} \mathcal{L}_2$. $\mathbf{M}_1(T)$, for a text T is defined as follows. Let $p_n = \mathbf{M}_2(\Theta(T)[n])$, and $\alpha = p_0, p_1, \ldots$. Let $\alpha' = \Psi(\alpha) = p'_0, p'_1, \ldots$. Then let $\mathbf{M}_1(T) = \lim_{n\to\infty} p'_n$.

It is easy to verify that $\leq^{\mathbf{TxtEx}}$ is reflexive and transitive.

3 *Q*-Classes

In this section we introduce classes of languages and corresponding degrees of intrinsic complexity that form the "scale" being used for estimating complexity of learning open semi-hulls and open hulls. First we define "ground" natural classes that are being used as "bricks" to build our hierarchy of degrees.

Definition 3. INIT $= \{L \subseteq N \mid (\exists i \in N)[L = \{x \in N \mid x \leq i\}]\}$.
COINIT $= \{L \subseteq N \mid (\exists i \in N)[L = \{x \in N \mid x \geq i\}]\}$.
HALF $= \{L \subseteq Z \mid (\exists i \in Z)[L = \{x \in Z \mid x \geq i\}]\}$.

Note that officially our definition for languages and r.e. sets as in the Section 2, only allows subsets of N. Since, one can easily code Z onto N, by slight abuse of convention, we can consider subsets of Z also as languages. We thus assume an implicit coding of Z onto N whenever we deal with languages and language classes involving HALF, without explicitly stating so.

While both classes INIT and COINIT are monotonically learnable, the types of conjectures being used to learn INIT and, respectively, COINIT are obviously different. For INIT the maximum element in the input gives a "code" for the language, whereas in COINIT the minimum element gives the code. Note that the maximum element used in INIT strategy is unbounded, whereas the minimum element for COINIT is bounded by 0. So, not surprisingly, the degrees of INIT and COINIT were proven in [23] to be different.

Classes HALF and COINIT are learnable by similar strategies, however, the minimum element in HALF is "unbounded". We will show below that HALF is different from both INIT and COINIT. Furthermore, we have shown that HALF can be viewed as a cross product of INIT and COINIT (that is HALF $\equiv^{\mathbf{TxtEx}}$ INIT $\times$ COINIT).

There are several other natural classes considered in the literature such as FINITE (which is equivalent to INIT), SINGLE, COSINGLE, etc. but we will not be concerned with them here since they will not be relevant to our results.

Now, following [22], we are going to combine classes INIT, COINIT, and HALF to form classes of "multidimensional" languages, where, to learn the "dimension" L_{k+1} of a language L, the learner must first learn the "parameters" $i_1, \ldots, i_k$ of the "dimensions" $L_1, \ldots, L_k$; then L_{k+1} is the projection $\{x_{k+1} | \langle i_1, \ldots, i_k, x_{k+1}, x_{k+2}, \ldots, x_n \rangle \in L\}$ with a simple sublanguage whose description is specified yet by $i_1, \ldots, i_k$. Once it has been determined which projection must be learned, the learner can use a predefined INIT, COINIT, or HALF-type strategy to learn the projection in question. For example, one can consider a class of "two-dimensional" languages (INIT, COINIT), where the first "dimension" $L_1 = \{x | \langle x, y \rangle \in L\}$ of any language L belongs to INIT, and if i is the "parameter" describing L_1 (that can be learned by an INIT-type strategy) then the projection $\{y | \langle i, y \rangle \in L\}$ is in COINIT.

Below for any tuples X and Y, let $X \cdot Y$ denote the concatenation of X and Y. That is if $X = \langle x_1, x_2, \ldots, x_n \rangle$ and $Y = \langle y_1, y_2, \ldots, y_m \rangle$ then $X \cdot Y = \langle x_1 \ldots, x_n, y_1, \ldots y_m \rangle$. Let BASIC $= \{$INIT, COINIT, HALF$\}$.

In part (c) of the following definition and in later situations in languages involving HALF we sometimes abuse notation slightly and allow elements of Z as components of the pairing function $\langle \cdots \rangle$. This is for ease of notation, and one could easily replace these by using some coding of Z onto N.

Definition 4. [22] Suppose $k \geq 1$. Let $Q \in \text{BASIC}^k$. Let $I \in N^k$. Then inductively on k, we define the languages L_I^Q and $T(L_I^Q)$ and $P(L_I^Q)$ as follows.
If $k = 1$, then
(a) if $Q =$ (INIT) and $I = (i)$, $i \in N$, then
$T(L_I^Q) = \{\langle x \rangle \mid x \in N, x < i\}$, $P(L_I^Q) = \{\langle i \rangle\}$, and $L_I^Q = T(L_I^Q) \bigcup P(L_I^Q)$.
(b) if $Q =$ (COINIT) and $I = (i)$, $i \in N$, then
$T(L_I^Q) = \{\langle x \rangle \mid x \in N, x > i\}$, $P(L_I^Q) = \{\langle i \rangle\}$, and $L_I^Q = T(L_i^Q) \bigcup P(L_i^Q)$.
(c) if $Q =$ (HALF) and $I = (i)$, $i \in Z$, then
$T(L_I^Q) = \{\langle x \rangle \mid x \in Z, x > i\}$, $P(L_I^Q) = \{\langle i \rangle\}$, and $L_I^Q = T(L_i^Q) \bigcup P(L_i^Q)$.

Now suppose we have already defined L_I^Q for $k \leq n$. We then define L_I^Q for $k = n + 1$ as follows. Suppose $Q = (q_1, \ldots, q_{n+1})$ and $I = (i_1, \ldots, i_{n+1})$. Let $Q_1 = (q_1)$ and $Q_2 = (q_2, \ldots, q_{n+1})$. Let $I_1 = (i_1)$ and $I_2 = (i_2, \ldots, i_{n+1})$. Then,
$T(L_I^Q) = \{X \cdot Y \mid X \in T(L_{I_1}^{Q_1})$, or $[X \in P(L_{I_1}^{Q_1})$ and $Y \in T(L_{I_2}^{Q_2})]\}$,
$P(L_I^Q) = \{X \cdot Y \mid X \in P(L_{I_1}^{Q_1})$ and $Y \in P(L_{I_2}^{Q_2})\}$, and
$L_I^Q = T(L_I^Q) \bigcup P(L_I^Q)$.

Intuitively, in the above definition $T(L_I^Q)$ denotes the "terminating" part of the language that is specified yet by $i_1, \ldots, i_n$ (and, thus, can be learned trivially), and $P(L_I^Q)$ denotes the "propagating" part of the language L_I^Q that could be used for adding a language in dimension "$n+1$." (See [22] for more details and motivation on the terminology of terminating and propagating.)

For ease of notation we often write $L^Q_{(i_1,i_2,\ldots,i_k)}$ as $L^Q_{i_1,i_2,\ldots,i_k}$.

Definition 5. [22] Let $k \geq 1$. Let $Q = (q_1, \ldots, q_k) \in \text{BASIC}^k$. Then the class $\mathcal{L}^Q$ is defined as

$\mathcal{L}^Q = \{L^Q_{i_1,i_2,\ldots,i_k} \mid$ if $q_j \in \{\text{INIT}, \text{COINIT}\}$ then $i_j \in N$ and if $q_j = \text{HALF}$, then $i_j \in Z\}$.

For technical convenience, for $Q = ()$, $I = ()$, we also define $T(L_I^Q) = \emptyset$, $P(L_Q^I) = \{\langle\rangle\}$, and $L_I^Q = T(L_I^Q) \bigcup P(L_I^Q)$, and $\mathcal{L}^Q = \{L_I^Q\}$.

Note that we have used a slightly different notation for defining the classes $\mathcal{L}^Q$ (for example instead of INIT, we now use $\mathcal{L}^{(\text{INIT})}$). This is for clarity of notation.

The immediate question is which classes Q represent different strong degrees.

Definition 6. Q is said to be a pseudo-subsequence of Q', iff there exists a subsequence Q'' of Q', such that Q'' is obtainable from Q by

(i) replacing some INIT with HALF,
(ii) replacing some COINIT with HALF,
(iii) replacing some HALF with (COINIT, INIT), or
(iv) replacing some HALF with (INIT, COINIT).

Theorem 1. *Suppose* $Q \in \text{BASIC}^k$ *and* $Q' \in \text{BASIC}^l$. *Then,* $\mathcal{L}^Q \leq^{\mathbf{TxtEx}} \mathcal{L}^{Q'}$ *iff* Q *is a pseudo-subsequence of* Q'.

4 Open Semi-hull

rat denotes the set of non-negative rationals. $\mathbf{rat}^+ = \mathbf{rat} - \{0\}$, denotes the set of positive rationals.

Any language $\text{SEMI\_HULL}^n_{\ldots}$ defined below is a geometrical figure "semi-hull," a collection of points in the first quadrant of the plane bounded by the y-axis and a "broken-line" that consists of a straight fragment l_0 of the x-axis (starting from origin) followed by a straight fragment l_1 that makes an angle $\delta_1 < 90°$ with the x-axis, followed by a fragment l_2 that makes an angle $\delta_2 > \delta_1$ with the x-axis, etc. (In above the angle is being measured anti-clockwise from the positive x-axis).

Definition 7. Suppose $a_1, \ldots, a_n \in N$ and $b_1, \ldots, b_n \in \mathbf{rat}^+$, where $0 < a_1 < a_2 < \ldots < a_n$.

$\text{SEMI\_HULL}^n_{a_1,b_1,a_2,b_2,\ldots,a_n,b_n} = \{(x,y) \in N^2 \mid y \geq \sum_{1 \leq i \leq n} b_i * (x \dot{-} a_i)\}$.

Note that $\text{SEMI\_HULL}^0 = N^2$. Also, note that though SEMI_HULL^n above are subsets of N^2, one can easily consider them as languages $\subseteq N$, by using pairing function. We assume such implicit coding whenever we are dealing with sets $\subseteq N^2$.

Parameters a_i in the above definition specify x-coordinates of "break" points of the border line,while the b_i specify the "slopes" that are being added to the "slope" of the border line after every "break" point.

To make our classes of languages learnable, we have to impose certain restrictions on the parameters a_i, b_i. First, we want both coordinates a and c of "break" points (a, c) to be integers. Secondly, for all languages in our classes, we fix a subset S from which "slopes" b_i may come from. (In the following definition S may be an arbitrary subset of $\mathbf{rat}^+$; however, later we will impose additional restrictions on S). The definition of *valid* sequences of parameters a_i, b_i accomplishes this goal.

Definition 8. Suppose $a_1, \ldots, a_n \in N$ and $b_1, \ldots, b_n \in \mathbf{rat}^+$, where $0 < a_1 < a_2 < \ldots < a_n$. Suppose $S \subseteq \mathbf{rat}^+$.

We say that $(a_1, b_1, \ldots, a_n, b_n)$ is *valid* iff for $1 \leq j \leq n$, $[\sum_{1 \leq i \leq n} b_i * (a_j \dot{-} a_i)] \in N$. Additionally, if each $b_i \in S$, then we say that $(a_1, b_1, \ldots, a_n, b_n)$ is *S-valid.*

Let $\text{VALID} = \{(a_1, b_1, \ldots, a_n, b_n) \mid (a_1, b_1, \ldots, a_n, b_n) \text{ is valid}\}$.
Let $\text{VALID}_S = \{(a_1, b_1, \ldots, a_n, b_n) \mid (a_1, b_1, \ldots, a_n, b_n) \text{ is } S\text{-valid}\}$.

Empty sequence () is considered both valid and S-valid. Also we require $a_1 > 0$. This is for technical convenience, and crucial for some of our results. Now we define the class of languages we are going to explore.

Definition 9. Suppose $S \subseteq \mathbf{rat}^+$. Then $\text{SEMI\_HULL}^{n,S} = \{\text{SEMI\_HULL}^n_{a_1,b_1,\ldots,a_n,b_n} \mid (a_1, b_1, \ldots, a_n, b_n) \in \text{VALID}_S\}$.

Now we are at the point when our results require additional constraint on the set S (of "slopes"). Intuitively, the set S satisfying the constraints "cover" the positive rational numbers, and can be algorithmically listed in a monotonic order on a two-sided-infinite tape. A natural example of set S satisfying the constraint below is the set $N \bigcup \{1/x | x \in N\}$. Although our results below hold for any fixed set S of rationals satisfying the constraint in question, we suggest the reader to keep in mind the above set when reading the proofs.

Definition 10. A set $S \subseteq \mathbf{rat}^+$ is said to be $\mathbf{rat}^+$-covering iff there exists a recursive bijection f from Z to S such that,
(i) for $i, j \in Z$, $i < j$ iff $f(i) < f(j)$.
(ii) for every $x \in \mathbf{rat}^+$, there exist $y, y' \in S$ such that $y < x < y'$.

(A natural choice for a set S (which doesn't satisfy the above constraint) seems to be the set $\mathbf{rat}^+$. However, in this case, a complete class of languages $\{L_y = \{x | x \in \mathbf{rat}^+, x \geq y\} \mid y \in \mathbf{rat}^+\}$ (see [22]) would be trivially reducible to any class of languages-figures considered in our paper, thus making all of them of the same complexity. The use of **rat**$^+$-covering sets S gives us opportunity to capture differences in learnability of different geometrical concepts observed in our paper).

Our results below hold for any **rat**$^+$-covering set S. However it is open at present whether SEMI_HULL^{n,S} $\equiv^{\mathbf{TxtEx}}$ SEMI_HULL$^{n,S'}$, for arbitrary **rat**$^+$-covering sets S and S'.

Our goal now is to establish an upper bound on the SEMI_HULL^{n,S} degrees in terms of Q-hierarchy. To find such a bound, we actually have to design a learning strategy for languages in SEMI_HULL^{n,S} that consists of q_i-type strategies for some $Q = (q_1, q_1, \ldots, q_k)$, and a grammar learned by every q_i is used by q_{i+1}. A natural strategy of this type would be the following $(q_1, q_2, \ldots, q_{2n-1}, q_{2n})$-strategy, where q_{2i+1} = INIT and q_{2i+2} = HALF for $i < n$: learn the first "break" point a_1 using an INIT-type strategy; once a_1 has been learned, learn the first "slope" b_1 at the point $(a_1, 0)$ using a $HALF$-type strategy; then learn the second "break" point $(a_2, b_1 * (a_2 - a_1))$ using an INIT-type strategy, etc. However, a much more "efficient" learning strategy is suggested by the theorem below. Informally one can visualize this strategy as follows. Assume that slope values come from the set $N \bigcup \{1/n \mid n \in N\}$. It may happen that in the beginning the learner receives points (x, y) indicating that the slope to be learned is greater or equal 1. Then the learner uses an INIT-like strategy to learn a "break" and a COINIT-like strategy (not a HALF-strategy as above!) to learn the slope: the slopes "tend" to 1 from above, and the learner uses this assumption. If the slope gets smaller than 1, the learner then uses a "combined" INIT-like strategy to learn the break point and the slope together: both of them change now in INIT-fashion.

There is a slight problem though in the above strategy. It may be possible that slope at some point seems less than 1, but later on when lots of new points $(i, 0)$ come from the input, slope again seems larger than 1. To prevent this from harming the learning process, the learner uses the "combined" INIT-strategy in a *safe* fashion. The actual proof of the theorem technically looks somewhat different, and the above method is a bit hidden. To make it easier for the reader to see the hidden strategy in the proof, we give the proof for $n = 1$ below. The general n case proof can be found in [21].

Theorem 2. *Suppose S is* **rat**$^+$-covering. *Suppose* $Q = (q_1, q_2, \ldots, q_{2n-1}, q_{2n})$, *where* q_{2i+1} = INIT *and* q_{2i+2} = COINIT, *for* $i < n$. *Then* SEMI_HULL^{n,S} $\leq^{\mathbf{TxtEx}}$ $\mathcal{L}^Q$.

Proof. We give a proof sketch for $n = 1$. The general case uses similar ideas as below but is a bit more complicated.

Suppose h is a 1–1 isomorphism from Z to S such that $h(i) < h(i + 1)$, for all $i \in Z$. For each S-valid (a, b), we first select a special point $(x_{a,b}, y_{a,b}) \in$ SEMI_HULL$^1_{a,b}$, which satisfy the following property:

(P1) if (a, b) and (a', b') are S-valid, and $\{(a, 0), (x_{a,b}, y_{a,b})\} \subseteq$ SEMI_HULL$^1_{a',b'}$, then $a < a'$ or $[a = a'$ and $b' \leq b]$.

It is easy to verify that such $(x_{a,b}, y_{a,b})$ can be easily selected. Note that we must have $x_{a,b} > a$ (otherwise (P1) cannot hold).

Define a directed graph $G = (V, E)$ as follows. $V = \{(a,b) \mid (a,b)$ is S-valid and $b \leq h(0)\}$, and $E = \{((a,b),(a',b')) \mid (a,b),(a',b') \in V$ and $\{(a,0),(x_{a,b},y_{a,b})\} \subseteq \mathrm{SEMI\_HULL}^1_{a',b'}\}$.

It can be shown that G is directed acyclic graph, and any vertex in G has only finitely many predecessors. This allows us to order vertices of G using a 1–1 function, code, such that for distinct $(a,b),(a',b') \in V$, if $\{(a,0),(x_{a,b},y_{a,b})\} \subseteq \mathrm{SEMI\_HULL}^1_{a',b'}$, then $\mathrm{code}(a,b) < \mathrm{code}(a',b')$.

Now, we extend code to all S-valid (a,b) as follows: $\mathrm{code}(a,b) = \mathrm{code}(a,h(0))$, for $b > h(0)$.

Claim. Suppose (a,b) and (a',b') are distinct and S-valid. Suppose $\{(a,0),(x_{a,b},y_{a,b})\} \subseteq \mathrm{SEMI\_HULL}^1_{a',b'}$.

Then, $\mathrm{code}(a,b) \leq \mathrm{code}(a',b')$, and if $\mathrm{code}(a,b) = \mathrm{code}(a',b')$, then $a = a'$ and $h(0) \leq b' < b$.

Proof. We consider the following cases.

Case 1: $b, b' \leq h(0)$.

Then by definition of code we have $\mathrm{code}(a,b) < \mathrm{code}(a',b')$.

Case 2: $b \leq h(0) < b'$.

Then, by (P1) we must have $a < a'$. Also, since $\{(a,0),(x_{a,b},y_{a,b})\} \subseteq \mathrm{SEMI\_HULL}^1_{a',b'} \subseteq \mathrm{SEMI\_HULL}^1_{a',h(0)}$, we have that $\mathrm{code}(a,b) < \mathrm{code}(a',h(0)) = \mathrm{code}(a',b')$.

Case 3: $b' \leq h(0) < b$.

In this case, $\{(a,0),(x_{a,b},y_{a,b})\} \subseteq \mathrm{SEMI\_HULL}^1_{a,b} \subseteq \mathrm{SEMI\_HULL}^1_{a,h(0)} \subseteq \mathrm{SEMI\_HULL}^1_{a',b'}$.

Thus, $\mathrm{code}(a,b) = \mathrm{code}(a,h(0)) \leq \mathrm{code}(a',b')$ (second inequality by definition of code). If $\mathrm{code}(a,h(0)) = \mathrm{code}(a',b')$, then we must have $a = a'$ and $b' = h(0) < b$.

Case 4: $h(0) < b, b'$.

Note that, by (P1) we must have $a \leq a'$. Thus, we have $\mathrm{code}(a,b) = \mathrm{code}(a,h(0)) \leq \mathrm{code}(a',h(0)) = \mathrm{code}(a',b')$. If $\mathrm{code}(a,b) = \mathrm{code}(a',b')$, then clearly, $a = a'$, and thus, we must have $b > b'$.

From the above cases, claim follows. □

For $b \in S$, define $g(b)$ as follows: $g(b) = 0$, if $b \leq h(0)$. Otherwise let $g(b) = i$, where $b = h(i)$.

Now our aim is to define Θ such that $\Theta(\mathrm{SEMI\_HULL}^1_{a,b}) = L^{(\mathrm{INIT},\mathrm{COINIT})}_{\mathrm{code}(a,b),g(b)}$. Note that such a Θ can be constructed by letting

$\Theta(L) = \bigcup\{L^{(\mathrm{INIT},\mathrm{COINIT})}_{\mathrm{code}(a,b),g(b)} \mid \{(a,0),(x_{a,b},y_{a,b})\} \subseteq L\}$.

It is easy to verify using Claim 4 that $\Theta(\mathrm{SEMI\_HULL}^1_{a,b}) = L^{(\mathrm{INIT},\mathrm{COINIT})}_{\mathrm{code}(a,b),g(b)}$. It is also easy to construct Ψ so that if α converges to a grammar for $L^{(\mathrm{INIT},\mathrm{COINIT})}_{\mathrm{code}(a,b),g(b)}$, then $\Psi(\alpha)$ converges to a grammar for $\mathrm{SEMI\_HULL}^1_{a,b}$. Theorem follows (for $n = 1$). ∎

Now we will show that the above theorem is in some sense optimal. That is, for $Q = (q_1, q_2, \ldots, q_{2n-1}, q_{2n})$, where $q_{2i+1} = \mathrm{INIT}$, and $q_{2i+2} = \mathrm{COINIT}$, for

$i < n$, and any $Q' \in$ BASIC*, if $\mathcal{L}^Q \not\leq^{\mathbf{TxtEx}} \mathcal{L}^{Q'}$, then $\mathrm{SEMI\_HULL}^{n,S} \not\leq^{\mathbf{TxtEx}} \mathcal{L}^{Q'}$. Thus, Q in above theorem cannot be improved if we use components only from BASIC (whether we can improve it by using some other basic components is open).

Theorem 3. *Suppose S is* **rat**$^+$-covering. *Let $Q = (q_1, \ldots, q_{2n})$, where $q_{2i+1} =$ INIT and $q_{2i+2} =$ COINIT, for $i < n$. Suppose $Q' \in$ BASIC* is such that $\mathcal{L}^Q \not\leq \mathcal{L}^{Q'}$. Then, $\mathrm{SEMI\_HULL}^{n,S} \not\leq^{\mathbf{TxtEx}} \mathcal{L}^{Q'}$.*

We now establish the best possible lower bound on the complexity of $\mathrm{SEMI\_HULL}^{n,S}$ in terms of Q-classes. One can ask the question: using a learner powerful enough to learn n-angle open semi-hulls, can a learner learn languages from the hierarchy based on BASIC? The next result shows that, using a learner able to learn n-angle open semi-hulls, one can learn all languages in (HALF, INIT, ..., INIT), where INIT is taken $n - 1$ times.

Theorem 4. *Suppose S is* **rat**$^+$-covering. *Let $n \in N^+$, and $Q = (q_1, q_2, \ldots, q_n)$, where $q_1 =$ HALF, and for $2 \leq i \leq n$, $q_i =$ INIT. Then, $\mathcal{L}^Q \leq^{\mathbf{TxtEx}} \mathrm{SEMI\_HULL}^{n,S}$.*

We now show that the above result is in some sense best possible with respect to Q-classes considered in this paper. For example, as Theorems 7 and 8 show, being able to learn classes $\mathrm{SEMI\_HULL}^{n,S}$ cannot help to learn languages even in classes (COINIT, COINIT) and (INIT, COINIT).

Theorem 5. *Suppose $n \in N$ and $Q = (q_1, q_2, \ldots, q_{n+1})$, where $q_i =$ INIT, for $1 \leq i \leq n + 1$. Suppose S is* **rat**$^+$-covering. *Then, $\mathcal{L}^Q \not\leq^{\mathbf{TxtEx}} \mathrm{SEMI\_HULL}^{n,S}$.*

Theorem 6. *Suppose $n \in N$ and $Q = (q_1, q_2, \ldots, q_{n+1})$, where $q_1 =$ COINIT, and $q_i =$ INIT, for $2 \leq i \leq n+1$. Suppose S is* **rat**$^+$-covering. *Then, $\mathcal{L}^Q \not\leq^{\mathbf{TxtEx}} \mathrm{SEMI\_HULL}^{n,S}$.*

Theorem 7. *Suppose $n \in N$ and S is* **rat**$^+$-covering. *Let $Q =$ (COINIT, COINIT). Then $\mathcal{L}^Q \not\leq^{\mathbf{TxtEx}} \mathrm{SEMI\_HULL}^{n,S}$.*

Theorem 8. *Suppose $n \in N$ and S is* **rat**$^+$-covering. *Let $Q =$ (INIT, COINIT). Then $\mathcal{L}^Q \not\leq^{\mathbf{TxtEx}} \mathrm{SEMI\_HULL}^{n,S}$.*

5 Complements of Open Semi Hull

We now define the classes of complements of SEMI_HULLs.

Definition 11. Suppose $a_1, \ldots, a_n \in N$ and $b_1, \ldots, b_n \in \mathbf{rat}^+$, where $0 < a_1 < a_2 < \ldots < a_n$.

$\mathrm{coSEMI\_HULL}^n_{a_1,b_1,a_2,b_2,\ldots,a_n,b_n} = \{(x, y) \in N^2 \mid y < \sum_{1 \leq i \leq n} b_i * (x \dot{-} a_i)\} = N^2 - \mathrm{SEMI\_HULL}^n_{a_1,b_1,a_2,b_2,\ldots,a_n,b_n}$.

Definition 12. Suppose $S \subseteq \mathbf{rat}^+$ is $\mathbf{rat}^+$-covering. $\text{coSEMI\_HULL}^{n,S} = \{\text{coSEMI\_HULL}^n_{a_1,b_1,\ldots,a_n,b_n} \mid (a_1,b_1,\ldots,a_n,b_n) \in \text{VALID}_S\}$.

We now obtain nearly the best possible upper bound on complexity of coSEMI_HULLs in terms of Q-degrees. Intuitive upper bound $\mathcal{L}^Q$ for $Q = (q_1, q_2, \ldots, q_{2n-1}, q_{2n})$ with q_{2i+1} = COINIT and q_{2i+2} = HALF can be easily established using the following learning strategy for $\text{coSEMI\_HULL}^{n,S}$: apply a COINIT-type strategy to learn the first "break" point a_1, then apply a HALF-type strategy to learn the first slope b_1, etc. However, the upper bound established below contains only $n+1$ components!

Theorem 9. *Suppose S is* $\mathbf{rat}^+$*-covering. Suppose $Q = (q_1, q_2, \ldots, q_{n+1})$, where q_1 =* INIT *and q_i =* COINIT, *for $2 \le i \le n+1$. Then* $\text{coSEMI\_HULL}^{n,S} \le^{\mathbf{TxtEx}} \mathcal{L}^Q$.

Theorem 10. *Suppose S is* $\mathbf{rat}^+$*-covering. Suppose $Q = (q_1, q_2, \ldots, q_{n+1})$, where q_2 =* INIT *and q_i =* COINIT, *for $1 \le i \le n+1$, $i \neq 2$. Then* $\text{coSEMI\_HULL}^{n,S} \le^{\mathbf{TxtEx}} \mathcal{L}^Q$.

We now show a lower bound for $\text{coSEMI\_HULL}^{n,S}$ having n components, and thus being very close to the upper bounds obtained above.

Theorem 11. *Suppose S is* $\mathbf{rat}^+$*-covering. Let $n \in N^+$, and $Q = (q_1, q_2, \ldots, q_n)$, where q_1 =* HALF, *and for $2 \le i \le n$, q_i =* COINIT.
Then, $\mathcal{L}^Q \le^{\mathbf{TxtEx}} \text{coSEMI\_HULL}^{n,S}$.

Note that upper and lower bounds for $\text{coSEMI\_HULL}^{n,S}$ given by Theorems 9, 10, and 11 do not match. The lower bound in Theorem 11 above is best possible (for Q-classes involving components from BASIC). However it is open whether the upper bound can be improved for general n. For $n = 1$, we do know that the upper bound can be improved to show that $\text{coSEMI\_HULL}^{1,S} \le^{\mathbf{TxtEx}}$ HALF (which is optimal by Theorem 11).

6 Open Hulls

Now consider the class of languages-"figures" that are intersections of SEMI_HULLs adjacent to the x-axis (that is with the first "break" point $(a_1, 0)$) and reverse SEMI_HULLs adjacent to the y-axis (with the first "break" point $(0, a'_1)$). These figures are the open hulls.

We give the formal definition below (preceded by the formal definition of the reverse SEMI_HULLs adjacent to the y-axis).

Definition 13. $\text{REV\_SEMI\_HULL}^n_{a_1,b_1,\ldots,a_n,b_n} = \{(x,y) \mid (y,x) \in \text{SEMI\_HULL}^n_{a_1,b_1,\ldots,a_n,b_n}\}$.
$\text{REV\_SEMI\_HULL}^{n,S} = \{\text{REV\_SEMI\_HULL}^n_{a_1,b_1,\ldots,a_n,b_n} \mid \text{SEMI\_HULL}^n_{a_1,b_1,\ldots,a_n,b_n} \in \text{SEMI\_HULL}^{n,S}\}$.

Definition 14. $\mathrm{OP\_HULL}^{n,m}_{a_1,b_1,\ldots,a_n,b_n;c_1,d_1,\ldots,c_m,d_m} = \mathrm{SEMI\_HULL}^{n}_{a_1,b_1,\ldots,a_n,b_n} \cap \mathrm{REV\_SEMI\_HULL}^{m}_{c_1,d_1,\ldots,c_m,d_m}$.
$\mathrm{OP\_HULL}^{n,m,S} = \{\mathrm{OP\_HULL}^{n,m,S}_{a_1,b_1,\ldots,a_n,b_n;c_1,d_1,\ldots,c_m,d_m} \mid \mathrm{SEMI\_HULL}^{n}_{a_1,b_1,\ldots,a_n,b_n} \in \mathrm{SEMI\_HULL}^{n,S}, \mathrm{REV\_SEMI\_HULL}^{n}_{c_1,d_1,\ldots,c_m,d_m} \in \mathrm{REV\_SEMI\_HULL}^{m,S}$, and $\sum_{1\le i\le n} b_i < \frac{1}{\sum_{1\le i\le m} d_i}\}$.

The latter condition, $\sum_{1\le i\le n} b_i < \frac{1}{\sum_{1\le i\le m} d_i}$, ensures that the languages in OP_HULLs are infinite, and thus the corresponding geometrical figures are *open* hulls (otherwise, the given classes will not be learnable).

Surprisingly, unlike SEMI_HULLs and coSEMI_HULL, upper and lower bounds for OP_HULLs match. The following theorem establishes the lower bound for the OP_HULLs.

Theorem 12. *Suppose S is* **rat**$^+$-covering. *Suppose $n \ge 1$, $m \ge 1$. Let $Q = (q_1,\ldots,q_n)$, where each $q_i =$ INIT. Then, (a) $\mathcal{L}^Q \le^{\mathbf{TxtEx}} \mathrm{OP\_HULL}^{n,m,S}$, and (b) $\mathcal{L}^Q \le^{\mathbf{TxtEx}} \mathrm{OP\_HULL}^{m,n,S}$.*

Now we show the upper bound for OP_HULLs.

Theorem 13. *Suppose S is* **rat**$^+$-covering. *Suppose $n \ge m \ge 1$. Let $Q = (q_1,\ldots,q_n)$, where each $q_i =$ INIT. Then, (a) $\mathrm{OP\_HULL}^{n,m,S} \le^{\mathbf{TxtEx}} \mathcal{L}^Q$, and (b) $\mathrm{OP\_HULL}^{m,n,S} \le^{\mathbf{TxtEx}} \mathcal{L}^Q$.*

$\mathrm{coOP\_HULL}^{n,m}_{a_1,b_1,\ldots,a_n,b_n;c_1,d_1,\ldots,c_m,d_m}$ can be naturally defined by taking the complements of $\mathrm{OP\_HULL}^{n,m}_{a_1,b_1,\ldots,a_n,b_n;c_1,d_1,\ldots,c_m,d_m}$.

The following theorems give the lower and upper bound for coOP_HULLs.

Theorem 14. *Suppose S is* **rat**$^+$-covering. *Suppose $n \ge 1$, $m \ge 1$. Let $Q = (q_1,\ldots,q_n)$, where each $q_i =$ COINIT. Then, (a) $\mathcal{L}^Q \le^{\mathbf{TxtEx}} \mathrm{coOP\_HULL}^{n,m,S}$, and (b) $\mathcal{L}^Q \le^{\mathbf{TxtEx}} \mathrm{coOP\_HULL}^{m,n,S}$.*

Theorem 15. *Suppose $n \ge m \ge 1$. Let $Q = (q_1,\ldots,q_n)$, where each $q_i =$ COINIT. Then, (a) $\mathrm{coOP\_HULL}^{n,m,S} \le^{\mathbf{TxtEx}} \mathcal{L}^Q$, and (b) $\mathrm{coOP\_HULL}^{m,n,S} \le^{\mathbf{TxtEx}} \mathcal{L}^Q$.*

7 Conclusions

A new complexity "scale" has been successfully applied for evaluating complexity of learning various geometrical "figures" from texts. Many upper bounds we have obtained are surprisingly lower than the ones suggested by "intuitive" learning strategies. Another surprising result is that upper and lower bounds match for OP_HULL and their complements, while there is a gap between upper and lower bounds for SEMI_HULLs that cannot be narrowed. One more interesting aspect of this picture is that upper bounds for OP_HULLs, the intersection of SEMI_HULLs, are much lower than for SEMI_HULLs themselves! In general, the picture of upper and lower bounds for OP_HULLs and their complements is much more uniform than for SEMI_HULLs and their complements: for the former, INITs just must be replaced with COINITs, while bounds for SEMI_HULLs and coSEMI_HULLs differ even in the number of components in Q-vectors.

There are many other interesting types of geometrical concepts whose complexity can be explored in terms of Q-classes. For example, one can evaluate complexity of learning SEMI_HULLs and all other figures observed in our paper dropping requirement of the first angle being adjacent to x or y-axis. Even more promising seems to be the class of finite unions of OP_HULLs (though proofs may become technically messy). In general, we are convinced that Q-classes (possibly using some other basic classes/strategies) are very promising tools for exploring complexity of learning "hard" languages from texts.

References

1. J. Bārzdiņš and R. Freivalds. On the prediction of general recursive functions. *Soviet Mathematics Doklady*, 13:1224–1228, 1972.
2. A. Blumer, A. Ehrenfeucht, D. Haussler, and M. Warmuth. Classifying learnable geometric concepts with the Vapnik-Chervonenkis dimension. In *Symposium on the Theory of Computation*, 1986.
3. N. Bshouty, S. Goldman, and D. Mathias. Noise-tolerant parallel learning of geometric concepts. In *Proceedings of the Eighth Annual Conference on Computational Learning Theory, Santa Cruz, California*, pages 345–352. ACM Press, 1995.
4. J. Case. The power of vacillation in language learning. *SIAM Journal on Computing*, 28(6):1941–1969, 1999.
5. J. Case and C. Lynes. Machine inductive inference and language identification. In M. Nielsen and E. M. Schmidt, editors, *Proceedings of the 9th International Colloquium on Automata, Languages and Programming*, volume 140 of *Lecture Notes in Computer Science*, pages 107–115. Springer-Verlag, 1982.
6. J. Case and C. Smith. Comparison of identification criteria for machine inductive inference. *Theoretical Computer Science*, 25:193–220, 1983.
7. Z. Chen. Learning unions of two rectangles in the plane with equivalence queries. In *Proceedings of the Sixth Annual Conference on Computational Learning Theory*, pages 243–252. ACM Press, 1993.
8. Z. Chen and W. Maass. On-line learning of rectangles. In *Proceedings of the Fifth Annual Workshop on Computational Learning Theory*, pages 16–28. ACM Press, 1992.
9. R. Daley and C. Smith. On the complexity of inductive inference. *Information and Control*, 69:12–40, 1986.
10. D. Dobkin and D. Gunopulos. Concept learning with geometric hypothesis. In *Proceedings of the Eighth Annual Conference on Computational Learning Theory, Santa Cruz, California*, pages 329–336. ACM Press, 1995.
11. J. Feldman. Some decidability results on grammatical inference and complexity. *Information and Control*, 20:244–262, 1972.
12. P. Fischer. More or less efficient agnostic learning of convex polygons. In *Proceedings of the Eighth Annual Conference on Computational Learning Theory, Santa Cruz, California*, pages 337–344. ACM Press, 1995.

13. R. Freivalds, E. Kinber, and C. Smith. On the intrinsic complexity of learning. *Information and Computation*, 123(1):64–71, 1995.
14. E. M. Gold. Language identification in the limit. *Information and Control*, 10:447–474, 1967.
15. P. Goldberg and S. Goldman. Learning one-dimensional geometric patterns under one-sided random misclassification noise. In *Proceedings of the Seventh Annual Conference on Computational Learning Theory*, pages 246–255. ACM Press, 1994.
16. P. Goldberg, S. Goldman, and H. David Mathias. Learing unions of boxes with membership and equivalence queries. In *Proceedings of the Seventh Annual Conference on Computational Learning Theory*, pages 198–207. ACM Press, 1994.
17. P. W. Goldberg, S. Goldman, and S. D. Scott. Pac learning of one-dimensional patterns. *Machine Learning*, 25:51–70, 1996.
18. S. Goldman, S. Kwek, and S. Scott. Agnostic learning of geometric patterns. In *Proceedings of the Eleventh Annual Conference on Computational Learning Theory*, pages 325–333. ACM Press, 1998. To appear in JCSS.
19. S. Goldman and S. D. Scott. A theoretical and empirical study of a noise-tolerant algorithm to learn geometric patterns. *Machine Learning*, 37:5–49, 1999.
20. T. Hegedus. Geometrical concept learning and convex polytopes. In *Proceedings of the Seventh Annual Conference on Computational Learning Theory*, pages 228–236. ACM Press, 1994.
21. S. Jain and E. Kinber. On intrinsic complexity of learning geometrical concepts from texts. Technical Report TRB6/99, School of Computing, National University of Singapore, 1999. Available at http://techrep.comp.nus.edu.sg/techreports/1999/TRB6-99.asp.
22. S. Jain, E. Kinber, and R. Wiehagen. Language learning from texts: Degrees of intrinsic complexity and their characterizations. In Nicolo Cesa-Bianchi and Sally Goldman, editors, *Proceedings of the Thirteenth Annual Conference on Computational Learning Theory*, pages 47–58. Morgan Kaufmann, 2000.
23. S. Jain and A. Sharma. The intrinsic complexity of language identification. *Journal of Computer and System Sciences*, 52:393–402, 1996.
24. S. Jain and A. Sharma. The structure of intrinsic complexity of learning. *Journal of Symbolic Logic*, 62:1187–1201, 1997.
25. E. Kinber. Monotonicity versus efficiency for learning languages from texts. In S. Arikawa and K. Jantke, editors, *Algorithmic Learning Theory: Fourth International Workshop on Analogical and Inductive Inference (AII '94) and Fifth International Workshop on Algorithmic Learning Theory (ALT '94)*, volume 872 of *Lecture Notes in Artificial Intelligence*, pages 395–406. Springer-Verlag, 1994.
26. E. Kinber and F. Stephan. Language learning from texts: Mind changes, limited memory and monotonicity. *Information and Computation*, 123:224–241, 1995.
27. S. Lange and T. Zeugmann. Learning recursive languages with a bounded number of mind changes. *International Journal of Foundations of Computer Science*, 4(2):157–178, 1993.
28. M. Machtey and P. Young. *An Introduction to the General Theory of Algorithms*. North Holland, New York, 1978.
29. D. Osherson and S. Weinstein. Criteria of language learning. *Information and Control*, 52:123–138, 1982.
30. H. Rogers. *Theory of Recursive Functions and Effective Computability*. McGraw-Hill, 1967. Reprinted, MIT Press 1987.
31. R. Wiehagen. On the complexity of program synthesis from examples. *Journal of Information Processing and Cybernetics (EIK)*, 22:305–323, 1986.

Toward a Computational Theory of Data Acquisition and Truthing

David G. Stork

Ricoh California Research Center
2882 Sand Hill Road Suite 115
Menlo Park, CA 94025-7022
stork@rii.ricoh.com

Abstract. *The creation of a pattern classifier requires choosing or creating a model, collecting training data and verifying or "truthing" this data, and then training and testing the classifier. In practice, individual steps in this sequence must be repeated a number of times before the classifier achieves acceptable performance. The majority of the research in computational learning theory addresses the issues associated with training the classifier (learnability, convergence times, generalization bounds, etc.). While there has been modest research effort on topics such as cost-based collection of data in the context of a particular classifier model, there remain numerous unsolved problems of practical importance associated with the collection and truthing of data. Many of these can be addressed with the formal methods of computational learning theory. A number of these issues, as well as new ones — such as the identification of "hostile" contributors and their data — are brought to light by the Open Mind Initiative, where data is openly contributed over the World Wide Web by non-experts of varying reliabilities. This paper states generalizations of formal results on the relative value of labeled and unlabeled data to the realistic case where a labeler is not a foolproof oracle but is instead somewhat unreliable and error-prone. It also summarizes formal results on strategies for presenting data to labelers of known reliability in order to obtain best estimates of model parameters. It concludes with a call for a rich, powerful and practical computational theory of data acquisition and truthing, built upon the concepts and techniques developed for studying general learning systems.*

Keywords: monitoring data quality, data truthing, open data collection, anomalous data detection, learning with queries, cost-based learning, Open Mind Initiative

1 Introduction

In broad outline, the creation of many practical systems to classify real-world patterns — such as acoustic speech, handwritten or omnifont optical characters, human faces, fingerprints, gestures, sonar images, and so on — involves the following steps:

D. Helmbold and B. Williamson (Eds.): COLT/EuroCOLT 2001, LNAI 2111, pp. 194–207, 2001.

Select a model. Select or design a computational model, specify its features, parameters and constraints or prior information about the unknown parameters

Collect and verify training data. Collect training data, verify or "truth" this data, and remove outliers and faulty data

Train. Train the model with this data, possibly employing regularization methods such as pruning, integrating multiple classifiers, or resampling methods such as boosting, and so on

Test. Test or estimate the performance of the classifier, either in the field, or more frequently in the lab using independent test data, to see if the classification performance is adequate for the application

These steps are not always followed in the sequence listed above (for instance, we may first collect our data before selecting a model), and in practice the steps are often repeated a number of times in an irregular order until the estimated performance of the classifier is acceptable.

The bulk of the research effort in computational learning theory, statistical learning theory and related discliplines has focused on model selection and training, and this has led to a wealth of powerful methods, including classifiers such as the nearest-neighbor method, neural nets, Support Vector Machines, and decision trees, regularization methods such as weight decay and pruning, general techniques such as multiclassifier integration and resampling, and theoretical results on learnability and convergence criteria, performance bounds, and much more [15].

But consider the databases of millions of labeled handwritten characters created by the National Institute of Standards and Technology (NIST), the immense volume of truthed postal data such as handwritten addresses and zip codes created by the Center for Excellence in Document Analysis and Recognition (CEDAR), or the transcriptions of tens of thousands of hours of speech created by the Linguistic Data Consortium (LDC), to mention but a few examples. These resources are invaluable to numerous groups developing classifiers and other intelligent software. The development of these databases requires a great deal of time, cost and effort, and relies on dozens of knowledge workers of varying expertise transcribing, checking, and cross-checking data in a model- and use-independent way.

Up to now, computational learning theory has contributed little to this vital process. In fact, most data acquisition teams rely on heuristics and trial and error, for instance in choosing the number of knowledge engineers that should truth a given dataset, how to monitor the reliability of individual engineers, and so on. Remarkably little of this information is published or otherwise shared. The goal of this paper is to begin to rectify this situation, by highlighting the need for large corpora of training data, describing some of the problems confronted in the creation of such datasets, suggesting results and techniques from computational learning theory that could be brought to bear, and providing some initial steps in the development of such a theory of data acquisition and truthing.

Section 2 reviews the need for data, or more specifically, the proposition that progress in classifier design will rely increasingly on larger and larger datasets and less and less on minor alterations to existing powerful learning techniques. This, then, underscores the need for theoretical effort on making more efficient the collection of high-quality datasets. Section 3 outlines some practical background and trends relevant to data acquisition and truthing. It describes in some detail a novel method of open data collection over the World Wide Web employed by the Open Mind Initiative. Section 4 illustrates several data collection and truthing scenarios and attendant practical problems ammenable to analysis through the tools of statistical and computational learning theory.

Section 5 reports two theoretical results relevant to data acquisition. The first is a generalization of the measure of the value of labeled and unlabeled data to the more realistic case when the labeler, rather than being a perfect oracle, instead has a probability of making a random labeling mistake. The second is a strategy for requesting labels from imperfect labelers that, under a number of natural conditions, optimizes an information criterion related to the quality of the resulting dataset. Conclusions and future directions are presented in Sect. 6.

2 The Need for Large Datasets

Nearly all software projects in pattern classification and artificial intelligence — such as search engines and computer vision systems — require large sets of training data. For instance, state-of-the-art speech recognition systems are trained with hundreds or thousands of hours of speech sounds transcribed or "labeled" by knowledge engineers; leading optical character recognition systems are trained with pixel images of several million characters along with their transcriptions; one commercial effort at building a knowledge base of common sense information has required 500 person-years of effort over 17 years so far, most of this in data entry [14].

There is theoretical and experimental evidence that given sufficiently large sets of training data a broad range of classifier methods yield similar high performance. From a probabilistic viewpoint, we know from Bayesian estimation theory that given a classifier model general enough to represent the true underlying class-conditional probability distributions, sufficiently large training sets can dominate or "swamp" poor prior information, thereby yielding accurate classifiers [1,7]. Moreover, just as the limitations imposed by the bias-variance dilemma in regression can be overcome with larger and larger data sets, so too the only way to overcome the analogous limitation imposed by the (boundary) bias-variance dilemma in classification is to increase the amount of training data [10]. Under reasonable conditions, virtually all sufficiently power training methods give improved estimates and classifiers as the amount of high-quality training data is increased.

Experimental evidence of the value of large data sets comes from numerous classification competitions, where systems trained with the largest data sets generally excel, and from corporations, which often expend more effort and resources on data collection and truthing than on classifier design and subtleties of training algorithms [3]. In particularly illuminating work, Ho and Baird trained each of three standard non-Bayesian classifiers with a very large dataset of isolated handwritten characters. They found that all three classifiers attained very nearly the same high accuracy and that the trained classifiers exhibited nearly the same pattern of misclassification errors [11]. They concluded, in short, that the information in sufficiently large training sets swamped biases and priors in their classifier models, and the implication is that this is a general result which holds so long as the fundamental classifier model is sufficiently general (low bias).

The above discussion is, of course, not an argument against efforts to find good models when building a classifier. Instead, it is a suggestion that builders of classifiers and AI systems should turn their attention to algorithms and theory that support the collection of large sets of accurately labeled data [12]. While computational learning theory may tell us how many patterns are needed for a given expect generalization error for example, such theory has provided little guidance on how to efficiently *collect* such data in a classifier- or use-independent way.

2.1 An Example

We now turn to an extreme illustration of poor generalization resulting from training parameterized model that is too impoverished to accurately approximate the true underlying distributions [7, pages 142–143]. While admittedly hardly a proof, this surprising example illustrates that even when we use a principled estimation method such as maximum-likelihood, we can get terrible results. Specifically, even though our model space contains a classifier that would yield near perfect results ($error = 0\%$), our estimation procedure produces a classifier with the worst possible generation ($error = 100\%$).

Consider a one-dimensional, two-category classification problem with equal priors $P(\omega_1) = P(\omega_2) = 0.5$, and the following class-conditional densities:

$$\begin{aligned} p(x|\omega_1) &= (1-k)\delta(x-1) + k\delta(x+X) \\ p(x|\omega_2) &= (1-k)\delta(x+1) + k\delta(x-X) \end{aligned} \tag{1}$$

where $\delta(\cdot)$ is the familiar Dirac delta function, which vanishes when its argument is non-zero and integrates to 1.0, as shown in Fig. 1. The scalar k (where $0 < k < 0.5$) is small, and will shrink toward zero in our construction; further, X is a distance from the origin, which will grow in our construction. Note that these two class-conditional densities are interchanged under the reflection symmetry operation $x \leftrightarrow -x$.

Suppose we model these distributions by Gaussians parameterized by a mean and variance, that is, $p(x|\omega_i) \sim N(\mu_i, \sigma_i^2)$. This is admittedly a poor model in this case, nevertheless such a model is often used when there is little or no information about the underlying distributions. The maximum-likelihood estimate of the mean μ_1 is merely the mean of the data in ω_1 [7], that is, $\hat{\mu}_1 = (k+1) - kX$, and

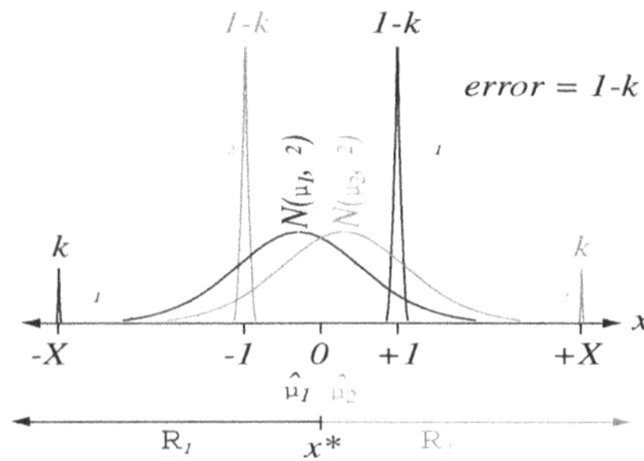

Fig. 1. A simple one-dimensional two-category classification problem in which a model's parameters are trained by maximum-likelihood methods on an infinitely large training set yields the worst possible classification (*error* = 100%), even though the model space contains the best possible classifier (*error* = 0%). The true or target (normalized) distribution for category ω_1 consists of a Dirac delta function at $x = +1$ of height $1 - k$, and a delta function at $x = -X$ of height k. The true distribution for category ω_2 is spatially symmetric to that of category ω_1, i.e., the one obtained under the interchange $x \leftrightarrow -x$, as given in Eq. 1 and shown in gray. The (poor) model for each distribution is a Gaussian, whose mean is estimated using an infinite amount of data sampled from $p(x|\omega_i)$ for $i = 1, 2$. For sufficiently large X, the estimated means obey $\hat{\mu}_1 < \hat{\mu}_2$, leading to an error of $1 - k$. If k is reduced and X increased accordingly, the training and generalization errors can be arbitrarily close to 100%.

analogously for $\hat{\mu}_2$. By the symmetry of the problem and estimation procedure, the (single) decision boundary will always be at $x^* = 0$.

For an arbitrary positive k, the estimated mean $\hat{\mu}_1$ is less than zero if $X > (k-1)/k$. Under equivalent conditions, the mean $\hat{\mu}_2$ is greater than zero. Informally speaking, in such a case the means have "switched positions" that is, $\hat{\mu}_2 > \hat{\mu}_1$. Thus the decision boundary is at $x^* = 0$ but the decision region for ω_1, i.e., $\mathcal{R}_1$, corresponds to all negative values of x, and $\mathcal{R}_2$ to all positive values of x. The error under this classification rule is clearly $1 - k$, which can be made arbitrarily close to 100% by letting $k \to 0$ and $X \to (k-1)/k + \epsilon$ where ϵ is an arbitrarily small positive number. Note that an infinite continuum of values of the parameters will yield a classifier with *error* = 0%, specifically any for which $\hat{\mu}_2 > \hat{\mu}_1$ and $|\hat{\mu}_2| = |\hat{\mu}_1|$. (In fact, there are yet other values of the means that yield classifiers with *error* = 0%, such as any that have equal variances, $\sigma_1^2 = \sigma_2^2$, and $\hat{\mu}_1 > \hat{\mu}_2$ with the intersection of the Gaussian densities lying between $x = -1$ and $x = +1$.)

This surprisingly poor classification performance is not an artifact of using limited training data or training to a poor local minimum in the likelihood function — in fact, neither of these are the case. Note too that even if the variances were parameters estimated from the data, because of the symmetry of the problem the decision boundary would remain at $x^* = 0$ and the *error* would be 100%. The informal lesson here is that even a well-founded estimation method such as maximum-likelihood can give poor classifiers if our model space is poorly matched to the problem (high bias). In such cases we should expand the expressiveness of the models; this generally requires that we train using larger data sets.

3 The Practice of Collecting and Truthing Data

Given the manifest need for large data sets, we naturally ask: What are some of the sources of such vital data? Optical character recognition companies employ knowledge engineers whose sole task is to optically scan printed pages and then transcribe and truth the identities of words or characters [3]. Likewise, the Linguistic Data Consortium has dozens of knowledge engineers who transcribe recorded speech in a variety of languages on a wide variety of topics. Entering data by hand this way is often expensive and slow, however. An alternative approach, traditional data mining [8], is inadequate for many problem domains in part because data mining provides *unlabeled* data or because the data is simply not in an appropriate form. For instance the web lacks pixel images of handwritten characters and explicit common sense data and thus such information cannot be extracted by data mining. Moreover, accurately *labeled* data can be used in powerful *supervised learning* algorithms, while if the data is unlabeled only less-powerful *unsupervised learning* algorithms can be used. For this reason, we naturally seek inexpensive methods for collecting labeled data. Such a goal is virtually identical to that for transcribing audiotapes and videotapes.

As we shall see below, the internet can be used in a new way to gather needed labeled data: facilitating the collection of information contributed by humans.

3.1 Trends in Open Software and Collaboration

Before we consider new methods for collecting and truthing data, we shall review some important trends. There are several compelling lessons from collaborative software projects that have major implications for systems supporting the collection of data. Consider the open source software movement, in which many programmers contribute software that is peer-reviewed and incorporated into large programs, such as the *Linux* operating system. Two specific trends must be noted. The first is that the average number of collaborators per project has increased over the past quarter century. For instance, in the late 1970s, most open collaborative software projects such as *emacs* involved several hundred programmers at most, while by the 1990s projects such as *Linux* involve over 100,000 software engineers. The second trend is that the average technical skill demanded of contributors has decreased over that same period. The programmers who contributed to *gcc* in the 1980s were experts in machine-level programming; the contributors to *Linux* know about file formats and device drivers; the contributors to the *Newhoo* collaborative open web directory need little if any technical background beyond an acquaintance with *HTML*.

3.2 The Open Mind Initiative

Let us review the following general facts and trends:

- pattern classifiers and intelligent software are improved with large sets of high-quality data
- open source software development techniques are applied increasingly to lower skilled collaborators
- open source development, and general collaborative projects, are expanding to larger groups as a result of the World Wide Web
- the internet can be used as an infrastructure for collecting data

These trends, and particularly the emergence of the World Wide Web, suggest that collaborative efforts can be extended to an extremely *large* pool of contributors (potentially anyone on the web), whose technical expertise can be *low* (merely the ability to point and click). These ideas were the inspiration underlying the creation of the Open Mind Initiative, the approach we now explore.

The central goal of the Open Mind Initiative (`www.OpenMind.org`) is to support non-expert web users contributing "informal" data needed for artificial intelligence and pattern recognition projects, as well as closely related tasks such as transcribing audio or video data. The Initiative thus extends the trends in open source software development to larger and larger groups of collaborators, allowing lower and lower levels of technical expertise. Moreover, the Initiative broadens the output of collaborative projects: while traditional open-source projects release software, the Initiative releases both software and data [17,18].

A prototypical open data collection project in the Initiative is illustrated in skeleton form in Fig. 2. The project site contains a large database of isolated handwritten characters, scanned from documents, but whose character identities are not known. Individual segmented characters from this database are presented on standard web browsers of contributors who then identify or "label" the pattern by clicking buttons on a simple interface. These labelings are automatically sent to the project site, where they are collected and used to train software that classifies handwritten digits.

Some data acquisition projects in the Initiative could employ novel human-machine interfaces based on games. For instance, imagine an Open Mind Initiative chatbot project in which data is collected while contributors play a modified version of *Dungeons and Dragons*. In this new game, players read short texts — which discuss potions to drink, swords to brandish, rooms to enter, tasks to accomplish — generated by automated text generation programs. As part of the game, players must indicate how "natural" these texts are. This valuable feedback, collected at the project site, provides information for adjusting the parameters in the text generation programs, thereby yielding more natural generated text. In such game-based projects, contributors download the game software (presumably written in *Java*) from the project site. The data captured on the contributor's machine is stored locally and sent to the project site at the end of a game session.

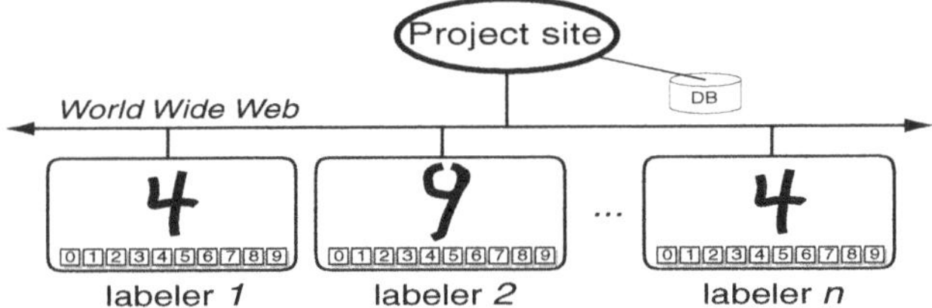

Fig. 2. This simplified, skeleton architecture shows the general approach in an open data collection project on isolated handwritten digit recognition. The unlabeled pixel images are presented on the browsers of non-expert web users, who indicate their judged category memberships by means of a button interface. Occasionally, the same pattern is presented to two or more independently selected contributors, to see if they agree; in this way, the reliability of contributors is monitored semi-automatically, and the quality of the data can be kept high.

While in most of the Initiative's projects contributors provide data through standard web browsers, in other projects contributors will require a more sophisticated human interface. For instance, in projects using a game interface, contributors will download the presentation and local cacheing software resident from the project site, and install it on their local machine. Data is collected while the contributor plays the game and is sent to the project home site at the end of a game session.

There are a number of incentives for people to contribute to Open Mind Initiative projects. Contributors seek benefit from the software (as in a text-to-speech generator); they enjoy game interfaces (as in online versions of *Dungeons and Dragons*); they seek public recognition for their contributions (as in *SETI@home*); they are interested in furthering the scientific goals of the project (as do amateur ornithologists through annual bird counts for the Audubon Society); they seek financial incentives such as lotteries, discounts, e-coupons or frequent-flier awards provided by third-party corporations [16].

The Open Mind Initiative differs from the Free Software Foundation and traditional open-source development in a number of ways. First, while open-source development relies on a hacker culture (e.g., roughly 10^5 programmers contributing to *Linux*), the Open Mind Initiative is instead based on a non-expert web user and business culture (e.g., 10^9 web users). While most of the work in open-source projects is directly on the final software to be released (e.g., source code), in the Initiative most of the effort is directed toward the tools, infrastructure and data gathering. Final decisions in open source are arbitrated by an expert or core group; in the Initiative contributed data is accepted or rejected automatically by software that is sensitive to anomalies or outliers. In some cases, data can be rejected semi-automatically, for instance by having data checked by two or more independently chosen contributors. Such "self-policing" not only helps to eliminate questionable or faulty *data*, it also helps to identify unreliable *contributors*, whose subsequent contributions can be monitored more closely or blocked altogether, as we shall mention below. It must be emphasized that the Open Mind Initiative's approach also differs significantly from traditional data mining. In particular, in data mining a fixed amount of unlabeled information is extracted from an existing database (such as the web), whereas in the Initiative a possibly boundless amount of labeled data is *contributed.*

The Open Mind Initiative has four projects in progress: handwriting recognition, speech recognition and a small, demonstration AI project, *Animals.* These have been tested on intranets and are being debugged and load tested for full web deployment. The fourth project site, Open Mind common sense, is open and accepting contributed data over the web. As of May 2001, it has collected 400,000 common sense facts from 7000 separate contributors through a range of "activities," such as DESCRIBE A PICTURE and RELATE TWO WORDS. To date, data monitoring in this project has been semi-automatic whereby contributors "self-police" the contributions of each other.

4 Challenges and Applications of a Theory of Data Acquisition and Truthing

Below are several scenarios and problems in data acquisition and truthing that are ammenable to computational theory, several are motivated by the challenges faced by the Open Mind Initiative. At base, many of these problems can be cast as learning the properties of the population of n labelers while simultaneously learning properties of the dataset.

- For open contributions of labels for handwritten characters, find the minimal conditions required to prove learnability of the character identities. This problem bears similarities to the approach of boosting, which will improve classification of weak learners [9]. Does the reliability of the contributors, weighted by the number of labels each provides, have to be greater than that of pure chance? Are there weaker conditions that nevertheless ensure learnability?
- A simple algorithm for improving the quality of contributed labels is "data voting," (or more generally "self-policing"), that is, presenting the same pattern to n_v labelers and accepting their majority vote. (This is related to the approach of collaborative filtering [4].) For a given total number of presentations of patterns to be labeled, if n_v is large, we collect a small amount of accurate data; conversely, if n_v is small, we get a large amount of less-accurate data. How do we set n_v to get a dataset that will lead to the most accurate classifiers? How does n_v change as the classifier is trained?
- How can we estimate the reliabilities of individual contributors while collecting data? How do we most efficiently identify "hostile" contributors, who seem to know the proper category identities, but deliberately submit false labels? (We assume that we can always associate a distinct identity with each contributor.)

- Given an estimate of such reliabilities and other properties of all n contributors, and given a set of unlabeled data and a partially trained classifier, how do we choose the single point from the data and a particular candidate labeler such that the returned label is expected to improve the classifier the most? This problem is more subtle than traditional active learning, which typically presumes the labeler is an omniscient oracle [6,19] (and see Sect. 5.2).
- How can we find the contributors who are "complementary," that is, where the weaknesses of one match the strengths of the other. For instance, in truthing handwritten OCR, one contributor might be very accurate on numerals, another on text letters. Clearly it would be most efficient to pair these contributors on a large text, than to use two who are both strong on numerals alone or on text alone.
- Optimal strategies for storing data and delaying decisions on whether to use it. A contributed point may seem like an outlier or hostile earlier in the data collection process, but no so, later in the context of more data.
- Consider the problem of transcribing a videotape by a number n of transcribers, each with a possibly different (estimated) accuracy and expertise. Suppose we have some measure of the $n \times (n-1)$ correlations between their labelings on representative texts. How do we find the smallest subset of labelers that will yield some criterion accuracy, say 99.5%?

At first consideration it appears that data collection such as in the Open Mind Initiative's handwriting project is an example of stochastic game theory. After all, we treat the contributors as random processes, with variable reliabilities, and the host seeks to minimize a cost. In fact, though, stochastic game theory addresses games in which opponents form strategies that must take into account random processes, such as the roll of dice in backgammon or sequence of cards dealt in poker [2]. There seems to be little or no work on computing optimal strategies in arrangments such as the Open Mind framework.

Collectively, questions of this sort are not properly data mining either, where there is a large fixed data set without human intervention. While closely related to cost-based training (where there is a cost for collecting data given a particular classifier or learning algorithm), in many cases we are building a dataset or transcribing a text and do not know which classification algorithm will later be applied.

5 Two Results in the Theory of Labeling

We now summarize two results, derived and explored more fully elsewhere, in the theory of data labelling [13].

5.1 The Fisher Information of Samples Labeled by an Unreliable Labeler

Recall first the statistical *score*, V, a random variable defined by

$$V = \frac{\partial}{\partial \theta} \ln p(\mathcal{D}; \theta), \tag{2}$$

where the data set $\mathcal{D}$ is sampled from the density $p(\mathbf{x};\theta)$ where θ is a scalar parameter. The *Fisher information* $J(\theta)$ is then the variance of the score, that is,

$$J(\theta) = \mathcal{E}_\theta \left[\frac{\partial}{\partial\theta} \ln p(\mathcal{D};\theta) \right]^2 . \tag{3}$$

The *Cramér-Rao* inequality states that the mean-squared error of an unbiased estimator $F(\mathcal{D})$ of the parameter θ is bounded from below by the reciprocal of the Fisher information, that is,

$$\mathrm{Var}[F] \geq \frac{1}{J(\theta)}. \tag{4}$$

Informally, we can view the Fisher information as the information about θ that is present in the sample $\mathcal{D}$. The Fisher information gives a lower bound on the error when we estimate θ from the data, though there is no guarantee that there must always exist an estimator that achieves this bound.

The Fisher information of the prior probability $P(\omega_1) \equiv P_1$ chosen from a density $p(\mathbf{x}|\omega_1)$ was shown by Castelli and Cover [5] in the labeled and unlabled cases to be

$$J(P_1) = \frac{1}{P_1(1-P_1)} \tag{5}$$

$$J(P_1) = \int \frac{(p_1(\mathbf{x}) - p_2(\mathbf{x}))^2}{P_1 p_1(\mathbf{x}) + (1-P_1)p_2(\mathbf{x})} d\mathbf{x} \tag{6}$$

respectively. Lam and Stork [13] have generalized these results to the more realistic case where labelers are unreliable. We model such unreliability as if the labeler had perfect information and employed Bayes decision rule but then, with probability α (where $0 \leq \alpha \leq 1$), reported a *different* label. Under these conditions, the Fisher information is:

$$J(P_1) = \int \left[\frac{(\alpha p_1(\mathbf{x}) - (1-\alpha)p_2(\mathbf{x}))^2}{\alpha P_1 p_1(\mathbf{x}) + (1-\alpha)(1-P_1)p_2(\mathbf{x})} + \frac{((1-\alpha)p_1(\mathbf{x}) - \alpha p_2(\mathbf{x}))^2}{(1-\alpha)P_1 p_1(\mathbf{x}) + \alpha(1-P_1)p_2(\mathbf{x})} \right] d\mathbf{x}. \tag{7}$$

The case $\alpha = 0$ is equivalent to the labeled case above. The case $\alpha = 1$ corresponds to a "hostile contributor" who always willfully provides the wrong label. In the two-category case, however, the hostile contributor is in fact very helpful. All we need is a single, reliable bit of information, provided by a trusted expert for instance, to identify the true labels from the hostile data.

5.2 An Optimal Strategy for Requesting Labels

A general labeling strategy is an algorithm for deciding which unlabeled data points are to be presented to which of a set of n labelers given some information about the labelers and the data in order to optimize some criterion. Consider the following specific case. Suppose we have two independent labelers, each known or assumed to have the same unreliability α. Suppose too that we have a set of unlabeled data in which each point is to be assigned one of two categories, ω_1 or ω_2. We have two unlabeled points, $\mathbf{x}_1$ and $\mathbf{x}_2$. Suppose we can exploit just two (total) labeling decisions from labelers, and our goal is to learn "as much as possible" under these conditions. Which pattern should be assigned to which labeler?

In this case, the natural measure of information to be learned is

$$
\begin{aligned}
I &= I(\omega|\mathbf{x}_1) + I(\omega|\mathbf{x}_2) \\
&= -\sum_{j=1}^{2} P(\omega_j|\mathbf{x}_1)\log_2 P(\omega_j|\mathbf{x}_1) - \sum_{j=1}^{2} P(\omega_j|\mathbf{x}_2)\log_2 P(\omega_j|\mathbf{x}_2),
\end{aligned} \tag{8}
$$

where $I(\omega|\mathbf{x}_i)$ is the information about the categories given a label on pattern $\mathbf{x}_i$ and the $P(\omega_j|\mathbf{x}_i)$ are probability estimates given by the current state of the classifier. The optimal strategy depends upon α and these estimated category memberships. Figure 3 summarizes the optimal strategy.

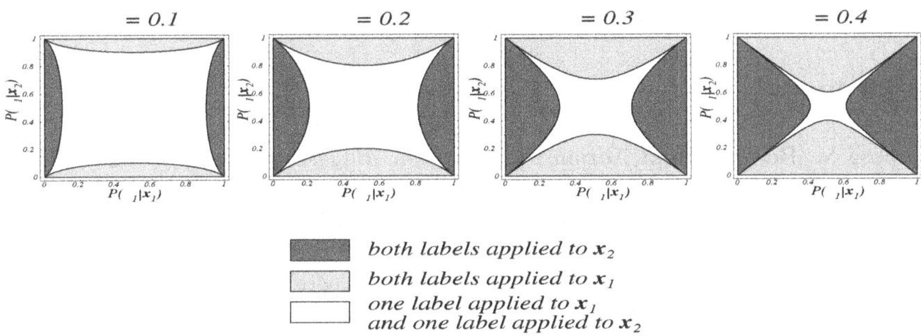

Fig. 3. The optimal data labeling strategy for two points $\mathbf{x}_1$ and $\mathbf{x}_2$ is illustrated for various levels of the contributor unreliability, described by α, and $P(\omega_1|\mathbf{x}_i)$ as given by a classifier. In the limit of small α, this strategy is to present one pattern to labeler 1 and one pattern to labeler 2. In the large-α case, the strategy is to present the most uncertain point (i.e., the one with $P(\omega_1|\mathbf{x}_i) \simeq 0.5$) to both labelers.

Examine the $\alpha = 0.1$ case. In this low-noise case, the labelers are reliable, and for most values of $P(\omega|\mathbf{x}_i)$ the optimal strategy is to request a label for $\mathbf{x}_1$ and for $\mathbf{x}_2$. However, if $P(\omega_1|\mathbf{x}_2)$ is very small (e.g., 0.05), then providing a label for $\mathbf{x}_2$ will not provide much information or refine our estimate of $P(\omega_1|\mathbf{x}_2)$. As such, our strategy in that case is to request both labelers to label $\mathbf{x}_1$, as shown by the light gray region.

In the high noise case, $\alpha = 0.4$, the range of values of estimated probabilities where we request separate points to be labeled separately is small. This is because we can gain more information by having two labels of a single point. In an extreme case $\alpha = 0.499$, not shown, then the labels are essentially the result of a coin toss, and provide no information. It is best, then, to apply both to the same point.

6 Future Work

There remains much work to be done on the computational theory of data acquisition and truthing. No doubt, there are formal similarities between subcases of the data acquisition and truthing problem and cases in more traditional computational learning. We should explore and exploit such formal similarities. Nevertheless, the manifest importance of collecting high-quality data sets in a number of application environments provides great opportunities for developing useful theory leading to improved real-world systems.

Acknowledgements

I thank Chuck Lam for his many useful discussions, analyses and comments on this paper.

References

1. José M. Bernardo and Adrian F. M. Smith. *Bayesian Theory.* John Wiley and Sons, New York, NY, 1994.
2. David Blackwell and M. A. Girshick. *Theory of Games and Statistical Decisions.* Dover Publications, New York, NY, 1979.
3. Mindy Bokser, 1999. Personal communication (Caere Corporation).
4. John S. Breese, David Heckerman, and Carl Kadie. Empirical analysis of predictive algorithms for collaborative filtering. In Gregory F. Cooper and Serafín Moral, editors, *Proceedings of the 14th Conference on Uncertainty in Artificial Intelligence (UAI-98)*, pages 43–52, San Francisco, 1998. Morgan Kaufmann.
5. Vittorio Castelli and Thomas M. Cover. The relative value of labeled and unlabeled samples in pattern recognition with an unknown mixing parameter. *Proc. IEEE Transactions on Information Theory*, IT-42(6):2102–2117, 1996.
6. David Cohn, Les Atlas, and Richard Ladner. Improving generalization with active learning. *Machine Learning*, 15(2):201–221, 1994.
7. Richard O. Duda, Peter E. Hart, and David G. Stork. *Pattern Classification.* Wiley, New York, NY, second edition, 2001.
8. Usama M. Fayyad, Gregory Piatetsky-Shapiro, Padhraic Smyth, and Ramaswamy Uthurusamy, editors. *Advances in knowledge discovery and data mining.* MIT Press, Cambridge, MA, 1996.
9. Yoav Freund. Boosting a weak learning algorithm by majority. In *Proceedings of the Third Workshop on Computational Learning Theory*, pages 202–216, San Mateo, CA, 1990. Morgan Kaufmann.

10. Jerome H. Friedman. On bias, variance, 0/1-loss, and the curse-of-dimensionality. *Data Mining and Knowledge Discovery*, 1(1):55–77, 1997.
11. Tin Kam Ho and Henry S. Baird. Large-scale simulation studies in pattern recognition. *IEEE Transactions on Pattern Analysis and Machine Intelligence*, PAMI-19(10):1067–1079, 1997.
12. Chuck Lam. *Open Data Acquisition: Theory and Experiments.* PhD thesis, Stanford University, Stanford, CA, 2002. in preparation.
13. Chuck Lam and David G. Stork. Optimal strategies for collecting and truthing data from contributors of varying reliabilities, 2001. submitted for publication.
14. Doug B. Lenat. CYC: A large-scale investment in knowledge infrastructure. *Communications of the ACM*, 38(11):33–38, 1995.
15. Tom M. Mitchell. *Machine Learning.* McGraw-Hill, New York, 1997.
16. David G. Stork. The Open Mind Initiative. *IEEE Intelligent Systems & their applications*, 14(3):19–20, 1999.
17. David G. Stork. Open data collection for training intelligent software in the Open Mind Initiative. In *Proceedings of the Engineering Intelligent Systems Conference (EIS 2000)*, Paisley, Scotland, 2000.
18. David G. Stork. An architecture supporting the collection and monitoring of data openly contributed over the World Wide Web. In *Proceedings of the Workshop on Enabling Technologies, Infrastructure for Collaborative Enterprises (WET ICE)*, Cambridge, MA, 2001.
19. Richard Valliant, Alan H. Dorfman, and Richard M. Royall. *Finite population sampling and inference: A prediction approach.* Wiley Series in Probability and Statistics. John Wiley and Sons, New York, NY, 2000.

Discrete Prediction Games with Arbitrary Feedback and Loss (extended abstract)

Antonio Piccolboni and Christian Schindelhauer *

[1] Email: piccolbo@yahoo.com
[2] Dept. of Math. and Comp. Science and Heinz-Nixdorf-Institut, Paderborn University, Germany. Email: schindel@upb.de

Abstract. We investigate the problem of predicting a sequence when the information about the previous elements (feedback) is only partial and possibly dependent on the predicted values. This setting can be seen as a generalization of the classical multi-armed bandit problem and accommodates as a special case a natural bandwidth allocation problem. According to the approach adopted by many authors, we give up any statistical assumption on the sequence to be predicted. We evaluate the performance against the best constant predictor (regret), as it is common in iterated game analysis.
We show that for any discrete loss function and feedback function only one of two situations can occur: either there is a prediction strategy that achieves in T rounds a regret of at most $O(T^{3/4}(\ln T)^{1/2})$ or there is a sequence which cannot be predicted by any algorithm without incurring a regret of $\Omega(T)$.
We prove both sides constructively, that is when the loss and feedback functions satisfy a certain condition, we present an algorithm that generates predictions with the claimed performance; otherwise we show a sequence that no algorithm can predict without incurring a linear regret with probability at least 1/2.

* Parts of this work are supported by a stipend of the "Gemeinsames Hochschulsonderprogramm III von Bund und Länder" through the DAAD.

1 Introduction

Our research was initially prompted by the following bandwidth allocation problem. On the link between two servers, a varying bandwidth is available. As it is common in an internetworking setting, little or no information is available about load patterns for the link and no cooperative behavior can be guaranteed. The goal is to send data as quickly as possible without exceeding the bandwidth available, assuming that some price is paid in case of congestion. Due to the limitations of typical protocols, the only feedback servers receive is whether congestion occurred or not (in the form, e.g., of a dropped packet). An algorithm choosing the bandwidth is fronting a trade off similar to the one that is the most distinctive trait of the multi-armed bandit problem: on one hand, trying to match the maximum bandwidth at any time step; on the other, choosing the bandwidth in order to collect more information about the load.

Another, even simpler, instance of this general setting arises from a simple quality control problem. In a manufacturing operation, the items produced can be either working or defective. Unfortunately, to asses the quality of an item it is necessary to destroy it. Both delivering a defective item and destroying a working one are undesirable events. Suppose that customer feedback is unavailable, late or unreliable. The only information available about the sequence of items produced so far is the one the destructive testing procedure provides, but we want to apply it as little as possible. When the plant is working properly, defective items are extremely rare so that little testing seems optimal, but a failure would be detected with a worrisome delay.

The goal we set for ourselves was to make these two examples, together with the multi-armed bandit problem and others, fit a general framework that encompasses different sequence prediction games where the prediction is based only on some "clues" about the past rounds of the game and good predictions are rewarded according to some weighting scheme. We model the available feedback on the sequence as a function of two arguments. One is the current sequence value itself, as it is common in system theory, and the other is the prediction. In system theory the classic problem is that of observability: is the feedback sufficient to find out the initial state of the system, whose transition function is assumed to be known? More closely related to our problem is that of learning from noisy observations, where the sequence is obfuscated by some noise process, as opposed to a deterministic transformation. The presence of the second argument, the prediction, makes our approach consistent with a large body of work in the sequence prediction literature, where the feedback is the reward. Decoupling the feedback and reward functions is the most notable feature of our approach.

Following a relatively recent trend in sequence prediction research (e.g. see [LW94,HKW95,Vov98,Sch99,CBFH+97,CBFHW93,HKW98,CBL99,FS97] and [ACBFS95,Vov99]), we make no assumptions whatsoever concerning the sequence to be predicted, meaning that we do not require, for instance, a statistical model of the sequence. For lack of a model, we need to assume that the sequence is arbitrary and therefore generated by an all-powerful device or adversary, which, among other things, is aware of the strategy a prediction algorithm is using. It might seem that competing with such a powerful opponent is hopeless. This is why, instead of the absolute performance of a prediction algorithm, it is customary to consider the regret w.r.t. the best predictor in some class. In this paper we make the choice of comparing our algorithm against the best constant predictor. Even if it seems a very restrictive setting, let us remind the reader that the best constant prediction is picked after the whole sequence is known, that is with a much better knowledge than any prediction algorithm has available and even more so in the incomplete feedback setting. Moreover, constant predictors are the focus of an important line of research on iterated games [Han57,FS97,ACBFS95]. Finally, the result can be readily extended to a finite class of arbitrary predictors along the same lines of [ACBFS95]. The details of this extension will be included in future versions of this paper.

Our research is closely related to the the one presented in [FS97], where the subject is, indeed, the problem of learning a repeated game from the point of view of one of the players —which can be thought of, indeed, as a predictor, once we accept that prediction can be rewarded in general ways and not according to a metric. In that work the authors designed the Multiplicative Weighting algorithm and proved that it has regret $O(\sqrt{T})$ when compared against the optimal constant strategy. This algorithm is used as a subroutine of ours. In their setting the predictor receives as input not the sequence at past rounds but the rewards every alternate prediction (not only the one made) would have received. Since this is all that matters to their algorithm, this setting is called *full information game* in [ACBFS95], even if, according to our definitions, the sequence and not the reward is the primary information. In the latter paper, a *partial information game* corresponds to the multi-armed bandit problem, in which only the reward relative to the prediction made is known to the predictor. What would have happened picking any of the other choices remains totally unknown. The best bound on the regret for this problem has been recently improved to $O(\sqrt{T})$ [Aue00].

In the present work we extend this result to our more general setting, provided that the feedback and loss functions jointly satisfy a simple but non-trivial condition. This case includes relevant special cases, such as the bandwidth allocation and quality control problems mentioned at the beginning of the present section, as well the classic multi-armed bandit problem and others. In this case it is possible to prove a bound of $O(T^{3/4})$ on the regret. The aforementioned condition is not specific to our algorithm: indeed we proved that, when it is not satisfied, any algorithm would incur a regret $\Omega(T)$, just as a prediction with no feedback at all.

Also closely related is the work presented in [WM00], where the same worst case approach to sequence prediction is assumed, but the sequence is available to a prediction algorithm only through noisy observations. Albeit very general, their results make some assumptions on the noise process, such as statistical independence between the noise components affecting observations at different time steps. Our feedback model encompasses also the situation of noisy observations, but gives up any statistical assumptions on the noise process too, in analogy with the notion of "malicious errors" in the context of PAC learning ([KL93]). That is we claim our work can be seen also as a worst case approach to the prediction of noisy sequences.

The paper is structured as follows. In Section 2 we formally describe the problem. In Section 3 we describe the basic algorithm and prove bounds on its performance. In Section 4 we review some examples and highlight some shortcomings of the basic algorithm and show how to overcome them. In Section 5 we present a general algorithm and prove that the algorithm is essentially the most general. In Section 6 we discuss our results.

2 The Model

We describe the problem as a game between a player choosing an action g_t and an adversary choosing the action y_t at time t. There are K possible actions available to the player, w.l.o.g., from the set $[K] = \{1, \ldots, K\}$, and R actions in the set $[R]$ from which the adversary can pick from. At every time step the player suffers a loss equal to $\ell(y_t, g_t) \in [0, 1]$.

The game is played in a sequence of trials $t = 1, 2, \ldots, T$. The adversary has full information about the history of the game, whereas the player only gets a feedback according to the function $f(y, g)$. Hence the $R \times K$-matrices L and F, with $L_{ij} = \ell(i, j)$ and $F_{ij} = f(i, j)$ completely describe an instance of the problem. At each round t the following events take place.

1. The adversary selects an integer $y_t \in [R]$.
2. Without knowledge of the adversary's choice, the player chooses an action by picking $g_t \in [K]$ and suffers a loss $x_{g_t}(t) = \ell(y_t, g_t)$.
3. The player observes $f_t = f(y_t, g_t)$.

Note that due to the introduction of the feedback function this is a generalization of the partial information game of [ACBFS95].

Let $W(T) := \sum_{t=1}^{T} x_{g_t}(t) = \sum_{t=1}^{T} \ell(y_t, g_t)$ be the total loss of player A choosing $g_1, \ldots, g_T$. We measure the performance of the player by the expected *regret* R_A, which is the difference between the total loss of A and the total loss of the best constant choice, that is:

$$R_A := \max_{y_1, \ldots, y_T} \mathbf{E} \left[\sum_{t=1}^{T} \ell(y_t, g_t) - \min_j \sum_{t=1}^{T} \ell(y_t, j) \right]$$

where each y_i is a function of $g_1, \ldots, g_{i-1}$. In some works the corresponding minmax problem is investigated, transforming the loss into a reward. The two settings are equivalent, as it is easy to check.

3 The Basic Algorithm

For the full information case the following *Multiplicative Weighting Algorithm* (see Fig. 1 and [FS97]) has been used in different settings and has been analyzed also in [ACBFS95].

Multiplicative Weighting (MW)
constant $\eta \in (0,1)$
begin
Initialize $p_i(1) := \frac{1}{K}$ for all $i \in [K]$.
for t **from** 1 **to** T **do**
Choose g_t according to probabilities $p_i(t)$.
Receive the loss vector $x(t)$.

$$Z_t := \sum_{i=1}^{K} \frac{p_i(t)}{\exp(\eta x_i(t))}.$$

$$p_i(t+1) := \frac{p_i(t)}{\exp(\eta x_i(t)) Z_t}, \text{ for all } i \in [K].$$

od
end

Fig. 1. The multiplicative weighting algorithm.

The analysis of [FS97] leads to a tight result for the full knowledge model. We will base our analysis on an adaptation of their main theorem. The following theorem establishes a bound on the performance of MW that holds for any loss function ℓ.

Theorem 1. *For* $\eta \in (0,1)$, *for any loss matrix* L *with* R *rows and* K *columns with entries in the range* $[0,1]$ *and for any sequence* $y_1, \ldots, y_T$ *the sequence of* $p(1), \ldots, p(T)$ *produced by algorithm MW satisfies*

$$\sum_{t=1}^{T} \sum_{i=1}^{K} \ell(y_t, i) p_i(t) \;\leq\; \min_j \sum_{t=1}^{T} \ell(y_t, j) + 2\eta T + \frac{\ln K}{\eta} \; .$$

Our algorithm relies on the existence of a $K \times K$ matrix G satisfying the following equation:

$$F\,G = L \; .$$

If such a G does not exist the basic algorithm fails, i.e. it cannot compute a strategy at all.

The algorithm can be described as follows. First, it estimates the loss vector using the matrix G and the feedback. This estimate is fed into the MW algorithm which returns a probability distribution on the player's actions. MW tends to choose an action with very low probability if the associated loss over the past history of the game is high. This is not acceptable in the partial information case, because actions are useful also from the point of view of the feedback. Therefore, and again in analogy with [FS97], the algorithm adjusts the distribution $p(t)$, output by the MW algorithm, to a new distribution $\hat{p}(t)$ such that $\hat{p}_i(t) \geq \frac{\gamma}{K}$ for each i. We will give an appropriate choice of γ and other parameters affecting the algorithm later on. What is new to this algorithm and what makes it much more general is the way the quantities $x_i(t)$ are estimated. More in detail, given

F and L and assuming there is a G such that $FG = L$, our basic algorithm works as shown in Fig. 2.

```
FeedExp3
begin
   Compute G such that F G = L.
   Choose η, γ ∈ (0,1) according to G.
   p_i(1) := 1/K for all i ∈ [K].
   for t from 1 to T do
      Select g_t to be j with probability p̂_j(t) := (1 − γ)p_j(t) + γ/K.
      Receive as feedback the number f_t.
      x̂_i(t) := F_{y_t,g_t} G_{g_t,i} / p̂_{g_t}(t), for all i ∈ [K].
      Z_t := Σ_{i=1}^{K} p_i(t) / exp(η x̂_i(t))
      p_i(t+1) := p_i(t) / (exp(η x̂_i(t)) Z_t), for all i ∈ [K].
   od
end
```

Fig. 2. The feedback exponential exploration and exploitation algorithm.

The following lemma shows that $\hat{x}(t)$ is an unbiased estimator of the loss vector $x(t)$.

Lemma 1. *For all i, t we have* $\mathbf{E}[\hat{x}_i(t)|g_1, \ldots, g_{t-1}] = x_i(t)$ and $\mathbf{E}[\hat{x}_i(t)] = \mathbf{E}[x_i(t)]$.

Proof. Note that

$$\mathbf{E}[\hat{x}_i(t)|g_1, \ldots, g_{t-1}] = \sum_{j=1}^{K} \hat{p}_j(x) \frac{F_{y_t,j}}{\hat{p}_j(x)} G_{j,i} = \sum_{j=1}^{K} F_{y_t,j} G_{j,i} = L_{y_t,i} = x_i(t) .$$

This implies

$$\mathbf{E}[\hat{x}_i(t)] = \mathbf{E}[\mathbf{E}[\hat{x}_i(t)|g_1, \ldots, g_{t-1}]] = \mathbf{E}[x_i(t)] .$$

Let $S_{y,i}(g) := F_{y,g} G_{g,i}$, for all $y \in [R]$, $g, i \in [K]$, $S^+ := \max_{y,g,i}\{S_{y,i}(g)\}$, $S^- := \min_{y,g,i}\{S_{y,i}(g)\}$ and $\rho := S^+ - S^-$ and $\sigma := \max(0, -S^-)$.

Lemma 2. *Let $\lambda, \delta \in (0,1)$. Then with probability at least $1-\delta$, for every action i, we have*

$$\sum_{t=1}^{T} \hat{x}_i(t) \leq (1+\lambda) \sum_{t=1}^{T} x_i(t) + \frac{\rho K \ln(K/\delta)}{\gamma \lambda} + \frac{\sigma \lambda T K}{\gamma \rho} .$$

Due to space limitation, we refer for a proof to the technical report [PS00]. It relies on a martingale argument similar to the ones used in the proof of Lemma 5.1 in [ACBFS95], but of course has to rest on weaker assumptions, in relation to the more general definition of $\hat{x}_i(t)$.

Lemma 3. *For any sequence $y_1, \ldots, y_T$ the sequence $\hat{p}(1), \ldots, \hat{p}(T)$ produced by FeedExp3 satisfies, for all j:*

$$\sum_{t=1}^{T}\sum_{i=1}^{K}\hat{x}_i(t)\hat{p}_i(t) \leq \sum_{t=1}^{T}\hat{x}_j(t) + \frac{2\eta\rho KT}{\gamma} + \frac{\rho K \ln K}{\gamma\eta} + \frac{\gamma}{K}\sum_{t=1}^{T}\sum_{i=1}^{K}\hat{x}_i(t) .$$

Proof. Consider a game where $p(t)$ denotes the probability distribution and the estimated loss $\hat{x}(t)$ is the real loss. Then, the FeedExp3-algorithm above reduces to a MW-algorithm, where $x(t)$ is replaced by $\hat{x}(t)$. Note that the range of the estimation vector now is $[KS^-/\gamma, KS^+/\gamma]$. So, we normalize the loss to $[0,1]$, by defining $\hat{x}'_i(t) := \frac{\gamma}{K\rho}\hat{x}_i(t) - S^-/\rho$, and apply Theorem 1. After rescaling, we use the fact that $\hat{p}_i(t) = (1-\gamma)p_i(t) + \frac{\gamma}{K}$.

Theorem 2. *If there exists G such that $F\ G = L$, then the expected regret $\mathbf{E}[R_{FeedExp3}(T)]$ of algorithm FeedExp3 after T steps is bounded by*

$$\mathbf{E}[R_{FeedExp3}(T)] = O(T^{3/4}(\ln T)^{1/2}K^{1/2})$$

for $T \geq K^2(\ln K)^2$ and with a constant factor linear in $\max\{\rho, \sigma/\rho\}$.

Proof. We first rewrite the expected loss $\mathbf{E}[W(T)]$ of algorithm FeedExp3 in a different way:

$$\begin{aligned}
\mathbf{E}[W(T)] &= \sum_{t=1}^{T}\mathbf{E}[x_{g_t}(t)] \\
&= \sum_{t=1}^{T}\mathbf{E}[\mathbf{E}[x_{g_t}(t)|g_1 \ldots g_{t-1}]] \\
&= \sum_{t=1}^{T}\mathbf{E}\left[\sum_{i=1}^{K}x_i(t)\hat{p}_i(t)\right] \\
&= \mathbf{E}\left[\sum_{t=1}^{T}\sum_{i=1}^{K}x_i(t)\hat{p}_i(t)\right] \\
&= \mathbf{E}\left[\sum_{t=1}^{T}\sum_{i=1}^{K}\mathbf{E}[\hat{x}_i(t)|g_1 \ldots g_{t-1}]\hat{p}_i(t)\right] \\
&= \mathbf{E}\left[\sum_{t=1}^{T}\sum_{i=1}^{K}\hat{x}_i(t)\hat{p}_i(t)\right] .
\end{aligned}$$

By Lemma 3 we have, for any j:

$$\sum_{t=1}^{T}\sum_{i=1}^{K}\hat{x}_i(t)\hat{p}_i(t) \leq \sum_{t=1}^{T}\hat{x}_j(t) + \frac{2\eta\rho KT}{\gamma} + \frac{\rho K \ln K}{\gamma\eta} + \frac{\gamma}{K}\sum_{t=1}^{T}\sum_{i=1}^{K}\hat{x}_i(t) .$$

Since the former inequality holds for any j, we can choose $j = g^*$ so as to minimize the right hand side of the last inequality, that is g^* is the best action, to obtain:

$$\sum_{t=1}^{T} \hat{x}_{g^*}(t) + \frac{2\eta\rho KT}{\gamma} + \frac{\rho K \ln K}{\gamma\eta} + \frac{\gamma}{K}\sum_{t=1}^{T}\sum_{i=1}^{K} \hat{x}_i(t).$$

Disregarding minor factors and applying Lemma 2 and the obvious bound $x_i(t) \leq 1$, we can further upper bound the latter expression with:

$$\sum_{t=1}^{T} x_{g^*}(t) + (\gamma + 2\lambda)T + \frac{2\eta\rho KT}{\gamma} + \frac{\rho K \ln K}{\gamma\eta} + \frac{2\rho K \ln(K/\delta)}{\gamma\lambda} + \frac{2\sigma\lambda TK}{\gamma\rho}.$$

This bound holds with probability δ. Therefore, to upper bound the expectation we started with, we need to add an error term δT. Furthermore, we set $\lambda = T^{-1/2}(\ln T)^{1/2}(\ln K)^{1/4}$, $\eta = T^{-1/2}(\ln K)^{1/2}$, $\gamma = T^{-1/4}K^{1/2}(\ln K)^{1/4}$ and $\delta = T^{-2}$.

$$\mathbf{E}\left[\sum_{t=1}^{T}\sum_{i=1}^{K} \hat{p}_i(t)x_i(t)\right] \leq \mathbf{E}\left[\sum_{t=1}^{T} x_{g^*}(t)\right] + O((\rho + \tfrac{\sigma}{\rho})T^{3/4}(\ln T)^{1/2}K^{1/2}).$$

4 Applications, Limits and Extensions

We are now equipped to show how the bandwidth allocation problem that initially prompted this research, as well as other important examples, can be solved using this algorithm, but we will also see that only some tweaking allows to solve other equally reasonable prediction problems. We will see in the next section that these "tricks" lead to a general algorithm, that, after some preprocessing, uses the basic algorithm to achieve sub-linear regret whenever this is feasible.

Let y be the available (unknown) bandwidth and g the allocated bandwidth. We can describe the available feedback as follows (*threshold feedback*):

$$f(y,g) = \begin{cases} 0 \text{ if } y < g \\ 1 \text{ otherwise}. \end{cases}$$

Therefore a feedback of 1 represents the successful transmission of a packet, a 0 its loss. This situation is not at all uncommon: namely, the most widespread networking protocol, TCP/IP, relies on this kind of information only. The corresponding feedback matrix F is a lower triangular matrix, with only 1's on the diagonal and below. F is invertible, allowing the application of the FeedExp3 algorithm, for any loss function, with the choice $G = F^{-1}L$.

In [KKPS00] the following loss model was introduced, under the name of *severe cost function*:

$$\ell(y,g) = \begin{cases} y \text{ if } y < g \\ y - g \text{ otherwise}. \end{cases}$$

When $g < y$ the value reflects the opportunity cost of sending a packet packet of size g when y was the maximum possible size. When $y > g$ the cost function takes into account the cost of compensating for packet loss, under the assumption that the protocol must wait for the first dropped packet to *time out* before resuming transmission.

The TCP solution to the allocation problem, abstracting from the details, is to decrease the allocated bandwidth by a constant factor whenever a packet loss is detected and to increase it by an additive term when the transmission is successful. It is clear that, when analyzed in an adversarial setting, TCP has linear regret if compared to the best constant choice.

The multi-armed bandit problem with partial information of [ACBFS95] corresponds to the case $F = L$. Under this condition, $G = I$ is a suitable choice. A somehow dual situation arises when $F = I$, that is when the feedback is a binary "hit or miss" information. Then $G = L$ is a suitable choice for G.

A more troublesome situation is the full feedback case. Even if in this case the more complex machinery presented in this paper is not necessary, since an expected regret of $O(T^{1/2} \log K)$ can be achieved by the MW algorithm [FS97], it is clear that a general algorithm for this class of problems must be able to solve this special case, too. A natural choice for F is $F_{ij} = i$, which implies $f_t = y_t$. Unfortunately, such a matrix has rank 1 and therefore the condition $FG = L$ can be satisfied only when L has a very special, and rather trivial, form. But more than the specific values of the entries of F, what defines "full feedback" is the fact that no two entries in every column of F have the same value, that is there is a bijection between the values in F_i and the range of y_t. If F satisfies this property, it is possible to compute y_t from f_t and hence we can say we are still in the full information case. Therefore, we are interested in finding a full rank matrix within the set of matrices just described, which all represent the full feedback case.

Another example is a slightly modified threshold feedback $f(y, g) = 0$, if $y \leq g$ and 1 otherwise. Then F becomes singular, but it is enough to reverse the arbitrary roles of 0 and 1 to get an equivalent problem, where this time F is invertible, and therefore, for any L, the equation $FG = L$ can be solved for G. Clearly we have to make our algorithm resilient to these simple formalization changes.

An acceptable transformation of F can be detailed as a set of functions for every column of F, from the range of the elements of F into some other range. The goal is to obtain a new matrix F', where every column is obtained applying one of the functions to the elements of a column of F, for which there is a G such that $F'G = L'$. It is clear that F' can have more columns than F, because every column can be transformed in different ways, but no fewer, since every action has to be represented. This corresponds to introducing new actions that are essentially replicas, but for each of which the feedback undergoes a different transformation. From the point of view of the loss, these additional actions are totally equivalent and therefore we need to extend L into a larger matrix L' by duplicating the appropriate columns. What we seek is a general way to expand F' so as to keep the number of columns reasonably small but making the linear span of F' all-inclusive, that is such that it cannot be enlarged by adding more columns obtained in a feasible way. This can be accomplished as follows. For every column F_i containing r_i distinct values (w.l.o.g. from the set $[r_i]$) we define r_i columns $F'_{R_i+1} \dots F'_{R_i+r_i}$, where $R_i = \sum_{j=1}^{i-1} r_i$, as follows: for $1 \le j \le r_i$, $F'_{R_i+j,k} = 1$ if $j = F_{i,k}$, and 0 otherwise. As to L', we set $L'_j = L_i$ if and only if $R_i < j \le R_i + r_i$. It is straightforward to check that the matrix F' obtained this way has the largest possible linear span among all the ones that can be obtained from F via the transformations detailed above. Also, since F is $R \times K$, F' is at most $R \times KR$. These are more columns than we need and would impact negatively the bounds on the regret: therefore we will pick the smallest subset of columns S which is still good for our purposes, that is that satisfies the following conditions:

- all the columns of L are represented in L' or, equivalently, all the actions in the original instance are represented, that is for every $i \in [K]$ there is a $j \in S$ such that $R_i < j \le R_i + r_i$;
- $\mathcal{L}(\{F'_i : i \in S\}) = \text{range}(F')$.

The final feedback and distance matrices can be obtained by dropping all the columns not in S from F' and L', and we will continue to use the same symbols for the submatrices defined this way. In the next section we will present a greedy algorithm which solves this problem.

Let us see how this helps in the full feedback case. Recall that a natural choice for F is $F_{ij} = i$. Therefore, the corresponding F' has maximum rank (some columns of F' form an $R \times R$ identity matrix), $F'G = L$ can be solved for G and the general algorithm can be applied successfully.

A further complication arises from *non-exploitable* actions. These are the ones which, for any adversarial strategy, do not turn out to be optimal. The problem here is that the condition $FG = L$ might be impossible to satisfy because of some columns related to non-exploitable actions. Consider, for instance:

$$F = \begin{pmatrix} 1\,1\,1 \\ 1\,1\,1 \\ 0\,1\,1 \end{pmatrix} \qquad L = \begin{pmatrix} 1\,1\,0 \\ 2\,1\,0 \\ 1\,0\,1 \end{pmatrix} .$$

Here column 1 of L is not in the linear span of F, but it is easy to see that actions 3 and 4 can be always preferred to the first. Therefore it might seem reasonable to simply drop the first column, as it is related to a non-exploitable action. It turns out, though, it is just action 1 that provides the necessary feedback to estimate the loss. It is clear that simply omitting non-exploitable actions is not a good strategy.

As with the feedback matrix F, the solution for these problems is to transform the loss matrix L into a new L' in a way that does not lower the regret.

If we add the same vector x to every column of L, we are not changing the problem instance in any substantial way, since the regret, our performance measure, is invariant w.r.t. this transformation. Therefore we are interested in those transformations that help fulfilling the condition $FG = L$. This time, it makes sense to try to obtain a matrix L' from L of minimum rank. Rank minimization is a difficult problem in general, but this special case turns out to be rather trivial.

Lemma 4. *Given three matrices L, L' and L'' such that for every i $L'_i = L_i - L_j$ and $L''_i = L_i - x$, we have that, for any vector x and index j, $\mathcal{L}(L') \subseteq \mathcal{L}(L'')$.*

Proof. Since $L_i - L_j = L_i - x - (L_j - x)$, the lemma follows.

Therefore choosing x equal to one of the columns of L minimizes the linear span of L'. In the following we will assume $L_1 = (0, \ldots, 0)$ w.l.o.g.

As to non-exploitable actions, we first need to formally define them. Let us define a partition[1] of the set of mixed strategies (for the adversary) as follows. Every element of the partition is centered around a column of L' and is defined as:

$$N(L_i) = \{v \in \mathcal{A} \mid \forall j: \; L_i \neq L_j \Rightarrow vL_i \leq vL_j\}$$

where the set $\mathcal{A} := \{v \in [0,1]^R \mid \sum_i v_i = 1\}$ denotes all possible mixed strategies of the adversary.

That is an element of this partition is the set of mixed adversarial strategies such that a certain prediction is preferred to any other. If $N(L_i)$ is empty, then i is a non-exploitable action. The rationale behind this definition is that no sensible algorithm will ever try this action for exploitation purposes (that is often), since there are other actions which bear a smaller loss. The interior of $N(L_i)$ is defined as follows:

$$S(L_i) = \{v \in \mathcal{A} \mid \forall j: \; L_i \neq L_j \Rightarrow vL_i < vL_j\} \; .$$

The following lemma shows that we can replace every mixed adversarial strategy on the surface of some element of the partition by another strategy not on the surface, with no penalty in performance.

Lemma 5. *For all mixed adversarial strategies $q \in \mathcal{A}$ there exists a column L_i with $S(L_i) \neq \emptyset$ such that $q \in N(L_i)$.*

Proof. We concentrate on elements in the set $\mathcal{F} := \bigcup_i N(L_i) \setminus S(L_i)$. Note that we have

$$\mathcal{F} \subseteq \bigcup_{i,j} \{v \in \mathcal{A} \mid v(L_i - L_j) = 0\} \; .$$

Therefore $\mathcal{F}$ is a subset of a union of at most K^2 subspaces of dimension $R-2$. Since $\mathcal{A}$ is a $R-1$ dimensional polytope, any ϵ-ball centered on a point $v \in N(L_i)$ contains elements not in $\mathcal{F}$. Such an element $v' \notin \mathcal{F}$ is contained in a set $L_{i'}$ with $S(L_{i'}) \neq \emptyset$. Since this is true for any ϵ-ball, then v belongs to the surface of $N(L_{i'})$ too, that is $vL_i = vL_{i'}$.

[1] Strictly speaking, it is not a partition, but the idea helps the intuition

Hence, we can extend the definition of non-exploitable action to columns with $S(L_i) = \emptyset$, since their choice gives no improvement over actions with $S(L_i) \neq \emptyset$.

In order to extend the applicability of the basic algorithm, we set all the entries in the columns corresponding to non-exploitable actions equal to the size of the maximum element in its column in L. This can only increase the regret w.r.t. the best constant strategy, because none of the actions associated to these columns can be part of any optimal strategy. Furthermore, it is easy to check that the columns obtained this way are in the linear span of F' for every F.

5 The General Algorithm

In Fig. 3 we show how to implement the construction of F' and L'. Let $[F_{i,j} = v]_{i=1,\ldots,R}$ denote the vector obtained replacing, in the jth column of F, every entry equal to v by 1 and all others by 0. The algorithm constructs F' and L' by appending columns derived from F and L to their right sides.

Augmented with this kind of preprocessing for the loss and feedback matrices, our algorithm covers all the examples we considered. A natural question is therefore whether the condition $F'G = L'$ is not only necessary for our algorithm to apply, but in general for any useful algorithm. The answer is positive, meaning that if the condition cannot be fulfilled, then any algorithm will undergo a loss $\Omega(T)$.

Theorem 3. *For any prediction game (F, L) we have either one of the following situations.*

- *The General Algorithm solves it with an expected regret of*

$$\mathbf{E}[R_{General}] \leq O(T^{3/4}(\ln T)^{1/2} \max(K, R^{1/2})) .$$

- *There is an adversarial strategy which causes any algorithm A to produce a regret of $\Omega(T)$ with probability $1/2$.*

Proof. In the previous section, we have already seen that we can map a sequence of actions for the prediction game (F', L') to the instance F, L in a way that does not essentially increase the regret. This proves the first part of the theorem. We can rephrase the second part as follows:

> Given an instance of the prediction game (F, L) let be F' and L' the matrices obtained through the transformations detailed in the previous section. If there is no G such that $F'G = L'$, then any prediction algorithm will undergo a loss $\Omega(T)$.

We associate a graph $H = (V, E)$ to the partition $\{N(L'_1), \ldots, N(L'_k)\}$ by defining $V = \{L_i : S(L'_i) \neq \emptyset\}$ and $(L'_i, L'_j) \in E$ if and only if $L'_i = L'_j$ or the sets $N(L'_i)$ and $N(L'_j)$ share a facet, i.e. a face of dimension $R-2$. Note that for all i the set $N(L'_i)$ describes a polytope of dimension $R-1$ or its interior $S(L'_i)$ is empty.

Let $\mathcal{L}(E)$ be the linear span of the set of differences between vectors at the endpoints of each edge in E. We have the following

```
The General Algorithm
  begin
    for j from 1 to K do
      for all values v in F_i do
        if [F_{i,j} = v]_{i=1,...,R} ∉ 𝓛(F'_1, ..., F'_z) then
          Append [F_{i,j} = v]_{i=1,...,R} to F'
          Append L_j to L'.
        fi
      od
      if L_j was not added to L' then
        Append (0, ..., 0)^T to F'
        Append L_j to L'.
      fi
    od
    K' := number of columns of F' and L'.
    Choose L'_b such that S(L'_b) ≠ ∅.
    for i from 1 to K' do
      L'_i := L'_i - L'_b
    od
    for i from 1 to K' do
      if S(L_i) = ∅ then
        L'_i := max_{j'} {L'_{j',i}} (1, ..., 1)^T
      fi
    od
    FeedExp3(F', L')
  end
```

Fig. 3. The General Algorithm

Lemma 6. $\mathcal{L}(E) = \mathcal{L}(\{L'_i : L'_i \in V\})$.

Proof. For each $L'_i \in V$, $L'_i = L'_i - L'_{i_1} + L'_{i_1} - L'_{i_2} + \ldots + L'_{i_p} - L'_1$, where $(L'_i, L'_{i_1}, \ldots, L'_{i_p}, L'_1)$ is a path connecting L'_i to L'_1, if such a path exists.

We need only to prove that H is connected. Given the two vertices L'_i and L'_j, we seek a path joining them. Consider the segment joining a point in the interior of $N(L'_i)$ to one in the interior of $N(L'_j)$. Since the set of mixed strategies is convex, every point in the segment is a mixed strategy. Let us pick an arbitrary orientation for this segment and consider the sequence of polytopes that share with the segment some interior point, and specifically two consecutive entries in the sequence, $N(L'_h)$ and $N(L'_k)$. If the segment goes from the first to the second through a facet, then the two corresponding vertices in the graph are joined by an edge. If not, that means that the two polytopes share only a face of dimension $R-3$ or lower, e.g. a vertex or an edge. In that case we need to pick a different point in, say, $N(L_j)$. This is always possible because $N(L_j)$ has dimension $R-1$ whereas the set of points collinear with the designated point in $N(L_i)$ and any point in any face of dimension $R-3$ or lower has dimension at most $R-2$.

Now, let us assume that there is no G such that $F'G = L'$. This implies that there is L'_i such that $L'_i \notin \mathcal{L}(F')$. Let us assume $S(L'_i) = \emptyset$. By definition of L', $L'_i = \alpha(1, \dots, 1)$ for some α. This implies, by definition of F', $L'_i \in \mathcal{L}(F')$, a contradiction. Therefore $S(L'_i) \neq \emptyset$ and, by lemma 6, $\mathcal{L}(E) \nsubseteq \mathcal{L}(F')$. Hence, for some $(L'_i, L'_j) \in E$, we have that $L'_i - L'_j \notin \mathcal{L}(F')$. Since the range of F' is the orthogonal complement to the null space of F'^T we have that, for some non-zero vector $n \in \mathrm{Ker}(F'^T)$, $n(L'_i - L'_j) \neq 0$. Let y be a point in the interior of the facet shared by $N(L'_i)$ and $N(L'_j)$. We have that $y + \alpha n$ and $y - \alpha n$ are both mixed strategies for some α. They are indistinguishable from the point of view of any algorithm because $(y + \alpha n)F' = (y - \alpha n)F' = yF'$, but they correspond to different optimal actions, and the regret implied by making the wrong choice is $|\alpha n(L'_i - L'_j)|$.

6 Conclusion and Open Problems

We solve the problem of discrete loss and feedback online prediction games in its general setting, presenting an algorithm which, on average, has sub-linear regret against the best constant choice, whenever this is achievable.

In the full knowledge case, it is well known that the average per step regret is bounded by $O(T^{-1/2})$. In [ACBFS95] it is shown that, if the feedback is identical to the loss, there is an algorithm whose average regret is bounded by $O(T^{-1/3})$ (omitting polylogarithmic terms), recently improved to $O(T^{-1/2})$ [Aue00]. In the present paper, we show that, for every "reasonable" feedback, the average per step regret is at most $O(T^{-1/4})$. Otherwise, no algorithm can do better than $\Omega(T)$.

While we proved that no algorithm can attain sub-linear regret on a larger class of instances than ours does, it is an open problem whether such general prediction games can be solved with a bound on the regret as good as the one obtained for the multi-armed bandit problem, in the most general setting or under some additional assumptions.

It is straightforward to transfer the upper bounds shown for the worst case regret against constant predictors to the finite pool of general predictors (a.k.a. "expert") model, in analogy with the argument of [ACBFS95], Section 7. However, the lower bound is not readily applicable to this case and therefore it is an open question whether our general algorithm achieves sub-linear regret whenever it is possible in this context.

Another interesting question is whether a uniform algorithm exists that works for any feedback and loss functions and achieves the best known performance for each feedback. Note that the algorithms presented in this work, even when given in input a feedback function corresponding to the "full knowledge" case, guarantees only an average per step regret of $O(T^{-1/4})$, whereas $O(T^{-1/2})$ is the best bound known.

7 Acknowledgements

We wish to thank Richard Karp for suggesting this line of research. Gadiel Seroussi, Marcelo Weinberg, Neri Merhav, Nicolò Cesa-Bianchi provided invaluable feedback about the paper and pointers to the literature. We are grateful to one of the anonymous referees who provided detailed comments, including a necessary fix to the proof of Theorem 2.

References

[ACBFS95] Peter Auer, Nicolò Cesa-Bianchi, Yoav Freund, and Robert E. Schapire. Gambling in a rigged casino: the adversarial multi-armed bandit problem. In *Proceedings of the 36th Annual Symposium on Foundations of Computer Science*, pages 322–331. IEEE Computer Society Press, Los Alamitos, CA, 1995.

[Aue00] Peter Auer. Using upper confidence bounds for online learning. In *Proceedings of the 41th Annual Symposium on Foundations of Computer Science*, pages 270–279. IEEE Computer Society Press, Los Alamitos, CA, 2000.

[CBFH+97] Nicolò Cesa-Bianchi, Yoav Freund, David P. Helmbold, David Haussler, Robert E. Schapire, and Manfred K. Warmuth. How to use expert advice. *Journal of the ACM*, 44(3):427–485, 1997.

[CBFHW93] Nicolò Cesa-Bianchi, Yoav Freund, David P. Helmbold, and Manfred Warmuth. On-line prediction and conversion strategies. In *EUROCOLT: EUROCOLT, European Conference on Computational Learning Theory, EuroCOLT,*. LNCS, 1993.

[CBL99] Nicolò Cesa-Bianchi and Gabor Lugosi. Minimax regret under log loss for general classes of experts. In *Proceedings of the 12th Annual Conference on Computational Learning Theory*. ACM Press, 1999.

[FS97] Y. Freund and R. Schapire. Adaptive game playing using multiplicative weights. *Games and Economic Behavior*, 1997. to appear.

[Han57] James Hannan. Approximation to bayes risk in repeated play. In M. Dresher, A. W. Tucker, and P. Wolfe, editors, *Contributions to the Theory of Games*, volume III, pages 97–139. Princeton University Press, 1957.

[HKW95] D. Haussler, J. Kivinen, and M. K. Warmuth. Tight worst-case loss bounds for predicting with expert advice. *Lecture Notes in Computer Science*, 904:69, 1995.

[HKW98] D. Haussler, J. Kivinen, and M. K. Warmuth. Sequential prediction of individual sequences under general loss functions. *IEEE Transactions on Information Theory*, 44, 1998.

[KKPS00] Richard Karp, Elias Koutsopias, Christos Papadimitriou, and Scott Shenker. Optimization Problems in Congestion Control In *Proceedings of the 41st Symposium on the Foundation of Computer Science*, 2000.

[KL93] M. Kearns and M. Li. Learning in the presence of malicious errors. *SIAM Journal on Computing,*, 22(4):807–837, August 1993.

[LW94] Nick Littlestone and Manfred K. Warmuth. The weighted majority algorithm. *Information and Computation*, 108(2):212–261, 1 February 1994.

[PS00] A. Piccolboni and C. Schindelhauer. Discrete prediction games with arbitrary feedback and loss. Technical Report A-00-18, Schriftenreihe der Institute für Informatik und Mathematik, Universität Lübeck, October 2000.

[Sch99] Robert E. Schapire. Drifting games. In *Proc. 12th Annu. Conf. on Comput. Learning Theory*, pages 114–124. ACM Press, New York, NY, 1999.

[Vov98] V. Vovk. A game of prediction with expert advice. *Journal of Computer and System Sciences*, 56(2):153–173, April 1998.

[Vov99] V. Vovk. Competitive on-line statistics. In *The 52nd Session of the International Statistical Institute*, 1999.

[WM00] T. Weissman and N. Merhav. Universal prediction of binary individual sequences in the presence of noise. accepted to IEEE Trans. Inform. Theory, September 2000.

Rademacher and Gaussian Complexities: Risk Bounds and Structural Results

Peter L. Bartlett[1] and Shahar Mendelson[2]

[1] BIOwulf Technologies
2030 Addison Street, Suite 102
Berkeley, CA 94704, USA
bartlett@barnhilltechnologies.com

[2] Research School of Information Sciences and Engineering
Australian National University
Canberra 0200, Australia
shahar@csl.anu.edu.au

Abstract. We investigate the use of certain data-dependent estimates of the complexity of a function class, called Rademacher and gaussian complexities. In a decision theoretic setting, we prove general risk bounds in terms of these complexities. We consider function classes that can be expressed as combinations of functions from basis classes and show how the Rademacher and gaussian complexities of such a function class can be bounded in terms of the complexity of the basis classes. We give examples of the application of these techniques in finding data-dependent risk bounds for decision trees, neural networks and support vector machines.

1 Introduction

In learning problems like pattern classification and regression, a considerable amount of effort has been spent on obtaining good error bounds. These are useful, for example, for the problem of model selection—choosing a model of suitable complexity. Typically, such bounds take the form of a sum of two terms: some sample-based estimate of performance and a penalty term that is large for more complex models. For example, in pattern classification, the following theorem is an improvement of a classical result of Vapnik and Chervonenkis [20].

Theorem 1. *Let F be a class of $\{\pm 1\}$-valued functions defined on a set $\mathcal{X}$. Let P be a probability distribution on $\mathcal{X} \times \{\pm 1\}$, and suppose that $(X_1, Y_1), \ldots, (X_n, Y_n)$ and (X, Y) are chosen independently according to P. Then, there is an absolute constant c such that for any integer n, with probability at least $1-\delta$ over samples of length n, every f in F satisfies*

$$P(Y \neq f(X)) \leq \hat{P}_n(Y \neq f(X)) + c\sqrt{\frac{\mathrm{VCdim}(F)}{n}},$$

where $\mathrm{VCdim}(F)$ denotes the Vapnik-Chervonenkis dimension of F, $\hat{P}_n(S) = (1/n)\sum_{i=1}^{n} \mathbf{1}_S(X_i, Y_i)$, and $\mathbf{1}_S$ is the indicator function of S,

D. Helmbold and B. Williamson (Eds.): COLT/EuroCOLT 2001, LNAI 2111, pp. 224–240, 2001.

In this case, the sample-based estimate of performance is the proportion of examples in the training sample that are misclassified by the function f, and the complexity penalty term involves the VC-dimension of the class of functions. It is natural to use such bounds for the model selection scheme known as complexity regularization: choose the model class containing the function with the best upper bound on its error. The performance of such a model selection scheme critically depends on how well the error bounds match the true error (see [2]). There is theoretical and experiment evidence that error bounds involving a fixed complexity penalty (that is, a penalty that does not depend on the training data) cannot be universally effective [4].

Recently, several authors have considered alternative notions of the complexity of a function class: the Rademacher and gaussian complexities (see [2,5,7,7, 13]).

Definition 1. *Let μ be a probability distribution on a set $\mathcal{X}$ and let $X_1, \ldots, X_n$ be independent samples selected according to μ. For a class F of functions mapping from $\mathcal{X}$ to $\mathbb{R}$, define the random variable*

$$\hat{R}_n(F) = \mathbf{E}\left[\sup_{f\in F}\left|\frac{2}{n}\sum_{i=1}^{n}\sigma_i f(X_i)\right| \middle| X_1, \ldots, X_n\right],$$

where $\sigma_1, \ldots, \sigma_n$ are independent uniform $\{\pm 1\}$-valued random variables. Then the Rademacher complexity of F is $R_n(F) = \mathbf{E}\hat{R}_n(F)$. Similarly, define the random variable

$$\hat{G}_n(F) = \mathbf{E}\left[\sup_{f\in F}\left|\frac{2}{n}\sum_{i=1}^{n}g_i f(X_i)\right| \middle| X_1, \ldots, X_n\right],$$

where $g_1, \ldots, g_n$ are independent gaussian $N(0,1)$ random variables. The gaussian complexity of F is $G_n(F) = \mathbf{E}\hat{G}_n(F)$.

Both $R_n(F)$ and $G_n(F)$ are intuitively reasonable as measures of complexity of the function class F: they quantify the extent to which some function in the class F can be correlated with a noise sequence of length n. The following lemma shows that these two complexity measures are closely related [19].

Lemma 1. *There are absolute constants c and C such that for every class F and every integer n, $cR_n(F) \leq G_n(F) \leq C \log n R_n(F)$.*

The following theorem is an example of the usefulness of these notions of complexity (see, e.g., [2]). The proof is a slight refinement of a proof of a more general result which we give below (Theorem 5); it is presented in Appendix A.

Theorem 2. *Let P be a probability distribution on $\mathcal{X} \times \{\pm 1\}$ and let F be a set of $\{\pm 1\}$-valued functions defined on $\mathcal{X}$. Then with probability at least $1-\delta$ over training samples $(X_i, Y_i)_{i=1}^n$ drawn according to P^n, every function f in F satisfies*

$$P(Y \neq f(X)) \leq \hat{P}_n(Y \neq f(X)) + \frac{R_n(F)}{2} + \sqrt{\frac{\ln(1/\delta)}{2n}}.$$

The following result shows that this theorem implies the upper bound of Theorem 1 in terms of VC-dimension, as well as a refinement in terms of VC-entropy. In particular, Theorem 2 can never be much worse than the VC results. Since the proof of Theorem 2 is a close analog of the first step of the proof of VC-style results (the symmetrization step), this is not surprising. In fact, the bounds of Theorem 2 can be considerably better than Theorem 1, since the first part of the following result is in terms of the *empirical* VC-dimension.

Theorem 3. *Fix a sample $X_1, \ldots, X_n$. For a function class $F \subseteq \{\pm 1\}^{\mathcal{X}}$, define the restriction of F to the sample as $F_{|X_i} = \{(f(X_1), \ldots, f(X_n)) : f \in F\}$. Define the empirical VC-dimension of F as $d = \mathrm{VCdim}\left(F_{|X_i}\right)$ and the empirical VC-entropy of F as $E = \log_2 \left|F_{|X_i}\right|$. Then $\hat{G}_n(F) = O\left(\sqrt{d/n}\right)$ and $\hat{G}_n(F) = O\left(\sqrt{E/n}\right)$.*

The proof of this theorem is based on an upper bound on $\hat{G}_n$ which is due to Dudley (quoted in Theorem 15 below), together with an upper bound on covering numbers due to Haussler (see [12]).

Koltchinskii and Panchenko [6] proved an analogous error bound in terms of *margins*. The margin of a real-valued function f on a labelled example $(x, y) \in \mathcal{X} \times \{\pm 1\}$ is $yf(x)$. For a function $h : \mathcal{X} \times \mathcal{Y} \to \mathbb{R}$ and a training sample $(X_1, Y_1), \ldots, (X_n, Y_n)$, we write $\hat{\mathbf{E}}_n h(X, Y) = (1/n) \sum_{i=1}^n h(X_i, Y_i)$.

Theorem 4. *Let P be a probability distribution on $\mathcal{X} \times \{\pm 1\}$ and let F be a set of $[-1, 1]$-valued functions defined on $\mathcal{X}$. Suppose that $\phi : \mathbb{R} \to [0, 1]$ satisfies $\phi(\alpha) \geq \mathbf{1}(\alpha \leq 0)$ and is Lipschitz with constant L. Then with probability at least $1 - \delta$ with respect to training samples $(X_i, Y_i)_{i=1}^n$ drawn according to P^n, every function in F satisfies*

$$P(Yf(X) \leq 0) \leq \hat{\mathbf{E}}_n \phi(Yf(X)) + 2LR_n(F) + \sqrt{\frac{\ln(2/\delta)}{2n}}.$$

This improves a number of results bounding error in terms of a sample average of a margin error plus a penalty term involving the complexity of the real-valued class (such as covering numbers and fat-shattering dimensions) [1, 10,17,18].

In the next section, we give a bound of this form that is applicable in a more general, decision-theoretic setting. Here, we have an input space $\mathcal{X}$, an action space $\mathcal{A}$ and an output space $\mathcal{Y}$. The training data $(X_1, Y_1), \ldots, (X_n, Y_n)$ are selected independently according to a probability measure P on $\mathcal{X} \times \mathcal{Y}$. There is a loss function $\mathcal{L} : \mathcal{Y} \times \mathcal{A} \to [0, 1]$, so that $\mathcal{L}(y, a)$ reflects the cost of taking a particular action $a \in \mathcal{A}$ when the outcome is $y \in \mathcal{Y}$. The aim of learning is to choose a function f that maps from $\mathcal{X}$ to $\mathcal{A}$, so as to minimize the expected loss $\mathbf{E}\mathcal{L}(Y, f(X))$.

For example, in multiclass classification, the output space $\mathcal{Y}$ is the space $\mathcal{Y} = \{1, \ldots, k\}$ of class labels. When using error correcting output codes [8,16] for this problem, the action space might be $\mathcal{A} = [0, 1]^m$, and for each $y \in \mathcal{Y}$

there is a codeword $a_y \in \mathcal{A}$. The loss function $\mathcal{L}(y, a)$ is equal to 0 if the closest codeword a_{y^*} has $y^* = y$ and 1 otherwise.

Section 2 gives bounds on the expected loss for decision-theoretic problems of this kind in terms of the sample average of a Lipschitz *dominating cost function* (a function that is pointwise larger than the loss function) plus a complexity penalty term involving a Rademacher complexity.

We also consider the problem of estimating $R_n(F)$ and $G_n(F)$ (for instance, for model selection). These quantities can be estimated by solving an optimization problem over F. However, for cases of practical interest, such optimization problems are difficult. On the other hand, in many such cases, functions in F can be represented as combinations of functions from simpler classes. This is the case, for instance, for decision trees, voting methods, and neural networks. In Section 3, we show how the complexity of such a class can be related to the complexity of the class of basis functions. Section 4 describes examples of the application of these techniques.

2 Risk Bounds

We begin with some notation. Given an independent sample $(X_i, Y_i)_{i=1}^n$ distributed as (X, Y), we denote by P_n the empirical measure supported on that sample and by μ_n the empirical measure supported on $(X_i)_{i=1}^n$. We say a function $\phi : \mathcal{Y} \times \mathcal{A} \to \mathbb{R}$ dominates a loss function $\mathcal{L}$ if for all $y \in \mathcal{Y}$ and $a \in \mathcal{A}$, $\phi(y, a) \geq \mathcal{L}(y, a)$. For a class of functions F, conv$F$ is the class of convex combinations of functions from F, $-F = \{-f : f \in F\}$, absconv$F$ is the class of convex combinations of functions from $F \cup -F$, and $cF = \{cf : f \in F\}$. If ϕ is a function defined on the range of the functions in F, let $\phi \circ F = \{\phi \circ f | f \in F\}$. Given a set A, we denote its characteristic function by $\mathbf{1}_A$ or $\mathbf{1}(A)$. Finally, constants are denoted by C or c. Their values may change from line to line, or even within the same line.

Theorem 5. *Consider a loss function $\mathcal{L} : \mathcal{Y} \times \mathcal{A} \to [0, 1]$ and a dominating cost function $\phi : \mathcal{Y} \times \mathcal{A} \to [0, 1]$. Let F be a class of functions mapping from $\mathcal{X}$ to $\mathcal{A}$ and let $(X_i, Y_i)_{i=1}^n$ be independently selected according to the probability measure P. Then, for any integer n and any $0 < \delta < 1$, with probability at least $1 - \delta$ over samples of length n, every f in F satisfies*

$$\mathbf{E}\mathcal{L}(Y, f(X)) \leq \hat{\mathbf{E}}_n \phi(Y, f(X)) + R_n(\tilde{\phi} \circ F) + \sqrt{\frac{8 \ln(2/\delta)}{n}},$$

where $\tilde{\phi} \circ F = \{(x, y) \mapsto \phi(y, f(x)) - \phi(y, 0) : f \in F\}$.

The proof uses McDiarmid's inequality [11].

Theorem 6 (McDiarmid's Inequality). *Let $X_1, ..., X_n$ be independent random variables taking values in a set A, and assume that $f : A^n \to \mathbb{R}$ satisfies*

$$\sup_{x_1, \ldots, x_n, x_i' \in A} |f(x_1, ..., x_n) - f(x_1, ..., x_{i-1}, x_i', x_{i+1}, ... x_n)| \leq c_i$$

for every $1 \le i \le n$*. Then, for every* $t > 0$*,*

$$P\Big\{|f(X_1, ..., X_n) - \mathbf{E}f(X_1, ..., X_n)| \ge \epsilon\Big\} \le 2e^{-2t/\sum_{i=1}^n c_i^2}.$$

Proof. (of Theorem 5) Since ϕ dominates $\mathcal{L}$, for all $f \in F$ we can write

$$\begin{aligned}\mathbf{E}\mathcal{L}(Y, f(X)) &\le \mathbf{E}\phi(Y, f(X)) \\ &\le \hat{\mathbf{E}}_n\phi(Y, f(X)) + \sup_{h\in\phi\circ F}\Big(\mathbf{E}h - \hat{\mathbf{E}}_n h\Big) \\ &= \hat{\mathbf{E}}_n\phi(Y, f(X)) + \sup_{h\in\tilde{\phi}\circ F}\Big(\mathbf{E}h - \hat{\mathbf{E}}_n h\Big) + \mathbf{E}\phi(Y,0) - \hat{\mathbf{E}}_n\phi(Y,0).\end{aligned}$$

When an (X_i, Y_i) pair changes, the random variable $\sup_{h\in\tilde{\phi}\circ F}\Big(\mathbf{E}h - \hat{\mathbf{E}}_n h\Big)$ can change by no more than $2/n$. McDiarmid's inequality implies that with probability at least $1 - \delta/2$,

$$\sup\Big(\mathbf{E}h - \hat{\mathbf{E}}_n h\Big) \le \mathbf{E}\sup\Big(\mathbf{E}h - \hat{\mathbf{E}}_n h\Big) + \sqrt{2\log(2/\delta)/n}\,.$$

A similar argument, together with the fact that $\mathbf{E}\hat{\mathbf{E}}_n\phi(Y,0) = \mathbf{E}\phi(Y,0)$, shows that with probability at least $1 - \delta$,

$$\mathbf{E}\mathcal{L}(Y, f(X)) \le \hat{\mathbf{E}}_n\phi(Y, f(X)) + \mathbf{E}\sup_{h\in\tilde{\phi}\circ F}\Big(\mathbf{E}h - \hat{\mathbf{E}}_n h\Big) + \sqrt{\frac{8\ln(2/\delta)}{n}}.$$

It remains to show that the second term on the right hand side is no more than $R_n(\tilde{\phi}\circ F)$. If $(X_1', Y_1'), \ldots, (X_n', Y_n')$ are independent random variables with the same distribution as (X, Y), then

$$\begin{aligned}\mathbf{E}\sup_{h\in\tilde{\phi}\circ F}\Big(\mathbf{E}h - \hat{\mathbf{E}}_n h\Big) &= \mathbf{E}\sup_{h\in\tilde{\phi}\circ F}\mathbf{E}\left[\frac{1}{n}\sum_{i=1}^n h(X_i', Y_i') - \hat{\mathbf{E}}_n h\,\middle|\,(X_i, Y_i)\right] \\ &\le \mathbf{E}\sup_{h\in\tilde{\phi}\circ F}\left(\frac{1}{n}\sum_{i=1}^n h(X_i', Y_i') - \hat{\mathbf{E}}_n h\right) \\ &= \mathbf{E}\sup_{h\in\tilde{\phi}\circ F}\frac{1}{n}\sum_{i=1}^n \sigma_i\left(h(X_i', Y_i') - h(X_i, Y_i)\right) \\ &\le 2\mathbf{E}\sup_{h\in\tilde{\phi}\circ F}\frac{1}{n}\sum_{i=1}^n \sigma_i h(X_i, Y_i) \\ &\le R_n(\tilde{\phi}\circ F).\end{aligned}$$

As an example, consider the case $\mathcal{A} = \mathcal{Y} = [0,1]$. It is possible to bound $R_n(F)$ in terms of expected covering numbers of F or its fat-shattering dimension. Indeed, the following result relates $G_n(F)$ to empirical versions of these notions of complexity, and implies that Theorem 5 can never give a significantly worse estimate than estimates in terms of these quantities. This result is essentially in [13]; although that paper gave a result in terms of the fat-shattering dimension, the same proof works for the empirical fat-shattering dimension.

Theorem 7. *Fix a sample $X_1, \dots, X_n$. Let F be a class of function whose range is bounded by 1. Assume that there is some $\gamma > 1$ such that for any $\epsilon > 0$, $\mathrm{fat}_\epsilon \left(F_{|X_i}\right) \le \gamma\epsilon^{-p}$. Then, there are absolute constants C_p, which depend only on p, such that*

$$\hat{G}_n(F) \le \begin{cases} C_p \gamma^{1/2} \log \gamma n^{-1/2} & \text{if } 0 < p < 2, \\ C_2 \left(\gamma^{1/2} \log \gamma\right) n^{-1/2} \log^2 n & \text{if } p = 2, \\ C_p \left(\gamma^{1/2} \log \gamma\right) n^{-1/p} & \text{if } p > 2. \end{cases}$$

3 Estimating the Rademacher and Gaussian Complexities of Function Classes

An important property of Rademacher and gaussian complexities is that they can be estimated from a single sample $(X_1, \dots, X_n)$. As an example, consider the following result, which follows from McDiarmid's inequality (see also [2]).

Theorem 8. *Let F be a class of functions mapping to $[-1, 1]$. For any integer n, with probability at least $1 - \delta$ over samples $X_1, \dots, X_n$,*

$$\left| R_n(F) - \hat{R}_n(F) \right| \le \sqrt{\frac{\log(1/\delta)}{2n}} .$$

In addition, $\hat{R}_n(F)$ can be estimated from one realization of the Rademacher variables $\sigma_1, \dots, \sigma_n$, and the same is true of $\hat{G}_n(F)$. This is a consequence of the following concentration results.

Theorem 9. *Let F be a class of real functions and fix some $x_1, ..., x_n$. Set $\tau^2 = \sup_{f \in F} \sum_{i=1}^n f^2(x_i)$. Then,*

$$P\left\{ \left| \frac{1}{n} \sup_{f \in F} \left| \sum_{i=1}^n \sigma_i f(x_i) \right| - \frac{1}{n} \mathbf{E} \sup_{f \in F} \left| \sum_{i=1}^n \sigma_i f(x_i) \right| \right| \ge \epsilon \right\} \le 2e^{-2n\epsilon^2/\tau^2} ,$$

$$P\left\{ \left| \frac{1}{n} \sup_{f \in F} \left| \sum_{i=1}^n g_i f(x_i) \right| - \frac{1}{n} \mathbf{E} \sup_{f \in F} \left| \sum_{i=1}^n g_i f(x_i) \right| \right| \ge \epsilon \right\} \le e^{-2n\epsilon^2/\pi^2\tau^2} .$$

The first (Rademacher) part of the theorem follows from McDiarmid's inequality, while the second is due to Maurey and Pisier [15].

Thus, it seems that the computation of $\hat{R}_n(F)$ and $\hat{G}_n(F)$ is particularly convenient. However, as mentioned before, their computation involves an optimization over the class F, which is hard for interesting function classes. The way we bypass this obstacle is to use that fact that same "large" classes can be expressed as combinations of functions from simpler classes. For instance, a decision tree can be expressed as a fixed boolean function of the functions appearing in each decision node, voting methods use thresholded convex combinations of functions from a simpler class, and neural networks are compositions of fixed squashing functions with linear combinations of functions from some class. Hence, we present several structural results that lead to bounds on the Rademacher and gaussian complexities of a function class F in terms of the complexities of simpler classes of functions from which F is constructed.

3.1 Simple Structural Results

We begin with the following observations regarding $R_n(F)$.

Theorem 10. *Let $F, F_1, \ldots, F_k$ and H be classes of real functions. Then*

1. *If $F \subseteq H$, $R_n(F) \leq R_n(H)$.*
2. $R_n(F) = R_n(\mathrm{conv} F) = R_n(\mathrm{absconv} F)$.
3. *For every $c \in \mathbb{R}$, $R_n(cF) = |c| R_n(F)$.*
4. *If $\phi : \mathbb{R} \to \mathbb{R}$ is Lipschitz with constant L_ϕ and satisfies $\phi(0) = 0$, then $R_n(\phi \circ F) \leq 2L_\phi R_n(F)$.*
5. *There is an absolute constant C such that for any uniformly bounded function h, $R_n(F + h) \leq R_n(F) + C\|h\|_\infty/\sqrt{n}$.*
6. *For $1 \leq q < \infty$, let $\mathcal{L}_{F,h,q} = \{|f - h|^q \,|f \in F\}$. There is an absolute constant C such that for any uniformly bounded function h, $R_n(\mathcal{L}_{F,h,q}) \leq q\left(R_n(F) + C\|h\|_\infty/\sqrt{n}\right)$.*
7. $R_n\left(\sum_{i=1}^k F_i\right) \leq \sum_{i=1}^k R_n(F_i)$.

Parts 1-3 are true for G_n, with exactly the same proof. The other observations hold for G_n with an additional factor of $\log n$ and may be established using the general connection between R_n and G_n (Lemma 1). Parts 5 and 6 allow us to estimate the Rademacher complexities of natural loss function classes.

Note that 7 is tight. To see this, let $F_1 = \cdots = F_k = F$. Then, by parts 1 and 3, $R_n\left(\sum_{i=1}^k F_i\right) \geq R_n(kF) = kR_n(F) = \sum_{i=1}^k R_n(F_i)$.

Proof. Parts 1 and 3 are immediate from the definitions. To see part 2, notice that for every $x_1, \ldots, x_n$ and $\sigma_1, \ldots, \sigma_n$,

$$
\begin{aligned}
\sup_{f \in \mathrm{absconv} F} \left| \sum_{i=1}^n \sigma_i f(x_i) \right| &= \sup_{f \in \mathrm{conv} F} \left| \sum \sigma_i f(x_i) \right| \\
&= \max\left(\sup_{f \in \mathrm{conv} F} \sum \sigma_i f(x_i), \sup_{f \in \mathrm{conv} F} - \sum \sigma_i f(x_i) \right) \\
&= \max\left(\sup_{f \in F} \sum \sigma_i f(x_i), \sup_{f \in F} - \sum \sigma_i f(x_i) \right) \\
&= \sup_{f \in F} \left| \sum \sigma_i f(x_i) \right| .
\end{aligned}
$$

The inequality of part 4 is due to Ledoux and Talagrand [9, Corollary 3.17]. As for part 5, note that there is an absolute constant C such that for every realization of $X_1, ..., X_n$,

$$
\begin{aligned}
\mathbf{E} \sup_{f \in F} \left| \sum_{i=1}^n \sigma_i \left(f(X_i) + h(X_i)\right) \right| &\leq \mathbf{E} \sup_{f \in F} \left| \sum_{i=1}^n \sigma_i f(X_i) \right| + \mathbf{E} \left| \sum_{i=1}^n \sigma_i h(X_i) \right| \\
&\leq \mathbf{E} \sup_{f \in F} \left| \sum_{i=1}^n \sigma_i f(X_i) \right| + C \left(\sum_{i=1}^n h(X_i)^2 \right)^{\frac{1}{2}} ,
\end{aligned}
$$

where the last inequality follows from Khintchin's inequality. Hence, $R_n(F+g) \leq R_n(F) + C \|h\|_\infty / \sqrt{n}$, as claimed.

To see part 6, notice that $\phi(x) = |x|^q$ is a Lipschitz function which passes through the origin with a Lipschitz constant q. By parts 4 and 5 of Theorem 10,

$$R_n(\mathcal{L}_{F,h,q}) \leq qR_n(F-h) \leq q\left(R_n(F) + C\frac{\|h\|_\infty}{\sqrt{n}}\right).$$

Finally, part 7 follows from the triangle inequality.

3.2 Lipschitz Functions on $\mathbb{R}^k$

Theorem 10 part 4 shows that composing real-valued functions in some class with a Lipschitz function changes the Rademacher complexity by no more than a constant factor. In this section, we prove a similar result for the gaussian complexity of a class of vector-valued functions. It is convenient to view a normalized version of G_n as the expectation of a gaussian vector with respect to a certain norm. To that end, we shall require several definitions from the theory of Banach spaces.

Let ℓ_2^n be an n dimensional Hilbert space, with inner product $\langle \cdot, \cdot \rangle$. Given a class F and a sample $S_n = \{X_1, ... X_n\}$, let μ_n be the empirical measure supported on S_n. We endow $\mathbb{R}^n$ with the Euclidean structure of $L_2(\mu_n)$, which is isometric to ℓ_2^n. Define $F/\mu_n = \{\sum_{i=1}^n f(X_i)\mathbf{1}_{X_i} | f \in F\}$. Since $(e_i)_{i=1}^n = (n^{1/2}\mathbf{1}_{X_i})_{i=1}^n$ is an orthonormal basis of $L_2(\mu_n)$, we can write

$$F/\mu_n = \left\{ \frac{1}{\sqrt{n}} \sum_{i=1}^n f(X_i) e_i | f \in F \right\}.$$

Definition 2. *For $F \subseteq \ell_2^n$, define the ℓ-norm of F as*

$$\ell(F) = \mathbf{E} \sup_{f \in F} \left| \left\langle f, \sum_{i=1}^n g_i e_i \right\rangle \right| ,$$

where the $g_1, \ldots, g_n$ are independent gaussian $N(0,1)$ random variables and $e_1, \ldots, e_n$ is an orthonormal basis of ℓ_2^n.

The following connection with the gaussian complexity is immediate.

Lemma 2. *For a class of functions F and empirical measure μ_n, $\ell(F/\mu_n) = (\sqrt{n}/2)\hat{G}_n(F)$.*

There is a well known connection between the ℓ-norm and the covering numbers of the set in ℓ_2^n. In the following theorem, the upper bound is due to Dudley, while the lower bound is due to Sudakov. The proof is in [15].

Theorem 11. *There are constants C and c, such that for all n and $F \subset \ell_2^n$,*

$$c \sup_{\epsilon > 0} \left(\epsilon \sqrt{\log \mathcal{N}(\epsilon, F, \ell_2^n)} \right) \leq \ell(F) \leq C \int_0^\infty \sqrt{\log \mathcal{N}(\epsilon, F, \ell_2^n)} d\epsilon .$$

The upper bound in the above theorem has the following discrete analog [14] that will be useful in the sequel.

Lemma 3. *There is a constant C such that for every two integers n and N, every $F \subset \ell_2^n$ and any real sequence $\epsilon_0 \geq \epsilon_1 \geq \cdots \geq \epsilon_N > 0$ with $\epsilon_0 \geq \sup_{f\in F} \|f\|_2$, we have $\ell(F) \leq C \left(\sum_{k=1}^{N} \epsilon_{k-1} \sqrt{\log \mathcal{N}(\epsilon_k, F, \ell_2^n)} \right) + 2n^{\frac{1}{2}} \epsilon_N$.*

In our discussion we will be interested in "direct sums" of real-valued classes. In this case, it is natural to turn to vector-valued L_2 spaces.

Definition 3. *Let B be a Banach space and set μ to be a measure on $\mathcal{X}$. Let $L_2(B,\mu)$ be the space of measurable B-valued functions with respect to the norm $\|f\|_{L_2(B,\mu)} = \left(\mathbf{E}\|f(x)\|_B^2\right)^{\frac{1}{2}}$.*

Note that if $B = \ell_2^m$, S_n is a sample and μ_n is the empirical measure supported on the sample, then $L_2(B,\mu_n)$ is isometric to $\ell_2^{m\times n}$. Indeed, for every $f \in L_2(B,\mu_n)$ set

$$f/\mu_n = \frac{1}{\sqrt{n}} \sum_{j=1}^{m} \sum_{i=1}^{n} f_j(x_i) v_{ij} \in \ell_2^{m\times n} \,,$$

where (v_{ij}) is an orthnormal basis in $\ell_2^{m\times n}$. Thus, the map $T : L_2(B,\mu_n) \to \ell_2^{m\times n}$ given by $Tf = f/\mu_n$ is an isometry, because we can write $\|f\|_{L_2(B,\mu_n)}^2 = (1/n)\sum_{i=1}^{n} \|f(x_i)\|_{\ell_2^m}^2 = \|f/\mu_n\|_{\ell_2^{m\times n}}^2$.

Let $F_1, \ldots F_m$ be classes of functions and let (u_j) be an orthonormal basis in ℓ_2^m. Set

$$F = \left\{ \sum_{j=1}^{m} f_j u_j | f_j \in F_j \right\} . \tag{1}$$

By the above observation, given an empirical measure μ_n, we may view $F \subset L_2(\ell_2^m, \mu_n)$ as a subset of $\ell_2^{m\times n}$, and we denote this set by F/μ_n.

Lemma 4. *For any F as in (1) and empirical measure μ_n,*

$$\ell(F/\mu_n) \leq \sum_{j=1}^{m} \ell(F_j/\mu_n) \,.$$

Proof. If μ_n is supported on $(X_1, \ldots, X_n)$ then by the definition of F/μ_n, $\ell(F/\mu_n)$ is

$$\mathbf{E} \sup_{f\in F} \frac{1}{\sqrt{n}} \left| \sum_{i=1}^{n} \sum_{j=1}^{m} g_{ij} f_j(X_i) \right| \leq \mathbf{E} \sum_{j=1}^{m} \sup_{f_j \in F_j} \left| \sum_{i=1}^{n} g_{ij} \frac{f_j(X_i)}{\sqrt{n}} \right| = \sum_{j=1}^{m} \ell(F_j/\mu_n) \,.$$

Now, we can formulate and prove the main result of this section, in which we estimate the ℓ-norm of a Lipschitz image of a direct sum of classes.

Theorem 12. *Let $\mathcal{A} = \mathbb{R}^m$ and let F be a class of functions mapping from $\mathcal{X}$ to $\mathcal{A}$. Suppose that there are real-valued classes $F_1, \ldots, F_m$ such that F is a subset of their direct sum. Assume further that $\phi : \mathcal{Y} \times \mathcal{A} \to \mathbb{R}$ is such that, for all $y \in \mathcal{Y}$, $\phi(y, \cdot)$ is a Lipschitz function with constant L which passes through the origin and is uniformly bounded. For $f \in F$, define $\phi \circ f$ as the mapping $(x, y) \mapsto \phi(y, f(x))$ and set $A = \sup_{f \in F} \|\phi \circ f\|_\infty$. Then, there is an absolute constant $C \geq 1$ such that for every integer $n \geq 3$ and every sample $(X_1, Y_1), \ldots, (X_n, Y_n)$,*

$$\ell\left((\phi \circ F)/P_n\right) \leq C \max\left(\frac{A}{\sqrt{n}}, L \sum_{j=1}^{m} \ell(F_j/\mu_n)\right) \log n \, ,$$

where P_n is the empirical measure supported on $(X_i, Y_i)_{i=1}^n$ and μ_n is the empirical distribution on $(X_i)_{i=1}^n$. Furthermore,

$$G_n(\phi \circ F) \leq C\left(\frac{A}{n} + L \sum_{j=1}^{m} G_n(F_j)\right) \log n \, .$$

Proof. For the first inequality, we can assume that $L \sum_{j=1}^m \ell(F_j/\mu_n) < A\sqrt{n}$, because if this is not the case, the uniform bound on $\phi \circ F$, together with Jensen's inequality, implies that $\ell\left((\phi \circ F)/P_n\right) \leq A\sqrt{n}$, and hence $\ell\left((\phi \circ F)/P_n\right)$ is no more than

$$A\sqrt{n} \leq \max\left(\frac{A}{\sqrt{n}}, L \sum_{j=1}^{m} \ell(F_j/\mu_n)\right) \leq C \log n \max\left(\frac{A}{\sqrt{n}}, L \sum_{j=1}^{m} \ell(F_j/\mu_n)\right) ,$$

provided that $n \geq e$.

By Lemma 3 there is an absolute constant $C \geq 1$ such that

$$\ell\left((\phi \circ F)/P_n\right) \leq C\left(\sum_{k=1}^{N} \epsilon_{k-1} \sqrt{\log \mathcal{N}(\epsilon_k, \phi \circ F, L_2(P_n))} + 2n^{\frac{1}{2}} \epsilon_N\right) ,$$

where (ϵ_i) is decreasing. Note that $\epsilon_0 = A$ is a 'legal' choice for ϵ_0 since $\phi \circ F$ consists of functions which are all bounded by A. Using the Lipschitz condition for ϕ, for every $x \in \mathcal{X}$, $y \in \mathcal{Y}$ and $f, h \in F$ $|\phi(y, f(x)) - \phi(y, h(x))| \leq L \|f(x) - h(x)\|_B$. Thus, for any probability measure P on $\mathcal{X} \times \mathcal{Y}$,

$$\|\phi \circ f - \phi \circ h\|_{L_2(P)} \leq L \|f - h\|_{L_2(B,\mu)} ,$$

where μ is the marginal distribution on $\mathcal{X}$. In particular, if P_n is an empirical measure on $\mathcal{X} \times \mathcal{Y}$ and μ_n is the corresponding empirical measure on $\mathcal{X}$, then for every $\epsilon > 0$, $\mathcal{N}(\epsilon, \phi \circ F, L_2(P_n)) \leq \mathcal{N}(\epsilon/L, F, L_2(B, \mu_n)) = \mathcal{N}(\epsilon/L, F/\mu_n, \ell_2^{m \times n})$. Applying Sudakov's lower bound (Theorem 11) and by Lemma 4,

$$\sqrt{\log \mathcal{N}(\epsilon/L, F/\mu_n, \ell_2^{m \times n})} \leq \frac{CL}{\epsilon} \ell(F/\mu_n) \leq \frac{CL}{\epsilon} \sum_{j=1}^{m} \ell(F_j/\mu_n) \, .$$

Set $\epsilon_k = r\epsilon_{k-1}$ for some $0 < r < 1$ to be named later. Define $S = \sum_{j=1}^m \ell(F_j/\mu_n)$. Then

$$\ell\left((\phi \circ F)/P_n\right) \leq C\left(\sum_{k=1}^N L\frac{\epsilon_{k-1}}{\epsilon_k}S + n^{\frac{1}{2}}\epsilon_N\right) \leq C\left(\frac{NL}{r}S + Ar^N\sqrt{n}\right) .$$

This is minimized when $r^{N+1} = LS/(A\sqrt{n})$, which is smaller than 1 by the assumption. Substituting this value of r gives

$$\ell\left((\phi \circ F)/P_n\right) \leq C(N+1)\left(A\sqrt{n}\right)^{1/(N+1)}(LS)^{N/(N+1)} . \tag{2}$$

If $LS < A/\sqrt{n}$, this quantity is less than $C(N+1)n^{1/(N+1)}(A/\sqrt{n})$. On the other hand, if $LS \geq A/\sqrt{n}$, (2) is no more than $C(N+1)n^{1/(N+1)}LS$. In either case, $\ell\left((\phi \circ F)/P_n\right) \leq C(N+1)n^{1/(N+1)}\max\left(A/\sqrt{n}, LS\right)$. Selecting $N = \lfloor \log n \rfloor$ gives the first part of the result.

To prove the second part, we bound the maximum by a sum,

$$\frac{\ell\left((\phi \circ F)/P_n\right)}{\sqrt{n}} \leq C\log n\left(\frac{A}{\sqrt{n}} + L\sum_{j=1}^m \frac{\ell(F_j/\mu_n)}{\sqrt{n}}\right),$$

and take the expectation of both sides.

Corollary 1. *Let $\mathcal{A}, F, F_1, \ldots, F_m, \phi$ be as in Theorem 12. Consider a loss function $\mathcal{L} : \mathcal{Y} \times \mathcal{A} \to [0,1]$ and suppose that ϕ dominates $\mathcal{L}$ and $\|\phi\|_\infty \leq 1$. Then, for any integer n there is a probability of at least $1-\delta$ that every f in F has*

$$\mathbf{E}\mathcal{L}(Y, f(X)) \leq \hat{\mathbf{E}}_n\phi(Y, f(X)) + c\left(L\log n\sum_{j=1}^m G_n(F_j) + \sqrt{\frac{\ln(2/\delta)}{n}}\right) .$$

3.3 Boolean Combinations of Functions

Theorem 13. *For a boolean function $g : \{\pm 1\}^k \to \{\pm 1\}$ and classes $F_1, \ldots, F_k$ of $\{\pm 1\}$-valued functions, $G_n(g(F_1, \ldots, F_k)) \leq C\left(\sum_{j=1}^k G_n(F_j) + 1/n\right)\log n$.*

Proof. First, we extend the boolean function g to a function $g : \mathbb{R}^k \to [-1,1]$ as follows: for $x \in \mathbb{R}^k$, define $g(x) = (1 - \|x-a\|)g(a)$ if $\|x - a\| < 1$ for some $a \in \{\pm 1\}^k$, and $g(x) = 0$ otherwise. The function is well-defined since all pairs of points in the k-cube are separated by distance at least 2. Clearly, $g(0) = 0$, and g is Lipschitz with constant 1. The theorem follows from Theorem 12, with $m = k$ and $\phi = g$.

4 Examples

The error bounds presented in previous sections can be used as the basis of a complexity regularization algorithm for model selection. This algorithm minimizes an upper bound on error involving the sample average of a cost function and a gaussian or Rademacher complexity penalty term. We have seen that these upper bounds in terms of gaussian and Rademacher complexities can never be significantly worse than bounds based, for example, on combinatorial dimensions. They can have a significant advantage over such bounds, since they measure the complexity of the class on the training data, and hence can reflect the properties of the particular probability distribution that generates the data. The computation of these complexity penalties involves an optimization over the model class. The structural results of the previous section give a variety of techniques that can simplify this optimization problem. For example, voting methods involve optimization over the convex hull of some function class H. By Theorem 10 part 2, we can estimate $G_n(\mathrm{conv}H)$ by solving a maximization problem over the base class H. In this section, we give some other examples illustrating this approach. In all cases, the resulting error bounds decrease at least as fast as $1/\sqrt{n}$.

4.1 Decision Trees

A binary-valued decision tree can be represented as a fixed boolean function of the decision functions computed at its nodes. Theorem 13 implies that the gaussian complexity of the class of decision trees of a certain size can be bounded in terms of the gaussian complexity of the class of node decision functions. Typically, this is simpler to compute. The following result gives a refinement of this idea, based on the representation (see, for example, [3]) of a decision tree as a thresholded linear combination of the indicator functions of the leaves.

Theorem 14. *Let P be a probability distribution on $\mathcal{X} \times \{-1,1\}$, and let H be a set of binary-valued functions defined on $\mathcal{X}$. Let T be the class of decision trees of depth no more than d, with decision functions from H. For a training sample $(X_1, Y_1, \ldots, X_n, Y_n)$ drawn from P^n and a decision tree from T, let $\tilde{P}_n(l)$ denote the proportion of all training examples which reach leaf l and are correctly classified. Then with probability at least $1-\delta$, every decision tree t from T with L leaves has* $\Pr(y \neq t(x))$ *no more than*

$$\hat{P}_n(y \neq t(x)) + \sum_l \min(\tilde{P}_n(l), cdG_n(H)\log n) + \sqrt{\frac{c\ln(L/\delta)}{2n}} \,.$$

Notice that the key term in this inequality is $O(dLG_n(H)\log n)$. It can be considerably smaller if many leaves have small empirical weight. This is the case, for instance, if $G_n(H) = O(n^{-1/2})$ and many leaves have weight less than $O\left(dn^{-1/2}\log n\right)$.

Proof. For a tree of depth d, the indicator function of a leaf is a conjunction of no more than d decision functions. More specifically, if the decision tree consists of decision nodes chosen from a class H of binary-valued functions, the indicator function of leaf l (which takes value 1 at a point x if x reaches l, and 0 otherwise) is a conjunction of d_l functions from H, where d_l is the depth of leaf l. We can represent the function computed by the tree as the sign of

$$f(x) = \sum_l w_l \sigma_l \bigwedge_{i=1}^{d_l} h_{l,i}(x),$$

where the sum is over all leaves l, $w_l > 0$, $\sum_l w_l = 1$, $\sigma_l \in \{\pm 1\}$ is the label of leaf l, $h_{l,i} \in H$, and the conjunction is understood to map to $\{0,1\}$. Let F be this class of functions. Choose a family $\{\phi_L : L \in \mathbb{N}\}$ of cost functions such that each ϕ_L dominates the step function $\mathbf{1}(yf(x) \le 0)$ and has a Lipschitz constant L. For each L, Theorem 4 implies that with probability at least $1-\delta$,

$$\Pr(yf(x) \le 0) \le \hat{\mathbf{E}}_n(\phi_L(yf(x))) + 2LR_n(F) + \sqrt{\frac{\ln(2/\delta)}{2n}}.$$

By setting $\delta_L = 6\delta/(\pi^2 L)$, applying this result to all positive integer values of L, and summing over L, we see that with probability at least $1-\delta$, every $f \in F$ and every ϕ_L has

$$\Pr(yf(x) \le 0) \le \hat{\mathbf{E}}_n(\phi_L(yf(x))) + 2LR_n(F) + \sqrt{\frac{\ln(\pi^2 L/3\delta)}{2n}}.$$

Define $\phi_L(\alpha)$ to be 1 if $\alpha \le 0$, $1 - L\alpha$ if $0 < \alpha \le 1/L$, and 0 otherwise, where L will be computed later. Let $\tilde{P}_n(l)$ denote the proportion of training examples which reach leaf l and are correctly classified ($y = \sigma_l$). Then we have

$$\begin{aligned}
&\hat{\mathbf{E}}_n(\phi_L(yf(x))) + 2LR_n(F) \\
&= \hat{P}_n(yf(x) \le 0) + \sum_l \tilde{P}_n(l)\phi_L(w_l) + 2LR_n(F) \\
&= \hat{P}_n(yf(x) \le 0) + \sum_l \tilde{P}_n(l)\max(0, 1 - Lw_l) + 2LR_n(F) \\
&= \hat{P}_n(yf(x) \le 0) + \sum_l \max(0, (1 - Lw_l)\tilde{P}_n(l)) + 2LR_n(F).
\end{aligned}$$

Now, choose $w_l = 0$ for $\tilde{P}_n(l) \le 2R_n(F)$, and $w_l = 1/L$ otherwise, where $L = |\{l : \tilde{P}_n(l) > 2R_n(F)\}|$. (Notice that choosing $w_l = 0$ for labelled examples for which $yf(x) > 0$ can only increase the bound.) Then we have

$$\begin{aligned}
\hat{P}_n(\phi(yf(x))) + 2LR_n(F) &\le \hat{P}_n(yf(x) \le 0) + \sum_l \mathbf{1}\left(\tilde{P}_n(l) \le 2R_n(F)\right)\tilde{P}_n(l) \\
&\quad + 2R_n(F)\sum_l \mathbf{1}\left(\tilde{P}_n(l) > 2R_n(F)\right) \\
&= \hat{P}_n(yf(x) \le 0) + \sum_l \min(\tilde{P}_n(l), 2R_n(F)).
\end{aligned}$$

Theorem 10 part 2, Theorem 13, and Lemma 1 together imply that $R_n(F) \le C\,(dG_n(H) + 1/n)\log n$, which implies the result.

4.2 Neural Networks and Kernel Methods

The following two lemmas give bounds on gaussian complexities for classes of bounded linear functions.

Lemma 5. *For $x \in \mathbb{R}^k$, define $F_1 = \left\{x \mapsto w \cdot x : w \in \mathbb{R}^k,\ \|w\|_1 \leq 1\right\}$. For any $x_1, \ldots, x_n \in \mathbb{R}^k$ we have $\hat{G}_n(F_1) \leq \frac{c}{n} \log k \max_{j,j'} \left(\sum_{i=1}^n (x_{ij} - x_{ij'})^2\right)^{1/2}$.*

Lemma 6. *Define $F_2 = \{x \mapsto w \cdot x : x, w \in \ell_2,\ \|w\| \leq 1\}$. For any $x_1, \ldots, x_n \in \ell_2$ we have $\hat{G}_n(F_2) \leq \frac{2}{n} \left(\sum_{i=1}^n \|x_i\|^2\right)^{1/2}$. Thus, if D is a diagonal operator on ℓ_2 with eigenvalues λ_j and the $x_1, \ldots, x_n$ lie in the image of the unit ball in ℓ_2 under D, then $\hat{G}_n(F_2) \leq 2\sqrt{\sum_j \lambda_j^2 / n}$.*

Note that the second part of this result gives a bound on the gaussian complexity for a support vector machine in terms of the eigenvalues of the kernel (see, for example, [21]).

The proofs use the following inequality for gaussian processes (see, e.g., [9, 15]).

Lemma 7 (Slepian's Lemma). *Let $Z_1, \ldots, Z_k$ be random variables such that for every $1 \leq j \leq k$, $Z_j = \sum_{i=1}^n a_{ij} g_i$, where $(g_i)_{i=1}^n$ are independent gaussian $N(0,1)$ random variables. Then, there is an absolute constant C such that*

$$\mathbf{E} \max_{1 \leq j \leq k} Z_j \leq c \log k \max_{j,j'} \sqrt{\mathbf{E}(Z_j - Z_{j'})^2}.$$

Proof. (of Lemma 5) From the definitions, $\hat{G}_n(F_1)$ is equal to

$$\mathbf{E} \sup_{f \in F} \frac{2}{n} \sum_{i=1}^n g_i f(x_i) = \mathbf{E} \sup_{w : \|w\|_1 \leq 1} \frac{2}{n} \sum_{i=1}^n g_i w \cdot x_i = \mathbf{E} \sup_{w : \|w\|_1 \leq 1} w \cdot \frac{2}{n} \sum_{i=1}^n g_i x_i \,.$$

Clearly, this inner product is maximized when w is at one of the extreme points of the ℓ_1 ball, which implies $\hat{G}_n(F_1) = \mathbf{E} \max_j (2/n) \sum_{i=1}^n g_i x_{ij}$, where $x_i = (x_{i1}, \ldots, x_{ik})$. Note that we can write $\hat{G}_n(F_1) = \frac{2}{n} \mathbf{E} \max_j Z_j$ where $Z_j = \sum_{i=1}^n g_i x_{ij}$. Since each Z_j is gaussian, we can apply Slepian's lemma to obtain

$$\begin{aligned}
\hat{G}_n(F_1) &\leq \frac{2c}{n} \log k \max_{j,j'} \sqrt{\mathbf{E}(Z_j - Z_{j'})^2} \\
&= \frac{2c}{n} \log k \max_{j,j'} \sqrt{\mathbf{E}\left(\sum_{i=1}^n g_i (x_{ij} - x_{ij'})\right)^2} \\
&= \frac{2c}{n} \log k \max_{j,j'} \sqrt{\sum_{i=1}^n (x_{ij} - x_{ij'})^2}.
\end{aligned}$$

Proof. *(of Lemma 6)* As in the proof of the previous lemma and by Jensen's inequality, $\hat{G}_n(F_2)$ is equal to

$$\mathbf{E} \sup_{w:\|w\|\leq 1} w \cdot \left(\frac{2}{n} \sum_{i=1}^n g_i x_i \right) = \frac{2}{n} \mathbf{E} \left\| \sum_{i=1}^n g_i x_i \right\| \leq \frac{2}{n} \sqrt{\mathbf{E} \left\| \sum_{i=1}^n g_i x_i \right\|^2} = \frac{2}{n} \sqrt{\sum_{i=1}^n \|x_i\|^2}.$$

For the second inequality of the theorem, note that if each x_i lies in the image of the unit ball under D then we can write it in the form $x_i = \sum_j \lambda_j a_{ij} e_j$, where $e_1, e_2, \ldots$ is an orthonormal basis of ℓ_2 and the a_{ij} satisfy $\sum_j a_{ij}^2 \leq 1$. Thus, by Jensen's inequality, $\hat{G}_n(F_2)$ is no more than

$$\frac{2}{n} \sqrt{\sum_{i=1}^n \left\| \sum_j \lambda_j a_{ij} e_j \right\|^2} = \frac{2}{n} \sqrt{\sum_{i=1}^n \sum_j \lambda_j^2 a_{ij}^2} = \frac{2}{n} \sqrt{\sum_j \lambda_j^2 \sum_{i=1}^n a_{ij}^2} \leq 2 \sqrt{\sum_j \lambda_j^2 / n}.$$

The following bound on the gaussian complexity of a two-layer neural network is immediate from Lemma 5.

Theorem 15. *Suppose that $\sigma : \mathbb{R} \to [-1, 1]$ has Lipschitz constant L and satisfies $\sigma(0) = 0$. Define the class computed by a two-layer neural network with 1-norm weight constraints as $F = \{x \mapsto \sum_i w_i \sigma(v_i \cdot x) : \|w\|_1 \leq 1, \|v_i\|_1 \leq B\}$. Then for $x_1, \ldots, x_n$ in $\mathbb{R}^k$,*

$$\hat{G}_n(F) \leq \frac{cLB \log k}{n} \max_{j,j'} \sqrt{\sum_{i=1}^n (x_{ij} - x_{ij'})^2}\,.$$

It is straightforward to extend this result to networks with more than two layers, and to networks with multiple outputs. Lemma 6 implies a similar result in terms of a 2-norm constraint on the hidden weights v_i.

A Proof of Theorem 2

We set $\mathcal{L}(Y, f(X)) = \mathbf{1}(Y \neq f(X))$ and proceed as in the proof of Theorem 5. For all $f \in F$,

$$P(Y \neq f(X)) = \mathbf{E}\mathcal{L}(Y, f(X)) \leq \hat{\mathbf{E}}_n \mathcal{L}(Y, f(X)) + \sup_{h \in \mathcal{L} \circ F} \left(\mathbf{E}h - \hat{\mathbf{E}}_n h \right)$$

In this case, when (X_i, Y_i) changes, the supremum changes by no more than $1/n$, so McDiarmid's inequality implies that with probability at least $1 - \delta$, every $f \in F$ satisfies

$$\mathbf{E}\mathcal{L}(Y, f(X)) \leq \hat{\mathbf{E}}_n \mathcal{L}(Y, f(X)) + \mathbf{E} \sup_{h \in \mathcal{L} \circ F} \left(\mathbf{E}h - \hat{\mathbf{E}}_n h \right) + \sqrt{\frac{\ln(1/\delta)}{2n}}.$$

The same argument as in the proof of Theorem 5 shows that

$$\begin{aligned}
\mathbf{E} \sup_{h \in \mathcal{L} \circ F} \left(\mathbf{E} h - \hat{\mathbf{E}}_n h \right) &\leq \mathbf{E} \sup_{h \in \mathcal{L} \circ F} \frac{2}{n} \sum_{i=1}^{n} \sigma_i h(X_i, Y_i) \\
&= \mathbf{E} \sup_{f \in F} \frac{2}{n} \sum_{i=1}^{n} \sigma_i \mathbf{1}(Y_i \neq f(X_i)) \\
&= \mathbf{E} \sup_{f \in F} \frac{2}{n} \sum_{i=1}^{n} \sigma_i (1 - Y_i f(X_i))/2 \\
&= \mathbf{E} \sup_{f \in F} \frac{1}{n} \sum_{i=1}^{n} \sigma_i f(X_i) \\
&= \frac{R_n(F)}{2},
\end{aligned}$$

where we have used the fact that $Y_i, f(X_i) \in \{\pm 1\}$, and that the conditional distribution of $\sigma_i Y_i$ is the same as the distribution of σ_i.

Acknowledgements

This work was done while Peter Bartlett was with the Research School of Information Sciences and Engineering at the Australian National University. Thanks to Arthur Gretton, Jonathan Baxter and Gábor Lugosi for helpful discussions. This work was partially supported by the Australian Research Council.

References

1. Peter L. Bartlett. The sample complexity of pattern classification with neural networks: the size of the weights is more important than the size of the network. *IEEE Transactions on Information Theory*, 44(2):525–536, 1998.
2. Peter L. Bartlett, Stéphane Boucheron, and Gábor Lugosi. Model selection and error estimation. *Machine Learning*, 2001. (To appear).
3. Mostefa Golea, Peter L. Bartlett, and Wee Sun Lee. Generalization in decision trees and DNF: Does size matter? In *NIPS 10*, pages 259–265, 1998.
4. Michael J. Kearns, Yishay Mansour, Andrew Y. Ng, and Dana Ron. An experimental and theoretical comparison of model selection methods. *Machine Learning*, 27:7–50, 1997.
5. V. Koltchinskii. Rademacher penalties and structural risk minimization. Technical report, Department of Mathematics and Statistics, University of New Mexico, 2000.
6. V. Koltchinskii and D. Panchenko. Empirical margin distributions and bounding the generalization error of combined classifiers. Technical report, Department of Mathematics and Statistics, University of New Mexico, 2000.
7. V. Koltchinskii and D. Panchenko. Rademacher processes and bounding the risk of function learning. Technical report, Department of Mathematics and Statistics, University of New Mexico, 2000.

8. E. B. Kong and T. G. Dietterich. Error-correcting output coding corrects bias and variance. In *Proc. 12th International Conference on Machine Learning*, pages 313–321. Morgan Kaufmann, 1995.
9. M. Ledoux and M. Talagrand. *Probability in Banach Spaces: isoperimetry and processes*. Springer, 1991.
10. Llew Mason, Peter L. Bartlett, and Jonathan Baxter. Improved generalization through explicit optimization of margins. *Machine Learning*, 38(3):243–255, 2000.
11. C. McDiarmid. On the method of bounded differences. In *Surveys in Combinatorics 1989*, pages 148–188. Cambridge University Press, 1989.
12. Shahar Mendelson. l-norm and its application to learning theory. *Positivity*, 2001. (To appear—see http://www.axiom.anu.edu.au/~shahar.).
13. Shahar Mendelson. Rademacher averages and phase transitions in Glivenko-Cantelli classes. (see http://www.axiom.anu.edu.au/~shahar), 2001.
14. Shahar Mendelson. Some remarks on covering numbers. (unpublished manuscript—see http://www.axiom.anu.edu.au/~shahar), 2001.
15. G. Pisier. *The volume of convex bodies and Banach space geometry*. Cambridge University Press, 1989.
16. Robert E. Schapire. Using output codes to boost multiclass learning problems. In *Machine Learning: Proc. Fourteenth International Conference*, pages 313–321, 1997.
17. Robert E. Schapire, Yoav Freund, Peter L. Bartlett, and Wee Sun Lee. Boosting the margin: a new explanation for the effectiveness of voting methods. *Annals of Statistics*, 26(5):1651–1686, October 1998.
18. John Shawe-Taylor, Peter L. Bartlett, Robert C. Williamson, and Martin Anthony. Structural risk minimisation over data-dependent hierarchies. *IEEE Transactions on Information Theory*, 44(5):1926–1940, 1998.
19. N. Tomczak-Jaegermann. *Banach-Mazur distance and finite-dimensional operator ideals*. Number 38 in Pitman Monographs and Surveys in Pure and Applied Mathematics. Pitman, 1989.
20. Vladimir N. Vapnik and A. Y. Chervonenkis. On the uniform convergence of relative frequencies of events to their probabilities. *Theory of Probability and its Applications*, 16(2):264–280, 1971.
21. R. C. Williamson, A. J. Smola, and B. Schölkopf. Generalization performance of regularization networks and support vector machines via entropy numbers of compact operators. *IEEE Transactions on Information Theory*, 2001. (To appear).

Further Explanation of the Effectiveness of Voting Methods: The Game between Margins and Weights

Vladimir Koltchinskii[1], Dmitriy Panchenko[1], and Fernando Lozano[2]

[1] Department of Mathematics and Statistics, The University of New Mexico, Albuquerque, NM, 87131, USA
{vlad, panchenk}@math.unm.edu

[2] Departamento de Ingeniería Electrónica, Universidad Javeriana, Cr. 7 40-62, Bogotá, Colombia
fernando.lozano@javeriana.edu.co

Abstract. In this paper we present new bounds on the generalization error of a classifier f constructed as a convex combination of base classifiers from the class $\mathcal{H}$. The algorithms of combining simple classifiers into a complex one, such as boosting and bagging, have attracted a lot of attention. We obtain new sharper bounds on the generalization error of combined classifiers that take into account both the empirical distribution of "classification margins" and the "approximate dimension" of the classifier, which is defined in terms of weights assigned to base classifiers by a voting algorithm. We study the performance of these bounds in several experiments with learning algorithms.

1 Introduction

Let $(X_1, Y_1), \ldots, (X_n, Y_n)$ be a sample of n labeled training examples defined on a probability space $(\Omega, \Sigma, \mathbb{P})$. We assume that the examples are independent identically distributed copies of a random couple (X, Y), X being an "instance" in a measurable space $(S, \mathcal{A})$ and Y being a "label" taking values in $\{-1, 1\}$. Let P denote the distribution of the couple (X, Y). Given a measurable function f from S into $\mathbb{R}$, we use $\text{sign}(f(x))$ as a predictor of the unknown label of an instance $x \in S$. We will call f a classifier of the examples from S. It is obvious that according to the above definition f predicts a label of x correctly if and only if $yf(x) > 0$. The quantity $m(x, y) = yf(x)$ will be called *the classification margin*. The probability $\mathbb{P}\{Yf(X) \le 0\} = P\{(x, y) : yf(x) \le 0\}$ defines *the generalization error* of the classifier f. The goal of learning (classification) is, given a set of training examples, to find a classifier f with a small generalization error.

Given a class of base (simple) classifiers $\mathcal{H}$, all voting algorithms produce a complex classifier that is a convex combination of base classifiers, i.e. belongs to the symmetric convex hull of $\mathcal{H}$:

$$\mathcal{F} := \text{conv}(\mathcal{H}) := \Big\{ \sum_{i=1}^{N} \lambda_i h_i : N \ge 1, \lambda_i \in \mathbb{R}, \sum_{i=1}^{N} |\lambda_i| \le 1,\ h_i \in \mathcal{H} \Big\}.$$

D. Helmbold and B. Williamson (Eds.): COLT/EuroCOLT 2001, LNAI 2111, pp. 241–255, 2001.

The explanation of the effectiveness of voting algorithms requires the construction of a good bound on the generalization error $P\{yf(x) \leq 0\}$ uniformly over $\mathcal{F}$. The results we present here follow the line of research that started with the paper of Schapire, Freund, Bartlett and Lee [13]. The main difficulty one encounters trying to prove a uniform bound on the generalization error of a classifier from the convex hull $\mathrm{conv}(\mathcal{H})$ is that even if the original class $\mathcal{H}$ had a finite VC-dimension, the convex hull can be significantly more complex. In this case the standard techniques of the VC-theory can not be used directly. Recall that the main idea of this approach is based on the following easy bound

$$P\{(x,y) : yf(x) \leq 0\} \leq P_n\{(x,y) : yf(x) \leq 0\} + \sup_{C \in \mathcal{C}} [P(C) - P_n(C)],$$

where P_n is the empirical distribution of the training examples, i.e. for any set $C \subset S \times \{-1,1\}$, $P_n(C)$ is the frequency of the training examples in the set C, $\mathcal{C} := \Big\{\{(x,y) : yf(x) \leq 0\} : f \in \mathcal{F}\Big\}$, and on further bounding the uniform (over the class $\mathcal{C}$) deviation of the empirical distribution P_n from the true distribution P. The methods that are used to construct such uniform deviation bounds belong to the theory of empirical processes and the crucial role is played by the VC-dimension, or by more sophisticated entropy characteristics of the class $\mathcal{C}$. For instance, if $m^{\mathcal{C}}(n)$ denotes the maximal number of subsets produced by intersecting a sample of size n with the class $\mathcal{C}$ (the so called shattering number), then the following bound holds (see [5], Theorem 12.6) for all $\varepsilon > 0$

$$\mathbb{P}\Big\{\exists f \in \mathcal{F} : P\{yf(x) \leq 0\} \geq P_n\{yf(x) \leq 0\} + \varepsilon\Big\} \leq 8m^{\mathcal{C}}(n)e^{-n\varepsilon^2/32}.$$

It follows from this bound that the training error measures the generalization error of a classifier $f \in \mathcal{F}$ with the accuracy $O\Big(\sqrt{\frac{V(\mathcal{C})\log n}{n}}\Big)$, where $V(\mathcal{C})$ is the VC-dimension of the class $\mathcal{C}$. In the case of classifiers with zero training error, the accuracy can be improved to $O\Big(\frac{V(\mathcal{C})\log n}{n}\Big)$. The above bounds, however, do not apply directly to the case of the class $\mathcal{F} = \mathrm{conv}(\mathcal{H})$, which is of interest in applications to bounding the generalization error of the voting methods, since in this case typically $V(\mathcal{C}) = +\infty$. Even when one deals with a finite number of base classifiers in a convex combination (which is the case, say, with boosting after finite number of rounds), the VC-dimensions of the classes involved are becoming rather large, so the above bounds do not explain the generalization ability of boosting and other voting methods observed in numerous experiments.

In [13] Schapire et al. (see also [1],[2]) developed a new class of bounds on generalization error of a convex combination of classifiers, expressed in terms of empirical distribution of margins. They showed that for a given $\alpha \in (0,1)$ with probability at least $1-\alpha$ for all $f \in \mathrm{conv}(\mathcal{H})$

$$P\{yf(x) \leq 0\} \leq \inf_{\delta}\Big[P_n\{yf(x) \leq \delta\} + \frac{C}{\sqrt{n}}\Big(\frac{V}{\delta^2}\log^2\frac{n}{V} + \log\frac{1}{\alpha}\Big)^{1/2}\Big], \qquad (1)$$

where V is the VC-dimension of $\mathcal{H}$. Choosing in the above bound the value of $\delta = \hat{\delta}(f)$ that solves the equation

$$\delta P_n\{yf(x) \le \delta\} = (V/n)^{1/2}$$

(which is nearly an optimal choice), one gets (ignoring the logarithmic factors) the generalization error of a classifier f from the convex hull of the order $O\Big(\frac{1}{\hat{\delta}(f)}\sqrt{\frac{V}{n}}\Big)$. Schapire et al. showed that in many experiments voting methods tended to classify the majority of examples not only correctly but with a high confidence, i.e. with a large margin, which means that one can expect $\hat{\delta}$ to be reasonably large and, therefore, the bound becomes meaningful.

In [8],[9] using the methods of theory of Empirical, Gaussian and Rademacher Processes (concentration inequalities, symmetrization, comparison inequalities) we generalized and refined this type of bounds. In our first result we do not immediately assume that $\mathcal{H}$ is a VC-class but propose to measure the complexity of the class in terms of what we call the Rademacher complexity function

$$R_n(\mathcal{H}) := \mathbb{E}\sup_{h\in\mathcal{H}} |n^{-1}\sum_{j=1}^{n} \varepsilon_j h(X_j)|,$$

where ε_j, $j = 1,\dots,n$ are i.i.d. Rademacher random variables. Then similarly to (1) we prove that for all $\alpha \in (0,1)$, with probability at least $1-\alpha$, $\forall f \in \operatorname{conv}(\mathcal{H})$

$$P\{yf(x) \le 0\} \le \inf_{\delta\in(0,1]}\Big[P_n(yf(x) \le \delta) + \frac{8}{\delta}R_n(\mathcal{H}) + \frac{1}{\sqrt{n}}\Big(\log\log_2\frac{2}{\delta}\Big)^{1/2} + \frac{1}{\sqrt{n}}\Big(\frac{1}{2}\log\frac{2}{\alpha}\Big)^{1/2}\Big]. \qquad (2)$$

The theory of empirical processes provides a number of bounds for $R_n(\mathcal{H})$ in terms of different characteristics of complexity of the class $\mathcal{H}$. For example, in the case when $\mathcal{H}$ is a VC-class with VC-dimension V one has the following bound ([16]) $R_n(\mathcal{H}) \le C\Big(\frac{V}{n}\Big)^{1/2}$ which shows that (2) improves (1).

Next, we suggested a way to improve these bounds even further. Again we save the case $\operatorname{conv}(\mathcal{H})$ where $\mathcal{H}$ is a VC-class as an example and work with the general assumption on the growth of random entropies of a class $\mathcal{F}$ to which the classifier belongs. Given a metric space (T,d), we denote $H_d(T;\varepsilon)$ the ε-entropy of T with respect to d, i.e. $H_d(T;\varepsilon) := \log N_d(T;\varepsilon)$, where $N_d(T;\varepsilon)$ is the minimal number of balls of radius ε covering T. If Q is a probability measure on $(S;\mathcal{A})$, $d_{Q,2}$ will denote the metric of the space $L_2(S;dQ)$: $d_{Q,2}(f;g) := (Q|f-g|^2)^{1/2}$. We assume that for some $\alpha \in (0,2)$

$$H_{d_{P_n,2}}(\mathcal{F};u) \le D_n^2 u^{-\alpha}, \quad u > 0 \quad \text{a.s.}, \qquad (3)$$

where $D_n = D_n(X_1,\dots,X_n)$ is a function of training examples such that $\mathbb{E}D_n < \infty$. If $\mathcal{F} = \operatorname{conv}(\mathcal{H})$ and $\mathcal{H}$ is a VC-class with VC-dimension V, then (3) holds with $\alpha = 2(V-1)/V$ and D_n is a constant that depends on the VC-dimension only (see [16]). To formulate one of the results that was obtained in [8] we need the following definitions. Given $\gamma > 0$, we define a γ-margin and an empirical γ-margin of the function f by

$$\delta_n(\gamma; f) := \sup\Big\{\delta \in (0,1) : \delta^\gamma P\{yf(x) \le \delta\} \le n^{-1+\frac{\gamma}{2}}\Big\},$$

$$\hat{\delta}_n(\gamma; f) := \sup\Big\{\delta \in (0,1) : \delta^\gamma P_n\{yf(x) \le \delta\} \le n^{-1+\frac{\gamma}{2}}\Big\}.$$

We proved in [8] that under the condition (3) for any $\gamma \ge 2\alpha/(2+\alpha)$ there exist constants $A, B > 0$ such that for n large enough

$$\forall f \in \mathcal{F} : A^{-1}\hat{\delta}_n(\gamma; f) \le \delta_n(\gamma; f) \le A\hat{\delta}_n(\gamma; f).$$

with probability at least

$$1 - B\log_2\log_2 n \exp\{-n^{\frac{\gamma}{2}}/2\}.$$

What this result says is that with high probability the "true" γ-margin and the empirical γ-margin are within a constant factor of each other. One can notice that the definition of the γ-margins contains the bound on the generalization error of a function f. It easily follows that with high probability for some constant A' and for an arbitrary $f \in \mathcal{F}$

$$P\{yf(x) \le 0\} \le \frac{A'}{n^{1-\gamma/2}\hat{\delta}_n(\gamma; f)^\gamma}. \tag{4}$$

It's easy to check that the quantity $(n^{1-\gamma/2}\hat{\delta}_n(\gamma; f)^\gamma)^{-1}$ is *decreasing* as γ decreases from 1 to 0. The previous bounds (1) and (2) corresponded to the worst case $\gamma = 1$. As we already mentioned above, if $\mathcal{F} = \mathrm{conv}(\mathcal{H})$ and $\mathcal{H}$ is a VC-class with VC-dimension V (this includes all voting methods), then $\alpha = 2(V-1)/V < 2$ and $\gamma = 2(V-1)/(2V-1) < 1$, improving the previous bounds.

Though qualitatively the γ-bounds constitute an improvement upon (1) and (2), when the VC-dimension V is large γ can be very close to 1. Our experiments [10] showed that, in the case of the classifiers obtained in consecutive rounds of boosting, the bounds on the generalization error in terms of γ-margins hold even for much smaller values of γ. This allows one to conjecture that such classifiers belong, in fact, to a class $\mathcal{F} \subset \mathrm{conv}(\mathcal{H})$ whose entropy might be much smaller than the entropy of the whole convex hull. The problem, though, is that it is practically impossible to identify such a class prior to experiments, leaving the question of how to choose the values of γ for which the bounds hold open.

2 Balancing Approximate Dimensions and Margins

In an attempt to capture a smaller subclass of the convex hull to which the classifier belongs we develop a new approach. Namely, we suggest an adaptive bound on the generalization error of a classifier produced by a specific procedure that in some sense tries to localize the location of the classifier inside the convex hull. We consider an unnested family of subsets of $\mathrm{conv}(\mathcal{H})$ that are defined in terms of weights (decay of weights) of the convex combination; the conditions on weights imply the bounds on the random entropy of these subclasses which in turn are used to prove the bounds on the generalization error. For example, the subset which corresponds to convex combinations with very few large weights must have a smaller complexity than the whole convex hull and, therefore, enjoy a sharper bound. The classifier represented by a convex combination may belong to many of these subsets which leads to a family of bounds. The adaptive bound suggested below is based on "optimizing" the bounds over the whole family.

Now we will give precise definitions and make these ideas rigorous. Let $\mathcal{H}$ be a VC-class of measurable functions from $(S, \mathcal{A})$ into $\{-1, 1\}$ with VC-dimension V. Let $\mathcal{F} \subset \mathrm{conv}(\mathcal{H})$. For a function $f \in \mathcal{F}$ and a number $\Delta \in [0,1]$, we define *the approximate Δ-dimension* of f as the smallest integer number $d \geq 0$ such that there exist $N \geq 1$, functions $h_j \in \mathcal{H}$, $j = 1, \ldots, N$ and numbers $\lambda_j \in \mathbb{R}$, $j = 1, \ldots, N$ satisfying the conditions $f = \sum_{j=1}^{N} \lambda_j h_j$, $\sum_{j=1}^{N} |\lambda_j| \leq 1$ and $\sum_{j=d+1}^{N} |\lambda_j| \leq \Delta$. The Δ-dimension of f will be denoted by $d(f;\Delta)$.

Let $\alpha := 2(V-1)/V$ and $\Delta_f = \{\Delta \in [0,1] : d(f;\Delta) \leq n\}$. Define

$$\varepsilon_n(f;\delta) := \inf_{\Delta \in \Delta_f} \Big[\frac{d(f;\Delta)}{n} \log \frac{ne^2}{\delta d(f;\Delta)} + \Big(\frac{\Delta}{\delta}\Big)^{\frac{2\alpha}{\alpha+2}} n^{-\frac{2}{\alpha+2}}\Big] \bigvee \frac{2\log n}{n}, \tag{5}$$

where $a \vee b := \max\{a, b\}$. Let

$$\hat{\delta}_n(f) := \sup\Big\{\delta \in (0, 1/2) : P_n\{yf(x) \leq \delta\} \leq \varepsilon_n(f;\delta)\Big\}.$$

Theorem 1. *There exist constants $A, B > 0$ such that for all $0 < t < n^{\frac{\alpha}{2+\alpha}}$*

$$\forall f \in \mathcal{F} \;\; P\{yf(x) \leq \frac{\hat{\delta}_n(f)}{4}\} \leq \; A\Big(\varepsilon_n(f; \frac{\hat{\delta}_n(f)}{2}) + \frac{t}{n}\Big)$$

with probability at least $1 - Be^{-t/4}$.

To understand this bound let us look at the definition of $\varepsilon_n(f;\delta)$. First of all, if instead of minimizing over Δ one sets $\Delta = 1$, then, since $d(f,1) = 0$, the bound becomes equivalent to the previous γ-bound (4), which means that the bound of the theorem improves the γ-bound. For a fixed Δ, the two terms in the definition of $\varepsilon_n(f;\delta)$ correspond to two parts of the combined classifier. The first term corresponds to the sum of $d(f,\Delta)$ base classifiers with the largest weights and the form of the bound basically coincides with the standard VC-dimension based bound in the zero error case. The second term corresponds to an "improper" convex combination of classifers with the smallest weights (the number of them is not limited), and the form of the bound is determined by the complexity of the whole convex hull, only scaled by a factor of Δ. It is clear that if a voting algorithm produces a convex combination in which there are very few classifiers with large weights, then the bound of the theorem can improve upon (4) significantly. Another way to say it is that the faster is the weight decay in the convex combination, the smaller is the complexity of the corresponding subset of the convex hull and the sharper is the bound.

As an example, we can assume that the algorithm produces a classifier with polynomial or exponential decay of the weights, which allows us to minimize (5) explicitly over Δ to see how the bound looks like. If $\mathcal{F} \subset \mathrm{conv}(\mathcal{H})$ is a class of functions such that for some $\beta > 0$

$$\sup_{f \in \mathcal{F}} d(f; \Delta) = O(\Delta^{-\beta}), \tag{6}$$

then with "high probability" for any classifier $f \in \mathcal{F}$ the upper bound on its generalization error becomes of the order

$$\frac{1}{n^{1-\gamma\beta/2(\gamma+\beta)} \hat{\delta}_n(f)^{\gamma\beta/(\gamma+\beta)}},$$

(which, of course, improves a more general bound in terms of γ-margins; the general bound corresponds to the case $\beta = +\infty$). The condition (6) means that the weights of the convex combination decrease polynomially fast, namely, $|\lambda_j| = O(j^{-\alpha})$, $\alpha = 1 + \beta^{-1}$. The case of exponential decrease of the weights is described by the condition

$$\sup_{f \in \mathcal{F}} d(f; \Delta) = O(\log \frac{1}{\Delta}). \tag{7}$$

In this case the upper bound becomes of the order $\frac{1}{n} \log^2 \frac{n}{\hat{\delta}_n(f)}$.

The complete proofs of the results require many more pages than it is available for us here. They can be found in our papers [8], [9] that are available online at www.boosting.org. Here we only give the sketch of the proof of Theorem 1, which is the main result of this paper. In the first and main part of the proof we consider a family of classes $\mathcal{F}_{d,\Delta}$ parametrized by two parameters d and Δ, and prove a uniform bound on the generalization error over any fixed class in this family. In the second part of the proof we make this bound adaptive, which means that if a function f belongs to more than one class in the family, then one can choose a class that provides the best bound.

Sketch of proof. Let us fix $\delta \in (0, 1/2]$. For any function f we denote $d(f) := d(f, \bar{\Delta})$, where $\bar{\Delta}$ is such that the infimum in the definition (5) is attained at $\bar{\Delta}$. For a fixed δ we consider a partition of $\mathcal{F}$ into two classes $\mathcal{F}_1^\delta$ and $\mathcal{F}_2^\delta = \mathcal{F} \setminus \mathcal{F}_1^\delta$, where $\mathcal{F}_1^\delta := \{f : d(f) = 0\}$ (note that $d(f)$ depends on δ). The fact that $f \in \mathcal{F}_1^\delta$ means that the weights of the classifier f are distributed "uniformly" and in this case the bound of Theorem 1 does not improve (4). The family of classes that we use to localize the classifier f is defined as follows:

$$\mathcal{F}_{d,\Delta} := \{f \in \mathcal{F}_2^\delta : d(f; \Delta) \le d\}.$$

If $f \in \mathcal{F}_{d,\Delta}$ and Δ is small then it means that the "voting power" is concentrated in the faction consisting of the first d base classifiers of the convex combination. First of all we estimate the complexity of this class. The definition of $\mathcal{F}_{d,\Delta}$ implies the following bound on the random entropy:

$$H_{d_{P_n,2}}(\mathcal{F}_{d,\Delta}; u) \leq K\Big[d \log \frac{e}{u} + \Big(\frac{\Delta}{u}\Big)^{\alpha}\Big] \text{ for } u \leq 1, \tag{8}$$

where K is a positive constant. To prove it one has to represent $\mathcal{F}_{d,\Delta}$ as

$$\mathcal{F}_{d,\Delta} \subseteq \mathcal{H}^d + \Delta \mathrm{conv}\mathcal{H}.$$

Next we use the complexity estimate (8) to prove a uniform bound on the generalization error of classifiers in $\mathcal{F}_{d,\Delta}$. The proof is based on an iterative application of Talagrand's concentration inequality for empirical processes (see [15], [12]) which allows us to measure the size of $\mathcal{F}_{d,\Delta}$ correctly and make a better inference about the generalization error of elements of this class. Let us first formulate the bound precisely. Let $1 \leq d \leq n$ and denote

$$\varepsilon_n(d;\delta;\Delta) := \Big[\frac{d}{n} \log \frac{ne^2}{\delta d} + \Big(\frac{\Delta}{\delta}\Big)^{\frac{2\alpha}{\alpha+2}} n^{-\frac{2}{\alpha+2}}\Big] \bigvee \frac{2 \log n}{n}.$$

We prove that there exist constants $A, B > 0$ such that the following event

$$\forall f \in \mathcal{F}_{d,\Delta} : P_n\{m \leq \delta\} \leq \varepsilon_n(d;\delta;\Delta) \text{ implies } P\{m \leq \frac{\delta}{2}\} \leq A\varepsilon_n(d;\delta;\Delta), \tag{9}$$

where $m(x,y) = yf(x)$, occurs with probability at least

$$1 - B\Big(\frac{\delta d}{n}\Big)^{d/4} \exp\Big\{-\frac{1}{4}\big(\sqrt{n}\frac{\Delta}{\delta}\big)^{2\alpha/(\alpha+2)}\Big\}.$$

To proceed from here, one has to carefully eliminate the dependence on d, Δ and δ, and as a result to get the adaptive bound of Theorem 1. This constitutes the second part of the proof.

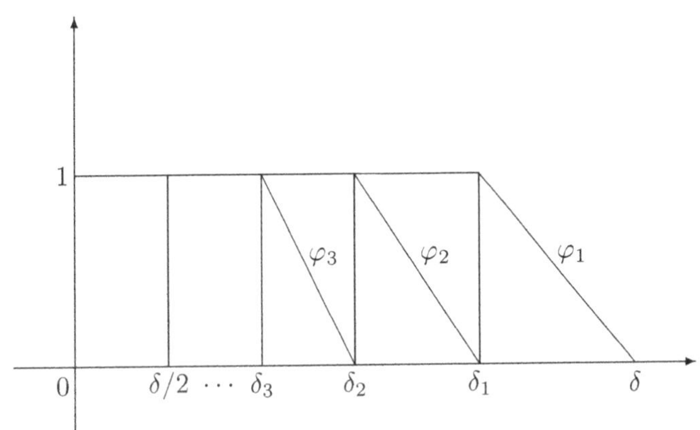

Let us now describe the iterative localization scheme that we used to prove (9). For a fixed δ, we choose (in a rather special way) a finite decreasing sequence $\delta_j, 1 \le j \le N$ such that $\delta_j < \delta$ and $\delta_N = \delta/2$. We consider the functions $\varphi_j, j \ge 1$ which are defined as shown in the figure above and which play the role of continuous approximations of indicator step functions $I(x \le \delta_j)$. For simplicity of notations, we will suppress the variable Y in the couple (X, Y) and assume that a function f denotes it's margin, instead of writing $yf(x)$. We start by assuming that the empirical distribution of the margin at the point δ is small, i.e. $P_n(f \le \delta) \ll 1$, and after N iterations arrive at the bound of the same magnitude for $P(f \le \delta/2)$, improving it at each step. Let us show how the iterative step is implemented. Skipping the first step we assume that we already showed that with high probability $P(f \le \delta_1) \le r_1 \ll 1$ (it can be done similarly to what we do below, just set $\sigma_1 := 1$). This means that f belongs to a (small) subset of $\mathcal{F}$, namely, $\mathcal{F}_1 = \{f \in \mathcal{F} : P(f \le \delta_1) \le r_1\}$. The following series of inequalities is clear (we use the notations $\|Z\|_{\mathcal{F}} := \sup_{f \in \mathcal{F}} |Z(f)|$, $Z : \mathcal{F} \mapsto \mathbb{R}$ and $\varphi(\mathcal{F}) := \{\varphi(f) : f \in \mathcal{F}\}$):

$$P(f \le \delta_2) \le P\varphi_2(f) \le P_n\varphi_2(f) + \|P_n - P\|_{\varphi_2(\mathcal{F}_1)} \le P_n(f \le \delta_1) + \|P_n - P\|_{\varphi_2(\mathcal{F}_1)}.$$

Now Talagrand's concentration inequality for empirical processes implies that for a fixed ε with high probability (at least $1 - e^{-n\varepsilon/2}$)

$$\|P_n - P\|_{\varphi_2(\mathcal{F}_1)} \le K(\mathbb{E}\|P_n - P\|_{\varphi_2(\mathcal{F}_1)} + \sqrt{\sigma_1^2\varepsilon} + \varepsilon)$$

for some constant $K > 0$ and $\sigma_1^2 = \sup_{\mathcal{F}_1} P\varphi_2^2(f) \le P(f \le \delta_1) \le r_1 \ll 1$ according to the bound from the previous step. Dudley's entropy bound (see [6]) implies in this case that

$$\mathbb{E}\|P_n - P\|_{\varphi_2(\mathcal{F}_1)} \le K\mathbb{E}\int_0^{\sigma_1} H_{d_{P_n,2}}^{1/2}(\varphi_2(\mathcal{F}_1), u)du,$$

which is further bounded using the entropy condition (8). Collecting all these estimates one can show that $P(f \le \delta_2) \le r_2 \le r_1$. Therefore, with high probability $f \in \mathcal{F}_2 = \{f \in \mathcal{F} : P(f \le \delta_2) \le r_2\}$, which in terms of generalization error is "smaller" than $\mathcal{F}_1$. As one can see this improvement was possible because of the fact that Talagrand's inequality measures the size of the class via σ_1. Now the similar argument can be iterated until the bound reaches (up to a multiplicative constant) the optimal fixed point of this recursive procedure, which is precisely formulated in (9).

3 Experiments

In this section we present the results of several experiments we conducted to test the ability of our bounds to predict the classification error of combined classifiers. Even though all the steps of the proofs of our results allow one to use explicit constants, the values of the constants will be too large due to the generality of the methods of empirical processes upon which our proof is heavily based. For example, the constants in Talagrand's concentration inequality are known (see [11]), but they are most likely far from being optimal. Therefore, we will simply use the quantities $(n^{1-\gamma/2}\hat{\delta}_n(\gamma; f)^\gamma)^{-1}$ and $\varepsilon_n(f; \hat{\delta}_n(f))$ instead of the upper bounds we actually proved, and we will refer to them as γ-bound and Δ-bound correspondingly.

We first describe the experiments with a "toy" problem which is simple enough to allow one to compute the generalization error exactly. Namely, we consider a one dimensional classification problem in which the space of instances S is an interval $[0,1]$ and, given a concept $C_0 \subset S$ which is a finite union of disjoint intervals, the label y is assigned to a point $x \in S$ according to the rule $y = f_0(x)$, where f_0 is equal to $+1$ on C_0 and to -1 on $S \setminus C_0$. We refer to this problem as the *intervals problem* (see also [7]). Note that for the class of decision stumps we have $V(\mathcal{H}) = 2$ (since $\mathcal{H} = \{I_{[0,b]} : b \in [0,1]\} \cup \{I_{[b,1]} : b \in [0,1]\}$), and according to the results above the values of γ in $[2/3, 1)$ provide valid bounds on the generalization error in terms of the γ-margins. In our experiments, the set C_0 was formed by 20 equally spaced intervals and the training set of size 1000 was generated by the uniform distribution on $[0,1]$. We ran Adaboost for 500 rounds and computed at each round the true generalization error of the combined classifier and the bounds for different values of γ.

In figure 1 we plot the true classification error and the γ-bounds for $\gamma = 1$, 0.8 and 2/3 against the number of iteration of Adaboost. The bound for $\gamma = 1$ corresponds to the previously known bounds (1) and (2) and as expected is inferior to the γ-bound for smaller values of γ. In figure 2 we compare the γ-bound for the best admissible $\gamma = 2/3$ with the Δ-bound of Theorem 1. As one can see when the number of iterations is small the Δ-bound takes advantage of the first "finite dimensional" term in the definition (5) since $d(f, \Delta)$ is small. When the number of iterations increases, the Δ-bound is gradually gravitating toward the more conservative γ-regime which means that the optimal value of Δ is increasing to 1. It seems unnatural that the bound increases while the true error decreases but as we will show later it can be simply a question of assigning different relative weights to two terms in the definition of the Δ-bound.

We also computed the bounds for more complex simulated data sets as well as for real data sets in which the same type of behavior was observed. We show the results for the Twonorm Data Set and the King Rook vs. King Pawn Data Set, using Adaboost and Bagging in figures 3-6. The Twonorm Data Set (taken from [4]) is a simulated 20 dimensional data set in which positive and negative training examples are drawn from the multivariate normal distributions with unit covariance matrix centered at $(2/\sqrt{20}, \ldots, 2/\sqrt{20})$ and $(-2/\sqrt{20}, \ldots, -2/\sqrt{20})$, respectively. The King Rook vs. King Pawn Data Set is a real data set from the UCI Irvine repository [3]. It is a 36 dimensional data set with 3196 samples.

As before, we used the decision stumps as base classifiers. An upper bound on $V(\mathcal{H})$ for the class $\mathcal{H}$ of decision stumps in R^d is given by the smallest n such that $2^{n-1} \geq (n-1)d + 1$. In each case we computed the Δ-bound and the γ-bounds for $\gamma = 1$ and for the smallest γ allowed by the theory ($\gamma_{\min}$). For

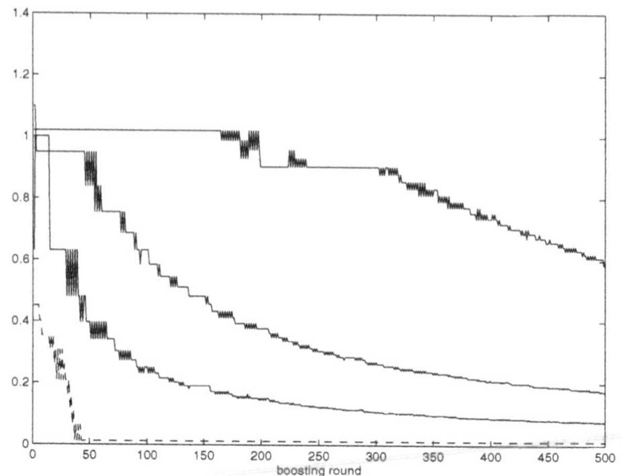

Fig. 1. Comparison of the generalization error (dashed line) with $(n^{1-\gamma/2}\hat{\delta}_n(\gamma; f)^{\gamma})^{-1}$ for $\gamma = 1, 0.8$ and $2/3$ (solid lines, top to bottom)

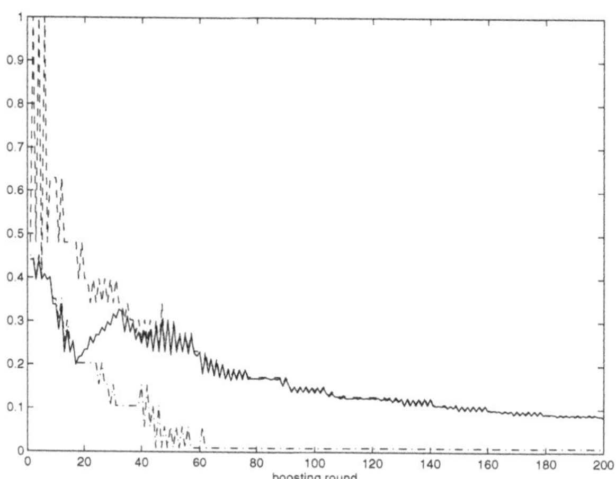

Fig. 2. Test error and bounds vs. number of classifiers for the intervals problem with a sample size of 1000. Test error (dot-dashed line), γ-margin bound with $\gamma = 2/3$ (dashed line), and Δ-bound (solid line).

the Twonorm Data Set, we estimated the generalization error by computing the empirical error on an indepedently generated set of 20000 observations. For the King Rook vs. King Pawn Data Set, we randomly selected 90% of the data for training and used the remaining 10% to compute the test error. The experiments were averaged over 10 repetitions. One can observe a similar two-regime behavior of the Δ-bound as in the intervals problem.

We also show that by slightly changing the definition of Δ-bound one can obtain in some cases a surprisingly accurate prediction of the shape of the generalization curve. The fact that both terms in the definition of $\varepsilon_n(f,\Delta)$ have weight 1 is related to lack of information about the values of the constants involved in the bounds. More subtle analysis can lead to a more general definition in which the weights of two terms might differ, for example

$$\varepsilon_{n,\zeta,K}(f;\delta) := K \inf_{\Delta \in \Delta_f} \left[\zeta \frac{d(f;\Delta)}{n} \log \frac{ne^2}{\delta d(f;\Delta)} + (1-\zeta)\left(\frac{\Delta}{\delta}\right)^{\frac{2\alpha}{\alpha+2}} n^{-\frac{2}{\alpha+2}}\right],$$

where $\zeta \in (0,1)$ and $K > 0$. Our goal in Theorem 1 was to understand the dependence of the bounds on the parameters of the problem and we were not concerned with the constants, but, in general, it would be more accurate to state the bound in this "weighted" form. In figures 7 and 8 we show the behavior of the modified Δ-bound for $\zeta = 0.1$ and 0.4. One can see that for a small value of ζ the "two-regime" behavior disappears and the bounds capture the shape of the true generalization curve (it should be emphasized that the value $\zeta = 0.1$ was determined based on an experiment with a toy example described above and was used for other data sets showing reasonable results in most of the experiments).

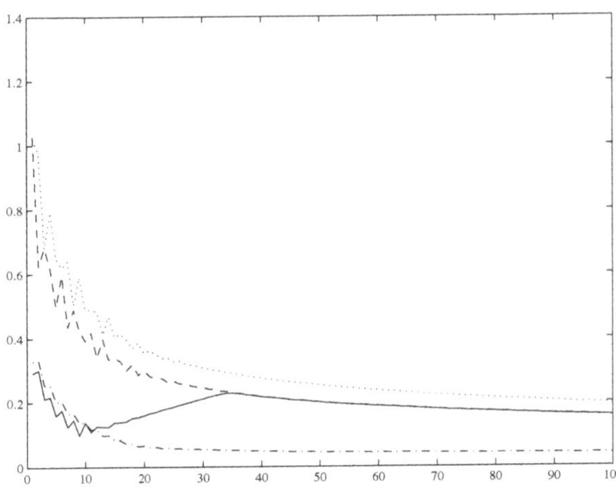

Fig. 3. Test error and bounds vs. number of classifiers for the twonorm data set using Adaboost. Test error (dot-dashed line), γ-margin bound with $\gamma = 1$ (dotted line), and $\gamma = \gamma_{\min}$ (dashed line), and Δ-bound (solid lines)

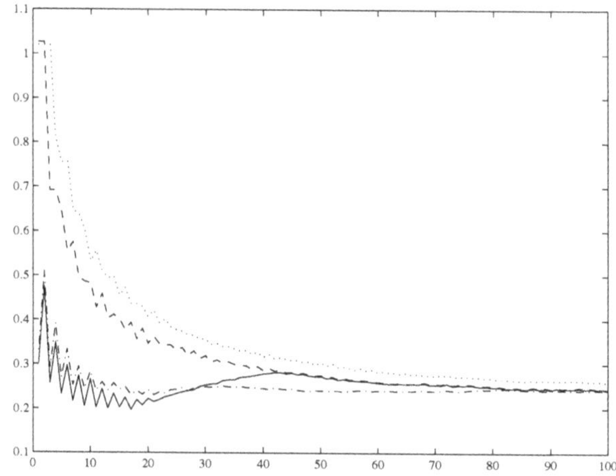

Fig. 4. Test error and bounds vs. number of classifiers for the twonorm data set using bagging. Test error (dot-dashed line), γ-margin bound with $\gamma = 1$ (dotted line), and $\gamma = \gamma_{\min}$ (dashed line), and Δ-bound (solid line)

4 Future Goals

An obvious goal of future research is to identify and, if possible, to optimize the constants in the bounds we proved. Another goal is to develop a more subtle definition of approximate dimension of classifiers in the convex hull that takes into account the closeness of base classifiers in convex combinations (for instance, the closeness in the empirical distance $d_{P_n,2}$). This can further reduce the dimensionality of the classifiers and result in better bounds on generalization error of voting algorithms.

References

1. Anthony, M. and Bartlett, P. (1999) Neural Network Learning: Theoretical Foundations. Cambridge University Press.
2. Bartlett, P. (1998) The Sample Complexity of Pattern Classification with Neural Networks: The Size of the Weights is More Important than the Size of the Network. *IEEE Transactions on Information Theory,* 44, 525–536.
3. Blake, C., Merz, C. (1998) UCI repository of machine learning databases. URL: http://www.ics.uci.edu/ mlearn/MLRepository.html.
4. Breiman, L. (1998) Arcing Classifiers. *The Annals of Statistics,* 26(3).
5. Devroye, L., Györfi, L. and Lugosi, L. (1996) A Probabilistic Theory of Pattern Recognition. Springer-Verlag, New York.
6. Dudley, R.M. (1999) Uniform Central Limit Theorems. Cambridge University Press.

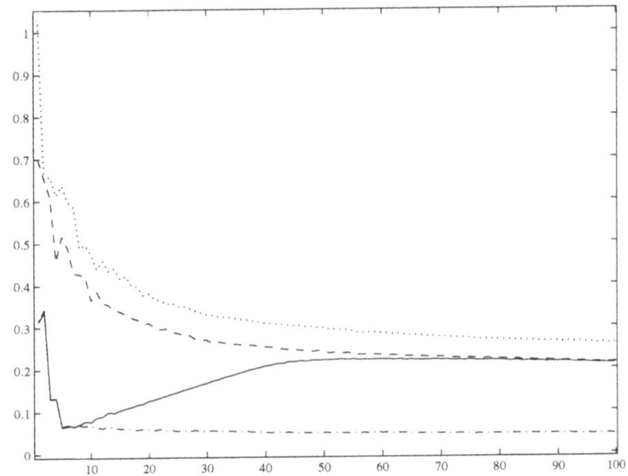

Fig. 5. Test error and bounds vs. number of classifiers for the King Rook vs. King Pawn data set using Adaboost. Test error (dot-dashed line), γ-margin bound with $\gamma = 1$ (dotted line), and $\gamma = \gamma_{\min}$ (dashed line), and Δ-bound (solid line)

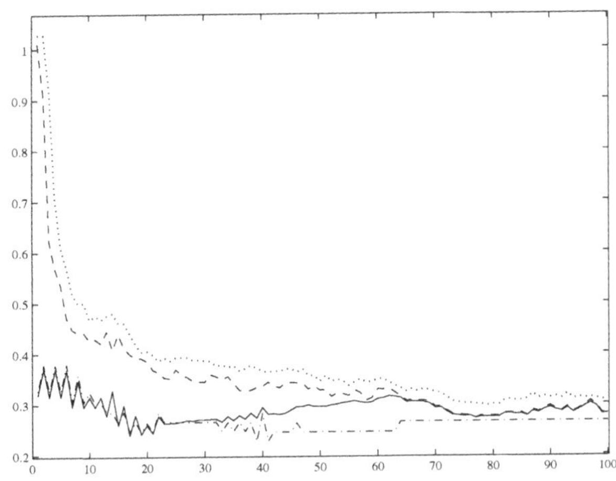

Fig. 6. Test error and bounds vs. number of classifiers for the King Rook vs. King Pawn data set using bagging Test error (dot-dashed lines), γ-margin bound with $\gamma = 1$ (dotted line), and $\gamma = \gamma_{\min}$ (dashed line), and Δ-bound (solid line)

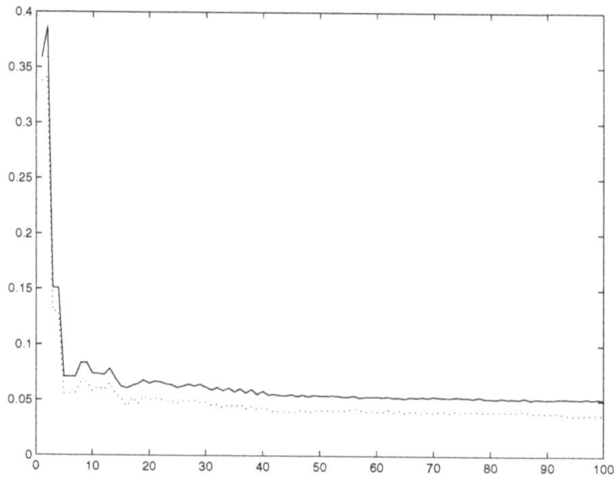

Fig. 7. Δ-Bound with $\zeta = 0.1$ (solid line), and test error (dotted line) for the King Rook vs. King Pawn data set

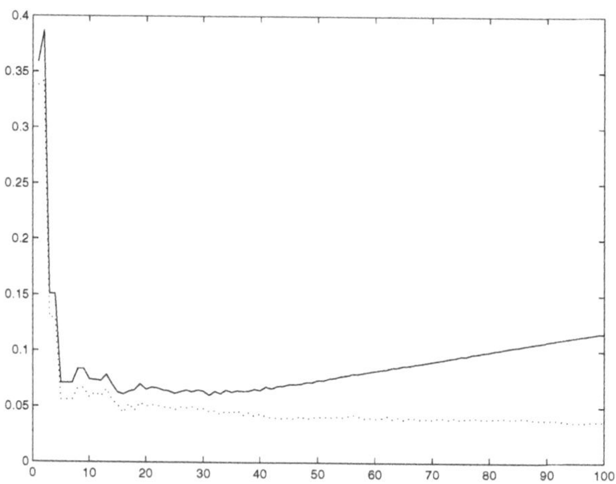

Fig. 8. Δ-Bound with $\zeta = 0.4$ (solid line), and test error (dotted line) for the King Rook vs. King Pawn data set

7. Kearns, M., Mansour, Y., Ng, A., Ron, D. (1997) An Experimental and Theoretical Comparison of Model Selection Methods. *Machine Learning,* 27(1)
8. Koltchinskii, V. and Panchenko, D. (2000) Empirical Margin Distributions and Bounding the Generalization Error of Combined Classifiers. To appear in *Ann. Statist.*
9. Koltchinskii, V., Panchenko, D. and Lozano, F. (2000) Bounding the Generalization Error of Convex Combinations of Classifiers: Balancing the Dimensionality and the Margins. Preprint.
10. Koltchinskii, V., Panchenko, D. and Lozano, F. (2000) Some New Bounds on the Generalization Error of Combined Classifiers. *Advances in Neural Information Processing Systems 13: Proc. of NIPS'2000.*
11. Massart, P. (2000) About the Constants in Talagrand's Concentration Inequalities for Empirical Processes. *Ann. Probab.*, 28(2).
12. Panchenko, D. (2001) A Note on Talagrand's Concentration Inequality. To appear in *Electron. J. Probab.*
13. Schapire, R., Freund, Y., Bartlett, P. and Lee, W.S. (1998) Boosting the Margin: A New Explanation of Effectiveness of Voting Methods. *Ann. Statist.* 26, 1651–1687.
14. Talagrand, M. (1996a) A New Look at Independence. *Ann. Probab.*, 24, 1-34.
15. Talagrand, M. (1996b) New Concentration Inequalities in Product Spaces. *Invent. Math.*, 126, 505-563.
16. van der Vaart, A.W. and Wellner, J.A. (1996) Weak Convergence and Empirical Processes. With Applications to Statistics. Springer-Verlag, New York.

Geometric Methods in the Analysis of Glivenko-Cantelli Classes

Shahar Mendelson

Computer Sciences Laboratory, RSISE, The Australian National University,
Canberra 0200, Australia
shahar@csl.anu.edu.au

Abstract. We use geometric methods to investigate several fundamental problems in machine learning. We present a new bound on the L_p covering numbers of Glivenko-Cantelli classes for $1 \leq p < \infty$ in terms of the fat-shattering dimension of the class, which does not depend on the size of the sample. Using the new bound, we improve the known sample complexity estimates and bound the size of the Sufficient Statistics needed for Glivenko-Cantelli classes.

1 Introduction

Estimating the covering numbers of a class of functions has always been important in the context of Learning Theory. This is due to the fact that almost all the sample complexity estimates and the characterization of Glivenko-Cantelli classes are based on the growth rate of the covering numbers as a function of the size of the sample. In fact, the strength of the combinatorial learning parameters (the VC dimension and the fat-shattering dimension) is that they enable one to bound the covering numbers of the class ([3,17]), usually with respect to the empirical L_∞ norms.

Let n be an integer and set S_n to be a sample which consists of at most n points. Sauer's lemma for VC classes and its real valued counterpart for classes with a finite fat-shattering dimension [3] provide a bound on the covering numbers of the set $F/S_n = \left\{ \left(f(\omega_1), ..., f(\omega_n) \right) \middle| f \in F, \omega_i \in S_n \right\}$ with respect to the L_∞ norm. These bounds imply that as the size of the sample is increased, the L_∞ covering numbers increase by a logarithmic factor in n.

For VC classes, it is possible to estimate the covering numbers with respect to other L_p norms and probability measures which are not necessarily supported on a finite set [18]. In particular, for $1 \leq p < \infty$ the covering numbers of F/S_n are uniformly bounded as a function of n. In the real valued case some progress was made, but only for empirical L_1 norms; in [4] it was shown that if F has a finite fat-shattering dimension then for every empirical measure μ_n its $L_1(\mu_n)$ covering numbers are linear in the fat-shattering dimension (up to a logarithmic factor). In this article we prove similar bounds for $1 < p < \infty$ and present several applications of the estimates. The most important application is an estimate on the so-called ℓ-norm of the sets F/S_n (defined below) when viewed as subsets

D. Helmbold and B. Williamson (Eds.): COLT/EuroCOLT 2001, LNAI 2111, pp. 256–272, 2001.

of L_2. The first application of the ℓ-norm estimates is a significant improvement in the known sample complexity estimates for Glivenko-Cantelli classes. The second application is a new bound on size of the *Sufficient Statistics* of Glivenko-Cantelli classes, which is the number of linear combinations of point evaluation functionals needed to identify a member of the given class.

We end this introduction with some definitions, notation and basic results we require in the sequel.

Recall that a class of functions is a Glivenko-Cantelli (GC) class if it satisfies the *uniform law of large numbers*. Formally, if F is a class of functions on a measurable set (Ω, Σ), it is a GC class if for every $\varepsilon > 0$,

$$\lim_{n\to\infty} \sup_{\mu} \mu\left\{ \sup_{m\geq n} \sup_{f\in F} \left| \frac{1}{m}\sum_{i=1}^{m} f(X_i) - \mathbb{E}_\mu f \right| \geq \varepsilon \right\} = 0 \ , \tag{1}$$

where the supremum is taken with respect to all probability measures μ, $(X_i)_{i=1}^{\infty}$ are independently sampled according to μ and $\mathbb{E}_\mu$ is the expectation with respect to μ.

We investigate the *GC sample complexity* of the class F which is a quantified version of (1); F is a GC class if and only if for every $\varepsilon > 0$ and $0 < \delta < 1$, there exists some integer n_0, such that for every probability measure μ and every $n \geq n_0$,

$$\mu\left\{ \sup_{f\in F} \left| \frac{1}{n}\sum_{i=1}^{n} f(X_i) - \mathbb{E}_\mu f \right| \geq \varepsilon \right\} \leq \delta \ . \tag{2}$$

For every $\varepsilon > 0$ and $0 \leq \delta < 1$, the smallest possible integer n_0 such that (2) is satisfied is called the Glivenko-Cantelli sample complexity associated with the pair ε, δ. If $\mathcal{H}$ is a class of functions on Ω, $g : \Omega \to [0,1]$ and $1 \leq q < \infty$, let $\{|h-g|^q \, |h \in \mathcal{H}\}$ be the q-loss class given by $\mathcal{H}$, g and q. The sample complexity the q-loss class is denoted by $S_q(\varepsilon, \delta, g, \mathcal{H})$.

If (X, d) is a metric space and if $F \subset X$, the ε-covering number of F, denoted by $N(\varepsilon, F, d)$, is the minimal number of open balls with radius $\varepsilon > 0$ (with respect to the metric d) needed to cover F. A set $A \subset X$ is said to be an ε-cover of F if the union of open balls $\bigcup_{a\in A} B(a,\varepsilon)$ contains F, where $B(a,\varepsilon)$ is the open ball of radius ε centered at a.

A set is called ε-separated if the distance between any two elements of the set is larger than ε. Set $D(\varepsilon, F)$ to be the maximal cardinality of an ε-separated set in F. $D(\varepsilon, F)$ are called the packing numbers of F (with respect to the fixed metric d). It is easy to see that for every $\varepsilon > 0$, $N(\varepsilon, F) \leq D(\varepsilon, F) \leq N(\varepsilon/2, F)$.

Given a Banach space X, denote its unit ball by $B(X)$. For any probability measure μ on the measurable space (Ω, Σ), let $\mathbb{E}_\mu$ be the expectation with respect to μ. $L_p(\mu)$ is the set of functions which satisfy $\mathbb{E}_\mu |f|^p < \infty$ and set $\|f\|_{L_p(\mu)} = (\mathbb{E}_\mu |f|^p)^{1/p}$. $L_\infty(\Omega)$ is the space of bounded functions on Ω with respect to the norm $\|f\|_\infty = \sup_{\omega\in\Omega} |f(\omega)|$. For every $\omega \in \Omega$, let δ_ω be the point evaluation functional, i.e., for every function f on Ω, $\delta_\omega(f) = f(\omega)$. We denote by μ_n an empirical measure supported on a set of n points, hence, $\mu_n =$

$\frac{1}{n}\sum_{i=1}^{n}\delta_{\omega_i}$. Given a set A, let $|A|$ be its cardinality, set χ_A to be its characteristic function and denote by A^c the complement of A. Finally, all absolute constants are assumed to be positive and are denoted by C or c. Their values may change from line to line or even within the same line.

The first combinatorial parameter used in learning theory was introduced by Vapnik and Chervonenkis for classes of $\{0,1\}$-valued functions [17]. Later, this parameter was generalized in various fashions. The parameter which we focus on is the *fat shattering dimension.*

Definition 1. *For every $\varepsilon > 0$, a set $A = \{\omega_1, ..., \omega_n\} \subset \Omega$ is said to be ε–shattered by F if there is some function $s : A \to \mathbb{R}$, such that for every $I \subset \{1, ..., n\}$ there is some $f_I \in \mathcal{F}$ for which $f_I(\omega_i) \geq s(\omega_i) + \varepsilon$ if $i \in I$, and $f_I(\omega_i) \leq s(\omega_i) - \varepsilon$ if $i \notin I$. Let*

$$\mathrm{fat}_\varepsilon(F) = \sup\Big\{|A| \,\Big|\, A \subset \Omega,\ A \text{ is } \varepsilon\text{–shattered by } F\Big\} .$$

f_I is called the shattering function of the set I and the set $\big\{s(\omega_i)|\omega_i \in A\big\}$ is called a witness to the ε-shattering.

The following result, due to Alon, Ben-David, Cesa-Bianchi and Haussler [3], enables one to estimate the $L_\infty(\mu_n)$ covering numbers of classes in terms of the fat shattering dimension.

Theorem 1. *Let F be a class of functions from Ω into $[0,1]$ and set $d = \mathrm{fat}_{\varepsilon/4}(F)$. Then, for every empirical measure μ_n on Ω,*

$$D\big(\varepsilon, F, L_\infty(\mu_n)\big) \leq 2\Big(\frac{4n}{\varepsilon^2}\Big)^{d\log\big(en/(d\varepsilon)\big)} .$$

In particular, the same estimate holds in $L_p(\mu_n)$ for any $1 \leq p < \infty$.

Although $\log D\big(\varepsilon, F, L_p(\mu_n)\big)$ is "almost linear" in $\mathrm{fat}_\varepsilon(F)$, this estimate is not dimension free, since it carries a factor of $\log^2 n$.

Let ℓ_2^n be a real n-dimensional inner product space, and denote the inner product by $\langle\ ,\ \rangle$. Given a set F, the symmetric convex hull of F is $\mathrm{absconv}(F) = \{\sum_{i=1}^{n} a_i f_i | n \in \mathbb{N}, f_i \in F, \sum_{i=1}^{n}|a_i| = 1\}$. The convex hull of F is $\mathrm{conv}(F) = \{\sum_{i=1}^{n} a_i f_i | n \in \mathbb{N}, f_i \in F,\ a_i \geq 0,\ \sum_{i=1}^{n} a_i = 1\}$.

If F is a class and μ_n is an empirical measure, we endow $\mathbb{R}^n$ with the Euclidean structure of $L_2(\mu_n)$, which is isometric to ℓ_2^n. If μ_n is the empirical measure supported on $\{\omega_1, ..., \omega_n\}$, let $F/\mu_n = \Big\{\sum_{i=1}^{n} f(\omega_i)\chi_{\{\omega_i\}} | f \in F\Big\} \subset L_2(\mu_n)$.

Throughout this article we make extensive use of probabilistic averaging techniques. To that end, we define the Gaussian averages of F/μ_n.

Definition 2. *Let F be a class of functions on Ω. Let $\{\omega_1, ..., \omega_n\} \subset \Omega$ be a fixed sample and let μ_n be the empirical measure supported on the sample. Set*

$$\ell(F/\mu_n) = \frac{1}{\sqrt{n}}\mathbb{E}\sup_{f\in F}\left|\sum_{i=1}^{n} g_i f(\omega_i)\right| ,$$

where $(g_i)_{i=1}^{n}$ are independent standard Gaussian random variables.

First, note that $\ell(\text{absconv}(F)/\mu_n) = \ell(F/\mu_n)$. Much less obvious and considerably more important is the following result, which provides an upper bound on $\ell(F/\mu_n)$ in terms of the covering numbers of F in $L_2(\mu_n)$. This bound was demonstrated by Dudley [6]

Theorem 2. *There is an absolute constant C such that for every integer n and every $F \subset L_2(\mu_n)$,*

$$\ell(F/\mu_n) \leq C \int_0^\infty \log^{\frac{1}{2}} \left(N(\varepsilon, F/\mu_n, L_2(\mu_n)\right) d\varepsilon \ .$$

In a similar fashion, it is possible to define the Rademacher averages associated with a class F and a sample $\{\omega_1, ..., \omega_n\}$.

Definition 3. *Let F be a class of functions on Ω. Let $\{\omega_1, ..., \omega_n\} \subset \Omega$ be a fixed sample and let μ_n be the empirical measure supported on the sample. Set*

$$R(F/\mu_n) = \frac{1}{\sqrt{n}} \mathbb{E} \sup_{f \in F} \left| \sum_{i=1}^n \varepsilon_i f(\omega_i) \right| \ ,$$

where $(\varepsilon_i)_{i=1}^n$ are independent Rademacher (i.e. symmetric $\{-1,1\}$-valued) random variables.

Remark 1. It is possible to show [16] that there is an absolute constant C such that for every class F, every integer n and every sample $\{\omega_1, ..., \omega_n\}$, $R(F/\mu_n) \leq C\ell(F/\mu_n)$.

2 The Covering Theorem and Its Applications

The main result presented in this section is an estimate on the covering numbers of a class, when considered as a subset of $L_p(\mu_n)$, for an empirical measure μ_n. The estimate is expressed in terms of the fat shattering dimension of the class. Controlling the covering numbers is important in this case, since this quantity appears in most deviation results used for sample complexity estimates. We present a bound which is dimension free (i.e., does not depend on the cardinality of the set on which the measure is supported) and is "almost" linear in $fat_\varepsilon(F)$. Thus far, the only way to obtain such a result in every L_p space was through the L_∞ estimates (Theorem 1). Unfortunately, those estimates carry a factor of $\log^2 |I|$, where I is the set on which the measure is supported. Hence, the estimate is not dimension free.

The proof is based on a idea which is due to Pajor [12] and is divided to two steps. We begin by showing that if μ_n is supported on $\{\omega_1, ..., \omega_n\}$ and if a set $F \subset B(L_\infty(\Omega))$ is "well separated" in $L_2(\mu_n)$, there is a "small" subset $I \subset \{\omega_1, ..., \omega_n\}$ such that F is "well separated" in $L_\infty(I)$. The next step in the proof is to apply the bound on the packing numbers of F in $L_\infty(I)$ in terms of the fat shattering dimension of F. Our result is stronger than Pajor's because we use a sharper upper bound on the packing numbers.

Lemma 1. *Let $F \subset B(L_\infty(\Omega))$ and suppose that μ_n is the empirical measure supported on $A = \{\omega_1, ..., \omega_n\}$. Fix $\varepsilon > 0$ and $p \geq 1$, set $d_p = D(\varepsilon, F, L_p(\mu_n))$ and assume that $d_p > 1$. Then, there is a constant c_p, which depends only on p, and a subset $I \subset A$, such that $|I| \leq c_p \varepsilon^{-p} \log d_p$, and $\log D(\varepsilon, F, L_p(\mu_n)) \leq \log D(\varepsilon/2, F, L_\infty(I))$.*

Proof. Fix any integer n and $p \geq 1$ and let $\{f_1, ..., f_{d_p}\} \subset F$ be ε-separated in $L_p(\mu_n)$. Hence, for every $i \neq j$, $\varepsilon^p < n^{-1} \sum_{k=1}^n |f_i(\omega_k) - f_j(\omega_k)|^p$. Let $L(i,j)$ be the set of indices on which $|f_i(\omega_k) - f_j(\omega_k)| \leq \varepsilon/2$. Note that for every $i \neq j$,

$$\begin{aligned} n\varepsilon^p &\leq \sum_{k=1}^n |f_i(\omega_k) - f_j(\omega_k)|^p \\ &= \sum_{k \in L(i,j)} |f_i(\omega_k) - f_j(\omega_k)|^p + \sum_{k \in L(i,j)^c} |f_i(\omega_k) - f_j(\omega_k)|^p \\ &\leq |L(i,j)| \left(\frac{\varepsilon}{2}\right)^p + 2^p(n - |L(i,j)|) \ . \end{aligned}$$

Thus,

$$|L(i,j)| \leq \left(1 - \left(\frac{2^p - 1}{4^p}\right)\varepsilon^p\right) n \ .$$

Let $(X_i)_{1 \leq i \leq t}$ be t independent random variables, uniformly distributed on $\{1, ..., n\}$. Clearly, for every pair $i < j$, the probability that for every $1 \leq k \leq t$, $X_k \in L(i,j)$ is smaller than $\left(1 - \left(\frac{2^p-1}{4^p}\right)\varepsilon^p\right)^t$. Therefore, the probability that there is a pair $i < j$ such that for every $1 \leq k \leq t$, $X_k \in L(i,j)$, is smaller than

$$\frac{d_p(d_p - 1)}{2} \left(1 - \left(\frac{2^p - 1}{4^p}\right)\varepsilon^p\right)^t =: \Theta \ .$$

If $\Theta < 1$, there is a set $I \subset \{\omega_1, ..., \omega_n\}$ such that $|I| \leq t$ and for every $i \neq j$, $\|f_i - f_j\|_{L_\infty(I)} \geq \varepsilon/2$, as claimed. Thus, all it requires is that $t \geq c_p \varepsilon^{-p} \log d_p$ where c_p is a constant which depends only on p.

Theorem 3. *If $F \subset B(L_\infty(\Omega))$, then for every $p \geq 1$ there is some constant c_p which depends only on p, such that for every empirical measure μ_n and every $\varepsilon > 0$,*

$$\log D(\varepsilon, F, L_p(\mu_n)) \leq c_p \mathrm{fat}_{\frac{\varepsilon}{8}}(F) \log^2 \left(\frac{2\mathrm{fat}_{\frac{\varepsilon}{8}}(F)}{\varepsilon}\right) \ .$$

Proof. Fix $\varepsilon > 0$. By Lemma 1 and Theorem 1 there is a subset $I \subset \{\omega_1, ..., \omega_n\}$ such that

$$|I| \leq c_p \frac{\log D(\varepsilon, F, L_p(\mu_n))}{\varepsilon^p} \ ,$$

and

$$\log D\big(\varepsilon, F, L_p(\mu_n)\big) \leq \log D\big(\frac{\varepsilon}{2}, F, L_\infty(I)\big) \leq$$
$$\leq c_p fat_{\frac{\varepsilon}{8}}(F) \log^2\Big(\frac{2\log D\big(\varepsilon, F, L_p(\mu_n)\big)}{\varepsilon^p}\Big) .$$

Therefore,

$$\log D\big(\varepsilon, F, L_p(\mu_n)\big) \leq c_p \mathrm{f}at_{\frac{\varepsilon}{8}}(F) \log^2\Big(\frac{2\mathrm{f}at_{\frac{\varepsilon}{8}}(F)}{\varepsilon}\Big) .$$

as claimed.

Note that the estimate we presented is optimal up to a logarithmic factor. This follows from the next general lower bound (see [2] for further details).

Theorem 4. *Let F be a class of functions. Then, for any $\varepsilon > 0$, every integer $n \geq \mathrm{f}at_{16\varepsilon}(F)$ and any $1 \leq p < \infty$,*

$$\sup_{\mu_n} N\big(\varepsilon, F, L_p(\mu_n)\big) \geq e^{fat_{16\varepsilon}(F)/8} .$$

Corollary 1. *Let $F \subset B\big(L_\infty(\Omega)\big)$. Then, for every $\varepsilon > 0$ and $1 \leq p < \infty$,*

$$\frac{fat_{16\varepsilon}(F)}{8} \leq \sup_n \sup_{\mu_n} \log N\big(\varepsilon, F, L_p(\mu_n)\big) \leq c_p \mathrm{f}at_{\frac{\varepsilon}{4}}(F) \log^2\Big(\frac{2\mathrm{f}at_{\frac{\varepsilon}{4}}(F)}{\varepsilon}\Big) ,$$

where c_p is a constant which depends only on p.

The behaviour of the supremum of the log-covering numbers plays an important part in the analysis of empirical processes. For example, Pollard's entropy condition, which is a condition sufficient to ensure that a class satisfies the Universal Central Limit Theorem, is given in terms of the integral of this supremum [18].

3 ℓ-Norm Estimates

The ℓ-norm of subsets of $L_2(\mu_n)$ spaces play an important part in our discussion. We will show that they may be used to estimate the number of Sufficient Statistics needed for a given class. Moreover, bounding the ℓ-norm yields a bound on the Rademacher averages associated with the class, which plays a major role in the analysis of the sample complexity of Glivenko-Cantelli classes.

We begin with the following lemma, which is based on the proof of the upper bound in Theorem 2 (see [14]).

Lemma 2. *Let μ_n be an empirical measure on Ω, put $F \subset B\big(L_\infty(\Omega)\big)$ and set $(\varepsilon_k)_{k=0}^\infty$ to be a monotone sequence decreasing to 0 such that $\varepsilon_0 = 1$. Then, there is an absolute constant C such that for every integer N,*

$$\ell(F/\mu_n) \leq C \sum_{k=1}^N \varepsilon_{k-1} \log^{\frac{1}{2}} N\big(\varepsilon_k, F, L_2(\mu_n)\big) + 2\varepsilon_N n^{\frac{1}{2}} .$$

In particular,

$$\ell(F/\mu_n) \le C \sum_{k=1}^{N} \varepsilon_{k-1} \mathrm{fat}^{\frac{1}{2}}_{\frac{\varepsilon_k}{8}}(F) \log\left(\frac{2\mathrm{fat}_{\frac{\varepsilon_k}{8}}(F)}{\varepsilon}\right) + 2\varepsilon_N n^{\frac{1}{2}} \ . \tag{3}$$

The latter part of Lemma 2 follows from its first part and Theorem 3. Before presenting the proof of Lemma 2, we require the following lemma, which is based on the classical inequality due to Slepian [14].

Lemma 3. *Let $(Z_i)_{i=1}^N$ be Gaussian random variables (i.e., $Z_i = \sum_{j=1}^m a_j g_j$ where (g_i) are independent standard Gaussian random variables). Then, there is some absolute constant C such that $\mathbb{E}\sup_i Z_i \le C \sup_{i,j} \|Z_i - Z_j\|_2 \log^{\frac{1}{2}} N$.*

Proof (of Lemma 2). We may assume that F is symmetric and contains 0. The proof in the non-symmetric case follows the same path. Let μ_n be an empirical measure supported on $\{\omega_1, \ldots \omega_n\}$. For every $f \in F$, let $Z_f = n^{-1/2} \sum_{i=1}^n g_i f(\omega_i)$, where $(g_i)_{i=1}^n$ are independent standard Gaussian random variables on the probability space (Y, P). Set $\mathcal{Z}_F = \{Z_f | f \in F\}$ and note that since $V : L_2(\mu_n) \to L_2(Y, P)$ is an isometry for which $V(F/\mu_n) = \mathcal{Z}_F$ then

$$N\big(\varepsilon, F/\mu_n, L_2(\mu_n)\big) = N\big(\varepsilon, \mathcal{Z}_F, L_2(P)\big) \ .$$

Let $(\varepsilon_k)_{k=0}^\infty$ be a monotone sequence decreasing to 0 such that $\varepsilon_0 = 1$, and set $H_k \subset \mathcal{Z}_F$ to be a $2\varepsilon_k$ cover of $\mathcal{Z}_F$. Thus, for every $k \in \mathbb{Z}$ and every $Z_f \in \mathcal{Z}_F$ there is some $Z_f^k \in H_k$ such that $\left\| Z_f - Z_f^k \right\|_2 \le 2\varepsilon_k$, and we select $Z_f^0 = 0$. Writing $Z_f = \sum_{k=1}^N (Z_f^k - Z_f^{k-1}) + Z_f - Z_f^N$ it follows that

$$\mathbb{E}\sup_{f\in F} Z_f \le \sum_{k=1}^N \mathbb{E}\sup_{f\in F}(Z_f^k - Z_f^{k-1}) + \mathbb{E}\sup_{f\in F}(Z_f - Z_f^N) \ .$$

By the definition of Z_f^k and Lemma 3, there is an absolute constant C for which

$$\begin{aligned}
\mathbb{E}\sup_{f\in F}(Z_f^k - Z_f^{k-1}) \le& \mathbb{E}\sup\big\{Z_i - Z_j | Z_i \in H_k, Z_j \in H_{k-1}, \|Z_i - Z_j\|_2 \le 4\varepsilon_{k-1}\big\} \\
\le& C \sup_{i,j} \|Z_i - Z_j\|_2 \log^{\frac{1}{2}} |H_k|\,|H_{k-1}| \\
\le& C\varepsilon_{k-1} \log^{\frac{1}{2}} N\big(\varepsilon_k, F, L_2(\mu_n)\big) \ .
\end{aligned}$$

Since $Z_f^N \in \mathcal{Z}_F$, there is some $f' \in F$ such that $Z_f^N = Z_{f'}$. Hence,

$$\left(\sum_{i=1}^n \left(\frac{f(\omega_i) - f'(\omega_i)}{\sqrt{n}}\right)^2\right)^{\frac{1}{2}} = \|Z_f - Z_{f'}\|_2 \le 2\varepsilon_N \ ,$$

which implies that for every $f \in F$ and every $y \in Y$,

$$|Z_f(y) - Z_f^N(y)| \le \sum_{i=1}^n \left| \frac{f(\omega_i) - f'(\omega_i)}{\sqrt{n}} g_i(y) \right| \le 2\varepsilon_N \Big(\sum_{i=1}^n g_i^2(y)\Big)^{\frac{1}{2}} \ .$$

Therefore, $\mathbb{E}\sup_{f\in F} Z_f - Z_f^N \le \varepsilon_N \mathbb{E}\big(\sum_{i=1}^n g_i^2\big)^{\frac{1}{2}} = 2\varepsilon_N\sqrt{n}$, and the claim follows.

Using this result it is possible to estimate the ℓ-norm of classes with a polynomial fat-shattering dimension.

Theorem 5. *Let $F \subset B\big(L_\infty(\Omega)\big)$ and assume that there is some $\gamma > 1$ such that for any $\varepsilon > 0$, $\mathrm{fat}_\varepsilon(F) \le \gamma\varepsilon^{-p}$. Then, there are absolute constants C_p, which depends only on p, such that for any empirical measure μ_n,*

$$\ell(F/\mu_n) \le \begin{cases} C_p\gamma^{\frac{1}{2}}\log\gamma & \text{if } 0<p<2 \\ C_2(\gamma^{\frac{1}{2}}\log\gamma)\log^2 n & \text{if } p=2 \\ C_p(\gamma^{\frac{1}{2}}\log\gamma)n^{\frac{1}{2}-\frac{1}{p}} & \text{if } p>2\ . \end{cases}$$

Proof. Let μ_n be an empirical measure on Ω. If $p<2$ then by Theorem 3,

$$\int_0^\infty \log^{\frac{1}{2}} N\big(\varepsilon, F, L_2(\mu_n)\big)d\varepsilon \le C_p\gamma^{\frac{1}{2}}\log\gamma\ ,$$

and the bound on the ℓ-norm follows from the upper bound in Theorem 2.

Assume that $p \ge 2$ and, using the notation of Lemma 2, select $\varepsilon_k = 2^{-k}$ and $N = p^{-1}\log n$. By (3),

$$\begin{aligned}\ell(F/\mu_n) &\le C_p(\gamma^{\frac{1}{2}}\log\gamma)\sum_{i=1}^N \varepsilon_k^{1-\frac{p}{2}}\log\frac{2}{\varepsilon_k} + 2\varepsilon_N n^{\frac{1}{2}} \\ &\le C_p(\gamma^{\frac{1}{2}}\log\gamma)\sum_{i=1}^N k2^{k(\frac{p}{2}-1)} + 2n^{\frac{1}{2}-\frac{1}{p}}\ .\end{aligned}$$

If $p=2$, the geometric sum is bounded by

$$C_p(\gamma^{\frac{1}{2}}\log\gamma)N^2 \le C_p(\gamma^{\frac{1}{2}}\log\gamma)\log^2 n\ ,$$

whereas is $p>2$ it is bounded by $C_p(\gamma^{\frac{1}{2}}\log\gamma)n^{\frac{1}{2}-\frac{1}{p}}$.

4 Complexity Estimates

Next, we investigate the sample complexity of Glivenko-Cantelli classes. The term "sample complexity" is often used in a slightly different way than the one we use in this article. Normally, when one talks about the sample complexity of a learning problem the meaning is the following: given a class $\mathcal{H}$ and some $1 \le q < \infty$, let $\ell_q^h(x,y) = |h(x)-y|^q$ and set $\mathcal{Y}$ to be a bounded subset of $\mathbb{R}$. A *learning rule* is a mapping which assigns to each sample of arbitrary length $z_n = (x_i, y_i)_{i=1}^n$, some $A_{z_n} \in \mathcal{H}$. Given a class $\mathcal{H}$ and $\mathcal{Y} \subset \mathbb{R}$, let the *learning sample complexity* be the smallest integer n_0 such that for every $n \ge n_0$, the following holds: there exists a learning rule A such that for every probability measure P on $\Omega \times \mathcal{Y}$,

$$P\left\{\mathbb{E}\left|A_{Z_n} - Y\right|^q \geq \inf_{h \in \mathcal{H}} \mathbb{E}\ell_q^h(X,Y) + \varepsilon\right\} < \delta \ ,$$

where Z_n is the sample $(X_i, Y_i)_{i=1}^n$ selected according to P. We denote the learning sample complexity associated with the range $\mathcal{Y}$ and the class $\mathcal{H}$ by $\mathcal{C}_q(\varepsilon, \delta, \mathcal{Y}, \mathcal{H})$.

It is possible to show [2] that if $\mathcal{Y} \subset [-M, M]$ then

$$\mathcal{C}_q(\varepsilon, \delta, \mathcal{Y}, \mathcal{H}) \leq \sup_{\|g\|_\infty \leq M} S_q(\varepsilon, \delta, g, \mathcal{H}) \ .$$

Hence, the GC sample complexity may be used to establish upper bounds on the sample complexity of learning problems.

We introduce a new parameter and show that it governs the GC sample complexity. This parameter is determined by the growth rate of the Rademacher averages associated with the class (see further details below), hence, by Theorem 2 and the fact that the Rademacher averages may be bounded using the ℓ-norm, it is possible to estimate the new parameter in terms of the covering numbers of the class.

4.1 Averaging Techniques

Let us start with a modified definition of the Rademacher averages associated with the class:

Definition 4. *Let F be a class of functions on Ω and let μ be a probability measure. Set*

$$R_n(F) = \sup_{(\omega_i)_{i=1}^n} \frac{1}{\sqrt{n}} \mathbb{E}_\varepsilon \sup_{f \in F} \left|\sum_{i=1}^n \varepsilon_i f(\omega_i)\right| , \quad \bar{R}_{n,\mu} = \frac{1}{\sqrt{n}} \mathbb{E}_\mu \mathbb{E}_\varepsilon \sup_{f \in F} \left|\sum_{i=1}^n \varepsilon_i f(X_i)\right| ,$$

where $(\varepsilon_i)_{i=1}^n$ are independent Rademacher random variables, μ is a probability measure and $(X_i)_{i=1}^n$ are independent, distributed according to μ.

Note that $R_n(F) = \sup_{\mu_n} R(F/\mu_n)$. Also, the relations between R_n and $\bar{R}_{n,\mu}$ are analogous to those between the VC dimension and the VC entropy; R_n is a "worst case" parameter, while $\bar{R}_{n,\mu}$ is an averaged version which takes into account the particular measure according to which one is sampling.

Rademacher averages appear naturally in the analysis of GC classes. Usually, the first step in estimating the deviation of the empirical means from the actual mean is to apply a symmetrization method [7]:

$$Pr\left\{\sup_{f \in F}\left|\frac{1}{n}\sum_{i=1}^n f(X_i) - \mathbb{E}f\right| \geq \varepsilon\right\} \leq 4Pr\left\{\sup_{f \in F}\left|\sum_{i=1}^n \varepsilon_i f(X_i)\right| \geq \frac{n\varepsilon}{4}\right\} = (*) \ .$$

The parameter we wish to introduce measures the growth rate of the Rademacher averages as a function of the size of the sample. We show that it may be used instead of the usual combinatorial parameters, e.g, the fat-shattering dimension, to obtain deviation estimates.

Definition 5. *Let $F \subset B\big(L_\infty(\Omega)\big)$. For every $\varepsilon > 0$, let*

$$\mathrm{rav}_\varepsilon(F) = \sup\{n \in \mathbb{N} | R_n(F) \geq \varepsilon\sqrt{n}\} \ .$$

To see the connection between $fat_\varepsilon(F)$ and $\mathrm{rav}_\varepsilon(F)$, assume that $\{\omega_1, ..., \omega_n\}$ is ε-shattered. Let $(\varepsilon_1, ..., \varepsilon_n) \in \{-1,1\}^n$ and set $I = \{i | \varepsilon_i = 1\}$. For every $J \subset \{\omega_1, ..., \omega_n\}$, let f_J be the function shattering J. Then, by the triangle inequality and selecting $f = f_I$, $f' = f_{I^c}$, it follows that

$$\frac{1}{\sqrt{n}} \sup_{f \in F} \left| \sum_{i=1}^n \varepsilon_i f(\omega_i) \right| \geq \frac{1}{2\sqrt{n}} \sup_{f, f' \in F} \left| \sum_{i=1}^n \varepsilon_i \big(f(\omega_i) - f'(\omega_i)\big) \right|$$

$$\geq \frac{1}{2\sqrt{n}} \left| \sum_{i=1}^n \varepsilon_i \big(f_I(\omega_i) - f_{I^c}(\omega_i)\big) \right| \geq \sqrt{n}\varepsilon \ .$$

Thus, if $\{\omega_1, ..., \omega_n\}$ is ε-shattered, then for every realization of the Rademacher random variables, $n^{-1/2} \sup_{f \in F} |\sum_{i=1}^n \varepsilon_i f(\omega_i)| \geq \sqrt{n}\varepsilon$, while $\mathrm{rav}_\varepsilon(F)$ is determined by averaging such realizations. Hence, $\mathrm{rav}_\varepsilon(F) \geq \mathrm{fat}_\varepsilon(F)$. It turn out that it is possible to find a general lower bound on $\mathrm{rav}_\varepsilon(F)$ in terms of $fat_\varepsilon(F)$ (see [10]).

The appeal in using the Rademacher averages instead of the fat-shattering dimension or other learning parameters is that the Rademacher averages remain unchanged if one takes the convex hull of the class, whereas $fat_\varepsilon(F)$ or the covering numbers may change dramatically by taking the convex hull. We shall use this property of the Rademacher averages to show that when assessing the GC sample complexity, there is no computational price to pay for taking the convex hull of the class.

Our first goal is to estimate the Rademacher averages of a loss class in terms of the Rademacher averages of the original class. The proof of the following claim is standard and is omitted.

Theorem 6. *Let F be a class of functions on Ω. Then,*

1. *$R_n\big(\mathrm{absconv}(F)\big) = R_n(F)$.*
2. *If Φ is a Lipschitz function such that $\Phi(0) = 0$ and L_Φ is its Lipschitz constant, then $R_n\big(\Phi(F)\big) \leq 2L_\phi R_n(F)$.*
3. *For any uniformly bounded function g let $F + g = \{f + g | f \in F\}$. There is an absolute constant C such that $R_n(F + g) \leq R_n(F) + C\|g\|_\infty$.*

From Theorem 6 we can derive the next corollary:

Corollary 2. *Let $\mathcal{H} \subset B\big(L_\infty(\Omega)\big)$ and $g \in B\big(L_\infty(\Omega)\big)$. If F_q is the q-loss function associated with the target g and $\mathrm{conv}(\mathcal{H})$, (i.e., each $f \in F_q$ is given by $f = |h - g|^q$, where $h \in \mathrm{conv}(\mathcal{H})$) then there is an absolute constant C such that*

$$R_n(F_q) \leq Cq\big(1 + R_n(\mathcal{H})\big) \ .$$

4.2 The Direct Approach

The first example of the direct approach we use to bound the rav, is for classes of linear functionals. This example is interesting in the context of Machine Learning since linear functionals are at the heart of the theory of Kernel Machines.

Recall that a Banach space has type p if there is a constant C such that for every integer n and every $x_1, ..., x_n \in X$,

$$\mathbb{E}_\varepsilon \left\| \sum_{i=1}^n \varepsilon_i x_i \right\| \leq C\Big(\sum_{i=1}^n \|x_i\|^p\Big)^{\frac{1}{p}} , \tag{4}$$

where, as always, $(\varepsilon_i)_{i=1}^n$ are independent symmetric $\{-1,1\}$-valued random variables. The smallest constant for which (4) holds is called the p type constant of X and is denoted by $T_p(X)$. Clearly, every Banach space has type $p=1$, and it is possible to show that X can not have type p for $p>2$. For example, Hilbert spaces have type 2 and $T_2 = 1$. For further details about the *type* of Banach spaces we refer the reader to [9,13].

Let X be a Banach space which has a nontrivial type $1 < p \leq 2$ with a type constant $T_p(X)$. Let $\mathcal{H} \subset B(X^*)$ when considered as a class of functions on $B(X)$. If $x_1, ..., x_n \in B(X)$ then

$$\begin{aligned}\mathbb{E}_\varepsilon \sup_{h\in\mathcal{H}} \left| \sum_{i=1}^n \varepsilon_i h(x_i) \right| &\leq \mathbb{E}_\varepsilon \sup_{x^*\in B(X^*)} \left| \sum_{i=1}^n \varepsilon_i x^*(x_i) \right| = \mathbb{E}_\varepsilon \left\| \sum_{i=1}^n \varepsilon_i x_i \right\| \\ &\leq T_p(X)\Big(\sum_{i=1}^n \|x_i\|^p\Big)^{\frac{1}{p}} .\end{aligned}$$

Since $\|x_i\| \leq 1$, $R_n(\mathcal{H}) \leq T_p(X) n^{\frac{1}{p}-\frac{1}{2}}$. Therefore, it follows that if $\|g\|_\infty \leq 1$ and if F_q is the q-loss associated with absconv$(\mathcal{H})$ and a target g then

$$\mathrm{rav}_\varepsilon(F_q) \leq C\big(qT_p(X)\big)^{\frac{p}{p-1}} \Big(\frac{1}{\varepsilon}\Big)^{\frac{p}{p-1}} .$$

The second example we present (which is very close in its nature to the first one) is that of Sobolev spaces.

Given a set $\Omega \subset \mathbb{R}^d$, let $W^{k,2}(\Omega)$ be the space of all the functions for which all the weak derivatives up to order k exist and belong to $L_2(\Omega)$.

Define $\|f\|_{W^{k,2}(\Omega)} = \sum_{|\alpha|\leq k} \|D^\alpha f\|_{L_2(\Omega)}$ and set $X = W_0^{k,2}(\Omega)$ to be the closure (with respect to the $\| \ \|_{W^{k,2}(\Omega)}$ norm) of the set of functions which vanish on the boundary of Ω and are continuously differentiable k times (see [1] for more details on Sobolev space).

It is possible to show that X is a Hilbert space, and therefore it has type 2 with $T_2(X) = 1$. Moreover, if $k > d/2$ then X is compactly embedded in the space of continuous functions on Ω. Hence, there is some $M > 0$ which depends on Ω such that for every $\omega \in \Omega$, $\|\delta_\omega\|_{X^*} \leq M$. Since X is a Hilbert space, each bounded linear functional is represented by an element of X, also denoted by δ_ω, which has the same norm as the functional.

Note that if $\mathcal{H}$ is a subset of unit ball of X then $R_n(\mathcal{H}) \leq M$. Indeed, for any sample $\{\omega_1, ..., \omega_n\}$,

$$\begin{aligned}\frac{1}{\sqrt{n}}\mathbb{E}_\varepsilon \sup_{h\in\mathcal{H}} \sum_{i=1}^n \varepsilon_i h(\omega_i) &= \frac{1}{\sqrt{n}}\mathbb{E}_\varepsilon \sup_{h\in\mathcal{H}} \sum_{i=1}^n \varepsilon_i \langle h, \delta_{\omega_i}\rangle = \frac{1}{\sqrt{n}}\mathbb{E}_\varepsilon \sup_{h\in\mathcal{H}} \langle \sum_{i=1}^n \varepsilon_i \delta_{\omega_i}, h\rangle \\ &\leq \frac{1}{\sqrt{n}}\mathbb{E}_\varepsilon \left\| \sum_{i=1}^n \varepsilon_i \delta_{\omega_i} \right\|_X \leq \frac{1}{\sqrt{n}} \Big(\sum_{i=1}^n \|\delta_{\omega_i}\|_X^2 \Big)^{\frac{1}{2}} \leq M \ .\end{aligned} \tag{5}$$

In particular,

$$rav_\varepsilon(F_q) \leq \frac{Cq^2(1+M)^2}{\varepsilon^2} \ .$$

Remark 2. Using a similar method one can estimate R_n of bounded subsets in the more general Sobolev spaces $W_0^{k,p}(\Omega)$.

4.3 Estimating rav Using Covering Numbers

We now present bounds on rav which are demonstrated via an indirect route, using the estimate on the ℓ-norm.

Recall that there is an absolute constant C such that for every F and every empirical measure μ_n supported on the sample $\{\omega_1, ..., \omega_n\}$, $R_n(F/\mu_n) \leq C\ell(F/\mu_n)$. Combining this fact with the ℓ-norm estimate in Theorem 5, one can prove the following result on $\mathrm{rav}_\varepsilon(\mathcal{H})$ when $\mathrm{fat}_\varepsilon(\mathcal{H})$ is polynomial in ε^{-1}.

Theorem 7. *Let $\mathcal{H} \subset B\big(L_\infty(\Omega)\big)$ and assume that $\mathrm{fat}_\varepsilon(\mathcal{H}) \leq \gamma\varepsilon^{-p}$ for some $\gamma > 1$ and every $\varepsilon > 0$. Then, there are constants C_p which depend only on p, such that for every $\varepsilon > 0$,*

$$\mathrm{rav}_\varepsilon(\mathcal{H}) \leq C_p \begin{cases} (\gamma \log^2 \gamma)\varepsilon^{-2} & \text{if } 0 < p < 2 \\ \gamma\varepsilon^{-2}\log^4 \gamma\varepsilon^{-1} & \text{if } p = 2 \\ (\gamma^{\frac{p}{2}} \log^p \gamma)\varepsilon^{-p} & \text{if } p > 2 \ . \end{cases} \tag{6}$$

4.4 GC Sample Complexity

Here, we present the GC sample complexity estimates in terms of $\mathrm{rav}_\varepsilon(F)$. We use a concentration result which yields an estimate on the deviation of the empirical means from the actual mean in terms of the Rademacher averages. We show that $\mathrm{rav}_\varepsilon(F)$ measures the sample complexity of the class F.

Recall the following concentration result, which is due to Talagrand [15]:

Theorem 8. *There are two absolute constants K and $a \leq 1$ with the following property: consider a class of functions F whose range is a subset of $[0,1]$, such that $\sup_{f\in F} \mathbb{E}(f - \mathbb{E}f)^2 \leq a$. If μ is any probability measure on Ω and*

$$\sqrt{n} \geq K\bar{R}_{n,\mu}, \qquad M \geq K\bar{R}_{n,\mu}$$

then

$$Pr\left\{\sup_{f\in F}|\mathbb{E}_{\mu_n}f-\mathbb{E}_\mu f|\geq Mn^{-\frac{1}{2}}\right\}\leq K\exp(-11M)\ .$$

Assume that members of $\mathcal{H}$ and g map Ω into $[0,1]$, and fix some $1\leq q<\infty$. Clearly, $F\equiv F_q$ is also a class of function whose range is a subset of $[0,1]$. Let a be as in Theorem 8, put $F^a=\{\sqrt{a}f|f\in F\}$ and note that $\sup_{f\in F^a}\mathbb{E}(f-\mathbb{E}f)^2\leq a$.

Lemma 4. *Let F and F^a be as in the above paragraph. There is an absolute constant C such that if $\varepsilon>0$ and n satisfy that*

$$n^{\frac{1}{2}}\geq KCa^{-\frac{1}{2}}\varepsilon^{-1}q\big(\bar{R}_{n,\mu}(\mathcal{H})+1\big)\ , \tag{7}$$

then

$$Pr\left\{\sup_{f\in F}|\mathbb{E}_{\mu_n}f-\mathbb{E}_\mu f|\geq\varepsilon\right\}\leq K\exp\big(-11an\varepsilon^2\big)\ .$$

Proof. Clearly,

$$Pr\left\{\sup_{f\in F}|\mathbb{E}_{\mu_n}f-\mathbb{E}_\mu f|\geq\varepsilon\right\}=Pr\left\{\sup_{f\in F^a}|\mathbb{E}_{\mu_n}f-\mathbb{E}_\mu f|\geq\frac{\sqrt{a}\varepsilon}{2}\right\}\ .$$

Let $M=a^{1/2}n^{1/2}\varepsilon$. Since $a,\varepsilon\leq1$, then if n satisfies (7) both conditions of Theorem 8 are automatically satisfies. The assertion follows directly from that theorem and the estimate on $\bar{R}_{n,\mu}(F_q)$ given in Corollary 2.

Theorem 9. *Assume that $\mathcal{H},g$ and q are as above and set F to be a q-loss class associated with $\mathcal{H}$ and g. Then, there is an absolute constant C such that for every $0<\varepsilon,\delta<1$ and every probability measure μ,*

$$Pr\left\{\sup_{f\in F}|\mathbb{E}_{\mu_n}f-\mathbb{E}_\mu f|\geq\varepsilon\right\}\leq\delta\ ,$$

provided that $n\geq C\max\{\mathrm{rav}_{C\varepsilon/q}(\mathcal{H}),\varepsilon^{-2}\log 1/\delta\}$.

4.5 Application: Smooth Functions

Let $\Omega\subset\mathbb{R}^d$ and set X to be the Sobolev space $W_0^{k,2}(\Omega)$. Assume that $k>d/2$ and that $\mathcal{H}\subset B(X)$. By the estimates on the Rademacher averages established in (5) one may obtain the GC sample complexity estimates for F_q.

Theorem 10. *Let $\mathcal{H}\subset B\big(W_0^{k,2}(\Omega)\big)$ and fix some g such that $\|g\|_\infty\leq1$. Then,*

$$S_q\big(\varepsilon,\delta,g,\mathrm{conv}(\mathcal{H})\big)\leq\frac{C_{q,\Omega}}{\varepsilon^2}\log\frac{1}{\delta}\ ,$$

where $C_{q,\Omega}$ is a constant which depends only on q and Ω.

4.6 Application: Classes with Polynomial Fat-Shattering Dimension

The most important application of the theory presented here is a considerable improvement we in the GC sample complexity for classes with polynomial fat-shattering dimension:

Theorem 11. *Let $\mathcal{H}$ be a class of functions whose range in contained in $[0,1]$, such that $\mathrm{fat}_\varepsilon(\mathcal{H}) \leq \gamma\varepsilon^{-p}$ for some $p > 0$. Then, for every $1 \leq q < \infty$ there are constants $C_{p,q,\gamma}$, which depend only on p, q, γ such that for any $g : \Omega \to [0,1]$,*

$$S_q(\varepsilon, \delta, g, \mathrm{conv}(\mathcal{H})) \leq C_{p,q,\gamma} \begin{cases} \varepsilon^{-2} \log \delta^{-1} & \text{if } 0 < p < 2 \\ \varepsilon^{-2}(\log^4 \varepsilon^{-1} + \log \delta^{-1}) & \text{if } p = 2 \\ \varepsilon^{-p} \log \delta^{-1} & \text{if } p > 2 \ . \end{cases} \tag{8}$$

Note that the best known estimates on the GC sample complexity were demonstrated in [3,5]. It was shown that if $\mathcal{H}$ is a GC class then

$$S_q(\varepsilon, \delta, g, \mathcal{H}) \leq C\frac{1}{\varepsilon^2}\left(\mathrm{fat}_{\frac{\varepsilon}{4}}(\mathcal{H}) \log^2 \frac{1}{\varepsilon} + \log \frac{1}{\delta}\right) . \tag{9}$$

If the fat-shattering dimension is polynomial, this result yields a bound which is $O(\varepsilon^{-(p+2)})$ up to logarithmic factors in ε^{-1} and δ^{-1}. Thus, (8) is a much better bound even regarding the sample complexity of $\mathcal{H}$ itself. If one were to try and estimate the sample complexity of a q-loss class associated with $\mathrm{conv}(\mathcal{H})$ using (9), the difference in the results is even more noticeable, since the fat-shattering dimension of the convex hull may be increased by a factor of ε^{-2}, whereas rav does not change.

5 Gelfand Numbers and Sufficient Statistics of GC Classes

In this final section we present another application of the ℓ-norm estimates. We investigate the number of linear constraints needed to pinpoint a function in a given class, up to a desired accuracy. Thus, the problem we face is as follows: given a class F and some $\varepsilon > 0$, we attempt to find a "small" set $\Gamma(\varepsilon) = (x_i^*)_{i=1}^m$ of linear functionals on F, (which may depend on ε) with the following properties:

1. For every $f \in F$ and every $1 \leq i \leq m$, $x_i^*(f)$ can be computed using empirical data.
2. If two functions $f, g \in F$ agree on every element in $\Gamma(\varepsilon)$ then $\|f - g\|_{L_2(\mu)}^2 < \varepsilon$.

The formal definition of ε-Sufficient Statistics is as follows:

Definition 6. *Let F be a class of functions defined on a set Ω and let μ be a probability measure on Ω. A set of linear empirical functionals $(x_i^*)_{i=1}^m$ is called ε-sufficient statistics with respect to $L_2(\mu)$ if for any $f, g \in F$ which satisfy that $x_i^*(g) = x_i^*(f)$ for every $1 \leq i \leq m$, $\|f - g\|_{L_2(\mu)}^2 < \varepsilon$.*

If F is a Glivenko-Cantelli class then the set $\Gamma(\varepsilon)$ may be constructed by taking the point evaluation functionals on a large enough sample. Indeed, if F is a Glivenko-Cantelli class, then the set $\{(f-g)^2 | f,g \in F\}$ is also a Glivenko-Cantelli class. Take n to be an integer such that there is an empirical measure μ_n which is supported on a sample S_n, and for every $f, g \in F$,

$$\left| \mathbb{E}_\mu (f-g)^2 - \mathbb{E}_{\mu_n} (f-g)^2 \right| < \varepsilon \ . \tag{10}$$

Set $\Gamma(\varepsilon)$ to be the set of point evaluation functionals $\{\delta_{\omega_i} | \omega_i \in S_n\}$. Thus, each element of $\Gamma(\varepsilon)$ is a linear functional on F and if f, g agree on each δ_{ω_i} (i.e., if $f(\omega_i) = g(\omega_i)$) then $\|f-g\|_{L_2(\mu)}^2 < \varepsilon$. Hence, $\Gamma(\varepsilon)$ is ε-sufficient statistics for F in $L_2(\mu)$.

Of course, there in no need to merely use point evaluation functionals. As explained in [11], even from the computational point of view it is possible to find a set of linear combinations of point evaluation functionals which are ε-sufficient statistics, using a random selection scheme. This idea is based on the so-called Gelfand numbers.

The Gelfand numbers are parameters which measure the "size" of a symmetric convex set. In some sense, it measures the "minimal width" of the symmetric convex hull of the set. Formally, given some $1 \leq k \leq n$ let H_k be a k-codimensional subspace of ℓ_2^n. A k-section of F is an intersection of F with some H_k. The k-th Gelfand number of $F \subset \ell_2^n$, denoted by $c_k(F)$, is the "smallest" possible diameter of a k-codimensional section of F. In our case, the Euclidean structure is that of $L_2(\mu_n)$, which is isometric to ℓ_2^n. Note that if the measure is supported on $\{\omega_1, ..., \omega_n\}$, a k-codimensional subspace is the intersection of the kernels of k linear functionals, every one of which is given by $x^* = \sum_{i=1}^n a_i \delta_{\omega_i}$. Assume that we can find a k-codimensional section of $\mathrm{absconv}(F)/\mu_n$ which has a diameter bounded by α, and let $x_1^*, ..., x_k^*$ be the linear functionals which define this section. Thus, each x_i^* is empirical, since $x_i^*(f)$ can be computed using the sample points, and if $x_i^*(f) = x_i^*(g)$ then $(f-g)/2 \in \mathrm{absconv}(F) \cap H_k$, implying that $\|f-g\|_{L_2(\mu_n)} \leq \alpha$. Therefore, if μ_n is an empirical measure such that (10) holds, then the set $\Gamma = (x_i^*)_{i=1}^k$ is $(\varepsilon + \alpha^2)$ sufficient statistics for F in $L_2(\mu)$.

It is possible to estimate the Gelfand numbers of a set $F \subset \ell_2^n$ using the ℓ-norm. This fact is due to Pajor and Tomczak-Jaegermann [14].

Theorem 12. *There is an absolute constant C such that for every integer n and every $F \subset \ell_2^n$, $\sup_{k \geq 1} k^{\frac{1}{2}} c_k(F) \leq C\ell(F)$.*

Since the ℓ-norm does not change by taking the symmetric convex hull, we can prove the following estimates, improving the bound presented in [11]

Theorem 13. *Let F be a class of functions which map Ω into $[0,1]$ and assume that there are $\gamma \geq 1$ and $p > 0$ such that for every $\varepsilon > 0$, $\mathrm{fat}_\varepsilon(F) \leq \gamma \varepsilon^{-p}$. For every probability measure μ and $\varepsilon > 0$ there is a set $\Gamma(\varepsilon)$ of ε-sufficient statistics* *such that*

$$|\Gamma(\varepsilon)| \leq C_{\gamma,p} \begin{cases} \varepsilon^{-1} & \text{if } 0 < p < 2 \\ \varepsilon^{-1} \log^2 \varepsilon^{-1} & \text{if } p = 2 \\ \varepsilon^{-(p-1)} & \text{if } p > 2 \ , \end{cases}$$

where $C_{\gamma,p}$ are constants which depend only on γ and p.

Proof. We present a proof only when $p > 2$. The proof in the other cases follows in a similar fashion.

Fix $\varepsilon > 0$, and let n be an integer such that

$$Pr\Big\{ \sup_{f,g \in F} \big| \mathbb{E}_\mu (f-g)^2 - \mathbb{E}_{\mu_n} (f-g)^2 \big| < \frac{\varepsilon}{2} \Big\} \geq \frac{1}{2} \ . \tag{11}$$

To find such an integer n, we use the GC sample complexity estimates. Indeed, let $\mathcal{H} = (F-F)^2 = \{(f-g)^2 | f,g \in F\}$ and note that since each member of F maps Ω into $[0,1]$ then $F - F \subset B\big(L_\infty(\Omega)\big)$. Clearly, $\phi(t) = t^2$ is a Lipshcitz function on $[-1,1]$ with a constant 2. Therefore, by Theorem 6,

$$R_n(\mathcal{H}) \leq 4R_n(F-F) = 8R_n\Big(\frac{1}{2}(F-F)\Big) = 8R_n(F) \ ,$$

where the last inequality holds because $\frac{1}{2}(F-F) \subset \text{absconv}(F)$. Thus, by Theorem 9 we may select $n = C_{p,\gamma}\varepsilon^{-p}$.

Since the set in (11) is nonempty, there is an empirical measure μ_n supported on $\{\omega_1, ..., \omega_n\}$ such that for every $f, g \in F$

$$\big| \mathbb{E}_\mu (f-g)^2 - \mathbb{E}_{\mu_n} (f-g)^2 \big| < \frac{\varepsilon}{2} \ .$$

Let $G \subset L_2(\mu_n)$ be the symmetric convex hull of F/μ_n. By the ℓ-norm estimate, for every integer $k \leq n$ there are k linear functionals on $L_2(\mu_n)$, denoted by $(x_i^*)_{i=1}^k$, such that if $f, g \in G$ satisfy that for every $1 \leq i < k$, $x_i^*(f) = x_i^*(g)$ then

$$\|f-g\|_{L_2(\mu_n)} \leq C_{p,\gamma} \frac{n^{\frac{1}{2}-\frac{1}{p}}}{\sqrt{k}} \ .$$

In particular, the same holds if $f, g \in F$. Thus, by the selection of n and μ_n, and for such f and g

$$\|f-g\|_{L_2(\mu)}^2 \leq \|f-g\|_{L_2(\mu_n)}^2 + \frac{\varepsilon}{2} < \frac{C_{p,\gamma}^2}{k}\Big(\frac{1}{\varepsilon}\Big)^{p-2} + \frac{\varepsilon}{2} \ .$$

Note that each $(x_i^*)_{i=1}^k$ is a linear combination of point evaluation functionals δ_{ω_i}. Thus, if $k = \lceil (C_{p,\gamma})^2 \varepsilon^{-(p-1)} \rceil$ then $\|f-g\|_{L_2(\mu)}^2 < \varepsilon$, implying that the set $(x_i^*)_{i=1}^k$ are ε-sufficient statistics, as claimed.

This result implies that the number of sufficient statistics is considerably smaller than the estimate one has by taking the point evaluation functionals. Indeed, if one is restricted to point evaluation functionals, then the number of such functionals needed is given by the sample complexity of the class $\{(f-g)^2 | f, g \in F\}$, which is $O(\varepsilon^{-\max\{2,p\}})$ when $\mathrm{fat}_\varepsilon(F) = O(\varepsilon^{-p})$. Note that when $p > 2$, this bound is optimal [10]. Hence, allowing linear combinations always yields considerably better bounds than those given by using only point evaluation functionals.

References

1. R.A. Adams: *Sobolev Spaces*, Pure and Applied Mathematics series 69, Academic Press 1975.
2. M.Anthony, P.L. Bartlett: *Neural Network Learning: Theoretical Foundations*, Cambridge University Press, 1999.
3. N. Alon, S. Ben–David, N. Cesa–Bianchi, D. Haussler: Scale sensitive dimensions, uniform convergence and learnability, J. of ACM 44(4), 615–631, 1997.
4. P.L. Bartlett, S.R. Kulkarni, S.E. Posner: Covering numbers for real valued function classes, IEEE transactions on information theory, 43(5), 1721–1724, 1997.
5. P.L. Bartlett, P. Long: More theorems about scale sensitive dimensions and learning, *Proceedings of the 8th annual conference on Computation Learning Theory*, 392-401, 1995.
6. R.M. Dudley: The sizes of compact subsets of Hilbert space and continuity of Gaussian processes, J. of Functional Analysis 1, 290-330, 1967.
7. R.M. Dudley, E. Giné, J. Zinn: Uniform and universal Glivenko–Cantelli classes, J. Theoret. Prob. 4, 485–510, 1991.
8. M. Ledoux, M. Talagrand: *Probability in Banach spaces*, Springer Verlag 1992.
9. J. Lindenstrauss, L. Tzafriri: *Classical Banach Spaces* Vol II, Springer Verlag.
10. S. Mendelson: Rademacher Averages and phase transitions in Glivenko-Cantelli classes, preprint.
11. S. Mendelson, N. Tishby: Statistical Sufficiency for Classes in Empirical L_2 Spaces, Proceedings of the 13th annual conference on Computational Learning Theory, 81-89, 2000.
12. A. Pajor: *Sous espaces ℓ_1^n des espaces de Banach*, 1985
13. G. Pisier: Probabilistic methods in the geometry of Banach spaces, *Probability and Analysis*, Lecture notes in Mathematics 1206, 167–241, Springer Verlag 1986.
14. G. Pisier: *The volume of convex bodies and Banach space geometry*, Cambridge University Press, 1989.
15. M. Talagrand: Sharper bounds for Gaussian and empirical processes, Annals of Probability, 22(1), 28-76, 1994.
16. N. Tomczak–Jaegermann: *Banach–Mazur distance and finite–dimensional operator Ideals*, Pitman monographs and surveys in pure and applied Mathematics 38, 1989
17. V. Vapnik, A. Chervonenkis: Necessary and sufficient conditions for uniform convergence of means to mathematical expectations, Theory Prob. Applic. 26(3), 532-553, 1971
18. A.W. Van–der–Vaart, J.A. Wellner: *Weak convergence and Empirical Processes*, Springer-Verlag, 1996.

Learning Relatively Small Classes

Shahar Mendelson

Computer Sciences Laboratory, RSISE, The Australian National University,
Canberra 0200, Australia
shahar@csl.anu.edu.au

Abstract. We study the sample complexity of proper and improper learning problems with respect to different L_q loss functions. We improve the known estimates for classes which have relatively small covering numbers (log-covering numbers which are polynomial with exponent $p < 2$) with respect to the L_q norm for $q \geq 2$.

1 Introduction

In this article we present sample complexity estimates for proper and improper learning problems of classes with respect to different loss functions, under the assumption that the classes are not "too large". Namely, we assume that their log-covering numbers are polynomial in ε^{-1} with exponent $p < 2$.

The question we explore is the following: let G be a class of functions defined on a probability space (Ω, μ) such that each $g \in G$ maps Ω into $[0, 1]$ and let T be an unknown function which is bounded by 1 (not necessarily a member of G). Recall that a learning rule L is a map which assigns to each sample $S_n = (\omega_1, ..., \omega_n)$ a function $L_{S_n} \in G$. The *learning sample complexity* associated with the q-loss, accuracy ε and confidence δ is the first integer n_0 such that for every $n \geq n_0$, every probability measure μ on (Ω, Σ) and every measurable function bounded by 1,

$$\mu^\infty \left\{ \mathbb{E}_\mu \left| L_{S_n} - T \right|^q \geq \inf_{g \in G} \mathbb{E}_\mu \left| g - T \right|^q + \varepsilon \right\} \leq \delta \ ,$$

where L is any learning rule and μ^∞ is the infinite product measure.

We were motivated by two methods previously used in the investigation of sample complexity [1]. Firstly, there is the standard approach which uses the Glivenko-Cantelli (GC) condition to estimate the sample complexity. By this we mean the following: let G be a class of functions on Ω, let T be the target concept (which, for the sake of simplicity, is assumed to be deterministic), set $1 \leq q < \infty$ and let $F = \{ |g - T|^q \, | g \in G \}$. The Glivenko-Cantelli sample complexity of the class F with respect to accuracy ε and confidence δ is the smallest integer n_0 such that for every $n \geq n_0$,

$$\sup_\mu \mu^\infty \left\{ \sup_{g \in G} \left| \mathbb{E}_\mu \left| g - T \right|^q - \mathbb{E}_{\mu_n} \left| g - T \right|^q \right| \geq \varepsilon \right\} \leq \delta \ ,$$

D. Helmbold and B. Williamson (Eds.): COLT/EuroCOLT 2001, LNAI 2111, pp. 273–288, 2001.

where μ_n is the empirical measure supported on the sample $(\omega_1, ..., \omega_n)$.

Therefore, if g is an "almost" minimizer of the empirical loss $\mathbb{E}_{\mu_n} |g - T|^q$ and if the sample is "large enough" then g is an "almost" minimizer with respect to the average loss. One can show that the learning sample complexity is bounded by the supremum of the GC sample complexities, where the supremum is taken over all possible targets T, bounded by 1. This is true even in the *agnostic* case, in which T may be random (for further details, see [1]).

Lately, it was shown [7] that if the log-covering numbers (resp. the fat shattering dimension) of G are of the order of ε^{-p} for $p \geq 2$, then the GC sample complexity of F is $\Theta(\varepsilon^{-p})$ up to logarithmic factors in ε^{-1}, δ^{-1}.

It is important to emphasize that the learning sample complexity may be established by other means rather than via the GC condition. Hence, it comes with no surprise that there are certain cases in which it is possible to improve this bound on the learning sample complexity. In [5,6] the following case was examined; let F be the loss class given by $\{|g - T|^2 - |T - P_G T|^2 \,|g \in G\}$, where $P_G T$ is a nearest point to T in G with respect to the $L_2(\mu)$ norm. Assume that there is an absolute constant C such that for every $f \in F$, $\mathbb{E}_\mu f^2 \leq C\mathbb{E}_\mu f$, i.e., that it is possible to control the variance of each loss function using its expectation. In this case, the learning sample complexity with accuracy ε and confidence δ is

$$O\Big(\frac{1}{\varepsilon}\Big(\mathrm{fat}_\varepsilon(F) \log^2 \frac{\mathrm{fat}_\varepsilon(F)}{\varepsilon} + \log \frac{1}{\delta}\Big)\Big) .$$

Therefore, if $\mathrm{fat}_\varepsilon(F) = O(\varepsilon^{-p})$ the learning sample complexity is bounded (up to logarithmic factors) by $O(\varepsilon^{-(1+p)})$. If $p < 1$, this estimate is better than the one obtained using the GC sample complexities.

As it turns out, the assumption above is not so far fetched; it is possible to show [5,6] that there are two generic cases in which $\mathbb{E}_\mu f^2 \leq C\mathbb{E}_\mu f$. The first case is when $T \in G$, because it implies that each $f \in F$ is nonnegative. The other case is when G is convex and $q = 2$. Thus, every loss function is given by $|g - T|^2 - |T - P_G T|^2$, where $P_G T$ is the nearest point to T in G with respect to the $L_2(\mu)$ norm.

Here, we combine the ideas used in [6] and in [7] to improve the learning complexity estimates. We show that if

$$\sup_n \sup_{\mu_n} \log N\big(\varepsilon, G, L_2(\mu_n)\big) = O(\varepsilon^{-p})$$

for $p < 2$ and if either $T \in G$ or if G is convex, then the learning sample complexity is $O(\varepsilon^{1+p/2})$ up to logarithmic factors in $\varepsilon^{-1}, \delta^{-1}$. Recently it was shown in [7,8] that for every $1 \leq q < \infty$ there is a constant c_q such that

$$\sup_n \sup_{\mu_n} \log N\big(\varepsilon, G, L_2(\mu_n)\big) \leq c_q \mathrm{fat}_{\frac{\varepsilon}{8}}(G) \log^2 \Big(\frac{2\mathrm{fat}_{\frac{\varepsilon}{8}}(G)}{\varepsilon}\Big) , \quad (1)$$

therefore, the estimates we obtain improve the $O\big(\varepsilon^{-(1+p)}\big)$ established in [6].

Our discussion is divided into three sections. In the second section we investigate the GC condition for classes which have "small" log-covering numbers. We focus the discussion on the case where the deviation in the GC condition is of the same order of magnitude as $\sup_{f \in F} \mathbb{E}_\mu f^2$. The proof is based on estimates on the Rademacher averages (defined below) associated with the class. Next, we explore sufficient conditions which imply that if F is the q-loss class associated with a convex class G, $\mathbb{E}_\mu f^2$ may be controlled by the $\mathbb{E}_\mu f$. We use a geometric approach to prove that if $q \geq 2$ there is some constant B such that for every q-loss function f, $\mathbb{E}_\mu f^2 \leq B(\mathbb{E}_\mu f)^{2/q}$. It turns out that those estimates are the key behind the proof of the learning sample complexity, which is investigated in the fourth and final section.

Next, we turn to some definitions and notation we shall use throughout this article.

If G is a class of functions, T is the target concept and $1 \leq q < \infty$, then for every $g \in G$ let $\ell_q(g)$ be its q-loss function. Thus,

$$\ell_q(g) = |g - T|^q - |g - P_G T|^q \quad ,$$

where $P_G T$ is a nearest element to T in G with respect to the L_q norm. We denote by F the set of loss functions $\ell_q(g)$.

Let G be a GC class. For every $0 < \varepsilon, \delta < 1$, denote by $S_G(\varepsilon, \delta)$ the GC sample complexity of the class G associated with accuracy ε and confidence δ. Let $C^q_{G,T}(\varepsilon, \delta)$ be the learning sample complexity of the class G with respect to the target T and the q-loss, for accuracy ε and confidence δ.

Given a Banach space X, let $B(X)$ be the unit ball of X. If $B \subset X$ is a ball, set $int(B)$ to be the interior of B and ∂B is the boundary of B. The *dual* of X, denoted by X^*, consists of all the bounded linear functionals on X, endowed with the norm $\|x^*\| = \sup_{\|x\|=1} |x^*(x)|$. If $x, y \in X$, the interval $[x, y]$ is defined by $[x, y] = \{tx + (1-t)y | 0 \leq t \leq 1\}$.

For any probability measure μ on a measurable space (Ω, Σ), let $\mathbb{E}_\mu$ be the expectation with respect to μ. $L_q(\mu)$ is the set of functions which satisfy $\mathbb{E}_\mu |f|^q < \infty$, and set $\|f\|_q = (\mathbb{E}|f|^q)^{1/q}$. $L_\infty(\Omega)$ is the space of bounded functions on Ω, with respect to the norm $\|f\|_\infty = \sup_{\omega \in \Omega} |f(\omega)|$. We denote by μ_n an empirical measure supported on a set of n points, hence, $\mu_n = \frac{1}{n}\sum_{i=1}^n \delta_{\omega_i}$, where δ_{ω_i} is the point evaluation functional at $\{\omega_i\}$.

If (X, d) is a metric space, set $B(x, r)$ to be the closed ball centered at x with radius r. Recall that if $F \subset X$, the ε-covering number of F, denoted by $N(\varepsilon, F, d)$, is the minimal number of open balls with radius $\varepsilon > 0$ (with respect to the metric d) needed to cover F. A set $A \subset X$ is said to be an ε-cover of F if the union of open balls $\bigcup_{a \in A} B(a, \varepsilon)$ contains F. In cases where the metric d is clear, we shall denote the covering numbers of F by $N(\varepsilon, F)$.

It is possible to show that the covering numbers of the q-loss class F are essentially the same as those of G.

Lemma 1. *Let $G \subset B\big(L_\infty(\Omega)\big)$ and let F be the q-loss class associated with G. Then, for any probability measure μ,*

$$\log N\big(\varepsilon, F, L_2(\mu)\big) \leq \log N\big(\varepsilon/q, G, L_2(\mu)\big) \; .$$

The proof of this lemma is standard and is omitted.

Next, we define the Rademacher averages of a given class of functions, which is the main tool we use in the analysis of GC classes.

Definition 1. *Let F be a class of functions and let μ be a probability measure on Ω. Set*

$$\bar{R}_{n,\mu} = \mathbb{E}_\mu \mathbb{E}_\varepsilon \sup_{f \in F} \frac{1}{\sqrt{n}} \left| \sum_{i=1}^n \varepsilon_i f(X_i) \right| ,$$

where ε_i are independent Rademacher random variables (i.e. symmetric, $\{-1,1\}$ valued) and (X_i) are independent, distributed according to μ.

It is possible to estimate $\bar{R}_{n,\mu}$ of a given class using its $L_2(\mu_n)$ covering numbers. The key result behind this estimate is the following theorem which is originally due to Dudley for Gaussian processes, and was extended to the more general setting of subgaussian processes [10]. We shall formulate it only in the case of Rademacher processes.

Theorem 1. *There is an absolute constant C such that for every probability measure μ, any integer n and every sample $(\omega_i)_{i=1}^n$*

$$\mathbb{E}_\varepsilon \sup_{f \in F} n^{-\frac{1}{2}} \left| \sum_{i=1}^n \varepsilon_i f(\omega_i) \right| \leq C \int_0^\delta \log^{\frac{1}{2}} N\big(\varepsilon, F, L_2(\mu_n)\big) d\varepsilon ,$$

where

$$\delta = \sup_{f \in F} \left(\frac{1}{n} \sum_{i=1}^n f^2(\omega_i) \right)^{\frac{1}{2}}$$

and μ_n is the empirical measure supported on the given sample $(\omega_1, ..., \omega_n)$.

Finally, throughout this paper, all absolute constants are assumed to be positive and are denoted by C or c. Their values may change from line to line or even within the same line.

We end the introduction with a statement of our main result.

Theorem 2. *Let $G \subset B\big(L_\infty(\Omega)\big)$ such that*

$$\sup_n \sup_{\mu_n} \log N\big(\varepsilon, G, L_2(\mu_n)\big) \leq \gamma \varepsilon^{-p}$$

for some $p < 2$ and let $T \in B\big(L_\infty(\Omega)\big)$ be the target concept. If $1 \leq q < \infty$ and either

(1) $T \in G$, or
(2) G is convex,

there are constants $C_{q,p,\gamma}$ which depend only on q, p, γ such that

$$\mathcal{C}^q_{G,T}(\varepsilon,\delta) \leq C_{q,p,\gamma}\Big(\frac{1}{\varepsilon}\Big)^{1+\frac{p}{2}}\Big(1+\log\frac{2}{\delta}\Big).$$

Also, if

$$\sup_n \sup_{\mu_n} N\big(\varepsilon, G, L_2(\mu_n)\big) \leq \Big(\frac{\gamma}{\varepsilon}\Big)^d$$

and either (1) or (2) hold, then

$$\mathcal{C}^q_{G,T}(\varepsilon,\delta) \leq C_{q,p,\gamma} d\Big(\frac{1}{\varepsilon}\log\frac{2}{\varepsilon}+\log\frac{2}{\delta}\Big).$$

There are numerous cases in which Theorem 2 applies. We shall name a few of them. In the proper case, Theorem 2 may be used, for example, if G is a VC class or a VC subgraph class [10]. Another case is if G satisfies that $\mathrm{fat}_\varepsilon(G) = O(\varepsilon^{-p})$ [7]. In both cases the covering numbers of G satisfy the conditions of the theorem. In the improper case, one may consider, for example, convex hulls of VC classes [10] and many Kernel Machines [11].

2 GC for Classes with "Small" Variance

Although the "normal" GC sample complexity of a class is $\Omega(\varepsilon^{-2})$ when one allows the deviation to be arbitrary small, it is possible to obtain better estimates when the deviation we are interested in is roughly the largest variance of a member of the class. As we demonstrate in the final section, this fact is very important in the analysis of learning sample complexities. The first step in that direction is the next result, which is due to Talagrand [9].

Theorem 3. *Assume that F is a class of functions into $[0,1]$. Let*

$$\sigma^2 = \sup_{f\in F} \mathbb{E}_\mu (f-\mathbb{E}_\mu f)^2, \quad S_n = n\sigma^2 + \sqrt{n}\bar{R}_{n,\mu} \ .$$

For every $L, S > 0$ and $t > 0$ define

$$\phi_{L,S}(t) = \begin{cases} \frac{t^2}{L^2 S} & \text{if } t \leq LS \\ \frac{t}{L}\big(\log\frac{et}{LS}\big)^{\frac{1}{2}} & \text{if } t \geq LS \ . \end{cases}$$

There is an absolute constant K such that if $t \geq K\sqrt{n}\bar{R}_{n,\mu}$, then

$$\mu\left\{\left\|\sum_{i=1}^n f(X_i) - n\mathbb{E}_\mu f\right\|_F \geq t\right\} \leq \exp\big(-\phi_{K,S}(t)\big) \ .$$

In the next two results, we present an estimate on the Rademacher averages $\bar{R}_{n,\mu}$ using data on the "largest" variance of a member of the class and on the covering numbers of F in empirical L_2 spaces. We divide the results to the case where the covering numbers are polynomial in ε^{-1} and the case where the log-covering numbers are polynomial is ε^{-1} with exponent $p < 2$.

Lemma 2. *Let F be a class of functions into $[0,1]$ and set $\tau^2 = \sup_{f\in F} \mathbb{E}_\mu f^2$. Assume that there are $\gamma \geq 1$ and $d \geq 1$ such that for every empirical measure μ_n,*

$$N(\varepsilon, F, L_2(\mu_n)) \leq (\gamma/\varepsilon)^d \ .$$

Then, there is a constant C_γ, which depends only on γ, such that

$$\bar{R}_{n,\mu} \leq C_\gamma \max\left\{ \frac{d}{\sqrt{n}} \log \frac{1}{\tau}, \sqrt{d}\tau \log^{\frac{1}{2}} \frac{1}{\tau} \right\} .$$

An important part of the proof is the following result, again, due to Talagrand [9], on the expectation of the diameter of F when considered as a subset of $L_2(\mu_n)$.

Lemma 3. *Let $F \subset B(L_\infty(\Omega))$ and set $\tau^2 = \sup_{f\in F} \mathbb{E}_\mu f^2$. Then, for every probability measure μ, every integer n, and every $(X_i)_{i=1}^n$ which are independent, distributed according to μ,*

$$\mathbb{E}_\mu \sup_{f\in F} \left| \sum_{i=1}^n f^2(X_i) \right| \leq n\tau^2 + 8\sqrt{n}\bar{R}_{n,\mu} \ .$$

Proof (of Lemma 2). Set $Y = n^{-1} \sup_{f\in F} \sum_{i=1}^n f^2(X_i)$. By Theorem 1 there is an absolute constant C such that for every sample $(X_1, ..., X_n)$

$$\begin{aligned} \frac{1}{\sqrt{n}} \mathbb{E}_\varepsilon \sup_{f\in F} \left| \sum_{i=1}^n \varepsilon_i f(X_i) \right| &\leq C \int_0^{\sqrt{Y}} \log^{\frac{1}{2}} N(\varepsilon, F, L_2(\mu_n)) d\varepsilon \\ &= C\sqrt{d} \int_0^{\sqrt{Y}} \log^{\frac{1}{2}} \frac{\gamma}{\varepsilon} d\varepsilon \ . \end{aligned}$$

It is easy to see that there is some absolute constant C_γ such that for every $0 < x \leq 1$,

$$\int_0^x \log^{\frac{1}{2}} \frac{\gamma}{\varepsilon} d\varepsilon \leq 2x \log^{\frac{1}{2}} \frac{C_\gamma}{x} \ ,$$

and $v(x) = x^{\frac{1}{2}} \log^{\frac{1}{2}}(C_\gamma/x)$ is increasing and concave in $(0, 10)$. Since $Y \leq 1$,

$$\mathbb{E}_\varepsilon \sup_{f\in F} \frac{1}{\sqrt{n}} \left| \sum_{i=1}^n \varepsilon_i f(X_i) \right| \leq C\sqrt{d} Y^{\frac{1}{2}} \log^{\frac{1}{2}} \frac{C_\gamma}{Y^{\frac{1}{2}}} \ .$$

Also, since $v(x)$ is increasing and concave in $(0, 10)$, and since $\mathbb{E}Y \leq 9$, then by Jensen's inequality, Lemma 3 and the fact that v is increasing, there is a constant C_γ which depends only on γ, such that

$$\mathbb{E}_\mu\Big(Y^{\frac{1}{2}}\log^{\frac{1}{2}}\frac{C_\gamma}{Y^{\frac{1}{2}}}\Big) = C_\gamma \mathbb{E}_\mu\Big(Y^{\frac{1}{2}}\log^{\frac{1}{2}}\frac{2}{Y}\Big) \leq C_\gamma(\mathbb{E}_\mu Y)^{\frac{1}{2}}\log^{\frac{1}{2}}\frac{2}{\mathbb{E}_\mu Y}$$
$$\leq C_\gamma\Big(\tau^2 + 8\frac{\bar{R}_{n,\mu}}{\sqrt{n}}\Big)^{\frac{1}{2}}\log^{\frac{1}{2}}\frac{2}{\tau^2+\frac{8\bar{R}_{n,\mu}}{\sqrt{n}}}$$
$$\leq C_\gamma\Big(\tau^2 + \frac{8\bar{R}_{n,\mu}}{\sqrt{n}}\Big)^{\frac{1}{2}}\log^{\frac{1}{2}}\frac{2}{\tau} \ .$$

Therefore,

$$\bar{R}_{n,\mu} \leq C_\gamma\sqrt{d}\Big(\tau^2 + \frac{8\bar{R}_{n,\mu}}{\sqrt{n}}\Big)^{\frac{1}{2}}\log^{\frac{1}{2}}\frac{2}{\tau} \ ,$$

and our claim follows from a straightforward computation.

Next, we explore the case in which the log-covering numbers are polynomial with exponent $p < 2$.

Lemma 4. *Let F be a class of functions into $[0,1]$ and set $\tau^2 = \sup_{f\in F}\mathbb{E}_\mu f^2$. Assume that there are $\gamma \geq 2$ and $p < 2$ such that for every empirical measure μ_n,*

$$\log N\big(\varepsilon, F, L_2(\mu_n)\big) \leq \gamma\varepsilon^{-p} \ .$$

Then, there is constant $C_{p,\gamma}$ which depend only on p and on γ such that

$$\bar{R}_{n,\mu} \leq C_{p,\gamma}\max\{n^{-\frac{1}{2}\frac{2-p}{2+p}}, \tau^{1-\frac{p}{2}}\} \ .$$

Proof. Again, let $Y = n^{-1}\sup_{f\in F}\sum_{i=1}^n f^2(X_i)$. For every realization of $(X_i)_{i=1}^n$, set μ_n to be the empirical measure supported on $X_1, ..., X_n$. By Theorem 1 for every fixed sample, there is an absolute constant C, such that

$$\frac{1}{\sqrt{n}}\mathbb{E}_\varepsilon\sup_{f\in F}\Big|\sum_{i=1}^n \varepsilon_i f(X_i)\Big| \leq C\int_0^{\sqrt{Y}}\log^{\frac{1}{2}} N\big(\varepsilon, F, L_2(\mu_n)\big)d\varepsilon$$
$$\leq \frac{C\gamma^{\frac{1}{2}}}{1-p/2}\Big(\frac{1}{n}\sup_{f\in F}\sum_{i=1}^n f^2(X_i)\Big)^{\frac{1}{2}(1-\frac{p}{2})} \ .$$

Taking the expectation with respect to μ and by Jensen's inequality and Lemma 3,

$$\bar{R}_{n,\mu} \leq C_{p,\gamma}\Big(\frac{1}{n}\mathbb{E}_\mu\sup_{f\in F}\sum_{i=1}^n f^2(X_i)\Big)^{\frac{1}{2}(1-\frac{p}{2})} \leq \Big(\tau^2 + \frac{8\bar{R}_{n,\mu}}{\sqrt{n}}\Big)^{\frac{1}{2}(1-\frac{p}{2})} \ .$$

Therefore,

$$\bar{R}_{n,\mu} \leq C_{p,\gamma}\Big(\tau^2 + \frac{8\bar{R}_{n,\mu}}{\sqrt{n}}\Big)^{\frac{1}{2}(1-\frac{p}{2})}$$

and the claim follows.

Combining Theorem 3, Lemma 2 and Lemma 4, we obtain the following deviation estimate:

Theorem 4. *Let F be a class of functions whose range is contained in $[0,1]$ and set $\tau^2 = \sup_{f \in F} \mathbb{E}_\mu f^2$.*

If there are $\gamma > 0$ and $d \geq 1$ such that

$$\log N\big(\varepsilon, F, L_2(\mu_n)\big) \leq d \log \gamma/\varepsilon$$

for every empirical measure μ_n and every $\varepsilon > 0$, then there is a constant C_γ, which depends only on γ, such that for every $k > 0$ and every $0 < \delta < 1$,

$$S_F(k\tau^2, \delta) \leq C_\gamma d \max\{k^{-1}, k^{-2}\}\Big(\frac{1}{\tau^2}\log\frac{2}{\tau} + \log\frac{2}{\delta}\Big) .$$

If there are $\gamma \geq 1$ and $p < 2$ such that

$$\log N\big(\varepsilon, F, L_2(\mu_n)\big) \leq \gamma \varepsilon^p$$

for every empirical measure μ_n and every $\varepsilon > 0$, then there are constants $C_{p,\gamma}$ which depend only on p and γ, such that for every $k > 0$ and every $0 < \delta < 1$,

$$S_F(k\tau^2, \delta) \leq C_{p,\gamma} \max\{k^{-1}, k^{-2}\}\Big(\frac{1}{\tau^2}\Big)^{1+\frac{p}{2}}\Big(1 + \log\frac{2}{\delta}\Big) .$$

Since the proof follows from a straightforward (yet tedious) calculation, we omit its details.

3 Dominating the Variance

The key assumption used in the proof of learning sample complexity in [6] was that there is some $B > 0$ such that for every loss function f, $\mathbb{E}_\mu f^2 \leq B\mathbb{E}_\mu f$. Though this is easily satisfied in proper learning (because each f is nonnegative), it is far from obvious whether the same holds in the improper setting. In [6] it was observed that if G is convex and F is the squared-loss class then $\mathbb{E}_\mu f^2 \leq B\mathbb{E}_\mu f$, and B depends on the L_∞ bound on the members of G and the target. The question we study is whether the same kind of bound can be established in other L_q norms. We will show that if $q \geq 2$ and if F is the q-loss function associated with G, there is some B such that for every $f \in F$, $\mathbb{E}_\mu f^2 \leq B(\mathbb{E}_\mu f)^{\frac{q}{2}}$. Our proof is based on a geometric characterization of the nearest point map onto a convex subset of L_q spaces. This fact was used in [6] for $q = 2$, but no emphasis was put on the geometric idea behind it. Our methods enable us to obtain the bound in L_q for $q \geq 2$.

Formally, let $1 \leq q < \infty$ and set G to be a compact convex subset of $L_q(\mu)$ such that each $g \in G$ maps Ω into $[0,1]$. Let F be the q-loss class associated with G and T, which is also assumed to have a range contained in $[0,1]$. Hence, each $f \in F$ is given by $f = |T-g|^q - |P_G T - T|^q$, where $P_G T$ is the nearest point to T in G with respect to the $L_q(\mu)$ norm.

Since we are interested in GC sets with "small" covering numbers in L_q for every $1 \leq q < \infty$ (e.g. $fat_\varepsilon(G) = O(\varepsilon^{-p})$ for $p < 2$), the assumption that G is compact in L_q follows if G is closed in L_q [7].

It is possible to show (see appendix A) that if $1 < q < \infty$ and if $G \subset L_q$ is convex and compact, the nearest point map onto G is a well defined map, i.e., each $T \in L_q$ has a unique best approximation in G.

We start our analysis by an proving an upper bound on $\mathbb{E}_\mu f^2$:

Lemma 5. *Let $g \in G$, assume that $1 < q < \infty$ and set $f = \ell_q(g)$. Then,*

$$\mathbb{E}_\mu f^2 \leq q^2 \mathbb{E}_\mu \left| g - P_G T \right|^2 .$$

Proof. Given any $\omega \in \Omega$, apply Lagrange's Theorem to the function $y = |x|^q$ for $x_1 = g(\omega) - T(\omega)$ and $x_2 = P_G T(\omega) - T(\omega)$. The result follows by taking the expectation and since $|x_1|, |x_2| \leq 1$.

The next step, which is to bound $\mathbb{E}_\mu f$ from below, is considerably more difficult. We shall require the following definitions which are standard in Banach spaces theory [2,4]:

Definition 2. *A Banach space is called strictly convex if for every $x, y \in X$ such that $\|x\|, \|y\| = 1$, $\|x + y\| < 2$. X is called uniformly convex if there is a positive function $\delta(\varepsilon)$ such that for every $0 < \varepsilon < 2$ and every $x, y \in X$ for which $\|x\|, \|y\| \leq 1$ and $\|x - y\| \geq \varepsilon$, $\|x + y\| \leq 2 - 2\delta(\varepsilon)$. Thus,*

$$\delta(\varepsilon) = \inf \left\{ 1 - \frac{1}{2} \|x + y\| \;\middle|\; \|x\|, \|y\| \leq 1, \; \|x - y\| \geq \varepsilon \right\} .$$

The function $\delta(\varepsilon)$ is called the modulus of convexity of X.

It is easy to see that X is strictly convex if and only if its unit sphere does not contain intervals. Also, if X is uniformly convex then it is strictly convex. Using the modulus of convexity one can provide a lower bound on the distance of an average of elements on the unit sphere of X and the sphere.

It was shown in [3] that for every $1 < q \leq 2$ the modulus of convexity of L_q is given by $\delta_q(\varepsilon) = (q-1)\varepsilon^2/8 + o(\varepsilon^2)$ and if $q \geq 2$ it is given by $\delta_q(\varepsilon) = 1 - \left(1 - (\varepsilon/2)^q\right)^{1/q}$.

The next lemma enables one to prove the lower estimate on $\mathbb{E}_\mu f$. The proof of the lemma is based on several ideas commonly used in the field of convex geometry, and is presented in appendix A

Lemma 6. *Let X be a uniformly convex, smooth Banach space with a modulus of convexity δ_X. Let $G \subset X$ be compact and convex, set $T \notin G$ and $d = \|T - P_G T\|$. Then, for every $g \in G$, $\delta_X(d_g^{-1} \|g - P_G T\|) \leq 1 - d/d_g$, where $d_g = \|T - g\|$.*

Corollary 1. *Let $q \geq 2$ and assume that G is a compact convex subset of the unit ball of $L_q(\mu)$, which consists of functions whose range is contained in $[0, 1]$.*

Let T be the target function which also maps Ω into $[0,1]$. If F is the q-loss class associated with G and T, there are constants C_q which depend only on q such that for every $g \in G$, $\mathbb{E}_\mu f^2 \leq C_q (\mathbb{E}_\mu f)^{2/q}$, where f is the q-loss function associated with g.

Proof. Recall that the modulus of uniform convexity of L_q for $q \geq 2$ is $\delta_q(\varepsilon) = 1 - \left(1 - (\varepsilon/2)^q\right)^{1/q}$. By Lemma 6 it follows that

$$1 - \left(\frac{\|g - P_G T\|}{2d_g}\right)^q \geq \left(\frac{d}{d_g}\right)^q .$$

Note that $\ell_q(g) = d_g^q - d^q$, hence

$$f = \ell_q(g) = d_g^q - d^q \geq 2^{-q} \mathbb{E}_\mu |g - P_G T|^q .$$

By Lemma 5 and since $\|f\|_2 \leq \|f\|_q$,

$$\mathbb{E}_\mu f^2 \leq q^2 \mathbb{E}_\mu |g - P_G T|^2 \leq q^2 \left(\mathbb{E}_\mu |g - P_G T|^q\right)^{\frac{2}{q}} \leq 4q^2 \left(\mathbb{E}_\mu f\right)^{\frac{2}{q}} .$$

4 Learning Sample Complexity

Unlike the GC sample complexity, the behaviour of the *learning sample complexity* is not monotone, in the sense that even if $H \subset G$, it is possible that the learning sample complexity associated with G may be *smaller* than that associated with F. This is due to the fact that a well behaved geometric structure of the class (e.g. convexity) enables one to derive additional data regarding the loss functions associated with the class. We will show that the learning sample complexity is determined by the GC sample complexity for a class of functions H such that $\sup_{h \in H} \mathbb{E}_\mu h^2$ is roughly the same as the desired accuracy.

We shall formulate results in two cases. The first theorem deals with proper learning (i.e. $T \in G$). In the second, we discuss improper learning. We present a proof only for the second theorem.

Let us introduce the following notation: for a fixed $\varepsilon > 0$ and given any empirical measure μ_n, let $f^*_{\mu_n}$ be some $f \in F$ such that $\mathbb{E}_{\mu_n} f^*_{\mu_n} \leq \varepsilon/2$. Thus, if $g \in G$ such that $\ell_q(g) = f^*_{\mu_n}$ then g is an "almost minimizer" of the empirical loss.

Theorem 5. *Assume that G is a class whose elements map Ω into $[0,1]$ and fix $T \in G$. Assume that $1 \leq q < \infty$, $\gamma > 1$, and let F be the q-loss class associated with G and T. Assume further that $p < 2$ and that for every integer n and any empirical measure μ_n, $\log N\left(\varepsilon, G, L_2(\mu_n)\right) \leq \gamma \varepsilon^{-p}$ for every $\varepsilon > 0$. Then, there is a constant $C_{p,q,\gamma}$ which depends only on p, q and γ such that if*

$$n \geq C_{p,q,\gamma} \left(\frac{1}{\varepsilon}\right)^{1+\frac{p}{2}} \left(1 + \log \frac{1}{\delta}\right) ,$$

then $Pr\left\{\mathbb{E}_\mu f^*_{\mu_n} \geq \varepsilon\right\} \leq \delta$.

Now, we turn to the improper case.

Theorem 6. *Let G, F and q be as in Theorem 5 and assume that $T \notin G$. Assume further that G is convex and that there is some B such that for every $f \in F$, $\mathbb{E}_\mu f^2 \leq B(\mathbb{E}_\mu f)^{q/2}$ Then, the assertion of Theorem 5 remains true.*

Remark 1. The key assumption here is that $\mathbb{E}_\mu f^2 \leq B(\mathbb{E}_\mu f)^{2/q}$ for every loss function f. Recall that in Section 3 we explored this issue. Combining Theorem 5 and Theorem 6 with the results of Section 3 gives us the promised estimate on the learning sample complexity.

Before proving the theorem we will need the following observations. Assume that $q \geq 2$ and let F be the q-loss class. First, note that

$$\begin{aligned} Pr\Big\{\mathbb{E}_\mu f^*_{\mu_n} \geq \varepsilon\Big\} &\leq Pr\Big\{\exists f \in F,\ \mathbb{E}_\mu f \geq \varepsilon,\ \mathbb{E}_\mu f^2 < \varepsilon,\ \mathbb{E}_{\mu_n} f \leq \varepsilon/2\Big\} \\ &\quad + Pr\Big\{\exists f \in F,\ \mathbb{E}_\mu f \geq \varepsilon,\ \mathbb{E}_\mu f^2 \geq \varepsilon,\ \mathbb{E}_{\mu_n} f \leq \varepsilon/2\Big\} \\ &= (1) + (2)\ . \end{aligned}$$

If $\mathbb{E}_\mu f \geq \varepsilon$ then

$$\mathbb{E}_\mu f \geq \frac{1}{2}(\mathbb{E}_\mu f + \varepsilon) \geq \frac{1}{2}\mathbb{E}_\mu f + \mathbb{E}_{\mu_n} f\ .$$

Therefore, $|\mathbb{E}_\mu f - \mathbb{E}_{\mu_n} f| \geq \frac{1}{2}\mathbb{E}_\mu f \geq \varepsilon/2$, and thus

$$\begin{aligned} (1) + (2) &\leq Pr\Big\{\exists f \in F,\ \mathbb{E}_\mu f^2 < \varepsilon,\ |\mathbb{E}_\mu f - \mathbb{E}_{\mu_n} f| \geq \frac{\varepsilon}{2}\Big\} \\ &\quad + Pr\Big\{\exists f \in F,\ \mathbb{E}_\mu f \geq \varepsilon,\ \mathbb{E}_\mu f^2 \geq \varepsilon,\ |\mathbb{E}_\mu f - \mathbb{E}_{\mu_n} f| \geq \frac{1}{2}\mathbb{E}_\mu f\Big\}\ . \end{aligned}$$

Let $\alpha = 2 - 2/q$ and set

$$H = \Big\{\frac{\varepsilon^\alpha f}{\mathbb{E}_\mu f} | f \in F,\ \mathbb{E}_\mu f \geq \varepsilon,\ \mathbb{E}_\mu f^2 \geq \varepsilon\Big\}\ . \tag{2}$$

Since $q \geq 2$ then $\alpha \geq 1$, and since $\varepsilon < 1$, each $h \in H$ maps Ω into $[0,1]$. Also, if $\mathbb{E}_\mu f^2 \leq B(\mathbb{E}_\mu f)^{q/2}$ then

$$\mathbb{E}_\mu h^2 \leq B\frac{\varepsilon^{2\alpha}}{(\mathbb{E}_\mu f)^{2-2/q}} \leq B\varepsilon^\alpha\ .$$

Therefore,

$$\begin{aligned} Pr\Big\{\mathbb{E}_\mu f^*_{\mu_n} \geq \varepsilon\Big\} &\leq Pr\Big\{\exists f \in F,\ \mathbb{E}_\mu f^2 < \varepsilon,\ |\mathbb{E}_\mu f - \mathbb{E}_{\mu_n} f| \geq \frac{\varepsilon}{2}\Big\} \\ &\quad + Pr\Big\{\exists h \in H,\ \mathbb{E}_\mu h^2 \leq B\varepsilon^\alpha,\ |\mathbb{E}_\mu h - \mathbb{E}_{\mu_n} h| \geq \frac{\varepsilon^\alpha}{2}\Big\} \end{aligned} \tag{3}$$

In both cases we are interested in a GC condition at a scale which is roughly the "largest" variance of the member of a class. This is the exact question which was investigated in Section 2.

The only problem in applying Theorem 4 directly to the class H is the fact that we do not have an a-priori bound on the covering numbers of that class. The question we need to tackle before proceeding is how to estimate the covering numbers of H, given that the covering numbers of F are well behaved. To that end we need to use the specific structure of F, namely, that it is a q-loss class associated with the class G.

We divide our discussion to two parts. First we deal with proper learning, in which each loss function is given by $f = |g - T|^p$ and no specific assumptions are needed on the structure of G. Then, we turn to the improper case, and assume that G is convex and F is the q-loss class for $1 \leq q < \infty$.

To handle both cases, we require the following simple definition:

Definition 3. *Let X be a normed space and let $A \subset X$. We say that A is star-shaped with center x if for every $a \in A$ the interval $[a, x] \subset A$. Given A and x, denote by $star(A, x)$ the union of all the intervals $[a, x]$, where $a \in A$.*

The next lemma shows that the covering numbers of $star(A, x)$ are almost the same as those of A.

Lemma 7. *Let X be a normed space and let $A \subset B(X)$. Then, for any $\|x\| \leq 1$ and every $\varepsilon > 0$, $N\big(2\varepsilon, star(A, x)\big) \leq 2N\big(\varepsilon, A\big)/\varepsilon$.*

Proof. Fix $\varepsilon > 0$ and let $y_1, ..., y_k$ be an ε-cover of A. Note that for any $a \in A$ and any $z \in [a, x]$ there is some $z' \in [y_i, x]$ such that $\|z' - z\| < \varepsilon$. Hence, an ε-cover of the union $\cup_{i=1}^{n} [y_i, z]$ is a 2ε-cover for $star(A, x)$. Since for every i, $\|x - y_i\| \leq 2$ it follows that each interval may be covered by $2\varepsilon^{-1}$ balls with radius ε and our claim follows.

Lemma 8. *Let G be a class of functions into $[0, 1]$, set $1 \leq q < \infty$ and denote $F = \{\ell_q(g) | g \in G\}$, where $T \in G$. Let $\alpha = 2 - 2/q$ and put $H = \{\frac{\varepsilon^\alpha f}{\mathbb{E}_\mu f} | f \in F\}$. Then, for every $\varepsilon > 0$ and every empirical measure μ_n,*

$$\log N\big(2\varepsilon, H, L_2(\mu_n)\big) \leq \log \frac{2}{\varepsilon} + \log N\big(\frac{\varepsilon}{q}, G, L_2(\mu_n)\big) \ .$$

Proof. Since every $h \in H$ is of the from $h = \alpha_f f$ where $0 < \alpha \leq 1$ then $H \subset star(F, 0)$. Thus, by Lemma 7,

$$\log N\big(2\varepsilon, H, L_2(\mu_n)\big) \leq \log \frac{2}{\varepsilon} + \log N\big(\varepsilon, F, L_2(\mu_n)\big) \ .$$

Our assertion follows from Lemma 1.

Now, we turn to the improper case.

Lemma 9. *Let G be a convex class of functions and let be F its q-loss class for some $1 \leq q < \infty$. Assume that α and H are as in Lemma 8. If there are $\gamma \geq 1$ and $p < 2$ such that for any empirical measure μ_n and every $\varepsilon > 0$, $\log N\big(\varepsilon, G, L_2(\mu_n)\big) \leq \gamma\varepsilon^{-p}$, then there are constants $c_{p,q}$ which depend only on p and q, such that for every $\varepsilon > 0$,*

$$\log N\big(\varepsilon, H, L_2(\mu_n)\big) \leq \log N\big(\frac{\varepsilon}{4q}, G, L_2(\mu_n)\big) + 2\log\frac{4}{\varepsilon} .$$

Proof. Again, every member of H is given by $\kappa_f f$, where $0 < \kappa_f < 1$. Hence,

$$H \subset \{\kappa\ell_q(g) | g \in G,\ \kappa \in [0,1]\} \equiv \mathcal{Q} .$$

By the definition of the q-loss function, it is possible to decompose $\mathcal{Q} = \mathcal{Q}_1 + \mathcal{Q}_2$, where

$$\mathcal{Q}_1 = \left\{\kappa\,|g - T|^q \,\middle|\, \kappa \in [0,1],\ g \in G\right\} \text{ and } \mathcal{Q}_2 = \left\{-\kappa\,|T - P_G T|^q \,\middle|\, \kappa \in [0,1]\right\} .$$

Note that T and $P_G T$ map Ω into $[0,1]$, hence $|T - P_G T|^q$ is bounded by 1 pointwise. Therefore, $\mathcal{Q}_2$ is contained in an interval whose length is at most 1, implying that for any probability measure μ,

$$N\big(\varepsilon, \mathcal{Q}_2, L_2(\mu)\big) \leq \frac{2}{\varepsilon} .$$

Let $V = \{|g - T|^q \,| g \in G\}$. Since every $g \in G$ and T map Ω into $[0,1]$ then $V \subset B\big(L_\infty(\Omega)\big)$. Therefore, by Lemma 1,

$$N\big(\varepsilon, V, L_2(\mu)\big) \leq N\big(\varepsilon/q, G, L_2(\mu)\big)$$

for every probability measure μ and every $\varepsilon > 0$. Also, $\mathcal{Q}_1 \subset \text{star}(V, 0)$, thus for any $\varepsilon > 0$,

$$N\big(\varepsilon, \mathcal{Q}_1, L_2(\mu)\big) \leq \frac{2N\big(\frac{\varepsilon}{2}, V, L_2(\mu)\big)}{\varepsilon} \leq \frac{2N\big(\frac{\varepsilon}{2q}, G, L_2(\mu)\big)}{\varepsilon} ,$$

which suffices, since one can combine the separate covers for $\mathcal{Q}_1$ and $\mathcal{Q}_2$ to form a cover for H.

Proof (of Theorem 6). The proof follows immediately from (3), Theorem 4 and Lemma 8 for the proper case and Lemma 9 in the improper case.

Remark 2. It is possible to prove an analogous result to Theorem 6 when the covering numbers of G are polynomial; indeed, if

$$\sup_n \sup_{\mu_n} \log N\big(\varepsilon, G, L_2(\mu_n)\big) \leq Cd\log\frac{\gamma}{\varepsilon}$$

then the sample complexity required is

$$C^q_{G,T}(\varepsilon, \delta) = C_{q,\gamma} d\Big(\frac{1}{\varepsilon}\log\frac{2}{\varepsilon} + \log\frac{2}{\delta}\Big) ,$$

where $C_{q,\gamma}$ depend only on γ and q.

A Convexity

In this appendix we present the definitions and preliminary results needed for the proof of Lemma 6. All the definitions are standard and my be found in any basic textbook in functional analysis, e.g., [4].

Definition 4. *Given $A, B \subset X$ we say that a nonzero functional $x^* \in X^*$ separates A and B if* $\inf_{a \in A} x^*(x) \geq \sup_{b \in B} x^*(b)$.

It is easy to see that x^* separates A and B if and only if there is some $\alpha \in \mathbb{R}$ such that for every $a \in A$ and $b \in B$, $x^*(b) \leq \alpha \leq x^*(a)$. In that case, the hyperplane $H = \{x | x^*(x) = \alpha\}$ separates A and B. We denote the closed "positive" halfspace $\{x | x^*(x) \geq \alpha\}$ by H^+ and the "negative" one by H^-. By the Hahn-Banach Theorem, if A and B are closed, convex and disjoint there is a hyperplane (equivalently, a functional) which separates A and B.

Definition 5. *Let $A \subset X$, we say that the hyperplane H supports A in $a \in A$ if $a \in H$ and either $A \subset H^+$ or $A \subset H^-$.*

By the Hahn-Banach Theorem, if $B \subset X$ is a ball then for every $x \in \partial B$ there is a hyperplane which supports B in x. Equivalently, there is some x^*, $\|x^*\| = 1$ and $\alpha \in \mathbb{R}$ such that $x^*(x) = \alpha$ and for every $y \in B$, $x^*(y) \geq \alpha$.

Given a line $V = \{tx + (1-t)y | t \in \mathbb{R}\}$, we say it supports a ball $B \subset X$ in z if $z \in V \cap B$ and $V \cap int(B) = \emptyset$. By the Hahn-Banach Theorem, if V supports B in z, there is a hyperplane which contains V and supports B in z.

Definition 6. *A Banach space X is called smooth if for any $x \in X$ there is a unique functional $x^* \in X^*$, such that $\|x^*\| = 1$ and $x^*(x) = \|x\|$.*

Thus, a Banach space is smooth if and only if for every x such that $\|x\| = 1$, there is a unique hyperplane which supports the unit ball in x. It is possible to show [4] that for every $1 < q < \infty$, L_q is smooth.

We shall be interested in the properties of the nearest point map onto a compact convex set in "nice" Banach spaces, which is the subject of the following lemma.

Lemma 10. *Let X be a strictly convex space and let $G \subset X$ be convex and compact. Then every $x \in X$ has a unique nearest point in G.*

Proof. Fix some $x \in X$ and set $R = \inf_{g \in G} \|g - x\|$. By the compactness of G and the fact that the norm is continuous, there is some $g_0 \in G$ for which the infimum is attained, i.e., $R = \|g_0 - x\|$.

To show uniqueness, assume that there is some other $g \in G$ for which $\|g - x\| = R$. Since G is convex then $g_1 = (g + g_0)/2 \in G$, and by the strict convexity of the norm, $\|g_1 - x\| < R$, which is impossible.

Lemma 11. *Let X be a strictly convex, smooth Banach space and let $G \subset X$ be compact and convex. Assume that $x \notin G$ and set $y = P_G x$ to be the nearest point to x in G. If $R = \|x - y\|$ then the hyperplane supporting the ball $B = B(x, R)$ at y separates B and G.*

Proof. Clearly, we may assume that $x = 0$ and that $R = 1$. Therefore, if x^* is the normalized functional which supports B at y, then for every $x \in B$, $x^*(x) \leq 1$. Let $H = \{x | x^*(x) = 1\}$, set H^- to be the open halfspace $\{x | x^*(x) < 1\}$ and assume that there is some $g \in G$ such that $x^*(g) < 1$. Since G is convex then for every $0 \leq t < 1$, $ty + (1-t)g \in G \cap H^-$. Moreover, since y is the unique nearest point to 0 in G and since X is strictly convex, $[g, y] \cap B = \{y\}$, otherwise there would have been some $g_1 \in G$ such that $\|g_1 - x\| < 1$. Hence, the line $V = \{ty + (1-t)g | t \in \mathbb{R}\}$ supports B in y. By the Hahn-Banach Theorem there is a hyperplane which contains V and supports B in y. However, this hyperplane can not be H because it contains g. Thus, B was two different supporting hyperplanes at y, contrary to the assumption that X is smooth.

In the following lemma, our goal is to be able to "guess" the location of some $g \in G$ based on the its distance from $T \notin G$. The idea is that since G is convex and since the norm of X is both strictly convex and smooth the intersection of a ball centered at the target and G are contained within a "slice" of a ball, i.e., the intersection of a ball and a certain halfspace. Formally, we claim the following:

Lemma 12. *Let X be a strictly convex, smooth Banach space and let $G \subset X$ be compact and convex. For any $T \notin G$ let $P_G T$ be the nearest point to T in G and set $d = \|T - P_G T\|$. Let x^* be the functional supporting $B(T, d)$ in $P_G T$ and put $H^+ = \{x | x^*(x) \geq d + x^*(T)\}$. Then, every $g \in G$, satisfies that $g \in B(T, d_g) \cap H^+$, where $d_g = \|g - T\|$.*

The proof of this corollary is straightforward and is omitted.

Finally, we arrive to the proof of the main claim. We estimate the diameter of the "slice" of G using the modulus of uniform convexity of X. This was formulated as Lemma 6 in the main text.

Lemma 13. *Let X be a uniformly convex, smooth Banach space with a modulus of convexity δ_X and let $G \subset X$ be compact and convex. If $T \notin G$ and $d = \|T - P_G T\|$ then for every $g \in G$,*

$$\delta_X\left(\frac{\|g - P_G T\|}{d_g}\right) \leq 1 - \frac{d}{d_g} ,$$

where $d_g = \|T - g\|$.

Proof. Clearly, we may assume that $T = 0$. Using the notation of Lemma 12,

$$\|g - P_G T\| \leq diam\big(B(T, d_g) \cap H^+\big) .$$

Let $\tilde{z}_1, \tilde{z}_2 \in \big(B(T, d_g) \cap H^+\big)$, put $\varepsilon = \|\tilde{z}_1 - \tilde{z}_2\|$ and set $z_i = \tilde{z}_i / d_g$. Hence, $\|z_i\| \leq 1$, $\|z_1 - z_2\| = \varepsilon / d_g$ and $x^*(z_i) \geq d / d_g$. Thus,

$$\frac{1}{2}\|z_1 + z_2\| \geq \frac{1}{2} x^*(z_1 + z_2) \geq \frac{d}{d_g} .$$

Hence,

$$\frac{d}{d_g} \leq \frac{1}{2}\|z_1 + z_2\| \leq 1 - \delta_X\left(\frac{\varepsilon}{d_g}\right) ,$$

and our claim follows.

References

1. M.Anthony, P.L. Bartlett: *Neural Network Learning: Theoretical Foundations*, Cambridge University Press, 1999.
2. B. Beauzamy: *Introduction to Banach spaces and their Geometry*, Math. Studies, vol 86, North-Holland, 1982
3. O. Hanner: On the uniform convexity of L^p and l^p, Ark. Math. 3, 239-244, 1956.
4. P. Habala, P. Hajék, V. Zizler: *Introduction to Banach spaces* vol I and II, matfyzpress, Univ. Karlovy, Prague, 1996.
5. W.S. Lee: *Agnostic learning and single hidden layer neural network*, Ph.D. thesis, The Australian National University, 1996.
6. W.S. Lee, P.L. Bartlett, R.C. Williamson: The Importance of Convexity in Learning with Squared Loss, IEEE Transactions on Information Theory 44 5, 1974-1980, 1998.
7. S. Mendelson: Rademacher averages and phase transitions in Glivenko–Cantelli classes, preprint.
8. S. Mendelson: Geometric methods in the analysis of Glivenko-Cantelli classes, this volume.
9. M. Talagrand: Sharper bounds for Gaussian and empirical processes, Annals of Probability, 22(1), 28-76, 1994.
10. A.W. Van–der–Vaart, J.A. Wellner: *Weak convergence and Empirical Processes*, Springer-Verlag, 1996.
11. R.C. Williamson, A.J. Smola, B. Schölkopf: Generalization performance of regularization networks and support vectors machines via entropy numbers of compact operators, to appear in IEEE transactions on Information Theory.

On Agnostic Learning with $\{0, *, 1\}$-Valued and Real-Valued Hypotheses

Philip M. Long

Genome Institute of Singapore
1 Research Link
IMA Building
National University of Singapore
Singapore 117604, Republic of Singapore

Abstract. We consider the problem of classification using a variant of the agnostic learning model in which the algorithm's hypothesis is evaluated by comparison with hypotheses that do not classify all possible instances. Such hypotheses are formalized as functions from the instance space X to $\{0, *, 1\}$, where $*$ is interpreted as "don't know". We provide a characterization of the sets of $\{0, *, 1\}$-valued functions that are learnable in this setting. Using a similar analysis, we improve on sufficient conditions for a class of real-valued functions to be agnostically learnable with a particular relative accuracy; in particular, we improve by a factor of two the scale at which scale-sensitive dimensions must be finite in order to imply learnability.

1 Introduction

In agnostic learning [13,17], an algorithm tries to find a hypothesis that generalizes nearly as well as is possible using any hypothesis in some class that is known a priori; this class is sometimes called the *comparison class.* This framework can be applied for analyzing algorithms for two-class classification problems; in this case, one can view hypotheses as functions from some domain X to $\{0, 1\}$.

In this paper, we consider a modified framework in which the members of the comparison class do not classify all elements of the domain, and are regarded to be wrong an any domain elements that they do not classify. Formally, hypotheses in this framework map X to $\{0, *, 1\}$, where $*$ is regarded as "don't know". This offers a clean way to make formal use of the intuition that points are unlikely to fall in the unclassified region, since results in this framework are strong to the extent that this is true.

For example, it can be used to formalize the assumption that there is a halfspace that is likely to classify instances correctly with a certain margin; such a halfspace has small error, even if instances falling close to its separating hyperplane are regarded as being classified incorrectly (i.e. are mapped to $*$). This viewpoint is implicit in the manner in which the "margin percentile bounds" for generalization of support vector machines [3,2,11] are formulated. These results bound the probability that there is some halfspace that classifies a large fraction

D. Helmbold and B. Williamson (Eds.): COLT/EuroCOLT 2001, LNAI 2111, pp. 289–302, 2001.

of a random sample correctly with a large margin, but fails to generalize well. Such results are interesting when it is likely, for a collection of random examples, that some halfspace gets most of the examples correct with a large margin, and this is the case when some halfspace is likely to classify individual random examples correctly with a large margin. A similar line of reasoning suggests that this assumption is implicit in Ben-David and Simon's [6] choice of analysis for their computationally efficient algorithm; indeed, agnostic learning of $\{0, *, 1\}$-valued functions in the model studied here abstracts the optimization criterion studied in their paper (see also [7]).

In this paper, we show that a generalization of the VC-dimension to $\{0, *, 1\}$-valued functions introduced in [4] provides a characterization of learnability in this setting, in that a class of functions is learnable if an only if its generalized VC-dimension is finite.

Next, we turn to the problem of learning with real-valued hypotheses. Scale-sensitive notions of the dimension of a class of real-valued functions have been used to characterize the learnability of classes of real-valued functions in different settings [1,5]: loosely, these results say that a class can be learned to any accuracy if and only if its dimension is finite at all scales. Previous work [4] considered the following question: at what scale does the dimension need to be finite for learning to a particular relative accuracy to be possible? This work left roughly a factor of two gap between the scales at which finite dimension is necessary and is sufficient. In this paper, we close this gap, improving by a factor of two the bound on the scale at which the dimension of a class of real-valued functions must be finite for it to be agnostically learnable.

The model of agnostic learning of $\{0, *, 1\}$-valued functions calls to mind the "sleeping experts" framework [12], but there are many differences, including the usual differences between batch and online learning settings. Blum, et al [8] studied a variant of the model of PAC learning with membership queries in which queries falling in a given region are answered with "don't know" and the distribution assigned zero weight to this "don't know" region.

2 Characterization of Agnostic Learnability with $\{0, *, 1\}$-Valued Hypothesis

2.1 Definitions

Say a set F of functions from X to $\{0, *, 1\}$ *shatters* elements $x_1, ..., x_d$ of X if

$$\{0,1\}^d \subseteq \{(f(x_1), ..., f(x_d)) : f \in F\}.$$

Define VCdim(F) [19,4] to be the size of the largest set shattered by F.

An *example* is an element of $X \times \{0, 1\}$ and a *sample* is a finite sequence of examples. A *hypothesis* is a function from X to $\{0, *, 1\}$. Define $\ell : \{0, *, 1\} \times \{0,1\} \to \{0,1\}$ by $\ell(\hat{y}, y) = 1$ iff $\hat{y} \neq y$. For a hypothesis h, and a probability distribution P over $X \times \{0, 1\}$, define the *error* of h with respect to P, to be $\mathrm{er}_P(h) = \mathbf{Pr}_{(x,y)\sim P}(h(x) \neq y)$.

A *learning strategy* is a mapping from samples to hypotheses. A *prediction strategy* [15] takes as input a sample and an element of X, and outputs an element of $\{0, 1\}$.

A set F of functions from X to $\{0, *, 1\}$ is said to be *agnostically learnable* if there is a learning strategy such that, for all $\epsilon, \delta > 0$, there is a natural number m such that, for any probability distribution P over $X \times \{0, 1\}$, if m examples are drawn independently at random according to P, and the resulting sample is passed to A which outputs a hypothesis h, then, with probability at least $1 - \delta$, $\mathrm{er}_P(h) \leq (\inf_{f \in F} \mathrm{er}_P(f)) + \epsilon$.

2.2 Overview of Some Technical Issues Involved

The model of agnostic learning of $\{0, *, 1\}$-valued functions falls within the general decision-theoretic framework proposed by Haussler [13]. In a special case of Haussler's framework, there is an instance space X, an action space A, an outcome space Y, a loss function $\ell : A \times Y \to \mathbf{R}^+$ and a comparison class F of functions mapping X to A. Given examples $(x_1, y_1), ..., (x_m, y_m)$ drawn independently at random according to a probability distribution P over $X \times Y$, a learning algorithm outputs a hypothesis h mapping X to A. Roughly, the goal is for $\mathbf{E}_{(x,y)\sim P}(\ell(h(x), y))$ to be close to $\inf_{f \in F} \mathbf{E}_{(x,y)\sim P}(\ell(f(x), y))$.

The model of this paper can be recovered by setting $A = \{0, *, 1\}$, $Y = \{0, 1\}$, and letting ℓ be the discrete loss, i.e. $\ell(\hat{y}, y) = 1$ if $\hat{y} \neq y$ and $\ell(\hat{y}, y) = 0$ if $\hat{y} = y$.

Unfortunately, some of the general analysis techniques [19,18,13] that have been applied in a wide range of concrete problems falling within this framework cannot be applied in the $\{0, *, 1\}$ case. The by now standard analysis considers a class of loss functions defined as follows. For each f, define $\ell_f : X \times Y \to \mathbf{R}^+$ to give the loss incurred by f, i.e. $\ell_f(x, y) = \ell(f(x), y)$. Then $\ell_F = \{\ell_f : f \in F\}$. The usual analysis proceeds by showing that conditions on F imply that ℓ_F is somehow "limited". For example, if $A = \{0, 1\}$, $Y = \{0, 1\}$ and ℓ is the discrete loss, then $\mathrm{VCdim}(\ell_F) \leq \mathrm{VCdim}(F)$. In our setting, it appears that nothing useful of this type is true; the set F of all functions from $\mathbf{N}$ to $\{0, *\}$ has $\mathrm{VCdim}(F) = 0$, but $\mathrm{VCdim}(\ell_F) = \infty$.

Instead, we use an approach from [10,4], in which given

$$(x_1, f(x_1)), ..., (x_m, f(x_m)),$$

and wanting to evaluate $h(x)$, the algorithm constructs a small cover of the restrictions of the functions in F to $x_1, ..., x_m, x$. In this context, loosely speaking, a cover of a set of functions is another set of functions for which each element of the set being covered is approximated well by some element of the set doing the covering. To analyze such an algorithm in this setting required a lemma about the existence of small covers. All bounds we know on covering numbers for learning applications proceed by first bounding packing numbers, and then appealing to a general bound on covering numbers in terms of packing numbers. (Roughly, a packing number of a set is the size of the largest pairwise distant subset.) It appears that this cannot work in this setting, because the relevant notion of "approximation" (defined below) is not a metric. The main technical novelty in this paper is a proof of a covering lemma that does not rely on packing.

2.3 The Covering Lemma

For this subsection, fix a finite set Z. Say that a function g from Z to $\{0, 1\}$ k-*covers* a function f from Z to $\{0, *, 1\}$ if $|\{z \in Z : f(z) \neq * \text{ and } f(z) \neq g(z)\}| \leq k$.

Say that a set G of $\{0, 1\}$-valued functions k-covers a set F of $\{0, *, 1\}$-valued functions if each function in F is k-covered by some function in G.

For technical reasons, it will be useful for a moment to consider learning when the *examples* can be labelled with $*$. In this context, an $*$ can be interpreted as "doesn't matter". For a hypothesis h, a function f from Z to $\{0, *, 1\}$, and a probability distribution D over Z, define the *error* of h with respect to f and D, to be

$$\mathrm{er}_{f,D}(h) = \mathbf{Pr}_{z \sim D}((h(z) \neq f(z)) \wedge (f(z) \neq *))$$

We will make use of the following known result about this model.

Lemma 1 ([4]). *Choose a set F of functions from Z to $\{0, *, 1\}$, and let d be the VC-dimension of F. There is a mapping A from finite sequences of elements of $Z \times \{0, *, 1\}$ to hypotheses such that, for any probability distribution D over Z, for any $f \in F$, and for any positive integer t, if $z_1, ..., z_t$ are chosen independently at random according to D, and A is applied to $(z_1, f(z_1)), ..., (z_t, f(z_t))$, and h is the resulting hypothesis, then $\mathbf{E}(\mathrm{er}_{f,D}(h)) \leq \frac{d}{t+1}$.*

Lemma 2. *Let $m = |Z|$. Choose a set F of functions from Z to $\{0, *, 1\}$ and let $d = \mathrm{VCdim}(F)$. Choose an integer k such that $1 \leq k \leq m$. There is a set G of $\{0, 1\}$-valued functions and a subset F' of F such that (a) $|F'| \geq |F|/2$, (b) G k-covers F', and (c) $|G| \leq 3^{\lceil 2dm/k \rceil}$.*

Proof: Define A as in Lemma 1. Let D be the uniform distribution over Z. Let P be the uniform distribution over F. Choose t (its value will be set later). Suppose that $z_1, ..., z_t$ are chosen independently at random according to D, f is chosen independently according to P, and $(z_1, f(z_1)), ..., (z_t, f(z_t))$ are passed to A; let $A(z_1, ..., z_t; f)$ be A's hypothesis (viewed as a random variable). Then Lemma 1 says that

$$\forall f \in F, \mathbf{E}_{z_1,...,z_t \sim D^t}(\mathrm{er}_{f,D}(A(z_1, ..., z_t; f))) < \frac{d}{t}.$$

Markov's inequality implies that

$$\forall f \in F, \mathbf{Pr}_{z_1,...,z_t \sim D^t}\left(\mathrm{er}_{f,D}(A(z_1, ..., z_t; f)) > \frac{2d}{t}\right) \leq 1/2.$$

Thus,

$$\mathbf{Pr}_{f \sim P, z_1,...,z_t \sim D^t}\left(\mathrm{er}_{f,D}(A(z_1, ..., z_t; f)) > \frac{2d}{t}\right) \leq 1/2.$$

Fubini's Theorem implies that

$$\mathbf{E}_{z_1,...,z_t \sim D^t}\left(\mathbf{Pr}_{f\sim P}(\mathrm{er}_{f,D}(A(z_1,...,z_t;f)) > \frac{2d}{t})\right) \le 1/2.$$

Thus,

$$\exists z_1,...,z_t,\ \mathbf{Pr}_{f\sim P}\left(\mathrm{er}_{f,D}(A(z_1,...,z_t;f)) > \frac{2d}{t}\right) \le 1/2. \qquad (1)$$

Choose such a sequence $z_1,...,z_t$. Let $G = \{A(z_1,...,z_t;f) : f \in F\}$, and let $F' = \left\{f \in F : \mathrm{er}_{f,D}(A(z_1,...,z_t;f)) \le \frac{2d}{t}\right\}$. Note that G $\frac{2dm}{t}$-covers F', and, by (1), $|F'| \ge |F|/2$. Suppose $t = \lceil 2dm/k \rceil$; then $\frac{2dm}{t} \le k$. There are only 3^t possible inputs to A with instances $x_1,...,x_t$. Thus, $|H| \le 3^t$, completing the proof. □

Theorem 1. *Let $m = |Z|$. Choose a set F of functions from Z to $\{0,*,1\}$ and let $d = \mathrm{VCdim}(F)$. Choose an integer k such that $1 \le k \le m$. There is a set G of $\{0,1\}$-valued functions that k-covers F and for which $|G| \le \lceil m \log_2 3 \rceil 3^{\lceil 2dm/k \rceil}$.*

Proof: Construct a sequence $G_1, G_2, ..., G_{\lceil \log_2 |F| \rceil}$ of sets of functions from X to $\{0,1\}$ by repeatedly applying Lemma 2 to k-cover at last half of the remaining functions in F, and then deleting the covered functions. Let $G = \cup G_i$. Then G k-covers F, and $|G| \le \lceil \log_2 |F| \rceil 3^{\lceil 2dm/k \rceil} \le \lceil m \log_2 3 \rceil 3^{\lceil 2dm/k \rceil}$.

2.4 Learning

Theorem 2. *A set F of functions from X to $\{0,*,1\}$ is learnable if and only if $\mathrm{VCdim}(F)$ is finite.*

The necessity follows from the corresponding result for the $\{0,1\}$ case [9]. The sufficiency is a direct consequence of the following theorem. The following proof closely follows that of Theorem 21 of [4]; the main difference is that it appeals to the new Theorem 1 of the present paper.

Theorem 3. *Choose a set F of functions from X to $\{0,*,1\}$ for which $\mathrm{VCdim}(F)$ is finite. Let $d = \mathrm{VCdim}(F)$.*

There is a prediction strategy A and constants c and m_0 such that, for any probability distribution P over $X \times \{0,*,1\}$, for any $m \ge m_0$, if $(x_1,y_1),...,(x_m,y_m)$ are drawn independently at random according to P, and $(x_1,y_1),...,(x_{m-1},y_{m-1})$ and x_m are given to A, which outputs $\hat{y}_m$, then

$$\mathbf{E}(\ell(\hat{y}_m, y_m)) - \inf_{f\in F} \mathrm{er}_P(f) \le c\left(\frac{d}{m}\right)^{1/3}.$$

Proof: Assume without loss of generality that m is even. Choose $\alpha > 0$ (its value will be set later).

Choose a function Φ that maps from X^m to the set of finite subsets of $\{0,1\}^m$ such that, for any $(x_1,...,x_m) \in X^m$, $\Phi(x_1,...,x_m)$ is one of the smallest sets that

αm-covers $\{(f(x_1), ..., f(x_m)) : f \in F\}$ and $\Phi(x_1, ..., x_m)$ is invariant under permutations of its arguments. (When defining "αm-covers" above, we are viewing an element of $\{0, *, 1\}^m$ as a function from $\{1, ..., m\}$ to $\{0, *, 1\}$.)

Consider the prediction strategy A that chooses $\hat{y} = (\hat{y}_1, ..., \hat{y}_m)$ from among the elements of $\Phi(x_1, ..., x_m)$ in order to minimize $\sum_{i=1}^{m/2} \ell(\hat{y}_i, y_i)$ (the error on the first half of the sample only), and outputs $\hat{y}_m$.

For $a \in \{0, 1\}^m$, $b \in \{0, *, 1\}^m$, define

$$\ell^{\text{first}}(a, b) = \frac{2}{m} \sum_{i=1}^{m/2} \ell(a_i, b_i),$$

$$\ell^{\text{last}}(a, b) = \frac{2}{m} \sum_{i=m/2+1}^{m} \ell(a_i, b_i),$$

and

$$\ell^{\text{all}}(a, b) = \frac{1}{m} \sum_{i=1}^{m} \ell(a_i, b_i).$$

Fix a distribution P on $X \times \{0, 1\}$, and suppose $(x_1, y_1), ..., (x_m, y_m)$ are chosen independently at random from P. Let $x = (x_1, ..., x_m)$ and $y = (y_1, ..., y_m)$. Choose $f^* \in F$ that satisfies $\text{er}_P(f^*) \leq \inf_{f \in F} \text{er}_P(f) + \alpha$. Since $\Phi(x)$ αm-covers $\{(f(x_1), ..., f(x_m)) : f \in F\}$

$$\exists t^* \in \Phi(x_1, ..., x_m), \ell^{\text{all}}(t^*, y) \leq \alpha + \ell^{\text{all}}((f^*(x_1), ..., f^*(x_m)), y). \tag{2}$$

(If $f^*(x_i) = *$, whatever the values of t_i and y_i, $\ell(t_i, y_i) \leq \ell(f^*(x_i), y_i)$.)

Applying the Hoeffding bound,

$$\mathbf{Pr}\left(\ell^{\text{all}}((f^*(x_1), ..., f^*(x_m)), y) > \text{er}_P(f^*) + \alpha\right) \leq e^{-2\alpha^2 m}. \tag{3}$$

Now, let U be the uniform distribution over $\{-1, 1\}^{m/2}$. Then, since Φ is invariant under permutations,

$$\mathbf{Pr}(\exists t \in \Phi(x)\ |\ell^{\text{first}}(t, y) - \ell^{\text{last}}(t, y)| > 2\alpha)$$
$$\leq \sup_{(x,y)} \mathbf{Pr}_{u \in U}\left(\exists t \in \Phi(x), \left|\tfrac{2}{m} \textstyle\sum_{i=1}^{m/2} u_i \left(\ell(t_i, y_i) - \ell(t_{i+m/2}, y_{i+m/2})\right)\right| > 2\alpha\right)$$

For any fixed $t \in \Phi(x)$, Hoeffding's inequality implies

$$\mathbf{Pr}_{u \in U}\left(\left|\frac{2}{m} \sum_{i=1}^{m/2} u_i \left(\ell(t_i, y_i) - \ell(t_{i+m/2}, y_{i+m/2})\right)\right| > 2\alpha\right) \leq 2e^{-\alpha^2 m}.$$

So with probability at least $1 - |\Phi(x)| 2e^{-\alpha^2 m}$, for all t in $\Phi(x)$,

$$|\ell^{\text{first}}(t, y) - \ell^{\text{last}}(t, y)| \leq 2\alpha.$$

This implies

$$|\ell^{\text{first}}(t,y) - \ell^{\text{all}}(t,y)| \leq \alpha$$

and

$$|\ell^{\text{last}}(t,y) - \ell^{\text{all}}(t,y)| \leq \alpha.$$

So, combining with (3), with probability at least $1 - (1 + 2|\Phi(x)|)e^{-\alpha^2 m}$, the $\hat{y} \in \Phi(x)$ with minimal $\ell^{\text{first}}(\hat{y}, y)$ satisfies

$$\begin{aligned} \ell^{\text{all}}(\hat{y},y) &\leq \ell^{\text{first}}(\hat{y},y) + \alpha \\ &\leq \ell^{\text{first}}(t^*,y) + \alpha \\ &\leq \ell^{\text{all}}(t^*,y) + 2\alpha \\ &\leq \ell^{\text{all}}((f^*(x_1),...,f^*(x_m)),y) + 3\alpha \\ &\leq \mathrm{er}_P(f^*) + 4\alpha \end{aligned}$$

and hence

$$\begin{aligned} \ell^{\text{last}}(\hat{y},y) &\leq \mathrm{er}_P(f^*) + 5\alpha \\ &\leq \inf_{f \in F} \mathrm{er}_P(f) + 6\alpha. \end{aligned}$$

That is,

$$\mathbf{Pr}\left(\ell^{\text{last}}(\hat{y},y) > \inf_{f \in F} \mathrm{er}_P(f) + 6\alpha\right) < (1 + 2|\Phi(x)|)e^{-\alpha^2 m}$$

which implies

$$\mathbf{E}(\ell^{\text{last}}(\hat{y},y)) - \inf_{f \in F} \mathrm{er}_P(f) < 6\alpha + (1 + 2|\Phi(x)|)e^{-\alpha^2 m}.$$

Thus, since any of $(x_{m/2+1}, y_{m/2+1}), ..., (x_m, y_m)$ was equally likely to have been the last,

$$\mathbf{E}(\ell(\hat{y}_m, y_m)) - \inf_{f \in F} \mathrm{er}_P(f) < 6\alpha + (1 + 2|\Phi(x)|)e^{-\alpha^2 m}.$$

Let $\alpha = \left(\frac{2c_1 d}{m}\right)^{1/3} + \sqrt{\frac{2 \ln m}{m}}$. Theorem 1 implies that there is are constants c_1 and m_0 such that for all $m \geq m_0$,

$$\mathbf{E}(\ell(\hat{y}_m, y_m)) - \inf_{f \in F} \mathrm{er}_P(f) < 6\alpha + \exp(c_1 d/\alpha - \alpha^2 m). \tag{4}$$

The following sequence of implications are immediate:

$$\begin{aligned} &\alpha \geq \left(\frac{2c_1 d}{m}\right)^{1/3} \text{ and } \alpha \geq \sqrt{\frac{2 \ln m}{m}} \\ &\alpha^2 m/2 \geq c_1 d/\alpha \text{ and } \alpha^2 m/2 \geq \ln \frac{1}{\alpha} \\ &\alpha^2 m \geq c_1 d/\alpha + \ln \frac{1}{\alpha} \\ &\exp(c_1 d/\alpha - \alpha^2 m) \leq \alpha. \end{aligned}$$

Applying (4), we get

$$\mathbf{E}(\ell(\hat{y}_m, y_m)) - \inf_{f \in F} \mathrm{er}_P(f) < 7\alpha.$$

Substituting the value of α completes the proof. □

Armed with Theorem 3, straightforward application of known techniques [14] (almost identical to the last paragraph of the proof of Theorem 21 in [4]) gets us the rest of the way to prove Theorem 2.

Proof (for Theorem 2): Theorem 3, together with Fubini's theorem, implies that there is a learning algorithm whose hypothesis h satisfies $\mathbf{E}(\mathrm{er}_P(h) - \inf_{f \in F} \mathrm{er}_P(f)) = c(d/t)^{1/3}$, where this expectation is with respect to t random examples. Markov's inequality implies that $\mathbf{Pr}(\mathrm{er}_P(h) - \inf_{f \in F} \mathrm{er}_P(f) > 2c(d/t)^{1/3}) \leq 1/2$. If we run the algorithm repeatedly $\approx \log_2 2/\delta$ times using t examples each time, with probability $1 - \delta/2$, one of resulting hypotheses will satisfy $\mathrm{er}_P(h) - \inf_{f \in F} \mathrm{er}_P(f) \leq 2c(d/t)^{1/3}$. Hoeffding's inequality implies that $\mathrm{poly}(t, 1/\delta)$ additional examples are sufficient to test of all the returned hypotheses, and find one that satisfies $\mathrm{er}_P(h) - \inf_{f \in F} \mathrm{er}_P(f) \leq 4c(d/t)^{1/3}$ with probability $1 - \delta$. □

2.5 Rounding

One might hope that all the $*$'s in a class of $\{0, *, 1\}$ valued functions can be "rounded" to 0 or 1 without increasing its VC-dimension. This would lead to a better bound than Theorem 3, and perhaps a simpler proof of Theorem 2. Unfortunately, it is not true.

Proposition 1. *There is a set X, and a set F of functions from X to $\{0, *, 1\}$ such that for any set G of functions from X to $\{0, 1\}$ that 0-covers F, $\mathrm{VCdim}(G) > \mathrm{VCdim}(F)$.*

Proof: Define F as in Figure 1. By inspection, $\mathrm{VCdim}(F) = 1$. It is not possible

	x_1	x_2	x_3
f_1	0	0	0
f_2	0	$*$	1
f_3	1	0	$*$
f_4	$*$	1	0
f_5	1	1	1

Fig. 1. F from Proposition 1 in table form.

for a single function to 0-cover two elements of F, since each pair of functions in F differ on some domain element on which neither evaluates to $*$. Thus, any G that 0-covers F must have $|G| \geq 5$, and therefore, by the Sauer-Shelah Lemma, $\mathrm{VCdim}(G) > 1$. □

3 Real-Valued Hypotheses

For a function f from X to $[0,1]$, a real threshold r and a non-negative margin γ, define $\psi_{r,\gamma}(f) : X \to \{0,*,1\}$ to indicate whether $f(x)$ is above or below r by a margin γ as follows

$$(\psi_{r,\gamma}(f))(x) = \begin{cases} 1 \text{ if } f(x) \geq r + \gamma \\ 0 \text{ if } f(x) \leq r - \gamma \\ * \text{ if } |f(x) - r| < \gamma. \end{cases}$$

For a class F of functions from X to $[0,1]$, let $\psi_{r,\gamma}(F) = \{\psi_{r,\gamma}(f) : f \in F\}$. Let $\mathrm{fatV}_F(\gamma) = \max_r \mathrm{VCdim}(\psi_{r,\gamma}(F))$. (This notion of dimension was proposed by Alon, et al [1].)

For this section, let us broaden the notion of an example to be an arbitrary element of $X \times [0,1]$ and redefine a learning and a prediction strategy accordingly. For a probability distribution P over $X \times [0,1]$ and a function h from X to $[0,1]$, let $\mathrm{er}_P(h) = \mathbf{E}_{(x,y)\sim P}(|h(x) - y|)$. For $\epsilon > 0$, we then say that a set F of functions from X to $[0,1]$ is *agnostically learnable to within* ϵ if there is a learning strategy A such that, for all $\delta > 0$, there is a natural number m such that, for any probability distribution P over $X \times [0,1]$, if m examples are drawn independently at random according to P, and the resulting sample is passed to A which outputs a hypothesis h, then, with probability at least $1-\delta$, $\mathrm{er}_P(h) \leq (\inf_{f\in F} \mathrm{er}_P(f)) + \epsilon$.

The following is the main result of this section.

Theorem 4. *For any set F of functions from X to $[0,1]$, if there is an $\alpha > 0$ such that $\mathrm{fatV}_F(\epsilon - \alpha)$ is finite, then F is agnostically learnable to within ϵ.*

This improves on the sufficient condition $(\exists \alpha > 0, \mathrm{fatV}_F(\epsilon/2 - \alpha) < \infty)$ from [4] by a factor of two on the scale at which the dimension of F is examined. The finiteness of $\mathrm{fatV}_F(\epsilon + \alpha)$ for some positive α has been shown to be necessary [4]. It implies a similar improvement on the sufficient condition stated in terms of Kearns and Schapire's [16] *fat-shattering function* [1,4], closing a factor of two gap there as well.

Say that a set F of functions from X to $[0,1]$ is agnostically predictable to within $\epsilon > 0$ if there is a sample size m and a prediction strategy A such that, for any probability distribution P over $X \times [0,1]$, if $(x_1, y_1), ..., (x_m, y_m)$ are drawn independently at random according to P, and $(x_1, y_1), ..., (x_{m-1}, y_{m-1}), x_m$ are passed to A, which outputs $\hat{y}_m$, then $\mathbf{E}(|\hat{y}_m - y_m|) - \inf_{f\in F} \mathrm{er}_P(f) \leq \epsilon$.

We will make use of the following lemma, implicit in [14,4].

Lemma 3. *For any X, and any set F of functions from X to $[0,1]$, if F is agnostically predictable to within $\epsilon > 0$, then F is agnostically learnable to within any $\epsilon' > \epsilon$.*

This enables us to prove Theorem 4 by analyzing a prediction strategy.

As in the previous section, we wanted a covering lemma whose proof doesn't go via packing; loosely speaking, here this is because one loses a factor of two converting between packing and covering.

3.1 Small Covers

Choose a finite set Z. For functions f and g from Z to $[0,1]$, let $\ell_1(f,g) = \frac{1}{|Z|}\sum_{z\in Z}|f(z)-g(z)|$. Say that a set G of functions from Z to $[0,1]$ ϵ-covers a set F of functions from Z to $[0,1]$ if for every $f \in F$, there is a $g \in G$ for which $\ell_1(f,g) \le \epsilon$. Let $\mathcal{N}(\epsilon, F)$ be the size of the smallest ϵ-cover of F.

For $\alpha > 0$ and $u \in \mathbf{R}$, let $Q_\alpha(u)$ denote the quantized version of u, with quantization width α. That is, define $Q_\alpha(u) = \alpha\lfloor u/\alpha \rfloor$. Let $Q_\alpha([0,1]) = \{Q_\alpha(u) : u \in [0,1]\}$. For a function f from Z to $\mathbf{R}$, define $Q_\alpha(f) : Z \to \mathbf{R}$ by $(Q_\alpha(f))(x) = Q_\alpha(f(x))$. Finally, for a set F of such functions, define $Q_\alpha(F) = \{Q_\alpha(f) : f \in F\}$.

Lemma 4. *For any set F of functions from Z to $[0,1]$, any $\epsilon > 0$, and $\alpha < \epsilon/2$, $\mathcal{N}(\epsilon, F) \le \mathcal{N}(\epsilon - \alpha, Q_\alpha(F))$.*

For functions h and f from X to $[0,1]$, and a probability distribution D over Z, define the *error* of h with respect to f and D, to be $\mathrm{er}_{f,D}(h) = \mathbf{Pr}_{z\sim D}(|h(z) - f(z)|)$.

Lemma 5 ([4]). *Choose a set F of functions from Z to $[0,1]$. There is a mapping A from finite sequences of elements of $Z \times [0,1]$ to hypotheses such that, for any probability distribution D over Z, for any $f \in F$, and for any positive integer m, if $z_1, ..., z_t$ are chosen independently at random according to D, A is applied to $(z_1, f(z_1)), ..., (z_t, f(z_t))$, and h is the resulting hypothesis, then $\mathbf{E}(\mathrm{er}_{f,D}(h)) \le \gamma + \frac{2\mathrm{fatV}_F(\gamma)}{t+1}$.*

Lemma 6. *Let $m = |Z|$. Choose $0 < \gamma < \epsilon \le 1$, $b \in \mathbf{N}$, and a set F of functions from Z to $Q_{1/b}([0,1])$. There is a set G of $\{0,1\}$-valued functions and a subset F' of F such that*

- *$|F'| \ge |F|/2$,*
- *G ϵ-covers F', and*
- *$|G| \le (b+1)^{\left\lceil \frac{2\mathrm{fatV}_F(\gamma)}{\epsilon-\gamma} \right\rceil}$.*

Proof: Define A as in Lemma 5. Let D be the uniform distribution over X, and let P be the uniform distribution over F. Choose a positive integer t (its value will be set later). Suppose that $z_1, ..., z_t$ are chosen independently at random uniformly according to D, f is chosen independently according to P, $(z_1, f(z_1)), ..., (z_t, f(z_t))$ are passed to A; let $A(z_1, ..., z_t; f)$ be A's hypothesis. Then Lemma 1 says that

$$\forall f \in F, \mathbf{E}_{z_1,...,z_t \sim D^t}(\mathrm{er}_{f,D}(A(z_1, ..., z_t; f))) < \gamma + \frac{2\mathrm{fatV}_F(\gamma)}{t}.$$

Arguing as in the proof of Lemma 2, we have

$$\exists z_1, ..., z_t,\ \mathbf{Pr}_{f\sim P}\left(\mathrm{er}_{f,D}(A(z_1, ..., z_t; f)) > \gamma + \frac{2\mathrm{fatV}_F(\gamma)}{t}\right) \le 1/2. \quad (5)$$

Choose such a sequence $z_1, ..., z_t$. Then if $G = \{A(z_1, ..., z_t; f) : f \in F\}$, and

$$F' = \left\{ f \in F : \mathrm{er}_{f,D}(A(z_1, ..., z_t; f)) \leq \gamma + \frac{2\mathrm{fatV}_F(\gamma)}{t} \right\},$$

then G $(\gamma + \frac{2\mathrm{fatV}_F(\gamma)}{t})$-covers F', and, by (5), $|F'| \geq |F|/2$. Suppose $t = \left\lceil \frac{2\mathrm{fatV}(\gamma)}{\epsilon-\gamma} \right\rceil$; then $\gamma + \frac{2\mathrm{fatV}_F(\gamma)}{t} \leq \epsilon$. There are only $(b+1)^t$ possible inputs to A with instances $z_1, ..., z_t$. Thus, $|H| \leq (b+1)^t$, completing the proof. □

Theorem 5. *Suppose* $m = |Z|$. *Choose a set* F *of functions from* Z *to* $[0, 1]$, *and* ϵ *and* $\alpha \in \mathbf{R}$ *for which* $0 < \alpha < \epsilon \leq 1$. *Then* $\mathcal{N}(\epsilon, F) \leq (m \log_2(3/\alpha + 2))(3/\alpha + 2)^{(6/\alpha+1)\mathrm{fatV}_F(\epsilon-\alpha)}$.

Proof: Let $b = \lceil 3/\alpha \rceil$. Then $\mathrm{fatV}(\epsilon - 3/b) \leq \mathrm{fatV}(\epsilon - \alpha)$. Construct a sequence $G_1, G_2, ..., G_{\lceil \log_2 |Q_{1/b}(F)| \rceil}$ of sets of functions from Z to $\{0, 1\}$ by repeatedly applying Lemma 6 to $(\epsilon - 1/b)$-cover at last half of the remaining functions in $Q_{1/b}(F)$, and then deleting the covered functions. Let $G = \cup G_i$. Then G $(\epsilon - 1/b)$-covers $Q_{1/b}(F)$, and

$$\begin{aligned} |G| &\leq (\log_2 |Q_{1/b}(F)|)(b+1)^{2b\mathrm{fatV}_{Q_{1/b}(F)}(\epsilon-2/b)} \\ &\leq (m \log_2(b+1))(b+1)^{2b\mathrm{fatV}_{Q_{1/b}(F)}(\epsilon-2/b)} \\ &\leq (m \log_2(b+1))(b+1)^{2b\mathrm{fatV}_F(\epsilon-3/b)}, \end{aligned}$$

since, straight from the definitions, $\mathrm{fatV}_{Q_{1/b}(F)}(\epsilon - 2/b) \leq \mathrm{fatV}_F(\epsilon - 3/b)$. Applying Lemma 4 completes the proof. □

3.2 Learning

Like the proof of Theorem 3, the following proof closely follows that of Theorem 21 of [4], except that it appeals to the new Theorem 5.

Theorem 6. *Choose a set* F *of functions from* X *to* $[0, 1]$, *and* $0 < \epsilon \leq 1$. *If there exists* $\alpha > 0$ *such that* $\mathrm{fatV}_F(\epsilon - \alpha)$ *is finite, then* F *is agnostically predictable to within* ϵ.

Proof: Let $d = \mathrm{fatV}_F(\epsilon - \alpha)$, $\kappa = \alpha/3$, and $\beta = \alpha/15$.

Choose a function Φ that maps from X^m to the set of finite subsets of $[0, 1]^m$ such that, for any $(x_1, ..., x_m) \in X^m$, $\Phi(x_1, ..., x_m)$ is one of the smallest sets that $(\epsilon - 2\kappa)$-covers $\{(f(x_1), ..., f(x_m)) : f \in F\}$ and $\Phi(x_1, ..., x_m)$ is invariant under permutations of its arguments. (Recall once again that here we are viewing an element of $[0, 1]^m$ as a function from $\{1, ..., m\}$ to $[0, 1]$.)

Consider the prediction strategy A that, given input

$$(x_1, y_1), ..., (x_{m-1}, y_{m-1}), x_m,$$

chooses $\hat{y} = (\hat{y}_1, ..., \hat{y}_m)$ from among the elements of $\Phi(x_1, ..., x_m)$ in order to minimize $\sum_{i=1}^{m/2} |\hat{y}_i - y_i|$, and outputs $\hat{y}_m$.

For $a \in [0,1]^m$, $b \in [0,1]^m$, define

$$\ell^{\text{first}}(a,b) = \frac{2}{m}\sum_{i=1}^{m/2} |a_i - b_i|,$$

$$\ell^{\text{last}}(a,b) = \frac{2}{m}\sum_{i=m/2+1}^{m} |a_i - b_i|,$$

and

$$\ell^{\text{all}}(a,b) = \frac{1}{m}\sum_{i=1}^{m} |a_i - b_i|.$$

Choose any probability distribution P over $X \times [0,1]$, and an even positive integer m. Suppose $(x_1, y_1), ..., (x_m, y_m)$ are drawn independently at random according to P, and $(x_1, y_1), ..., (x_{m-1}, y_{m-1})$ and x_m are given to A, which outputs $\hat{y}_m$. Let $x = (x_1, ..., x_m)$ and $y = (y_1, ..., y_m)$. Choose $f^* \in F$ that satisfies $\text{er}_P(f^*) \le \inf_{f \in F} \text{er}_P(f) + \beta$. Since $\Phi(x)$ $\epsilon - 2\kappa$-covers $\{(f(x_1), ..., f(x_m)) : f \in F\}$

$$\exists t^* \in \Phi(x_1, ..., x_m), \ell^{\text{all}}(t^*, y) \le \epsilon - 2\kappa + \ell^{\text{all}}((f^*(x_1), ..., f^*(x_m)), y). \quad (6)$$

Applying the Hoeffding bound,

$$\mathbf{Pr}\left(\ell^{\text{all}}((f^*(x_1), ..., f^*(x_m)), y) > \text{er}_P(f^*) + \beta\right) \le e^{-2\beta^2 m}. \quad (7)$$

Now, let U be the uniform distribution over $\{0,1\}^{m/2}$. Then, since Φ is invariant under permutations,

$$\begin{aligned}&\mathbf{Pr}(\exists t \in \Phi(x)\ |\ell^{\text{first}}(t,y) - \ell^{\text{last}}(t,y)| > 2\beta)\\ &\le \sup_{(x,y)} \mathbf{Pr}_{u \in U}\left(\exists t \in \Phi(x) \left|\tfrac{2}{m}\textstyle\sum_{i=1}^{m/2} u_i \left(\ell(t_i, y_i) - \ell(t_{i+m/2}, y_{i+m/2})\right)\right| > 2\beta\right)\end{aligned}$$

For any fixed $t \in \Phi(x)$, Hoeffding's inequality implies

$$\mathbf{Pr}_{u \in U}\left(\left|\frac{2}{m}\sum_{i=1}^{m/2} u_i \left(\ell(t_i, y_i) - \ell(t_{i+m/2}, y_{i+m/2})\right)\right| > 2\beta\right) \le 2e^{-\beta^2 m}.$$

So with probability at least $1 - |\Phi(x)| 2e^{-\beta^2 m}$, for all t in $\Phi(x)$,

$$|\ell^{\text{first}}(t,y) - \ell^{\text{last}}(t,y)| \le 2\beta.$$

This implies

$$|\ell^{\text{first}}(t,y) - \ell^{\text{all}}(t,y)| \le \beta$$

and

$$|\ell^{\text{last}}(t,y) - \ell^{\text{all}}(t,y)| \le \beta.$$

So, combining with (7), with probability at least $1-(1+2|\Phi(x)|)e^{-\beta^2 m}$, the $\hat{y}\in\Phi(x)$ with minimal $\ell^{\text{first}}(\hat{y},y)$ satisfies

$$\begin{aligned}\ell^{\text{all}}(\hat{y},y) &\le \ell^{\text{first}}(\hat{y},y)+\beta\\ &\le \ell^{\text{first}}(t^*,y)+\beta\\ &\le \ell^{\text{all}}(t^*,y)+2\beta\\ &\le \ell^{\text{all}}((f^*(x_1),...,f^*(x_m)),y)+\epsilon-2\kappa+2\beta\\ &\le \mathrm{er}_P(f^*)+\epsilon-2\kappa+3\beta\end{aligned}$$

and hence

$$\begin{aligned}\ell^{\text{last}}(\hat{y},y) &\le \mathrm{er}_P(f^*)+\epsilon-2\kappa+4\beta\\ &\le \inf_{f\in F}\mathrm{er}_P(f)+\epsilon-2\kappa+5\beta.\end{aligned}$$

That is,

$$\mathbf{Pr}\left(\ell^{\text{last}}(\hat{y},y) > \inf_{f\in F}\mathrm{er}_P(f)++\epsilon-2\kappa+5\beta\right) < (1+2|\Phi(x)|)e^{-\beta^2 m}$$

which implies

$$\mathbf{E}(\ell^{\text{last}}(\hat{y},y)) - \inf_{f\in F}\mathrm{er}_P(f) < \epsilon-2\kappa+5\beta+(1+2|\Phi(x)|)e^{-\beta^2 m}$$

and hence, since any of $(x_{m/2+1},y_{m/2+1}),...,(x_m,y_m)$ was equally likely to have been the last,

$$\mathbf{E}(|\hat{y}_m-y_m|) - \inf_{f\in F}\mathrm{er}_P(f) < \epsilon-2\kappa+5\beta+(1+2|\Phi(x)|)e^{-\beta^2 m}.$$

Substituting $\kappa/5$ for β,

$$\mathbf{E}(|\hat{y}_m-y_m|) - \inf_{f\in F}\mathrm{er}_P(f) < \epsilon-\kappa+(1+2|\Phi(x)|)e^{-\kappa^2 m/25}. \tag{8}$$

Recall that $d=\mathrm{fatV}(\epsilon-\alpha)=\mathrm{fatV}(\epsilon-3\kappa)$, and $\Phi(x)$ is a minimum sized $\epsilon-2\kappa$ cover of $\{(f(x_1),...,f(x_m)):f\in F\}$; Theorem 5 and (8) imply that

$$\begin{aligned}&\mathbf{E}(|\hat{y}_m-y_m|) - \inf_{f\in F}\mathrm{er}_P(f)\\ &\le \epsilon-\kappa+(1+2(m\log_2(3/\kappa+2))(3/\kappa+2)^{(6/\kappa+1)d})e^{-\kappa^2 m/25}.\end{aligned}$$

Thus, if m is large enough, $\mathbf{E}(|\hat{y}_m-y_m|)-\inf_{f\in F}\mathrm{er}_P(f)\le\epsilon$; this completes the proof. □

Acknowledgements

We'd like to express warm thanks to Peter Bartlett, Shai Ben-David, Nadav Eiron, David Haussler and Yishay Mansour for valuable conversations.

We acknowledge the support of National University of Singapore Academic Research Fund Grant RP252–000–070–107.

References

1. N. Alon, S. Ben-David, N. Cesa-Bianchi, and D. Haussler. Scale-sensitive dimensions, uniform convergence, and learnability. *Journal of the Association for Computing Machinery*, 44(4):616–631, 1997.
2. M. Anthony and P. L. Bartlett. *Neural Network Learning: Theoretical Foundations.* Cambridge University Press, 1999.
3. P. L. Bartlett. The sample complexity of pattern classification with neural networks: the size of the weights is more important than the size of the network. *IEEE Transactions on Information Theory*, 44(2):525–536, 1998.
4. P. L. Bartlett and P. M. Long. Prediction, learning, uniform convergence, and scale-sensitive dimensions. *Journal of Computer and System Sciences*, 56(2):174–190, 1998.
5. P. L. Bartlett, P. M. Long, and R. C. Williamson. Fat-shattering and the learnability of real-valued functions. *Journal of Computer and System Sciences*, 52(3):434–452, 1996.
6. S. Ben-David and H. U. Simon. Efficient learning of linear perceptrons. *Advances in Neural Information Processing Systems 14*, 2000.
7. Shai Ben-David, Nadav Eiron, and Hans U. Simon. The computational complexity of densest region detection. *Proceedings of the 2000 Conference on Computational Learning Theory*, 2000.
8. A. Blum, P. Chalasani, S. Goldman, and D. K. Slonim. Learning with unreliable boundary queries. *Proceedings of the 1995 Conference on Computational Learning Theory*, pages 98–107, 1995.
9. A. Blumer, A. Ehrenfeucht, D. Haussler, and M. K. Warmuth. Learnability and the Vapnik-Chervonenkis dimension. *JACM*, 36(4):929–965, 1989.
10. K.L. Buescher and P.R. Kumar. Learning stochastic functions by smooth simultaneous estimation. *Proceedings of the 5th Annual ACM Workshop on Computational Learning Theory*, pages 272–279, 1992.
11. N. Cristianini and J. Shawe-Taylor. *An introduction to support vector machines and other kernel-based learning methods.* Cambridge University Press, 2000.
12. Y. Freund, R. E. Schapire, Y. Singer, and M.K. Warmuth. Using and combining predictors that specialize. *Proceedings of the Twenty-Ninth Annual ACM Symposium on the Theory of Computing*, 1997.
13. D. Haussler. Decision theoretic generalizations of the PAC model for neural net and other learning applications. *Information and Computation*, 100(1):78–150, 1992.
14. D. Haussler, M. Kearns, N. Littlestone, and M. K. Warmuth. Equivalence of models for polynomial learnability. *Information and Computation*, 95:129–161, 1991.
15. D. Haussler, N. Littlestone, and M. K. Warmuth. Predicting $\{0,1\}$-functions on randomly drawn points. *Information and Computation*, 115(2):129–161, 1994.
16. M. J. Kearns and R. E. Schapire. Efficient distribution-free learning of probabilistic concepts. *Journal of Computer and System Sciences*, 48(3):464–497, 1994.
17. M. J. Kearns, R. E. Schapire, and L. M. Sellie. Toward efficient agnostic learning. *Machine Learning*, 17:115–141, 1994.
18. V. N. Vapnik. *Estimation of Dependencies based on Empirical Data.* Springer Verlag, 1982.
19. V. N. Vapnik and A. Y. Chervonenkis. On the uniform convergence of relative frequencies of events to their probabilities. *Theory of Probability and its Applications*, 16(2):264–280, 1971.

When Can Two Unsupervised Learners Achieve PAC Separation?

Paul W. Goldberg*

Dept. of Computer Science, University of Warwick, Coventry CV4 7AL, U.K.
pwg@dcs.warwick.ac.uk

Abstract. In this paper we study a new restriction of the PAC learning framework, in which each label class is handled by an unsupervised learner that aims to fit an appropriate probability distribution to its own data. A hypothesis is derived by choosing, for any unlabeled instance, the label whose distribution assigns it the higher likelihood.

The motivation for the new learning setting is that the general approach of fitting separate distributions to each label class, is often used in practice for classification problems. The set of probability distributions that is obtained is more useful than a collection of decision boundaries. A question that arises, however, is whether it is ever more tractable (in terms of computational complexity or sample-size required) to find a simple decision boundary than to divide the problem up into separate unsupervised learning problems and find appropriate distributions.

Within the framework, we give algorithms for learning various simple geometric concept classes. In the boolean domain we show how to learn parity functions, and functions having a constant upper bound on the number of relevant attributes. These results distinguish the new setting from various other well-known restrictions of PAC-learning. We give an algorithm for learning monomials over input vectors generated by an unknown product distribution. The main open problem is whether monomials (or any other concept class) distinguish learnability in this framework from standard PAC-learnability.

1 Introduction

A standard approach to classification problems (see e.g. Duda and Hart [10]) is the following. For each class, find a *discriminant function* that maps elements of the input domain to real values. These functions can be used to label any input element $\mathbf{x}$ by giving it the class label whose associated discriminant function takes the largest value on $\mathbf{x}$. The discriminant functions are usually estimates of the probability densities of points having some class label, weighted by the class prior (relative frequency of that class label).

In learning theory e.g. PAC learning [2] or more recently support vectors [7] the approach is to find decision boundaries that optimize some performance guarantee. (The guarantee is usually based on observed classification performance in

* Partially supported by the IST Programme of the EU under contract number IST-1999-14186 (ALCOM-FT).

D. Helmbold and B. Williamson (Eds.): COLT/EuroCOLT 2001, LNAI 2111, pp. 303–319, 2001.

conjunction with other features of the boundary such as syntactic or combinatorial complexity, or the number of support vectors and margin of separation.) The general approach clearly requires examples with different labels to be taken in conjunction with each other when finding a decision boundary. By contrast, discriminant functions are constructed from individual label classes in isolation.

There are practical advantages to applying an unsupervised learning method to each label class, and obtaining estimates of the distribution over that label class. In contrast with decision boundaries, we obtain for any input vector $\mathbf{x}$, the values of the probability densities of label classes at $\mathbf{x}$, which provide a conditional distribution over the class label of $\mathbf{x}$. A predicted class label for $\mathbf{x}$ can then take into account variable misclassification penalties, or changes in the assumed class priors. There are of course other ways to obtain such distributions, for example using logistic regression, or more generally (for k-class classification) neural networks with k real-valued outputs re-scaled using the softmax activation function (see Bishop [3] for details). Learning using an unsupervised learner for each class has other advantages over these techniques, notably the first two of the following observations.

1. For applications such as handwritten digit recognition, it is more natural to model the data generation process in terms of 10 separate probability distributions, than as a collection of thresholds between different digits.
2. Label classes can be added without re-training the system. So for example if the euro symbol were added to a character set, then given a good estimate of the probability distribution over images of euro symbols, this can be used in conjunction with pre-existing models for how other symbols are generated.
3. The approach can treat situations where class overlap occurs (as is usually the case in practice). Standard PAC algorithms do not address this problem (although there have been extensions such as "probabilistic concepts" [18] that do so, and of course versions of support vector networks also allow decision boundaries that do not necessarily agree with all observed data).

Another difficulty with decision boundaries arises specifically in the context of multiclass classification. It has been noted [1] that multiclass classifiers are often constructed using multiple 2-class classifiers. How to combine them is a challenging topic that has itself received much recent attention, see for example [13,1]. In practical studies such as [19] that build a multi-class classifier from a collection of 2-class classifiers, a distinction is made between separating each class from the union of the others (*1-v-r* classifiers, where 1-v-r stands for one-versus-rest) and pairwise separation (*1-v-1* classifiers). Neither is entirely satisfactory – for example it may be possible to perform linear 1-v-1 separation for all pairs of classes, but not linear 1-v-r separation, while a problem with 1-v-1 classification (as studied in [19]) is the difficulty of combining the collection of pairwise classifiers to get an overall classification, in a principled way, for example ensuring that all classes are treated the same way. In [19], the first test for any unlabeled input is to apply the separator that distinguishes 0 from 9. Thus 0 and 9 are being treated differently from other digits (which in turn are also treated differently from each other.)

1.1 Main Research Questions

In view of the advantages we have noted of using unsupervised learners to solve classification problems, we propose to search for a gap between the tractability of classification problems and the tractability of classification problems subject to the restriction that each class be learned with its own unsupervised learner. Does there exist a learning problem for which we can both obtain a positive result for finding a decision boundary, and a negative result for the problem of fitting appropriate probability distributions to the classes so that maximum likelihood gives rise to a decision boundary with the same performance guarantees?

We consider this question in the basic Probably Approximately Correct (PAC) setting of [20,21], since it is well-understood. In PAC learning, the usual algorithmic challenge is to separate the two classes of examples. It would be remarkable if it turned out that PAC-learnability were equivalent to PAC-learnability using unsupervised learners, in view of the way the PAC criterion seems to lead to a search for class separation. The main drawback of studying PAC-learnability is the loss of realism associated with class separability.

There are not many papers on unsupervised learning in the computational learning theory literature; the topic was introduced in [17], see also [8,11,12,9]. The algorithms we describe here differ substantially from these previous ones (as well as from the algorithms in the much more extensive general literature on unsupervised learning). The reason is that our aim is not really to approximate a distribution over inputs. Rather, it is to construct a discriminant function in such a way that we expect it to work well in conjunction with the corresponding discriminant function constructed on data with the opposite class label.

From a theoretical perspective, we address a natural question in asking how much it hampers learning not to have simultaneous access to examples with different labels. The topic appears to raise new and interesting research problems. The main theoretical question (which we leave open) is of course: are all PAC learnable problems also learnable in this framework, and if not, how does the set of learnable problems compare with other subsets of PAC learnable problems, for example Statistical Query (SQ) learnability [16]. (In the case of SQ learning, we find that parity functions are learnable in this framework but from [16] they are not learnable using SQs.)

1.2 Formalizing the Learning Framework

In PAC learning there is a source of data consisting of instances generated by a probability distribution D over a domain X, labeled using an unknown function $f : X \longrightarrow \{0,1\}$. Thus f divides members of X into two sets $f^{-1}(0)$ and $f^{-1}(1)$, and the learner's objective is to find good approximations to those sets. As usual we will let ϵ and δ denote the target error and uncertainty respectively.

We use the standard convention of referring to the two classes of inputs associated with the two class labels as the "positive examples" and the "negative examples". Each learner has access to a source of examples having one of the two class labels. More precisely, one learner may (in unit time) draw a sample from D restricted to the positive examples, and the other may sample from D restricted to the negative examples. This formalism loses any information about the class priors, *i.e.* the relative frequency of positive and negative examples, but PAC learnability is in fact equivalent to PAC learnability where the class priors are concealed from the learner. (Formally, this is the equivalence of the standard PAC framework with the "two-button" version, where the learner has access to a "positive example oracle" and a "negative example oracle" [14]. The two-button version conceals the class priors and only gives the learner access to the distribution as restricted to each class label.)

We assume that neither unsupervised learner knows whether it is receiving the positive or the negative examples. Consequently both learners must apply the same algorithm. Note that for a concept class that is closed under complementation, output labels are of no help to the learners. For a concept class that is not closed under complementation (such as rectangles), observe that it is PAC learnable if and only if its closure under complementation is PAC learnable. Hence any learning algorithm in our framework which required class labels to be provided to each of the two learners, would lack a robustness property that standard PAC algorithms have. That observation also indicates that the main question of distinguishability from standard PAC-learnability is independent of the assumption that class labels (positive/negative) are provided. Note however that for some concept classes (notably monomials, section 3.1) we can (without much difficulty) find algorithms in our setting that use labeled examples, but we have so far not found any algorithm that works with unlabeled examples.

The class label which the pair of learners assign to input x is the one associated with the data sent to the learner that assigned x the higher likelihood. If x is given the same likelihood by both distributions generated by the learners, the tie is broken at random.

1.3 Notation and Terminology

We refer to the unsupervised learners as learners A and B, and we also assume by convention that learner A is the one receiving the positive examples, however as we have noted above, learner A (and likewise B) is not told its identity.

Theorem 1 below justifies the design of algorithms in which instead of insisting that the outputs of the unsupervised learners define probability distributions, we allow unrestricted discriminant functions from domain X to the real numbers $\mathbf{R}$. The comparison of the two values assigned to any $x \in X$ is used to determine the class label that the hypothesis classifier assigns to x. In what follows we refer to the "score" assigned to an input vector $\mathbf{x}$ by an unsupervised learner to mean the value taken by its discriminant function on input $\mathbf{x}$.

We will say that learner A (respectively B) "claims" an input x if it gives x a higher likelihood or score than learner B (respectively A). We say that a learner "rejects" an input if it assigns a likelihood of 0, or alternatively a score of minimal value (it is convenient to use $-\infty$ to denote such a score). Thus if a learner rejects an input, it will be claimed by the other learner provided that the other learner does not also reject that input.

2 General Results

In this section we give some general results about the two unsupervised learners framework. (Then in section 3 we give some algorithms for specific PAC learning problems. The results of section 3 also serve to distinguish our learning setting from other restrictions of the PAC setting in terms of what concept classes may be learned.) We show first that if hypotheses may be any real-valued discriminant functions, then the algorithm may be modified so that the hypotheses are probability distributions, and the separation is still PAC. There is no particular reason to suppose that probability distributions obtained in this way will approximate the underlying distributions generating the instances, according to previously-studied metrics such as variation distance or KL-distance.

Theorem 1. *Let X be a domain of inputs. If there is a PAC algorithm in which each unsupervised learner may assign any real number to an element of X, then there is a PAC algorithm in which the learners must choose numbers that integrate or sum to 1 over the domain (i.e. are a probability distribution).*

Proof. Let $\mathcal{A}$ be an algorithm that returns any discriminant function. So in a problem instance, $\mathcal{A}$ is applied twice, once to A's data and once to B's data, and we obtain functions $f_A : X \longrightarrow \mathbf{R}$ and $f_B : X \longrightarrow \mathbf{R}$. (So for example any $x \in X$ with $f_A(x) > f_B(x)$ would be labeled as positive by the overall hypothesis, under our convention that A receives the positive examples.)

Our approach is to re-scale any function returned by the algorithm so that the outcome of any comparison is preserved, but the new functions sum or integrate to 1. In a case where, for example, $\sum_{x \in X} f_A(x) = 1$ and $\sum_{x \in X} f_B(x) = 2$, this initially appears problematic: f_B has to be scaled down, but then the new values of f_B may become less than f_A. Note however that we can modify f_A by choosing an arbitrary $\hat{x}$ in A's data, and adding 1 to $f_A(\hat{x})$. This can only improve the resulting classifier (it may cause $\hat{x}$ to be claimed by A where previously it was claimed by B). Now the new f_A together with f_B can both be rescaled down by a factor of 2, and comparisons are clearly preserved.

Making the above idea general, suppose that algorithm $\mathcal{A}$ takes a sample of data S and returns a function $f : X \longrightarrow \mathbf{R}$. Modify $\mathcal{A}$ as follows. Define $g(x) = e^{f(x)}/(1 + e^{f(x)})$, so the range of g is $(0, 1)$. Let $P(X)$ be a probability distribution over X that does not vanish anywhere. Let $s = \sum_{x \in X} g(x)P(x)$, or $\int_{x \in X} g(x)P(x)dx$ for continuous X. s is well-defined and lies in the range $(0, 1)$. Now for a discrete domain X, the probability distribution returned by the modified $\mathcal{A}$ is $D'(x) = g(x)P(x)$ for all $x \in X$ except for some arbitrary $\hat{x} \in S$, where $D'(\hat{x}) = g(x)P(x) + 1 - s$. For a continuous domain the probability distribution is the mixture of the continuous density $D'(x) = g(x)P(x)$ with coefficient s and a point probability mass located at some $\hat{x} \in S$ with probability $1 - s$. ◇

In view of the above result, we subsequently give algorithms for hypotheses that may output unrestricted real numbers. The next two results about PAC-learning with two unsupervised learners provide some further information about how it compares with other variants of PAC-learning in terms of which concept classes become learnable. First, note that the framework can be extended to a misclassification noise situation by letting each learner have examples that are (correctly or incorrectly) assigned the class label associated with that learner.

Theorem 2. *Any concept class that is PAC-learnable in the presence of uniform misclassification noise can be learned by two unsupervised learners in the presence of uniform misclassification noise if the input distribution is known to both learners.*

Proof. Let D be the known distribution over the input domain X. Let $\mathcal{C}$ be a concept class that is PAC-learnable with uniform misclassification noise. We may assume that $\mathcal{C}$ is closed under complementation (we have noted that if it is not closed under complementation we can take it closure under complementation which should still be PAC learnable).

Each learner takes a set of N examples, where N is chosen such that a standard PAC algorithm would have error bound ϵ^2. Let D^+ (resp. D^-) be the probability that an example generated by D belongs to target T (resp. $X \setminus T$). Let ν be the noise rate. With probability $\frac{(1-\nu)D^+}{(1-\nu)D^+ + \nu D^-}$ an example received by A belongs to target T; meanwhile with probability $\frac{(1-\nu)D^-}{(1-\nu)D^- + \nu D^+}$ an example received by B comes from $X \setminus T$.

Each learner labels all its examples as positive, and then generates a set of N examples from D, each of which is labeled positive with some probability $p < \frac{1}{2}$, otherwise negative. For learner A, the union of these two sets consists of a set of examples from a new probability distribution D', labeled by the same target concept T. It may be verified that the examples from T have misclassification noise with noise rate

$$\frac{(1-p)(D^+(1-\nu) + D^-\nu)}{(1-p)(D^+(1-\nu) + D^-\nu) + 1 - \nu}$$

and the examples from $X \setminus T$ have misclassification noise with noise rate

$$\frac{\nu + p(D^+(1-\nu) + D^-\nu)}{\nu + (D^+(1-\nu) + D^-\nu)}.$$

It may be verified from these expressions that there is a unique value of p in the range $[0, \frac{1}{2}]$ for which these two noise rates are equal, and for that value of p they are both strictly less than $\frac{1}{2}$.

Hence for some value of p we obtain data with uniform misclassification noise. An appropriate p can be found by trying all values $p = r\epsilon$ for $r = 0, \ldots, 1/2\epsilon$, and checking whether the hypothesis obtained (using a standard noise-tolerant PAC algorithm) is consistent with uniform misclassification noise.

The same reasoning applies to learner B using $X \setminus T$ as the target concept.

Let H be the set of examples labeled positive by the resulting hypothesis. Each learner assigns discriminant function values as follows. If the observed value of $D'(H)$ is at least $1-\epsilon$, use a value of $\frac{1}{2}$ for all elements of X. Otherwise use a value of 1 for elements of H and a value of 0 for elements of $X \setminus H$.

Let D'_A and D'_B be the D''s for learners A and B.

$D(T)$ is the probability that a random example from D belongs to T. Assuming $D(T) < 1-\epsilon$, we can say that error $O(\epsilon^2)$ with respect to D'_A implies error $O(\epsilon)$ with respect to D. If alternatively $D(T) \geq 1-\epsilon/2$, the hypothesis H found by A will have a probability $D'(H) > 1-\epsilon$ as observed on the data. A learner finding such a hypothesis then gives all examples a score of $\frac{1}{2}$, allowing B's scores to determine the overall classification. A similar argument applies for low values of $D(T)$, *i.e.* $\leq \epsilon/2$, (where we expect B to assign scores of $\frac{1}{2}$). ◇

It is probably not the case that noise-free distribution-specific learnability with two unsupervised learners is actually equivalent to standard PAC-learnability with uniform misclassification noise. This is because, given the Noisy Parity Assumption (that it is hard to PAC-learn parity functions in the presence of random misclassification noise given the uniform distribution over input vectors), noise-free distribution-specific learning with two unsupervised learners is tractable (see corollary 2) in a situation where the uniform misclassification noise situation is intractable.

The following result is a sufficient condition for learning with unsupervised learners:

Theorem 3. *If a concept class is closed under complementation and learnable from positive examples only, then it is learnable with two unsupervised learners.*

Proof. Let $X = X_A \cup X_B$ be the partition of the domain X where X_A is the set of positive examples and X_B the negative examples. Closure under complementation implies that X_B as well as X_A is a member of the concept class.

Both learners apply an algorithm that learns from positive examples only. Consequently A's hypothesis must be a subset of X_A and B's hypothesis must be a subset of X_B. A and B use discriminant functions f_A and f_B that are the indicator functions of their hypotheses. As a result, if f_A and f_B both have error at most ϵ, then A and B correctly claim all but a fraction ϵ of examples from X_A and X_B respectively. ◇

As a consequence we have

Corollary 1. *Boolean functions over a constant number of variables are learnable using unsupervised learners.*

Proof. The class of functions is clearly closed under complementation.

To learn the class from positive examples, suppose k is the number of variables in the target formula. Given a set S of boolean vectors that constitutes the observed data (assumed to be positive examples), label a new vector $\mathbf{v}$ as positive if and only if for each set of k attributes in $\mathbf{v}$, there is a member of S that agrees with $\mathbf{v}$ on those attributes.

It can be readily verified that for constant k, the time and sample complexity of the above rule is polynomial in the total number of variables. ◇

The following result distinguishes our learning setting from learnability with uniform misclassification noise, or learnability with a restricted focus of attention. A *parity function* [15] has an associated subset of the variables, and an associated "target parity" (even or odd), and evaluates to 1 provided that the parity of the number of "true" elements of that subset agrees with the target parity, otherwise the function evaluates to 0.

Corollary 2. *The class of parity functions is learnable by unsupervised learners.*

Proof. Once again it is clear that the class is closed under complementation.

To learn a parity function from positive examples only, then similar to the algorithm of [15], each unsupervised learner finds the affine subspace of $GF(2)^n$ spanned by its examples, and assigns a score of 1 to elements of that subspace and a score of 0 to all elements of the domain. $\diamondsuit$

3 Examples of Concrete Learning Problems

The algorithms in this section give an idea of the new technical challenges, and also distinguish the learning setting from various others. We have already distinguished the learning setting from learnability with uniform misclassification noise or learnability with a restricted focus of attention, and the result of section 3.2 distinguishes it from learnability with one-sided error or learnability from positive or negative examples only.

3.1 Monomials

Recall that a monomial is a boolean function consisting of the conjunction of a set of literals (where a literal is either a boolean attribute or its negation). Despite the simplicity of this class of functions, we have not resolved its learnability in the two unsupervised learners framework, even for monotone (*i.e.* negation-free) monomials. If the unsupervised learners are told which of them has the positive and which the negative examples, then the problem does have a simple solution (a property of any class of functions that is learnable from either positive examples only or else negative examples only). The "negative" unsupervised learner assigns a score of $\frac{1}{2}$ to all boolean vectors. The "positive" unsupervised learner uses its data to find a PAC hypothesis, and assigns a score of 1 to examples satisfying that hypothesis, and 0 to other examples.

Discussion of the Distribution-independent Learning Problem. Given a monomial f, let $pos(f)$ denote its satisfying assignments. The problem that arises when the unsupervised learners are not told which one is receiving the positive examples, is that the distribution over the negative examples could in fact produce boolean vectors that satisfy some monomial m that differs from target monomial t, but if $D(pos(m) \cap pos(t)) > \epsilon$ this may give excessive error. This problem can of course be handled in the special case where the monomial is over a constant number k of literals, and corollary 1 applies.

Learnability of Monomials over Vectors of Attributes Generated by a Product Distribution. In view of the importance of the concept class of monomials, we consider whether they are learnable given that the input distribution D belongs to a given class of probability distributions. This situation is intermediate between knowing D exactly (in which case by theorem 2 the problem would be solved since monomials are learnable in the presence of uniform misclassification noise) and the distribution-independent setting. We assume now that the class priors are known approximately, since we no longer have the equivalence of the one-button and two-button versions of PAC learnability. Formally, assume each learner can sample from D, but if the example drawn belongs to the other learner's class then the learner is told only that the example belonged to the other class, and no other information about it. Hence each learner has an "observed class prior", the observed probability that examples belong to one's own class.

Suppose that D is known to be a product distribution. Let $x_1, \ldots, x_n$ be the boolean attributes in examples. Let d_i, $i = 1, \ldots, n$, be the probability that the i-th attribute equals 1. For attribute x_i for which one of the literals x_i or $\overline{x_i}$ is in the target monomial t (we assume that they are not both in t), let p_i be the probability that the literal is satisfied, so $p_i = d_i$ for an un-negated literal, otherwise $p_i = 1 - d_i$.

We say that attribute x_i is "useful" if x_i or $\overline{x_i}$ is in t, and also $p_i \in [\epsilon, 1-\epsilon/n]$. Note that if $p_i < \epsilon$ then the probability that any example is positive is also $< \epsilon$, and if $p_i > 1 - \epsilon/n$ then only a very small fraction of examples can be negative due to their value of x_i.

The Algorithm.

We use the fact that for D a product distribution, D restricted to the positive examples of a monomial is also a product distribution. We apply a test (step 3 of the algorithm) to see whether the observed data appears to come from a product distribution. The test identifies negative data when there is more than one useful attribute. The discriminant function (computed in step 4) also handles the case when at most one attribute is useful.

1. Draw a sample S of size $O((n/\epsilon)^3 \log(\frac{1}{\delta}))$.
2. If the observed class prior of the examples is $\leq \epsilon/2$, reject all examples. Otherwise do the following.
3. (product distribution test) For each literal l that is satisfied by at least a fraction ϵ/n of elements of S, let S_l denote elements of S which satisfy l, and for each literal $l' \neq l$ check whether the fraction of examples satisfying l' differs by at least ϵ/n^2 from the fraction of examples belonging to S_l that satisfy l'. If any such l' exists, the test "fails" and we assume that the negative examples are being seen, and give all examples a score of $1/2$. Otherwise (the test is "passed") proceed to step 4:
4. Let L be the set of literals satisfied by *all* elements of S.
   a) If an example satisfies all the literals in L *and* fails to satisfy all literals that are satisfied by a fraction $< \epsilon/2n$ of elements of S, give that example a score of 1.

b) Otherwise, if the example still satisfies L, assign a score of $1/2$.
c) Otherwise assign a score of 0.

Note: step 3 is a test with "one-sided error" in the sense that we may reasonably expect all product distributions to pass the test, but there exist distributions other than product distributions that may also pass. However, we show below that when a product distribution restricted to the negative data of a monomial passes the test, then (with probability $\geq 1 - \delta$) there is at most one useful attribute.

Proving That the Algorithm is PAC. There must be at least one useful attribute in order for the frequency of both positive and negative examples to exceed ϵ. We consider two cases: first when there is only one useful attribute, second, when there is more than one.
Case 1: In this case, we expect the distributions over both the positive and negative examples to be close to product distributions, so that the test of step 3 of the algorithm will be passed in both A's case and B's case. Learner A (with probability $1-O(\delta)$) gives a score of 1 to examples that satisfy the useful literal l, with the exception of a small fraction of them due to the additional requirement in step 4a. Meanwhile, learner B assigns a score of $\leq \frac{1}{2}$ to all examples satisfying l, since l is not satisfied by any of B's data. Hence learner A claims all but a fraction $< \epsilon/2$ of the positive data. By a similar argument, learner B claims all but a fraction $< \epsilon/2$ of the negative data.
Case 2: When there are two useful attributes, the positive examples are still generated by a product distribution, so A's data pass the test of step 3. Meanwhile, with probability $> 1 - \delta$, B's data fail this test, since when we choose literal l in target t that happens to be useful, and remove elements of S which satisfy l, then the conditional probability that any other useful literal is satisfied, changes by $> \epsilon/n^2$. (A Chernoff bound analysis assures that the change will be detected with probability $1 - \delta/2$.) All examples are then given scores of $1/2$, and this allows A to claim positives and leave B the negatives.

3.2 Unions of Intervals

Let the domain be the real numbers $\mathbf{R}$, and assume that the target concept is a union of k intervals in $\mathbf{R}$. We show that this concept class is learnable by two unsupervised learners. This result shows that learnability with two unsupervised learners is distinct from learnability from positive examples only, or from negative examples only.

Each learner does the following. Let S be the set of real values that constitutes its data. Define discriminant function f as

$$f(r) = -\Big(\min_{s\in S, s>r}(s) - \max_{s\in S, s<r}(s)\Big) \;\text{ if } r \notin S$$

$$f(r) = 1 \;\text{ if } r \in S.$$

This choice of discriminant function ensures that when A's and B's scores are combined, the set of all points that are claimed by A consists of a union of at most k intervals, and this set contains A's data but not B's data. Hence we have a consistent hypothesis of V-C dimension no more than the target concept, so this method is PAC (with runtime polynomial in k, ϵ^{-1} and δ^{-1}). Note that the value of k needs to be prior knowledge for the purpose of identifying a sufficient sample size. This is in contrast with PAC learning in the standard setting, where an appropriate sample size can be identified using the standard on-line approach of comparing the number of examples seen so far with the complexity of the simplest consistent classifier, and continuing until the ratio is large enough.

3.3 Rectangles in the Plane with Bounded Aspect Ratio

Let α denote the length of the target rectangle divided by the width, and we give a PAC-learning algorithm that is polynomial in α as well as the standard PAC parameters. We do not have a PAC algorithm that works without the bound on the aspect ratio. A notable feature of this learning problem is that it seems to require quite a complex method, despite the simplicity of the concept class. Extensions are discussed in the next section.

The general idea is that each learner partitions the domain into rectangles containing equal numbers of its data points, and given a query point $\mathbf{q}$, compares the coordinates of $\mathbf{q}$ with other points in the partition element within which $\mathbf{q}$ falls. A high score is given when there exist points in that partition element with similar coordinate values.

The Algorithm. Each learner does the following.

1. Generate a sample of size $N = \Theta(\alpha \log(\delta^{-1})/\epsilon^9)$.
2. Build a partition P of the domain $\mathbf{R}^2$ as follows:
   a) Partition the domain into $1/\epsilon^2$ pieces using lines normal to the y-axis, such that each piece contains the same number of data points.[1]
   b) Partition each element of the above partition into $1/\epsilon^2$ pieces using lines normal to the x-axis, such that each piece contains the same number of data points.
3. For query point $\mathbf{q} \in \mathbf{R}^2$ the score assigned to $\mathbf{q}$ is computed as follows.
   a) Let $P_{\mathbf{q}} \in P$ be the rectangle in P containing $\mathbf{q}$.
   b) Let $S(P_{\mathbf{q}})$ be the sample points that lie inside $P_{\mathbf{q}}$. (So $|S(P_{\mathbf{q}})| = \Theta(\alpha \log(\delta^{-1})/\epsilon^5))$
   c) Sort $S(P_{\mathbf{q}}) \cup \{\mathbf{q}\}$ by x-coordinate. If $\mathbf{q}$ is among the first $(\frac{1}{\epsilon})^{-1}$ elements or among the last $(\frac{1}{\epsilon})^{-1}$ elements, then reject $\mathbf{q}$, *i.e.* assign $\mathbf{q}$ a score of $-\infty$ and terminate.
   d) If $\mathbf{q}$ was not rejected, define the x-cost of $\mathbf{q}$ to be the difference between the x-coordinates of the two neighbors of $\mathbf{q}$.
   e) Sort $S(P_{\mathbf{q}}) \cup \{\mathbf{q}\}$ by y-coordinate. If $\mathbf{q}$ is among the first $(\frac{1}{\epsilon})^{-1}$ elements or among the last $(\frac{1}{\epsilon})^{-1}$ elements, then reject $\mathbf{q}$.

[1] Throughout we ignore rounding error in situations where for example an equal partition is impossible; such rounding will only change quantities by a constant.

f) If $\mathbf{q}$ was not rejected, define the y-cost of $\mathbf{q}$ to be the difference between the y-coordinates of the two neighbors of $\mathbf{q}$.
g) Finally, the score assigned to $\mathbf{q}$ is the negation of the sum of the x-cost and y-cost.

Proving That the Algorithm is PAC. Let P_A be the partition constructed by A and let P_B be the partition constructed by B. Let μ_A (respectively μ_B) be the measure on $\mathbf{R}^2$ induced by the input distribution D restricted to target T (respectively T', the complement of T) and re-normalised, so that we have $\mu_A(\mathbf{R}^2) = \mu_B(\mathbf{R}^2) = 1$. So, given region $R \subseteq \mathbf{R}^2$, $\mu_A(R)$ is the probability that a random input x lies within R conditioned on x being an element of T. Let $\hat{\mu}_A$ and $\hat{\mu}_B$ denote the measures μ_A and μ_B as observed by A and B respectively on the random examples used in the algorithm. The well-known V-C theory of [4] says that for a concept class $\mathcal{C}$ of V-C dimension v, given a sample of size[2] $O(v \log(\delta^{-1}\epsilon^{-1})/\epsilon)$, we have that with probability $1-\delta$,

$$|\hat{\mu}(C) - \mu(C)| \leq \epsilon \text{ for all } C \in \mathcal{C}$$

where μ is a probability measure and $\hat{\mu}$ is the measure as observed on the sample. Noting that axis-aligned rectangles in $\mathbf{R}^2$ have V-C dimension 4, we deduce that if learners A and B draw samples of size $O(\log(\delta^{-1}\epsilon^{-1})/\epsilon)$, then with probability $1-\delta$,

$$|\hat{\mu}_A(R) - \mu_A(R)| \leq \epsilon \text{ and}$$

$$|\hat{\mu}_B(R) - \mu_B(R)| \leq \epsilon, \text{ for all rectangles } R.$$

The following fact emerges automatically from the V-C bounds:

Remark 1. N is chosen such that if learners A and B use samples of size N, then with probability $1 - O(\delta)$ we have that for all rectangles R:

$$|\hat{\mu}_A(R) - \mu_A(R)| \leq \epsilon^9$$

$$|\hat{\mu}_B(R) - \mu_B(R)| \leq \epsilon^9.$$

From the construction of partition P we note:

Remark 2. P_A and P_B are each of size $(1/\epsilon)^4$, and each element of P_A (respectively P_B) contains $\Theta(\alpha \log(\delta^{-1})(1/\epsilon)^5)$ of A's (respectively B's) data points.

From remark 2, given rectangle $R \in P_A$, $\hat{\mu}_A(R) = \epsilon^4$, and consequently $|\mu_A(R) - \epsilon^4| \leq \epsilon^9$ with high probability, using remark 1. Clearly all rectangles in P_A intersect target rectangle T (similarly members of P_B intersect T'). Now consider the potential problem of rectangles in P_B that contain positive examples. We continue by upper-bounding the number of those rectangles, and

[2] This is weaker than the known bound — we are using a weak bound to simplify the presentation.

upper-bounding the amount of damage each one can do (due to claiming data examples that should be claimed by A).

Let $P_A^* \subseteq P_A$ be elements of P_A which intersect T' (so are not proper subsets of T). Similarly let P_B^* denote elements of P_B which intersect T. We show that the number of elements of P_A^* and P_B^* is substantially smaller than the cardinalities of P_A and P_B.

Remark 3. Any axis-aligned line cuts $(\frac{1}{\epsilon})^2$ elements of P_A and similarly $(\frac{1}{\epsilon})^2$ elements of P_B.

Corollary 3. *The boundary of T intersects at most $O((\frac{1}{\epsilon})^2)$ elements of P_A and similarly at most $O((\frac{1}{\epsilon})^2)$ elements of P_B.*

In particular, it intersects at most $4.(\frac{1}{\epsilon})^2$ elements of either partition.

So partition P_B has $(\frac{1}{\epsilon})^4$ elements each containing $(\frac{1}{\epsilon})^5$ data points, and only $O((\frac{1}{\epsilon})^2)$ of them intersect T. Now we consider how an element $R \in P_B$ could intersect T. We divide the kinds of overlap into

1. An edge overlap, where one edge and no vertices of T are overlapped by R.
2. A two-edge overlap, where 2 opposite edges and no corner of T are overlapped by R.
3. Any overlap where R contains a corner of T.

We treat these as separate cases. Note that since there are ≤ 4 overlaps of type 3 we may obtain relatively high bounds on the error they introduce, by comparison with the edge and two-edge overlaps, of which there may be up to $(\frac{1}{\epsilon})^2$. Throughout we use the following notation. Let $\mathbf{x}$ be a point in target rectangle T which is being assigned scores using A's and B's partitions. Let $\mathbf{x} \in$ rectangle $R_A \in P_A$ and $\mathbf{x} \in R_B \in P_B$, so that R_A intersects T.

Case 1: (edge overlap) R_B has an edge overlap with T. Consider steps 3c and 3e of the algorithm. When $\mathbf{x}$ is being compared with the points in R_B it will have either an x-coordinate or a y-coordinate which is maximal or minimal for data points observed in R_B. One of these steps of the algorithm will cause B to reject $\mathbf{x}$. But $\mathbf{x}$ will only have a probability $O(\epsilon^5)$ of having a maximal or minimal coordinate value amongst points in R_A (since R_A contains $(\frac{1}{\epsilon})^5$ data points and $\mathbf{x}$ is generated by the same distribution that generated those data points).

Case 2: (two-edge overlap) There are at most $(\frac{1}{\epsilon})^2$ two-edge overlaps possible. Suppose that in fact R_B overlaps the top and bottom edges of T (the following argument will apply also to the other sub-case). Hence all the two-edge overlaps do in fact overlap the top and bottom edges of T. Let x_T and y_T denote the lengths of T as measured in the x and y directions, so we have $x_T/y_T \in [1/\alpha, \alpha]$. Then the y-cost of R_B is at least y_T. Meanwhile, all but a fraction ϵ of boxes in P_A will give a y-cost of $\leq \epsilon \cdot y_T$. Also, all but a fraction ϵ of boxes in P_A will have x-costs at most $\epsilon \cdot x_T$. Using our aspect ratio assumption, this is at most $\epsilon\alpha y_T$. Hence, for points in all but a fraction ϵ of boxes in P_A, the y-cost will dominate, and the score assigned by B will exceed A's score.

Case 3: (corner overlap) Suppose R_B overlaps a corner of T. We show that R_B introduces error $O(\epsilon)$, and since there are at most 4 such rectangles, this case is then satisfactory. For R_B to introduce error $> \epsilon$, it must overlap a fraction $\Omega(\epsilon)$ of rectangles in P_A, hence $> (\frac{1}{\epsilon})^3$ rectangles in P_A. In this situation, R_B contains $\Omega((\frac{1}{\epsilon})^3)$ recangles in P_A in its interior. On average, both the x and y coordinates of sample points in these interior rectangles will be $\Omega(\frac{1}{\epsilon})$ closer to each other than the points in R_B. This means that only an ϵ-fraction of points in these elements of P_A will have coordinates closer to points in R_B, than to some other point in the same element of P_A. Hence all but an ϵ-fraction of these points will be claimed by A.

Discussion, possible extensions. Obviously we would like to know whether it is possible to have PAC learnability without the restriction on the aspect ratio of the target rectangle. The restriction is arguably benign from a practical point of view. Alternatively, various reasonable "well-behavedness" restrictions on the input distribution would probably allow the removal of the aspect ratio restriction, and also allow simpler algorithms.

The extension of this result to unions of k rectangles in the plane is fairly straightforward, assuming that the aspect ratio restriction is that both the target region and its complement are expressible as a union of k rectangles all with bound α on the aspect ratio. The general idea being used is likely to be extendable to any constant dimension, but then the case analysis (on the different ways that a partition element may intersect the region with the opposite class label) may need to be extended. If so it should generalize to unions of boxes[3] in fixed dimension (as studied in [6] in the setting of query learning, a generalization is studied in [5] in PAC learning). Finally, if boxes are PAC learnable with two unsupervised learners in time polynomial in the dimension, then this would imply learnability of monomials, considered previously.

3.4 Linear Separators in the Plane

Given a set S of points in the plane, it would be valid for an unsupervised learner to use a probability distribution whose domain is the convex hull[4] of S, *provided that only a "small" fraction of elements of S are actually vertices of that convex hull.* For a general PAC algorithm we have to be able to handle the case when the convex hull has most or all of the points at its vertices, as can be expected to happen for an input distribution whose domain is the boundary of a circle, for example. Our general approach is to start out by computing the convex hull P and give maximal score to points inside P (which are guaranteed to have the same class label as the observed data). Then give an intermediate score to points in a polygon Q containing P, where Q has fewer edges. We argue that the way Q is chosen ensures that most points in Q are indeed claimed by the learner.

---

[3] A *box* means the intersection of a set of halfspaces whose bounding hyperplanes are axis-aligned, *i.e.* each hyperplane is normal to one of the axes.

[4] The *convex hull* of a finite set S of points is the smallest convex polygon (more generally, polytope) that contains S. Clearly all the vertices of the convex hull of S are members of S.

The Algorithm. The general idea is to choose a discriminant function in such a way that we can show that the boundary between the classes is piecewise linear with $O(\sqrt{N})$ pieces, where N is sample size. This sublinear growth ensures a PAC guarantee, since we have an "Occam" hypothesis — the V-C dimension of piecewise linear separators in the plane with $O(\sqrt{N})$ pieces is itself $O(\sqrt{N})$.

1. Draw a sample S of size $N = \Theta(\log(\delta^{-2}\epsilon^{-2})/\epsilon^2)$.
2. Let polygon P be the convex hull of S.
3. Let Q be a polygon having $\leq 2 + \sqrt{N}$ edges such that
   a) Every edge of Q contains an edge of P
   b) Adjacent edges of Q contain edges of P that are $\leq \sqrt{N}$ apart in the adjacency sequence of P's edges.
4. Define discriminant function h as follows.
   a) For points in P use a score of 1.
   b) For each region contained between P and 2 adjacent edges of Q, give points in that region a score of the negation of the area of that region.
   c) Reject all other points (not in Q).

Regarding step 3: Q can be found in polynomial time; we allow Q to have $2 + \sqrt{N}$ edges since P may have 2 acute vertices that force pairs of adjacent edges of Q to contain adjacent edges of P.

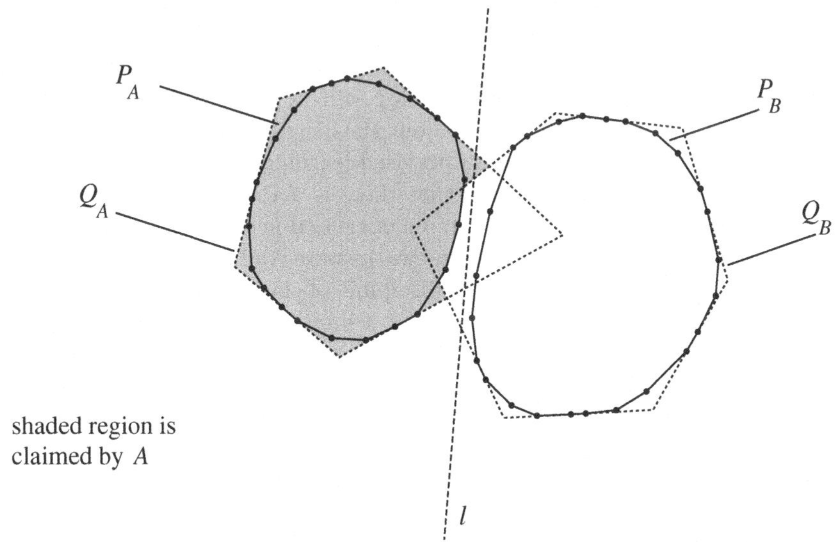

Fig. 1.

Proving That the Algorithm is PAC. Figure 1 illustrates the construction. Let P_A and P_B be the convex hulls initially found by learners A and B respectively. They define subsets of the regions claimed by A and B respectively. Let Q_A and Q_B be the polygons Q constructed by A and B respectively. Let l be a line separating P_A and P_B. Observe that Q_A and Q_B respectively can each only have at most two edges that cross l, and at most one vertex on the opposite side of l from P_A and P_B respectively, using the fact that each edge of Q_A contains an edge of P_A, and similarly for Q_B and P_B.

Hence only one of the regions enclosed between P_A and two adjacent edges of Q_A can cross line l, and potentially be used to claim part of the interior of Q_B. If this region contains more than one of the similar regions in Q_B, then it will not in fact claim those regions of Q_B, since the score assigned to its interior will be lower. Omitting the details, it is not hard to show using these observations that the region claimed by A is enclosed by a polygon with $O(\sqrt{N})$ edges, and similarly for B. N was chosen such that the V-C bound of section 3.3 ensures PAC-ness with parameters ϵ and δ.

4 Conclusion and Open Problems

The standard requirement of PAC learning that algorithms must work for any input distribution D, appears to give rise to very novel algorithmic challenges, even for fairly elementary computational learning problems. At the same time however, the resulting algorithms do not appear to be applicable to the sort of class overlap situations that motivated the learning setting. Probably it will be necessary to model learning situations with an additional assumption that D should belong to some given class of distributions, as we did in section 3.1. Our formalisation of this learning setting will hopefully provide insights into what assumptions need to be made about the distribution of inputs, in order for standard practical methods of unsupervised learning to be applied.

The main open question is whether there is a PAC-learnable concept class that is not PAC-learnable in the two unsupervised learners framework. It would be remarkable if the two learning frameworks were equivalent, in view of the way the PAC criterion seems to impose a discipline of class separation on algorithms. Regarding specific concept classes, the most interesting one to get an answer for seems to be the class of monomials, a special case of nearly all boolean concept classes studied in the literature. It may be possible to extend the approach in section 3.1 to the assumption that D is a mixture of two product distributions, a class of distributions shown to be learnable in [8,11].

Related open questions are: does there exist such a concept class for computationally unbounded learners (where the only issue is sufficiency of information contained in a polynomial-size sample). Also, can it be shown that *proper* PAC-learnability holds for some concept class but not in the two unsupervised learners version. (So, we have given algorithms for various learning problems that are known to be properly PAC-learnable, but the hypotheses we construct do not generally belong to the concept classes.)

References

1. E.L. Allwein, R.E. Schapire and Y. Singer (2000). Reducing Multiclass to Binary: A Unifying Approach for Margin Classifiers. *Journal of Machine Learning Research* **1**, 113-141.
2. M. Anthony and N. Biggs (1992). *Computational Learning Theory*, Cambridge Tracts in Theoretical Computer Science, Cambridge University Press, Cambridge.
3. C.M. Bishop (1995). *Neural Networks for Pattern Recognition*, Oxford University Press.
4. A. Blumer, A. Ehrenfeucht, D. Haussler and M.K. Warmuth (1989). Learnability and the Vapnik-Chervonenkis Dimension, J.ACM **36**, 929-965.
5. N.H. Bshouty, S.A. Goldman, H.D. Mathias, S.Suri and H. Tamaki (1998). Noise-Tolerant Distribution-Free Learning of General Geometric Concepts. *Journal of the ACM* **45**(5), pp. 863-890.
6. N.H. Bshouty, P.W. Goldberg, S.A. Goldman and H.D. Mathias (1999). Exact learning of discretized geometric concepts. *SIAM J. Comput.* **28**(2) pp. 674-699.
7. N. Cristianini and J. Shawe-Taylor (2000). *An Introduction to Support Vector Machines.* Cambridge University Press.
8. M. Cryan, L. Goldberg and P. Goldberg (1998). Evolutionary Trees can be Learned in Polynomial Time in the Two-State General Markov Model. *Procs. of 39th FOCS symposium*, pp. 436-445.
9. S. Dasgupta (1999). Learning mixtures of Gaussians. *40th IEEE Symposium on Foundations of Computer Science.*
10. R.O. Duda and P.E. Hart. *Pattern Classification and Scene Analysis.* Wiley, New York (1973).
11. Y. Freund and Y. Mansour (1999). Estimating a mixture of two product distributions. *Procs. of 12th COLT conference*, pp. 53-62.
12. A. Frieze, M. Jerrum and R. Kannan (1996). Learning Linear Transformations. *37th IEEE Symposium on Foundations of Computer Science*, pp. 359-368.
13. V. Guruswami and A. Sahai (1999). Multiclass Learning, Boosting, and Error-Correcting Codes. *Procs. of 12th COLT conference*, pp. 145-155.
14. D. Haussler, M. Kearns, N. Littlestone and M.K. Warmuth (1991). Equivalence of Models for Polynomial Learnability. *Information and Computation*, 95(2), pp. 129-161.
15. D. Helmbold, R. Sloan and M.K. Warmuth (1992). Learning Integer Lattices. *SIAM Journal on Computing*, 21(2), pp. 240-266.
16. M.J. Kearns (1993). Efficient Noise-Tolerant Learning From Statistical Queries, *Procs. of the 25th Annual Symposium on the Theory of Computing*, pp. 392-401.
17. M. Kearns, Y. Mansour, D. Ron, R. Rubinfeld, R.E. Schapire and L. Sellie (1994). On the Learnability of Discrete Distributions, *Proceedings of the 26th Annual ACM Symposium on the Theory of Computing*, pp. 273-282.
18. M.J. Kearns and R.E. Schapire (1994). Efficient Distribution-free Learning of Probabilistic Concepts, *Journal of Computer and System Sciences*, **48**(3) 464-497. (see also FOCS '90)
19. J.C. Platt, N. Cristianini and J. Shawe-Taylor (2000). Large Margin DAGs for Multiclass Classification, *Procs. of 12th NIPS conference.*
20. L.G. Valiant (1984). A Theory of the Learnable. *Commun. ACM* **27**(11), pp. 1134-1142.
21. L.G. Valiant (1985). Learning disjunctions of conjunctions. *Procs. of 9th International Joint Conference on Artificial Intelligence.*

Strong Entropy Concentration, Game Theory, and Algorithmic Randomness

Peter Grünwald*

EURANDOM
Postbus 513
5600 MB Eindhoven
The Netherlands pdg@cwi.nl

Abstract. We give a characterization of Maximum Entropy/Minimum Relative Entropy inference by providing two 'strong entropy concentration' theorems. These theorems unify and generalize Jaynes' 'concentration phenomenon' and Van Campenhout and Cover's 'conditional limit theorem'. The theorems characterize exactly in what sense a 'prior' distribution Q conditioned on a given constraint and the distribution $\tilde{P}$ minimizing $D(P\|Q)$ over all P satisfying the constraint are 'close' to each other. We show how our theorems are related to 'universal models' for exponential families, thereby establishing a link with Rissanen's MDL/stochastic complexity. We then apply our theorems to establish the relationship (A) between entropy concentration and a game-theoretic characterization of Maximum Entropy Inference due to Topsøe and others; (B) between maximum entropy distributions and sequences that are random (in the sense of Martin-Löf/Kolmogorov) with respect to the given constraint. These two applications have strong implications for the use of Maximum Entropy distributions in *sequential prediction tasks*, both for the logarithmic loss and for general loss functions. We identify circumstances under which Maximum Entropy predictions are almost optimal.

1 Introduction

Jaynes' Maximum Entropy (MaxEnt) Principle is a well-known principle for inductive inference [5,7,24,15,25,4,10,19]. It has been applied to statistical and machine learning problems ranging from protein modeling so stock market prediction [17]. One of its characterizations (some would say 'justifications') is the so-called *concentration phenomenon* [13,14]. Here is an informal version of this phenomenon, in Jaynes' words:

* Also: CWI, Kruislaan 413, 1098 SJ Amsterdam. The author would like to thank Richard Gill and Phil Dawid for very useful discussions regarding resp. conditioning on measure 0-events and the concentration phenomenon. Part of this research was performed while the author was at the Computer Science Department of Stanford University, financed by an NWO (Netherlands Organization of Scientific Research) TALENT Grant.

D. Helmbold and B. Williamson (Eds.): COLT/EuroCOLT 2001, LNAI 2111, pp. 320–336, 2001.

> "If the information incorporated into the maximum-entropy analysis includes all the constraints actually operating in the random experiment, then the distribution predicted by maximum entropy is overwhelmingly the most likely to be observed experimentally." [16, Page 1124]

For the case in which a prior distribution over the domain at hand is available, Van Campenhout and Cover [25,4] have proven the related *conditional limit theorem*. In Part I of this paper (Sections 2-4), we provide a strong generalization of both the concentration phenomenon and the conditional limit theorem. In Part II (Section 5) we apply this. We first show how our theorems can be used to construct universal models for exponential families, thereby establishing a link with Rissanen's Minimum Description Length Principle. We then extend an existing game-theoretic characterization of Maximum Entropy due to Topsøe [24]. Finally we combine the results of Part I with the theory of algorithmic (Martin-Löf/Kolmogorov) randomness. This allows us to substantiate the often-heard informal claim that 'adopting the Maximum Entropy distribution leads to good predictions if the data are random with respect to the given constraint' and to make precise informal notions like '*all* constraints *actually* operating in an environment' as used in Jaynes' statement above. We end by discussing implications of our results in Part II for (sequential) *prediction*. We identify circumstances in which Maximum Entropy distributions lead to almost optimal predictions. The proofs of Theorem 1 and Theorem 3 are in the paper; proofs of other theorems, as well as extended discussion, can be found in the technical report [12].

2 Informal Overview

Maximum Entropy. Let X be a random variable taking values in some set $\mathcal{X}$, which (only for the time being!) we assume to be finite: $\mathcal{X} = \{1, \ldots, m\}$. Let P, Q be distributions for $\mathcal{X}$ with probability mass functions p and q. We define $\mathbf{H}_Q(P)$, *the Q-entropy of P*, as

$$\mathbf{H}_Q(P) = -E_P[\log \frac{p(x)}{q(x)}] = -D(P||Q) \tag{1}$$

In the usual MaxEnt setting[1], we are given a 'prior' distribution Q and a *moment constraint*:

$$E[T(X)] = \tilde{t} \tag{2}$$

where T is some function $T : \mathcal{X} \to \mathbf{R}^k$ for some $k > 0$. We define, if it exists, $\tilde{P}$ to be the unique distribution over $\mathcal{X}$ that maximizes the Q-entropy over all distributions (over $\mathcal{X}$) satisfying (2):

$$\tilde{P} = \arg \max_{\{P: E_P[T(X)] = \tilde{t}\}} \mathbf{H}_Q(P) = \arg \min_{\{P: E_P[T(X)] = \tilde{t}\}} D(P||Q) \tag{3}$$

[1] More general formulations with arbitrary convex constraints exist [5], but here we stick to constraints of form (2).

The MaxEnt Principle then tells us that, in absence of any further knowledge about the 'true' or 'posterior' distribution according to which data are distributed, our best guess for it is $\tilde{P}$. In practical problems we are usually not given a constraint of form (2). Rather we are given an *empirical constraint* of the form

$$\frac{1}{n}\sum_{i=1}^{n} T(X_i) = \tilde{t} \quad \text{which we always abbreviate to '}\overline{T^{(n)}} = \tilde{t}\text{'} \tag{4}$$

The MaxEnt Principle is then usually applied as follows: suppose we are given an empirical constraint of form (4). We then have to make predictions about new data coming from the same source. In absence of knowledge of any 'true' distribution generating this data, we should make our predictions based on the MaxEnt distribution $\tilde{P}$ for the moment constraint (2) corresponding to empirical constraint (4). $\tilde{P}$ is extended to several outcomes by taking the product distribution.

The Concentration Phenomenon and The Conditional Limit Theorem. Why should this procedure make any sense? Here is one justification. If $\mathcal{X}$ is finite, and in the absence of any prior knowledge beside the constraint, one usually picks the uniform distribution for Q. In this case, Jaynes' 'concentration phenomenon' applies[2]. It says that for all $\epsilon > 0$,

$$Q^n(\sup_{j\in\mathcal{X}} |\frac{1}{n}\sum_{i=1}^{n} I_j(X_i) - \tilde{P}(X = j)| > \epsilon \mid \overline{T^{(n)}} = \tilde{t}) = O(e^{-cn}) \tag{5}$$

for some constant c depending on ϵ. Here Q^n is the n-fold product distribution of Q, and I is the indicator function: $I_j(x) = 1$ if $x = j$ and 0 otherwise. In words, for the overwhelming majority among the sequences satisfying the constraint, the empirical frequencies are close to the maximum entropy probabilities. It turns out that (5) still holds if Q is non-uniform. For an illustration we refer to Example 1. A closely related result (Theorem 1, [25]) is the Van Campenhout-Cover conditional limit theorem[3], which says that

$$\lim_{\substack{n\to\infty \\ n\tilde{t}\in\mathbf{N}}} Q^1(\cdot \mid \overline{T^{(n)}} = \tilde{t}) = \tilde{P}^1(\cdot) \tag{6}$$

where $Q^1(\cdot \mid \overline{T^{(n)}} = \tilde{t})$ and $\tilde{P}^1(\cdot)$ refer to the marginal distribution of X_1 under $Q(\cdot \mid \overline{T^{(n)}} = \tilde{t})$ and $\tilde{P}$ respectively.

Our Results. Both theorems above say that for some sets $\mathcal{A}$,

$$Q^n(\mathcal{A} \mid \overline{T^{(n)}} = \tilde{t}) \approx \tilde{P}^n(\mathcal{A}) \tag{7}$$

[2] We are referring here to the version in [13]. The theorem in [14] extends this in a direction different from the one we consider here.

[3] This theorem too has later been extended in several directions different from the one considered here [6]; see the discussion at the end of Section 4.

In the concentration phenomenon, the set $\mathcal{A} \subset \mathcal{X}^n$ is about the frequencies of individual outcomes in the sample. In the conditional limit theorem $\mathcal{A} \subset \mathcal{X}^1$ only concerns the first outcome. One might conjecture that (7) holds asymptotically in a much wider sense, namely for *just about any set whose probability one may be interested in.* For examples of such sets see Example 1. In Theorems 1 and 2 we show that (7) indeed holds for a very large class of sets; moreover, we give an explicit indication of the error one makes if one approximates $Q(\mathcal{A} \mid \overline{T^{(n)}} = \tilde{t})$ by $\tilde{P}(\mathcal{A})$. In this way we unify and strengthen both the concentration phenomenon and the conditional limit theorem. To be more precise, let $\{\mathcal{A}_n\}$, with $\mathcal{A}_i \subset \mathcal{X}^i$ be a sequence of 'typical' sets for $\tilde{P}$ in the sense that $\tilde{P}^n(\mathcal{A}_n)$ goes to 1 sufficiently fast. Then broadly speaking Theorem 1 shows that $Q^n(\mathcal{A}_n \mid \overline{T^{(n)}} = \tilde{t})$ goes to 1 too, 'almost' as fast as $\tilde{P}^n(\mathcal{A}_n)$. Theorem 2, our main theorem, says that, if m is an arbitrary increasing sequence with $\lim_{n\to\infty} m/n = 0$, then for *every* (measurable) sequence $\{\mathcal{A}_m\}$ (i.e. not just the typical ones), with $\mathcal{A}_m \subset \mathcal{X}^m$, $\tilde{P}^n(\mathcal{A}_m) \to Q^n(\mathcal{A}_m \mid \overline{T^{(n)}} = \tilde{t})$. Then, in Section 5, we first connect this to the notion of 'universal models' as arising in the MDL (Minimum Description Length) approach to inductive inference. We next show in what sense our strong concentration phenomena really provide a 'justification', not just a characterization, of MaxEnt. We show first (Theorem 3) that our concentration phenomenon implies that the MaxEnt distribution $\tilde{P}$ *uniquely* achieves the best minimax logarithmic loss achievable for sequential prediction of samples satisfying the constraint. We also show (Theorem 4) that for sequences that are algorithmically *random* relative to the constraint, $\tilde{P}$ achieves good loss also for loss functions other than the logarithmic loss.

3 Mathematical Preliminaries

The Sample Space. From now on we assume a sample space $\mathcal{X} \subseteq \mathbf{R}^l$ for some $l > 0$ and let X be the random vector with $X(x) = x$ for all $x \in \mathcal{X}$. We reserve the symbol Q to refer to a distribution for X called the *prior distribution* (formally, Q is a distribution over $(\mathcal{X}, \sigma(X))$ where $\sigma(X)$ is the Borel-σ-algebra generated by X). We will be interested in sequences of i.i.d. random variables $X_1, X_2, \ldots$, all distributed according to Q. Whenever no confusion can arise, we use Q also to refer to the joint (product) distribution of $\times_{i\in\mathbf{N}} X_i$. Otherwise, we use Q^m to denote the m-fold product distribution of Q. The sample $(X_1, \ldots, X_m)$ will also be written as $X^{(m)}$.

The Constraint Functions T. Let $T = (T_{[1]}, \ldots, T_{[k]})$ be a k-dimensional random vector that is $\sigma(X)$-measurable. We refer to the event $\{x \in \mathcal{X} \mid T(x) = t\}$ both as '$T(X) = t$' and as '$T = t$'. Similarly we write $T_i = t$ as an abbreviation of $T(X_i) = t$ and $T^{(n)}$ as short for $(T(X_1), \ldots, T(X_n))$. The *average* of n observations of T will be denoted by $\overline{T^{(n)}} := n^{-1} \sum_{i=1}^{n} T(X_i)$. We assume that the support of $\mathcal{X}$ is either countable (in which case the prior distribution Q admits a probability mass function) or that it is a connected subset of $\mathbf{R}^l$ for some $l > 1$ (in which case we assume that Q has a bounded continuous density with respect to Lebesgue measure). In both cases, we denote the probability mass function/density by q. If $\mathcal{X}$ is countable, we shall further assume that T is of the *lattice form* (which it will be in most applications):

Definition 1. **[9, Page 490]** *A k-dimensional lattice random vector $T = (T_{[1]}, \ldots, T_{[k]})$ is a random vector for which there exists real-valued $b_1, \ldots, b_k$ and $h_1, \ldots, h_k$ such that, for $1 \leq j \leq k$, $\forall x \in \mathcal{X} : T_{[j]}(x) \in \{b_j + sh_j \mid s \in \mathbf{N}\}$. We call the largest h_i for which this holds the* span *of $T_{[i]}$.*

If X is continuous, we shall assume that T is 'regular':

Definition 2. *We say a k-dimensional random vector is of* regular continuous form *if its distribution under Q admits a bounded continuous density with respect to Lebesgue measure.*

Maximum Entropy. Throughout the paper, log is used to denote logarithm to base 2. Let P, Q be distributions for $\mathcal{X}$. We define $\mathbf{H}_Q(P)$, *the Q-entropy of P*, as

$$\mathbf{H}_Q(P) = -D(P||Q) \tag{8}$$

This is defined even if P or Q have no densities, see [5]. Assume we are given a constraint of form (2), i.e. $E_P[T(X)] = \tilde{t}$. Here $T = (T_{[1]}, \ldots, T_{[k]}), \tilde{t} = (\tilde{t}_{[1]}, \ldots, \tilde{t}_{[k]})$. We define, if it exists, $\tilde{P}$ to be the unique distribution over $\mathcal{X}$ that maximizes the Q-entropy over all distributions (over $(\mathcal{X}, \sigma(X))$) satisfying (2). That is, $\tilde{P}$ is given by (3). If Condition 1 below holds, then $\tilde{P}$ exists and is given by the exponential form (9), as expressed in the proposition below. In the condition, the notation $a^T b$ refers to the dot product between a and b.

Condition 1: There exists $\tilde{\beta} \in \mathbf{R}^k$ such that $Z(\tilde{\beta}) = \int_{x \in \mathcal{X}} \exp(-\tilde{\beta}^T T(x)) dQ(x)$ is finite and the distribution $\tilde{P}$ with density (with respect to Q)

$$\tilde{p}(x) := \frac{1}{Z(\tilde{\beta})} e^{-\tilde{\beta}^T T(x)} \tag{9}$$

satisfies $E_{\tilde{P}}[T(X)] = \tilde{t}$.

Proposition 1 ([5]). *Assume Condition 1 holds for Constraint (2). Then it holds for only one $\tilde{\beta} \in \mathbf{R}^k$ and* $\inf \{D(P||Q) \mid P : E_P[T(X)] = \tilde{t}\}$ *is attained by (and only by) the $\tilde{P}$ given by (9).*

If Condition 1 holds, then $\tilde{t}$ determines both $\tilde{\beta}$ and $\tilde{P}$. In our theorems, we shall simply assume that Condition 1 holds. A sufficient (by no means necessary!) requirement for Condition 1 is for example that Q has bounded support; see [5] for a more precise characterization. We will also assume in our theorems the following natural condition:

Condition 2: The 'T-covariance matrix' Σ with $\Sigma_{ij} = E_{\tilde{P}}[T_{[i]}T_{[j]}] - E_{\tilde{P}}[T_{[i]}]E_{\tilde{P}}[T_{[j]}]$ is invertible.

Σ is guaranteed to exist by Condition 1 (see any book with a treatment of exponential families, for example, [18]) and will be singular only if either $\tilde{t}_j$ lies at the boundary of the range of $T_{[j]}$ for some j or if some of the $T_{[j]}$ are affine combinations of the others. In the first case, the constraint $T_{[j]} = \tilde{t}_j$ can be replaced by restricting the sample space to $\{x \in \mathcal{X} \mid T_{[j]}(x) = \tilde{t}_j\}$ and considering the remaining constraints for the new sample space. In the second case, we can remove some of the $T_{[i]}$ from the constraint without changing the set of distributions satisfying it, making Σ once again invertible.

4 The Concentration Theorems

Theorem 1. (the concentration phenomenon for typical sets, lattice case) *Assume we are given a constraint of form (2) such that T is of the lattice form and $h = (h_1, \ldots, h_k)$ is the span of T and such that conditions 1 and 2 hold. Then there exists a sequence $\{c_i\}$ satisfying*

$$\lim_{n\to\infty} c_n = \frac{\prod_{j=1}^k h_j}{\sqrt{(2\pi)^k \det \Sigma}}$$

such that

1. *Let $\mathcal{A}_1, \mathcal{A}_2, \ldots$ be an arbitrary sequence of sets with $\mathcal{A}_i \subset \mathcal{X}^i$. For all n with $Q(T_n = \tilde{t}) > 0$, we have:*

$$\tilde{P}(\mathcal{A}_n) \geq n^{-k/2} c_n Q(\mathcal{A}_n \mid \overline{T^{(n)}} = \tilde{t}). \tag{10}$$

Hence if $\mathcal{B}_1, \mathcal{B}_2, \ldots$ is a sequence of sets with $\mathcal{B}_i \subset \mathcal{X}^i$ whose probability tends to 1 under $\tilde{P}$ in the sense that $1 - \tilde{P}(\mathcal{B}_n) = O(f(n)n^{-k/2})$ for some function $f : \mathbf{N} \to \mathbf{R}$; $f(n) = o(1)$, then $Q(\mathcal{B}_n | \overline{T^{(n)}} = \tilde{t})$ tends to 1 in the sense that $1 - Q(\mathcal{B}_n | \overline{T^{(n)}} = \tilde{t}) = O(f(n))$.

2. *If for all n, $\mathcal{A}_n \subseteq \{x^{(n)} \mid n^{-1} \sum_{i=1}^n T(x_i) = \tilde{t}\}$ then (10) holds with equality.*

Theorem 1 has applications for coding/compression, Minimum Description Length inference and prediction. These are discussed in Section 5. The relation of the Theorem to Jaynes' original concentration phenomenon is discussed at the end of this section.

Proof. We need the following theorem[4]:

[4] Feller gives the local central limit theorem only for 1-dimensional lattice random variables with $E[T] = 0$ and $\text{var}[T] = 1$; extending the proof to k-dimensional random vectors with arbitrary means and covariances is, however, completely straightforward: see XV.7 (page 494) of [9].

Theorem. **('local central limit theorem for lattice random variables', [9], page 490)** Let $T = (T_{[1]}, \ldots, T_{[k]})$ be a lattice random vector and $h_1, \ldots, h_k$ be the corresponding spans as in Definition 1; let $E_P[T(X)] = t$ and suppose that P satisfies Condition 2 with T-covariance matrix Σ. Let $X_1, X_2, \ldots$ be i.i.d. with common distribution P. Let V be a closed and bounded set in $\mathbf{R}^k$. Let $v_1, v_2, \ldots$ be a sequence in V such that for all n, $P(\sum_{i=1}^n (T_i - t)/\sqrt{n} = v_n) > 0$. Then as $n \to \infty$,

$$\frac{n^{k/2}}{\prod_{j=1}^k h_j} P(\frac{\sum_{i=1}^n (T_i - t)}{\sqrt{n}} = v_n) - \aleph(v_n) \to 0.$$

Here $\aleph$ is the density of a k-dimensional normal distribution with mean vector $\mu = t$ and covariance matrix Σ.

The theorem shows that there exists a sequence $d_1, d_2, \ldots$ with $\lim_{n\to\infty} d_n = 1$ such that, for all n with $P(\sum_{i=1}^n (T_i - t) = \mathbf{0}) > 0$,

$$\frac{\frac{n^{k/2}}{\prod_{j=1}^k h_j} P(\frac{\sum_{i=1}^n (T_i - t)}{\sqrt{n}} = \mathbf{0})}{\aleph(0)} = \frac{\sqrt{(2\pi n)^k \det \Sigma}}{\prod_{j=1}^k h_j} P(\frac{1}{n}\sum_{i=1}^n T_i = t) = d_n \qquad (11)$$

The proof now becomes very simple. First note that $\tilde{P}(\mathcal{A}_n \mid \overline{T^{(n)}} = \tilde{t}) = Q(\mathcal{A}_n \mid \overline{T^{(n)}} = \tilde{t})$ (write out the definition of conditional probability and realize that $\exp(-\tilde{\beta}^T T(x)) = \exp(-\tilde{\beta}^T \tilde{t}) =$ constant for all x with $T(x) = \tilde{t}$. Use this to show that

$$\begin{aligned} \tilde{P}(\mathcal{A}_n) \geq \tilde{P}(\mathcal{A}_n, \overline{T^{(n)}} = \tilde{t}) &= \tilde{P}(\mathcal{A}_n \mid \overline{T^{(n)}} = \tilde{t}) \tilde{P}(\overline{T^{(n)}} = \tilde{t}) \\ &= Q(\mathcal{A}_n \mid \overline{T^{(n)}} = \tilde{t}) \tilde{P}(\overline{T^{(n)}} = \tilde{t}). \end{aligned} \qquad (12)$$

Clearly, with $\tilde{P}$ in the rôle of P, the local central limit theorem is applicable to random vector T. Then, by (11), $\tilde{P}(\overline{T^{(n)}} = \tilde{t}) = (\prod_{j=1}^k h_j)/\sqrt{(2\pi n)^k \det \Sigma} d_n$. Defining $c_n := \tilde{P}(\overline{T^{(n)}} = \tilde{t}) n^{k/2}$ finishes the proof of item 1. For item 2, notice that in this case (12) holds with equality; the rest of the proof remains unchanged.

Example 1. The 'Brandeis dice example' is a toy example frequently used by Jaynes and others in discussions of the MaxEnt formalism [13]. Let $\mathcal{X} = \{1, \ldots, 6\}$ and X be the outcome in one throw of some given die. We initially believe (e.g. for reasons of symmetry) that the distribution of X is uniform. Then $Q(X = j) = 1/6$ for all j and $E_Q[X] = 3.5$. We are then told that the average number of spots is $E[X] = 4.5$ rather than 3.5. As calculated by Jaynes, the MaxEnt distribution $\tilde{P}$ given this constraint is given by

$$(\tilde{p}(1), \ldots, \tilde{p}(6)) = (0.05435, 0.07877, 0.11416, 0.16545, 0.23977, 0.34749). \quad (13)$$

By the Chernoff bound, for every $j \in \mathcal{X}$, every $\epsilon > 0$, $\tilde{P}(|n^{-1}\sum_{i=1}^n I_j(X_i) - \tilde{p}(j)| > \epsilon) < 2\exp(-nc)$ for some constant $c > 0$ depending on ϵ; here

$I_j(X)$ is the indicator function for $X = j$. Theorem 1 then implies that $Q(|n^{-1}\sum_{i=1}^{n} I_j(X_i) - \tilde{p}(j)| > \epsilon | \overline{T^{(n)}} = \tilde{t}) = O(\sqrt{n}e^{-nc}) = O(e^{-nc'})$ for some $c' > 0$. In this way we recover Jaynes' original concentration phenomenon (5): the fraction of sequences satisfying the constraint with frequencies close to MaxEnt probabilities $\tilde{p}$ is overwhelmingly large. Suppose now we receive new information about an additional constraint: $P(X = 4) = P(X = 5) = 1/2$. This can be expressed as a moment constraint by $E[(I_4(X), I_5(X))^T] = (0.5, 0.5)^T$. We can now either use $\tilde{P}$ defined as in (13) in the rôle of prior Q and impose the new constraint $E[(I_4(X), I_5(X))^T] = (0.5, 0.5)^T$, or use uniform Q and impose the combined constraint $E[T] = E[(T_{[1]}, T_{[2]}, T_{[3]})^T] = (4.5, 0.5, 0.5)^T$, with $T_{[1]} = X, T_{[2]} = I_4(X), T_{[3]} = I_5(X)$. In both cases we end up with a new MaxEnt distribution $\tilde{\tilde{p}}(4) = \tilde{\tilde{p}}(5) = 1/2$. This distribution, while still consistent with the original constraint $E[X] = 4.5$, rules out the vast majority of sequences satisfying it. However, we can apply our concentration phenomenon again to the new MaxEnt distribution $\tilde{\tilde{P}}$. Let $\mathcal{I}_{j,j',\epsilon}$ denote the event that

$$|\frac{1}{n}\sum_{i=1}^{n} I_j(X_i) - \frac{\sum_{i=1}^{n-1} I_{j'}(X_i) I_j(X_{i+1})}{\sum_{i=1}^{n-1} I_{j'}(X_i)}| > \epsilon.$$

According to $\tilde{\tilde{P}}$, we still have that $X_1, X_2, \ldots$ are i.i.d. Then by the Chernoff bound, for each $\epsilon > 0$, for $j, j' \in \{4, 5\}$, $\tilde{\tilde{P}}(\mathcal{I}_{j,j',\epsilon})$ is exponentially small. Theorem 1 then implies that $Q^n(\mathcal{I}_{j,j'\epsilon} \mid \overline{T^{(n)}} = (4.5, 0.5, 0.5)^T)$ is exponentially small too: for the overwhelming majority of samples satisfying the combined constraint, the sample will look just as if it had been generated by an i.i.d. process, even though $X_1, \ldots, X_n$ are obviously not *completely* independent under $Q^n(\cdot | \overline{T^{(n)}} = (4.5, 0.5, 0.5)^T)$.

There also exists a version of Theorem 1 for continuous-valued random vectors. This is given, along with the proof, in technical report [12].

There are a few limitations to Theorem 1: (1) we must require that $\tilde{P}(\mathcal{A}_n)$ goes to 0 or 1 as $n \to \infty$; (2) the continuous case needed a separate statement, which is caused by the more fundamental (3) it turns out that the proof technique used cannot be adapted to point-wise conditioning on $\overline{T^{(n)}} = \tilde{t}$ in the continuous case, see [12]. Theorem 2 overcomes all these problems. The price we pay is that, when conditioning on $\overline{T^{(n)}} = \tilde{t}$, the sets $\mathcal{A}_m$ must only refer to $X_1, \ldots, X_m$ where m is such that $m/n \to 0$; for example, $m = \lceil n/\log n \rceil$ will work. Whenever in the case of continuous-valued T we write $Q(\cdot \mid \overline{T^{(n)}} = t)$ or $\tilde{P}(\cdot \mid \overline{T^{(n)}} = t)$ we refer to the continuous version of these quantities. These are easily shown to exist, see [12]. Recall that (for $m < n$) $Q^m(\cdot \mid \overline{T^{(n)}} = \tilde{t})$ refers to the marginal distribution of $X_1, \ldots, X_m$ conditioned on $\overline{T^{(n)}} = \tilde{t}$. It is implicitly understood in the theorem that in the lattice case, n ranges only over those values for which $Q(\overline{T^{(n)}} = \tilde{t}) > 0$.

Theorem 2. (Main Theorem: the Strong Concentration Phenomenon/ Strong Conditional Limit Theorem) *Let $\{m_i\}$ be an increasing sequence* *with* $m_i \in \mathbf{N}$, *such that* $\lim_{n\to\infty} m_n/n = 0$. *Assume we are given a constraint of form (2) such that* T *is of the regular continuous form or of the lattice form and suppose that Conditions 1 and 2 are satisfied. Then as* $n \to \infty$, $Q^{m_n}(\cdot \mid \overline{T^{(n)}} = \tilde{t})$ *converges weakly*[5] *to* $\tilde{P}^{m_n}(\cdot)$.

The proof (using the same key idea, but involving much more work than the proof of Theorem 1) is in technical report [12].

Related Results. Theorem 1 is related to Jaynes' original concentration phenomenon, the proof of which is based on Stirling's approximation of the factorial. Another closely related result (also based on Stirling's approximation) is in Example 5.5.8 of [20]. Both results can be easily extended to prove the following weaker version of Theorem 1, item 1: $\tilde{P}(\mathcal{A}_n) \geq n^{-|\mathcal{X}|} c_n Q(\mathcal{A}_n | \overline{T^{(n)}} = \tilde{t})$ where c_n tends to some constant. Note that in this form, the theorem is void for infinite sample spaces. In [14] the original concentration phenomenon is extended in a direction somewhat different from Theorem 1; it would be interesting to study the relations.

Theorem 2 is similar to the original 'conditional limit theorems' (Theorems 1 and 2) of Van Campenhout and Cover [25]. We note that the preconditions for our theorem to hold are weaker and the conclusion is stronger than for the original conditional limit theorems, the main novelty being that Theorem 2 supplies us with an explicit bound on how fast m can grow as n tends to infinity. The conditional limit theorem was later extended by Csiszár [6]. His setting is considerably more general than ours (e.g. allowing for general convex constraints rather than just moment constraints), but his results also lack an explicit estimate of the rate at which m can increase with n. Csiszár [6] and Cover and Thomas [4] (where a simplified version of the conditional limit theorem is proved) both make the connection to large deviation results, in particular Sanov's theorem. As shown in the latter reference, weak versions of the conditional limit theorem can be interpreted as immediate consequences of Sanov's theorem.

5 Applications

For simplicity we restrict ourselves in this section to countable sample spaces $\mathcal{X}$ and we identify probability mass functions with probability distributions. Subsections 5.1 and 5.2 make frequent use of coding-theoretic concepts which we now briefly review (Sections 5.3 and 6 can be read without knowledge of coding/information theory).

Recall that by the Kraft Inequality [4], for every prefix code with lengths L over symbols from a countable alphabet $\mathcal{X}^n$, there exists a (possibly sub-additive) probability mass function p over $\mathcal{X}^n$ such that for all $x^{(n)} \in \mathcal{X}^n$,

[5] That is, for all sequences $\{\mathcal{A}_m\}$ where each $\mathcal{A}_m$ is a measurable continuity set $\mathcal{A}_m \subseteq \mathcal{X}^m$, $Q^{m_n}(\mathcal{A}_{m_n} \mid \overline{T^{(n)}} = \tilde{t}) \to \tilde{P}^{m_n}(\mathcal{A}_{m_n})$. A 'continuity set' $\mathcal{A}_m$ is a set such that the $\tilde{P}^m$-probability of the *boundary* of the set $\mathcal{A}_m$ is 0; in our case, *all* measurable sets $\mathcal{A}_m$ are continuity sets. See Theorem 2.1 of [3].

$L(x^{(n)}) = -\log p(x^{(n)})$. We will call this p the 'probability (mass) function corresponding to L'. Similarly, for every probability mass function p over $\mathcal{X}^n$ there exists a (prefix) code with lengths $L(x^{(n)}) = \lceil -\log p(x^{(n)}) \rceil$. Neglecting the round-off error, we will simply say that for every p, there exists a code with lengths $L(x^{(n)}) = -\log p(x^{(n)})$. We call the code with these lengths 'the code corresponding to p'. By the information inequality [4], this is also the most efficient code to use if data $X^{(n)}$ were actually distributed according to p.

We can now see that Theorem 1, item 2, has important implications for coding. Consider the following special case of Theorem 1, which obtains by taking $\mathcal{A}_n = \{x^{(n)}\}$ and logarithms:

Corollary 1. (the concentration phenomenon, coding-theoretic formulation) *Assume we are given a constraint of form (2) such that T is of the lattice form and $h = (h_1, \ldots, h_k)$ is the span of T and such that conditions 1 and 2 hold. For all n, all $x^{(n)}$ with $n^{-1} \sum_{i=1}^{n} T(x_i) = \tilde{t}$, we have*

$$\begin{aligned} -\log \tilde{p}(x^{(n)}) &= -\log q(x^{(n)} \mid \tfrac{1}{n} \textstyle\sum_{i=1}^{n} T(X_i) = \tilde{t}) + \\ &+ \tfrac{k}{2} \log 2\pi n + \log \sqrt{\det \Sigma} - \textstyle\sum_{j=1}^{k} \log h_j + o(1) = \\ &- \log q(x^{(n)} \mid \tfrac{1}{n} \textstyle\sum_{i=1}^{n} T(X_i) = \tilde{t}) + \tfrac{k}{2} \log n + O(1). \end{aligned} \tag{14}$$

In words, this means the following: let $x^{(n)}$ be a sample distributed according to Q, Suppose we are given the information that $n^{-1} \sum_{i=1}^{n} T(x_i) = \tilde{t}$. Then, by the information inequality, the most efficient code to encode $x^{(n)}$ is the one based on $q(\cdot | \overline{T^{(n)}} = \tilde{t})$ with lengths $-\log q(x^{(n)} \mid \overline{T^{(n)}} = \tilde{t})$. Yet if we encode $x^{(n)}$ using the code with lengths $-\log \tilde{p}(\cdot)$ (which would be the most efficient had $x^{(n)}$ been generated by $\tilde{p}$) then the number of extra bits we need is only of the order $(k/2) \log n$. That means, for example, that the number of additional bits we need *per outcome* goes to 0 as n increases. These and other consequences of Corollary 1 will be exploited in the next three subsections.

5.1 Connection to MDL, Stochastic Complexity, Two-Part Codes

Universal Models play a fundamental rôle in modern versions of the MDL (Minimum Description Length) approach to inductive inference and model selection [2,22]. For details about universal models and codes as well as all coding-theoretic concepts appearing in this section, we refer to [2]. The material in the present section is not needed to understand later sections.

Let $\mathcal{M}_k = \{P_\theta(\cdot) \mid \theta \in \Gamma_k\}$, where $\Gamma_k \subseteq \mathbf{R}^k$ is a k-dimensional parametric class of i.i.d. distributions for sample space $\mathcal{X}$. Let C be a code for alphabet $\mathcal{X}^n$, with lengths L_C and define the *regret* $R_C(\cdot)$ such that for all $x^{(n)}$,

$$L_C(x^{(n)}) = -\log p_{\hat{\theta}(x^{(n)})}(x^{(n)}) + R_C(x^{(n)}),$$

where $\hat{\theta}(x^{(n)})$ is the (ML) Maximum Likelihood estimator in $\mathcal{M}_k$ for data $x^{(n)}$, assumed to exist. Roughly speaking, a *universal code* for sequences of length n is a code C such that the regret $r_C(x^{(n)})$ is small uniformly for all or (in some sense) 'most' $x^{(n)}$. A *universal model* is the probability distribution corresponding to a universal code.

It is well-known [2,22] that, under mild regularity conditions, there exist universal codes C for $\mathcal{M}_k$ with lengths $L_C(x^{(n)}) = -\log p_{\hat{\theta}(x^{(n)})}(x^{(n)}) + \frac{k}{2}\log n + O(1)$, leading to regret

$$R_C(x^{(n)}) = \frac{k}{2}\log n + O(1) \tag{15}$$

Usually (15) holds uniformly for all sequences $x_1, x_2, \ldots$. (we sometimes need to restrict ourselves to a compact subset of Γ_k in order to make (15) uniformly true). It is also known that (15) is in some sense (up to $O(1)$) the best regret that can be achieved [21,2]. Therefore, *every* code that achieves (15) is usually called a 'universal code', and its corresponding distribution 'universal model'. Until very recently there were four known ways to construct a universal model for a given class $\mathcal{M}_k$: the two-part code, the Bayesian mixture-code , the Shtarkov-normalized-maximum-likelihood (NML) code and the predictive or 'prequential' code, see [2]. These four methods, while superficially very different, all share the same asymptotic lengths (15). Under further regularity conditions on $\mathcal{M}_k$ and if the code C that is used is allowed to depend on sample size n, (15) the Shtarkov-NML and two-part codes can be refined to give [2]:

$$R_C(x^{(n)}) = \frac{k}{2}\log\frac{n}{2\pi} + \log\int_{\Gamma_k}\sqrt{\det I(\theta)}d\theta + o(1), \tag{16}$$

where $I(\theta)$ is the (expected) Fisher information matrix of θ. Quite recently, Rissanen [23] showed that the regret (16) is the best that can be achieved under at least three different definitions of optimality. $L_C(x^{(n)}) = -\log p_{\hat{\theta}(x^{(n)})}(x^{(n)}) + R_C(x^{(n)})$, with $R_C(x^{(n)})$ given by (16), is called the 'stochastic complexity of $x^{(n)}$ relative to $\mathcal{M}_k$'.

In the same recent reference [23], Rissanen implicitly introduced a new type of universal code that achieves regret (16). We illustrate this kind of code for the simple case where $\mathcal{M}_k$ is a k-dimensional exponential family with finite sample space $\mathcal{X}$. Let then $\mathcal{M}_k = \{P_\theta(\cdot) \mid \theta \in \Gamma_k\}$ be a k-parameter exponential family for $\mathcal{X}$ with Γ_k the mean-value parameter space, q the background measure and sufficient statistic $T = (T_{[1]}, \ldots, T_{[k]})$. Then $p_\theta = \tilde{p}$ with $\tilde{p}$ given by (9), and $E_{p_\theta}[T] = \tilde{t} = \theta$.

We will encode $x^{(n)}$ in a way similar to (but, as we shall see, still essentially different from) the two-part coding technique [2]: we first code (describe) a distribution for $\mathcal{X}^n$ and then code the data 'with the help of' this distribution. In our case, for data $x^{(n)}$, we first encode the ML estimator $\hat{\theta}(x^{(n)})$ using some code C_1 with lengths L_1. We then encode $x^{(n)}$ itself using some code C_2, making use of the fact that its ML estimator is $\hat{\theta}(x^{(n)})$. By the Kraft inequality this can be done using $L_2(x^{(n)} \mid \hat{\theta}(x^{(n)})) = -\log q(x^{(n)} \mid \overline{T^{(n)}} = \hat{\theta}(x^{(n)})) = -\log q(x^{(n)} \mid \hat{\theta}(x^{(n)}))$ bits. This leads to a code C^* that allows us to encode all $x^{(n)} \in \mathcal{X}^n$ by concatenating the code words of $\hat{\theta}(x^{(n)})$ (under C_1) and $x^{(n)}|\hat{\theta}(x^{(n)})$ (under C_2).

Since $\mathcal{X}$ is finite, $n^{-1}\sum_{i=1}^{n} T_{[j]}(X_i)$ can only take on $n \cdot |\mathcal{X}|$ distinct values. Therefore, we can choose C_1 such that $L_1(\hat{\theta}(x^{(n)})) = k \log n + k \log |\mathcal{X}|$. By Corollary 1 the code $L_2(\cdot|\cdot)$ has lengths

$$L_2(x^{(n)} \mid \hat{\theta}(x^{(n)})) = -\log p_{\hat{\theta}(x^{(n)})}(x^{(n)}) - \frac{k}{2} \log n - O(1). \tag{17}$$

Summing L_1 and L_2, we see that the total code length $L^*(x^{(n)})$ for *arbitrary* $x^{(n)}$ is bounded by $\frac{k}{2} \log n - \log p_{\hat{\theta}(x^{(n)})}(x^{(n)}) + O(1)$. Therefore, the regret satisfies (15) which suggests that C^* is a universal code for $\mathcal{M}_k$. Indeed, in the technical report [12] we sketch how, by changing C_1, we can even refine C^* such that the regret (16) is achieved.

Other relations between MDL and Maximum Entropy have been investigated by Feder [8] and Li and Vitányi [20]. In the next section we will see how Theorem 1 leads to yet another relation between minimum code length and Maximum Entropy.

5.2 Empirical Constraints and Game Theory

Recall we assume countable $\mathcal{X}$. The σ-algebra of such $\mathcal{X}$ is always tacitly taken to be the power set of $\mathcal{X}$. The σ-algebra thus being implicitly understood, we can define $\mathcal{P}(\mathcal{X})$ to be the set of all probability distributions over $\mathcal{X}$. For a product $\mathcal{X}^\infty = \times_{i \in \mathbf{N}} \mathcal{X}$ of a countable sample space $\mathcal{X}$, we define $\mathcal{P}(\mathcal{X}^\infty)$ to be the set of all distributions over the product space with the associated product σ-algebra.

In [24,10], a characterization of Maximum Entropy distributions quite different from the present one was given. It was shown that, under regularity conditions,

$$= \sup_{p^* : E_{p^*}[T] = \tilde{t}} \inf_{p} E_{p^*}[-\log \frac{p(X)}{q(X)}] = \inf_{p} \sup_{p^* : E_{p^*}[T] = \tilde{t}} E_{p^*}[-\log \frac{p(X)}{q(X)}] \tag{18}$$

where both p and p^* are understood to be members of $\mathcal{P}(\mathcal{X})$ and $\mathbf{H}_q(\tilde{p})$ is defined as in (1). By this result, the MaxEnt setting can be thought of as a game between Nature, who can choose any p^* satisfying the constraint, and Statistician, who only knows that Nature will choose a p^* satisfying the constraint. Statistician wants to minimize his worst-case expected logarithmic loss (relative to q), where the worst-case is over all choices for Nature. It turns out that the minimax strategy for Statistician in (18) is given by $\tilde{p}$. That is,

$$\tilde{p} = \arg \inf_{p} \sup_{p^* : E_{p^*}[T] = \tilde{t}} E_{p^*}[-\log \frac{p(x)}{q(x)}]. \tag{19}$$

This gives a decision-theoretic justification of using MaxEnt probabilities which seems quite different from our concentration phenomenon. Or is it? Realizing that in practical situations we deal with empirical constraints of form (4) rather than (2) we may wonder what distribution $\hat{p}$ is minimax in the empirical version of problem (19). In this version Nature gets to choose an individual sequence rather than a distribution[6]. To make this precise, let

$$\mathcal{C}_n = \{x^{(n)} \in \mathcal{X}^n \mid n^{-1} \sum_{i=1}^{n} T(x_i) = \tilde{t}\}. \tag{20}$$

Then, for n with $\mathcal{C}_n \neq \emptyset$, $\hat{p}_n$ (if it exists) is defined by

$$\hat{p}_n := \arg \inf_{p \in \mathcal{P}(\mathcal{X}^n)} \sup_{x^{(n)} \in \mathcal{C}_n} -\log \frac{p(x_1, \ldots, x_n)}{q(x_1, \ldots, x_n)} = \arg \sup_{p \in \mathcal{P}(\mathcal{X}^n)} \arg \inf_{x^{(n)} \in \mathcal{C}_n} \frac{p(x^{(n)})}{q(x^{(n)})} \tag{21}$$

$\hat{p}_n$ can be interpreted in two ways: (1) it is the distribution that assigns 'maximum probability' (relative to q) to all sequences satisfying the constraint; (2) as $-\log(\hat{p}(x^{(n)})/q(x^{(n)})) = \sum_{i=1}^{n}(-\log \hat{p}(x_i|x_1, \ldots, x_{i-1}) + \log q(x_i|x_1, \ldots, x_{i-1}))$, it is also the p that minimizes cumulative worst-case logarithmic loss relative to q when used for sequentially predicting $x_1, \ldots, x_n$.

One immediately verifies that $\hat{p}_n = q^n(\cdot \mid \overline{T^{(n)}} = \tilde{t})$: the solution to the empirical minimax problem is just the conditioned prior, which we know by Theorems 1 and 2 is in some sense very close to $\tilde{p}$. However, for no single n, $\tilde{p}$ is exactly equal to $q^n(\cdot \mid \overline{T^{(n)}} = \tilde{t})$. Indeed, $q^n(\cdot \mid \overline{T^{(n)}} = \tilde{t})$ assigns zero probability to any sequence of length n not satisfying the constraint. This means that using q in prediction tasks against the logarithmic loss will be problematic if the constraint only holds approximately (as we will discuss in more detail in the journal version of this paper) and/or if n is unknown in advance. In the latter case, it is impossible to use $q(\cdot \mid \overline{T^{(n)}} = \tilde{t})$ for prediction without modification. The reason is that there exist sequences $x^{(n_2)}$ of length $n_2 > n_1$ satisfying the constraint such that $q(x^{(n_2)}|x^{(n_1)} \in \mathcal{C}_{n_1}) = 0$. We may guess that in this case (n not known in advance), the MaxEnt distribution $\tilde{p}$, rather than $q(\cdot|\overline{T^{(n)}} = \tilde{t})$ is actually the optimal distribution to use for prediction. The following theorem shows that this is indeed so:

Theorem 3. *Let $\mathcal{X}$ be a countable sample space. Assume we are given a constraint of form (2) such that T is of the lattice form, and such that Conditions 1 and 2 are satisfied. Let $\mathcal{C}_n$ be as in (20). Then the infimum in*

$$\inf_{p \in \mathcal{P}(\mathcal{X}^\infty)} \sup_{\{n \,:\, \mathcal{C}_n \neq \emptyset\}} \sup_{x^{(n)} \in \mathcal{C}_n} -\frac{1}{n} \log \frac{p(x_1, \ldots, x_n)}{q(x_1, \ldots, x_n)} \tag{22}$$

is achieved by the Maximum Entropy distribution $\tilde{p}$, and is equal to $\mathbf{H}_q(\tilde{p})$.

Proof. Let $\mathcal{C} = \cup_{i=1}^{\infty} \mathcal{C}_i$. We need to show that for all n, for all $x^{(n)} \in \mathcal{C}$,

$$\mathbf{H}_q(\tilde{p}) = -\frac{1}{n} \log \frac{\tilde{p}(x^{(n)})}{q(x^{(n)})} = \inf_{p \in \mathcal{P}(\mathcal{X}^\infty)} \sup_{\{n \,:\, \mathcal{C}_n \neq \emptyset\}} \sup_{x^{(n)} \in \mathcal{C}_n} -\frac{1}{n} \log \frac{p(x^{(n)})}{q(x^{(n)})} \tag{23}$$

[6] To our knowledge, we are the first to analyze this 'empirical' game.

Equation (23) implies that $\tilde{p}$ reaches the inf in (22) and that the inf is equal to $\mathbf{H}_q(\tilde{p})$. The leftmost equality in (23) is a standard result about exponential families of form (9); see for example, [11, Proposition 4.1] or [22]. To prove the rightmost equality in (23), let $x^{(n)} \in \mathcal{C}_n$. Consider the conditional distribution $q(\cdot \mid x^{(n)} \in \mathcal{C}_n)$. Note that, for every distribution p_0 over $\mathcal{X}^n$, $p_0(x^{(n)}) \leq q(x^{(n)}|x^{(n)} \in \mathcal{C}_n)$ for at least one $x^{(n)} \in \mathcal{C}_n$. By Theorem 1 (or rather Corollary 1), for this $x^{(n)}$ we have

$$-\frac{1}{n}\log\frac{p_0(x^{(n)})}{q(x^{(n)})} \geq -\frac{1}{n}\log\frac{\tilde{p}(x^{(n)})}{q(x^{(n)})} - \frac{k}{2n}\log n - O(\frac{1}{n}),$$

and we see that for every distribution p_0 over $\mathcal{X}^\infty$,

$$\sup_{\{n\,:\,\mathcal{C}_n\neq\emptyset\}} \sup_{x^{(n)}\in\mathcal{C}_n} -\frac{1}{n}\log\frac{p_0(x^{(n)})}{q(x^{(n)})} \geq \sup_{\{n\,:\,\mathcal{C}_n\neq\emptyset\}} \sup_{x^{(n)}\in\mathcal{C}_n} -\frac{1}{n}\log\frac{\tilde{p}(x^{(n)})}{q(x^{(n)})},$$

which shows the rightmost equality in (23).

5.3 Maximum Entropy and Algorithmic Randomness

In the algorithmic theory of randomness, [20], one (broadly speaking) identifies *randomness of individual sequences* with incompressibility of such sequences. In this section we show that a sequence that is 'random relative to a given constraint' is 'almost' random with respect to the MaxEnt distribution $\tilde{P}$ for the constraint. The reader who is not familiar with Martin-Löf randomness is urged to move on to Theorem 4 which demonstrates the consequences of this fact for prediction based on MaxEnt distributions.

Throughout this section we assume $\mathcal{X}$ to be finite and Q to be uniform, so maximizing the entropy reduces to the 'original' Maximum (Shannon) Entropy formalism. Let $\mathcal{U} := \cup_{i=1}^{\infty}\mathcal{X}^i$. For $\mathbf{x}, \mathbf{y} \in \mathcal{U}$, $K(\mathbf{x}|\mathbf{y})$ will stand for the prefix Kolmogorov complexity of sequence $\mathbf{x}$ conditional on $\mathbf{y}$; $K(\mathbf{x})$ stands for $K(\mathbf{x}|\lambda)$ where λ is the empty sequence. For a finite set $\mathcal{C} \subset \mathcal{U}$, $K(\mathbf{x}|\mathcal{C})$ is the prefix complexity of $\mathbf{x}$ conditional on $\mathbf{x} \in \mathcal{C}$. Kolmogorov complexity is defined here with respect to some fixed universal reference prefix Turing Machine. For precise definitions of all these concepts, see Section 3.1 and Exercise 2.2.12. of [20].

Theorem. (**Theorem 3.6.1 and Corollary 4.5.2 of [20]**) *An infinite sequence $(x_1, x_2, \ldots) \in \mathcal{X}^\infty$ is Martin-Löf random with respect to the uniform distribution iff there exists a constant c such that for all n, $K(x_1, \ldots, x_n) \geq n - c$.*

Here, we take this characterization of Martin-Löf randomness as basic. We will extend the notion of randomness to *sequences conditional on constraints* in an obvious manner. Let $\{\mathcal{C}_n\}$ be a sequence of constraints, where $\mathcal{C}_n \subseteq \mathcal{X}^n$ (we identify constraints with the set of sequences satisfying them). The theorem above suggests the following definition:

Definition 3. *An infinite sequence $(x_1, x_2, \ldots) \in \mathcal{X}^\infty$ is called random with respect to the sequence of constraints $\{\mathcal{C}_n\}$ (relative to the uniform distribution) iff there exists a constant c such that for all n with $\mathcal{C}_n \neq \emptyset$, we have $K(x^{(n)}|\mathcal{C}_n) \geq \log|\mathcal{C}_n| - c$.*

In our situation, the constraint is of form (20). Because of this simple form and since $\mathcal{X}$ is finite, there exists a fixed-length program that, for each n, when input $\langle n, \mathbf{x}\rangle$ with $\mathbf{x} \in \mathcal{X}^n$, outputs 1 iff $\mathbf{x} \in \mathcal{C}_n$ and 0 otherwise. Therefore the definition reduces to $(x_1, x_2, \ldots)$ *is random iff* $\exists c \forall n : \mathcal{C}_n \neq \emptyset \Rightarrow K(x^{(n)}|n) \geq \log |\mathcal{C}_n| - c$.

By Theorem 1, if $(x_1, x_2, \ldots)$ is random with respect to the constraints $\{\mathcal{C}_n\}$, then for all $x^{(n)} \in \mathcal{C}_n$,

$$K(x^{(n)}|n) \geq \log |\mathcal{C}_n| - O(1) = -\log \tilde{p}(x^{(n)}) - \frac{k}{2} \log n - O(1). \qquad (24)$$

In words: (see Corollary 4.5.2 of [20]) *If* $(x_1, x_2, \ldots)$ *is random with respect to the constraints* $\{\mathcal{C}_n\}$ *(relative to the uniform distribution) then* $(x_1, x_2, \ldots)$ *is 'almost' Martin-Löf random with respect to the maximum entropy distribution* $\tilde{p}$.

Equation 24 suggests that for the overwhelming majority of sequences satisfying the constraint (namely, those that are random with respect to the constraint), sequentially predicting outcomes in the sequence on the basis of the MaxEnt distribution leads to almost optimal results, no matter what loss function we use. The following theorem shows that this is indeed so. It holds for general prior distributions Q and is proved in technical report [12]. Consider a loss function $\text{LOSS} : \mathcal{X} \times \Delta \rightarrow [0, \infty]$ where Δ is some space of *predictions* or *decisions*. A *prediction (decision) strategy* δ^* is a function $\delta^* : \cup_{i=0}^{\infty} \mathcal{X}^i \rightarrow \Delta$. $\delta^*(x_1, \ldots, x_n)$ is to be read as 'the prediction/decision for X_{n+1} based on initial data $(x_1, \ldots, x_n)$'. We assume

Condition 3. $\mathcal{X}$ is finite. $\text{LOSS}(x; \cdot)$ is continuous in its second argument for all $x \in \mathcal{X}$. Δ is a compact convex subspace of $\mathbf{R}^l$ for some $l > 0$.

Under this condition, there exists at least one δ attaining $\inf E_{\tilde{P}}[\text{LOSS}(X; \delta)]$. Fix any such optimal (under $\tilde{P}$) decision and denote it $\tilde{\delta}$.

Theorem 4. *Suppose that* T *is of lattice form and suppose Conditions 1, 2 and 3 hold. Then (letting* n *reach over all numbers such that* $Q(\overline{T^{(n)}} = \tilde{t}) > 0$*), for all decision strategies* δ^**, for all* $\epsilon > 0$*, there exists a* $c > 0$ *such that*

$$Q(\frac{1}{n}(\sum_{i=1}^{n} \text{LOSS}(x_i; \tilde{\delta}) - \sum_{i=1}^{n} \text{LOSS}(x_i; \delta^*(x_1, \ldots, x_{i-1}))) > \epsilon \mid \overline{T^{(n)}} = \tilde{t}) = O(e^{-cn}). \qquad (25)$$

6 Consequences for Prediction

We summarize the implications of our results for prediction of individual sequences based on Maximum Entropy distributions. In this section $\mathcal{X}$ is finite and Q stands for the uniform distribution. Suppose then you have to make predictions about a sequence $(x_1, \ldots, x_n)$. You know the sequence satisfies the given constraint (i.e. for some n, $x^{(n)} \in \mathcal{C}_n$, with $\mathcal{C}_n$ as in (20)), but you do not know the length n of the sequence in advance. We distinguish between the special case of the log loss function $\text{LOSS}(x; p) = -\log p(x)$ and the general case of arbitrary (computable) loss functions.

1. **(log loss)** The MaxEnt distribution $\tilde{p}$ is worst-case optimal with respect to log loss, where the worst-case is over all sequences of all lengths satisfying the constraint. This is a consequence of Theorem 3.
2. **(log loss)** Whatever sample $x^{(n)} \in \mathcal{C}_n$ arrives, the average log loss you make per outcome when you predict outcomes using $\tilde{p}$ is determined in advance and will be exactly equal to $\mathbf{H}_q(\tilde{p}) = E_{\tilde{p}}[-\log \tilde{p}(X)]$. This is also a consequence of Theorem 3.
3. **(log loss)** For the overwhelming majority of sequences satisfying the constraint, $\tilde{p}$ will be asymptotically almost optimal with respect to log loss in the following sense: the excess loss of $\tilde{p}$ over *every* other prediction strategy (including strategies depending on past data) is at most a sub-linear function of n. This is a consequence of Theorem 4. In Example 1, an example of an exceptional sequence for which $\tilde{p}$ is not optimal would be any sequence consisting of 50% fours and 50% fives.
4. **(general loss)** For *every* regular loss function LOSS (satisfying Condition 3), predicting using $\tilde{\delta}$, (that is, *acting as if the sample had been generated by* $\tilde{p}$) leads to almost optimal predictions for the overwhelming majority of sequences satisfying the constraint, in the following sense: the excess loss of $\tilde{\delta}$ over *every* other prediction strategy is at most a sub-linear function of n. This is a consequence of Theorem 4.

We stress that the fact that items (3) and (4) hold for the overwhelming majority of sequences certainly does *not* imply that they will hold on actual, real-world sequences! Often these will exhibit more regularity than the observed constraint, and then $\tilde{\delta}$ is not necessarily optimal any more.

There are two important points we have neglected so far: (1) in practice, the given constraints will often only hold approximately. (2) the results of this paper have important implications for Maximum Likelihood and Bayesian prediction of sequences based on model classes that are exponential families [1]. The reason is that the Maximum Entropy model for constraint $E[T] = \tilde{t}$ is the Maximum *Likelihood* model for the (exponential family) model class given by (9) for *every* sequence of data $x^{(n)}$ with $n^{-1}\sum_{i=1}^{n} T(x_i) = \tilde{t}$ (see e.g. [4] or [11]) . The connection will be further discussed in the journal version of this paper.

References

1. K. Azoury and M. Warmuth. Relative loss bounds for on-line density estimation with the exponential family of distributions. In *Proceedings of the Fifteenth Conference on Uncertainty in Artificial Intelligence (UAI '99)*, pages 31–40. Morgan Kaufmann, 1999.
2. A. Barron, J. Rissanen, and B. Yu. The minimum description length principle in coding and modeling. *IEEE Transactions on Information Theory*, 44(6):2743–2760, 1998.
3. P. Billingsley. *Convergence of Probability Measures*. Wiley, 1968.
4. T.M. Cover and J.A. Thomas. *Elements of Information Theory*. Wiley Interscience, New York, 1991.

5. I. Csiszár. *I*-divergence geometry of probability distributions and minimization problems. *The Annals of Probability*, 3(1):146–158, 1975.
6. I. Csiszár. Sanov property, generalized *i*-projection and a conditional limit theorem. *The Annals of Probability*, 12(3):768–793, 1984.
7. I. Csiszár. Why least squares and maximum entropy? An axiomatic approach to inference for linear inverse problems. *The Annals of Statistics*, 19(4):2032–2066, 1991.
8. M. Feder. Maximum entropy as a special case of the minimum description length criterion. *IEEE Transactions on Information Theory*, 32(6):847–849, 1986.
9. W. Feller. *An Introduction to Probability Theory and Its Applications*, volume 2. Wiley, 1968. Third edition.
10. P. D. Grünwald. Maximum entropy and the glasses you are looking through. In *Proceedings of the Sixteenth Conference on Uncertainty in Artificial Intelligence (UAI 2000)*. Morgan Kaufmann Publishers, 2000.
11. P.D. Grünwald. *The Minimum Description Length Principle and Reasoning under Uncertainty*. PhD thesis, University of Amsterdam, The Netherlands, October 1998. Available as ILLC Dissertation Series 1998-03; see www.cwi.nl/~pdg.
12. P.D. Grünwald. Strong entropy concentration, coding, game theory and randomness. Technical Report 010, EURANDOM, 2001.
13. E.T. Jaynes. Where do we stand on maximum entropy? In R.D. Levine and M. Tribus, editors, *The Maximum Entropy Formalism*, pages 15–118. MIT Press, Cambridge, MA, 1978.
14. E.T. Jaynes. On the rationale of maximum-entropy methods. *Proceedings of the IEEE*, 70(939-951), 1982.
15. E.T. Jaynes. *Papers on Probability, Statistics and Statistical Physics*. Kluwer Academic Publishers, second edition, 1989.
16. E.T. Jaynes. Probability theory: the logic of science. Available at ftp://bayes.wustl.edu/Jaynes.book/, 1996.
17. J. N. Kapur and H. K Kesavan. *Entropy Optimization Principles with Applications*. Academic Press, Inc., 1992.
18. R.E. Kass and P.W. Voss. *Geometrical Foundations of Asymptotic Inference*. Wiley Interscience, 1997.
19. J. Lafferty. Additive models, boosting and inference for generalized divergences. In *Proceedings of the Twelfth Annual Workshop on Computational Learning Theory (COLT '99)*, 1999.
20. M. Li and P.M.B. Vitányi. *An Introduction to Kolmogorov Complexity and Its Applications*. Springer-Verlag, New York, revised and expanded second edition, 1997.
21. N. Merhav and M. Feder. A strong version of the redundancy-capacity theorem of universal coding. *IEEE Transactions on Information Theory*, 41(3):714–722, 1995.
22. J. Rissanen. *Stochastic Complexity in Statistical Inquiry*. World Scientific Publishing Company, 1989.
23. J. Rissanen. Strong optimality of the normalized ML models as universal codes, 2001. To appear in *IEEE Transactions on Information Theory*.
24. F. Topsøe. Information theoretical optimization techniques. *Kybernetika*, 15(1), 1979.
25. J. van Campenhout and T. Cover. Maximum entropy and conditional probability. *IEEE Transactions on Information Theory*, IT-27(4):483–489, 1981.

Pattern Recognition and Density Estimation under the General i.i.d. Assumption

Ilia Nouretdinov, Volodya Vovk, Michael Vyugin, and Alex Gammerman

Computer Learning Research Centre
Department of Computer Science
Royal Holloway, University of London
Egham, Surrey TW20 0EX, England
{ilia,vovk,misha,alex}@cs.rhul.ac.uk

Abstract. Statistical learning theory considers three main problems, pattern recognition, regression and density estimation. This paper studies solvability of these problems (mainly concentrating on pattern recognition and density estimation) in the "high-dimensional" case, where the patterns in the training and test sets are never repeated. We show that, assuming an i.i.d. data source but without any further assumptions, the problems of pattern recognition and regression can often be solved (and there are practically useful algorithms to solve them). On the other hand, the problem of density estimation, as we formalize it, cannot be solved under the general i.i.d. assumption, and additional assumptions are required.

1 Introduction

We consider the following special case of the standard problem of machine learning: given a training set

$$\Pi = ((x_1, y_1), \dots, (x_l, y_l)) \tag{1}$$

consisting of labelled instances (x_i, y_i) and given a test unlabelled instance x_{l+1}, predict x_{l+1}'s label y_{l+1}. (This is a special case because we assume that there is only one test instance.) It is assumed that every labelled instance (x_i, y_i), $i = 1, \dots, l+1$, is generated by some unknown probability distribution P (one and the same for all instances) independently of other instances; we will call this the *i.i.d. assumption* (and we will say *general i.i.d. assumption* to emphasize that no other assumptions are made). Sometimes we will say that x_i are *patterns*; a typical example is where x_i are hand-written digits and y_i are their classifications, $y_i \in \{0, 1, \dots, 9\}$. Let $\mathbf{X}$ be the set of all possible patterns and $\mathbf{Y}$ be the set of all possible labels; therefore, P is a probability distribution in $\mathbf{X} \times \mathbf{Y}$.

According to Vapnik [10] there are three main problems of statistical learning theory:

- *pattern recognition* (or *classification*), in which the label space $\mathbf{Y}$ is finite (and usually quite small, such as $\{0, 1\}$);

D. Helmbold and B. Williamson (Eds.): COLT/EuroCOLT 2001, LNAI 2111, pp. 337–353, 2001.

- *regression*, where $\mathbf{Y} = \mathbb{R}$ is the real line;
- *density estimation*, where the task is not just to predict y_{l+1} but to give a probability distribution for different values of y_{l+1}.

The goal of this paper is to draw a first rough boundary between what can and what cannot be done under the general i.i.d. assumption. It turns out that the first two problems can be solved (this is well known) but the third problem cannot (in non-trivial cases).

As usual, the positive results (solvability of pattern recognition and regression problems) do not require any general theory; however, to state the negative result (impossibility of density estimation) in the most natural way we will use the algorithmic notion of randomness (for details, see [5] and Section 2)[1]. The algorithmic theory of randomness asserts that there is a universal statistical test for checking whether a given data sequence can be generated by a given probability distribution; and a sequence $(z_1, \ldots, z_n)$ (in the case that interests us every z_i is a labelled instance, $z_i = (x_i, y_i) \in \mathbf{Z} := \mathbf{X} \times \mathbf{Y}$) is said to be random w.r. to a probability distribution P if the universal test does not detect disagreement between $(z_1, \ldots, z_n)$ and P. We say that a sequence is i.i.d. random (or just random) if it is random w.r. to some product distribution P^n. More accurately, for finite sequences ω the crisp notion of randomness has to be replaced by a function $d_P(\omega)$, called randomness level, measuring the degree to which ω is random w.r. to P: $d_P(\omega) = 1$ means complete randomness and $d_P(\omega) = 0$ means complete lack of randomness; here P is either a probability distribution in $\mathbf{Z}^n$ (where n is the length of ω) or a probability distribution in $\mathbf{Z}$ (in which case $d_P(\omega)$ is defined to be the same as $d_{P^n}(\omega)$). These definitions are also applicable to "partial" data sequences such as (Π, x_{l+1}) (where the classification of the last instance is not given).

Let X and Y be random variables taking values in $\mathbf{X}$ and $\mathbf{Y}$ respectively such that (X, Y) is distributed as P. If $\mathbf{Y}$ is finite, we will often use $P(y \mid x)$, where $x \in \mathbf{X}$ and $y \in \mathbf{Y}$, as the shorthand for the probability that $Y = y$ given $X = x$.

In this paper we are mainly interested in the case $\mathbf{Y} = \{0, 1\}$. Our informal statement of the problems of pattern recognition and density estimation is as follows. Suppose the training set Π is i.i.d. random; consider all probability distributions P in $\mathbf{Z}$ such that the training set Π is δ-random w.r. to P:

$$\operatorname{Rand}(\Pi, x_{l+1}, \delta) := \{P : d_P(\Pi, x_{l+1}) > \delta\} . \tag{2}$$

Typically δ is a conventional threshold, such as 1%, and $\operatorname{Rand}(\Pi, x_{l+1}, \delta)$ is the set of all probability distributions that can generate Π and x_{l+1} (all other distributions are rejected by the universal statistical test at the level δ). Consider the interval

$$[a, b] := [\inf P(1 \mid x_{l+1}), \sup P(1 \mid x_{l+1})] , \tag{3}$$

[1] In principle, it is possible to understand the main result of this paper without algorithmic randomness: the reader can proceed directly to Corollary 1 in Appendix B, and read only the definitions of notions used there.

where P ranges over $\mathrm{Rand}(\Pi, x_{l+1}, \delta)$. The problem of pattern recognition is feasible for the training set Π, test pattern x_{l+1} and significance level δ if

- either b is close to 0, in which case we can confidently predict $y_{l+1} = 0$ (all probability distributions P compatible with the training set agree that $P(1 \mid x_{l+1})$ is close to 0),
- or a is close to 1, in which case we can confidently predict $y_{l+1} = 1$ (all probability distributions P compatible with the training set agree that $P(1 \mid x_{l+1})$ is close to 1).

The problem of density estimation is feasible if a and b are close to each other, i.e., all probability distributions P compatible with the training set have similar $P(1 \mid x_{l+1})$.

Remark 1. The term "density" is most often applied to densities w.r. to the Lebesgue measure. We consider, instead, densities with respect to counting measures, such as the counting measure μ on the set $\{0, 1\}$ (recall that $\mu\{0\} = \mu\{1\} = 1$). This is sufficient for our purpose of demonstrating impossibility of density estimation: it is clear that we cannot hope to be able to estimate densities w.r. to the Lebesgue measure if we cannot do the much simpler task of estimating densities w.r. to counting measures.

In this paper we are interested in the "high-dimensional" case, where, in particular, the same pattern never occurs twice among the given patterns $x_1, \ldots, x_{l+1}$ (for example, in a data set of gray-scale 16×16 handwritten digits, we do not expect two images to be *precise* copies of each other). Of course, the training set will usually contain patterns similar, in some sense, to the test pattern, and a natural idea would be to use these similar patterns to estimate the probability that the classification of the test pattern is 1. However, since i.i.d. is our only assumption, similarity of patterns does not imply at all that classifications are likely to coincide or be close in any sense. It might even seem surprising that pattern recognition is possible for real-world high-dimensional data sets under the general i.i.d. assumption. This is, however, demonstrated in [8], and can also be seen from older results of PAC theory, such as Littlestone and Warmuth's Theorem 4.25 (and its corollary Theorem 6.8) in [2]. The latter asserts that

$$b \leq \frac{1}{l-d}\left(d \ln \frac{el}{d} + \ln \frac{l}{\delta}\right) \tag{4}$$

if Support Vector Machine (see Vapnik [11]) predicts 0 with d support vectors, and

$$a \geq 1 - \frac{1}{l-d}\left(d \ln \frac{el}{d} + \ln \frac{l}{\delta}\right) \tag{5}$$

if SVM predicts 1 with d support vectors (this is true for a specific statistical test, but will be true for the universal test if δ is replaced with δ/c for some constant c). Littlestone and Warmuth's result can be generalized to regression problems as well: see, e.g., [6] and [2] (Theorems 4.26, 4.28 and 4.30). The results of [8] are stated in a different framework, but in Section 3 we establish connections between the two frameworks.

Remark 2. Our only use of the requirement that the data set is "high-dimensional" is that we do not expect repeated patterns in it. Actually the latter condition will often be satisfied in low-dimensional cases as well: e.g., if x_i are real numbers generated according to a continuous distribution. Therefore, in the rest of the paper we will use a more neutral expression, "diverse data set".

The main result of this paper is that, for a diverse data set and under the general i.i.d. assumption, density estimation is feasible only in the trivial case where already pattern recognition is feasible: if the interval $[a, b]$ is non-empty, a slight increase in δ will make it contain 0 or 1. (In the algorithmic theory of randomness, δ matters only to within a constant factor, so a slight increase corresponds to multiplying by a universal constant c.) Therefore, non-trivial density estimation, where $[a, b] \subseteq (0, 1)$, can only be possible for a narrow range of δ. (And analysis of the proof will show that one cannot hope to get $[a, b] \subseteq (0, 1)$ even for a narrow range of δ in non-pathological cases: see Corollary 1 on p. 353.) These results elaborate on a remark in [13].

Remark 3. Since we consider diverse data sets, standard statistical techniques such as the Glivenko–Cantelli theorem (see, e.g., Vapnik [11], Theorem 1.1 on p. 42) are not applicable in this context. The Glivenko–Cantelli theorem considers the case where x_i are absent and y_i take values in $\mathbb{R}$; it is equivalent and will be more convenient for us to assume that all x_i are equal to some predefined "null" element of $\mathbf{X}$. Therefore, our main assumption, that all x_i's are different, is violated; the Glivenko–Cantelli situation is opposite: all x_i coincide. When all x_i coincide and $\mathbf{Y}$ is finite, density estimation is also simple: we can estimate $P\{Y = y \mid X = x_{l+1}\} = P\{Y = y\}$ by the relative frequency of the classification y in the training set (see, e.g., [3]). Extending the Glivenko–Cantelli theorem in the Vapnik–Chervonenkis direction (Vapnik [11], Theorem 4.5 on p. 149) does not help either: since we are interested in estimating conditional probability given $X = x_{l+1}$, the corresponding VC dimension will be infinite or too big to give non-trivial accuracy of estimation.

2 Mathematical Background

We will use the algorithmic notion of randomness only in the case where $\mathbf{Y} = \{0, 1\}$ and $\mathbf{X}$ is a finite set. Our statements are applied to different finite sets $\mathbf{X}$ which are supposed to be subsets of some countable set $\mathbf{W}$ (big enough to contain all objects of interest to us; e.g., $\mathbf{W}$ might be the set of all finite sequences of ASCII symbols). We assume that $\mathbf{W}$ is a "constructive space", in the sense that all its elements have individual names. Each finite $\mathbf{X} \subset \mathbf{W}$ can be effectively given by listing all its elements; we assume that such a description of $\mathbf{X}$ is given as an input to all algorithms we are going to consider.

Let $\mathbf{Z} := \mathbf{X} \times \mathbf{Y}$; denote the set of all probability distributions in a measurable space A as $\mathcal{P}(A)$. Notice that $\mathcal{P}(A)$ is a finite-dimensional space when A is finite (e.g., when $A = \mathbf{Z}^n$). The following are standard definitions of the algorithmic theory of randomness. A real-valued function $f(u)$ is called *semicomputable from above* (resp. *from below*) if there exists a computable function $F(i, u)$, i ranging over the positive integers, such that:

- for all i and u, $F(i, u) \geq F(i + 1, u)$ (resp. $F(i, u) \leq F(i + 1, u)$),
- for all u, $f(u) = \lim_{i \to \infty} F(i, u)$.

A function $t : \cup_n(\mathbf{Z}^n \times \mathcal{P}(\mathbf{Z}^n)) \times \mathbf{W} \to [0, 1]$ is called a *conditional statistical test* if, for any n, $P \in \mathcal{P}(\mathbf{Z}^n)$, $w \in \mathbf{W}$ and $\gamma \in [0, 1]$:

$$P\{\omega = (z_1, \ldots, z_n) : t(\omega, P, w) \leq \gamma\} \leq \gamma.$$

(It is conventional in the algorithmic theory of randomness to give this definition "on the log-scale", in terms of $-\log t$.) Similarly, a *statistical test* (unconditional) can be defined as a function $t : \cup_n(\mathbf{Z}^n \times \mathcal{P}(\mathbf{Z}^n)) \to [0, 1]$ such that, for any n, $P \in \mathcal{P}(\mathbf{Z}^n)$ and $\gamma \in [0, 1]$:

$$P\{\omega \in \mathbf{Z}^n : t(\omega, P) \leq \gamma\} \leq \gamma \tag{6}$$

(in principle, this notion is superfluous, since we can use conditional tests with a fixed condition).

A conditional statistical test d is called a *universal conditional statistical test* if it is semicomputable from above and, for any other semicomputable from above conditional statistical test t, there exists a constant $c > 0$ such that $d(\omega, P, w) \leq ct(\omega, P, w)$ for any n, $\omega \in \mathbf{Z}^n$, $P \in \mathcal{P}(\mathbf{Z}^n)$ and $w \in \mathbf{W}$. A universal conditional test exists by a theorem due to Kolmogorov and Martin-Löf [15,14]. We fix a universal conditional test d and call $d_P(\omega \mid w) := d(\omega, P, w)$ the *randomness level* of ω w.r. to P when w is known. We also fix some element $w_0 \in W$ (the "null" element) and call $d_P(\omega) := d_P(\omega \mid w_0)$ the (unconditional) *randomness level* of ω w.r. to P. We will usually give our definitions for unconditional level, although sometimes they will be used in the conditional case as well. Notation such as $d_{P^n}(\omega)$ will be sometimes simplified to $d_P(\omega)$; we will also write $t_P(\omega)$ for arbitrary statistical tests (not necessarily universal).

If $\mathcal{Q}$ is a family of probability distributions in $\mathbf{Z}^n$, we define the randomness level of $\omega \in \mathbf{Z}^n$ w.r. to $\mathcal{Q}$ as the supremum

$$d_{\mathcal{Q}}(\omega) := \sup_{P \in \mathcal{Q}} d_P(\omega)$$

(ω is considered random w.r. to a family if it is random w.r. to at least one distribution in the family). According to *Levin's theorem*, when $\mathcal{Q}$ ranges over (constructively) closed families (possibly with different n), $d_{\mathcal{Q}}(\omega)$ is semicomputable from above and is valid in the sense that always

$$\sup_{P \in \mathcal{Q}} P\{\omega : d_{\mathcal{Q}}(\omega) \leq \gamma\} \leq \gamma;$$

moreover, it is the minimal, up to a constant factor, function satisfying these properties.

If Π is the training set (1), x_{l+1} is a test pattern and $P \in \mathcal{P}(\mathbf{Z})$, we define the randomness level of Π extended by adding the test pattern as the supremum over all possible classifications of the test pattern:

$$d_P(\Pi, x_{l+1}) := \sup_{y \in \mathbf{Y}} d_P(\Pi, (x_{l+1}, y)).$$

Analogously to Levin's theorem, thus defined function d on the extended sequences in $\mathbf{Z}^l \times \mathbf{X}$, $l = 1, 2, \ldots$, is, up to a constant factor, the minimal upper semicomputable function such that the probability of the event $d_P(\Pi, x_{l+1}) \leq \gamma$ never exceeds γ, provided the data items (x_i, y_i) are generated from P independently. We will also be using the notation $d_{\mathcal{Q}}(\Pi, x_{l+1})$ for $\sup_{P \in \mathcal{Q}} d_P(\Pi, x_{l+1})$ (we refrain from restating this definition).

We will be especially interested in the randomness level with respect to the family $\mathcal{Q}$ of all probability distributions P^n in $\mathbf{Z}^n$, $P \in \mathcal{P}(\mathbf{Z})$; in this case we will write $d_{\mathrm{iid}}(\cdot)$ instead of $d_{\mathcal{Q}}(\cdot)$.

3 Pattern Recognition

As we saw in the introductory section (see p. 339), the problem of pattern recognition is sometimes (when the number of support vectors is small) solvable in the diverse case. In principle, this answers the main question of this paper for pattern recognition, and so this section is to some degree an aside. However, one feature of the solution offered by PAC theory is so worrying that it deserves to be discussed at length.

This worrying feature of PAC theory is the looseness of the bounds it establishes. Littlestone and Warmuth's bound stated in Section 1 is one of the tightest, but even it usually does not give practically meaningful results. E.g., for the US Postal Service database (described in [11], Section 12.2), the error bound for one out of ten classifiers is something like

$$\frac{1}{l-d}\left(d \ln \frac{el}{d} + \ln \frac{l}{\delta}\right) \approx \frac{1}{7291 - 274} 274 \ln \frac{7291e}{274} \approx 0.17,$$

even if we ignore the term $\ln \frac{l}{\delta}$ (274 is the average number of support vectors for polynomials of degree 3, which give the best predictive performance; see Table 12.2 in [11]). Since there are ten classifiers, the bound on the total probability of mistake becomes 1.7, which is not useful. Even if Littlestone and Warmuth's result were applicable to multi-class classifiers, we would still obtain

$$\frac{1}{l-d}\left(d \ln \frac{el}{d} + \ln \frac{l}{\delta}\right) \approx \frac{1}{7291 - 1677} 1677 \ln \frac{7291e}{1677} \approx 0.74$$

(1677 is the total number of support vectors for all ten classifiers for polynomial kernels; see [11], Table 12.5), not much better than the trivial bound 1. Other standard theorems known to us give even worse results (see, e.g., [2]).

Of course, there are practically useful algorithms for pattern recognition: e.g., Vapnik ([11], Section 12.2) describes algorithms achieving an error rate close to 3% for the USPS data set. The problem with such algorithms is that they produce "bare predictions": at the moment of making a prediction one does not know anything about its accuracy. The purpose of bounds such as (4) and (5) is to complement a bare prediction for y_{l+1} with some measure of confidence: e.g., if the right-hand side of (5) is 95%, the probability that $y_{l+1} = 1$ is at least 95% (assuming an event of probability δ did not happen). As we saw, the solution offered by PAC bounds, while theoretically elegant, is unlikely to be practically useful.

Papers [4,8,13,9,6,7] report practically meaningful results (see below) for pattern recognition and regression with confidence. To distinguish the approach of those papers from other approaches (such as PAC and Bayesian) we will call it the "randomness approach"; the attribute "randomness" will similarly be used to indicate that the concept belongs to the randomness approach. The randomness approach has two varieties of results: "universal" randomness results (involving the universal statistical test) and "specific" randomness results (involving specific non-universal statistical tests).

The specific randomness approach is very simple and in the spirit of the classical nonparametric statistics (for a discussion of simple parametric cases, see [1], Section 7.5), in contrast to the sophisticated PAC techniques. Its main idea, in the case of pattern recognition, is as follows: a prediction $\hat{y}_{l+1}$ for y_{l+1} is considered to be reliable if the alternative classifications $y_{l+1} \neq \hat{y}_{l+1}$ are excluded by some statistical test, which is required to be valid (i.e., is required to satisfy (6)) under any i.i.d. distribution. (In the universal randomness approach, this statistical test is the universal test.) "Excluded" means that the statistical test takes value less than some threshold; we will take 1% as the threshold. As the validity condition (6) (with $\gamma = 0.01$) shows, it is possible that the true classification will be excluded, but the probability of this does not exceed 1%.

The recent paper [7] constructs a statistical test based on the Nearest Neighbours procedure which, for the USPS data set mentioned above, gives reliable predictions for 95% of the test examples (see Table 1 in [7]). In other words, in 95% of all test examples we can exclude all classifications but one at the significance level 1%; using the terminology introduced in [4,8,13], we can also say that in 95% of cases the confidence of our prediction is 99% or more. The use of a statistical test based on the Nearest Neighbours is not essential here; similar results can be obtained using, e.g., Support Vector Machine as the underlying algorithm.

We can see that the randomness framework used in [4,8,13,9,6,7] is different from that of this paper (see Section 1). However, the following simple theorem shows that there is a close connection (we are again assuming $\mathbf{Y} = \{0, 1\}$): if $y_{l+1} = 1$ leads to a low randomness level, $P(1 \mid x_{l+1})$ is low, and vice versa (we state this only for the label 1; the statement for 0 is symmetrical).

Theorem 1. *Let Π be a training set of size l and x_{l+1} be a test pattern. There exists a constant $c > 0$ such that:*

– *For any constant $\epsilon > 0$ and probability distribution $P \in \mathcal{P}(\mathbf{Z})$,*

$$d_P(\Pi, (x_{l+1}, 1) \mid \epsilon) \leq \epsilon \Longrightarrow P(1 \mid x_{l+1}) \leq \frac{c\epsilon}{d_P(\Pi, x_{l+1} \mid \epsilon)}. \tag{7}$$

– *For any constant $\epsilon > 0$ and probability distribution $P \in \mathcal{P}(\mathbf{Z})$,*

$$P(1 \mid x_{l+1}) \leq \epsilon \Longrightarrow d_P(\Pi, (x_{l+1}, 1) \mid \epsilon) \leq c\epsilon d_P(\Pi, x_{l+1} \mid \epsilon). \tag{8}$$

Proof. Equation (7) can be rewritten as

$$d_P(\Pi, (x_{l+1}, 1) \mid \epsilon) \leq \epsilon \Longrightarrow d_P(\Pi, x_{l+1} \mid \epsilon) \leq c\epsilon / P(1 \mid x_{l+1});$$

therefore, it is sufficient to show that the function equal to $\epsilon/P(1 \mid x_{l+1})$ if $d_P(\Pi, (x_{l+1}, 1) \mid \epsilon) \leq \epsilon$ and to 1 otherwise is a statistical test. Its semicomputability from above obviously follows from semicomputability from above of $d_P(\Pi, (x_{l+1}, 1) \mid \epsilon)$; the validity follows from

$$P\{(\Pi, x_{l+1}) : d_P(\Pi, (x_{l+1}, 1) \mid \epsilon) \leq \epsilon \,\&\, \epsilon/P(1 \mid x_{l+1}) \leq \gamma\} \leq \gamma.$$

Equation (8) follows from the fact that the function equal to $\epsilon d_P(\Pi, x_{l+1} \mid \epsilon)$ if $P(1 \mid x_{l+1}) \leq \epsilon$ and $y_{l+1} = 1$ and equal to 1 otherwise is a statistical test in $\mathbf{Z}^{l+1}$. □

Let us see what this theorem means in practice. First we need to restate the theorem in terms of specific tests. Its proof shows that for any statistical test t (we will take as t essentially the statistical test constructed in [7]) there exists a statistical test T such that we have the analogue of (7) with $c = 1$:

$$t_P(\Pi, (x_{l+1}, 1) \mid \epsilon) \leq \epsilon \Longrightarrow P(1 \mid x_{l+1}) \leq \frac{\epsilon}{T_P(\Pi, x_{l+1} \mid \epsilon)};$$

analogously,

$$t_P(\Pi, (x_{l+1}, 0) \mid \epsilon) \leq \epsilon \Longrightarrow P(0 \mid x_{l+1}) \leq \frac{\epsilon}{T_P(\Pi, x_{l+1} \mid \epsilon)}.$$

This can be easily extended to more than 2 labels. Let us take $\epsilon = 0.01$ and the test (which does not depend on P and ϵ at all) constructed in [7] as $t(\omega) = t_P(\omega \mid w)$. As we already mentioned, for the 95% of the USPS test examples we have

$$t(\Pi, (x_{l+1}, j)) \leq 0.01$$

for all $j \in \{0, \ldots, 9\}$ but one (this only j will be denoted $\hat{y}_{l+1}$). The multi-class extension of Theorem 1 shows that for any probability distribution satisfying

$$T_P(\Pi, x_{l+1} \mid 0.01) > 0.1$$

(this will hold with probability 90% or more if P is the true distribution generating the data) we will have

$$P(y_{l+1} \neq \hat{y}_{l+1} \mid x_{l+1}) < 0.01/0.1 = 0.1.$$

We can see that the P-probability of mistake will be bounded by 0.1 (unless an event of probability 0.1 happens); not an impressive result for such a clean data set as USPS, but still much better than 1.7 found above.

Our interpretation of the calculation in the previous paragraph is that PAC's approach of bounding the probability of error for typical training sets might be too ambitious for practical problems. We believe that reporting confidence and credibility (as defined in [8] and [13]) is usually much more informative.

Remark 4. At the beginning of this section we discussed the weakness, from the practical point of view, of the error bound in Littlestone and Warmuth's theorem. In this remark we will briefly discuss similar weaknesses of other results of PAC theory and statistical learning theory. The confidence measures provided by the randomness approach can always be extracted from the given data set alone. This is also true about Littlestone and Warmuth's theorem and most results reported in [2], but not true about many other well-known results. For example, Theorem 10.7 in [11] (p. 415) gives the error bound

$$ER(\alpha_l) \leq \frac{E \min\left(\mathcal{K}_{l+1}, \left(\frac{\mathcal{D}_{l+1}}{\rho_{l+1}}\right)^2\right)}{l+1};$$

this bound might be tighter than that in Littlestone and Warmuth's theorem, but there is no way to see from the data set (Π, x_{l+1}) at hand what the expected value in the right-hand side is going to be. All other theorems in [11] and [12] giving error bounds for the Support Vector Machine are of this type. Another common problem preventing one from evaluating theoretical error bounds is using unspecified constants and imposing conditions on the underlying probability distribution that are impossible to verify given only the data set (Π, x_{l+1}) (see [2] for numerous examples).

4 Density Estimation

The following theorem shows that non-trivial estimates of $P(1 \mid x_{l+1})$ are impossible: there will always exist a probability distribution under which (Π, x_{l+1}) is as random as under any other distribution ($d_P(\Pi, x_{l+1}) \geq d_{\text{iid}}(\Pi, x_{l+1})/c$) and for which $P(1 \mid x_{l+1})$ is trivial (0 or 1).

Theorem 2. *There exists a constant $c > 0$ which satisfies the following. If Π is a training set without repeating patterns and x_{l+1} is a test pattern different from all training patterns, there exists a probability distribution $P \in \mathcal{P}(\mathbf{Z})$ such that*

$$d_P(\Pi, x_{l+1}) \geq d_{\text{iid}}(\Pi, x_{l+1})/c \;\&\; P(1 \mid x_{l+1}) \in \{0, 1\}.$$

Proof sketch Let Q be a probability distribution in $\mathbf{Z}$ such that (Π, x_{l+1}) is random w.r.t. to Q. We represent the distribution Q as a mixture of the distributions P which are "simple" for Q (in the sense that that the marginal distributions in $\mathbf{X}$ for P and Q coincide and $P(1 \mid x)$ is always 0 or 1). Intuitively, our construction corresponds to the following picture: to generate a sample $(x_1, y_1), \ldots, (x_{l+1}, y_{l+1})$ (assuming no two x_i coincide) according to the distribution Q, we can first choose randomly $f : X \to \{0, 1\}$ according to the conditional distributions of Q (i.e., we set $f(x) := 1$ with probability $Q(1 \mid x)$, independently for all $x \in X$), and then compute $y_i = f(x_i)$ from x_i generated from the marginal distribution of Q. With every such f we associate the distribution P with the same marginal as Q and with $P(1 \mid x) = f(x)$ for all $x \in X$. The randomness of (Π, x_{l+1}) w.r.t. to Q then implies the randomness of (Π, x_{l+1}) w.r.t. to one of the simple P. There are some technical complications connected with the fact that this argument only works for the samples where x_i are not repeated, whereas randomness tests have to be defined for all samples. For details, see Appendix A. □

In the previous section we discussed practical implications of Theorem 1. Since Theorem 2 is a negative result, we cannot discuss its practical implication at the same level of concreteness. It shows, however, that attempts to design general density estimation algorithms are doomed unless the patterns are at least occasionally repeated (the extreme case being Glivenko–Cantelli) or we have some prior information about the density $P(j \mid x_{l+1})$ (say, a smooth, in some sense, dependence on x_{l+1}).

As usual for "universal" results (i.e., results using the universal randomness test), Theorem 2 involves an undefined constant, c. This makes its direct application problematic: imagine that, say, $c = 100$. The proof of Theorem 2 shows, however, that, roughly speaking, c can be taken equal to 1. For details, see Appendix B (especially Corollary 1 on p. 353).

5 Regression

The main subjects of this paper are pattern recognition and density estimation, but in this section we briefly discuss regression, stating an analogue of Theorem 1. Because of the looseness of PAC bounds, we will again deduce the feasibility of regression for diverse data sets from the existence of randomness regression procedures that work in the diverse case; our main reference in this section will be the recent paper [6]. (Besides their looseness, the PAC results tend to make extra assumptions about the i.i.d. distribution generating the data: e.g., all theorems in Section 4.5 "Generalization for Regression" of [2] assume the boundedness of support for the generating distribution. Such assumptions cannot be verified by looking at the data set; cf. Remark 4 above.)

Let F be a *region estimator*, in the sense that F is a function defined on the sequences

$$(\Pi, x_{l+1}) = ((x_1, y_1), \ldots, (x_l, y_l), x_{l+1}) \in (\mathbf{X} \times \mathbf{Y})^l \times \mathbf{X},$$

for all $l = 1, 2, \ldots$, which takes values in the Borel subsets of the real line:

$$F(\Pi, x_{l+1}) \subseteq \mathbb{R}.$$

We have two natural measures of quality of region estimators. First we can say that a region estimator F is *(ϵ, δ)-valid*, where ϵ and δ are (small) positive constants, if, for any l, any Π (as per (1)), any $x_{l+1} \in X$ and any $P \in \text{Rand}(\Pi, x_{l+1}, \delta)$ (see (2)),

$$P(F(\Pi, x_{l+1})) \geq 1 - \epsilon.$$

This is the notion we are interested in in this paper. The usual randomness definition (used in [6]) is, however, as follows: we say that F is a $(1-\epsilon)$-region estimator, where ϵ is a (small) positive constant, if, for any l and any $P \in \mathcal{P}(\mathbf{Z})$,

$$P^{l+1}\left\{(\Pi, x_{l+1}, y_{l+1}) : y_{l+1} \in F(\Pi, x_{l+1})\right\} \geq 1 - \epsilon$$

(Π is defined by (1)).

Paper [6] constructs $(1-\epsilon)$-region estimators that work well for artificial and standard benchmark data sets in the situation where the patterns x_i are never repeated. Therefore, to demonstrate the feasibility of regression in the framework of this paper ((ϵ, δ)-validity), we only need to establish the connection between these two notions of quality for region estimators. The following theorem establishes this connection in the needed direction. Since we defined randomness level only in the case $\mathbf{Y} = \{0, 1\}$, we state it as a theorem of existence of a statistical test; notice that we do not require $\mathbf{Y} = \mathbb{R}$.

Theorem 3. *There exists a conditional statistical test t which satisfies the following. For any $\epsilon > 0$, any $(1-\epsilon)$-region estimator F, any l, any training set Π of size l, any test pattern x_{l+1}, and any probability distribution $P \in \mathcal{P}(\mathbf{Z})$,*

$$P(F(\Pi, x_{l+1}) \mid x_{l+1}) \geq 1 - \frac{\epsilon}{t_P(\Pi, x_{l+1} \mid \epsilon)}. \tag{9}$$

Proof. The inequality in (9) can be rewritten as

$$P(F^c(\Pi, x_{l+1}) \mid x_{l+1}) \leq \frac{\epsilon}{t_P(\Pi, x_{l+1} \mid \epsilon)}$$

(E^c stands for the complement of E) and, therefore, as

$$t_P(\Pi, x_{l+1} \mid \epsilon) \leq \frac{\epsilon}{P(F^c(\Pi, x_{l+1}) \mid x_{l+1})}.$$

We can see that it is sufficient to show that the function in the right-hand side of this inequality is a statistical test:

$$P\left\{\frac{\epsilon}{P(F^c(\Pi, x_{l+1}) \mid x_{l+1})} \leq \gamma\right\} \leq \gamma.$$

If this inequality were violated,

$$P\left\{P(F^c(\Pi, x_{l+1}) \mid x_{l+1}) \geq \frac{\epsilon}{\gamma}\right\} > \gamma,$$

we would have

$$P^{l+1}\left\{(\Pi, x_{l+1}, y_{l+1}) : y_{l+1} \notin F(\Pi, x_{l+1})\right\} > \epsilon,$$

which contradicts F being a $(1-\epsilon)$-region estimator. □

The notion of (ϵ, δ)-validity of region estimators can be adapted to non-universal tests: "(ϵ, δ)-valid w.r. to a statistical test t" is defined in the same way as "(ϵ, δ)-valid" but using t instead of the randomness level d. Theorem 3 shows that if ϵ and δ are fixed positive constant and F is a $(1-\epsilon)$-region estimator, it will be an $(\epsilon/\delta, \delta)$-valid w.r. to $t(\cdot \mid \epsilon)$ region estimator. In particular, it will be a $(\sqrt{\epsilon}, \sqrt{\epsilon})$-valid region estimator.

Remark 5. The problem of regression, as understood in this section, is to predict $y_{l+1} \in \mathbb{R}$ (giving, e.g., a predictive region $F(\Pi, x_{l+1})$, hopefully containing y_{l+1}). There is another understanding of the problem of regression, however. According to Vapnik [11] (p. 26), the problem of *regression estimation* is to estimate the *regression function*

$$r(x) := \mathbf{E}(Y \mid X = x),$$

which maps $x \in \mathbf{X}$ to the expected value (w.r. to the true distribution P generating the pairs (x_i, y_i)) of Y conditional on $X = x$; in our current context, the problem of regression estimation is to estimate the value $r(x_{l+1})$ of the regression function at the test pattern. We can see that the problem of regression estimation is simpler than the problem of density estimation (where we are required to estimate the full conditional distribution of Y given $X = x_{l+1}$ rather than its mean value). However, in the special case $\mathbf{Y} = \{0, 1\}$ considered in Section 4 the difference disappears; therefore, our results show that the problem of density estimation is infeasible in the diverse case even for binary y_i, unless $r(x_{l+1})$ is close to 0 or 1.

6 Open Problems

The following are open problems naturally arising from the results of this paper:

- Prove impossibility of density estimation in the case where the training set can contain repeating patterns but there are no patterns identical to the test one.
- It is clear that density estimation is possible when the training set contains many patterns identical to the test one (cf. Remark 3 above). It would be interesting to prove a general result containing this positive result and Theorem 2 as special cases.
- As discussed in Section 3, it is important (if possible) to find practically meaningful PAC error bounds for diverse data sets (ideally, approaching the quality of the measures of confidence offered by the randomness approach). This might require abandoning the most appealing feature of the usual PAC bounds: logarithmic dependence on δ (as in (4) and (5)).

7 Conclusion

In this paper we argued that, in the "diverse" case where the patterns x_i are never repeated in the given data set:

- The problems of pattern recognition and regression can be feasible (moreover, they are often feasible in practice).
- The problem of density estimation is never feasible even in the case $\mathbf{Y} = \{0, 1\}$ (see Section 4 and Corollary 1).

Acknowledgements

This work was partially supported by EPSRC through grants GR/M14937 ("Predictive complexity: recursion-theoretic variants") and GR/M16856 ("Comparison of Support Vector Machine and Minimum Message Length methods for induction and prediction"). We are grateful to the Programme Committee for numerous suggestions which greatly helped us to improve the presentation.

References

1. David R. Cox and David V. Hinkley. *Theoretical Statistics.* Chapman and Hall, London, 1974.
2. Nello Cristianini and John Shawe-Taylor. *An Introduction to Support Vector Machines and Other Kernel-based Methods.* Cambridge, Cambridge University Press, 2000.
3. Alex Gammerman and A. R. Thatcher. Bayesian diagnostic probabilities without assuming independence of symptoms. *Yearbook of Medical Informatics*, pp. 323–330, 1992.
4. Alex Gammerman, Vladimir Vapnik, and Volodya Vovk. Learning by transduction. In *Proceedings of the Fourteenth Conference on Uncertainty in Artificial Intelligence*, pp. 148–156, San Francisco, CA, 1998. Morgan Kaufmann.
5. Ming Li and Paul Vitányi. *An Introduction to Kolmogorov Complexity and Its Applications.* Springer, New York, 2nd edition, 1997.
6. Ilia Nouretdinov, Tom Melluish, and Volodya Vovk. Ridge Regression Confidence Machine. In *Proceedings of the 18th International Conference on Machine Learning*, 2001.
7. Kostas Proedrou, Ilia Nouretdinov, Volodya Vovk, and Alex Gammerman. Transductive confidence machines for pattern recognition. Technical Report CLRC-TR-01-02, Computer Learning Research Centre, Royal Holloway, University of London, 2001. Available from the CLRC web site, `http://www.clrc.rhul.ac.uk`.
8. Craig Saunders, Alex Gammerman, and Volodya Vovk. Transduction with confidence and credibility. In *Proceedings of the 16th International Joint Conference on Artificial Intelligence*, pp. 722–726, 1999.
9. Craig Saunders, Alex Gammerman, and Volodya Vovk. Computationally efficient transductive machines. In *Proceedings of ALT'00*, 2000.
10. Vladimir N. Vapnik. *The Nature of Statistical Learning Theory.* Springer, New York, 1995.
11. Vladimir N. Vapnik. *Statistical Learning Theory.* Wiley, New York, 1998.

12. Vladimir N. Vapnik and Olivier Chapelle. Bounds on error expectation for Support Vector Machines. In Alex J. Smola, Peter Bartlett, B. Schölkopf, and C. Schuurmans, editors, *Advances in Large Margin Classifiers*, pp. 5–26. MIT Press, 1999.
13. Volodya Vovk, Alex Gammerman, and Craig Saunders. Machine-learning applications of algorithmic randomness. In *Proceedings of the 16th International Conference on Machine Learning*, pp. 444–453, 1999.
14. Volodya Vovk and Vladimir V. V'yugin. On the empirical validity of the Bayesian method. *Journal of Royal Statistical Society* B, 55:253–266, 1993.
15. Alexander K. Zvonkin and Leonid A. Levin. The complexity of finite objects and the development of the concepts of information and randomness by means of the theory of algorithms. *Russian Mathematical Surveys*, 25:83–124, 1970.

Appendix A. Proof of Theorem 2

First we give several definitions. Any probability distribution P in $\mathbf{Z} := \mathbf{X} \times \mathbf{Y}$ (remember that $\mathbf{Y} = \{0,1\}$) defines a probability distribution $\mathbf{m}_P$ in the set $\mathbf{X}$ and a function $\mathbf{f}_P : \mathbf{X} \to [0,1]$ in the following way: for any $E \subseteq \mathbf{X}$,

$$\mathbf{m}_P(E) := P\{(x,y) : x \in E, y \in \mathbf{Y}\}$$

(i.e., $\mathbf{m}_P$ is the marginal distribution of P) and

$$\mathbf{f}_P(x) := P(1 \mid x) := \frac{P\{(x,1)\}}{P\{(x,0)\} + P\{(x,1)\}}$$

(i.e., $\mathbf{f}_P(x)$ is the conditional probability that $Y = 1$ given $X = x$; when $P\{(x,0)\} + P\{(x,1)\} = 0$, we can set, for example, $\mathbf{f}_P(x) := 1/2$).

Conversely, any probability distribution m in $\mathbf{X}$ and function $f : \mathbf{X} \to [0,1]$ define a probability distribution $\mathbf{P}_{m,f}$ in $\mathbf{Z}$ with the marginal distribution m and the conditional probabilities f:

$$\mathbf{m}_{\mathbf{P}_{m,f}} = m, \quad m\{x\} \neq 0 \Longrightarrow \mathbf{f}_{\mathbf{P}_{m,f}}(x) = f(x).$$

Consider any probability distribution P in $\mathbf{Z}$. We will say that a probability distribution R in $\mathbf{Z}$ is *simple for* P if $\mathbf{m}_R = \mathbf{m}_P$ and $\mathbf{f}_R(x) \in \{0,1\}$ for any $x \in \mathbf{X}$ such that $\mathbf{m}_R\{x\} > 0$. We say that R is *simple* if it is simple for some P (i.e., if $\mathbf{f}_R(x) \in \{0,1\}$ for any $x \in \mathbf{X}$ such that $\mathbf{m}_R\{x\} > 0$).

For any $n = 1, 2, \ldots$, define

$$\overline{\mathbf{Z}^n} := \{((x_1,y_1),\ldots,(x_n,y_n)) \in \mathbf{Z}^n : \forall i,j : x_i = x_j \Rightarrow y_i = y_j\}$$

(in particular, all data sequences with no repeated patterns are in $\overline{\mathbf{Z}^n}$).

For any probability distribution P in $\mathbf{Z}$ we define a measure (not necessarily a probability distribution) $\overline{P^n}$ on $\mathbf{Z}^n$ as the restriction of P^n to $\overline{\mathbf{Z}^n}$:

$$\overline{P^n}\{\omega\} := \begin{cases} P^n\{\omega\} & \text{if } \omega \in \overline{\mathbf{Z}^n}, \\ 0 & \text{otherwise.} \end{cases}$$

Notice that for a simple $R \in \mathcal{P}(\mathbf{Z})$ we always have $\overline{R^n} = R^n$. More generally, for any $P \in \mathcal{P}(\mathbf{Z}^n)$ we define $\overline{P}$ to be the restriction of P to $\overline{\mathbf{Z}^n}$.

We will derive the statement of the theorem from the following lemma.

Lemma 1. *There exists a constant $c > 0$ such that for any n, any $\omega \in \overline{\mathbf{Z}^n}$ and any probability distribution $P \in \mathcal{P}(\mathbf{Z})$, there exists another probability distribution $R \in \mathcal{P}(\mathbf{Z})$ which is simple for P and satisfies*

$$d_R(\omega) \geq d_P(\omega)/c.$$

To prove this result, we need another two lemmas. In the first of these, we use randomness level w.r. to a measure which is not necessarily a probability distribution; this generalized definition is analogous to the definition for probability distributions.

Lemma 2. *There exists a constant $c > 0$ such that, for any n, $\omega \in \overline{\mathbf{Z}^n}$ and $P \in \mathcal{P}(\mathbf{Z})$,*

$$d_{\overline{P^n}}(\omega) \geq d_{P^n}(\omega)/c.$$

Proof. We will prove the statement of the lemma for all $Q \in \mathcal{P}(\mathbf{Z}^n)$, not just for the powers P^n. Define $t_Q(\omega) = d_{\overline{Q}}(\omega)$ if $\omega \in \overline{\mathbf{Z}^n}$ and $t_Q(\omega) = 1$ otherwise. It is easy to check that t is a statistical test, and by the definition of the universal test we have, for $\omega \in \overline{\mathbf{Z}^n}$,

$$d_{\overline{Q}}(\omega) = t_Q(\omega) \geq d_Q(\omega)/c. \qquad \square$$

Lemma 3. *For any n, $\omega \in \mathbf{Z}^n$ and $P \in \mathcal{P}(\mathbf{Z})$,*

$$\overline{P^n}(\omega) = \sum_{g:X\to\{0,1\}} \overline{\mathbf{P}^n_{\mathbf{m}_P,g}}(\omega)\pi_P(g),$$

where

$$\pi_P(g) = \prod_{x\in X} \mathbf{f}_P(x)^{[g(x)]} \qquad \textit{and} \qquad a^{[b]} = \begin{cases} a & \text{if } b = 1, \\ 1-a & \text{if } b = 0. \end{cases}$$

Notice that $\sum_{g:X\to\{0,1\}} \pi_P(g) = 1$.

Proof. Let $\omega = ((x_1, y_1), \ldots, (x_n, y_n))$; without loss of generality we assume $\omega \in \overline{\mathbf{Z}^n}$. We have

$$\overline{\mathbf{P}^n_{\mathbf{m}_P,g}}(\omega) = \mathbf{m}_P(x_1)\ldots\mathbf{m}_P(x_n)y_1^{[g(x_1)]}\ldots y_n^{[g(x_n)]};$$

therefore,

$$\sum_g \overline{\mathbf{P}^n_{\mathbf{m}_P,g}}(\omega)\pi_P(g) = \mathbf{m}_P(x_1)\ldots\mathbf{m}_P(x_n)\sum_g y_1^{[g(x_1)]}\ldots y_n^{[g(x_n)]}\prod_{x\in X}\mathbf{f}_P(x)^{[g(x)]}$$

$$= \mathbf{m}_P(x_1)\ldots\mathbf{m}_P(x_n) \sum_{g:g(x_i)=y_i,\forall i}\ \prod_{x\in X}\mathbf{f}_P(x)^{[g(x)]} = \mathbf{m}_P(x_1)\ldots\mathbf{m}_P(x_n)$$

$$\times \left(\sum_{g:X\setminus\{x_1,\dots,x_n\}\to\{0,1\}} \prod_{x\in X\setminus\{x_1,\dots,x_n\}} \mathbf{f}_P(x)^{[g(x)]} \prod_{i=1}^{n} \mathbf{f}_P(x_i)^{[y_i]} \right)$$

$$= \mathbf{m}_P(x_1)\dots\mathbf{m}_P(x_n) \prod_{i=1}^{n} \mathbf{f}_P(x_i)^{[y_i]} = \overline{P^n}(\omega). \qquad \square$$

We will derive the statement of Lemma 1 from Lemmas 2 and 3.

Proof of Lemma 1. Define

$$t_{\overline{P^n}}(\omega) = \sup_{R \text{ is simple for } P} d_{\overline{R^n}}(\omega). \tag{10}$$

We will show that this function is a statistical test in the following sense: the validity condition (6) is satisfied for measures of the form $\overline{P^n}$ and t is semicomputable from above inside its domain. First notice that it satisfies the condition

$$\overline{R^n}\{\omega = (z_1, \dots, z_n) : t_{\overline{P^n}}(\omega) \le \gamma\} \le \gamma$$

for any R which is simple for P. Using Lemma 3, we obtain that it also satisfies the required validity condition

$$\overline{P^n}\{\omega = (z_1, \dots, z_n) : t_{\overline{P^n}}(\omega) \le \gamma\} \le \gamma,$$

since $\overline{P^n}$ is a mixture of $\overline{R^n}$. Semicomputability from above follows from the fact that for fixed $\overline{P^n}$ and ω the supremum in (10) involves only finitely many R. It can be shown (a simple argument omitted) that $t_{\overline{P^n}}$ can be extended to a statistical test t_Q (where Q are not necessarily of the form $\overline{P^n}$).

Hence, $t_{\overline{P^n}}(\omega) \ge d_{\overline{P^n}}(\omega)/c_1$ for some constant $c_1 > 0$, and there exists such R (on which the supremum is reached) that

$$d_{R^n}(\omega) = d_{\overline{R^n}}(\omega) \ge d_{\overline{P^n}}(\omega)/c_1,$$

and, by Lemma 2, we have

$$d_{\overline{P^n}}(\omega) \ge d_{P^n}(\omega)/c_2. \qquad \square$$

The statement of the theorem can be easily derived from Lemma 1. Indeed, there exists a measure $P \in \mathcal{P}(\mathbf{Z})$ such that $d_P(\Pi, x_{l+1}) = d_{\text{iid}}(\Pi, x_{l+1})$; without loss of generality we assume $d_{\text{iid}}(\Pi, x_{l+1}) > 0$. Then by Lemma 1 there exists a measure R which is simple for P and such that $d_R(\Pi, x_{l+1}) \ge d_{\text{iid}}(\Pi, x_{l+1})/c$ for some constant $c > 0$. Because the distribution R is simple for P, we have $R(1 \mid x_{l+1}) \in \{0, 1\}$ (the case $\mathbf{m}_P\{x_{l+1}\} = 0$ is excluded by $d_{\text{iid}}(\Pi, x_{l+1}) > 0$).

Appendix B. Specific form of Theorem 2

In this appendix we will see that the following specific (i.e., not involving the universal test) version of Theorem 2 holds.

Theorem 4. *For any statistical test t there exists a statistical test T such that the following holds. If Π is a training set without repeating patterns and x_{l+1} is a test pattern different from all training patterns, then for any probability distribution $P \in \mathcal{P}(\mathbf{Z})$ there exists a probability distribution $R \in \mathcal{P}(\mathbf{Z})$ which is simple for P and satisfies*

$$t_R(\Pi, x_{l+1}) \geq T_P(\Pi, x_{l+1}).$$

The proof immediately follows from the following specific version of Lemma 1.

Lemma 4. *For any statistical test t there exists a statistical test T such that the following holds. For any n, any $\omega \in \overline{\mathbf{Z}^n}$ and any probability distribution $P \in \mathcal{P}(\mathbf{Z})$, there exists a probability distribution $R \in \mathcal{P}(\mathbf{Z})$ which is simple for P and satisfies*

$$t_R(\omega) \geq T_P(\omega).$$

Proof. This proof follows the proof of Lemma 1. Define

$$t'_{\overline{P^n}}(\omega) = \sup_{R \text{ is simple for } P} t_{\overline{R^n}}(\omega).$$

We already know that this is a statistical test (the universality of d was not used in the proof of Lemma 1). There exists such R (on which the supremum is reached) that

$$t_{R^n}(\omega) = t_{\overline{R^n}}(\omega) = t'_{\overline{P^n}}(\omega).$$

It remains to define $T_P(\omega)$ as $t'_p(\omega)$ if $\omega \in \overline{\mathbf{Z}^n}$ and as 1 otherwise. □

To see the relevance of Theorem 4 to the practical problem of density estimation, define (analogously to (2))

$$\mathrm{Rand}_t(\Pi, x_{l+1}, \delta) := \{P : t_P(\Pi, x_{l+1}) > \delta\},$$

where t is any (not necessarily the universal) statistical test; this is the set of probability distributions that the statistical test t deems compatible with the data set (Π, x_{l+1}). We also define

$$\mathrm{DE}_t(\Pi, x_{l+1}, \delta) := \left[\inf_{P \in \mathrm{Rand}_t(\Pi, x_{l+1}, \delta)} P(1 \mid x_{l+1}), \sup_{P \in \mathrm{Rand}_t(\Pi, x_{l+1}, \delta)} P(1 \mid x_{l+1})\right]$$

(set to $\emptyset$ if $\mathrm{Rand}_t(\Pi, x_{l+1}, \delta) = \emptyset$); this is the interval (denoted $[a, b]$ in Section 1) for possible values of the conditional probability that $y_{l+1} = 1$. One performs non-trivial density estimation when $\mathrm{DE}_t(\Pi, x_{l+1}, \delta)$ is an interval that does not contain 0 and 1. Theorem 4 shows that non-trivial density estimation is impossible, in the following sense.

Corollary 1. *For any statistical test t there exists a statistical test T such that the following holds. If Π is a training set without repeating patterns and x_{l+1} is a test pattern different from all training patterns, then*

$$\mathrm{DE}_t(\Pi, x_{l+1}, \delta) \subseteq (0, 1) \Longrightarrow \mathrm{DE}_T(\Pi, x_{l+1}, \delta) = \emptyset.$$

Therefore, we can do non-trivial density estimation at significance level δ only in trivial cases where all i.i.d. distributions can be excluded at the level δ.

A General Dimension for Exact Learning*

José L. Balcázar[1], Jorge Castro[1], and David Guijarro[2]**

[1] Dept. LSI, Universitat Politècnica de Catalunya,
Campus Nord, 08034 Barcelona, Spain
{balqui,castro}@lsi.upc.es
[2] Mannes Technology Consulting
Pl. Tirant lo Blanc 7, 08005 Barcelona, Spain
david@mannes-tech.com

Abstract. We introduce a new combinatorial dimension that gives a good approximation of the number of queries needed to learn in the exact learning model, no matter what set of queries is used. This new dimension generalizes previous dimensions providing upper and lower bounds for all sorts of queries, and not for just example-based queries as in previous works. Our new approach gives also simpler proofs for previous results. We present specific applications of our general dimension for the case of unspecified attribute value queries, and show that unspecified attribute value membership and equivalence queries are not more powerful than standard membership and equivalence queries for the problem of learning DNF formulas.

1 Introduction

This paper is about query complexity, i.e. counting the number of queries needed to learn in any exact query learning model such as those defined in [1]. We do not deal with time complexity issues but, instead, concentrate our efforts in giving a *unique* combinatorial notion that characterizes the query complexity for *any* set of queries.

In the exact learning model there is a special type of queries whose answers can be always modeled with sets of examples: the example-based queries. In this case, there is a lot of work done for specific cases: certificates [11] and consistency dimension [4] for membership and equivalence queries, approximate fingerprints [2,7] and strong consistency dimension [4] for equivalence queries and extended teaching dimension [10] for membership queries. Furthermore, there is a unifying concept, the abstract identification dimension (AIdim) [3], that gives a unique characterization for any set of example-based queries.

However, there are queries that do not fit in the notion of example-based queries; for instance, restricted equivalence [1] (equivalence queries that do not

* Work supported in part by the EC through the Esprit Program EU BRA program under project 20244 (ALCOM-IT), the EC Working Group EP27150 (NeuroColt II) and the spanish government grant PB98-0937-C04-04.

** Part of this work was done while this author was still in LSI, UPC.

D. Helmbold and B. Williamson (Eds.): COLT/EuroCOLT 2001, LNAI 2111, pp. 354–367, 2001.

supply a counterexample) and unspecified attribute value queries [9] (UAVs). There are works on lower bounds for UAVs [5,12] but, as far as we know, there is no general learning dimension for UAVs comparable to AIdim in the case of example-based queries.

In this work we introduce a new combinatorial notion, Gdim, that gives a good approximation of the number of queries needed to learn with any set of queries in the exact learning model. We show that AIdim is the natural derivation of Gdim in the case of example-based queries. And finally, we present two applications of Gdim for UAVs: (a) the first characterizations of the UAV protocols with membership and equivalence queries and for membership queries alone, which are a straightforward but nice generalization of their standard counterparts and (b) the number of standard membership and equivalence queries needed to learn DNF formulas, which we prove to be polynomially bounded by the number of UAV membership and equivalence queries. This last result shows that, in a query complexity sense, UAVs do not help in learning DNF formulas.

2 Notation and the Abstract Setting for Exact Learning

We focus on exact learning of Boolean functions and we fix all along the paper n as the number of variables. A Boolean function of arity n is a function from $\{0,1\}^n \to \{0,1\}$. The set of all Boolean functions of arity n is denoted by B_n.

An element x of $\{0,1\}^n$ is called an *assignment*. A pair (x, b), where $b \in \{0,1\}$ is a binary label, is called *example for function* $f \in B_n$ if $f(x) = b$. A *sample* is a collection of examples for some function $f \in B_n$. We denote by $\|X\|$ the cardinality of set X.

A partial assignment α is a word from $\{0,1,\star\}^n$. A complete assignment $x \in \{0,1\}^n$ satisfies a partial assignment α if they coincide in the positions where α is not $\star$. The hypercube H_α of a partial assignment α is the set of all complete assignments that satisfy α. Given $b \in \{0,1\}$, the expression $\alpha \cup v \leftarrow b$ denotes the partial assignment such that for any variable u it holds $u(\alpha \cup v \leftarrow b) = u(\alpha)$ when $u \neq v$ and $u(\alpha \cup v \leftarrow b) = b$ if $u = v$. We also denote by t_α the term that, when applied to a complete assignment x, evaluates to 1 if x satisfies α and to 0 otherwise and by c_α the clause such that $c_\alpha = \overline{t}_\alpha$.

Each function $f \in B_n$ can be formalized as an assignment in $\{0,1\}^{2^n}$. In this way, we identify the set of Boolean functions from $B_n \to \{0,1\}$ with B_{2^n}. Functions in B_{2^n} have a variable for each assignment y in $\{0,1\}^n$, which we denote by λ_y. We will make the following natural interpretation: $f \in B_n$ satisfies the positive (resp. negated) literal with variable λ_y when $(y,1)$ (resp. $(y,0)$) is an example of f; this is naturally denoted by $\lambda_y(f)$. For $S \subseteq B_{2^n}$ and $f \in B_n$, the expression $S(f)$ is $\bigwedge_{\Lambda \in S} \Lambda(f)$.

We use an abstract generalization of the exact learning model via queries of Angluin [1]. In our abstract setting, queries are atomic objects. Answers provide some partial knowledge of the target. Since our target concepts are always Boolean functions of arity n, we assume that such partial knowledge is always modeled as a function in B_{2^n} that is interpreted as a property that the target function satisfies. That is, answers correspond to functions in B_{2^n}.

Thus, in any abstract learning protocol we have two participants: the set Q of queries and the set of all possible answers. Since the set of answers will be specifically defined by each learning protocol, we only write explicitly the dependence of the protocol on Q. A protocol *Protocol*(Q) is a subset of $\{\langle q, \Lambda\rangle \mid q \in Q, \Lambda \in B_{2^n}\}$.

For instance, if we want to talk about learning with the usual equivalence queries with hypothesis coming from a subset $H \subseteq B_n$, we define $\mathit{Protocol}_{\equiv}(H)$ as the set

$$\{\langle h, \lambda_y\rangle \mid h \in H, y \in \{0,1\}^n, h(y) = 0\} \cup \{\langle h, \overline{\lambda}_y\rangle \mid h \in H, y \in \{0,1\}^n, h(y) = 1\}$$

$$\cup$$

$$\{\langle h, (\bigwedge_y \lambda_y) \wedge (\bigwedge_z \overline{\lambda}_z)\rangle \mid h \in H,\ y, z \in \{0,1\}^n, h(y) = 1, h(z) = 0\}$$

where the first two sets correspond to counterexamples and the last set to YES answers.

Angluin defined in [1] equivalence queries without counterexamples. These queries, called *restricted* equivalence queries, have as possible answers YES or NO. We can consider this protocol in our setting as follows. For restricted equivalence queries with hypothesis $H \subseteq B_n$ the set $\mathit{Protocol}_{\equiv_r}(H)$ is

$$\{\langle h, (\bigwedge_y \lambda_y) \wedge (\bigwedge_z \overline{\lambda}_z)\rangle \mid h \in H,\ y, z \in \{0,1\}^n, h(y) = 1, h(z) = 0\}$$

$$\cup$$

$$\{\langle h, (\bigvee_y \overline{\lambda}_y) \vee (\bigvee_z \lambda_z)\rangle \mid h \in H,\ y, z \in \{0,1\}^n, h(y) = 1, h(z) = 0\}$$

where the first set corresponds to a YES answer and the second one to a NO answer. Observe that this protocol cannot be formalized in the framework presented in [3].

For a protocol P and a query q, P_q denotes the set of all answers associated, in P, to query q; formally, $P_q = \{\Lambda \mid \langle q, \Lambda\rangle \in P\}$. For $f \in B_n$ we use P_q^f to denote the set of answers to query q in P that are satisfied by f; formally, $P_q^f = \{\Lambda \mid \Lambda \in P_q \wedge \Lambda(f)\}$. We require all protocols P to be *complete* for the set of queries Q, which means that for all $q \in Q$ and for all $f \in B_n$, $P_q^f \neq \emptyset$. We also use P^f to denote the set $\{\langle q, \Lambda\rangle \mid q \in Q \wedge \langle q, \Lambda\rangle \in P \wedge \Lambda(f)\}$. The notation is extended to apply it to subsets of P.

An *answering scheme* T of a protocol P is a subset of P that for all $q \in Q$ the set of answers T_q is non empty. The set of all answering schemes of P is denoted as $\mathcal{T}(P)$. The notation is also extended to apply it to answering schemes of answering schemes. For any answering scheme T, T_Q denotes the set $\{\Lambda \mid q \in Q \wedge \langle q, \Lambda\rangle \in T\}$, i.e. the set of potential answers to all queries.

A protocol whose answers are always Boolean functions that can be expressed as terms, i.e. conjunctions of literals, is a *conjunctive* protocol. The answers of conjunctive protocols provide a partial knowledge of the target concept that can be modeled as the values of the target function on a subdomain. Thus, each answer is just a sample of the target. We note that queries that give this kind of answers are sometimes called example-based queries (see [8], for example). Some of the most popular protocols such as membership queries, equivalence queries and subset queries are conjunctive.

3 Exact Learning and the General Dimension

The learning game is defined as follows. A teacher answers with respect to $f \in B_n$ and using $P = Protocol(Q)$ if for each query $q \in Q$, it outputs some $\Lambda \in P_q^f$. A function class $C \subseteq B_n$ is learnable with d queries under $P = Protocol(Q)$ if there exists an algorithm A such that for any $f \in C$ and for any teacher B that answers with respect to f using P, the only remaining function in C that satisfies the answers received after at most d interactions is f. For a class $C \subseteq B_n$ and a protocol $P = Protocol(Q)$ we define the *learning complexity*, $\mathrm{LC}(C, P)$, as the smallest $d \geq 0$ such that C is learnable with d queries under P. If no such integer exists then $\mathrm{LC}(C, P) = \infty$.

A combinatorial parameter that captures the learning complexity can be defined using a chain of alternating quantifiers of queries and answers. We describe it here, as a way of introducing the idea, and also for the sake of comparison with the much nicer "flat" version we will describe below.

Given a protocol P with query set Q and a target class $C \subseteq B_n$ we define the *alternating dimension* as the smallest integer $d \geq 0$ such that

$$(\exists q_1 \in Q)(\forall \Lambda_1 \in P_{q_1}) \ldots (\exists q_d \in Q)(\forall \Lambda_d \in P_{q_d})(\|\{c \in C | \bigwedge \Lambda_i(c)\}\| \leq 1)$$

If no such integer exists then $\mathrm{Adim}(C, P) = \infty$.

Now, the following theorem can be easily proved by a fully standard adversary argument:

Theorem 1. *For any protocol P and any class $C \subseteq B_n$,*

$$LC(C, P) = Adim(C, P)$$

In the next part of the section we present a nicer dimension without alternating quantifiers that gives an approximation, up to a logarithm of the cardinality of the target class, of the learning complexity.

Given a target class $C \subseteq B_n$ and a protocol P on a query set Q, we define the *general dimension*, $\mathrm{Gdim}(C, P)$, as the minimum integer $d \geq 0$ such that

$$(\forall T \in \mathcal{T}(P))\,(\exists S \subseteq T_Q)\,(\|S\| \leq d \wedge \|\{c \in C | S(c)\}\| \leq 1)$$

If no such integer exists then $\mathrm{Gdim}(C, P) = \infty$.

That is, no matter what answering scheme is chosen there exists some set of at most d answers such that at most one function in the target class satisfies all those answers.

The following lemma will be central in the proof of our main result in this section and is interesting in its own right.

Lemma 1. *Let $D \subseteq C \subseteq B_n$ such that $\|D\| > 1$, $P = Protocol(Q)$ and $Gdim(C, P) = d$. There exists $q \in Q$ such that for any $\Lambda \in P_q$, at least $\frac{\|D\|-1}{d}$ functions from D do not satisfy Λ.*

Proof. (sketch) Suppose that for each $q \in Q$ there exists some $\Lambda_q \in P_q$ such that less than $\frac{\|D\|-1}{d}$ functions do not satisfy Λ_q. A contradiction with $\mathrm{Gdim}(C, P) = d$ can be easily obtained simply considering the answering scheme T with $T_q = \{\Lambda_q\}$. •

Our main contribution of this section is the following characterization:

Theorem 2. *For any concept class $C \subseteq B_n$ and any protocol P on a query set Q,*

$$Gdim(C, P) \leq LC(C, P) \leq Gdim(C, P)\lceil \ln \|C\| \rceil$$

Proof. (sketch) We will start showing that if $\mathrm{Gdim}(C, P) > k$ then any learning algorithm must ask more than k queries. Let T be the answering scheme such that

$$(\forall S \subseteq T_Q)(\|S\| \leq k \Rightarrow \|\{c \in C | S(c)\}\| > 1)$$

obtained by negation of the definition of Gdim. We answer all queries from a learner using T. After k interactions, the learner knows a set of given answers $S \subseteq T_Q$, and by the choice of T, there exist two different functions in C that satisfy all answers in S.

Now we show the upper bound. Let $\mathrm{Gdim}(C, P) = k$. The case $k = 0$ is easy. If $k = 1$ the theorem follows easily because Lemma 1 guarantees that $\mathrm{LC}(C, P) = 1$. Otherwise, let $\mathcal{V}$ be the version space consisting of functions in C that satisfy all the answers received so far (initially $\mathcal{V} = C$). Now we make the query whose existence is guaranteed by Lemma 1 when $D = \mathcal{V}$ such that no matter what the answer is, at least $\frac{\|\mathcal{V}\|-1}{k}$ functions from $\mathcal{V}$ do not satisfy that answer. A standard calculus shows that the number of such queries needed to reduce the number of surviving candidates to 1 is bounded by $k\lceil \ln \|C\| \rceil$. •

Observe that the algorithm implicit in the previous proof is simpler than its counterpart in [3] because it relies on a more abstract lemma. The key difference is that while the algorithm of [3] needed to make a majority vote strategy the present algorithm does not.

Next we show a necessary and sufficient condition for $\mathrm{Gdim}(C, P)$ being ∞ and a trivial upper bound when the dimension is finite (proof omitted).

Theorem 3. *For any $C \subseteq B_n$ and for any $P = Protocol(Q)$,*

1. *$Gdim(C, P) \neq \infty$ if and only if for all $f, g \in C$ with $f \neq g$, there exists $q \in Q$ such that $P_q^f \cap P_q^g = \emptyset$.*
2. *If $Gdim(C, P) \neq \infty$ and $C \neq \emptyset$ then $Gdim(C, P) \leq \|C\| - 1$.*

4 Abstract Identification Dimension Revisited

We present now how to relate Gdim with the abstract identification dimension (AIdim) [3]. This concept is defined now by weakening the universal quantifier over answering schemes in the definition of Gdim and relaxing it to cover only answering schemes for which the conjunction of all of its answers is satisfiable by some function in B_n.

Formally, given a class $C \subseteq B_n$ and a protocol P on the query set Q, AIdim(C, P) is the minimum integer $d \geq 0$ such that

$$(\forall f \in B_n)\,(\forall T \in \mathcal{T}(P^f))\,(\exists S \subseteq T_Q)\,(\|S\| \leq d \wedge \|\{h \in C \big| S(h)\}\| \leq 1)$$

If no such integer exists then AIdim$(C, P) = \infty$.

In [3], we showed that AIdim is a crucial notion in the sense that it unifies all learning dimensions of example-based query models. However, AIdim cannot replace Gdim as a general notion of learning dimension. There are protocols where AIdim does not characterize learning complexity. For instance, consider the following example.

Example 1. Let us consider P as the protocol of restricted equivalence queries with hypothesis in B_n. For any class $C \subseteq B_n$, it holds AIdim$(C, P) \leq 1$. We note that any answering scheme T in $\mathcal{T}(P^f)$ has, as answer to the query f, the conjunction $(\bigwedge_{f(y)=1} \lambda_y) \wedge (\bigwedge_{f(y)=0} \overline{\lambda}_y)$ that represents a YES answer. Exactly one function satisfies this answer, f itself.

However, it is well known that if C has N functions and $N > 0$, the learning complexity is $N - 1$. In fact, the following answering scheme T shows that Gdim$(C, P) > N - 2$: each query is answered in T negatively (with the clause). Note that each of those answers is unsatisfied by one function from B_n, namely the function being queried. Therefore each of those answers is falsified by at most one function from C which implies that with $N - 2$ answers there will be at least two satisfying functions from C. ○

The next theorem shows how AIdim corresponds with Gdim in conjunctive protocols. We recall that conjunctive protocols are the formalization in our abstract framework of the example-based query models.

Theorem 4. *Let P be a conjunctive protocol and $C \subseteq B_n$. Then*

$$Gdim(C, P) \leq \max(2, AIdim(C, P))$$

Proof. Let T be any answering scheme. If for some function $f \in B_n$ it holds $T \in \mathcal{T}(P^f)$, we simply choose as set $S \subseteq T_Q$ in the definition of Gdim the set S promised by AIdim(C, P). If T cannot be satisfied by any function in B_n then there are two answers that already are not satisfied by any function. This is so because (a) a conjunction cannot be satisfied if and only if it contains two complemented literals and (b) the conjunction of conjunctive answers is still a conjunction. So this proves that Gdim$(C, P) \leq \max(2, \text{AIdim}(C, P))$. •

Observe that it is always the case that $\text{AIdim}(C, P) \leq \text{Gdim}(C, P)$ which is tantamount to say that they are equal if $\text{AIdim}(C, P) \geq 2$. When $\text{AIdim}(C, P) \leq 1$, Gdim and AIdim can be different. Consider the target class of all Boolean functions B_n and the protocol of equivalence queries with counterexamples where the set of hypothesis is also B_n. It is easy to prove that in this case AIdim is 1 and Gdim is 2.

The main difference between AIdim and Gdim relies in the fact that AIdim only considers answering schemes that contain answers that all together are satisfiable by, at least, one function. Theorem 4 shows that for conjunctive protocols we only need to take into account adversary strategies that give answers according to some function and discard all other possibilities because they can be discovered to be cheating with just two answers. This contrasts with the results shown in Example 1 where the learner has to make too many queries (more than a constant) to discover a cheating teacher and therefore we cannot rule out the answering schemes that are not satisfiable.

5 Unspecified Attribute Value Protocols

In this section we present our results for a concrete query set: the Unspecified Attribute Value (UAV) queries from [9,5,6]. Following [9], given a function $f \in B_n$ and a partial assignment $\alpha \in \{0, 1, \star\}^n$, we define $f(\alpha) = 1$ if and only if f is the constant 1 in H_α. Similarly, we define $f(\alpha) = 0$ if and only if f is the constant 0 in H_α. Otherwise, we say that $f(\alpha) =?$ (for unknown).

For a target concept f and a partial assignment α, the UAV membership query α returns YES when $f(\alpha) = 1$, NO if $f(\alpha) = 0$, and ? otherwise. In response to a UAV equivalence query with hypothesis h, the learner either is told that $h \equiv f$ or else is given a counterexample α, along with its classification, for which $f(\alpha) \neq h(\alpha)$. Note that the target function is a ternary function and all three values are distinct. So, for example, if $h(\alpha) = 1$ and $f(\alpha) =?$ then α could serve as a counterexample for h.

Below we formalize these queries in our framework and we show several results using our machinery.

5.1 Unspecified Attribute Value Membership Queries

Let H_α be the hypercube associated to the partial assignment α. The three possible answers to the UAV membership query α are modeled as follows

- YES corresponds to $\bigwedge_{y \in H_\alpha} \lambda_y$,
- NO corresponds to $\bigwedge_{y \in H_\alpha} \overline{\lambda}_y$,
- ? corresponds to $(\bigvee_{y \in H_\alpha} \lambda_y) \wedge (\bigvee_{y \in H_\alpha} \overline{\lambda}_y)$.

In a similar way as we did in the previous section we can get rid of the answering schemes that are not satisfiable. Let $PUAV_\in$ be the protocol for UAV membership queries.

Theorem 5. *For any $C \subseteq B_n$,*

$$Gdim(C, PUAV_{\in}) \leq \max(3, AIdim(C, PUAV_{\in}))$$

Proof. As in the proof of Theorem 4 it is enough to show that any answering scheme T can be discovered to be unsatisfiable with at most 3 answers. Since T must be complete it must contain answers for all UAV queries on complete assignments (that do not contain $\star$s). If any of those answers is the corresponding function for ? then this single answer shows already the unsatisfiability (it will be $\lambda_y \wedge \overline{\lambda}_y$ for some complete assignment y).

Otherwise we have a unique function that satisfies all the answers of the UAV membership queries with complete assignments. Call this function f. Now we proceed in a bottom up manner. We consider the answers to the UAV queries that contain $\star$s both from T and from f and we consider them by levels: first the queries with only one $\star$, then with two, and so on and so forth. We know, by the assumption made on the unsatisfiability of T, that at some point and for some query α the answer from T and the answer from f are different while all the answers to queries inside H_α coincide. Now let us consider some cases:

1. If T answers YES or NO to the query α and f YES or NO or ? (but not the same as T), then two answers suffice: the answer to α and some answer to a complete assignment in H_α.
2. If T answers ? and f answers YES or NO, then three answers suffice: the answer to α and the two answers to $\alpha \cup v \leftarrow 1$ and $\alpha \cup v \leftarrow 0$, for any variable v such that $v(\alpha) = \star$. •

The *extended teaching dimension* [10] (see also [11] and [3]) characterizes the number of queries needed to learn in the standard membership queries learning protocol. We present below the counterpart of the extended teaching dimension for the $PUAV_{\in}$ protocol.

We need some new notation first. For a function $f \in B_n$ and a partial assignment $\alpha \in \{0, 1, \star\}^n$ we say that f is single valued on α if f is constant on H_α. We denote by SV_f the set of all pairs (α, b) such that f is single valued on α and $f(\alpha) = b$. Given $S \subseteq SV_f$ and $g \in B_n$ we define $S(g)$ as

$$((\bigwedge_{y \in H_\alpha \wedge (\alpha,1) \in S} \lambda_y) \wedge (\bigwedge_{z \in H_\beta \wedge (\beta,0) \in S} \overline{\lambda}_z))(g).$$

Let $C \subseteq B_n$. We define the *UAV extended teaching dimension*, uavetdim(C), as the smallest integer $d \geq 0$ such that

$$(\forall f \in B_n)\,(\exists S \subseteq SV_f)\,((\|S\| \leq d) \wedge (\|\{c \in C | S(c)\}\| \leq 1)).$$

Note that this is a straightforward generalization of the extended teaching dimension where complete assignments have been replaced by single valued hypercubes. A similar approach will be taken in 5.3 below.

Theorem 6. *For any $C \subseteq B_n$,*

$$AIdim(C, PUAV_{\in}) \leq uavetdim(C) \leq 2AIdim(C, PUAV_{\in})$$

Proof. First observe that any choice of S in the definition of uavetdim(C) is a valid choice for AIdim($C, PUAV_\in$) which implies directly the first inequality.

To prove the second inequality consider a function $f \in B_n$, an answering scheme T in $PUAV_\in^f$ and $\langle \alpha, ? \rangle \in T$. Let A be the set of target concepts that are not single valued on H_α. Let x and y two assignments that satisfy α and such that $f(x) \neq f(y)$. Clearly, the set of target concepts which agree with function f on x and y is a subset of A. This implies that we can substitute any ? answer by two conjunctive answers (YES or NO) to two UAV queries and the set of surviving functions from C does not grow. So if the set S of answers that shows AIdim($C, PUAV_\in$) $= d$ contains some ? answers, we can replace each of them by two YES and NO answers corresponding to two examples in SV_f, which concludes the proof. •

Note that all this trick has consisted in removing the non conjunctive answers. The following corollary is immediate.

Corollary 1. *For any class $C \subseteq B_n$,*

$$\frac{uavetdim(C)}{2} \leq LC(C, PUAV_\in) \leq (uavetdim(C) + 2)\lceil \ln \|C\| \rceil$$

Our point is that with the abstract dimension uavetdim the proofs of many results are simplified a lot as we show in the next examples.

Example 2. Let P be the protocol of standard membership and equivalence queries with hypothesis in H (see [3]). The *certificate size* or *consistency dimension* [11] [4] of a target class C ($C \subseteq H \subseteq B_n$), denoted by cdim($C, H$), is the smallest integer $d \geq 0$ such that

$$(\forall f \in B_n)(f \notin H \Rightarrow (\exists S \subseteq P_Q^f)(\|S\| \leq d \wedge \{c \in C | S(c)\} = \emptyset)).$$

It is known that cdim(C, H) is a good approximation of LC(C, P).

The CDNF size of a Boolean function is the maximum among their CNF and DNF sizes. We fix the hypothesis class H as the set of functions with CDNF size at most m. Let $C \subseteq H$ be any target class. The next theorem states that cdim(C, H) is related to uavetdim(C).

Theorem 7. *For classes C and H just defined, it holds*

$$uavetdim(C) \leq \max(2m, cdim(C, H))$$

Proof. Let f be any function in B_n. If $f \in H$ we choose as set S in the definition of uavetdim a set of cardinality at most $2m$ whose elements are

$$\{(\alpha, 1) | f = \bigvee t_\alpha\} \cup \{(\beta, 0) | f = \bigwedge c_\beta\}.$$

Here, t_α and c_β are the term and the clause defined in section 2.

If $f \notin H$ we can choose as S the set of literals (examples) promised by the definition of cdim. •

As a consequence of this theorem we have,

Corollary 2. *If C is polynomially query learnable by membership and equivalence queries in the CDNF size, then C is polynomially UAV-MQ query learnable.*

A stronger version of this Corollary is shown in [6], where a time efficient transformation is also proved. ○

Example 3. We consider $C \subseteq B_n$ as the set of functions with CDNF size at most m. In [6] is shown that the target class C is polynomially query learnable in the protocol $PUAV_{\in}$. The proof is based on Corollary 2 and in a result in [11] that shows that C is polynomially query learnable by membership and equivalence queries. We give here an direct proof of this fact using our abstract machinery. First, we introduce some new notation.

Given a partial assignment α and a function $f \in B_n$ we denote by $f_{[\alpha]}$ the projection of $f \in B_n$ with respect to α. On input x, $f_{[\alpha]}(x) = f(x_\alpha)$ where x_α is the assignment in H_α of minimum Hamming distance with respect to x.

Theorem 8. *Let C be the class of functions in B_n with CDNF size at most m, it holds*

$$uavetdim(C) \leq 4m$$

Proof. (sketch) Let f be a function in B_n. If f has CDNF size at most $2m$, we proceed as in the first part of the proof of Theorem 7.

If f has CDNF size greater than $2m$ we use a projection trick. We choose a partial assignment α such that the CDNF size of $f_{[\alpha]}$, denoted by $|f_{[\alpha]}|_{\text{cdnf}}$, is greater than $2m$ and for some variable v both projections $f_{[\alpha\cup v\leftarrow 0]}$ and $f_{[\alpha\cup v\leftarrow 1]}$ have CDNF size bounded by $2m$. Because of $f_{[\alpha]} = (\overline{v} \wedge f_{[\alpha\cup v\leftarrow 0]}) \vee (v \wedge f_{[\alpha\cup v\leftarrow 1]})$, and $f_{[\alpha]} = (\overline{v} \vee f_{[\alpha\cup v\leftarrow 1]}) \wedge (v \vee f_{[\alpha\cup v\leftarrow 0]})$, at least one of the two projections must have CDNF size greater than m. Therefore there exists $b \in \{0,1\}$ such that $|f_{[\alpha\cup v\leftarrow b]}|_{\text{cdnf}} > m$. Let β be the partial assignment $\alpha \cup v \leftarrow b$, let $t_{\gamma_1}, \ldots, t_{\gamma_i}$ be the terms of $t_\beta \wedge f_{[\beta]}$ and let $c_{\delta_1}, \ldots, c_{\delta_j}$ the clauses of $c_\beta \vee f_{[\beta]}$. As $|f_{[\beta]}|_{\text{cdnf}} \leq 2m$ we can assume that $i + j \leq 4m$. Now we choose as set S in the definition of uavetdim the set whose elements are $(\gamma_1, 1), \ldots, (\gamma_i, 1)$ and $(\delta_1, 0), \ldots, (\delta_j, 0)$. These labeled examples reveal the values of f in H_β and rule out all functions in C because of: (1) $f_{[\beta]} \notin C$, (2) The projection $g_{[\beta]}$ of any function g that agrees with f on H_β is $f_{[\beta]}$ and (3) C is projection closed. ○

5.2 Unspecified Attribute Value Equivalence Queries

We can formalize the UAV equivalence queries with hypothesis coming from $H \subseteq B_n$ as the protocol $PUAV_{\equiv}(H)$ whose answers to query $h \in H$ are:

- Positive counterexamples: $\bigwedge_{y\in H_\alpha} \lambda_y$ where α is such that $h(\alpha) \neq 1$.
- Negative counterexamples: $\bigwedge_{y\in H_\alpha} \overline{\lambda_y}$ where α is such that $h(\alpha) \neq 0$.
- ? counterexamples: $(\bigvee_{y\in H_\alpha} \lambda_y) \wedge (\bigvee_{y\in H_\alpha} \overline{\lambda_y})$ where α is such that $h(\alpha) \neq ?$.
- YES answer: $(\bigwedge_{h(y)=1} \lambda_y) \wedge (\bigwedge_{h(z)=0} \overline{\lambda_z})$.

With respect to AIdim this protocol has a different behavior from $PUAV_{\in}$. The example below shows that AIdim is not a proper notion of dimension for $PUAV_{\equiv}(H)$.

Example 4. We consider as target class $C = SING_n$, as hypothesis class $H = B_n$ and we denote by P the protocol $PUAV_{\equiv}(H)$. It is not difficult to see that AIdim$(C,P) = 1$. Each answering scheme T in $\mathcal{T}(P^f)$ has the formula $(\bigwedge_{f(y)=1} \lambda_y) \wedge (\bigwedge_{f(z)=0} \overline{\lambda}_z)$ as answer to the hypothesis f. At most one function in C satisfies this answer, f itself.

However, the following adversary shows that LC(C,P) is $2^n - 1$. Each UAV-EQ query with hypothesis $h \neq 0$ is answered $(x, 0)$ being x a complete assignment such that $h(x) = 1$. If h is the constant 0 the adversary returns $(\star^n, ?)$. Note that each of these answers discards at most one function in $SING_n$. ∘

5.3 UAV Queries and the Learnability of DNF Boolean Formulas

Finally, we study the protocol $PUAV_{\in,\equiv}(H)$ that considers UAV membership and UAV equivalence queries with hypothesis in $H \subseteq B_n$. First, we observe that once again AIdim is a proper notion of dimension for $PUAV_{\in,\equiv}(H)$. As in this protocol we can do UAV membership queries, minor changes on the proof of Theorem 5 also shows

Theorem 9. *Let P be the protocol $PUAV_{\in,\equiv}(H)$. For any $C \subseteq B_n$,*

$$Gdim(C,P) \leq \max(3, AIdim(C,P))$$

The *certificate size* or *consistency dimension* [11] [4], formally defined in Example 2, characterizes the query complexity in the protocol of standard membership and equivalence queries. Theorem 9 is the key that allows us to extend this notion into the protocol $PUAV_{\in,\equiv}(H)$. Similarly as we did in 5.1 introducing the UAV extended teaching dimension, we define the *UAV consistency dimension* for a target class $C \subseteq B_n$ and hypothesis class H, $C \subseteq H \subseteq B_n$, as the smallest integer $d \geq 0$ such that

$$(\forall f \in B_n)(f \notin H \Rightarrow (\exists S \subseteq SV_f)(\|S\| \leq d \wedge \{c \in C \,|\, S(c)\} = \emptyset)).$$

We denote by uavcdim(C,H) this number. Again, this is a direct generalization of the consistency dimension.

Theorem 10. *Let P be the protocol $PUAV_{\in,\equiv}(H)$. For any target class $C \subseteq B_n$ and hypothesis class $H \subseteq B_n$ such that $C \subseteq H$, if uavcdim$(C,H) > 0$ then*

$$AIdim(C,P) \leq uavcdim(C,H) \leq 2AIdim(C,P) + 1$$

Proof. (sketch) We consider the first inequality. Let $f \in B_n$ be any function. If $f \in H$, the only answer of P^f to the equivalence query with hypothesis f discards all functions but at most one in C. Otherwise we choose the set of answers promised by the definition of uavcdim(C, H) to rule out all functions in C.

We prove now the second inequality. Let $f \notin H$ be a Boolean function and let S be the set of answers that shows AIdim$(C, P) = d$. Using the same trick as in the proof of Theorem 6, we can replace each ? answer in S by two answers YES and NO, and in such a way that the set of functions ruled out does not decrease. Finally, if there is still one function c in C such that $S(c)$, we can get rid of c adding to S a labeled example (literal) that shows $f \neq c$. •

The learnability of DNF formulas using membership and equivalence queries is an important open problem. In [9,5] is shown that $PUAV_{\in,\equiv}$ is stronger than the standard protocol for membership and equivalence queries. One may think that replacing the standard protocol by $PUAV_{\in,\equiv}$ some progress could be obtained. Below we show that for DNF the consistency and UAV consistency dimensions are close. So, as the learnability problem is equivalent in both protocols (recall that we are talking about query complexity only), we do not get any essential advantage of using UAV membership queries. We fix C as the class of m-term DNF where $m \geq 4$, and we present a chain of technical lemmas that lead to the proof of that result.

Lemma 2. *Let $\alpha_1, \ldots, \alpha_l$ and $\beta_1, \ldots, \beta_k$ partial assignments such that no function in C can evaluate 1 on $\cup_i H_{\alpha_i}$ and 0 on $\cup_j H_{\beta_j}$. Then, there exists a set S of complete assignments, $S \subseteq \cup_i H_{\alpha_i}$ such that*

$$(\forall \gamma \in \{0, 1, \star\}^n)(\|H_\gamma \cap S\| > \|S\|n/m \Rightarrow H_\gamma \cap (\cup_j H_{\beta_j}) \neq \emptyset)$$

Proof. For the sake of contradiction assume that for all $S \subseteq \cup_i H_{\alpha_i}$ there exists a partial assignment γ such that $\|H_\gamma \cap S\| > \|S\|n/m$ and $H_\gamma \cap (\cup_j H_{\beta_j}) = \emptyset$.

Let $S_1 = \cup_i H_{\alpha_i}$ and let γ_1 be the the partial assignment promised above. Then, the term t_{γ_1} (see definition in Section 2) evaluates 1 in H_{γ_1} and 0 in $\cup_j H_{\beta_j}$. Now, we consider $S_2 = S_1 - (H_{\gamma_1} \cap S_1)$ and we repeat the process. After m iterations we have a m-term DNF $t_{\gamma_1} \vee \ldots \vee t_{\gamma_m}$ that evaluates 1 on $\cup_i H_{\alpha_i}$ and 0 on $\cup_j H_{\beta_j}$. •

Lemma 3. *Let T be a set of complete assignments and let $\beta_1, \ldots, \beta_k$ be partial assignments such that*

$$(\forall \gamma \in \{0, 1, \star\}^n)(\|H_\gamma \cap T\| \geq \|T\|/(m^2 n) \Rightarrow H_\gamma \cap (\cup_j H_{\beta_j}) \neq \emptyset),$$

then there exists a set $S \subseteq T$ of cardinality $\|S\| \leq m^2 n/3$ such that

$$(\forall \gamma \in \{0, 1, \star\}^n)(\|H_\gamma \cap S\| \geq \|S\|/m \Rightarrow H_\gamma \cap (\cup_j H_{\beta_j}) \neq \emptyset).$$

Proof. We choose $S \subseteq T$ of size $\lfloor m^2 n/3 \rfloor$ at random and let p be the probability of the event

$$(\exists \gamma \in \{0, 1, \star\}^n)(\|H_\gamma \cap S\| \geq \|S\|/m \wedge H_\gamma \cap (\cup_j H_{\beta_j}) = \emptyset).$$

By the union bound p is at most $3^n q$, where q is the probability of the event $\|H_\gamma \cap S\| \geq \|S\|/m \wedge H_\gamma \cap (\cup_j H_{\beta_j}) = \emptyset$ for a fixed $\gamma \in \{0,1,\star\}^n$. By hypothesis,

$$H_\gamma \cap (\cup_j H_{\beta_j}) = \emptyset \Rightarrow \|H_\gamma \cap T\| < \|T\|/(m^2 n).$$

The bound $\binom{n}{k} p^k$ for the probability of obtaining at least k heads in n trials of a p biased coin shows that q is at most

$$\binom{\|S\|}{\lceil \|S\|/m \rceil} \left(\frac{1}{m^2 n}\right)^{\lceil \|S\|/m \rceil}.$$

This bound for q shows that $p < 1$. •

Lemma 4. *Given $y \in \{0,1\}^n$ and $\beta \in \{0,1,\star\}^n$ there exists $y^\beta \in H_\beta$ such that:*

$$(\forall \gamma \in \{0,1,\star\}^n)(y \in H_\gamma \wedge H_\gamma \cap H_\beta \neq \emptyset \Rightarrow y^\beta \in H_\gamma).$$

Proof. Consider the translation $\sigma_y : \{0,1\}^n \to \{0,1\}^n$ defined by $\sigma_y(x) = x \oplus y \oplus 1^n$. Note that $\sigma_y \circ \sigma_y$ is the identity function. Let z^β the maximum of the hypercube $\sigma_y(H_\beta)$ and let $y^\beta = \sigma_y(z^\beta)$. Note that y^β belongs to H_β.

Let γ be a partial assignment such that $y \in H_\gamma$ and $H_\gamma \cap H_\beta \neq \emptyset$. As we see below, these assumptions force $y^\beta \in H_\gamma$:

$$y^\beta \in H_\gamma \Leftrightarrow t_\gamma(y^\beta) = 1 \Leftrightarrow t_\gamma \circ \sigma_y(z^\beta) = 1.$$

We note that $t_\gamma \circ \sigma_y(z^\beta) = 1$ must be true because of: (1) $y \in H_\gamma$ implies $t_\gamma \circ \sigma_y$ is a monotone term, (2) z^β is the maximum of the hypercube $\sigma_y(H_\beta)$ and (3) $H_\gamma \cap H_\beta \neq \emptyset$ implies that $t_\gamma \circ \sigma_y$ is not the null function in $\sigma_y(H_\beta)$. •

Theorem 11. *Let C be the class of m-term DNF and let D be the class of s-term DNF where $m > s^2 n^2$ and $s \geq 4$. Let H be any hypothesis class such that $C \subseteq H$. It holds*

$$cdim(D, H) \leq (s^2 n/3) uavcdim(C, H)$$

Proof. (sketch) Let $f \in B_n$ be a Boolean function and let $\{(\alpha_i, 1) | 1 \leq i \leq k\} \cup \{(\beta_j, 0) | 1 \leq j \leq l\}$ be the set of pairs in SV_f promised by the UAV consistency dimension. Thus, no function in C can evaluate 1 on $\cup_i H_{\alpha_i}$ and 0 on $\cup_j H_{\beta_j}$.

Apply Lemma 2 on $\alpha_1, \ldots, \alpha_k$ and $\beta_1, \ldots, \beta_l$, and afterwards, Lemma 3 replacing m by s (note that fraction n/m from Lemma 2 is less than $1/(s^2 n)$). We obtain a set $S \subseteq \cup_i H_{\alpha_i}$ of complete assignments of cardinality bounded by $s^2 n/3$ such that no term can evaluate 1 on a fraction $1/s$ of S and 0 on $\cup_j H_{\beta_j}$. Finally, for each pair $y \in S$ and $\beta_j, 1 \leq j \leq l$, we choose the assignment y^{β_j} promised by Lemma 4. It is easy to see that no function in D can evaluate 1 on S and 0 on $\{y^{\beta_j} | y \in S \wedge 1 \leq j \leq l\}$. •

6 Acknowledgments

The last subsection of the paper strongly benefits from conversations with Vijay Raghavan during his sabbatical in Barcelona.

References

1. Dana Angluin. Queries and concept learning. *Machine Learning*, 2:319–342, 1988.
2. Dana Angluin. Negative results for equivalence queries. *Machine Learning*, 5:121–150, 1990.
3. Jose Luis Balcázar, Jorge Castro, and David Guijarro. A new abstract combinatorial dimension of exact learning via queries. In *Proc. 13th Annu. Conference on Comput. Learning Theory*, pages 248–254. Morgan Kaufmann, San Francisco, 2000. Revised version to appear in *JCSS*.
4. José Luis Balcázar, Jorge Castro, David Guijarro, and Hans Ulrich Simon. The consistency dimension and distribution-dependent learning from queries. In *ALT'99*, volume 1720, pages 77–92. LNAI. Springer, 1999. Revised version to appear in *TCS*.
5. Andreas Birkendorf, Norbert Klasner, Christian Kuhlmann, and Hans Ulrich Simon. Structural results about exact learning with unspecified attribute values. *J. of Comput. Syst. Sci.*, 60(2):258–277, 2000. Special Issue for COLT '98.
6. Nader H. Bshouty and David K. Wilson. On learning in the presence of unspecified attribute values. In *Proc. 12th Annu. Conf. on Comput. Learning Theory*, pages 81–87. ACM Press, New York, NY, 1999.
7. Ricard Gavaldà. On the power of equivalence queries. In *Computational Learning Theory: Eurocolt '93*, pages 193–203. Oxford University Press, 1994.
8. Sally Goldman and Michael Kearns. On the complexity of teaching. *Journal of Computer and System Sciences*, 50:20–31, 1995.
9. Sally A. Goldman, Stephen S. Kwek, and Stephen D. Scott. Learning from examples with unspecified attribute values. In *Proc. 10th Annu. Conf. on Comput. Learning Theory*, pages 231–242. ACM Press, New York, NY, 1997.
10. Tibor Hegedüs. Generalized teaching dimension and the query complexity of learning. In *8th Annu. Conf. on Comput. Learning Theory*, pages 108–117, New York, 1995. ACM Press.
11. Lisa Hellerstein, Krishnan Pillaipakkamnatt, Vijay Raghavan, and Dawn Wilkins. How many queries are needed to learn? *Journal of the ACM*, 43(5):840–862, 1996.
12. Norbert Klasner and Hans Ulrich Simon. General lower bounds on the query complexity within the exact learning model. *Discrete Applied Mathematics*, 107:61–81, 2000.

Data-Dependent Margin-Based Generalization Bounds for Classification*

Balázs Kégl[1], Tamás Linder[2], and Gábor Lugosi[3]

[1] Department of Computer Science and Operations Research
University of Montreal,
CP 6128 succ. Centre-Ville,
Montréal, Canada H3C 3J7
kegl@iro.umontreal.ca

[2] Department of Mathematics and Statistics,
Queen's University,
Kingston, Ontario, Canada K7L 3N6
linder@mast.queensu.ca

[3] Department of Economics,
Pompeu Fabra University,
Ramon Trias Fargas 25-27,
08005 Barcelona, Spain
lugosi@upf.es

Abstract. We derive new margin-based inequalities for the probability of error of classifiers. The main feature of these bounds is that they can be calculated using the training data and therefore may be effectively used for model selection purposes. In particular, the bounds involve quantities such as the empirical fat-shattering dimension and covering number measured on the training data, as opposed to their worst-case counterparts traditionally used in such analyses, and appear to be sharper and more general than recent results involving empirical complexity measures. In addition, we also develop an alternative data-based bound for the generalization error of classes of convex combinations of classifiers involving an empirical complexity measure that is more easily computable than the empirical covering number or fat-shattering dimension. We also show an example of efficient computation of the new bounds.

1 Introduction

Suppose the feature space $\mathcal{X}$ is a measurable set and the observation X and its label Y form a pair (X, Y) of random variables taking values in $\mathcal{X} \times \{0, 1\}$. Let $\mathcal{F}$ be a class of real measurable functions on $\mathcal{X}$. For $f \in \mathcal{F}$, let $L(f)$ denote the probability of error of the prediction rule obtained by thresholding $f(X)$ at $1/2$, that is,

$$L(f) = \mathbf{P}\big(\operatorname{sgn}(f(X) - 1/2) \neq Y\big)$$

* This research was supported in part by the Natural Sciences and Engineering Research Council (NSERC) of Canada and DGI grant BMF2000-0807.

D. Helmbold and B. Williamson (Eds.): COLT/EuroCOLT 2001, LNAI 2111, pp. 368–384, 2001.

where

$$\operatorname{sgn}(t) = \begin{cases} 1 & \text{if } t \geq 0 \\ 0 & \text{if } t < 0. \end{cases}$$

The margin of f on $(x, y) \in \mathcal{X} \times \{0, 1\}$ is defined by

$$\operatorname{margin}(f(x), y) = \begin{cases} f(x) - 1/2 & \text{if } y = 1 \\ 1/2 - f(x) & \text{if } y = 0. \end{cases}$$

Let the data $D_n = ((X_1, Y_1), \ldots, (X_n, Y_n))$ consist of independent and identically distributed (i.i.d.) copies of (X, Y). For $f \in \mathcal{F}$ and $\gamma > 0$, define the sample error of f on D_n with respect to γ as

$$\widehat{L}_n^\gamma(f) = \frac{1}{n} \sum_{i=1}^{n} I_{\{\operatorname{margin}(f(X_i), Y_i) < \gamma\}}$$

where I_A denotes the indicator of an event A.

It is well known that in many cases $L(f)$ may be upper bounded by the margin error $\widehat{L}_n^\gamma(f)$ plus a quantity that typically decreases with increasing γ, see, e.g., Bartlett [6], Anthony and Bartlett [2], Shawe-Taylor *et al.* [15]. In particular, covering numbers and fat-shattering dimensions of $\mathcal{F}$ at scale γ have been used to obtain useful bounds on the probability of error of classifiers. In this paper we develop improved, data-dependent bounds. We show that the empirical versions of the fat-shattering dimensions and covering numbers may also be used to bound the probability of error. Our bounds are closely related to results of Shawe-Taylor and Williamson [16] who obtained generalization bounds in terms of the margin error $\widehat{L}_n^\gamma(f)$ and empirical covering numbers, but the new bounds are sharper and more general. The improvement was made possible by some recent concentration inequalities for combinatorial entropies [7].

The rest of the paper is organized as follows: In Sections 2 and 3 we present the main data-dependent upper bounds for the probability of misclassification. In Section 4 we also develop an alternative data-based bound which provides a more easily computable data-dependent bound on the generalization error of classes of convex combinations of classifiers. In section 5 we provide a nontrivial example of a function class for which the data-dependent quantities appearing in the main inequalities of Section 2 may be computed efficiently. Section 6 contains proofs of selected theorems.

2 Bounding by the Random Fat-Shattering Dimension

For $\gamma > 0$, a sequence $x_1^n = (x_1, \ldots, x_n) \in \mathcal{X}^n$ is said to be γ-shattered by $\mathcal{F}$ if there is an $(r_1, \ldots, r_n) \in \mathbb{R}^n$ such that for each $(b_1, \ldots, b_n) \in \{0, 1\}^n$ there is an $f \in \mathcal{F}$ satisfying for all $i = 1, \ldots, n$,

$$f(x_i) \geq r_i + \gamma \text{ if } b_i = 1, \text{ and } f(x_i) \leq r_i - \gamma \text{ if } b_i = 0$$

or, equivalently,

$$(2b_i - 1)(f(x_i) - r_i) \geq \gamma. \quad (1)$$

The (empirical) fat-shattering dimension (γ-dimension) of $\mathcal{F}$ in a sequence $x_1^n = (x_1, \ldots, x_n) \in \mathcal{X}^n$ is defined for any $\gamma > 0$ by

$$\mathrm{fat}_{\mathcal{F},x_1^n}(\gamma) = \max\{m : \mathcal{F}\ \gamma\text{-shatters a subsequence of length } m \text{ of } x_1^n\}.$$

Note that for $X_1^n = (X_1, \ldots, X_n)$, $\mathrm{fat}_{\mathcal{F},X_1^n}(\gamma)$ is a random quantity whose value depends on the data. The (worst-case) fat-shattering dimension

$$\overline{\mathrm{fat}}_{\mathcal{F},n}(\gamma) = \sup_{x_1^n \in \mathcal{X}^n} \mathrm{fat}_{\mathcal{F},x_1^n}(\gamma)$$

was used by Kearns and Schapire [11], Alon *et al.* [1], Shawe-Taylor *et al.* [15], and Bartlett [6] to derive useful bounds. In particular, Anthony and Bartlett [2] show that if $d = \overline{\mathrm{fat}}_{\mathcal{F},n}(\gamma/8)$, then for any $0 < \delta < 1/2$, with probability at least $1 - \delta$, all $f \in \mathcal{F}$ satisfies

$$L(f) < \widehat{L}_n^\gamma(f) + 2.829\sqrt{\frac{1}{n}\left(d\log_2\left(\frac{32en}{d}\right)\ln(128n)\right)} + 2.829\sqrt{\frac{\ln(4/\delta)}{n}}. \quad (2)$$

(Throughout this paper $\log_b$ denotes the logarithm to the base b and ln denotes the natural logarithm.)

Before stating the first two main theorems, we need to introduce the notion of covering and packing numbers. Let (S, ρ) be a metric space. For $\epsilon > 0$, the ϵ-covering number $N_\rho(\epsilon, S)$ of S is defined as the minimum number of open balls of radius ϵ in S whose union covers S. (If no such finite cover exists, we formally define $N_\rho(\epsilon, S) = \infty$.)

A set $W \subset S$ is said to be ϵ-separated if $\rho(x, y) \geq \epsilon$ for all distinct $x, y \in W$. The ϵ-packing number $M_\rho(\epsilon, S)$ is defined as the maximum cardinality of an ϵ separated subset of S.

For $x_1^n = (x_1, \ldots, x_n) \in \mathcal{X}^n$ and a family $\mathcal{G}$ of functions mapping $\mathcal{X}$ into $\mathbb{R}$, let $\mathcal{G}_{x_1^n}$ denote the subset of $\mathbb{R}^n$ given by

$$\mathcal{G}_{x_1^n} = \{(g(x_1), \ldots, g(x_n)) : g \in \mathcal{G}\}.$$

Let ρ_∞ denote the l_∞ metric on $\mathbb{R}^n$, given for any $u_1^n, v_1^n \in \mathbb{R}^n$ by $\rho_\infty(u_1^n, v_1^n) = \max_{1\leq i\leq n} |u_i - v_i|$ and, for $\epsilon > 0$ and $x_1^n \in \mathcal{X}^n$, define $\mathcal{N}_\infty(\epsilon, \mathcal{G}, x_1^n) = N_{\rho_\infty}(\epsilon, \mathcal{G}_{x_1^n})$ and $\mathcal{M}_\infty(\epsilon, \mathcal{G}, x_1^n) = M_{\rho_\infty}(\epsilon, \mathcal{G}_{x_1^n})$. For $\gamma > 0$, let $\pi_\gamma : \mathbb{R} \to [1/2 - \gamma, 1/2 + \gamma]$ be the "hard-limiter" function

$$\pi_\gamma(t) = \begin{cases} 1/2 - \gamma & \text{if } t \leq 1/2 - \gamma \\ t & \text{if } 1/2 - \gamma < t < 1/2 + \gamma \\ 1/2 + \gamma & \text{if } t \geq 1/2 + \gamma \end{cases}$$

and set $\pi_\gamma(\mathcal{F}) = \{\pi_\gamma \circ f : f \in \mathcal{F}\}$.

The next result improves (2) in various ways. The most important improvement is that we are able to replace the worst-case fat-shattering dimension $\overline{\mathrm{fat}}_{\mathcal{F},n}(\gamma/8)$ by its empirical counterpart $\mathrm{fat}_{\mathcal{F},X_1^n}(\gamma/8)$. Since for certain "lucky" distributions of the data the improvement is significant, such an empirical bound can play a crucial role in model selection.

Theorem 1. *Let $\mathcal{F}$ be a class of real measurable functions on $\mathcal{X}$, let $\gamma > 0$, and set $d(X_1^n) = \mathrm{fat}_{\mathcal{F},X_1^n}(\gamma/8)$. Then for any $0 < \delta < 1/2$, the probability that all $f \in \mathcal{F}$ satisfies*

$$L(f) < \widehat{L}_n^\gamma(f) + 2.355\sqrt{\tfrac{1}{n}\left(1 + d(X_1^n)\log_2\left(\tfrac{16en}{d(X_1^n)}\right)\log_2(64n)\right)} + 6.364\sqrt{\tfrac{\ln(2/\delta)}{n}}$$

is greater than $1-\delta$. Also, the probability that all $f \in \mathcal{F}$ satisfies

$$L(f) < \widehat{L}_n^\gamma(f) + 2.829\sqrt{\frac{\ln \mathcal{N}_\infty(\gamma/8, \mathcal{F}, X_1^n)}{n}} + 6.364\sqrt{\frac{\ln(2/\delta)}{n}}$$

is greater than $1-\delta$.

The following result, improves Theorem 1 if $\widehat{L}_n^\gamma(f)$ is very small.

Theorem 2. *Consider the notation of Theorem 1. Then for any $0 < \delta < 1/2$ and $\alpha > 0$, the probability that all $f \in \mathcal{F}$ satisfies*

$$L(f) < (1+\alpha)\,\widehat{L}_n^\gamma(f) + \tfrac{28}{n}\cdot\tfrac{1+\alpha}{\alpha}\left(1 + d(X_1^n)\log_2\left(\tfrac{16en}{d(X_1^n)}\right)\log_2(64n) + 4.1\ln\tfrac{8}{\delta}\right)$$

is greater than $1-\delta$. Also, with probability greater than $1-\delta$, for all $f \in \mathcal{F}$,

$$L(f) \le (1+\alpha)\,\widehat{L}_n^\gamma(f) + \frac{40}{n}\cdot\frac{1+\alpha}{\alpha}\left(\ln \mathcal{N}_\infty(\gamma/8, \mathcal{F}, X_1^n) + 4.1\ln\frac{8}{\delta}\right).$$

The proofs of Theorems 1 and 2 are found in Section 6.

The result of Shawe-Taylor and Williamson [16] assumes $\widehat{L}_n^\gamma(f) = 0$ and in that case states an inequality similar to the second inequality of Theorem 2, though we were able to get rid of some extra logarithmic factors present in the main result of [16].

3 An Alternative Data-Based Bound

In this section we propose another new data-dependent upper bound for the probability of error. The estimate is close, in spirit, to the recently introduced estimates of Koltchinskii and Panchenko [12] based on Rademacher complexities, and the maximum discrepancy estimate of Bartlett, Boucheron, and Lugosi [4].

Assume that n is even, and, for each $f \in \mathcal{F}$, consider the empirical error

$$\widehat{L}_{n/2}^{(2)}(f) = \frac{2}{n}\sum_{i=n/2+1}^{n} I_{\{\mathrm{sgn}(f(X_i)-1/2)\neq Y_i\}}$$

measured on the second half of the data. This may be compared with the sample error of f, with respect to margin γ, measured on the first half of the data

$$\widehat{L}^{\gamma}_{n/2}(f) = \frac{2}{n}\sum_{i=1}^{n/2} I_{\{\mathrm{margin}(f(X_i),Y_i)<\gamma\}} \,.$$

We have the following data-based estimate for the probability of error of any classifier in $\mathcal{F}$:

Theorem 3. *Let $\mathcal{F}$ be a class of real measurable functions on $\mathcal{X}$, let $\gamma > 0$. Then for any $0 < \delta < 1/2$, the probability that all $f \in \mathcal{F}$ satisfies*

$$L(f) < \widehat{L}^{\gamma}_n(f) + \sup_{f'\in\mathcal{F}}\left(\widehat{L}^{(2)}_{n/2}(f') - \widehat{L}^{\gamma}_{n/2}(f')\right) + 3\sqrt{\frac{\ln(2/\delta)}{2n}}$$

is at least $1-\delta$.

The proof uses ideas similar to Theorem 6 of [4].

Remark 1. Theorem 3 is, modulo a small constant factor, always at least as good as Theorem 1. This may be seen by observing that by concentration of $\sup_{f\in\mathcal{F}}\left(\widehat{L}^{(2)}_{n/2}(f) - \widehat{L}^{\gamma}_{n/2}(f)\right)$ (which can be easily quantified using the bounded difference inequality [14]),

$$\sup_{f\in\mathcal{F}}\left(\widehat{L}^{(2)}_{n/2}(f) - \widehat{L}^{\gamma}_{n/2}(f)\right) \approx \mathbf{E}\sup_{f\in\mathcal{F}}\left(\widehat{L}^{(2)}_{n/2}(f) - \widehat{L}^{\gamma}_{n/2}(f)\right)$$

with very large probability. This is essentially the same quantity as $\mathbf{E}\sup_{f\in\mathcal{F}}\left(L'_n(f) - \widehat{L}^{\gamma}_n(f)\right)$ appearing in the proof of Theorem 2; only the sample size n has now been replaced by $n/2$.

4 Convex Hulls

In this section we consider an important class of special cases. Let $\mathcal{H}$ be a class of "base" classifiers, that is, a class of functions $h : \mathcal{H} \to \{0,1\}$. Then we may define the class $\mathcal{F}$ of all (finite) convex combinations of elements of $\mathcal{H}$ by

$$\mathcal{F} = \left\{ f(x) = \sum_{i=1}^{N} w_i h_i(x) : N \geq 1, w_1, \ldots, w_N \geq 0, \sum_{i=1}^{N} w_i = 1, h_1, \ldots, h_N \in \mathcal{H} \right\}. \tag{3}$$

Voting methods such as bagging and boosting choose a classifier from a class of classifiers of the above form. A practical disadvantage of the upper bounds appearing in Theorems 1, 2, and 3 is that their computation may be prohibitively complex. For example, the bound of Theorem 3 involves optimization over the whole class $\mathcal{F}$. In the argument below we show, using ideas of Koltchinskii and

Panchenko [12], that at the price of weakening the bound of Theorem 3 we may obtain a data-dependent bound whose computation is significantly less complex than that of the bound of Theorem 3. Observe that to calculate the upper bound of the theorem below, it suffices to optimize over the "small" class of base classifiers $\mathcal{H}$.

Theorem 4. *Let $\mathcal{F}$ be a class of the form (3). Then for any $0 < \delta < 1/2$ and $\gamma > 0$, the probability that all $f \in \mathcal{F}$ satisfy*

$$L(f) < \widehat{L}_n^{\gamma}(f) + \frac{1}{\gamma} \sup_{h \in \mathcal{H}} \left(\widehat{L}_{n/2}^{(2)}(h) - \widehat{L}_{n/2}^{(1)}(h) \right) + \left(3 + \sqrt{2} + \frac{\sqrt{2}}{\gamma} \right) \sqrt{\frac{\ln(4/\delta)}{2n}}$$

is at least $1 - \delta$, where $\widehat{L}_{n/2}^{(1)}(h) = \frac{2}{n} \sum_{i=1}^{n/2} I_{\{\mathrm{sgn}(h(X_i)-1/2) \neq Y_i\}}$.

The proof is based on arguments of [12] and concentration inequalities.

Remark 2. To interpret this new bound note that, for all $\delta > 0$, by the bounded difference inequality [14], with probability at least $1 - \delta$,

$$\sup_{h \in \mathcal{H}} \left(\widehat{L}_{n/2}^{(2)}(h) - \widehat{L}_{n/2}^{(1)}(h) \right) \leq \mathbf{E} \sup_{h \in \mathcal{H}} \left(\widehat{L}_{n/2}^{(2)}(h) - \widehat{L}_{n/2}^{(1)}(h) \right) + \sqrt{\frac{2 \log(1/\delta)}{n}}.$$

The expectation on the right-hand side may be further bounded by the Vapnik-Chervonenkis inequality (see [9] for this version):

$$\mathbf{E} \sup_{h \in \mathcal{H}} \left(\widehat{L}_{n/2}^{(2)}(h) - \widehat{L}_{n/2}^{(1)}(h) \right) \leq \sqrt{\frac{8 \mathbf{E} \log S_{\mathcal{H}}(X_1^n)}{n}}$$

where $S_{\mathcal{H}}(X_1^n)$ is the random shatter coefficient, that is, the number of different ways the data points $X_1, \ldots, X_n$ can be classified by elements of the base class $\mathcal{H}$. We may convert this bound into another data-dependent bound by recalling that, by [7, Theorem 4.2], $\log S_{\mathcal{H}}(X_1^n)$ is strongly concentrated around its mean. Putting the pieces together, we obtain that, with probability at least $1 - \delta$, all $f \in \mathcal{F}$ satisfy

$$L(f) < \widehat{L}_n^{\gamma}(f) + \frac{4}{\gamma} \sqrt{\frac{\log S_{\mathcal{H}}(X_1^n)}{n}} + \left(3 + \sqrt{2} + \frac{5\sqrt{2} + 2}{\gamma} \right) \sqrt{\frac{\ln(8/\delta)}{2n}} .$$

Remark 3. The bound of Theorem 4 may be significantly weaker than that of Theorem 3. As an example, consider the case when $\mathcal{X} = [0, 1]$, and let $\mathcal{H}$ be the class of all indicator functions of intervals in $\mathbb{R}$. In this case, [2, Theorem 12.11] shows that $\overline{\mathrm{fat}}_{\mathcal{F},n}(\gamma) \leq 2/\gamma + 1$, and therefore Theorem 1 (and even (2)) yields a bound of the order $O\left(\sqrt{\log^2 n / (\gamma n)} \right)$. Thus, the dependence of the bound of Theorem 4 on γ is significantly worse than those of Theorems 1 and 3. This is the price we pay for computational feasibility.

5 Measuring Empirical Fat-Shattering Dimension: An Example

As noted in the previous section, the empirical fat-shattering dimension and the alternative bound of Theorem 3 may be difficult to compute in general. However, in certain special cases, the computation is practically feasible. In this section we offer a simple example of a class $\mathcal{F}$ for which the empirical fat-shattering dimension may be calculated efficiently in polynomial time. While we realize that the practical importance of this example is limited, our purpose is to point out that the bounds of Theorems 1 and 3 may be important tools in practice and may give significant improvements over their non-data-dependent counterparts.

Consider the problem of measuring the empirical fat-shattering dimension of a simple function class, the class of convex combinations of one-dimensional "piecewise-linear sigmoids" with bounded slope. Our results here show that, at least in one-dimension, it is possible to measure the empirical fat-shattering dimension in polynomial time, and that the empirical fat-shattering dimension measured on a given data set can be considerably lower than the worst-case fat-shattering dimension.

Consider the family $\mathcal{G}_\alpha$ of one-dimensional piecewise-linear sigmoids with bounded slope. Formally, for $x_a, x_b, y_a, y_b \in \mathbb{R}$ such that $x_a < x_b$, let

$$g^{(x_a,x_b,y_a,y_b)}(x) = \begin{cases} y_a & \text{if } x \le x_a \\ y_b & \text{if } x \ge x_b \\ y_a + \frac{y_b - y_a}{x_b - x_a}(x - x_a) & \text{otherwise} \end{cases}$$

and let $\mathcal{G}_\alpha = \{g^{(x_a,x_b,y_a,y_b)} : \left|\frac{y_b-y_a}{x_b-x_a}\right| \le 2\alpha\}$. Let $\mathcal{F}_\alpha$ be the set of functions constructed by (3) using $\mathcal{G}_\alpha$ as the set of base classifiers. The next lemma will serve as a basis for a constructive algorithm that can measure $\text{fat}_{\mathcal{F}_\alpha, x_1^n}(\gamma)$ on any data set $x_1^n = \{x_1, \ldots, x_n\} \subset \mathbb{R}$.

Lemma 1. *An ordered set $x_1^n = \{x_1, \ldots, x_n\} \subset \mathbb{R}, x_i < x_{i+1}, i = 1, \ldots, n-1$, is γ-shattered by $\mathcal{F}_\alpha$ if and only if*

$$\sum_{i=2}^{n} \frac{1}{d_i} \le \frac{\alpha}{\gamma} \tag{4}$$

where $d_i = x_i - x_{i-1}$.

The proof of Lemma 1 is found in Section 6.

Lemma 1 shows that to find the empirical fat-shattering dimension of a data set x_1^n, we have to find the largest subset of x_1^n for which (4) holds. Suppose that the points of x_1^n are indexed in increasing order, and let $d_{ij} = x_i - x_j$. First consider the problem of finding a subsequence of x_1^n of length k that minimizes the cost $\sum_{i=1}^{k-1} \frac{1}{d_{j_{i+1}, j_i}}$ over all subsequences of length k. Let $S(k; p, r) = (x_p = x_{j_1}, \ldots, x_{j_{k+1}} = x_r)$ denote the optimal subsequence of length $k+1$ between

x_p and x_r, and let $C(k;p,r) = \sum_{i=1}^{k} \frac{1}{d_{j_i,j_{i+1}}}$ be the cost of $S(k;p,r)$. Observe that any subsequence $(x_{j_i}, \ldots, x_{j_{i+\ell-1}})$ of $S(k;p,r)$ of length ℓ is optimal over all subsequences of length ℓ between x_{j_i} and $x_{j_{i+\ell-1}}$, so $C(k;p,r)$ can be defined recursively as

$$C(k;p,r) = \begin{cases} \frac{1}{d_{p,r}} & \text{if } k = 1 \\ \min\limits_{q:p+k-1 \le q \le r-1} \left(C(k-1;p,q) + C(1;q,r)\right) & \text{if } k > 1. \end{cases}$$

Observe also that if $C(k-1;1,r)$ is known for all the $O(n)$ different indices r, then $C(k;1,r)$ can be calculated in $O(n^2)$ time for all r. Thus, by using a dynamic programming approach, we can find the sequence $C(1;1,n), C(2;1,n), \ldots, C(k;1,n)$ in $O(n^2 k)$ time. To compute $\mathrm{fat}_{\mathcal{F}_\alpha, x_1^n}(\gamma)$, notice that $\mathrm{fat}_{\mathcal{F}_\alpha, x_1^n}(\gamma) = k$ if and only if $C(k-1;1,n) \le \frac{\alpha}{\gamma}$ and either $C(k;1,n) > \frac{\alpha}{\gamma}$ or $k = n$. The algorithm is given formally in Figure 1.

```
FatLinearSigmoid(X, α, γ)

n ← X.length
for p ← 1 to n − 1 do
    for r ← p + 1 to n do
        C[1, p, r] ← 1/(X[r] − X[p])
k ← 1
while C[k, 1, n] ≤ α/γ do
    k ← k + 1
    if k = n then
        return k
     for r ← k + 1 to n do
        C[k, 1, r] ← ∞
        for q ← k to r − 1 do
            c ← C[k − 1, 1, q] + C[1, q, r]
            if c < C[k, 1, r] then
                C[k, 1, r] ← c
 return k
```

Fig. 1. FatLinearSigmoid(X, α, γ) computes $\mathrm{fat}_{\mathcal{F}_\alpha, x_1^n}(\gamma)$ in $O(n^2 \,\mathrm{fat}_{\mathcal{F}_\alpha, x_1^n})$ time. The input array X contains the data points in increasing order.

It is clear from Lemma 1 that the worst-case fat-shattering dimension $\overline{\mathrm{fat}}_{\mathcal{F}_\alpha, n}(\gamma) = \infty$ for all $\gamma > 0$ if the data points may take any value in $\mathbb{R}$. Thus, the data-dependent dimension $\mathrm{fat}_{\mathcal{F}_\alpha, x_1^n}(\gamma)$ presents a qualitative improvement. If the data points $x_1, \ldots, x_n$ are restricted to fall in the an interval of length A then it follows from Lemma 1 and the inequality between arithmetic and harmonic means that $\overline{\mathrm{fat}}_{\mathcal{F}_\alpha, n}(\gamma) = \left\lfloor \sqrt{A\alpha/\gamma} \right\rfloor + 1$. This upper bound is achieved by equispaced data points. Even in this case, the empirical fat-shattering dimension may be significantly smaller than its worst-case upper bound, and the difference is larger if the data points are very unevenly distributed. To experimentally quantify this intuition, we compared the fat-shattering dimension of data sets drawn from different distributions over $[0, 1]$. Figure 2(a) shows that even in the case of uniform distribution, for high α/γ ratio we gain approximately 20% over the data-independent fat-shattering dimension. As the points become more and more unevenly distributed (Gaussian distributions with decreasing standard deviations), the difference between the data-independent and data-dependent fat-shattering dimensions increases.

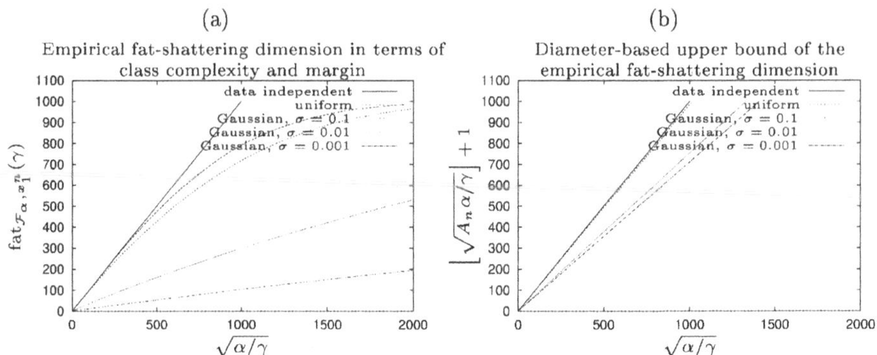

Fig. 2. The first figure shows the empirical fat-shattering dimensions of different data sets as a function of the class complexity α and the margin γ. The second figure indicates the upper bound (5) based on the empirical diameter A_n of the data. The solid lines in both figures show the data-independent fat-shattering dimension $\overline{\text{fat}}_{\mathcal{F}_\alpha,n}(\gamma) = \left\lfloor\sqrt{A\alpha/\gamma}\right\rfloor + 1$ achieved by equispaced data points. We generated data sets of 1000 points drawn from the uniform distribution in $[0, 1]$, and from the mixture of two identical Gaussians with means $1/4$ and $3/4$, and standard deviations indicated by the figure. The Gaussian mixtures were truncated to $[0, 1]$ to keep their data-independent fat-shattering dimension finite.

The empirical diameter $A_n = \max_i x_i - \min_i x_i$ can also be used to bound the data-dependent fat-shattering dimension from above since

$$\text{fat}_{\mathcal{F}_\alpha,x_1^n}(\gamma) \le \left\lfloor\sqrt{A_n\alpha/\gamma}\right\rfloor + 1. \tag{5}$$

The computation of (5) is, of course, trivial. Figure 2(b) shows that if the empirical diameter A_n is significantly smaller then the a-priori diameter A, the bound (5) can provide an improvement over the data-independent fat-shattering dimension. Such simple upper bounds for the empirical fat-shattering dimension may be useful in practice and may be easy to obtain in more general situations as well. However, if the data is unevenly distributed in the empirical support $[\min_i x_i, \max_i x_i]$, $\text{fat}_{\mathcal{F}_\alpha,x_1^n}(\gamma)$ can be much smaller than the empirical diameter-based bound (5).

6 Selected Proofs

Proof of Theorem 1

The following result from [2] is instrumental in proving Theorem 1. The version given here improves on the constants of the inequality given in [2].

Theorem 5. *Suppose $\mathcal{F}$ is a set of real-valued functions defined on $\mathcal{X}$. Then for any positive integer n and $\gamma > 0$,*

$$\mathbf{E} \sup_{f \in \mathcal{F}} \left(L(f) - \widehat{L}_n^\gamma(f) \right) \leq \mathbf{E} \sqrt{\frac{2 \ln \mathcal{N}_\infty(\gamma/2, \pi_\gamma(\mathcal{F}), X_1^{2n})}{n}} .$$

The following well-known lemma is used in the proof (see, e.g., [9]):

Lemma 2. *Let $\sigma > 0$, $N \geq 2$, and let $Z_1, \ldots, Z_N$ be real-valued random variables such that for all $s > 0$ and $1 \leq i \leq N$, $\mathbf{E}\left[e^{sZ_i}\right] \leq e^{s^2\sigma^2/2}$. Then*

$$\mathbf{E}\left[\max_{i \leq N} Z_i\right] \leq \sigma\sqrt{2 \ln N} .$$

Proof of Theorem 5. Let (X_i, Y_i), $i = n+1, \ldots, 2n$, be i.i.d. copies of (X, Y), independent of D_n, and define, for each $f \in \mathcal{F}$,

$$L_n'(f) = \frac{1}{n} \sum_{i=n+1}^{2n} I_{\{\mathrm{sgn}(f(X_i)-1/2) \neq Y_i\}} .$$

Then

$$\begin{aligned}
\mathbf{E} \sup_{f \in \mathcal{F}} \left(L(f) - \widehat{L}_n^\gamma(f) \right) &= \mathbf{E} \sup_{f \in \mathcal{F}} \mathbf{E}\left[L_n'(f) - \widehat{L}_n^\gamma(f) \middle| D_n \right] \\
&\leq \mathbf{E}\left[\mathbf{E}\left[\sup_{f \in \mathcal{F}} \left(L_n'(f) - \widehat{L}_n^\gamma(f) \right) \middle| D_n \right]\right] \\
&= \mathbf{E} \sup_{f \in \mathcal{F}} \left(L_n'(f) - \widehat{L}_n^\gamma(f) \right) .
\end{aligned}$$

To bound this quantity, consider a minimal $\gamma/2$-cover $\mathcal{G}$ of $\pi_\gamma(\mathcal{F})$. Thus, $\mathcal{G}$ is a set of functions with $|\mathcal{G}| = \mathcal{N}_\infty(\gamma/2, \pi_\gamma(\mathcal{F}), X_1^{2n})$ elements such that for any $f \in \mathcal{F}$ there exists a $g \in \mathcal{G}$ such that $\max_{i \leq 2n} |\pi_\gamma(f(X_i)) - g(X_i)| < \gamma/2$. Observe that if f and g are such that $\max_{i \leq 2n} |\pi_\gamma(f(X_i)) - g(X_i)| < \gamma/2$, then

$$I_{\{\mathrm{sgn}(f(X_i)-1/2) \neq Y_i\}} \leq I_{\{\mathrm{margin}(g(X_i), Y_i) < \gamma/2\}} , \quad i = 1, \ldots, 2n$$

and

$$I_{\{\mathrm{margin}(f(X_i), Y_i) < \gamma\}} \geq I_{\{\mathrm{margin}(g(X_i), Y_i) < \gamma/2\}} , \quad i = 1, \ldots, 2n .$$

Thus, we see that

$$\begin{aligned}
&\mathbf{E}\sup_{f\in\mathcal{F}}\left(L'_n(f)-\widehat{L}^\gamma_n(f)\right)\\
&=\mathbf{E}\sup_{f\in\mathcal{F}}\frac{1}{n}\left(\sum_{i=n+1}^{2n} I_{\{\mathrm{sgn}(f(X_i)-1/2)\neq Y_i\}}-\sum_{i=1}^{n} I_{\{\mathrm{margin}(f(X_i),Y_i)<\gamma\}}\right)\\
&\le\mathbf{E}\max_{g\in\mathcal{G}}\frac{1}{n}\left(\sum_{i=n+1}^{2n} I_{\{\mathrm{margin}(g(X_i),Y_i)<\gamma/2\}}-\sum_{i=1}^{n} I_{\{\mathrm{margin}(g(X_i),Y_i)<\gamma/2\}}\right).
\end{aligned}$$

The proof is finished by applying Lemma 2 if we observe that, by Hoeffding's inequality (Hoeffding [10]), for each $g\in\mathcal{G}$, the zero-mean random variable

$$Z(g)=\sum_{i=1}^{n}\left(I_{\{\mathrm{margin}(g(X_{n+i}),Y_{n+i})<\gamma/2\}}-I_{\{\mathrm{margin}(g(X_i),Y_i)<\gamma/2\}}\right)$$

satisfies $\mathbf{E}\left[e^{sZ(g)}\right]\le e^{ns^2/2}$. □

Proof of Theorem 1 The quantized version of a real number u, with step-size $\alpha>0$ is

$$Q_\alpha(u)=\alpha\left\lfloor\frac{u-1/2}{\alpha}\right\rfloor+1/2$$

where $\lfloor t\rfloor$ denotes the greatest integer less than or equal to t. (Similarly, $\lceil t\rceil$ denotes the least integer greater than or equal to t.) Let $\mathcal{H}=\pi_\gamma(\mathcal{F})$ and define

$$Q_\alpha(\mathcal{H})=\{Q_\alpha\circ h : h\in\mathcal{H}\}.$$

By a well-known relation between covering and packing numbers, for all $x_1^n\in\mathcal{X}^n$,

$$\mathcal{N}_\infty(\gamma/2,\mathcal{H},x_1^n)\le\mathcal{M}_\infty(\gamma/2,\mathcal{H},x_1^n). \tag{6}$$

Moreover, it is not hard to show (see [2, Lemma 12.3]) that for all $x_1^n\in\mathcal{X}^n$ and $0<\alpha\le\gamma/2$,

$$\mathcal{M}_\infty(\gamma/2,\mathcal{H},x_1^n)\le\mathcal{M}_\infty(\gamma/2,Q_\alpha(\mathcal{H}),x_1^n) \tag{7}$$

and thus

$$\mathcal{M}_\infty(\gamma/2,\mathcal{H},x_1^n)\le\mathcal{M}_\infty(\gamma/2,Q_{\gamma/2}(\mathcal{H}),x_1^n). \tag{8}$$

Setting $T(x_1^n)=\mathcal{M}_\infty(\gamma/2,Q_{\gamma/2}(\mathcal{H}),x_1^n)$, Theorem 5 implies

$$\mathbf{E}\sup_{f\in\mathcal{F}}\left(L(f)-\widehat{L}^\gamma_n(f)\right)\le\sqrt{\frac{2\mathbf{E}\ln T(X_1^{2n})}{n}}\,. \tag{9}$$

for all $\gamma>0$.

Now observe that each $h \in \mathcal{H}$ maps $\mathcal{X}$ into $[1/2-\gamma, 1/2+\gamma]$, $Q_{\gamma/2}$ maps $[1/2-\gamma, 1/2+\gamma]$ into $C = \{1/2, 1/2 \pm \gamma/2, 1/2 \pm \gamma\}$, and hence each $g \in Q_{\gamma/2}(\mathcal{H})$ maps $\mathcal{X}$ into C. Thus by the special choice $\alpha = \gamma/2$ of the quantization step-size, $T(x_1^n)$ is just the cardinality of the set $Q_{\gamma/2}(\mathcal{H})_{x_1^n} \subset \mathbb{R}^n$. More explicitly,

$$T(x_1^n) = \left|\{(g(x_1), \dots, g(x_n)) \in C^n : g \in Q_{\gamma/2}(\mathcal{H})\}\right| \tag{10}$$

implying (since $|C| = 5$) that $\log_5 T(x_1^n)$ is a combinatorial entropy in the sense of [7]. Thus by [7, Theorem 2], the random variable $\log_5 T(X_1^n)$ satisfies the concentration inequality

$$\mathbf{P}\left(\log_5 T(X_1^n) \le \mathbf{E}[\log_5 T(X_1^n)] - t\right) \le \exp\left(-\frac{t^2}{2\mathbf{E}[\log_5 T(X_1^n)]}\right). \tag{11}$$

Thus, for any $u > 0$ and $v > 0$, using (9), we obtain

$$\begin{aligned}
&\mathbf{P}\left(\sup_{f\in\mathcal{F}}\left(L(f) - \widehat{L}_n^\gamma(f)\right) \ge \sqrt{\frac{8\ln T(X_1^n)}{n}} + \sqrt{\frac{8v}{n}} + u\right) \\
&\qquad \le \mathbf{P}\left(\sup_{f\in\mathcal{F}}\left(L(f) - \widehat{L}_n^\gamma(f)\right) \ge \mathbf{E}\sup_{f\in\mathcal{F}}\left(L(f) - \widehat{L}_n^\gamma(f)\right) + u\right) \\
&\qquad\quad + \mathbf{P}\left(\sqrt{\frac{2\mathbf{E}\ln T(X_1^{2n})}{n}} > \sqrt{\frac{8\ln T(X_1^n)}{n}} + \sqrt{\frac{8v}{n}}\right).
\end{aligned}$$

The first probability on the right-hand side may be bounded by e^{-2nu^2}, by a simple application of the bounded difference inequality (see, e.g., McDiarmid [14]). To bound the second probability of the right-hand side, first note that $T(X_1^{2n}) \le T(X_1^n)T(X_{n+1}^{2n})$, and therefore $\mathbf{E}\ln T(X_1^{2n}) \le 2\mathbf{E}\ln T(X_1^n)$. Combining this with the lower-tail inequality (11) gives

$$\begin{aligned}
&\mathbf{P}\left(\sqrt{\frac{2\mathbf{E}\ln T(X_1^{2n})}{n}} > \sqrt{\frac{8\ln T(X_1^n)}{n}} + \sqrt{\frac{8v}{n}}\right) \\
&\qquad \le \mathbf{P}\left(\sqrt{\frac{4\mathbf{E}\ln T(X_1^n)}{n}} > \sqrt{\frac{8\ln T(X_1^n)}{n}} + \sqrt{\frac{8v}{n}}\right) \\
&\qquad \le \mathbf{P}\left(\mathbf{E}[\ln T(X_1^n)] > 2\ln T(X_1^n) + 2v\right) \\
&\qquad \le \exp\left(-\frac{1}{\ln 5}\frac{\left(\frac{1}{2}\mathbf{E}[\ln T(X_1^n)] + v\right)^2}{2\mathbf{E}[\ln T(X_1^n)]}\right) \\
&\qquad < e^{-v/4}.
\end{aligned} \tag{12}$$

Setting $u = \sqrt{(1/(2n))\ln(2/\delta)}$ and $v = 4\ln(2/\delta)$ in these bounds, we obtain

$$\mathbf{P}\left(\sup_{f\in\mathcal{F}}\left(L(f) - \widehat{L}_n^\gamma(f)\right) \ge \sqrt{\frac{8\ln T(X_1^n)}{n}} + (\sqrt{32} + 1/\sqrt{2})\sqrt{\frac{\ln(2/\delta)}{n}}\right) < \delta. \tag{13}$$

To obtain the second inequality of Theorem 1, simply observe that for all $x_1^n \in \mathcal{X}^n$,

$$\begin{aligned}
T(x_1^n) &= \mathcal{M}_\infty(\gamma/2, Q_{\gamma/2}(\mathcal{H}), x_1^n) \\
&\leq \mathcal{M}_\infty(\gamma/2, Q_{\gamma/8}(\mathcal{H}), x_1^n) \quad (\text{since } Q_{\gamma/2}(\mathcal{H}) \subset Q_{\gamma/8}(\mathcal{H})) \\
&\leq \mathcal{N}_\infty(\gamma/4, Q_{\gamma/8}(\mathcal{H}), x_1^n) \\
&\leq \mathcal{N}_\infty(\gamma/8, \mathcal{H}, x_1^n) \\
&\qquad (\text{since for all } u, v \in \mathbb{R}, |Q_{\gamma/8}(u) - Q_{\gamma/8}(v)| \leq |u - v| + \gamma/8) \\
&\leq \mathcal{N}_\infty(\gamma/8, \mathcal{F}, x_1^n). \qquad (14)
\end{aligned}$$

In the last part of the proof we relate $T(X_1^n) = \mathcal{M}_\infty(\gamma/2, Q_{\gamma/2}(\mathcal{H}), X_1^n)$ to $\mathrm{fat}_{\mathcal{F},X_1^n}(\gamma/8)$ using the following result:

Lemma 3 ([2, Lemma 12.9]). *Let $\mathcal{G}$ be a family of real functions functions mapping $\mathcal{X}$ into the finite set $\{0, 1, \ldots, b\}$. Then for all $x_1^n \in \mathcal{X}^n$,*

$$\mathcal{M}_\infty(2, \mathcal{G}, x_1^n) \leq 2(nb^2)^{\lceil \log_2 y \rceil}$$

where, with $d = \mathrm{fat}_{\mathcal{G},x_1^n}(1)$,

$$y = \sum_{i=1}^{d} \binom{n}{i} b^i.$$

Now notice that $Q_{\gamma/4}(Q_{\gamma/2}(\mathcal{H})) = Q_{\gamma/4}(\mathcal{H})$, and hence by (7)

$$\mathcal{M}_\infty(\gamma/2, Q_{\gamma/2}(\mathcal{H}), x_1^n) \leq \mathcal{M}_\infty(\gamma/2, Q_{\gamma/4}(\mathcal{H}), x_1^n).$$

Since each $g \in Q_{\gamma/4}(\mathcal{H})$ is a mapping from $\mathcal{X}$ into the finite set $\{1/2 + j\gamma/4 : j = 0, \pm 1, \ldots, \pm 4\}$, after simple shifting and rescaling, Lemma 3 with $b = 8$ and $d = \mathrm{fat}_{Q_{\gamma/4}(\mathcal{H}),x_1^n}(\gamma/4)$ implies

$$\mathcal{M}_\infty(\gamma/2, Q_{\gamma/4}(\mathcal{H}), x_1^n) \leq 2(64n)^{\lceil \log_2 y \rceil}$$

where

$$y = \sum_{i=1}^{d} \binom{n}{i} b^i \leq b^d \left(\frac{en}{d}\right)^d = \left(\frac{8en}{d}\right)^d$$

and hence

$$\lceil \log_2 y \rceil \leq d \log_2 \left(\frac{16en}{d}\right).$$

It can be shown (see [2, equation (12.4)]) that for all $0 < \alpha < 2\epsilon$,

$$\mathrm{fat}_{Q_\alpha(\mathcal{H}),x_1^n}(\epsilon) \leq \mathrm{fat}_{\mathcal{H},x_1^n}(\epsilon - \alpha/2)$$

and thus

$$\text{fat}_{Q_{\gamma/4}(\mathcal{H}),x_1^n}(\gamma/4) \le \text{fat}_{\mathcal{H},x_1^n}(\gamma/8) \le \text{fat}_{\mathcal{F},x_1^n}(\gamma/8)$$

where the second inequality holds because $\mathcal{H} = \pi_\gamma(\mathcal{F})$. Setting $d(X_1^n) = \text{fat}_{\mathcal{F},x_1^n}(\gamma/8)$, we obtain

$$\ln T(X_1^n) \le \ln 2 \left(1 + d(X_1^n) \log_2\left(\frac{16en}{d(X_1^n)}\right) \log_2(64n)\right). \tag{15}$$

Substituting this bound into (13) completes the proof of Theorem 1. □

Proof of Theorem 2

The proof combines elements of the proof of Theorem 1 with a version of a classical "relative difference" inequality of Vapnik and Chervonenkis [17]. The first lemma is such an inequality which takes margin error into account. Bartlett [6] gives a similar inequality with the only difference that his result involves worst-case covering numbers. We omit the proof of this lemma as its proof is almost identical to that of [6, Theorem 6]. (The proof is based on Anthony and Shawe-Taylor's proof [3] of the above-mentioned inequality of Vapnik and Chervonenkis [17].)

Lemma 4. *Using the notation of the proof of Theorem 1, for any $\gamma > 0$ and $\epsilon > 0$,*

$$\mathbf{P}\left(\sup_{f\in\mathcal{F}} \frac{L(f) - \widehat{L}_n^\gamma(f)}{\sqrt{L(f)}} > \epsilon\right) \le 4\mathbf{E}\mathcal{N}_\infty(\gamma/2, \pi_\gamma(\mathcal{F}), X_1^{2n})e^{-n\epsilon^2/4}.$$

Proof of Theorem 2. First observe that for any $\alpha > 0$,

$$\mathbf{P}\left(\exists f \in \mathcal{F} : L(f) > (1+\alpha)\,\widehat{L}_n^\gamma(f) + \epsilon^2\frac{1+\alpha}{\alpha}\right) \le \mathbf{P}\left(\sup_{f\in\mathcal{F}} \frac{L(f) - \widehat{L}_n^\gamma(f)}{\sqrt{L(f)}} > \epsilon\right)$$

(see Bartlett and Lugosi [5] for the elementary argument). Thus, Lemma 4 implies that, with probability at least $1 - \delta/2$, for all $f \in \mathcal{F}$,

$$L(f) \le (1+\alpha)\,\widehat{L}_n^\gamma(f) + \frac{4}{n} \cdot \frac{1+\alpha}{\alpha}\left(\ln \mathbf{E}\mathcal{N}_\infty(\gamma/2, \pi_\gamma(\mathcal{F}), X_1^{2n}) + \ln\frac{8}{\delta}\right).$$

As in the proof of Theorem 1, we upper bound $\mathcal{N}_\infty(\gamma/2, \pi_\gamma(\mathcal{F}), X_1^{2n})$ by $T(X_1^{2n})$. Recall that by (12), for any $v > 0$,

$$\mathbf{P}\left(\mathbf{E}[\ln T(X_1^{2n})] > 4\ln T(X_1^n) + 4v\right) < e^{-v/4}.$$

Also, by [7, Theorem 4.2], $\log_5 T(X_1^n)$ satisfies the concentration inequality

$$\log_5 \mathbf{E}[T(X_1^n)] \le \frac{4}{\ln 5}\mathbf{E}[\log_5 T(X_1^n)]$$

and therefore $\ln \mathbf{E}[T(X_1^{2n})] \le 2.5\,\mathbf{E}[\ln T(X_1^{2n})]$. Thus, setting $v = 4\ln(2/\delta)$ and using the union bound, we obtain that with probability at least $1-\delta$, for all $f \in \mathcal{F}$,

$$L(f) \le (1+\alpha)\,\widehat{L}_n^{\gamma}(f) + \frac{4}{n}\cdot\frac{1+\alpha}{\alpha}\left(10\ln T(X_1^n) + 41\ln\frac{8}{\delta}\right).$$

Substitute (15) and (14) into the inequality above to recover the two inequalities of Theorem 2. □

Proof of Lemma 1

First we show that if (4) holds, $\mathcal{F}_\alpha$ γ-shatters x_1^n. Let $(b_1,\ldots,b_n) \in \{0,1\}^n$ be an arbitrary binary vector, and let $\tilde{b}_i = 2b_i - 1$ for $i = 1,\ldots,n$. For $j = 2,\ldots,n$ we define $w_j = \frac{\frac{1}{d_j}}{\sum_{i=2}^n \frac{1}{d_i}}$ and $g_j = g^{(x_{j-1},x_j,-\tilde{b}_j\alpha d_j+r,-\tilde{b}_{j-1}\alpha d_j+r)}$ where $r = \frac{\alpha}{\sum_{j=2}^n \frac{1}{d_j}}\sum_{i=1}^n \tilde{b}_i$. By the definitions of $\mathcal{G}_\alpha$ and d_i it is clear that $g_j \in \mathcal{G}_\alpha$ for $j = 2,\ldots,n$. Since $\sum_{j=2}^n w_j = 1$, $f(x) = \sum_{j=2}^n w_j g_j(x) \in \mathcal{F}_\alpha$.

We show by induction that $\tilde{b}_i f(x_i) = \frac{\alpha}{\sum_{j=2}^n \frac{1}{d_j}}$ for all $i = 1,\ldots,n$. This together with (4) means that $\tilde{b}_i f(x_i) \ge \gamma$ for all $i = 1,\ldots,n$; hence (1) is satisfied with $r_i = 0$ for all $i = 1,\ldots,n$. For x_1 we have

$$\begin{aligned}
\tilde{b}_1 f(x_1) &= \tilde{b}_1 \sum_{i=2}^n w_i g_i(x_1) \\
&= \tilde{b}_1 \sum_{i=2}^n \frac{\frac{1}{d_i}}{\sum_{j=2}^n \frac{1}{d_j}}(-\tilde{b}_i\alpha d_i + r) \\
&= -\tilde{b}_1 \frac{\alpha}{\sum_{j=2}^n \frac{1}{d_j}}\sum_{i=2}^n \tilde{b}_i + \tilde{b}_1 r \frac{1}{\sum_{j=2}^n \frac{1}{d_j}}\sum_{i=2}^n \frac{1}{d_i} \\
&= -\tilde{b}_1 \frac{\alpha}{\sum_{j=2}^n \frac{1}{d_j}}\sum_{i=2}^n \tilde{b}_i + \tilde{b}_1 r \\
&= -\tilde{b}_1 \frac{\alpha}{\sum_{j=2}^n \frac{1}{d_j}}\sum_{i=2}^n \tilde{b}_i + \tilde{b}_1 \frac{\alpha}{\sum_{j=2}^n \frac{1}{d_j}}\sum_{i=1}^n \tilde{b}_i \\
&= \frac{\alpha}{\sum_{j=2}^n \frac{1}{d_j}}.
\end{aligned}$$

In the inductive step we assume that $\tilde{b}_{i-1} f(x_{i-1}) = \frac{\alpha}{\sum_{j=2}^n \frac{1}{d_j}}$. Since the only base function that can change between x_{i-1} and x_i is g_i, we have

$$\begin{aligned}
\tilde{b}_i f(x_i) &= \tilde{b}_i f(x_{i-1}) + \tilde{b}_i w_i\left(g_i(x_i) - g_i(x_{i-1})\right) \\
&= \tilde{b}_i f(x_{i-1}) + \tilde{b}_i w_i\left(-\tilde{b}_{i-1}\alpha d_i + \tilde{b}_i\alpha d_i\right) \\
&= \tilde{b}_i f(x_{i-1}) + w_i\alpha d_i(1 - \tilde{b}_i\tilde{b}_{i-1}).
\end{aligned}$$

If $\tilde{b}_{i-1} = \tilde{b}_i$ then $\tilde{b}_i f(x_i) = \tilde{b}_i f(x_{i-1}) = \tilde{b}_{i-1} f(x_{i-1}) = \frac{\alpha}{\sum_{j=2}^{n} \frac{1}{d_j}}$. If $\tilde{b}_{i-1} \neq \tilde{b}_i$ then

$$\begin{aligned}
\tilde{b}_i f(x_i) &= -\tilde{b}_{i-1} f(x_{i-1}) + 2 w_i \alpha d_i \\
&= -\frac{\alpha}{\sum_{j=2}^{n} \frac{1}{d_j}} + 2 \frac{\alpha}{\sum_{j=2}^{n} \frac{1}{d_j}} \\
&= \frac{\alpha}{\sum_{j=2}^{n} \frac{1}{d_j}}.
\end{aligned}$$

Next we show that if $\mathcal{F}_\alpha$ γ-shatters x_1^n, (4) holds. Consider the two alternating labelings $\tilde{b}_i^+ = -\tilde{b}_i^- = (-1)^i, i = 1, \ldots, n$. If $\mathcal{F}_\alpha$ γ-shatters x_1^n then by (1), there exists $f^+, f^- \in \mathcal{F}_\alpha$ such that for a given real vector $(r_1, \ldots, r_n)$,

$$\begin{aligned}
\tilde{b}_i^+ f^+(x_i) &\geq \tilde{b}_i^+ r_i + \gamma, \\
\tilde{b}_i^- f^-(x_i) &\geq \tilde{b}_i^- r_i + \gamma,
\end{aligned}$$

for $i = 1, \ldots, n$, so by setting $f(x) = \frac{1}{2}(f^+(x) - f^-(x))$,

$$(-1)^i f(x_i) \geq \gamma.$$

By the definition of $\mathcal{G}_\alpha$, if $g \in \mathcal{G}_\alpha$ then $-g \in \mathcal{G}_\alpha$, so $f \in \mathcal{F}_\alpha$, which means that f can be written in the form

$$f = \sum_{j=1}^{N} w_j g^{(x_{a_j}, x_{b_j}, y_{a_j}, y_{b_j})}$$

where $\sum_{j=1}^{N} w_j = 1$. Let $\alpha_j = \frac{1}{2} \left| \frac{y_b - y_a}{x_b - x_a} \right|$ and $s_j = \operatorname{sgn}\left(\frac{y_b - y_a}{x_b - x_a} \right)$ for $j = 1, \ldots, N$. Since $(-1)^i (f(x_i) - f(x_{i-1})) \geq 2\gamma$ for all $i = 2, \ldots, n$, and since f is continuous, there must be a point x_i' between x_{i-1} and x_i where $(-1)^i$ times the (left) derivative of f is not less then $\frac{2\gamma}{x_i - x_{i-1}}$. Therefore,

$$(-1)^i f'(x_i') = (-1)^i \sum_{j: x_{a_j} < x_i' \leq x_{b_j}} w_j 2 s_j \alpha_j \geq \frac{2\gamma}{d_i}$$

for $i = 2, \ldots, n$. Taking the sum of both sides from $i = 2$ to n yields

$$\begin{aligned}
\gamma \sum_{i=2}^{n} \frac{1}{d_i} &\leq \sum_{i=2}^{n} (-1)^i \sum_{j: x_{a_j} < x_i' \leq x_{b_j}} w_j s_j \alpha_j \\
&= \sum_{j=1}^{N} w_j s_j \alpha_j \sum_{i: x_{a_j} < x_i' \leq x_{b_j}} (-1)^i \\
&\leq \sum_{j=1}^{N} w_j \alpha_j \qquad (\text{since } x_2' < \ldots < x_n') \\
&\leq \alpha.
\end{aligned}$$

□

Acknowledgements. We thank Miklós Csűrös for helpful comments and discussions.

References

1. N. Alon, S. Ben-David, N. Cesa-Bianchi, and D. Haussler. Scale-sensitive dimensions, uniform convergence, and learnability. *Journal of the ACM*, 44:615–631, 1997.
2. M. Anthony and P. L. Bartlett. *Neural Network Learning: Theoretical Foundations*. Cambridge University Press, Cambridge, 1999.
3. M. Anthony and J. Shawe-Taylor. A result of Vapnik with applications. *Discrete Applied Mathematics*, 47:207–217, 1993.
4. P. Bartlett, S. Boucheron, and G. Lugosi. Model selection and error estimation. *Machine Learning*, to appear, 2001.
5. P. Bartlett and G. Lugosi. An inequality for uniform deviations of sample averages from their means. *Statistics and Probability Letters*, 44:55–62, 1999.
6. P.L. Bartlett. The sample complexity of pattern classification with neural networks: the size of the weights is more important than the size of the network. *IEEE Transactions on Information Theory*, 44:525–536, 1998.
7. S. Boucheron, G. Lugosi, and P. Massart. A sharp concentration inequality with applications. *Random Structures and Algorithms*, 16:277–292, 2000.
8. L. Devroye, L. Györfi, and G. Lugosi. *A Probabilistic Theory of Pattern Recognition*. Springer-Verlag, New York, 1996.
9. L. Devroye and G. Lugosi. *Combinatorial Methods in Density Estimation*. Springer-Verlag, New York, 2000.
10. W. Hoeffding. Probability inequalities for sums of bounded random variables. *Journal of the American Statistical Association*, 58:13–30, 1963.
11. M. Kearns and R.E. Schapire. Efficient distribution-free learning of probabilistic concepts. *Journal of Computer Systems Sciences*, 48:464–497, 1994.
12. V. Koltchinskii and D. Panchenko. Empirical margin distributions and bounding the generalization error of combined classifiers. *manuscript*, 2000.
13. M. Ledoux and M. Talagrand. *Probability in Banach Space*. Springer-Verlag, New York, 1991.
14. C. McDiarmid. On the method of bounded differences. In *Surveys in Combinatorics 1989*, pages 148–188. Cambridge University Press, Cambridge, 1989.
15. J. Shawe-Taylor, P.L. Bartlett, R.C. Williamson, and M. Anthony. Structural risk minimization over data-dependent hierarchies. *IEEE Transactions on Information Theory*, 44:1926–1940, 1998.
16. J. Shawe-Taylor and R.C. Williamson. Generalization performance of classifiers in terms of observed covering numbers. In H. U. Simon P. Fischer, editor, *Computational Learning Theory: Proceedings of the Fourth European Conference, EuroCOLT'99*, pages 153–167. Springer, Berlin, 1999. Lecture Notes in Artificial Intelligence 1572.
17. V. N. Vapnik and A. Ya. Chervonenkis. *Theory of Pattern Recognition*. Nauka, Moscow, 1974. (in Russian); German translation: *Theorie der Zeichenerkennung*, Akademie Verlag, Berlin, 1979.

Limitations of Learning via Embeddings in Euclidean Half-Spaces*

Shai Ben-David[1], Nadav Eiron[2], and Hans Ulrich Simon[3]

[1] Department of Computer Science, Technion, Haifa 32000, Israel
shai@cs.technion.ac.il
[2] IBM Almaden Research Center, 650 Harry Road, San Jose, CA 95120, USA†
nadav@us.ibm.com
[3] Fakultät für Mathematik, Ruhr-Universität Bochum, D-44780 Bochum, Germany
simon@lmi.ruhr-uni-bochum.de

Abstract. This paper considers the embeddability of general concept classes in Euclidean half spaces. By embedding in half spaces we refer to a mapping from some concept class to half spaces so that the labeling given to points in the instance space is retained. The existence of an embedding for some class may be used to learn it using an algorithm for the class it is embedded into. The Support Vector Machines paradigm employs this idea for the construction of a general learning system.

We show that an overwhelming majority of the family of finite concept classes of constant VC dimension d cannot be embedded in low-dimensional half spaces. (In fact, we show that the Euclidean dimension must be almost as high as the size of the instance space.) We strengthen this result even further by showing that an overwhelming majority of the family of finite concept classes of constant VC dimension d cannot be embedded in half spaces (of arbitrarily high Euclidean dimension) with a large margin. (In fact, the margin cannot be substantially larger than the margin achieved by the trivial embedding.) Furthermore, these bounds are robust in the sense that allowing each image half space to err on a small fraction of the instances does not imply a significant weakening of these dimension and margin bounds.

Our results indicate that any universal learning machine, which transforms data into the Euclidean space and then applies linear (or large margin) classification, cannot enjoy any meaningful generalization guarantees that are based on either VC dimension or margins considerations.

* This work has been supported in part by the ESPRIT Working Group in Neural and Computational Learning II, NeuroCOLT2, No. 27150. The authors gratefully acknowledge the support of the German-Israeli Foundation for Scientific Research and Development Grant I-403-001.06/95. The third author was supported by the Deutsche Forschungsgemeinschaft Grant SI 498/4-1.

† Some of this research was carried out while the this author was a graduate student at the Computer Science Department, Technion, Haifa, Israel.

D. Helmbold and B. Williamson (Eds.): COLT/EuroCOLT 2001, LNAI 2111, pp. 385–401, 2001.

1 Introduction

Half spaces, or hyper-planes, have been at the center of the computational learning theory research since the introduction of the Perceptron algorithm by Rosenblatt [11,12,8]. This interest in half spaces has led to a multitude of results concerning the learnability of these classes. In an attempt to harness the results achieved for this concept class in more general cases, one may consider a (more or less) universal learning paradigm that works by embedding other concept classes in half spaces. E.g., Support Vector Machines (SVMs) are based on the idea of embedding complex concept classes into half spaces and then applying efficient half-spaces learning algorithms.

However, there may be a cost to pay for learning via such embeddings. The best known sample-independent bounds on the generalization ability of a hypothesis generated by a learning algorithm depend on the VC-dimension of the concept class from which hypotheses are drawn. For half-spaces this equals the Euclidean dimension over which these half-spaces are defined. The first question addressed by this research is:

> Given a training sample and a concept class, what is the minimal dimension of half-spaces into which they can be embedded?

SVM theory offers a partial remedy to this problem. The margins of a hypothesis half-space w.r.t. a given training sample can be used to compute a bound on the generalization quality of the hypothesis. If classification occurs with large enough margins then good generalization can be guaranteed regardless of the Euclidean dimension of these half-spaces (e.g., [13,6,7]). This leads us to the second question that we discuss:

> Given a training sample and a concept class, can the sample and the class of concepts be embedded in some class of half-spaces (of arbitrarily high Euclidean dimension) in such a way that there will be some significant margin separating the images of the sample points from the half-spaces that are the images of the concepts of the class?

In this work we obtain strong negative answers to both questions. We prove that for 'most classes' no embedding can obtain either a dimension or margins that are significantly better than those obtained by the trivial embedding. For classes that exhibit this kind of behavior, the generalization that can be guaranteed by SVM's is too weak to be of any practical value. Such examples exist also for classes of small VC-dimension, in which case learning by empirical risk minimization over the original class would yield much better generalization bounds.

Before we elaborate any further on our results, let us explain the basic framework that we work in. Consider an SVM specialist faced with some learning task. The first significant decision she makes is the choice of kernel (or embedding) to be used for mapping the original feature vectors of the training set into a Euclidean space (where later half-space learning algorithms will be applied). Assuming no prior knowledge on the nature of the learning task, one can readily see that the best possible embeddings are those mapping each example into a separate Euclidean dimension. We call such an embedding a *trivial embedding*. It is easy to see that trivial embeddings cannot yield any useful generalization. The other extreme case is when the learner bases her choice of embedding on the full knowledge of the sample labels. In this case the redundant function that maps all positively labeled examples to one point and all the negatively labeled examples to another, achieves perfect loading of the data, alas, once again it yields no generalization. Practical reality is somewhere between these two extremes: the learner does assume some prior knowledge and uses it for the choice of embedding. It is not at all clear how to model this prior knowledge. In this work we consider the case where the prior knowledge available to the learner is encapsulated as a collection of possible dichotomies of the domain feature vectors. The learner assumes that the correct labeling of the examples is close to one of these dichotomies. This modeling is very common in COLT research, and the collection of dichotomies is known as the *concept class*. Given such a class, the learner wishes to find an embedding of the instance space into a Euclidean space, so that every dichotomy in the class will be realized by a half-space over the images of the examples.

We assume that both the instance space and the concept class are finite, and denote their cardinalities by n and m respectively.

In section 3 we show that, as n and m grow unboundedly, an overwhelming majority of the family of finite concept classes of any constant VC dimension, d, cannot be embedded in the class of r-dimensional half spaces, unless $r > n^{1-1/d-1/2^d}$ (assuming $m \geq n$). Note that, for large values of d, this lower bound approaches the trivial upper bound n achieved by the trivial embedding. Thus, for large values of d, our lower bound is (almost) tight for fairly trivial reasons. For some small values of d, namely $d = 4$ or $d = 6$, we are also able to prove (in a less trivial manner) that our lower bound is essentially tight.

In section 4 we address the issue of the margins obtainable by embeddings. We show that an overwhelming majority of the family of finite concept classes of constant VC dimension d cannot be embedded in the class of half spaces (of arbitrarily high dimension) with margin μ, unless μ (as a function in m, n and assuming $m \geq n$) is asymptotically smaller than $\sqrt{\ln(nm)/n^{1-1/d-1/2^d}}$. Note that, for large values of d, this upper bound on μ approaches the trivial lower bound $1/\sqrt{n}$ achieved by the trivial embedding.

Furthermore, we show that our impossibility results remain qualitatively the same if the notion of embedding is relaxed, so that for every concept in the original class there exist a half-space that classifies *almost all* of the embedded points like the original concept (rather than demanding the existence of a half space that achieves perfect fit with the concept dichotomy).

Our results indicate that any universal learning machine, which transforms data to a Euclidean space and then applies linear (or large margin) classification, cannot preserve good generalization bounds in general. Although we address only two generalization bounds (namely, the VC dimension and margin bounds), we believe that the phenomena that we demonstrate applies to other generalization bounds as well. Our results may be interpreted as showing that for an 'average' (or 'random' or 'common') concept class of samll VC dimension, an embedding of the class into a class of linearly separable dichotomies, inevitably introduces a significant degree of over-fitting.

To clarify the implications of our results, we would like to mention that these results do not, of course, render learning machines of this type (like SVMs) useless. In fact, if most of the *important* classes could be nicely embedded, who cares about the vast majority? Instead, our results indicate that the design of a "universal" learning machine (based on embeddings in half spaces) is an overly ambitious goal if it is pursued without further restrictions.

Most of our results are based on counting arguments and therefore only show the *existence* of 'hard-to-embed' classes (and that, indeed, they are the common case). However, in Section 4.1 we discuss the (non-)embeddability of specific concept classes.

We believe that the design of analytic tools, that allow the study of embeddability of a given concept class, will deepen the understanding of the embeddability question further. (See [4,5] as first steps in this direction.)

2 Definitions

The central notion discussed in this paper is the notion of embedding of one concept class into another.

Definition 1. *A concept class $\mathcal{C} \subseteq 2^{\mathcal{X}}$ over a domain $\mathcal{X}$ is embeddable in another concept class $\mathcal{C}' \subseteq 2^{\mathcal{X}'}$ over a domain $\mathcal{X}'$ iff there exists a function $\psi : \mathcal{X} \mapsto \mathcal{X}'$ such that*

$$\forall f \in \mathcal{C}, \exists g \in \mathcal{C}', \forall x \in \mathcal{X} \ f(x) = g(\psi(x)).$$

We also present some results on approximate embeddings. These are embeddings in which some of the points in every concept class may be mis-classified by the embedding. Formally:

Definition 2. *A concept class $\mathcal{C} \subseteq 2^{\mathcal{X}}$ over a domain $\mathcal{X}$ is η-approximately embeddable in another concept class $\mathcal{C}' \subseteq 2^{\mathcal{X}'}$ over a domain $\mathcal{X}'$ iff there exist a function $\psi : \mathcal{X} \mapsto \mathcal{X}'$ such that*

$$\forall f \in \mathcal{C}\ , \exists g \in \mathcal{C}' \ |\{x \in \mathcal{X} : g(\psi(x)) \neq f(x)\}| \leq \eta|\mathcal{X}|.$$

We use binary matrices to represent concept classes of boolean functions. A class $\mathcal{C}$ is represented by a matrix F of size $m \times n$, where $|\mathcal{C}| = m$, $|\mathcal{X}| = n$, and $F_{i,j}$ is the value of the ith concept on the instance j.

Definition 3. *Let $\mathcal{D}(m, n, d)$ denote the family of binary matrices with m rows and n columns that have VC dimension smaller than d.*

Definition 4. *Let $\mathcal{E}(m, n, r)$ denote the family of binary matrices with m rows and n columns that can be embedded into the class of half spaces of Euclidean dimension r.*

Our basic approach will be to derive a lower bound on the Euclidean dimension r from the inequality $|\mathcal{D}(m, n, d)| \leq |\mathcal{E}(m, n, r)|$ (or slight variations of this inequality).

Another notion that is in the focus of this paper is the notion of the margins of a half space with respect to a sample.

Definition 5. *The* margin *of a homogeneous half space with normal vector w over a set $\mathcal{X}$ is defined as:*

$$\min_{x \in \mathcal{X}} \frac{|w \cdot x|}{\|w\| \|x\|}$$

When speaking of margins we will usually normalize w to be of length one, and assume all points x are on the unit sphere, in which case the margin becomes simply $\min_{x \in \mathcal{X}} |w \cdot x|$. The definition of a margin is naturally extended to a set of half spaces $\mathcal{C}$, by defining the margin of $\mathcal{C}$ to be the minimum margin achieved by any $w \in \mathcal{C}$.

We conclude this collection of definitions with two technical notions that shall be needed in our proofs in Section 3.

Definition 6. *For natural numbers m, n, s, t, we define the following parameters:*

- *$\mathcal{Z}(m, n, s, t)$ denotes the family of binary matrices with m rows and n columns that do not contain a generalized rectangle of all 1's (a 1-monochromatic rectangle) of size $s \times t$.*
- *$z(m, n, s, t)$ denotes the maximum number of 1-entries in any matrix in $\mathcal{Z}(m, n, s, t)$.*

Note that we may interpret $z(m, n, s, t)$ as the maximum number of edges in a bipartite graph G, whose vertex classes have size m and n, respectively, subject to the condition that G does not contain a complete bipartite $s \times t$ subgraph.

The following observation relates these combinatorial notions to classes of small VC dimesion.

Lemma 1. $\mathcal{Z}(m, n, 2^d, d) \subseteq \mathcal{D}(m, n, 2d)$.

Proof. Consider a matrix F that shatters a set $Y = \{y_1 \dots y_{2d}\}$ of size $|Y| = 2d$. By the definition, it means that F contains concepts with every possible assignment in those $2d$ places, including 2^d concepts that assign 1 to $y_1 \dots y_d$ and any other combination to the rest of the y's. These concepts define a 1-monochromatic rectangle in F with 2^d rows and d columns. Therefore, any matrix that does not contain such a rectangle has VC dimension smaller than $2d$.

3 An Asymptotic Lower Bound on the Euclidean Dimension Needed by Embeddings in Half Spaces

This section presents our results concerning the minimal dimension required to embed general concept classes of fixed VC dimension in half spaces. Our proofs use known results for a combinatorial problem known as "the problem of Zarankiewicz".

In order to provide lower bounds on the dimensions of half spaces needed for embeddings, we shall show that there are many classes of any fixed VC dimension. We shall compare these bounds with known upper bounds on the number of classes that can be embedded into half spaces in any fixed dimension Euclidean space.

The problem of determining $z(m,n,s,t)$ was first suggested (for specific values of s,t), by Zarankiewicz [14], and later became known as "the problem of Zarankiewicz". Bollobás [3] provides the following bounds, which are valid for all $2 \leq s \leq m$, $2 \leq t \leq n$:

$$z(m,n,s,t) < (s-1)^{1/t}(n-t+1)m^{1-1/t} + (t-1)m \tag{1}$$

$$z(m,n,s,t) \geq l(m,n,s,t) \triangleq \left\lfloor \left(1 - \frac{1}{s!t!}\right) m^{1-\alpha} n^{1-\beta} \right\rfloor \tag{2}$$

where

$$\alpha = \alpha(s,t) \triangleq \frac{s-1}{st-1} \text{ and } \beta = \beta(s,t) \triangleq \frac{t-1}{st-1}. \tag{3}$$

Since the class $\mathcal{Z}(m,n,s,t)$ of matrices (viewed as bipartite graphs) is closed under edge deletion, the following inequality obviously holds:

$$|\mathcal{Z}(m,n,s,t)| \geq 2^{z(m,n,s,t)} \geq 2^{l(m,n,s,t)} = 2^{\left\lfloor (1-\frac{1}{s!t!}) m^{1-\alpha} n^{1-\beta} \right\rfloor} \tag{4}$$

Assume that at least a fraction $0 < \lambda \leq 1$ of the matrices in $\mathcal{Z}(m,n,s,t)$ is embeddable in the class of r-dimensional half spaces. It follows that

$$|\mathcal{E}(m,n,r)| \geq \lambda 2^{z(m,n,s,t)} \geq \lambda 2^{l(m,n,s,t)}. \tag{5}$$

If inequality (5) is violated for every $r < r_0$, we may conclude that less than a fraction λ of the matrices in $\mathcal{Z}(m,n,s,t)$ can be embedded in the class of half spaces unless we embed into at least r_0 Euclidean dimensions. We will use this basic counting argument several times in what follows.

On the other hand, there are known bounds on the number of matrices of size $m \times n$ that may be embedded into half spaces.

Theorem 1 (Alon et al. [1]). *For every n, m, r:*

$$|\mathcal{E}(m,n,r)| \leq \min_{h \leq mn} \left(8 \left\lceil \frac{mn}{h} \right\rceil\right)^{(n+m)r+h+m} \tag{6}$$

The remainder of this section is devoted to a first application of the basic counting argument. For sake of simplicity, we restrict ourselves to the case $m = n$. The (more or less straightforward) generalizations to the case $m \geq n$ will be presented in the full paper.

We consider the parameters s, t or d as arbitrary but fixed constants and work towards statements that are asymptotically valid when n approaches infinity. More specifically, let γ be an arbitrary but fixed constant such that $\alpha+\beta < \gamma < 1$, let $h = n^{2-\gamma}$, and $\lambda = 2^{-l(n,n,s,t)/2}$. Then (5) and (6) lead (after some algebraic manipulations) to the following inequality:

$$(2r + n^{1-\gamma} + 1)\log\left(8\lceil n^{\gamma}\rceil\right) \geq \frac{1}{2}\left\lfloor\left(1 - \frac{1}{s!t!}\right)n^{1-\alpha-\beta}\right\rfloor$$

From this inequality, the following is immediate:

Theorem 2. *Let $s, t \geq 2$ be arbitrary but fixed constants. Then, for all sufficiently large n, the following holds. Only a vanishing fraction $2^{-l(n,n,s,t)/2}$ of the matrices from the family $\mathcal{Z}(n,n,s,t)$ is embeddable in the class of half spaces of Euclidean dimension r unless*

$$r = \Omega\left(\frac{n^{1-\alpha(s,t)-\beta(s,t)}}{\log n}\right) = \omega\left(n^{1-1/s-1/t}\right).$$

With some additional effort, Theorem 2 can be generalized to approximate embeddings:

Corollary 1. *Let $s, t \geq 2$ be arbitrary but fixed constants, and let γ be an arbitrary constant such that $\alpha(s,t) + \beta(s,t) < \gamma < 1$. ($\gamma = 1/s + 1/t$ would be a possible choice.) Then, for all sufficiently large n, the following holds. Only a vanishing fraction $2^{-l(n,n,s,t)/2}$ of the matrices from the family $\mathcal{Z}(n,n,s,t)$ is $n^{-\gamma}$-approximately embeddable in the class of half spaces of Euclidean dimension r unless*

$$r = \Omega\left(\frac{n^{1-\alpha(s,t)-\beta(s,t)}}{\log n}\right) = \omega\left(n^{1-1/s-1/t}\right).$$

Proof. Suppose that K is an arrangement of n halfspaces and n vectors in $\mathbb{R}^r$ that represents a matrix F of $\mathcal{Z}(n,n,s,t)$. Then K represents a matrix F' $n^{-\gamma}$-approximately if, for all $i = 1, \ldots, n$, the Hamming distance between the ith row in F and the ith row in F' is at most $n^{-\gamma}n = n^{1-\gamma}$. The number of the matrices that are $n^{-\gamma}$-approximately represented by K is therefore upper-bounded by

$$\left(n^{n^{1-\gamma}}\right)^n = n^{n^{2-\gamma}}.$$

In order to complete the proof, we may therefore perform similar calculations as before, except that we have to expand the upper bound in Theorem 1 by the additional factor $n^{n^{2-\gamma}}$. These calculations lead to an Euclidean dimension r that exhibits the same asymptotic growth as before.

Combined with Lemma 1, this implies:

Corollary 2. *Let $d \geq 2$ be arbitrary but fixed. Let γ be an arbitrary constant such that $\alpha(2^d,d) + \beta(2^d,d) < \gamma < 1$. ($\gamma = 1/d + 1/2^d$ would be a possible choice.) Then, for all sufficiently large n, the following holds. Only a vanishing fraction $2^{-l(n,n,2^d,d)/2}$ of the concept classes from the family $\mathcal{D}(n,n,2d)$ is $n^{-\gamma}$-approximately embeddable in the class of half spaces of Euclidean dimension r unless*

$$r = \Omega\left(\frac{n^{1-\alpha(2^d,d)-\beta(2^d,d)}}{\log n}\right) = \omega\left(n^{1-1/2^d-1/d}\right).$$

4 Upper Bounds on the Margin Attainable by Embeddings in Half Spaces

In this section we prove some upper bounds on the margin that an embedding of an arbitrary class into half spaces may yield. We are going to employ two different techniques: a bound based on a concrete parameter of the class, and a combinatorial counting argument over the family of classes.

4.1 A Concrete Bound as a Function of Online Mistake Bounds

We present a rather simple technique that yields non-trivial upper bounds on the margins that can be obtained for certain specific classes. The idea is to use the online learning complexity of the class.

Recall that the online (or Mistake Bound) learning task for a class C of functions from some domain X to $\{0,1\}$ is defined as a game between a 'teacher' and a 'student'. The teacher picks some function $c \in C$. Now the game runs in steps. At each step i the teacher picks some $x_i \in X$ and presents it to the student. The student returns a label $l_i \in \{0,1\}$ and passes it to the teacher, who then tells the student the value $c(x_i)$ and picks x_{i+1}. The cost of such a run of the game is $|\{i : l_i \neq c(x_i)\}|$. The Mistake Bound complexity of a class C is the minimum over all students strategies of the maximum over all teacher strategies of the cost of the run that is produced by these playing strategies. We denote it by MB(C).

Now, how does it relate to embeddings and margins? Let us recall the following well known result:

Theorem 3 (Novikoff [9]). *Let $S = ((x_1, b_1), \ldots, (x_s, b_s))$ be a sequence of $\{0,1\}$ labeled points in the unit ball in $\mathbb{R}^n$. If there exists a hyperplane that separates $\{x_i : b_i = 0\}$ from $\{x_i : b_i = 1\}$ with margin $\geq \gamma$, then the online Perceptron algorithm makes at most $\left(\frac{2}{\gamma}\right)^2$ many mistakes on S.*

Tying these notions together we readily get:

Theorem 4. *Pick any $\gamma > 0$. If a class C can be embedded in half-spaces (in any dimension) so that every dichotomy that is induced by a member of C can be realized by a half-space that has margin $\geq \gamma$ (with respect to the images of the points in the instance space over which C is defined), then $MB(C) \leq 4/\gamma^2$.*

Proof. The trick is to apply Novikoff's theorem about the Perceptron algorithm. Let $\psi : X \mapsto \mathbb{R}^n$ be an embedding that achieves margins above γ for the class C. Now let the learner use the following strategy: upon receiving a point x_{i+1} run the perceptron algorithm on $(\psi(x_1), c(x_1)), \ldots (\psi(x_i), c(x_i))$ and let l_{i+1} be the label given to $\psi(x_{i+1})$ by the half-space that the perceptron algorithm produces. By Novikoff's theorem, if there exists a half-space that separates the images of the points that c labels 1 from the images of the points that c labels 0 with margin $\geq \gamma$, then the perceptron algorithm (and therefore, our student) will make at most $4/\gamma^2$ mistakes.

The above simple result can be readily applied to demonstrate that some of the simplest classes cannot be embedded in half-spaces with good margins. For example, let I^n be the class of all initial segments of $(1, \ldots, n)$. Note that the VC dimension of I^n is 1 regardless of the value of n. Just the same, it is not hard to see that $\mathrm{MB}(I^n) = \lfloor \log(n) \rfloor$.

Corollary 3. *For any embedding of n points to some unit ball in a Euclidean space, if every dichotomy in I^n can be realized as a half-space over the images of the points, then there exists some $c \in I^n$ so that the image of the dichotomy it defines cannot be realized by a half-space with margin below $2/\sqrt{\log(n)}$.*

In spite of the simplicity of the above result, it has quite striking consequences for learning methods. Namely, for some of the most simple concept classes, while Empirical Risk Minimization suffices for learning them efficiently (due to their constant VC dimension and simple structure), once they are embedded into half-spaces, the generalization bound that relies on margins will grow to infinity with the size of the instance space!

Note however that, as the mistake bound of a class C is always bounded from above by $\log(|C|)$ (due to the Halving algorithm), the above idea cannot be used for obtaining larger upper bounds on the values of obtainable margins.

In the following subsection, we turn to a counting technique, that yields stronger bounds, but shows only existence of classes (rather then providing bounds for concrete classes).

4.2 Strong Margin Bounds for the Majority of Classes

In this section we are going to translate the lower bounds of Section 3 on the dimension of embeddings, into bounds on obtainable margins. The translation is done via the random projections technique. We use the following result:

Lemma 2. (Arriaga and Vempala [2]) *Let $u \in \mathbb{R}^r$ be arbitrary but fixed. Let $R = (R_{i,j})$ be a random $(k \times r)$-matrix such that the entries $R_{i,j}$ are i.i.d. according to the normal distribution $N(0,1)$. Consider the* random projection $u_R \triangleq \frac{1}{\sqrt{k}}(Ru) \in \mathbb{R}^k$. *Then the following holds for every constant $\mu > 0$:*

$$\Pr_R \left[\left| \|u_R\|^2 - \|u\|^2 \right| \geq \mu \|u\|^2 \right] \leq 2e^{-\mu^2 k/8}.$$

Corollary 4. *Let $w, x \in \mathbb{R}^r$ be arbitrary but fixed. Let $R = (R_{i,j})$ be a random $(k \times r)$-matrix such that the entries $R_{i,j}$ are i.i.d. according to the normal distribution $N(0,1)$. Then the following holds for every constant $\mu > 0$:*

$$\Pr_R \left[|w_R \cdot x_R - w \cdot x| \geq \frac{\mu}{2} \left(\|w\|^2 + \|x\|^2 \right) \right] \leq 4e^{-\mu^2 k/8}.$$

Proof. Consider the events

$$\left| \|w_R + x_R\|^2 - \|w + x\|^2 \right| < \mu \|w + x\|^2 \tag{7}$$

$$\left| \|w_R - x_R\|^2 - \|w - x\|^2 \right| < \mu \|w - x\|^2 . \tag{8}$$

According to Lemma 2 (applied to $u = w + x$ and $u = w - x$, respectively), the probability of a violation of (7) or (8) is upper-bounded by $4e^{-\mu^2 k/8}$. It suffices therefore to derive $|w_R \cdot x_R - w \cdot x| < \frac{\mu}{2}(\|w\|^2 + \|x\|^2)$ from (7) and (8). From

$$\|w + x\|^2 = \|w\|^2 + 2w \cdot x + \|x\|^2 \text{ and } \|w - x\|^2 = \|w\|^2 - 2w \cdot x + \|x\|^2, \quad (9)$$

we conclude that

$$\|w + x\|^2 - \|w - x\|^2 = 4w \cdot x. \quad (10)$$

Clearly, the analogous relation holds for the random projections:

$$\|w_R + x_R\|^2 - \|w_R - x_R\|^2 = 4w_R \cdot x_R. \quad (11)$$

Applying (10), (11), the triangle inequality, (7), (8), and (9) (in this order), we accomplish the proof as follows:

$$\begin{aligned}
|w_R \cdot x_R - w \cdot x| &= \frac{1}{4}\left|\|w_R + x_R\|^2 - \|w + x\|^2 + \|w - x\|^2 - \|w_R - x_R\|^2\right| \\
&\le \frac{1}{4}\left(\left|\|w_R + x_R\|^2 - \|w + x\|^2\right| + \left|\|w_R - x_R\|^2 - \|w - x\|^2\right|\right) \\
&< \frac{\mu}{4}\left(\|w + x\|^2 + \|w - x\|^2\right) \\
&= \frac{\mu}{2}\left(\|w\|^2 + \|x\|^2\right).
\end{aligned}$$

From Lemma 2 and Corollary 4, the following results are easily obtained:

Corollary 5. *Let $\mathcal{C}$ be a set of $m = |\mathcal{C}|$ homogeneous half spaces of dimension r, and let $\mathcal{X}$ be a set of $n = |\mathcal{X}|$ points in $\mathbb{R}^r$, such that the margin of $\mathcal{C}$ over $\mathcal{X}$ is μ. Let R be a random $(k \times r)$-matrix such that the entries $R_{i,j}$ are i.i.d. according to the normal distribution $N(0,1)$. Then the following holds:*

1. $\Pr_R\left[\exists w \in \mathcal{C}, \exists x \in \mathcal{X} \ : \ sgn(w \cdot x) \neq sgn(R^T w \cdot R^T x)\right] \le 4mne^{-\mu^2 k/8}$.
2. *If $\mu > \sqrt{8\ln(4mn)/k}$, then $\mathcal{C}$ can be embedded in the class of k-dimensional half spaces.*[1]

Note that this result is independent of the original dimension r, and depends only on the margin μ and the dimension into which we embed, k. From Corollaries 5 and 2, we immediately obtain the main result of this section:

Theorem 5. *Let $d \ge 2$ be arbitrary but fixed. Then, for all sufficiently large n, the following holds. Only a vanishing fraction $2^{-l(n,n,2^d,d)/2}$ of the concept classes from the family $\mathcal{D}(n,n,2d)$ is embeddable in the class of half spaces (of arbitrarily large dimension) with a margin μ unless*

$$\mu = O\left(\sqrt{\frac{\ln(n)\log(n)}{n^{1-\alpha(2^d,d)-\beta(2^d,d)}}}\right) = o\left(\sqrt{\frac{\ln(n)}{n^{1-1/2^d-1/d}}}\right).$$

[1] Note that $\mu > \sqrt{8\ln(4mn)/k}$ is equivalent to $4mne^{-\mu^2 k/8} < 1$. The second statement is therefore an immediate consequence of the first statement.

We briefly note (without proof) that one can derive the following result from Corollary 5 and the counting arguments given in the paper [1] of Alon, Frankl, and Rödl.

Theorem 6. *For all sufficiently large n, the following holds. Only a vanishing fraction of the Boolean matrices of size $n \times n$ is embeddable in the class of half spaces (of arbitrarily large dimension) with a margin μ unless*

$$\mu = O\left(\sqrt{\frac{\ln(n)}{n}}\right).$$

5 Tight Bounds for Classes of Low VC Dimension

We turn now to the question of what positive results can be achieved to complement our negative results on the dimension required for embedding. The type of results we seek is:

> For some fixed d, all matrices (or classes) of size $n \times n$ and VC-dimension $2d$ may be embedded in half spaces of dimension $r(d, n)$, for some function $r(d, n) = O(n^{1-1/2^d-1/d})$.

Obviously, such a result would be interesting primarily for low values of d, where the difference between $r(d, n)$ and n (the dimension required by the trivial embedding) is significant. While we cannot present a general positive result, we do show that, for specific values of s, t, there exist subfamilies of $\mathcal{Z}(n, n, s, t)$ that can be embedded into half spaces of a dimension matching the corresponding lower bound. Although this result is weaker than can ideally be hoped for, it shows that there are non-trivial cases, where the smallest Euclidean dimension needed to embed a family of matrices can be determined quite accurately.

The main results in this section are as follows:

Theorem 7. *For all n, the class of matrices $\mathcal{Z}(n, n, 2, 2)$ contains a subfamily $\mathcal{F}_{2\times 2}(n)$ that can be embedded in half spaces of dimension $O(n^{1/2})$. Furthermore, this class cannot be embedded into half spaces of dimension $o(n^{1/2}/\log(n))$.*

Theorem 8. *For all n, the family of matrices $\mathcal{Z}(n, n, 3, 3)$ contains a subfamily $\mathcal{F}_{3\times 3}(n)$ that can be embedded in half spaces of dimension $O(n^{2/3})$. Furthermore, this class cannot be embedded into half spaces of dimension $o(n^{2/3}/\log(n))$.*

The proofs of these theorems are given in section 5.1 and 5.2. As in section 3, the lower bounds are obtained by the basic counting argument. The upper bounds are obtained by exploiting the relationship between communication complexity and embeddings (see [10]). Section 5.1 presents the subfamilies $\mathcal{F}_{2\times 2}(n)$ and $\mathcal{F}_{3\times 3}(n)$ and applies the basic counting argument to them. Section 5.2 presents the corresponding embeddings.

5.1 Lower Bounds for Classes of Low VC Dimension

We would like to demonstrate that the bound we achieve for the Zarankiewicz matrices can be matched by an actual embedding for matrices of this type. The reason such results can only be expected for specific (small) values of s and t is that, as commented in [3], the general lower bound for the Zarankiewicz problem is far from being tight. We therefore consider specific values of s, t for which better lower bounds are known. Furthermore, for these cases, constructions of the graphs that demonstrate the lower bound on $z(m, n, s, t)$ are also known (unlike the general lower bound, whose proof is not constructive). We consider two such specific cases, and show that for these cases we can construct an embedding into dimension close to our lower bound (using the improved results for the Zarankiewicz problem available for these cases).

The first case we tackle concerns the class of graphs $\mathcal{Z}(n, n, 2, 2)$, namely, bipartite graphs with two vertex sets of equal cardinality that do not contain a quadrilateral. For this specific case, [3] shows the following construction:

Let q be a prime power, and let $\mathrm{PG}(2, q)$ be the projective plane over a field of order q. Let V_1 be the set of points in $\mathrm{PG}(2, q)$ and V_2 be the set of lines in $\mathrm{PG}(2, q)$. An edge (v_1, v_2) is included in the graph iff the point v_1 is incident to the line v_2. It is immediate to verify that this graph indeed does not contain quadrilaterals (as any two points can only be incident to a single line).

The number of points, as well as the number of lines, in the projective plane, assuming we take $q = p$, a prime, is:

$$n = \frac{p^3 - 1}{p - 1} = p^2 + p + 1.$$

It is well-known that each point is incident to exactly $p - 1$ lines. We conclude that, for each prime p and $n = p^2 + p + 1$, there exists a Boolean $(n \times n)$-matrix F_n with $(p - 1)n$ 1-entries that does not contain a 1-monochromatic rectangle of size 2×2. Note that the latter property is preserved by flipping 1-entries to 0. Denote by $\mathcal{F}_{2\times 2}(n)$ the family of all matrices of size $n \times n$, where $n = p^2 + p + 1$, that are constructed from F_n by flipping some of the 1-entries into zeros. We conclude that $\mathcal{F}_{2\times 2}(n) \subseteq \mathcal{Z}(n, n, 2, 2)$ and

$$z(n, n, 2, 2) \geq n(p - 1) \geq n^{3/2}(1 - o(1))$$

A straightforward application of our basic counting argument shows that $r = \Omega(n^{1/2}/\log n)$ Euclidean dimensions are needed to embed each matrix from $\mathcal{F}_{2\times 2}(n)$ in the class of r-dimensional half spaces. In the next subsection, we show that $O(n^{1/2})$ Euclidean dimensions are enough.

Another specific construction that appears in [3] is tailored to the case $s = t = 3$. Again the construction is via geometry spaces over finite fields. This time the affine geometry space $\mathrm{AG}(3, p)$ of dimension 3 over the field $\mathrm{GF}(p)$ is used. For the construction we choose an element q in $\mathrm{GF}(p)$ which is a quadratic residue if and only if -1 is not a quadratic residue. We then define $S(x)$, for a point $x \in \mathrm{AG}(3,p)$, to be the sphere consisting of points y that satisfy:

$$\sum_{i=1}^{3}(x_i - y_i)^2 = q. \tag{12}$$

We can now construct a bipartite graph, with $n = p^3$ vertices in each of the vertex sets V_1 and V_2. We connect the edge between vertices $x \in V_1$ and $y \in V_2$ iff $x \in S(y)$ (or, equivalently, $y \in S(x)$). The resulting matrix, say F'_n, contains no 1-monochromatic rectangle of size 3×3. The number of 1-entries in F'_n is $p^5 - p^4$. Let us denote the family of matrices of size $n \times n$ obtained from F'_n by flipping some of 1-entries into zeros by $\mathcal{F}_{3\times 3}(n)$. Again, we have, $\mathcal{F}_{3\times 3}(n) \subseteq \mathcal{Z}(n,n,3,3)$, and a straightforward application of our basic counting argument shows that $r = \Omega(n^{2/3}/\log n)$ Euclidean dimensions are needed to embed each matrix from $\mathcal{F}_{3\times 3}(n)$ in the class of r-dimensional half spaces. In the next subsection, we show that $O(n^{2/3})$ Euclidean dimensions are enough.

5.2 Constructing Embeddings through Communication Protocols

To construct embeddings we use a well-known connection between probabilistic communication complexity and embedding in half spaces. We use the model of unbounded error, two sided, communication complexity (see [10]). In this model, two players P_0 and P_1 are trying to compute a Boolean function $f(x,y)$, where P_0 is given $x \in \{0,1\}^n$ as input and P_1 is given $y \in \{0,1\}^n$ as input. Each player has unlimited computational power, and may realize any distribution on the messages it transmits to the other player. A protocol is said to calculate a function $f(x,y)$, if for any possible input pair (x,y), with probability exceeding 1/2 (over the randomness of the players), the protocol will output the value of $f(x,y)$. For a communication protocol $\mathcal{A}$, we denote $C(\mathcal{A})$ its communication complexity, defined as the maximum over all possible inputs of the number of bits exchanged between P_0 and P_1 during the run of the protocol. For a function f, we define its unbounded error communication complexity to be:

$$C_f \stackrel{\triangle}{=} \min_{\mathcal{A}_f} C(\mathcal{A}_f)$$

where the minimum is taken over all protocols $\mathcal{A}_f$ that correctly compute f.

The function f to be computed in such a communication protocol may also be represented by a square binary matrix F, where the entry $F(x,y)$ contains the value of $f(x,y)$. Paturi and Simon prove the following result (which is cited here with terminology adapted to this paper):

Theorem 9. (Paturi and Simon [10]) *Let F be the matrix of a Boolean function f. Let r be the smallest dimension in which there is an embedding of the class represented by F into hyper-planes. Then, the unbounded error probabilistic communication complexity C_f for the function f satisfies:*

$$\lceil \log(r) \rceil \le C_f \le \lceil \log(r) \rceil + 1$$

Therefore, each communication protocol in this model for a function f with matrix F implicitly represents an embedding of F into the class of half spaces of dimension exponential in the communication complexity of the protocol (and vice versa). Let us now present communication protocols for the functions whose matrices were introduced in the previous subsection.

Recall that $F_n \in \mathcal{F}_{2\times2}(n)$ denotes the matrix from the family $\mathcal{F}_{2\times2}(n)$, $n = p^2+p+1$, that indicates the incidences between points and lines in PG$(2,p)$. Assume processor P_0 has as input a (binary encoding of the) point x in PG$(2,p)$, while P_1 has as input a (binary encoding of the) line y in PG$(2,p)$. Our protocol for the matrix F_n is based on the following observation:

F_n has a 1 in position (x,y) if and only if the point x is incident to the line y. If we represent a point (a 1-dimensional vector subspace of $(\mathrm{GF}(p))^3$) by a vector in that subspace, and a line (a 2-dimensional vector subspace of $(\mathrm{GF}(p))^3$) by a vector that is orthogonal to the subspace, we have that x is incident to y if and only if $x \cdot y = 0$ (where "$\cdot$" denotes the inner product of the vector space $(\mathrm{GF}(p))^3$).

We can therefore use the following probabilistic communication protocol for the matrix F_n:

Protocol 1

1. Processor P_0 normalizes its input: if $x_1 \neq 0$, let $\hat{x} = x/x_1$. Otherwise, let $\hat{x} = x$.
2. Processor P_0 sends the value of $\hat{x}_1$ (one bit).
3. Processor P_0 sends the value of $\hat{x}_2$.
4. Processor P_1 solves the equation $\sum_{i=1}^{3} \hat{x}_i y_i = 0$ for $\hat{x}_3$. Denote this solution by z.
5. The processors run the protocol, EQ, for testing the equality of z and $\hat{x}_3$ (see [10]) and output the same bit as the EQ-protocol.

Theorem 10. *Protocol 1 is a probabilistic communication protocol for the matrix F_n that uses $3 + \lceil \log(p) \rceil = \frac{1}{2}\log(n) + O(1)$ bits of communication.*

Proof. The correctness of the protocol is immediate: in step 4, processor P_1 has the values for y_1, y_2, y_3, $\hat{x}_1$, and $\hat{x}_2$ and can therefore solve the linear equation. From the observation above, a 1 in the matrix F_n corresponds to a solution of this equation. The EQ-protocol is then used to check whether $\hat{x}$ indeed solves this equation.

As for communication complexity, communicating the value of $\hat{x}_1$ takes just 1 bit (since its value is either 0 or 1). Communicating the value of $\hat{x}_2$ takes $\lceil \log(p) \rceil$ bits, and the EQ-protocol of Paturi and Simon requires two additional bits.

Note that a slight modification of this protocol can be used in the case that some of the 1-entries in the matrix were changed to zeros:
In step 4 above, a check should be made to see if the entry represented by the solution to this equation is 0. If this is the case, we can immediately output zero, even without running the EQ-protocol.

It follows that each matrix of the family $\mathcal{F}_{2,2}(n)$ can be computed by a protocol that exchanges $\frac{1}{2}\log n + O(1)$ bits. According to Theorem 9, each matrix from the family $\mathcal{F}_{2,2}(n)$ can be embedded into half spaces of dimension $O(n^{1/2})$. Theorem 7 immediately follows.

Let us now move to matrices from the class $\mathcal{F}_{3\times 3}(n)$, $n = p^3$, described in subsection 5.1. Recall that F'_n is the matrix from $\mathcal{F}_{3\times 3}(n)$ that has a 1-entry in position (x, y) iff x and y satisfy relation (12). Assume, once more, that processor P_0 has as input a point $x \in \mathrm{AG}(3,p)$ while processor P_1 has as input a point $y \in \mathrm{AG}(3,p)$.

Before we describe a protocol for this matrix, let us mention a protocol for a problem we call EQ2 (for Equality-2). In this problem, processor P_0 is given an l-bit number x and processor P_1 is given two different l-bit numbers[2] (z, z'). The function EQ2 is given by

$$\mathrm{EQ2}(x, z, z') = 1 \iff (x = z \vee x = z').$$

Note that we assumed $z \neq z'$.

Lemma 3. *There exists a probabilistic communication protocol for EQ2 that uses* 5 *bits of communication (regardless of* l*).*

Proof. Paturi and Simon provided a two-dimensional half space embedding for the matrix induced by the equality function, EQ, that checks whether two given l-bit numbers x and z are equal. Clearly, this embedding can be converted into a three-dimensional homogeneous half space embedding of EQ or, alternatively, $\neg$EQ. In other words, we may represent x as $(\xi_1, \xi_2, \xi_3) \in \mathbb{R}^3$ and z as $(\zeta_1, \zeta_2, \zeta_3) \in \mathbb{R}^3$ such that

$$x = z \iff \sum_{i=1}^{3} \xi_i \zeta_i < 0 \text{ and } x \neq z \iff \sum_{i=1}^{3} \xi_i \zeta_i > 0.$$

Making use of $z \neq z'$, it follows that

$$(x = z \vee x = z') \iff \sum_{i=1}^{3}\sum_{j=1}^{3} \xi_i \xi_j \zeta_i \zeta'_j = \left(\sum_{i=1}^{3} \xi_i \zeta_i\right) \cdot \left(\sum_{j=1}^{3} \xi_j \zeta'_j\right) < 0. \quad (13)$$

Equation (13) shows that the matrix induced by the function EQ2 can be embedded in the class of 9-dimensional half spaces. According to Theorem 9, there must be a probabilistic communication protocol that uses at most 5 bits of communication.

We refer to the protocol for function EQ2 as the EQ2-protocol in what follows. Now that we have the EQ2-protocol (exchanging at most 5 bits), we are ready to introduce our protocol for the matrix F'_n:

[2] While the model of Paturi and Simon require inputs to both processors to be of the same length, we may assume that P_0 is given two l-bit numbers, and ignores one of them in its computation.

Protocol 2

1. Processor P_0 sends the values of x_1 and x_2 to processor P_1.
2. Given x_1, x_2, y_1, y_2, y_3, Processor P_1 solves equation (12) for x_3 and finds (at most) two solutions. If no solutions exist, output 0. Otherwise, denote the solutions by z and z'. Processor P_1 informs P_0 whether $z = z'$ or $z \neq z'$ (one bit).
3. If $z = z'$, the processors run the EQ-protocol such as to check whether $x_3 = z$. If $z \neq z'$, the processors run the EQ2-protocol such as to check whether $x_3 = z$ or $x_3 = z'$. They output the same bit as the EQ-protocol or the EQ2-protocol, respectively, does.

Theorem 11. *Protocol 2 is a probabilistic communication protocol for the matrix F'_n, and uses $6 + 2\lceil\log(p)\rceil = (2/3)\log n + O(1)$ bits of communication.*

Proof. The communication complexity of Protocol 2 is immediate: Processor P_0 sends x_1 and x_2, which are both elements of GF(p) and therefore require $\lceil\log(p)\rceil$ bits each. Processor P_1 sends one bit in order to inform P_0 of whether $z = z'$ or not. Afterwards, the processors either run the EQ-protocol (at the expense of 2 bits) or the EQ2-protocol (at the expense of 5 bits). This sums up to at most $6 + 2\lceil\log(p)\rceil$ bits of communication.

The correctness of the protocol is also immediate. Equation (12), solved by P_1 in step 2 of the protocol, coincides with the equation that was used to define the 1-entries of the matrix F'_n.

Again, a slight modification of the protocol may be used for matrices in $\mathcal{F}_{3\times3}(n)$ that had some of their 1-entries flipped to 0:
Either P_1 knows, after receiving x_1 and x_2, that the result is 0 (if all solutions to the equation of step 2 correspond to entries that have been flipped to 0), or it knows that one of the two possible solutions to this equation (say, w.l.o.g., z'), corresponds to an entry that was flipped to 0. In the latter case, the EQ-protocol can be used to check whether $x_3 = z$.
It follows that each matrix of the family $\mathcal{F}_{3,3}(n)$ can be computed by a protocol that exchanges $(2/3)\log n + O(1)$ bits. According to Theorem 9, each matrix from the family $\mathcal{F}_{3,3}(n)$ can be embedded into half spaces of dimension $O(n^{2/3})$. Theorem 7 immediately follows.

References

1. N. Alon, P. Frankl, and V. Rödl. Geometrical realization of set systems and probabilistic communication complexity. In *Proceedings of the 26th Symposium on Foundations of Computer Science*, pages 277–280. IEEE Computer Society Press, 1985.
2. Rosa I. Arriaga and Santosh Vempala. An algorithmic theory of learning: Robust concepts and random projection. In *Proceedings of the 40'th Annual Symposium on the Foundations of Computer Science*, pages 616–623, 1999.
3. Béla Bollobás. *Extremal Graph Theory.* Academic Press, 1978.

4. Juergen Forster. A linear bound on the unbounded error probabilistic communication complexity. In *Proceedings of the 16th Annual Conference on Computational Complexity*. IEEE Computer Society Press, 2001. To appear.
5. Juergen Forster, Niels Schmitt, and Hans Ulrich Simon. Estimating the optimal margins of embeddings in Euclidean half spaces. This proceedings.
6. Yoav Freund and Robert Schapire. Large margin classification using the perceptron algorithm. *Machine Learning*, 37(3):277–296, 1999.
7. Llew Mason, Peter L. Bartlett, and Jonathan Baxter. Improved generalization through explicit optimization of margins. *Machine Learning*, 38(3):243–255, 2000.
8. Marvin L. Minsky and Seymour A. Papert. *Perceptrons*. The MIT Press, Cambrigde MA, third edition, 1988.
9. A. B. J. Novikoff. On convergence proofs for perceptrons. In *Proceedings of the Symposium of Mathematical Theory of Automata*, pages 615–622, 1962.
10. Ramamohan Paturi and Janos Simon. Probabilistic communication complexity. *Journal of Computer and System Sciences*, 33(1):106–123, 1986.
11. F. Rosenblatt. The perceptron: A probabilistic model for information storage and organization in the brain. *Psych. Rev.*, 65:386–407, 1958.
12. F. Rosenblatt. *Principles and Neurodynamics: Perceptrons and the Theory of Brain Mechanisms*. Spartan Books, Washington, D.C., 1962.
13. Vladimir Vapnik. *Statistical Learning Theory*. Wiley Series on Adaptive and Learning Systems for Signal Processing, Communications, and Control. John Wiley & Sons, 1998.
14. K. Zarankiewicz. Problem P 101. *Colloq. Math.*, 2:301, 1951.

Estimating the Optimal Margins of Embeddings in Euclidean Half Spaces

Jürgen Forster, Niels Schmitt, and Hans Ulrich Simon

Lehrstuhl Mathematik & Informatik, Fakultät für Mathematik,
Ruhr-Universität Bochum, 44780 Bochum, Germany
{forster,nschmitt,simon}@lmi.ruhr-uni-bochum.de

Abstract. Concept classes can canonically be represented by matrices with entries 1 and -1. We use the singular value decomposition of this matrix to determine the optimal margins of embeddings of the concept classes of singletons and of half intervals in homogeneous Euclidean half spaces. For these concept classes the singular value decomposition can be used to construct optimal embeddings and also to prove the corresponding best possible upper bounds on the margin. We show that the optimal margin for embedding n singletons is $\frac{n}{3n-4}$ and that the optimal margin for half intervals over $\{1,\ldots,n\}$ is $\frac{\pi}{2\ln n} + \Theta\left(\frac{1}{(\ln n)^2}\right)$. For the upper bounds on the margins we generalize a bound given in [6]. We also discuss the concept classes of monomials to point out limitations of our approach.

1 Introduction

Recently there has been a lot of interest in maximal margin classifiers. Learning algorithms that calculate the hyperplane with the largest margin on a sample and use this hyperplane to classify new instances have shown excellent empirical performance (see [5]). Often the instances are mapped (implicitly when a kernel function is used) to some possibly high dimensional space before the hyperplane with maximal margin is calculated. If the norms of the instances are bounded and a hyperplane with large margin can be found, a bound on the VC-dimension can be applied (Vapnik [12]; [5], Theorem 4.16). A small VC-dimension means that a concept class can be learned with a small sample (Vapnik and Chervonenkis [13]; Blumer et. al. [4]; [8], Theorem 3.3).

The success of maximal margin classifiers raises the question which concept classes can be embedded in half spaces with a large margin. For every concept class there is a trivial embedding into half spaces. Ben-David, Eiron and Simon [2] show that most concept classes cannot be embedded with a margin that is much larger than the trivial margin. They use counting arguments that do not give upper bounds on the margins of particular concept classes. Vapnik [12] also showed an upper bound on the margin in terms of the VC-dimension. A stronger result was shown by Forster [6]: A concept class $\mathcal{C}$ over an instance space X can be represented by the matrix $M \in \{-1,1\}^{X\times\mathcal{C}}$ for which the entry M_{xc} is 1

D. Helmbold and B. Williamson (Eds.): COLT/EuroCOLT 2001, LNAI 2111, pp. 402–415, 2001.

if $x \in c$ and -1 otherwise. He showed that a concept class $(X, \mathcal{C})$ can only be embedded in homogeneous half spaces with margin at most $\frac{\|M\|}{\sqrt{|X|\,|Y|}}$, where $\|M\|$ denotes the operator norm of M. It is not hard to see that for every matrix $M \in \{-1,1\}^{X \times Y}$:

$$\max(\sqrt{|X|}, \sqrt{|Y|}) \leq \|M\| \leq \sqrt{|X|\,|Y|} \ .$$

(See for example Krause [9], Lemma 1.1.) The equality $\|M\| = \sqrt{|Y|}$ holds if and only if the rows of M are orthogonal, $\|M\| = \sqrt{|X|}$ holds if and only if the columns of M are orthogonal, and $\|M\| = \sqrt{|X|\,|Y|}$ holds if and only if $\text{rank}(M) = 1$. The Hadamard matrices $H_n \in \mathbb{R}^{2^n \times 2^n}$ are examples of matrices with orthogonal rows and columns. They are recursively defined by

$$H_0 = 1 \ , \qquad H_{n+1} = \begin{pmatrix} H_n & H_n \\ H_n & -H_n \end{pmatrix} \ .$$

From the upper bound $\frac{\|M\|}{\sqrt{|X|\,|Y|}}$ on the margin it follows easily that for the concept classes for which the matrix M has orthogonal rows or orthogonal columns the trivial embedding has the optimal margin.

In this paper we give a straightforward generalization of Forster's result to the case where the entries of the matrix M can be arbitrary real numbers. For finite sets X, Y we say that a matrix $M \in \mathbb{R}^{X \times Y}$ can be realized by an arrangement of homogeneous half spaces with margin γ if there are vectors u_x, v_y for $x \in X$, $y \in Y$ that lie in the unit ball of some $\mathbb{R}^k$ (where k can be arbitrarily large) such that M_{xy} and $\langle u_x, v_y \rangle$ have the same sign and $|\langle u_x, v_y \rangle| \geq \gamma$ for all $x \in X$, $y \in Y$.

A vector v_y can be interpreted as a normal vector of the boundary of the homogeneous half space $\{z \in \mathbb{R}^k \mid \langle v_y, z \rangle \geq 0\}$. Then $\langle u_x, v_y \rangle > 0$ means that the vector u_x lies in the interior of this half space. The sign of M_{xy} determines whether u_x must lie in the half space or not. The requirement $|\langle u_x, v_y \rangle| \geq \gamma$ means that the point u_x has distance at least γ from the boundary of the half space. Analogously we can interpret the vectors u_x as normal vectors of half spaces and the vectors v_y as points.

It is crucial that we require the vectors to lie in a unit ball (or that they are bounded) because otherwise we could increase the margin by simply stretching all vectors. Note that it is not really a restriction to assume that the half spaces are homogeneous: There is a standard way to transform an embedding with inhomogeneous half spaces into an embedding with homogeneous half spaces that has at least half the old margin.

For every matrix $M \in \mathbb{R}^{X \times Y}$ there exists an optimal embedding: We can assume without loss of generality that the vectors of any embedding lie in the unit ball of $\mathbb{R}^X$. (Because the linear span of the vectors u_x has dimension at most $|X|$ and we can project the vectors v_y to this span without changing the scalar products $\langle u_x, v_y \rangle$.) The margin of the embedding is continuous in the vectors u_x, v_y, and the unit ball of $\mathbb{R}^X$ is compact. Thus the maximal margin is attained.

We introduce a new tool from functional analysis, the singular value decomposition, to estimate the optimal margins of concept classes. The singular value decomposition can not only be used to construct embeddings, but also to show upper bounds on the margins of all embeddings. We show that for two types of concept classes, namely singletons and half intervals, our techniques can be used to calculate the best possible margins exactly. However, we also show that these techniques fail for the concept classes of monomials.

The paper is organized as follows: In Section 2 we fix some notation for the rest of the paper. In Section 3 we show that a matrix $M \in \mathrm{IR}^{X \times Y}$ can only be embedded in homogeneous half spaces with margin at most $\frac{\|M\|\sqrt{|X|}}{\sqrt{\sum_{y \in Y}\left(\sum_{x \in X}|M_{xy}|\right)^2}}$. In Section 4 we show how the singular value decomposition can be used to apply the upper bound from Section 3. In Sections 5 and 6 we use the results from the previous sections to calculate the optimal margins for the concept classes of singletons and of half intervals. In Section 7 we discuss the concept class of monomials.

2 Notation

For a finite set X, IR^X is the vector space of real functions ("vectors") on X. The Euclidean norm of a vector $a \in \mathrm{IR}^X$ is $\|a\|_2 := \sqrt{\sum_{x \in X} a_x^2}$, the supremum norm is $\|a\|_\infty := \max_{x \in X} |a_x|$. As usual we write $\mathrm{IR}^n = \mathrm{IR}^{\{1,\ldots,n\}}$. The vectors $x \in \mathrm{IR}^n$ are column vectors. For two finite sets X, Y we write $\mathrm{IR}^{X \times Y}$ for the set of real matrices with rows indexed by the elements of X and columns indexed by the elements of Y. The transposition of a matrix $A \in \mathrm{IR}^{X \times Y}$ is denoted by $A^\top \in \mathrm{IR}^{Y \times X}$. For $x \in X$ we define $e_x \in \mathrm{IR}^X$ to be the canonical base of IR^X for which

$$(e_x)_y = \begin{cases} 1 \ , & x = y \ , \\ 0 \ , & x \neq y \ , \end{cases}$$

for $y \in X$. For a complex vector $x \in \mathbb{C}^n$, $\bar{x}$ is the complex conjugate and x^* the complex conjugate transpose of x. I_X is the identity matrix. A nonsingular matrix $A \in \mathrm{IR}^{X \times X}$ is called orthogonal if $A^{-1} = A^\top$. The operator norm of a matrix $A \in \mathrm{IR}^{X \times Y}$ is

$$\|A\| = \sup_{\substack{x \in \mathrm{IR}^X \\ \|x\| \leq 1}} \|Ax\| = \max_{\substack{x \in \mathrm{IR}^X \\ \|x\| \leq 1}} \|Ax\| \ .$$

The supremum is attained because $\|Ax\|$ is a continuous function of x and the unit ball $\{x \in \mathrm{IR}^X \mid \|x\| \leq 1\}$ is compact. It is well know that $\|A\|^2 = \|A^\top A\| = \|AA^\top\|$ for any matrix $A \in \mathrm{IR}^{X \times Y}$.

The signum function sign : $\mathrm{IR} \to \mathrm{IR}$ is given by

$$\mathrm{sign}(x) = \begin{cases} 1 \ , & x > 0 \ , \\ 0 \ , & x = 0 \ , \\ -1 \ , & x < 0 \ . \end{cases}$$

3 An Upper Bound on the Margins of Embeddings

It was previously known that the margin of any embedding of a matrix $M \in \{-1,1\}^{X\times Y}$ in homogeneous Euclidean half spaces is at most $\frac{\|M\|}{\sqrt{|X||Y|}}$ (see Forster [6], Theorem 3). In Theorem 1 we prove a straightforward generalization of this result to matrices $M \in \mathbb{R}^{X\times Y}$ with arbitrary entries.

In the proof of Theorem 1 we will use the following simple fact: For any two symmetric positive semi-definite matrices $A, B \in \mathbb{R}^{X\times X}$ the sum of the products of the entries is nonnegative. This can be seen as follows. Because of the Spectral Theorem there are eigenvectors $d_1, \ldots, d_{|X|} \in \mathbb{R}^X$ and eigenvalues $\lambda_1, \ldots, \lambda_{|X|} \geq 0$ of A such that $A = \sum_{i=1}^{|X|} \lambda_i d_i d_i^\top$. It follows that

$$\sum_{x,\tilde{x}\in X} A_{x\tilde{x}} B_{x\tilde{x}} = \sum_{x,\tilde{x}\in X} \sum_{i=1}^{|X|} \lambda_i (d_i)_x (d_i)_{\tilde{x}} B_{x\tilde{x}} = \sum_{i=1}^{|X|} \underbrace{\lambda_i}_{\geq 0} \underbrace{d_i^\top B d_i}_{\geq 0} \geq 0 \ .$$

Theorem 1. *Let $M \in \mathbb{R}^{X\times Y}$ be a matrix. Any embedding (in the sense described in Section 1) of M in homogeneous Euclidean half spaces has margin at most*

$$\frac{\sqrt{|X|}\,\|M\|}{\sqrt{\sum_{y\in Y}\left(\sum_{x\in X}|M_{xy}|\right)^2}} \ .$$

Proof. Let an embedding u_x, v_y of M with margin γ be given. For every $y \in Y$ we have that

$$\gamma \sum_{x\in X} |M_{xy}| \leq \sum_{x\in X} M_{xy} \langle u_x, v_y\rangle = \left\langle \sum_{x\in X} M_{xy} u_x, v_y \right\rangle \overset{\|v_y\|\leq 1}{\leq} \left\| \sum_{x\in X} M_{xy} u_x \right\| \ . \tag{1}$$

We square this inequality and sum over $y \in Y$:

$$\begin{aligned} \gamma^2 \sum_{y\in Y} \left(\sum_{x\in X} |M_{xy}|\right)^2 &\overset{(1)}{\leq} \sum_{y\in Y} \left\| \sum_{x\in X} M_{xy} u_x \right\|^2 \\ &= \sum_{y\in Y} \sum_{x,\tilde{x}\in X} M_{xy} \cdot M_{\tilde{x}y} \cdot \langle u_x, u_{\tilde{x}}\rangle = \sum_{x,\tilde{x}\in X} \left(MM^\top\right)_{x\tilde{x}} \langle u_x, u_{\tilde{x}}\rangle \\ &\overset{(*)}{\leq} \sum_{x,\tilde{x}\in X} \left(\|M\|^2 I_X\right)_{x\tilde{x}} \langle u_x, u_{\tilde{x}}\rangle = \|M\|^2 \sum_{x\in X} \|u_x\|^2 \leq |X|\,\|M\|^2 \ . \end{aligned}$$

Here inequality $(*)$ holds because $A := \|M\|^2 I_X - MM^\top$ and $B := (\langle u_x, u_{\tilde{x}}\rangle)_{x,\tilde{x}\in X}$ are symmetric positive semi-definite matrices, i.e. $\sum_{x,\tilde{x}\in X} A_{x\tilde{x}} B_{x\tilde{x}} \geq 0$. □

If we apply Theorem 1 to a matrix $M \in \{-1,1\}^{X\times Y}$ with entries -1 and 1 we get the upper bound $\frac{\|M\|}{\sqrt{|X|\,|Y|}}$ from Forster [6], Theorem 3. For an arbitrary matrix $M \in \mathbb{R}^{X \times Y}$ we also get the upper bound

$$\frac{\sqrt{|Y|}\,\|M\|}{\sqrt{\sum_{x\in X}\left(\sum_{y\in Y}|M_{xy}|\right)^2}}$$

on the margin if we apply Theorem 1 to $M^\top$.

4 The Singular Value Decomposition

The problem of embedding a matrix $M \in \mathbb{R}^{X \times Y}$ in Euclidean half spaces with a large margin can be stated as follows: We are looking for two matrices B, C with rows of norm 1 such that the signs of the entries of $BC^\top$ are equal to the signs of the entries of M, and such that the smallest absolute value of the entries of $BC^\top$ is as large as possible.

One possibility of writing M as a product of matrices is the *singular value decomposition* of M: Let r be the rank of M. Then there always exist matrices $U \in \mathbb{R}^{X \times r}$ and $V \in \mathbb{R}^{Y \times r}$ with orthonormal columns and nonnegative numbers $s_1, \ldots, s_r$, called the *singular values* of M, such that $M = U\mathrm{diag}(s_1, \ldots, s_r)V^\top$ (see [7].) Obviously the matrices

$$B = U\mathrm{diag}(\sqrt{s_1}, \ldots, \sqrt{s_r}) \ , \quad C = V\mathrm{diag}(\sqrt{s_1}, \ldots, \sqrt{s_r})$$

satisfy $M = BC^\top$. If we normalize the rows of B and C we get an embedding of M. Surprisingly, we can show that for the concept classes of singletons and of half intervals this embedding has the best possible margin. For both of these concept classes we can also use the singular value decomposition to show the optimal upper bound on the margin: We can simply apply Theorem 1 to the matrix $UV^\top$. Trying this matrix can be a good idea because it is orthogonal, which means that all its singular values are equal, they are "optimally balanced". Of course we have to check that the entries of $UV^\top$ have correct signs, since this is not true for all matrices M.

Theorem 2. *Let $M \in \{-1,1\}^{X \times Y}$ be a matrix with singular value decomposition $U\mathrm{diag}(s_1, \ldots, s_r)V^\top$. Let $\hat{u}$, $\hat{v}$ be the vectors whose entries are the squared Euclidean norms of the rows of the matrices $U\mathrm{diag}(\sqrt{s_1}, \ldots, \sqrt{s_r})$ and $V\mathrm{diag}(\sqrt{s_1}, \ldots, \sqrt{s_r})$, i.e.*

$$\hat{u} := \left(\sum_{j=1}^{r} s_j U_{xj}^2\right)_{x\in X} \in \mathbb{R}^X \ , \qquad \hat{v} := \left(\sum_{j=1}^{r} s_j V_{yj}^2\right)_{y\in Y} \in \mathbb{R}^Y \ .$$

Then the embedding

$$u_x := \frac{1}{\sqrt{\hat{u}_x}}(\sqrt{s_j}U_{xj})_{j=1,\ldots,r} \in \mathbb{R}^r \ , \qquad x \in X \ ,$$

$$v_y := \frac{1}{\sqrt{\hat{v}_y}}(\sqrt{s_j}V_{yj})_{j=1,\ldots,r} \in \mathbb{R}^r \ , \qquad y \in Y \ ,$$

of the matrix M has margin

$$\frac{1}{\sqrt{\|\hat{u}\|_\infty \|\hat{v}\|_\infty}} \leq \frac{\sqrt{|X|\,|Y|}}{\sum_{j=1}^r s_j} \ . \tag{2}$$

If the entries of M and of $UV^\top$ have the same signs, then every embedding of M in homogeneous Euclidean half spaces has margin at most

$$\min\left(\frac{\sqrt{|X|}}{\|\hat{v}\|_2}, \frac{\sqrt{|Y|}}{\|\hat{u}\|_2}\right) \leq \frac{\sqrt{|X||Y|}}{\sum_{j=1}^r s_j} \ . \tag{3}$$

If additionally all norms of the rows of $U\mathrm{diag}(\sqrt{s_1},\ldots,\sqrt{s_r})$ and all norms of the rows of $V\mathrm{diag}(\sqrt{s_1},\ldots,\sqrt{s_r})$ are equal, then the above embedding of M that uses the singular value decomposition of M has margin

$$\frac{1}{\sqrt{\|\hat{u}\|_\infty \|\hat{v}\|_\infty}} = \frac{\sqrt{|X|\,|Y|}}{\sum_{j=1}^r s_j} \ ,$$

and this margin is optimal.

Proof. Obviously $\|u_x\| = 1 = \|v_y\|$ holds, and from $\langle u_x, v_y\rangle = \frac{M_{xy}}{\sqrt{\hat{u}_x \hat{v}_y}}$ it follows that the margin of the embedding is $1/\sqrt{\|\hat{u}\|_\infty \|\hat{v}\|_\infty}$. The upper bound $\sqrt{|X|}/\|\hat{v}\|_2$ on the margin follows if we apply Theorem 1 to the matrix $UV^\top$ because $\|UV^\top\| \leq \|U\|\|V\| = 1$ and because of

$$\begin{aligned}\sum_{x\in X} |(UV^\top)_{xy}| &= \sum_{x\in X} M_{xy}(UV^\top)_{xy} \\ &= \sum_{x\in X}\sum_{j=1}^r s_j U_{xj}V_{yj}\sum_{k=1}^r U_{xk}V_{yk} = \sum_{j=1}^r s_j V_{yj}^2 = \hat{v}_y \ .\end{aligned}$$

Here the first equality holds because the entries of M and $UV^\top$ have the same signs, for the second equality we used that $M = U\mathrm{diag}(s_1,\ldots,s_r)V^\top$, and for the third equality we used that the rows of U are orthonormal. Both the sum of the components of $\hat{u}$ and the sum of those of $\hat{v}$ are equal to $\sum_{j=1}^r s_j$. From this it follows that

$$\begin{aligned}\|\hat{u}\|_2 &\geq \frac{\sum_{j=1}^r s_j}{\sqrt{|X|}} \ , \quad \|\hat{v}\|_2 \geq \frac{\sum_{j=1}^r s_j}{\sqrt{|Y|}} \ , \\ \|\hat{u}\|_\infty &\geq \frac{\sum_{j=1}^r s_j}{|X|} \ , \quad \|\hat{v}\|_\infty \geq \frac{\sum_{j=1}^r s_j}{|Y|} \ ,\end{aligned}$$

and this implies the inequalities in (2) and (3). If all the components of $\hat{u}$ are equal and all the components of $\hat{v}$ are equal, then equality holds in (2) and (3).

□

It is easy to see that Theorem 2 gives an embedding with optimal margin for matrices that have orthogonal rows or orthogonal columns. Note that it was already observed by Forster [6] that the margin of the trivial embedding is optimal in this case. In the following two sections we show that Theorem 2 can also be used to construct optimal embeddings for the concept classes of singletons and of half intervals.

5 The Optimal Margins of Singleton Concept Classes

Given a parameter $n \in \mathbb{N}$, we look at the concept class of singletons. It has the matrix

$$\mathrm{SINGLETONS}_n = \begin{pmatrix} 1 & -1 & \cdots & -1 \\ -1 & \ddots & \ddots & \vdots \\ \vdots & \ddots & \ddots & -1 \\ -1 & \cdots & -1 & 1 \end{pmatrix} \in \{-1,1\}^{n \times n} \ .$$

It is obvious that this matrix can be embedded with constant margin: We can get an embedding in inhomogeneous half spaces if we choose the points to be the canonical unit vectors of $\mathbb{R}^n$ and choose the half spaces that have the the canonical unit vectors as normal vectors and that have thresholds $\frac{1}{2}$. This leads to a margin of $\frac{1}{2}$. Ben-David, Eiron and Simon [3] observed that the optimal margin that can be achieved with inhomogeneous half spaces is $\frac{1}{2} + \frac{1}{2n}$.

We show that Theorem 2 can be used to calculate the optimal margin for embeddings with homogeneous half spaces. The matrix $\mathrm{SINGLETONS}_n$ is symmetric and has the eigenvalue 2 with eigenspace $\mathrm{null}(M - 2I_n) = \{x \in \mathbb{R}^n \mid \sum_{k=1}^n x_k = 0\}$ and the eigenvalue $2-n$ with eigenvector $(1,\dots,1)^\top$. The eigenvectors

$$a_j = \frac{1}{\sqrt{j^2+j}}(\underbrace{1,\dots,1}_{j \text{ times}}, -j, 0, \dots, 0)^\top \ , \qquad j = 1,\dots,n-1 \ ,$$

$$a_n = \frac{1}{\sqrt{n}}(1,\dots,1)^\top \ ,$$

of M give an orthonormal basis of $\mathbb{R}^n$. From this it follows that a singular value decomposition of M is given by

$$\underbrace{\begin{pmatrix} a_1 & \cdots & a_n \end{pmatrix}}_{U} \underbrace{\mathrm{diag}(2,\dots,2,n-2)}_{\mathrm{diag}(s_1,\dots,s_n)} \underbrace{\begin{pmatrix} a_1 & \cdots & a_{n-1} & -a_n \end{pmatrix}^\top}_{V}$$

(to check this we can apply the above to the vectors $a_1,\dots,a_n$.) Obviously the entries of

$$UV^\top = \frac{1}{2}M + \left(\frac{n}{2} - 2\right) a_n a_n^\top = \begin{pmatrix} 1-\frac{2}{n} & -\frac{2}{n} & \cdots & -\frac{2}{n} \\ -\frac{2}{n} & \ddots & \ddots & \vdots \\ \vdots & \ddots & \ddots & -\frac{2}{n} \\ -\frac{2}{n} & \cdots & -\frac{2}{n} & 1-\frac{2}{n} \end{pmatrix}$$

have the same signs as the corresponding entries of SINGLETONS_n and we can apply Theorem 2. From

$$\sum_{j=1}^{r} s_j U_{kj}^2 = \sum_{j=1}^{r} s_j V_{kj}^2 = 2 - \frac{2}{k} + 2 \underbrace{\sum_{j=k}^{n-1} \overbrace{\frac{1}{j(j+1)}}^{=\frac{1}{j}-\frac{1}{j+1}}}_{=\frac{1}{k}-\frac{1}{n}} + 1 - \frac{2}{n} = 3 - \frac{4}{n} = \frac{3n-4}{n}$$

for $k = 1, \ldots, n$ it follows that

Theorem 3. *The maximal margin of a realization of the matrix* SINGLETONS_n *with homogeneous Euclidean half spaces is*

$$\frac{n}{3n-4} = \frac{1}{3} + \frac{4}{9n-12} = \frac{1}{3} + \Theta\left(\frac{1}{n}\right) .$$

6 The Optimal Margins of Half Interval Concept Classes

For a parameter $n \in \mathbb{N}$, the concept class of half intervals has the following matrix:

$$\text{HALF-INTERVALS}_n = \begin{pmatrix} 1 & -1 & \cdots & -1 \\ \vdots & \ddots & \ddots & \vdots \\ \vdots & & \ddots & -1 \\ 1 & \cdots & \cdots & 1 \end{pmatrix} \in \{-1, 1\}^{n \times n} .$$

As observed by Ben-David [1], we can use Novikoff's Theorem [11] to get an upper bound on the margins of embeddings of this matrix in half spaces: If we have an embedding with margin γ, then it follows from Novikoff's Theorem that the concept class can be learned with at most γ^{-2} EQ-queries. The learning complexity of HALF-INTERVALS_n with arbitrary EQ-queries is $\lfloor \log_2 n \rfloor$ (see Maass and Turan [10], Proposition 4.2.) This shows that $\gamma^{-2} \geq \lfloor \log_2 n \rfloor$, or equivalently $\gamma \leq \frac{1}{\sqrt{\lfloor \log_2 n \rfloor}}$.

We can show a much stronger result: From Theorem 2 we get an exact formula for the optimal margin. In the following we consider only the case that n is even, but the case n odd is very similar.

We start by calculating the complex eigenvalues and eigenspaces of $M = \text{HALF-INTERVALS}_n$. Let μ be a complex root of -1, i.e. $\mu \in \mathbb{C}$, $\mu^n = -1$. Then the vector $x_\mu := (\mu^{k-1})_{k=1,\ldots,n} \in \mathbb{C}^n$ is an eigenvector of M for the eigenvalue $\frac{2\mu}{\mu-1}$:

$$Mx_\mu = \left(\sum_{j=1}^{k} \mu^{j-1} - \sum_{j=k+1}^{n} \mu^{j-1} \right)_{k=1,\ldots,n} = \left(\frac{1-\mu^k}{1-\mu} - \frac{\mu^k+1}{1-\mu} \right)_{k=1,\ldots,n}$$

$$= \left(\frac{-2\mu^k}{1-\mu} \right)_{k=1,\ldots,n} = \frac{2\mu}{\mu-1} x_\mu .$$

Because the eigenvectors x_μ are pairwise orthogonal and because of $\|x_\mu\|^2 = n$ this means that we can write M as

$$M = \sum_{\mu \in \mathbb{C}:\mu^n=-1} \frac{2\mu}{n(\mu-1)} x_\mu x_\mu^* \ .$$

(To check this we can apply the above to the vectors x_μ for the n complex roots μ of -1.) Now the entries of M can be written as

$$\begin{aligned}
M_{jk} &= \frac{2}{n} \sum_{\mu \in \mathbb{C}:\mu^n=-1} \frac{\mu}{\mu-1} \mu^{j-1} \mu^{1-k} = \frac{2}{n} \sum_{\mu \in \mathbb{C}:\mu^n=-1} \frac{\mu^{j-k+1}}{\mu-1} \\
&\overset{\mu=e^{i\pi(2l-1)/n}}{=} \frac{2}{n} \sum_{l=1}^{n} \frac{e^{i\pi(2l-1)(j-k+1)/n}}{e^{i\pi(2l-1)/n}-1} \\
&= \frac{2}{n} \sum_{l=1}^{n/2} \left(\frac{e^{i\pi(2l-1)(j-k+1)/n}}{e^{i\pi(2l-1)/n}-1} + \frac{e^{-i\pi(2l-1)(j-k+1)/n}}{e^{-i\pi(2l-1)/n}-1} \right) \\
&= \frac{2}{n} \sum_{l=1}^{n/2} \frac{e^{i\pi(2l-1)(2j-2k+1)/2n} - e^{-i\pi(2l-1)(2j-2k+1)/2n}}{e^{i\pi(2l-1)/2n} - e^{-i\pi(2l-1)/2n}} \\
&= \frac{2}{n} \sum_{l=1}^{n/2} \frac{\sin \frac{\pi(2l-1)(2j-2k+1)}{2n}}{\sin \frac{\pi(2l-1)}{2n}} \\
&= \frac{2}{n} \sum_{l=1}^{n/2} \left(\sin \frac{\pi(2l-1)}{2n} \right)^{-1} \left(\sin \frac{\pi(2l-1)j}{n} \cos \frac{\pi(2l-1)(2k-1)}{2n} \right. \\
&\qquad \left. - \cos \frac{\pi(2l-1)j}{n} \sin \frac{\pi(2l-1)(2k-1)}{2n} \right) .
\end{aligned}$$

Thus we can write $M = UDV^\top$, where $U, D, V \in \mathbb{R}^{n \times n}$ are given by

$$\begin{aligned}
U &= \left(\sqrt{\frac{2}{n}} \sin \frac{\pi(2l-1)j}{n} \ ; \ \sqrt{\frac{2}{n}} \cos \frac{\pi(2l-1)j}{n} \right)_{\substack{j=1,\dots,n \\ l=1,\dots,n/2}} \\
D &= \operatorname{diag} \left(\left(\sin \frac{\pi(2l-1)}{2n} \right)^{-1} , \left(\sin \frac{\pi(2l-1)}{2n} \right)^{-1} \right)_{l=1,\dots,n/2} \\
V &= \left(\sqrt{\frac{2}{n}} \cos \frac{\pi(2l-1)(2k-1)}{2n} \ ; \ -\sqrt{\frac{2}{n}} \sin \frac{\pi(2l-1)(2k-1)}{2n} \right)_{\substack{k=1,\dots,n \\ l=1,\dots,n/2}} .
\end{aligned}$$

It is not hard to check that the rows of U and V are orthonormal, i.e. $UDV^\top$ is a singular value decomposition of M. The entries of $UV^\top$ have the same signs as those of HALF-INTERVALS$_n$, because for all $j, k \in \{1, \dots, n\}$ (for shortness let $\alpha := \frac{\pi(2j-2k+1)}{2n}$):

$$(UV^\top)_{jk} = \frac{2}{n}\sum_{l=1}^{n/2}\left(\sin\frac{\pi(2l-1)j}{n}\cos\frac{\pi(2l-1)(2k-1)}{2n} - \cos\frac{\pi(2l-1)j}{n}\sin\frac{\pi(2l-1)(2k-1)}{2n}\right)$$

$$= \frac{2}{n}\sum_{l=1}^{n/2}\underbrace{\sin\left(\frac{\pi(2l-1)(2j-2k+1)}{2n}\right)}_{=\mathrm{Im}(\exp(i(2l-1)\alpha))} = \frac{2}{n}\mathrm{Im}\left(e^{i\alpha}\sum_{l=0}^{n/2-1}\left(e^{2i\alpha}\right)^l\right)$$

$$= \frac{2}{n}\mathrm{Im}\left(\underbrace{\frac{e^{i\alpha}}{1-e^{2i\alpha}}}_{=\frac{1}{e^{-i\alpha}-e^{i\alpha}}=\frac{i}{2\sin\alpha}}(1-\underbrace{e^{in\alpha}}_{=\pm i})\right) = \frac{1}{n\sin\alpha}\ .$$

is positive if and only if $j \geq k$. Now we can apply Theorem 2, and because the sums

$$\sum_{l=1}^{n} D_{ll}U_{jl}^2 = \sum_{l=1}^{n} D_{ll}V_{kl}^2 = \frac{1}{n}\sum_{l=1}^{n} D_{ll}$$

are equal for all j, k (the above equalities follow immediately from the special structure of the matrices U, D, V) we get

Theorem 4. *The maximal margin of a realization of the concept class of half intervals with matrix HALF-INTERVALS$_n$ in Euclidean homogeneous half spaces is*

$$n\left(\sum_{l=1}^{n}\left(\sin\frac{\pi(2l-1)}{2n}\right)^{-1}\right)^{-1} = \frac{\pi}{2\ln n} + \Theta\left(\frac{1}{(\ln n)^2}\right)\ .$$

Proof. We still have to show that the optimal margin is asymptotically $\frac{\pi}{2\ln n}$. We use that $\sin\frac{\pi}{2n} \geq \frac{1}{n}$ for all positive integers n. (This follows from the concavity of the sine function on $[0, \pi/2]$.) Because of

$$2\sum_{l=1}^{n/2}\left(\sin\frac{\pi(2l-1)}{2n}\right)^{-1} \leq \underbrace{\frac{2}{\sin\frac{\pi}{2n}}}_{\leq 2n} + 2\int_1^{n/2}\left(\sin\frac{\pi(2x-1)}{2n}\right)^{-1}dx$$

$$\overset{y=\frac{\pi(2x-1)}{2n}}{\leq} \frac{2n}{\pi}\int_{\frac{\pi}{2n}}^{\frac{\pi}{2}-\frac{\pi}{2n}}\frac{1}{\sin x}\,dx + 2n = \frac{2n}{\pi}\left[\ln\frac{\sin x}{1+\cos x}\right]_{\frac{\pi}{2n}}^{\frac{\pi}{2}-\frac{\pi}{2n}} + 2n$$

$$= \frac{2n}{\pi}\left(\ln\underbrace{\frac{\cos\frac{\pi}{2n}}{1+\sin\frac{\pi}{2n}}}_{\leq 1} - \ln\underbrace{\frac{\sin\frac{\pi}{2n}}{1+\cos\frac{\pi}{2n}}}_{\geq\frac{1}{2n}}\right) + 2n \leq \frac{2n}{\pi}\ln(2n) + 2n$$

the optimal margin is at least $\left(\frac{2}{\pi}\ln(2n)+2\right)^{-1}$. Because of

$$
\begin{aligned}
2\sum_{l=1}^{n/2}\left(\sin\frac{\pi(2l-1)}{2n}\right)^{-1} &\geq 2\int_1^{(n+1)/2}\left(\sin\frac{\pi(2x-1)}{2n}\right)^{-1}dx \\
&\overset{y=\frac{\pi(2x-1)}{2n}}{=} \frac{2n}{\pi}\int_{\frac{\pi}{2n}}^{\frac{\pi}{2}}\frac{1}{\sin x}\,dx = \frac{2n}{\pi}\left[\ln\frac{\sin x}{1+\cos x}\right]_{\frac{\pi}{2n}}^{\frac{\pi}{2}} \\
&= -\frac{2n}{\pi}\ln\underbrace{\frac{\sin\frac{\pi}{2n}}{1+\cos\frac{\pi}{2n}}}_{\leq\frac{\pi}{2n}} \geq \frac{2n}{\pi}\ln\frac{2n}{\pi}
\end{aligned}
$$

the optimal margin is at most $\left(\frac{2}{\pi}\ln\frac{2n}{\pi}\right)^{-1}$. □

7 Monomials

For the concept class of monomials over n Boolean variables $x_1,\ldots,x_n$ the instances are all possible assignments to these variables and the concepts are all conjunctions of the literals $x_1,\neg x_1,\ldots,x_n,\neg x_n$. The matrix MONOMIALS$_n$ = M_n of this concept class is recursively given by

$$
M_0=(1)\ ,\qquad M_n=\begin{pmatrix} M_{n-1} & -1 \\ M_{n-1} & M_{n-1} \\ -1 & M_{n-1}\end{pmatrix}\in\{-1,1\}^{3^n\times 2^n}\ .
$$

For $n=0$ we have only the empty monomial which is always true. For $n\geq 1$ the first 2^{n-1} columns of M_n correspond to the assignments of the variables for which x_n is true and the last 2^{n-1} columns correspond to the assignments for which x_n is false. The first 3^{n-1} rows correspond to the monomials m containing the literal x_n, the next 3^{n-1} rows to the monomials containing neither x_n nor $\neg x_n$, and the last rows to the monomials containing $\neg x_n$.

There is an embedding of MONOMIALS$_n$ in inhomogeneous half spaces with margin $1/n$: We map each monomial m to a half space given by a normal vector u_m and threshold t_m. The j-th component of $u_m\in\mathbb{R}^n$ is 1 if m contains the positive literal x_j, -1 if m contains $\neg x_j$, and 0 otherwise. If l_m is the number of literals contained in m, we define the threshold t_m as $l_m-1\in\mathbb{R}$. For each assignment a of the variables $x_1,\ldots,x_n$ we define a vector $v_a\in\mathbb{R}^n$ by $(v_a)_j=1$ if a assigns true to x_j and $(v_y)_j=-1$ otherwise. Given a monomial m, the scalar product $\langle u_m,v_a\rangle$ attains its maximal value $l_m=t_m+1$ for the assignments a that fulfill m. For all other assignments a we have $\langle u_m,v_a\rangle\leq l_m-2=t_m-1$. This means that $\langle u_m,v_a\rangle>t_m$ if and only if a fulfills m and $|\langle u_m,v_a\rangle|\geq 1$. After dividing the vectors by $\sqrt{n}$ and dividing the thresholds by n we have an embedding with margin $1/n$.

The best margin of an embedding of MONOMIALS$_n$ with homogeneous half spaces is at most $1/\sqrt{n}$ because the matrix MONOMIALS$_n$ has n orthogonal rows: We consider only the monomials that consist of a single positive literal. The corresponding rows of $\mathrm{MONOMIALS}_n$ are orthogonal because two distinct literals differ on exactly half of all of the assignments to the variables $x_1, \ldots, x_n$.

We want to argue now that the embedding of Theorem 2 does not give good margins for the concept classes of monomials. For this we calculate the sum of the singular values of M_n. Consider the matrix

$$A_n = \frac{1}{2}(M_n + 1_{3^n \times 2^n}) \in \{0,1\}^{3^n \times 2^n}$$

which results from M_n if we replace the -1 entries of M_n by zeros. For this matrix it holds that

$$A_0^\top A_0 = (1) \ , \qquad A_n^\top A_n = \begin{pmatrix} 2A_{n-1}^\top A_{n-1} & A_{n-1}^\top A_{n-1} \\ A_{n-1}^\top A_{n-1} & 2A_{n-1}^\top A_{n-1} \end{pmatrix} \in \mathbb{R}^{2^n \times 2^n} \ .$$

For $n = 0$, obviously $x_1^{(0)} = (1)$ is an eigenvector of $A_0^\top A_0$ for the eigenvalue $\lambda_1^{(0)} = 1$. It is easy to see that if $x_j^{(n-1)}$ is an eigenvector of $A_{n-1}^\top A_{n-1}$ for the eigenvalue $\lambda_j^{(n-1)}$ then

$$x_j^{(n)} = \begin{pmatrix} x_j^{(n-1)} \\ -x_j^{(n-1)} \end{pmatrix} \ , \qquad x_{2^{n-1}+j}^{(n)} = \begin{pmatrix} x_j^{(n-1)} \\ x_j^{(n-1)} \end{pmatrix}$$

are linearly independent eigenvectors of $A_n^\top A_n$ for the eigenvalues $\lambda_j^{(n)} = \lambda_j^{(n-1)}$ and $\lambda_{2^{n-1}+j}^{(n)} = 3\lambda_j^{(n-1)}$.

The singular values of A_n are the square roots of the eigenvalues of $A_n^\top A_n$. Thus each singular value $s_j^{(n-1)}$ of A_{n-1} produces two singular values $s_j^{(n)} = s_j^{(n-1)}$ and $s_{2^{n-1}+j}^{(n)} = \sqrt{3}\, s_j^{(n-1)}$ for A_n. Because of $s_1^{(0)} = 1$ the sum of the singular values of A_n is $\sum_{j=1}^{2^n} s_j^{(n)} = (1+\sqrt{3})^n$.

Because each column of A_n contains exactly 2^n ones, it follows that

$$\begin{aligned} M_n^\top M_n &= (2A_n - 1_{3^n \times 2^n})^\top (2A_n - 1_{3^n \times 2^n}) \\ &= 4A_n^\top A_n - 2A_n^\top 1_{3^n \times 2^n} - 2 \cdot 1_{2^n \times 3^n} A_n + 1_{2^n \times 3^n} 1_{3^n \times 2^n} \\ &= 4A_n^\top A_n + (3^n - 4 \cdot 2^n) \cdot 1_{2^n \times 2^n} \ . \end{aligned}$$

By construction it follows inductively that each vector $x_j^{(n)}$ for $1 \leq j < 2^n$ contains as many 1s as -1s, i.e. $1_{2^n \times 2^n} x_j^{(n)} = 0$. Thus $x_j^{(n)}$ is an eigenvector of $M_n^\top M_n$ for the eigenvalue $4\lambda_j^{(n)}$ for $1 \leq j < 2^n$.

The vector $x_{2^n}^{(n)}$ contains only 1*s*, thus $1_{2^n \times 2^n} x_{2^n}^{(n)} = 2^n x_{2^n}^{(n)}$. Because of $\lambda_{2^n}^{(n)} = 3^n$, this vector is an eigenvector of $M_n^\top M_n$ for the eigenvalue

$$4\lambda_{2^n}^{(n)} + 2^n(3^n - 4 \cdot 2^n) = 4 \cdot 3^n + 6^n - 4^{n+1} \ .$$

The singular values of M_n are the square roots of the eigenvalues of $M_n^\top M_n$. Thus the sum of the singular values of M_n is almost equal to twice the sum of the singular values of A_n. We just have to add a term that takes care of the special case of the largest eigenvalue of $M_n^\top M_n$: The sum of the singular values of $M_n^\top M_n$ is

$$S := 2\big((1+\sqrt{3})^n - \sqrt{3}^n\big) + \sqrt{4 \cdot 3^n + 6^n - 4^{n+1}}\ .$$

Now it follows from Theorem 2 that the margin of the embedding obtained with the singular value decomposition method for MONOMIALS$_n$ is at most

$$\frac{\sqrt{3^n 2^n}}{S} = O\Big(\Big(\frac{\sqrt{6}}{1+\sqrt{3}}\Big)^n\Big)\ .$$

Because of $\sqrt{6}/(1+\sqrt{3}) \approx 0.8966 < 1$ this margin is exponentially small in n. We have already seen that there is an embedding of MONOMIALS$_n$ with margin $1/n$. This means that the upper bound of Theorem 2 on the optimal margin does not hold for all matrices. In particular, for large n not all entries of the matrix $UV^\top$ given by a singular value decomposition of MONOMIALS$_n$ have the correct signs.

Acknowledgments

Many thanks to Shai Ben-David for interesting discussions. Jürgen Forster was supported by the Deutsche Forschungsgemeinschaft grant SI 498/4–1. This research was also supported by a grant from the G.I.F., the German-Israeli Foundation for Scientific Research and Development.

References

1. Ben-David, S.. (2000). Personal Communication.
2. Ben-David, S., Eiron, N., & Simon, H. U. (2000). Limitations of learning via embeddings in Euclidean Hals-Spaces. *The Fourteenth Annual Conference on Computational Learning Theory* and *The Fifth European Conference on Computational Learning Theory.*
3. Ben-David, S., Eiron, N., & Simon, H. U. (2000). Unpublished manuscript.
4. Blumer, A., Ehrenfeucht, A., Haussler, D., & Warmuth, M. K. (1989). Learnability and the Vapnik-Chervonenkis dimension. *Journal of the ACM, 100*, 157–184.
5. Christianini, N., & Shawe-Taylor, J. (2000). *An Introduction to Support Vector Machines.* Cambridge, United Kingdom: Cambridge University Press.
6. Forster, J. (2001). A Linear Lower Bound on the Unbounded Error Probabilistic Communication Complexity. *Sixteenth Annual IEEE Conference on Computational Complexity.*
7. Horn, R. A., & Johnson, C. R. (1985). *Matrix Analysis.* Cambridge, United Kingdom: Cambridge University Press.
8. Kearns, M. J., & Vazirani, U. V. (1994). *An Introduction to Computational Learning Theory.* Cambridge, Massachusetts: Massachusetts Institute of Technology.
9. Krause, M. (1996). Geometric arguments yield better bounds for threshold circuits and distributed computing. *Theoretical Computer Science, 156*, 99–117.

10. Maass, W. & Turan, G. (1992). Lower Bound Methods and Separation Results for On-Line Learning Models. *Machine Learning, 9*, 107–145.
11. Novikoff, A. B. (1962). On convergence proofs on perceptrons. *Symposium on the Mathematical Theory of Automata, 12*, 615–622. Polytechnic Institute of Brooklyn.
12. Vapnik, V. (1998). *Statistical Learning Theory.* New York: John Wiley & Sons, Inc.
13. Vapnik, V. N., & Chervonenkis, A. Y. (1971). On the uniform convergence of relative frequencies of events to their probabilities. *Theory of Probability and its Applications, 16*, 264–280.

A Generalized Representer Theorem

Bernhard Schölkopf[1,2,3], Ralf Herbrich[1,2], and Alex J. Smola[1]

[1] Australian National University, Department of Engineering, Canberra ACT 0200, Australia
bs@conclu.de, rherb@microsoft.com, alex.smola@anu.edu.au
[2] Microsoft Research Ltd., 1 Guildhall Street, Cambridge, UK
[3] New address: Biowulf Technologies, Floor 9, 305 Broadway, New York, NY 10007, USA

Abstract. Wahba's classical representer theorem states that the solutions of certain risk minimization problems involving an empirical risk term and a quadratic regularizer can be written as expansions in terms of the training examples. We generalize the theorem to a larger class of regularizers and empirical risk terms, and give a self-contained proof utilizing the feature space associated with a kernel. The result shows that a wide range of problems have optimal solutions that live in the finite dimensional span of the training examples mapped into feature space, thus enabling us to carry out kernel algorithms independent of the (potentially infinite) dimensionality of the feature space.

1 Introduction

Following the development of support vector (SV) machines [23], positive definite kernels have recently attracted considerable attention in the machine learning community. It turns out that a number of results that have now become popular were already known in the approximation theory community, as witnessed by the work of Wahba [24]. The present work brings together tools from both areas. This allows us to formulate a generalized version of a classical theorem from the latter field, and to give a new and simplified proof for it, using the geometrical view of kernel function classes as corresponding to vectors in linear feature spaces.

The paper is organized as follows. In the present first section, we review some basic concepts. The two subsequent sections contain our main result, some examples and a short discussion.

1.1 Positive Definite Kernels

The question under which conditions kernels correspond to dot products in linear spaces has been brought to the attention of the machine learning community by Vapnik and coworkers [1,5,23]. In functional analysis, the same problem has been studied under the heading of Hilbert space representations of kernels. A good monograph on the functional analytic theory of kernels is [4]. Most of the material in the present introductory section is taken from that work. Readers familiar with the basics of kernels can skip over the remainder of it.

D. Helmbold and B. Williamson (Eds.): COLT/EuroCOLT 2001, LNAI 2111, pp. 416–426, 2001.

Suppose we are given empirical data

$$(x_1, y_1), \ldots, (x_m, y_m) \in \mathcal{X} \times \mathbf{R}. \tag{1}$$

Here, the target values y_i live in $\mathbf{R}$, and the patterns x_i are taken from a domain $\mathcal{X}$. The only thing we assume about $\mathcal{X}$ is that is a nonempty set. In order to study the problem of learning, we need additional structure. In kernel methods, this is provided by a similarity measure

$$k : \mathcal{X} \times \mathcal{X} \to \mathbf{R}, \quad (x, x') \mapsto k(x, x'). \tag{2}$$

The function k is called a kernel [20]. The term stems from the first use of this type of function in the study of integral operators, where a function k giving rise to an operator T_k via

$$(T_k f)(x) = \int_{\mathcal{X}} k(x, x') f(x')\, dx' \tag{3}$$

is called the kernel of T_k. Note that we will state most results for the more general case of complex-valued kernels;[1] they specialize to the real-valued case in a straightforward manner. Below, unless stated otherwise, indices i and j will be understood to run over the training set, i.e. $i, j = 1, \ldots, m$.

Definition 1 (Gram matrix). *Given a kernel k and patterns $x_1, \ldots, x_m \in \mathcal{X}$, the $m \times m$ matrix*

$$K := (k(x_i, x_j))_{ij} \tag{4}$$

is called the Gram matrix *of k with respect to $x_1, \ldots, x_m$.*

Definition 2 (Positive definite matrix). *An $m \times m$ matrix K over the complex numbers $\mathbf{C}$ satisfying*

$$\sum_{i=1}^{m} \sum_{j=1}^{m} c_i \bar{c}_j K_{ij} \geq 0 \tag{5}$$

for all $c_1, \ldots, c_m \in \mathbf{C}$ is called positive definite.

Definition 3 (Positive definite kernel). *Let $\mathcal{X}$ be a nonempty set. A function $k : \mathcal{X} \times \mathcal{X} \to \mathbf{C}$ which for all $m \in \mathbf{N}, x_1, \ldots, x_m \in \mathcal{X}$ gives rise to a positive definite Gram matrix is called a* positive definite (pd) kernel.[2]

Real-valued kernels are contained in the above definition as a special case. However, it is not sufficient to require that (5) hold for real coefficients c_i. If we want to get away with real coefficients only, we additionally have to require that the

[1] We use the notation $\bar{c}$ to denote the complex conjugate of c.

[2] One might argue that the term *positive definite kernel* is slightly misleading. In matrix theory, the term *definite* is sometimes used to denote the case where equality in (5) only occurs if $c_1 = \cdots = c_m = 0$. Simply using the term *positive kernel*, on the other hand, could be confused with a kernel whose *values* are positive.

kernel be symmetric. The complex case is slightly more elegant; in that case, (5) can be shown to imply symmetry, i.e. $k(x_i, x_j) = \overline{k(x_j, x_i)}$.

Positive definite kernels can be regarded as generalized dot products. Indeed, any dot product is a pd kernel; however, linearity does not carry over from dot products to general pd kernels. Another property of dot products, the Cauchy-Schwarz inequality, does have a natural generalization: if k is a positive definite kernel, and $x_1, x_2 \in \mathcal{X}$, then

$$|k(x_1, x_2)|^2 \leq k(x_1, x_1) \cdot k(x_2, x_2). \tag{6}$$

1.2 ... and Associated Feature Spaces

We define a map from $\mathcal{X}$ into the space of functions mapping $\mathcal{X}$ into $\mathbf{C}$, denoted as $\mathbf{C}^{\mathcal{X}}$, via [4]

$$\phi : \mathcal{X} \to \mathbf{C}^{\mathcal{X}}, \quad x \mapsto k(\cdot, x). \tag{7}$$

Here, $\phi(x) = k(\cdot, x)$ denotes the function that assigns the value $k(x', x)$ to $x' \in \mathcal{X}$. Applying ϕ to x amounts to representing it by its similarity to *all* other points in the input domain $\mathcal{X}$. This seems a very rich representation, but it turns out that the kernel allows the computation of a dot product in that representation.

We shall now construct a dot product space containing the images of the input patterns under ϕ. To this end, we first need to endow it with the linear structure of a vector space. This is done by forming linear combinations of the form

$$f(\cdot) = \sum_{i=1}^{m} \alpha_i k(\cdot, x_i), \quad g(\cdot) = \sum_{j=1}^{m'} \beta_j k(\cdot, x'_j). \tag{8}$$

Here, $m, m' \in \mathbf{N}$, $\alpha_1, \ldots, \alpha_m, \beta_1, \ldots, \beta_{m'} \in \mathbf{C}$ and $x_1, \ldots, x_m, x'_1, \ldots, x'_{m'} \in \mathcal{X}$ are arbitrary. A dot product between f and g can be constructed as

$$\langle f, g \rangle := \sum_{i=1}^{m} \sum_{j=1}^{m'} \bar{\alpha}_i \beta_j k(x_i, x'_j). \tag{9}$$

To see that this is well-defined, although it explicitly contains the expansion coefficients (which need not be unique), note that $\langle f, g \rangle = \sum_{j=1}^{m'} \beta_j \overline{f(x'_j)}$, using $k(x'_j, x_i) = \overline{k(x_i, x'_j)}$. The latter, however, does not depend on the particular expansion of f. Similarly, for g, note that $\langle f, g \rangle = \sum_i \bar{\alpha}_i g(x_i)$. This also shows that $\langle \cdot, \cdot \rangle$ is anti-linear in the first argument and linear in the second one. It is symmetric, since $\langle f, g \rangle = \overline{\langle g, f \rangle}$. Moreover, given functions $f_1, \ldots, f_n$, and coefficients $\gamma_1, \ldots, \gamma_n \in \mathbf{C}$, we have

$$\sum_{i=1}^{n} \sum_{j=1}^{n} \bar{\gamma}_i \gamma_j \langle f_i, f_j \rangle = \left\langle \sum_{i=1}^{n} \gamma_i f_i, \sum_{j=1}^{n} \gamma_j f_j \right\rangle \geq 0, \tag{10}$$

hence $\langle \cdot, \cdot \rangle$ is actually a pd kernel on our function space.

For the last step in proving that it even is a dot product, one uses the following interesting property of ϕ, which follows directly from the definition: for all functions (8),

$$\langle k(\cdot, x), f \rangle = f(x), \tag{11}$$

i.e., k is the *representer of evaluation*. In particular, $\langle k(\cdot, x), k(\cdot, x') \rangle = k(x, x')$, the *reproducing kernel property* [2,4,24], hence (cf. (7)) we indeed have $k(x, x') = \langle \phi(x), \phi(x') \rangle$. Moreover, by (11) and (6) we have

$$|f(x)|^2 = |\langle k(\cdot, x), f \rangle|^2 \leq k(x, x) \cdot \langle f, f \rangle. \tag{12}$$

Therefore, $\langle f, f \rangle = 0$ implies $f = 0$, which is the last property that was left to prove in order to establish that $\langle \cdot, \cdot \rangle$ is a dot product.

One can complete the space of functions (8) in the norm corresponding to the dot product, i.e., add the limit points of sequences that are convergent in that norm, and thus gets a Hilbert space H_k, usually called a *reproducing kernel Hilbert space (RKHS)*. The case of real-valued kernels is included in the above; in that case, H_k can be chosen as a real Hilbert space.

2 The Representer Theorem

As a consequence of the last section, one of the crucial properties of kernels is that even if the input domain $\mathcal{X}$ is only a set, we can nevertheless think of the pair $(\mathcal{X}, k)$ as a (subset of a) Hilbert space. From a mathematical point of view, this is attractive, since we can thus study various data structures (e.g., strings over discrete alphabets [26,13,18]) in Hilbert spaces, whose theory is very well developed. From a practical point of view, however, we now face the problem that for many popular kernels, the Hilbert space is known to be infinite-dimensional [24]. When training a learning machine, however, we do not normally want to solve an optimization problem in an infinite-dimensional space.

This is where the main result of this paper will be useful, showing that a large class of optimization problems with RKHS regularizers have solutions that can be expressed as kernel expansions in terms of the training data. These optimization problems are of great interest for learning theory, both since they comprise a number of useful algorithms as special cases and since their statistical performance can be analyzed with tools of learning theory (see [23,3], and, more specifically dealing with regularized risk functionals, [6]).

Theorem 1 (Nonparametric Representer Theorem). *Suppose we are given a nonempty set $\mathcal{X}$, a positive definite real-valued kernel k on $\mathcal{X} \times \mathcal{X}$, a training sample $(x_1, y_1), \ldots, (x_m, y_m) \in \mathcal{X} \times \mathbf{R}$, a strictly monotonically increasing real-valued function g on $[0, \infty[$, an arbitrary cost function $c : (\mathcal{X} \times \mathbf{R}^2)^m \to \mathbf{R} \cup \{\infty\}$, and a class of functions*

$$\mathcal{F} = \left\{ f \in \mathbf{R}^{\mathcal{X}} \,\middle|\, f(\cdot) = \sum_{i=1}^{\infty} \beta_i k(\cdot, z_i), \beta_i \in \mathbf{R}, z_i \in \mathcal{X}, \|f\| < \infty \right\}. \tag{13}$$

Here, $\|\cdot\|$ is the norm in the RKHS H_k associated with k, i.e. for any $z_i \in \mathcal{X}, \beta_i \in \mathbf{R}$ $(i \in \mathbf{N})$,

$$\left\| \sum_{i=1}^{\infty} \beta_i k(\cdot, z_i) \right\|^2 = \sum_{i=1}^{\infty} \sum_{j=1}^{\infty} \beta_i \beta_j k(z_i, z_j). \tag{14}$$

Then any $f \in \mathcal{F}$ minimizing the regularized risk functional

$$c\left((x_1, y_1, f(x_1)), \ldots, (x_m, y_m, f(x_m))\right) + g\left(\|f\|\right) \tag{15}$$

admits a representation of the form

$$f(\cdot) = \sum_{i=1}^{m} \alpha_i k(\cdot, x_i). \tag{16}$$

Let us give a few remarks before the proof. In its original form, with mean squared loss

$$c((x_1, y_1, f(x_1)), \ldots, (x_m, y_m, f(x_m))) = \frac{1}{m} \sum_{i=1}^{m} (y_i - f(x_i))^2, \tag{17}$$

or hard constraints on the outputs, and $g(\|f\|) = \lambda \|f\|^2$ $(\lambda > 0)$, the theorem is due to [15]. Note that in our formulation, hard constraints on the solution are included by the possibility of c taking the value ∞. A generalization to non-quadratic cost functions was stated by [7], cf. the discussion in [25] (note, however, that [7] did not yet allow for coupling of losses at different points). The present generalization to $g(\|f\|)$ is, to our knowledge, new. For a machine learning point of view on the representer theorem and a variational proof, cf. [12].

The significance of the theorem is that it shows that a whole range of learning algorithms have solutions that can be expressed as expansions in terms of the training examples. Note that monotonicity of g is necessary to ensure that the theorem holds. It does not ensure that the regularized risk functional (15) does not have multiple local minima. For this, we would need to require convexity of g and of the cost function c. If we discarded the strictness of the monotonicity of g, it would no longer follow that each minimizer (there might be multiple ones) of the regularized risk admits an expansion (16); however, it would still follow that there is always another solution minimizing (15) that *does* admit the expansion. In the SV community, (16) is called the *SV expansion*.

Proof. As we have assumed that k maps into $\mathbf{R}$, we will use (cf. (7))

$$\phi : \mathcal{X} \to \mathbf{R}^{\mathcal{X}}, \quad x \mapsto k(\cdot, x). \tag{18}$$

Since k is a reproducing kernel, evaluation of the function $\phi(x)$ on the point x' yields

$$(\phi(x))(x') = k(x', x) = \langle \phi(x'), \phi(x) \rangle \tag{19}$$

for all $x, x' \in \mathcal{X}$. Here, $\langle \cdot, \cdot \rangle$ denotes the dot product of H_k.

Given $x_1, \ldots, x_m$, any $f \in \mathcal{F}$ can be decomposed into a part that lives in the span of the $\phi(x_i)$ and a part which is orthogonal to it, i.e.

$$f = \sum_{i=1}^{m} \alpha_i \phi(x_i) + v \tag{20}$$

for some $\alpha \in \mathbf{R}^m$ and $v \in \mathcal{F}$ satisfying, for all j,

$$\langle v, \phi(x_j) \rangle = 0. \tag{21}$$

Using the latter and (19), application of f to an arbitrary training point x_j yields

$$f(x_j) = \left\langle \sum_{i=1}^{m} \alpha_i \phi(x_i) + v, \phi(x_j) \right\rangle = \sum_{i=1}^{m} \alpha_i \langle \phi(x_i), \phi(x_j) \rangle, \tag{22}$$

independent of v. Consequently, the first term of (15) is independent of v. As for the second term, since v is orthogonal to $\sum_{i=1}^{m} \alpha_i \phi(x_i)$, and g is strictly monotonic, we get

$$\begin{aligned} g(\|f\|) &= g\left(\left\| \sum_i \alpha_i \phi(x_i) + v \right\| \right) = g\left(\sqrt{ \left\| \sum_i \alpha_i \phi(x_i) \right\|^2 + \|v\|^2 } \right) \\ &\geq g\left(\left\| \sum_i \alpha_i \phi(x_i) \right\| \right), \end{aligned} \tag{23}$$

with equality occuring if and only if $v = 0$. Setting $v = 0$ thus does not affect the first term of (15), while strictly reducing the second term — hence, any minimizer must have $v = 0$. Consequently, any solution takes the form $f = \sum_i \alpha_i \phi(x_i)$, i.e., using (19),

$$f(\cdot) = \sum_{i=1}^{m} \alpha_i k(\cdot, x_i). \tag{24}$$

The theorem is proven.

The extension to the case where we also include a parametric part is slightly more technical but straightforward. We state the corresponding result without proof:

Theorem 2 (Semiparametric Representer Theorem). *Suppose that in addition to the assumptions of the previous theorem we are given a set of M real-valued functions $\{\psi_p\}_{p=1}^{M}$ on $\mathcal{X}$, with the property that the $m \times M$ matrix $(\psi_p(x_i))_{ip}$ has rank M. Then any $\tilde{f} := f + h$, with $f \in \mathcal{F}$ and $h \in \operatorname{span}\{\psi_p\}$, minimizing the regularized risk*

$$c\Big((x_1, y_1, \tilde{f}(x_1)), \ldots, (x_m, y_m, \tilde{f}(x_m)) \Big) + g\left(\|f\| \right) \tag{25}$$

admits a representation of the form

$$\tilde{f}(\cdot) = \sum_{i=1}^{m} \alpha_i k(x_i, \cdot) + \sum_{p=1}^{M} \beta_p \psi_p(\cdot), \tag{26}$$

with unique coefficients $\beta_p \in \mathbf{R}$ for all $p = 1, \ldots, M$.

Remark 1 (Biased regularization). A straightforward extension of the representer theorems can be obtained by including a term $-\langle f_0, f \rangle$ into (15) or (25), respectively, where $f_0 \in H_k$. In this case, if a solution to the minimization problem exists, it admits an expansion which differs from the above ones in that it additionally contains a multiple of f_0. To see this, decompose the vector v used in the proof of Theorem 1 into a part orthogonal to f_0 and the remainder.

In the case where $g(\|f\|) = \frac{1}{2}\|f\|^2$, this can be seen to correspond to an effective overall regularizer of the form $\frac{1}{2}\|f - f_0\|^2$. Thus, it is no longer the size of $\|f\|$ that is penalized, but the difference to f_0.

Some explicit applications of Theorems 1 and 2 are given below.

Example 1 (SV regression). For SV regression with the ε–insensitive loss [23] we have

$$c\left((x_i, y_i, f(x_i))_{i=1,\ldots,m}\right) = \frac{1}{\lambda} \sum_{i=1}^{m} \max\left(0, |f(x_i) - y_i| - \varepsilon\right) \tag{27}$$

and $g(\|f\|) = \|f\|^2$, where $\lambda > 0$ and $\varepsilon \geq 0$ are fixed parameters which determine the trade-off between regularization and fit to the training set. In addition, a single ($M = 1$) constant function $\psi_1(x) = b$ ($b \in \mathbf{R}$) is used as an offset that is not regularized by the algorithm [25].

In [22], a semiparametric extension was proposed which shows how to deal with the case $M > 1$ algorithmically. Theorem 2 applies in that case, too.

Example 2 (SV classification). Here, the targets satisfy $y_i \in \{\pm 1\}$, and we use

$$c\left((x_i, y_i, f(x_i))_{i=1,\ldots,m}\right) = \frac{1}{\lambda} \sum_{i=1}^{m} \max\left(0, 1 - y_i f(x_i)\right), \tag{28}$$

the regularizer $g(\|f\|) = \|f\|^2$, and $\psi_1(x) = b$. For $\lambda \to 0$, we recover the hard margin SVM, i.e., the minimizer must correctly classify each training point (x_i, y_i). Note that after training, the actual classifier will be $\operatorname{sgn}(f(\cdot) + b)$.

Example 3 (SVMs minimizing actual risk bounds). The reason why SVM algorithms such as the ones discussed above use the regularizer $g(\|f\|) = \|f\|^2$ are practical ones. It is usually argued that theoretically, we should really be minimizing an upper bound on the expected test error, but in practice, we use a quadratic regularizer, traded off with an empirical risk term via some constant. One can show that in combination with certain loss functions (hard constraints, linear loss, quadratic loss, or suitable combinations thereof), this regularizer leads to a convex quadratic programming problem [5,23]. In that case, the standard Kuhn-Tucker machinery of optimization theory [19] can be applied to derive a so-called dual optimization problem, which consists of finding the expansion coefficients $\alpha_1, \ldots, \alpha_m$ rather than the solution f in the RKHS.

From the point of view of learning theory, on the other hand, more general functions g might be preferable, such as ones that are borrowed from uniform convergence bounds. For instance, we could take inspiration from the basic pattern recognition bounds of [23] and use, for some small $\eta > 0$, the (strictly monotonic) function

$$g(\|f\|) := \sqrt{\frac{R^2\|f\|^2\left(\log\frac{2m}{R^2\|f\|^2}+1\right)-\log(\eta/4)}{m}}. \tag{29}$$

More sophisticated functions based on other bounds on the test error are conceivable, as well as variants for regression estimation (e.g., [3,6]).

Unlike Wahba's original version, the generalized representer theorem can help dealing with these cases. It asserts that the solution still has an expansion in terms of the training examples. It is thus sufficient to minimize the risk bound over expansions of the form (16) (or (26)). Substituting (16) into (15), we get an (m-dimensional) problem in coefficient representation (without having to appeal to methods of optimization theory)

$$\begin{aligned}\min_{\alpha_1,\ldots,\alpha_m\in\mathbf{R}} \; & c\left((x_1,y_1,\sum_{i=1}^m \alpha_i k(x_1,x_i)),\ldots,(x_m,y_m,\sum_{i=1}^m \alpha_i k(x_m,x_i))\right)\\ & + g\left(\sqrt{\sum_{i=1}^m\sum_{j=1}^m \alpha_i\alpha_j k(x_i,x_j)}\right).\end{aligned} \tag{30}$$

If g and c are convex, then so will be the dual, thus we can solve it employing methods of convex optimization (such as interior point approaches often used even for standard SVMs). If the dual is non-convex, we will typically only be able to find local minima.

Independent of the convexity issue, the result lends itself well to gradient-based on-line algorithms for minimizing RKHS-based risk functionals [10,9,17, 11,8,16]: for the computation of gradients, we only need the objective function to be differentiable; convexity is not required. Such algorithms can thus be adapted to deal with more general regularizers.

Example 4 (Bayesian MAP estimates). The well-known correspondence to Bayesian methods is established by identifying (15) with the negative log posterior [14,12]. In this case, $\exp(-c((x_i, y_i, f(x_i))_{i=1,\ldots,m}))$ is the likelihood of the data, while $\exp(-g(\|f\|))$ is the prior over the set of functions. The well-known Gaussian process prior (e.g. [24,27]), with covariance function k, is obtained by using $g(\|f\|) = \lambda\|f\|^2$ (here, $\lambda > 0$, and, as above, $\|\cdot\|$ is the norm of the RKHS associated with k). A Laplacian prior would be obtained by using

$g(\|f\|) = \lambda\|f\|$. In all cases, the minimizer of (15) corresponds to a function with maximal a posteriori probability (MAP).

Example 5 (Kernel PCA). PCA in a kernel feature space can be shown to correspond to the case of

$$c((x_i, y_i, f(x_i))_{i=1,\dots,m}) = \begin{cases} 0 & \text{if } \frac{1}{m}\sum_{i=1}^{m}\left(f(x_i) - \frac{1}{m}\sum_{j=1}^{m} f(x_j)\right)^2 = 1 \\ \infty & \text{otherwise} \end{cases} \tag{31}$$

with g an arbitrary strictly monotonically increasing function [21]. The constraint ensures that we are only considering linear feature extraction functionals that produce outputs of unit empirical variance. Note that in this case of unsupervised learning, there are no labels y_i to consider.

3 Conclusion

We have shown that for a large class of algorithms minimizing a sum of an empirical risk term and a regularization term in a reproducing kernel Hilbert space, the optimal solutions can be written as kernel expansions in terms of training examples. This has been known for specific algorithms; e.g., for the SV algorithm, where it is a direct consequence of the structure of the optimization problem, but not in more complex cases, such as the direct minimization of some bounds on the test error (cf. Example 3). The representer theorem puts these individual findings into a wider perspective, and we hope that the reader will find the present generalization useful by either gaining some insight, or by taking it as a practical guideline for designing novel kernel algorithms: as long as the objective function can be cast into the form considered in the generalized representer theorem, one can recklessly carry out algorithms in infinite dimensional spaces, since the solution will always live in a specific subspace whose dimensionality equals at most the number of training examples.

Acknowledgements. Thanks to Bob Williamson, Grace Wahba, Jonathan Baxter, Peter Bartlett, and Nello Cristianini for useful comments. This work was supported by the Australian Research Council. AS was supported by DFG grant SM 62/1-1.

References

1. M. A. Aizerman, É. M. Braverman, and L. I. Rozonoér. Theoretical foundations of the potential function method in pattern recognition learning. *Automation and Remote Control*, 25:821–837, 1964.
2. N. Aronszajn. Theory of reproducing kernels. *Transactions of the American Mathematical Society*, 68:337–404, 1950.

3. P. L. Bartlett and J. Shawe-Taylor. Generalization performance of support vector machines and other pattern classifiers. In B. Schölkopf, C. J. C. Burges, and A. J. Smola, editors, *Advances in Kernel Methods — Support Vector Learning*, pages 43–54, Cambridge, MA, 1999. MIT Press.
4. C. Berg, J. P. R. Christensen, and P. Ressel. *Harmonic Analysis on Semigroups.* Springer-Verlag, New York, 1984.
5. B. E. Boser, I. M. Guyon, and V. N. Vapnik. A training algorithm for optimal margin classifiers. In D. Haussler, editor, *Proceedings of the 5th Annual ACM Workshop on Computational Learning Theory*, pages 144–152, Pittsburgh, PA, July 1992. ACM Press.
6. O. Bousquet and A. Elisseeff. Algorithmic stability and generalization performance. In T. K. Leen, T. G. Dietterich, and V. Tresp, editors, *Advances in Neural Information Processing Systems 13.* MIT Press, 2001.
7. D. Cox and F. O'Sullivan. Asymptotic analysis of penalized likelihood and related estimators. *Annals of Statistics*, 18:1676–1695, 1990.
8. L. Csató and M. Opper. Sparse representation for Gaussian process models. In T. K. Leen, T. G. Dietterich, and V. Tresp, editors, *Advances in Neural Information Processing Systems 13.* MIT Press, 2001.
9. Y. Freund and R. E. Schapire. Large margin classification using the perceptron algorithm. In J. Shavlik, editor, *Machine Learning: Proceedings of the Fifteenth International Conference*, San Francisco, CA, 1998. Morgan Kaufmann.
10. T.-T. Frieß, N. Cristianini, and C. Campbell. The kernel adatron algorithm: A fast and simple learning procedure for support vector machines. In J. Shavlik, editor, *15th International Conf. Machine Learning*, pages 188–196. Morgan Kaufmann Publishers, 1998.
11. C. Gentile. Approximate maximal margin classification with respect to an arbitrary norm. Unpublished.
12. F. Girosi, M. Jones, and T. Poggio. Regularization theory and neural networks architectures. *Neural Computation*, 7(2):219–269, 1995.
13. D. Haussler. Convolutional kernels on discrete structures. Technical Report UCSC-CRL-99-10, Computer Science Department, University of California at Santa Cruz, 1999.
14. G. S. Kimeldorf and G. Wahba. A correspondence between Bayesian estimation on stochastic processes and smoothing by splines. *Annals of Mathematical Statistics*, 41:495–502, 1970.
15. G. S. Kimeldorf and G. Wahba. Some results on Tchebycheffian spline functions. *J. Math. Anal. Applic.*, 33:82–95, 1971.
16. J. Kivinen, A. J. Smola, P. Wankadia, and R. C. Williamson. On-line algorithms for kernel methods. in preparation, 2001.
17. A. Kowalczyk. Maximal margin perceptron. In A. J. Smola, P. L. Bartlett, B. Schölkopf, and D. Schuurmans, editors, *Advances in Large Margin Classifiers*, pages 75–113, Cambridge, MA, 2000. MIT Press.
18. H. Lodhi, J. Shawe-Taylor, N. Cristianini, and C. Watkins. Text classification using string kernels. Technical Report 2000-79, NeuroCOLT, 2000. Published in: T. K. Leen, T. G. Dietterich and V. Tresp (eds.), *Advances in Neural Information Processing Systems 13*, MIT Press, 2001.
19. O. L. Mangasarian. *Nonlinear Programming.* McGraw-Hill, New York, NY, 1969.
20. J. Mercer. Functions of positive and negative type and their connection with the theory of integral equations. *Philosophical Transactions of the Royal Society, London*, A 209:415–446, 1909.

21. B. Schölkopf, A. Smola, and K.-R. Müller. Kernel principal component analysis. In B. Schölkopf, C. J. C. Burges, and A. J. Smola, editors, *Advances in Kernel Methods - Support Vector Learning*, pages 327–352. MIT Press, Cambridge, MA, 1999.
22. A. Smola, T. Frieß, and B. Schölkopf. Semiparametric support vector and linear programming machines. In M. S. Kearns, S. A. Solla, and D. A. Cohn, editors, *Advances in Neural Information Processing Systems 11*, pages 585–591, Cambridge, MA, 1999. MIT Press.
23. V. Vapnik. *The Nature of Statistical Learning Theory*. Springer, NY, 1995.
24. G. Wahba. *Spline Models for Observational Data*, volume 59 of *CBMS-NSF Regional Conference Series in Applied Mathematics*. SIAM, Philadelphia, 1990.
25. G. Wahba. Support vector machines, reproducing kernel Hilbert spaces and the randomized GACV. In B. Schölkopf, C. J. C. Burges, and A. J. Smola, editors, *Advances in Kernel Methods — Support Vector Learning*, pages 69–88, Cambridge, MA, 1999. MIT Press.
26. C. Watkins. Dynamic alignment kernels. In A. J. Smola, P. L. Bartlett, B. Schölkopf, and D. Schuurmans, editors, *Advances in Large Margin Classifiers*, pages 39–50, Cambridge, MA, 2000. MIT Press.
27. C. K. I. Williams. Prediction with Gaussian processes: From linear regression to linear prediction and beyond. In M. I. Jordan, editor, *Learning and Inference in Graphical Models*. Kluwer, 1998.

A Leave-One-out Cross Validation Bound for Kernel Methods with Applications in Learning

Tong Zhang

IBM T.J. Watson Research Center
Yorktown Heights, NY 10598
tzhang@watson.ibm.com

Abstract. In this paper, we prove a general leave-one-out style cross-validation bound for Kernel methods. We apply this bound to some classification and regression problems, and compare the results with previously known bounds. One aspect of our analysis is that the derived expected generalization bounds reflect both approximation (bias) and learning (variance) properties of the underlying kernel methods. We are thus able to demonstrate the universality of certain learning formulations.

1 Introduction

Kernel methods such as Gaussian processes for regression and support vector machines for classification have become popular recently. Although in effect these methods may use infinite dimensional features in the corresponding reproducing kernel Hilbert spaces (RKHS), the kernel representation makes the computation feasible. An important aspect of kernel methods is their good generalization abilities despite of their large underlying feature spaces. This means that these learning methods can accurately predict outputs associated with previously unobserved data.

A popular method to study such generalization ability is the so-called Vapnik-Chervonenkis (VC) style analysis [10]. This method depends on the uniform convergence of observed errors of the hypothesis family to their true errors. The rate of uniform convergence depends on an estimate of certain sample-dependent covering numbers (growth numbers) for the underlying hypothesis family. Although this framework is quite general and powerful, it also has many disadvantages. For example, the derived generalization bounds are often very loose.

Because of various disadvantages of VC analysis, other methods to estimate generalization performance have been introduced. One interesting idea is to bound the leave-one-out error of a learning algorithm. This is useful since if the training data are independently drawn from a fixed underlying distribution, then the expected leave-out-out error equals the expected test error, which measures the generalization ability of the learning method. Leave-one-out bounds have received much attention recently. For example, see [3,5,6,10] and references

D. Helmbold and B. Williamson (Eds.): COLT/EuroCOLT 2001, LNAI 2111, pp. 427–443, 2001.

therein. Also in [5,10], the leave-one-out analysis has already been employed to study the generalization ability of support vector classification. In this paper, we extend their results by deriving a general leave-one-out bound for a class of convex dual kernel learning machines and apply it to classification and regression problems. We compare our bounds with previous results.

We organize the paper as follows. In Section 2, we introduce the general kernel learning machine formulation and review the corresponding RKHS representation. We then derive a general leave-one-out bound for the estimated parameter that is the foundation of our analysis. Section 3 and Section 4 contain specific results of this analysis on some classification and regression problems. Concluding remarks are given in Section 5.

2 Kernel Learning Machines and Leave-One-out Approximation Bound

2.1 Kernel Representation

In many machine learning problems, we are given a training set of input variable x and output variable y. Our goal is to find a function that can predict y based on x. Typically, one needs to restrict the hypothesis function family size so that a stable estimate within the function family can be obtained from a finite number of samples. Let the training samples be $(x_1, y_1), \ldots, (x_n, y_n)$. We assume that the hypothesis function family that predicts y based on x can be specified with the following kernel method:

$$p(\alpha, x) = \sum_{i=1}^{n} \alpha_i K(x_i, x), \tag{1}$$

where $\alpha = [\alpha_i]_{i=1,\ldots,n}$ is a parameter vector that needs to be estimated from the data. K is a symmetric positive kernel. That is, $K(a, b) = K(b, a)$, and the $n \times n$ Gram matrix $G = [K(x_i, x_j)]_{i,j=1,\ldots,n}$ is always positive semi-definite.

Definition 1. *Let* $H_0 = \{\sum_{i=1}^{\ell} \alpha_i K(x_i, x) : \ell \in N, \alpha_i \in R\}$. H_0 *is an inner product space with norm defined as*

$$\|\sum_i \alpha_i K(x_i, \cdot)\| = (\sum_{i,j} \alpha_i \alpha_j K(x_i, x_j))^{1/2}.$$

Let H *be the closure of* H_0 *under the norm* $\|\cdot\|$, *which forms a Hilbert space, called the reproducing kernel Hilbert space of* K.

In recent machine learning literature, kernel representation (1) has frequently been discussed under the assumptions of the Mercer's theorem, which gives a feature space representation of H (for example, see [2], chapter 3). Although this representation provides some useful insights into the underlying feature space the kernel induces, it is technically non-essential. Also one often does not need to use the Mercer's theorem in order to obtain a feature space representation (for example, one may use Taylor expansion). In addition, there has not been any quantitative result on approximation properties of H by using the feature space representation. Therefore in this paper, we do not consider feature spaces. We take a more general approach that only relies on simple properties of a positive symmetric kernel function K. Such an approach has been used in approximation theory.

We shall also define a useful quantity that characterizes the learning property of using the kernel representation (1) to approximate any target function $p(x)$.

Definition 2. *Denote by X_n a sequence of samples $x_1, \ldots, x_n$. We use $G(X_n)$ to denote the Gram matrix $[K(x_i, x_j)]_{i,j=1,\ldots,n}$.*

For any function $p(x)$ and symmetric positive kernel K, we define

$$\|p(X_n)\| = \inf \{+\infty\} \cup \{s : \forall \alpha, p(X_n)^T \alpha \leq s(\alpha^T G(X_n)\alpha)^{1/2}\},$$

where α denotes an n-dimensional vector.

We also define $\|p(x)\|_{[n]} = \sup_{X_n} \|p(X_n)\|$, where X_n consists of a sequence of n samples.

Intuitively, $\|p(X_n)\|$ can be regarded as the interpolation of function p at X_n with minimal $\|\cdot\|$ norm. We list the following basic facts of norm $\|\cdot\|$ without proof. These facts are not difficult to prove, and are useful in our later analysis.

Proposition 1. *Let K be a symmetric positive kernel, and consider samples $X_n = \{x_1, \ldots, x_n\}$. For any function $p(x)$, the following two situations may happen:*

- *$p(X_n)$ is not in the range of the Gram matrix $G(X_n)$: $\|p(X_n)\| = +\infty$.*
- *$p(X_n)$ can be represented as $p(X_n) = G(X_n)\alpha$: $\|p(X_n)\| = (\alpha^T G(X_n)\alpha)^{1/2}$.*

In particular, if $G(X_n)$ is invertible, then $\|p(X_n)\| = (p(X_n)^T G(X_n)^{-1} p(X_n))^{\frac{1}{2}}$.

Proposition 2. *Let K be a symmetric positive kernel. $\forall p(x) \in H$, and variable x:*

$$|p(x)| \leq \|p(\cdot)\| K(x,x)^{1/2},$$

and

$$\|p(x)\|_{[n]} \leq \|p(\cdot)\|.$$

As we shall see later, the quantity $\|p(x)\|_{[n]}$ is related to the quality of approximating $p(x)$ using kernel representation (1). In fact, our learning bounds containing this quantity directly yield general approximation bounds. This is also a new quantity that has not been considered in the traditional approximation literature. For example, the approximation property of kernel representation is typically studied using standard analytical techniques such as Fourier analysis (see [7,11] and references therein). Such results usually depend on many complicated quantities as well as the data dimensionality. Compared with these previous results, our bounds using $\|p(x)\|_{[n]}$ are much simpler and more general.

However, we do not discuss specific approximation consequences of our analysis, but rather concentrate on the general learning aspect.

When the target function p is not in H, we do not give conditions to bound $\|p(x)\|_{[n]}$. Note that techniques used in approximation theory to analyze the stability of $G(X_n)$ can be applied here. The stability of the system can be measured by the condition number of $G(X_n)$ (in 2-norm) or the 2-norm of $G(X_n)^{-1}$. See [8] and references there-in for related analysis. The new quantity $\|p(x)\|_{[n]}$ is clearly related to the 2-norm of $G(X_n)^{-1}$ (the latter gives an upper bound) which measures the stability. However, the stability concept as used in approximation theory only has numerical consequences but no consequence in approximation rate or learning accuracy. On the other hand, the quantity $\|p(x)\|_{[n]}$ determines the rate of approximation (or learning) of using the kernel representation (1). Although it is a well-known fact that the norm of $G(X_n)^{-1}$ degrades as the number of samples increases, one may introduce smoothness conditions on p so that $\|p(x)\|_{[n]}$ behaves nicely for a wide range of function families.

2.2 Leave-One-out Bound for Dual Kernel Learning

We consider the following general formulation of dual kernel learning machines that can be used to estimate $p(\alpha, \cdot)$ in (1) from the training data:

$$\hat{\alpha} = \arg\min_{\alpha}[\sum_{i=1}^{n} f(\alpha_i, x_i, y_i) + \frac{1}{2}\sum_{i=1}^{n}\sum_{j=1}^{n} \alpha_i \alpha_j K(x_i, x_j)]. \tag{2}$$

We assume that $f(a, b, c)$ is a convex function of a. For simplicity, we assume that a solution of (2) exists, but may not be unique.

To be able to treat classification and regression under the same general framework, we shall consider convex functions from the general convex analysis point of view, as in [9]. Especially we allow a convex function to take the $+\infty$ value which is equivalent to a constraint.

Consider a convex function $p(u) : R^d \to R^+$, where R is the real line, and R^+ denotes the extended real line $R \cup \{+\infty\}$. However, we assume that convex functions do not achieve $-\infty$. We also assume that any convex function $p(u)$ in this paper contains at least one point u_0 such that $p(u_0) < +\infty$. Convex functions that satisfy these conditions are called *proper* convex functions. This definition is very general: virtually all practically interesting convex functions are proper. We only consider *closed* convex functions. That is, $\forall u$, $p(u) = \lim_{\epsilon\to 0^+} \inf\{p(v) : \|v - u\| \le \epsilon\}$. This condition essentially means that the convex set above the graph of u: $\{(u, y) : y \ge p(u)\}$ is closed.

In this paper, we use $\nabla p(u)$ to denote a *subgradient* of a convex function p at u, which is a vector that satisfies the following condition:

$$\forall u', \quad p(u') \ge p(u) + \nabla p(u)^T (u' - u).$$

The set of all subgradients of p at u is called the *subdifferential* of p at u and is denoted by $\partial p(u)$.

Denote by $L_n(\alpha)$ the objective function

$$\sum_{i=1}^{n} f(\alpha_i, x_i, y_i) + \frac{1}{2}\sum_{i=1}^{n}\sum_{j=1}^{n} \alpha_i\alpha_j K(x_i, x_j)$$

in (2). In this paper, we also assume that (2) has a solution $\hat{\alpha}_n$ and the value $L_n(\hat{\alpha}_n)$ is finite. However, we do not assume that the solution is unique. Although we do not attempt to give general conditions that ensure the existence of solution (to make the paper more focused on the main topic of leave-one-out analysis), we would like to point out that for most specific learning formulations we considered later in the paper, the existence of solution is guaranteed.

Since the solution $\hat{\alpha}_n$ of (2) achieves the minimum of $L_n(\alpha)$, we have (see page 264 in [9]) $0 \in \partial_{\alpha_i} L_n(\hat{\alpha})$ for all i (the sub-differential is with respect to each α_i). By Theorem 23.8 in [9], for each i, we can find a subgradient of $f(\alpha_i, x_i, y_i)$ at $\hat{\alpha}_i$ with respect to α_i such that

$$\nabla_{\alpha_i} f(\hat{\alpha}_i, x_i, y_i) + \sum_{j=1}^{n} \hat{\alpha}_j K(x_i, x_j) = 0. \qquad (i = 1, \ldots, n) \tag{3}$$

We may now prove the following fundamental leave-one-out bound for kernel methods:

Lemma 1. *Let $\hat{\alpha}$ be the solution of (2), and let $\hat{\alpha}^{[k]}$ be the solution of (2) with the k-th datum removed from the training set, then*

$$\|p(\hat{\alpha}, \cdot) - p(\hat{\alpha}^{[k]}, \cdot)\| \le |\hat{\alpha}_k| K(x_k, x_k)^{1/2}.$$

Proof. For notational simplicity, we assume $k = n$. Using (3), we have for all $i \le n-1$:

$$\nabla_{\alpha_i} f(\hat{\alpha}_i, x_i, y_i)(\hat{\alpha}_i^{[k]} - \hat{\alpha}_i) + \sum_{j=1}^{n} \hat{\alpha}_j K(x_i, x_j)(\hat{\alpha}_i^{[k]} - \hat{\alpha}_i) = 0.$$

By the definition of subgradient, we have

$$\nabla_{\alpha_i} f(\hat{\alpha}_i, x_i, y_i)(\hat{\alpha}_i^{[k]} - \hat{\alpha}_i) \le f(\hat{\alpha}_i^{[k]}, x_i, y_i) - f(\hat{\alpha}_i, x_i, y_i),$$

which can now be equivalently written as:

$$f(\hat{\alpha}_i, x_i, y_i) - \sum_{j=1}^{n} \hat{\alpha}_j K(x_i, x_j)(\hat{\alpha}_i^{[k]} - \hat{\alpha}_i) \le f(\hat{\alpha}_i^{[k]}, x_i, y_i).$$

Summing over i, we have

$$\sum_{i=1}^{n-1}[f(\hat{\alpha}_i, x_i, y_i) - \sum_{j=1}^{n} \hat{\alpha}_j K(x_i, x_j)(\hat{\alpha}_i^{[k]} - \hat{\alpha}_i)] + \frac{1}{2}\sum_{i=1}^{n-1}\sum_{j=1}^{n-1} \hat{\alpha}_i^{[k]}\hat{\alpha}_j^{[k]} K(x_i, x_j)$$

$$\leq \sum_{i=1}^{n-1} f(\hat{\alpha}_i^{[k]}, x_i, y_i) + \frac{1}{2} \sum_{i=1}^{n-1} \sum_{j=1}^{n-1} \hat{\alpha}_i^{[k]} \hat{\alpha}_j^{[k]} K(x_i, x_j)$$

$$\leq \sum_{i=1}^{n-1} f(\hat{\alpha}_i, x_i, y_i) + \frac{1}{2} \sum_{i=1}^{n-1} \sum_{j=1}^{n-1} \hat{\alpha}_i \hat{\alpha}_j K(x_i, x_j).$$

The second inequality above follows from the definition of $\hat{\alpha}^{[k]}$. Rearrange the above inequality, and denote $\hat{\alpha}_n^{[k]} = 0$, we obtain:

$$\frac{1}{2} \sum_{i=1}^{n} \sum_{j=1}^{n} K(x_i, x_j)(\hat{\alpha}_i^{[k]} - \hat{\alpha}_i)(\hat{\alpha}_j^{[k]} - \hat{\alpha}_j) \leq \frac{1}{2} \hat{\alpha}_n^2 K(x_n, x_n).$$

Using Lemma 1, we can easily obtain the following general leave-one-out bound. We will study the consequence of this bound in regression and classification in subsequent sections.

Theorem 1. *Under the assumptions of Lemma 1, Let $L(p, x, y)$ be any loss function. The leave-one-out cross-validation error with respect to $L(p, x, y)$ satisfies the following inequality:*

$$\sum_{k=1}^{n} L(p(\hat{\alpha}^{[k]}, x_k), x_k, y_k) \leq \sum_{k=1}^{n} \sup_{|t_k| \leq 1} L(p(\hat{\alpha}, x_k) + t_k |\hat{\alpha}_k| K(x_k, x_k), x_k, y_k). \quad (4)$$

We would like to mention that the proof of Lemma 1 implies the stability of parameter estimation in the sense that removing a training datum does not change the estimated predictor $p(\hat{\alpha}, \cdot)$ very much. The concept of convergence of the estimated parameter has been widely used in traditional numerical mathematics and statistics. However, it has only recently been applied to analyzing learning problems. For example, techniques related to what we use here have also been applied in [12,13]. In fact, the proof of Lemma 1 is essentially the dual version of the technique which was used in [12]. The convergence of the estimated parameter is also related to the algorithmic stability concept in [1,6]. The former implies the latter but not conversely. Consequently, better bounds can usually be obtained if we can show the convergence of the estimated parameter.

Bounds given in [1,6] are in the style of the convergence of the empirical loss of the estimated parameter to the true loss of the estimated parameter, which usually yields an expected difference of $O(1/\sqrt{n})$ (when we assume that the regularization parameter λ in [1] is fixed). However, this rate does not have consequences in judging the quality of the estimated parameter. For example, bounds in this paper imply that for problems such as ridge regression in [1] with fixed λ, the (expected) difference between the generalization errors of the estimated parameter and that of the best possible parameter in the hypothesis class is typically $O(1/n)$. This rate is comparable to bounds obtained in [3]. However, unlike our bounds, their bounds for regression problems are dimensional dependent. Such results are not useful for kernel methods considered in this paper.

It is also possible to use Lemma 1 to derive sequential validation bounds as in [12] for kernel methods considered in this paper. A specific consequence will be loss bounds for ridge regression that extend similar results in [4]. This type of sequential validation bounds complement the leave-one-out analysis studied in this paper.

2.3 Duality

In this section, we briefly discuss a convex duality of (2), which becomes useful in our later discussions. For function $f(u, b, c)$ in (2), we define its dual with respect to the first parameter as

$$g(v, b, c) = \sup_u [uv - f(u, b, c)].$$

We have the following strong duality theorem (its special situation appeared in [5]).

Theorem 2. *For any solution $\hat{\alpha}$ of (2), the function $p(\hat{\alpha}, x)$ is a solution of the following primal optimization problem:*

$$\arg \min_{p(\cdot)\in H} [\sum_{i=1}^{n} g(-p(x_i), x_i, y_i) + \frac{1}{2}\|p(\cdot)\|^2]. \tag{5}$$

The converse is also true if the Gram matrix $G(X_n)$ is non-singular.

Proof. To prove the theorem, we first note that the solution of (5) is a solution of

$$\arg \min_{p(\cdot)\in H_{X_n}} [\sum_{i=1}^{n} g(-p(x_i), x_i, y_i) + \frac{1}{2}\|p(\cdot)\|^2], \tag{6}$$

where H_{X_n} is the subspace of H spanned by $K(x_i, \cdot)$ $(i = 1, \ldots, n)$. This is because that for any $p \in H$, let p_{X_n} be the orthogonal projection of p onto the subspace X_n, then $p(x_i) = p_{X_n}(x_i)$ for all i and $\|p_{X_n}\| \leq \|p\|$ with the equality holds only when $p \in H_{X_n}$.

Now, let $\hat{\alpha}$ be a solution of (2) which satisfies (3). By the relationship of duality and subgradient in [9], Section 23, we can rewrite (3) as:

$$\hat{\alpha}_i - \nabla_1 g(-p(\hat{\alpha}, x_i), x_i, y_i) = 0. \qquad (i = 1, \ldots, n) \tag{7}$$

Where $\nabla_1 g(v, b, c)$ denotes a subgradient of g with respect to v. Now multiply the two sides by $K(x_i, x_\ell)$, and sum over i, we have

$$\sum_{i=1}^{n} \hat{\alpha}_i K(x_i, x_\ell) - \sum_{i=1}^{n} \nabla_1 g(-p(\hat{\alpha}, x_i), x_i, y_i) K(x_i, x_\ell) = 0. \qquad (\ell = 1, \ldots, n) \tag{8}$$

For any α, we multiply (8) by $\alpha_\ell - \hat{\alpha}_\ell$, and sum over ℓ to obtain:

$$\sum_{i=1}^{n} \hat{\alpha}_i (p(\alpha, x_i) - p(\hat{\alpha}, x_i)) - \sum_{i=1}^{n} \nabla_1 g(-p(\hat{\alpha}, x_i), x_i, y_i)(p(\alpha, x_i) - p(\hat{\alpha}, x_i)) = 0. \tag{9}$$

Using the definition of subgradient, (9) implies

$$\frac{1}{2}(\|p(\alpha,\cdot)\|^2 - \|p(\hat{\alpha},\cdot)\|^2) + \sum_{i=1}^{n}(g(-p(\alpha,x_i),x_i,y_i) - g(-p(\hat{\alpha},x_i),x_i,y_i)) \geq 0.$$

That is, $\hat{\alpha}$ achieves the minimum of (6).

Since the above steps can be reversed when the Gram matrix $G(X_n)$ is non-singular, the converse is also true.

Note that the proof also implies that even when $G(X_n)$ is singular, a solution $p(x)$ of (5) can still be written as $p(\hat{\alpha},x)$ where $\hat{\alpha}$ is a solution of (2). In addition, the sum of the optimal values of (5) and (2) is zero. However this fact is not important in this paper.

3 Regression

In this section, we apply Theorem 1 to some regression formulations. We define

$$D_\epsilon(p,y) = \max(|p-y| - \epsilon, 0)$$

for all $\epsilon \geq 0$. In Theorem 1, let

$$L(p,x,y) = D_\epsilon(p,y)^s,$$

which is a standard regression loss. Our goal is to find a function $p(x)$ to minimize the expected loss

$$Q(p(\cdot)) = E_{(x,y)} D_\epsilon(p(x),y)^s,$$

where E denotes the expectation with respect to an unknown distribution. The training samples $(x_1,y_1),\ldots,(x_n,y_n)$ are independently drawn from the same underlying distribution.

In this case, we have the following leave-one-out cross-validation bound from Theorem 1:

Lemma 2. *Under the conditions of Lemma 1, the following bound on leave-one-out error is valid for all $s \geq 1$:*

$$(\sum_{k=1}^{n} D_\epsilon(p(\hat{\alpha}^{[k]},x_k),y_k)^s)^{\frac{1}{s}} \leq (\sum_{k=1}^{n} D_\epsilon(p(\hat{\alpha},x_k),y_k)^s)^{\frac{1}{s}} + (\sum_{k=1}^{n} |\hat{\alpha}_k K(x_k,x_k)|^s)^{\frac{1}{s}}.$$

Proof. Note that

$$\sup_{|t|\leq 1} D_\epsilon(p + t\Delta p, y) \leq D_\epsilon(p,y) + |\Delta p|.$$

Let $L(p,x,y) = D_\epsilon(p,y)^s$. The right-hand-side of equation (4) can be bounded as

$$\sum_{k=1}^{n}(D_\epsilon(p(\hat{\alpha},x_k),y_k) + |\hat{\alpha}_k| K(x_k,x_k))^s.$$

The lemma then follows from the Minkowski inequality.

The above lemma gives a generic bound for regression where the right-hand side can be estimated from the data. From the theoretical point of view, it is useful to further investigate the behavior of the right hand side.

We consider the following formulation of regression with g in (5) as

$$g(-p(x), x, y) = \frac{C^s}{s} D_\epsilon(p(x), y)^s, \tag{10}$$

where $C > 0$ is a regularization parameter, $s \in (1, +\infty)$, and $\epsilon \geq 0$ is a parameter to control the sparsity of computed α. In this case, f in (2) becomes

$$f(\alpha, x, y) = \frac{C^{-t}}{t} |\alpha|^t - \alpha y + \epsilon|\alpha|, \tag{11}$$

where $1/s + 1/t = 1$.

For simplicity, we assume that $K(x,x)^{1/2} \leq M$ for all x through-out the rest of the section. Although this condition simplifies the analysis, it is not technically essential if we allow the parameter s in Lemma 2 to be different from s in equation (10). For example, see [13] for such derivations.

With f in (2) given by (11), we obtain from equation (7):

$$|\hat{\alpha}_i| = C^s \max(|p(\hat{\alpha}, x_i) - y_i| - \epsilon, 0)^{s-1} \qquad (i = 1, \ldots, n).$$

Therefore $\forall i$:

$$|\hat{\alpha}_i|^t = C^{st} D_\epsilon(p(\hat{\alpha}, x_i), y_i)^s.$$

Summing over i, we obtain:

$$\sum_{k=1}^{n} |\hat{\alpha}_k K(x_k, x_k)|^t \leq C^{st} \sum_{k=1}^{n} D_\epsilon(p(\hat{\alpha}, x_k), y_k)^s M^{2t}.$$

Using Jensen's inequality and simple algebra, it is easy to obtain the following inequality:

$$\frac{1}{n^{\max(1/s,1/t)}} (\sum_{k=1}^{n} |\hat{\alpha}_k K(x_k, x_k)|^s)^{1/s} \leq (\frac{1}{n} \sum_{k=1}^{n} |\hat{\alpha}_k K(x_k, x_k)|^t)^{1/t}.$$

Substituting into Lemma 2, we obtain the following leave-one-out bound:

Lemma 3. *Under the conditions of Lemma 1 with f given by (11), we have*

$$(\sum_{k=1}^{n} D_\epsilon(p(\hat{\alpha}^{[k]}, x_k), y_k)^s)^{1/s} \leq (\sum_{k=1}^{n} D_\epsilon(p(\hat{\alpha}, x_k), y_k)^s)^{1/s} + C^s M^2 n^{\max(1/s-1/t,0)} (\sum_{k=1}^{n} D_\epsilon(p(\hat{\alpha}, x_k), y_k)^s)^{1/t}.$$

Theorem 3. *Under the conditions of Lemma 1 with f given by (11). If $1 < s \leq 2$, and let*

$$\bar{Q}(x_1, y_1, \ldots, x_n, y_n) = \frac{1}{n} \sum_{k=1}^{n} D_\epsilon(p(\hat{\alpha}, x_k), y_k)^s.$$

We have

$$E^{\frac{1}{s}} Q(p(\hat{\alpha}^{[k]}, \cdot)) \leq E^{\frac{1}{s}} \bar{Q}(x_1, y_1, \ldots, x_n, y_n) + C^s M^2 E^{\frac{1}{t}} \bar{Q}(x_1, y_1, \ldots, x_n, y_n),$$

where E denotes the expectation over n random samples $(x_1, y_1), \ldots, (x_n, y_n)$.

Proof. Using Lemma 3 and the Minkowski inequality, we have

$$(E \sum_{k=1}^{n} D_\epsilon(p(\hat{\alpha}^{[k]}, x_k), y_k)^s)^{1/s} \leq (E \sum_{k=1}^{n} D_\epsilon(p(\hat{\alpha}, x_k), y_k)^s)^{1/s} +$$
$$C^s M^2 n^{(\frac{1}{s} - \frac{1}{t})} E^{\frac{1}{s}} (\sum_{k=1}^{n} D_\epsilon(p(\hat{\alpha}, x_k), y_k)^s)^{\frac{s}{t}}.$$

Now apply the Jensen's inequality to the second term on the right hand side, we obtain

$$C^s M^2 n^{1/s - 1/t} E^{1/s} (\sum_{k=1}^{n} D_\epsilon(p(\hat{\alpha}, x_k), y_k)^s)^{s/t}$$
$$\leq C^s M^2 n^{1/s - 1/t} (E \sum_{k=1}^{n} D_\epsilon(p(\hat{\alpha}, x_k), y_k)^s)^{1/t}.$$

Also note that

$$E \sum_{k=1}^{n} D_\epsilon(p(\hat{\alpha}^{[k]}, x_k), y_k)^s = nE\, D_\epsilon(p(\hat{\alpha}^{[k]}, x_k), y_k)^s = nE\, Q(p(\hat{\alpha}^{[k]}, \cdot)).$$

We thus obtain the theorem.

Corollary 1. *Under the conditions of Lemma 1 with f given by (11). Assume $1 < s \leq 2$, and let*

$$Q_n = \inf_{p(\cdot)} [Q(p(\cdot)) + \frac{sC^{-s}}{2n} \|p(\cdot)\|_{[n]}^2],$$

where p is an arbitrary function. The expected generalization error is bounded by

$$E^{1/s} Q(p(\hat{\alpha}^{[k]}, \cdot)) \leq Q_n^{1/s} + C^s M^2 Q_n^{1/t},$$

where E denotes the expectation over n random samples $(x_1, y_1), \ldots, (x_n, y_n)$.

Proof. Note that $\forall p$,

$$\bar{Q}(x_1, y_1, \ldots, x_n, y_n) \leq \frac{1}{n} \sum_{k=1}^{n} D_\epsilon(p(x_k), y_k)^s + \frac{sC^{-s}}{2n} \|p(X_n)\|^2.$$

Taking expectation, we see that Q_n is an upper bound of $E\,\bar{Q}(x_1, y_1, \ldots, x_n, y_n)$ in Theorem 3.

The bound given in Corollary 1 shows that using a regression method with $s < 2$ is more robust as far as parameter estimation is concerned. This is because even if $Q_n^{1/s}$ is large, the variance term $C^s M^2 Q_n^{1/t}$ can still be small if t is large.

As we have mentioned earlier, the analysis in [1] studied the difference between the true loss and the empirical loss for the estimated parameter. It is not very suitable for our problem formulation since a direct application would have led to an upper bound on the expected generalization (for the special case of $s = 2$) as $E^{1/s}\, Q(p(\hat{\alpha}^{[k]}, \cdot)) \leq Q_n^{1/s} + O(\sqrt{n} C^s)$. Also in the case of $s = 2$, the convergence rate implied by our bound in Corollary 1 is compatible with loss bounds obtained in [4] for some ridge regression like online algorithms. As we have mentioned earlier, it is also possible to derive similar loss bounds by using Lemma 1 and techniques in [13].

Now, assume $1 < s \leq 2$ and let $\epsilon = 0$. We also take $p \in H$ in the definition of Q_n in Corollary 1. Then we have the following consequences:

- $\inf_{p \in H} E_{x,y}\, |p(x) - y|^s = 0$: In this case, with any fixed C, we have

$$\lim_{n \to \infty} E\, E_{x,y}\, |p(\hat{\alpha}, x) - y|^s = 0.$$

- $\inf_{p \in H} E_{x,y}\, |p(x) - y|^s > 0$: Choose C such that $C \to 0$ but $C^s n \to \infty$ as $n \to \infty$, then

$$\lim_{n \to \infty} E\, E_{x,y}\, |p(\hat{\alpha}, x) - y|^s = \inf_{p \in H} E_{x,y}\, |p(x) - y|^s.$$

In the above, the first is the noiseless case, and the second is the noisy case. However, in both cases, we do not need to assume that there is a target function $p \in H$ that achieves the minimum of $\inf_{p \in H} E_{x,y}\, |p(x) - y|^s$. For example, we may have a function $\tilde{p}(x)$ such that $E_{x,y}\, |\tilde{p}(x) - y|^s = \inf_{p \in H} E_{x,y}\, |p(x) - y|^s$, but $\tilde{p}(x)$ does not belong to H. The function may lie in the closure of H under another topology, such as the point-wise convergence topology. For some kernel functions, this closure of H may contain all continuous functions. In this case, Corollary 1 implies that when $n \to \infty$, the kernel learning machine formulation (2) is able to learn all continuous target functions even under observation noise. We call this property universal learning. We are able to demonstrate the universal property since our results incorporate both approximation and learning aspects under a single framework.

4 Classification

In this section, we apply Theorem 1 to some binary classification formulations. In this case, $y = \pm 1$. The decision rule is to predict y as 1 if $p(x) \geq 0$ and -1 if $p(x) < 0$. We define the classification error function of this prediction as:

$$I(p, y) = \begin{cases} 0 & \text{if } py > 0, \\ 1 & \text{if } py \leq 0. \end{cases}$$

The following result is a direct consequence of Theorem 1. A similar bound can be found in [5].

Lemma 4. *Under the conditions of Lemma 1, the following bound on leave-one-out classification error is valid:*

$$\sum_{k=1}^{n} I(p(\hat{\alpha}^{[k]}, x_k), y_k) \leq \sum_{k=1}^{n} I(p(\hat{\alpha}, x_k) - |\hat{\alpha}_k| y_k K(x_k, x_k), y_k).$$

The above bound, although useful computationally, does not provide useful theoretical insights. In this section, we show how to estimate the right hand side of the above bound using techniques similar to our analysis of regression problems. One difficulty is the non-convexity of the classification error function. We use a convex upper bound of $I(p, y)$ to remedy the problem. There are many possible choices. However, for simplicity, we only consider powers of $D_+(p, y) = \max(0, 1 - py)$, which is related to support vector machines. We shall mention that other functions (such as logistic or exponential functions, etc) are also suitable. There is nothing in our analysis that makes support vector machines special or theoretically superior. Some examples of margin-style classification error bounds with general loss functions are given in [13]. The same technique can be applied here to derive similar bounds.

Lemma 5. *Under the conditions of Lemma 1, the following bound on leave-one-out classification error is valid for all $s \geq 1$:*

$$\sum_{k=1}^{n} I(p(\hat{\alpha}^{[k]}, x_k), y_k) \leq [(\sum_{k=1}^{n} D_+(p(\hat{\alpha}, x_k), y_k)^s)^{1/s} + (\sum_{k=1}^{n} |\hat{\alpha}_k K(x_k, x_k)|^s)^{1/s}]^s.$$

Proof. In Lemma 4, we consider an upper bound $D_+(p, y)^s$ of $I(p, y)$ on the right hand side. Note that $D_+(p + \Delta p, y) \leq D_+(p, y) + |\Delta p|$. We apply the Minkowski inequality, the right hand side of Lemma 4 can be bounded as

$$[(\sum_{k=1}^{n} D_+(p(\hat{\alpha}, x_k), y_k)^s)^{1/s} + (\sum_{k=1}^{n} |\hat{\alpha}_k K(x_k, x_k)|^s)^{1/s}]^s.$$

To further investigate theoretical properties of support vector machines, we need to bound the right hand side of Lemma 5 in a way similar to the regression analysis.

We consider the following SVM formulation of classification with g in (5) as

$$g(-p(x), x, y) = \frac{C^s}{s} D_+(p(x), y)^s, \tag{12}$$

where $C > 0$ is a regularization parameter, and $1 \leq s < \infty$. In this case, f in (2) becomes

$$f(\alpha, x, y) = \frac{C^{-t}}{t} |\alpha|^t - \alpha y, \quad (\alpha y \geq 0) \tag{13}$$

where $1/s + 1/t = 1$. Note that if $s = 1$, then $t = +\infty$. Equation (13) can be equivalently written as:

$$f(\alpha, x, y) = \begin{cases} -\alpha y \text{ if } \alpha y \in [0, C], \\ +\infty \quad \text{otherwise.} \end{cases} \tag{14}$$

For simplicity, we also assume that $K(x, x)^{1/2} \leq M$ for all x through-out the rest of the section. Again, this condition is not essential in our analysis.

With f in (2) given by (13), we obtain from equation (7):

$$\hat{\alpha}_i y_i = C^s \max(1 - p(\hat{\alpha}, x_i) y_i, 0)^{s-1} \qquad (i = 1, \ldots, n). \tag{15}$$

Note that if $s = 1$, then the right-hand-side of equation (15) is not uniquely defined at $p(\hat{\alpha}, x_i) y_i = 1$. The equation becomes $\hat{\alpha}_i y_i \in [0, C]$ in this case.

In the following, we would like to bound the average size of $|\hat{\alpha}_i|$. We discuss two possible ways for doing so.

The first method is similar to the regression analysis. We assume that $s > 1$ so that $t < +\infty$:

$$|\hat{\alpha}_i|^t = C^{st} D_+(p(\hat{\alpha}, x_i), y_i)^s.$$

Using the same derivation as that in Section 3, we sum over i and apply Jensen's inequality to obtain the following result from Lemma 5:

Lemma 6. *Under the conditions of Lemma 1 with f given by (13), we have*

$$\left(\sum_{k=1}^{n} I(p(\hat{\alpha}^{[k]}, x_k), y_k)\right)^{1/s} \leq \left(\sum_{k=1}^{n} D_+(p(\hat{\alpha}, x_k), y_k)^s\right)^{1/s} + C^s M^2 n^{\max(1/s - 1/t, 0)} \left(\sum_{k=1}^{n} D_+(p(\hat{\alpha}, x_k), y_k)^s\right)^{1/t}.$$

Using the same proof of Theorem 3, we obtain the following bound on expected generalization error.

Theorem 4. *Under the conditions of Lemma 1 with f given by (13). If $1 < s \leq 2$, and let*

$$\bar{Q}(x_1, y_1, \ldots, x_n, y_n) = \frac{1}{n} \sum_{k=1}^{n} D_+(p(\hat{\alpha}, x_k), y_k)^s.$$

The expected generalization error satisfies

$$(E\,I(p(\hat{\alpha}^{[k]},x_k),y_k))^{1/s} \leq (E\,\bar{Q}(x_1,y_1,\ldots,x_n,y_n))^{1/s} + C^s M^2 (E\,\bar{Q}(x_1,y_1,\ldots,x_n,y_n))^{1/t},$$

where E denotes the expectation over n random samples $(x_1,y_1),\ldots,(x_n,y_n)$.

The proof of the following result is the same as that of Corollary 1.

Corollary 2. *Under the conditions of Lemma 1 with f given by (13). Furthermore, if $1 < s \leq 2$, and let*

$$Q_n = \inf_{p(\cdot)}[E_{x,y}\,D_+(p(x),y)^s + \frac{sC^{-s}}{2n}\|p(\cdot)\|_{[n]}^2],$$

where p is an arbitrary function. We have

$$(E\,I(p(\hat{\alpha}^{[k]},x_k),y_k))^{1/s} \leq (Q_n)^{1/s} + C^s M^2 Q_n^{1/t},$$

where E denotes the expectation over n random samples $(x_1,y_1),\ldots,(x_n,y_n)$.

The second method to bound the average size of $|\hat{\alpha}_i|$ is by using the following inequality. From (15), we obtain

$$\hat{\alpha}_i y_i(1-p(\hat{\alpha},x_i)y_i) \leq C^s \max(1-p(\hat{\alpha},x_i)y_i,0)^s \qquad (i=1,\ldots,n).$$

Summing over i, we obtain:

$$\sum_{i=1}^n \hat{\alpha}_i y_i(1-p(\hat{\alpha},x_i)y_i) \leq \sum_{i=1}^n C^s D_+(p(\hat{\alpha},x_i),y_i)^s.$$

That is,

$$\sum_{i=1}^n \hat{\alpha}_i y_i - \|p(\hat{\alpha},\cdot)\|^2 \leq \sum_{i=1}^n C^s D_+(p(\hat{\alpha},x_i),y_i)^s.$$

Note that $\hat{\alpha}_i y_i = |\hat{\alpha}_i|$ for all i. Therefore

$$\sum_{k=1}^n |\hat{\alpha}_k K(x_k,x_k)| \leq (\|p(\hat{\alpha},\cdot)\|^2 + \sum_{i=1}^n C^s D_+(p(\hat{\alpha},x_i),y_i)^s)M^2.$$

For simplicity, we only consider the case of $s=1$. By applying this inequality, we obtain the following leave-one-out bound from Lemma 5.

Lemma 7. *Under the conditions of Lemma 1 with f given by (14), we have*

$$\sum_{k=1}^n I(p(\hat{\alpha}^{[k]},x_k),y_k) \leq (1+CM^2)\sum_{k=1}^n D_+(p(\hat{\alpha},x_k),y_k) + \|p(\hat{\alpha},\cdot)\|^2 M^2.$$

Since for any function p,

$$\sum_{k=1}^{n} D_+(p(x_k), y_k) + \frac{C^{-1}}{2}\|p(X_n)\|^2$$

is an upper bound of

$$\sum_{k=1}^{n} D_+(p(\hat{\alpha}, x_k), y_k) + \frac{C^{-1}}{2}\|p(\hat{\alpha}, \cdot)\|^2,$$

we obtain the following theorem:

Theorem 5. *Under the conditions of Lemma 1 with f given by (14), we have*

$$\sum_{k=1}^{n} I(p(\hat{\alpha}^{[k]}, x_k), y_k) \leq \inf_{p(\cdot)}[(1+2CM^2)\sum_{k=1}^{n} D_+(p(x_k), y_k) + \frac{\frac{1}{C}+2M^2}{2}\|p(X_n)\|^2],$$

where p is an arbitrary function.

Taking expectation E over the training data, we see that the expected generalization error satisfies the following bound:

Corollary 3. *Under the conditions of Lemma 1 with f given by (14), we have*

$$E\, I(p(\hat{\alpha}^{[k]}, x_k), y_k) \leq \inf_{p(\cdot)}[(1+2CM^2)E_{x,y}D_+(p(x), y) + \frac{C^{-1}+2M^2}{2n}\|p\|^2_{[n]}],$$

where E denotes the expectation over n random samples $(x_1, y_1), \ldots, (x_n, y_n)$. p denotes an arbitrary function.

If the problem is separable, Theorem 5 implies a leave-one-out bound of

$$\sum_{k=1}^{n} I(p(\hat{\alpha}^{[k]}, x_k), y_k) \leq \frac{C^{-1}+2M^2}{2}\|p(X_n)\|^2$$

for all function p such that $p(x_i)y_i \geq 1$ for all $i = 1, \ldots, n$. We can let $C \to +\infty$, then the formulation becomes the optimal margin hyperplane (separable SVM) method, and the above bound becomes

$$\sum_{k=1}^{n} I(p(\hat{\alpha}^{[k]}, x_k), y_k) \leq \|p(\hat{\alpha}, \cdot)\|^2 M^2.$$

This bound is identical to Vapnik's bound for optimal margin hyperplane method in [10]. The bound implies that the optimal margin method can find a decision function that has classification error approaches zero as the sample size $n \to +\infty$ when the problem can be separated by a function in H with a large margin.

We can further consider the case that the problem is separable but not by any function in H (or not by a large margin). As we have pointed out in Section 3, there may be a function $p \notin H$ (but p belongs to H's closure under certain topology) so that $p(x)y > 0$ almost everywhere. In general, we assume in this case

$$\inf_{p \in H} E_{x,y} \max(1 - p(x)y, 0) = 0.$$

It is clear from Corollary 3 that the optimal margin hyperplane method may not estimate a classifier $p(\hat{\alpha}, \cdot)$ that has expected classification error approaches zero when $n \to +\infty$. That is, the method is not universal even for separable problems. This is not surprising since when $n \to \infty$, $\|p(\hat{\alpha}, \cdot)\|$ may also go to $+\infty$ at the same rate of n. On the other hand, by Corollary 3, with fixed regularization parameter C, $\lim_{n \to +\infty} E_{x,y} I(p(\hat{\alpha}, x), y) = 0$. This means that the soft-margin SVM with fixed C is a universal learning method for the separable formulation. A similar conclusion can be drawn from Corollary 2 with $1 < s \leq 2$. Note that we cannot obtain any quantitative universal learning result for non-separable problems since the SVM formulation minimizes an upper bound of classification error rather than the classification error itself.

5 Summary

In this paper, we derived a general leave-one-out approximation bound for kernel methods. The approximation bound leads to a very general leave-one-out cross-validation bound for an arbitrary loss function. We have applied the derived bound to some regression and classification problems. Our bounds reflect both learning and approximation aspects of the underlying problems. Based on these results, we are able to demonstrate universal learning properties of certain kernel methods. Our analysis also suggests that even for noiseless problems in regression, or separable problems for classification, it is still helpful to use penalty type regularization. This is because in these cases, formulations with fixed regularization parameters are universal.

In this paper, we show that the minimal interpolation norm $\|p(x)\|_{[n]}$ of a function $p(x)$ determines the rate of learning $p(x)$ with the corresponding $\|\cdot\|$ kernel function. However, we do not investigate the behavior of $\|p(x)\|_{[n]}$ for any specific functional class and any specific kernel formulation. It will be interesting to study such issues, which may lead to useful insights into various kernel formulations.

References

1. Olivier Bousquet and André Elisseeff. Algorithmic stability and generalization performance. In *Advances in Neural Information Processing Systems 13*, pages 196–202, 2001.
2. Nello Cristianini and John Shawe-Taylor. *An Introduction to Support Vector Machines and other Kernel-based Learning Methods.* Cambridge University Press, 2000.
3. Jüergen Forster and Manfred Warmuth. Relative expected instantaneous loss bounds. In *COLT 00*, pages 90–99, 2000.

4. Jüergen Forster and Manfred Warmuth. Relative loss bounds for temporal-difference learning. In *ICML 00*, pages 295–302, 2000.
5. T. Jaakkola and D. Haussler. Probabilistic kernel regression models. In *Proceedings of the 1999 Conference on AI and Statistics*, 1999.
6. Michael Kearns and Dana Ron. Algorithmic stability and sanity-check bounds for leave-one-out cross-validation. *Neural Computation*, 11(6):1427–1453, 1999.
7. H. N. Mhaskar, F. J. Narcowich, and J. D. Ward. Approximation properties of zonal function networks using scattered data on the sphere. *Adv. Comput. Math.*, 11(2-3):121–137, 1999. Radial basis functions and their applications.
8. F. J. Narcowich, N. Sivakumar, and J. D. Ward. Stability results for scattered-data interpolation on Euclidean spheres. *Adv. Comput. Math.*, 8(3):137–163, 1998.
9. R. Tyrrell Rockafellar. *Convex analysis.* Princeton University Press, Princeton, NJ, 1970.
10. V.N. Vapnik. *Statistical learning theory.* John Wiley & Sons, New York, 1998.
11. Holger Wendland. Error estimates for interpolation by compactly supported radial basis functions of minimal degree. *J. Approx. Theory*, 93(2):258–272, 1998.
12. Tong Zhang. Convergence of large margin separable linear classification. In *Advances in Neural Information Processing Systems 13*, pages 357–363, 2001.
13. Tong Zhang. A sequential approximation bound for some sample-dependent convex optimization problems with applications in learning. In *COLT*, 2001.

Learning Additive Models Online with Fast Evaluating Kernels*

Mark Herbster

Department of Computer Science
University College London
Gower Street
London WC1E 6BT, UK
M.Herbster@cs.ucl.ac.uk

Abstract. We develop three new techniques to build on the recent advances in online learning with kernels. First, we show that an exponential speed-up in prediction time per trial is possible for such algorithms as the Kernel-Adatron, the Kernel-Perceptron, and ROMMA for specific additive models. Second, we show that the techniques of the recent algorithms developed for online linear prediction when the best predictor changes over time may be implemented for kernel-based learners at no additional asymptotic cost. Finally, we introduce a new online kernel-based learning algorithm for which we give worst-case loss bounds for the ϵ-insensitive square loss.

* Mark Herbster was supported by ESPRC grant GR/M15972.

D. Helmbold and B. Williamson (Eds.): COLT/EuroCOLT 2001, LNAI 2111, pp. 444–460, 2001.

Introduction

The aim of this research is to make online learning with kernels more practical. We do this in three ways. Initially, in Part 1 we present an algorithmic innovation which speeds computation time for certain kernels designed for additive modeling. This works with a broad class of algorithms such as those in [14, 13,25,15] and the algorithms presented in Part 2. Specifically, with an additive spline kernel, on trial t we may predict and then update our hypothesis with $O(\log t)$ computations as opposed to the usual $O(t)$ computation time. In Part 2 we present a unified analysis of two algorithms, one for classification and one for regression. The classification algorithm is a simple variant of the well-known Perceptron [34] algorithm. We then present a novel algorithm for regression with the useful property that it updates *conservatively*. We give a simple total loss bound for this algorithm with the ϵ-insensitive square loss. Finally, in Part 2 we show that the recent results of [21] may be applied and implemented efficiently for online learning with kernels; this allows us to prove *local* loss bounds. These bounds differ from total loss bounds in that they hold for any segment of the sequence. Thus they are particularly relevant to online learning.

As discussed above the paper is divided into two parts. Each part is wholly self-contained. However, the techniques presented in both parts are easily combined.

1 Fast Kernel Evaluation for Additive Models

Reproducing kernels were initially introduced in the machine literature for use with the perceptron algorithm in [1]. The current popularity of kernel-based methods is due to the successful integration of the "optimal separating hyperplane" method [41] with a kernel transformation to create the support vector machine [7]. Recently there has a been a renewed interest in online kernel-based algorithms both as a proxy for batch learning and in their own right. The use of online kernel algorithms for batch learning [13,14,25,33] has been proposed for two essential reasons: first, their simplicity of implementation; and second, whereas typical batch methods require memory quadratic in the dataset size, typical online algorithms require memory linear in the dataset size. Thus for the largest of datasets online algorithms may be the best option. A key obstacle facing online kernel-based learners is the fact that on trial t prediction typically requires $O(t)$ time. In this part of the paper we tread a middle ground, in that we restrict the hypothesis class of kernel-based learners to a class of *additive* models, but in compensation on trial t we may predict in $O(\log t)$ time, a per-trial exponential speed-up. Another major problem with online kernel-based learners is that the internal hypothesis representation on trial t is potentially of $O(t)$ size; thus an important goal of online kernel-based learners is to restrict the representation to a finite size. In this paper we do not address this problem, but in preliminary research [38] a broad framework was presented for online kernel-based learners motivated by a regularized stochastic gradient descent update; it was also pointed out that the online regularization led to weight decay and thus potentially to bounds for an algorithm with finite memory size.

Additive modeling is a well-known technique from statistics [17] (also see [16]) where we suppose the underlying hypothesis class is essentially additive, i.e.,

$$f(\boldsymbol{x}) = \sum_{i=1}^{d} f_i(x_i)$$

for d-dimensional data. In effect we attempt to learn a different smooth function for each dimension. If we expect lower order correlations among the components, it may be reasonable to explicitly expand the coordinate vectors by multiplication. However, the technique presented in this section is inappropriate for highly correlated data, as in the classic postal digit recognition task [24].

The kernels and data structures presented in this part are compatible with a number of online kernel-based learners such as presented in [13,14,25][1]. The key features that are required to make use of techniques of this part is an online algorithm that changes its dual representation a single term at a time, and that the computations lead to a single term being changed are not "too complex". In Part 2 we give two sample algorithms which are compatible with the speed-up technique presented in this part.

For simplicity we illustrate the idea in the batch setting. The well-known dual representation of a kernel learner's hypothesis is

$$f(x) = \sum_{i=1}^{m} \alpha_i K(x_i, x), \tag{1}$$

a regression prediction is simply $f(x)$, whereas for classification the prediction is $\operatorname{sign}(f(x))$. In either case the straightforward method of evaluating $f(x)$ requires m steps. In this paper we show that for certain kernels only $O(\log m)$ steps are needed after a preprocessing step. For example, consider the single coordinate radial basis kernel $K(p,q) = e^{-\sigma|p-q|}$. Now consider that a batch learning procedure has determined the $2m$ parameters $\alpha_1, \ldots, \alpha_m, x_1, \ldots, x_m$ of the hypothesis f. In Figure 1 we show that $f(x)$ as represented in Equation (1) may be repeatedly evaluated for any x in $O(\log m)$ steps after a $O(m \log m)$ preprocessing step. Thus rapid evaluation of the dual form (Equation (1)) with $K(p,q) = e^{-\sigma|p-q|}$ requires $O(m)$ space but only $O(\log m)$ time. For the sake of comparison this kernel may be viewed as intermediate between the the kernels $e^{-\sigma(p-q)}$ and $e^{-\sigma(p-q)^2}$. The first kernel is a special case of kernels in the form $K_k(p,q) = k(p)k(q)$, which after preprocessing may be evaluated in $O(1)$ time and represented in $O(1)$ space, since

$$f(x) = \sum_{i=1}^{m} \alpha_i K_k(x_i, x) = \left[\sum \alpha_i k(x_i)\right] k(x).$$

[1] For both the Kernel-Perceptron and ROMMA, we refer to their non-voted versions.

Preprocessing:

1. Sort in ascending order $x_1, \ldots, x_m$ then relabel as $x'_1 < \ldots < x'_m$ and set $x'_0 = -\infty$.
2. Set $\alpha'_j = \alpha_i$ when $x'_j = x_i$ for $i = 1, \ldots, m$.
3. Set $\text{lhs}_{\{e^{\sigma p}\}}[i] = \sum_{j=1}^{i} \alpha'_j e^{\sigma x'_j}$ for $i = 0, \ldots, m$.
4. Set $\text{rhs}_{\{e^{-\sigma p}\}}[i] = \sum_{j=i+1}^{m} \alpha'_j e^{-\sigma x'_j}$ for $i = 0, \ldots, m$.

Evaluation:
We may evaluate f on an arbitrary x as follows:

1. With a binary search let $j^* = \max\{j : x_j \leq x\}$.
2. Let $f(x) = \text{lhs}_{\{e^{\sigma p}\}}[j^*]e^{-\sigma x} + \text{rhs}_{\{e^{-\sigma p}\}}[j^*]e^{\sigma x}$.

Fig. 1. Evaluating $f(x) = \sum_{i=1}^{m} \alpha_i e^{\sigma|x_i - x|}$ in $O(\log m)$ time

Whereas for the kernel $e^{-\sigma(p-q)^2}$ it is an open problem if Equation (1) can be evaluated for any x in less than $O(m)$ steps with a polynomial preprocessing step[2].

A spline kernel $K : (0, \infty) \times (0, \infty) \rightarrow \Re$ of order z with an infinite number of knots [39,22] is defined by

$$K_d(p, q) = \sum_{r=0}^{z} \frac{\binom{z}{r}}{2z - r + 1} \min(p, q)^{2z-r+1} |q - p|^r + \sum_{r=0}^{z} p^r q^r. \tag{2}$$

In the short version of the paper we will only consider linear splines ($z = 1$) which fit the data with a piecewise cubic polynomial between knots. The linear spline kernel is then

$$K_1(p, q) = 1 + pq + \frac{1}{2}|q - p| \min(p, q)^2 + \frac{1}{3} \min(p, q)^3 \tag{3}$$

$$= 1 + pq + \begin{cases} \frac{1}{2}p^2 q - \frac{5}{6}p^3 & p \leq q \\ \frac{1}{2}pq^2 - \frac{5}{6}q^3 & p > q. \end{cases} \tag{4}$$

Following the schema of Figure 1, we may perform evaluations of the dual representation (see Equation (1)) in $O(\log m)$ time after an $O(m \log m)$ preprocessing step by creating 4 cached values for each data point and two globally cached values. Thus assuming the notation of steps 1 and 2 of Figure 1, we define for $i = 0, \ldots, m$,

$$\begin{array}{ll} \text{lhs}_{\{\frac{1}{2}p^2\}}[i] = \frac{1}{2}\sum_{j=1}^{i} \alpha'_j (x'_j)^2 \ ; & \text{lhs}_{\{-\frac{5}{6}p^3\}}[i] = -\frac{5}{6}\sum_{j=1}^{i} \alpha'_j (x'_j)^3 \\ \text{rhs}_{\{\frac{1}{2}p\}}[i] = \frac{1}{2}\sum_{j=i+1}^{m} \alpha'_j x'_j \ ; & \text{rhs}_{\{-\frac{5}{6}\}}[i] = -\frac{5}{6}\sum_{j=i+1}^{m} \alpha'_j \\ \text{gs}_{\{1\}} = \sum_{j=1}^{m} \alpha'_j \ ; & \text{gs}_{\{p\}} = \sum_{j=1}^{m} \alpha'_j x'_j. \end{array}$$

[2] All three kernels are reproducing kernels, however the Hilbert space induced by the kernel $e^{-\sigma(p-q)}$ is 1-dimensional. While the other two induced Hilbert spaces are infinite-dimensional.

We can then evaluate Equation (1) with linear splines in $O(\log m)$ time by finding j^* (see Figure 1), then computing

$$f(x) = \text{gs}_{\{1\}} + \text{gs}_{\{p\}}x + \text{lhs}_{\{\frac{1}{2}p^2\}}[j^*]x + \text{lhs}_{\{-\frac{5}{6}p^3\}}[j^*] + \text{rhs}_{\{\frac{1}{2}p\}}[j^*]x^2 + \text{rhs}_{\{-\frac{5}{6}\}}[j^*]x^3.$$

The key to our method, very loosely, is that the kernel must be separable into left-hand sides and right-hand sides such that a linear combination of either side is quick to evaluate; a technical discussion follows. Let $\chi_p(q) = \begin{cases} 1 & q \leq p \\ 0 & q > p \end{cases}$, denote a heavyside function. Then given a kernel[3] $K(p,q) : \Re \times \Re \rightarrow \Re$ we split it into "left" and "right" functions, $k_p^L = K(p,\cdot)\chi_p(\cdot)$ and $k_p^R = K(p,\cdot)(1-\chi_p(\cdot))$; thus $K(a,b) = K_a^L(b) + K_a^R(b)$. Define the vector space $F_x^L = \text{span}\ \{k_y^L \chi_x : y \in [x,\infty) \in \Re\}$. Suppose there exists a vector space F^L with basis $\phi_1^L, \ldots, \phi_d^L$ such that $F_x^L \subset \text{span}\ \{\phi_i^L \chi_x : i = 1,\ldots,d\}$ for all $x \in \Re$ (further suppose F_x is of the least dimension such that the former holds). Then we say that the Hilbert space $\mathcal{H}_K$ induced by K has *left dimension* d; the *right dimension* is defined analogously. Without loss of generality assume that both the left and right dimension are d; then $K(p,\cdot)$ may be expanded in terms of the left and right bases, i.e.,

$$K(p,\cdot) = [\sum_{i=1}^{d} \beta_i^L \phi_i^L(\cdot)]\chi_p(\cdot) + [\sum_{j=1}^{d} \beta_j^R \phi_j^R(\cdot)](1-\chi_p(\cdot))$$

and if the constants (implicitly dependent on p) $\beta_1^L, \ldots, \beta_d^L, \beta_1^R, \ldots, \beta_d^R$ are easily computed then the techniques described below may be applied to compute (1) on trial m in $O(d \log m)$ steps.

The extension of this method to additive multicoordinate kernels is straightforward. Given a 1-coordinate kernel $K(p,q)$ the additive c-coordinate kernel is simply

$$K(\boldsymbol{p},\boldsymbol{q}) = \sum_{i=1}^{c} K(p_i,q_i).$$

Since each coordinate is additively independent we can apply the above technique in each coordinate independently, which leads to a cost of $O(cd \log m)$ to evaluate a point after preprocessing.

In an online setting it is possible to use a balanced binary tree (e.g., a red-black tree) as the base data structure, to evaluate Equation (1) for the above kernels in $O(d \log m)$ steps; then if the sum consists of m terms a new term may be added to the structure in $O(d \log m)$ steps. The following is a sketch of how this may be done. In the balanced binary tree each node $i = 1,\ldots,m$ will contain a *key* x_i, and $2d$ *values* $\alpha_i \beta_{i,j}^L, \alpha_i \beta_{i,j}^R$ for each $(j = 1,\ldots,d,\{L,R\})$. For each of the values there is also an *augmented value* which is the sum of the values $\alpha_{i'}\beta_{i',j}$ in the subtree rooted at i (in [9, Theorem 15.1] it is demonstrated that these augmented values may be implemented at no additional asymptotic

[3] The domain may be any ordered set for concreteness we choose $\Re$.

cost for operations on the balanced tree). Given the existence of these augmented value sums, the $2d$ *derived sums* $\sum_{i:x_i \leq x} \alpha_i \beta^L_{i,j}$ and $\sum_{i:x_i > x} \alpha_i \beta^R_{i,j}$ may each then be computed $O(d \log m)$ steps. Thus evaluation of (1) and the addition of a new term may be accomplished in $O(d \log m)$ steps. We provide further details in the full paper.

2 Online Algorithms

2.1 Preliminaries

A Hilbert space, in this paper, denotes a complete inner product space, which may be finite or infinite dimensional; thus $\Re^n$ is a Hilbert space. The notation $\langle \boldsymbol{v}, \boldsymbol{w} \rangle$ indicates the inner product between $\boldsymbol{v}$ and $\boldsymbol{w}$. The set $\mathcal{H}$ always denotes an arbitrary Hilbert space.

2.2 Introduction

We consider the following on-line learning model based on a model introduced by Littlestone [27,26,28]. Learning proceeds in trials $t = 1, 2, \ldots, \ell$. The algorithm maintains a parameter vector (hypothesis), denoted by $\boldsymbol{w}_t$. In each trial the algorithm receives a *pattern* $\mathbf{x}_t$. It then produces some action or a prediction denoted $\hat{y}_t$, a function of current pattern $\mathbf{x}_t$ and hypothesis $\boldsymbol{w}_t$. Finally, the algorithm receives an *outcome* y_t, and incurs a loss $L(y_t, \hat{y}_t)$ measuring the discrepancy between y_t and $\hat{y}_t$.

In this part we give algorithms for classification and regression. For classification we predict with $\hat{y}_t = \text{sign}(\langle \boldsymbol{w}_t, \mathbf{x}_t \rangle)$, while for regression $\hat{y}_t = \langle \boldsymbol{w}_t, \mathbf{x}_t \rangle$ and we assign loss with

$$L_{\text{m}}(y_t, \hat{y}_t) = \begin{cases} 0 & y_t = \hat{y}_t \\ 1 & y_t \neq \hat{y}_t \end{cases} \tag{5}$$

$$L_{\text{sq},\epsilon}(y_t, \hat{y}_t) = \begin{cases} 0 & |y_t - \hat{y}_t| \leq \epsilon \\ (|y_t - \hat{y}_t| - \epsilon)^2 & |y_t - \hat{y}_t| > \epsilon \end{cases} \tag{6}$$

for the mistake counting loss and the ϵ-insensitive square loss for classification and regression, respectively. The mistake counting loss is a natural measure of discrepancy. The ϵ-insensitive square loss may appear less natural, but consider the following example. Suppose that a robot arm must place a peg into a hole slightly larger than the peg. If the peg is placed in the hole there is no loss; otherwise it is necessary to pay the squared distance from the boundary of the hole to reorient the arm. Thus the ϵ-insensitive square loss is potentially appropriate for situations where there is a natural tolerance for the "correct" response. The ϵ-insensitive linear or quadratic loss is often used in batch learning for support vector regression [40].

In the usual methodology of worst-case loss bounds the total loss of the algorithm is expressed as a function of the total loss of any member in a comparison class of predictors [27]. Surprisingly, such bounds are achievable even when there are no probabilistic assumptions made on the sequence of examples; some prominent results are found in [26,42,8,18,23,19,44]. In this paper we consider a simplification of the above goal, i.e., we give bounds on the loss of algorithm in terms of any member of the *realizable* set of predictors, rather than the whole comparison class. The realizable set are those predictors that "perfectly" fit the data. For classification the realizable set are those predictors that separate the data with a given minimum margin. For regression, it is the set of predictors for which the ϵ-insensitive square loss is zero over the data sequence. The *realizabilty* condition is certainly a limitation on the bounds, particularly in the classification case. However, it is less of a limitation in the regression case, as there necessarily exists an ϵ such that the data will be realizable. In both cases, however, the realizability restriction is less onerous with the *kernel* transformation, since the hypotheses' classes are then much richer and there is the recent technique in [37] to incorporate noise tolerance into a kernel by mixing it with a delta function.

The key tool which we use to repeatedly construct updates for our algorithms is *projection* as is defined below.

Definition 1. *Given a Hilbert space $\mathcal{H}$, the projection of a point $\boldsymbol{w} \in \mathcal{H}$ onto a closed convex nonempty set $\Gamma \subset \mathcal{H}$ is defined by:*

$$\mathcal{P}_{\Gamma}(\boldsymbol{w}) = \underset{\boldsymbol{u}\in\Gamma}{arg\,min}\, \|\boldsymbol{u} - \boldsymbol{w}\|. \tag{7}$$

The existence and uniqueness of projection is well-known (e.g. [35, Theorem 4.1]); in this paper the needed projections are always simple to compute. In the full version we give proofs for the methods of computation given for various projections. Given the definition of the projection above, we may give the following well-known version of the Pythagorean Theorem.

Theorem 1. *Given a Hilbert space $\mathcal{H}$, a point $\boldsymbol{w} \in \mathcal{H}$, a closed convex set $\Gamma \subset \mathcal{H}$, and $\boldsymbol{u} \in \Gamma$, then*

$$\|\boldsymbol{u} - \boldsymbol{w}\|^2 \geq \|\boldsymbol{u} - \mathcal{P}_{\Gamma}(\boldsymbol{w})\|^2 + \|\mathcal{P}_{\Gamma}(\boldsymbol{w}) - \boldsymbol{w})\|^2. \tag{8}$$

In the special case where Γ is an affine set the above becomes an equality.

A hyperplane is an example of an affine set. The Pythagorean Theorem is the main tool used to prove bounds for the algorithms given in this part.

2.3 Online Algorithms for Regression and Classification

In this section we give two online algorithms (see Figure 2) for classification and regression, and prove worst-case loss bounds. These algorithms are based on the Prototypical projection algorithm (see Figure 3) which is a relatively well-known technique from the convex optimization community. An early reference for a version of this algorithm is found in the work of Von Neumann [31]. Bauschke and Borwein [5] present a broadly generalized version of this algorithm and a

Algorithms for arbitrary Hilbert Space $\mathcal{H}$		
	Classification	**ϵ-insensitive Regression**
Input:	$\{(\boldsymbol{x}_1,y_1),\ldots,(\boldsymbol{x}_\ell,y_\ell)\}\in(\mathcal{H},\{-1,1\})^\ell$	$\{(\boldsymbol{x}_1,y_1),\ldots,(\boldsymbol{x}_\ell,y_\ell)\}\in(\mathcal{H},\Re)^\ell$
Initialization:	$\boldsymbol{w}_1=\boldsymbol{0}$	$\boldsymbol{w}_1=\boldsymbol{0}$, choose $\epsilon>0$
Prediction:	Upon receiving the tth instance $\boldsymbol{x}_t$, set $\overline{y}_t=\langle\boldsymbol{w}_t,\boldsymbol{x}_t\rangle$ then give the prediction:	
	$\hat{y}_t=\text{sign}(\overline{y}_t)$	$\hat{y}_t=\overline{y}_t$
Update:	Project $\boldsymbol{w}_t$ onto the tth feasible set $\mathcal{U}_t$, $\boldsymbol{w}_{t+1}=\mathcal{P}_{\mathcal{U}_t}(\boldsymbol{w}_t)$	
Feasible set:	$\mathcal{U}_t=\{\boldsymbol{v}:\langle\boldsymbol{v},\mathbf{x}_t\rangle y_t\geq 1\}$	$\mathcal{U}_t=\{\boldsymbol{v}:\langle\boldsymbol{v},\mathbf{x}_t\rangle\in[y_t-\epsilon,y_t+\epsilon]\}$
Update Eq:	if $\overline{y}_t y_t\geq 1$ then $\boldsymbol{w}_{t+1}=\boldsymbol{w}_t$ else $\boldsymbol{w}_{t+1}=\boldsymbol{w}_t+\frac{y_t-\overline{y}_t}{\Vert\boldsymbol{x}_t\Vert^2}\boldsymbol{x}_t$ (9)	if $\overline{y}_t\in[y_t-\epsilon,y_t+\epsilon]$ then $\boldsymbol{w}_{t+1}=\boldsymbol{w}_t$ else $s=\text{sign}(\overline{y}_t-(y_t-\epsilon))$ $\boldsymbol{w}_{t+1}=\boldsymbol{w}_t+\frac{y_t+s\epsilon-\overline{y}_t}{\Vert\boldsymbol{x}_t\Vert^2}\boldsymbol{x}_t$ (10)
Algorithms for data mapped to RKHS $\mathcal{H}_K$ via kernel $K:\mathcal{E}\times\mathcal{E}\to\Re$		
Input:	$\{(x_1,y_1),\ldots,(x_\ell,y_\ell)\}\in(\mathcal{E},\{-1,1\})^\ell$	$\{(x_1,y_1),\ldots,(x_\ell,y_\ell)\}\in(\mathcal{E},\Re)^\ell$
Initialization:	$\boldsymbol{w}_1=\boldsymbol{0}$ $(\alpha_1=0)$	$\boldsymbol{w}_1=\boldsymbol{0}$ $(\alpha_1=0)$, choose $\epsilon>0$
Prediction:	Upon receiving the tth instance x_t, set $\overline{y}_t=\boldsymbol{w}_t(\boldsymbol{x}_t)=\sum_{i=1}^{t-1}\alpha_i K(x_i,x_t)$ then give the prediction:	
	$\hat{y}_t=\text{sign}(\overline{y}_t)$	$\hat{y}_t=\overline{y}_t$
Update:	Project $\boldsymbol{w}_t$ onto the tth feasible set $\mathcal{U}_t$, $\boldsymbol{w}_{t+1}=\mathcal{P}_{\mathcal{U}_t}(\boldsymbol{w}_t)$	
Feasible set:	$\mathcal{U}_t=\{\boldsymbol{v}:\boldsymbol{v}(x_t)y_t\geq 1\}$	$\mathcal{U}_t=\{\boldsymbol{v}:\boldsymbol{v}(x_t)\in[y_t-\epsilon,y_t+\epsilon]\}$
Update Eq:	if $\overline{y}_t y_t\geq 1$ then $\alpha_t=0$ else $\alpha_t=\frac{y_t-\overline{y}_t}{K(x_t,x_t)}$ (11)	if $\overline{y}_t\in[y_t-\epsilon,y_t+\epsilon]$ then $\alpha_t=0$ else $s=\text{sign}(\overline{y}_t-(y_t-\epsilon))$ $\alpha_t=\frac{y_t+s\epsilon-\overline{y}_t}{K(x_t,x_t)}$ (12)
	$\boldsymbol{w}_{t+1}=\boldsymbol{w}_t+\alpha_t K(x_t,\cdot)$	

Fig. 2. Projection algorithms for classification and regression

review of its many applications. The first application of this algorithm in the machine learning literature was by Faber and Mycielski [11] to proving worst-case square loss bounds for regression in the noise-free case; Cesa-Bianchi et. al. [8] generalized this work to noisy data with the GD algorithm. In this section we will discuss the application of the prototypical projection algorithm to classification and regression, producing a simple variant of the Perceptron algorithm [34] and a new online algorithm for regression with noisy data.

The following lemma regarding the convergence of the prototypical projection algorithm is well-known.

Lemma 1. *Given a sequence of convex set $\{\mathcal{U}_1,\ldots,\mathcal{U}_\ell\}$ and a start vector $\boldsymbol{w}_1$ as input to the prototypical projection algorithm (see Figure 3) the following*

Input: A sequence of closed convex sets $\{\mathcal{U}_1, \ldots, \mathcal{U}_\ell\} \subset \mathcal{H}^\ell$ and a point $w_1 \in \mathcal{H}$ where $\mathcal{H}$ is a Hilbert space.
Update: $w_{t+1} = \mathcal{P}_{\mathcal{U}_t}(w_t)$

Fig. 3. Prototypical projection algorithm

inequality holds

$$\sum_{t=1}^{\ell} \|w_t - w_{t+1}\|^2 \leq \|u - w_1\|^2 \tag{13}$$

for all $u \in \bigcap_{t=1}^{\ell} \mathcal{U}_t$.

Proof. On any trial t the Pythagorean Theorem 1 implies the inequality

$$\|w_{t+1} - w_t\|^2 \leq \|u - w_t\|^2 - \|u - w_{t+1}\|^2$$

for all u such that $u \in \mathcal{U}_t$. Summing the previous inequality over all trials $t = 1, \ldots, \ell$ we have

$$\sum_{t=1}^{\ell} \|w_{t+1} - w_t\|^2 \leq \|u - w_1\|^2 - \|u - w_{\ell+1}\|^2$$

for all $u \in \bigcap_{t=1}^{\ell} \mathcal{U}_t$. Dropping the final term of the above inequality proves the lemma.

An implication of the above lemma is that if $\bigcap_{t=1}^{\ell} \mathcal{U}_t$ is nonempty, and if we repeatedly cycle through the input $\{\mathcal{U}_1, \ldots, \mathcal{U}_\ell\}$, then the Cauchy sequence $\{w_1, w_2, \ldots\}$ generated by the prototypical projection algorithm necessarily converges to a point in the above intersection.

We use the prototypical projection algorithm to produce online learning algorithms by associating the *feasible set* sequence $\{\mathcal{U}_1, \ldots, \mathcal{U}_\ell\}$ with the example sequence $\{(x_1, y_1), \ldots, (x_\ell, y_\ell)\}$. Each feasible set $\mathcal{U}_t$ consists of those hypothesis vectors which are "compatible" with the last example. In the projection algorithm for classification, the feasible set is the halfspace of vectors $\mathcal{U}_t = \{v : \langle v, \mathrm{x}_t \rangle y_t \geq 1\}$ which classify the last example correctly with a margin[4] greater than 1. For regression with the ϵ-insensitive square loss the feasible set is the "hyper-rectangle" of vectors $\mathcal{U}_t = \{v : \langle v, \mathrm{x}_t \rangle \in [y_t - \epsilon, y_t + \epsilon]\}$. These are the vectors which classify the last example correct up to an absolute error of most epsilon. In order to prove bounds for these algorithms, we lower bound each term of the sum in Equation (13) with a term that is the ratio of the loss

[4] Margin here has a different meaning than typically used in discussion of the Perceptron algorithm or the Maximal margin algorithm. Generally the margin is allowed to vary while the norm of the classifier is fixed to less than 1. In our discussion the margin is fixed to be larger than 1 while the norm of the classifier is allowed to vary. We choose these semantics to indicate the parallels between classification and regression.

of the algorithm on that example with the squared norm of the instance. Thus applying the lower bounds which are given in the Lemmas 2 and 3 in combination with Lemma 1 proves the worst-case loss bounds for classification and ϵ-insensitive regression in Theorems 2 and 3 respectively.

Lemma 2. *On any trial t the mistake-counting loss of the projection algorithm for classification may be bounded by*

$$\frac{L_m(y_t, \hat{y}_t)}{\|\mathbf{x}_t\|^2} \leq \|\boldsymbol{w}_{t+1} - \boldsymbol{w}_t\|^2 \tag{14}$$

Proof. Consider two cases. First, if $L_{\mathrm{m}}(y_t, \hat{y}_t) = 0$ the lemma is trivial, otherwise we have

$$\frac{|y_t - \overline{y}_t|^2}{\|\mathbf{x}_t\|^2} = \|\boldsymbol{w}_{t+1} - \boldsymbol{w}_t\|^2$$

by Update (9). Since $L_{\mathrm{m}}(y_t, \hat{y}_t) \leq |y_t - \overline{y}_t|^2$ when $y_t \neq \hat{y}_t$, the lemma is proven.

Lemma 3. *On any trial t the ϵ-insensitive square loss of the projection algorithm for regression may be bounded by*

$$\frac{L_{sq,\epsilon}(y_t, \hat{y}_t)}{\|\mathbf{x}_t\|^2} \leq \|\boldsymbol{w}_{t+1} - \boldsymbol{w}_t\|^2 \tag{15}$$

Theorem 2. *Given a sequence of examples $\{(\boldsymbol{x}_1, y_1), \ldots, (\boldsymbol{x}_\ell, y_\ell)\} \in (\mathcal{H}, \{-1, 1\})^\ell$ and a start vector $\boldsymbol{w}_1 \in \mathcal{H}$, let $R = \max_{t=1,..,\ell} \|\boldsymbol{x}_t\|$ then the cumulative mistakes of the projection algorithm for classification is bounded by*

$$\sum_{t=1}^{\ell} L_m(y_t, \hat{y}_t) \leq R^2 \|\boldsymbol{u} - \boldsymbol{w}_1\|^2 \tag{16}$$

for all $\boldsymbol{u}$ such that $\langle \boldsymbol{u}, \boldsymbol{x}_t \rangle y_t \geq 1$ for $t = 1, \ldots, \ell$.

This algorithm for classification is a simple variant of Rosenblatt's perceptron algorithm [34], and the bound proven, though differing in form, is the same as that proven by Novikoff [32]. This algorithm is equivalent to the perceptron if the data is always normalized and we also update when correct but $y_t \overline{y}_t < 1$. As given in the conditions of theorem the algorithm only provides a bound when the data is linearly separable; recently, however, Freund and Schapire [13] have proven a bound for the perceptron algorithm (in $\Re^n$) when the data is linearly inseparable; this technique is further extended in [37] for inseparable data in more general kernel spaces.

Theorem 3. *Given a sequence of examples $\{(\boldsymbol{x}_1, y_1), \ldots, (\boldsymbol{x}_\ell, y_\ell)\} \in (\mathcal{H}, \Re)^\ell$ and a start vector $\boldsymbol{w}_1 \in \mathcal{H}$, let $R = \max_{t=1,\ldots,\ell} \|\boldsymbol{x}_t\|$. Then the cumulative ϵ-insensitive square loss of the projection algorithm for regression is bounded by*

$$\sum_{t=1}^{\ell} L_{sq,\epsilon}(y_t, \hat{y}_t) \leq R^2 \|\boldsymbol{u} - \boldsymbol{w}_1\|^2 \tag{17}$$

for all $\boldsymbol{u}$ such that $\langle \boldsymbol{u}, \boldsymbol{x}_t \rangle \in [y_t - \epsilon, y_t + \epsilon]$ for $t = 1, \ldots, \ell$.

For the special case when $\epsilon = 0$ this theorem was first proven in [11]. The GD algorithm [8] is also designed for online regression on noisy data, a salient feature of the GD algorithm is that given an upper bound on R (as defined above) the algorithm may be tuned so that a worst-case bound on the usual square loss is given for any data sequence, whereas the projection algorithm for regression requires for its bound the assumption that $\sum_{t=1}^{\ell} \mathcal{U}_t$ is non-empty.

Two useful properties of the projection algorithm for regression are that it is convergent (see the discussion following Lemma 1), and that like the perceptron algorithm it is *conservative*, i.e., for a given example we only update if $|y_t - \hat{y}_t| \geq \epsilon$. This feature is particularly important when applying the algorithm in conjunction with a kernel transformation, since on any given example when there is a nonvacuous update (see Equation (12) in Figure 2) the representation of the hypothesis grows, and this increases the computation time for future predictions.

2.4 Methods for Local Loss Bounds

In the traditional methodology of total loss bounds the performance over the whole sequence is bounded; but nothing is known about the performance over any particular contiguous subsequence of trials except in a very weak average sense. However, for many online learning applications what is needed is a *local* guarantee, i.e., a statement of this form: given an unbounded sequence of trials the loss over trials s to s' is bounded by X. Local bounds are thus appropriate when the best predictor for the example sequence is changing over time. There have been a number of papers [28,20,3,43,6,21] which prove loss bounds in terms of a measure of the amount of change of the best predictor over time. These bounds have been called *shifting* or *switching* bounds. The local bounds of this section are direct simplifications of the shifting bounds in [21]. Here we give local bounds rather than shifting bounds, however, since less introductory machinery is required, the bounds are easier to interpret, and weaker assumptions on the example sequence are possible in the theorem statements.

Examining the Theorems 2 and 3 it is clear that statements of the form

$$\sum_{t=s}^{s'} L(y_t, \hat{y}_t) \leq \|\boldsymbol{w}_s - \boldsymbol{u}\|^2 R^2, \tag{18}$$

for all $\boldsymbol{u} \in \bigcap_{t=s}^{s'} \mathcal{U}_t$ where $R = \max_{t=s,\ldots,s'} \|\mathbf{x}_t\|$ are provable. However, the weakness of bounds of the above form is that $\boldsymbol{w}_s$ is wholly unknown without reference to the example sequence prior to trial s. We resolve this by introducing an additional update step (first introduced in [21]) into the Prototypical projection algorithm which constrains the hypotheses vectors $\boldsymbol{w}_1, \ldots$ to an origin centered hypersphere Γ_γ with radius γ (see Figure 4) by projection. The projection corresponding to the new update may be computed as follows:

$$\mathcal{P}_{\Gamma_\gamma}(\boldsymbol{w}) = \begin{cases} \boldsymbol{w} & \boldsymbol{w} \in \Gamma_\gamma \\ \gamma \frac{\boldsymbol{w}}{\|\boldsymbol{w}\|} & \boldsymbol{w} \notin \Gamma_\gamma . \end{cases} \tag{19}$$

We can now prove the analogue of Lemma 1.

Input: A constraint parameter $\gamma > 0$, a sequence of closed convex sets $\{\mathcal{U}_1, \ldots\} \subset \mathcal{H}^\infty$ and a point $\boldsymbol{w}_1 \in \Gamma_\gamma$ where $\Gamma_\gamma = \{\boldsymbol{v} : \|\boldsymbol{v}\| \leq \gamma\} \subset \mathcal{H}$ and $\mathcal{H}$ is a Hilbert space.
Update 1: $\boldsymbol{w}'_t = \mathcal{P}_{\mathcal{U}_t}(\boldsymbol{w}_t)$
Update 2: $\boldsymbol{w}_{t+1} = \mathcal{P}_{\Gamma_\gamma}(\boldsymbol{w}'_t)$

Fig. 4. Constrained prototypical projection algorithm

Lemma 4. *Given a constraint parameter* $\gamma > 0$, *a sequence of convex sets* $\{\mathcal{U}_1, \ldots\}$ *and a start vector* $\boldsymbol{w}_1 \in \Gamma_\gamma$ *where* $\Gamma_\gamma = \{\boldsymbol{v} : \|\boldsymbol{v}\| \leq \gamma\}$ *as input to the constrained prototypical projection algorithm (see Figure 4); then for any positive integers* s *and* s' *the inequality*

$$\sum_{t=s}^{s'} \|\boldsymbol{w}_t - \boldsymbol{w}'_t\|^2 \leq (\gamma + \|\boldsymbol{u}\|)^2 \tag{20}$$

holds for all $\boldsymbol{u} \in \bigcap_{t=s}^{s'} \mathcal{U}_t$ *such that* $\|\boldsymbol{u}\| \leq \gamma$.

Proof. On any trial t the Pythagorean Theorem 1 implies the following two inequalities:

$$\|\boldsymbol{w}'_t - \boldsymbol{w}_t\|^2 \leq \|\boldsymbol{u} - \boldsymbol{w}_t\|^2 - \|\boldsymbol{u} - \boldsymbol{w}'_t\|^2$$

for all $\boldsymbol{u}$ such that $\boldsymbol{u} \in \mathcal{U}_t$, and

$$0 \leq \|\boldsymbol{u} - \boldsymbol{w}'_t\|^2 - \|\boldsymbol{u} - \boldsymbol{w}_{t+1}\|^2$$

for all $\boldsymbol{u}$ such that $\boldsymbol{u} \in \Gamma_\gamma$. Combining the above two inequalities gives

$$\|\boldsymbol{w}'_t - \boldsymbol{w}_t\|^2 \leq \|\boldsymbol{u} - \boldsymbol{w}_t\|^2 - \|\boldsymbol{u} - \boldsymbol{w}_{t+1}\|^2$$

for all $\boldsymbol{u}$ such that $\boldsymbol{u} \in \mathcal{U}_t \bigcap \Gamma_\gamma$. Summing the previous inequality over all trials $t = s, \ldots, s'$ we have

$$\sum_{t=s}^{s'} \|\boldsymbol{w}'_t - \boldsymbol{w}_t\|^2 \leq \|\boldsymbol{u} - \boldsymbol{w}_s\|^2 - \|\boldsymbol{u} - \boldsymbol{w}_{s'+1}\|^2$$

for all $\boldsymbol{u} \in [\bigcap_{t=s}^{s'} \mathcal{U}_t] \bigcap \Gamma_\gamma$. Maximizing the first term and dropping the second term of the right hand side of the above inequality proves the lemma.

We designate the modification of projection algorithms in Figure 2 with the additional constraint update (see Equation (19)) as *constrained* projection algorithms for classification and regression. The following two theorems give local loss bounds for these algorithms by combining the Lemma above with Lemmas 2 and 3.

Theorem 4. *Given a sequence of examples* $\{(\boldsymbol{x}_1, y_1), \ldots\} \in (\mathcal{H}, \{-1, 1\})^\infty$, *a constraint parameter* $\gamma > 0$, *a start vector* $\boldsymbol{w}_1 \in \Gamma_\gamma \subset \mathcal{H}$, *and two positive integers* s *and* s', *where* $\Gamma_\gamma = \{\boldsymbol{v} : \|\boldsymbol{v}\| \leq \gamma\}$ *and* $R = \max_{t=s,\ldots,s'} \|\boldsymbol{x}_t\|$ *then* *the cumulative mistakes of the constrained projection algorithm for classification between trials s and s' is bounded by*

$$\sum_{t=s}^{s'} L_m(y_t, \hat{y}_t) \leq R^2(\gamma + \|\boldsymbol{u}\|)^2 \tag{21}$$

for all $\boldsymbol{u}$ such that $\langle \boldsymbol{u}, \boldsymbol{x}_t \rangle y_t \geq 1$ for $t = s, \ldots, s'$ and $\|\boldsymbol{u}\| \leq \gamma$.

Theorem 5. *Given a sequence of examples $\{(\boldsymbol{x}_1, y_1), \ldots\} \in (\mathcal{H}, \Re)^\infty$, a constraint parameter $\gamma > 0$, a start vector $\boldsymbol{w}_1 \in \Gamma_\gamma \subset \mathcal{H}$, two positive integers s and s', where $\Gamma_\gamma = \{\boldsymbol{v} : \|\boldsymbol{v}\| \leq \gamma\}$ and $R = \max_{t=s,\ldots,s'} \|\boldsymbol{x}_t\|$ then the cumulative ϵ-insensitive square loss of the constrained projection algorithm for regression between trials s and s' is bounded by*

$$\sum_{t=s}^{s'} L_{sq,\epsilon}(y_t, \hat{y}_t) \leq R^2(\gamma + \|\boldsymbol{u}\|)^2 \tag{22}$$

for all $\boldsymbol{u}$ such that $\langle \boldsymbol{u}, \boldsymbol{x}_t \rangle \in [y_t - \epsilon, y_t + \epsilon]$ for $t = s, \ldots, s'$ and $\|\boldsymbol{u}\| \leq \gamma$.

2.5 Incorporating Kernels

Reproducing kernel preliminaries. We assume that the reader is already familiar with kernel-based methods (for an overview see [10]). This section is for notation and a cursory review of kernel concepts. For our purposes, given an abstract set $\mathcal{E}$ a kernel is a function $K : \mathcal{E} \times \mathcal{E} \rightarrow \Re$ where, for every finite set $\{x_1, \ldots, x_n\} \subset \mathcal{E}^n$ and every set of scalars $\{\alpha_1, \ldots, \alpha_n\} \subset \Re^n$ the following holds:

$$\sum_{i=1}^{n} \sum_{j=1}^{n} \alpha_i \alpha_j K(x_i, x_j) \geq 0.$$

Such a kernel is known in the literature as a reproducing kernel [2], a positive definite kernel [29] and as a positive hermitian matrix [30]. An immediate consequence of the above property is that the kernel is symmetric, i.e., $K(x, y) = K(y, x)$. The associated Hilbert space $\mathcal{H}_K$ is the completion of the span of the set $\{K(x, \cdot) : x \in \mathcal{E}\}$ where the associated inner product between elements with finite representations $f = \sum_{i=1}^{n} \alpha_i K(x_i, \cdot)$, $f' = \sum_{i=1}^{n'} \alpha'_i K(x'_i, \cdot)$ is given by

$$\langle f, f' \rangle = \sum_{i=1}^{n} \sum_{j=1}^{n'} \alpha_i \alpha'_j K(x_i, x'_j). \tag{23}$$

When the representations are not finite, the appropriate limits are taken. The key property of $\mathcal{H}_K$ which we will use repeatedly is the reproducing property, which states that, given any $f \in \mathcal{H}_K$ and any $x \in \mathcal{E}$ then

$$\langle f(\cdot), K(x, \cdot) \rangle = f(x). \tag{24}$$

The kernel may be viewed as a function that computes an inner product in a *feature space* [10]. None of the results in this paper depend explicitly on the existence of a feature space representation, thus it is not introduced.

The kernel transformation algorithmic details and bounds. Given a data set $\{(x_1, y_1), \ldots, (x_\ell, y_\ell)\} \in (\mathcal{E}, \Re)^\ell$, a reproducing kernel $K : \mathcal{E} \times \mathcal{E} \to \Re$, and an algorithm A which accepts as input an example sequence $\{(\boldsymbol{x}_1, y_1), \ldots, (\boldsymbol{x}_\ell, y_\ell)\} \in (\mathcal{H}, \Re)^\ell$, the new algorithm A_K simply executes algorithm A on the data set $\{(K(x_1, \cdot), y_1), \ldots, (K(x_\ell, \cdot), y_\ell)\}$. The kernel algorithms in Figure 2 follow directly by syntactic substitution of $K(x, \cdot)$ for $\boldsymbol{x}$ and application of the reproducing Property (24). The transformation of Theorems 2, 3, 4 and 5 follow from similar substitutions. We give as an example the transformation of Theorem 3 below, but we omit the other transforms since they follow the same schema.

Theorem 6. *Given a sequence of examples $\{(x_1, y_1), \ldots, (x_\ell, y_\ell)\} \in (\mathcal{E}, \Re)^\ell$ and a start vector $\boldsymbol{w}_1 \in \mathcal{H}_K$, let $R = \max_{t=1,\ldots,\ell} K(x_t, x_t)$, then the cumulative ϵ-insensitive square loss of the kernel projection algorithm for regression is bounded by*

$$\sum_{t=1}^{\ell} L_{sq,\epsilon}(y_t, \hat{y}_t) \leq R^2 \|\boldsymbol{u} - \boldsymbol{w}_1\|^2 \tag{25}$$

for all functions $\boldsymbol{u} \in \mathcal{H}_K$ such that $\boldsymbol{u}(x_t) \in [y_t - \epsilon, y_t + \epsilon]$ for $t = 1, \ldots, \ell$.

Recently strong total loss bounds have been proven for ridge regression [12,44,4], in [36] a method to perform kernel ridge regression is given. Unfortunately the loss bounds for ridge regression with kernels do not transform since the proofs rely on properties of $\Re^n$. A transformation of those bounds is an interesting open problem.

Computational issues. When implementing the projection algorithms for regression and classification, significant computational shortcuts can be taken when the patterns of the example sequence are from $\Re^n$. This is because when summing two vectors $\boldsymbol{x}$ and $\boldsymbol{y}$ from $\Re^n$, the resultant $\boldsymbol{x}+\boldsymbol{y}$ has the same sized representation as $\boldsymbol{x}$ or $\boldsymbol{y}$ under a simplified model of computation, i.e., size$(\boldsymbol{x}+\boldsymbol{y}) =$ size$(\boldsymbol{x})$ $=$ size$(\boldsymbol{y})$. Whereas when the elements are drawn from an arbitrary Hilbert space, as with kernel-based algorithms, size$(\boldsymbol{x} + \boldsymbol{y}) =$ size$(\boldsymbol{x})$ + size$(\boldsymbol{y})$. Thus for data from $\Re^n$ the projections algorithms take $O(n)$ time per trial. Whereas the kernel-based projection algorithms require for typical kernels and typical implementations $O(m)$ kernel computations on trial t (in order to predict), if there have been $m \leq t$ nonvacuous updates. In Part 1, there are presented particular kernels for which we require only $O(\log m)$ computation time on trial t after m nonvacuous updates.

The implementation of the constraint update, $\mathcal{P}_{\Gamma_\gamma}(\boldsymbol{w})$ (see Equation 19) requires $O(n)$ time when $\boldsymbol{w} \in \Re^n$. The naive implementation of the constraint update for the kernel-based algorithms requires t^2 kernel computations after t nonvacuous updates since the function $\boldsymbol{w}$ has a representation of length t, i.e., $\boldsymbol{w}_{t+1} = \sum_{i=1}^{t} \alpha_i K(x_i, \cdot)$ since the inner product (see Equation (23)) is

$$\|\boldsymbol{w}_{t+1}\|^2 = \langle \boldsymbol{w}_{t+1}, \boldsymbol{w}_{t+1} \rangle = \sum_{i=1}^{t} \sum_{j=1}^{t} \alpha_i \alpha_j K(x_i, x_j).$$

However, we may use a simple recurrence to track the value of $\|\boldsymbol{w}_{t+1}\|$, since after an update we have only one new α value, i.e.,

$$\|\boldsymbol{w}_{t+1}\|^2 = \|\boldsymbol{w}_t\|^2 + \sum_{i=1}^{t-1} \alpha_i \alpha_t K(x_i, x_t) + \sum_{j=1}^{t-1} \alpha_t \alpha_j K(x_t, x_j) + \alpha_t^2 K(x_t, x_t)$$
$$= \|\boldsymbol{w}_t\|^2 + 2\alpha_t \overline{y}_t + \alpha_t^2 K(x_t, x_t).$$

Since in order to predict we already compute $\overline{y}_t$, we may keep track of $\|\boldsymbol{w}_{t+1}\|$ at no additional asymptotic cost. Implementing the constraint update then only requires the additional step of shrinking $\boldsymbol{w}_t$ by $\rho_t \in (0,1]$ (see Equation 19). Rather than explicitly multiplying each term of $\boldsymbol{w}_t$ by ρ_t, we maintain the scale constant $\rho^{(t)} = \prod_{i=1}^t \rho_i$ ($\rho^0 = 1$), all arithmetic is then done with the scale constant implicitly. Thus it can be seen that the projection update leads to a version of weight decay, since at the start of trial t we have

$$\boldsymbol{w}_t = \sum_{i=1}^{t-1} \prod_{j=i}^{t-1} \rho_j \alpha_i K(x_i, \cdot),$$

internally, however, we maintain the representation

$$\boldsymbol{w}_t = \rho^{(t-1)} \sum_{i=1}^{t-1} \frac{1}{\rho^{(i-1)}} \alpha_i K(x_i, \cdot)$$

so that the constraint update may be implemented in $O(1)$ time rather than $O(t)$ time.

Acknowledgments: The author would like to thank Nello Cristianini for useful discussions and Mary Dubberly for the proofreading of an early draft. A portion of this research was undertaken while at the Computer Learning Research Centre at Royal Holloway University.

References

1. M. A. Aizerman, E. M. Braverman, and L. I. Rozonoér. Theoretical foundations of the potential function method in pattern recognition learning. *Automation and Remote Control*, 25:821–837, 1964.
2. N. Aronszajn. Theory of reproducing kernels. *Trans. Amer. Math. Soc.*, 68:337–404, 1950.
3. P. Auer and M. K. Warmuth. Tracking the best disjunction. *Journal of Machine Learning*, 32(2):127–150, August 1998. Special issue on concept drift.
4. Katy S. Azoury and M. K. Warmuth. Relative loss bounds for on-line density estirnation with the exponential family of distributions. In Kathryn B. Laskey and Henri Prade, editors, *Proceedings of the 15th Conference on Uncertainty in Artificial Intelligence (UAI-99)*, pages 31–40, S.F., Cal., July 30–August 1 1999. Morgan Kaufmann Publishers.
5. Heinz H. Bauschke and Jonathan M. Borwein. On projection algorithms for solving convex feasibility problems. *SIAM Review*, 38(3):367–426, September 1996.

6. A. Blum and C. Burch. On-line learning and the metrical task system problem. *Machine Learning*, 39(1):35–58, 2000.
7. B. E. Boser, I. M. Guyon, and V. N. Vapnik. A training algorithm for optimal margin classifiers. In *Proc. 5th Annu. Workshop on Comput. Learning Theory*, pages 144–152. ACM Press, New York, NY, 1992.
8. N. Cesa-Bianchi, P. Long, and M.K. Warmuth. Worst-case quadratic loss bounds for on-line prediction of linear functions by gradient descent. *IEEE Transactions on Neural Networks*, 7(2):604–619, May 1996.
9. T. H. Cormen, C. E. Leiserson, and R. L. Rivest. *Introduction to Algorithms*. MIT Press, Cambridge, MA, 1990.
10. N. Cristianini and J. Shawe-Taylor. *An Introduction to Support Vector Machines*. Cambridge University Press, Cambridge, UK, 2000.
11. V. Faber and J. Mycielski. Applications of learning theorems. *Fundamenta Informaticae*, 15(2):145–167, 1991.
12. D. P. Foster. Prediction in the worst case. *The Annals of Statistics*, 19(2):1084–1090, 1991.
13. Yoav Freund and Robert E. Schapire. Large margin classification using the perceptron algorithm. *Machine Learning*, 37(3):277–296, 1999.
14. Thilo-Thomas Frieß, Nello Cristianini, and Colin Campbell. The Kernel-Adatron algorithm: a fast and simple learning procedure for Support Vector machines. In *Proc. 15th International Conf. on Machine Learning*, pages 188–196. Morgan Kaufmann, San Francisco, CA, 1998.
15. C. Gentile. A new approximate maximal margin classification algorithm. In T. K. Leen, T. G. Dietterich, and V. Tresp, editors, *Advances in Neural Information Processing Systems*, volume 13, 2001.
16. Federico Girosi, Michael Jones, and Tomaso Poggio. Regularization theory and neural networks architectures. *Neural Computation*, 7(2):219–269, 1995.
17. T. Hastie and R. Tibshirani. Generalized additive models, 1990.
18. D. Haussler, J. Kivinen, and M. K. Warmuth. Sequential prediction of individual sequences under general loss functions. IEEE Transactions on Information Theory, 44(2):1906–1925, September 1998.
19. D. P. Helmbold, J. Kivinen, and M. K. Warmuth. Relative loss bounds for single neurons. *Journal of Machine Learning*, 2001. To appear.
20. Mark Herbster and Manfred Warmuth. Tracking the best expert. In *Proc. 12th International Conference on Machine Learning*, pages 286–294. Morgan Kaufmann, 1995.
21. Mark Herbster and Manfred K. Warmuth. Tracking the best regressor. In *Proc. 11th Annu. Conf. on Comput. Learning Theory*, pages 24–31. ACM Press, New York, NY, 1998.
22. G. S. Kimeldorf and G. Wahba. Some results on tchebycheffian spline functions. *J. Math. Anal. Applications*, 33(1):82–95, 1971.
23. J. Kivinen and M. K. Warmuth. Additive versus exponentiated gradient updates for linear prediction. *Information and Computation*, 132(1):1–64, January 1997.
24. Y. LeCun, L. Jackel, L. Bottou, A. Brunot, C. Cortes, J. Denker, H. Drucker, I. Guyon, U. Muller, E. Sackinger, P. Simard, and V. Vapnik. Comparison of learning algorithms for handwritten digit recognition, 1995.
25. Y. Li. and P. Long. The relaxed online maximum margin algorithm. *Machine Learning*, 2001.
26. N. Littlestone. Learning when irrelevant attributes abound: A new linear-threshold algorithm. *Machine Learning*, 2:285–318, 1988.

27. N. Littlestone. *Mistake Bounds and Logarithmic Linear-threshold Learning Algorithms.* PhD thesis, Technical Report UCSC-CRL-89-11, University of California Santa Cruz, 1989.
28. N. Littlestone and M. K. Warmuth. The weighted majority algorithm. *Information and Computation*, 108(2):212–261, 1994.
29. J. Mercer. Functions of a positive and negative type and their connection with the threory of integral equations. *Philosophical Transactions Royal Society London Ser. A.*, 209, 1909.
30. E. H. Moore. *General Analysis. Part I.* American Philosophical Society, Philadelphia, 1935.
31. J. Von Neumann. *Functional Operators, Vol II. The Geometry of orthogonal spaces*, volume 22. Princeton University Press, 1950.
32. A. Novikoff. On convergence proofs for perceptrons. In *Proc. Sympos. Math. Theory of Automata (New York, 1962)*, pages 615–622. Polytechnic Press of Polytechnic Inst. of Brooklyn, Brooklyn, N.Y., 1963.
33. J. Platt. Fast training of support vector machines using sequential minimal optimization. In B. Schölkopf, C. J. C. Burges, and A. J. Smola, editors, *Advances in Kernel Methods — Support Vector Learning*, pages 185–208, Cambridge, MA, 1999. MIT Press.
34. F. Rosenblatt. The perceptron: A probabilistic model for information storage and organization in the brain. *Psych. Rev.*, 65:386–407, 1958. (Reprinted in *Neurocomputing* (MIT Press, 1988).).
35. Walter Rudin. *Real and Complex Analysis.* McGraw-Hill, New York, 3 edition, 1986.
36. G. Saunders, A. Gammerman, and V. Vovk. Ridge regression learning algorithm in dual variables. In *Proc. 15th International Conf. on Machine Learning*, pages 515–521. Morgan Kaufmann, San Francisco, CA, 1998.
37. John Shawe-Taylor and Nello Cristianini. Further results on the margin distribution. In *Proc. 12th Annu. Conf. on Comput. Learning Theory*, pages 278–285. ACM Press, New York, NY, 1999.
38. A. Smola. Large scale and online learning with kernels. Talk given Dec 5, 2000 at Royal Holloway University, based on joint work with J. Kivinen, P. Wankadia, and R. Williamson.
39. V. Vapnik. *Statistical Learning Theory.* John_Wiley, 1998.
40. V. Vapnik, S. Golowich, and A. Smola. Support vector method for function approximation, regression estimation, and signal processing. In M. Mozer, M. Jordan, and T. Petsche, editors, *Advances in Neural Information Processing Systems 9*, pages 281–287, Cambridge, MA, 1997. MIT Press.
41. V. N. Vapnik and A. Y. Chervonenkis. *Teoriya raspoznavaniya obrazov. Statisticheskie problemy obucheniya. [Theory of Pattern Recognition].* Izdat. "Nauka", Moscow, 1974.
42. V. Vovk. Aggregating strategies. In *Proc. 3rd Annu. Workshop on Comput. Learning Theory*, pages 371–383. Morgan Kaufmann, 1990.
43. V. Vovk. Derandomizing stochastic prediction strategies. In *Proc. 10th Annu. Workshop on Comput. Learning Theory.* ACM Press, New York, NY, 1997.
44. Volodya Vovk. Competitive on-line linear regression. In Michael I. Jordan, Michael J. Kearns, and Sara A. Solla, editors, *Advances in Neural Information Processing Systems*, volume 10. The MIT Press, 1998.

Geometric Bounds for Generalization in Boosting

Shie Mannor and Ron Meir

Department of Electrical Engineering
Technion, Haifa 32000
Israel
(shie,rmeir)@(tx,ee).technion.ac.il

Abstract. We consider geometric conditions on a labeled data set which guarantee that boosting algorithms work well when linear classifiers are used as weak learners. We start by providing conditions on the error of the weak learner which guarantee that the empirical error of the composite classifier is small. We then focus on conditions required in order to insure that the linear weak learner itself achieves an error which is smaller than $1/2 - \gamma$, where the advantage parameter γ is strictly positive and *independent* of the sample size. Such a condition guarantees that the generalization error of the boosted classifier decays to its minimal value at a rate of $1/\sqrt{m}$, where m is the sample size. The required conditions, which are based solely on geometric concepts, can be easily verified for any data set in time $O(m^2)$, and may serve as an indication for the effectiveness of linear classifiers as weak learners for a particular data set.

1 Introduction

Many learning algorithms proposed in recent years are based on the idea of constructing a complex composite classifier by combining a sequence of so-called 'weak' classifiers. A weak classifier for binary classification problems is required to achieve a weighted empirical error which is strictly and consistently smaller than 1/2 for *any* probability distribution. While an error of 1/2 is trivially achieved, such a result is not useful for learning, since it does not endow the weak learner with a significant margin which can be boosted to yield a classifier that generalizes well. The basic issue which we address in this work, extending our recent results in [10], deals with providing sufficient conditions which guarantee that the margin attained by the weak learner is sufficiently large to be effectively boosted. We loosely refer to such a weak learner as an *effective weak learner.*

There have been several attempts in the literature to provide conditions for the existence of an effective weak learner. The first results along these lines dealt with Boolean functions, and defined a certain correlation measure between a hypothetical target function and the class of weak learners, which guaranteed that an effective weak learner exists [4,8]. The main distinction between these

D. Helmbold and B. Williamson (Eds.): COLT/EuroCOLT 2001, LNAI 2111, pp. 461–472, 2001.

results and ours is that we focus on real-valued inputs and on purely geometric quantities, which depend solely on the data itself and not on a hypothetical target function. Moreover, the conditions we provide can be easily checked using the data itself, without further assumptions. The results discussed in this work are based on the framework introduced in [10] which builds on the work of Alexander [1,2]. We extend these results by considerably weakening the conditions and tightening the bounds. In particular, we provide conditions on the data set which guarantee that a linear classifier exists whose weighted empirical error is bounded from above by $1/2-\gamma$ where the advantage γ is strictly positive and *independent* of the sample size.

2 Boosting Error Bounds

In order to motivate our work, we recall some of the main results in the field of boosting. In particular, we focus on the training and generalization error bounds, which will serve as motivation for our analysis.

2.1 Generalization Error

We begin by quoting a recent result from the work of Koltchinskii *et al.* [9], which extends the results of Schapire *et al.* [11]. Let $\mathcal{H}$ be a class of binary classifiers of VC-dimension $d_{\mathcal{H}}$, and denote by $\text{co}(\mathcal{H})$ the convex hull of $\mathcal{H}$, namely

$$\text{co}(\mathcal{H}) = \left\{ f : f(\mathbf{x}) = \sum_i \alpha_i h_i(\mathbf{x}),\ \alpha_i \geq 0, \sum_i \alpha_i = 1 \right\} .$$

Given a sample $S = \{(\mathbf{x}_1, y_1), \ldots, (\mathbf{x}_m, y_m)\}$, $\mathbf{x}_i \in \mathbb{R}^d$ and $y_i \in \{-1, +1\}$, of m examples drawn independently at random from some probability distribution D over $\mathbb{R}^d \times \{-1, +1\}$, Koltchinskii *et al.* [11] show that, with probability at least $1 - \delta$, for *every* $f \in \text{co}(\mathcal{H})$ and $\theta > 0$,

$$\mathbf{P}_D[Yf(X) \leq 0] \leq \mathbf{P}_S[Yf(X) \leq \theta] + O\left(\frac{1}{\theta} \sqrt{\frac{d_{\mathcal{H}}}{m}} \right) + O\left(\sqrt{\frac{\log \frac{1}{\delta}}{m}} \right) , \tag{1}$$

where the empirical *margin-error* $\mathbf{P}_S[Yf(X) \leq \theta]$ denotes the fraction of training points for which $y_i f(\mathbf{x}_i) \leq \theta$, namely

$$\mathbf{P}_S[Yf(X) \leq \theta] = \frac{1}{m} \sum_{i=1}^{m} I[y_i f(\mathbf{x}_i) \leq \theta] , \tag{2}$$

where $I[E]$ is the indicator function for the event E. The term $\mathbf{P}_D[Yf(X) \leq 0]$ is simply the probability of misclassification of the classifier $h(\mathbf{x}) = \text{sgn}(f(\mathbf{x}))$. Observe that one of the improvements of (1) with respect to the bound in [11] is that the second term decays at a rate of $1/\sqrt{m}$ rather than $\sqrt{\log m/m}$. Moreover, the bound may be extended to classes for which the VC-dimension is infinite (although the fat-shattering dimension is finite). The essence of the bound (1) takes the form of a *luckiness argument* [13], in that *if* a large margin can be guaranteed with respect to the data (i.e., $P_S[Yf(X) \le \theta]$ can be made small for large values of θ) then the complexity penalty term (the second term on the r.h.s. of (1)) is small, since it depends on the VC-dimension of $\mathcal{H}$, rather than on the VC-dimension of co($\mathcal{H}$) which may be significantly larger. It should be immediately clear from the bound that once θ depends on m, one can no longer guarantee a rate of convergence of order $1/\sqrt{m}$. This observation motivates us to search for situations where θ may be chosen to be independent of m, while still guaranteeing that the empirical margin error (2) is small.

2.2 Training Error

Boosting algorithms (e.g., [5,7,11,12]) operate by successively constructing a sequence of weak learners based on a re-weighted version on the data. The final (composite) hypothesis is then formed by taking a weighted combination of the weak learners. Denote the weighted empirical error of the t-th weak learner h_t by ϵ_t, where

$$\epsilon_t = \sum_{i=1}^{m} P_i I[h_t(\mathbf{x}_i) \neq y_i],$$

and P_i are the weights assigned by the boosting algorithm. We introduce the 'advantage' parameter γ_t by $\epsilon_t = 1/2 - \gamma_t$. In other words, γ_t measures the advantage of the weak learner over a trivial learner which achieves an error of 1/2.

Consider the AdaBoost algorithm introduced in [6]. We begin by considering conditions under which the margin-error (2) can be guaranteed to be small. Denoting the combined classifier at step T by f_T, Schapire *et al.* [11] obtained a bound on the empirical error $\mathbf{P}_S[Yf_T(X) \le \theta]$,

$$\mathbf{P}_S[Yf_T(X) \le \theta] \le \prod_{t=1}^{T} (1-2\gamma_t)^{\frac{1-\theta}{2}} (1+2\gamma_t)^{\frac{1+\theta}{2}}. \qquad (3)$$

In [11] conditions were provided for the convergence of the upper bound to zero as a function of the number of boosting iteration. In particular, it was shown that if $\sum_{t=1}^{\infty} \gamma_t^2 \to \infty$, then the empirical error (corresponding to $\theta = 0$ in (2)) converges to zero. We are interested in conditions guaranteeing that $\mathbf{P}_S[Yf_T(X) \le \theta]$ is small, not necessarily zero. Let

$$\bar{\gamma}_\theta = \frac{\theta}{2} + \frac{1}{\sqrt{2}} \sqrt{\log 2 - H\left(\frac{1-\theta}{2}\right)}, \qquad (4)$$

where $H(u) = -u \log u - (1-u)\log(1-u)$, $0 \le u \le 1$, is the binary entropy function. Logarithms in this paper are taken with respect to the natural basis. With these definitions we have the following result.

Theorem 1. *Let the advantage of the weak classifier obtained at step t of AdaBoost be $\gamma_t = \bar{\gamma}_\theta + \delta_t$, where $\bar{\gamma}_\theta$ is given in (4). Then the empirical margin error of the composite classifier obtained at step T is bounded from above by*

$$\mathbf{P}_S[Yf_T(X) \leq \theta] \leq \exp\left\{ -2(2\bar{\gamma}_\theta - \theta)\sum_{t=1}^{T} \delta_t - 2\sum_{t=1}^{T} \delta_t^2 \right\}.$$

This error is bounded by a finite value smaller than 1 if

$$\liminf_{T\to\infty} \sum_{t=1}^{T} \delta_t \geq c > 0, \tag{5}$$

and converges to zero if either $c = \infty$, or if c is finite and $\sum_{t=1}^{T} \delta_t^2$ converges to infinity.

The proof of Theorem 1 can be found in the appendix.

Remark 1. It is interesting to observe that δ_t in Theorem 1 may be positive or negative. In other words, there is no need for the advantage γ_t to always exceed some finite value. The margin-error remains bounded even if γ_t fluctuates around some finite value. For example, let δ_t be an alternating sequence of the form $(-1)^t f_t$, $t = 1, 2, \ldots$, where f_t is non-negative and monotonically decreasing. Then $\sum_{t=1}^{T} \delta_t$ converges to a finite non-negative limit if δ_1 is positive.

3 Bounding the Error of a Linear Weak Learner

In view of the claims following (2), we wish to consider situations where the parameter θ in (1) can be chosen to be *independent* of the sample size m. In this section we establish geometric conditions which guarantee that this is the case. Since the parameters θ and γ are related through $\gamma_t = \bar{\gamma}_\theta + \delta_t$, we will obtain conditions on the weak learner. We begin by defining the precise set-up for our problem, and recall some basic concepts from [10], which are in turn based on [1,2]. From this point we limit ourselves to linear weak learners, i.e., classifiers of the form

$$h(\mathbf{x}) = \mathrm{sgn}(\mathbf{w}^T\mathbf{x} + b) \quad \text{where } \mathbf{w} \in \mathbb{R}^d,\ b \in \mathbb{R}.$$

3.1 An Exact Setting

Let the i-th sample be denoted by $z_i = (\mathbf{x}_i, y_i)$, and let $P_i^{(m)}$ be a non-negative weight assigned to z_i such that $\sum_{i=1}^{m} P_i^{(m)} = 1$, $m = 1, 2, \ldots$. We define a filtration of samples by: $S_1 \subseteq S_2 \subseteq \cdots$ where $S_m = (z_1, \ldots, z_m)$. A classifier ξ is defined as a function $\xi : \mathbb{R}^d \to \{-1, 1\}$. The weighted empirical error $\epsilon(P^{(m)}, \xi)$ of a classifier ξ is defined as $\epsilon(P^{(m)}, \xi) = \sum_{i=1}^{m} P_i^{(m)} I[y_i \neq \xi(\mathbf{x}_i)]$. Note that $\epsilon(P^{(m)}, \xi)$ is a sequence of numbers between zero and one. We are interested in the behavior of $\epsilon(P^{(m)}, \xi)$ for certain classes of filtrations. In Section 3.3 below we consider conditions on the filtration which guarantee that the minimal value of $\epsilon(P^{(m)}, \xi)$ does not depend on the number of points m.

3.2 Preliminary Results and Definitions

In this section we consider a fixed sample of m points. To keep the notation simple we denote the sample by S (rather than S_m), and the probability assignment by P (rather than $P^{(m)}$). Consider a set of probabilities $\{P_i\}_{i=1}^m$ assigned to each element of the sample S, and let

$$\nu_i = y_i P_i .$$

In the sequel we assume that the set of weights $\{P_i\}$ is symmetric, namely $P^+ = P^-$, where P^+/P^- are the total weights of the positively/negatively labeled points. Lemma 4.1 in [10] shows that there is no loss of generality in this assumption in the following sense. If there exists a classifier ξ achieving an error smaller than $1/2 - \gamma$ on any symmetric distribution P, then a classifier exists with error smaller than $1/2 - \gamma/2$ for an arbitrary distribution.

Following [1] let ν and Φ be discrete signed measures on $\mathbb{R}^d$ and $\mathbb{R}$, respectively, and let $\nu \star \Phi$ be the product measure over $\mathbb{R}^d \times \mathbb{R}$. The measure ν is assumed to be supported on the data set $X = \{\mathbf{x}_1, \ldots, \mathbf{x}_m\} \in \mathbb{R}^d$, while Φ is supported on the n points $\{r_1, \ldots, r_n\} \in \mathbb{R}$. We use the notation $\nu(\mathbf{x}_i) = \nu_i$ and $\Phi_k = \Phi(r_k)$. Assume further that both measures obey the conditions:

$$\sum_{i=1}^{m} \nu_i = \sum_{j=1}^{n} \phi_i = 0 \quad ; \quad \sum_{i=1}^{m} |\nu_i| = \sum_{j=1}^{n} |\phi_i| = 1 \,. \tag{6}$$

Finally, for any two points $\mathbf{x}_i$ and $\mathbf{x}_j$ let $\Delta_{ij} = \|\mathbf{x}_i - \mathbf{x}_j\|$, where $\|\mathbf{x}\|$ is the Euclidean L_2 norm of the vector $\mathbf{x}$, and define

$$F_\Phi(\Delta_{ij}) = -\sum_{k=1}^{n} \sum_{l=1}^{n} \left(\Delta_{ij}^2 + |r_k - r_l|^2\right)^{1/2} \phi_k \phi_l \,. \tag{7}$$

A non-trivial result concerning $F_\Phi(\rho)$ follows from Theorem 6 in [2]. In particular, it is shown that $F_\Phi(\rho)$ is a *non-negative* and *monotonically decreasing* function of ρ.

Consider the class of linear classifiers, and let $\epsilon^*(P) = 1/2 - \gamma^*(P)$ be the minimal weighted error achieved in the class with respect to the data set S and the distribution P, and denote by L the radius of the smallest ball containing all the data points. A fundamental result in [1] (see also Section 4 in [10]) is that

$$\gamma^*(P) \geq \sqrt{-(C_d/2L) I(\nu \star \Phi)} \qquad (\nu_i = y_i P_i), \tag{8}$$

where the constant C_d depends only on the dimension d (C_d behaves like $1/\sqrt{d}$ for large d) and where

$$-I(\nu \star \Phi) = F_\Phi(0) \sum_i \nu_i^2 + \sum\sum_{i \neq j} F_\Phi(\Delta_{ij}) \nu_i \nu_j \,. \tag{9}$$

Note that ν is a signed measure, and thus the term $\nu_i \nu_j$ may be negative. Moreover, a direct consequence of Eq. (6a) in [1] is that $-I(\nu \star \Phi)$ is non-negative.

In [10] we computed a lower bound on $-I(\nu \star \Phi)$ by constructing a specific measure Φ for which $F_\Phi(\rho)$ decays rapidly with ρ. However, for that construction to be useful it was mandatory that a minimal distance exists between the positively and negatively labeled points. Moreover, the bound vanishes if this distance is zero. Such a result is clearly not robust in that two aberrant data points may result in a very weak bound. Moreover, the lower bound on $\gamma^*(P)$ in [10] depended explicitly on the sample size m, whereas here we provide geometric conditions which guarantee that the optimal advantage $\gamma^*(P)$ is *independent* of the sample size for any distribution P.

3.3 Attaining an Error Independent of the Sample-Size

Denote the positive and negative subsets of points by X^+ and X^- respectively. Consider a partition of the data into homogeneous subsets of points, where by homogeneous we mean that each subset contains only equally labeled points. Further, let $X^+ = X_1^+ \cup \cdots \cup X_{K^+}^+$ where $X_i^+ \cap X_j^+ = \emptyset$, $i \neq j$, and similarly for X^-. Denote the number of data points belonging to the subset X_k^+ by $m_{+,k}$, and similarly for X_ℓ^- and $m_{-,\ell}$.

Denote the set of indices corresponding to elements in the subset $X_k^\pm$ by $\mathcal{I}_k^\pm$. By re-arranging the double sum in (9), and recalling that $\Delta_{ij} = \|\mathbf{x}_i - \mathbf{x}_j\|$ and $\nu_i = y_i P_i$, one can easily show that

$$
\begin{aligned}
-I(\nu \star \Phi) = {} & F_\Phi(0) \sum_i P_i^2 - \sum_{k=1}^{K^+} \sum_{\ell=1}^{K^-} \sum_{i \in \mathcal{I}_k^+} \sum_{j \in \mathcal{I}_\ell^-} F_\Phi(\Delta_{ij}) P_i P_j \\
& + \sum_{k \neq \ell}^{K^+} \sum^{K^+} \sum_{i \in \mathcal{I}_k^+} \sum_{j \in \mathcal{I}_\ell^+} F_\Phi(\Delta_{ij}) P_i P_j + \sum_{k=1}^{K^+} \sum \sum_{\substack{i \neq j \\ i,j \in \mathcal{I}_k^+}} F_\Phi(\Delta_{ij}) P_i P_j \\
& + \sum_{k \neq \ell}^{K^-} \sum^{K^-} \sum_{i \in \mathcal{I}_k^-} \sum_{j \in \mathcal{I}_\ell^-} F_\Phi(\Delta_{ij}) P_i P_j + \sum_{k=1}^{K^-} \sum \sum_{\substack{i \neq j \\ i,j \in \mathcal{I}_k^-}} F_\Phi(\Delta_{ij}) P_i P_j .
\end{aligned} \tag{10}
$$

The advantage of this representation is that it makes the negative terms explicit, as all terms on the r.h.s. of (10), except for the second term, are non-negative.

In order to proceed in obtaining a simple geometric characterization of sufficient conditions for a bound independent of m, we assume that the weights in each subset of the partition are equal. While we use this assumption at this point as a simplifying assumption aimed at reducing the complexity of the computations, we point out that this assumption is obeyed during the iteration of the AdaBoost algorithm. In particular, beginning with a uniform distribution over points, at each step an additional linear classifier is constructed and added to the pool of existing weak learners. Each additional linear classifier (hyperplane) splits the sample S and the previously obtained regions. However, equally labeled points which are on the same side of the hyperplane are correctly/incorrectly classified together by the new weak learner. Since the update of the boosting weights depends only on the latter factor, equally labeled points belonging to the same region after the split possess the same weights.

We use the notation $P_i = \tilde{P}_{+,k}$ for all $\mathbf{x}_i \in X_k^+$. Then

$$\begin{aligned} -I(\nu \star \Phi) = {} & F_\Phi(0) \sum_{i=1}^{m} P_i^2 - \sum_{k=1}^{K^+} \sum_{\ell=1}^{K^-} \tilde{P}_{+,k} m_{+,k} \tilde{P}_{-,\ell} m_{-,\ell} F_\Phi(\rho_{k,\ell}^{+-}) \\ & + \sum_{k \neq \ell}^{K^+} \sum^{K^+} \tilde{P}_{+,k} m_{+,k} \tilde{P}_{+,\ell} m_{+,\ell} F_\Phi(\rho_{k,\ell}^{++}) + \sum_{k=1}^{K^+} \tilde{P}_{+,k}^2 m_{+,k}^2 F_\Phi(\rho_k^+) \\ & + \sum_{k \neq \ell}^{K^-} \sum^{K^-} \tilde{P}_{-,k} m_{-,k} \tilde{P}_{-,\ell} m_{-,\ell} F_\Phi(\rho_{k,\ell}^{--}) + \sum_{k=1}^{K^-} \tilde{P}_{-,k}^2 m_{-,k}^2 F_\Phi(\rho_k^-) \end{aligned} \tag{11}$$

Here $\rho_{k,\ell}^{+-}$ is defined through

$$m_{+,k} m_{-,\ell} F_\Phi(\rho_{k,\ell}^{+-}) = \sum_{i \in \mathcal{I}_k^+} \sum_{j \in \mathcal{I}_\ell^-} F_\Phi(\Delta_{ij}) \qquad (\Delta_{ij} = \|\mathbf{x}_i - \mathbf{x}_j\|) \, ,$$

where the continuity of $F_\Phi(u)$ and the mean-value theorem guarantee the existence of $\rho_{k,\ell}^{+-}$. Observe that $\rho_{k,\ell}^{+-}$ represents a non-Euclidean dissimilarity measure between the sets X_k^+ and X_ℓ^-. An analogous expression holds for the other terms $\rho_{k,\ell}^{++}$, ρ_k^+, $\rho_{k,\ell}^{--}$ and ρ_k^-.

The only bothersome term in (11) is, of course, the negative one. We treat each term separately. Again using the continuity of $F_\Phi(\rho)$ and the mean-value theorem, there exists a non-negative number $\tilde{\rho}^{+-}$ such that

$$F_\Phi(\tilde{\rho}^{+-}) = \sum_{k=1}^{K^+} \sum_{\ell=1}^{K^-} \tilde{P}_{+,k} m_{+,k} \tilde{P}_{-,\ell} m_{-,\ell} F_\Phi(\rho_{k,\ell}^{+-}) \Big/ \sum_{k=1}^{K^+} \sum_{\ell=1}^{K^-} \tilde{P}_{+,k} m_{+,k} \tilde{P}_{-,\ell} m_{-,\ell} \, . \tag{12}$$

The term $\tilde{\rho}^{+-}$ is an average dissimilarity measure between the positive and negative subsets of the partition. A similar argument can be applied to the other terms in (11), leading to

$$F_\Phi(\tilde{\rho}^{++}) = \sum_{k \neq \ell}^{K^+} \sum^{K^+} \tilde{P}_{+,k} m_{+,k} \tilde{P}_{+,\ell} m_{+,\ell} F_\Phi(\rho_{k,\ell}^{++}) \Big/ \sum_{k \neq \ell}^{K^+} \sum^{K^+} \tilde{P}_{+,k} m_{+,k} \tilde{P}_{+,\ell} m_{+,\ell} \, ,$$

$$F_\Phi(\tilde{\rho}^{+}) = \sum_{k=1}^{K^+} \tilde{P}_{+,k}^2 m_{+,k}^2 F_\Phi(\rho_k^+) \Big/ \sum_{k=1}^{K^+} \tilde{P}_{+,k}^2 m_{+,k}^2 \, .$$

Similar expressions hold for $\tilde{\rho}^{--}$ and $\tilde{\rho}^{-}$.

Let $\tilde{m}_+ = \sum_{k=1}^{K^+} \tilde{P}_{+,k} m_{+,k}$ (and similarly for $\tilde{m}_-$), and observe that

$$\sum_{k \neq \ell}^{K^+} \sum^{K^+} \tilde{P}_{+,k} m_{+,k} \tilde{P}_{+,\ell} m_{+,\ell} = \tilde{m}_+^2 - \sum_{k=1}^{K^+} \tilde{P}_{+,k}^2 m_{+,k}^2 \, .$$

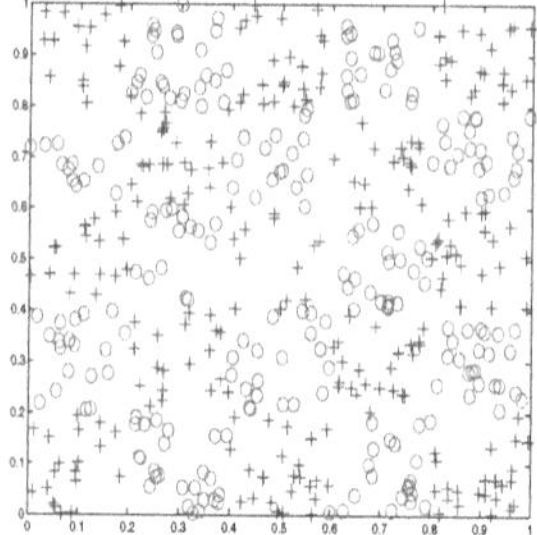

Fig. 1. A two-dimensional data set distributed over a 5×5 chess-board.

Simple algebra leads to the expression

$$-I(\nu \star \Phi) = F_\Phi(0) \sum_{i=1}^{m} P_i^2 - \tilde{m}_+ \tilde{m}_- F_\Phi(\tilde{\rho}^{+-}) + \tilde{m}_+^2 F_\Phi(\tilde{\rho}^{++}) + \tilde{m}_-^2 F_\Phi(\tilde{\rho}^{--})$$

$$+ \left[F_\Phi(\tilde{\rho}^+) - F_\Phi(\tilde{\rho}^{++})\right] \sum_{k=1}^{K^+} \tilde{P}_{+,k}^2 m_{+,k}^2 + \left[F_\Phi(\tilde{\rho}^-) - F_\Phi(\tilde{\rho}^{--})\right] \sum_{\ell=1}^{K^-} \tilde{P}_{-,\ell}^2 m_{-,\ell}^2 . \tag{13}$$

Note that $\tilde{\rho}^+$ is related to the average size of the positive subsets of the partition, while $\tilde{\rho}^{++}$ is related to the average distance between the positive subsets. The term 'average size' here should be understood in the sense of (12). Keeping in mind the monotonic decrease of $F_\Phi(\rho)$ with ρ we conclude that the last two terms are non-negative. Observe that this can always be guaranteed by choosing $K^\pm$ to be large enough (in which case $\tilde{\rho}^\pm$ can be made arbitrarily small). Clearly then a sufficient condition for the non-negativity of $-I(\nu \star \Phi)$ is that $\tilde{m}_+^2 F_\Phi(\tilde{\rho}^{++}) + \tilde{m}_-^2 F_\Phi(\tilde{\rho}^{--}) \geq \tilde{m}_+ \tilde{m}_- F_\Phi(\tilde{\rho}^{+-})$. We wish to consider situations under which $-I(\nu \star \Phi)$, and therefore $\gamma^*(P)$, may be bounded from below by a quantity which is *independent* of the sample size m. As a simple example, consider the data set depicted in Figure 1, corresponding to a 5×5 chess-board configuration of equally weighted points. The measure Φ chosen for this example (see (6,7)) is supported on $\{-1/4, 0, 1/4\}$ where $\Phi(-1/4) = -1/4$, $\Phi(0) = 1/2$ and $\Phi(1/4) = -1/4$. The value of $\tilde{m}_+^2 F_\Phi(\tilde{\rho}^{++}) + \tilde{m}_-^2 F_\Phi(\tilde{\rho}^{--}) - \tilde{m}_+ \tilde{m}_- F_\Phi(\tilde{\rho}^{+-})$ is positive and equal to 0.0032.

Under these circumstances we find that

$$-I(\nu \star \Phi) \geq F_\Phi(0) \sum_{i=1}^{m} P_i^2 + \Delta_\Phi^+ \sum_{k=1}^{K^+} \tilde{P}_{+,k}^2 m_{+,k}^2 + \Delta_\Phi^- \sum_{\ell=1}^{K^-} \tilde{P}_{-,\ell}^2 m_{-,\ell}^2 , \tag{14}$$

where

$$\Delta_\Phi^\pm = \left[F_\Phi(\tilde{\rho}^\pm) - F_\Phi(\tilde{\rho}^{\pm\pm})\right] .$$

A simple lower bound may be obtained by searching for the probability distribution $\tilde{P}$ which minimizes the final two terms in (14), subject to the constraint that the probabilities sum to one. This problem can be easily solved using Lagrange multipliers. Skipping the details of the algebra in this extended abstract, and recalling that $\gamma^*(P) \geq \sqrt{-(C_d/2L)I(\nu \star \Phi)}$, we conclude that for any P

$$\gamma^*(P) \geq \frac{\sqrt{C_d/2L}}{\sqrt{K^+/\Delta_\Phi^\pm + K^-/\Delta_\Phi^\mp}} + \left(\frac{C_d}{2L} F_\Phi(0) \sum_{i=1}^m P_i^2\right)^{1/2}, \tag{15}$$

where we have used the inequality $\sqrt{a+b} \geq (\sqrt{a}+\sqrt{b})/\sqrt{2}$. The most important conclusion from this result is that the first term in (15) does not depend on the sample size m. The dependence of the bound on the geometry of the problem is particularly interesting. First, observe that the bound decreases with an increase in the number of regions $K^\pm$ in the partition. In the limit when the number of regions is of the same order of magnitude as the sample size, we obtain a bound which of the order $\Omega(1/\sqrt{m})$. However, if at least one of the positive/negative subsets is composed of a small number of regions (namely, K^+ or K^- is small), a tighter bound is obtained. The dependence on the term $\Delta_\Phi^\pm = F_\Phi(\tilde{\rho}^\pm) - F_\Phi(\tilde{\rho}^{\pm\pm})$ is also interesting. Recall that this term is related to the difference between the average size of each of the uni-labeled clusters and the average distance between clusters. Large values of $\Delta_\Phi^\pm$ indicate highly populated small subsets, which are relatively far apart. Under these circumstances we expect that the advantage γ^* is large. We summarize our conclusions in the following theorem.

Theorem 2. *Let $S = \{(\mathbf{x}_1, y_1), \ldots, (\mathbf{x}_m, y_m)\}$, $\mathbf{x}_i \in \mathbb{R}^d$ and $y_i \in \{-1, +1\}$ be a sample of m points, to each of which is associated a non-negative weight P_i, $\sum_{i=1}^m P_i = 1$. Assume further that the weights are symmetric, namely $\sum_{i=1}^m y_i P_i = 0$. Partition S into $K^+(K^-)$ subsets of positive (negative) points such that the weights assigned to points in each subset are equal. If the configuration satisfies the condition*

$$\tilde{m}_+^2 F_\Phi(\tilde{\rho}^{++}) + \tilde{m}_-^2 F_\Phi(\tilde{\rho}^{--}) \geq \tilde{m}_+ \tilde{m}_- F_\Phi(\tilde{\rho}^{+-}),$$

then the optimal margin $\gamma^*(P)$ is lower bounded as in (15).

As mentioned following (10), in the context of boosting one may think of $K^\pm$ as the number of regions obtained during the boosting process. It may happen that in some cases the number of regions obtained during boosting is so large, as to render the bound (15) useless. It turns out that even in this case the bound (15) can be useful if the distribution P becomes skewed, concentrating mainly on a small number of points, in which case the term $\|P\|_2^2 = \sum_{i=1}^m P_i^2$ becomes large relative to $1/m$. While it is difficult to prove that this is the case in general, we have run many simulations of AdaBoost and found that $\|P\|_2^2$ increases with the number of boosting iterations, becoming much larger than $1/m$, the initial value at the beginning of the process when all weights are equal to $1/m$. In Figure 2 we plot the value of $\|P\|_2^2$ as a function of the number of boosting iterations, for

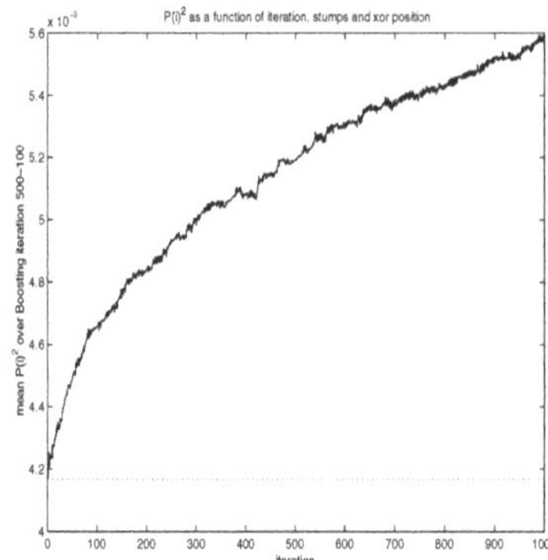

Fig. 2. The value of $\|P\|_2^2$ as a function of the number of boosting iterations.

a two-dimensional noisy data set. The plots were obtained using stumps as weak learners, although similar behavior was observed using other types of classifiers and data sets. We do not as yet have a good theoretical explanation for it.

Finally, we briefly discuss the implications of the results of the present section to the choice of θ in (1). Recall that the empirical margin error $\mathbf{P}_S[Yf(X) \leq \theta]$ is bounded by a constant smaller than 1 if (5) holds, where the advantage parameter γ_t at the t-th boosting step is given by $\gamma_t = \bar{\gamma}_\theta + \delta_t$, and $\bar{\gamma}_\theta$ is given in (4). Under the conditions of Theorem 2, we have that $\gamma_t \geq \zeta$, where ζ is a constant independent of the sample size. Combining both results we see that the condition that needs to be obeyed by θ is that $\bar{\gamma}_\theta \geq \zeta - \delta_t$. Since $\bar{\gamma}_\theta \geq \theta$, a slightly weaker condition is that $\theta \geq \zeta - \delta_t$. For example, if $\delta_t \geq \eta > 0$ for all t (an admittedly strong condition), we immediately obtain a simple connection between θ and ζ, the latter parameter characterizing the geometry of the data. In other words, a weak learner advantage larger than ζ guarantees that the empirical margin-error $\mathbf{P}_S[Yf(X) \leq \theta]$ of the combined classifier converges to zero if $\theta \geq \zeta - \eta$. A more elaborate analysis of this issue is be deferred to the full paper.

4 Discussion

We have provided explicit conditions on a data set which guarantee that the weighted empirical error of a linear classifier is bounded by $1/2 - \gamma$, where γ is bounded below by a term which is independent of the sample size. Such a result guarantees that the AdaBoost algorithm produce asymptotically zero error. Moreover, under certain conditions on θ a small value of the empirical margin error (2) may be guaranteed. Such a result provides conditions under which fast convergence rate of the generalization error bound (1) is assured.

Several open issues remain for future work. First, while we have provided sufficient conditions which guarantee a sample-size independent bound on the error of a linear weak learner, it is not clear how stringent they are. Second, our results assume that the weights are equal on each subset of the partition. It would useful to eliminate this assumption. Third, the dynamics of the function $\sum_{i=1}^{m} P_i^2$ as a function of the number of boosting iterations seems extremely interesting and pertinent to our bounds. A good theoretical understanding of its behavior would shed light on some of the intricacies of the boosting algorithm. Finally, nothing was assumed about the measure Φ except for the conditions (6). An interesting question relates to optimizing this measure based on the data set.

Acknowledgments

This work was partially supported by the Technion fund for promotion of research.

References

1. R. Alexander. Geometric methods in the study of irregularities of distribution. *Combinatorica*, 10(2):115–136, 1990.
2. R. Alexander. Principles of a new method in the study of irregularities of distribution. *Invent. Math.*, 103:279–296, 1991.
3. L. Devroye and Györfi. *Nonparametric Density Estimation: The L1 View.* John Wiley, New York, 1985.
4. Y. Freund. Boosting a weak learning algorithm by majority. *Information and Computation*, 121:256–285, 1995.
5. Y. Freund and R.E. Schapire. Experiments with a new boosting algorithm. In *Proceeding of the Thirteenth International Conference on Machine Learning*, pages 148–156, 1996.
6. Y. Freund and R.E. Schapire. Game theory, on-line prediction and boosting. In *Proceedings of the Ninth Annual Conference on Computational Learning Theory, 1996*, pages 325–332, 1996.
7. J. Friedman, T. Hastie, and R. Tibshirani. Additive logistic regression: a statistical view of boosting. *The Annals of Statistics*, 38(2):337–374, 2000.
8. M. Goldman, L. Håstad, and A. Razborov. Majority gates vs. general weighted threshold gates. *Jour. of Comput. Complexity*, 1(4):277–300, 1992.
9. V. Koltchinskii, D. Panchenko, and F. Lozano. Some new bounds on the generlization error of combined classifiers. In T. Dietterich, editor, *Advances in Neural Information Processing Systems 14*, Boston, 2001. MIT Press.
10. S. Mannor and R. Meir. On the existence of weak learners and applications to boosting. *Machine Learning*, 2001. To appear.
11. R.E. Schapire, Y. Freund, P. Bartlett, and W.S. Lee. Boosting the margin: a new explanation for the effectiveness of voting methods. *The Annals of Statistics*, 26(5):1651–1686, 1998.
12. R.E. Schapire and Y. Singer. Improved boosting algorithms using confidence-rated predictions. *Machine Learning*, 37(3):297–336, 1999.
13. J. Shaw-Taylor, P.L. Bartlett, R.C. Williamson, and M Anthony. Structural risk minimization over data-dependent hierarchies. *IEEE Trans. Inf. Theory*, 44(5):1926–1940, September 1998.

Appendix

Proof of Theorem 1

Taking logarithms on both side of (1) we have

$$\log \mathbf{P}_S[Yf_T(X) \le \theta] \le \sum_{t=1}^{T} \left[\left(\frac{1-\theta}{2} \right) \log(1-2\gamma_t) + \left(\frac{1+\theta}{2} \right) \log(1+2\gamma_t) \right].$$

Let $X \in \{0,1\}$ be a binary random variable, and consider two distributions p and q_t, where

$$p(X=1) = \left(\frac{1-\theta}{2} \right) \quad ; \quad q_t(X=1) = \left(\frac{1-2\gamma_t}{2} \right).$$

Then, simple algebra yields the result

$$\log \mathbf{P}_S[Yf_T(X) \le \theta] \le -\sum_{t=1}^{T} D(p\|q_t) + T\left[\log 2 - H\left(\frac{1-\theta}{2}\right)\right],$$

where $D(p\|q_t) = \sum_x p(x)\log[p(x)/q_t(x)]$ is the Kullback-Leibler divergence between p and q_t. Using the bound, $D(p\|q) \ge \frac{1}{2}\left(d_1(p,q)\right)^2$ (e.g., [3], p.222), where $d_1(p,q) = \sum_x |p(x) - q(x)|$ denotes the L_1 distance between probability distributions p and q, we find that

$$\log \mathbf{P}_S[Yf_T(X) \le \theta] \le -\frac{1}{2}\sum_{t=1}^{T}(2\gamma_t - \theta)^2 + T\left[\log 2 - H\left(\frac{1-\theta}{2}\right)\right],$$

Set $\gamma_t = \bar{\gamma}_\theta + \delta_t$, where $\bar{\gamma}_\theta$ is chosen to satisfy the equation $\frac{1}{2}(2\bar{\gamma}_\theta - \theta)^2 = \log 2 - H\left(\frac{1-\theta}{2}\right)$, implying that $\bar{\gamma}_\theta$ is given by (4). It is easy to see that $\bar{\gamma}_\theta$ is monotonically increasing with θ and that $\bar{\gamma}_\theta \ge \theta$ with equality if, and only if, $\theta = 0$. We then find that

$$\log \mathbf{P}_S[Yf_T(X) \le \theta] \le -2(2\bar{\gamma}_\theta - \theta)\sum_{t=1}^{T}\delta_t - 2\sum_{t=1}^{T}\delta_t^2 .$$

For any $\theta > 0$ we have $2\bar{\gamma}_\theta - \theta > 0$ implying that a sufficient condition guaranteeing that $\log \mathbf{P}_S[Yf_T(X) \le \theta]$ is bounded from above by a finite *negative* value (namely $\mathbf{P}_S[Yf_T(X) \le \theta]$ is strictly smaller than 1) is that

$$\liminf_{T\to\infty} \sum_{t=1}^{T} \delta_t \ge c > 0,$$

for some positive constant c. When $c = \infty$, we see that $\mathbf{P}_S[Yf_T(X) \le \theta] \to 0$ in the limit $T \to \infty$. Note that this condition is trivially obeyed if $\delta_t \ge \eta$ for some positive constant η.

Smooth Boosting and Learning with Malicious Noise

Rocco A. Servedio

Division of Engineering and Applied Sciences, Harvard University
Cambridge, MA 02138
rocco@deas.harvard.edu

Abstract. We describe a new boosting algorithm which generates only smooth distributions which do not assign too much weight to any single example. We show that this new boosting algorithm can be used to construct efficient PAC learning algorithms which tolerate relatively high rates of malicious noise. In particular, we use the new smooth boosting algorithm to construct malicious noise tolerant versions of the PAC-model p-norm linear threshold learning algorithms described in [23]. The bounds on sample complexity and malicious noise tolerance of these new PAC algorithms closely correspond to known bounds for the online p-norm algorithms of Grove, Littlestone and Schuurmans [14] and Gentile and Littlestone [13]. As special cases of our new algorithms we obtain linear threshold learning algorithms which match the sample complexity and malicious noise tolerance of the online Perceptron and Winnow algorithms. Our analysis reveals an interesting connection between boosting and noise tolerance in the PAC setting.

1 Introduction

Any realistic model of learning from examples must address the issue of noisy data. In 1985 Valiant introduced the notion of PAC learning in the presence of *malicious noise*. This is a worst-case model of errors in which some fraction of the labeled examples given to a learning algorithm may be corrupted by an adversary who can modify both example points and labels in an arbitrary fashion (a detailed description of the model is given in Section 3). The frequency of such corrupted examples is known as the *malicious noise rate*.

Learning in the presence of malicious noise is in general quite difficult. Kearns and Li [16] have shown that for many concept classes it is impossible to learn to accuracy ϵ if the malicious noise rate exceeds $\frac{\epsilon}{1+\epsilon}$. In fact, for many interesting concept classes (such as the class of linear threshold functions), the best efficient algorithms known can only tolerate malicious noise rates significantly lower than this general upper bound. Despite these difficulties, the importance of being able to cope with noisy data has led many researchers to study PAC learning in the presence of malicious noise (see e.g. [1,2,3,6,7,20]).

In this paper we give a new *smooth boosting* algorithm which can be used to transform a malicious noise tolerant weak learning algorithm into a PAC

D. Helmbold and B. Williamson (Eds.): COLT/EuroCOLT 2001, LNAI 2111, pp. 473–489, 2001.

algorithm which learns successfully in the presence of malicious noise. We use this smooth boosting algorithm to construct a family of PAC algorithms for learning linear threshold functions in the presence of malicious noise. These new algorithms match the sample complexity and noise tolerance of the online p-norm algorithms of Grove, Littlestone and Schuurmans [14] and Gentile and Littlestone [13], which include as special cases the well-known Perceptron and Winnow algorithms.

1.1 Smooth Boosting and Learning with Malicious Noise

Our basic approach is quite simple, as illustrated by the following example. Consider a learning scenario in which we have a weak learning algorithm L which takes as input a finite sample S of m labeled examples. Algorithm L is known to have some tolerance to malicious noise; specifically, L is guaranteed to generate a hypothesis with nonnegligible advantage provided that the frequency of noisy examples in its sample is at most 10%. We would like to learn to high accuracy in the presence of malicious noise at a rate of 1%.

The obvious approach in this setting is to use a boosting algorithm, which will generate some sequence of distributions $\mathcal{D}_1, \mathcal{D}_2, \ldots$ over S. This approach can fail, though, if the boosting algorithm generates distributions which are very skewed from the uniform distribution on S; if distribution $\mathcal{D}_i$ assigns weights as large as $\frac{20}{m}$ to individual points in S, for instance, then the frequency of noisy examples for L in stage i could be as high as 20%. What we need instead is a *smooth* boosting algorithm which only constructs distributions $\mathcal{D}_i$ over S which never assign weight greater than $\frac{10}{m}$ to any single example. By using such a smooth booster we are assured that the weak learner will function successfully at each stage, so the overall boosting process will work correctly.

While the setting described above is artificial, we note that indirect empirical evidence has been given supporting the smooth boosting approach for noisy settings. It is well known [8,21] that commonly used boosting algorithms such as `AdaBoost` [11] can perform poorly on noisy data. Dietterich [8] has suggested that this poor performance is due to `AdaBoost`'s tendency to generate very skewed distributions which put a great deal of weight on a few noisy examples. This overweighting of noisy examples cannot occur under a smooth boosting regimen.

In Section 2 we give a new boosting algorithm, `SmoothBoost`, which is guaranteed to generate only smooth distributions as described above. We show in Section 5 that the distributions generated by `SmoothBoost` are optimally smooth.

`SmoothBoost` is not the first boosting algorithm which attempts to avoid the skewed distributions of `AdaBoost`; algorithms with similar smoothness guarantees have been given by Domingo and Watanabe [9] and Impagliazzo [15]. Freund [10] has also described a boosting algorithm which uses a more moderate weighting scheme than `AdaBoost`. In Section 2.3 we show that our `SmoothBoost` algorithm has several other desirable properties, such as constructing a large margin final hypothesis, which are essential for the noisy linear threshold learning application of Section 3. We discuss the relationship between `SmoothBoost` and the algorithms of [9,10,15] in Section 2.4.

1.2 Learning Linear Threshold Functions with Malicious Noise

We use the SmoothBoost algorithm in Section 3 to construct a family of PAC-model malicious noise tolerant algorithms for learning linear threshold functions. A similar family was constructed by Servedio in [23] using AdaBoost instead of SmoothBoost as the boosting component. It was shown in [23] that for linearly separable data these PAC model algorithms have sample complexity bounds which are essentially identical to those of the online p-norm linear threshold learning algorithms of Grove, Littlestone and Schuurmans [14], which include as special cases ($p = 2$ and $p = \infty$) the well-studied online Perceptron and Winnow algorithms.

Gentile and Littlestone [13] have given mistake bounds for the online p-norm algorithms when run on examples which are not linearly separable, thus generalizing previous bounds on noise tolerance for Perceptron [12] and Winnow [19]. A significant drawback of the AdaBoost-based PAC-model p-norm algorithms of [23] is that they do not appear to succeed in the presence of malicious noise. We show in Section 4 that for all values $2 \leq p \leq \infty$, our new PAC algorithms which use SmoothBoost match both the sample complexity and the malicious noise tolerance of the online p-norm algorithms. Our construction thus provides malicious noise tolerant PAC analogues of Perceptron and Winnow (and many other algorithms as well).

2 Smooth Boosting

In this section we describe a new boosting algorithm, SmoothBoost, which has several useful properties. SmoothBoost only constructs smooth distributions which do not put too much weight on any single example; it can be used to generate a large margin final hypothesis; and it can be used with a weak learning algorithm which outputs real-valued hypotheses. All of these properties are essential for the noisy linear threshold learning problem we address in Section 3.

2.1 Preliminaries

We fix some terminology from [15] first. A *measure* on a finite set is a function $M : S \to [0, 1]$. We write $|M|$ to denote $\sum_{x \in S} M(x)$. Given a measure M, there is a natural induced distribution $\mathcal{D}_M$ defined by $\mathcal{D}_M(x) = M(x)/|M|$. This definition yields

Observation 1 $L_\infty(\mathcal{D}_M) \leq \frac{1}{|M|}$.

Let $\mathcal{D}$ be a distribution over a set $S = \langle x^1, y_1 \rangle, \ldots, \langle x^m, y_m \rangle$ of labeled examples with each $y_j \in \{-1, 1\}$ and let h be a real-valued function which maps $\{x^1, \ldots, x^m\}$ into $[-1, 1]$. If $\frac{1}{2} \sum_{j=1}^{m} \mathcal{D}(j)|h(x^j) - y_j| \leq \frac{1}{2} - \gamma$ then we say that the *advantage* of h under $\mathcal{D}$ is γ. We say that an algorithm which takes S and $\mathcal{D}$ as input and outputs an h which has advantage at least $\gamma > 0$ is a *weak learning algorithm* (this is somewhat less general than the notion of weak learning which

Input: parameters $0 < \kappa < 1$, $0 \leq \theta \leq \gamma < \frac{1}{2}$
sample $S = \langle x^1, y_1 \rangle, \ldots, \langle x^m, y_m \rangle$ where each $y_i \in \{-1, 1\}$
weak learner WL which takes input $(S, \mathcal{D}_t)$ and outputs
$h_t : \{x^1, \ldots, x^m\} \rightarrow [-1, 1]$

Output: hypothesis $h(x) = \text{sign}(f(x))$

1. **forall** $j = 1, \ldots, m$ **set** $M_1(j) = 1$
2. **forall** $j = 1, \ldots, m$ **set** $N_0(j) = 0$
3. **set** $t = 1$
4. **until** $|M_t|/m < \kappa$ **do**
5. **forall** $j = 1, \ldots, m$ **set** $\mathcal{D}_t(j) = M_t(j)/|M_t|$
6. run $\texttt{WL}(S, \mathcal{D}_t)$ to get h_t such that $\frac{1}{2}\sum_{j=1}^{m} \mathcal{D}_t(j)|h_t(x^j) - y_j| \leq \frac{1}{2} - \gamma$
7. **forall** $j = 1, \ldots, m$ **set** $N_t(j) = N_{t-1}(j) + y_j h_t(x^j) - \theta$
8. **forall** $j = 1, \ldots, m$ **set** $M_{t+1}(j) = \begin{cases} 1 & \text{if } N_t(j) < 0 \\ (1-\gamma)^{N_t(j)/2} & \text{if } N_t(j) \geq 0 \end{cases}$
9. **set** $t = t + 1$
10. **set** $T = t - 1$
11. **return** $h = \text{sign}(f(x))$ where $f(x) = \frac{1}{T}\sum_{i=1}^{T} h_i(x)$

Fig. 1. The SmoothBoost algorithm.

was originally introduced by Kearns and Valiant in [17] but is sufficient for our purposes). Finally, let $g(x) = \text{sign}(f(x))$ where $f : X \rightarrow [-1, 1]$ is a real-valued function. We say that the *margin* of g on a labeled example $\langle x, y \rangle \in X \times \{-1, 1\}$ is $yf(x)$; intuitively, this is the amount by which g predicts y correctly. Note that the margin of g on $\langle x, y \rangle$ is nonnegative if and only if g predicts y correctly.

2.2 The SmoothBoost Algorithm

The SmoothBoost algorithm is given in Figure 1. The parameter κ is the desired error rate of the final hypothesis, the parameter γ is the guaranteed advantage of the hypotheses returned by the weak learner, and θ is the desired margin of the final hypothesis. SmoothBoost runs the weak learning algorithm several times on a sequence of carefully constructed distributions and outputs a thresholded sum of the hypotheses thus generated. The quantity $N_t(j)$ in line 7 may be viewed as the cumulative amount by which the hypotheses $h_1, \ldots, h_t$ beat the desired margin θ on the labeled example $\langle x^j, y_j \rangle$. The measure M_{t+1} assigns more weight to examples where N_t is small and less weight to examples where N_t is large, thus forcing the weak learner to focus in stage $t + 1$ on examples where previous hypotheses have done poorly. Note that since any measure maps into $[0, 1]$ there is a strict bound on the amount of weight which can be assigned to any example.

2.3 Proof of Correctness

Several useful properties of the SmoothBoost algorithm are easy to verify. The algorithm is called SmoothBoost because each distribution it constructs is guaranteed to be "smooth," i.e. no single point receives too much weight:

Lemma 1. *Each $\mathcal{D}_t$ defined in step 5 of* SmoothBoost *has* $L_\infty(\mathcal{D}_t) \leq \frac{1}{\kappa m}$.

Proof. Follows directly from Observation 1 and the condition in line 4. □

Another useful property is that the final hypothesis h has margin at least θ on all but a κ fraction of the points in S :

Theorem 1. *If* SmoothBoost *terminates then f satisfies* $\frac{|\{j \,:\, y_j f(x^j) \leq \theta\}|}{m} < \kappa$.

Proof. Since $N_T(j) = T(y_j f(x^j) - \theta)$, if $y_j f(x^j) \leq \theta$ then $N_T(j) \leq 0$ and hence $M_{T+1}(j) = 1$. Consequently we have

$$\frac{|\{j \,:\, y_j f(x^j) \leq \theta\}|}{m} \leq \frac{\sum_{j=1}^m M_{T+1}(j)}{m} = \frac{|M_{T+1}|}{m} < \kappa$$

by the condition in line 4. □

Note that since $\theta \geq 0$ Theorem 1 implies that the final SmoothBoost hypothesis is correct on all but a κ fraction of S.

Finally we must show that the algorithm terminates in a reasonable amount of time. The following theorem bounds the number of times that SmoothBoost will execute its main loop:

Theorem 2. *If each hypothesis h_t returned by* WL *in line 6 has advantage at least γ under $\mathcal{D}_t$ (i.e. satisfies the condition of line 6) and θ is set to $\frac{\gamma}{2+\gamma}$, then* SmoothBoost *terminates with* $T < \frac{2}{\kappa\gamma^2\sqrt{1-\gamma}}$.

As will be evident from the proof, slightly different bounds on T can be established by choosing different values of θ in the range $[0, \gamma]$. We take $\theta = \frac{\gamma}{2+\gamma}$ in the theorem above both to obtain a margin of $\Omega(\gamma)$ and to obtain a clean bound in the theorem. Theorem 2 follows from the bounds established in the following two lemmas:

Lemma 2. $\sum_{j=1}^m \sum_{t=1}^T M_t(j) y_j h_t(x^j) \geq 2\gamma \sum_{t=1}^T |M_t|$.

Lemma 3. *If* $\theta = \frac{\gamma}{2+\gamma}$, *then* $\sum_{j=1}^m \sum_{t=1}^T M_t(j) y_j h_t(x^j) < \frac{2m}{\gamma\sqrt{1-\gamma}} + \gamma \sum_{t=1}^T |M_t|$.

Combining these bounds we obtain $\frac{2m}{\gamma\sqrt{1-\gamma}} > \gamma \sum_{t=1}^T |M_t| \geq \gamma\kappa m T$ where the last inequality is because $|M_t| \geq \kappa m$ for $t = 1, \ldots, T$.

Proof of Lemma 2: Since $h_t(x^j) \in [-1, 1]$ and $y_j \in \{-1, 1\}$, we have $y_j h_t(x^j) = 1 - |h_t(x^j) - y_j|$, and thus

$$\sum_{j=1}^m \mathcal{D}_t(j) y_j h_t(x^j) = \sum_{j=1}^m \mathcal{D}_t(j)(1 - |h_t(x^j) - y_j|) \geq 2\gamma.$$

This implies that

$$\sum_{j=1}^{m}\sum_{t=1}^{T} M_t(j)y_j h_t(x^j) = \sum_{t=1}^{T} |M_t| \sum_{j=1}^{m} \mathcal{D}_t(j)y_j h_t(x^j) \geq \sum_{t=1}^{T} 2\gamma|M_t|.$$

□

The proof of Lemma 3 is given in Appendix A.

2.4 Comparison with Other Boosting Algorithms

The SmoothBoost algorithm was inspired by an algorithm given by Impagliazzo in the context of hard-core set constructions in complexity theory [15]. Klivans and Servedio [18] observed that Impagliazzo's algorithm can be reinterpreted as a boosting algorithm which generates distributions $\mathcal{D}_t$ which, like the distributions generated by SmoothBoost, satisfy $L_\infty(\mathcal{D}_t) \leq \frac{1}{\kappa m}$. However, our SmoothBoost algorithm differs from Impagliazzo's algorithm in several important ways. The algorithm in [15] uses additive rather than multiplicative updates for $M_t(j)$, and the bound on T which is given for the algorithm in [15] is $O(\frac{1}{\kappa^2\gamma^2})$ which is worse than our bound by essentially a factor of $\frac{1}{\kappa}$. Another important difference is that the algorithm in [15] has no θ parameter and does not appear to output a large margin final hypothesis. Finally, the analysis in [15] only covers the case where the weak hypotheses are binary-valued rather than real-valued.

Freund and Schapire's well-known boosting algorithm AdaBoost is somewhat faster than SmoothBoost, requiring only $T = O(\frac{\log(1/\kappa)}{\gamma^2})$ stages [11]. Like SmoothBoost, AdaBoost can be used with real-valued weak hypotheses and can be used to output a large margin final hypothesis [22]. However, AdaBoost is not guaranteed to generate only smooth distributions, and thus does not appear to be useful in a malicious noise context.

Freund has recently introduced and studied a sophisticated boosting algorithm called BrownBoost [10] which uses a gentler weighting scheme than AdaBoost. Freund suggests that BrownBoost should be well suited for dealing with noisy data; however it is not clear from the analysis in [10] whether BrownBoost-generated distributions satisfy a smoothness property such as the $L_\infty(\mathcal{D}_t) \leq \frac{1}{\kappa m}$ property of SmoothBoost, or whether BrownBoost can be used to generate a large margin final hypothesis. We note that the BrownBoost algorithm is much more complicated to run than SmoothBoost, as it involves solving a differential equation at each stage of boosting.

SmoothBoost is perhaps most similar to the modified AdaBoost algorithm MadaBoost which was recently defined and analyzed by Domingo and Watanabe [9]. Like SmoothBoost, MadaBoost uses multiplicative updates on weights and never allows weights to exceed 1 in value. Domingo and Watanabe proved that MadaBoost takes at most $T \leq \frac{2}{\kappa\gamma^2}$ stages, which is quite similar to our bound in Theorem 2. (If we set $\theta = 0$ in SmoothBoost, a slight modification of the proof of Theorem 2 gives a bound of roughly $\frac{4}{3\kappa\gamma^2}$, which improves the Madaboost bound by a constant factor.) However, the analysis for MadaBoost given in [9] only covers only the case of binary-valued weak hypotheses, and does not establish that `MadaBoost` generates a large margin final hypothesis. We also note that our proof technique of simultaneously upper and lower bounding $\sum_{j=1}^{m}\sum_{t=1}^{T} M_t(j)y_j h_t(x^j)$ is different from the approach used in [9].

3 Learning Linear Threshold Functions with Malicious Noise

In this section we show how the `SmoothBoost` algorithm can be used in conjunction with a simple noise tolerant weak learning algorithm to obtain a PAC learning algorithm for learning linear threshold functions with malicious noise.

3.1 Geometric Preliminaries

For $\overline{x} = (x_1, \ldots, x_n) \in \Re^n$ and $p \geq 1$ we write $\|\overline{x}\|_p$ to denote the p-norm of $\overline{x}$, namely $\|\overline{x}\|_p = \left(\sum_{i=1}^{n} |x_i|^p\right)^{1/p}$. The ∞-norm of $\overline{x}$ is $\|\overline{x}\|_\infty = \max_{i=1,\ldots,n} |x_i|$. We write $B_p(R)$ to denote the p-norm ball of radius R, i.e. $B_p(R) = \{\overline{x} \in \Re^n : \|\overline{x}\|_p \leq R\}$.

For $p, q \geq 1$ the q-norm is *dual* to the p-norm if $\frac{1}{p} + \frac{1}{q} = 1$; so the 1-norm and the ∞-norm are dual to each other and the 2-norm is dual to itself. For the rest of the paper p and q always denote dual norms. The following facts (see e.g. [25] pp. 203-204) will be useful:

Hölder Inequality: $|\overline{u} \cdot \overline{v}| \leq \|\overline{u}\|_p \|\overline{v}\|_q$ for all $\overline{u}, \overline{v} \in \Re^n$ and $1 \leq p \leq \infty$.

Minkowski Inequality: $\|\overline{u}+\overline{v}\|_p \leq \|\overline{u}\|_p + \|\overline{v}\|_p$ for all $\overline{u}, \overline{v} \in \Re^n$ and $1 \leq p \leq \infty$.

Finally, recall that a *linear threshold function* is a function $f : \Re^n \rightarrow \{-1, 1\}$ such that $f(\overline{x}) = \text{sign}(\overline{u} \cdot \overline{x})$ for some $\overline{u} \in \Re^n$.

3.2 PAC Learning with Malicious Noise

Let $EX_{MAL}^{\eta}(\overline{u}, \mathcal{D})$ be a *malicious example oracle with noise rate* η that behaves as follows when invoked: with probability $1 - \eta$ the oracle returns a *clean* example $\langle \overline{x}, \text{sign}(\overline{u} \cdot \overline{x}) \rangle$ where $\overline{x}$ is drawn from the probability distribution $\mathcal{D}$ over $B_p(R)$. With probability η, though, $EX_{MAL}^{\eta}(\overline{u}, \mathcal{D})$ returns a *dirty* example $\langle \overline{x}, y \rangle \in B_p(R) \times \{-1, 1\}$ about which nothing can be assumed. Such a malicious example $\langle \overline{x}, y \rangle$ may be chosen by a computationally unbounded adversary which has complete knowledge of $\overline{u}$, $\mathcal{D}$, and the state of the learning algorithm when the oracle is invoked.

The goal of a learning algorithm in this model is to construct an approximation to the target concept $\text{sign}(\overline{u} \cdot \overline{x})$. More formally, we say that a Boolean function $h : \Re^n \rightarrow \{-1, 1\}$ is an *ϵ-approximator for $\overline{u}$ under $\mathcal{D}$* if $\Pr_{\overline{x} \in \mathcal{D}}[h(\overline{x}) \neq \text{sign}(\overline{u} \cdot \overline{x})] \leq \epsilon$. The learning algorithm is given an accuracy parameter ϵ and a confidence parameter δ, has access to $EX_{MAL}^{\eta}(\overline{u}, \mathcal{D})$, and must output a hypothesis h which, with probability at least $1 - \delta$, is an ϵ-approximator for $\overline{u}$ under

$\mathcal{D}$. The *sample complexity* of a learning algorithm in this model is the number of times it queries the malicious example oracle.

(A slightly stronger model of PAC learning with malicious noise has also been proposed [1,6]. In this model first a clean sample of the desired size is drawn from a noise-free oracle; then each point in the sample is independently selected with probability η; then an adversary replaces each selected point with a dirty example of its choice; and finally the corrupted sample is provided to the learning algorithm. This model is stronger than the original malicious noise model since each dirty example is chosen by the adversary with full knowledge of the entire sample. All of our results also hold in this stronger model.)

A final note: like the Perceptron algorithm, the learning algorithms which we consider will require that the quantity $\overline{u}\cdot\overline{x}$ be bounded away from zero (at least most of the time). We thus say that a distribution $\mathcal{D}$ is *ξ-good for $\overline{u}$* if $|\overline{u}\cdot\overline{x}| \geq \xi$ for all $\overline{x}$ which have nonzero probability under $\mathcal{D}$, and we restrict our attention to learning under ξ-good distributions. (Of course, dirty examples drawn from $EX^{\eta}_{MAL}(\overline{u},\mathcal{D})$ need not satisfy $|\overline{u}\cdot\overline{x}| \geq \xi$.)

3.3 A Noise Tolerant Weak Learning Algorithm

As shown in Figure 2, our weak learning algorithm for linear threshold functions, called WLA, takes as input a data set S and a distribution $\mathcal{D}$ over S. The algorithm computes the vector $\overline{z}$ which is the average location of the (label-normalized) points in S under $\mathcal{D}$, transforms $\overline{z}$ to obtain a vector $\overline{w}$, and predicts using the linear functional defined by $\overline{w}$. As motivation for the algorithm, note that if every example pair $\langle\overline{x},y\rangle$ satisfies $y=\text{sign}(\overline{u}\cdot\overline{x})$ for some $\overline{u}$, then each point $y\overline{x}$ would lie on the same side of the hyperplane defined by $\overline{u}$ as $\overline{u}$ itself, and hence the average vector $\overline{z}$ defined in Step 1 of the algorithm intuitively should point in roughly the same direction as $\overline{u}$.

In [23] it is shown that the WLA algorithm is a weak learning algorithm for linear threshold functions in a noise-free setting. The following theorem shows that if a small fraction of the examples in S are affected by malicious noise, WLA will still generates a hypothesis with nonnegligible advantage provided that the input distribution $\mathcal{D}$ is sufficiently smooth.

Theorem 3. *Fix $2 \leq p \leq \infty$ and let $S = \langle\overline{x}^1,y_1\rangle,\ldots,\langle\overline{x}^m,y_m\rangle$ be a set of labeled examples with each $\overline{x}^j \in B_p(R)$. Let $\mathcal{D}$ be a distribution over S such that $L_\infty(\mathcal{D}) \leq \frac{1}{\kappa m}$. Suppose that $\xi > 0$ and $\overline{u}\in\Re^n$ are such that $\xi \leq R\|\overline{u}\|_q$ and at most $\eta' m$ examples in S do not satisfy $y_j(\overline{u}\cdot\overline{x}^j)\geq\xi$, where $\eta' \leq \frac{\kappa\xi}{4R\|\overline{u}\|_q}$. Then* WLA$(p,S,\mathcal{D})$ *returns a hypothesis $h: B_p(R)\rightarrow[-1,1]$ which has advantage at least $\frac{\xi}{4R\|\overline{u}\|_q}$ under $\mathcal{D}$.*

Proof: By Hölder's inequality, for any $\overline{x}\in B_p(R)$ we have

$$|h(\overline{x})| = \frac{|\overline{w}\cdot\overline{x}|}{\|\overline{w}\|_q R} \leq \frac{\|\overline{w}\|_q\|\overline{x}\|_p}{\|\overline{w}\|_q R} \leq 1,$$

and thus h indeed maps $B_p(R)$ into $[-1,1]$.

Input: parameter $p \geq 2$
sample $S = \langle \overline{x}^1, y_1 \rangle, \ldots, \langle \overline{x}^m, y_m \rangle$ where each $y_i \in \{-1, 1\}$
distribution $\mathcal{D}$ over S
upper bound R on $\|\overline{x}\|_p$

Output: hypothesis $h(\overline{x})$

1. **set** $\overline{z} = \sum_{j=1}^m \mathcal{D}(j) y_j \overline{x}^j$
2. **for all** $i = 1, \ldots, n$ **set** $w_i = \text{sign}(z_i)|z_i|^{p-1}$
3. **return** hypothesis $h(\overline{x}) \equiv \overline{v} \cdot \overline{x}$ where $\overline{v} = \frac{\overline{w}}{\|\overline{w}\|_q R}$

Fig. 2. The p-norm weak learning algorithm WLA.

Now we show that h has the desired advantage. Since $h_t(\overline{x}^j) \in [-1, 1]$ and $y_j \in \{-1, 1\}$, we have $|h(\overline{x}^j) - y_j| = 1 - y_j h(\overline{x}^j)$, so

$$\frac{1}{2}\sum_{j=1}^{m} \mathcal{D}(j)|h(\overline{x}^j) - y_j| = \frac{1}{2}\sum_{j=1}^{m} \mathcal{D}(j)(1 - y_j h(\overline{x}^j)) = \frac{1}{2} - \left(\frac{\sum_{j=1}^m \mathcal{D}(j) y_j (\overline{w} \cdot \overline{x}^j)}{2\|\overline{w}\|_q R} \right).$$

To prove the theorem it thus suffices to show that $\frac{\sum_{j=1}^m \mathcal{D}(j) y_j (\overline{w} \cdot \overline{x}^j)}{\|\overline{w}\|_q} \geq \frac{\xi}{2\|\overline{u}\|_q}$. The numerator of the left side is $\overline{w} \cdot \left(\sum_{j=1}^m \mathcal{D}(j) y_j \overline{x}^j \right) = \overline{w} \cdot \overline{z} = \sum_{i=1}^n |z_i|^p = \|\overline{z}\|_p^p$. Using the fact that $(p-1)q = p$, the denominator is

$$\|\overline{w}\|_q = \left(\sum_{i=1}^n \left(|z_i|^{p-1} \right)^q \right)^{1/q} = \left(\sum_{i=1}^n |z_i|^p \right)^{1/q} = \|\overline{z}\|_p^{p/q}.$$

We can therefore rewrite the left side as $\|\overline{z}\|_p^p / \|\overline{z}\|_p^{p/q} = \|\overline{z}\|_p$, and thus our goal is to show that $\|\overline{z}\|_p \geq \frac{\xi}{2\|\overline{u}\|_q}$. By Hölder's inequality it suffices to show that $\overline{z} \cdot \overline{u} \geq \frac{\xi}{2}$, which we now prove.

Let $S_1 = \{ \langle \overline{x}^j, y_j \rangle \in S : y_j (\overline{u} \cdot \overline{x}^j) \geq \xi \}$ and let $S_2 = S \setminus S_1$. The definition of S_1 immediately yields $\sum_{j \in S_1} \mathcal{D}(j) y_j (\overline{u} \cdot \overline{x}^j) \geq \mathcal{D}(S_1)\xi$. Moreover, since each $\|\overline{x}^j\|_p \leq R$, by Hölder's inequality we have $y_j(\overline{u} \cdot \overline{x}^j) \geq -\|\overline{x}^j\|_p \cdot \|\overline{u}\|_q \geq -R\|\overline{u}\|_q$ for each $\langle \overline{x}^j, y_j \rangle \in S_2$. Since each example in S_2 has weight at most $\frac{1}{\kappa m}$ under $\mathcal{D}$, we have $\mathcal{D}(S_2) \leq \frac{\eta'}{\kappa}$, and hence

$$\begin{aligned}
\overline{z} \cdot \overline{u} &= \sum_{j=1}^m \mathcal{D}(j) y_j (\overline{u} \cdot \overline{x}^j) = \sum_{j \in S_1} \mathcal{D}(j) y_j (\overline{u} \cdot \overline{x}^j) + \sum_{j \in S_2} \mathcal{D}(j) y_j (\overline{u} \cdot \overline{x}^j) \\
&\geq \mathcal{D}(S_1)\xi - \mathcal{D}(S_2) R \|\overline{u}\|_q \geq \left(1 - \frac{\eta'}{\kappa}\right)\xi - \frac{\eta' R \|\overline{u}\|_q}{\kappa} \\
&\geq \frac{3\xi}{4} - \frac{\xi}{4} = \frac{\xi}{2},
\end{aligned}$$

where the inequality $(1 - \frac{\eta'}{\kappa}) \geq \frac{3}{4}$ follows from the bound on η' and the fact that $\xi \leq R\|\overline{u}\|_q$. □

3.4 Putting It All Together

The algorithm for learning $\text{sign}(\overline{u} \cdot \overline{x})$ with respect to a ξ-good distribution $\mathcal{D}$ over $B_p(R)$ is as follows:

- Draw from $EX^{\eta}_{MAL}(\overline{u}, \mathcal{D})$ a sample $S = \langle \overline{x}^1, y_1 \rangle, \ldots, \langle \overline{x}^m, y_m \rangle$ of m labeled examples.
- Run `SmoothBoost` on S with parameters $\kappa = \frac{\epsilon}{4}$, $\gamma = \frac{\xi}{4R\|\overline{u}\|_q}$, $\theta = \frac{\gamma}{2+\gamma}$ using `WLA` as the weak learning algorithm.

We now determine constraints on the sample size m and the malicious noise rate η under which this is a successful and efficient learning algorithm.

We first note that since $\mathcal{D}$ is ξ-good for $\overline{u}$, we have that $\xi \leq R\|\overline{u}\|_q$. Furthermore, since $\kappa = \frac{\epsilon}{4}$, Lemma 1 implies that each distribution $\mathcal{D}_t$ which is given to `WLA` by `SmoothBoost` has $L_\infty(\mathcal{D}_t) \leq \frac{4}{\epsilon m}$. Let $S_C \subseteq S$ be the clean examples and $S_D = S \setminus S_C$ the dirty examples in S. If $\eta \leq \frac{\epsilon\xi}{32R\|\overline{u}\|_q}$ and $m \geq \frac{96R\|\overline{u}\|_q}{\epsilon\xi} \log \frac{2}{\delta}$, then a simple Chernoff bound implies that with probability at least $1 - \frac{\delta}{2}$ we have $|S_D| \leq \frac{\epsilon\xi}{16R\|\overline{u}\|_q} m$. Thus, we can apply Theorem 3 with $\eta' = \frac{\epsilon\xi}{16R\|\overline{u}\|_q}$; so each weak hypothesis $h_t(\overline{x}) = \overline{v}^t \cdot \overline{x}$ generated by `WLA` has advantage $\frac{\xi}{4R\|\overline{u}\|_q}$ under $\mathcal{D}_t$. Consequently, by Theorems 1 and 2, `SmoothBoost` efficiently outputs a final hypothesis $h(\overline{x}) = \text{sign} f(\overline{x})$ which has margin less than θ on at most an $\frac{\epsilon}{4}$ fraction of S. Since $|S_C|$ is easily seen to be at least $\frac{m}{2}$, we have that the margin of h is less than θ on at most an $\frac{\epsilon}{2}$ fraction of S_C. This means that we can apply powerful methods from the theory of data-dependent structural risk minimization [5,24] to bound the error of h under $\mathcal{D}$.

Recall that the final `SmoothBoost` hypothesis is $h(\overline{x}) = \text{sign}(f(\overline{x}))$ where $f(\overline{x}) = \overline{v} \cdot \overline{x}$ is a convex combination of hypotheses $h_t(\overline{x}) = \overline{v}^t \cdot \overline{x}$. Since each vector $\overline{v}^t$ satisfies $\|\overline{v}^t\|_q \leq \frac{1}{R}$, by Minkowski's inequality we have that $\|\overline{v}\|_q \leq \frac{1}{R}$ as well. The following theorem is proved in [23]:

Theorem 4. *Fix any value* $2 \leq p \leq \infty$ *and let* $\mathcal{F}$ *be the class of functions* $\{\overline{x} \mapsto \overline{v} \cdot \overline{x} : \|\overline{v}\|_q \leq \frac{1}{R}, \overline{x} \in B_p(R)\}$. *Then* $fat_{\mathcal{F}}(\mu) \leq \frac{2 \log 4n}{\mu^2}$, *where* $fat_{\mathcal{F}}(\mu)$ *is the* fat-shattering dimension of $\mathcal{F}$ at scale μ *as defined in, e.g., [4,5,24].*

The following theorem is from [5]:

Theorem 5. *Let* $\mathcal{F}$ *be a collection of real-valued functions over some domain* X, *let* $\mathcal{D}$ *be a distribution over* $X \times \{-1, 1\}$, *let* $S = \langle \overline{x}^1, y_1 \rangle, \ldots, \langle \overline{x}^m, y_m \rangle$ *be a sequence of labeled examples drawn from* $\mathcal{D}$, *and let* $h(\overline{x}) = \text{sign}(f(\overline{x}))$ *for some* $f \in \mathcal{F}$. *If* h *has margin less than* θ *on at most* k *examples in* S, *then with probability at least* $1 - \delta$ *we have that* $\Pr_{\langle \overline{x}, y \rangle \in \mathcal{D}}[h(\overline{x}) \neq y]$ *is at most*

$$\frac{k}{m} + \sqrt{\frac{2}{m}(d \ln(34e/m) \log(578m) + \ln(4/\delta))}, \tag{1}$$

where $d = fat_{\mathcal{F}}(\theta/16)$.

We have that h has margin less than θ on at most an $\frac{\epsilon}{2}$ fraction of the clean examples S_C, so we may take k/m to be $\frac{\epsilon}{2}$ in the above theorem. Now if we apply Theorem 4 and solve for m the inequality obtained by setting (1) to be at most ϵ, we obtain

Theorem 6. *Fix $2 \leq p \leq \infty$ and let $\mathcal{D}$ be a distribution over $B_p(R)$ which is ξ-good for $\overline{u}$. The algorithm described above uses $m = \tilde{O}\left(\left(\frac{R\|\overline{u}\|_q}{\xi\epsilon}\right)^2\right)$ examples and outputs an ϵ-approximator for $\overline{u}$ under $\mathcal{D}$ with probability $1-\delta$ in the presence of malicious noise at a rate $\eta = \Omega\left(\epsilon \cdot \frac{\xi}{R\|\overline{u}\|_q}\right)$.*

4 Comparison with Online Algorithms

The bounds given by Theorem 6 on sample complexity and malicious noise tolerance of our algorithms based on `SmoothBoost` are remarkably similar to the bounds which can be obtained through a natural PAC conversion of the online p-norm algorithms introduced by Grove, Littlestone and Schuurmans [14] and studied by Gentile and Littlestone [13]. Grove, Littlestone and Schuurmans (Theorem 6.1) proved that the online p-norm algorithm makes at most $O\left(\left(\frac{R\|\overline{u}\|_q}{\xi}\right)^2\right)$ mistakes on linearly separable data. Subsequently Gentile and Littlestone [13] extended the analysis from [14] and considered a setting in which the examples are not linearly separable. Their analysis (Theorem 6) shows that if an example sequence containing K malicious errors is provided to the online p-norm algorithm, then the algorithm will make at most

$$O\left(\left(\frac{R\|\overline{u}\|_q}{\xi}\right)^2 + K \cdot \frac{R\|\overline{u}\|_q}{\xi}\right)$$

mistakes. To obtain PAC-model bounds on the online p-norm algorithms in the presence of malicious noise, we use the following theorem due to Auer and Cesa-Bianchi [3] (Theorem 6.2):

Theorem 7. *Fix a hypothesis class $\mathcal{H}$ of Vapnik-Chervonenkis dimension d. Let A be an online learning algorithm with the following properties: (1) A only uses hypotheses which belong to $\mathcal{H}$, (2) if A is given a noise-free example sequence then A makes at most m_0 mistakes, and (3) if A is given an example sequence with K malicious errors then A makes at most $m_0 + BK$ mistakes. Then there is a PAC algorithm A' which learns to accuracy ϵ and confidence δ, uses $\tilde{O}(\frac{B^2}{\epsilon^2} + \frac{m_0}{\epsilon} + \frac{d}{\epsilon})$ examples, and can tolerate a malicious noise rate $\eta = \frac{\epsilon}{2B}$.*

Applying this theorem, we find that these PAC conversions of the online p-norm algorithms have sample complexity and malicious noise tolerance bounds which are essentially identical to the bounds given for our `SmoothBoost`-based algorithm.

5 SmoothBoost Is Optimally Smooth

It is evident from the proof of Theorem 6 that the smoothness of the distributions generated by SmoothBoost relates directly to the level of malicious noise which our linear threshold learning algorithm can tolerate. On the other hand, as mentioned in Section 1, Kearns and Li have shown that for a broad range of concept classes no algorithm can learn to accuracy ϵ in the presence of malicious noise at a rate $\eta > \frac{\epsilon}{1+\epsilon}$. Using the Kearns-Li upper bound on malicious noise tolerance, we prove in this section that SmoothBoost is optimal up to constant factors in terms of the smoothness of the distributions which it generates. This demonstrates an interesting connection between bounds on noise-tolerant learning and bounds on boosting algorithms.

Recall that if SmoothBoost is run on a set of m examples with input parameters κ, γ, θ, then each distribution $\mathcal{D}_t$ which SmoothBoost constructs will satisfy $L_\infty(\mathcal{D}_t) \leq \frac{1}{\kappa m}$. The proof is by contradiction; so suppose that there exists a boosting algorithm called SuperSmoothBoost which is similar to SmoothBoost but which has an even stronger guarantee on its distributions. More precisely we suppose that SuperSmoothBoost takes as input parameters κ, γ and a labeled sample S of size m, has access to a weak learning algorithm WL, generates a sequence $\mathcal{D}_1, \mathcal{D}_2, \ldots$ of distributions over S, and outputs a Boolean-valued final hypothesis h. As in Section 2.3, we suppose that if the weak learning algorithm WL always returns a hypothesis h_t which has advantage γ under $\mathcal{D}_t$, then SuperSmoothBoost will eventually halt and the final hypothesis h will agree with at least a $1-\kappa$ fraction of the labeled examples in S. Finally, we suppose that each distribution $\mathcal{D}_t$ is guaranteed to satisfy $L_\infty(\mathcal{D}_t) \leq \frac{1}{64\kappa m}$.

Consider the following severely restricted linear threshold learning problem: the domain is $\{-1,1\}^2 \subset \Re^2$, so any distribution $\mathcal{D}$ can assign weight only to these four points. Moreover, we only allow two possibilities for the target concept $\text{sign}(\overline{u} \cdot \overline{x})$: the vector $\overline{u}$ is either $(1,0)$ or $(0,1)$. The four points in $\{-1,1\}^2$ are classified in all four possible ways by these two concepts, and hence the concept class consisting of these two concepts is a *distinct* concept class as defined by Kearns and Li [16]. It is clear that every example belongs to $B_\infty(1)$ (i.e. $R=1$), that $\|\overline{u}\|_1 = 1$, and that any distribution $\mathcal{D}$ over $\{-1,1\}^2$ is 1-good for $\overline{u}$ (i.e. $\xi = 1$).

Consider the following algorithm for this restricted learning problem:

- Draw from $EX^{\eta}_{MAL}(\overline{u}, \mathcal{D})$ a sample $S = \langle \overline{x}^1, y_1\rangle, \ldots, \langle \overline{x}^m, y_m\rangle$ of m labeled examples.
- Run SuperSmoothBoost on S with parameters $\kappa = \frac{\epsilon}{4}$, $\gamma = \frac{\xi}{4R\|\overline{u}\|_q} = \frac{1}{4}$ using WLA with $p = \infty$ as the weak learning algorithm.

Suppose that the malicious noise rate η is 2ϵ. As in Section 3.4, a Chernoff bound shows that for $m = O(\frac{1}{\epsilon}\log\frac{1}{\delta})$, with probability at least $1-\frac{\delta}{2}$ we have that the sample S contains at most $4\epsilon m$ dirty examples. By the SuperSmoothBoost smoothness property and our choice of κ, we have that $L_\infty(\mathcal{D}_t) \leq \frac{1}{16\epsilon m}$. Theorem 3 now implies that each WLA hypothesis h_t has advantage at least $\frac{\xi}{4R\|\overline{u}\|_q} = \frac{1}{4}$

with respect to $\mathcal{D}_t$. As in Section 3.4, we have that with probability at least $1-\frac{\delta}{2}$ the final hypothesis h output by SuperSmoothBoost disagrees with at most an $\frac{\epsilon}{2}$ fraction of the clean examples S_C.

Since the domain is finite (in fact of size four) we can bound generalization error directly. A simple Chernoff bound argument shows that if m is sufficiently large, then with probability at least $1-\delta$ the hypothesis h will be an ϵ-approximator for $\text{sign}(\overline{u} \cdot \overline{x})$ under $\mathcal{D}$. However, Kearns and Li have shown (Theorem 1 of [16]) that no learning algorithm for a distinct concept class can learn to accuracy ϵ with probability $1-\delta$ in the presence of malicious noise at rate $\eta \geq \frac{\epsilon}{1+\epsilon}$. This contradiction proves that the SuperSmoothBoost algorithm cannot exist, and hence the distributions generated by SmoothBoost are optimal up to constant factors.

6 Conclusions and Further Work

One goal for future work is to improve the SmoothBoost algorithm given in Section 2. As noted in Section 5, the smoothness of the generated distributions is already essentially optimal; however it may be possible to improve other aspects of the algorithm such as the number of stages of boosting which are required. Is there an algorithm which matches the smoothness of SmoothBoost but, like AdaBoost, runs for only $O(\frac{\log(1/\kappa)}{\gamma^2})$ stages? Another possible improvement would be to eliminate the θ (margin) parameter of SmoothBoost; a version of the algorithm which automatically chooses an appropriate margin parameter would be useful in practical situations.

7 Acknowledgements

We thank Avrim Blum for a helpful discussion concerning the malicious noise tolerance of the Perceptron algorithm. We also thank Les Valiant for suggesting that the techniques in this paper could be used to prove a lower bound on the smoothness of an arbitrary boosting algorithm.

References

1. J. Aslam and S. Decatur. Specification and simulation of statistical query algorithms for efficiency and noise tolerance, *J. Comput. Syst. Sci.* **56** (1998), 191-208.
2. P. Auer. Learning nested differences in the presence of malicious noise, *Theoretical Computer Science* **185**(1) (1997), 159-175.
3. P. Auer and N. Cesa-Bianchi. On-line learning with malicious noise and the closure algorithm, *Ann. Math. and Artif. Intel.* **23** (1998), 83-99.
4. P. Bartlett, P. Long and R. Williamson. Fat-shattering and the learnability of real-valued functions, *J. Comput. Syst. Sci.*, **52**(3) (1996), 434-452.
5. P. Bartlett and J. Shawe-Taylor. Generalization performance of support vector machines and other pattern classifiers, *in* B. Scholkopf, C.J.C. Burges, and A.J. Smola, eds, *Advances in Kernel Methods - Support Vector Learning,* (1999), 43-54.

6. N. Cesa-Bianchi, E. Dichterman, P. Fischer, E. Shamir and H.U. Simon. Sample-efficient strategies for learning in the presence of noise, *J. ACM* **46**(5) (1999), 684-719.
7. S. Decatur. Statistical queries and faulty PAC oracles, *in* "Proc. Sixth Work. on Comp. Learning Theory" (1993), 262-268.
8. T.G. Dietterich. An experimental comparison of three methods for constructing ensembles of decision trees: Bagging, boosting, and randomization. *Machine Learning,* **40**(2) (2000), 139-158.
9. C. Domingo and O. Watanabe. MadaBoost: a modification of AdaBoost. *in* "Proc. 13th Conf. on Comp. Learning Theory" (2000), 180-189.
10. Y. Freund. An adaptive version of the boost by majority algorithm, *in* "Proc. Twelfth Conf. on Comp. Learning Theory" (1999), 102-113.
11. Y. Freund and R. Schapire. A decision-theoretic generalization of on-line learning and an application to boosting, *J. Comput. Syst. Sci.* **55**(1) (1997), 119-139.
12. Y. Freund and R. Schapire. Large margin classification using the perceptron algorithm, *in* "Proc. 11th Conf. Comp. Learning Theory" (1998), 209-217.
13. C. Gentile and N. Littlestone. The robustness of the p-norm algorithms, *in* "Proc. 12th Ann. Conf. on Comp. Learning Theory" (1999), 1-11.
14. A. Grove, N. Littlestone and D. Schuurmans. General convergence results for linear discriminant updates, *in* "Proc. 10th Ann. Conf. on Comp. Learning Theory" (1997), 171-183.
15. R. Impagliazzo. Hard-core distributions for somewhat hard problems, *in* "Proc. 36th Symp. on Found. of Comp. Sci." (1995), 538-545.
16. M. Kearns and M. Li. Learning in the presence of malicious errors, *SIAM J. Comput.* **22**(4) (1993), 807-837.
17. M. Kearns, L. Valiant. Cryptographic limitations on learning boolean formulae and finite automata, *J. ACM* **41**(1) (1994), 67-95. Also "Proc. 21st Symp. on Theor. of Comp." (1989), 433-444.
18. A. Klivans and R. Servedio. Boosting and hard-core sets, *in* "Proc. 40th Ann. Symp. on Found. of Comp. Sci." (1999), 624-633.
19. N. Littlestone. Redundant noisy attributes, attribute errors, and linear-threshold learning using winnow, *in* "Proc. Fourth Workshop on Computational Learning Theory," (1991), 147-156.
20. Y. Mansour and M. Parnas. Learning conjunctions with noise under product distributions, *Inf. Proc. Let.* **68**(4) (1998), 189-196.
21. R.E. Schapire. Theoretical views of boosting, *in* "Proc. 10th Int. Conf. on Algorithmic Learning Theory" (1999), 12-24.
22. R. Schapire, Y. Freund, P. Bartlett and W.S. Lee. Boosting the margin: a new explanation for the effectiveness of voting methods, *Annals of Statistics* **26**(5) (1998), 1651-1686.
23. R. Servedio. PAC analogues of perceptron and winnow via boosting the margin, *in* "Proc. 13th Conf. on Comp. Learning Theory," 2000.
24. J. Shawe-Taylor, P.L. Bartlett, R.C. Williamson and M. Anthony. Structural risk minimization over data-dependent hierarchies, *IEEE Trans. Inf. Theory,* **44**(5) (1998), 1926-1940.
25. A. Taylor and W. Mann. *Advanced Calculus,* Wiley & Sons, 1972.
26. L.G. Valiant. Learning disjunctions of conjunctions, *in* "Proc. 9th Internat. Joint Conf. on Artif. Intel." (1985), 560-566.

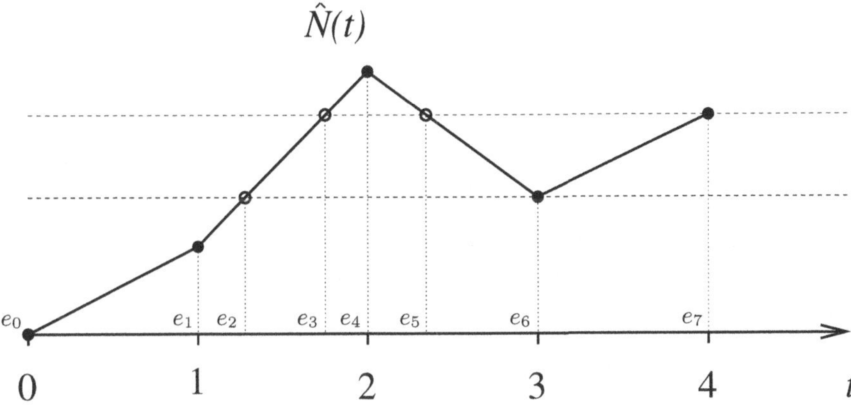

Fig. 3. A plot of $\hat{N}$ with $T = 4$. Note that $\hat{N}$ is piecewise linear with joins at integer values of t. A possible pairing of segments matches $[e_2, e_3]$ with $[e_5, e_6]$ and $[e_3, e_4]$ with $[e_4, e_5]$, leaving $[e_0, e_1]$, $[e_1, e_2]$ and $[e_6, e_7]$ unpaired. In this example $\hat{N}$ is increasing on each unpaired segment.

A Proof of Lemma 3

By the definition of $N_t(j)$, we have

$$\sum_{j=1}^{m}\sum_{t=1}^{T} M_t(j) y_j h_t(x^j) = \sum_{j=1}^{m}\sum_{t=1}^{T} M_t(j)(N_t(j) - N_{t-1}(j) + \theta)$$
$$= \theta \sum_{t=1}^{T} |M_t| + \sum_{t=1}^{T}\sum_{j=1}^{m} M_t(j)(N_t(j) - N_{t-1}(j)). \quad (2)$$

It thus suffices to show that if $\theta = \frac{\gamma}{2+\gamma}$, then for each $j = 1, \ldots, m$ we have

$$\sum_{t=1}^{T} M_t(j)(N_t(j) - N_{t-1}(j)) < \frac{2}{\gamma\sqrt{1-\gamma}} + (\gamma - \theta)\sum_{t=1}^{T} M_t(j) \quad (3)$$

since summing this inequality over $j = 1, \ldots, m$ and substituting into (2) proves the lemma. Fix any $j \in \{1, \ldots, m\}$; for ease of notation we write N_t and M_t in place of $N_t(j)$ and $M_t(j)$ for the rest of the proof.

If $N_t = N_{t-1}$ for some integer t then the term $M_t(N_t - N_{t-1})$ contributes 0 to the sum in (3), so without loss of generality we assume that $N_t \neq N_{t-1}$ for all integers t. We extend the sequence $(N_0, N_1, \ldots, N_T)$ to a continuous piecewise linear function $\hat{N}$ on $[0, T]$ in the obvious way, i.e. for t an integer and $\epsilon \in [0, 1]$ we have $\hat{N}(t + \epsilon) = N_t + \epsilon(N_{t+1} - N_t)$. Let

$$E = \{e \in [0, T] : \hat{N}(e) = N_t \text{ for some integer } t = 0, 1, \ldots, T\}.$$

The set E is finite so we have $0 = e_0 < e_1 \cdots < e_r = T$ with $E = \{e_0, \ldots, e_r\}$ (see Figure 3). Since for each integer $t \geq 1$ the interval $(t-1, t]$ must contain some e_i, we can reexpress the sum $\sum_{t=1}^{T} M_t(N_t - N_{t-1})$ as

$$\sum_{i=1}^{r} M_{\lceil e_i \rceil} \left(\hat{N}(e_i) - \hat{N}(e_{i-1}) \right). \tag{4}$$

We say that two segments $[e_{a-1}, e_a]$ and $[e_{b-1}, e_b]$ *match* if $\hat{N}(e_{a-1}) = \hat{N}(e_b)$ and $\hat{N}(e_{b-1}) = \hat{N}(e_a)$. For example, in Figure 3 the segment $[e_2, e_3]$ matches $[e_5, e_6]$ but does not match $[e_6, e_7]$. We pair up matching segments until no more pairs can be formed. Note that if any unpaired segments remain, it must be the case that either $\hat{N}$ is increasing on each unpaired segment (if $N_T > 0$) or $\hat{N}$ is decreasing on each unpaired segment (if $N_T < 0$). Now we separate the sum (4) into two pieces, i.e. $\sum_{i=1}^{r} M_{\lceil e_i \rceil}(\hat{N}(e_i) - \hat{N}(e_{i-1})) = P + U$, where P is the sum over all paired segments and U is the sum over all unpaired segments. We will show that $P < (\gamma - \theta) \sum_{t=1}^{T} M_t$ and $U < \frac{2}{\gamma\sqrt{1-\gamma}}$, thus proving the lemma.

First we bound P. Let $[e_{a-1}, e_a]$ and $[e_{b-1}, e_b]$ be a pair of matching segments where $\hat{N}$ is increasing on $[e_{a-1}, e_a]$ and decreasing on $[e_{b-1}, e_b]$. The contribution of these two segments to P is

$$\begin{aligned} M_{\lceil e_a \rceil} \left(\hat{N}(e_a) - \hat{N}(e_{a-1}) \right) &+ M_{\lceil e_b \rceil} \left(\hat{N}(e_b) - \hat{N}(e_{b-1}) \right) \\ &= (M_{\lceil e_a \rceil} - M_{\lceil e_b \rceil}) \left(\hat{N}(e_a) - \hat{N}(e_{a-1}) \right). \end{aligned} \tag{5}$$

Since each segment $[e_{a-1}, e_a]$ is contained in $[t-1, t]$ for some integer t, we have that $\lceil e_a \rceil - 1 \leq e_{a-1} < e_a \leq \lceil e_a \rceil$. The linearity of $\hat{N}$ on $[\lceil e_a \rceil - 1, \lceil e_a \rceil]$ implies that

$$N_{\lceil e_a \rceil - 1} \leq \hat{N}(e_{a-1}) < \hat{N}(e_a) \leq N_{\lceil e_a \rceil} \leq N_{\lceil e_a \rceil - 1} + 1 - \theta \tag{6}$$

where the last inequality is because $y_j h_t(x^j) \leq 1$ in line 7 of `SmoothBoost`. Similarly, we have that $\lceil e_b \rceil - 1 \leq e_{b-1} < e_b \leq \lceil e_b \rceil$, and hence

$$N_{\lceil e_b \rceil - 1} \geq \hat{N}(e_{b-1}) > \hat{N}(e_b) \geq N_{\lceil e_b \rceil} \geq N_{\lceil e_b \rceil - 1} - 1 - \theta. \tag{7}$$

Since $\hat{N}(e_a) = \hat{N}(e_{b-1})$ inequalities (6) and (7) imply that $N_{\lceil e_a \rceil - 1} \geq N_{\lceil e_b \rceil - 1} - 2$. The definition of M now implies that $M_{\lceil e_b \rceil} \geq (1 - \gamma) M_{\lceil e_a \rceil}$. Since $\hat{N}(e_a) - \hat{N}(e_{a-1}) > 0$, we thus have that (5) is at most

$$\gamma M_{\lceil e_a \rceil} \left(\hat{N}(e_a) - \hat{N}(e_{a-1}) \right) \leq \gamma(1 - \theta) M_{\lceil e_a \rceil}(e_a - e_{a-1}) \tag{8}$$

where the inequality follows from (6) and the linearity of $\hat{N}$ on $[e_{a-1}, e_a]$. Since $\hat{N}(e_a) - \hat{N}(e_{a-1}) = \hat{N}(e_{b-1}) - \hat{N}(e_b)$, we similarly have that (5) is at most

$$\begin{aligned} \gamma M_{\lceil e_a \rceil} \left(\hat{N}(e_{b-1}) - \hat{N}(e_b) \right) &\leq \frac{\gamma}{1-\gamma} M_{\lceil e_b \rceil} \left(\hat{N}(e_{b-1}) - \hat{N}(e_b) \right) \\ &\leq \frac{\gamma}{1-\gamma} (1 + \theta) M_{\lceil e_b \rceil}(e_{b-1} - e_b). \end{aligned} \tag{9}$$

Using the fact that $\theta = \frac{\gamma}{2+\gamma}$ and some algebra, inequalities (8) and (9) imply that (5) is at most

$$\frac{\gamma(1+\gamma)}{2+\gamma}\left(M_{\lceil e_a \rceil}(e_a - e_{a-1}) + M_{\lceil e_b \rceil}(e_{b-1} - e_b)\right). \tag{10}$$

If we sum (10) over all pairs of matching segments the resulting quantity is an upper bound on P. In this sum, for each value of $t = 1, \ldots, T$, the coefficient of M_t will be at most $\frac{\gamma(1+\gamma)}{2+\gamma} = \gamma - \theta$. (This bound on the coefficient of M_t holds because for each t, the total length of all paired segments in $[t-1, t]$ is at most 1). Consequently we have $P < (\gamma - \theta)\sum_{t=1}^{T} M_t$ as desired.

Now we show that U, the sum over unpaired segments, is at most $\frac{2}{\gamma\sqrt{1-\gamma}}$. If $\hat{N}$ is decreasing on each unpaired segment then clearly $U < 0$, so we suppose that $\hat{N}$ is increasing on each unpaired segment. Let $[e_{c_1-1}, e_{c_1}], \ldots, [e_{c_d-1}, e_{c_d}]$ be all the unpaired segments. As in Figure 2 it must be the case that the intervals $[\hat{N}(e_{c_i-1}), \hat{N}(e_{c_i}))$ are all disjoint and their union is $[0, N_T)$. By the definition of M, we have $U = \sum_{i=1}^{d}(1-\gamma)^{(N_{\lceil e_{c_i} \rceil}-1)/2}\left(\hat{N}(e_{c_i}) - \hat{N}(e_{c_i-1})\right)$. As in the bound for P, we have

$$N_{\lceil e_{c_i} \rceil - 1} \le \hat{N}(e_{c_i-1}) < \hat{N}(e_{c_i}) \le N_{\lceil e_{c_i} \rceil} \le N_{\lceil e_{c_i} \rceil - 1} + 1 - \theta < N_{\lceil e_{c_i} \rceil - 1} + 1$$

and hence

$$\begin{aligned} U &\le \sum_{i=1}^{d}(1-\gamma)^{(\hat{N}(e_{c_i})-1)/2}\left(\hat{N}(e_{c_i}) - \hat{N}(e_{c_i-1})\right) \\ &= (1-\gamma)^{-1/2}\sum_{i=1}^{d}(1-\gamma)^{\hat{N}(e_{c_i})/2}\left(\hat{N}(e_{c_i}) - \hat{N}(e_{c_i-1})\right). \end{aligned}$$

Since $\hat{N}$ is increasing, for each i we have

$$(1-\gamma)^{\hat{N}(e_{c_i})/2}\left(\hat{N}(e_{c_i}) - \hat{N}(e_{c_i-1})\right) < \int_{z=\hat{N}(e_{c_i-1})}^{\hat{N}(e_{c_i})}(1-\gamma)^{z/2}dz.$$

Since the disjoint intervals $[\hat{N}(e_{c_i-1}), \hat{N}(e_{c_i}))$ cover $[0, N_T)$ we thus have

$$\begin{aligned} U &< (1-\gamma)^{-1/2}\int_{z=0}^{N_T}(1-\gamma)^{z/2}dz \\ &< (1-\gamma)^{-1/2}\int_{z=0}^{\infty}(1-\gamma)^{z/2}dz \\ &= \frac{-2}{\sqrt{1-\gamma}\ln(1-\gamma)} < \frac{2}{\gamma\sqrt{1-\gamma}} \qquad \text{for } 0 < \gamma < 1/2. \end{aligned}$$

(Lemma 3) ■

On Boosting with Optimal Poly-Bounded Distributions

Nader H. Bshouty[1] and Dmitry Gavinsky[2]

[1] Technion - Israel Institute of technology, Haifa 32000, Israel,
bshouty@cs.technion.ac.il
[2] Technion - Israel Institute of technology, Haifa 32000, Israel,
demitry@cs.technion.ac.il

Abstract. In the paper, we construct a framework which allows to bound polynomially the distributions produced by certain boosting algorithms, without significant performance loss.
Further, we study the case of Freund and Schapire's *AdaBoost* algorithm, bounding its distributions to near-polynomial w.r.t. the example oracle's distribution. An advantage of *AdaBoost* over other boosting techniques is that it doesn't require an a-priori accuracy lower bound for the hypotheses accepted from the weak learner during the learning process.
We turn *AdaBoost* into an on-line boosting algorithm (boosting "by filtering"), which can be applied to the wider range of learning problems. In particular, now *AdaBoost* applies to the problem of *DNF-learning*, answering affirmatively the question posed by Jackson.
We also construct a hybrid boosting algorithm, in that way achieving the lowest bound possible for booster-produced distributions (in terms of $\tilde{O}$), and show a possible application to the problem of DNF-learning w.r.t. the uniform.

1 Introduction

Boosting is a learning method which shows computational equivalence between two learning models: the model of *distribution-free (strong) PAC-learning* and that of *distribution-free weak PAC-learning* (the PAC-model was first introduced by Valiant in [V84], the strong and the weak cases were distinguished by Kearns and Valiant in [KV94]).

General framework for boosting algorithms is the following. Suppose we are dealing with some binary concept class, say C, which is a subclass of all functions from $\{0,1\}^n$ to $\{0,1\}$.

In the distribution-free (strong) PAC-learning model, our (the learner's) task is to produce an approximation to a concept $c \in C$, "known" to the oracle. Each time it is called, the oracle provides us with an instance $x \in \{0,1\}^n$, chosen accordingly to some fixed but unknown distribution D and with the corresponding labeling $c(x)$ of the instance. The learner's aim is to provide, with probability at least $1-\delta$, a *final hypothesis* $h(x)$ which $1-\epsilon$-approximates the concept c w.r.t. the distribution D. Here ϵ and δ are received parameters.

D. Helmbold and B. Williamson (Eds.): COLT/EuroCOLT 2001, LNAI 2111, pp. 490–506, 2001.

In the framework of boosting, the learner is supplied with some auxiliary algorithm *WL* (the *weak learner*) which satisfies the following conditions (accordingly to the distribution-free weak PAC-learning model). Given an access to the standard PAC-oracle answering accordingly to some target function $f \in C$ over distribution D_i, produces a hypothesis h_i s.t.

$$\Pr_{D_i}[f(x) = h_i(x)] \geq \frac{1}{2} + \gamma$$

for some γ, $\frac{1}{\gamma} = O(poly(n))$. [1] Algorithm *WL* provides the desired accuracy $\frac{1}{2} + \gamma$ with given confidence factor δ, runs in time polynomial in $\log(1/\delta)$ and other standard complexity parameters (n, the size of the target representation, etc.).

The booster is allowed to use *WL* as a subroutine, by sequentially providing distributions D_i and receiving corresponding weak hypotheses h_i; afterwards it combines the accepted weak hypotheses in some manner, thus producing the strong PAC-hypothesis. This "combination" of the booster and the weak learner should possess all qualities required from the learner by the standard distribution-free PAC model (see above) and its complexity bounds should be polynomial in all standard complexity parameters.

Sometimes, an additional restriction is applied to the booster: all the distributions D_i it produces should be *polynomially near-D*, i.e., for all i and all $x \in \{0,1\}^n$ it holds that

$$D_i(x) \leq D(x) \cdot poly(n).$$ [2]

In this paper we show that sometimes a boosting algorithm whose produced distributions are not polynomially near-D can be converted into an algorithm possessing this property. As an example, we will consider the case of the *AdaBoost* algorithm which was first introduced by Freund and Schapire in [FS97]. This algorithm doesn't need a-priori lower bound on the accuracy of weak hypotheses accepted throughout the learning. Different weak hypotheses play "different roles" in the final hypothesis, accordingly to their individual accuracies w.r.t. the target concept. In this sense, *AdaBoost* makes a "more optimal" use of the information accepted from the weak learner than other boosting algorithms which use an a-priori accuracy lower bound.

Originally, *AdaBoost* was designed to work *by sampling*, i.e., in two stages. In the first stage the algorithm collects a "sufficient" number of learning examples and in the second stage it performs the learning over this examples collection only. Using our technique, we transform the algorithm into booster *by filtering*, i.e., no pre-collection is performed in this case and the learning is performed over the whole set of instances. This allows to apply *AdaBoost* to DNF-learning, which affirmatively answers the question posed by Jackson in [J97].

[1] In this paper, the meaning of the notation $poly(n)$ is that there exist some polynomial that satisfies the condition.

[2] In certain cases, this restriction makes sense when the target distribution D is polynomially near-uniform, like the case of DNF-learning considered in Section 6. In this case, all the distributions D_i are also polynomially near-uniform.

Eventually, we construct a hybrid boosting algorithm, whose produced distributions is even more "flat", achieving the lowest bound possible for near-uniform distributions produced by a booster, in terms of $\tilde{O}$.

For the sake of demonstration, we apply this algorithm to DNF-learning w.r.t. the uniform distribution. The performance achieved is somewhat weaker then that of Klivans and Servedio's algorithm shown in [KS99], but the case provides a good example of learning problem where the "flatness" is critical to the solution complexity. It is possible that a more detailed study of the case could lead to some improvement.

2 Definitions and Notation

We will call a boosting algorithm producing only polynomially near-D distributions *a polynomially near-D boosting algorithm*[3].

Let B be any boosting algorithm learning some concept class C using a weak learning algorithm *WL*. Let us consider the way B is producing its final hypothesis using weak hypotheses received during the boosting iterations. As an example, consider the Freund and Schapire's *AdaBoost* algorithm [FS97], whose final hypothesis is a weighted majority vote of all the weak hypotheses seen during the boosting process.

In this final hypothesis structure, one interesting feature can be observed: if we insert some "additional" relative error ϵ' into any of the weak hypotheses, this change can, in the worst case, add the same relative error ϵ' to the final hypothesis. In other words, an inaccuracy present in some instance of any weak hypothesis can cause an inaccurate result accepted only in the same instance of the final hypothesis.

We will call a final hypothesis structure possessing this quality and a boosting algorithms producing such hypotheses *accuracy preserving.*

3 Providing Near-D Bounds to Distributions

In this section, for simplicity we will not take into account the fact that *WL* has some probability to fail (δ mentioned above), i.e., *WL* will be treated as a deterministic algorithm.

Consider some accuracy preserving boosting algorithm B. Recall that the overall number T of weak hypotheses is polynomially bounded. If we allow an "additional" error ϵ' in each one of the weak hypotheses, it will result, in the worst case, in $T \cdot \epsilon'$ additional inaccuracy in the final hypothesis[4].

Suppose that the booster in a certain stage of the game provides not polynomially bounded distribution D_i to the weak learner. Let's assume that we

[3] In further references the word *polynomially* will be omitted sometimes.

[4] Notice that any modification made in some iteration is not allowed to affect the following iterations, otherwise some "side effects" can be caused by the change.

can estimate $D_i(x)$ for all instances x[5]. So we will act in the following manner: first we estimate the total weight (w.r.t. D_i) of the instances x whose weight is above $p_0(n) \cdot D(x)$, where $p_0(n)$ is a polynomial to be fixed later[6]. If this weight exceeds $\frac{3}{4}$, we will not call the weak learner but return an "empty" hypothesis (e.g., const. 1) to the booster; otherwise we will just "suppress" all instances whose weight exceeds $p_0(n) \cdot D(x)$.

Let's call the distribution produced this way at the i'th stage D_i'; it can be seen that if WL was executed during the i'th stage then

$$D_i'(x) = \begin{cases} \frac{D_i(x)}{Pr_{D_i}[D_i(x) \leq p_0(n) \cdot D(x)]} & if\ D_i(x) \leq p_0(n) \cdot D(x) \\ 0 & otherwise \end{cases} . \tag{1}$$

There is no such instance x that receives a weight higher than $4p_0(n) \cdot D(x)$ after the modification, and the resulting distribution is therefore near-D.

In the later case there is no such instance x that receives a weight higher than $4p_0(n) \cdot D(x)$ after the modification, and the resulting distribution is therefore near-D.

First of all, as mentioned above, we should provide a "stable work" of the booster during the succeeding stages. To do that, we will modify the booster a bit. Successful learning can be ensured *if and only if* all weak hypothesis seen by the booster are $(\frac{1}{2} + \gamma)$-accurate at least.

Assume that at the i'th stage the booster received some hypothesis h_i (which is $(\frac{1}{2} + \gamma)$-accurate w.r.t. D_i', but not necessary w.r.t. D_i). Define:

$$h_i'(x) = \begin{cases} h_i(x)\ if\ D_i(x) \leq p_0(n) \cdot D(x) \\ f(x)\ \ otherwise \end{cases} . \tag{2}$$

The modified booster must proceed on receiving h_i like the original one would on receiving h_i'; the possibility of this modification obviously also depends on the internal structure of the boosting algorithm. Note that this will "localize" the influence of the each distribution alteration to a single boosting stage.

Let's examine the properties of the new algorithm. First of all, we can see that all the h_i'-s are well correlated with f. If WL wasn't executed in the i'th iteration then

$$\Pr_{D_i}[h_i'(x) = f(x)] \geq \frac{3}{4} > \frac{1}{2} + \gamma.$$ [7]

Otherwise it holds that

$$\Pr_{D_i}[h_i'(x) = f(x)] \geq \frac{1}{2} + \gamma,$$

[5] This assumption, like some further constructions, employs a prior "knowledge" about the boosting algorithm; in this paper we are not handling the booster as a "black box".

[6] The bound is polynomial in all the standard complexity parameters, and is as well in n, assuming that the complexity parameters themselves are polynomial in n. Notice also that in practice we will sometimes use the Chernoff bound to perform estimations; this will affect slightly some constructions of this section.

[7] In general, $\frac{1}{2} + \mathbf{const} > \frac{1}{2} + \gamma$ seems to be a reasonable assumption.

which naturally follows from (1) and (2).

Therefore, the only "damage" brought to the booster's performance by the above-mentioned modification is that resulting from the differences between h_i-s and corresponding h'_i-s being substituted into the final hypothesis. For any iteration i it holds that

$$\begin{aligned} &|\mathrm{Pr}_D[h'_i = f] - \mathrm{Pr}_D[h_i = f]| \leq \\ &\leq \mathrm{Pr}_D[h'_i \neq h_i] \leq \mathrm{Pr}_D\left[D_i(x) > p_0(n) \cdot D(x)\right] < \tfrac{1}{p_0(n)} \triangleq \epsilon'. \end{aligned} \tag{3}$$

Let's denote the modified version of the boosting algorithm by B'; call the initial weak learner W, which can be viewed as an oracle in this case. Denote by $F_{p_0}(W)$ the weak learning oracle simulated by the technique described above and by $F'_{p_0}(W)$ the "virtual" version of the $F_{p_0}(W)$ where all h_i-s (the produced weak hypotheses) are replaced by corresponding h'_i-s. Denote by $B^{\Upsilon}(\epsilon, \delta)$ the final hypothesis returned by the boosting algorithm B using Υ as a weak learner and given accuracy and confidence parameters ϵ and δ respectively. Assume that the overall number of boosting iterations is T, B is accuracy preserving and denote by $\mathrm{Err}(B)$ the value of $\mathrm{Pr}_D\left[B(x) \neq f(x)\right]$. The lemma follows:

Lemma 1.

$$Err(B'^{F_{p_0}(W)}(\epsilon, \delta)) \leq Err(B^{F'_{p_0}(W)}(\epsilon, \delta)) + \frac{T}{p_0(n)}.$$

4 The Case of *AdaBoost*

In this section we will apply the technique described in the previous section to the case of the *AdaBoost* algorithm ([FS97]). In general, $h_i(x)$ (a weak hypothesis) is not necessary a binary function, it can be a real-valued hypothesis; in fact, we only assume that this function has $[0, 1]$ range. Therefore, we will consider the value of

$$\mathop{\mathbf{E}}_{D} |h_f(x) - f(x)|$$

as the error of the final hypothesis $h_f(x)$ (instead of $\mathrm{Pr}_D[h_f(x) \neq f(x)]$ used so far).

Recall that the final hypothesis produced by *AdaBoost* is accuracy preserving. At the same time, the number of iterations required by *AdaBoost* to achieve desired accuracy depends upon all ϵ_i-s - the errors of the weak hypotheses seen during the boosting process. However, being provided with an upper bound for those (some $\gamma_{\min}$ s.t. for every iteration i it holds: $\epsilon_i \leq \frac{1}{2} - \gamma_{\min}$), the overall number of iterations can be bounded. As shown in [FS97], in this case the number of iterations T satisfies:

$$T \leq \left\lceil \frac{1}{2{\gamma_{\min}}^2} \ln \frac{1}{\epsilon} \right\rceil.$$

In this section we will consider two possible applications of the above "polynomializing" technique: to the case of boosting by sampling (which is very similar to the "original" *AdaBoost*) and to the case of boosting by filtering. The latter is made possible by the technique introduced in this paper[8].

4.1 Boosting by Sub-sampling

The main idea behind boosting by sampling is the following. The algorithm collects a training set; the further learning is performed over this training set only. The set is obviously polynomial by size (which intuitively reduces the "need for Chernoff", as the necessary statistical measurements can be performed straightforward over the whole training set). After achieving a certain accuracy of the final hypothesis on the training set (which is often the absolute coincidence), theoretic-informational techniques are applied to measure the overall accuracy of the same hypothesis (Occam, VC-dim, etc.).

We call our algorithm *QuickSamp*$(n, WL, \gamma_{\min}, S, m)$. We denote by m the size of the training set $S = \{(x_1, f(x_1)), ..., (x_m, f(x_m))\}$. In this case the distribution D is defined to be uniform over the set S, therefore the (final) hypothesis is correct on S when it has error smaller than $1/m$.

The algorithm is shown in Figure 3 in the appendix section. As mentioned before, the algorithm is very similar to *AdaBoost*; its analysis can also be found in the appendix section. We will not make further use of the result achieved in this section; it is considered only to represent the approach introduced in this paper[9].

4.2 Boosting by Filtering

In this section we no longer assume that *WL* is deterministic; now it is provided with an argument δ', which is the allowed probability to fail.

The meaning of the term of *boosting by filtering* is that the booster takes the whole instances set as its domain. The examples accepted by the booster are not stored (like the set S used by *QuickSamp*) but are either forwarded to the current session of *WL* or "rejected" (i.e., are not used at all). This approach has two obvious advantages over boosting by sampling: the space complexity is lowered because we are not storing the examples and no generalization error is present. At the same time, the analysis and the algorithm itself become slightly more involved, as now we cannot collect "statistics" by running through all the instances of the sample and need to use some estimation schemes (e.g., Chernoff bound).

We call the *QuickSamp*'s "twin" working by filtering *QuickFilt* (see Figure 1 and Figure 2). The arguments of this new algorithm are $(n, EX, WL, \gamma_{\min}, \epsilon, \delta)$; the changes in comparison with *QuickSamp* are that D, S and m are no longer

[8] In general, boosting by filtering is possible only if all distributions produced by the booster are polynomially near-D.

[9] The advantages of the "polynomializing" are minimized in this case by the fact that the distribution D is (always) not polynomially near-uniform, and therefore the distributions provided by the booster are not near-uniform as well.

needed, they are "replaced" by example oracle EX (producing learning examples accordingly to the target distribution D); other new arguments are ϵ which is the error allowed for the final hypothesis and δ which denotes the allowed probability for *QuickFilt* to fail (i.e., $\delta = 1-\mathit{confidence}$).

QuickFilt$(n, \boldsymbol{EX}, \boldsymbol{WL}, \gamma_{\min}, \epsilon, \delta)$

1. **set** $\gamma_{\min} = \min\{\gamma_{\min}, \frac{1}{30}\}$; $T_{\max} = \left\lceil \frac{1}{2{\gamma_{\min}}^2} \ln\left(\frac{6}{\epsilon}\right) \right\rceil$
2. **set** $B = \frac{5T_{\max}}{\delta}$; $C = \frac{4T_{\max}}{\epsilon}$
3. **set** $\Delta_\epsilon = \min\{\frac{\epsilon}{64T_{\max}}, \frac{1}{15}\}$; $k_\sigma = 1\frac{1}{2}$; $\Delta_\sigma = 1 - \frac{1}{k_\sigma}$
4. **set** $\epsilon_c = 1$; $i = 0$
5. **while** $(\epsilon_c \geq \frac{5\epsilon}{6})$
6. **set** $i = i + 1$
7. **set** $\sigma_i = \mathit{Evaluate}(X =_{x_j \sim D} \mathit{Get\_w}(i+1, j),$ $\frac{\lambda}{b-a} = \frac{\Delta_\sigma}{2C \cdot k_\sigma^2}, \delta = \frac{1}{B})$
8. **call** WL*$(\delta' = \frac{1}{B})$, providing it with distribution generated by $D_i$gen; denote the returned weak hypothesis by h_i*
9. **define** $\widehat{h'_i}(x) \triangleq \begin{cases} h_i(x) \ \mathit{if}\ w_j \leq C \cdot k_\sigma \sigma_i \\ f(x) \ \ \mathit{otherwise} \end{cases}$
10. **call** ReviewDestroy
11. **set** $\beta_i = \frac{\epsilon_i}{1-\epsilon_i}$
12. **define** $h'_f(x) = \begin{cases} 1 \ \mathit{if}\ \sum_{t=1}^{i} (\log \frac{1}{\beta_t}) h_t(x) \geq \frac{1}{2} \sum_{t=1}^{i} \log \frac{1}{\beta_t} \\ 0 \ \mathit{otherwise} \end{cases}$
13. **set** $\epsilon_c = \mathit{Evaluate}(X =_{x \sim D} |h'_f(x) - f(x)|, \frac{\lambda}{b-a} = \frac{\epsilon}{6}, \delta = \frac{1}{B})$
14. **endwhile**
15. *Output the final hypothesis:* $h_f(x) = h'_f(x)$

Fig. 1. The *QuickFilt*$(n, EX, WL, \gamma_{\min}, \epsilon, \delta)$ hypothesis boosting algorithm.

Denote by $\mathbf{Av}[X_i]$ the mean value of $\{X_i\}$ [10]. The analysis of the algorithm can be found in the appendix section. It shows that with probability at least δ, the algorithm *QuickFilt* halts and returns the final hypothesis which $(1-\epsilon)$-approximates the target function. Moreover, in the same case the running time of the algorithm is:

$$\tilde{O}\left(\frac{1}{\mathbf{Av}[\overline{\gamma_i'^2}]} \cdot T[WL(\delta {\gamma_{\min}}^2)] + \right.$$
$$\left. + \frac{1}{\epsilon {\gamma_{\min}}^2 (\mathbf{Av}[\overline{\gamma_i'^2}])^2} \cdot Q[WL(\delta {\gamma_{\min}}^2)] + \frac{1}{\epsilon^2 {\gamma_{\min}}^4 (\mathbf{Av}[\overline{\gamma_i'^2}])^2} \right),$$

and the query complexity is

$$\tilde{O}\left(\frac{1}{\epsilon {\gamma_{\min}}^2\, \mathbf{Av}[\overline{\gamma_i'^2}]} \cdot Q[WL(\delta {\gamma_{\min}}^2)] \right),$$

[10] If X is a random value, we consider the set of its instances accepted during specific algorithm execution.

$D_i gen$
do
  get $(x_j, f(f_j))$ *from* EX; *chose* $r \sim \mathbf{U}_{0,1}$
  if $(r < \frac{w_j}{2C \cdot k_\sigma^3 \sigma_i})$ **then return** $(x_j, f(f_j))$
enddo

Get_w(i, j)
set $w_j = 1, k = 1$
while $(k < i)$
  set $w_j = \begin{cases} w_j \cdot \beta_k^{1-a_i|h_k(x_j)-f(x_j)|-b_i} & if\ w_j \leq C \cdot k_\sigma \sigma_k \\ w_j \cdot \beta_k & otherwise \end{cases}$
  set $k = k + 1$
endwhile
return $w_j^i = w_j$

ReviewDestroy
set $\widehat{\epsilon_i} = Evaluate(X =_{x \sim D_i gen} |\widehat{h}_i'(x) - f(x)|, \frac{\lambda}{b-a} = \Delta_\epsilon, \delta = \frac{1}{B})$
if $(\epsilon_i < \frac{1}{3} + \Delta_\epsilon)$ **then**
  set $a_i = \frac{\frac{2}{3} - \Delta_\epsilon}{1 - \widehat{\epsilon_i}}$; $b_i = 1 - a_i$; $\epsilon_i = \frac{1}{3} + \Delta_\epsilon$
else
  set $a_i = 1$; $b_i = 0$; $\epsilon_i = \widehat{\epsilon_i}$
endif
define $h_i'(x) \triangleq a_i \widehat{h}_i'(x) + b_i(1 - f(x))$

Evaluate$(X, \frac{\lambda}{b-a}, \delta)$
set $m = \left\lceil \frac{\ln(\frac{2}{\delta})}{2(\frac{\lambda}{b-a})^2} \right\rceil$
return $\frac{\sum_{i=1}^m X_i}{m}$

Fig. 2. Subroutines used in the *QuickFilt* hypothesis boosting algorithm.

where $T[\,WL(\delta')]$ and $Q[\,WL(\delta')]$ are correspondingly time and query complexity[11] of a single *WL* execution with confidence parameter δ'. All distributions provided by *QuickFilt* to *WL* satisfy for all x:

$$D_i(x) \leq \frac{9}{\epsilon {\gamma_{\min}}^2} \ln\left(\frac{6}{\epsilon}\right) \cdot D(x).$$

4.3 Implementation Considerations

Note that both *QuickSamp*'s and *QuickFilt*'s time complexity depends on two different "γ-related" attributes: $\gamma_{\min}$ and $\mathbf{Av}[\gamma_i^2]$. In fact, in both cases $\gamma_{\min}$ is used only to pre-estimate the overall number of boosting iterations. This number, in fact, depends on $\mathbf{Av}[\gamma_i^2]$ only; therefore, in both cases $\gamma_{\min}$ may be replaced

[11] Both expressions assumed to be polynomials in $1/\delta'$

by $\mathbf{Av}[\gamma_i^2]$ (or its lower bound), whenever a suitable estimation for that can be found. But unfortunately, in most cases such an estimation cannot be found.

We shall now introduce the Freund's boosting algorithm and then make use of it in order to create a "boosting tandem" possessing still better performance characteristics.

5 Towards "Flat" Boosting

Using the result of the previous section it is possible to directly apply the *QuickFilt* algorithm to DNF-learning; this approach would posses all advantages of *AdaBoost*-application mentioned above, in particular, it would make a "rational use" of all the weak hypotheses seen. On the other hand, another approach is possible, which further "unbends" the distributions produced by the booster.

Historically, the *AdaBoost* algorithm has a predecessor, which is described by Freund in [F95]. This algorithm (denote it by F), while not capable of utilizing the "additional" accuracy, has some advantages over *AdaBoost*. One of them is that all distributions produced by F are "initially" polynomially bounded; moreover, this bound depends on the value of ϵ only and is independent of γ. The later feature can be utilized to further lower the bound for poly-near-D distributions provided by *QuickFilt* (this will also improve the complexity of the algorithm).

We will replace the weak learner *WL* in *QuickFilt* by F executed with $\epsilon \equiv \mathbf{const}$. This allows us to make D_i-s produced by the algorithm to be near-uniform bounded by

$$O\left(\frac{1}{\epsilon}\ln\left(\frac{1}{\epsilon}\right)\right) = \tilde{O}\left(\frac{1}{\epsilon}\right),$$

while no result better than $O\left(\frac{1}{\epsilon}\right)$ is possible [12].

5.1 Freund's Boosting Algorithm

Algorithm F is a modification of the original boosting algorithm introduced by Freund in [F95]; we will shortly describe it here. This version of the algorithm was used in [J97]. We denote by WL_F the weak learning algorithm accepted by F, by γ_F the corresponding γ value (note that now we assume some uniform γ is hold by all the weak hypotheses produced), by δ_F and ϵ_F the confidence and the accuracy required from F correspondingly. We will use the corresponding

[12] To see that, recall that we are dealing with a "context free" boosting model, i.e. a booster may be executed with any concept class, being provided with a proper weak learner for the same class. However, considering the class of all binary functions over n binary inputs, one can easily see that the weak learner could totally "conceal" the value of the target in any specific area of total weight ϵ from the booster under assumptions that all queries made by the booster are k-near-D for some $k < (\frac{1}{2} - \gamma)\frac{1}{\epsilon}$.

notation of $T[WL_F(\delta')]$ and $Q[WL_F(\delta')]$ for the time and query complexity of WL_F, still assuming that both are polynomials in δ'.

The algorithm works by collecting

$$T_F \triangleq \frac{1}{2{\gamma_F}^2} \ln \frac{4}{\epsilon_F}$$

weak hypotheses and representing their majority vote as the strong hypothesis. The whole algorithm is very similar to *AdaBoost*; the two main differences are that the final hypothesis is represented by unweighted majority vote and that the algorithm uses a different scheme for generating of intermediate distributions. The distributions produced are $O(\epsilon^{-3})$-near-D, and the confidence δ_{WL_F} required from WL_F satisfies

$$\delta_{WL_F} \geq \delta_F / O\left({\gamma_F}^{-2} \ln\left(\epsilon_F^{-1}\right)\right) .$$

Freund shows in [F95] that the algorithm is correct. Its query complexity is

$$O(poly(\epsilon_F)T_F) = O({\gamma_F}^{-2} poly(\epsilon_F))$$

times the number of examples required by a single WL_F execution and its time complexity is

$$O({\gamma_F}^{-2} poly(\epsilon_F)) \ + \ [\textit{the time consumed by } T_F \textit{ calls to } WL_F].$$

5.2 *F* + *QuickFilt* Hybrid's Analysis

In this section we will make the notation clearer by adding subscript $_{QF}$ to parameters and variables which belong to *QuickFilt*. As mentioned before, we are going to use the F and *QuickFilt* algorithms with $\epsilon_F \equiv \mathbf{const}$, $\gamma_{QF} \equiv \mathbf{const}$ and $\delta_F \triangleq \delta_{QF}{\gamma_{QF}}^2$ [13]. Therefore the corresponding expressions for query and time complexity of F are

$$O\left({\gamma_F}^{-2} \cdot Q[WL_F(\delta_F {\gamma_F}^2)]\right)$$

and

$$O\left({\gamma_F}^{-2} \cdot T[WL_F(\delta_F {\gamma_F}^2)]\right) .$$

The query complexity of the booster resulting from the two booster's (F+ *QuickFilt*) combination is

$$\tilde{O}\left(\epsilon^{-1}\gamma^{-2} \cdot Q[WL_F(\delta_{QF} {\gamma_F}^2)]\right) ,$$

and the time complexity is

$$\tilde{O}\left(\epsilon^{-2} + \gamma^{-2} \cdot T[WL_F(\delta_{QF}{\gamma_F}^2)] + \epsilon^{-1}\gamma^{-2} \cdot Q[WL_F(\delta_{QF}{\gamma_F}^2)]\right) .$$

[13] I.e., the *QuickFilt* algorithm will be executed given $\gamma_{\min} \equiv \mathbf{const}$, provided with F as a weak learner; in this way we create "chain" of 3 algorithms *QuickFilt*, F and WL_F, each taking the following as a subroutine.

Notice that the distributions produced by F are poly-near-D having the same bounding polynomial, up to a constant factor, as the distributions passed from *QuickFilt* to F. Therefore, the distributions produced by the boosting tandem are near-D satisfying

$$\forall i: \; D_i(x) = O\left(\epsilon^{-1}\ln(\epsilon^{-1})D(x)\right) = \tilde{O}\left(\epsilon^{-1}D(x)\right).$$

6 Learning DNF over the PAC-Model with Membership Oracle under Polynomially Near-Uniform Distribution

In this section we assume that the target distribution D of the booster is polynomially near-uniform holding

$$\forall x \in \{0,1\}^n: \; D(x) \leq \frac{1}{2^n} \cdot p_D(n)$$

for some polynomial p_D. Notice that in this case the boosting tandem described in the previous section produces poly-near-uniform distributions.

One of the boosting problems where the near-uniform bound is critical for the solution's efficiency is learning of DNF over the model of (strong) PAC-learning with membership queries w.r.t. the near-uniform distributions. There exist some limitations for boosting algorithms which can be used in DNF-learning scheme similar to that described in [J97], which result from the features of the weak learning algorithm used, which, in the case of [J97] is the *KM* algorithm described in [KM93].

For the purposes of this paper we will use another weakly learning algorithm introduced by Bshouty, Jackson and Tamon in [BJT99], which was designed having DNF-learning scheme in mind; this algorithm is developed from another one, described by Levin in [L93]. We will denote the algorithm introduced in [BJT99] simply by W. Algorithm W possesses all the features of *KM* which are critical for DNF-learning but has some complexity advantages over *KM*.

Like *KM*, W is capable of finding "heavy" Fourier coefficients of the target w.r.t. the uniform only; therefore the following reduction is used. Instead of weakly learning the target binary function $f(x)$ under some non-uniform distribution D_i we will consider the following real-valued function $g(x)$:

$$g(x) \triangleq 2^n D_i(x) \cdot f(x),$$

which, as shown in [J97], has "heavy" Fourier constituents (parity functions) which weakly approximate $f(x)$ w.r.t. the distribution D_i. Algorithm W must be provided with some bound θ which describes the magnitude of the Fourier coefficients desired, which in our case represents the approximation accuracy of the returned parities. We supply W with example oracle for the function

$$g'(x) \triangleq \frac{g(x)}{\max_x\{2^n D_i(x)\}}$$

(which can be easily simulated knowing $f(x)$ and $\max_x\{2^n D_i(x)\}$) and with

$$\theta' \triangleq \frac{\theta}{\max_x\{2^n D_i(x)\}}.$$

The complexity of W depends polynomially on θ^{-1}, therefore the produced distributions D_i should by polynomially near-uniform, as follows from the construction above. Furthermore, W needs to be provided with a so-called distribution oracle, or, in other words, the booster should be able to report the probabilistic weight assigned to a specific point. Regarding the later condition, it was shown in [J97] that F is capable of estimating up to some constant multiplicative factor the produced distributions, being supplied with a distribution oracle of its own target distribution. Such estimation is obviously possible for *QuickFilt* as well (which follows from the algorithm analysis represented in the appendix section). Jackson shows that such accuracy is sufficient and doesn't affect adversely the performance of KM; the same holds for W.

In the case of weak DNF approximation using parity functions, the value of ${\gamma_F}^{-1}$ is hold within $O(s)$, where s is the number of DNF-terms contained in the formula. Another observation relevant to DNF-learning using W is that the query complexity may be significantly reduced by reuse of the same set of instances throughout the iterations. That can be done because *oblivious* sampling is used by the algorithm; that is, the samples are chosen without regard to the target function [14]. This considerations turn the query complexity of the boosting tandem (described in Section 5.2) to

$$\tilde{O}\left(\epsilon^{-1} \cdot Q[W]\right),$$

and its time complexity to

$$\tilde{O}\left(\epsilon^{-2} + s^2 \cdot T[W] + \epsilon^{-1} \cdot Q[W]\right). \text{ [15]}$$

The distributions supplied to W are $\epsilon^{-1}p_D(n)$-near-uniform, the W's complexity in this case is $\tilde{O}(n\theta'^{-2})$ queries and $\tilde{O}(n\theta'^{-2})$ time. Denote:

$$d_\infty(D_i) \triangleq \max_x\{2^n D_i(x)\}.$$

As follows from the construction of $g'(x)$, it holds that

$$\theta'^{-1} = O(d_\infty(D_i) \cdot \gamma^{-1}) = O\left(s\epsilon^{-1}p_D(n)\right),$$

and

$$Q[W] = T[W] = \tilde{O}\left(ns^2\epsilon^{-2}p_D^2(n)\right)$$

[14] Notice that in this case the boosting analysis is still applied to the whole set of instances, and, aside from the memory required to store the set of examples, the case entirely corresponds to the boosting in filtering mode.

[15] Here we make two simplification: first, we remove the dependency of $T[W]$ and of $Q[W]$ upon the confidence required, which is done because the impact is logarithmic in the case of W; second, we don't really distinguish between membership and PAC query complexity; in fact, the upper bound on both is considered.

(recall that $p_D(n)$ is a bound on the target distribution's "non-uniformity").

The resulting DNF-learning complexity is

$$\tilde{O}\left(ns^2\epsilon^{-3} \cdot p_D^2(n)\right)$$

queries and

$$\tilde{O}\left(np_D^2(n) \cdot (s^4\epsilon^{-2} + s^2\epsilon^{-3})\right)$$

time [16].

A Appendix

A.1 *QuickSamp*'s Analysis

The whole subroutine *SampEX* can be viewed as a weak learner, in which case the only difference between this booster and *AdaBoost* is line 8, where we "re-define" the hypothesis for the further references. Notice that in line 8 we don't really construct $h_i'(x)$ (we couldn't do that for we don't have $f(x)$ at our disposal), but for the further operation we only need to know whether $h_i'(x) = f(x)$.

The *SampEX* subroutine implements the "distribution bounding" ideas introduced in this paper. In line 6 of the subroutine we need to efficiently sample accordingly to $D_i'(x)$ defined in line 5, which can be done easily; for example see *Bsamp* algorithm from [F95].

Lemma 2. *Suppose the subroutine* SampEX *returned without making a call to* WL *(line* 3 *of* SampEX*)* T_1 *times and* WL *was executed* T_2 *times* $(T = T_1 + T_2)$*. Suppose also that* WL *was called in the iterations* $k_1, ..., k_{T_2}$ *and it returned hypotheses* $h_{k_1}, ..., h_{k_{T_2}}$ *s.t. for every* k_i *it holds that* $Err_{D'_{k_i}}(h_{k_i}) = \epsilon'_{k_i}$*. Then the error w.r.t.* D *of the final hypothesis* h_f *generated by* QuickSamp *is bounded above by*

$$\epsilon_f \le \prod_{i=1}^{T_2} 2\sqrt{\epsilon'_{k_i}(1-\epsilon'_{k_i})} \cdot \left(\frac{\sqrt{3}}{2}\right)^{T_1} + \frac{T_1 + T_2}{C} .$$

Theorem 1. *Suppose* QuickSamp *was executed with arguments (n,* WL*,* $\gamma_{\min}$*, S, m). Suppose also that the subroutine* SampEX *returned without making a call to* WL *(line 3 of* SampEX*)* T_1 *times and* WL *was executed* T_2 *times* $(T = T_1 + T_2)$*. Suppose also that* WL *was called in the iterations* $k_1, ..., k_{t_2}$ *and it returned hypotheses* $h_{k_1}, ..., h_{k_{T_2}}$ *s.t. for all* k_i $(1 \le i \le t_2)$ *it holds:*

$$\underset{D'_{k_i}}{Err}(h_{k_i}) = \epsilon'_{k_i} \le \frac{1}{2} - \gamma_{\min}.$$

Then the algorithm QuickSamp *halts and returns the final hypothesis which makes a correct prediction over the instances of S.*

[16] It is shown in [BJT99] that the algorithm can easily be modified into *attribute-efficient*, i.e., the complexity, when represented in terms of $\tilde{O}$, is independent of n but depends on r- the number of attributes that are relevant to the target. The resulting complexity bounds are the same with n being replaced by r.

QuickSamp$(n, \boldsymbol{WL}, \gamma_{\min}, S, m)$

define $D(x) = \begin{cases} 1/m \ if \ x \in S \\ 0 \quad otherwise \end{cases}$

set $\epsilon = 1/m$; $\gamma_{\min} = \min\{\gamma_{\min}, 1/4\}$; $C = \left\lceil \frac{1}{\epsilon {\gamma_{\min}}^2} \ln\left(\frac{2}{\epsilon}\right) \right\rceil$

set $\epsilon_c = 1$; $i = 0$; $w_1 = ... = w_m = 1$

while $(\epsilon_c \geq \frac{\epsilon}{2})$

  set $i = i + 1$; $\sigma = \sum_{j=1}^{m} w_j \cdot D(x_j)$

  define $D_i(x_j) = \frac{w_j \cdot D(x_j)}{\sigma}$

  call SampEX

  define $h_i'(x) \triangleq \begin{cases} h_i(x) \ if \ D_i(x) \leq C \cdot D(x) \\ f(x) \ otherwise \end{cases}$

  set $\epsilon_i = \sum_{x_j \in S} D_i(x_j) \cdot |h_i'(x_j) - f(x_j)|$; $\beta_i = \frac{\epsilon_i}{1-\epsilon_i}$

  set $\forall j \in \{1...m\} : w_j = w_j \cdot \beta_i^{1-|h_i'(x_j)-f(x_j)|}$

  set $\epsilon_c = \epsilon_c \cdot 2\sqrt{\epsilon_i(1-\epsilon_i)}$

endwhile

Output the final hypothesis:

$h_f(x) = \begin{cases} 1 \ if \ \sum_{t=1}^{i} (\log \frac{1}{\beta_t}) h_t(x) \geq \frac{1}{2} \sum_{t=1}^{i} \log \frac{1}{\beta_t} \\ 0 \ otherwise \end{cases}$

SampEX

define $E = \{x_j \in S \mid w_j > C \cdot \sigma\}$; $\mu = D_i(E)$

if $(\mu \geq \frac{3}{4})$ **then**

  $h_i \equiv 1$

else

  set $D_i'(x) = \begin{cases} D_i(x) \cdot \frac{1}{1-\mu} \ if \ x \in E \\ 0 \quad otherwise \end{cases}$

  call WL, *providing it with distribution* D_i'*;* *denote the returned weak hypothesis by* h_i

endif

Fig. 3. The *QuickSamp*$(n, WL, \gamma_{\min}, S, m)$ hypothesis boosting algorithm.

Denote by $T[WL](n)$ the time complexity of WL running over the instance space $\{0,1\}^n$, and by $Q[WL](n)$ its query complexity (i.e., the number of requested examples).

Theorem 2. *Suppose that all the conditions of Theorem 1 hold. Then all distributions* D_i' *supplied by* QuickSamp *to* WL *satisfy:*

$$D_i'(x) \leq \frac{4}{\epsilon {\gamma_{\min}}^2} \ln\left(\frac{2}{\epsilon}\right) \cdot D(x)$$

for all x*, and the running time of* QuickSamp$(n, \mathrm{WL}, \gamma_{\min}, S, m)$ *is*

$$O\left(\frac{\ln(\frac{1}{\epsilon})}{\mathbf{Av}[\gamma_i^2]} \cdot (mQ[\mathrm{WL}](n) + T[\mathrm{WL}](n))\right) = \\ = \tilde{O}\left(\frac{1}{\mathbf{Av}[\gamma_i^2]} \cdot (mQ[\mathrm{WL}](n) + T[\mathrm{WL}](n))\right).$$

Notice that in this section we still assumed *WL* to be a deterministic algorithm; in practice, *WL* usually desires an additional argument δ', which is its probability to fail. In this case, *QuickSamp* will accept an additional argument δ, the confidence measure desired, and *WL* will always be executed with confidence factor $\delta' = \frac{\delta}{C}$, which is polynomial in δ, $\frac{1}{\epsilon}$ and n.

A.2 *QuickFilt*'s Analysis

The *QuickFilt* algorithm has a subroutine called *Evaluate*, used to estimate expectancies of random variables, based on the Hoeffding bound. The routine $Evaluate(X, \frac{\lambda}{b-a}, \delta)$ estimates the expectancy of X with accuracy $1-\lambda$ and confidence $1-\delta$, and has time complexity of

$$O\left(\frac{\ln\left(\frac{1}{\delta}\right)}{\left(\frac{\lambda}{b-a}\right)^2}\right).$$

Notice that *QuickFilt* "limits" the allowed accuracy of weak hypotheses, which can be seen in the *ReviewDestroy* subroutine. That is done to properly bound some intermediate values, which simplifies the error estimation; on the other hand, this doesn't affect the time complexity (in terms of O) of the algorithm. Note also that the aforementioned bounding is applied to the "virtual" hypotheses $\widehat{h'_i}$ only (i.e., the final hypotheses is built using the original h_i-s, but the weights update is held using the hypotheses h'_i resulting from the *ReviewDestroy* execution, which, in certain cases, are slightly "damaged").

In the case of filtering, we cannot permanently keep the values of w_j as we did in *QuickSamp*; now we use the *Get_w* subroutine to calculate the values of w^i_j (i and j are this subroutine's arguments). The values of w^i_j are defined exactly as they were before, in the case of *QuickSamp*.

For the *QuickFilt*'s analysis, we use the notation of $\overline{value}$ to denote the "true" values, as distinct from those resulting from the estimations produced by the algorithm; e.g., by β_i we denote the value that is assigned to the variable of the same name during a specific algorithm's execution, while $\overline{\beta_i}$ is the value that would be accepted using the "actual" value of ϵ_i ($\overline{\epsilon_i}$), i.e., $\overline{\beta_i} = \frac{\overline{\epsilon_i}}{1-\overline{\epsilon_i}}$. $\mathrm{Err}(value)$ denotes the estimation inaccuracy, i.e., $\mathrm{Err}(value) = |value - \overline{value}|$.

We denote by D_i the distribution produced by $D_i gen$.

Claim. Each time lines 8-11 of *QuickFilt* are executed, with probability $1 - \frac{2}{B}$ at least the following is true. The resulting weak hypothesis h'_i satisfies:

$$\frac{1}{2} - \gamma_{\min} \geq \overline{\epsilon_i} \geq \frac{1}{3}, \;\; \mathrm{Err}(\epsilon_i) \leq \Delta_\epsilon, \;\; \mathrm{Err}(\beta_i) \leq 4\Delta_\epsilon \tag{4}$$

w.r.t. D_i. Also it holds that

$$\frac{1}{2} - \gamma_{\min} \geq \epsilon_i \geq \frac{1}{3} + \Delta_\epsilon \;\; \textit{and} \;\; \frac{1}{2} < \beta_i < 1. \tag{5}$$

Moreover, if h_i returned by WL satisfies $\mathbf{E}_{D_i}|h_i(x) - f(x)| \geq \frac{1}{3} + 2\Delta_\epsilon$, then it holds that

$$\mathop{\mathbf{E}}_{D_i}|h'_i(x) - f(x)| \leq \mathop{\mathbf{E}}_{D_i}|h_i(x) - f(x)|,$$

and if $\mathbf{E}_{D_i}|h'_i(x) - f(x)| > \mathbf{E}_{D_i}|h_i(x) - f(x)|$ then

$$\mathop{\mathbf{E}}_{D_i}|h'_i(x) - f(x)| \leq \frac{1}{3} + 2\Delta_\epsilon.$$

Now we show that all distributions produced by the *QuickFilt* are polynomially near uniform.

Claim. There exists a probability, $1 - \frac{T}{B}$ at least (where T is the overall number of boosting iterations performed), that each time WL is called, the distribution D_i is near-uniform bounded by $2C \cdot k_\sigma^2 D$, i.e.,

$$\forall i, j: \; D_i(x_j) \leq 2C \cdot k_\sigma^2 D(x_j)$$

and that all the estimations of $\overline{\sigma_i}$ performed in line 7 of *QuickFilt* are accurate up to the multiplicative factor k_σ (i.e., $k_\sigma^{-1}\overline{\sigma_i} \leq \sigma_i \leq k_\sigma \overline{\sigma_i}$). Moreover, for each i D_i satisfies:

$$\forall j: D_i(x_j) = \frac{w_j^i}{\sum_{x_j} w_j^i} \cdot D(x_j) = \frac{w_j^i}{\overline{\sigma_i}} \cdot D(x_j). \tag{6}$$

As mentioned before, it was shown in [J97] that F is capable of estimating up to some constant multiplicative factor the produced distributions, being supplied with a distribution oracle of its own target distribution. Note that such estimation is possible for *QuickFilt* as well, this follows from Equation (6): recall that the estimations of $\overline{\sigma_i}$ is assumed to be accurate up to the multiplicative factor k_σ.

Theorem 3. *Suppose* QuickFilt *was executed with arguments (n, EX,* WL, *$\gamma_{\min}$, ϵ, δ). Suppose also that each time* WL *was called with argument δ' being supplied with distribution D_i, it returned a hypothesis h_i s.t.*

$$\Pr[\mathop{\mathbf{E}}_{D_i}|h_i(x) - f(x)| \leq \frac{1}{2} - \gamma_{\min}] \geq \delta'.$$

Then there exists a probability, δ at least, that algorithm QuickFilt *halts and returns the final hypothesis which makes $(1-\epsilon)$-correct prediction over the instance space.*

Let's denote by $T[WL(\frac{1}{B})](n, d_\infty)$ the time complexity of $WL(\delta' = \frac{1}{B})$ running over the instance space $\{0,1\}^n$ and being supplied with a distribution D', satisfying

$$\forall x \in \{0,1\}^n: \; D'(x) \leq \frac{1}{2^n} \cdot d_\infty,$$

and by $Q[WL(\frac{1}{B})](n, d_\infty)$ its query complexity (i.e., the number of examples requested by WL).

Theorem 4. *Suppose that all conditions of Theorem 3 hold. Suppose also that the target distribution D is near-uniform with bound $p_D(n)$, i.e.,*

$$\forall x: \; D(x) \leq \frac{1}{2^n} \cdot p_D(n).$$

Then the running time of QuickFilt$(n,\ EX,\ \mathrm{WL},\ \gamma_{\min},\ \epsilon,\ \delta)$ *is*

$$\tilde{O}\Bigg(\frac{1}{\mathbf{Av}[\overline{\gamma_i'^2}]} \cdot T[\mathrm{WL}(\delta{\gamma_{\min}}^2)](n, \tfrac{1}{\epsilon{\gamma_{\min}}^2} p_D(n)) + \\ + \frac{1}{\epsilon{\gamma_{\min}}^2 (\mathbf{Av}[\overline{\gamma_i'^2}])^2} \cdot Q[\mathrm{WL}(\delta{\gamma_{\min}}^2)](n, \tfrac{1}{\epsilon{\gamma_{\min}}^2} p_D(n)) + \\ + \frac{1}{\epsilon^2{\gamma_{\min}}^4 (\mathbf{Av}[\overline{\gamma_i'^2}])^2} \Bigg),$$

and its query complexity is

$$\tilde{O}\left(\frac{1}{\epsilon{\gamma_{\min}}^2\, \mathbf{Av}[\overline{\gamma_i'^2}]} \cdot Q[\mathrm{WL}(\delta{\gamma_{\min}}^2)](n, \frac{1}{\epsilon{\gamma_{\min}}^2} p_D(n)) \right).$$

References

[BJT99] N. Bshouty, J. Jackson, C. Tamon. More efficient PAC-learning of DNF with membership queries under the uniform distribution. *Twelfth Annual Conference on Computational Learning Theory*, 1999, pp. 286-295.

[F95] Y. Freund. Boosting a weak learning algorithm by majority. *Information and Computation*, 1995, 121(2), pp. 256-285.

[FS97] Y. Freund, R. E. Schapire. A decision-theoretic generalization of on-line learning and an application to boosting. *Journal of Computer and System Sciences*, 1997, 55(1), pp. 119-139.

[J97] J. Jackson. An efficient membership-query algorithm for learning DNF with respect to the uniform distribution. *Journal of Computer and System Sciences*, 1997, 55(3),pp. 414-440.

[KM93] E. Kushilevitz, Y. Mansour. Learning Decision Trees using the Fourier Spectrum. *SIAM Journal on Computing*, 1993, 22(6) pp. 1331-1348.

[KS99] A. R. Klivans, R. A. Servedio. Boosting and Hard-Core Sets. *Proc. of 40th Foundations of Computer Science (FOCS)*, 1999, pp. 624-633.

[KV94] M. Kearns, L. Valiant. Cryptographic limitations on learning boolean formulae and finite automata. *Journal of the ACM*, 1994, 41(1) pp. 67-95.

[L93] L. Levin. Randomness and Non-determinism. *Journal of Symbolic Logic*, 1993, 58(3), pp. 1102-1103.

[V84] L. Valiant. A theory of learnable. *Comm. ACM*, 1984, 27, pp. 1134-1142.

Agnostic Boosting

Shai Ben-David[1], Philip M. Long[2], and Yishay Mansour[3]

[1] Department of Computer Science
Technion
Haifa 32000
Israel
shai@cs.technion.ac.il
[2] Genome Institute of Singapore
1 Research Link
IMA Building
National University of Singapore
Singapore 117604, Republic of Singapore
plong@comp.nus.edu.sg
[3] Department of Computer Science
Tel-Aviv University
Tel-Aviv, Israel
mansour@math.tau.ac.il

Abstract. We extend the boosting paradigm to the realistic setting of agnostic learning, that is, to a setting where the training sample is generated by an arbitrary (unknown) probability distribution over examples and labels. We define a β-weak agnostic learner with respect to a hypothesis class F as follows: given a distribution P it outputs some hypothesis $h \in F$ whose error is at most $\mathbf{er}_P(F) + \beta$, where $\mathbf{er}_P(F)$ is the minimal error of an hypothesis from F under the distribution P (note that for some distributions the bound may exceed a half).

We show a boosting algorithm that using the weak agnostic learner computes a hypothesis whose error is at most $\max\{c_1(\beta)\mathbf{er}(F)^{c_2(\beta)}, \epsilon\}$, in time polynomial in $1/\epsilon$. While this generalization guarantee is significantly weaker than the one resulting from the known PAC boosting algorithms, one should note that the assumption required for β-weak agnostic learner is much weaker. In fact, an important virtue of the notion of weak agnostic learning is that in many cases such learning is achieved by efficient algorithms.

1 Introduction

Boosting has proven itself as a powerful tool both from a theoretical and a practical perspective of Machine Learning [11]. From a theoretical perspective, it gives a very clean and elegant model in which one can develop new algorithmic ideas and even hope to analyze some existing heuristics. From a practical perspective, although the weak learning assumption can rarely be proven, the boosting algorithms have had a dramatic impact on practitioners. In a sense,

D. Helmbold and B. Williamson (Eds.): COLT/EuroCOLT 2001, LNAI 2111, pp. 507–516, 2001.

this work can be viewed as a step towards providing a theoretical explanation to this phenomenon. We prove that under certain conceivable conditions, boosting has some nontrivial performance guarantees even when no weak learners exist.

The Probably Approximately Correct (PAC) model [12] developed two separate models. The first one assumes that the target function belongs to the class studied, which was the original PAC assumption, and tries to drive the error as close to zero as possible. The second allows an arbitrary target function, but rather than shooting for absolute success, compares the error of the learner's hypothesis to that of the best predictor in some pre-specified comparison class of predictors. This model is also known as agnostic learning [8]. When one tries to consider which model is more realistic, it has to be the case that the agnostic model wins. We rarely know if there is a clear target function, let alone if it belongs to some simple class of hypotheses.

The aim of this paper is to study the boosting question in an agnostic setting. The first step has to be to define an analogue of the weak learning assumption. In the original formulation, a fixed but unknown target function generated labels, and a weak learner was assumed to achieve error less than $1/2 - \gamma$ for any distribution over the instances.

We define a β-weak agnostic learner with respect to a hypothesis class F as follows: given any distribution P over instance-label pairs it outputs some hypothesis $h \in F$ whose error is at most $\mathbf{er}_P(F) + \beta$. Since error of $1/2$ can be trivially achieved (let us assume that every concept class we consider contains both the constant 1 and the constant 0 functions), this implies that in order for the answer of the weak learner to convey interesting information it has to be the case that $\mathbf{er}_P(F)$ is less than $1/2 - \beta$.

Note that the β-weak agnostic learner assumption is only an assumption about the learner and not about the hypothesis class F, that is, such learners exist for every hypothesis class, even if we take $\beta = 0$. The interesting aspect of such weak learners is their complexity (both sample complexity and computational complexity).

The search for a 'strong' hypothesis in the agnostic setting is NP hard. More precisely, there are no known learning algorithm that, for a non-trivial hypothesis class F, finds in time polynomial in $1/\epsilon$ a hypothesis in F that has error below $\mathbf{er}_P(F) + \epsilon$. Furthermore, for many interesting classes F, for small enough β (in the order of 0.005), unless P=NP there exist no β-weak agnostic learner ([2], [3]). However, no currently known result rules out the existence of agnostic β-weak learners for these classes once β is sufficiently large (say, $\beta > 0.1$). Furthermore, the hardness results cited above rule out only the existence of efficient finders of good hypothesis *within* a class F. Since the output of a boosting algorithm is a member of a larger class of functions - the convex hull of F, all currently known hardness results are consistent with the existence of efficient algorithms that solve the agnostic learning task for non-trivial classes via boosting.

The question is what can one hope to achieve under the β-weak agnostic learner assumption. It seems unreasonable to expect that agnostic weak learners can be always transformed into strong learners, as weak learners exist also for trivial classes, say F that includes only a single hypothesis. On the other hand, clearly we can find a hypothesis whose error is $\mathbf{er}_P(F)+\beta$, but can we do better?

In this paper we answer this question in the affirmative. We show that given a parameter ϵ, there is an efficient algorithm that, using a β-weak agnostic learner as an oracle, can construct a predictor whose error is at most

$$c_1(\beta)\mathbf{er}_P(F)^{c_2(\beta)} + \epsilon,$$

where $c_2(\beta) = 2(1/2 - \beta)^2/\ln(1/\beta - 1)$, and $c_1(\beta)$ is a constant which depends only on β. Note that for small values of $\mathbf{er}_P(F)$ we outperform the naive bound.

Our algorithm simply runs AdaBoost [6] for a certain number of pre-specified steps. The interesting part is to show that one can exhibit a significant gain in the accuracy this way. By no means do we think that this is the ultimate answer. A major open problem of this research is whether one can achieve a bound of $O(\mathbf{er}_P(F) + \epsilon)$ using a β-weak agnostic learner.

To motivate our results and model we consider agnostic learning of a general hypothesis class of VC dimension d. Assume that the error-minimization task - finding a member of the class that minimizes the error over a sample of size m - is performed in $T(m)$ time. The naive way to produce a hypothesis h such that $\mathbf{er}_P(h) \leq \mathbf{er}_P(F) + \epsilon$, is to sample $m = \tilde{O}(d/\epsilon^2)$ examples, and try to find the best hypothesis from our class. The running time of such a learner is therefore of order $T(\frac{d}{\epsilon^2})$. Our approach would be to create β-weak agnostic learner, for some fixed β. For that purpose we need to sample only $m' = \tilde{O}(d)$, and the running time of the minimization is $T(\tilde{O}(d))$, independent of ϵ. Applying our boosting result we get a learner that runs in time $T(\tilde{O}(d)) \times poly(1/\epsilon)$ for some polynomial $poly()$, and finds a hypothesis such that $\mathbf{er}_P(h) \leq c_1(\beta)\mathbf{er}_P(F)^{c_2(\beta)} + \epsilon$. The main benefit is that the running time depends fairly weakly on ϵ. This benefit becomes apparent as $\mathbf{er}_P(F)$ approaches zero. (A similar result, for the case of $\mathbf{er}_P(F) = 0$, is implicit in [10,5]. While they consider the sample complexity, their ideas can be used also for the computational complexity.)

2 Preliminaries

Fix a set X. An *example* is an element of $X \times \{-1, 1\}$ and a *sample* is a finite sequence of examples. A *hypothesis* is a function from X to $\{-1, 1\}$. For a hypothesis h, and a probability distribution P over $X \times \{-1, 1\}$, define the *error* of h with respect to P, to be

$$\mathbf{er}_P(h) = \mathbf{E}_{(x,y)\sim P}(h(x) \neq y)).$$

Similarly, for a sample S, let $\mathbf{er}_S(h)$ be the fraction of examples (x, y) in S for which $h(x) \neq y$. For a set F of functions from X to $\{-1, 1\}$, define $\mathbf{er}_P(F) = \inf_{h\in F} \mathbf{er}_P(h)$.

A *learning strategy* is a mapping from samples to hypotheses; If it is computable, then it is a *learning algorithm*.

For some domain X and a comparison class F of functions from X to $\{-1,1\}$, a *β-weak agnostic learning oracle*, given as input an oracle for sampling according to some probability distribution P over $X \times \{-1,1\}$, returns a hypothesis h such that

$$\mathbf{er}_P(h) \le \mathbf{er}_P(F) + \beta.$$

The following definition places a mild requirement that is satisfied by most common concept classes.

Definition 1. *Let F be a class of functions from some domain X to $\{-1,1\}$.*

- *The* F-consistency problem *is defined as follows:*
  Input: *A finite labeled sample S.*
  Output: *A hypothesis $h \in F$ such that $\mathbf{er}_S(h) = 0$, if such h exists, and* NO *otherwise.*
- *We say that a class F is* con-decidable *if the F - consistency problem is decidable.*

Notation: Let $H_2(p)$ be the binary entropy function, i.e. $H_2(p) = -p\log_2(p) - (1-p)\log(1-p)$. It is well known that for $k \le n/2$, $\sum_{i=0}^{k}\binom{n}{i} \le 2^{H_2(k/n)n}$.

3 Existence of Efficient Agnostic Weak Learners

It should be clear from the definition that, for every hypothesis class F of finite VC-dimension, for every fixed β, a β-weak agnostic learning strategy always exists – simply chose h to minimize $\mathbf{er}_S(h)$ for a sufficiently large sample S drawn independently at random according to P. The interesting question that arises in this context is the computational complexity of weak learning algorithms.

Theorem 1. *Let F be a con-decidable class with VC-dim$(F) = d < \infty$. Then, for every $\beta > 0$ there exist a β - weak learner for F that succeeds with probability $\ge 1-\delta$ and runs in time*

$$O\left(t_F(s(\beta,d)) \times \exp\left(H_2(\mathbf{er}_P(F) + \beta/2)s(\beta,d)\right)\ln\left(\frac{1}{\delta}\right)\right),$$

where $t_F : \mathbf{N} \mapsto \mathbf{N}$ is the running time of an algorithm for the consistency problem for the class F, and $s(\beta,d) = c\frac{d}{\beta^2}$, for some constant c.

Proof. Let d denote the VC-dimension of the class F. Having access to an oracle sampling according to a distribution P, the weak learner starts by asking for a sample S of size $s(\beta,d)$. By the standard VC-dimension uniform convergence bounds, such sample size guarantees that with probability exceeding $1/2$, for every $h \in F$, $|\mathbf{er}_S(h) - \mathbf{er}_P(h)| \le \beta/2$.

Next, the weak learner performs an exhaustive search for Argmin$\{\mathbf{er}_S(h) : h \in F\}$. One way of carrying out such a search is as follows:

Given a sample S of size m, the algorithm considers all subsets $T \subset S$ in order of their size, breaking ties arbitrarily. Once it finds a hypothesis $h \in F$ that classifies all the examples in $S - T$ correctly, it returns this h. It follows that the running time of the algorithm can be bounded by $t_F(|S|) \times \exp(H_2(\mathbf{er}_P(F) + \beta/2)|S|)$. Finally, using a standard 'test and re-sample' trick, for a multiplicative factor of order $\ln(1/\delta)$, the confidence parameter can be boosted from 1/2 to $1-\delta$ (see e.g., [10]). □

Corollary 1. *If F is s con-decidable class having a constant VC-dimension, then, for every $\beta > 0$ there exist a β - weak agnostic learner for F that runs in time $O(\ln(1/\delta))$ and succeeds with probability $\geq 1 - \delta$.*

4 Agnostic Boosting

In this section we prove our main theorem about boosting using β-weak agnostic learner. Theorem 1 above essentially states that for classes of finite VC dimension there are learning algorithms that run in time exponential in a parameter β (and some other parameters) and outputs a hypothesis whose expected error is within an additive factor β from the best hypothesis in the class. The boosting results of this section show that, as long as the additive approximation factor β (or, as it is commonly denoted, ϵ) is above some threshold, there are learning algorithms whose running time is only polynomial in ϵ. The threshold for which we can prove these results is a function only of $\mathbf{er}_P(F)$ and goes to zero as $\mathbf{er}_P(F)$ does.

The algorithm that we analyze is a slight variant of AdaBoost [6]. It uses the oracle for sampling according to P to generate oracles for sampling under a sequence $D_1, D_2, ...$ of filtered distributions, and passes these to the weak learner, which in response returns a sequence $h_1, h_2, ...$ of weak hypotheses.

The main intuition is as follows. The generalization guarantee that the algorithm has to achieve is sufficiently weak as to allow a trivial hypothesis for input probability distributions that drive the error rate of a weak learner close to 1/2. Consequently, we only have to address input distributions relative to which a β-weak agnostic learner is guaranteed to have small error. In order to carry out the usual analysis of boosting, we have to make sure that this assumption remains valid for the new distributions that are generated by the boosting algorithm. We therefore work out an upper bound on the rate at which the boosting distributions may change. We can keep iterating the boosting steps as long as we do not generate distributions that are too far from the input sample distribution. The final step of our analysis is a calculation of the amount of progress that boosting can achieve under this constraint.

Theorem 2. *Fix a domain X, and a class F of functions from X to $\{-1, 1\}$. There is an algorithm A such that, for any probability distribution P over $X \times \{-1, 1\}$, if A is given access to a β-weak agnostic learning oracle for F, and a source of random examples of P, then for any $\epsilon > 0$, in polynomial in $1/\epsilon$ time, with probability at least 1/2, algorithm A returns a hypothesis h such that*

$$\mathbf{er}_P(h) \leq c_1(\beta)\mathbf{er}_P(F)^{c_2(\beta)} + \epsilon,$$

where $c_2(\beta) = 2(1/2 - \beta)^2 / \ln(1/\beta - 1)$*, and* $c_1(\beta)$ *is a constant which depends only on* β*.*

Proof. We will begin by assuming that the algorithm is also given $\mathbf{er}_P(F)$ as input. We will discuss how to remove this assumption at the end of the proof (in short, standard guessing and hypothesis testing techniques suffice).

We now spell out algorithm A, which is simply AdaBoost [6], with some of the parameters fixed. Let

$$T = \min\left\{ \left\lceil \frac{\ln((1/2 - \beta)/\mathbf{er}_P(F))}{\ln(1/\beta - 1)} \right\rceil, \left\lceil \frac{1}{(1/2-\beta)^2} \ln \frac{1}{\epsilon} \right\rceil \right\}.$$

and

$$\eta_i = (1/2 - \beta) - (1/\beta - 1)^i \mathbf{er}_P(F).$$

This implies that $\eta_i \geq 0$ for $i \leq T$. Also

$$\alpha_i = \frac{1}{2} \ln \frac{1/2 + \eta_i}{1/2 - \eta_i}$$

which implies that

$$e^{2\alpha_i} = \frac{1/2 + \eta_i}{1/2 - \eta_i} \leq \frac{1}{\beta} - 1.$$

Algorithm A starts by setting D_0 to be P, then for $t = 0, ..., T$, it

- passes D_t to the weak learning algorithm,
- gets h_t in return
- generates D_{t+1} in two steps by first, for each $(x, y) \in X \times \{-1, 1\}$, setting

$$D'_{t+1}(x,y) = \begin{cases} e^{\alpha_t} D_t(x,y) & \text{if } h_t(x) \neq y \\ e^{-\alpha_t} D_t(x,y) & \text{otherwise} \end{cases}$$

  then normalizing by setting $Z_{t+1} = \sum_{(x,y)} D'_{t+1}(x,y)$ and $D_{t+1}(x,y) = D'_{t+1}(x,y)/Z_t$.

Finally, it outputs a function h obtained through a majority vote over $h_1, ..., h_T$. Note that

$$Z_t \geq \sum_{(x,y)} e^{-\alpha_{t-1}} D_{t-1}(x,y) \geq e^{-\alpha_{t-1}}.$$

This implies that for any (x, y), $D_{t+1}(x, y) \leq e^{2\alpha_t} D_t(x, y)$. By induction, for each $t \leq T$,

$$D_t(x,y) \leq e^{2\sum_{i=0}^{t} \alpha_i} P(x,y)$$

Since, by assumption, $\mathbf{er}_{D_t}(h_t) \leq \mathbf{er}_{D_t}(F) + \beta$, this implies that

$$\mathbf{er}_{D_t}(h_t) \leq e^{2\sum_{i=0}^{t} \alpha_i} \mathbf{er}_P(F) + \beta \leq 1/2 - \eta_t.$$

and A achieves an edge of at least η_t in round t. The performance of AdaBoost [6] guarantees that

$$\mathbf{er}_P(h) \le e^{-2\sum_{i=0}^{T}\eta_i^2}.$$

Recall that,

$$\begin{aligned}
\sum_{i=0}^{T}\eta_i^2 &= \sum_{i=0}^{T}\left[(\frac{1}{2}-\beta)-(\frac{1}{\beta}-1)^i\mathbf{er}_P(F)\right]^2 \\
&= (\frac{1}{2}-\beta)^2 T - 2(\frac{1}{2}-\beta)\mathbf{er}_P(F)\frac{(\frac{1}{\beta}-1)^{T+1}-1}{\frac{1}{\beta}-2} \\
&\quad +\mathbf{er}_P^2(F)\frac{(\frac{1}{\beta}-1)^{2(T+1)}-1}{(\frac{1}{\beta}-1)^2-1} \\
&= (\frac{1}{2}-\beta)^2 T + c(\beta)
\end{aligned}$$

where the last identity uses the fact that $(1/\beta-1)^T \le (1/2-\beta)/\mathbf{er}_P(F)$. In the case that $T = \left\lceil \frac{1}{(1/2-\beta)^2}\ln\frac{1}{\epsilon}\right\rceil$, then $\mathbf{er}_P(h) \le \epsilon$, completing the proof. In the case that $T = \left\lceil \frac{\ln((1/2-\beta)/er_P(F)}{\ln(1/\beta-1)}\right\rceil$, then

$$\mathbf{er}_P(h) \le \exp\left(-2(\frac{1}{2}-\beta)^2\frac{\ln((\frac{1}{2}-\beta)/er_P(F)}{\ln(1/\beta-1)}\right) = c_1(\beta)\left(\mathbf{er}_P(F)\right)^{2\frac{(\frac{1}{2}-\beta)^2}{\ln(\frac{1}{\beta}-1)}}$$

for some constant $c_1(\beta)$ which depends only on β.

It is easy to see how to simulate the distributions $D_1, ..., D_T$, given access to a source of examples for P, in polynomial time, using the rejection method [9], since always $e^{-\sum_{i=1}^{T}\alpha_i} \ge (1/\beta-1)^{-T/2}$. Therefore, since T is bounded by a logarithm in $1/\epsilon$, the time for Algorithm A is polynomially bounded.

Recall that we assumed that Algorithm A "knew" $\mathbf{er}_P(F)$. One can construct an algorithm that does not need to know $\mathbf{er}_P(F)$ from A as follows. Note that Algorithm A can use an upper bound b on $\mathbf{er}_P(F)$, and achieve $\mathbf{er}_P(h) \le c_1(\beta)b^{c_2(\beta)} + \gamma$ in poly$(1/\gamma)$ time. Define $\phi : [0,1] \to [0, c_1(\beta)]$ by $\phi(x) = c_1(\beta)x^{c_2(\beta)}$. Consider the Algorithm B that uses as guesses for b all values of $\phi^{-1}(z)$ for multiples z of $\epsilon/4$, sets $\gamma = \epsilon/4$, calls Algorithm A for each of these values, then uses hypothesis testing as in [7] to estimate which of those roughly $4/\epsilon$ hypotheses is the best. One of the poly$(1/\epsilon)$ runs would produce a hypothesis with error at most $c_1(\beta)\mathbf{er}_P(F)^{c_2(\beta)} + \epsilon/2$, and hypothesis testing can be applied to find from among a set of hypothesis with one such good one a hypothesis with error at most $c_1(\beta)\mathbf{er}_P(F)^{c_2(\beta)} + \epsilon$. □

We can now apply the bound of Theorem 1 on the time complexity of weak learners to the above boosting result to obtain:

Corollary 2. *Let F be a con-decidable class so that VC-dim$(F) = d < \infty$. For every $\beta > 0$, there is an algorithm A such that, for any probability distribution*

P over $X \times \{-1,1\}$, if A is given access to a source of random examples of P, A runs in time

$$O(t_F(s(\beta, d, \frac{1}{\ln(\ln(1/\epsilon))})) \times \exp(H_2(\mathbf{er}_P(F)+\beta/2)s(\beta, d, \frac{1}{\ln(\ln(1/\epsilon))}) \times \ln(1/\epsilon))$$

(where $t_F : \mathbf{N} \mapsto \mathbf{N}$ is the running time of an algorithm for the consistency problem for the class F, and $s(\beta, d, \delta) = \frac{c}{\beta^2}\left(d + \ln(\frac{1}{\delta})\right)$, for some constant c).

Also, with probability at least 1/2, algorithm A returns a hypothesis h such that

$$\mathbf{er}_P(h) \le c_1(\beta)\mathbf{er}_P(F)^{c_2(\beta)} + \epsilon,$$

where $c_2(\beta) = 2(1/2-\beta)^2/\ln(1/\beta - 1)$, and $c_1(\beta)$ is a constant which depends only on β.

Proof Sketch. We apply the boosting algorithm to the agnostic weak learning algorithm of Theorem 1. However, one has to make sure that the success probability of the weak learner is high enough to endure the T many iterations required by the boosting algorithm. For that purpose, we have to chose the δ of the weak learner to be of order $(\ln(\ln(1/\epsilon)))^{-1}$. □

Corollary 3. *Let F be a con-decidable class of functions from some domain X to $\{-1,1\}$. If the VC dimension of F is finite then, for every $\beta > 0$, there is an algorithm A such that, for any probability distribution P over $X \times \{-1,1\}$, if A is given access to a source of random examples of P, then for any $\epsilon > 0$, in polynomial in $1/\epsilon$ time, with probability at least 1/2, algorithm A returns a hypothesis h such that*

$$\mathbf{er}_P(h) \le c_1(\beta)\mathbf{er}_P(F)^{c_2(\beta)} + \epsilon,$$

where $c_2(\beta) = 2(1/2-\beta)^2/\ln(1/\beta - 1)$, and $c_1(\beta)$ is a constant which depends only on β.

5 Learning with Large-Margin Half-Spaces

As a first application of the above results we briefly present a learning algorithm for learning with margin half-spaces. In this learning problem the instance space is the n-dimensional Euclidean unit ball and the learner is assessed by comparison with the best half-space, but where examples falling within a given distance γ of a separating hyper-plane in the comparison class are counted as wrong.

The motivation for such learning is that, as agnostically learning with half-spaces is computationally infeasible (see [3]), a hypothesis half-space that is computed an efficient learner is bound to make more mistakes that the best possible hyper-plane. However, it may be argued that making mistakes near the boundary of a separating hyper-plane is less costly than erring on points that are classified with large margins. The margin half-space learning model can be viewed as a model that adopts this view by ignoring mistakes on points that are within γ margins of a comparison half-space.

Previous work [4] provided an algorithm for this problem whose hypothesis h satisfies $\mathbf{er}_P(h) \leq \mathbf{er}_P(H_{\gamma,n}) + \epsilon$ in $(1/\epsilon)^{O(1/\gamma^2)}$ time.

Using the basic margin generalization bound (see [1]) it is not difficult to prove the following weak learner result.

Let B^n be the unit ball in $\mathbf{R}^n$ and, for a probability distribution P over $\mathbf{B}^n \times \{-1, 1\}$, let $\mathbf{er}_P(H_{\gamma,n})$ denote the minimal P- expected error of any half-space in $\mathbf{R}^n$, when points that have margin less than γ to the half-space are counted as errors.

Theorem 3. *Choose $\gamma, \epsilon > 0$. There is a polynomial-time learning algorithm A and a polynomial p such that, for any natural number n, any $\delta > 0$, and any probability distribution P over $\mathbf{B}^n \times \{-1, 1\}$ (where B^n is the unit ball in $\mathbf{R}^n$), if $p(n, 1/\delta)$ examples are drawn according to P and passed to algorithm A, then with probability at least $1 - \delta$, the output h of algorithm A satisfies*

$$\mathbf{er}_P(h) \leq \mathbf{er}(H_{\gamma,n}) + \epsilon.$$

We can now apply our boosting technique, namely Theorem 2, to obtain:

Theorem 4. *Choose $\gamma > 0$. There is a learning algorithm that runs in time poly($c_1^{O(1/\gamma^2)}$,$1/\epsilon$) time, while achieving $\mathbf{er}_P(h) \leq c_2 \mathbf{er}_P(H_{\gamma,n})^{c_3} + \epsilon$, where c_1, c_2 and c_3 are constants.*

Acknowledgments

We thank Peter Bartlett and Nadav Eiron for valuable conversations.

Phil Long acknowledges the support of National University of Singapore Academic Research Fund Grant RP252–000–070–107.

Yishay Mansour acknowledges the support of the Israeli Science Foundation.

References

1. P. L. Bartlett. The sample complexity of pattern classification with neural networks: the size of the weights is more important than the size of the network. *IEEE Transactions on Information Theory*, 44(2):525–536, 1998.
2. P. L. Bartlett and S. Ben-David. Hardness Results for Neural Network Approximation Problems. *Proceedings of the 4th European Conference on Computational Learning Theory (EuroCOLT'99)*, pp 50-62. A revised version will appear in JCSS.
3. S. Ben-David, N. Eiron, and P. Long. On the difficulty of approximately maximizing agreement. *Proceedings of the 13th Annual Conference on Computational Learning Theory, COLT00*, pages 266–274, 2000.
4. S. Ben-David and H. U. Simon. Efficient learning of linear perceptrons. In *NIPS*, 2000.
5. Yoav Freund. *Data Filtering and Distribution Modeling Algorithms for Machine Learning.* PhD thesis, University of California at Santa Cruz, 1993. Retrievable from: ftp.cse.ucsc.edu/pub/tr/ucsc-crl-93-37.ps.Z.

6. Yoav Freund and Robert E. Schapire. A decision-theoretic generalization of on-line learning and an application to boosting. In *Computational Learning Theory: Second European Conference, EuroCOLT '95*, pages 23–37. Springer-Verlag, 1995.
7. D. Haussler, M. Kearns, N. Littlestone, and M. K. Warmuth. Equivalence of models for polynomial learnability. *Information and Computation*, 95:129–161, 1991.
8. M. J. Kearns, R. E. Schapire, and L. M. Sellie. Toward efficient agnostic learning. *Machine Learning*, 17:115–141, 1994.
9. D. E. Knuth. *The Art of Computer Programming, Volume II: Semi numerical Algorithms*. Addison-Wesley, 1981.
10. Robert E. Schapire. *The Design and Analysis of Efficient Learning Algorithms*. PhD thesis, M. I. T., 1991.
11. Robert E. Schapire. Theoretical views of boosting and applications. In *Tenth International Conference on Algorithmic Learning Theory*, 1999.
12. L. G. Valiant. A theory of the learnable. *Communications of the ACM*, 27(11):1134–1142, 1984.

A Theoretical Analysis of Query Selection for Collaborative Filtering

Wee Sun Lee[1] and Philip M. Long[2]

[1] Department of Computer Science
National University of Singapore
Singapore 117543, Republic of Singapore
[2] Genome Institute of Singapore
1 Research Link
IMA Building
National University of Singapore
Singapore 117604, Republic of Singapore

Abstract. We consider the problem of determining which of a set of experts has tastes most similar to a given user by asking the user questions about his likes and dislikes. We describe a simple and fast algorithm for a theoretical model of this problem with a provable approximation guarantee, and prove that solving the problem exactly is NP-Hard.

1 Introduction

Recommender systems (also known as collaborative filtering systems) use the opinions of past users to make recommendations to new users. The design of many such systems is based on the assumption that people with similar opinions about some things are likely to have similar opinions about others (see [10, 4]). The user is typically asked to rate a few items before any new item is recommended. Once a sufficient number of items have been rated, the system can use those ratings to estimate which previous users of the system are most similar to the current user overall. The opinions of these previous users can then used to generate recommendations; methods based on weighted majority prediction [8] and correlation coefficients [9] usually work quite well for this.

In this paper, we investigate a different aspect of the problem: how to select the initial items for the user to rate. These items are not presented as recommendations, but are asked only for the purpose of learning about the user. Since these are troublesome to the user, a high priority must be placed on asking few of these questions. (This is in contrast to the work on "approximate nearest neighbor searching" [3,7,5], where all the components of the point being searched are assumed to be given.) If later questions are decided based on the answers to earlier questions, the questions must also be generated in real time.

We allow the ratings to come from any finite set Y, and assume that the algorithm is given an integer-valued loss function ℓ on Y to measure the distance

D. Helmbold and B. Williamson (Eds.): COLT/EuroCOLT 2001, LNAI 2111, pp. 517–528, 2001.

between different ratings. We require that the loss function ℓ be a metric, that is, it satisfies the properties: $\ell(x, y) \geq 0$, $\ell(x, y) = 0$ if and only if $x = y$, $\ell(x, y) = \ell(y, x)$ and $\ell(x, y) \leq \ell(x, z) + \ell(z, y)$ for any $z \in Y$. Common loss functions that satisfy these properties include the $0 - 1$ loss and the absolute loss. The distance between users will then be measured by the sum, over all items, of the loss between their ratings on a given item.

The emphasize the role that they play, we refer to the previous users as *experts*; our approximation bounds will be in terms of the number of such experts. Therefore, it may be worthwhile to cluster the previous users in a preprocessing step, and use the cluster centers as the experts.

Before proceeding to the general case, we illustrate our techniques in a highly idealized setting. We assume that there are only two possible ratings, that the distance between ratings is 1 if they are different and 0 if they are the same, and that some expert agrees with the user on all items. In this case, the problem can be described in terms of the *membership query model* [1].

In the membership query model [1], the learning algorithm is trying to learn an unknown $\{0, 1\}$-valued function f (called the "target") chosen from a known concept class F. The algorithm is allowed to ask the value of $f(x)$ for domain elements x of its choosing, and must eventually halt and output the identity of f.

In the idealized case described above, the problem of finding the perfect expert can be viewed as the problem of learning using membership queries. The different items would be the domain X, the likes and dislikes of the user is the function f to be learned, and asking the user its opinion about an item can be interpreted as a membership query. The experts are then the concept class F. Viewed this way, the problem we are faced with is that of, given a concept class F as input, designing a membership query algorithm for F.

We begin by showing that the very simple and fast "query-by-committee" [11] algorithm, which maintains a list of possible targets, and chooses the query for which the remaining possibilities are most evenly divided, learns any class F with an approximately optimal number of membership queries in the worst case. Specifically, if $\mathrm{opt}(F)$ is the optimal worst-case bound on the number of membership queries for learning arbitrary elements of F, then the query-by-committee algorithm learns F while making at most $\mathrm{opt}(F)(\ln(|F|/\mathrm{opt}(F)) + 1) + 1$ queries. We also show that it is NP-Hard to design a polynomial-time algorithm that, given F as input and an membership oracle for an element f of F, is guaranteed to learn f using $\mathrm{opt}(F)$ queries.

Next, we look at the more general case. To study this case, we use a variant of the membership query model similar to that proposed by Angluin, Krikis, Sloan and Turán [2]. Here, the range of the target f (our model of the user) and the functions in F (the experts) is an arbitrary finite set Y. As mentioned above, the algorithm is given an integer-valued metric ℓ on $Y \times Y$, and the distance between functions f and g is measured by $\sum_{x \in X} \ell(f(x), g(x))$. The target function f is not necessarily in F, but the algorithm is given a parameter η such that there is a function g in F at a distance at most η from f. The algorithm must output some element of F within distance η (there may be more than one). Let us refer to the optimal worst-case bound on the number of queries for this model by $\mathrm{opt}(F, \eta)$.

The algorithm we analyze for this problem also maintains a list of elements of F that are "alive"; here, these are elements that might possibly be within distance η of the target function f. Loosely speaking, it repeatedly chooses a domain element for which any response will discredit the remaining possibilities in total by a large amount.

To analyze this algorithm, we make use of a quantity that we call the η-degree of F. In the recommender system application, this can be interpreted as a measure of the diversity of opinion among the experts; for example, if any possible target f is at a distance at most η from a unique element of F, then the η-degree of F is 0. The motivation for this measure is strongest if we imagine that F is the result of a clustering preprocessing step. Note that, informally, if F consists of the centers of tight clusters, and users typically belong to one such cluster, being much closer to one element of F than to any other should often be expected in practice. Tight clustering is the implicit assumption underlying the design of many collaborative filtering systems.

One can view the definition of η-degree as follows: imagine centering balls of radius η at the elements of F, and constructing a graph where the vertices are these balls, and there are edges between pairs of vertices that overlap. The η-degree of F is the edge degree of that graph.

Our generalization of the query-by-committee algorithm is guaranteed to find an element of F within distance η after at most

$$2\mathrm{opt}(F, \eta) \ln \frac{|F|}{1 + \deg(F, \eta)} + \eta(1 + \deg(F, \eta))$$

queries. Thus, if each possible target is within distance η of a unique element of F, $2\mathrm{opt}(F, \eta) \ln |F| + \eta$ queries suffice.

2 Membership Queries

Fix some finite domain X. For some function f from X to $\{0, 1\}$, a membership oracle for f, when queried about an element x of X, returns $f(x)$. For an algorithm A with access to a membership oracle for f, let $Q(A, f)$ be the number of queries asked by A before it outputs the identity of f. For a class F of functions from X to $\{0, 1\}$, let $Q(A, F)$ be the maximum of $Q(A, f)$ over all $f \in F$. Let $\mathrm{opt}(F)$ be the minimum of $Q(A, F)$ over all algorithms A (note that there is no limitation on the time taken by A).

In this section, we show that there is an algorithm that takes F as input, and, given access to an oracle for an arbitrary element f of F, learns f with a nearly optimal number of queries in polynomial time.

The algorithm analyzed in this section is the "query-by-committee" [11] algorithm. (Our analysis of it builds on Johnson's analysis of his approximation algorithm for Set Cover [6].) It maintains a list of the elements of F consistent with the answers received so far, and asks the query x that divides the elements the most evenly, i.e. for which the number of "alive" functions g for which $g(x) = 1$ and the number for which $g(x) = 0$ are as close as possible. After receiving $f(x)$, those possibilities that are inconsistent with this value are deleted, and the algorithm continues. When only one possibility remains, the algorithm halts and outputs it.

The key lemma in our analysis is the following.

Lemma 1. *For any domain X, and any finite set F of at least two functions from X to $\{0,1\}$, there is an x for which* $\min_{y\in\{0,1\}} |\{f \in F : f(x) = y\}| \geq (|F| - 1)/\mathrm{opt}(F)$.

Proof: Let A be an optimal membership query algorithm for F. Assume for contradiction that for all $x \in X$, either $|\{f \in F : f(x) = 1\}| < (|F| - 1)/\mathrm{opt}(F)$, or $|\{f \in F : f(x) = 0\}| < (|F| - 1)/\mathrm{opt}(F)$.

Our strategy will be to use the fact that any possible query that A could ask has an answer that eliminates few possibilities to argue that after asking a certain number of queries, A cannot know the function to be learned. We will design an adversary that repeatedly gives the answer to A that eliminates the fewest possibilities.

Let $F_0 = F$ (in general, F_t will be the possibilities remaining after t queries have been asked). Let x_1 be the first query asked by A. Choose y_1 to minimize $|\{f \in F : f(x_1) = y_1\}|$. Let $F_1 = \{f \in F : f(x_1) = y_1\}$. Then, by assumption, $|F_1| - 1 > |F| - 1 - (|F| - 1)/\mathrm{opt}(F)$.

Continuing, let each x_t be the tth query asked, and choose y_t to minimize $|\{f \in F : f(x_t) = y_t\}|$, and let $F_t = \{f \in F : f(x_1) = y_1, ..., f(x_t) = y_t\}$. For each such t, $|F_t| - 1 > |F_{t-1}| - 1 - (|F| - 1)/\mathrm{opt}(F)$. Telescoping,

$$|F_{\mathrm{opt}(F)}| - 1 > (1 - \mathrm{opt}(F)/\mathrm{opt}(F))(|F| - 1) = 0. \tag{1}$$

Thus, after $\mathrm{opt}(F)$ queries, there is more than one element of F consistent with the information received by A, a contradiction. □

Theorem 1. *For any finite set X, and any finite set F of at least two functions from X to $\{0,1\}$, the query-by-committee algorithm, given F and a membership oracle for any arbitrary $f \in F$, outputs f after asking at most*

$$\mathrm{opt}(F)\left(1 + \ln \frac{|F| - 1}{\mathrm{opt}(F)}\right) + 1$$

queries.

Proof: Choose F, and a target $f \in F$. Suppose the query-by-committee algorithm asks T queries before learning f, and for each $0 \leq t \leq T$, let F_t be the set of functions in F consistent with the information received after the first t queries. Lemma 1 implies that for all $t \leq T$,

$$\begin{aligned} |F_t| - 1 &\leq (1 - 1/\mathrm{opt}(F_{t-1}))(|F_{t-1}| - 1) \\ &\leq (1 - 1/\mathrm{opt}(F))(|F_{t-1}| - 1). \end{aligned} \tag{2}$$

We also have

$$|F_t| \leq |F_{t-1}| - 1. \tag{3}$$

Let S be largest index for which $|F_S| - 1 \geq \text{opt}(F)$. Then (2) implies

$$\left(1 - \frac{1}{\text{opt}(F)}\right)^S (|F| - 1) \geq \text{opt}(F)$$

and, applying the fact that $\forall x, 1 - x \leq e^{-x}$ and solving for S, we get

$$S \leq \text{opt}(F) \ln \frac{|F| - 1}{\text{opt}(F)}.$$

Also, (3), together with the fact that $|F_{T-1}| > 1$, implies that

$$T - S < \text{opt}(F) + 1,$$

completing the proof. □

2.1 Hardness Result

We now show that the problem of, given F, learning an arbitrary element of f with $\text{opt}(F)$ membership queries is NP-Hard. Since this is a special case of our model of the query selection problem for collaborative filtering, this problem is NP-hard also. Our proof is via a reduction from the set covering problem.

An instance (X', F') of the *set covering problem* consists of a finite set X' and a family F' of subsets of X' such that every element of X' belongs to at least one subset of F'. The problem is to find the minimum-sized subset $C \subseteq F'$, such that every element of X' belongs to at least one subset of C.

For any instance of the set covering problem where $|X'| = n$ and $|F'| = m$, we will construct an optimal query problem whose solution will give the solution to the set covering problem. We first describe a closely related optimal query problem. An instance of the optimal query problem can be given as an $|F| \times |X|$ matrix. We construct an initial matrix M of size $n \times m$, where an element of X' in the set covering problem corresponds to an element in F of our optimal query problem while an element of F' in the set covering problem corresponds to an element of X in our optimal query problem. For each subset $s \in F'$, the ith entry in the corresponding column of matrix M is set to 1 if the element of X' corresponding to the ith row is a member of s, otherwise it is set to 0. Assume that we augment the matrix M with an all zero row which we set as the target for a query algorithm. Each query corresponds to a member of F' and will eliminate all the rows with 1's at that column. When the target is identified, all the rows except the all zero row will have been eliminated. The subset of F' corresponding to the subset of queries will thus form a cover for X'.

However, our optimal query algorithm is guaranteed to give only the optimal *worst case* number of queries which does not necessarily correspond to the smallest cover. In order to ensure that the optimal *worst case* queries gives us the optimal cover, we solve the optimal query problem for an augmented matrix M'. We first augment the matrix M with n columns that are zero in every entry. Then we augment the augmented matrix with $n+1$ rows. The last row of the matrix consist of all zero elements while the $n+i$th row ($i = 1, \ldots, n$) consist of all zeros except for element $m+i$ which is set to 1. Call the doubly augmented matrix M'. We will show that if an optimal query algorithm for the matrix M' uses at most $n+q$ queries, then the optimal cover for the corresponding covering problem has size q.

The all zero row will be used as the target of an optimal query algorithm. Each query corresponding to the one of the first m columns corresponds to a member of F'. Hence the subset of F' corresponding to queries from the first m columns will form a cover of X'. We call this subset the cover *generated* by the query algorithm. Note that the rows $n+1$ to $2n$ cannot be eliminated by any query except the query to the column where they have entry 1 and that such a query will eliminate only one row. Hence to uniquely identify the target, n of the queries must be to the last n columns. We now need to show that the cover generated by the optimal query algorithm is an optimal cover.

Lemma 2. *The cover generated by an optimal query algorithm for matrix M' is a cover of the smallest size.*

Proof: Let A be an optimal query algorithm. Assume that the cover generated by A is not a cover of the smallest size. Hence it is possible to reduce the number of queries needed to identify the all zero row target by generating a smaller cover. Let B be an algorithm that uses the fewest number of queries to identify the all zero row target. We transform B into another algorithm B'. The algorithm B' has the property that any query on the last n columns always happens after the queries to the first m columns. This can be done by delaying the queries on the last n columns while retaining the ordering of the other queries. Since a query to column $m+i$ can eliminate only row $n+i$, the effect of the delays is to potentially reduce the number of queries required for the first n rows while potentially increasing the number of queries required for the other rows. The number of queries required for the all zero rows remain the same.

The algorithm B' will take the optimal number of queries for identifying the all zero row target and no more than n queries to identify any of the first n rows. This is because rows $n+1$ to $2n+1$ are identically zero when restricted to the first m columns, giving effectively a matrix with $n+1$ distinct rows. At least $n+1$ queries is needed by any algorithm to identify the all zero row target and the all zero row target always takes more queries than rows $n+1$ to $2n$. Hence, algorithm B' has better worst case performance than algorithm A contradicting the optimality of algorithm A. □

3 General Case

Choose a finite nonempty set Y, a positive integer M, and a metric ℓ mapping $Y \times Y$ to the nonnegative integers.

For functions f and g from X to Y define the distance $d(f,g)$ between f and g by

$$d(f,g) = \sum_{x \in X} \ell(f(x), g(x)).$$

Let $F^{\oplus\eta}$ consist of all $g : X \to \{0,1\}$ such that there is an $f \in F$ for which $d(f,g) \leq \eta$.

In this model, the adversary picks a function f from $F^{\oplus\eta}$ (which we will call the target), and provides an evaluation oracle for f to the algorithm; this oracle responds to a query of x with $f(x)$. The algorithm then must output $h \in F$ such that $d(f,h) \leq \eta$ (there may be more than one such possibility). The worst case number of queries for an algorithm A in this setting is $Q(A, F, \eta)$, and the optimal number of queries is $\mathrm{opt}(F, \eta)$.

For a function $f : X \to Y$, and $U \subseteq X$, denote the restriction of f to U by $f_{|U}$.

For a set F of functions from X to Y, define the η-degree of F, denoted by $\deg(F, \eta)$, to be the maximum, over all $g \in F$, of $|\{f \in F : 0 < d(f,g) \leq 2\eta\}|$. For $\mu : F \to \mathbf{Z}^+$, define $\phi(F, \mu)$ to be the maximum, over all $g \in F$, of

$$\sum_{f \in F : d(f,g) \leq \mu(f) + \mu(g)} \mu(f).$$

For technical reasons, we will consider a related model. In this model, instead of η, the learning algorithm is given a priori a function $\mu : F \to \mathbf{Z}^+$ called a *quota function*, and access to an evaluation oracle for some $f : X \to Y$ such that there is an $g \in F$ with $d(f,g) \leq \mu(g)$. The algorithm then must output an $h \in F$ such that $d(f,h) \leq \mu(h)$. Let $\mathrm{opt}(F, \mu)$ be the optimal worst-case number of queries for learning in this model.

Algorithm Our algorithm works in time polynomial in $|X|$, $|Y|$, and $|F|$. (Note that the latter is significantly less than $|F^{\oplus\eta}|$.)

Our algorithm (let's call it B_F), is defined recursively as follows. Suppose at some point in time B_F has previously asked queries $x_1, ..., x_{t-1}$, which were answered with $y_1, ..., y_{t-1}$ respectively. Let

$$F_t = \{f_{|X - \{x_1, \ldots, x_{t-1}\}} : f \in F, \sum_{s<t} \ell(f(x_s), y_s) \leq \eta\}.$$

Informally F_t consists of the restrictions of those elements of F that are "still alive" to the unexplored portion of X. If $|F_t| = 1$, it halts, and outputs an extension h of the single element of F_t to all of X that minimizes $\sum_{s<t} \ell(h(x_s), y_s)$. Otherwise, it chooses x_t from $X - \{x_1, ..., x_{t-1}\}$ in order to maximize

$$\min_{y \in Y} \sum_{f \in F_t} \ell(f(x_t), y_t).$$

The following is the main lemma in our analysis of this algorithm.

Lemma 3. *Choose a finite X, a finite Y, a finite set F of at least 2 functions from X to Y, and $\mu : F \to \mathbf{Z}^+$. There is an $x \in X$ for which*

$$\min_{y \in Y} \sum_{f \in F} \ell(f(x_t), y_t) \geq \frac{1}{\mathrm{opt}(F, \mu)} \left(\left(\sum_{f \in F} (1 + \mu(f)) \right) - \phi(F, \mu) \right)$$

Proof: Let A be an optimal membership query algorithm for learning F with a quota function μ in the model of this section. Let $T = \mathrm{opt}(F, \mu)$. Assume without loss of generality that A always asks exactly T queries before halting and outputting a function in F. Assume for contradiction that

$$\forall x, \exists y, \sum_{f \in F} \ell(f(x), y) < \frac{1}{T} \left(\left(\sum_{f \in F} (1 + \mu(f)) \right) - \phi(F, \mu) \right). \tag{4}$$

Generate $(x_1, y_1), ..., (x_T, y_T)$ recursively as follows. For each t, let x_t be A's query when its previous queries $x_1, ..., x_{t-1}$ were answered with $y_1, ..., y_{t-1}$ respectively. Choose

$$y_t = \mathrm{argmin}_u \sum_{f \in F} \ell(f(x_t), u). \tag{5}$$

First, we claim that $(x_1, y_1), ..., (x_T, y_T)$ are "legal", in the sense that there is at least one potential target function f such that $f(x_1) = y_1, ..., f(x_T) = y_T$ for which there is a $g \in F$ with $d(f, g) \leq \mu(g)$. To see this, note that (4) and (5) imply

$$\begin{aligned} \sum_{g \in F} \sum_{t=1}^{T} \ell(g(x_t), y_t) &= \sum_{t=1}^{T} \sum_{g \in F} \ell(g(x_t), y_t) \\ &< \left(\sum_{g \in F} (1 + \mu(g)) \right) - \phi(F, \mu) \qquad (6) \\ &\leq \left(\sum_{g \in F} (1 + \mu(g)) \right). \end{aligned}$$

Thus, there is a $g \in F$ such that $\sum_{t=1}^{T} \ell(g(x_t), y_t) \leq \mu(g)$. So if f is defined by $f(x_1) = y_1, ..., f(x_T) = y_T$ and $f(x) = g(x)$ for $x \notin \{x_1, ..., x_T\}$, f satisfies the requirements of a target function.

Suppose A outputs h. Loosely speaking, any $f \in F$ that is too far from h had better be eliminated as a possible target by $(x_1, y_1), ..., (x_T, y_T)$, since otherwise an adversary could choose f as a target. Specifically, for any $f \in F$ such that $d(h, f) > \mu(h) + \mu(f)$, it must be the case that $\sum_{t=1}^{T} \ell(f(x_t), y_t) > \mu(f)$, since otherwise, an adversary could modify f to get a target function with distance at most $\mu(f)$ from f, and therefore distance greater than $\mu(h)$ from h. Thus

$$\sum_{f \in F} \sum_{t=1}^{T} \ell(f(x_t), y_t) \geq \sum_{f \in F : d(f,h) > \mu(f) + \mu(h)} (1 + \mu(f))$$

$$\geq \left(\sum_{f\in F}(1+\mu(f))\right) - \sum_{f\in F:d(f,h)\leq\mu(f)+\mu(h)} \mu(f)$$

$$\geq \left(\sum_{f\in F}(1+\mu(f))\right) - \phi(F,\mu),$$

contradicting (6) and completing the proof. □

Now we're ready for our theorem about B_F.

Theorem 2. *Choose X, a set F of functions from X to Y, and an integer $\eta \geq 1$. Then $Q(B_F, F, \eta) \leq 2\mathrm{opt}(F,\eta)\ln(|F|/(1+\deg(F,\eta))) + \eta(1+\deg(F,\eta))$.*

Proof: Consider a run of algorithm B_F in which it asks queries $x_1, ..., x_T$, which are answered with $y_1, ..., y_T$. For each t, let

$$F_t = \{f_{X-\{x_1,...,x_{t-1}\}} : f \in F, \sum_{S<t} \ell(f(x_s), y_s) \leq \eta\}.$$

For each t, define $\mu_t : F_t \to \mathbf{Z}^+$ by

$$\mu_t(f) = \eta - \min\{\sum_{s<t} \ell(g(x_s), y_s) : g \in F, g_{|X-\{x_1,...,x_{t-1}\}} = f\}.$$

Informally, $\mu_t(f)$ is the amount of loss left before f is eliminated as a possible target.

We divide our analysis of B_F into two stages. Let

$$S = \max\left\{t : \sum_{f\in F_t}(1+\mu_t(f)) \geq 2\eta(1+\deg(F,\eta))\right\}.$$

Choose $t \leq S$. By Lemma 3,

$$\sum_{f\in F_{t+1}} (1+\mu_{t+1}(f))$$
$$\leq \left(\sum_{f\in F_t}(1+\mu_t(f))\right) - \sum_{f\in F_t} \ell(f(x_t), y_t)$$
$$\leq \left(\sum_{f\in F_t}(1+\mu_t(f))\right) - \frac{1}{\mathrm{opt}(F_t,\mu_t)}\left(\left(\sum_{f\in F_t}(1+\mu_t(f))\right) - \phi(F_t,\mu_t)\right). \quad (7)$$

We will now prove that

$$\phi(F_t, \mu_t) \leq \eta(1+\deg(F,\eta)). \quad (8)$$

For each $f \in F_t$, let $f^E \in F$ be obtained by extending f to X so as to minimize $\sum_{s<t} \ell(f^E(x_s), y_s)$. Recall that

$$\phi(F_t, \mu_t) = \max_{g \in F_t} \sum_{f \in F_t : d(f,g) \leq \mu_t(f) + \mu_t(g)} \mu_t(f).$$

Choose $g_* \in F_t$ achieving this maximum. We have

$$\begin{aligned}
\eta(1 + \deg(F, \eta)) &= \eta \max_{g \in F} |\{f \in F : d(f, g) \leq 2\eta\}| \\
&\geq \eta |\{f \in F : d(f, g_*^E) \leq 2\eta\}| \\
&= \sum_{f \in F : d(f, g_*^E) \leq 2\eta} \eta \\
&\geq \sum_{f \in F_t : d(f^E, g_*^E) \leq 2\eta} \eta. \qquad (9)
\end{aligned}$$

For any $f, g \in F_t$,

$$\begin{aligned}
d(f^E, g^E) &= \sum_{x \in X} \ell(f^E(x), g^E(x)) \\
&= d(f, g) + \sum_{s<t} \ell(f^E(x_s), g^E(x_s)) \\
&\leq d(f, g) + \sum_{s<t} \ell(f^E(x_s), y_s) + \ell(g^E(x_s), y_s) \\
&\leq d(f, g) + 2\eta - (\mu_t(f) + \mu_t(g))
\end{aligned}$$

since, by definition, for all $f \in F_t$, $\sum_{s<t} \ell(f^E(x_s), y_s) \leq \eta - \mu_t(f)$. Thus (9) implies

$$\begin{aligned}
\eta(1 + \deg(F, \eta)) &\geq \sum_{f \in F_t : d(f, g_*) \leq \mu_t(f) + \mu_t(g_*)} \eta \\
&\geq \sum_{f \in F_t : d(f, g_*) \leq \mu_t(f) + \mu_t(g_*)} \mu_t(f),
\end{aligned}$$

proving (8).

Putting (8) together with (7), we have

$$\begin{aligned}
&\sum_{f \in F_{t+1}} (1 + \mu_{t+1}(f)) \\
&\leq \left(\sum_{f \in F_t} (1 + \mu_t(f)) \right) - \frac{1}{2\mathrm{opt}(F_t, \mu_t)} \sum_{f \in F_t} (1 + \mu_t(f)) \\
&= \left(1 - \frac{1}{2\mathrm{opt}(F_t, \mu_t)} \right) \sum_{f \in F_t} (1 + \mu_t(f))
\end{aligned}$$

$$\leq \left(1 - \frac{1}{2\text{opt}(F,k)}\right) \sum_{f \in F_t} (1 + \mu_t(f)).$$

Thus,

$$\sum_{f \in F_S} (1 + \mu_S(f)) \leq \left(1 - \frac{1}{2\text{opt}(F,\eta)}\right)^S |F|(\eta + 1).$$

But, by definition, $\sum_{f \in F_S}(1 + \mu_S(f)) \geq 2\eta(1 + \deg(F,\eta))$, and so

$$\begin{aligned}
2\eta(1 + \deg(F,\eta)) &\leq \left(1 - \frac{1}{2\text{opt}(F,\eta)}\right)^S |F|(\eta + 1) \\
2\eta(1 + \deg(F,\eta)) &\leq \exp\left(-\frac{S}{2\text{opt}(F,\eta)}\right) |F|(\eta + 1) \\
\ln 2 + \ln \eta + \ln(1 + \deg(F,\eta)) &\leq -\frac{S}{2\text{opt}(F,\eta)} + \ln|F| + \ln(\eta + 1) \\
S &\leq 2\text{opt}(F,\eta) \ln(|F|/(1 + \deg(F,\eta))).
\end{aligned}$$

For all $t \leq T$, since $|F_t| > 1$, and $\ell(u,v) \geq 1$ for $u \neq v$,

$$\sum_{f \in F_{t+1}} (1 + \mu_{t+1}(f)) \leq \left(\sum_{f \in F_t} (1 + \mu_t(f))\right) - 1. \tag{10}$$

Since $\sum_{f \in F_{S+1}}(1 + \mu_{S+1}(f)) < 2\eta(1 + \deg(F,\eta))$ and $\sum_{f \in F_T}(1 + \mu_T(f)) \geq 1$, (10) implies that $T - S \leq 2\eta(1 + \deg(F,\eta))$. This completes the proof. □

4 Acknowledgements

We gratefully acknowledge the support of National University of Singapore Academic Research Fund grant R252–000–070–107.

References

1. D. Angluin. Queries and concept learning. *Machine Learning*, 2:319–342, 1988.
2. D. Angluin, M. Krikis, R. H. Sloan, and G. Turán. Malicious omissions and errors in answers to membership queries. *Machine Learning*, 28:211–255, 1997.
3. S. Arya, D. M. Mount, N. S. Netanyahu, R. Silverman, and A. Wu. An optimal algorithm for approximate nearest neighbor searching. *Proc. 5th ACM-SIAM Sympos. Discrete Algorithms*, pages 573–582, 1994.
4. J.S. Breese, D. Heckerman, and C. Kadie. Empirical analysis of predictive algorithms for collaborative ltering. *Proceedings of the Fourteenth Conference on Uncertainty in Articial Intelligence*, pages 43–52, 1998.
5. P. Indyk and R. Motwani. Approximate nearest neighbors: Towards removing the curse of dimensionality. *Proceedings of the 30th ACM Symposium on the Theory of Computing*, pages 604–613, 1998.

6. D. S. Johnson. Approximation algorithms for combinatorial problems. *Journal of Computer and System Sciences*, 9:256–278, 1974.
7. E. Kushilevitz, R. Ostrovsky, and Y. Rabani. Efficient search for approximate nearest neighbor in high dimensional spaces. *Proceedings of the 30th ACM Symposium on the Theory of Computing*, pages 614–623, 1998.
8. Atsuyoshi Nakamura and Naoki Abe. Collaborative filtering using weighted majority pr ediction algorithms. In *Proceedings of the Fifteenth International Confere nce on Machine Learning*, 1998.
9. P. Resnick, N. Iacovou, M. Suchak, P. Ber gstrom, and J. Riedl. Grouplens: An open architecture for collaborative filtering of netnews. In *Proceedings of the ACM 1994 Conference on Computer Supported Cooperative Work*, 1994.
10. P. Resnick and H. R. Varian. Recommender systems. *Communications of the ACM*, 40:56–58, 1997.
11. H. S. Seung, M. Opper, and H. Sompolinsky. Query by committee. *Proceedings of the 1992 Workshop on Computational Learning Theory*, pages 287–294, 1992.

On Using Extended Statistical Queries to Avoid Membership Queries*

Nader H. Bshouty and Vitaly Feldman

Department of Computer Science
Technion, Haifa, 32000, Israel
{bshouty, felvit}@cs.technion.ac.il

Abstract. The Kushilevitz-Mansour (KM) algorithm is an algorithm that finds all the "heavy" Fourier coefficients of a boolean function. It is the main tool for learning decision trees and DNF expressions in the PAC model with respect to the uniform distribution. The algorithm requires an access to the membership query (MQ) oracle.
We weaken this requirement by producing an analogue of the KM algorithm that uses extended statistical queries (SQ) (SQs in which the expectation is taken with respect to a distribution given by a learning algorithm). We restrict a set of distributions that a learning algorithm may use for its SQs to be a set of specific constant bounded product distributions. Our analogue finds all the "heavy" Fourier coefficients of degree lower than $c \log n$ (we call it BS). We use BS to learn decision trees and by adapting Freund's boosting technique we give algorithm that learns DNF in this model. Learning in this model implies learning with persistent classification noise and in some cases can be extended to learning with product attribute noise.
We develop a characterization for learnability with these extended SQs and apply it to get several negative results about the model.

1 Introduction and Overview

The problems of learning decision trees and DNF expressions are among the most well studied problems of computational learning theory. In this paper we address learning of these classes in the popular PAC model with respect to the uniform distribution. The first algorithm that learns decision trees in this setting was given by Kushilevitz and Mansour in [13]. The main tool that they used is the algorithm for finding all the Fourier coefficients of a boolean function larger than given threshold (it is usually referred as the KM algorithm). Later Jackson in [10] used this algorithm and Freund's boosting technique to build his famous algorithm for learning DNF expressions. These outstanding results became possible through utilization of *membership query* (MQ) oracle. That is, in order to use these algorithms we need an access to values of the learned function at any

* This research was supported by the fund for the promotion of research at the Technion. Part of research was done at the university of Calgary, Calgary, Alberta, Canada.

D. Helmbold and B. Williamson (Eds.): COLT/EuroCOLT 2001, LNAI 2111, pp. 529–545, 2001.

given point. Angluin and Kharitonov in [3] proved that under standard cryptographic assumptions every class that is learnable in the distribution-independent PAC model with MQs is also learnable without MQs, i.e., MQs are not helpful in this model. On the other hand, there is no known algorithm that learns the above-mentioned classes in the PAC model with respect to the uniform distribution without use of MQs. The access to MQ oracle is not available in most of applications and thus we suggest a way to weaken the requirement of MQs that results from the following approach.

Learning in the basic PAC model (without MQs) represents learning without any control over the points in which the value of the target function will be known. On the other side, membership queries represent the total control over these points. It may be the case that a learning algorithm has more than no control and less than total control over the choice of points. We reflect this situation by allowing the learning algorithm to get points sampled with respect to the distribution given by the learning algorithm. Set of distributions $\mathcal{D}$ that a learning algorithm may use measures the amount of control the learning algorithm has [1] Naturally, this defines learnability with respect to given $\mathcal{D}$ or learnability in the PAC-$\mathcal{D}$. In this paper we discuss SQ-$\mathcal{D}$ — the statistical query (SQ) analogue of the above model. This is an extension of SQ model introduced by Kearns in [12] in which a learning algorithm may get statistical queries with respect to any distribution from $\mathcal{D}$. An important property of this model is that under some limitations on $\mathcal{D}$ it can be simulated using MQs with persistent noise (this model is particularly interesting as defining a type of *agnostic learning* (see [14] for more details)). This gives us a general framework for producing persistent noise tolerant algorithms. Shamir and Shwartzman in [17] were first to consider extending the notion of SQ as a way to produce (persistent) noise tolerant algorithms. Their extension allows estimating expectation of real-valued functionals of arbitrary range and order higher than one. Their approach was developed in [11] and permits use of several distributions. Thus SQ-$\mathcal{D}$ is, in some sense, included in their extension. The framework they have developed focuses on use of second-order SQs to offset persistent classification noise in Jackson's algorithm for learning DNF. On the other hand, we stress limiting the set $\mathcal{D}$ as a way to avoid MQs.

We consider the set $\mathcal{D}_\rho$ containing all the product distributions with each input bit being 1 with probability $\rho, 1/2$ or $1-\rho$ for a constant $0 < \rho < 1/2$. Learnability with respect to this set of distributions represents a situation when a learning algorithm has some influence on each input bit (or attribute) of the next sampled value. That is, if a learning algorithm chooses distribution with i-th bit being 1 with probability ρ - this bit will be more probably be 0 than 1 ($1-\rho > \rho$); choosing $1-\rho$ represents symmetrical situation and choosing $1/2$ means 0 or 1 with equal probability. Amount of this influence is given by ρ and is limited by restrictions on ρ. It is easy to see that boundary values of ρ represent

[1] It should be noted that any specific set $\mathcal{D}$ does not necessarily reflect any practical situation. But we think that this approach generalizes the notion of control over the choice sample points.

regular the PAC learning with respect to uniform distribution. ($\rho = 1/2$) and the PAC model with MQs ($\rho = 0$).

We give a weaker analogue of the `KM` algorithm for SQ–$\mathcal{D}_\rho$ that finds all the "heavy" target function Fourier coefficients of degree lower than $c \log n$ (we call it the *Bounded Sieve*). We show that the Bounded Sieve (`BS`) is, in fact, sufficient for learning the class of decision trees and weakly learning the class of DNF formulae. Then, by employing Freund's boosting algorithm, we can strongly learn DNF in SQ–$\mathcal{D}_\rho$. To prove this fact we first need to adapt the Freund's technique to SQ–$\mathcal{D}_\rho$. Our adaptation is simple and more efficient than the one previously given in [1] (for regular SQ model).

Since $\mathcal{D}_\rho$ meets the above-mentioned limitation our algorithms can be simulated using MQs with persistent classification noise. We then show how to modify `BS` so that it could handle another non-trivial noise - product attribute noise in MQs. This type of noise was previously considered in [18], [8] and [5]. In these papers attribute noise appeared in randomly sampled points (i.e., in the regular PAC model). We extend this noise model to learning with MQs. Particularly, for every sample point x (random or received through MQ) oracle flips every bit i of x with probability p_i and returns the value of target function at the resulting point (unless classification noise is also present). This type of noise may reflect the situation when communication with oracle is done using faulty channel or querying very specific point is difficult (or even impossible) to attain. Specifically, we handle any *known* attribute noise rates bounded away from $1/2$ by a constant.

In the second part of this paper we show some negative results about the newly introduced model. We start by developing a characterization of classes weakly learnable in regular SQ model and extend it to the SQ-$\mathcal{D}$. In fact, we will show that concept classes are weakly learnable in the SQ model if and only if they are weakly learnable by SQ algorithms of a very restricted form. Besides giving an interesting insight into the nature of weakly SQ-learnable classes, this form provides an information theoretic characterization of weakly SQ-learnable classes. This characterization is used similarly to the SQ-DIM characterization which was given in [4]. We have decided to use our characterization for its simplicity and easy extendability to SQ-$\mathcal{D}$. The characterization will enable us to show that the class of all parity functions having at most $k(n)$ variables is not weakly learnable in SQ-$\mathcal{D}_\rho$ if $k(n)$ is greater than $O(\log n)$. This fact complements the Bounded Sieve which obviously learns every such class for $k(n) = O(\log n)$. Another interesting application of this characterization will help us to show that although the model we have introduced is powerful enough to learn DNF expressions it still cannot learn a class of parity functions learnable in the PAC model with classification noise (to show this we rely on the result proved in [6]). We also show that the class of all parity functions is not weakly learnable with respect to any "non-biased" distribution (i.e., not containing points with probability greater than $\frac{1}{poly(n)}$) even in SQ-$\mathcal{D}$ for $\mathcal{D}$ containing all "non-biased" distributions. This gives another evidence that the class of all parity functions is hard for any statistics based learning.

2 Definitions and Notation

Throughout this paper we refer to several well-studied and well-known models of learning. Particularly, the PAC model, use of membership queries, the statistical query model and two relevant models of classification noise (random independent and random persistent). Many parts of our analysis rely heavily on the use of the well-known Fourier transform technique. This beautiful technique was introduced to learning theory by Linial et al. in [15]. An extended survey of the technique and the KM algorithm can be found in [16].

Below we describe notation we will use in this paper. Most of it follows the common practice and is provided for reference purposes.

2.1 General Notation

We consider an input space $X = \{0,1\}^n$. A *concept* is a boolean function on X. For convenience, when applying the Fourier transform technique, we define boolean functions to have output in $\{-1,+1\}$. A *concept class* $\mathcal{F}$ is a set of concepts. For any vector x we denote by x_i an i-th element (or bit) of x and by $x_{[i,j]}$ we denote $x_i x_{i+1} \ldots x_j$. We use $[a]^k$ to denote a vector of k elements equal to a.

U is used to denote the uniform distribution over X. We say that a function g $\epsilon-$approximates f with respect to distribution D if $Pr_D[f = g] \geq 1-\epsilon$. It is easy to see that this is equivalent to saying that $\mathbf{E}_D[fg] \geq 1-2\epsilon$. For any real-valued function ϕ we define $L_\infty(\phi) = max_{x\in X}|\phi(x)|$. If $p(n) = O(q(n))$ and $q'(n)$ is $q(n)$ with all the logarithmic factors removed we write $p(n) = \tilde{O}(q(n))$. Similarly we define $\tilde{\Omega}$ for lower bounds. This extends to k-ary functions in obvious way.

2.2 Estimating Expected Values

We will frequently need to estimate the expected value of a random variable. Although the SQ model itself provides us with such estimates, sometimes a random variable will be a result of a statistical query. In such a case we usually cannot use SQ to estimate the expectation of the variable. Thus we will find the expectation by sampling the variable and averaging the results. The justification for the method results from Hoeffding's lemma. According to the lemma if we sample randomly and independently a random variable Y with values in $[a,b]$ then to reach the accuracy of at least μ with confidence of at least δ it is sufficient to take $H(\mu, b-a, \delta) = O(\log(1/\delta)(b-a)^2\frac{1}{\mu^2})$ samples of Y.

Another implication of the fact that a value of random variable is a result of SQ is that we get the value within some tolerance ρ. It is easy to see that in such a case the above procedure will return the expectation within $\rho+\mu$.

3 Extending the SQ Model

We are now going to consider an extension of the SQ model. In this new model we allow the learning algorithm to supply a distribution with respect to which it wants to calculate the expectation. More formally, let $\mathcal{D}$ be a set of distributions over X containing distribution D.

Learning algorithm in the *SQ-$\mathcal{D}$* model is supplied with the STAT$(f, \mathcal{D})$ oracle, where f is the target concept. The query to this oracle is a triple (ψ, r, D') where $\psi : \{0,1\}^n \times \{-1,+1\} \to \{-1,+1\}$ is a query function, $r \in [0,1]$ is a tolerance (as in SQ model) and D' is a distribution from $\mathcal{D}$. To such a query the oracle responds with the value v satisfying $|\mathbf{E}_{D'}[\psi(x, f(x))] - v| \leq r$. Respectively, we say that concept class $\mathcal{F}$ is (weakly) learnable in SQ-$\mathcal{D}$ model with respect to D if it is (weakly) learnable by a polynomial algorithm (as defined in the regular SQ model) with access to the newly defined oracle.

It is important to note that if we do not restrict $\mathcal{D}$ we can simulate membership queries using distributions with all the weight concentrated in one point. Our second observation is that this model is equivalent to the regular SQ model for $\mathcal{D} = \{D\}$. A more interesting property of this model is that given oracles for the distributions in $\mathcal{D}$ (or being able to sample according to these distributions) it is easy to simulate the statistical query oracle using membership queries.

An important property of the model is that a learning algorithm can be further extended to learning in the presence of random classification noise. Transformation to learning in this model is done by offsetting the effect of the noise on the query (see [12] for more details). Since we are simulating using membership queries we are actually interested in learning with persistent classification noise. Offsetting noise in this model can be a more complicated task. However, if the probability of seeing the same point in sample of every $D' \in \mathcal{D}$ is negligible (relative to learning parameters) we can offset the noise in the same way as before. This probability is negligible if and only if the probability to see each specific point in D' is negligible. Formally, if we denote by $L_\infty(\mathcal{D}) = max_{D' \in \mathcal{D}}\{L_\infty(D')\}$ we get the following theorem.

Theorem 1. *Let $\mathcal{F}$ be a concept class and $\mathcal{D}$ be a set of distributions with oracle available for every $D' \in \mathcal{D}$. If $\mathcal{F}$ is learnable in SQ-$\mathcal{D}$ with respect to D and $L_\infty(\mathcal{D}) < \rho^n$ for a constant $0 < \rho < 1$, then $\mathcal{F}$ is learnable with respect to D given access to MQs corrupted by random persistent classification noise.*

4 Learning with Respect to the Uniform Distribution Using Product Distributions

4.1 Definitions and Prerequisites

In this section we will examine $\mathcal{D}$ that contains all the product distributions such that every input bit is 1 with probability ρ , $1/2$ or $1-\rho$, i.e., for every input bit x_i, $\mathbf{Pr}[x_i = 1] = p_i$ independently of all the other inputs and $p \in \{\rho, 1/2, 1-\rho\}^n$ (we call such p a *probability vector*). We assume that ρ is a constant satisfying $1/2 > \rho > 0$. For every $p \in \{\rho, 1/2, 1-\rho\}^n$ denote by D_p the product distribution defined by this probability vector. Denote by

$$\mathcal{D}_\rho = \{D_p \mid p \in \{\rho, 1/2, 1-\rho\}^n\} .$$

This distribution class will be used to learn with respect to the uniform distribution which itself is contained in $\mathcal{D}_\rho$ for any ρ. It is important to note that according to Theorem 1 learning in SQ–$\mathcal{D}_\rho$ implies learning with persistent noise since $L_\infty(\mathcal{D}_\rho) = (1-\rho)^n$.

In further algorithms we will need to get statistics not only about boolean functions but also about any real-valued function involving $f(x)$. For this purpose we will rely on the following simple lemma.

Lemma 1. *There exists a procedure* `RVMEAN` *such that for every bounded real-valued function* $\phi : \{0,1\}^n \times \{-1,1\} \to [-b,b]$, *tolerance* r *and distribution* $D' \in \mathcal{D}$, `RVMEAN`(ϕ, b, r, D') *returns a value* v *satisfying*

$$|\mathbf{E}_{D'}\phi(x, f(x)) - v| \leq r \ .$$

Its time complexity is $O(\log b/r)$. *The required tolerance is bounded from below by* $\frac{r^2}{4b\log b/r}$ *and complexity of the query functions is the complexity of computation of* ϕ *plus* $O(n)$.

4.2 An Analogue of the `KM` Algorithm

Our learning algorithms will be based on a weaker analogue of the `KM` algorithm implemented in the SQ-$\mathcal{D}_\rho$ model. It will find all the "heavy" Fourier coefficients of degree lower than ℓ in time polynomial in 2^ℓ thus allowing only the Fourier coefficients with degree bounded by $c\log n$ to be found efficiently.

Particularly, for the target function f, given parameters n, θ, ℓ and δ it will, with probability at least $1-\delta$, find the set of $S \subseteq \{0,1\}^n$ with the following properties:

1. For all a, if $|\hat{f}(a)| \geq \theta$ and $w(a) \leq \ell$ then $a \in S$
2. For all $a \in S$, $|\hat{f}(a)| \geq \theta/2$.

We say that such a set possesses the *large Fourier coefficient property for function* f, *threshold* θ *and degree* ℓ (this property can be defined for any real-valued function).

The `KM` algorithm is based on the subroutine that estimates the sum of squares of all the coefficients for vectors starting with given prefix. In the same fashion our algorithm will be based on ability to estimate weighted sum of squares of all the coefficients for vectors starting with given prefix. Particularly, for $0 \leq k \leq n$ and $\alpha \in \{0,1\}^k$ denote

$$S^\rho_\alpha(f) = \sum_{b\in\{0,1\}^{n-k}} \hat{f}^2(\alpha b)(1-2\rho)^{2w(b)} \ .$$

Lemma 2. *There exists an SQ-*$\mathcal{D}_\rho$ *randomized algorithm* $\mathcal{C}$ *that for any target function* f, *prefix vector* α *of length at most* n *and confidence* δ, $\mathcal{C}(n, \alpha, \tau, \delta)$ *returns, with probability at least* $1-\delta$, *a value estimating* $S^\rho_\alpha(f)$ *within* τ. *It runs in* $O(\tau^{-2}\log(1/\delta))$ *time and tolerance of its queries is bounded from below by* $\tau/6$.

Proof: Let k denote the length of α and let $p = [\frac{1}{2}]^k[\rho]^{n-k}$ and $\alpha_0 = \alpha[0]^{n-k}$. Denote by $p \oplus x$ probability vector for which $(p \oplus x)_i = p_i$ if $x_i = 0$ and $(p \oplus x)_i = 1 - p_i$ if $x_i = 1$. It is easy to see that if $p \in \{\rho, 1/2, 1-\rho\}^n$ then $p \oplus x \in \{\rho, 1/2, 1-\rho\}^n$ and that $D_{p \oplus x}(y) = D_p(x \oplus y)$. The algorithm is based on the following equation

$$S_\alpha^\rho(f) = \mathbf{E}_{x \sim U}\left[\mathbf{E}_{y \sim D_{p\oplus x}}[f(y)\chi_{\alpha_0}(x \oplus y)]\right]^2 .$$

To prove it denote

$$\pi(x) \triangleq \mathbf{E}_{y \sim D_{p\oplus x}}[f(y)\chi_{\alpha_0}(x \oplus y)] .$$

Since by Parseval equality for every function f, $\mathbf{E}_{x\sim U}[f^2(x)] = \sum_{a\in\{0,1\}^n} \hat{f}^2(a)$, it is enough to prove that

$$\pi(x) = \sum_{b\in\{0,1\}^{n-k}} \hat{f}(\alpha b)(1-2\rho)^{w(b)}\chi_{\alpha b}(x) .$$

This can be proved as follows

$$\begin{aligned}
\pi(x) = \mathbf{E}_{y \sim D_{p\oplus x}}[f(y)\chi_{\alpha_0}(x \oplus y)] &= \sum_{y\in\{0,1\}^n} f(y)\chi_{\alpha_0}(x\oplus y)D_{p\oplus x}(y) \\
&= \sum_{y\in\{0,1\}^n} f(y)\chi_{\alpha_0}(x\oplus y)D_p(x\oplus y) \\
&= \sum_{z\in\{0,1\}^n} f(x\oplus z)\chi_{\alpha_0}(z)D_p(z) \\
&= \mathbf{E}_{z\sim D_p}[f(x\oplus z)\chi_{\alpha_0}(z)] \\
&= \mathbf{E}_{z\sim D_p}\left[\sum_{a\in\{0,1\}^n} \hat{f}(a)\chi_a(x\oplus z)\chi_{\alpha_0}(z)\right] \\
&= \mathbf{E}_{z\sim D_p}\left[\sum_{a\in\{0,1\}^n} \hat{f}(a)\chi_a(x)\chi_{a\oplus\alpha_0}(z)\right] \\
&= \sum_{a\in\{0,1\}^n} \hat{f}(a)\chi_a(x)\mathbf{E}_{z\sim D_p}[\chi_{a\oplus\alpha_0}(z)].
\end{aligned}$$

But since $p = [\frac{1}{2}]^k[\rho]^{n-k}$ and $\alpha_0 = \alpha[0]^{n-k}$,

$$\mathbf{E}_{z\sim D_p}[\chi_{a\oplus\alpha_0}(z)] = \prod_{i\in\{1,..n\}} 1 - p_i + p_i(-1)^{a_i\oplus\alpha_{0,i}} = \prod_{i\in\{1,..n\},a_i\oplus\alpha_{0,i}=1} (1-2p_i) =$$

$$\left(\prod_{i\in\{1,..k\},a_i\neq\alpha_i} 0\right)\left(\prod_{i\in\{k+1,..n\},a_i=1} (1-2\rho)\right),$$

i.e., if $a = \alpha b$ then $\mathbf{E}_{z \sim D_p}[\chi_{a \oplus \alpha_0}(z)] = (1-2\rho)^{w(b)}$, otherwise $\mathbf{E}_{z \sim D_p}[\chi_{a \oplus \alpha_0}(z)] = 0$. This finishes the proof of the required identity.

All we need now is to estimate $\mathbf{E}_{x \sim U}[\pi^2(x)]$. By the definition of $\pi(x)$, for every x_i, we can estimate $\pi(x_i)$ within $\tau/6$ using a statistical query $(f(x)\chi_{\alpha_0}(x_i \oplus x), \tau/6, D_{p \oplus \alpha_0})$ and we can assume that the estimate has absolute value of at most 1. Hence by squaring this estimate we get an estimate for $\pi^2(x_i)$ within $\tau/2$. Now, by applying Hoeffding's lemma we get that using $H(\tau/2, 1, \delta)$ random samples will give us the required estimate. Since asking a query requires $O(1)$ time, the complexity of the algorithm is $O(\tau^{-2} \log(1/\delta))$. □

With algorithm $\mathcal{C}$ we are now ready to describe the Bounded Sieve.

Theorem 2. *There exists an SQ-$\mathcal{D}_\rho$ randomized algorithm* $\mathtt{BS}_\rho$ *that for any target concept f, threshold $\theta > 0$, confidence $\delta > 0$ and degree bound $0 \leq \ell \leq n$,* $\mathtt{BS}_\rho(n, \theta, \ell, \delta)$ *returns, with probability at least $1-\delta$, the set with the large Fourier coefficient property for function f, threshold θ and degree ℓ. Its running time is $\tilde{O}(n(2^\ell)^{-6\log(1-2\rho)}\theta^{-6}\log(1/\delta))$. Tolerance of queries is bounded from below by $(2^\ell)^{2\log(1-2\rho)}\theta^2/24$.*

Proof: If there is at least one coefficient greater than θ with degree lower than ℓ for the parity function of vector starting with α then $S_\alpha^\rho(f)$ is at least $(1-2\rho)^{2\ell}\theta^2 = 2^{2\log(1-2\rho)\ell}\theta^2 = 2^{-c_0\ell}\theta^2$ for a positive constant $c_0 = -2\log(1-2\rho)$. All the coefficients for the vectors starting with α can be separated into two disjoint sets — those for the vectors that start with $\alpha 0$ and those for the vectors that start with $\alpha 1$. With these observations and the procedure for estimating $S_\alpha^\rho(f)$ we can write a recursive subroutine $\mathtt{SA}$ that for every α returns all the vectors from the required set that start with α. $\mathtt{SA}$ is called recursively only when $S_\alpha^\rho(f) \geq 3b/4 - b/4 = b/2$. Since $\sum_{\alpha \in \{0,1\}^k} S_\alpha^\rho(f) \leq \sum_a \hat{f}^2(a) = 1$, $\mathtt{SA}$ will be invoked at most $2 \cdot 2^{c_0\ell}\theta^2$ times for each length of α, i.e., there will be at most $2n2^{2c_0\ell}\theta^{-2}$ calls to $\mathtt{SA}$. To find all the required coefficients we invoke $\mathtt{SA}$ for an empty prefix. Lemma 2 gives the required complexity bounds. □

In our future applications we will need to find the Fourier coefficients not only of a boolean target f but also of any real-valued function involving $f(x)$. Thus we extend $\mathtt{BS}$ as follows.

Theorem 3. *Let $\phi : \{0,1\}^n \times \{-1,1\} \to \mathbb{R}$ be any real-valued function. There exists an SQ-$\mathcal{D}_\rho$ randomized algorithm* $\mathtt{BS}'_\rho$ *that for every target concept f, positive threshold θ, confidence $\delta > 0$, degree bound $0 \leq \ell \leq k$ and β that bounds $L_\infty(\phi)$,* $\mathtt{BS}'_\rho(n, \phi, \beta, \theta, \ell, \delta)$ *returns, with probability at least $1-\delta$, the set with the large Fourier coefficient property for function ϕ, threshold θ and degree ℓ. It runs in $\tilde{O}(n(2^\ell)^{-6\log(1-2\rho)}\theta^{-6}\beta^2\log(1/\delta))$ time and tolerance of queries is bounded from below by $\tilde{\Omega}(\beta^{-2}(2^\ell)^{2\log(1-2\rho)}\theta^2)$. Complexity of query functions is bounded by $O(\tau) + O(n)$, where τ is the complexity of computation of ϕ.*

According to Lemma 1, using the procedure $\mathtt{RVMEAN}$ we can make statistical queries for ϕ in the same fashion as for f. Thus the previous proof with insignificant modifications is applicable in this case.

4.3 Learning Decision Trees

Below we will show the first application of the $\mathtt{BS}_\rho$ algorithm. We prove that the class of decision trees is learnable in SQ-$\mathcal{D}_\rho$ model. For this and ongoing applications we take $\rho = \frac{1}{4}$. This makes $-\log(1-2\rho)$ to be 1. Let DT-size(f) denote the size (number of leaves) of minimal decision tree representation of f.

Theorem 4. *There exists an SQ-$\mathcal{D}_{\frac{1}{4}}$ randomized algorithm* `DT-learn` *that for any target concept f, $s =$DT-size(f), $\epsilon > 0$ and $\delta > 0$,* `DT-learn`(n, s, ϵ, δ) *with probability at least $1 - \delta$ returns ϵ-approximation to f. The algorithm runs in $\tilde{O}(ns^6\epsilon^{-6}\log(1/\delta))$ time. Tolerance of its queries is $\Omega(\epsilon^2 s^{-2})$.*

Proof: A simple corollary of two facts that are proven in [16] is that it is possible to approximate decision tree only by considering its "heavy" coefficients (this fact is used to learn DT's in [13]) and these coefficients have degree bounded by function logarithmic in size (of DT) and accuracy. This ensures that we can learns DTs by a single call to `BS` and estimation of coefficients for returned parity functions. □

4.4 Weak DNF Learning

Another simple application the Bounded Sieve algorithm is weak DNF learning in SQ-$\mathcal{D}_{\frac{1}{4}}$. It is based on the fact that every DNF expression has a "heavy" Fourier coefficient of "low" degree. Below we prove generalization of this fact that will also be required for our future application.

Lemma 3. *Let f be a boolean function, s be a DNF-size(f) and D be a distribution over X. There exists a parity function χ_a such that $E_D[f\chi_a] \geq \frac{1}{2s+1}$ and $w(a) \leq \log((2s+1)L_\infty(2^n D))$.*

Proof: By Fact 8 in [10] there exists a parity function χ_a such that $E_D[f\chi_a] \geq \frac{1}{2s+1}$. Let $A = \{i \mid a_i = 1\}$. As it can be seen from the proof of the fact, $A \subseteq T$, where T is a term of f (a set of literals and a boolean function it represents) and $\mathbf{Pr}_D[T = 1] \geq \frac{1}{2s+1}$. On the other hand,

$$\mathbf{Pr}_D[T = 1] = \sum_{x, T(x)=1} D(x) < 2^{-|T|} 2^n L_\infty(D) \ .$$

Thus $w(a) = |A| \leq |T| \leq \log((2s+1)L_\infty(2^n D))$. □

Let DNF-size(f) denote the size (number of terms) of minimal DNF representation of f.

Theorem 5. *There exists an SQ-$\mathcal{D}_{\frac{1}{4}}$ randomized algorithm* `UWDNF` *that for any target concept f, $s =$DNF-size(f), $\epsilon > 0$ and $\delta \geq 0$,* `UWDNF`(n, s, δ) *returns, with probability at least $1 - \delta$, $(\frac{1}{2} - \frac{1}{6s})$-approximation to f. The algorithm runs in $\tilde{O}(ns^6\log(1/\delta))$ time. Tolerance of its queries is $\Omega(s^{-2})$. The weak hypothesis is parity function (possibly negated).*

Proof: By Lemma 3 call to $\mathtt{BS}_{\frac{1}{4}}(n, \theta = \frac{1}{2s+1}, \ell = \log(2s+1), \delta)$ returns, with probability at least $1-\delta$, a set containing at least one vector. Among the returned vectors we can easily find vector b such that χ_b or its negation will give an $(\frac{1}{2} - \frac{1}{6s})$-approximation to the target. By Theorem 2 the running time of this invocation will be $\tilde{O}(ns^6 \log(1/\delta))$ and tolerance of queries is $\Omega(s^{-2})$.

5 Strongly Learning DNF in SQ-$\mathcal{D}_{\frac{1}{4}}$

Certainly, the next interesting question is whether we can strongly learn DNF in SQ-$\mathcal{D}_{\frac{1}{4}}$. We answer this question positively by following the way used by Jackson in his proof of DNF learnability. The proof consists of two components. The first one is weak DNF learning with respect to any given distribution (although efficient only on distributions that are polynomially close to uniform). The second one is Freund's boosting technique that boosts the weak learner to a strong learner. First we present the required weak learner.

Theorem 6. *Let f be a boolean function, s =DNF-size(f) and let D_f be a computable probability distribution over the sample space. The computation of $D_f(x)$ may involve the value of $f(x)$. There exists a randomized SQ-$\mathcal{D}_{\frac{1}{4}}$ algorithm $\mathtt{WDNF}_{\frac{1}{4}}$ such that for the target function f, confidence $\delta > 0$ and β that bounds $L_\infty(2^n D_f)$, $\mathtt{WDNF}_{\frac{1}{4}}(n, s, D_f, \beta, \delta)$ finds, with probability at least $1-\delta$, a boolean function h that $(\frac{1}{2} - \frac{1}{6s})$-approximates f. The running time of the algorithm is $\tilde{O}(n\beta^8 s^{12} \log(1/\delta))$. The tolerance of its queries is lower bounded by $\tilde{\Omega}(\beta^{-4}s^{-4})$. Complexity of its query functions is the time complexity of D_f plus $O(n)$. The weak hypothesis is parity function(possibly negated).*

Proof: As it is proved in Lemma 3 for every DNF expression f there exists a parity function χ_b such that $|\mathbf{E}_{D_f}[f\chi_b]| \geq \frac{1}{2s+1}$ and

$$w(b) \leq \log((2s+1)L_\infty(2^n D_f)) \leq \log((2s+1)\beta) .$$

$\mathbf{E}_{D_f}[f\chi_b] = \mathbf{E}[2^n D_f f \chi_b]$ thus in order to find a parity function that weakly approximates f with respect to D_f we can find the "heavy" Fourier coefficients of function $2^n D_f f$. This means that by invoking

$$\mathtt{BS}'_{\frac{1}{4}}(n, \phi = 2^n D_f f, \beta, \theta = \frac{1}{2s+1}, \ell = \log((2s+1)\beta), \delta)$$

and then proceeding as in `UWDNF` we can find the required weak approximator. By Theorem 3 we get that all the complexities are as stated.

The next step is adapting Freund's boosting technique for SQ-$\mathcal{D}_\rho$ model. The main advantage of Freund's booster `F1` utilized by Jackson is that it requires only weak learning with respect to polynomially computable distributions that are polynomially close to the uniform distribution (i.e., $L_\infty(D) \leq p(n, s, \epsilon)$ for some polynomial p).

Below we are going to give the brief account of the Freund's boosting technique and in particular his `F1` algorithm for the PAC learning with respect to distribution D. Detailed discussion of the technique can be found in [7] and in [10].

As input, F1 is given positive ϵ, δ, and γ, a weak learner WL that produces $(\frac{1}{2}-\gamma)$–approximate hypotheses for functions in a function class $\mathcal{F}$, and an example oracle $\mathrm{EX}(f, D)$ for some $f \in \mathcal{F}$. The WL is assumed to take the example oracle for some distribution D' and confidence parameter δ' as inputs and produce $(\frac{1}{2}-\gamma)$–approximate hypothesis with probability at least $1-\delta'$. Given these inputs, F1 steps sequentially through k stages (k is given below). At each stage i, $0 \le i \le k-1$ F1 generates distribution function D_i, runs WL on simulated oracle $\mathrm{EX}(f, D_i)$ and (with high probability) gets a $(\frac{1}{2}-\gamma)$–approximate hypothesis w_i. Finally, F1 generates its hypothesis using majority function MAJ of all the w_i.

For every i, value of $D_i(x)$ can be found easily using values of the previous hypotheses at point x and $f(x)$. Thus with our weak learner used to learn with respect to D_i the technique will gives us the required strongly approximating hypothesis. In Figure 1 we give a straightforward implementation of the adaptation.

Input: Example oracle $STAT(f, \mathcal{D}_{\frac{1}{4}})$; DNF-size s of f; $\epsilon > 0$; $\delta > 0$
Output: h such that, with probability at least $1-\delta$, $\mathbf{Pr}_U[f = h] \ge 1-\epsilon$

$\gamma = 1/6s$; $k \leftarrow \frac{1}{2}\gamma^{-2}\ln(4/\epsilon)$
$w_0 \leftarrow$UWDNF$_{\frac{1}{4}}(n, s, \delta/k)$
for $i \leftarrow 1, ..., k-1$ **do**
  $r_i(x) \equiv |\{0 \le j < i | w_j(x) = f(x)\}|$
  $B(j; n, p) \equiv \binom{n}{j} p^j (1-p)^{n-j}$
  $\tilde{\alpha}_r^i \equiv B(\lfloor k/2 \rfloor - r; k-j-1, 1/2+\hat{\gamma})$ if $i - k/2 < r \le k/2$, $\tilde{\alpha}_r^i \equiv 0$ otherwise
  $\alpha_r^i \equiv \tilde{\alpha}_r^i / \max_{r'=0,\ldots,i-1}\{\tilde{\alpha}_{r'}^i\}$
  $\theta \equiv \epsilon^3/57$
  $E_\alpha \leftarrow$RVMEAN$(\alpha_{r_i(x)}^i, 1, \theta/3, U)$
  if $E_\alpha \le \frac{2}{3}\theta$ **then**
    $k \leftarrow i$
    break do
  endif
  $D_i'(x) \equiv U(x)\alpha_{r_i(x)}^i / E_\alpha$
  $w_i \leftarrow$WDNF$_{\frac{1}{4}}(n, s, D_i', 3/(2\theta), \delta/k)$
enddo
$h(x) \equiv MAJ(w_0(x), w_1(x), ..., w_{k-1}(x))$
return h

Fig. 1. Adaptation of Freund's algorithm for boosting a weak learner in the PAC model to SQ-$\mathcal{D}_{\frac{1}{4}}$

As in Jackson's adaptation of F1 we neglected the fact that D_i' is only the estimate of the correct D_i since E_α is only the estimation of the true expectation. To be more precise, there is a constant $c_i \in [1/2, 3/2]$ such that for all x, $D'_i(x) = c_i D_i(x)$. Now consider the functional impact of supplying this approximate distribution rather than true distribution to $\mathtt{WDNF}_{\frac{1}{4}}$. $\mathtt{WDNF}_{\frac{1}{4}}$ uses its given distribution for exactly one purpose: to find the "heavy" Fourier coefficients of the function $2^n D_f f$. Since the Fourier transform is a linear operator (i.e., $\hat{cg}(a) = c\hat{g}(a)$) we can be certain that $2^n D'_i f$ has a Fourier coefficient with absolute value of at least $\frac{1}{6s}$. Thus by slightly modifying $\mathtt{WDNF}_{\frac{1}{4}}$ we can handle this problem. As a result of the modification $\mathtt{WDNF}_{\frac{1}{4}}$ will return hypothesis that $(\frac{1}{2} - \frac{1}{12s})$- approximates target function. These modifications may increase the running time of the algorithm only by a small constant and thus do not affect our analysis.

Our last concern is the complexity of this algorithm. Total number of phases executed will be $O(s^2 \log \epsilon^{-1})$. Clearly the "heaviest" part of each phase is the execution of the weak learner. By Theorem 6 the running time of each call to $\mathtt{WDNF}_{\frac{1}{4}}$ is $\tilde{O}(ns^{12}\epsilon^{-24} \log(1/\delta))$. Thus the total running time of the algorithm is $\tilde{O}(ns^{14}\epsilon^{-24} \log(1/\delta))$. The tolerance of queries is $\tilde{\Omega}(s^{-4}\epsilon^{12})$. The complexity of query functions is as complexity of $\alpha^i_{r_i(x)}$ plus $O(n)$. All the $O(k^2) = \tilde{O}(s^4)$ possible values of $\alpha^i_{r_i(x)}$ can be evaluated in advance, i.e., complexity of query functions will be $O(n)$. The dependence on ϵ can be significantly reduced using a recent hybrid boosting algorithm by Bshouty and Gavinsky. In this algorithm for every stage i, $L_\infty(D_i) = \tilde{O}(\epsilon^{-1})$. The algorithm can be adapted to SQ-$\mathcal{D}$ in the same way as Freund's algorithm. Thus dependence of running time on ϵ becomes ϵ^{-8} and dependence of tolerance becomes ϵ^4.

6 Learning with Attribute Noise in Membership Queries

Now we would like to show that it is possible to implement BS using membership queries with random product attribute noise of known rate.

6.1 Noise Model

For a constant probability vector $p \in (0,1)^n$ and D_p the product distribution defined by p, we define noisy membership oracle $\mathrm{MEM}^p(f)$ as follows. For a query x, $\mathrm{MEM}^p(f)$ chooses randomly (and independently of any previous queries) b according to the distribution D_p and returns $f(b \oplus x)$. This type of noise is called random product attribute noise. It was previously considered as appearing in example oracle $\mathrm{EX}(f, D)$ (see [18],[8] and [5] for more details). The oracle $\mathrm{EX}^p(f, U)$ can be easily simulated using $\mathrm{MEM}^p(f)$ and thus we will not use it in our applications.

We may also add a classification noise to the oracle and define $\mathrm{MEM}^{p,\eta}(f)$. This classification noise does not have to be persistent as a learner cannot get a label of the same point twice (with any non-negligible probability).

6.2 Offsetting Attribute Noise in BS

Let $p \in (0,1)^n$ be a probability vector and $\tau > 0$ be a constant such that for all i, $|p_i - 1/2| \geq \tau$.

Theorem 7. *Given p as above, the Bounded Sieve can be efficiently implemented using access to $MEM^p(f)$ oracle.*

Proof: A query to the oracle $\mathrm{MEM}^p(f)$ at point y returns $f(y \oplus b)$ where b is chosen randomly according to the distribution D_p, thus by the Hoeffding's formula we can get an estimate for

$$f^p(y) \triangleq \mathbf{E}_{b \sim D_p} f(y \oplus b).$$

Obviously $L_\infty(f^p) \leq 1$ thus by further sampling we can estimate (with any desired accuracy σ and probability $1-\delta$) the values

$$S^{\rho}_{\alpha}(f^p) = \mathbf{E}_{x \sim U}\left[\mathbf{E}_{y \sim D_{p \oplus x}}[f^p(y)\chi_{\alpha_0}(x \oplus y)]\right]^2 \text{ and } \hat{f^p}(a) = \mathbf{E}_{x \sim U}[f^p(x)\chi_a(x)]$$

as it is done in procedure $\mathcal{C}$ (see Lemma 2)(the running time will be polynomial in σ^{-1} and $\log(1/\delta)$). By using this estimate as in the original BS we can find the set with the large Fourier coefficients property for function f^p, threshold ϑ and degree ℓ in time polynomial in $n, \vartheta^{-1}, 2^\ell$ and $\log(1/\delta)$. But

$$\begin{aligned} f^p(y) = \mathbf{E}_{b \sim D_p} f(y \oplus b) &= \sum_{a \in \{0,1\}^n} \hat{f}(a)\mathbf{E}_{b \sim D_p}\chi_a(y \oplus b) \\ &= \sum_{a \in \{0,1\}^n} [\hat{f}(a)\mathbf{E}_{b \sim D_p}\chi_a(b)]\chi_a(y) \ , \end{aligned}$$

i.e., we have that for all a, $\hat{f^p}(a) = \hat{f}(a)\mathbf{E}_{b \sim D_p}\chi_a(b)$. We can easily calculate the value

$$c_a \triangleq \mathbf{E}_{b \sim D_p}\chi_a(b) = \prod_{a_i = 1}(1 - 2p_i) \ .$$

By the properties of p, $|c_a| \geq (2\tau)^{w(a)}$. Thus if we run the above algorithm for the threshold $\vartheta = (2\tau)^\ell\theta$ we will get the set S' that contains the set with the large Fourier coefficient property for the function f, threshold θ and degree ℓ. Size of S' is bounded by $(2\tau)^{-2\ell}\theta^{-2}$. In order to estimate the values of the coefficient $\hat{f}(a)$ with accuracy σ we estimate the coefficient $\hat{f^p}(a)$ with accuracy $\sigma|c_a| > (2\tau)^\ell\sigma$ and return $c_a^{-1}\hat{f^p}(a)$. Thus we can refine the set S' and return the set with the large Fourier coefficient property for the function f, threshold θ and degree ℓ. All the parts of the described algorithm run in time polynomial in $n, (2\tau)^{-\ell}\theta^{-1}$ and 2^ℓ, i.e., for a constant τ it is polynomial in n, θ^{-1} and 2^ℓ. □

Remark 1. When using $\mathrm{MEM}^{p,\eta}(f)$ oracle instead of $\mathrm{MEM}^p(f)$ in the above algorithm we can immediately offset the classification noise in a standard way (multiplying the expectation by $\frac{1}{1-2\eta}$).

By sole use of BS we can efficiently learn decision trees and weakly learn DNF expressions as described in Theorems 4 and 5.

7 Characterizing SQ-$\mathcal{D}$ Learnable Concept Classes

7.1 The Characterization

We start by showing a new and simple way to characterize weakly SQ–learnable concept classes. This characterization will then be extended to SQ-$\mathcal{D}$.

Our characterization is based on the fact that every SQ can be substituted by two SQs that are independent of the target function (i.e., query function ϕ does not depend on f) and two SQs for which query function equals $g(x)f(x)$ for some boolean function g. This fact is proven by the following equation :

$$\mathbf{E}_D[\psi(x, f(x))] = \mathbf{E}_D\left[\psi(x,-1)\frac{1-f(x)}{2} + \psi(x,1)\frac{1+f(x)}{2}\right] =$$

$$\frac{1}{2}\mathbf{E}_D[\psi(x,1)f(x)] - \frac{1}{2}\mathbf{E}_D[\psi(x,-1)f(x)] + \frac{1}{2}\mathbf{E}_D[\psi(x,1)+\psi(x,-1)] \; .$$

Thus we may assume that learning algorithms in SQ use only these types of queries. Moreover, we may assume that queries that are independent of target are not asked since their values may be estimated in advance. From this inspections we can directly obtain the following theorem.

Theorem 8. *Let $\mathcal{F}$ be a concept class weakly SQ–learnable with respect to D, particularly there exists an algorithm $\mathcal{A}$ that for $f \in \mathcal{F}$, such that size(f) = s, uses at most $p(n,s)$ queries of tolerance lower bounded by $\frac{1}{r(n,s)}$ to produce $(\frac{1}{2} - \frac{1}{q(n,s)})$-approximation to f. Let $r'(n,s) \triangleq max\{2r(n,s), q(n,s)\}$. There exists a collection of sets $\{W_s\}$ such that $|W_s| \leq p(n,s)+1$ and for every $f \in \mathcal{F}$, there exists $g \in W_{size(f)}$ that $(\frac{1}{2} - \frac{1}{r'(n,size(f))})$-approximates f with respect to D (or $\{W_s\}$ $(\frac{1}{2} - \frac{1}{r'(n,s)})$-approximates $\mathcal{F}$ with respect to D for short).*

Proof: According to the above discussion we may assume that all the queries that $\mathcal{A}$ asks are for query functions of the form fg. We build the set W_s as follows. We simulate algorithm $\mathcal{A}(n,s)$ and for every query (fg_i, ρ) we add g_i to W_s and return the value 0 as a result of the query. We continue the simulation till it violates any of the complexity bounds of $\mathcal{A}$ or $\mathcal{A}$ stops and returns final hypothesis h. In the last case we also add h to W_s. First, by the definition of $S_{n,s}$, $|S_s| \leq p(n,s)+1$. Now, assume that $\{W_s\}$ does not $(\frac{1}{2} - \frac{1}{r'(n,s)})$–approximate $\mathcal{F}$, i.e., there exists $f \in \mathcal{F}$ such that s = size(f) and for every $g \in W_s$, $|\mathbf{E}_D[fg]| < \frac{2}{r'(n,s)}$. This means that in our simulation for building W_s we gave answers that are valid for oracle STAT(f,D). Thus by the validity of $\mathcal{A}$ it returns hypothesis h that $(\frac{1}{2} - \frac{1}{q(n,s)})$-approximates f, i.e., $h \in W_s$. This contradicts the assumption that $|\mathbf{E}_D[fh]| < \frac{2}{r'(n,s)} \leq \frac{2}{q(n,s)}$. □

Remark 2. When the size of description of every function in $\mathcal{F}$ is bounded by some fixed polynomial in n, we can omit the s parameter in all the discussion and get a single set W of polynomial (in n) size that $(\frac{1}{2} - \frac{1}{r'(n)})$-approximates $\mathcal{F}$.

This characterization can be easily extended to SQ-$\mathcal{D}$ in the following way. Every query (fg, ρ, D') to STAT$(f, \mathcal{D})$ has its own distribution $D' \in \mathcal{D}$. Thus along with every function in the approximating collection of sets we need to record the distribution with respect to which function in $\mathcal{F}$ is approximated. Formally, we define sets in collection to contain function-distribution pairs and get the following theorem.

Theorem 9. *Let $\mathcal{F}$ be a class learnable in SQ-$\mathcal{D}$. For p and r' defined as in Theorem 8 there exists a collection of sets (of pairs) $\{W_s\}$ such that $|W_s| \leq p(n,s)+1$ and for every $f \in \mathcal{F}$ and $s = size(f)$ there exists $(g, D') \in W_s$ such that $D' \in \mathcal{D}$ and g $(\frac{1}{2} - \frac{1}{r'(n,s)})$-approximates f with respect to D' (or $\{W_s\}$ $(\frac{1}{2} - \frac{1}{r'(n,s)})$-approximates $\mathcal{F}$ with respect to $\mathcal{D}$ for short).*

7.2 Applications

Although the characterization we gave for SQ is not equivalent to SQ-DIM given in [4] it is applied in the very similar way. In fact, is easy to see that the main result of application of SQ-DIM (concerning the SQ-learnability of class containing superpolynomial number of parity functions) can be as well easily obtained using our characterization.

Our characterization of SQ-$\mathcal{D}$ learnable classes can be used to show the limitations of SQ-$\mathcal{D}_\rho$ model. $\mathtt{BS}_\rho$ learns the class of all parity function containing at most $O(\log n)$ variables (with respect to U). On the other hand, we will show that class of all parity function containing at most $c(n)\log n$ variables for an unbounded $c(n)$ cannot be learned in SQ-$\mathcal{D}_\rho$. For this purpose we denote by $A^k = \{0,1\}^k[0]^{n-k}$, and let PAR^k denote the class of all parity functions for vectors in A^k, i.e., all parity functions based on the first k variables. In fact, we give somewhat stronger result.

Theorem 10. *Let $c(n)$ any unbounded function. $PAR^{c(n)\log n}$ is not weakly learnable in SQ-$\mathcal{D}_\rho$ for any unbounded $c(n)$.*

Proof: Assume that the theorem is not true. By Theorem 9 (with Remark 2) there exist polynomials $p(n)$ and $r(n)$ and set of pairs W such that $|W| \leq p(n)$ and for every $f \in$PAR there exists $(g, D') \in W$, where $D' \in \mathcal{D}_\rho$, such that $\mathbf{E}_{D'}[g\chi_a] \geq 1/r(n)$. This means that $\sum_{1\leq i\leq |W|} \mathbf{E}^2_{D_i}[g_i\chi_a] \geq 1/r^2(n)$. And thus

$$\sum_{a\in A^k} \sum_{1\leq i\leq |W|} \mathbf{E}^2_{D_i}[g_i\chi_a] \geq |A^k|/r^2(n) .$$

This means that there exists i such that

$$\sum_{a\in A^k} \mathbf{E}^2_{D_i}[g_i\chi_a] \geq |A^k|/(|W|r^2(n)) \geq |A^k|/(p(n)r^2(n)) .$$

Or, if we denote by U^k a uniform distribution over A^k, then we get that

$$\mathbf{E}_{a\sim U^k}\left[\mathbf{E}^2_{D_i}[g_i\chi_a]\right] \geq 1/(p(n)r^2(n)) . \quad (1)$$

On the other hand,

$$\mathbf{E}_{a\sim U^k}\left[\mathbf{E}^2_{D_i}[g_i\chi_a]\right] = \mathbf{E}_{x\sim D_i}[\mathbf{E}_{y\sim D_i}[g_i(x)g_i(y)\mathbf{E}_{a\sim U^k}[\chi_a(x\oplus y)]]] \ .$$

But

$$\lambda(x) \triangleq \mathbf{E}_{a\sim U^k}[\chi_a(x)] = \mathbf{E}_{a\sim U^k}[\chi_{x_{[1,k]}}(a_{[1,k]})] = \begin{cases} 0 \ x_{[1,k]} \neq [0]^k \\ 1 \ x_{[1,k]} = [0]^k \end{cases}$$

We denote by D_i^k distribution induced by D_i over $[0]^k\{0,1\}^{n-k}$. Using the fact that D_i is a product distribution we can write the expression we are evaluating as follows

$$\mathbf{E}_{x\sim D_i}\left[\sum_{y\in\{0,1\}^n} D_i(y)g_i(x)g_i(y)\lambda(x\oplus y)\right] =$$

$$\mathbf{E}_{x\sim D_i}\left[\sum_{y\in 0^k\{0,1\}^{n-k}} \mathbf{Pr}_{D_i}[x_{[1,k]} = [0]^k]D_i^k(y_{[k+1,n]})g_i(x)g_i(y)\right] =$$

$$\mathbf{Pr}_{D_i}[x_{[1,k]} = [0]^k]\mathbf{E}_{x\sim D_i}\left[\mathbf{E}_{y\sim D_i^k}[g_i(x)g_i(y)]\right] \leq$$

$$\mathbf{Pr}_{D_i}[x_{[1,k]} = [0]^k] \leq (1-\rho)^k \qquad (2)$$

For $k = c(n)\log n$, $(1-\rho)^k = n^{-c_0 c(n)}$ for a positive constant c_0. As $c(n)$ is unbounded, equation 1 contradicts equation 2. □

The last theorem may also be used to prove that the set of concept classes learnable in the PAC model with classification noise of constant rate is not contained in the set of concept classes weakly learnable in SQ-$\mathcal{D}_{\frac{1}{4}}$. This result can be obtained by combining our result with the following theorem for $k = \log n \log\log n$ (see Theorem 2 in [6])

Theorem 11. *PAR^k for noise rate η equal to any constant less than $\frac{1}{2}$, can be learned with respect to the uniform distribution using number of samples and total computation time $2^{O(k/\log k)}$.*

Another interesting application of our characterization is to demonstrate that PAR - the class of all parity functions possesses some inherent hardness for any statistics based learning. For this purpose we give the following definition. We say that a distribution class $\mathcal{D}$ is *biased* if there exist a polynomial $p(n)$ such that $L_\infty(\mathcal{D}) \geq \frac{1}{p(n)}$. We may notice that if a distribution class $\mathcal{D}$ is biased then a non-uniform learning algorithm may get a value the target function at the "biased" point. This ability contradicts the idea of statistical learning and, on the other hand, is the main element of known algorithms for learning of parity functions.

Theorem 12. *Let $\mathcal{D}$ be a class of distributions. If $\mathcal{D}$ is not biased then for every $D\in\mathcal{D}$, PAR is not weakly learnable in SQ-$\mathcal{D}$ model with respect D.*

References

1. Javed Aslam, Scott Decatur. General bounds on statistical query learning and PAC learning with noise via hypothesis boosting. In *Proceedings of 34-th Annual Symposium on Foundations of Computer Science*, pp. 282–291, 1993.
2. Dana Angluin, Philip Laird. Learning from noisy examples. In *Machine Learning,* 2(4) pp.343–370, 1988.
3. Dana Angluin, Michael Kharitonov. When won't membership queries help? In *Proceedings of the 23-rd Annual ACM Symposium on Theory of Computing*, 1991, pp. 454–454.
4. Avrim Blum, Merrick Furst, Jeffrey Jackson, Michael Kearns, Yishay Mansour, Steven Rudich. Weakly learning DNF and characterizing statistical query learning using Fourier analysis. In *Proceedings of the 26-th Annual ACM Symposium on the Theory of Computing*, pp. 253–262, 1994.
5. Nader Bshouty, Jeffrey Jackson, Christino Tamon. Uniform-distribution attribute noise learnability. In *Proceedings of the 12-th Annual Conference on COLT*, pp. 75–80, 1999.
6. Avrim Blum, Adam Kalai, Hal Wasserman. Noise-tolerant learning, the parity problem and the Statistical Query model. In *Proceedings of the 32-th Annual ACM Symposium on Theory of Computing*, pp. 435–440, 2000.
7. Yoav Freund. Boosting a weak learning algorithm by majority. In *Proceedings of the Third Annual Workshop on COLT*, pp. 202–216, 1990.
8. Sally Goldman, Robert Sloan. Can PAC learning algorithms tolerate random attribute noise? In *Algorithmica*, 14(1) pp. 70–84, 1995.
9. Sally Goldman, Michael Kearns, Robert Shapire. Exact identification of circuits using fixed points of amplification functions, In *SIAM Journal on Computing, 22 (1993)*, pp. 705–726.
10. Jeffrey Jackson. An efficient membership-query algorithm for learning DNF with respect to the uniform distribution. In *Proceedings of the 35th Annual Symposion on Foundations of Computer Science*, pp. 42–53, 1993.
11. Jeffrey Jackson, Eli Shamir, Clara Shwartzman. Learning with queries corrupted by classification noise. In *Proceedings of Fifth Israel Symposium on Theory of Computing and Systems*, pp. 45–53, 1997.
12. Michael Kearns. Efficient noise-tolerant learning from statistical queries. In *Proceedings of the Forth Annual Workshop on COLT*, pp. 392–401, 1993.
13. Eyal Kushilevitz, Yishay Mansour. Learning decision trees using the Fourier spectrum. In *Proceedings of the 23-rd Annual Symposium on Theory of Computing,* pages 455–464.
14. Michael Kearns, Robert Shapire, Linda Sellie. Toward efficient agnostic learning. In *Proceedings of the Fifth Annual Workshop on COLT*, pp. 341–352, 1992.
15. Nathan Linial, Yishay Mansour, Noam Nisan. Constant depth circuits, Fourier transform, and learnability. *In Proceedings of the 31-st Symposium on the Foundations of Computer Science,* pp. 574–579, 1989.
16. Yishay Mansour. Learning Boolean Functions via the Fourier Transform. In *Theoretical Advances in Neural Computation and Learning*, (V.P. Roychodhury and K-Y. Siu and A. Orlitsky, ed.), 391–424, 1994.
17. Eli Shamir, Clara Shwartzman. Learning by extended statistical queries and its relation to PAC learning. In *Proceedings of Second European Conference, EuroCOLT '95*, pp. 357–366, 1995.
18. George Shakelford, Dennis Volper. Learning $k-$DNF with noise in the attributes. In *Proceedings of the 1988 Workshop on COLT*, pp. 97–103, 1988.

Learning Monotone DNF from a Teacher That Almost Does Not Answer Membership Queries

Nader H. Bshouty[1*] and Nadav Eiron[2**]

[1] Department of Computer Science, Technion – Israel Institute of Technology, Haifa 32000, Israel. bshouty@cs.technion.ac.il

[2] IBM Almaden Research Center, 650 Harry Road, San Jose, CA, 95120, USA nadav@us.ibm.com

Abstract. We present results concerning the learning of Monotone DNF (MDNF) from Incomplete Membership Queries and Equivalence Queries. Our main result is a new algorithm that allows efficient learning of MDNF using Equivalence Queries and Incomplete Membership Queries with probability of $p = 1 - 1/\text{poly}(n,t)$ of failing. Our algorithm is expected to make

$$O\left(\left(\frac{tn}{1-p}\right)^2\right)$$

queries, when learning a MDNF formula with t terms over n variables. Note that this is polynomial for any failure probability $p = 1 - 1/\text{poly}(n,t)$. The algorithm's running time is also polynomial in t, n, and $1/(1-p)$. In a sense this is the best possible, as learning with $p = 1 - 1/\omega(\text{poly}(n,t))$ would imply learning MDNF, and thus also DNF, from equivalence queries alone.

* The research was supported by the fund for the promotion of research at the Technion. Part of this research was done at the University of Calgary, Calgary, Alberta, Canada.

** Some of the research described in this paper was conducted while this author was a graduate student at the Department of Computer Science, Technion – Israel Institute of Technology, Haifa, Israel.

D. Helmbold and B. Williamson (Eds.): COLT/EuroCOLT 2001, LNAI 2111, pp. 546–557, 2001.

1 Introduction

Angluin's exact learning model [1], using equivalence queries and membership queries, has attracted much attention in COLT literature so far. One of its biggest disadvantages, however, is its requirement of the membership oracle to be able to supply, on demand, the value of the target function at any point of its domain. To relax this requirement, the model of Incomplete Membership Queries was suggested by Angluin and Slonim [2]. In this model, some of the points cannot be queried: an MQ query for such a point returns the result "I don't know" instead of the value of the target function. Points for which MQs are not answered are chosen randomly and independently of each other. So far, this model was known to allow learning of functions not learnable by EQs alone, only if many of the MQs were answered (see, for example, [2], [6] and [5]).

In this work we show that even when the MQ oracle has a polynomially small probability of supplying an answer, Monotone DNF can still be efficiently learned. As Monotone DNF is not efficiently learnable from equivalence queries alone, this shows that even adding a very "weak" membership oracle to the equivalence oracle gives additional power to the learning algorithm. The idea behind our algorithm is that, at any stage, it is possible to find polynomially many points on which MQs may be asked, such that any one of them being answered would allow us to, again, generate polynomially many new points on which MQs may be asked. Our result improves upon the previous results that required a constant fraction of the queries to be answered for successful learning [5]. Note that this is the best possible, since an efficient learning algorithm that uses an incomplete membership oracle with sub-polynomial probability of answering queries should expect to never receive any answers to MQs, as it will make only polynomially many queries. Thus, efficient exact learning with an Incomplete Membership Oracle with probability less than polynomial of answering queries is equivalent to learning from EQs alone, and it is well known that learning MDNF from EQs alone implies the learning of DNF from EQs alone.

We also present a more accurate analysis of the Angluin-Slonim algorithm [2], that shows that this algorithm can actually learn MDNF with an Incomplete MQ oracle that has success probability that is poly-logarithmically small in the target size. This improves on the previous results known for the performance of that algorithm.

The rest of this paper is organized as follows: Section 2 formally defines the framework within which our results are presented, including the learning models used and the type of problems addressed. Section 3 briefly introduces our results. Section 4 includes a detailed presentation our main positive result, showing that Monotone DNF can be efficiently learned using Equivalence Queries and Incomplete Membership Queries of polynomially small probability of success. We conclude with discussion of our results and some open problems in Section 5. The improved analysis of the Angluin-Slonim algorithm is brought in the appendix.

2 Preliminaries

2.1 Exact Learning

The exact learning model was introduced by Angluin [1], with many variants of it defined over the years (for instance, in [7,8,3,4]). We first define some of the basic terms used in exact learning; We concern ourselves with learning boolean concepts. A learning algorithm is trying to identify a *target function* $f : \mathcal{X} \mapsto \{0,1\}$, which is known to have been chosen from a *concept class* $\mathcal{C}$, of boolean functions over an instance space, or domain $\mathcal{X}$. The learning process is successful if the algorithm outputs a hypothesis function h that is equivalent to f. The learning algorithm may query oracles. One type of oracle used is the Equivalence Oracle EQ. This oracle receives as input some hypothesis $h : \mathcal{X} \mapsto \{0,1\}$, and either answers 'YES', if $h \equiv f$, or else, answers with some counter-example $x \in \mathcal{X}$ for which $f(x) \neq h(x)$. A concept class $\mathcal{C}$ is said to be exactly learnable from equivalence queries, if there exists an algorithm such that for all $f \in \mathcal{C}$ and any equivalence oracle, the algorithm, using the equivalence oracle, will output, in polynomial time, a hypothesis h that is equivalent to f.

Another often-used oracle in exact learning is the membership oracle MQ. The membership oracle is given as input a point $x \in \mathcal{X}$, and returns as a result the value of the target function at the given point $f(x)$. The criterion for successful learning remains the same.

2.2 Monotone DNF

The concept class which we concern ourselves with is the class of Monotone DNF formulas. A Monotone DNF formula f over n variables $x_1, \ldots, x_n$ is the disjunction of terms, denoted $T_1, \ldots, T_t$. Each term is a monotone monomial in the variables over which the formula is defined.

We may regard an assignment x to the n variables as a binary vector. We further consider the lattice defined over these vectors by the component-wise "and" and "or" operators. This lattice implies the ordering such that $x \leq y$ iff $x_i \leq y_i$ for all $i \in \{1, \ldots, n\}$. Once this partial order is defined, we may uniquely define any monotone term by the minimal assignment that satisfies it. We refer to such an assignment as the *minterm* of a monotone term, and denote the monotone term whose minterm is x by $T(x)$. We denote by $\mathrm{wt}(x)$ the Hamming weight of the assignment x. Given a pair of assignments x and y, we define the distance between them, $\mathrm{dist}(x, y) \stackrel{\triangle}{=} \mathrm{wt}(x + y)$ where $x + y$ is the sum of x and y as vectors over $\mathrm{GF}(2)$. x and y are called d-close if $\mathrm{dist}(x, y) \leq d$. We say y is a descendant of x if $y < x$. For a natural number d, the d-descendants of x are all assignments y such that y is a descendant of x, and x and y are d-close.

2.3 Incomplete Membership Queries

One of the learning models with which we concern ourselves uses incomplete membership queries, originally introduced in [2]. This is a variant of the exact learning model, in which the learner is given access to an oracle MQ^p, called the Incomplete Membership Oracle of Probability p (where clear from the context, we will call it just the "Incomplete Membership Oracle", and drop the superscript p from the notation), in addition to the equivalence oracle EQ. MQ^p is a probabilistic function mapping the instance space $\mathcal{X}$ to the set $\{0, 1, \text{I don't know}\}$. When given as input a point $x \in \mathcal{X}$, MQ^p first checks to see if this point was ever given to it before. If so, it answers with the same answer it gave on the previous time. If not, it tosses a biased coin with probability p of landing on "heads". If it lands "heads", MQ^p answers "I don't know". Otherwise, it answers with $f(x)$.

3 Statement of Main Results

In this paper we present two new main results regarding the learnability of MDNF with an Incomplete MQ oracle. The first result is the following:

Theorem 1. *There exists an algorithm that, with probability at least $1 - \delta$, learns Monotone DNF from EQs plus incomplete MQs of probability p in time polynomial in n, the size of the target, $1/(1-p)$ and $\log 1/\delta$.*

Section 4 presents such a learning algorithm and its analysis. Note that, by using $p = 1 - 1/\mathrm{poly}(n, |f|)$, Theorem 1 implies:

Corollary 1. *It is possible to efficiently exact-learn Monotone DNF formulas from EQs and Incomplete MQs, even if MQs are answered with polynomially small probability.*

The second result, refers to the algorithm Angluin and Slonim [2] suggested for learning MDNF:

Theorem 2. *For any $p < 1 - 1/2^{\log^\alpha n}$ for any constant $\alpha < 1$, the time complexity of Angluin-Slonim's algorithm is*

$$tn^{O\left(\frac{\log \frac{1}{1-p}}{\log \log n}\right)}.$$

In particular, the algorithm runs in polynomial time for any

$$p = 1 - \frac{1}{poly(\log n)}.$$

The proof of this theorem is presented in the appendix.

4 A New Algorithm for Learning Monotone DNF with Incomplete Membership Queries

In this section we present an algorithm (see Figure 1) that exact-learns the class of Monotone DNF, using an Equivalence Oracle, and an Incomplete Membership Oracle. The algorithm we present runs in time polynomial in the size of the

Algorithm LearnFromIncomplete:

1. Initialization: $N \leftarrow \emptyset$, $P \leftarrow \emptyset$.
2. $x \leftarrow \mathrm{EQ}(0)$.
   If $x =$"YES" – output $f(x) \equiv 0$ and terminate.
3. Otherwise, let $B \leftarrow \{x\}$.
4. As long as no EQ was answered "YES", do:
   a) Remove from P all points x for which there exist $x' \in N$ such that $x' \geq x$ or for which there exists $x' \in B$ such that $x' \leq x$.
   b) Let $H \leftarrow \bigvee_{x \in P \cup B} T(x)$
      Ask $x \leftarrow \mathrm{EQ}(H)$.
      If $x =$ YES, output H and halt.
      If $H(x) = 1$, let $N \leftarrow N \cup \{x\}$, and goto 4a.
   c) For all $x' \in B$:
      let $z \leftarrow x \wedge x'$,
      let $b \leftarrow \mathrm{MQ}^p(z)$.
      If $b = 1$, insert z to B, remove x' from B.
      If $b = 0$, let $N \leftarrow N \cup \{z\}$.
      If $b =$"I don't know", let $P \leftarrow P \cup \{z\}$.
   d) If none of the MQs in step 4c were answered positively, insert x into B.

Fig. 1. LearnFromIncomplete – An algorithm for Learning Monotone DNF

target function (that is n – the number of variables, and t – the number of terms), $\log 1/\delta$, where δ is a confidence parameter, and $1/(1-p)$ where p is the probability that the Incomplete Membership Oracle does not answer a query.

First, we give an informal explanation of the algorithm: The algorithm works by maintaining three sets of points in $\mathcal{X}$. The set N contains points that are known to be negative. The set B contains points that are known to be positive. The set P contains points that are generated by taking the conjunction of a pair of points from B (which implies $|P| = O(|B|^2)$). Points in P for which the classification is known are moved to either B or N, depending on the classification. The algorithm also removes "redundent" points from B and N (a point x is redundent if it is covered by another point in the same set that implies x's classification).

The algorithm initializes N and P to be empty, and B to contain some positive point. It then progresses by presenting the function whose minterms are $B \cup P$ to the EQ oracle. If a negative counter-example is returned, it must imply that some point in P actually belongs in N. In that case, the algorithm will remove that point from P, and try the EQ again. If the result of the EQ is a positive counter-example, the algorithm will ask Incomplete MQs on all conjunctions of the new point with a point from B. The results are then stored in one of the three sets depending on the result of the queries. A formal analysis of the algorithm follows.

In the sequel, we assume that the target function f has t terms whose minterms are $M_1, \ldots, M_t$ (i.e., $f = \bigvee_{i=1}^{t} T(M_i)$). Furthermore, we denote by

B_i the following subset of B:

$$B_i \triangleq \{x \in B \;:\; x \geq M_i\}\,.$$

Lemma 1. *In each complete iteration of Step 4 of LearnFromIncomplete at least one of the following happens: Either a point x is inserted into B such that for all $i \in \{1, \ldots, t\}$, if $x \geq M_i$ then $B_i = \emptyset$, or, at least one MQ is asked on a point y such that for some i for which $y \geq M_i$, y has Hamming weight strictly less than that of any point in B_i. Furthermore, in the second case, this y was never queried before.*

Proof. The algorithm is such that the only way to finish an iteration of step 4 is if an equivalence query returns a positive counterexample. If the EQ returns a positive counter example x that satisfies that for all i, if $M_i \leq x$ then no other point exists in B_i then we are done with the proof. We therefore assume that we receive a positive counter example x such that there is some M_i such that $M_i \leq x$. Furthermore, let $x' \in B_i$ be a point with minimal Hamming weight in B_i. Consider the point $x \wedge x'$. Since x and x' both satisfy $T(M_i)$, we have that $f(x \wedge x') = 1$. Furthermore, since $T(x')$ was part of the hypothesis we used as input for the EQ oracle, we know that x is not above x' in the lattice order. Hence $x' \wedge x < x'$.

All that remains to be seen is that this point was never queried before. Indeed, had it been queried before, the result would have been either positive (in which case either $x' \wedge x$ itself, or some point below it would have been inserted into B), or it would have been answered with "I don't know", in which case it would have been inserted into P, and never be removed from it, as its true label is 1. In both cases, $T(x \wedge x')$ would have been one of the terms in the hypothesis passed to the EQ oracle, in contradiction with the fact that x is a positive counter example. Hence, $x' \wedge x$ was never passed to the Incomplete Membership Oracle before.

Lemma 2. *With probability at least $1-\delta$, Algorithm LearnFromIncomplete terminates after at most*

$$O\left(\frac{tn}{1-p}\log\frac{1}{\delta}\right)$$

iterations.

Proof. Consider the two options that we have for completing an iteration of step 4, according to Lemma 1: If the point we receive is covered only by minterms M_is for which their B_is were empty, then for at least one of these minterms, from now on, there will always be a point in B that belongs to it (i.e., for at least one B_i that was empty, it will never be empty anymore). Therefore, at most t iterations of step 4 may be such that all minterms below the counter-example returned from the EQ oracle do not have other points above them in B (i.e., the first case of Lemma 1 happens).

Consider the other option by which an iteration of step 4 may be completed, according to Lemma 1: Let i be as in the statement of Lemma 1. Let x' be a point with minimal Hamming weight in B_i. If the MQ on $x' \wedge x$ will be answered by the Incomplete Membership Oracle (which will happen with probability $1-p$, independent of other points in the run of the algorithm), the minimal Hamming weight for points in B_i will be strictly reduced. Since all points in B_i must have Hamming weight not less than that of M_i, and since no point can have Hamming weight greater than n, the minimal Hamming weight for a point in B_i may be lowered at most n times. Thus, for each $i \in \{1, \ldots, t\}$, at most n "successful" iterations, in which the query on $x' \wedge x$ is answered, may occur during the running of the algorithm. Since each iteration is "successful" for at least one term, with probability $1-p$, we have, by the Chernoff inequality, that after

$$O\left(\frac{tn}{1-p} \log \frac{1}{\delta}\right)$$

iterations, with probability $1-\delta$ we had nt successful iterations, meaning all minimal points in all the sets B_i are the minterms M_i themselves, which means the target was found, and the algorithm will terminate.

Lemma 3. *With probability at least $1-\delta$, each iteration of Step 4 Algorithm LearnFromIncomplete makes takes time at most:*

$$O\left(\left(\frac{tn}{1-p} \log \frac{1}{\delta}\right)^2\right).$$

Proof. In each iteration of Step 4, $|B|$ grows by at most 1. Hence, by Lemma 2, with probability at least $1-\delta$, $|B|$ will never be more than

$$O\left(\frac{tn}{1-p} \log \frac{1}{\delta}\right).$$

In each iteration, MQs are asked for every element in B (which takes $O(|B|)$ time). For each MQ asked, an element may be inserted into P. Thus the maximal size of P is $O(|B|^2)$ (since there are $|B|$ iterations, with possibly $|B|$ elements inserted in each one). Then, in the loop of Step 4a – Step 4b, in each iteration, at least one element is removed from P. Thus, there are at most $O(|B|^2)$ EQs made in that stage, before P is emptied, and a negative counter-example must be returned. All in all, the running time of a single iteration is $O(|B|^2)$. This completes the proof of this lemma.

Lemma 4. *Throughout the running of Algorithm LearnFromIncomplete, with probability at least $1-\delta$, at most*

$$O\left(\left(\frac{tn}{1-p} \log \frac{1}{\delta}\right)^2\right)$$

queries (both EQs and MQs) are made.

Proof. Clearly, in each iteration, at most $|B|$ MQs are made. Since $|B|$ is at most the total number of iterations, it follows from Lemma 2 that, w.h.p., at most

$$O\left(\left(\frac{tn}{1-p}\log\frac{1}{\delta}\right)^2\right)$$

membership queries are asked during the running of the algorithm. For each EQ asked, either a point is added to B (if a positive counter-example is returned), or a point is added to N (if a negative counter-example is returned). However, when a point is added to N, it causes at least one point to be removed from P. Thus, the total number of equivalence queries cannot be more than $|B|+|B|^2$ (as there are at most $|B|$ EQs answered positively, and at most $|P| \leq |B|^2$ answered negatively). Again, from Lemma 2, this gives the required bound on the number of equivalence queries.

The proof of Theorem 1 now becomes an immediate application of Lemmas 2 and 3.

5 Conclusion

In this work we have shown that, even when limited to answering a very small fraction of the queries (in a sense, the smallest fraction that can still be used by an efficient algorithm at all), the Membership Query Oracle adds significant power to the learner. We demonstrated how an Incomplete MQ oracle can still be used to allow exact learning of Monotone DNF. Two natural questions arise:

1. Which algorithms may be modified to work with such an Incomplete Membership Oracle? Specifically, can other interesting classes, such as Decision Trees be efficiently learned with such an Incomplete Membership Oracle?
2. Are there any concept classes for which it may be proven that learning with an EQ oracle and an Incomplete MQ oracle that gives answers with polynomially small probability is not possible, but for which efficient learning algorithms for learning with an EQ oracle and a standard MQ oracle exist? This may be restated in the following way: Can we prove that an Incomplete MQ oracle of polynomial probability is strictly weaker than a standard MQ oracle?

References

1. D. Angluin. Queries and concept learning. *Machine Learning*, 2(4):319–342, April 1988.
2. Dana Angluin and Donna K. Slonim. Randomly fallible teachers: Learning monotone DNF with an incomplete membership oracle. *Machine Learning*, 14:7–26, 1994.
3. P. Auer. On-line learning of rectangles in noisy environments. In *Proc. 6th Annu. Conf. on Comput. Learning Theory*, pages 253–261. ACM Press, New York, NY, 1993.

4. Peter Auer and Nicolò Cesa-Bianchi. On-line learning with malicious noise and the closure algorithm. *Annals of Mathematics and Artificial Intelligence*, 23(1/2):83–99, 1998. Special issue for AII '94 and ALT '94.
5. Z. Chen. A note on learning DNF formulas using equivalence and incomplete membership queries. In *Proc. 5th Int. Workshop on Algorithmic Learning Theory*, pages 272–281. Springer-Verlag, 1994.
6. S. A. Goldman and H. D. Mathias. Learning k-term DNF formulas with an incomplete membership oracle. In *Proc. 5th Annu. Workshop on Comput. Learning Theory*, pages 77–84. ACM Press, New York, NY, 1992.
7. N. Littlestone. *Mistake Bounds and Logarithmic Linear-threshold Learning Algorithms.* PhD thesis, Technical Report UCSC-CRL-89-11, University of California Santa Cruz, 1989.
8. N. Littlestone and M. K. Warmuth. The weighted majority algorithm. *Inform. Comput.*, 108(2):212–261, 1994.

Appendix: A New Analysis of the Angluin-Slonim Algorithm

We present a new analysis of the algorithm of Angluin and Slonim described in [2]. Their algorithm proceeds by using the EQ oracle to receive a positive counter-example, and then using the procedure **Reduce** attempt to locate a min-term of the target that covers that counter-example.

```
Reduce(x, d)
Let D be the set of all d-descendants of v
For each y ∈ D in breadth-first order
        If MQ(y) = 1 then
                Return Reduce(y, d)
Return v.
```

In this procedure we start from a positive example x of f (f is the target function) and at each iteration we move to a new positive example y that is a d-descendant of v. When no positive example is found we return from the procedure.

Angluin and Slonim show the following: Let x be any positive example $0 < p < 1$. If $d = O(\log(1/(1-p)))$ then with probability at least $1/2$, **Reduce**(x, d) returns an assignment u that is d-close to a minterm of the target formula. Therefore adding all the d-descendants of u to the hypothesis will guarantee getting a new minterm of the target with probability at least $1/2$.

The algorithm also adds to the hypothesis all the assignments queried by **Reduce** that result in an answer "I don't know". This guarantees that none of those assignments will be queried twice. Some of those assignments are negative and will be removed by the negative counterexamples we get from the equivalence queries. (See [2, pp. 18–20] for more details of the algorithm.)

The following Lemma follows from [2, Lemma 1 and 2] and the analysis of [2, Lemma 3].

Lemma 5. *Let f be a monotone DNF formula. Assume we have an incomplete membership oracle for f with failure probability p, and some queries have already been made to the oracle. Assume that x is a positive example of f such that no descendant of x that is a positive example of f has yet been subject of a membership query to the oracle. Let d be a positive integer, and let*

$$g(k,d) = \binom{k+1}{d} + \binom{k+1}{d-1} + \cdots + \binom{k+1}{1}.$$

Let **Reduce** *be called with arguments x and d and let w denote the assignments returned. Then the probability that some minterm u of f that is below w satisfies $dist(u,w) > k$ is at most*

$$\frac{p^{g(k,d)}}{1-p}.$$

We now prove our main Lemma

Lemma 6. *The probability that w is a minterm of f is at least*

$$(1-p)^k\left(1-\frac{p^{g(k,d)}}{1-p}\right)$$

for any k.

Proof. Let $x = x_1$ and $x_2, x_3, \ldots, x_l = w$ be the assignments that **Reduce** passes through in step (5) of the algorithm. Let U be the set of all points in $\{0,1\}^n$ such that for any $u \in U$ every minterm of f that is below u is of distance at most k from u. For $u \in U$ let A_u be a random variable that is 1 if $x_1 = u$ or for some $i > 1$ we have $x_i = u$ and $x_{i-1} \notin U$, and 0 otherwise and let $A = \sum_{u \in U} A_u$. Let B be a random variable that is 1 if w is a minterm and 0 otherwise. We first prove the following

1. If $B = 1$ then $A_u = 1$ for exactly one $u \in U$.
2. $E[A] \geq 1 - \frac{p^{g(k,d)}}{1-p}$.
3. $E[B|A_u] \geq (1-p)^k$ for every $u \in U$.

To prove (1) we have: If $B = 1$ then $x_l = w$ is a minterm of f and $x_l \in U$. If $x_1 \in U$ then $A_{x_1} = 1$ and it is the only one that is equal to 1. Otherwise let i be the least integer such that $x_i \in U$ and $x_{i-1} \notin U$. Then $A_{x_i} = 1$ and it is the only one that is equal to 1.

(2) is true because if $w \in U$ then $A_{x_i} = 1$ for some $x_i \in U$ and then $A = 1$. Therefore, by Lemma 5

$$E[A] \geq \Pr[w \in U] \geq 1 - \frac{p^{g(k,d)}}{1-p}.$$

To prove (3) notice that $E[B|A_u]$ is the probability that **Reduce**(u,d) returns a minterm. Since $u \in U$ we have $\mathrm{dist}(u,y) \leq k$ for any minterm y of f that is below u. We consider the path $u \to u^{(0)} \to u^{(1)} \to \cdots \to u^{(k')}$ that is produced from running Angluin's algorithm for monotone DNF in [1] (with perfect membership queries) with the positive counterexample u. This is the same path that **Reduce**(u, d) would take if $p = 0$. We will find the probability that **Reduce**(u, d) will take this path. Notice first that this probability is at most $E[B|A_u]$. Now since $k' \leq k$ and the success probability of moving from $u^{(i)}$ to $u^{(i+1)}$ in **Reduce** is $1 - p$, the probability that this path is taken is exactly $(1-p)^{k'} \geq (1-p)^k$. Therefore,

$$E[B|A_u] \geq (1-p)^k.$$

Now we are ready to prove the Lemma. By (1)–(3) we have

$$\begin{aligned}
\Pr[w \text{ is a minterm}] &= E[B] \\
&= E\left[\sum_{u \in U} A_u B\right] && \text{By (1)} \\
&= \sum_{u \in U} E[A_u B] \\
&= \sum_{u \in U} E[A_u] E[B|A_u] \\
&\geq \min_u E[B|A_u] \sum_{u \in U} E[A_u] \\
&= \min_u E[B|A_u] E[A] && \text{and by (2) and (3)} \\
&\geq (1-p)^k \left(1 - \frac{p^{g(k,d)}}{1-p}\right)
\end{aligned}$$

In [2] Angluin and Slonim show that the expected time and total number of queries needed for the algorithm is

$$tn^{O\left(\log \frac{1}{1-p}\right)}.$$

We are now ready to present the proof of Theorem 2:

Proof. (Theorem 2) Since the success probability of getting a minterm is

$$w = (1-p)^k \left(1 - \frac{p^{g(k,d)}}{1-p}\right)$$

the expected number of queries is tn^d/w. Now we choose

$$\begin{aligned}
d &= \frac{\log \frac{1}{1-p} + \log \ln \frac{2}{1-p}}{\log \log n + \log c - \log \log \frac{1}{1-p}} \\
&= \frac{\log \left(\frac{1}{1-p} \ln \frac{2}{1-p}\right)}{\log \left(c \frac{\log n}{\log \frac{1}{1-p}}\right)}
\end{aligned}$$

and

$$k = cd\frac{\log n}{\log \frac{1}{1-p}}$$

for some constant $c < 1$.

Now

$$\begin{aligned} p^{g(k,d)} &\le (1-(1-p))^{\left(\frac{k}{d}\right)^d} \\ &\le e^{-(1-p)\left(\frac{k}{d}\right)^d} \\ &= e^{-(1-p)\left(c\frac{\log n}{\log \frac{1}{1-p}}\right)^d} \\ &= e^{-\ln \frac{2}{1-p}} = \frac{1}{2}(1-p) \end{aligned}$$

and therefore

$$1 - \frac{p^{g(k,d)}}{1-p} \ge \frac{1}{2}$$

and

$$w = \frac{1}{2}(1-p)^k = \frac{1}{2}n^{-cd}.$$

Hence we have

$$\frac{tn^d}{w} = 2tn^{(1+c)d}.$$

Now since $p < 1 - 1/2^{\log^{\alpha} n}$ we have $\log\log\frac{1}{1-p} < \alpha \log\log n$ and therefore

$$d = O\left(\frac{\log \frac{1}{1-p}}{\log\log n}\right).$$

and

$$\frac{tn^d}{w} = tn^{O\left(\frac{\log \frac{1}{1-p}}{\log\log n}\right)}.$$

On Learning Monotone DNF under Product Distributions

Rocco A. Servedio

Division of Engineering and Applied Sciences, Harvard University
Cambridge, MA 02138
rocco@deas.harvard.edu

Abstract. We show that the class of monotone $2^{O(\sqrt{\log n})}$-term DNF formulae can be PAC learned in polynomial time under the uniform distribution from random examples only. This is an exponential improvement over the best previous polynomial-time algorithms in this model, which could learn monotone $o(\log^2 n)$-term DNF, and is the first efficient algorithm for monotone $(\log n)^{\omega(1)}$-term DNF in any nontrivial model of learning from random examples. We also show that various classes of small constant-depth circuits which compute monotone functions on few input variables are PAC learnable in polynomial time under the uniform distribution. All of our results extend to learning under any constant-bounded product distribution.

1 Introduction

A *disjunctive normal form* formula, or DNF, is a disjunction of conjunctions of Boolean literals. The *size* of a DNF is the number of conjunctions (also known as *terms*) which it contains. In a seminal 1984 paper [30] Valiant introduced the distribution-free model of Probably Approximately Correct (PAC) learning from random examples and posed the question of whether polynomial-size DNF are PAC learnable in polynomial time. Over the past fifteen years the DNF learning problem has been widely viewed as one of the most important – and challenging – open questions in computational learning theory. This paper substantially improves the best previous results for a well-studied restricted version of the DNF learning problem.

1.1 Previous Work

The lack of progress on Valiant's original question – are polynomial-size DNF learnable from random examples drawn from an arbitrary distribution in polynomial time? – has led many researchers to study restricted versions of the DNF learning problem. As detailed below, the restrictions which have been considered include

- allowing the learner to make *membership queries* for the value of the target function at points selected by the learner;

D. Helmbold and B. Williamson (Eds.): COLT/EuroCOLT 2001, LNAI 2111, pp. 558–573, 2001.

- requiring that the learner succeed only under restricted distributions on examples, such as the uniform distribution, rather than all distributions;
- requiring that the learner succeed only for restricted subclasses of DNF formulae such as monotone DNF with a bounded number of terms.

A *SAT-k* DNF is a DNF in which each truth assignment satisfies at most k terms. Khardon [22] gave a polynomial time membership query algorithm for learning polynomial-size SAT-1 DNF under the uniform distribution; this result was later strengthened by Blum et al. [4] to SAT-k DNF for any constant k. Bellare [6] gave a polynomial time membership query algorithm for learning $O(\log n)$-term DNF under the uniform distribution. This result was strengthened by Blum and Rudich [7] who gave a polynomial time algorithm for exact learning $O(\log n)$-term DNF using membership and equivalence queries; several other polynomial-time algorithms for $O(\log n)$-term DNF have since been given in this model [3,9,10,25]. Mansour [27] gave a $n^{O(\log \log n)}$-time membership query algorithm which learns polynomial-size DNF under the uniform distribution. In a celebrated result, Jackson [18] gave a polynomial-time membership query algorithm for learning polynomial-size DNF under constant-bounded product distributions. His algorithm, the efficiency of which was subsequently improved by several authors [11,23], is the only known polynomial time algorithm for learning the unrestricted class of polynomial size DNF in any learning model.

In the standard PAC model without membership queries positive results are known for various subclasses of DNF under restricted distributions. A *read-k* DNF is one in which each variable appears at most k times. Kearns *et al.* [20,21] showed that read-once DNF are PAC learnable under the uniform distribution in polynomial time. Hancock [15] extended this result to read-k DNF for any constant k. Verbeurgt [31] gave an algorithm for learning arbitrary polynomial-size DNF under the uniform distribution in time $n^{O(\log n)}$, and Linial *et al.* [26] gave an algorithm for learning any AC^0 circuit (constant depth, polynomial size, unbounded fanin AND/OR gates) under the uniform distribution in $n^{poly(\log n)}$ time.

A *monotone* DNF is a DNF with no negated variables. It is well known that in the distribution-independent setting, learning monotone DNF is equivalent to learning general DNF [20]. However this equivalence does not hold for restricted distributions such as the uniform distribution, and many researchers have studied the problem of learning monotone DNF under restricted distributions. Hancock and Mansour [16] gave a polynomial time algorithm for learning monotone read-k DNF under constant-bounded product distributions. Verbeurgt [32] gave a polynomial time uniform distribution algorithm for learning poly-disjoint one-read-once monotone DNF and read-once factorable monotone DNF. Kucera *et al.* [24] gave a polynomial-time algorithm which learns monotone k-term DNF under the uniform distribution using hypotheses which are monotone k-term DNF. This was improved by Sakai and Maruoka [29] who gave a polynomial-time algorithm for learning monotone $O(\log n)$-term DNF under the uniform distribution using hypotheses which are monotone $O(\log n)$-term DNF. In [9] Bshouty gave a polynomial-time uniform-distribution algorithm for learning a class which includes monotone $O(\log n)$-term DNF. Later Bshouty and Tamon [12] gave a polynomial-time algorithm for learning a class which includes monotone $O(\log^2 n/(\log\log n)^3)$-term DNF under constant-bounded product distributions.

1.2 Our Results

We give an algorithm for learning monotone DNF under the uniform distribution. If the desired accuracy level ϵ is constant as a function of n (the number of variables), then the algorithm learns $2^{O(\sqrt{\log n})}$-term monotone DNF over n variables in poly(n) time. (We note that the algorithm of [12] for learning monotone DNF with $O((\log n)^2/(\log\log n)^3)$ terms also requires that ϵ be constant in order to achieve poly(n) runtime.) This is the first polynomial time algorithm which uses only random examples and successfully learns monotone DNF with more than a polylogarithmic number of terms. We also show that essentially the same algorithm learns various classes of small constant-depth circuits which compute monotone functions on few variables. All of our results extend to learning under any constant-bounded product distribution.

Our algorithm combines ideas from Linial *et al.*'s influential paper [26] on learning AC^0 functions using the Fourier transform and Bshouty and Tamon's paper [12] on learning monotone functions using the Fourier transform. By analyzing the Fourier transform of AC^0 functions, Linial et al. showed that almost all of the Fourier "power spectrum" of any AC^0 function is contained in "low" Fourier coefficients, i.e. coefficients which correspond to small subsets of variables. Their learning algorithm estimates each low Fourier coefficient by sampling and constructs an approximation to f using these estimated Fourier coefficients. If c is the size bound for low Fourier coefficients, then since there are $\binom{n}{c}$ Fourier coefficients corresponding to subsets of c variables the algorithm requires roughly n^c time steps. Linial *et al.* showed that for AC^0 circuits c is essentially poly($\log n$); this result was later sharpened for DNF formulae by Mansour [27].

Our algorithm extends this approach in the following way: Let $C \subset AC^0$ be a class of Boolean functions which we would like to learn. Suppose that C has the following properties:

1. For every $f \in C$ there is a set S_f of "important" variables such that almost all of the power spectrum of f is contained in Fourier coefficients corresponding to subsets of S_f.
2. There is an efficient algorithm which identifies the set S_f from random examples.

(Such an algorithm, which we give in Section 3.1, is implicit in [12] and requires only that f be monotone.) We can learn an unknown function f from such a class C by first identifying the set S_f, then estimating the low Fourier coefficients which correspond to small subsets of S_f and using these estimates to construct an approximation to f. To see why this works, note that since f is in AC^0 almost all of the power spectrum of f is in the low Fourier coefficients; moreover, property

(1) implies that almost all of the power spectrum of f is in the Fourier coefficients which correspond to subsets of S_f. Consequently it must be the case that almost all of the power spectrum of f is in low Fourier coefficients which correspond to subsets of S_f. Thus in our setting we need only estimate the $\binom{|S_f|}{c}$ Fourier coefficients which correspond to "small" subsets of variables in S_f. If $|S_f| \ll n$ then this is much more efficient than estimating all $\binom{n}{c}$ low Fourier coefficients.

In Section 2 we formally define the learning model and give some necessary facts about Fourier analysis over the Boolean cube. In Section 3 we give our learning algorithm for the uniform distribution, and in Section 4 we describe how the algorithm can be modified to work under any constant-bounded product distribution.

2 Preliminaries

We write $[n]$ to denote the set $\{1, \ldots, n\}$ and use capital letters for subsets of $[n]$. We write $|A|$ to denote the number of elements in A. Barred lowercase letters denote bitstrings, i.e. $\overline{x} = (x_1, \ldots, x_n) \in \{0,1\}^n$. In this paper Boolean circuits are composed of AND/OR/NOT gates where AND and OR gates have unbounded fanin and negations occur only on inputs. We view Boolean functions on n variables as real valued functions which map $\{0,1\}^n$ to $\{-1,1\}$. A Boolean function $f : \{0,1\}^n \rightarrow \{-1,1\}$ is *monotone* if changing the value of an input bit from 0 to 1 never causes the value of f to change from 1 to -1.

If $\mathcal{D}$ is a distribution and f is a Boolean function on $\{0,1\}^n$, then as in [12, 16] we say that the *influence of x_i on f with respect to $\mathcal{D}$* is the probability that $f(\overline{x})$ differs from $f(\overline{y})$, where $\overline{y}$ is $\overline{x}$ with the i-th bit flipped and $\overline{x}$ is drawn from $\mathcal{D}$. For ease of notation let $f_{i,0}$ denote the function obtained from f by fixing x_i to 0 and let $f_{i,1}$ be defined similarly. We thus have

$$I_{\mathcal{D},i}(f) = \Pr_{\mathcal{D}}[f_{i,0}(\overline{x}) \neq f_{i,1}(\overline{x})] = \frac{1}{2} E_{\mathcal{D}}[|f_{i,1} - f_{i,0}|].$$

For monotone f this can be further simplified to

$$I_{\mathcal{D},i}(f) = \frac{1}{2} E_{\mathcal{D}}[f_{i,1} - f_{i,0}] = \frac{1}{2} \left(E_{\mathcal{D}}[f_{i,1}] - E_{\mathcal{D}}[f_{i,0}] \right). \tag{1}$$

We frequently use Chernoff bounds on sums of independent random variables [14]:

Theorem 1. *Let $x_1, \ldots, x_m$ be independent identically distributed random variables with $E[x_i] = p$, $|x_i| \leq B$, and let $s_m = x_1 + \cdots + x_m$. Then*

$$m \geq \frac{2B^2}{\epsilon^2} \ln \frac{2}{\delta} \qquad \textit{implies that} \qquad \Pr\left[\left| \frac{s_m}{m} - p \right| > \epsilon \right] \leq \delta.$$

2.1 The Learning Model

Our learning model is a distribution-specific version of Valiant's Probably Approximately Correct (PAC) model [30] which has been studied by many researchers, e.g. [4,6,11,12,13,16,18,22,24,26,27,31,32]. Let C be a class of Boolean functions over $\{0,1\}^n$, let $\mathcal{D}$ be a probability distribution over $\{0,1\}^n$, and let $f \in C$ be an unknown target function. A learning algorithm A for C takes as input an accuracy parameter $0 < \epsilon < 1$ and a confidence parameter $0 < \delta < 1$. During its execution the algorithm has access to an *example oracle* $EX(f, \mathcal{D})$ which, when queried, generates a random labeled example $\langle \overline{x}, f(\overline{x}) \rangle$ where $\overline{x}$ is drawn according to $\mathcal{D}$. The learning algorithm outputs a hypothesis h which is a Boolean function over $\{0,1\}^n$; the error of this hypothesis is defined to be $\mathrm{error}(h, f) = \Pr_{\mathcal{D}}[h(\overline{x}) \neq f(\overline{x})]$. We say that A *learns* C *under* $\mathcal{D}$ if for every $f \in C$ and $0 < \epsilon, \delta < 1$, with probability at least $1 - \delta$ algorithm A outputs a hypothesis h which has $\mathrm{error}(h, f) \leq \epsilon$.

2.2 The Discrete Fourier Transform

Let $\mathcal{U}$ denote the uniform distribution over $\{0,1\}^n$. The set of all real valued functions on $\{0,1\}^n$ may be viewed as a 2^n-dimensional vector space with inner product defined as

$$\langle f, g \rangle = 2^{-n} \sum_{\overline{x} \in \{0,1\}^n} f(\overline{x}) g(\overline{x}) = E_{\mathcal{U}}[fg]$$

and norm defined as $\|f\| = \sqrt{\langle f, f \rangle}$. Given any subset $A \subseteq [n]$, the Fourier basis function $\chi_A : \{0,1\}^n \to \{-1,1\}$ is defined by $\chi_A(\overline{x}) = (-1)^{|A \cap X|}$, where X is the subset of $[n]$ defined by $i \in X$ iff $x_i = 1$. It is well known that the 2^n basis functions χ_A form an orthonormal basis for the vector space of real valued functions on $\{0,1\}^n$; we refer to this basis as *the* χ *basis*. In particular, any function f can be uniquely expressed as $f(\overline{x}) = \sum_A \hat{f}(A)\chi_A(\overline{x})$, where the values $\hat{f}(A)$ are known as the Fourier coefficients of f with respect to the χ basis. Since the functions χ_A form an orthonormal basis, the value of $\hat{f}(A)$ is $\langle f, \chi_A \rangle$; also, by linearity we have that $f(\overline{x}) + g(\overline{x}) = \sum_A (\hat{f}(A) + \hat{g}(A))\chi_A(\overline{x})$. Another easy consequence of orthonormality is Parseval's identity

$$E_{\mathcal{U}}[f^2] = \|f\|^2 = \sum_{A \subseteq [n]} \hat{f}(A)^2.$$

If f is a Boolean function then this value is exactly 1. Finally, for any Boolean function f and real-valued function g we have [12,26]

$$\Pr_{\mathcal{U}}[f \neq \mathrm{sign}(g)] \leq E_{\mathcal{U}}[(f - g)^2] \tag{2}$$

where $\mathrm{sign}(z)$ takes value 1 if $z \geq 0$ and takes value -1 if $z < 0$.

3 Learning under Uniform Distributions

3.1 Identifying Relevant Variables

The following lemma, which is implicit in [12], gives an efficient algorithm for identifying the important variables of a monotone Boolean function. We refer to this algorithm as `FindVariables`.

Lemma 1. *Let $f : \{0,1\}^n \to \{-1,1\}$ be a monotone Boolean function. There is an algorithm which has access to $EX(f,\mathcal{U})$, runs in poly$(n, 1/\epsilon, \log 1/\delta)$ time steps for all $\epsilon, \delta > 0$, and with probability at least $1-\delta$ outputs a set $S_f \subseteq [n]$ such that*

$$i \in S_f \text{ implies } \sum_{A:i\in A} \hat{f}(A)^2 \geq \epsilon/2 \quad \text{and} \quad i \notin S_f \text{ implies } \sum_{A:i\in A} \hat{f}(A)^2 \leq \epsilon.$$

Proof. Kahn *et al.* ([19] Section 3) have shown that

$$I_{\mathcal{U},i}(f) = \sum_{A:i\in A} \hat{f}(A)^2. \tag{3}$$

To prove the lemma it thus suffices to show that $I_{\mathcal{U},i}(f)$ can be estimated to within accuracy $\epsilon/4$ with high probability. By Equation (1) from Section 2 this can be done by estimating $E_{\mathcal{U}}[f_{i,1}]$ and $E_{\mathcal{U}}[f_{i,0}]$. Two applications of Chernoff bounds finish the proof: the first is to verify that with high probability a large sample drawn from $EX(f,\mathcal{U})$ contains many labeled examples which have $x_i = 1$ and many which have $x_i = 0$, and the second is to verify that a collection of many labeled examples with $x_i = b$ with high probability yields an accurate estimate of $E_{\mathcal{U}}[f_{i,b}]$. □

3.2 The Learning Algorithm

Our learning algorithm, which we call `LearnMonotone`, is given below:

- Use `FindVariables` to identify a set S_f of important variables.
- Draw m labeled examples $\langle \overline{x}^1, f(\overline{x}^1)\rangle, \ldots, \langle \overline{x}^m, f(\overline{x}^m)\rangle$ from $EX(f,\mathcal{U})$. For every $A \subseteq S_f$ with $|A| \leq c$ set $\alpha_A = \frac{1}{m}\sum_{i=1}^m f(\overline{x}^i)\chi_A(\overline{x}^i)$. For every A such that $|A| > c$ or $A \not\subseteq S_f$ set $\alpha_A = 0$.
- Output the hypothesis sign$(g(\overline{x}))$, where $g(\overline{x}) = \sum_A \alpha_A \chi_A(\overline{x})$.

The algorithm thus estimates $\hat{f}(A)$ for $A \subseteq S_f, |A| \leq c$ by sampling and constructs a hypothesis using these approximate Fourier coefficients. The values of m and c and the parameter settings for `FindVariables` are specified below.

3.3 Learning Monotone $2^{O(\sqrt{\log n})}$-Term DNF

Let $f : \{0,1\}^n \rightarrow \{-1,1\}$ be a monotone t-term DNF. The proof that algorithm `LearnMonotone` learns f uses a DNF called f_1 to show that `FindVariables` identifies a small set of variables S_f and uses another DNF called f_2 to show that f can be approximated by approximating Fourier coefficients which correspond to small subsets of S_f.

Let f_1 be the DNF which is obtained from f by removing every term which contains more than $\log \frac{32tn}{\epsilon}$ variables. Since there are at most t such terms each of which is satisfied by a random example with probability less than $\epsilon/32tn$, we have $\Pr_{\mathcal{U}}[f(\overline{x}) \neq f_1(\overline{x})] < \frac{\epsilon}{32n}$ (this type of argument was first used by Verbeurgt [31]). Let $R \subseteq [n]$ be the set of variables which f_1 depends on; it is clear that $|R| \leq t \log \frac{32tn}{\epsilon}$. Moreover, since $I_{\mathcal{U},i}(f_1) = 0$ for $i \notin R$, equation (3) from Section 3.1 implies that $\hat{f}_1(A) = 0$ for $A \nsubseteq R$.

Since f and f_1 are Boolean functions, $f - f_1$ is either 0 or 2, so $E_{\mathcal{U}}[(f - f_1)^2] = 4 \Pr_{\mathcal{U}}[f \neq f_1] < \epsilon/8n$. By Parseval's identity we have

$$\begin{aligned} E_{\mathcal{U}}[(f - f_1)^2] &= \sum_A (\hat{f}(A) - \hat{f}_1(A))^2 \\ &= \sum_{A \subseteq R} (\hat{f}(A) - \hat{f}_1(A))^2 + \sum_{A \nsubseteq R} (\hat{f}(A) - \hat{f}_1(A))^2 \\ &= \sum_{A \subseteq R} (\hat{f}(A) - \hat{f}_1(A))^2 + \sum_{A \nsubseteq R} (\hat{f}(A))^2 \\ &< \epsilon/8n. \end{aligned}$$

Thus $\sum_{A \nsubseteq R} \hat{f}(A)^2 < \frac{\epsilon}{8n}$, and consequently we have

$$i \notin R \text{ implies } \sum_{A : i \in A} \hat{f}(A)^2 < \frac{\epsilon}{8n}. \tag{4}$$

We set the parameters of `FindVariables` so that with high probability

$$i \in S_f \quad \text{implies} \quad \sum_{A : i \in A} \hat{f}(A)^2 \geq \epsilon/8n \tag{5}$$

$$i \notin S_f \quad \text{implies} \quad \sum_{A : i \in A} \hat{f}(A)^2 \leq \epsilon/4n. \tag{6}$$

Inequalities (4) and (5) imply that $S_f \subseteq R$, so $|S_f| \leq t \log \frac{32tn}{\epsilon}$. Furthermore, since $A \nsubseteq S_f$ implies $i \in A$ for some $i \notin S_f$, inequality (6) implies

$$\sum_{A \nsubseteq S_f} \hat{f}(A)^2 \leq \epsilon/4. \tag{7}$$

The following lemma is due to Mansour ([27] Lemma 3.2):

Lemma 2 (Mansour). *Let f be a DNF with terms of size at most d. Then for all $\epsilon > 0$*

$$\sum_{|A|>20d\log(2/\epsilon)} \hat{f}(A)^2 \leq \epsilon/2.$$

One approach at this point is to use Mansour's lemma to approximate f by approximating the Fourier coefficients of all subsets of S_f which are smaller than $20d\log(2/\epsilon)$, where $d = \log\frac{32tn}{\epsilon}$ is the maximum size of any term in f_1. However, this approach does not give a good overall running time because d is too large. Instead we consider another DNF with smaller terms than f_1 which also closely approximates f. By using this stronger bound on term size in Mansour's lemma we get a better final result.

More precisely, let f_2 be the DNF obtained from f by removing every term which contains at least $\log\frac{32t}{\epsilon}$ variables. Let $c = 20\log\frac{128t}{\epsilon}\log\frac{8}{\epsilon}$. Mansour's lemma implies that

$$\sum_{|A|>c} \hat{f}_2(A)^2 \leq \epsilon/8. \tag{8}$$

Moreover, we have $\Pr_{\mathcal{U}}[f \neq f_2] \leq \epsilon/32$ and hence

$$4\Pr_{\mathcal{U}}[f \neq f_2] = E_{\mathcal{U}}[(f - f_2)^2] = \sum_A(\hat{f}(A) - \hat{f}_2(A))^2 \leq \epsilon/8. \tag{9}$$

Let α_A and $g(\overline{x})$ be as defined in `LearnMonotone`. Using inequality (2) from Section 2.2, we have

$$\Pr[\mathrm{sign}(g) \neq f] \leq E_{\mathcal{U}}[(g - f)^2] = \sum_A(\alpha_A - \hat{f}(A))^2 = X + Y + Z,$$

where

$$X = \sum_{|A|\leq c, A\not\subseteq S_f} (\alpha_A - \hat{f}(A))^2,$$

$$Y = \sum_{|A|>c} (\alpha_A - \hat{f}(A))^2,$$

$$Z = \sum_{|A|\leq c, A\subseteq S_f} (\alpha_A - \hat{f}(A))^2.$$

To bound X, we observe that $\alpha_A = 0$ for $A \not\subseteq S_f$, so by (7) we have

$$X = \sum_{|A|\leq c, A\not\subseteq S_f} \hat{f}(A)^2 \leq \sum_{A\not\subseteq S_f} \hat{f}(A)^2 \leq \epsilon/4.$$

To bound Y, we note that $\alpha_A = 0$ for $|A| > c$ and hence $Y = \sum_{|A|>c}\hat{f}(A)^2$. Since $\hat{f}(A)^2 \leq 2(\hat{f}(A) - \hat{f}_2(A))^2 + 2\hat{f}_2(A)^2$, we have

$$Y \leq 2\sum_{|A|>c} (\hat{f}(A) - \hat{f}_2(A))^2 + 2\sum_{|A|>c} \hat{f}_2(A)^2$$

$$\le 2\sum_{A}(\hat{f}(A) - \hat{f}_2(A))^2 + \epsilon/4$$
$$\le \epsilon/2$$

by inequalities (8) and (9) respectively.

It remains to bound $Z = \sum_{|A|\le c, A\subseteq S_f}(\alpha_A - \hat{f}(A))^2$. As in Linial *et al.* [26] this sum can be made less than $\epsilon/4$ by taking m sufficiently large so that with high probability each estimate α_A differs from the true value $\hat{f}(A)$ by at most $\sqrt{\epsilon/4|S_f|^c}$. A straightforward Chernoff bound argument shows that taking $m = \mathrm{poly}(|S_f|^c, 1/\epsilon, \log(1/\delta))$ suffices.

Thus, we have $X + Y + Z \le \epsilon$. Recalling our bounds on $|S_f|$ and c, we have proved:

Theorem 2. *Under the uniform distribution, for any $\epsilon, \delta > 0$, the algorithm* `LearnMonotone` *can be used to learn t-term monotone DNF in time polynomial in n, $(t \log \frac{tn}{\epsilon})^{\log \frac{t}{\epsilon} \log \frac{1}{\epsilon}}$ and $\log(1/\delta)$.*

Taking $t = 2^{O(\sqrt{\log n})}$ we obtain the following corollary:

Corollary 1. *For any constant ϵ algorithm* `LearnMonotone` *learns $2^{O(\sqrt{\log n})}$-term monotone DNF in poly$(n, \log(1/\delta))$ time under the uniform distribution.*

As noted earlier, Bshouty and Tamon's algorithm [12] for learning monotone DNF with $O((\log n)^2/(\log\log n)^3)$ terms also requires that ϵ be constant in order to achieve poly(n) runtime.

3.4 Learning Small Constant-Depth Monotone Circuits on Few Variables

Let C be the class of depth d, size M circuits which compute monotone functions on r out of n variables. An analysis similar to that of the last section (but simpler since we do not need to introduce auxiliary functions f_1 and f_2) shows that algorithm `LearnMonotone` can be used to learn C. As in the last section the `FindVariables` procedure is used to identify the "important" relevant variables, of which there are now at most r. Instead of using Mansour's lemma, we use the main lemma of Linial *et al.* [26] to bound the total weight of high-order Fourier coefficients for constant-depth circuits:

Lemma 3 (Linial *et al.*). *Let f be a Boolean function computed by a circuit of depth d and size M and let c be any integer. Then*

$$\sum_{|A|>c} \hat{f}(A)^2 \le 2M2^{-c^{1/d}/20}.$$

Taking $m = \mathrm{poly}(r^c, 1/\epsilon, \log(1/\delta))$ and $c = \Theta((\log(M/\epsilon))^d)$ in `LearnMonotone` we obtain:

Theorem 3. *Fix $d \geq 1$ and let $C_{d,M,r}$ be the class of depth d, size M circuits which compute monotone functions on r out of n variables. Under the uniform distribution, for any $\epsilon, \delta > 0$, algorithm* `LearnMonotone` *learns class $C_{d,M,r}$ in time polynomial in n, $r^{(\log(M/\epsilon))^d}$ and $\log(1/\delta)$.*

One interesting corollary is the following:

Corollary 2. *Fix $d \geq 1$ and let C_d be the class of depth d, size $2^{O((\log n)^{1/(d+1)})}$ circuits which compute monotone functions on $2^{O((\log n)^{1/(d+1)})}$ variables. Then for any constant ϵ algorithm* `LearnMonotone` *learns class C_d in poly$(n, \log(1/\delta))$ time.*

While this class C_d is rather limited from the perspective of Boolean circuit complexity, from a learning theory perspective it is fairly rich. We note that C_d strictly includes the class of depth d, size $2^{O((\log n)^{1/(d+1)})}$ circuits on $2^{O((\log n)^{1/(d+1)})}$ variables which contain only unbounded fanin AND and OR gates. This follows from results of Okol'nishnikova [28] and Ajtai and Gurevich [1] (see also [8] Section 3.6) which show that there are monotone functions which can be computed by AC^0 circuits but are not computable by AC^0 circuits which have no negations.

4 Product Distributions

A *product distribution* over $\{0,1\}^n$ is characterized by parameters $\mu_1, \ldots, \mu_n$ where $\mu_i = \Pr[x_i = 1]$. Such a distribution $\mathcal{D}$ assigns values independently to each variable, so for $\overline{a} \in \{0,1\}^n$ we have $\mathcal{D}(\overline{a}) = \left(\prod_{a_i=1} \mu_i\right)\left(\prod_{a_i=0}(1-\mu_i)\right)$. The uniform distribution is a product distribution with each $\mu_i = 1/2$. The standard deviation of x_i under a product distribution is $\sigma_i = \sqrt{\mu_i(1-\mu_i)}$. A product distribution $\mathcal{D}$ is *constant-bounded* if there is some constant $c \in (0,1)$ independent of n such that $\mu_i \in [c, 1-c]$ for all $i = 1, \ldots, n$. We let β denote $\max_{i=1,\ldots,n}(1/\mu_i, 1/(1-\mu_i))$. Throughout the rest of this paper $\mathcal{D}$ denotes a product distribution.

Given a product distribution $\mathcal{D}$ we define a new inner product over the vector space of real valued functions on $\{0,1\}^n$ as

$$\langle f, g\rangle_{\mathcal{D}} = \sum_{\overline{x}\in\{0,1\}^n} \mathcal{D}(\overline{x}) f(\overline{x}) g(\overline{x}) = E_{\mathcal{D}}[fg]$$

and a corresponding norm $\|f\|_{\mathcal{D}} = \sqrt{\langle f, f\rangle_{\mathcal{D}}}$. We refer to this norm as *the $\mathcal{D}$-norm*. For $i = 1, \ldots, n$ let $z_i = (x_i - \mu_i)/\sigma_i$. Given $A \subseteq [n]$, let ϕ_A be defined as $\phi_A(\overline{x}) = \prod_{i\in A} z_i$. As noted by Bahadur [5] and Furst *et al.* [13], the 2^n functions ϕ_A form an orthonormal basis for the vector space of real valued functions on $\{0,1\}^n$ with respect to the $\mathcal{D}$-norm, i.e. $\langle \phi_A, \phi_B\rangle_{\mathcal{D}}$ is 1 if $A = B$ and is 0 otherwise. We refer to this basis as *the ϕ basis*. The following fact is useful:

Fact 1 (Bahadur; Furst et. al) *The ϕ basis is the basis which would be obtained by Gram-Schmidt orthonormalization (with respect to the $\mathcal{D}$-norm) of the χ basis performed in order of increasing $|A|$.*

By the orthonormality of the ϕ basis, any real function on $\{0,1\}^n$ can be uniquely expressed as $f(\overline{x}) = \sum_A \tilde{f}(A)\phi_A(\overline{x})$ where $\tilde{f}(A) = \langle f, \phi_A\rangle_{\mathcal{D}}$ is the Fourier coefficient of A with respect to the ϕ basis. Note that we write $\tilde{f}(A)$ for the ϕ basis Fourier coefficient and $\hat{f}(A)$ for the χ basis Fourier coefficient. Also by orthonormality we have Parseval's identity

$$E_{\mathcal{D}}[f^2] = \|f\|_{\mathcal{D}}^2 = \sum_{A\subseteq[n]} \tilde{f}(A)^2$$

which is 1 for Boolean f. Finally, for Boolean f and real-valued g we have ([13] Lemma 10)

$$\Pr_{\mathcal{D}}[f \neq \mathrm{sign}(g)] \leq E_{\mathcal{D}}[(f-g)^2]. \tag{10}$$

Furst *et al.* [13] analyzed the ϕ basis Fourier spectrum of AC^0 functions and gave product distribution analogues of Linial *et al.*'s results on learning AC^0 circuits under the uniform distribution. In Section 4.1 we sharpen and extend some results from [13], and in Section 5 we use these sharpened results together with techniques from [13] to obtain product distribution analogues of our algorithms from Section 3.

4.1 Some ϕ Basis Fourier Lemmas

A *random restriction* $\rho_{p,\mathcal{D}}$ is a mapping from $\{x_1,\ldots,x_n\}$ to $\{0,1,*\}$ where x_i is mapped to $*$ with probability p, to 1 with probability $(1-p)\mu_i$, and to 0 with probability $(1-p)(1-\mu_i)$. If f is a Boolean function then $f\lceil\rho$ represents the function $f(\rho_{p,\mathcal{D}}(\overline{x}))$ whose variables are those x_i which are mapped to $*$ and whose other x_i are instantiated as 0 or 1 according to $\rho_{p,\mathcal{D}}$.

The following is a variant of Håstad's well known switching lemma [17]:

Lemma 4. *Let $\mathcal{D}$ be a product distribution with parameters μ_i and β as defined above, let f be a CNF formula where each clause has at most d literals, and let $\rho_{p,\mathcal{D}}$ be a random restriction. Then with probability at least $1-(4\beta pd)^s$,*

1. *the function $f\lceil\rho$ can be expressed as a DNF formula where each term has at most s literals;*
2. *the terms of such a DNF all accept disjoint sets of inputs.*

Proof sketch: The proof is a minor modification of arguments given in Section 4 of [2]. □

The following corollary is a product distribution analogue of ([26] Corollary 1):

Corollary 3. *Let $\mathcal{D}$ be a product distribution with parameters μ_i and β, let f be a CNF formula where each clause has at most d literals, and let $\rho_{p,\mathcal{D}}$ be a random restriction. Then with probability at least $1-(4\beta pd)^s$ we have that $\widetilde{f\lceil\rho}(A)=0$ for all $|A|>s$.*

Proof. Linial *et al.* [26] show that if $f\lceil\rho$ satisfies properties (1) and (2) of Lemma 4 then $\widehat{f\lceil\rho}(A)=0$ for all $|A|>s$. Hence such a $f\lceil\rho$ is in the space spanned by $\{\chi_A : |A|\le s\}$. By Fact 1 and the nature of Gram-Schmidt orthonormalization, this is the same space which is spanned by $\{\phi_A : |A|\le s\}$, and the corollary follows. □

Corollary 3 is a sharpened version of a similar lemma, implicit in [13], which states that under the same conditions with probability at least $1-(5\beta pd/2)^s$ we have $\widetilde{f\lceil\rho}(A)=0$ for all $|A|>s^2$. Armed with the sharper Corollary 3, using arguments from [13] it is straightforward to prove

Lemma 5. *For any Boolean function f, for any integer t,*

$$\sum_{|A|>t}\tilde{f}(A)^2\le 2\Pr_{\rho_{p,D}}[\widetilde{f\lceil\rho}(A)\neq 0 \text{ for some } |A|>tp/2].$$

Boolean duality implies that the conclusion of Corollary 3 also holds if f is a DNF with each term of length at most d. Taking $p=1/8\beta d$ and $s=\log\frac{4}{\epsilon}$ in this DNF version of Corollary 3 and $t=16\beta d\log\frac{4}{\epsilon}$ in Lemma 5, we obtain the following analogue of Mansour's lemma (Lemma 2) for the ϕ basis:

Lemma 6. *Let f be a DNF with terms of size at most d. Then for all $\epsilon>0$*

$$\sum_{|A|>16\beta d\log(4/\epsilon)}\tilde{f}(A)^2\le\epsilon/2.$$

Again using arguments from [13], Corollary 3 can also be used to prove the following version of the main lemma from [13]:

Lemma 7. *Let f be a Boolean function computed by a circuit of depth d and size M and let c be any integer. Then*

$$\sum_{|A|>c}\tilde{f}(A)^2\le 2M2^{-c^{1/d}/8\beta}.$$

The version of this lemma given in [13] has $1/(d+2)$ instead of $1/d$ in the exponent of c. This new tighter bound will enable us to give stronger guarantees on our learning algorithm's performance under product distributions than we could have obtained by simply using the lemma from [13].

5 Learning under Product Distributions

5.1 Identifying Relevant Variables

We have the following analogue to Lemma 2 for product distributions:

Lemma 8. *Let $f : \{0,1\}^n \to \{-1,1\}$ be a monotone Boolean function. There is an algorithm which has access to $EX(f, \mathcal{D})$, runs in poly$(n, \beta, 1/\epsilon, \log 1/\delta)$ time steps for all $\epsilon, \delta > 0$, and with probability at least $1-\delta$ outputs a set $S_f \subseteq [n]$ such that*

$$i \in S_f \text{ implies } \sum_{A:i\in A} \tilde{f}(A)^2 \geq \epsilon/2 \qquad \text{and} \qquad i \notin S_f \text{ implies } \sum_{A:i\in A} \tilde{f}(A)^2 \leq \epsilon.$$

The proof uses the fact ([12] Lemma 4.1) that $4\sigma_i^2 I_{\mathcal{D},i}(f) = \sum_{A:i\in A} \tilde{f}(A)^2$ for any Boolean function f and any product distribution $\mathcal{D}$. The algorithm uses sampling to approximate each μ_i (and thus σ_i) and to approximate $I_{\mathcal{D},i}(f)$. We call this algorithm `FindVariables2`.

5.2 The Learning Algorithm

We would like to modify `LearnMonotone` so that it uses the ϕ basis rather than the χ basis. However, as in [13] the algorithm does not know the exact values of μ_i so it cannot use exactly the ϕ basis; instead it approximates each μ_i by a sample value μ_i' and uses the resulting basis, which we call the ϕ' basis. In more detail, the algorithm is as follows:

- Use `FindVariables2` to identify a set S_f of important variables.
- Draw m labeled examples $\langle \overline{x}^1, f(\overline{x}^1)\rangle, \ldots, \langle \overline{x}^m, f(\overline{x}^m)\rangle$ from $EX(f, \mathcal{D})$. Compute $\mu_i' = \frac{1}{m}\sum_{j=1}^m x_i^j$ for $1 \leq i \leq n$. Define $z_i' = (x_i - \mu_i')/\sqrt{\mu_i'(1-\mu_i')}$ and $\phi_A' = \prod_{i\in A} z_i'$.
- For every $A \subseteq S_f$ with $|A| \leq c$ set $\alpha_A' = \frac{1}{m}\sum_{j=1}^m f(\overline{x}^j)\phi_A'(\overline{x}^j)$. If $|\alpha_A'| > 1$ set $\alpha_A' = \text{sign}(\alpha_A')$. For every A such that $|A| > c$ or $A \not\subseteq S_f$ set $\alpha_A' = 0$.
- Output the hypothesis sign$(g(\overline{x}))$, where $g(\overline{x}) = \sum_A \alpha_A' \chi_A(\overline{x})$.

We call this algorithm `LearnMonotone2`. As in [13] we note that setting α_A' to ± 1 if $|\alpha_A'| > 1$ can only bring the estimated value closer to the true value of $\tilde{f}(A)$.

5.3 Learning Monotone $2^{O(\sqrt{\log n})}$-Term DNF

For the most part only minor changes to the analysis of Section 3.3 are required. Since a term of size greater than d is satisfied by a random example from $\mathcal{D}$ with probability less than $(\frac{\beta-1}{\beta})^d$, we now take $\log_{\frac{\beta}{\beta-1}} \frac{32tn}{\epsilon} = \Theta(\beta \log \frac{tn}{\epsilon})$ as the term size bound for f_1. Proceeding as in Section 3.3 we obtain $|S_f| = O(\beta t \log \frac{tn}{\epsilon})$. We similarly set a term size bound of $\Theta(\beta \log \frac{t}{\epsilon})$ for f_2. We use the ϕ basis

Parseval identity and inequality (10) in place of the χ basis identity and inequality (2) respectively. Lemma 6 provides the required analogue of Mansour's lemma for product distributions; using the new term size bound on f_2 we obtain $c = \Theta(\beta^2 \log \frac{t}{\epsilon} \log \frac{1}{\epsilon})$.

The one new ingredient in the analysis of LearnMonotone2 comes in bounding the quantity $Z = \sum_{|A| \le c, A \subseteq S_f} (\alpha'_A - \tilde{f}(A))^2$. In addition to the sampling error which would be present even if μ'_i were exactly μ_i, we must also deal with error due to the fact that α'_A is an estimate of the ϕ' basis coefficient rather than the ϕ basis coefficient $\tilde{f}(A)$. An analysis entirely similar to that of Section 5.2 of [13] shows that taking $m = \text{poly}(c, |S_f|^c, \beta^c, 1/\epsilon, \log(1/\delta))$ suffices. We thus have

Theorem 4. *Under any product distribution $\mathcal{D}$, for any $\epsilon, \delta > 0$, algorithm* LearnMonotone2 *can be used to learn t-term monotone DNF in time polynomial in n, $(\beta t \log \frac{tn}{\epsilon})^{\beta^2 \log \frac{t}{\epsilon} \log \frac{1}{\epsilon}}$, and* $\log(1/\delta)$.

Since a constant-bounded product distribution $\mathcal{D}$ has $\beta = \Theta(1)$, we obtain

Corollary 4. *For any constant ϵ and any constant-bounded product distribution $\mathcal{D}$, algorithm* LearnMonotone2 *learns $2^{O(\sqrt{\log n})}$-term monotone DNF in poly$(n, \log(1/\delta))$ time.*

5.4 Learning Small Constant-Depth Monotone Circuits on Few Variables

Using Lemma 7 and an analysis similar to the above, we obtain

Theorem 5. *Fix $d \ge 1$ and let C be the class of depth d, size M circuits which compute monotone functions on r out of n variables. Under any product distribution $\mathcal{D}$, for any $\epsilon, \delta > 0$, algorithm* LearnMonotone2 *learns class C in time polynomial in n, $r^{(\beta \log \frac{M}{\epsilon})^d}$ and* $\log(1/\delta)$.

Corollary 5. *Fix $d \ge 1$ and let C be the class of depth d, size $2^{O((\log n)^{1/(d+1)})}$ circuits which compute monotone functions on $2^{O((\log n)^{1/(d+1)})}$ variables. Then for any constant ϵ and any constant-bounded product distribution $\mathcal{D}$, algorithm* LearnMonotone2 *learns class C in poly$(n, \log(1/\delta))$ time.*

6 Open Questions

The positive results reported in this paper for $2^{O(\sqrt{\log n})}$-term DNF provide some hope that it may be possible to obtain a polynomial time algorithm for learning polynomial size monotone DNF under the uniform distribution from random examples only. We note that in the non-monotone case much less is known; in particular, it would be a significant step forward to give a polynomial time algorithm for learning arbitrary $t(n)$-term DNF under the uniform distribution, from random examples only, for any $t(n) = \omega(1)$.

7 Acknowledgements

We thank Les Valiant for his advice and enouragement.

References

1. M. Ajtai and Y. Gurevich. Monotone versus positive, *J. ACM* **34**(4) (1987), 1004-1015.
2. P. Beame. A switching lemma primer. Tech. report UW-CSE-95-07-01, University of Washington, November 1994.
3. A. Beimel, F. Bergadano, N. Bshouty, E. Kushilevitz and S. Varricchio. On the applicationf of multiplicity automata in learning, *in* "Proc. 37th Ann. Symp. on Foundations of Computer Science" (1996), 349-358.
4. A. Blum, M. Furst, J. Jackson, M. Kearns, Y. Mansour, and S. Rudich. Weakly learning DNF and characterizing statistical query learning using Fourier analysis, *in* "Proc. 26th Ann. Symp. on Theory of Computing" (1994), 253-262.
5. R. Bahadur. A representation of the joint distribution of responses to n dichotomous items, *in* Herbert Solomon, ed., *Studies in Item Analysis and Prediction,* pp. 158-168, Stanford University Press, 1961.
6. M. Bellare. A technique for upper bounding the spectral norm with applications to learning, *in* "Proc. Fifth Ann. Workshop on Comp. Learning Theory" (1992), 62-70.
7. A. Blum and S. Rudich. Fast learning of k-term DNF formulas with queries, *J. Comp. Syst. Sci.* **51**(3) (1995), 367-373.
8. R. Boppana and M. Sipser. The complexity of finite functions, in *Handbook of Theoretical Computer Science,* vol. A, MIT Press, 1990.
9. N. Bshouty. Exact learning via the monotone theory. *Information and Computation* **123**(1) (1995), 146-153.
10. N. Bshouty. Simple learning algorithms using divide and conquer, *Information Processing Letters*
11. N. Bshouty, J. Jackson, and C. Tamon. More efficient PAC-learning of DNF with membership queries under the uniform distribution, *in* "Proc. 12th Ann. Conf. on Comp. Learning Theory" (1999), 286-295.
12. N. Bshouty and C. Tamon. On the Fourier spectrum of monotone functions, *J. ACM* **43**(4) (1996), 747-770.
13. M. Furst, J. Jackson, and S. Smith. Improved learning of AC^0 functions, *in* "Proc. Fourth Ann. Workshop on Comp. Learning Theory" (1991), 317-325.
14. T. Hagerup and C. Rub. A guided tour to Chernoff bounds, *Inf. Proc. Lett.* **33** (1989), 305-308.
15. T. Hancock. The complexity of learning formulas and decision trees that have restricted reads, Ph.D. thesis, Harvard University, TR-15-92 (1992).
16. T. Hancock and Y. Mansour. Learning monotone k-μ DNF formulas on product distributions, *in* "Proc. 4th Ann. Workshop on Comp. Learning Theory" (1991), 179-183.
17. J. Håstad. *Computational Limitations for Small Depth Circuits.* Ph.D. thesis, MIT Press, 1986.
18. J. Jackson. An efficient membership-query algorithm for learning DNF with respect to the uniform distribution, *J. Comput. Syst. Sci.* **55** (1997), 414-440.

19. J. Kahn, G. Kalai, and N. Linial. The influence of variables on Boolean functions, *in* "Proc. 29th Ann. Symp. on Found. of Comp. Sci." (1988), 68-80.
20. M. Kearns, M. Li, L. Pitt, and L. Valiant. On the learnability of Boolean formulae, *in* "Proc. 19th Ann. ACM Symp. on Theory of Computing" (1987), 285-295.
21. M. Kearns, M. Li, and L. Valiant. Learning boolean formulas, *J. ACM* **41**(6) (1994), 1298-1328.
22. R. Khardon. On using the Fourier transform to learn disjoint DNF, *Information Processing Letters* **49** (1994), 219-222.
23. A. Klivans and R. Servedio. Boosting and hard-core sets, *in* "Proc. 40th Ann. Symp. on Found. of Comp. Sci." (1999), 624-633.
24. L. Kucera, A. Marchetti-Spaccamela and M. Protassi. On learning monotone DNF formulae under uniform distributions, *Inf. and Comput.* **110** (1994), 84-95.
25. E. Kushilevitz. A simple algorithm for learing $O(\log n)$-term DNF. *Information Processing Letters* **61**(6) (1997), 289-292.
26. N. Linial, Y. Mansour and N. Nisan. Constant depth circuits, Fourier transform and learnability, J. ACM **40**(3) (1993), 607-620.
27. Y. Mansour. An $O(n^{\log\log n})$ learning algorithm for DNF under the uniform distribution, *J. Comput. Syst. Sci.* **50** (1995), 543-550.
28. E. Okol'nishnikova. On the influence of negations on the complexity of a realization of monotone Boolean functions by formulas of bounded depth, *Metody Diskret. Analiz.* **38** (1982), 74-80 (in Russian).
29. Y. Sakai and A. Maruoka. Learning monotone log-term DNF formulas under the uniform distribution, *Theory Comput. Systems* **33** (2000), 17-33. A preliminary version appeared in "Proc. Seventh Conf. on Comp. Learning Theory" (1994), 165-172.
30. L. G. Valiant. A theory of the learnable, *Comm. ACM* **27**(11) (1984), 1134-1142.
31. K. Verbeurgt. Learning DNF under the uniform distribution in quasi-polynomial time, *in* "Proc. 3rd Ann. Workshop on Comp. Learning Theory" (1990), 314-326.
32. K. Verbeurgt. Learning sub-classes of monotone DNF on the uniform distribution, *in* "Proc. 9th Conf. on Algorithmic Learning Theory" (1998), 385-399.

Learning Regular Sets with an Incomplete Membership Oracle

Nader Bshouty and Avi Owshanko

Departments of computer science
Technion 32000 Haifa, Israel
{bshouty, avshash}@cs.technion.ac.il

Abstract. This paper gives an "efficient" algorithm for learning deterministic finite automata by using an equivalence oracle and an incomplete membership oracle. This solves an open problem that was posed by Angluin and Slonim in 94.[1]

1 Introduction

One of the fundemental learning problems is learning finite automata. This is an important problem, with many reductions. One such (important) reduction is the problem of learning $O(\log n)$−Term DNF [13] [7]. The first "efficient algorithm" solving this problem was published in 87 by D. Angluin [1]. That algorithm used two omniscient oracles - one to give short counterexamples (the equivalence oracle), and one foranswering queries (the membership oracle). Later, Kearns and Valient showed a reduction from the automaton learning problem with the equivalence oracle only to that of finding quadratic roots [11]. It was also shown by Angluin [3] that it is impossible to learn an automaton using only equivalence queries with automata hypotheses.

The model we use is situated between the "exact learning with equivalence queries only" model and the "exact learning with membership and equivalence queries" model, introduced by Angluin and Slonim [4] in 1994. The main difference between model and the standard membership model is that the membership oracle is not omniscient, i.e. it does not know the answers to all the queries. The membership oracle has a fixed probability p to know the answer to some query. If the oracle does not know the answer, then it returns a special answer "I don't know" (the membership oracle never lies), keeping the oracle consistent. If the oracle did not answer a query, it will never know the answer.

Not many positive results were published for this model. One result is learning Monontone DNF with a constant probability of an answer ($p \leq c < 1$), given by Angluin and Slonim [4]. The algorithm we show in this paper solves one of the open problems posed in that paper. The more general problem of learning

[1] This research was supported by the fund for the promotion of reseach at the Technion. Part of research was done at the university of Calgary, Calgary, Alberta, Canada.

D. Helmbold and B. Williamson (Eds.): COLT/EuroCOLT 2001, LNAI 2111, pp. 574–588, 2001.

monontone DNF with unbound probability of an answer p was solved by Bshouty and Einon [9]. Other contributions concerning the learning of DNF formulas were made by Goldman and Mathias [16] concerning learning $k-term$ DNF formulas, and by Chen [10], discussing restricted classes of DNF.

Organization: In section 2 we present some background on the learning model and regular sets. Section 3 gives some definitions we use later. In section 4 we show a simple learning algorithm using standard equivalence oracle and a failable membership oracle, with a bound number of errors. In section 5 we give the learning algorithm for regular sets, and conclude in section 6. Appendix A gives a more detailed description of an algorithm for adding execptions (errors) to an automaton (briefly described in section 3). Appendix B. gives a detailed description of the algorithm. Appendix C. gives proofs for some lemmas.

2 The Learning Model and Concept Classes

2.1 The Learning Models

In this paper, the learning criteria we consider is *exact learning* and the concept class C is the set of regular languages.

We represent the class of regular languages by the set of Deterministic Finite Automata. The deterministic finite automaton A (called here automaton) is the tuple (S, Σ, s_0, μ, F), where S is a finite set of states, Σ is the alphabet (for this paper, $\Sigma = \{0,1\}$), $s_0 \in S$ is the initial state, $\mu : S \times \Sigma \to S$ is the transition function and F is the set of accepting states.

We say that $\pi = s_0 s_1 \dots s_k \in S^{k+1}$ is the *path* corresponding to the word $\gamma = \sigma_0 \dots \sigma_{k-1} \in \Sigma^k$ if s_0 is the initial state of A and for every i, $\mu(s_i, \sigma_i) = s_{i+1}$. Note that because μ is a function and s_0 is unique, then each word γ has exactly one corresponding path π in A.

We say that a word γ is a *member* of $Lan(A)$ if the last state of the corresponding path π is accepting. i.e. $s_k \in F$.

In the exact learning model, there is a regular language $L \in C$ called the *target language*. The goal of the learning algorithm is to halt and output an automaton A, such that $Lan(A) = L$.

The learning algorithm may perform a *membership query* by supplying a word $\gamma \in \{0,1\}^*$ as input to the *membership oracle*. The oracle answers whether γ is a member of L or not. For our algorithm, we regard this oracle as a procedure Membership Query, $MQ(\gamma)$.

The learning algorithm may perform an *equivalence query* by supplying any automaton A as input to the *equivalence oracle*. The oracle can either answer "YES", signifying that A represents the language L, or give a *counterexample* γ, such that $\gamma \in L \triangle Lan(A)$ (where $\triangle$ is the symmetric difference). For our algorithm, we regard this oracle as a procedure Equivalence Query, $EQ(A)$.

We measure the complexity of algorithms w.r.t. the size of the smallest automaton which describes the language L and w.r.t. b, the length of the longest counterexample. We say that a class of regular languages C is *exactly learnable* in polynomial time if there is an algorithm that outputs for each L in C an automaton A such that $Lan(A) = L$ in polynomial time (i.e. after a polynomial number of operations). An assumption we make is that the length of counterexamples is polinomialy bound in m. That is, the equivalence oracle does not give a counterexample of length greater than $poly(m)$.

Two additional learning models we use are: the *t-malicious membership oracle*, which is a membership oracle that makes no more than t wrong classifications for all of the domain Σ^*. For our algorithm, we regard this oracle as a procedure Malicious Membership Query, $MMQ(\gamma)$.

The *p-incomplete membership oracle* is a membership oracle that returns the correct answer with probability p and otherwise returns the answer "I do not know". An additional constraint is that the oracle is consistent, hence if the oracle ever returns "I do not know" for some γ, it will never return anything else. For our algorithm, we regard this oracle as a procedure Incomplete Membership Query, $IMQ(\gamma)$. For the incomplete membership model, we use an "on-line" adversary. That is, the choice of a counterexample may depend on the target hypothesis, all previous answers (by the membership oracle) and full knowledge of the algorithm. The choice of counterexamples may not depend on the answers to membership queries not yet made. This is the same adversary as in the original model [4].

We say that an algorithm is *"efficient"* if it stops with a correct hypothesis with probability greater than $(1 - \delta)$, in polynomial time of $m, b, \frac{1}{\delta}, \frac{1}{p}$.

3 Preliminaries

In this section, we give some notations and assumptions that are used in this paper.

We first assume that the equivalence oracle does not give the same counterexample twice. To justify this assumption, we show an algorithm (in appendix A) for combining the counterexamples with any hypothesis automaton and get an automaton consistent with the set of counterexamples. Because we resort to similar techniques in section 5, we show this algorithms, instead of just stating that regular sets are closed under exceptions.

Lemma 1. *Given an automaton A, and a (non-empty) set of labeled words $M \subset \Sigma^* \times \{Yes, No\}$, we can combine them into an automaton A^M such that for each $\gamma \in \Sigma^*$*

- *if γ is labeled Yes in M then γ is in $Lan(A^M)$*
- *if γ is labeled No in M then γ is not in $Lan(A^M)$*
- *if γ is not labeled in M then γ is in $Lan(A^M)$ iff γ is in $Lan(M)$*

The algortihm to build this automaton is given in Appendix A.

We call the set M the *exception set* and we call each member of M an *exception*.

We let $\gamma\beta$ denote concatenating the word β to the word γ, ϵ denotes the zero length word. Given an automaton A, $|A|$ denotes the size of set of states S.

Throughout this paper we let m denote $|A|$ — the size of the (smallest) target automaton.

4 Exact Learning of Regular Languages with a t-Malicious Membership Oracle

This problem can be solved using the method given by Angluin, Kriķis, Sloan and Turán [5]. We can use that result because the language of regular sets is closed under exeptions (as was shown in previous section). We still show some proofs so that we can use tighter bounds. Note that we do not set any limits on the length of exceptions for the learning algorithm, only on the length of counterexamples. This fact lets us ignore the length of errors we emulate in the next section.

4.1 Preview

Consider Angluin's algorithm for learning regular languages with equivalence queries and membership queries (we use Kearns and Vazirani version [12]). Recall that in this algorithm, each state s_i is represented as some word γ_i that is a member of the states representative set Γ. State s_i is the last state in γ_i corresponding path. We also have some distinction set D. For each two different words $\gamma_i, \gamma_j \in \Gamma$, there is some $\beta \in D$ that distinguishes between them, i.e. $MQ(\gamma_i\beta) \neq MQ(\gamma_j\beta)$. Also recall that after each counterexample γ, we add to Γ some new state represented by γ_k. The new state we add is a prefix of the current counterexample γ. Now consider what would happen if we were to run Angluin's algorithm with a t-malicious membership oracle. The algorithm will run until it gets a counterexample countering some membership query or until the algorithm stops. If the algorithm stops, then it has a correct hypothesis. If we get a counterexample countering a membership oracle answer $MMQ(\gamma)$, we can correct the membership oracle and start the algorithm again. We call each such correction a "reset". After (at most) t "resets" we corrected all the mistakes and the algorithm runs with no mistakes and so stops with a correct hypothesis. Next we show that $|\Gamma|$ is no larger than $tb + m$. Note that if $t = 0$, we have that Γ is of size m. Suppose we reach the point where we have a group of states Γ of size $tb + m + 1$. At this point, we have, at least, $m + 1$ words in Γ that are not a prefix of a wrong answer. We denote this subgroup by Γ^T. Because A has only m distinct states, we can find two different words $\gamma_i, \gamma_j \in \Gamma^T$ that end at the same state. As already stated, we can also find some word $\beta \in D$ such that $MMQ(\gamma_i\beta) \neq MMQ(\gamma_j\beta)$. Because γ_j is not a prefix of a wrong answer, $MMQ(\gamma_i\beta) = MQ(\gamma_i\beta)$. The same holds for γ_j. From that we get that $MQ(\gamma_i\beta) \neq MQ(\gamma_j\beta)$. But if γ_i and γ_j end at the same state s, then we should get $MQ(\gamma_i\beta) = MQ(\gamma_j\beta)$ and so we have a contradiction. Because we add one member to Γ for each equivalence query we ask, there are no more than $tb + m$ EQs between two "resets". That is $tb+m-1$ equivalence queries for the algorithm and the last one for countering a wrong answer by the membership oracle. The number of "resets" is therefore bound by t, note that after each "reset" we have one less error. Hence we limit the number of EQs to $\frac{(t+1)}{2}(tb+m) \le t(tb+m)$, and bound the number of of MMQs by $t(tb+m)^2\log(b)$.

5 Exact Learning of Regular Languages in the Incomplete Model with an Online Adversary

In this section, we present a divide and conquer algorithm (as was defined by Bshouty in [8]) to learn regular languages in the incomplete model that we defined in section 2.

5.1 Preview

The following text provides some intuition for the algorithm. Suppose we have a set $S_i \subset \Sigma^*$ such that each path corresponding to $\gamma \in S_i$ ends at the state s_i. Furthermore, suppose that the equivalence oracle returns counterexamples that have a prefix from S_i (this constraint will be removed later). We can now learn the automaton A_i, that is the target automaton A, but with initial state s_i, using Angluin's algorithm for learning regular sets. Each time we get some counterexample $\gamma\beta$ to A, where $\gamma \in S_i$. We treat it as counterexample β to automaton A_i. Each time we need to ask $MQ(\beta)$ for A_i, we query $\gamma\beta$ for all γ in S_i, until we get an answer that is not an "I do not know". We are guarantied that we get the correct answer, as the path corresponding to γ ends at s_i. If there are no two words γ_j and γ_k in S_i, such that γ_j is a prefix of γ_k, then all queries are independent and we improve the probability that we will not be able to classify a word β to $(1-p)^{|S_i|}$ (since only one success is needed for a classification).

Given such a large S_i we can run Angluin's algorithm and get an automaton with a very high probability. Unfortunately, nobody gives us such a set S_i. Our algorithm tries to find such sets for some states and emulate them as initial states. To do that we must find sets that "cover" all of our domain, except some small number of words. We do that by building a prefix-closed tree, where each leaf-word is assigned to some *cover set* S_i (a leaf-word is the word that results from traveling the path to that leaf). However, due to the way the S_i are constructed, lack of knowledge and dependencies between member sets, some misclassifications are possible. At this point we let each cover set emulate a different automaton and build the appropriate general automaton. Each time we get a counterexample, it counters either one of the words inside the tree or it counters some cover set. The size of our tree is polynomial (in b, $\frac{1}{p}$ and $\ln(\frac{1}{\delta})$). Now we look at the cover set counterexamples. For each cover set S_i, we run Angluin's algorithm until the next equivalence query and then wait. When all cover sets enter a wait state, we ask an equivalence query (using the full automaton). The counterexample we receive can either give us an answer to some previously asked (incomplete) membership query, or it gives a counterexample for some cover set. We can now continue running the algorithms for this set, until the next equivalence query. We might find some witness β that lets us discard some word γ from the set S_i due to contradiction in the set S_i. In that case we build a new covering, and start the algorithm from the beginning. We show that the number of such "resets" is polynomial in $b, \ln(\frac{1}{\delta})$ and $\frac{1}{p}$. We also show that the number of expected mistakes between two "resets" is polynomialy bound by $b, \ln(\frac{1}{\delta})$ and $\frac{1}{p}$. So we have an algorithm that runs in expected polynomial time.

5.2 Learning the Automaton

We start with some definitions. Two words γ and υ are said to be *consistent* w.r.t. some distinction set $D \subseteq \{0,1\}^*$ if for each $\beta \in D$, $IMQ(\gamma\beta) =$ "I do not know" or $IMQ(\upsilon\beta) =$ "I do not know" or $IMQ(\gamma\beta) = IMQ(\upsilon\beta)$. A word γ is said to be a *true prefix* of υ if γ is a prefix of υ and $\gamma \neq \upsilon$. We define an order $\prec$ over the cover sets, so that $S_i \prec S_j$ if and only if $|S_i| < |S_j|$ or ($|S_i| = |S_j|$ and $i < j$). For a word $\gamma \in \Sigma^*$, we let $[\gamma]$ denote the largest cover set S_i with respect to the order $\prec$, such that $\gamma \in S_i$. We let $POST(\beta)$ denote the set that holds β and all of βs postfixes.
Now we give a short description of the algorithm. A full description can be found in Appendix B.

The goal of our algorithm is to find some good, large enough cover sets. A good cover set is a set of words, such that the corresponding paths of all words end at the same state. For the work of the algorithm, we use four sets:

- The prefix set $\Upsilon \subset \{0,1\}^*$ is the set holding all the words that can be members of a cover set. This set is prefix closed.
- The state set $\Gamma \subseteq \Upsilon$ represents the identified different states. Each word γ in Γ ends in a different state.
- The distinction set $D \subseteq \{0,1\}^*$ is the set holding all postfixes of queries asked during the running of the algorithm.
- The covering $\{S_i\}$ is a set of cover sets. Each cover set S_i is a subset of Υ. The union of all cover sets is Υ. All leaves of Υ (i.e. words that are not true prefixes of any other words in Υ) are members of (at least) one large cover set (a set larger than some constant k). All members of cover set S_i are consistent with the word $\gamma_i \in \Gamma$ w.r.t. D. Note that the cover sets are not necessarily disjoint.
- A fifth set is introduced only to simplify the proofs, and therefore will be ignored for now. $TERM \subseteq D$ holds only words that distinguish between two members of Υ.
- We also maintain a label table which keeps all counterexamples and answers to membership queries. Each time we get some counterexample or an answer to some membership query, we add the answer to the table. Each time we ask a membership query, we first check the table, and only if the table does not hold an answer, we ask the membership oracle.

The sets listed above are initialized by setting Υ, Γ and D to be $\{\epsilon\}$ (the zero length word). We initialize $TERM$ to be the empty set. At the start of each iteration, we increase the prefix set and fix the covering by calling the procedure *partition* (see the procedure in Appendix B). Procedure *partition* receives all sets, and tries to find some consistent covering, such that all leaves of the prefix set Υ are members of a large enough cover sets. As long as there is some leaf that is not a member of a large cover set, we split this leaf. We split a leaf γ by adding both $\gamma 0$ and $\gamma 1$ to Υ, making γ an inner vertex. After each such split, we try to build a new large cover set. The procedure stops when there are no more leaf words that are not members of a large cover set.

We build our initial hypothesis for this iteration using procedure *Build − Cover − Automaton* (see the procedure in Appendix B). First, we build the tree of the set Υ, in such a way that every inner vertex $v \in \Upsilon$ has an edge labeled 0 to the vertex $v0$ and an edge labeled 1 to the vertex $v1$. Note that both $v0$ and $v1$ are members of Υ. Next, we build an initial automaton hypothesis for each cover set S_i. This is done as in Angluin's algorithm. We let two edges, one labeled 0 and the other 1, to lead from S_i into S_i. Next we connect each leave v with the set $[v]$ (recall that $[v]$ is some S_j). We connect them with two edges, one labeled 0 and the other 1.

Next, we start our learning loop for this iteration. Each cover set S_i runs Angluin's algorithm. At the start of each loop, all cover sets are waiting for a counterexample. We ask the equivalence oracle for a counterexample. If we get none, we go to wrapup phase. If we have some counterexample d, either d is a member of Υ, in which case we fix the label and ask another equivalence query, or there is some v, a prefix of d, such that v is a leaf of Υ. Hence we have $d = v\beta$. If d is an answer to a previous query (that was answered "I don't know"), we fix the label table and go to the next loop. If not, it must be a counterexample β to the cover set $[v]$. If this is the case, we can continue to run Angluin's algorithm, until the next equivalence query. Each time the algorithm asks a membership query, we activate the procedure $EmulateMQ(S_i, \beta)$.

In procedure $EmulateMQ(S_i, \beta)$, we first add $POST(\beta)$ to D. We then check if all $\{S_i\}$ are still consistent w.r.t. D. If not, we do a "reset", i.e., we throw away all inconsistent words from all inconsistent cover set S_i and start the next phase. We also add a word d that caused "reset" to $TERM$. If all coverings are still consistent, then we return the answer that one member $\lambda \in S_i$ answered for $IMQ(\lambda\beta)$. If all answers were "I don't know", we return an arbitrary answer "NO".

This is the end of both the phase loop and the learning loop, and we start the wrapup phase. At the start of this phase, we probably have a very large hypothesis automaton $\tilde{A}$ that agrees with the target automaton A on all words of length b or shorter. Because we want to learn A, we now start minimizing $\tilde{A}$. If $b > m^2 + m$, we can restart Angluin's algorithm for learning DFAs using an equivalence oracle and a membership oracle, but with our hypothesis $\tilde{A}$ serving as both oracles. We return the shortest counterexample, until the shortest counterexample is longer than m^2. Our final hypothesis will be A due to charactaristics of DFAs.

5.3 Proofs

This section previews the proof of the proposed algorithm for "efficiently" learns class of regular languages in the incomplete model.

First, we prove that the algorithm is correct. Our algorithm consists of two phases, the first is learning the language L with length b as a limit, and the second phase is learning the correct automaton. Because we can get to the second phase only after we received an "equivalent" reply from the equivalence oracle, we really learned the target langauge L, with b as a word limit. Now we learn again the language, but with correct answers only, (no longer than b). By construction, to learn an automaton of size m, we only ask mebmership queries of length not greater than m digits beyond the longest counterexample. If we give only short counterexamples (of length m^2 or less), and if $b \geq m^2+m$, then at the end of the second phase we get a correct automaton. Notice that if we have two different automatons of length m or shorter, we can always find some counterexample of length m^2 or shorter. Hence our second phase stops with a correct answer.

Next we go over group complexity. Our first question is how large can Υ get. We can only increase Υ by splitting a word v (adding both 0 and 1 to it) such that $|[v]| \leq k$. Hence, only states which appear fewer than k times in Υ may be split. (two different words that end at the same state can never disagree with each other). We therefore can split only k words for each state in the target automaton A. Because $|A| = m$, we conclude that we have (at most) km splits. Each split adds 2 words to Υ, so the size of Υ can not exceed $2kn+1$. For termination calculations, we also added some set $TERM$. We add a word to $TERM$ only when it distinguishes between two different words v_1 and v_2 in Υ that have no word $t \in TERM$ yet which differentiates them. It follows immediatly that $|TERM| \leq (|\Upsilon|-1)^2$, or $|TERM| \leq 4k^2m^2$.

We count mistakes next. We define two kinds of mistakes: *"knowledge mistkes"* and *"misclassifications mistakes"*. A knowledge mistake occures when all members of a set $[v]$ return "I do not know". A miscalassification mistake occurs when a member of a set $[v]$ returns a wrong answer, while v returns "I do not know". We get both kind of mistked only for members of Υ. Because Υ is prefix closed and because $|\Upsilon| \leq 2km+1$, we can count mistkes using words shorter than $2km+2$.

The probability that one state v_1 can lie to v_2 on t queries (i.e. cause "misclassifications mistakes"), is $(1-p)^t$. The reason is that every query we ask for v_1, we also ask for v_2 (because we add v_2 to Γ only if is no prefix of any other v_1 in Υ). To calculate "knowledge mistkes" we need a bit more advanced calculations. We assume that the number of membership queries is bound by k^{20}. Now, given k members of Υ, how many "misclassifications mistakes" can our only adversay cause, and we find that this number is quite low with high probability.

The bottom line of all our calculations is that if we take k to be the maximum between: b, $2\frac{1}{p}\ln(\frac{1}{\delta})$,$100\frac{1}{p}^2$ and 400, we get a bound of less than k^{20} membership and equivalence queries, for probability of $(1-\delta)$. This are very large numbers, but we use them only for proof of polynomial bound. Much tighter bounds can be achieved (with more mathematical effort). Hence we conclude that with high probability, our algorithm stops after a polynomial number of operations.

6 Conclusions and Open Problems

We have shown an "efficient" algorithm to learn a regular language using an equivalence oracle and an incomplete membership oracle. Using this result, we can learn any problem that was reducted to regular language, such as learning an $O(\log n)-$Term DNF [13] using the same model.

A problem that is still open is whether we can improve our algorithm so that it will be able to handle multiplicity automata, in the same way that was done in [6], for the omniscient model. We believe that if we can find a consistent cover set for words in the multiplicity automaton, we can generalize algorithm [6] in the same way as we have generalized [1].

Another open problem is whether we can generalize our algorithm in such a way so that we will be able to apply it to a whole family of learning algorithms in the standard model.

In future work we plan to improve this algorithm so it will manage errors in answers (with variable probability p).

Another future improvement will show that this algorithm can handle an "off-line" adversary — an adversary that knows all the membership oracle's answers in advance. We have a proof, and intend to publish it in the near future.

Acknowledgment

Ron Sivan for helping in the writing of this article.
Orr Dunkelman for helping in the writing of this article.

References

1. D. Angluin. (1987). Learning Regular Sets from Queries and Counterexamples. *Information and Computation*, 75:87-106.
2. D. Angluin. (1988). Queries and Concept Learning. *Machine Learning*, 2:319-342.
3. D. Angluin. (1990). Negative Results for Equivalence Queries. *Machine Learning*, 5:121-150.
4. D. Angluin and D. K. Slonim. (1994). Randomly Fallible Teachers: Learning Monotone DNF with an Incomplete Membership Oracle. *Machine Learning*, 14:7-26.
5. D. Angluin, M. Kriķis, R. H. Sloan and G. Turán. (1997). Malicious Omissions and Errors in Answers to Membership Queries. *Machine Learning*, 28:211-255.
6. A. Beimel, F. Bergadoano, N.H. Bshouty and E.Kushilevitz. (1996) On the Application of Multiplicity automaton in Learning. *FOCS96*, 349-358.
7. A. Blum, R. Khardon, E. Kushilevitz, L. Pitt and D. Roth. (1994). On Learning Read-k-Satisfy-j DNF. *COLT94*, 110-117.
8. N. H. Bshouty (1997). Simple Learning Algorithms using Divide and Conquer. *Computational Complexity*, 6:174-194.

9. N. H. Bshouty and N. Einon. Learning Monotone DNF from a Teacher that almost does not answer membership queries Manuscript.
10. Z. Chen. (1994). A note on learning DNF formulas using Equivalence and Incomplete Membership Queries. *AII/ALT*, 272-281.
11. M.Kearns and L.Valient. (1994). Cryptographic Limitations on Learning Boolean Formulae and Finite automaton. *Journal of the Association for Computing Machinery*, 41:67-95.
12. M. Kearns and U. Vazirani. "An introduction to Computational Learning Theory". MIT Press, 1994.
13. E. Kushilevitz. (1996). A Simple Algorithm for Learning $O(\log n)-$Term DNF. *COLT96*, 266-269.
14. R.L.Rivest and R.E.Schapire. (1993). Inference of Finite automaton Using Homing Sequences. *Information and Computation*, 103(2):299-347.
15. R.H.Sloan and G. Turan. (1994). Learning with Queries but Incomplete Information. *In Proceedings of the Seventh Annual ACM Conference on Computational Learning Theory*, 237-245
16. S.A.Goldman and H.D.Mathias. (1992). Learning k-term DNF formulas with an incomplete membership oracle. *In Proceedings of the Fifth Annual ACM Workshop on Computational Learning Theory*, 77-84.

Appendix A: The Exception Automaton

Here we show the exception automaton for lemma 1:

Given an automaton A, and a (non-empty) set of labeled words $M \subset \{0,1\}^* \times \{Yes, No\}$, we can combine them into an automaton A^M such that for each $\gamma \in \{0,1\}^*$

- $(\gamma, Yes) \in M \rightarrow \gamma \in Lan(A^M)$
- $(\gamma, No) \in M \rightarrow \gamma \notin Lan(A^M)$
- $((\gamma, Yes) \notin M \wedge (\gamma, No) \notin M) \rightarrow (\gamma \in Lan(M) \Leftrightarrow \gamma \in Lan(A^M))$

Given such exception list, we build the automaton as following:

- Init Γ to be the set of words labeled in M.
- Add to Γ all prefixes of every word $\gamma \in \Gamma$.
- Let S^M be $S \cup \Gamma$ (We assume that $S \cap \Gamma = \phi$).
- $\Sigma^M = \{0,1\}$
- Let s_0^M be ϵ (if $|M| > 0$ then $\epsilon \in \Gamma$).
- The definition of $\mu^M(s^M, \sigma)$:
  - If $s^M \in S$, then $\mu^M(s^M, \sigma) = \mu(s^M, \sigma)$.
  - If $s^M \in \Gamma$ and $s^M\sigma \in \Gamma$, then $\mu^M(s^M, \sigma) = s^M\sigma$.
  - Let $\pi = s_0 \ldots s_k$ be the path corresponding to the word $s^M\sigma$ in A. If $s^M \in \Gamma$ and $s^M\sigma \notin \Gamma$, then $\mu^M(s^M, \sigma) = s_k$.
- Init F^M to be F.
- For each $\gamma \in \Gamma$ do:
  - If $(\gamma, Yes) \in M$, add γ to F^M.
  - If $((\gamma, Yes) \notin M \wedge (\gamma, No) \notin M)$, let $\pi = s_0 \ldots s_k$ be the path corresponding to the word γ. If $s_k \in F$, add γ to F^M.

It is easy to see that this automaton really yields the original automaton with the given exception list.

Appendix B: The Learning Algorithm

Here we give better algorithms description and proofs for the claims in section 5.

Procedure *Partition*$(\Upsilon, D, \Gamma, \{S_i\})$:

1. For each $\gamma_i \in \Gamma$, initialize S_i to be $\{\gamma_i\}$.
2. For each $\upsilon \in \Upsilon \setminus \Gamma$:
   a) Add υ to all S_i, such that υ is consistent with γ_i w.r.t. D.
   b) If no such γ_i exists:
      i. Add υ to Γ.
      ii. Goto 1. * we restart the procedure*\
3. Initialize Λ to be Υ.
4. Remove from Λ all λs such that λ is a true prefix of some $\upsilon \in \Lambda$.
5. Remove from Λ all λs such that $|[\lambda]| > k$.
6. While $\Lambda \neq \phi$:
   a) Choose some $\lambda \in \Lambda$
   b) If λ is a member of Γ, remove λ from Γ and assign $[\lambda] \leftarrow \phi$.
   c) If there are more than k members of Υ that are consistent with λ w.r.t. D:
      i. Remove from Γ all members γ_i that are consistent with λ w.r.t. D. Assign $S_i \leftarrow \phi$.
      ii. Add λ to Γ.
   d) Else
      i. Add $\lambda 0$ and $\lambda 1$ to Υ and to Λ.
      ii. Remove λ from Λ.
      iii. Assign $\lambda 0$ and $\lambda 1$ to all possible cover sets as before.
   e) As long as exits some β in Λ such that β is not a member of any cover set S_i, add β to Γ, init a new cover set S_j and assign to S_j all $\lambda \in \Lambda$ such that λ is consistent with β w.r.t. D.
   f) Remove from Λ all λs such that $|[\lambda]| > k$.

Procedure *Emulate* $- MQ(S_i, \beta)$**:**

1. Assign $D \rightarrow D \cup POST(\beta)$.
2. If there exist a λ in some S_j such that λ is not consistent with γ_j w.r.t. $POST(\beta)$:
   a) For each inconsistent member λ in S_j and the (new) distinction word $d \in POST(\beta)$:
      i. Add d to $TERM$. * We use this set only to get simple proofs. *\
   b) return "Reset".
3. If $IMQ(\gamma_i\beta) \neq$ "I do not know", Return $IMQ(\gamma_i\beta)$.
4. Else, find the some $\upsilon \in S_i$ such that $IMQ(\upsilon\beta) \neq$ "I do not know"
5. Return $IMQ(\upsilon\beta)$.
6. If all members of S_i returned "I don't know" then return "NO".

Procedure *Build* $-$ *Cover* $-$ *automaton*$(\{S_i\})$**:**

1. Assign a vertex for each $\upsilon \in \Upsilon$.
2. Label each vertex υ by $IMQ(\upsilon)$ (i.e. accepting or not). If $IMQ(\upsilon) =$ "I do not know", label υ as not accepting.
3. For each vertex $\upsilon 0$ in Υ, add an edge from υ to $\upsilon 0$ labeled by 0.
4. For each vertex $\upsilon 1$ in Υ, add an edge from υ to $\upsilon 1$ labeled by 1.
5. Add a vertex for each group $[\gamma_i]$.
6. Label each vertex $[\gamma_i]$ by *Emulate* $- MQ([\gamma_i], \epsilon)$
7. For each vertex $[\gamma_i]$, add two edges from $[\gamma_i]$ to $[\gamma_i]$, one labeled 0 and one labeled 1.
8. For each vertex $\upsilon \in \Upsilon$, such that υ is not a true prefix of any $\lambda \in \Upsilon$, add two edges from υ to $[\upsilon]$ labeled with 0 and 1.
9. Return the automaton.

Procedure *Learn − automaton − with − IMQs*:

1. Initialization:
   a) $\Gamma \leftarrow \{\epsilon\}$
   b) $D \leftarrow \{\epsilon\}$
   c) $TERM \leftarrow \{\epsilon\}$
   d) $\Upsilon \leftarrow \{\epsilon\}$
   e) $\{S_i\} \leftarrow \phi$
   f) call $Partition(\Upsilon, D, \Gamma, \{S_i\})$
   g) $A \leftarrow Build - Cover - automaton(\{S_i\})$
2. $\gamma \leftarrow EQ(A)$
3. While There exists a counter example d: * This is the learning loop *\
   a) If $d \in \Upsilon$, change d's label and call $Partition(\Upsilon, D, \Gamma, \{S_i\})$.
   b) Else
      i. Find υ, the longest prefix of d, such that $\upsilon \in \Upsilon$.
      ii. Let $d = \upsilon\lambda$. If $MQ(d) = emulate - MQ([\upsilon], \lambda)$
         A. give λ as a counter example to the automaton of $[\upsilon]$ and run the algorithm from the section 4 on $[\upsilon]$ up to the first EQ.
         B. Each time the algorithm asks $MQ(\beta)$, answer with $Emulate - MQ([\upsilon], \beta)$
         C. If $Emulate - MQ$ returns "reset", goto 3.c.
         D. If the emulation changed some edge that goes out of $[\upsilon]$, change all the corresponding edges from the words $\lambda \in \Upsilon$, such that $[\lambda] = S_i$ (they always go to the same states as S_i).
   c) If there was a "reset": \ * Go to next phase *\
      i. call $Partition(\Upsilon, D, \Gamma, \{S_i\})$
      ii. $A \leftarrow Build - Cover - automaton(\{S_i\})$
   d) $\gamma \leftarrow EQ(A)$
4. Run the previous algorithm with A as an oracle that returns the shortest counterexamples. Stop when the shortest counterexample (given by A) is of length greater than b.

Appendix C: Some Proofs

In this appendix we give proofs for the bounds on the number of mistakes, both *"knowledge mistkes"* and *"misclassifications mistakes"*. We do not give the full proofs, but only guidelines.

Lemma 2. *Our algorithm has no more than k^3 "misclassifications mistakes" between any member of Γ and Υ, with probability greater than $(1-\frac{\delta}{2})$.*

Proof. We start by bounding the probability of k^3 such mistakes between $\gamma \in \Gamma$ and $\upsilon \in \Upsilon$. Because γ is no prefix of any other member of Υ, we can assume that when we ask γ about β such that $MQ(\gamma\beta) \neq MQ(\upsilon\beta)$, we already know the answer to $MMQ(\upsilon\beta)$. We count here only βs such that $MMQ(\upsilon\beta)$ is not "I do not know" (because υ tries to lie to γ).

So, the probability that υ lies to γ k^3 times is $(1-p)^{k^3}$. From the way we have chosen k, it follows that $(1-p)^{k^3} \leq e^{-k^3 p} \leq \frac{\delta}{2} e^{-k^2}$.

Υ holds only words of length no longer than $2km+1$. Hence we need only consider 2^{2km+1} words. Γ is partial to Υ, so we can also consider only 2^{2km+1} words for Γ. The number of couples from Γ and Υ is bound by $2^{4km+2} \leq 2^{k^2}$. So the probability that we might find a couples from Γ and Υ with more than k^3 misclassifications is bound by $\frac{\delta}{2} e^{-k^2} \cdot 2^{k^2} \leq \frac{\delta}{2}$

Lemma 3. *Our algorithm has no more than k^5 "knowledge mistakes" for any k members of Υ, for less than k^{20} $MMQs$, with probability greater than $(1-\frac{\delta}{2})$.*

Proof. We first try to calculate the probability for k members of Υ to have no knowledge on k^3 different words. In other words, given some set Υ' of size k, what is the largest set D, such that we have no knowledge of any query in $\Upsilon' \cdot D$, when we are allowed only k^{20} MMQs.

In the i'th iteration, we ask query β_i. We need to calculate the probability that d_i is a member of D. For β_i to be a member of D, we need k answers of "I do not know" for some set of size k such that β is a member in. We have at most k such different sets (beacuse Υ' is of size k). Assuming all such sets are new (if we asked about any member previously, then that set is already accounted for), we have a probability of $(1-(1-p)^k)^k \geq 1-k(1-p)^k$ for failure. That is $1-(1-p)^k$ for each set (best case they are independent). The other side of the coin that that we have k or less new members of D with probability less than $k(1-p)^k \leq ke^{-kp}$. The probability for more than k^5 mistakes here (that is k^4 successes for our adversary) is less than $(\frac{k^{20}ke^{-kp}e}{k^4})^{k^4}$. We chose k such that $\frac{k^{20}ke^{-kp}e}{k^4} \leq \frac{1}{2}$. Hence we get a probability of less than 2^{-k^4} for more than k^5 knowledge mistakes for a given set Υ' (when we have an online adversary), with less than k^{20} MMQs.

Because Υ' is a subset of Υ, and because Υ has no more than 2^{2km+1} members, then we have less than 2^{k^3} such possible sets. Hence the probability for our adversary to cause us more than k^5 knowledge mistakes is bound by $2^{-k^4} 2^{k^3} \leq \frac{\delta}{2}$. And so we conclude.

Learning Rates for Q-Learning

Eyal Even-Dar and Yishay Mansour

School of Computer Science, Tel-Aviv University
evend@cs.tau.ac.il mansour@cs.tau.ac.il

Abstract. In this paper we derive convergence rates for Q-learning. We show an interesting relationship between the convergence rate and the learning rate used in the Q-learning. For a polynomial learning rate, one which is $1/t^{\omega}$ at time t where $\omega \in (1/2, 1)$, we show that that the convergence rate is polynomial in $1/(1-\gamma)$, where γ is the discount factor. In contrast we show that for a linear learning rate, one which is $1/t$ at time t, the convergence rate has an exponential dependence on $1/(1-\gamma)$. In addition we show a simple example that proves that this exponential behavior is inherent for a linear learning rate.

1 Introduction

In Reinforcement Learning, an agent wanders in an unknown environment and tries to maximize its long term return by performing actions and receiving rewards. The challenge is to understand how a current action will affect future rewards. A good way to model this task is Markov Decision Process (MDP), which has become the dominating approach in Reinforcement Learning [SB98, BT96].

An MDP includes states, which abstract the environment, actions, which are the available actions to the agent, and for each state and action a distribution of next states, the state reached after performing the action in the given state. In addition there is a reward function that assigns a stochastic reward for each state and action. The return combines a sequence of the rewards to a single value that the agent tries to optimize. A discounted return has a parameter $\gamma \in (0, 1)$ where the reward received in step k is discounted by γ^k.

One of the challenges of Reinforcement Learning is when the MDP is not known, and we can only observe the trajectory of states, actions and rewards generated by the agent wandering in the MDP. There are two basic conceptual approaches to the learning problem. The first is model base, where we first reconstruct a model of the MDP, and then find an optimal policy for the approximate model. The second approach are implicit methods that updates the information after each step, and based on this have an estimate to the optimal policy. The most popular of those methods in Q-learning [Wat89].

Q-learning is an off-policy method that can be run on top of any strategy wandering in the MDP. It uses the information observed to approximate the optimal function, from which one can construct the optimal policy. There are various proofs that Q-learning does converge to the optimal Q function, under

D. Helmbold and B. Williamson (Eds.): COLT/EuroCOLT 2001, LNAI 2111, pp. 589–604, 2001.

very mild conditions, [BT96,Tsi94,WD92,MS96,JJS94,BM00]. The conditions have to do with the exploration policy and the learning rate. For the exploration one needs to require that each state action be performed infinitely often. The learning rate controls how fast we modify our estimates. One expects to start with a high learning rate, which allows fast changes, and lowers the learning rate at time progresses. The basic conditions are that the sum of the learning rates goes to infinity (so that any value could be reached) and that the sum of the squares of the learning rates is finite (which is require to show that the convergence is with probability one).

We use the proof technique of [BT96], which is based on convergence of stochastic processes, to derive convergence rates for Q-learning. The most interesting outcome of our investigation is the relationship between the form of the learning rates and the rate of convergence. We study two models of updating in Q-learning. The first is the synchronous model, where all state action pairs are updated simultaneously. The second is the asynchronous model, where at each step we update a single state action pair. We distinguish between two sets of learning rates. A linear learning rate is of the form $1/t$ at time t, and a polynomial learning rate, which is of the form $1/t^{\omega}$, where $\omega \in (1/2, 1)$ is a parameter.

We show for synchronous model that using a polynomial learning rate the convergence rate is polynomial in $1/(1-\gamma)$, while for a linear learning rate the convergence rate is exponential in $1/(1-\gamma)$. We also show an exponential behavior for linear learning rate. The lower bound simply shows that if the initial value is one and all the rewards are zero, it takes $O((1/\epsilon)^{1/(1-\gamma)})$ updates, using a linear learning rate, until we reach a value of ϵ.

The convergence rate of Q-learning in a batch setting, where many samples are averaged for each update, was analyzed in [KS98]. A batch setting does not have a learning rate and it has much of the flavor of model based techniques, since each update is an average of many samples.

The convergence of Q-learning with linear learning rate was studied in [Sze97] for special MDPs, where the next state distribution is the same for each state. (This setting is much closer to the PAC model, since there is no influence between the action performed and the states reached, and the states are distributed i.i.d.). For this model [Sze97] shows a convergence rate, which is exponential in $1/(1-\gamma)$. In [BGS99] an exponential lower bound in the number of the states is given for undiscounted return.

2 The Model

We define a Markov Decision process (MDP) as follows

Definition 2.1. *A Markov Decision process (MDP) M is a 4-tuple (S, U, P, R), where S is a set of the states, U is a set of actions ($U(i)$ is the set of actions available at state i), $P_{i,j}^{M}(a)$ is the transition probability from state i to state j when performing action $a \in U(i)$ in state i, and $R_M(a, s)$ is the reward received when performing action a in state s.*

We assume that $R_M(a,s)$ is non-negative and bounded by R_{max}, i.e, $\forall s,a: 0 \le R_M(a,s) \le R_{max}$. For simplicity we assume that the reward $R_M(a,s)$ is deterministic, however all our results apply when $R_M(a,s)$ is stochastic.

A strategy for an MDP assigns, at each time t, for each state s a probability for performing action $a \in U(s)$, given a history $F_{t-1} = \{s_1, a_1, r_1, ..., s_{t-1}, a_{t-1}, r_{t-1}\}$ which includes the states, actions and rewards observed until time $t-1$. A policy is memory-less strategy, i.e., it depends only on the current state and not on the history. A deterministic policy assigns each state a unique action.

While following a policy π we perform at time t action a_t at state s_t and observe a reward r_t (distributed according to $R_M(a,s)$), and the next state s_{t+1} distributed according to $P^M_{s_t,s_{t+1}}(a_t)$. We combine the sequence of rewards to a single value called the return, and our goal is to maximize the return. In this work we focus on *discounted return*, which has a parameter $\gamma \in (0,1)$, and the discounted return of policy π is $V^\pi_M = \sum_{t=0}^\infty \gamma^t r_t$, where r_t is the reward observed at time t. Since all the rewards are bounded by R_{max} the discounted return is bounded by $V_{max} = \frac{R_{max}}{1-\gamma}$.

We define a value function for each state s, under policy π, as $V^\pi_M(s) = E[\sum_{i=0}^\infty r_i \gamma^i]$, where the expectation is over a run of policy π starting at state s. We define a state-action value function $Q^\pi_M(s,a) = R_M(a,s) + \gamma \sum_{\bar{s}} P_{s,\bar{s}}(a) V^\pi_M(\bar{s})$, whose value is the return of initially performing action a at state s and then following policy π. Since $\gamma < 1$ we can define another parameter $\beta = (1-\gamma)/3$, which will be useful for our results. Note that as β decreases V_{max} increases.

Let π^* be an optimal policy which maximizes the return from any start state. (It is well known that there exists an optimal strategy, which is a deterministic policy [Put94].) This implies that for any policy π and any state s we have $V^{\pi^*}_M(s) \ge V^\pi_M(s)$, and $\pi^*(s) = argmax_a(R_M(a,s) + \gamma(\sum_{s'} P^M_{s,s'}(a) \max_b Q(s',b))$. The optimal policy is also the only fixed point of the operator, $(TQ)(s,a) = R_M(a,s) + \gamma \sum_{s'} P_{s,s'}(a) \max_b Q(s',b)$. We use V^*_M and Q^*_M for $V^{\pi^*}_M$ and $Q^{\pi^*}_M$, respectively. We say that a policy π is an ϵ-approximation of the optimal policy if $\|V^*_M - V^\pi_M\|_\infty \le \epsilon$.

The *covering time*, denoted by L, is a bound on the number of steps needed, from any start state, until all state-action pairs are performed. Note that the covering time is a function of both the MDP and the underlying strategy. Initially we assume that from any start state, within L steps all state-action pairs are performed. Later, we relax the assumption and assume that with probability at least $\frac{1}{2}$, from any start state in L steps all state-action pairs are performed.

The Parallel Sampling Model, $PS(M)$, as was introduced in [KS98]. The $PS(M)$ is an ideal exploration policy. A single call to $PS(M)$ returns for every pair (s,a) the next state s', distributed according to $P^M_{s,s'}(a)$ and a reward r distributed according to $R_M(a,s)$. The advantage of this model is that it allows ignoring the exploration and focusing on the learning. In some sense $PS(M)$ can be viewed as a perfect exploration policy.

Notations: The notation $g = \tilde{\Omega}(f)$ implies that there are constants c_1 and c_2 such that $g \ge c_1 f \ln^{c_2}(f)$. All the norms $\|\cdot\|$, unless otherwise specified, are L_∞ norms, i.e., $\|(x_1, \ldots, x_n)\| = \max_i x_i$.

3 Q-Learning

The Q-Learning algorithm [Wat89] estimates the state-action value function (for discounted return) as follows:

$$Q_{t+1}(s,a) = (1-\alpha_t(s,a))Q_t(s,a) + \alpha_t(s,a)(r_t(s,a) + \gamma \max_{a\in U(s')} Q_t(s',a)), \quad (1)$$

where s' is the state reached from state s when performing action a at time t. Let $T^{i,u}$ be the set of times, where action u was performed at state i, then $\alpha_t(\bar{s},\bar{a}) = 0$ for $t \notin T^{\bar{s},\bar{a}}$. It is known Q-Learning converges to Q^* if each state action pair is performed infinitely often and $\alpha_t(s,a)$ satisfies for each (s,a) pair: $\sum_{t=1}^{\infty} \alpha_t(s,a) = \infty$ and $\sum_{t=1}^{\infty} \alpha_t^2(s,a) < \infty$ ([BT96,Tsi94,WD92,MS96,JJS94]).

Q-Learning is an asynchronous process in the sense that it updates a single entry each step. Next we describe two variants of Q-Learning, which are used in the proofs. The first algorithm is *synchronous Q-Learning*, which performs the updates by using the $PS(M)$. Specifically:
$\forall s,a: Q_0(s,a) = 0$
$\forall s,a: Q_{t+1}(s,a) = (1-\alpha_t^\omega)Q_t(s,a) + \alpha_t^\omega(R_M(a,s) + \gamma \max_{a\in U(\bar{s})} Q_t(\bar{s},a))$,
where $\bar{s}$ is the state reached from state s when performing action a. The learning rate is $\alpha_t^\omega = \frac{1}{(t+1)^\omega}$, for $\omega \in (1/2,1]$. We distinguish between a *linear learning rate*, which is $\omega = 1$, and a *polynomial learning rate*, which is $\omega \in (\frac{1}{2},1)$.

The *asynchronous Q-Learning algorithm*, is simply regular Q-learning as define in (1). We add the assumption that the underlying strategy has a covering time of L. The updates are as follows:

$$\forall s,a: Q_0(s,a) = 0$$
$$\forall s,a: Q_{t+1}(s,a) = (1-\alpha_t^\omega(s,a))Q_t(s,a) + \alpha_t^\omega(s,a)(R_M(a,s) + \gamma \max_{b\in U(\bar{s})} Q_t(\bar{s},b))$$

Let $\#(s,a,t)$ be one plus the number of times, until time t, that we visited state s and performed action a. The learning rate $\alpha_t^\omega(s,a) = \frac{1}{[\#(s,a,t)]^\omega}$, if at time t we perform action a in state s and $\alpha_t^\omega(s,a) = 0$ otherwise. Again, $\omega = 1$ is a linear learning rate, and $\omega \in (\frac{1}{2},1)$ is a polynomial learning rate.

4 Our Main Results

Our main results are upper bounds on the convergence rates of Q-Learning algorithms and showing their dependence on the learning rate. The basic case is the synchronous Q-learning. We show that for a polynomial learning rate we have a complexity, which is polynomial in $1/(1-\gamma) = 1/(3\beta)$. In contrast, linear learning rate has an exponential dependence on $1/\beta$. Our results exhibit a sharp difference between the two learning rates, although they both converge in probability one. This distinction, which is highly important, can be observed only when we study the convergence rate, rather than convergence in the limit.

The bounds for asynchronous Q-Learning are similar. The main difference is the introduction of a covering time L. For polynomial learning rate we derive a bound polynomial in $1/\beta$, and for linear learning rate our bound is exponential in $\frac{1}{\beta}$. We also show a lower bound for linear learning rate, which is exponential in $\frac{1}{\beta}$. This implies that our upper bounds are tight, and that the gap between the two bounds is real.

We first prove the results for the synchronous Q-Learning algorithm, where we update all the entries of the Q function at each time step, i.e., the updates are synchronous. The following theorem derives the bound for polynomial learning rate.

Theorem 4.1. *Let Q_T be the value of the synchronous Q-learning algorithm using polynomial learning rate at time T. Then $||Q_T - Q^*|| \leq \epsilon$, given that*

$$T = \Omega\left(\left(\left(\frac{V_{max}^2 \ln(\frac{|S|\,|A|V_{max}}{\delta\beta\epsilon})}{\beta^2\epsilon^2}\right)^{\frac{1-\omega}{\omega}} + \frac{1}{\beta}\ln\frac{V_{max}}{\epsilon}\right)^{\frac{1}{1-\omega}}\right)$$

The above bound is somewhat complicated. To simplify, assume that ω is a constant and consider first only its dependence on ϵ. This gives us $\Omega((\ln(1/\epsilon)/\epsilon^2)^{1/\omega} + (\ln(1/\epsilon))^{1/(1-\omega)})$ which is optimized when ω approaches one. Considering the dependence only on β, recall that $V_{max} = R_{max}/(3\beta)$, therefore the complexity is $\tilde{\Omega}(1/\beta^{4/\omega} + 1/\beta^{1/(1-\omega)})$ which is optimized for $\omega = 4/5$. The following theorem bounds the time for linear learning rate.

Theorem 4.2. *Let Q_T be the value of the synchronous Q-learning algorithm using linear learning rate at time T. Then $||Q_T - Q^*|| \leq \epsilon$, given that*

$$T = \Omega\left((\frac{V_{max}}{\epsilon})^{\frac{1}{\beta}} \frac{V_{max}^2 \ln(\frac{|S|\,|A|V_{max}}{\delta\beta\epsilon})}{(\beta\epsilon)^2}\right).$$

Next we state our results to asynchronous Q-learning. The bounds are similar to those of synchronous Q-learning, but have the extra dependency on the covering time L.

Theorem 4.3. *Let Q_T be the value of the asynchronous Q-learning algorithm using polynomial learning rate at time T. Then $||Q_T - Q^*|| \leq \epsilon$, given that*

$$T = \Omega\left(\left(\left(\frac{L^{1+2\omega} V_{max}^2 \ln(\frac{|S|\,|A|V_{max}}{\delta\beta\epsilon})}{\beta^2\epsilon^2}\right)^{\frac{1-\omega}{\omega}} + \frac{L}{\beta}\ln\frac{V_{max}}{\epsilon}\right)^{\frac{1}{1-\omega}}\right)$$

The dependence on the covering time, in the above theorem, is $\Omega(L^{2+1/\omega} + L^{1/(1-\omega)})$, which is optimized for $\omega = \sqrt{2}/2$. For the linear learning rate the dependence is much worse, since it has to be that $L \geq |S| \cdot |A|$, as is stated in the following theorem.

Theorem 4.4. *Let Q_T be the value of the asynchronous Q-learning algorithm using linear learning rate at time T. Then $||Q_T - Q^*|| \leq \epsilon$, given that*

$$T = \Omega\left((3L+1)^{\frac{1}{\beta}\ln\frac{V_{max}}{\epsilon}} \frac{LV_{max}^2 \ln(\frac{|S|\,|A|V_{max}}{\delta\beta\epsilon})}{(\beta\epsilon)^2} \right)$$

The following Theorem shows that a linear learning rate may require an exponential dependence on $1/(3\beta) = 1/(1-\gamma)$, thus showing that the gap between linear learning rate and polynomial learning rate is real and does exist for some MDPs. (The proof is in Appendix A.)

Theorem 4.5. *There exists an MDP such that Q-Learning with linear learning rate after $T = \Omega((\frac{1}{\epsilon})^{\frac{1}{1-\gamma}})$ steps has $||Q_T - Q^*_M|| > \epsilon$.*

5 Background from Stochastic Algorithms

Before we derive our proofs we first introduce the proof given in [BT96] for the convergence of stochastic iterative algorithms, and then show that Q-Learning algorithms fall in this category. In this section we review the proof for the convergence in the limit, and in the next section we will analyze the rate at which different Q-learning algorithms converge. (We will try to keep the background as close as possible to our needs for this paper.)

This section considers a general type of *iterative stochastic algorithms*, which is performed as follows:

$$X_{t+1}(i) = (1 - \alpha_t(i))X_t(i) + \alpha_t(i)((H_tX_t)(i) + w_t(i)), \tag{2}$$

where w_t is a bounded random variable with zero expectation and each H_t is assumed to belong to a family $\mathcal{H}$ of mappings.

Definition 5.1. *An iterative stochastic algorithm is well behaved if:*

1. *The step size $\alpha_t(i)$ satisfy (1) $\sum_{t=0}^{\infty} \alpha_t(i) = \infty$, (2) $\sum_{t=0}^{\infty} \alpha_t^2(i) < \infty$ and (3) $\alpha_t(i) \in (0,1)$.*
2. *There exists a constant A that bounds $w_t(i)$ for any history F_t, i.e., $\forall t, i : |w_t(i)| \leq A$*
3. *There exists $\gamma \in [0,1)$ and a vector X^* such that for any X we have $||H_tX - X^*|| \leq \gamma||X - X^*||$.*

The following fact (proven in [BT96]) shows the connection with the Q-learning algorithms.

Fact 5.1 *Synchronous Q-learning and Asynchronous Q-learning are both well behaved stochastic iterative algorithms.*

The main theorem states that a well behaved stochastic iterative algorithm converges in the limit.

Theorem 5.2. *Let X_t be the sequence generated by a well behaved stochastic iterative algorithm. Then X_t converges to X^* with probability* 1.

The following is an outline of the proof given in [BT96]. Without loss of generality, assume that $X^* = 0$ and $\|X_0\| \leq A$. The value of X_t is bounded since for any history F_t we have $\|w_t\| \leq A$, and since $\|X_0\| \leq A$, hence, for any t we have $\|X_t\| \leq A$.

Recall that $\beta = \frac{1-\gamma}{3}$. Let $D_1 = A$ and $D_{k+1} = (1-\beta)D_k$ for $k \geq 1$. Clearly the sequence D_k converges to zero. We prove by induction that for every k there exists some time τ_k such that for any $t \geq \tau_k$ we have $\|X_t\| \leq D_k$. Note that this will guarantee that at time $t \geq \tau_k$ for any i the value $X_t(i)$ is in the interval $[-D_k, D_k]$.

The proof is by induction. Assume that there is such a time τ_k and we show that there exists a time τ_{k+1} such that for $t \geq \tau_{k+1}$ we have $\|X_t\| \leq D_{k+1}$. Since D_k converges to zero this proves that X_t converges to zero, which equals X^*. For the proof we define for $t \geq \tau$ the quantity

$$W_{t+1,\tau}(i) = (1-\alpha_t)W_{t,\tau}(i) + \alpha_t w_t(i),$$

where $W_{\tau;\tau}(i) = 0$. The value of $W_{t;\tau}$ bounds the contributions of $w_j(i)$, $j \in [\tau, t]$, to the value of X_t (starting from time τ). We also define for $t \geq \tau_k$,

$$Y_{t+1;\tau}(i) = (1-\alpha_t(i))Y_{t;\tau}(i) + \alpha_t(i)\gamma D_k + \alpha_t \beta D_k$$

where $Y_{\tau_k;\tau_k} = D_k$. Notice that $Y_{t;\tau_k}$ is a deterministic process. The following lemma gives the motivation for the definition of $Y_{t;\tau_k}$ (the proof can be found in [BT96]).

Lemma 5.1. *For every i, we have*

$$-Y_{t;\tau_k}(i) + W_{t;\tau_k}(i) \leq X_t(i) \leq Y_{t;\tau_k}(i) + W_{t;\tau_k}(i)$$

Proof. From the definition of $Y_{t;\tau}$ and the assumption that $\sum_{t=0}^{\infty} \alpha_t = \infty$ it follows that $Y_{t;\tau}$ converges to $\gamma D_k + \beta D_k$ as t goes to infinity. In addition $W_{t;\tau_k}$ converges to zero as t goes to infinity. Therefore there exists a time τ_{k+1} such that $Y_{t;\tau} \leq (\gamma+\beta)D_k + \beta D_k/2$, and $|W_{t;\tau_k}| \leq \beta D_k/2$. This fact, together with Lemma. 5.1, yields that for $t \geq \tau_{k+1}$,

$$\|X_t\| \leq (\gamma + 2\beta)D_k = D_{k+1},$$

which completes the proof. □

6 Synchronous Q-Learning

In this section we sketch the proof of Theorem 4.1. The proof of Theorem 4.2 is similar in spirit and can be found in Appendix B. Our main focus will be the value of $r_t = \|Q_t - Q^*\|$, and our aim is to bound the time until $r_t \leq \epsilon$. We use a sequence of values D_i, such that $D_{k+1} = (1-\beta)D_k$ and $D_1 = V_{max}$. As in Section 5, we will consider times τ_k such that for any $t \geq \tau_k$ we have $r_t \leq D_k$. We call the time between τ_k and τ_{k+1} the kth iteration. (Note the distinction between a step of the algorithm and an iteration, which is a sequence of many steps.)

Our proof has two parts. The first (and simple) part is bounding the number of iterations until $D_i \leq \epsilon$. The bound is derived in the following fact.

Fact 6.1 *For $m \geq \frac{1}{\beta}\ln(V_{max}/\epsilon)$ we have $D_m \leq \epsilon$*

The second (and much more involve) part is to bound the number of steps in an iteration. We use the following quantities introduced in Section 5. Let $W_{t+1,\tau}(s,a) = (1-\alpha_t^\omega)W_{t,\tau}(s,a) + \alpha_t^\omega w_t(s,a)$, where $W_{\tau;\tau}(s,a) = 0$ and

$$w_t(s,a) = R(s,a) + \gamma \max_{v \in U(s')} Q_t(s',v) - \sum_{j=1}^{|S|} P_{s,j}(u)\left(R(s,a) + \gamma \max_{v \in U(j)} Q_t(j,v)\right),$$

where s' is the state reached after performing action a at state s. Let

$$Y_{t+1;\tau_k}(s,a) = (1-\alpha_t^\omega)Y_{t;\tau_k}(s,a) + \alpha_t^\omega \gamma D_k + \alpha_t^\omega \beta D_k,$$

where $Y_{\tau_k;\tau_k}(s,a) = D_k$. Our first step is to rephrase Lemma 5.1 for our setting.

Lemma 6.1. *For every state s action a and time τ_k, we have*

$$-Y_{t;\tau_k}(s,a) + W_{t;\tau_k}(s,a) \leq Q_t(s,a) - Q^*(s,a) \leq Y_{t;\tau_k}(s,a) + W_{t;\tau_k}(s,a)$$

The above lemma suggests (once again) that in order to bound the error r_t one can bound $Y_{t;\tau_k}$ and $W_{t;\tau_k}$ separately, and the two bounds imply a bound on r_t. We first bound the Y_t term, which is deterministic process, and then we bound the term, $W_{t;\tau}$, which is stochastic. We start with Q-learning using a polynomial learning rate and show that the duration of iteration k, which starts at time τ_k and ends at time τ_{k+1}, is bounded by τ_k^ω. For synchronous Q-learning with polynomial learning rate we define $\tau_{k+1} = \tau_k + \tau_k^\omega$, where τ_1 will be specified latter.

Lemma 6.2. *Consider synchronous Q-learning with a polynomial learning rate and assume that for any $t \geq \tau_k$ we have $Y_{t;\tau_k}(s,a) \leq D_k$. Then for any $t \geq \tau_k + \tau_k^\omega = \tau_{k+1}$ we have $Y_{t;\tau_k}(s,a) \leq D_k(\gamma + \beta + \frac{2}{e}\beta)$*

Proof. Let $Y_{\tau_k;\tau_k}(s,a) = (\gamma+\beta)D_k - \rho_{\tau_k}$, where $\rho_{\tau_k} = (1-(\gamma+\beta))D_k$. We can now write

$$Y_{t+1;\tau_k}(s,a) = (1-\alpha_t^\omega)Y_{t;\tau_k}(s,a) + \alpha_t^\omega(\gamma+\beta)D_k = (\gamma+\beta)D_k + (1-\alpha_t^\omega)\rho_t.$$

Therefore, $\rho_{t+1} = \rho_t(1-\alpha_t^\omega)$. We would like show that after time $\tau_{k+1} = \tau_k + \tau_k^\omega$ for any $t \geq \tau_{k+1}$ we have $\rho_t \leq \beta D_k$. By definition we can rewrite ρ_t as,

$$\rho_t = (1-(\gamma+\beta))D_k \prod_{l=1}^{t-\tau_k}(1-\alpha_{l+\tau_k}^\omega) = 2\beta D_k \prod_{l=1}^{t-\tau_k}(1-\frac{1}{(l+\tau_k)^\omega}),$$

where the last identity follows from the fact that $\alpha_t^\omega = 1/t^\omega$. Since the α_t^ω's are monotonically decreasing

$$\rho_t \le 2\beta D_k (1 - \frac{1}{\tau_k^\omega})^{t-\tau_k}.$$

For $t \ge \tau_k + \tau_k^\omega$ we have

$$\rho_t \le 2\beta D_k (1 - \frac{1}{\tau_k^\omega})^{\tau_k^\omega} \le \frac{2}{e}\beta D_k.$$

Hence, $Y_{t;\tau_k}(s,a) \le (\gamma + \beta + \frac{2}{e}\beta) D_k$. □

Next we bound the term $W_{t;\tau_k}(s,a)$ by $(1-\frac{2}{e})\beta D_k$. The sum of the bounds for $W_{t;\tau_k}(s,a)$ and $Y_{t;\tau_k}(s,a)$ would be $(\gamma + 2\beta) D_k = (1-\beta) D_k = D_{k+1}$, as desired.

Definition 6.1. *Let* $W_{t;\tau_k}(s,a) = (1-\alpha_t^\omega) W_{t-1;\tau_k}(s,a) + \alpha_t^\omega w_t(s,a)$ $= \sum_{i=\tau+1}^{t} \eta_i^{k,t} w_{\tau_k+i}(s,a)$, *where* $\eta_i^{k,t} = \alpha_{i+\tau_k}^\omega \prod_{j=\tau_k+i+1}^{t} (1-\alpha_j^\omega)$.

We have bounded the term $Y_{t;\tau_k}$, for $t = \tau_{k+1}$. This bound holds for any $t \ge \tau_{k+1}$, since the sequence $Y_{t;\tau_k}$ is monotonically decreasing. In contrast the term $W_{t;\tau_k}$ is stochastic. Therefore it is not sufficient to bound $W_{\tau_{k+1};\tau_k}$, but we need to bound $W_{t;\tau_k}$ for $t \ge \tau_{k+1}$. However it is sufficient to consider $t \in [\tau_{k+1}, \tau_{k+2}]$. The following lemma bounds the coefficients in that interval.

Lemma 6.3. *For any* $t \in [\tau_{k+1}, \tau_{k+2}]$ *and* $i \in [\tau_k, t]$, *we have* $\eta_i^{k,t} = \Theta(\frac{1}{\tau_k{}^\omega})$,

The following lemma provides a bound for the stochastic error caused by the term $W_{t;\tau_k}$.

Lemma 6.4. *Consider synchronous Q-learning with a polynomial learning rate. With probability at least* $1 - \frac{\delta}{m}$ *we have* $|W_{t;\tau_k}| \le (1-\frac{2}{e})\beta D_k$ *for any* $t \in [\tau_{k+1}, \tau_{k+2}]$, *i.e.*

$$Pr\left[\forall t \in [\tau_{k+1}, \tau_{k+2}] : \quad |W_{t;\tau_k}| \le (1-\frac{2}{e})\beta D_k\right] \ge 1 - \frac{\delta}{m}$$

given that $\tau_k = \Theta((\frac{V_{max}^2 \ln(V_{max}|S|\,|A|m/(\delta\beta D_k))}{\beta^2 D_k^2})^{1/\omega})$

Proof. Note that by definition $w_{\tau_k+i}(s,a)$ has zero mean and is bounded by V_{max} for any history. Since $\eta_i^{k,t} = \Theta(1/\tau_k^\omega)$ and $t - \tau_k = \Theta(\tau_k^\omega)$, we can define a random variables $\tilde{w}_{i+\tau_k}(s,a) = (t-\tau_k)\eta_i^{k,t} w_{i+\tau_k}(s,a)$, which have zero mean and are bounded by $\Theta(V_{max})$. Using a Chernoff bound for every state-action pair we can derive that,

$$\begin{aligned} Pr\left[W_{t;\tau_k}(s,a) \ge \tilde{\epsilon}\right] &= Pr\left[\sum_{i=\tau_k}^{t} w_i(s,a)\eta_{i-\tau_k}^{k,t} \ge \tilde{\epsilon}\right] \\ &= Pr\left[\frac{1}{t-\tau_k}\sum_{i=\tau_k}^{t} \tilde{w}_i(s,a) \ge \tilde{\epsilon}\right] \le e^{-c\tau_k^\omega \tilde{\epsilon}^2/V_{max}^2}, \end{aligned}$$

for some constant $c > 0$. Set $\tilde{\delta}_k = e^{-c\tau_k^\omega \tilde{\epsilon}^2/V_{max}^2}$, which holds for $\tau_k^\omega = \Theta(\ln(1/\tilde{\delta})$ $V_{max}^2/\tilde{\epsilon}^2)$. Using the union bound we have,

$$Pr\left[\forall t \in [\tau_{k+1}, \tau_{k+2}] : W_{t;\tau_k}(s,a) \leq \tilde{\epsilon}\right] \leq \sum_{t=\tau_{k+1}}^{\tau_{k+2}} Pr\left[W_{t;\tau_k}(s,a) \leq \tilde{\epsilon}\right],$$

thus taking $\tilde{\delta}_k = \frac{\delta}{m(\tau_{k+2}-\tau_{k+1})|S||A|}$ assures that with probability at least $1 - \frac{\delta}{m}$ the statement hold at every state-action pair and time $t \in [\tau_{k+1}, \tau_{k+2}]$. As a result we have,

$$\tau_k = \Theta\left((\frac{V_{max}^2 \ln(|S|\ |A|\ m\tau_k^\omega/\delta)}{\tilde{\epsilon}^2})^{1/\omega} \right) = \Theta\left((\frac{V_{max}^2 \ln(|S|\ |A|\ mV_{max}/\delta\tilde{\epsilon})}{\tilde{\epsilon}^2})^{1/\omega} \right)$$

Setting $\tilde{\epsilon} = (1 - 2/e)\beta D_k$ gives the desire bound. □

We have bounded for each iteration the time needed to achieve the desired precision level with probability $1 - \frac{\delta}{m}$. The following lemma provides a bound for the error in all the iterations.

Lemma 6.5. *Consider synchronous Q-learning using a polynomial learning rate. With probability* $1-\delta$, *for every iteration* $k \in [1, m]$ *and time* $t \in [\tau_{k+1}, \tau_{k+2}]$ *we have* $W_{t;\tau_k} \leq (1 - \frac{2}{e})\beta D_k$, *i.e.,*

$$Pr\left[\forall k \in [1,m],\ \forall t \in [\tau_{k+1}, \tau_{k+2}] :\ \ |W_{t;\tau_k}| \leq (1 - \frac{2}{e})\beta D_k\right] \geq 1 - \delta,$$

given that $\tau_0 = \Theta((\frac{V_{max}^2 \ln(V_{max}|S|\ |A|/(\delta\beta\epsilon))}{\beta^2\epsilon^2})^{1/\omega})$

We have bounded both the size of each iteration, as a function of its starting time, and the number of the iterations needed. The following lemma solves the recurrence $\tau_{k+1} = \tau_k + \tau_k^\omega$, which bounds the total time required. (The proof follows from Lemma 7.3.)

Lemma 6.6. *Let*

$$a_{k+1} = a_k + a_k^\omega = a_0 + \sum_{i=0}^{k} a_i^\omega .$$

For any constant $\omega \in (0,1)$, $a_k = O((a_0^{1-\omega} + k)^{\frac{1}{1-\omega}})$.

The proof of Theorem 4.1 follows from Lemma 6.6, Lemma 6.4 and Lemma 6.2.

7 Asynchronous Q-Learning

The major difference between synchronous and asynchronous Q-learning is that in the asynchronous Q-learning updates only one state action pair at each time while the synchronous Q-learning updates all the state action pairs each time unit. This causes two difficulties, the first is that different updates use different values of the Q function in their update, this problem is fairly easy to handle given the machinery introduced. The second, and more basic, is that each state action pair should occur enough times, so that the update can progress. To overcome this we introduce the notion of covering time, denoted by L. We first extend the analysis of the synchronous Q-learning to asynchronous Q-learning, in which each run has covering time L with probability one, this implies that for any start state in L steps all state action pairs are performed. Latter we relax the probability such that the condition holds with probability 1/2, and show that with high probability we have a covering time of $L \log T$ for a run of length T. Note that our notion of covering time does not assume a stationary distribution of the exploration strategy, it may be the case that at some periods of time certain state action pairs are more frequent while in other periods different state action pairs are more frequent. In fact we do not even assume that the sequence of state action pairs is generated by a strategy, it can be an arbitrary sequence of state action pairs with their reward and next state.

Definition 7.1. *Let $n(s, a, t_1, t_2)$ be the number of times that (s, a) was performed in the time interval $[t_1, t_2]$.*

We first give the results for asynchronous Q-learning using polynomial learning rate. (A similar proof to linear learning rate can be found in Appendix D). We use in this section the same notations as in Section 6 for D_k, τ_k, $Y_{t;\tau_k}$ and $W_{t;\tau}$, with a different set of values for τ_k. Our main goal is to show that the size of the kth iteration is $L\tau_k^{\omega}$. The covering time property guarantees that in $L\tau_k^{\omega}$ steps each pair of state action is performed at least τ_k^{ω} times. For this reason we define for asynchronous Q-learning with polynomial learning rate the sequence $\tau_{k+1} = \tau_k + L\tau_k^{\omega}$, where τ_1 will be specified latter. As in Section 6 we first bound the value of $Y_{t;\tau_k}$ (proof omitted).

Lemma 7.1. *Consider asynchronous Q-learning with a polynomial learning rate and assume that for any $t \geq \tau_k$ we have $Y_{t;\tau_k}(s, a) \leq D_k$. Then for any $t \geq \tau_k + L\tau_k^{\omega} = \tau_{k+1}$ we have $Y_{t;\tau_k}(s, a) \leq D(\gamma + \beta + \frac{2}{e}\beta)$*

The following lemma bounds the value of $W_{t;\tau}$.

Lemma 7.2. *Consider asynchronous Q-learning with a polynomial learning rate. With probability at least $1 - \frac{\delta}{m}$ we have for every state-action pair $|W_{t;\tau_k}(s, a)| \leq (1 - \frac{2}{e})\beta D_k$ for any $t \in [\tau_{k+1}, \tau_{k+2}]$, i.e.*

$$Pr\left[\forall t \in [\tau_{k+1}, \tau_{k+2}] : \ |W_{t;\tau_k}| \leq (1 - \frac{2}{e})\beta D_k\right] \geq 1 - \frac{\delta}{m}$$

given that $\tau_k = \Theta((\frac{L^{1+2\omega} V_{max}^2 \ln(V_{max}|S|\,|A|m/(\delta\beta D_k))}{\beta^2 D_k^2})^{1/\omega})$

Proof. We sketch the proof. Note that by definition w_{τ_k+i} has zero mean and is bounded by V_{max} for any history. In a time interval of length τ, by definition of the covering time, each state action pair is performed at least τ/L times, therefore, $\eta_i^{k,t}(s,a) \leq (L/\tau_k)^{\omega}$. Let $\ell = n(s,a,\tau_k,t)$ by definition $\ell = \Theta(L\tau_k^{\omega})$, we can define a random variable $\tilde{w}_{i+\tau_k}(s,a) = \ell\eta_i^{k,t}(s,a)w_{i+\tau_k}(s,a)$, which has zero mean and is bounded by $O(V_{max}\ell(L/\tau_k)^{\omega})$. Using a Chernoff bound for every state action pair we can derive that,

$$Pr\left[W_{t;\tau_k}(s,a) \geq \tilde{\epsilon}\right] = Pr\left[\sum_{i=\tau_k}^{t} w_i(s,a)\eta_{i-\tau_k}^{k,t} \geq \tilde{\epsilon}\right]$$

$$= Pr\left[\frac{1}{n(s,a,\tau_k,t)}\sum_{i=\tau_k}^{t} \tilde{w}_i(s,a) \geq \tilde{\epsilon}\right]$$

$$\leq e^{-c\frac{\ell\tilde{\epsilon}^2\tau_k^{2\omega}}{\ell^2 L^{2\omega}V_{max}^2}} \leq e^{-c\frac{\tilde{\epsilon}^2\tau_k^{\omega}}{L^{1+2\omega}V_{max}^2}},$$

for some constant $c > 0$. We can set $\tilde{\delta}_k = e^{-c\tau_k^{\omega}\tilde{\epsilon}^2/(L^{1+2\omega}V_{max}^2)}$ which holds for $\tau_k^{\omega} = \Theta(\ln(1/\tilde{\delta})L^{1+2\omega}V_{max}^2/\tilde{\epsilon}^2)$. Using the union bound we have,

$$Pr\left[\forall t \in [\tau_{k+1},\tau_{k+2}] : W_{t;\tau_k}(s,a) \leq \tilde{\epsilon}\right] \leq \sum_{t=\tau_{k+1}}^{\tau_{k+2}} Pr\left[W_{t;\tau_k}(s,a) \leq \tilde{\epsilon}\right],$$

thus taking $\tilde{\delta}_k = \frac{\delta}{m(\tau_{k+2}-\tau_{k+1})|S||A|}$ assures certainty level of $1 - \frac{\delta}{m}$ for each state-actions pairs. As a result we have,

$$\tau_k^{\omega} = \Theta\left(\frac{L^{1+2\omega}V_{max}^2\ln(|S|\,|A|\,m\tau_k^{\omega}/\delta)}{\tilde{\epsilon}^2}\right) = \Theta\left(\frac{L^{1+2\omega}V_{max}^2\ln(|S|\,|A|\,mV_{max}/(\delta\tilde{\epsilon}))}{\tilde{\epsilon}^2}\right)$$

Setting $\tilde{\epsilon} = (1-2/e)\beta D_k$ give the desire bound. □

The following lemma solves the recurrence $\sum_{i=0}^{m} L\tau^{\omega} + \tau_0$ and derives the time complexity. (The proof can be found is Appendix C.)

Lemma 7.3. *Let*

$$a_{k+1} = a_k + La_k^{\omega} = a_0 + \sum_{i=0}^{k} La_i^{\omega}$$

Then for any constant $\omega \in (0,1)$, $a_k = O((a_0^{1-\omega} + Lk)^{\frac{1}{1-\omega}})$

The proof of Theorem 4.3 follows from Lemmas 7.1, 7.2 and 7.3. In the following lemma we relax the condition of the covering time.

Lemma 7.4. *Assume that from any start state with probability 1/2 in L steps we perform all state action pairs. Then with probability* $1-\delta$, *from any start state we perform all state action pairs in* $L\log(\frac{T}{L}\frac{1}{\delta})$ *steps, for a run of length* T.

References

[BGS99] F. Beleznay, T. Grobler, and Cs. Szepesvari. Comparing value-function estimation algorithms in undiscounted problems. Technical Report TR-99-02, Mindmaker Ltd, 1999.

[BM00] V.S. Borkar and S.P. Meyn. The o.d.e method for convergence of stochstic approximation and reinforcement learning. *Siam J. control*, 38 (2):447–69, 2000.

[BT96] Dimitri P. Bertsekas and Jhon N. Tsitsklis. *Neuro-Dynamic Programming.* Athena Scientific, Belmont, MA, 1996.

[JJS94] T. Jaakkola, M. I. Jordan, and S. P. Singh. On the convergence of stochastic iterative dynamic programming algorithms. *Neural Computation, 6*, 1994.

[KS98] Michael Kearns and Stinder Singh. Finite-sample convergence rates for q-learning and indirect algorithms. In *Neural Information Processing Systems 10*, 1998.

[MS96] Littman M. and Cs. Szepesvari. A generalized reinforcement learning model: convergence and applications. In *In International Conference on Machine Learning*, 1996.

[Put94] M.L Puterman. *Markov Decision Processes - Discrete Stochastic Dynamic Programming.* Jhon Wiley & Sons. Inc., New York, NY, 1994.

[SB98] Richard S. Sutton and Andrew G. Bato. *Reinforcement Learning.* Mit press, 1998.

[Sze97] Cs. Szepesvari. The asymptotic convergence-rate of q-learning. In *Neural Information Processing Systems 10*, pages 1064 – 1070, 1997.

[Tsi94] Jhon N. Tsitsklis. Asynchronous stochastic approximation and q-learning. *Machine Learning*, 16:185–202, 1994.

[Wat89] C. Watkins. *Learning from Delayed Rewards.* PhD thesis, Cambridge University, 1989.

[WD92] C. Watking and P. Dyan. Q-learning. *Machine Learning*, 8(3/4):279 –292, 1992.

A Lower Bound for Q-Learning Using Linear Learning Rate

In this section we show a lower bound for Q-Learning with linear learning rate, which is $O((\frac{1}{\epsilon})^{\frac{1}{1-\gamma}})$. We consider the following MDP, denoted M_0, that has a single state s, a single action a, and a deterministic reward $R_{M_0}(s,a) = 0$. Since there is only one action in the MDP we denote $Q_t(s,a)$ as $Q_t(s)$. We initialize $Q_0(s) = 1$ and observe the time until $Q_t(s) \le \epsilon$.

Lemma A.1. *Consider running synchronous Q-learning with linear learning rate on MDP M_0, when initializing $Q_0(s) = 1$. Then for $t = O((\frac{1}{\epsilon})^{\frac{1}{1-\gamma}})$ we have $Q_t \ge \epsilon$.*

Proof. First we prove by induction on t that

$$Q_t(s) = \prod_{i=1}^{t-1} \frac{i+\gamma}{i+1}.$$

For $t = 2$ we have $Q_1(s) = (1 - 1/2)Q_0(s) + (1/2)\gamma Q_0(s) = (1+\gamma)/2$. Assume the hypothesis holds for $t-1$ and prove it for t. by definition,

$$Q_t(s) = (1 - \frac{1}{t})Q_{t-1}(s) + \frac{1}{t}\gamma Q_{t-1}(s) = \frac{t-1+\gamma}{t}Q_{t-1}(s).$$

In order to help us estimate this quantity we use the Γ function. Let

$$\Gamma(x+1,k) = \frac{1 \cdot 2 \cdots k}{(x+1)\cdot(x+2)\cdot \cdots \cdot (x+k)}k^x$$

The limit of $\Gamma(1+x,k)$, as k goes to infinity, is constant for any x. We can rewrite $Q_t(s)$ as

$$Q_t(s) = \frac{1}{\Gamma(\gamma+1,t)}\frac{t^\gamma}{t+1} = \Theta(t^{\gamma-1})$$

Therefore, there is a time $t = c(\frac{1}{\epsilon})^{\frac{1}{1-\gamma}}$, for some constant $c > 0$, such that $Q_t(s) \geq \epsilon$. □

B Synchronous Q-Learning with Linear Learning Rate

In this section we derive the results for A-learning with linear learning rate. The proof is very similar in spirit and we give here the analogue lemmas to the ones in Section 6. First, the number of iterations required for synchronous Q-learning with linear learning rate is the same as for polynomial learning rate. Therefore, we need to analyze the number of steps in an iteration.

Lemma B.1. *Consider synchronous Q-learning with a polynomial learning rate and assume that for any $t \geq \tau_k$ we have $Y_{t;\tau_k}(s,a) \leq D_k$. Then for any $t \geq 4\tau_k = \tau_{k+1}$ we have $Y_{t;\tau_k}(s,a) \leq D_k(\gamma + \beta + \frac{1}{2}\beta)$*

Proof. Let $Y_{\tau_k;\tau_k}(s,a) = (\gamma+\beta)D_k - \rho_{\tau_k}$, where $\rho_{\tau_k} = (1-(\gamma+\beta))D_k$. We can now write

$$Y_{t+1;\tau_k}(s,a) = (1-\alpha_t^1)Y_{t;\tau_k}(s,a) + \alpha_t^1(\gamma+\beta)D_k = (\gamma+\beta)D_k + (1-\alpha_t^1)\rho_t.$$

Therefore, $\rho_{t+1} = \rho_t(1-\alpha_t^1)$. We would like show that after time $4\tau_k = \tau_{k+1}$ for any $t \geq \tau_{k+1}$ we have $\rho_t \leq \beta D_k$. By definition we can rewrite ρ_t as,

$$\rho_t = (1-(\gamma+\beta))D_k \prod_{l=1}^{t-\tau_k}(1-\alpha_{l+\tau_k}^1) = 2\beta D_k \prod_{l=1}^{t-\tau_k}(1-\frac{1}{l+\tau_k}),$$

where the last identity follows from the fact that $\alpha_t = 1/t$. Simplifying the expression, and setting $t = 4\tau_k$, we have,

$$\rho_t \leq 2D_k\beta\frac{\tau_k}{t} \leq 2D_k\beta = \frac{D_k\beta}{2}$$

Hence, $Y_{t;\tau_k}(s,a) \leq (\gamma+\beta+\frac{1}{2}\beta)D_k$. □

In a similar way to Lemma 6.4 we show,

Lemma B.2. *Consider synchronous Q-learning with a linear learning rate. With probability at least* $1 - \frac{\delta}{m}$ *we have* $|W_{t;\tau_k}| \leq \frac{1}{2}\beta D_k$ *for any* $t \in [\tau_{k+1}, \tau_{k+2}]$, *i.e.*

$$Pr\left[\forall t \in [\tau_{k+1}, \tau_{k+2}]: \quad |W_{t;\tau_k}| \leq \frac{1}{2}\beta D_k\right] \geq 1 - \frac{\delta}{m}$$

given that $\tau_k = \Theta(\frac{V_{max}^2 \ln(V_{max}|S|\,|A|m/(\delta\beta D_k))}{\beta^2 D_k^2})$

Theorem 4.4 follows from Lemmas B.2 and B.1, and the fact that $a_{k+1} = 4a_k = 4^k a_1$.

C Proof of Lemma 7.3

Proof of Lemma 7.3 We define the following series

$$b_{k+1} = \sum_{i=0}^{k} L b_i^{\omega} + b_0$$

with an initial condition

$$b_0 = L^{\frac{1}{1-\omega}}.$$

We show by induction that $b_k \leq (L(k+1))^{\frac{1}{1-\omega}}$ for $k \geq 1$. For $k = 0$

$$b_0 = L^{\frac{1}{1-\omega}}(0+1)^{\frac{1}{1-\omega}} \leq L^{\frac{1}{1-\omega}}$$

We assume that the induction hypothesis holds $k-1$ and prove it for k,

$$b_k = b_{k-1} + L b_{k-1}^{\omega} \leq (Lk)^{\frac{1}{1-\omega}} + L(Lk)^{\frac{\omega}{1-\omega}} \leq L^{\frac{1}{1-\omega}} k^{\frac{\omega}{1-\omega}}(k+1) \leq (L(k+1))^{\frac{1}{1-\omega}}$$

and the claim is proved.

Now we lower bound b_k by $(L(k+1)/2)^{1/(1-\omega)}$. For $k = 0$ we have,

$$b_0 = L^{\frac{1}{1-\omega}} \geq (\frac{L}{2})^{\frac{1}{1-\omega}}$$

Assume that the induction hypothesis holds for $k-1$ and prove for k,

$$\begin{aligned} b_k &= b_{k-1} + L b_{k-1}^{\omega} \\ &= (Lk/2)^{\frac{1}{1-\omega}} + L(Lk/2)^{\frac{\omega}{1-\omega}} \\ &= L^{\frac{1}{1-\omega}}((k/2)^{\frac{1}{1-\omega}} + (k/2)^{\frac{\omega}{1-\omega}}) \\ &\geq L^{\frac{1}{1-\omega}}((k+1)/2)^{\frac{1}{1-\omega}}. \end{aligned}$$

For $a_0 > L^{\frac{1}{1-\omega}}$ we can view the series as starting at $b_k = a_0$. From the lower bound we know that the start point has moved $\Theta(a_0^{1-\omega}/L)$. Therefore we have a total complexity of $O((a_0^{1-\omega} + Lk)^{\frac{1}{1-\omega}})$. □

D Asynchronous Q-Learning Using Linear Learning Rate

In this section we consider asynchronous Q-learning with a linear learning rate. The sequence of times in this case is $\tau_{k+1} = \tau_k + 3L\tau_k$. Due to lack of space we only state the lemmas that bound $Y_{t;\tau}$ and then bound $W_{t;\tau}$.

Lemma D.1. *Consider asynchronous Q-learning with a polynomial learning rate and assume that for any $t \geq \tau_k$ we have $Y_{t;\tau_k}(s,a) \leq D_k$. Then for any $t \geq \tau_k + 3L\tau_k = \tau_{k+1}$ we have $Y_{t;\tau_k}(s,a) \leq (\gamma + \beta + \frac{1}{2}\beta)D_k$*

Lemma D.2. *Consider asynchronous Q-learning with a linear learning rate. With probability at least $1 - \frac{\delta}{m}$ we have for every state-action pair $|W_{t;\tau_k}(s,a)| \leq (1 - \frac{1}{2})\beta D_k$ for any $t \geq \tau_{k+1}$, i.e.*

$$Pr\left[\forall t \geq \tau_{k+1} : \;\; W_{t;\tau_k}(s,a) \leq (1 - \frac{2}{e})\beta D_k\right] \geq 1 - \frac{\delta}{m}$$

given that $\tau_k = \Theta((\frac{LV_{max}^2 \ln(V_{max}|S|\,|A|m/(\delta\beta D_k))}{\beta^2 D_k^2}))$

Theorem 4.4 follows from Lemmas D.1, D.2 and the fact that $a_{k+1} = a_k + 3La_k = (3L+1)^k$.

Optimizing Average Reward Using Discounted Rewards

Sham Kakade

Gatsby Computational Neuroscience Unit
17 Queen Square
London WC1N 3AR
United Kingdom
sham@gatsby.ucl.ac.uk
http://www.gatsby.ucl.ac.uk/~sham/index.html

Abstract. In many reinforcement learning problems, it is appropriate to optimize the average reward. In practice, this is often done by solving the Bellman equations using a discount factor close to 1. In this paper, we provide a bound on the average reward of the policy obtained by solving the Bellman equations which depends on the relationship between the discount factor and the mixing time of the Markov chain. We extend this result to the direct policy gradient of Baxter and Bartlett, in which a discount parameter is used to find a biased estimate of the gradient of the average reward with respect to the parameters of a policy. We show that this biased gradient is an exact gradient of a related discounted problem and provide a bound on the optima found by following these biased gradients of the average reward. Further, we show that the exact Hessian in this related discounted problem is an approximate Hessian of the average reward, with equality in the limit the discount factor tends to 1. We then provide an algorithm to estimate the Hessian from a sample path of the underlying Markov chain, which converges with probability 1.

1 Introduction

Sequential decision making problems are usually formulated as dynamic programming problems in which the agent must maximize some measure of future reward. In many domains, it is appropriate to optimize the average reward. Often, discounted formulations with a discount factor γ close to 1 are used as a proxy to an average reward formulation. It is natural to inquire about the consequences of using a discount factor close to one. How does the quality of the policy, measured in an average reward sense, degrade as the discount factor is reduced? What are the benefits in using a smaller discount factor?

This papers focuses on the former issue by extending the results of Baxter and Bartlett[2,1]. A key relationship proved in [2] shows that the discounted reward, scaled by $1-\gamma$, is approximately the average reward, which suggests that maximizing discounted reward will be approximately maximizing average

D. Helmbold and B. Williamson (Eds.): COLT/EuroCOLT 2001, LNAI 2111, pp. 605–615, 2001.

reward. We show if $\frac{1}{1-\gamma}$ is large compared to the mixing time of the Markov chain, then we would expect any policy that solves the Bellman equations to have a large average reward.

This interpretation of using discounted rewards to maximize average reward extends to the case of maximizing the average reward by following a gradient. We show that the approximate gradient of Baxter and Bartlett is an exact gradient of a related discounted, start state problem and provide a similar bound on the quality of the optima reached using this approximate gradient. These results naturally lead to an algorithm for computing an approximation to the Hessian. A slightly different, independent derivation of the Hessian is given in [3].

2 The Reinforcement Learning Problem

We consider the standard formulation of reinforcement learning, in which an agent interacts with a finite Markov decision process (MDP). An MDP is a tuple (S, A, R, P) where: S is finite set of states $S = \{1, \ldots, n\}$, A is a finite set of actions, R is a reward function $R : S \to [0, R_{max}]$[1], and P is the transition model in which $p_{ij}(u)$ is the probability of transitioning to state j from state i under action u.[2]

The agent's decision making procedure is characterized by a stochastic policy $\mu : S \to A$, where $\mu_u(i)$ is the probability of taking action u in state i. For each policy μ there corresponds a Markov chain with a transition matrix $P(\mu)$, where $[P(\mu)]_{ij} = \sum_u p_{ij}(u)\mu_u(i)$. We assume that these Markov chains satisfy the following assumption:

Assumption 1. *Each $P(\mu)$ has a unique stationary distribution $\pi(\mu) \equiv [\pi(\mu, 1), \ldots, \pi(\mu, n)]'$ satisfying:*

$$\pi(\mu)'P(\mu) = \pi(\mu)'$$

(where $\pi(\mu)'$ denotes the transpose of $\pi(\mu)$).

The *average reward* is defined by:

$$\eta(\mu) \equiv \lim_{N\to\infty} \frac{1}{N} \sum_i \pi(\mu, i) E_\mu\{\sum_{t=0}^{N-1} r(i_t)|i_0 = i\}$$

where i_t is the state at time t. The average reward can be shown to equal:

$$\eta(\mu) = \pi(\mu)'r$$

[1] It is a straightforward to extend these results to the case where the rewards are dependent on the actions, $R(s, a)$.

[2] We ignore the start state distribution, since the average reward is independent of the starting distribution under the current assumption of a unique stationary distribution.

where $r = [r(1), ..., r(n)]'$ (see [4]). The goal of the agent is to find a policy μ^* that returns the maximum average reward over all policies.

We define the γ-*discounted reward* from some starting state i as:

$$J_\gamma(\mu, i) \equiv E_\mu\{\sum_{t=0}^{\infty} \gamma^t r(i_t) | i_0 = i\}$$

where $\gamma \in [0, 1)$. These value functions satisfy the following consistency condition [8]:

$$J_\gamma(\mu) = r + \gamma P(\mu) J_\gamma(\mu) \tag{1}$$

(again we use the vector notation $J_\gamma(\mu) = [J_\gamma(\mu, 1), ..., J_\gamma(\mu, n)]'$). The *expected discounted reward* is defined as $\pi(\mu)' J_\gamma(\mu)$, where the expectation is taken over the stationary distribution . As shown in [6], the expected discounted reward is just a multiple of the average reward:

$$\pi(\mu)' J_\gamma(\mu) = \frac{\eta(\mu)}{1-\gamma} \,. \tag{2}$$

Thus, optimizing the expected discounted reward for any γ is equivalent to optimizing the average reward. Also, for all states i, $\lim_{\gamma \to 1}(1-\gamma)J_\gamma(i) = \eta$ (see [4]).

In discounted dynamic programming, we are concerned with finding a vector $J_\gamma \in \Re^n$ that satisfies the Bellman equations:

$$J_\gamma = \max_\mu (r + \gamma P(\mu) J_\gamma) \,. \tag{3}$$

Let $\mu^{\gamma *}$be a policy such that $J_\gamma(\mu^{\gamma *})$ satisfies this equation (there could be more than one such policy). Although the policy $\mu^{\gamma *}$ simultaneously maximizes the discounted reward starting from every state, it does not necessarily maximize the average discounted reward, which is sensitive to the stationary distribution achieved by this policy (see equation 2). The policies that solve the Bellman equations could lead to poor stationary distributions that do not maximize the average reward.

3 Appropriateness of Maximizing Discounted Reward

We extend the results of Baxter and Bartlett to show that if $\frac{1}{1-\gamma}$ is large compared to the mixing time of the Markov chain of the optimal policy then the solutions to the Bellman equations will have an average reward close to the maximum average reward. We use the following relation (shown by Baxter and Bartlett [2], modulo a typo), for any policy:

$$(1-\gamma)J_\gamma(\mu) = \eta(\mu)e + S(\mu)\, diag(0, \frac{1-\gamma}{1-\gamma|\lambda_2(\mu)|}, \ldots, \frac{1-\gamma}{1-\gamma|\lambda_n(\mu)|}) S(\mu)^{-1} r \tag{4}$$

where $e = [1, 1, \ldots, 1]'$ and $S(\mu) = (s_1 s_2 \cdots s_n)$ is the matrix of right eigenvectors of $P(\mu)$ with the corresponding eigenvalues $\lambda_1(\mu) = 1 >| \lambda_2(\mu)| \geq \cdots \geq$

$|\lambda_n(\mu)|$ (assuming that $P(\mu)$ has n distinct eigenvalues). This equation follows from separating $J_\gamma = \sum_{t=0}^{\infty} \gamma^t P^t r$ into the contribution associated with $\lambda_1 = 1$ and that coming from the remaining eigenvalues. Note that for γ near 1, the scaled discounted value function for each state is approximately the average reward, with an approximation error of order $1-\gamma$.

Throughout the paper, $\|A\|_2$ denotes the spectral norm of a matrix A, defined as $\|A\|_2 \equiv \max_{x:\|x\|=1} \|Ax\|$, where$\|x\|$ denotes the Euclidean norm of x, and $\kappa_2(A)$ denotes the spectral condition number of a nonsingular matrix A, defined as $\kappa_2(A) \equiv \|A\|_2 \|A^{-1}\|_2$.

Theorem 1. *Let $\mu^{\gamma *}$be a policy such that $J_\gamma(\mu^{\gamma *})$ satisfies the Bellman equations (equation 3) and let μ^* be a policy such that $\eta(\mu^*)$ be the maximum average reward over all policies. Assume $P(\mu^*)$ has n distinct eigenvalues. Let $S = (s_1 s_2 \cdots s_n)$ be the matrix of right eigenvectors of $P(\mu^*)$ with the corresponding eigenvalues $\lambda_1 = 1 >| \lambda_2| \geq \cdots \geq |\lambda_n|$. Then*

$$\eta(\mu^{\gamma *}) \geq \eta(\mu^*) - \kappa_2(S)\|r\| \frac{1-\gamma}{1-\gamma|\lambda_2|}\,.$$

Proof. Since $J_\gamma(\mu^{\gamma *})$ satisfies the Bellman equations, we have

$$\forall \mu \quad J_\gamma(\mu^{\gamma *}) \geq J_\gamma(\mu)$$

where the vector inequality is shorthand for the respective component wise inequality. As a special case, the inequality holds for a policy μ^* that maximizes the average reward, *ie* $J_\gamma(\mu^{\gamma *}) \geq J_\gamma(\mu^*)$. It follows from equation 2 and equation 4 (applied to μ^*) that

$$\begin{aligned}
\eta(\mu^{\gamma *}) &= (1-\gamma)\pi(\mu^{\gamma *})' J_\gamma(\mu^{\gamma *}) \\
&\geq (1-\gamma)\pi(\mu^{\gamma *})' J_\gamma(\mu^*) \\
&= \eta(\mu^*)\pi(\mu^{\gamma *})'e + \pi(\mu^{\gamma *})' S \operatorname{diag}(0, \frac{1-\gamma}{1-\gamma|\lambda_2|}, \ldots, \frac{1-\gamma}{1-\gamma|\lambda_n|}) S^{-1} r \\
&\geq \eta(\mu^*) - |\pi(\mu^{\gamma *})' S \operatorname{diag}(0, \frac{1-\gamma}{1-\gamma|\lambda_2|}, \ldots, \frac{1-\gamma}{1-\gamma|\lambda_n|}) S^{-1} r|
\end{aligned}$$

where we have used $\pi(\mu^{\gamma *})'e = 1$. The dependence of S and λ_i on μ^* is suppressed. Using the Cauchy-Schwartz inequality, we have

$$\begin{aligned}
\eta(\mu^{\gamma *}) &\geq \eta(\mu^*) - \|S\pi(\mu^{\gamma *})\| \, \|\operatorname{diag}(0, \frac{1-\gamma}{1-\gamma|\lambda_2|}, \ldots, \frac{1-\gamma}{1-\gamma|\lambda_n|}) S^{-1} r\| \\
&\geq \eta(\mu^*) - \|S\pi(\mu^{\gamma *})\| \, \|\operatorname{diag}(0, \frac{1-\gamma}{1-\gamma|\lambda_2|}, \ldots, \frac{1-\gamma}{1-\gamma|\lambda_n|})\|_2 \|S^{-1} r\|\,.
\end{aligned}$$

It is easy to show that $\|\operatorname{diag}(d_1, \ldots, d_n)\|_2 = \max_i |d_i|$. Using $\|\pi\| \leq 1$, it follows from the definition of the spectral norm and spectral condition number that $\|S\pi(\mu^{\gamma *})\| \, \|S^{-1}r\| \leq \kappa_2(S)\|r\|$. □

The previous theorem shows that if $1-\gamma$ is small compared to $1-|\lambda_2|$, then the solution to the Bellman equations will be close to the maximum average reward. Under assumption 1, from any initial state, the distribution of states of the Markov chain will converge at an exponential rate to the stationary distribution, and the rate of this will depend on the eigenvalues of the transition matrix. The second largest eigenvalue, $|\lambda_2|$, will determine an upper bound on this mixing time.

4 Direct Gradient Methods

A promising recent approach to finding the gradient of the average reward was presented by Baxter and Bartlett [2], where a discount parameter controls the bias and variance of the gradient estimate (also see a related approach by Marbach and Tsitsiklis [5]). We now relate this approximate gradient to an exact gradient for a modified discounted problem and provide a bound on the quality of the local optima reached by following this approximate gradient. To ensure the existence of certain gradients and the boundedness of certain random variables, we assume

Assumption 2. *The derivatives, ∇P_{ij} and $\nabla \mu_u(\theta, i)$, exist and the ratios, $\frac{\nabla P_{ij}}{P_{ij}}$ and $\frac{\nabla \mu_u(\theta,i)}{\mu_u(\theta,i)}$, are bounded by a constant for all $\theta \in \Re^k$.*

Let $\theta \in R^k$ be the parameters of a policy $\mu(\theta) : S \to A$, where $\mu_u(\theta, i)$ is the chance of taking action u in state i. These parameters implicitly parameterize the average reward, the stationary distribution, and the transition matrix, which we denote by $\eta(\theta)$, $\pi(\theta)$, and $P(\theta)$. Also let $J_\gamma(\theta)$ be the discounted value function under $P(\theta)$. The key result of Baxter and Bartlett shows that the exact gradient of the average reward, $\nabla\eta(\theta)$, can be approximated by

$$\nabla\eta(\theta) \approx \gamma\pi(\theta)'\nabla P(\theta) J_\gamma(\theta) \equiv \tilde{\nabla}_\gamma \eta(\theta)$$

where this approximation becomes exact as $\gamma \to 1$. We denote this approximate gradient by $\tilde{\nabla}_\gamma\eta(\theta)$ (the tilde makes it explicitly clear that $\tilde{\nabla}_\gamma$ is not differentiating with respect to γ). Further, they give an algorithm that estimates $\tilde{\nabla}_\gamma\eta(\theta)$ from a sample trajectory.

Before we state our theorem, we define $\nu_\gamma(\theta, \rho)$ to be the expected discounted reward received from a starting state chosen from the distribution ρ under $P(\theta)$, *ie*

$$\nu_\gamma(\theta, \rho) \equiv \rho' J_\gamma(\theta) \; .$$

Theorem 2. *Let $\nu_\gamma(\tilde{\theta}, \pi(\theta)) \equiv \pi(\theta)' J_\gamma(\tilde{\theta})$. Then*

$$(1-\gamma)\nabla_{\tilde{\theta}} \nu_\gamma(\tilde{\theta}, \pi(\theta))|_{\tilde{\theta}=\theta} = \tilde{\nabla}_\gamma \eta(\theta) \tag{5}$$

where $\nabla_{\tilde{\theta}}$ is the gradient with respect to $\tilde{\theta}$.

Proof. It follows from the fact that $\pi(\theta)$ is independent of $\tilde{\theta}$ that

$$\begin{aligned}\nabla_{\tilde{\theta}}\nu_\gamma(\tilde{\theta},\pi(\theta)) &= \pi(\theta)'\nabla_{\tilde{\theta}}J_\gamma(\tilde{\theta}) \\ &= \pi(\theta)'\nabla_{\tilde{\theta}}(r+\gamma P(\tilde{\theta})J_\gamma(\tilde{\theta})) \\ &= \pi(\theta)'(\nabla_{\tilde{\theta}}P(\tilde{\theta})J_\gamma(\tilde{\theta})+\gamma P(\tilde{\theta})\nabla_{\tilde{\theta}}J_\gamma(\tilde{\theta}))\,.\end{aligned}$$

Using $\pi(\theta)'P(\theta)=\pi(\theta)'$,

$$\begin{aligned}\nabla_{\tilde{\theta}}\nu_\gamma(\tilde{\theta},\pi(\theta))|_{\tilde{\theta}=\theta} &= \pi(\theta)'\nabla P(\theta)J_\gamma(\theta)+\gamma\pi(\theta)'P(\theta)\nabla_{\tilde{\theta}}J_\gamma(\tilde{\theta})|_{\tilde{\theta}=\theta} \\ &= \tilde{\nabla}_\gamma\eta(\theta)+\gamma\pi(\theta)'\nabla_{\tilde{\theta}}J_\gamma(\tilde{\theta})|_{\tilde{\theta}=\theta} \\ &= \tilde{\nabla}_\gamma\eta(\theta)+\gamma\nabla_{\tilde{\theta}}\nu_\gamma(\tilde{\theta},\pi(\theta))|_{\tilde{\theta}=\theta}\,.\end{aligned}$$

Collecting terms proves equation 5. □

Note that the approximate gradient at θ_1 is equivalent to the exact gradient in a start state problem under the starting distribution $\pi(\theta_1)$, whereas the approximate gradient at θ_2 is equivalent to the exact gradient in the start state problem with a different starting distribution, $\pi(\theta_2)$. If the approximate gradient is 0 at some point $\theta^{\gamma*}$ then this point will also be an extremum of the related problem, which allows us to make the following statement. In the following theorem, the basin of attraction of a maximum x of $f(x)$ is the set of all points which converge to x when taking infinitesimal steps in the direction of the gradient.

Theorem 3. *Let $\theta^{\gamma*}$ be a point such that $\nabla\nu_\gamma(\theta,\pi(\theta^{\gamma*}))|_{\theta=\theta^{\gamma*}}=0$. Assume that this extremum is a local maximum and let Ω be the basin of attraction of this maximum with respect to $\nu_\gamma(\theta,\pi(\theta^{\gamma*}))$. Let $\theta^*\in\Omega$ such that $\eta(\theta^*)$ is the maximum average reward over all θ in Ω. Assume $P(\mu^*)$ has n distinct eigenvectors. Let $S=(s_1 s_2\cdots s_n)$ be the matrix of right eigenvectors of $P(\theta^*)$ with the corresponding eigenvalues $\lambda_1=1>|\lambda_2|\geq\cdots\geq|\lambda_n|$. Then*

$$\eta(\theta^{\gamma*})\geq\eta(\theta^*)-\kappa_2(S)\|r\|\frac{1-\gamma}{1-\gamma|\lambda_2|}\,.$$

Proof. By assumption that this is a local maximum,

$$\forall\theta\in\Omega\quad\pi(\theta^{\gamma*})'J_\gamma(\theta^{\gamma*})\geq\pi(\theta^{\gamma*})'J_\gamma(\theta)\,.$$

Let θ^* be a point in Ω which returns $\eta(\theta^*)$, the maximum average reward in Ω. As a special case, we have $\pi(\theta^{\gamma*})'J_\gamma(\theta^{\gamma*})\geq\pi(\theta^{\gamma*})'J_\gamma(\theta^*)$. Using equation 2,

$$\begin{aligned}\eta(\theta^{\gamma*}) &= (1-\gamma)\pi(\theta^{\gamma*})'J_\gamma(\theta^{\gamma*}) \\ &\geq(1-\gamma)\pi(\theta^{\gamma*})'J_\gamma(\theta^*)\,.\end{aligned}$$

The remainder of the argument parallels the proof given in Theorem 1. □

The previous theorem gives a constraint on the quality of the maximum reached *if and when* the approximate gradient ascent converges. Note that this bound is essentially identical to the bound on the average reward of the policy obtained by solving the Bellman equations.

5 Direct Hessian Methods

Theorem 2 suggests that the natural choice for an approximate Hessian is $(1-\gamma)\nabla^2\nu_\gamma(\tilde{\theta},\pi(\theta))|_{\tilde{\theta}=\theta}$. We define

$$\tilde{\nabla}^2_\gamma\eta(\theta) \equiv (1-\gamma)\nabla^2_{\tilde{\theta}}\nu_\gamma(\tilde{\theta},\pi(\theta))|_{\tilde{\theta}=\theta} \,.$$

We make the following assumption.

Assumption 3. *The Hessians, $\nabla^2 P_{ij}$ and $\nabla^2\mu_u(\theta,i)$, exist and the ratios, $\frac{\nabla^2 P_{ij}}{P_{ij}}$ and $\frac{\nabla^2\mu_u(\theta,i)}{\mu_u(\theta,i)}$, are bounded by a constant for all $\theta\in\Re^k$.*

Theorem 4. *For all $\theta\in\Re^k$,*

$$\nabla^2\eta(\theta) = \lim_{\gamma\to 1}\tilde{\nabla}^2_\gamma\eta(\theta) \,.$$

Proof. Let $\partial_k \equiv \frac{\partial}{\partial\theta_k}$. Using equation 2 and suppressing the θ dependence,

$$\begin{aligned}
\lim_{\gamma\to 1}[\nabla^2\eta(\theta)]_{mn} &= \lim_{\gamma\to 1}(1-\gamma)\partial_m\partial_n(\pi' J_\gamma) \\
&= \lim_{\gamma\to 1}(1-\gamma)([\partial_m\partial_n\pi']J_\gamma + [\partial_m\pi'][\partial_n J_\gamma] + [\partial_n\pi'][\partial_m J_\gamma] \\
&\quad +\pi'[\partial_m\partial_n J_\gamma]) \\
&= \eta(\theta)\partial_m\partial_n\pi' e + \partial_n\eta\partial_m\pi' e + \partial_m\eta\partial_n\pi' e + \lim_{\gamma\to 1}(1-\gamma)\pi'\partial_m\partial_n J_\gamma \\
&= \lim_{\gamma\to 1}(1-\gamma)\pi'\partial_m\partial_n J_\gamma
\end{aligned}$$

where we have used $\lim_{\gamma\to 1}(1-\gamma)J_\gamma = \eta e$ (see [4]), $\lim_{\gamma\to 1}(1-\gamma)\partial_k J_\gamma = \partial_k\eta e$ (which is straightforward to prove), and $\partial_k\pi' e = \partial_k 1 = 0$. Following from the definition of ν_γ, $[\nabla^2_{\tilde{\theta}}\nu_\gamma(\tilde{\theta},\pi(\theta))|_{\tilde{\theta}=\theta}]_{mn} = \pi(\theta)'[\nabla^2 J_\gamma(\theta)]_{mn}$. □

The previous theorem shows that in the limit as γ tends to 1 the exact Hessian in the start state problem is the Hessian of the average reward. The following theorem gives an expression for $\tilde{\nabla}^2_\gamma\eta(\theta)$, which we later show how to estimate from Monte-Carlo samples.

Theorem 5. *For all θ and $\gamma\in[0,1)$,*

$$[\tilde{\nabla}^2_\gamma\eta(\theta)]_{mn} = \gamma\pi'([\partial_m\partial_n P]J_\gamma + [\partial_m P][\partial_n J_\gamma] + [\partial_n P][\partial_m J_\gamma]) \tag{6}$$

where

$$\partial_k J_\gamma = \sum_{t=1}^{\infty}\gamma^t[P^{t-1}\nabla P J_\gamma]_k \,. \tag{7}$$

Algorithm 1: HMDP (Hessian for a Markov Decision Process)

Obtain an arbitrary state i_0
Set $z_0 = \Delta_0 = 0 \in \Re^k$ and set $\tilde{z}_0 = y_0 = H_0 = 0 \in \Re^k \times \Re^k$
for $t = 0$ to $t = T-1$ **do**
  Generate control u_t according to $\mu_{u_t}(\theta, x_t)$
  Observe $r(x_{t+1})$ and x_{t+1}(generated according to $P_{x_t x_{t+1}}(u_t)$)
  $y_{t+1} = \gamma(y_t + \frac{\nabla\mu_{u_t}(\theta,x_t)}{\mu_{u_t}(\theta,x_t)} z_t' + z_t \frac{\nabla\mu_{u_t}(\theta,x_t)'}{\mu_{u_t}(\theta,x_t)})$
  $z_{t+1} = \gamma(z_t + \frac{\nabla\mu_{u_t}(\theta,x_t)}{\mu_{u_t}(\theta,x_t)})$
  $\tilde{z}_{t+1} = \gamma(\tilde{z}_t + \frac{\nabla^2\mu_{u_t}(\theta,x_t)}{\mu_{u_t}(\theta,x_t)})$
  $\Delta_{t+1} = \Delta_t + r(x_{t+1}) z_{t+1}$
  $H_{t+1} = H_t + r(x_{t+1})\tilde{z}_{t+1} + r(x_{t+1}) y_{t+1}$
end for
gradient $\Delta_T \leftarrow \Delta_T / T$
Hessian $H_T \leftarrow H_T / T$

Proof. Suppressing the θ dependence where it is clear,

$$\begin{aligned}
[\nabla^2_{\tilde{\theta}} \nu_\gamma(\tilde{\theta}, \pi(\theta))|_{\tilde{\theta}=\theta}]_{mn} &= \pi(\theta)'[\nabla^2_{\tilde{\theta}} J_\gamma(\tilde{\theta})|_{\tilde{\theta}=\theta}]_{mn} \\
&= \pi(\theta)'[\nabla^2_{\tilde{\theta}}(r + \gamma P(\tilde{\theta}) J_\gamma(\tilde{\theta}))|_{\tilde{\theta}=\theta}]_{mn} \\
&= \gamma\pi'(\partial_m\partial_n P J_\gamma + \partial_m P \partial_n J_\gamma + \partial_n P \partial_m J_\gamma + P\partial_m\partial_n J_\gamma) \\
&= \gamma\pi'(\partial_m\partial_n P J_\gamma + \partial_m P \partial_n J_\gamma + \partial_n P \partial_m J_\gamma) \\
&\quad + \gamma[\nabla^2_{\tilde{\theta}} \nu_\gamma(\tilde{\theta}, \pi(\theta))|_{\tilde{\theta}=\theta}]_{mn}
\end{aligned}$$

where we have used the stationarity of π' in the last line. Collecting terms proves equation 6. Using equation 1,

$$\begin{aligned}
\nabla J_\gamma &= \nabla(r + \gamma P J_\gamma) \\
&= \gamma \nabla P J_\gamma + \gamma P \nabla J_\gamma \,.
\end{aligned}$$

Equation 7 follows from unrolling the previous equation (see [7] for an equivalent proof of equation 7) □

Algorithm 1 introduces HMDP, which estimates the approximate Hessian $\tilde{\nabla}^2_\gamma \eta$ from a single sample path. It also includes the gradient algorithm of Baxter and Bartlett (with an additional factor of γ that [2] ignores). We outline the proof out its asymptotic correctness.

Theorem 6. *The HMDP sequence $\{H_T\}$ has the following property:*

$$\lim_{T\to\infty} H_T = \tilde{\nabla}^2_\gamma \eta \,.$$

Proof. The first term in equation 6, $\gamma\pi'\nabla^2 PJ_\gamma$, is estimated in the algorithm by $\frac{1}{T}\sum_{t=0}^{T-1}\tilde{z}_t r(i_t)$. The proof of the asymptotic correctness of this term parallels the proof in [2] that $\frac{1}{T}\sum_{t=0}^{T-1} z_t r(i_t)$ is an asymptotically correct estimate of $\gamma\pi'\nabla PJ_\gamma$ (see Algorithm 1 for definitions of $\tilde{z}_t$ and z_t).

We can write the other terms of equation 6 as

$$\gamma\pi'\partial_m P\partial_n J_\gamma = \gamma\sum_{i,,j,u}\pi(i)p_{ij}(u)\mu_u(\theta,i)\frac{\partial_m\mu_u(\theta,i)}{\mu_u(\theta,i)}\partial_n J_\gamma(\theta\, j)$$

where we have used $\partial_m P_{ij} = \sum_u p_{ij}(u)\mu_u(\theta,i)\frac{\partial_m\mu_u(\theta,i)}{\mu_u(\theta,i)}$. Let $x_0, x_1,\ldots$ be a sample trajectory corresponding to our Markov chain with x_0 chosen from the stationary distribution, which implies x_t is also a sample from the stationary distribution. Let $u_0, u_1, \ldots$ be the corresponding actions. Thus, $\gamma\frac{\partial_m\mu_{u_t}(\theta,x_t)}{\mu_{u_t}(\theta,x_t)}\times \partial_n J_\gamma(\theta, x_{t+1})$ is an unbiased estimate of $\gamma\pi'\partial_m P\partial_n J_\gamma$ for any t.

As shown in [7] (also see equation 7),

$$\partial_n J_\gamma(\theta,x_{t+1}) = \sum_{i,j,u}\sum_{\tau=t+1}^{\infty}\gamma^{\tau-t}P(X_\tau = i|X_{t+1}=x_{t+1})p_{ij}(u) \times\mu_u(\theta,i)\frac{\partial_n\mu_u(\theta,i)}{\mu_u(\theta,i)}J_\gamma(\theta,j)$$

where X_τ is a random variable for the state of the system at time τ. For any t, $\sum_{\tau=t+1}^{\infty}\gamma^{\tau-t}\frac{\partial_n\mu_{u_\tau}(\theta,x_\tau)}{\mu_{u_\tau}(\theta,x_\tau)}J_\gamma(x_{\tau+1})$ is an unbiased estimate of $\partial_n J_\gamma(\theta,x_{t+1})$.

It follows from the Markov property that for any t,

$$\gamma\frac{\partial_m\mu_{u_t}(\theta,x_t)}{\mu_{u_t}(\theta,x_t)}\sum_{\tau=t+1}^{\infty}\gamma^{\tau-t}\frac{\partial_n\mu_{u_\tau}(\theta,x_\tau)}{\mu_{u_\tau}(\theta,x_\tau)}J_\gamma(\theta,x_{\tau+1})$$

is an unbiased sample of $\gamma\pi'\partial_m P\partial_n J_\gamma$. Since each x_t is a sample from the stationary distribution, the average

$$\frac{\gamma}{T}\sum_{t=0}^{T-1}\gamma\frac{\partial_m\mu_{u_t}(\theta,x_t)}{\mu_{u_t}(\theta,x_t)}\sum_{\tau=t+1}^{\infty}\gamma^{\tau-t}\frac{\partial_n\mu_{u_\tau}(\theta,x_\tau)}{\mu_{u_\tau}(\theta,x_\tau)}J_\gamma(\theta,x_{\tau+1})$$

almost surely converges to $\gamma\pi'\partial_m P\partial_n J_\gamma$ as $T\to\infty$. The previous expression depends on the exact values of $J_\gamma(\theta,x_t)$, which are not known. However, each $J_\gamma(\theta,x_t)$ can be estimated from the sample trajectory, and it is straightforward to show that

$$\frac{\gamma}{T}\sum_{t=0}^{T-1}\frac{\partial_m\mu_{u_t}(\theta,x_t)}{\mu_{u_t}(\theta,x_t)}\sum_{\tau=t+1}^{\infty}\gamma^{\tau-t}\frac{\partial_n\mu_{u_\tau}(\theta,x_\tau)}{\mu_{u_\tau}(\theta,x_\tau)}\sum_{\tilde{\tau}=\tau+1}^{\infty}\gamma^{\tilde{\tau}-\tau-1}r(x_{\tilde{\tau}}) \tag{8}$$

almost surely converges to $\gamma\pi'\partial_m P\partial_n J_\gamma$ as $T\to\infty$. Using the ergodic theorem, the assumption that x_0 is chosen according to the stationary distribution can be relaxed to x_0 is an arbitrary state, since $\{X_t\}$ is asymptotically stationary (under assumption 1). Hence, equation 8 almost surely converges to $\gamma\pi'\partial_m P\partial_n J_\gamma$ for any start state x_0.

Unrolling the equations for H_T in the HMDP shows that

$$\frac{\gamma}{T}\sum_{t=0}^{T-2}\frac{\partial_m\mu_{u_t}(\theta,x_t)}{\mu_{u_t}(\theta,x_t)}\sum_{\tau=t+1}^{T-1}\gamma^{\tau-t}\frac{\partial_n\mu_{u_\tau}(\theta,x_\tau)}{\mu_{u_\tau}(\theta,x_\tau)}\sum_{\tilde{\tau}=\tau+1}^{T}\gamma^{\tilde{\tau}-\tau-1}r(x_{\tilde{\tau}})$$

is the estimate for $\gamma\pi'\partial_m P\partial_n J_\gamma$. It is straightforward to show that the error between the previous equation and equation 8 goes to 0 as $T\to\infty$. □

6 Discussion

Equation 4 suggests that the discount factor can be seen as introducing a bias-variance trade off. This equation shows that the scaled value function for every state is approximately the average reward, with an approximation error of $O(1-\gamma)$. Crudely, the variance of Monte-Carlo samples of the value function for each state is $\frac{1}{1-\gamma}$, since this is the horizon time over which rewards are added. Solving the Bellman equations will be simultaneously maximizing each biased estimate $J_\gamma(\mu,i)\approx\eta(\mu)$. We used the error in this approximation to bound the quality, measured by the average reward, of the policy obtained by solving the Bellman equations. This bound shows that good policies can be obtained if $\frac{1}{1-\gamma}$ is sufficiently larger than the mixing time of the Markov chain. This bound does not answer the question of which value of $\gamma<1$ is large enough such that the policy that solves the Bellman equations is the optimal policy. This stems from using the worst case scenario for the error of the average reward approximation when deriving our bound, in which the stationary distribution is parallel to the second term in equation 4.

The idea of approximately maximizing the average reward using discounted rewards carries over to gradient methods. We have shown that Baxter and Bartlett's approximation to the gradient of the average reward is an exact gradient of a related discounted start state problem, and proved a similar bound on the quality of policies obtained by following this biased gradient. In [1], Bartlett and Baxter show that the bias of this approximate gradient is $O(1-\gamma)$ and the variance is $O(\frac{1}{1-\gamma})$.

Some average reward formulations exist and are essentially identical to discounted formulations with a discount factor sufficiently close to 1. Tsitsiklis and Van Roy [10] show that average reward temporal differencing (TD) (see [9]), with a discount factor sufficiently close to 1, is identical to discounted TD given appropriate learning rates and biases — converging to the same limit with the same transient behavior. An equivalent expression to the approximate gradient in the limit as $\gamma\to 1$ is given by Sutton *et al's* exact average reward gradient [7], which uses a reinforcement comparison term to obtain finite state-action values.

We have also presented an algorithm (HMDP) for computing arbitrarily accurate approximations to the Hessian from a single sample path. As suggested by [2], extensions include modifying the algorithm to compute the Hessian in a Partially Observable Markov Decision Process and in continuous state, action, and control spaces. Experimental and theoretical results are needed to better understand the approximation and estimation error of HMDP.

Acknowledgments

We thank Peter Dayan for discussions and comments on the paper. Funding is from the NSF and the Gatsby Charitable Foundation.

References

1. P. Bartlett and J. Baxter. Estimation and approximation bounds for gradient-based reinforcement learning. Technical report, Australian National University, 2000.
2. J. Baxter and P. Bartlett. Direct gradient-based reinforcement learning. Technical report, Australian National University, Research School of Information Sciences and Engineering, July 1999.
3. J. Baxter and P. Bartlett. Algorithms for infinite-horizon policy-gradient estimation. *Journal of Artificial Intelligence Research*, 2001. (forthcoming).
4. D. P. Bertsekas. *Dynamic Programming and Optimal Control, Volumes 1 and 2.* Athena Scientific, 1995.
5. P. Marbach and J. Tsitsiklis. Simulation-based optimization of markov reward processes. Technical report, Massachusetts Institute of Technology, 1998.
6. S. Singh, T. Jaakkola, and M. I. Jordan. Learning without state-estimation in partially observable markovian decision processes. *Proc. 11th International Conference on Machine Learning*, 1994.
7. R. Sutton, D. McAllester, S. Singh, and Y. Mansour. Policy gradient methods for reinforcement learning with function approximation. *Neural Information Processing Systems*, 13, 2000.
8. R. S. Sutton and A. G. Barto. *Reinforcement Learning: An Introduction.* MIT Press, 1998.
9. John N. Tsitsiklis and Benjamin Van Roy. Average cost temporal-difference learning. *Automatica*, 35:319–349, 1999.
10. John N. Tsitsiklis and Benjamin Van Roy. On average versus discounted reward temporal-difference learning. *Machine Learning*, 2001. (forthcoming).

Bounds on Sample Size for Policy Evaluation in Markov Environments

Leonid Peshkin and Sayan Mukherjee

MIT Artificial Intelligence Laboratory
545 Technology Square
Cambridge, MA 02139
{pesha,sayan}@ai.mit.edu

Abstract. Reinforcement learning means finding the optimal course of action in Markovian environments without knowledge of the environment's dynamics. Stochastic optimization algorithms used in the field rely on estimates of the value of a policy. Typically, the value of a policy is estimated from results of simulating that very policy in the environment. This approach requires a large amount of simulation as different points in the policy space are considered. In this paper, we develop value estimators that utilize data gathered when using one policy to estimate the value of using another policy, resulting in much more data-efficient algorithms. We consider the question of accumulating a sufficient experience and give PAC-style bounds.

1 Introduction

Research in reinforcement learning focuses on designing algorithms for an agent interacting with an environment, to adjust its behavior in such a way as to optimize a long-term return. This means searching for an optimal behavior in a class of behaviors. Success of learning algorithms therefore depends both on the richness of information about various behaviors and how effectively it is used. While the latter aspect has been given a lot of attention, the former aspect has not been addressed scrupulously. This work is the attempt to adapt solutions developed for similar problems in the field of statistical learning theory.

The motivation for this work comes from the fact that, in reality, the process of interaction between the learning agent and the environment is costly in terms of time, money or both. Therefore, it is important to carefully allocate available interactions, to use all available information efficiently and to have an estimate of how informative the experience overall is with respect to the class of possible behaviors. The interaction between agent and environment is modeled by a Markov decision process (MDP) [7,25]. The learning system does not know the correct behavior, or the true model of the environment it interacts with. Given the sensation of the environment state as an input, the agent chooses the action according to some rule, often called a *policy*. This action constitutes the output. The effectiveness of the action taken and its effect on the environment is communicated to the agent through a scalar value (*reinforcement signal*).

D. Helmbold and B. Williamson (Eds.): COLT/EuroCOLT 2001, LNAI 2111, pp. 616–629, 2001.

The environment undergoes some transformation—changes the current state into a new state. A few important assumptions about the environment are made. In particular, the so-called Markov property is assumed: given the current state and action, the next state is independent of the rest of the history of states and actions. Another assumption is a *non-deterministic* environment, which means that taking the same action in the same state could lead to a different next state and generate a different payoff signal. It is an objective of the agent to find a behavior which optimizes some long-run measure of payoff, called *return*.

There are many efficient algorithms for the case when the agent has perfect information about the environment. An optimal policy is described by mapping the last observation into an action and can be computed in polynomial time in the size of the state and action spaces and the effective time horizon [2]. However in many cases the environment state is described by a vector of several variables, which makes the environment state size exponential in the number of variables. Also, under more realistic assumptions, when a model of environment dynamics is unknown and the environment's state is not observable, many problems arise. The optimal policy could potentially depend on the whole history of interactions and for the undiscounted finite horizon case computing it is PSPACE-complete [18]. In realistic settings, the class of policies is restricted and even among the restricted set of policies, the absolute best policy is not expected to be found due to the difficulty of solving a global multi-variate optimization problem. Rather, the only option is to explore different approaches to finding near-optimal solutions among local optima.

The issue of finding a near-optimal policy from a given class of policies is analogous to a similar issue in supervised learning. There we are looking for a near-optimal hypothesis from a given class of hypotheses [28]. However, there are crucial differences in these two settings. In supervised learning we assume that there is some target function, that labels the examples, and some distribution that generates examples. A crucial property is that the distribution is the same for all the hypotheses. This implies both that the same set of samples can be evaluated on any hypothesis, and that the observed error is a good estimate of the true error.

On the other hand, there is no fixed distribution generating experiences in reinforcement learning. Each policy induces a different distribution over experiences. The choice of a policy defines both a "hypothesis" and a distribution. This raises the question of how one re-uses the experience obtained while following one policy to learn about another. The other policy might generate a very different set of samples (experiences), and in the extreme case the support of the two distributions might be disjoint.

In the pioneering work by Kearns et al. [9], the issue of generating enough information to determine the near-best policy is considered. Using a random policy (selecting actions uniformly at random), they generate a set of history trees. This information is used to define estimates that uniformly converge to the true values. However, this work relies on having a generative model of the environment, which allows simulation of a reset of the environment to any state and execute any action to sample an immediate reward. Also, the reuse of information is partial—an estimate of a policy value is built only on a subset of experiences, "consistent" with the estimated policy.

Mansour [11] has addressed the issue of computational complexity in the setting of Kearns et al. [9] by establishing a connection between *mistake bounded algorithms* (adversarial on-line model [10]) and computing a near-best policy from a given class with respect to a finite-horizon return. Access to an algorithm that learns the policy class with some maximal permissible number of mistakes is assumed. This algorithm is used to generate "informative" histories in the POMDP, following various policies in the class, and determine a near-optimal policy. In this setting a few improvements in bounds are made.

In this work we present a way of reusing all of the accumulated experience without having access to a generative model of the environment. We make use of the technique known as "importance sampling" [26] or "likelihood ratio estimation" [5] to different communities. We discuss properties of different estimators and provide bounds for the uniform convergence of estimates on the policy class. We suggest a way of using these bounds to select among candidate classes of policies with various complexity, similar to structural risk minimization [28].

The rest of this paper is organized as follows. Section 2 discusses reinforcement learning as a stochastic optimization problem. In Section 3 we define our notation. Section 4 presents the necessary background in sampling theory and presents our way of estimating the value of policies. The algorithm and PAC-style bounds are given in Section 5.

2 Reinforcement Learning as Stochastic Optimization

There are various approaches to solving RL problems. *Value search* algorithms find the optimal policy by using dynamic-programming methods to compute the value function—utility of taking a particular action in a particular world state—then deducing the optimal policy from the value function. *Policy search* algorithms (e.g. REINFORCE [30]) work directly in the policy class, trying to maximize the expected reward without the help of Bellman's optimality principle.

Policy search methods rely on estimating the value of the policy (or the gradient of the value) at various points in a policy class and attempt to solve the *optimization issue*. In this paper we ignore the optimization issue and concentrate on the *estimation issue*—how much and what kind of experience one needs to generate in order to be able to construct uniformly good value estimators over the whole policy class. In particular we would like to know what the relation is between the number of sample experiences and the confidence of value estimates across the policy class.

Two different approaches to optimization can be taken. One involves using an algorithm, driven by newly generated policy value (or gradient thereof) estimates at each iteration to update the hypothesis about the optimal policy after each interaction (or few interactions) with the environment. We will call this *on-line* optimization. Another is to postpone optimization until all possible interaction with the environment is exhausted, and combine all information available in order to estimate (*off-line*) the whole "value surface".

In this paper we are not concerned with the question of optimization. We concentrate on the second case with the goal of building a module that contains a non-parametric model of optimization surface. Given an arbitrary policy such a module outputs an estimate of its value, as if the policy was tried out in the environment. Once such module is built and guarantees on good estimates of policy value are obtained across the policy class, we may use our favorite optimization algorithm. Gradient descent methods, in particular REINFORCE [30, 31] have been used recently in conjunction with policy classes constrained in various ways, e.g., with external memory [21], finite state controllers [14] and in multi-agent settings [20]. Furthermore, the idea of using importance sampling in the reinforcement learning has been explored [13,24]. However only on-line optimization was considered.

One realistic off-line scenario in reinforcement learning is when the data processing and optimization (learning) module is separated (physically) from the data acquisition module (agent). Say we have an ultra-light micro-sensor connected to a central computer . The agent then has to be instructed initially how to behave when given a chance to interact with the environment for a limited number of times, then bring/transmit the collected data back. Naturally during such limited interaction only a few possible behaviors can be tried out. It is extremely important to be able to generalize from this experience in order to make a judgment about the quality of behaviors which were not tried out. This is possible when some kind of similarity measure in the policy class can be established. If the difference between the values of two policies could be estimated, we could estimate the value of one policy based on experience with the other.

3 Background and Notation

MDP. The class of problems described above can be modeled as Markov decision processes (MDPs). An MDP is a 4-tuple $\langle S, A, T, R \rangle$, where: S is the set of states; A is the set of actions; $T : S \times \mathcal{A} \rightarrow \mathcal{P}(S)$ is a mapping from states of the environment and actions of the agent to probability distributions[1] over states of the environment; and $R : S \times A \rightarrow R$ is the payoff function (*reinforcement*), mapping states of the environment and actions of the agent to immediate reward.

POMDP. The more complex case is when the agent is no longer able to reliably determine which state of the MDP it is currently in. The process of generating an observation is modeled by an observation function $B(s(t))$. The resulting model is a *partially observable Markov decision process* (POMDP). Formally, a POMDP is defined as a tuple $\langle S, O, A, B, T, R \rangle$ where: S is the set of states; O is the set of observations; A is the set of actions; B is the observation function $B : S \rightarrow \mathcal{P}(O)$; $T : S \times \mathcal{A} \rightarrow \mathcal{P}(S)$ is a mapping from states of the environment and actions of the

[1] Let $\mathcal{P}(\Omega)$ denote the set of probability distributions defined on some space Ω.

agent to probability distributions over states of the environment; $R: S \times A \rightarrow \mathcal{R}$ is the payoff function, mapping states of the environment and actions of the agent to immediate reward. In a POMDP, at each time step: an agent observes $o(t)$ corresponding to $B(s(t))$ and performs an action $a(t)$ according to its policy, inducing a state transition of the environment; then receives the reward $r(t)$. We assume that the rewards $r(s,a)$ are bounded by r_{max} for any s and a.

History. We denote by H_t the set of all possible experience sequences of length t: $H_t = \{\langle o(1), a(1), r(1), \ldots, o(t), a(t), r(t), o(t+1)\rangle\}$, where $o(t) \in O$ is the observation of agent at time t; $a(t) \in A$ is the action the agent has chosen to take at time t; and $r(t) \in \mathcal{R}$ is the reward received by agent at time t. In order to specify that some element is a part of the history h at time τ, we write, for example, $r(\tau, h)$ and $a(\tau, h)$ for the τth reward and action in the history h.

Policy. Generally speaking, in a POMDP, a policy π is a rule specifying the action to perform at each time step as a function of the whole previous history: $\pi : H \rightarrow \mathcal{P}(A)$. *Policy class Π* is any set of policies. We assume that the probability of the elementary event is bounded away from zero: $0 \leq \underline{c} \leq \Pr(a|h, \pi)$, for any $a \in A$, $h \in H$ and $\pi \in \Pi$.

Return. A history h includes several immediate rewards $\langle r(1) \ldots r(i) \ldots \rangle$, that can be combined to form a return $R(h)$. In this paper we focus on returns which may be computed (or approximated) using the first T steps, and are bounded in absolute value by R_{max}. This includes two well-studied return functions—the undiscounted finite horizon return and the discounted infinite-horizon return. The first is $R(h) = \sum_{t=1}^{T} r(t,h)$, where T is the finite-horizon length. In this case $R_{max} = T r_{max}$. The second is the discounted infinite horizon return [25] $R(h) = \sum_{t=0}^{\infty} \gamma^t r(t,h)$, with a geometric discounting by the factor $\gamma \in (0; 1)$. In this case we can approximate R using the first $T_\epsilon = \log_\gamma \frac{\epsilon}{R_{max}}$ immediate rewards. Using T_ϵ steps we can approximate R within ϵ since $R_{max} = \frac{r_{max}}{1-\gamma}$ and $\sum_{t=0}^{\infty} \gamma^t r(t) - \sum_{t=0}^{T_\epsilon} \gamma^t r(t) < \epsilon$. It is important to approximate the return in T steps, since the length of the horizon is a parameter in our bounds.

Value. Any policy $\pi \in \Pi$ defines a conditional distribution $\Pr(h|\pi)$ on the class of all histories H. The value of policy π is the expected return according to the probability induced by this policy on histories space:

$$V(\pi) = \mathrm{E}_\pi \left[R(h) \right] = \sum_{h \in H} \left[R(h) \Pr(h|\pi) \right],$$

where for brevity we introduced notation E_π for $\mathrm{E}_{\Pr(h|\pi)}$. It is an *objective* of the agent to find a policy π^* with optimal value: $\pi^* = \mathrm{argmax}_\pi V(\pi)$. We assume that policy value is bounded by V_{max}. That means of course that returns are also bounded by V_{max} since value is a weighted sum of returns.

4 Sampling

For the sake of clarity we are introducing concepts from sampling theory using functions and notation for relevant reinforcement learning concepts. Rubinstein [26] provides a good overview of this material.

"Crude" sampling. If we need to estimate the value $V(\pi)$ of policy π, from independent, identically distributed (i.i.d.) samples induced by this policy, after taking N samples $h_i, i \in (1..N)$ we have:

$$\hat{V}(\pi) = \frac{1}{N}\sum_i R(h_i) \ .$$

The expected value of this estimator is $V(\pi)$ and it has variance $\mathrm{Var}\Big[\hat{V}(\pi)\Big]$:

$$\frac{1}{N}\sum_{h\in H} R(h)^2 \Pr(h|\pi) - \frac{1}{N}\left[\sum_{h\in H} R(h)\Pr(h|\pi)\right]^2 = \frac{1}{N}\mathrm{E}_\pi\left[R(h)^2\right] - \frac{1}{N}V^2(\pi) \ .$$

Indirect sampling. Imagine now that for some reason we are unable to sample from the policy π directly, but instead we can sample from another policy π'. The intuition is that if we knew how "similar" those two policies were to one another, we could use samples drawn according to the distribution π' and make an adjustment according to the similarity of the policies. Formally we have:

$$\begin{aligned} V(\pi) = & \ \textstyle\sum_{h\in H} R(h_i)\Pr(h|\pi) = \sum_{h\in H} R(h_i)\frac{\Pr(h|\pi')}{\Pr(h|\pi')}\Pr(h|\pi) \\ & = \textstyle\sum_{h\in H} R(h_i)\frac{\Pr(h|\pi)}{\Pr(h|\pi')}\Pr(h|\pi') = \mathrm{E}_{\pi'}\left[R(h_i)\frac{\Pr(h|\pi)}{\Pr(h|\pi')}\right] \ , \end{aligned}$$

where an agent might not be (and most often is not) able to calculate $\Pr(h|\pi)$.

Lemma 1. *It is possible to calculate* $\frac{\Pr(h|\pi)}{\Pr(h|\pi')}$ *for any* $\pi, \pi' \in \Pi$ *and* $h \in H$.

Proof. The Markov assumption in POMDPs warrants that

$$\begin{aligned} \Pr(h|\pi) &= \Pr(s(0))\prod_{t=1}^{T}\Pr(o(t)|s(t))\Pr(a(t)|o(t),\pi)\Pr(s(t+1)|s(t),a(t)) \\ &= \left[\Pr(s(0))\prod_{t=1}^{T}\Pr(o(t)|s(t))\Pr(s(t+1)|s(t),a(t))\right]\left[\prod_{t=1}^{T}\Pr(a(t)|o(t),\pi)\right] \\ &= \Pr(h_e)\Pr(h_a|\pi) \ . \end{aligned}$$

$\Pr(h_e)$ is the probability of the part of the history, dependent on the environment, that is unknown to the agent and can be only sampled. $\Pr(h_a|\pi)$ is the probability of the part of the history, dependent on the agent, that is known to the agent and can be computed (and differentiated). Therefore we can compute

$$\frac{\Pr(h|\pi)}{\Pr(h|\pi')} = \frac{\Pr(h_e)\Pr(h_a|\pi)}{\Pr(h_e)\Pr(h_a|\pi')} = \frac{\Pr(h_a|\pi)}{\Pr(h_a|\pi')} \ .$$

□

We can now construct an indirect estimator $\hat{V}_{\pi'}(\pi)$ from i.i.d. samples $h_i, i \in (1..N)$ according to the distribution $\Pr(h|\pi')$:

$$\hat{V}_{\pi'}(\pi) = \frac{1}{N} \sum_i R(h_i) w_\pi(h_i, \pi') \ , \tag{1}$$

where for convenience, we denote the fraction $\frac{\Pr(h|\pi)}{\Pr(h|\pi')}$ by $w_\pi(h, \pi')$. This is an unbiased estimator of $V(\pi)$ with variance

$$\begin{aligned} \mathrm{Var}\left[\hat{V}_{\pi'}(\pi)\right] &= \tfrac{1}{N}\left\{\sum_{h \in H} \left(R(h) w_\pi(h, \pi')\right)^2 \Pr(h|\pi') - V(\pi)^2\right\} \\ &= \tfrac{1}{N}\left\{\sum_{h \in H} \frac{(R(h)\Pr(h|\pi))^2}{\Pr(h|\pi')} - V(\pi)^2\right\} \\ &= \tfrac{1}{N}\mathrm{E}_\pi\left[R(h)^2 w_\pi(h, \pi')\right] - \tfrac{1}{N}V(\pi)^2 \ . \end{aligned} \tag{2}$$

This estimator $\hat{V}_{\pi'}(\pi)$ is usually called in statistics [26] an *importance sampling* (IS) estimator because the probability $\Pr(h|\pi')$ is chosen to emphasize parts of the sampled space that are important in estimating V. The technique of IS was originally designed to increase the accuracy of Monte Carlo estimates by reducing their variance [26]. Variance reduction is always a result of exploiting some knowledge about the estimated quantity.

Optimal sampling policy. It can be shown [8], for example by optimizing the expression 2 with Lagrange multipliers, that the optimal sampling distribution is $\Pr(h|\pi') = \frac{R(h)\Pr(h|\pi)}{V(\pi)}$, which gives an estimator with *zero* variance. Not surprisingly this distribution can not be used, since it depends on prior knowledge of a model of the environment (transition probabilities, reward function), which contradicts our assumptions, and on the value of the policy which is what we need to calculate. However all is not lost. There are techniques which approximate the optimal distribution, by changing the sampling distribution during the trial, while keeping the resulting estimates unbiased via reweighting of samples, called "adaptive importance sampling" and "effective importance sampling" (see, for example, [15,32,17]). In the absence of any information about $R(h)$ or estimated policy, the optimal sampling policy is the one which selects actions uniformly at random: $\Pr(a|h) = \frac{1}{2}$. For the horizon T, this gives us the upper bound which we denote η:

$$w_\pi(h, \pi') \le 2^T (1 - \underline{c})^T = \eta \ . \tag{3}$$

Remark 1. One interesting observation is that it is possible to get a better estimate of $V(\pi)$ while following another policy π'. Here is an illustrative example: imagine that reward function $R(h)$ is such that it is *zero* for all histories in some sub-space H_0 of history space H. At the same time policy π, which we are trying to estimate spends almost all the time there, in H_0. If we follow π in our exploration, we are wasting samples/time! In this case, we can really call what happens *"importance sampling"*, unlike usually when it is just "reweighting", not connected to "importance" *per se*. That is why we advocate using the name *"likelihood ratio"* rather than *"importance sampling"*.

Remark 2. So far, we talked about using a single policy to collect all samples for estimation. We also made an assumption that all considered distributions have equal support. In other words, we assumed that any history has a non-zero probability to be induced by any policy. Obviously it could be beneficial to execute a few different sampling policies, which might have disjoint or overlapping support. There is literature on this so-called stratification sampling technique [26]. Here we just mention that it is possible to extend our analysis by introducing a prior probability on choosing a policy out of a set of sampling policies, then executing this sampling policy. Our sampling probability will become: $\Pr(h) = \Pr(\pi') \Pr(h|\pi')$.

5 Algorithm and Bounds

Table 1 presents the computational procedure for estimating the value of any policy from the policy class off-line. The sampling stage consists of accumulating histories h_i, $i \in [1..N]$ induced by a sampling policy π' and calculating returns on these histories $R(h_i)$. After the first stage is done, the procedure can simulate the interaction with the environment for any policy search algorithm, by returning an estimate for arbitrary policy.

Table 1. Policy evaluation

Sampling stage:
- Chose a sampling policy π';
- Accumulate the set of histories h_i, $i \in [1..N]$ induced by π';
- Calculate the set of returns $R(h_i)$, $i \in [1..N]$;

Estimation stage:
- Input: policy $\pi \in \Pi$
- Calculate $w_\pi(h_i, \pi')$ for $i \in [1..N]$;
- Output: estimate $\hat{V}(\pi)$ according to equation 1: $\frac{1}{N}\sum_i R(h_i)w_\pi(h_i,\pi')$

5.1 Sample Complexity

We first compute deviation bounds for the IS estimator for a single policy from its expectation using Bernstein's inequality:

Theorem 1. *(Bernstein [3]) Let $\xi_1, \xi_2, \ldots$ be independent random variables with identical mean* $\mathrm{E}\xi$*, bounded by some constant $|\xi_i| \le a$, $a > 0$. Also let* $\mathrm{Var}(M_N) = \mathrm{E}\xi_1^2 + \ldots + \mathrm{E}\xi_N^2 \le L$*. Then the partial sums $M_N = \xi_1 + \ldots + \xi_N$ obey the following inequality for all $\epsilon > 0$:*

$$\Pr\left(\left|\frac{1}{N}M_N - E\xi\right| > \epsilon\right) \le 2\exp\left(-\frac{1}{2}\frac{\epsilon^2 N}{L + a\epsilon}\right).$$

Lemma 2. *With probability* $(1-\delta)$ *the following holds true. The estimated value* $\hat{V}(\pi)$ *based on* N *samples is close to the true value* $V(\pi)$ *for some policy* π *:*

$$\left|V(\pi)-\hat{V}(\pi)\right| \leq \frac{V_{max}}{N}\left(\log(1/\delta)\eta+\sqrt{2\log(1/\delta)(\eta-1)+\log(1/\delta)^2\eta^2}\right).$$

Proof. In our setup, $\xi_i = R(h_i)w_\pi(h_i,\pi')$, and $\mathrm{E}\xi = \mathrm{E}_{\pi'}\left[R(h_i)w_\pi(h_i,\pi')\right] = \mathrm{E}_\pi\left[R(h_i)\right] = V(\pi)$; and $a = V_{max}\eta$ by equation 3. According to equation 2 $L = \mathrm{Var}(M_N) = \mathrm{Var}\hat{V}_{\pi'}(\pi) \leq \frac{V_{max}^2}{N}(\eta-1)$. So we can use Bernstein's inequality and we get the following deviation bound for a policy π:

$$\Pr\left(\left|V(\pi)-\hat{V}(\pi)\right|>\epsilon\right) \leq 2\exp\left[-\frac{1}{2}\frac{\epsilon^2 N}{\frac{V_{max}^2(\eta-1)}{N}+V_{max}\eta\epsilon}\right]=\delta, \quad (4)$$

After solving for ϵ, we get the statement of Lemma 2. □

Note that this result is for a single policy. We need a convergence result *simultaneously* for all policies in the class Π. We proceed using classical uniform convergence results for covering numbers as a measure of complexity.

Remark 3. We use covering numbers (instead of VC dimension as Kearns et al. [9]) both as a measure of the metric complexity of a policy class in a union bound and as a parameter for bounding the likelihood ratio. Another advantage is that metric entropy is a more refined measure of capacity than VC dimension since the VC dimension is an upper bound on the growth function which is an upper bound on the metric entropy [28].

Definition 1. *Let* Π *be class of policies that form a metric space with metric* $D_\infty(\pi,\pi')$ *and* $\varepsilon > 0$*. The covering number* $\mathcal{N}(\Pi,D,\varepsilon)$ *is defined as the minimal integer* ℓ *such that there exist* ℓ *disks in* Π *with radius* ε *covering* Π*. If no such partition exists for some* $\varepsilon > 0$ *then the covering number is infinite. The metric entropy is defined as* $\mathcal{K}(\Pi,D,\varepsilon) = \log\mathcal{N}(\Pi,D,\varepsilon)$.

Theorem 2. *With probability* $1-\delta$ *the difference* $|V(\pi)-\hat{V}(\pi)|$ *is less than* ϵ *simultaneously for all* $\pi\in\Pi$ *for the sample size:*

$$N = O\left(\frac{V_{max}}{\epsilon}2^T(1-\underline{c})^T(\log(1/\delta)+\mathcal{K})\right).$$

Proof. Given a class of policies Π with finite covering number $\mathcal{N}(\Pi,D,\epsilon)$, the upper bound $\eta = 2^T(1-\underline{c})^T$ on the likelihood ratio, and $\epsilon > 0$,

$$\Pr\left(\sup_{\pi\in\Pi}\left|V(\pi)-\hat{V}(\pi)\right|>\epsilon\right) \leq 8\mathcal{N}\left(\Pi,D,\frac{\epsilon}{8}\right)\exp\left[-\frac{1}{128}\frac{\epsilon^2 N}{\frac{V_{max}^2(\eta-1)}{N}+\frac{V_{max}\eta\epsilon}{8}}\right].$$

Note the relationship to equation 4. The only essential difference is in the covering number, which takes into account the extension from a single policy π to the class Π. This requires the sample size N to increase accordingly to achieve the given confidence level. The derivation is similar to uniform convergence result of Pollard [22](see pages 24-27), using Bernstein's inequality instead of Hoeffding's. Solving for N gives us the statement of the theorem. □

Let us compare our result with a similar result for algorithm by Kearns et al. [9]:

$$N = O\left(\left(\frac{V_{max}}{\epsilon}\right)^2 2^{2T} VC(\Pi) \log(T) \left(T + \log(V_{max}/\epsilon) + \log(1/\delta)\right)\right) \quad (5)$$

both dependences are exponential in the horizon, however in our case the dependence on $(\frac{V_{max}}{\epsilon})$ is linear rather than quadratic. The metric entropy $\log(\mathcal{N})$ takes the place of the VC dimension $VC(\Pi)$ in terms of class complexity. This reduction in a sample size could be explained by the fact that the former algorithm uses all trajectories for evaluation of any policy, while the latter uses just a subset of trajectories.

Remark 4. Let us note that a weaker bound which is remarkably similar to the equation 5 could be obtained [19] using Mc-Diarmid [12] theorem, applicable for a more general case:

$$N = O\left(\left(\frac{V_{max}}{\epsilon}\right)^2 2^{2T} (1 - \underline{c})^{2T} \left(\mathcal{K} + \log(1/\delta)\right)\right).$$

The proof is based on the fact that replacing one history h_i in the set of samples $h_i, i \in (1..N)$ for the estimator $\hat{V}_{\pi'}(\pi)$ of equation 1, can not change the value of the estimator by more than $\frac{V_{max}\eta}{N}$.

5.2 Bounding the Likelihood Ratio

We would like to find a way to estimate a policy which minimizes sample complexity. Remember that we are free to choose a sampling policy. We have discussed what it means for one sampling policy π to be optimal with respect to another. Here we would like to consider what it means for a sampling policy π to be optimal with respect to a policy class Π. Choosing the optimal sampling policy allows us to improve bounds with regard to exponential dependence on the horizon T. The idea is that if we are working with a policy class of a finite metric dimension, the likelihood ratio can be upper bounded through the covering number due to the limit in combinatorial choices. The trick is to consider sample complexity for the case of the sampling policy being optimal in the information -theoretic sense.

This derivation is very similar to the one of an upper bound on the minimax regret for predicting probabilities under logarithmic loss [4,16]. The upper bounds on logarithmic loss we use were first obtained by Opper and Haussler [16] and then generalized by Cesa-Bianchi and Lugosi [4]. The result of Cesa-Bianchi and Lugosi is more directly related to the reinforcement learning problem since it applies to the case of arbitrary rather than *static* experts, which corresponds to learning a policy. First, we describe the sequence prediction problem and result of Cesa-Bianchi and Lugosi, then show how to use this result in our setup.

In a sequential prediction game T symbols $h_a^T = \langle a(1), \ldots, a(T) \rangle$ are observed sequentially. After each observation $a(t-1)$, a learner is asked how likely it is for each value $a \in A$ to be the *next* observation. The learner goal is to assign a probability distribution $\Pr(a(t)|h_a^{t-1}; \pi')$ based on the previous values. When at the next time step t, the actual new observation $a(t)$ is revealed, the learner suffers a loss $-\log(\Pr(a(t)|h_a^{t-1}; \pi')$. At the end of the game, the learner has suffered a total loss $-\sum_{t=1}^{T} \log \Pr(a(t)|h_a^{t-1}; \pi')$. Using the join distribution $\Pr(h_a^T|\pi') = \prod_{t=1}^{T} \Pr(a(t)|h_a^{t-1}; \pi')$ we are going to write the loss as $-\log \Pr(h_a^T|\pi')$. When it is known that the sequences h_a^T are generated by some probability distribution π from the class Π, we might ask what is the worst *regret*: the difference in the loss between the learner and the best expert in the target class Π on the worst sequence:

$$R_T = \inf_{\pi'} \sup_{h_a^T} \left\{ -\log \Pr(h_a^T|\pi') + \sup_{\pi \in \Pi} \log \Pr(h_a^T|\pi) \right\}.$$

Using the explicit solution to the minimax problem due to Shtarkov [27] Cesa-Bianchi and Lugosi prove the following theorem:

Theorem 3. *(Cesa-Bianchi and Lugosi [4] theorem 3) For any policy class Π:*

$$R_T \leq \inf_{\epsilon > 0} \left(\log \mathcal{N}(\Pi, D, \epsilon) + 24 \int_0^{\epsilon} \sqrt{\log \mathcal{N}(\Pi, D, \tau)} d\tau \right),$$

where covering number and metric entropy for the class Π, are defined using the distance measure $D_\infty(\pi, \pi') \doteq \sup_{a \in A} |\log \Pr(a|\pi) - \log \Pr(a|\pi')|$.

It is now easy to relate the problem of bounding the likelihood ratio to the worst case regret. Intuitively, we are asking what is the worst case likelihood ratio if we have the optimal sampling policy. Optimality means that our sampling policy will induce action sequences with probabilities close to the estimated policies. Remember that likelihood ratio depends only on actions sequence h_a in the history h according to the Lemma 1. We need to upper bound the maximum value of the ratio $\frac{\Pr(h_a|\pi)}{\Pr(h_a|\pi')}$, which corresponds to $\inf_{\pi'} \sup_{h_a} \left(\frac{\Pr(h_a|\pi)}{\Pr(h_a|\pi')} \right)$.

Lemma 3. *By the definition of the maximum likelihood policy* $\sup_{\pi \in \Pi} \Pr(h_a|\pi)$ *we have:*

$$\inf_{\pi'} \sup_{h_a} \left(\frac{\Pr(h_a|\pi)}{\Pr(h_a|\pi')} \right) \leq \inf_{\pi'} \sup_{h_a} \left\{ \frac{\sup_{\pi \in \Pi} \Pr(h_a|\pi)}{\Pr(h_a|\pi')} \right\}.$$

Henceforth we can directly apply the results of Cesa-Bianchi and Lugosi and get a bound of e^{R_T}. Note the logarithmic dependence of the bound on R_T with respect to the covering number $\mathcal{N}$. Moreover, since actions a belong to the finite set of actions A, many of the remarks of Cesa-Bianchi and Lugosi regarding finite alphabets apply [4]. In particular, for most "parametric" classes—which can be parametrized by a bounded subset of $\mathcal{R}^n$ in some "smooth" way [4]—the metric entropy scales as follows: for some positive constants k_1 and k_2,

$$\log \mathcal{N}(\Pi, D, \epsilon) \leq k_1 \log \frac{k_2 \sqrt{T}}{\epsilon}.$$

For such policies the minimax regret can be bounded by

$$R_T \leq \frac{k_1}{2} \log T + o(\log T),$$

which makes the likelihood ratio bound of $\eta = O((T)^{\frac{k_1}{2}})$. In this case exponential dependence on the horizon is eliminated and the sample complexity bound becomes

$$N = O\left(\frac{V_{max}}{\epsilon} T^{\frac{k_1}{2}} \left(\mathcal{K} + \log 1/\delta\right)\right).$$

6 Discussion and Future Work

In this paper, we developed value estimators that utilize data gathered when using one policy, to estimate the value of using another policy, resulting in data-efficient algorithms. We considered the question of accumulating a sufficient experience and gave PAC-style bounds. Note that for these bounds to hold the covering number of the class of policies Π should be finite.

Armed with the theorem 2 we are ready to answer a very important question of how to choose among several candidate policy classes. Our reasoning here is similar to that of structural risk minimization principal by Vapnik [28]. The intuition is that given a very limited data, one might prefer to work with a primitive class of hypotheses with good confidence, rather than getting lost in a sophisticated class of hypotheses due to low confidence. Formally, we would have the following method: given a set of policy classes $\Pi_1, \Pi_2, \ldots$ with corresponding covering numbers $\mathcal{N}_1, \mathcal{N}_2, \ldots$, a confidence δ and a number of available samples N, compare error bounds $\epsilon_1, \epsilon_2, \ldots$ according to the theorem 2. Another way to utilize the result of theorem 2 is to find what is the minimal experience necessary to be able to provide the estimate for any policy in the class with a given confidence. This work also provides insight for a new optimization technique. Given the value estimate, the number of samples used, and the covering number of the policy class, one can search for optimal policies in a class using a new cost function $\hat{V}(\pi) + \Phi(\mathcal{N}, \delta, N) \leq V(\pi)$. This is similar in spirit to using structural risk minimization instead of empirical risk minimization.

The capacity of the class of policies is measured by bounds on covering numbers in our work or by VC-dimension in the work of Kearns *et al.* [9]. The worst case assumptions of these bounds often make them far too loose for practical use. An alternative would be to use more empirical or data dependent measures of capacity, *e.g.* the empirical VC dimension [29] or maximal discrepancy penalties on splits of data [1], which tend to give more accurate results.

We are currently working on extending our results for the *weighted importance sampling* (WIS) estimator [23,26] which is a biased but consistent estimator and has a better variance for the case of small number of samples. This can be done using martingale inequalities by Mc-Diarmid [12] to parallel Bernstein's result. There is room for employing various alternative sampling techniques, in order to approximate the optimal sampling policy, for example one might want to interrupt uninformative histories, which do not bring any return for a while. Another place for algorithm sophistication is sample pruning for the case when the set of histories gets large. A few most representative samples can reduce the computational cost of estimation.

Acknowledgements. Theodoros Evgeniou introduced L.P. to the field of statistical learning theory. Leslie Kaelbling, Tommi Jaakkola, Michael Schwarz, Luis Ortiz and anonymous reviewers gave helpful remarks.

References

1. P. Bartlett, S. Boucheron, and G. Lugosi. Model selection and error estimation. In *Proceedings of the Thirteenth Annual Conference on Computational Learning Theory*. ACM Press, New York, NY, 2000.
2. Richard Bellman. *Dynamic Programming*. Princeton University Press, Princeton, New Jersey, 1957.
3. S.N. Bernstein. *The Theory of Probability*. Gostehizdat, Moscow, 1946.
4. Nicolò Cesa-Bianchi and Gábor Lugosi. Worst-case bounds for the logarithmic loss of predictors. *Machine Learning*, 43(3):247–264, 2001.
5. Peter Glynn. Importance sampling for stochastic simulations. *Management Science*, 35(11):1367–1392, 1989.
6. D. Haussler. Decision theoretic generalizations of the pac model. *Inf. and Comp.*, 100:78–150, 1992.
7. Leslie Pack Kaelbling, Michael L. Littman, and Andrew W. Moore. Reinforcement learning: A survey. *Journal of Artificial Intelligence Research*, 4, 1996.
8. H. Kahn and A. Marshall. Methods of reducing sample size in Monte Carlo computations. *Journal of the Operations Research Society of America*, 1:263–278, 1953.
9. Michael Kearns, Yishay Mansour, and Andrew Y. Ng. Approximate planning in large POMDPs via reusable trajectories. In *Advances in Neural Information Processing Systems*, 1999.
10. Nick Littlestone. Learning quickly when irrelevant attributes abound: A new linear threshold algorithm. *Machine Learning*, 2(4):245–318, 1988.
11. Yishay Mansour. Reinforcement learning and mistake bounded algorithms. In *Proc. 12th Annu. Conf. on Comput. Learning Theory*, pages 183–192. ACM Press, New York, NY, 1999.
12. C. McDiarmid. *Surveys in Combinatorics*, chapter On the method of bounded differences, pages 148–188. Cambridge University Press, 1989.
13. Nicolas Meuleau, Leonid Peshkin, and Kee-Eung Kim. Exploration in gradient-based reinforcement learning. Technical Report 1713, MIT, 2000.
14. Nicolas Meuleau, Leonid Peshkin, Kee-Eung Kim, and Leslie P. Kaelbling. Learning finite-state controllers for partially observable environments. In *Proceedings of the Fifteenth Conference on Uncertainty in Artificial Intelligence*, pages 427–436. Morgan Kaufmann, 1999.
15. M. Oh and J. Berger. Adaptive importance sampling in Monte Carlo integration, 1992.
16. M. Opper and D. Haussler. Worst case prediction over sequences in under log loss. In *The Mathematics of Information coding, Extraction, and Distribution*. Springer Verlag, 1997.

17. Luis Ortiz and Leslie P. Kaelbling. Adaptive importance sampling for estimation in structured domains. In *Proceedings of the Sixteenth Conference on Uncertainty in Artificial Intelligence*, pages 446–454, San Francisco, CA, 2000. Morgan Kaufmann Publishers.
18. Christos H. Papadimitriou and John N. Tsitsiklis. The complexity of Markov decision processes. *Mathematics of Operations Research*, 12(3):441–450, 1987.
19. Leonid Peshkin. *Architectures for policy search.* PhD thesis, Brown University, Providence, RI 02912, 2001. in preparation.
20. Leonid Peshkin, Kee-Eung Kim, Nicolas Meuleau, and Leslie P. Kaelbling. Learning to cooperate via policy search. In *Sixteenth Conference on Uncertainty in Artificial Intelligence*, pages 307–314, San Francisco, CA, 2000. Morgan Kaufmann.
21. Leonid Peshkin, Nicolas Meuleau, and Leslie P. Kaelbling. Learning policies with external memory. In I. Bratko and S. Dzeroski, editors, *Proceedings of the Sixteenth International Conference on Machine Learning*, pages 307–314, San Francisco, CA, 1999. Morgan Kaufmann.
22. D. Pollard. *Convergence of Stochastic Processes.* Springer, 1984.
23. M. Powell and J. Swann. Weighted uniform sampling - a Monte Carlo technique for reducing variance. *Journal of the Institute of Mathematics and Applications*, 2:228–236, 1966.
24. D. Precup, R. S. Sutton, and S. Singh. Eligibility traces for off-policy policy evaluation. In *Proceedings of the Seventeenth International Conference on Machine Learning*, 2000.
25. M.L. Puterman. *Markov Decision Processes.* John Wiley & Sons, New York, 1994.
26. R.Y. Rubinstein. *Simulation and the Monte Carlo Method.* Wiley, New York, NY, 1981.
27. J. Shtarkov. Universal sequential coding of single measures. *Problems of Information Transmission*, pages 175–185, 1987.
28. V. Vapnik. *Statistical Learning Theory.* Wiley, 1998.
29. V. Vapnik, E. Levin, and Y. Le Cun. Measuring the VC-dimension of a learning machine. *Neural Computation*, 1994.
30. R. J. Williams. Simple statistical gradient-following algorithms for connectionist reinforcement learning. *Machine Learning*, 8(3):229–256, 1992.
31. Ronald J. Williams. Reinforcement learning in connectionist networks: A mathematical analysis. Technical Report ICS-8605, Institute for Cognitive Science, University of California, San Diego, La Jolla, California, 1986.
32. Y. Zhou. *Adaptive Importance Sampling for Integration.* PhD thesis, Stanford University, Palo-Alto, CA, 1998.

Author Index

Lecture Notes in Artificial Intelligence (LNAI)

Lecture Notes in Computer Science

Vol. 2071: R. Harper (Ed.), Types in Compilation. Proceedings, 2000. IX, 207 pages. 2001.

Vol. 2072: J. Lindskov Knudsen (Ed.), ECOOP 2001 – Object-Oriented Programming. Proceedings, 2001. XIII, 429 pages. 2001.

Vol. 2073: V.N. Alexandrov, J.J. Dongarra, B.A. Juliano, R.S. Renner, C.J.K. Tan (Eds.), Computational Science – ICCS 2001. Part I. Proceedings, 2001. XXVIII, 1306 pages. 2001.

Vol. 2074: V.N. Alexandrov, J.J. Dongarra, B.A. Juliano, R.S. Renner, C.J.K. Tan (Eds.), Computational Science – ICCS 2001. Part II. Proceedings, 2001. XXVIII, 1076 pages. 2001.

Vol. 2075: J.-M. Colom, M. Koutny (Eds.), Applications and Theory of Petri Nets 2001. Proceedings, 2001. XII, 403 pages. 2001.

Vol. 2076: F. Orejas, P.G. Spirakis, J. van Leeuwen (Eds.), Automata, Languages and Programming. Proceedings, 2001. XIV, 1083 pages. 2001.

Vol. 2077: V. Ambriola (Ed.), Software Process Technology. Proceedings, 2001. VIII, 247 pages. 2001.

Vol. 2078: R. Reed, J. Reed (Eds.), SDL 2001: Meeting UML. Proceedings, 2001. XI, 439 pages. 2001.

Vol. 2081: K. Aardal, B. Gerards (Eds.), Integer Programming and Combinatorial Optimization. Proceedings, 2001. XI, 423 pages. 2001.

Vol. 2082: M.F. Insana, R.M. Leahy (Eds.), Information Processing in Medical Imaging. Proceedings, 2001. XVI, 537 pages. 2001.

Vol. 2083: R. Goré, A. Leitsch, T. Nipkow (Eds.), Automated Reasoning. Proceedings, 2001. XV, 708 pages. 2001. (Subseries LNAI).

Vol. 2084: J. Mira, A. Prieto (Eds.), Connectionist Models of Neurons, Learning Processes, and Artificial Intelligence. Proceedings, 2001. Part I. XXVII, 836 pages. 2001.

Vol. 2086: M. Luck, V. Mařík, O. Stěpánková, R. Trappl (Eds.), Multi-Agent Systems and Applications. Proceedings, 2001. X, 437 pages. 2001. (Subseries LNAI).

Vol. 2089: A. Amir, G.M. Landau (Eds.), Combinatorial Pattern Matching. Proceedings, 2001. VIII, 273 pages. 2001.

Vol. 2091: J. Bigun, F. Smeraldi (Eds.), Audio- and Video-Based Biometric Person Authentication. Proceedings, 2001. XIII, 374 pages. 2001.

Vol. 2092: L. Wolf, D. Hutchison, R. Steinmetz (Eds.), Quality of Service – IWQoS 2001. Proceedings, 2001. XII, 435 pages. 2001.

Vol. 2093: P. Lorenz (Ed.), Networking – ICN 2001. Proceedings, 2001. Part I. XXV, 843 pages. 2001.

Vol. 2094: P. Lorenz (Ed.), Networking – ICN 2001. Proceedings, 2001. Part II. XXV, 899 pages. 2001.

Vol. 2095: B. Schiele, G. Sagerer (Eds.), Computer Vision Systems. Proceedings, 2001. X, 313 pages. 2001.

Vol. 2096: J. Kittler, F. Roli (Eds.), Multiple Classifier Systems. Proceedings, 2001. XII, 456 pages. 2001.

Vol. 2097: B. Read (Ed.), Advances in Databases. Proceedings, 2001. X, 219 pages. 2001.

Vol. 2098: J. Akiyama, M. Kano, M. Urabe (Eds.), Discrete and Computational Geometry. Proceedings, 2000. XI, 381 pages. 2001.

Vol. 2099: P. de Groote, G. Morrill, C. Retoré (Eds.), Logical Aspects of Computational Linguistics. Proceedings, 2001. VIII, 311 pages. 2001. (Subseries LNAI).

Vol. 2101: S. Quaglini, P. Barahona, S. Andreassen (Eds.), Artificial Intelligence in Medicine. Proceedings, 2001. XIV, 469 pages. 2001. (Subseries LNAI).

Vol. 2102: G. Berry, H. Comon, A. Finkel (Eds.), Computer-Aided Verification. Proceedings, 2001. XIII, 520 pages. 2001.

Vol. 2103: M. Hannebauer, J. Wendler, E. Pagello (Eds.), Balancing Reactivity and Social Deliberation in Multi-Agent Systems. VIII, 237 pages. 2001. (Subseries LNAI).

Vol. 2105: W. Kim, T.-W. Ling, Y-J. Lee, S.-S. Park (Eds.), The Human Society and the Internet. Proceedings, 2001. XVI, 470 pages. 2001.

Vol. 2106: M. Kerckhove (Ed.), Scale-Space and Morphology in Computer Vision. Proceedings, 2001. XI, 435 pages. 2001.

Vol. 2109: M. Bauer, P.J. Gymtrasiewicz, J. Vassileva (Eds.), User Modelind 2001. Proceedings, 2001. XIII, 318 pages. 2001. (Subseries LNAI).

Vol. 2110: B. Hertzberger, A. Hoekstra, R. Williams (Eds.), High-Performance Computing and Networking. Proceedings, 2001. XVII, 733 pages. 2001.

Vol. 2111: D. Helmbold, B. Williamson (Eds.), Computational Learning Theory. Proceedings, 2001. IX, 631 pages. 2001. (Subseries LNAI).

Vol. 2118: X.S. Wang, G. Yu, H. Lu (Eds.), Advances in Web-Age Information Management. Proceedings, 2001. XV, 418 pages. 2001.

Vol. 2119: V. Varadharajan, Y. Mu (Eds.), Information Security and Privacy. Proceedings, 2001. XI, 522 pages. 2001.

Vol. 2121: C.S. Jensen, M. Schneider, B. Seeger, V.J. Tsotras (Eds.), Advances in Spatial and Temporal Databases. Proceedings, 2001. XI, 543 pages. 2001.

Vol. 2126: P. Cousot (Ed.), Static Analysis. Proceedings, 2001. XI, 439 pages. 2001.